The Law, Privileges, Proceedings
and Usage of Parliament

The Law and Privileges, Procedures
and Usage of Parliament

Erskine May's
Treatise on
The Law, Privileges, Proceedings
and Usage of Parliament

Twenty-first Edition

Editor

C. J. Boulton, CB
Clerk of the House of Commons

Assistant Editors

House of Commons

J. F. Sweetman, TD   **D. W. Limon**
H. M. Barclay   W. R. McKay
A. J. Hastings   R. J. Willoughby

House of Lords

B. P. Keith

London Butterworths 1989

United Kingdom	Butterworth & Co. (Publishers) Ltd., 88 Kingsway, **London** WC2B 6AB and 4 Hill Street, **Edinburgh** EH2 3JZ
Australia	Butterworths Pty Ltd., **Sydney, Melbourne, Brisbane, Adelaide, Perth, Canberra** and **Hobart**
Canada	Butterworths Canada Ltd., **Toronto** and **Vancouver**
Ireland	Butterworth (Ireland) Ltd., **Dublin**
New Zealand	Butterworths of New Zealand Ltd., **Wellington** and **Auckland**
Puerto Rico	Equity de Puerto Rico, Inc., **Hato Rey**
Singapore	Malayan Law Journal Pte Ltd., **Singapore**
U.S.A.	Butterworth Legal Publishers, **Austin**, Texas; **Boston**, Massachusetts; **Clearwater**, Florida (D & S Publishers); **Orford**, New Hampshire (Equity Publishing); **St Paul**, Minnesota; and **Seattle**, Washington

A CIP Catalogue record for this book is available from the British Library.

[*Publishing history if required*]

ISBN 0 406 11471 4

Printed in Great Britain by
Thomson Litho Ltd, East Kilbride, Scotland

To
The Right Honourable
Bernard Weatherill, MP
Speaker of the House of Commons
and to
The Speakers and Officers
of Commonwealth Parliaments
all of whom guard the precious
heritage of Parliamentary government

PREFACE

Erskine May should, like Shakespeare's justice, be full not only of wise saws but also of modern instances. This requirement is particularly important since Parliamentary practice in the United Kingdom develops to a large extent by way of precedent and rulings from the Chair, rather than within the constraints of a codified 'written constitution'. To this end, it is a daily task for Clerks to consider whether any developments at the previous sitting of the House merit inclusion in the next edition of this work. Now, six years after the publication of the twentieth edition, it has fallen to me to present the results of that consideration and to make such other changes to the form and emphasis of the work as I feel are required. I need not say what a privilege I deem it to be to have been entrusted with this responsibility.

Readers familiar with previous editions will find certain changes intended to improve clarity, and to give greater emphasis to current rather than former practice.

An Introduction has been added to Part I describing the general basis and authority for Parliamentary procedure, and this replaces the former chapter entitled 'Content and sources of Parliamentary procedure'.

The chapters on Privilege have been re-cast by putting the older historical background into one introductory chapter and revising it in the light of modern scholarship. As in much of the rest of the work, the need to retain the former 'small type' passages has been considered, and where this was held to be justified they have largely been absorbed into the main text. There has been a thorough re-casting of the chapter on the courts and privilege, and some modern cases (including a number from overseas) have been added. A recent case before the Privileges Committee has touched on such issues as privilege in relation to the precincts of Parliament; the House and injunctions; the definition of 'proceedings in Parliament'; and privilege and national security. Mention is also made of the statutory creation of Parliamentary copyright.

In Part II of the work, the chapter entitled 'The Arrangement of Sessional Business' has been substantially rewritten and now appears as chapter 15 under the title 'The control and distribution of time in the House of Commons'. In chapter 17, the section on the Previous Question (thought to be a procedure passing into desuetude) takes account of recent precedents.

Chapter 19 on methods of curtailing debate has been radically revised and reordered and in chapter 18 the section on Members' Interests has been considerably expanded.

In the chapters on public bills there has been a considerable re-writing to reflect current practice and emphases; for instance, the passage on Instructions takes account of the fact that the Chair's power to select Instructions has made them useless for purposes of obstruction, and the flow of rulings on them has in consequence dried up.

The financial chapters have been shortened and simplified. The previous edition took account of the procedural changes introduced shortly before its publication. The new presentation takes account of the fact that since those changes the Autumn Statement, the Public Expenditure Survey and the system of cash limits have assumed a greater significance in the Parliamentary control of finance than the formal passing of the Supply Estimates.

This edition has been prepared at a time when attention has been focussed on the extent to which the functions and even the sovereignty of Parliament have been affected by the United Kingdom's membership of the European Communities. The opportunity has been taken to present a short account of the functions of the main institutions of the Communities. Particular reference is made to those functions which are scrutinised in some way by the two Houses, and to the procedures through which this scrutiny is carried out.

While the same editorial treatment has been applied throughout the work, there are no significant changes in the procedures of the House of Lords to which special attention need be drawn here.

Reference is made to the thorough review of Private Bill Procedure carried out by a Joint Select Committee which reported in July 1988.

In November 1986 the Public Business Standing Orders of the House of Commons were completely re-arranged and re-numbered. This edition contains, in an Appendix, the complete Standing Orders in their revised form.

Erskine May is inevitably a work of reference rather than a work of literature intended for consecutive reading. It is important, therefore, that those who consult it should be given every assistance in finding an appropriate passage. They sometimes do so in circumstances of great urgency. To this end, much thought has been given to the expansion of the index within practicable bounds and it is hoped that this will be one of the more noticeable improvements of the current edition. Bold type (explained at the beginning of the index) has been introduced; there are more sub-headings; and items relating to Lords and Commons procedures have been separated to a greater extent than hitherto. The Table of Contents continues to be a valuable supplement to the index in finding a particular reference.

It remains for me to record my warm thanks to the Assistant Editors whose names appear on the title page, and to all the other members of the Clerk's Department and other Departments of both Houses who have so willingly taken part in the preparation of this edition. Mr S. J. Patrick prepared the index. I am also particularly grateful for the co-operation of Sir John Sainty KCB, Clerk of the Parliaments. I finally express my thanks to the publishers and printers for their handling of much intractable material, and to the Trustees of the Erskine May Memorial Trust and their Secretary, Mr C. B. Winnifrith, for giving me the opportunity to produce this latest edition of a classic work.

April 1989   C.J.B.

Contents

Chapter 3   Disqualification for membership of either House

Chapter 4   Power and jurisdiction of Parliament

Chapter 5   The privilege of Parliament

Chapter 6   Privilege of freedom of speech

Chapter 7   Privilege of freedom from arrest or molestation

Chapter 10   Complaints of breach of privilege or contempt

Chapter 11   The courts and privilege

PART II   PROCEEDINGS IN PARLIAMENT: PUBLIC BUSINESS

Chapter 12   Precincts and organisation of Parliament

Chapter 13   A new Parliament and opening and close of session

Chapter 14   A Sitting: general arrangements in the House of Commons

Chapter 15   The control and distribution of time in the House of Commons

Chapter 20   Organisation and conduct of business in the House of Lords

Chapter 21   Proceedings of Parliament in passing public bills

Chapter 22   Delegated legislation

Chapter 23   Formal communications between Crown and Parliament and between Lords and Commons

Chapter 25   Witnesses and Parliament

Chapter 26   Financial procedure—general

Chapter 32   Parliament, the European Communities and international assemblies

PART III   PROCEEDINGS IN PARLIAMENT: PRIVATE BUSINESS

Chapter 33   Preliminary view of private bills

Chapter 34   Preliminary proceedings in both Houses on private bills

Chapter 35 Petitions in favour of, against, or relating to private bills in the House of Commons; and the Court of Referees

Chapter 36 Proceedings in the House of Commons on private bills

Contents

Chapter 37 Proceedings in the House of Lords on private and personal bills; Royal Assent and classification of private Acts

Chapter 38 Provisional orders and special procedure orders

Chapter 39   Private legislation procedure (Scotland)

Appendix   House of Commons standing orders relative to public business (July 1989)

Contents

Table of abbreviations

A & E Ad & El	Adolphus and Ellis's Reports, King's Bench and Queen's Bench, 1834–1842
Anson	Law and Custom of the Constitution, volume 1, 5th edition, 1922.
B	Bidder's Locus Standi Reports, 1920–1936.
B & Ald	Barnewall and Alderson's Reports, King's Bench, 1817–1822.
Bac Abr	Bacon's Abridgment.
Bar & Aust	Barron and Austin's Election Cases, 1842.
Beav	Beavan's Reports, Rolls Court, 1838–66.
Bl Com	Blackstone's Commentaries.
Brit Mus Harl	The Harleian Manuscripts in the British Museum.
Bro Parl Cas	J. Brown's Cases in Parliament, 1702–1800.
Bulst	Bulstrode's Reports, King's Bench, folio, 3 parts in 1 volume, 1610–1626.
Burnet	Bishop Burnet's History of his own Time, 6 volumes, 2nd edition enlarged, 1833.
Burr	Burrow's Reports, King's Bench, 1756–1772.
C	Paper presented to Parliament by Royal Command, 1870–1900.
Cd	Paper presented to Parliament by Royal Command, 1900–1918.
CJ ( )	Journals of the House of Commons (followed by sessional year or years).
Cm	Paper presented to Parliament by Royal Command, 1986–.
Campbell, Ch Just	Lives of the Chief Justices of England, by John, Lord Campbell, 3 volumes, 1849–1857.
Campbell, Lives	Lives of the Lord Chancellors and Keepers of the Great Seal of England, by John, Lord Campbell, 8 volumes, 1845–1869.
Car & Kir	Carrington and Kirwan's Reports, Nisi Prius, 1843–1853.
Car & M	Carrington and Marshman's Reports, Nisi Prius, 1841–1842.
Carth	Carthew's Reports, King's Bench, folio, 1 volume, 1687–1700.
Cav Deb	Sir Henry Cavendish's Debates of the House of Commons, 1768–1771, in 2 volumes, 1841–1842.
Ch (preceded by date)	Law Reports, Chancery Division, since 1890.
Ch App	Law Reports, Chancery Appeals, 1865–1875.

Ch D	Law Reports, Chancery Division, 1875–1890.
Chandler, Deb	Debates of the House of Commons, by Richard Chandler, 15 volumes, 1670–1743.
Chatham Corr	Chatham's Correspondence, 1741–78, 4 volumes.
Chit	Chitty's Practice Reports, King's Bench, 1770–1822.
Cl & Fin	Clark and Finelly's Reports, House of Lords, 1831–1846.
Clarendon	A History of the Rebellion and Civil Wars in England, by Edward, Earl of Clarendon, Oxford, 1849.
C & R Clif & Rick	Clifford and Rickards' Locus Standi Reports, 1873–1884.
C & S Clif & Steph	Clifford and Stephens' Locus Standi Reports, 1867–1872.
Clifford	History of Private Bill Legislation, by Frederick Clifford, 2 volumes, 1887.
Cmd	Papers presented to Parliament by Royal Command, 1919–1956.
Cmnd	Papers presented to Parliament by Royal Command, 1956–1986.
Co Inst	Institutes of the Laws of England, by Sir Edward Coke.
Colchester	Diary and Correspondence of Charles Abbot, Lord Colchester, 3 volumes, 1861.
Co Litt	Commentary upon Littleton by Sir Edward Coke, 19th edition, 1832.
Constable	Treatise on Provisional Orders applicable to Scotland under the Private Legislation Procedure (Scotland) Act, by Constable, Beveridge and Macmillan, 1900.
Co Rep	Reports of Sir Edward Coke, 13 parts, 1572–1616.
Cotton	An exact abridgement of the Records of the Tower of London, by Sir Robert Cotton, 1689.
Coxe's Walpole	Memoirs of the Life of Sir Robert Walpole, by William Coxe.
Cowp	Cowper's Reports, King's Bench, 1774–1778.
Dasent, Speakers	Speakers of the House of Commons, by Arthur Irwin Dasent, 1911.
Decision (serial number)	Decisions from the Chair, compiled by the Clerk of the House of Commons, privately printed.
Denison	Notes from my Journal when Speaker of the House of Commons, by the late John Evelyn Denison, 1900.
D'Ewes	Journals of all the Parliaments, during the reign of Queen Elizabeth, by Sir Simonds d'Ewes, 1682.
Digest	English and Empire Digest, 44 volumes, 1200–1929 and current.
Doug El Cas	Douglas' Election Cases, 1774–1776.
Dow Dow & Ry (KB)	Dowling and Ryland's Reports, King's Bench, 1822–1827.
East	East's Reports, King's Bench, 1800–1812.

Elsynge	The Manner of Holding Parliaments in England, by Henry Elsynge, Cler Parl, 1768.
Epit HC	Epitome of the Reports from the Committees of Public Accounts, 1857 to 1969, and of the Treasury Minutes thereon.
Esp	Espinasse's Reports, Nisi Prius, 1793–1810.
Exch	Exchequer Reports (Welsby, Hurlstone, and Gordon), 1849–1856.
F & F	Foster and Finlason's Reports, Nisi Prius, 1856–67.
Fortescue	De Laudibus Legum Angliae, by Sir John Fortescue (circa 1470).
Freem	Freeman's Reports, Chancery, King's Bench and Common Pleas, 1660–1706.
GO	General Orders under the Private Legislation Procedure (Scotland) Act 1936.
Gibson, Codex	Codex juris eccles. Anglicani, by E. Gibson, 2 volumes, 1761.
Grey, Deb	Debates of the House of Commons from 1667 to 1694, collected by the Honourable Anchitell Grey, 10 volumes, 1769.
HC	House of Commons; followed by numeral and date, Parliamentary Paper printed by Order of House, with page and sessional year.
HC Deb	Parliamentary Debates (Official Report), 5th and 6th series, House of Commons, 1909–(current).
HL	House of Lords. If followed by numeral and date, Parliamentary Paper printed by Order of House, with page and sessional year.
HL Cases	Clark's Report. House of Lords, 1847–1866.
HL Deb	Parliamentary Debates (Official Report), 5th series, House of Lords, 1909–(current).
Hakewill	Modus tenendi parliamentum or the old manner of holding parliaments in England, by W. Hakewill, 1660.
Hale, Jurisd. Lords	Jurisdiction of the Lords' House of Parliament considered according to ancient records, by Lord Chief Justice Hale, 1796.
Hatsell	Precedents of Proceedings in the House of Commons, 4 volumes, 1818, by John Hatsell, Clerk of the House.
Holinshed	Chronicles of England, Scotland and Ireland, 6 volumes, 1807–1808.
Inst	See Co Inst (above).
IR Eq	Irish Reports, Equity, Fourth Series, 1866–1877.
JP	Justice of the Peace, 1837–(current).
K & J	Kay and Johnson's Reports, VC, 1854–1858.

KB (preceded by date)	Law Reports, King's Bench Division.
Keb	Keble's Reports, folio 1661–1677.
Keny	Kenyon's Notes of Cases, King's Bench, 1753–1759.
LR Appeal	Law Reports, Appeal Cases, 1876–(current).
LJ	Journals of the House of Lords (followed by sessional year or years).
LJ (CH)	Law Journal, Chancery, 1822–1946.
LJ (EX)	Law Journal, Exchequer, 1830–1875.
LRCP	Law Reports, Common Pleas, 1865–1875.
LR Eq	Law Reports, Equity cases, 1865–75.
LR Ir	Law Reports (Ireland), Chancery and Common Law 1877–1893.
LRQB	Law Reports, Queen's Bench, 1865–1875.
LSR	Locus Standi Reports, 1936–1960 and 1960–1983.
LT	Law Times Reports, 1859–1947.
Ld Raym	Lord Raymond's Reports, King's Bench and Common Pleas, 1694–1732.
Lev	Levinz's Reports, King's Bench and Common Pleas, 1660–1696.
Lex Parl	Lex Parliamentaria or a Treatise of the Law and Custom of Parliaments, 2nd edition (by George Petyt).
Liv Tract	'Liverpool Tractate', edited by Strateman, 1937.
Lut	Sir E. Lutwyche's Entries and Reports, Common Pleas, 2 volumes, 1682–1704.
M & S	Maule and Selwyn's Reports, King's Bench, 1813–1817.
Macaulay, Hist	History of England from the accession of James II, by Thomas Babington Macaulay, 5 volumes, 1849–1861.
Mac & G	Macnaghten and Gordon's Reports, Chancery, 1849–1852.
Macqueen	Appellate Jurisdiction of the House of Lords and Privy Council, by John Macqueen, 1842.
Marsh	Marshall's Reports, Common Pleas, 1813–1816.
Marvell	Works of Andrew Marvell, esquire, 3 volumes, 1776.
Mass.	Law Reports of Massachusetts.
May Const Hist	Constitutional History of England since the accession of George the Third, by Sir Thomas Erskine May, K.C.B., D.C.L., edited and continued to 1911 by Francis Holland, 3 volumes, 1912.
Mod Rep	Modern Reports, 1669–1755.
Moo ⎱ PC Moore ⎰	Reports of cases before Judicial Committee of Privy Council, 24 volumes, 1836–1873.
Morr	Morrell's Reports, Bankruptcy, 1884–1893.
Off J	Journal of Proceedings upon Applications for Provisional Orders under the Private Legislation Procedure (Scotland) Acts, 1899 and 1936.

PAC	Reports of Committee of Public Accounts (House of Commons).
PD	Law Reports, Probate, Divorce, and Admiralty Division, 1875–1890.
PLR	Private Legislation (Scotland) Reports, by Constable, Macmillan and Beveridge.
PR & D	Power, Rodwell and Dew's Election Cases, 1848–58.
Parl Deb	Parliamentary Debates (authorized edition), First to Fourth Series, 1803–1908.
Parl Hist	Parliamentary History of England from the earliest period to the year 1803.
Parl Reg	Parliamentary Register, 89 volumes, 1774–1803.
Peck	Peckwell's Election Cases, 1803–1806.
Perceval	Life of the Right Hon. Spencer Perceval, by Spencer Walpole, 2 volumes, 1874.
Pike	Constitutional History of the House of Lords, 1894.
Ph	Phillips' Reports, Chancery, 1841–1849.
Pollex	Pollexfen's Reports, King's Bench, 1670–1682.
Prynne, Register	Brief Register, Kalendar, and Survey of the Several Kinds, Forms of all Parliamentary Writs, by William Prynne, 1659–1664.
QB (preceded by date)	Law Reports, Queen's Bench Division.
QBD	Law Reports, Queen's Bench Division, 1875–1890.
Rapin	History of England, by de Rapin-Thoyras, translated by N. Tindal, 2 volumes, 1733.
Redlich	Redlich and Ilbert, Procedure of the House of Commons, 3 volumes, 1908.
Rep Dignity of Peer	Reports of Lords' Committee on the Dignity of a Peer of the Realm, Parl Pap (HC), sess. 1826, 1st Report, No. 391; Appendix No. 1, Part I. No. 392; Part II. No. 393; 2nd, 3rd, and 4th Reports, No. 394.
R & M Rick & M	Rickards and Michael's Locus Standi Reports, 1885–1889.
R & S Rick & S	Rickards and Saunders' Locus Standi Reports, 1890–1894.
Rogers	Rogers on Elections, vol. 1, Registration; vol. 2, Parliamentary Elections and Petitions
RP Rot Parl	Rotuli Parliamentorum, etc, 6 Edward I to 19 Henry VII.
Rushworth	Historical Collections, 1618–1648, 3 volumes.
S	See Smethurst (below)
SCC (preceded by date)	Court of Session Cases (Scotland).
SI	Statutory Instruments, published by authority.
SO	Standing Orders of Each House; when followed by 'No.' indicates Standing Orders relating to Public Business; but when followed immediately by figures, indicates Standing Orders relating to Private Business in each House.
SR & O	Statutory Rules and Orders, published by authority.

Salk	Salkeld's Reports, King's Bench, 1689–1712.
Saund	Saunders' Reports, King's Bench, 1666–1672.
S & A Saund & A	Saunders and Austin's Locus Standi Reports, 1895–1904.
S & B Saund & B	Saunders and Bidder's Locus Standi Reports, 1905–1919.
Sch	Schedule (to an Act of Parliament).
Scobell	Memorials of the Manner of passing bills, by Henry Scobell, esquire, Cler Parl (in Miscellanea Parliamentaria, 1685).
Show	Shower's Reports, King's Bench, 1678–1695.
Sidmouth	Life and Correspondence of the Rt. Hon. Henry Addington, 1st Viscount Sidmouth, by the Honourable George Pellew DD, 3 volumes, 1847.
S Smethurst	Treatise on Locus Standi, 2nd edition, 1867.
State Papers	State Papers published under the authority of His Majesty's Commission, King Henry VIII, 11 volumes, 1830–1852.
State Tr	State Trials, 1163–1820. New Series, 1820–1858.
Stat. of the Realm	Statutes of the Realm (Record Commission), 1810 et seq.
Stg Co Deb	Official Report of Debates of Commons Standing Committees.
Story	Commentaries on the Constitution of the United States, by Joseph Story LLD, 3rd edition, 2 volumes, 1858.
Stra	Strange's Reports, 1716–1747.
Sty	Style's Reports, King's Bench, folio, 1646–1655.
Sugden	A treatise of the Law of Property as administered by the House of Lords, by Sir Edward Sugden, 1849.
Suppl to Votes	Supplement to the Votes and Proceedings of the House of Commons.
TLR	The Times Law Reports, 1884–1952.
Taunt	Taunton's Reports, Common Pleas, 1807–1819.
TR Term Rep	Term Reports (Durnford and East), folio, 1785–1800.
Todd	Parliamentary Government in England, by Alpheus Todd. New edition by Spencer Walpole, 1892.
Vent	Ventris' Reports, folio, 1668–1691.
WLR	Weekly Law Reports.
WR	Weekly Reporter, 1852–1906.
West, Inq	An Inquiry into the Manner of creating Peers (by Richard West), 1719.
Williams	Historical Development of Private Bill Procedure and Standing Orders in the House of Commons, by O. Cyprian Williams, 2 volumes, 1949.
Wils	G. Wilson's Reports, King's Bench and Common Pleas, folio, 1742–1774.

PART I

Constitution, powers and privileges of Parliament

INTRODUCTION

'The law, privileges, proceedings and usages of Parliament' in a nation with a long history and an unwritten constitution must be discovered largely by observing its practice, rather than by consulting fundamental texts and the decisions of a Supreme Court. The 'law of Parliament' includes those aspects of Parliamentary activity that depend for their effectiveness on recognition by the courts, and such law—although it may be unwritten—is only changed by way of statute. But most Parliamentary procedure and usage derives from the admitted right of each House to regulate its own proceedings, a right which led a former Clerk of the Commons to observe, 'What does it signify about precedents? The House can do what it likes. Who can stop it?'[1]

Thus, to understand the working of Parliament, it is necessary to be familiar with recent practice as well as with the formal rules. By citing the latest decisions and describing current developments, Erskine May seeks to provide as complete an account as is practicable of the role and functioning of Parliament at the present day. This Introduction indicates the kinds of authority on which the rules of procedure are based. First it describes their broad purpose.

Many Parliamentary procedures originated in the period when the Commons, at least, regarded themselves as in opposition to the Crown and devised ways of checking and controlling the actions of Ministers. Today, by contrast, the Crown's Ministers are entitled to assume that they enjoy the general support of a majority of the House of Commons, and the purpose of many of the rules is to safeguard the rights of a minority of the House: to guard against the development of an 'elective dictatorship' which some have predicted. The sheer pressure of business in a House of Commons of 650 Members in a non-federal constitution has led to the adoption of many rules that limit opportunities for debate. Such rules include time-limits on many items of business and on the length of individual speeches on certain occasions, and limits on the number of days on which certain business (for example, Estimates of Expenditure) may be taken. But other allocations of time have been for the purpose of safeguarding the rights of minorities and of individuals. These include, in particular, the provision of allotted days for the Opposition and other minority parties, and the allocation of days for Private Members' bills and motions. Above all, the balance between the right of Governments to obtain their business and the right of the House as a whole to examine it, and to require the opportunity to amend it and propose alternatives before ultimately approving it, is maintained through the discretionary powers given to the Speaker. By calling to its Chair a Member who thereupon permanently distances himself from his former political background, the House of Commons has evolved a method of entrusting to a

---

1 John Ley, Clerk 1820–1850.

colleague the oversight of 'fair play'. This has enabled the Speaker to be given power to select which amendments will be debated; to decide whether or not he will allow the Closure of Debate, or a dilatory motion, to be moved; and, from day to day, to decide which Members should be called in debate so as to provide a representative expression of the House's opinions. Such authority, which is also reflected in the powers and conduct of the chairmen of committees, is the principal defence against the arbitrary use of the executive's majority position.

The rules themselves are of different kinds and derive from different sources—from practice; from standing orders and *ad hoc* orders and resolutions; from rulings from the Chair; and (occasionally) from statute. Each of these elements is now described.

(1) Practice. Practice is that part of procedure which developed spontaneously in the course of the transaction of business in each House. The authority for many of the old-established forms and rules of practice is unrecorded. Some of them were no doubt invented in Parliament itself, but others have been traced to analogies in the medieval courts of law and in the councils of the Church. This older practice is sometimes distinguished as 'ancient usage', and needs no other authority than proof of its de facto existence. It may be defined as the usual and regular method of proceeding not (so far as is known) instituted by express authority, but which is recorded as being already in operation in the volumes of the early Journals. The readings of bills and the use of select committees are examples of ancient usage. But there is also a deliberately authorized practice. Some of the rules of practice were laid down by the House in the form of orders or resolutions, recorded in the Journals, mainly during the seventeenth century. Of these, some purport to lay down new rules or invent new forms of machinery, such as the Committee of the whole House. But most of them are declaratory in form, and made with the evident intention of giving an authoritative exposition of already existing practice rather than of making new practice. Practice was developed by precedents, which were established in much the same way and are still treated with similar respect in Parliament, as judicial precedents in the courts. When a case occurred which could not be decided on any existing rule, the House appointed a committee to 'search the Journals for precedents of what hath been done in like cases', or ordered proceedings from the Journals in analogous cases to be read at the Table; and, after a careful consideration of the precedents thus collected, the case was settled, to become itself a precedent for future occasions. Or, if the circumstances of the case were too peculiar, an entry was made in the Journals that it should not be drawn into a precedent. The great period of practice was in the first half of the seventeenth century; although it looked back to an imaginary golden age in the fifteenth century, its spirit was thoroughly practical and took such hold of Parliament that it survived unchanged in the House of Commons till after the Reform Act of 1832, and still forms the groundwork of procedure. Many forms were common to both Houses, and continue unchanged in the procedure of the House of Lords.

The principal common characteristic of the rules of practice was to provide ample opportunity for debate[1] and for initiative in choosing subjects for

---

1 Cf Balfour's remark in defence of his reforms of 1902: 'In the middle of the 18th century and
  indeed to a very much later period, the difficulty was not to check the flow of oratory, but to
  induce it to flow at all' (Redlich i, 64).

debate, and ample safeguards against business being taken without due notice so that decisions could not be reached without opportunities for full consideration being given.

Manuals and textbooks of the practice of Parliament and particularly of the House of Commons were published in the sixteenth, seventeenth and eighteenth centuries.[1] But these books were couched in general terms, and in order to understand the details of the old practice, it is necessary to study the Journals of the two Houses and any records of debates which were published before the institution of the series of Hansard's Reports, or which have been preserved in manuscript.

The methods by which practice was made—the formation of precedents, the recording of decisions by the House in individual cases—are still in full operation, and in the House of Commons have been supplemented by a new and fertile method, which was hardly operative before the period of the standing orders (in which the judicial position of the Speaker has been greatly enhanced) namely, the giving of rulings by the Speaker and other occupants of the chair. Thus there is a modern as well as an ancient practice; the function of modern practice, besides that of applying (usually in a restrictive sense) the rules of the ancient usage to changing conditions, is to supplement the standing orders and to harmonize them with each other and with the general body of practice. A field in which there have been many opportunities for constructive interpretation in the light of modern conditions is the ancient financial procedure of the House of Commons.

Nevertheless the rules of practice still provide the framework of procedure, for the work of the standing orders has been far less to lay down new rules than to modify existing rules. For the House of Lords, a statement of practice is contained in 'The Companion to the Standing Orders', which is periodically revised and issued with the authority of the Procedure Committee. A 'Brief Guide' summarising the main procedures is also issued from time to time. For the House of Commons, a summary of procedure called 'The Manual of Procedure in the Public Business' is compiled for the use of Members in a periodically revised form, and laid upon the Table of the House by Mr Speaker.

(2) The standing orders. The second main basis of procedure is provided by the standing orders, which, as indicated above, have to be read in conjunction with the practice of the House and do not form a complete code of procedure. All but a very few of the Commons' standing orders have been passed since 1832. Their chief characteristic is that they are intended to

---

1 See, for example, from the early 1560's, Sir Thomas Smith's *De republica Anglorum*, ed Mary Dewar (1982); from about 1572, Hooker's 'Order and Usage of keeping a Parliament in England' *in Parliament in Elizabethan England*, V F Snow (1977); between 1581 and 1584, Lambarde's *Notes on the Orders, Proceedings, Punishments and Privileges of the House of Commons*, ed P L Ward (1977); about 1611, *the Manner how Statutes are enacted in Parliament*, William Hakewill (1641); probably a similar date, 'Policies in Parliament', ed C S Sims in *Huntinton Library Quarterly* vol 15 (1951–52) p 45; Henry Elsying the elder's *Manner of holding Parliaments in England*, completed in 1625 but not published till 1660 (ed Thomas Tyrwhitt, 1768); *Memorials of the Method and Manner of proceedings in Parliament in passing bills*, Henry Scobell (1656, 1685); *Lex Parliamentaria*, Petyt (1690); *The Liverpool Tractate*, ed C Strateman (1937) on procedure in the 1760's; and John Hatsell's *Precedents of Proceedings in the House of Commons* (1781 and 1818). A survey of the continuing influence of the mediaeval *Modus tenendi Parliamentum* is to be found in *Parliamentary Texts of the late Middle Ages*, N Pronay and J Taylor (1980).

expedite the progress of business by reducing the opportunities for debate
and checking its luxuriance. The relation between practice and the standing
orders in the modern procedure of the House of Commons is further
illustrated below.

Although a standing order differs from every other order of the House in
having an express duration beyond the end of the session in which it is
passed, no special procedure is, as a rule, involved in its passage except that
after it has been agreed to on motion a further order is made declaring it to
be a standing order of the House. Standing orders are not safeguarded by
any special procedure against amendment, repeal or suspension, whether
explicitly or by an order contrary to their purport. Ordinary notice only is
requisite for the necessary motion; and some standing orders have included
arrangements for the suspension of their own provisions by a bare vote,
without amendment or debate. The practice has sometimes been followed in
recent years of making standing orders, limited in their duration until the
end of the current Parliament, for the purpose of appointing and nominating
certain select committees which earlier would have been set up by order of
the House each session.

Orders and resolutions. Orders and resolutions relating to procedure,
whose duration is expressly or by implication limited to that of the session in
which they are made, are usually made for such purposes as to give precedence to specified kinds of business or to subject specified proceedings to
specially stringent restrictions, rather than for the regulation of general
procedure, except in periods of emergency as in time of war.

Certain orders and resolutions (known loosely as 'sessional orders') are
renewed regularly on the first day of each session in the House of Commons,
and are to all intents and purposes standing orders except that they do not
regulate the procedure of the House itself, but in the main prescribe rules for
the conduct of persons, who are not Members, in their relation to the House.
Another use for orders limited to a single session is to experiment with new
rules which are intended to be permanent if they prove satisfactory in
working. Thus, Standing Order No 15 (Prayers against statutory instruments etc. (negative procedure) (see p 243)) had a preliminary period of trial
as a sessional order before it became a standing order in 1957.

Orders and resolutions which affect the procedure of either House without any period of duration being fixed are often regarded as having permanent validity, although according to the custom of Parliament their
effectiveness is concluded by prorogation. Many such resolutions, the validity of which is even now recognized, may be found in the Journals of the
seventeenth century. These have been referred to already as providing one
of the bases of practice; and in a later age they would no doubt have
been passed as standing orders. Examples of these are orders of 1604
against speaking tediously, impertinently and beside the question,[1] and the
resolutions of the same year that a Member may not speak twice to the same
question, and that the same question be not proposed again during the same
session; and resolutions prohibiting speaking after the voices have been fully
taken, and directing the formal reading of a bill at the opening of the session.
Even since the beginning of the 'standing order period', examples are to be

1 Hatsell 230, CJ (1547–1628) 172, 946.

found of orders and resolutions made by the House of Commons with permanent effect; for example the order of 1836 prohibiting the printing and publication of the evidence of a committee before it has been reported to the House; the resolution of the same session with regard to parliamentary agents; the resolution of 1947 against contractual arrangements tending to limit Members' freedom of action in Parliament (see p 85); and the resolutions of 1963 and 1972 setting out the rules relating to matters that are sub judice (see p 377).

(3) Rulings from the Chair. The third source of procedure in the House of Commons is to be found in rulings from the Chair (there is no equivalent in the House of Lords, where the Speaker and Chairman may not give rulings (see pp 173–174)). If ancient usage corresponds to the common law and the standing orders to the statute law, the rulings of the Speaker in the House, and of the Chairman in Committee of the whole House, afford an obvious parallel to the decisions of judges in the courts. The House of Commons has its own body of case-law. This consists principally of rulings given by Mr Speaker in answer to questions raising points of order on current business. Such rulings are, as stated above, the principal source of modern *practice*. They are constantly needed for the purpose of applying the standing orders to doubtful or new cases; and for harmonizing the standing orders with older practice and with each other. A field in which there have been many occasions for constructive interpretation and adaptation to modern conditions is provided by the ancient financial procedure of the House, including the 'public money' standing orders which date from the early eighteenth century.

The procedure for obtaining a ruling from the Chair is generally as follows. Notice is given to the Speaker by the Member who desires to raise a point of order, so that the ruling, publicly delivered in the House, may take account of any relevant precedents and of all the considerations involved. Such a ruling forms a precedent, often fitting into its place in a series of precedents from which a general rule may be eventually drawn for all future practice in a particular range of procedure. In addition to the formal rulings which he gives after notice, the Speaker is frequently called upon to give decisions on points suddenly arising in the course of business, eg, on supplementary questions or relevancy in debate. The Chairman and Deputy Chairmen of Ways and Means and members of Mr Speaker's panel of chairmen have similarly to give decisions in Committee of the whole House and in standing committees. All such decisions are to be found recorded in the Official Report of Debates. But sometimes rulings are given privately on matters before they are brought before the House; and, when such a ruling has the effect of bringing a proposal into order or of excluding it finally as out of order, there has until recently been no opportunity for it to be delivered publicly in the House. On 5 November 1981, however, the Speaker announced that, in future, when he gave a private ruling which in his judgment was of general interest or could serve as a precedent for the future, the substance of the ruling would be published in the Official Report immediately before replies to written questions.[1]

---

1 HC Deb (1981–82) 12, c 113. For an example of this, see HC Deb (1981–82) 14, c 970.

(4) Statutory modification of procedure. The element of procedure which derives its authority from statute is comparatively small. With the exception of an early statute for regulating places in the Lords[1] and certain statutes affecting the prorogation of Parliament, statutory modification of existing procedure is not found before the nineteenth century. Examples since then are an Act of 1850 (13 & 14 Vict c 21), the first section of which annulled the rule of practice that a bill could not be introduced at variance with the provisions of an Act passed during the same session; the Private Legislation Procedure (Scotland) Act 1936; the Statutory Orders (Special Procedure) Acts 1945 and 1965; the Statutory Instruments Act 1946 (and analogous provision under the Northern Ireland Act 1974); and the Parliament Acts 1911 and 1948. The first four of these Acts prescribed common procedure for both Houses, and the last two the procedure consequent upon disagreement between them. Also the Exchequer and Audit Departments Acts 1866 and 1921, the Public Accounts and Charges Act 1891, and the Provisional Collection of Taxes Acts 1913 and 1968, have directly or indirectly affected the financial procedure of the House of Commons; and the Representation of the People Act 1949, has delegated to the courts the jurisdiction over controverted elections formerly exercised by the House itself. The Royal Assent Act 1967 repealed a statute and modified the practice of both Houses with regard to the signification of the royal assent to Bills.

The four sources of procedure just mentioned are of different degrees of authority. A statute overrides, and cannot be superseded by, an order or regulation of one House or of both jointly. An express order can supersede another such order of the same House; thus a sessional order can set aside, and an ad hoc order can suspend, a standing order. Any form of express order takes precedence of a rule of practice. In the Commons the function of the Chair is declaratory and interpretative. But the Speaker is in a sense a law-giver too; for, by the application of principles and precedents to new circumstances, he may establish a general rule in the course of deciding a particular case.

---

1 31 Hen 8, c 10. Now largely obsolete and in part repealed. See Standing Orders of the House of Lords, App.

CHAPTER 1

The constituent parts of Parliament

INTRODUCTORY

The origins of Parliament lie in the great assemblies of magnates which from the early Middle Ages were called together by the King to advise him and to hear and acknowledge his decisions. The word 'parliament' is first officially used in the thirteenth century to describe a similar assembly, an enlarged meeting of the King's Council, at which barons, prelates and ministers were present. In the late thirteenth century Parliament was concerned with judicial, administrative and legislative matters, and gave assent to taxation. At that period the King often summoned knights of the shire and burgesses to Parliament as well as barons and prelates; by the mid fourteenth century he invariably did so.[1]

The functions of the Parliament of the United Kingdom today have evolved over many centuries, and in their present form they chiefly comprise legislation, consent to taxation and control of public expenditure, debate on government policy and scrutiny of government administration, and appellate jurisdiction.

Parliament is composed of the Sovereign, the House of Lords and the House of Commons. These several powers collectively form the legislature; and as distinct members of the constitution they exercise functions and enjoy privileges peculiar to each.

The Sovereign

The Crown is hereditary, subject, however, to special limitations by Parliament; and the King or Queen has always enjoyed, by prescription, custom and law, the chief place in Parliament and the sole executive power. The right of succession and the prerogatives of the Crown itself are, however, subject to limitations and change by legislative process with the consent and authority of the sovereign;[2] and in the exercise of the prerogatives and powers of the Crown the sovereign now, by constitutional convention, depends on the advice of Ministers of the Crown, who only continue to serve in that capacity so long as they retain the confidence of Parliament, and whose advice is tendered by virtue either of their several responsibilities or of their membership of the Privy Council.

Limitations of prerogative. Many changes have been effected at different times in the legal succession to the Crown; that occurring at the Revolution

---

1 See Sayles *The King's Parliament of England*; Davies and Benton *The English Parliament in the Middle Ages*.
2 For additions made by statute to the royal style and title, see the Royal Titles Acts 1876, 1901 and 1953, and see Index of the Statutes, tit. Crown. See also, The Title of the Sovereign (Cmd 8748).

of 1688 being a notable example. The power of Parliament over the Crown is distinctly affirmed by the statute law, and recognized as an important principle of the constitution.

The Act of Settlement (1700–1) affirms 'that the laws of England are the birthright of the people thereof; and all the Kings and Queens[1] who shall ascend the throne of this realm ought to administer the government of the same according to the said laws; and all their officers and ministers ought to serve them respectively according to the same'. The Succession to the Crown Act 1707 declares it high treason for any one to maintain and affirm, by writing, printing, or preaching, 'that the Kings or Queens of this realm, by and with the authority of Parliament, are not able to make laws and statutes of sufficient force and validity to limit and bind the Crown, and the descent, limitation, inheritance, and government thereof'. The relationship between the Crown and Parliament had earlier been defined in the Bill of Rights, which declared, inter alia, that 'the pretended power of suspending or dispensing with laws, or the execution of laws, without consent of Parliament, is illegal', and that 'levying money for or to the use of the Crown, by pretence of prerogative, without grant of Parliament for longer time or in other manner than the same is or shall be granted, is illegal'.[2]

Prerogative in connection with Parliament. The prerogatives of the Crown, in connection with the legislature, are of paramount importance. The legal existence of Parliament results from the exercise of royal prerogative (see p 58). As 'supreme governor, as well in all spiritual or ecclesiastical things or causes as temporal',[3] the Queen appoints the archbishops and bishops who, as 'Lords Spiritual', form part of the House of Lords. All titles of honour are the gift of the Crown, and thus the 'Lords Temporal' also, who form the remainder of the upper House, have been created by royal prerogative, and their number may be increased at pleasure. To a Queen's writ, also, the House of Commons owe their election as the representatives of the people. To these fundamental powers are added others of scarcely less importance, which will be described in the appropriate place.

The Crown also has a close relationship with the presiding officer of each House. The Speaker of the Lords is the Lord Chancellor and is appointed by the Crown. The Speaker of the Commons, though elected by them, is submitted to the approbation of the Crown (pp 226–227).

The House of Lords

The Lords Spiritual and Temporal sit together, and jointly constitute the House of Lords.[4] As members of the House they enjoy the same rights and privileges.[5]

---

1 For a statutory confirmation of the ancient right of females to inherit the Crown, see 1 Mar Sess 2, c 1; and 1 Mar Sess 3, c 1; 1 Eliz c 3. For the form in which the accession of a sovereign is recognized, see CJ (1837) 488; ibid (1901) 2; ibid (1910) 148; ibid (1935–36) 49; ibid (1936–37) 58; ibid (1951–52) 88.
2 1688, c 2, arts 1 and 4.
3 Act 1 Eliz c 1, s 19; Gibson, Codex, 1. 45. Concerning the use of the title 'Supreme Head of the Church,' see 4 Co Inst 344; Hooker, Eccl Pol book viii c 4; Zurich Letters (Parker Society), i. 29. 33; and the preamble of 2 & 3 Ann c 20.
4 There is no limit to the number of Lords Temporal. In July 1989 there were 1160 such Lords on the roll making, together with the 26 Lords Spiritual, a total of 1186.
5 Lords Spiritual do not enjoy privilege of peerage (SO No 6); for the privilege of peerage, see p 70.

Lords Spiritual. The Lords Spiritual are the archbishops and bishops of the Church of England having seats in Parliament by ancient usage and by statute.[1] In 1847, on the creation of the bishopric of Manchester, it was enacted that the number of bishops sitting in Parliament should not be increased in consequence, and a similar provision has been made in the case of bishoprics which have been created subsequently.[2]

The following bishops now have seats in the House of Lords: the archbishops of Canterbury and York; the bishops of London, Durham and Winchester; twenty-one other bishops of the Church of England according to seniority of appointment to diocesan sees.[3] A bishop may resign his see and therewith his seat.[4] Bishops appointed since 1975 are obliged to retire at 70.

Lords Temporal. The Lords Temporal may be divided into three categories. The first is composed of the hereditary peers and peeresses of England, Scotland, Great Britain and the United Kingdom.[5] They are subdivided into five degrees—dukes, marquesses, earls, viscounts and barons—but the distinction is one of rank and does not affect their rights as lords of Parliament. The second comprises the barons and baronesses created for life under the Life Peerages Act 1958.[6] The third consists of the barons created for life under the Appellate Jurisdiction Act 1876, as amended. They are appointed to serve as salaried Lords of Appeal in Ordinary and they remain members of the House after their retirement from office. The maximum

1 They were excluded by Act 16 Cha 1, c 27, and did not resume their seats after the Restoration, in the Convention Parliament, but were restored in the next Parliament, by statute 13 Cha 2, c 2. The four bishops added to the House of Lords, at the Union, to represent the episcopal body of Ireland, were withdrawn after 1 January 1871 on the disestablishment of the Irish Church by the Irish Church Act 1869. On the disestablishment of the Church in Wales on 31 March 1920 (see s 2 of the Welsh Church (Temporalities) Act 1919) bishops of that Church ceased, under s 2(2) of the Welsh Church Act 1914, to be qualified to sit or vote as Lords of Parliament, and no bishop of the Church in Wales is, as such, to be summoned to the House of Lords. The vacancies caused by the withdrawal of the bishops of the Church in Wales who had seats in Parliament were supplied by the issue of writs of summons to bishops not disqualified by the Act who had not previously received writs of summons. Ibid s 2(3).
2 The Ecclesiastical Commissioners Act 1847, s 2; St Albans, 1875 (38 & 39 Vict c 34); Truro, 1876 (39 & 40 Vict c 54); Liverpool, Newcastle, Southwell, and Wakefield, 1878 (41 & 42 Vict c 68); Bristol, 1884 (47 & 48 Vict c 66); Southwark and Birmingham, 1904 (4 Edw 7, c 30); Chelmsford, St Edmundsbury and Ipswich, and Sheffield, 1913 (3 and 4 Geo 5, c 36); Bradford and Coventry, 1917 (7 & 8 Geo 5, c 57); Portsmouth and Guildford, 1923 (14 & 15 Geo 5, Measure No 2); Blackburn, 1923 (14 & 15 Geo 5, Measure No 4); Derby, 1923 (14 & 15 Geo 5, Measure No 5); Leicester, 1925 (15 & 16 Geo 5, Measure No 2).
3 Bishoprics Act 1878, s 5. The Bishop of Sodor and Man has no seat in Parliament, not having originally held his temporalities directly from the Crown.
4 Bishops (Retirement) Measure 1951, s 2.
5 The Peerage Act 1963 discontinued the system, established by the Act of Union of 1707, by which the peers of Scotland elected sixteen of their number to sit in the House of Lords as representatives. It also removed the disqualification which had previously barred hereditary peeresses from membership of the House. See also Report by Joint Committee on House of Lords Reform, 1963 (HL 23 (1962–63), HC 38 (1962–63)).
6 Following the decision in the Wensleydale peerage case (LJ (1856) 38; May *Const Hist* i, 196–201), legislation was necessary to make it possible for life peers to be members of the House. The Appellate Jurisdiction Act 1876 was the first such legislation.

number of Lords of Appeal in Ordinary is at present fixed at eleven.[1] It may be raised by order in council subject to affirmative resolutions by both Houses.

Disclaimer of peerage. Any person who succeeds to a peerage in the peerage of England, Scotland, Great Britain or the United Kingdom may by an instrument of disclaimer delivered to the Lord Chancellor within twelve months[2] of his succession (or of attaining the age of twenty-one if he is under that age when he succeeds) disclaim that peerage for his life.[3] The effect of such disclaimer, which is irrevocable, is to divest that person (and, if he is married, his wife) of all right or interest to or in the peerage, and all titles, rights, offices, privileges and precedence attaching thereto, and to relieve him of all obligations and disabilities (including any disqualification in respect of membership of the House of Commons and elections to that House) arising therefrom. It does not accelerate the succession to that peerage nor affect its devolution on his death. No other hereditary peerage may be conferred upon the person by whom it is disclaimed but a life peerage may be so conferred, and no writ in acceleration may be issued in respect of the disclaimed peerage to the person entitled to it on his death.

Peers of Ireland. By virtue of the Act of Union of 1800 the Peers of Ireland elected twenty-eight of their number to sit in the House of Lords as representatives. Elections were, however, discontinued after 1922. In 1966 the House agreed to a report of the Committee for Privileges to the effect that the provisions of the Act of Union relating to the election of representative peers ceased to be effective on the passing of the Irish Free State Agreement Act 1922 and the right to elect such peers no longer exists.[4] Peers of Ireland may petition the House to have their claims to succession established. Such petitions are referred to the Lord Chancellor who reports his decision to the House.[5] Since 1963 a peer of Ireland has been entitled to be elected a member of the House of Commons for any constituency in the United Kingdom and to vote at parliamentary elections.[6]

Expenses of members of the House of Lords

Members of the House of Lords do not, as such, receive a salary. They are entitled to recover travel and certain other expenses incurred in connection with their parliamentary duties. Members, including those in receipt of a salary paid from public funds, ie Ministers, office-holders in the House of Lords and Lords of Appeal in Ordinary, may recover the cost of travelling from and to their permanent place of residence for the purpose of attending sittings of the House or meetings of committees (excluding judicial business). Subject to certain conditions, the cost of journeys made on parliamen-

---

1 Administration of Justice Act 1968, s 1. The original number was four. This was increased to six in 1913, to seven in 1929, and to nine in 1947 (Appellate Jurisdiction Acts 1876, ss 6 and 14; 1913, s 1; 1929, s 2; 1947, s 1). See p 66–67.
2 One month in the case of members of and candidates for the House of Commons, see p 30.
3 Peerage Act 1963.
4 LJ (1966–67), 263; Report by Committee for Privileges on the Petition of the Irish Peers (HL 53 (1966–67)).
5 SO No 75.
6 Peerage Act 1963, s 5.

tary duties elsewhere within the United Kingdom may also be recovered. In such cases the cost of public transport is reimbursed or a mileage allowance is paid for journeys made by car. Except for Ministers and certain office-holders, Lords are also entitled to recover, up to a specified maximum, the cost of overnight accommodation, subsistence and secretarial expenses certified by them as incurred for the purpose of their parliamentary duties at sittings of the House or its committees. Secretarial expenses may also be recovered for periods when the House does not sit. A disabled Lord may recover the additional expenses of attending the House incurred by reason of his disablement. The Chairman and Principal Deputy Chairman of Committees and members of the House in receipt of a salary under the Ministerial and other Salaries Act 1975 may recover secretarial expenses incurred by them on parliamentary duty within a specified annual maximum.[1]

The arrangements for the reimbursement of Lords' expenses are supervised by the Leave of Absence and Lords' Expenses Committee (see pp 168–169).

Salary of the Lord Chancellor as Speaker of the House. Since 1832 the Lord Chancellor has received part of his remuneration in the form of a salary as Speaker of the House. This salary is at present (1 July 1989) £12,810, the Lord Chancellor's total remuneration being £91,500.[2]

Salaries of the Chairman and the Principal Deputy Chairman of Committees. Salaries of £37,047 and £33,537 are payable to the Chairman and Principal Deputy Chairman of Committees respectively (1 July 1989).[3]

Salaries of the Leader of the Opposition and the Chief Opposition Whip. Salaries were first granted to the Leader of the Opposition and the Chief Opposition Whip in 1965. These salaries are at present (1 July 1989) £30,647 and £27,377 respectively.[4]

THE HOUSE OF COMMONS

Although knights and burgesses were not always summoned to early Parliaments, they were invariably summoned by the mid fourteenth century. By that period too the Lords and the Commons deliberated separately. It was usual for King, Lords and Commons to meet initially together; afterwards the Lords and the Commons deliberated in separate rooms; finally the Commons or their spokesmen rejoined the King and the Lords. The Commons used the Painted Chamber of the Palace of Westminster or the chapter house of Westminster Abbey for their separate deliberations. From the late fourteenth century they also met in the Abbey's refectory. They moved to

---

1 LJ (1945–46) 282; LJ (1965–57) 244; LJ (1960–61) 256; LJ (1964–65) 91; LJ (1969–70) 93–94; LJ (1971–72) 105; LJ (1974–75) 864; LJ (1979–80) 190, 647; LJ (1981–82) 347; LJ (1983–84) 85, 746–747; LJ (1985–86) 551; LJ (1987–88) 89, 576.
2 LJ (1831–32) 436; 1975 c 27, s 1(2); SI 1989/681.
3 Each receives in addition a London supplement of £1,222; LJ (1987–88) 255.
4 1965 c 11, s 2; 1975 c 27, Sch 2; SI 1988/2253.

St Stephen's Chapel in 1547 (see pp 163–164).[1] There were spokesmen for
the Commons from the thirteenth century but the spokesman who is first
known to have been chosen by the Commons and who is traditionally seen as
the first Speaker was Sir Peter de la Mare in 1376. His successor Sir Thomas
Hungerford was the first Speaker to be recorded on the Parliament Rolls. It
is not known whether early Speakers acted as presiding officers. The first
reference to a Clerk of the Commons, Robert de Melton, occurs in 1363.[2]

Member of Parliament. In the reign of Henry VIII the title 'Member of our
Parliament' was applied indifferently to the Members of either House of
Parliament, but since the Restoration the title of Member of Parliament has
been used as the designation of a Member of the House of Commons.[3] Until
1872 the ancient terms of knights, citizens, and burgesses, barons of the
cinque ports and burgesses of the universities, were used in the writs and
returns; but by the Parliamentary and Municipal Elections Act 1872 these
distinctions were discontinued and all are alike termed members in the writs
and returns.

History of Parliament Trust. There is in course of preparation under the
authority of the History of Parliament Trust a comprehensive history of the
membership of the House of Commons from 1386 to 1832. The Trust was
established in 1940 and since 1951 it has received a grant-in-aid.[4] Its members include (ex officio) the Lord Chairman of Committees, the Chairman of
Ways and Means, the Chief Secretary to the Treasury, the Clerk of the
Parliaments and the Clerk of the House of Commons, together with senior
Members of both Houses and others. Ten sections of the history are projected, to be prepared under the supervision of an editorial board of his-
torians.[5]

Representation in the House of Commons

Representation in the House of Commons is governed principally by the
Representation of the People Act 1983 and the Parliamentary Constituencies Act 1986 which consolidated the House of Commons (Redistribution of Seats) Acts 1949 to 1979. A brief description follows of the
legislation which preceded these Acts and of the previous history of representation in the House.

---

1 For a full account of the various meeting places of the Commons until their removal to St
   Stephen's Chapel in 1547, See Dasent, *Speakers*, 41. On the restoration of the Palace of
   Westminster after the fire, 16 October 1834, the Chambers allotted to the Houses of
   Parliament were first used by the Lords, 15 April 1847, LJ (1847) 123; by the Commons,
   30 May 1850, CJ (1850) 377. See also Sir Goronwy Edwards *The Second Century of the
   English Parliament* and Davies and Denton '*The English Parliament in the Middle Ages*'.
2 J S Roskell *Parliamentary Politics in Late Mediaeval England*; P Laundy *The Office of
   Speaker*.
3 State Papers, iii. 395; Gardiner's Commonwealth and Protectorate, i. 296, n 2. See, however,
   HL Deb (1916) 22, c 82.
4 HC Deb (1950–51) 484, c 1067.
5 The sections for 1558–1603, 1715–1754 and 1754–1790 have already been published by HM
   Stationery Office and the sections for 1509–1558, 1660–1690 and 1790–1820 have been
   published by Martin Secker and Warburg Ltd which has also reprinted the section for
   1754–1790.

Number of the Commons at different times. The number of members admitted to the House of Commons has varied considerably at different periods. In the early fifteenth century there were nominally over 250 members of the commons; there were two knights from 37 counties (Cheshire and Durham not being represented), two citizens or burgesses from each of 80 or so cities or boroughs which were by custom represented, and 14 members from the Cinque Ports. It is, however, impossible to say how many actually attended any Parliament. At the beginning of Henry VIII's reign there were about 300 seats available.[1] In that reign 27 members were added by statute for Wales[2] and four for the county and city of Chester,[3] and in Charles II's reign four for the county and city of Durham.[4] Between the reigns of Henry VIII and Charles II 180 new members were added by royal charter.[5] In 1673 Newark was the last constituency to be enfranchised in this way. There were then 513 members in England and Wales.[6]

After Union with Scotland and Ireland. Forty-five Members were assigned to Scotland, as her proportion of Members in the British Parliament, on the union of that kingdom with England; and one hundred to Ireland at the commencement of the nineteenth century, when her Parliament became incorporated with that of the United Kingdom. By these successive additions the number was increased to 658; and notwithstanding the changes effected in the distribution of the elective franchise by the Reform Acts in 1832, that number continued unaltered, except by the disfranchisement of certain cities and boroughs for corruption, until the year 1885, when the number of the House was raised to 670 by the operation of the Redistribution of Seats Act of that year. By the Representation of the People Act 1918 the number of Members was increased to 707, but the reduction of the number of Members for constituencies in Northern Ireland from 52 to 13 under the Government of Ireland Act 1920, and the cessation of representation of constituencies in Southern Ireland consequential on the establishment of the Irish Free State, reduced the number of members of the House of Commons to 615. As a result of the House of Commons (Redistribution of Seats) Act 1944, which made temporary provision for the subdivision of certain abnormally large constituencies (specified in the Second Schedule to the Act),[7] the number of Members was increased by 25 to 640. This number was reduced by the Representation of the People Act 1948, to 625, subject to variation by Order in Council on the recommendation of the Boundary Commissions; such Orders in Council were made under the authority of the House of Commons (Redistribution of Seats) Act 1949 and since 1986 under the Parliamentary Constituencies Act 1986 (see

---

1 See Davies and Denton *The English Parliament in the Middle Ages* p 117, and *History of Parliament 1509–1558.*
2 27 Hen 8, c 26.
3 34 Hen 8, c 13.
4 25 Cha 2, c 9.
5 Christian's Notes to Blackstone; 2 Hatsell 413.
6 *History of Parliament 1660–1690* p 104.
7 This partial measure of redistribution was recommended by the Speaker's Conference on Electoral Reform and Redistribution of Seats 1944, in their first report. (Letter from Mr Speaker to the Prime Minister, 24 May 1944; Cmd 6534.)

pp 24–26). Since the General Election of June 1983 the number of constituencies has been 650.[1]

Although under rule 1 of Schedule 2 of the Parliamentary Constituencies Act 1986 it is stated that the number of constituencies in Great Britain should not be substantially greater than or less than 613, there has been a steady increase in the number of seats since 1948. Other rules for the redistribution of seats set down in Schedule 2 of the 1986 Act make it extremely difficult for the Boundary Commissioners to create 613 seats with electorates of the same size. Rule 4, for example, states that, so far as is practicable, local authority boundaries should be respected, and rule 7 states that the Boundary Commissioners should take account of 'the inconveniences attendant on alterations of constituencies . . .' and of 'any local ties which would be broken by such alterations'. Accordingly the creation of new constituencies, because of the growth of population in some areas, has not been offset to the same extent by the reduction of seats where population has fallen.

Representation for England and Wales. From 1673 to 1832 there were 513 Members in England and Wales. Following the English Reform Act (the Representation of the People Act 1832) the number was reduced from 513 to 500. The number of knights of the shire was increased to 159. Many boroughs were disenfranchised while new boroughs were created; after the Act the two universities and the several cities and boroughs elected 341 Members.

Further changes were effected by the Representation of the People Act 1867, the Representation of the People (Scotland) Act 1868, and the Redistribution of Seats Act 1885. Under the Representation of the People Act 1918 England and Wales returned, for 58 parliamentary counties 254 Members; for 137 parliamentary boroughs 266 Members; and for twelve universities 8 Members; making a total number of 528 for England and Wales. This number was temporarily increased to 553 under the provisions of the House of Commons (Redistribution of Seats) Act 1944, but was reduced to 542, with provision for variation on the recommendation of the Boundary Commission, by the Representation of the People Act 1948, which abolished University representation and adjusted the boundaries of many constituencies. As a result of changes recommended by the Boundary Commission (pp 24–26), the number of constituencies since the General Election of June 1983 has been 561.[2]

Representation for Scotland. The number of Members for Scotland was increased by the Scottish Reform Act (the Representation of the People (Scotland) Act 1832) from 45 to 53, 30 of whom were commissioners of shires, and 23 commissioners of burghs, representing towns, burghs, or districts of small burghs. Further changes were effected by the Representation of the People (Scotland) Act 1868 and the Redistribution of Seats Act 1885. Under the Representation of the People Act 1918 Scotland returned for 21 parliamentary counties, 38 Members; for 13 parliamentary boroughs, 33 Members, and for 4 universities in 1 university constituency, 3 Members;

---

1 Following the Reports of the Boundary Commissions in 1982–83.
2 The number was increased to 561 by the Parliamentary Constituencies Orders for England and Wales (SI 1983/417 and 418).

making a total representation for Scotland of 74 Members. This representation was not affected by the House of Commons (Redistribution of Seats)
Act 1944, but the abolition of University representation effected by the
Representation of the People Act 1948 reduced the number to 71, with
provision for variation on the recommendation of the Boundary Commission. Since the General Election of June 1983 there have been 72
constituencies.

Representation for Ireland. By the Irish Reform Act (the Representation
of the People (Ireland) Act 1832) the number of Representatives for Ireland
in the British Parliament was increased from 100 to 105. The representation
of Ireland in the Parliament of the United Kingdom was reduced by the
Government of Ireland Act 1920, in the case of Southern Ireland constituencies to 33 Members, 4 being Members for boroughs, 26 being Members
for counties, and 3 being Members for universities, and in the case of
Northern Ireland to 13 Members, 4 being Members for boroughs, 8 for
counties, and 1 being returned by the Queen's University of Belfast.[1] This
reduction was not to take place before the dissolution of the parliament then
existing.[2] The Irish Free State (Agreement) Act 1922 provided (section 1
(4)) that after its passing no writ should be issued for the election of a
Member to serve in the House of Commons for a constituency in Ireland
other than a constituency in Northern Ireland, with the result that the
representation of Ireland was reduced to 13 Members, returned by constituencies in Northern Ireland. The temporary provisions of the House of
Commons (Redistribution of Seats) Act 1944 did not affect this representation, but the abolition of University representation effected by the Representation of the People Act 1948 reduced the number to 12. Under the
House of Commons (Redistribution of Seats) Act 1979, the Boundary
Commission for Northern Ireland were required, in framing their first
report after the passing of the Act, to divide the Province into not fewer than
16 nor more than 18 constituencies. Since the General Election of June 1983
there have been 17 constituencies.[3]

Financial status of the House of Commons

The statutory arrangements for the appointment and management of the
permanent staff of the Department of the House of Commons were reorgan-
ised as a result of the passing of the House of Commons (Administration)
Act 1978. The Act provided for the appointment of a House of Commons
Commission, including Members directly appointed by the House, whose
functions included that of employer of the permanent staff of the House.[4]
The Commission present their own Estimates to the House for the expenses
of the House Departments and for 'any other expenses incurred for the
service of the House of Commons'. Although many services, including those
of Her Majesty's Stationery Office (for printing and publication services)
and of the Department of the Environment (for building maintenance and

1 See s 19 and Sch V.
2 See s 73(1).
3 The former constituencies were still in force at the General Election in 1979, and their
 number was increased to 17 by the Parliamentary Constituencies (Northern Ireland) Order
 1982 (SI 1982/1838).
4 See pp 192–193.

repairs), continue to be provided on 'allied service' terms, the 1978 Act has provided the framework for the development of a substantial degree of financial autonomy for the House of Commons in the control of its own internal affairs.

Payment of members

Constituencies were liable from the thirteenth century for the expense of maintaining their Members during their attendance upon Parliament.[1] This liability continued into the sixteenth century and was referred to in the Act to establish constituencies in Wales in Henry VIII's reign,[2] but as early as the beginning of the seventeenth century it had ceased to be observed, save in a few isolated cases.

In the nineteenth century there was a movement for the payment of Members out of national funds. Motions in favour of the proposal were brought before the House of Commons on a number of occasions[3] and in 1895 a resolution in favour of the payment of a reasonable allowance to Members was agreed to.[4]

In 1911 the House decided that Members who were not in receipt of salaries as Ministers, officers of the House or officers of His Majesty's Household should be paid a salary of £400 a year.[5] Similar provision was made in subsequent sessions. Deductions were not made from Members' salaries when they were serving in the Armed Forces in the two World Wars.[6]

The payment to Members was held to be salary or income within the meaning of the Bankruptcy Acts.[7] An income payments order under the Insolvency Act 1986[8] may be made, requiring the whole or part of it to be paid to the trustee of the bankrupt's estate either directly or by the bankrupt.

A Member of Parliament is classified as an office-holder and therefore also as an 'employed earner', for the purpose of the Social Security Acts.[9]

Increase in payment of Members. The adequacy of the salary of £400 a year was called in question by a Select Committee as early as 1920,[10] but no action was taken until June 1937, when, after debate and division, the House resolved that the salary should be increased to £600 a year.[11] In 1946, following the report of a similar select committee, the salary was further increased to £1,000.[12] A sessional allowance of £2 per day on days when the

---

1 Prynne, 4th Register, 53, 495, 4 Co Inst 46. Hallam, Mid Ages, iii. 114, n. H Cam *Liberties and Communities* p 237.
2 26 Henry VIII, c 26.
3 Parl Deb (1830) 22, c 689; CJ (1839) 339; ibid (1888) 348; ibid (1892) 135; ibid (1893–94) 160.
4 CJ (1895) 108.
5 CJ (1911) 400, 406; Appropriation Act 1911, Sch B, Pt 7.
6 HC Deb (1914–15) 70, cc 1257–1258, 1701, 1745; ibid (1916) 81, c 1388; CJ (1916) 49. See also Revised Estimate, HC 75 (1916); HC Deb (1939–40) 35, c 212.
7 *Hollinshead v Hazelton* [1916] 1 AC 428.
8 1986, c 45, s 310.
9 1975, c 14, n 2(1)(a).
10 HC 255 (1920). See also CJ (1921) 173; HC Deb (1921) 142, c 1087; HC 110 (1921).
11 CJ (1936–37) 309; HC Deb (1936–37) 325, c 1049.
12 HC 93 (1945–46); CJ (1945–46) 275, 345. At the same time Ministerial Salaries Act 1946 authorized a salary of £500 a year to Members who, as Ministers of the Crown or as Leader of the Opposition, received salaries of less than £5,000 a year.

House sat (except Fridays) was introduced in Session 1953–54 in addition to the salary.[1] It was replaced by an annual allowance of £750 in 1957.[2] After the report of an extra-parliamentary committee the salary of Members was increased to £3,250 in 1964.[3] In 1970 the task of reviewing parliamentary remuneration was entrusted to the newly-established Review Body on Top Salaries.[4] Its recommendations were implemented with only minor modifications and from 1972 the salary was established at £4,500. Periodical increases brought it to £14,510 in 1982. In 1983 the House decided to set the levels of pay for the next five years, and then, from 1 January 1988, to link it to the civil service grade which earned £18,500 per annum in 1983, which was 89 per cent of the maximum point of Senior Principal (now Grade 6) civil servants.[5] The policy was confirmed in the next Parliament in July 1987.[6] From 1 January 1989 Members have been paid £24,107 per annum.

In addition to his salary a Member can claim subsistence allowances up to a specified maximum per year in respect of 'additional expenses necessarily incurred (by him) in staying overnight away from his only or main residence for the purpose of performing his parliamentary duties'.[7] Since 1 April 1989 the maximum limit for this allowance has been £9,468 per annum. Members sitting for inner London constituencies cannot claim this allowance but instead receive a fixed taxable supplement of £1,222 a year (at 1 April 1989) in recognition of the higher cost of living in London; and Members for outer London constituencies may opt to receive this supplement rather than claim under the subsistence allowance scheme.

An allowance to meet the costs of office expenses and secretarial and research assistance can also be claimed. It was introduced in October 1967.[8] In 1984 increases in the allowance were linked to increases in civil service senior personal secretaries' pay.[9] In 1986 the government's proposal that the allowance should be £13,211 was defeated and the House set it at £19,000 whilst maintaining the link to the rise in senior personal secretaries' pay.[10] On 1 April 1988 it was £22,588. Since March 1980 an allowance not exceeding 10 per cent of secretaries' actual pay and not exceeding 10 per cent of the office costs allowance may be paid to an approved pension scheme.

Members are subject to income tax on their total salary payments, but are entitled to claim a deduction for allowable expenses.[11]

Salaries of Members who are Officers of the House, Ministers of the Crown, Leader of the Opposition, Opposition Whips

Under the Ministerial and other Salaries Act 1975, Mr Speaker, Ministers of the Crown, the Leader of the Opposition and Opposition Whips receive a salary which was set down by the Act and which can be and has been

---

1 HC Deb (1953–54) 529, c 2347; CJ (1953–54) 289.
2 HC Deb (1956–57) 572, cc 1308–1310; CJ (1956–57) 247.
3 HC Deb (1963–64) 686, cc 1441–1444; Cmnd 2516.
4 Cmnd 4836; CJ (1971–72), 87–89.
5 CJ (1983–84) 77–78, 100–102.
6 Votes and Proceedings 21 July 1987.
7 CJ (1974) 312.
8 CJ (1969–70) 94.
9 CJ (1983–84) 714.
10 CJ (1985–86) 506.
11 HC Deb (1956–57) 573, c 230; ibid (1964–65) 704, cc 812–816.

amended by Order in Council following a resolution by both Houses or in the case of Mr Speaker by a resolution of the House of Commons. The salaries of the Chairman of Ways and Means and the Deputy Chairmen are voted annually in the estimates of the House of Commons. All the holders of the above posts receive in addition a salary as a Member of Parliament which is set at 67 per cent of a Grade 6 Civil Servant and which from 1 January 1989 was £18,148.[1]

Salary of Mr Speaker. An Act of 1790 first authorized the payment of a fixed salary 'for the better support of the Dignity of the Speaker of the House of Commons'.[2] The payment of £6000 laid down by the Act was reduced to £5000 in 1834.[3] No further change was made until 1965 when the salary was increased to £8500; and in 1972, following the report of the Review Body on Top Salaries (see above) the salary was further increased to £13,000 by s1(3) of the Ministerial and other Salaries Act 1972.[4] Since 1 January 1989 it has been £36,209 and his total salary including that which he receives as a Member of Parliament is therefore £54,357. To ensure the independence of Mr Speaker, his salary is a charge upon the Consolidated Fund and so not subject to annual approval by Parliament.[5] When he vacates his office he is usually created a peer and is granted a pension under Part II of the Parliamentary and other Pensions Act 1972,[6] and in any case he invariably relinquishes his membership of the House. Under the 1972 Act the widow of the Speaker is also entitled to a pension.[7]

Salaries of Chairman and Deputy Chairmen of Ways and Means. Salaries are payable to the Chairman and Deputy Chairmen of Ways and Means in respect of their offices. They are usually increased at the same time as those salaries determined under the Ministerial and other Salaries Act 1975. On 1 January 1989 they were £24,209 and £21,199 respectively. Their total salaries including that element received as a Member of Parliament were £40,798 and £37,788 respectively.

Salaries of Leader of Opposition and Opposition Whips. A salary was first granted to the Leader of the Opposition (see p 200) by the Ministers of the Crown Act 1937, and since 1 January 1989 has been £31,559, making a total salary, including that portion received as a Member of Parliament, of £49,207.[8] Since 1965 provision has been made for payment of a salary to the Chief Opposition Whip, and in 1972 this provision was extended to cover not more than two Assistant Opposition Whips.[9] The amounts of these salaries since 1 January 1989 have been currently £24,209 for the Chief Opposition Whip and £15,349 for the Assistant Opposition Whips making their total salaries £42,357 and £33,497.

---

1 See Votes and Proceedings 21 July 1987.
2 30 Geo III, c 10.
3 4 & 5 Will IV, c 70.
4 1965, c 11, s3; 1972, c 3, s1(3) (re-enacted as 1975, c 27, s1(3)).
5 House of Commons (Speaker) Act 1832 (2 & 3 Will IV, c 105, s 1).
6 1972, c 48.
7 1972, c 48, s 27.
8 1937, c 38, s5; 1975, c 27, Sch 2.
9 1965, c 11, s2; 1972, c 3, Sch 2; 1975, c 27, Sch 2.

Conditions of payment. The salary of a Member becomes payable when he takes the oath or makes the affirmation required by law,[1] and begins from the day following that on which the poll is held.[2] A Member who has not taken the oath within six months of the return of his writ to the Clerk of the Crown is not entitled to claim any salary prior to the date when he takes the oath.[3] When a Member dies or is appointed to an office of profit under the Crown, his salary ceases to be payable from the end of the day on which his death or appointment occurs. A Member who is made a Judge receives his salary up to, but not including, the date of his letters patent or warrant of appointment. The salary of a Member who is created a peer is payable up to and including the day on which his letters patent are granted. A Member who succeeds to a peerage receives his salary up to and including the day on which the previous holder of the title died. A Member suspended from the service of the House under the provisions of Standing Order No 43 (see p 397) does not forfeit his salary during the period of his suspension.

A person who is a Member at the time of a dissolution of Parliament continues to receive his salary until the end of the day of the poll in the consequent general election. A resettlement grant of up to 12 months' salary is payable to a person under the age of 65 who ceases to be a Member following a General Election.[4]

Travelling expenses of Members

Since 1924 Members have been entitled to first- or third- (now second-) class travel vouchers between London and their constituencies including steamship passages.[5] In 1935 air travel by certain approved airlines was allowed.[6] In 1969 travelling expenses were extended to cover travel by road by public transport, in 1971 to cover a Member's travel on parliamentary duties within his constituency[7] and since 1980 to cover his travel outside his constituency, but within the United Kingdom, on parliamentary business.[8] Provision is also made for up to 15 return journeys per year by a Member's spouse, or

---

1 HC Deb (1917–18) 90, c 1691. An exceptional course was taken in 1945, see HC Deb (1945–46) 413, c 276.
2 HC Deb (1958–59) 605, c 1569; ibid (1970–71) 803, c 335.
3 HC Deb (1924) 170, c 2556.
4 CJ (1971–72), 88–89.
5 Following the recommendations of the Select Committee on Members' Expenses, 1920 (HC 255 (1920); CJ (1921) 173, HC Deb (1921) 142, c 1087, HC 110 (1921); HC 56 (1924), HC Deb (1924) 172, c 663).
6 Subject to Members paying the excess over the first-class rail fare (HC Deb (1934–35) 304, c 748–749). From 1936 free first-class sleeping berth accommodation was added (HC Deb (1935–36) 315, c 1858) to these facilities. In November 1945 a resolution was passed to extend the free travel arrangements to cover flights by scheduled air services and to include journeys between a Member's home and his constituency and between his home and London (HC Deb (1945–46) 415, c 2477). In 1946 free railway season tickets were introduced for Members who travel from their homes to Westminster at least four times a week when the House is sitting (HC Deb (1945–46) 423, c 1235). The facilities were further extended in March 1953 to include travel between airport and air station in the coaches usually provided for those services (CJ (1952–53) 137), in July 1968 to include travel by chartered air services or private aeroplane 'provided that the cost to public funds is no greater than the cost of travel by public transport' (HC Deb (1967–68) 754, c 1175; ibid 769, c 1134).
7 HC Deb (1969–70) 793, c 1693; CJ (1971–72) 88; and between his constituency and the local or regional office of Government Departments etc.
8 HC Deb (1979–80) c 424.

children under 18, between London and the Member's home or constituency,[1] and up to 9 return journeys per year by a Member's staff, if such staff are paid by the Fees Office out of the Member's office costs allowance.[2]

On 18 May 1961 the House resolved to introduce, as an alternative to the other arrangements for travel, a car allowance not exceeding the corresponding first-class rail fare, based on the petrol consumption of private cars used by Members at their own expense for the normal authorized journeys. This basis of calculation was later replaced by a flat rate car allowance.[3] In 1984 it was decided that the allowance should be linked to the size of the car engine.[4] From 1 April 1988 the rates were: for the first 20,000 miles per year for engine capacity of 1300 cc or less 22.7p per mile: of more than 1300 cc and not more than 2300 cc 34.1p per mile: and of more than 2300 cc 53.5p per mile. Additional mileages over 20,000 per annum are paid at rates of 12.5p per mile, 16.1p per mile and 26.8p per mile respectively. Claims for payment of this allowance must be submitted within six months unless extenuating circumstances can be shown.[5]

The allowances for journeys between Westminster and a Member's constituency are tax free, but in certain circumstances the allowances for journeys between his home and Westminster or his home and his constituency are taxable. The application of the rules and practice governing the payment of Members' travelling expenses is determined by Mr Speaker on the advice of the House of Commons (Services) Committee (see p 657).

Members' Fund

The House of Commons Members' Fund Act 1939 provided for the making of grants to those who have been Members of the House and to their widows and children 'having regard to the financial circumstances of the persons to or in respect of whom the payments are made'. It created a fund by authorizing the deduction of twelve pounds per annum from the salaries of all Members of the House; and made provision for the appointment of trustees to administer the fund.[6] The House of Commons Members' Fund Act 1948, increased the annual payments to past Members and their widows, extended the benefits of the scheme to widowers and authorized grants to alleviate special cases of hardship. The benefits were again increased by resolutions of the House on 17 November 1955[7] , 7 March 1957[8] and 17 May 1961.[9]

The House of Commons Members' Fund and Parliamentary Pensions Act 1981 extended the scope of the Fund and enables payments to be made by

---

1 CJ (1970–71) 380; (1971–72) 88, etc.
2 CJ (1983–84) 79.
3 CJ (1960–61) 235; (1964–65) 88; Cmnd 2156, p 17; HC Deb (1964–65) 704, c 731; CJ (1974) 312, etc.
4 CJ (1983–84) 714–715.
5 CJ (1971–72) 89.
6 For the appointment of trustees, see CJ (1938–39) 482, HC Deb (1938–39) 353, c 1279.
7 CJ (1955–56) 129–30.
8 CJ (1956–57) 122.
9 To assist in the payment of the increased benefits the Exchequer made a grant of £10,000 a year to the Fund and, by a resolution of 18 July 1957, the amount deducted from the salaries of Members was increased to £18 a year. A resolution of 17 May 1961 empowered the Trustees to make increased payments to former Members 'having regard to length of service and need', and increased the deduction from salaries to £24 a year; and the Exchequer grant was increased to a sum not exceeding £22,000 a year, CJ (1956–57) 264; SI 1961/988; CJ (1960–61) 232.

the Trustees to ex-Members who have attained 65 years of age or who are infirm, provided that they have completed ten years' or more service and were not Members after 15 October 1964, and to their widows or widowers, subject to certain conditions. The Trustees may, in special circumstances, make payments where the period of service is less than ten years. The Act provides for an annual rate of payment of £1,000 to an ex-Member and £500 to the widow or widower of an ex-Member, but the House of Commons may from time to time vary the rates by resolution. To fund the extended benefits provided under the 1981 Act the Exchequer grant was increased to a maximum of £215,000 per annum (SI 1981/748).

Many of the functions of the Members' Fund were superseded by the introduction of the contributory pension scheme (see below); but the need to maintain payments in respect of Members who retired before its introduction has made it necessary for the Fund to remain in being.

Parliamentary Contributory Pension Fund

In 1954 a Select Committee on Members' expenses recommended that there should be a non-contributory scheme for Members' pensions to be awarded according to length of service without regard to need.[1] The trustees of the Members' Fund, to whom this recommendation was referred, proposed instead a self-supporting contributory pensions scheme.[2] No action was taken on these proposals until in 1965 a similar scheme was enacted in the Ministerial Salaries and Members' Pension Act 1965.[3] The scheme was radically revised and extended by the Parliamentary and other Pensions Act 1972 which was amended by the Parliamentary and other Pensions and Salaries Act 1976; the Parliamentary Pensions Act 1978;[4] the House of Commons Members' Fund and Parliamentary Pensions Act 1981; the Parliamentary Pensions etc Act 1984[5] and the Parliamentary and other Pensions Act 1987.[6] The latter is an enabling measure under which the detailed arrangements may be contained in subordinate legislation.

The Fund derives its income from its investments; from contributions from Members, Ministers and office-holders, other than those who have elected not to participate, and from Exchequer contributions. The contribution paid by participants is 9 per cent of salary; the Exchequer contribution is expressed as a multiple (determined from time to time by the Government Actuary) of the ordinary contributions paid by participants. (In the year 1988/89 the multiple was two.) The fund is managed by a board of Trustees appointed by the House from among its own Members, the Members appointed being the Trustees of the Members' Fund, together with two other Members.

As presently constituted, the Fund provides a pension to Members who leave the House at or after reaching the normal retirement age (65 years); the pension is calculated at the rate of one-fiftieth of relevant terminal salary for each year of service (one-sixtieth for service rendered before 20 July

---

1 HC 72 (1953–54).
2 HC 105 (1954–55).
3 Following the report of the Committee on the Remuneration of Ministers and Members of Parliament (Cmnd 2516). HC Deb (1964–65) 702, c 37.
4 1978, c 56.
5 1984, c 52.
6 1987, c 45.

1983). Provisions are made for the payment of pension, subject to certain conditions as to age and length of service, to a Member who leaves the House at a general election and who has not then attained the normal retirement age. A Member who retires on grounds of ill health may receive an immediate pension. A Member who, otherwise than on grounds of ill health, leaves the House before reaching the normal retirement age may, as an alternative to a deferred pension payable from retirement age, elect to transfer his accrued rights to any approved pension scheme he may subsequently enter.

The Fund also provides benefits for the widow(er)s and children of Members and ex-Members.

CHAPTER 2

Elections

THE ELECTORATE

The persons entitled to vote at a parliamentary election in any constituency are those resident there on the qualifying date for inclusion in the electoral register, who are not subject to any legal incapacity to vote, are either British subjects or citizens of the Republic of Ireland, are on the date of the poll of the age of eighteen years or over and are registered in the electoral register.[1] In Northern Ireland residence in Northern Ireland for the whole of a three-months period ending on the qualifying date is required.[2]

Persons reaching 18 years of age after the date on which the register comes into operation on 16 February each year but on or before the following 15 February are entitled to have their names included in the register with the date on which they will attain the age of 18; and they are entitled to vote at an election at which the day fixed for the poll is on or after that date.

Members of the forces, persons employed in the service of the Crown or by the British Council in posts outside the United Kingdom, and their spouses, if residing outside the United Kingdom with them, have a service qualification and may make a service declaration before the qualifying date for the register (10 October) which entitles them to be registered under the address contained in the declaration.[3]

Under the Representation of the People Act 1985 British citizens who are resident outside the United Kingdom can qualify as overseas electors, in respect of the constituency for which they were last registered, for a period of five years after they leave. Overseas electors must make a declaration similar to the service declaration.[4]

Any question as to a person's residence is determined in accordance with the general principles formerly applied under the Representation of the People Act 1918, and in particular regard is to be had to the purpose and other circumstances, as well as to the fact, of the person's presence at or absence from the address in question. But a person is not disqualified for registration through an absence of up to six months in the course of his employment, even if his house has been let in the expectation of his absence for that reason, or if it has been let for nine weeks or less for other reasons, provided he intends to resume residence before the end of that period.[5] There are special provisions applying to a person who is a merchant seaman: he may be registered as an elector in respect of an address at which he would

---

1 Representation of the People Act 1983, s 1(1).
2 Ibid s 1(2).
3 Ibid ss 14–17.
4 Representation of the People Act 1985, s 1.
5 Representation of the People Act 1983 s 5.

be residing but for his occupation, and a hostel or club for merchant seamen can be regarded as a place of residence for registration purposes.[1]

Disqualification of electors

Peers[2] other than Irish peers,[3] aliens, and persons under eighteen years of age, or of unsound mind, convicted persons during the period of their detention in a penal institution in pursuance of their sentence,[4] and persons found guilty of corrupt or illegal practices at elections, are all incapable of voting.

Constituencies

Under section 1 of the Parliamentary Constituencies Act 1986 it is provided that for the purpose of parliamentary elections there shall be the county and borough constituencies, each returning a single member, which are described in Orders in Council made under that Act. Under the same Act it is provided that for the purpose of the continuous review of the distribution of seats there shall be four permanent Boundary Commissions, one each for England, Scotland, Wales and Northern Ireland; each boundary commission is to keep under review the representation in the House of Commons of the part of the United Kingdom with which it is concerned, and is to report at intervals of not less than ten or more than fifteen years what changes, if any, it recommends in the division of its part of the United Kingdom into constituencies, in accordance with general principles set out in the Second Schedule of the 1986 Act, taking account of the inconveniences attendant on alterations of constituencies and of any local ties which would be broken by such alterations.[5] A Boundary Commission may also make recommendations at any time about any particular constituency or constituencies. The Speaker is nominated Chairman of each Commission and all other Members of the House of Commons are excluded from membership of a Commission.

---

1 Ibid s 6.
2 See sessional resolutions of the Commons, eg CJ (1967–68) 3; also debates in the Lords (Parl Deb (1852–53) 128, c 791; ibid (1857–58) 151, cc 926, 927); and opinion of the attorney general ibid (1882) 275, c 12. In 1872, the legal question of the right of peers to vote, or to be entered upon the register of voters, was conclusively decided by the Court of Common Pleas. The Earl of Beauchamp and the Marquess of Salisbury, having had their names struck off the register by the revising barrister, appealed to the Court of Common Pleas. The court unanimously decided that, in law, as derived from authorities and from the determination of election committees, as well as by resolutions of the House of Commons, peers had no right to vote; and the appeal was accordingly dismissed with costs, 15 November 1872, 8 LRCP 245. This decision was followed in the case of a peer who claimed a right to vote at an election of a Member for the University of Cambridge, *Marquis of Bristol v Beck* (1907) 96 LT 55, 71 JP 99, 23 TLR 224. See also the Report of the Committee of Privileges in the case of the Earl of Roden, who before his succession to the title, had been placed on the parliamentary register for the South Down division of County Down, and voted at an election in that division after succeeding to the title, as his name remained on the register, HC 153 (1911). A Government spokesman said in the House of Lords on 29 June 1983: 'The Question of whether Lords Spiritual can vote at parliamentary elections has never been expressly considered by the courts'. However, bishops do not by tradition vote.
3 S 5 of the Peerage Act 1963.
4 Representation of the People Act 1983, s 3.
5 Sch 2 of the Parliamentary Constituencies Act 1986.

The Parliamentary Constituencies Act 1986 consolidated the House of Commons (Redistribution of Seats) Acts 1949 to 1979. The 1949 Act had substantially re-enacted the provisions for regular re-examination of constituency boundaries originally enacted under the House of Commons (Redistribution of Seats) Act 1944. Formerly redistribution of seats had been to a large extent consequential upon revision of the franchise, and Boundary Commissions had been appointed ad hoc, and, on the completion of their work, had ceased to exist. But under the 1944 Act, provision was made for the first time for regular re-examination of constituency boundaries, unconnected with any extension of the franchise, and merely to take account of the movement of population.

When a Boundary Commission makes a report recommending changes in the boundaries of constituencies, the Secretary of State for the Home Department, the Secretary of State for Scotland or the Secretary of State for Northern Ireland must lay before Parliament a draft of an Order in Council for giving effect to the recommendations with or without modification; where the recommendations are modified a statement of the reasons for the modifications must be laid at the same time. If the motion to approve the draft is negatived or withdrawn in either House the Secretary of State may lay an amended draft before Parliament. The Order in Council has no effect until after the dissolution of the Parliament which approved the draft.[1]

The initial comprehensive recommendations of the Boundary Commissions were the basis of the boundaries enacted by the Representation of the People Act 1948, and were given statutory form following a recommendation of the Speaker's Conference on Electoral Reform and Redistribution of 1944 that the comprehensive recommendations should be the subject of a Bill and not of an Order in Council.

The first periodical reviews of the Boundary Commissions were completed in 1954 and the recommendations in the reports of the Commissions which were laid before Parliament in November 1954 were, following the approval of each House of Parliament, implemented by Order in Council.

Following the presentation to Parliament of the second periodical reports of the Boundary Commissions in June 1969, a Bill (the House of Commons (Redistribution of Seats) (No 2) Bill) was introduced into the House of Commons whose purpose was to suspend the normal procedure for the alteration of constituencies 'pending consideration of proposals for local government reorganization in the different parts of the United Kingdom'. Considerable amendments were made to the Bill in the House of Lords, and no agreement between the Houses was reached before the end of the session. In the following session draft Orders in Council to give effect to the reports were laid before Parliament but the House of Commons agreed to resolutions that they be not approved.[2] The same draft orders were approved on 28 October 1970, in the next Parliament. Draft Orders in Council to give effect to the third periodical reports of the Boundary Commissions were approved in 1983 before the General Election of that year.[3]

---

1 Parliamentary Constituencies Act 1986, s 4.
2 CJ (1969–70) 30.
3 CJ (1982–83) 189, 209, 217 and 267.

In December 1954 two attempts were made to obtain the intervention of the Courts in the procedure for obtaining the approval of Her Majesty in Council to draft Orders under the House of Commons (Redistribution of Seats) Act 1949. In the first instance, which concerned a draft Order in Council which had been laid before Parliament, but not yet approved by either House, the plaintiffs sought an order enjoining the Boundary Commissioners concerned to inform the Home Secretary that their report was a nullity because they had not observed the rules for redistributing seats contained in Schedule 2 of the Act. The order was refused on the ground that Parliament, not the courts, was the judge of whether a mistake had been made in the application of the rules.[1]

The second application to the Courts was made in respect of a draft Order in Council which had been approved by both Houses, but had not yet been submitted to Her Majesty by the Home Secretary. An interim injunction was requested restraining the Home Secretary from so submitting the order, as it was claimed that it was not an order proper to be submitted in accordance with the Act, being based on recommendations made as a result of the Commission having misdirected themselves in the application of the rules. An interim injunction was granted but was discharged on appeal, the Court of Appeal holding that wide discretion was given by the Act to the Commissioners in applying the rules, and that they had not in fact departed from the rules in making their recommendations. The Act did not in any event contemplate that the Courts should be competent to determine whether a particular line which had commended itself to the Commissioners was one which the Court thought best.[2]

In January 1983 the Court of Appeal dismissed two appeals against the refusal of the Divisional Court to prohibit the submission of the Commission's report to the Home Secretary. In the first case, it was contended that the Commission had misconstrued their statutory duties, with consequential disproportionate variations in the size of new constituencies. But the court was not satisfied that a sufficient case had been made and declared that the application had failed on merits. In the second case, it was alleged that the Commission had not dissociated themselves from an error made in the course of a local inquiry. The Court found no grounds for requiring the Commission to reconsider the matter.[3]

It is provided in the Parliamentary Constituencies Act 1986, that the validity of any Order in Council purporting to be made under the Act shall not be called in question in any legal proceedings whatsoever.[4]

Registration of electors

The Representation of the People Act 1983 provides that registers of parliamentary electors shall be prepared once a year, instead of twice a year as formerly.[5] The same Act provides that the qualifying date is 10 October for Great Britain and 15 September for Northern Ireland, for inclusion in the register to be published not later than 15 February in the following year, and

---

1 *Hammersmith Corpn and others v The Boundary Commission for England* (1954) Times, 15 December.
2 *Harper v Secretary of State for the Home Department* [1955] Ch 238.
3 TLR 26 January 1983.
4 S 4(7).
5 S 13(1).

to be used for any election at which the date of the poll falls within the period of twelve months beginning with 16 February.

All persons who claim to vote at a parliamentary election must be registered before voting.[1] At a general election a person is not entitled to vote in more than one constituency, or more than once in the same constituency at any parliamentary election.[2]

Registration officers

In England and Wales the council of every district and London borough is required to appoint one of its officers to be registration officer, responsible for the preparation and publication of the electoral register for any constituency or part of a constituency coterminous with or contained in the district or borough. In Scotland the corresponding appointment is made by the council of every region and islands area, who may select an officer of the council for an adjoining region or islands area or an officer appointed by a combination of such councils. In Northern Ireland the duties of registration officer for the United Kingdom parliamentary constituencies are performed by the Chief Electoral Officer.[3] Appeal on any decision of the registration officer on any claim for registration or objection to a person's registration lies to a county court, and thence on a point of law to the Court of Appeal, whose decision is final. In Scotland the sheriff court is substituted for the county court, and the court of three judges of the Court of Session for the Court of Appeal.[4]

Postal and proxy voting

An elector votes in person unless he is entitled to an absent vote at the election.[5] An elector is entitled to vote by post or by proxy at an election if he is shown in the absent voters list for the election. A person is eligible for an absent vote in the election for an indefinite period for the following principal reasons:

(a) if he is or will be registered as a service voter;
(b) if he cannot reasonably be expected to go in person to the polling station allotted to him or to vote unaided there by reason of blindness or other physical incapacity;
(c) if he cannot reasonably be expected to go there by reason of the general nature of his occupation etc;
(d) if he is or will be registered as overseas elector.[6]

An elector is eligible for an absent vote at a particular election if the registration officer is satisfied that he cannot reasonably be expected to vote

---

1 Representation of the People Act 1983, s 1(3).
2 Ibid s 1(4).
3 Ibid s 8.
4 Ibid ss 56 and 57.
5 Representation of the People Act 1985, s 5; there is an exception: if entitled to vote by proxy, a person applies for a ballot paper from the appropriate polling station for the purpose of voting there; before a ballot paper has been issued for him to vote by proxy, he may vote in person.
6 Representation of the People Act 1985, s 6(2).

in person at the polling station alloted to him.[1] Holidaymakers were the main beneficiaries of this change introduced by the 1985 Act. A person applying to vote by post must provide an address in the United Kingdom as the address to which his ballot paper is to be sent.[2]

The Representation of the People Act 1985 recites the duties of the registration officer to allow applications to be treated as an absent voter and to keep a record of absent voters and of those for whom proxies have been appointed (as well as of the names and addresses of the persons so appointed) and to determine claims and objections.[3] The appeal against his decision is the same as that in connection with registration of voters (see above). Copies of the register of electors are deposited in the British Library.

The holding of elections

Elections of Members of the House of Commons are held by returning officers in obedience to the Queen's writ out of Chancery. The statutory provisions which determine who are the returning officers for England and Wales, for Scotland and for Northern Ireland are to be found in sections 24 to 26 of the Representation of the People Act 1983.

The time-table for elections is contained in Schedule 1 to the Representation of the People Act 1983 as amended by the Representation of the People Act 1985. At a general election all polls must be held on one day, namely the eleventh day after the last day for delivery of nomination papers. The last day for receiving nominations should be the same in all constituencies, namely, the sixth day after the date of the proclamation summoning the new parliament.

For a by-election the returning officer must give notice of the election not later than four in the afternoon on the second day after that on which the writ is received. Nomination papers are delivered (between 10 am and 4 pm) on any day after the date of publication of the notice of election until a day fixed by the returning officer which must be not earlier than the third day after the date of publication of the notice of election nor later than the seventh day after that on which the writ is received.

In the case of all by-elections the poll takes place on such day as the returning officer may appoint, not being earlier than the ninth nor later than the eleventh day after the last day for delivery of nomination papers.

In reckoning time for all election proceedings, Saturdays, Sundays, Christmas Eve, Christmas Day, Maundy Thursday, Good Friday and other Bank Holidays, and days appointed for public thanksgiving or mourning are to be disregarded.

In the event of the death of a candidate after the publication of the statement of persons nominated as candidates and before the result of the election is declared, the returning officer countermands the notice of the poll or, if polling has begun, directs that it be abandoned; thereafter proceedings start afresh as if the writ had been received 28 days after the day on which proof was given to the returning officer of the death.[4]

Election campaigns

The law on election campaigns is comprehensively set out in Part II of the Representation of the People Act 1983 as amended by the Representation of the People Act 1985.

---

1 Ibid s 7.
2 Ibid ss 6 and 7.
3 Ibid ss 6–9.
4 Representation of the People Act 1983, Sch 1, r 60.

The maximum expense which may be incurred by a candidate or his agent is £3,370 plus 3·8p for every entry in the electoral register in a county constituency and £3,370 plus 2·9p for every entry in a borough constituency.[1]

The personal expenses of the candidate are not taken into account in calculating the maximum. Shortly after a new Parliament is elected, an address is presented to the Sovereign for a Return showing the expenses of each candidate at the General Election, together with the number of votes polled by each candidate, the number of polling districts and stations, the number of electors and the number of persons entitled to vote by post.[2] The Commons also pass a sessional resolution regarding bribery at elections.[3] On 10 December 1779 the Commons resolved that it was 'highly criminal in any Minister or Ministers, or other servants under the Crown of Great Britain, directly or indirectly to use the powers of office in the election of representatives to serve in Parliament, etc.'[4] For the detailed provisions of the law and practice reference may be made to the statutes themselves or to text-books.[5]

NEW WRITS

Whenever vacancies occur in the House of Commons from any legal cause, after the original issue of writs for a new Parliament by the Crown, writs are issued out of Chancery by a warrant from the Speaker, which he issues, when the House is sitting, upon the order of the House of Commons. The causes of vacancy are the death of Members or their succession to a peerage, the acceptance of a disqualifying office, the elevation of Members to the peerage, bankruptcy, mental illness, the establishment of any other legal disqualification for sitting and voting in the House of Commons, and the determination of election judges that elections or returns are void. The various disqualifications for membership of the House of Commons are described in greater detail in the following chapter.

Vacancies during a session

When the House is sitting, and the death of a Member, or other cause of vacancy, is known, Mr Speaker may be ordered by the House, upon a motion made by any Member, to issue his warrant to the Clerk of the Crown for a new writ for the place represented by the Member whose seat is thus vacated.

A new writ is moved as a matter of privilege, without notice (see p 276).

It was resolved on 5 April 1848 'that in all cases where the seat of any Member has been declared void on the grounds of bribery or treating, no

---

1 Representation of the People (Variation of Limit of Candidates Expenses) Order 1987.
2 Eg HC 374 (1979–80).
3 Eg CJ (1985–86) 3.
4 CJ (1778–80) 507.
5 Parker's *Conduct of Parliamentary Elections*, ed R J Clayton, Assistant Legal Adviser, Home Office.

motion for the issue of a new writ shall be made without previous notice being given in the votes.'[1] When such notice was dropped it was required to be renewed like the other dropped notices.[2] In 1853 and 1854 it was ordered that no such motion should be made without seven days' previous notice in the votes.[3] This required period of notice was reduced to two days in resolutions passed periodically between 1857 and 1911.[4] No such resolution has been passed since 1911 but notice has been given even in the absence of a resolution enjoining it.[5] Such notices are appointed for consideration before the orders of the day and notices of motions.

Period for presenting petitions

Where a vacancy has occurred prior to, or immediately after, the first meeting of a new Parliament, the writ will not be issued until the time for presenting election petitions has expired.[6] Nor will a writ be issued if the seat which has been vacated be claimed on behalf of another candidate. In such cases it has been ruled that the writ should be withheld until after the trial of the claim[7] or until the petition has been withdrawn.[8] Where a void election only is alleged the new writ may be issued at any time after the vacancy occurs.[9]

Vacancy by peerage

Peer by descent. If a Member succeeds to a peerage he has one month under the Peerage Act 1963 in which to lodge a disclaimer, if he so wishes (section 2 (1)). (In the case of candidates for election succeeding to a peerage between the issue of a writ for the election and polling day the period is one month after the election (section 2 (2)). If no disclaimer has been lodged when that period expires, or if the Member applies for a writ of summons to the House of Lords before it expires, his seat thereupon becomes vacant and a motion for a new writ may be made (see also pp 41–43).

A select committee appointed in 1894 to inquire into the vacating of seats, reported that the House usually waited for proof of succession to a peerage by one of its Members, such proof being furnished by the issue of the writ of summons, before it agreed to the motion for a new writ;[10] but that if there was any delay in this matter the House would, if it thought fit, inquire into the fact of the Member's succession and act on such evidence as it thought

1 CJ (1847–48) 432.
2 Parl Deb (1847–48) 99, c 1289.
3 CJ (1852–53) 315; ibid (1854) 388.
4 CJ (1857) 283; ibid (1875) 23; ibid (1880) 213; ibid (1882) 20; ibid (1886) 149; ibid (1893–94) 14; ibid (1901) 15; ibid (1906) 226; ibid (1910) 161; ibid (1911) 49. See also debate on the issue of new writs, 31 January 1893, Parl Deb (1893–94) 8, c 62.
5 One clear day's notice was given in 1907 and 1924, CJ (1907) 14, Parl Deb (1907) 169, c 317; CJ (1924) 202. But see also CJ (1923) 155.
6 For interpretation of this rule, see CJ (1922) 356; ibid (1924) 17; HC Deb (1950) 472, c 1721–30.
7 Athlone Election, 1859.
8 Durham Election (Mr Grainger) CJ (1852–53) 161; Louth Election (Mr Chichester Fortescue) 1866.
9 Southampton and Carlow writs, 29 December 1852. See also Parl Deb (1859) 154, cc 450, 454; 155, c 865; Chester Writ, 3 May 1880, CJ (1880) 125.
10 It is still normal for the motion to refer to the former Member as having been 'called up to the House of Peers'.

sufficient;[1] and it has been stated by the Committee of Privileges that, in their opinion, it is the law that the fact of succession to a peerage disqualifies from membership of the House of Commons and this disqualification does not depend on receipt of a writ of summons.[2]

Peer by creation. If a Member be created a peer, his seat is not vacated until the letters patent conferring the dignity have passed the great seal.[3] When it is advisable to issue the writ without delay in the case of a Member created a peer, the Member accepts the Chiltern Hundreds before his patent is made out[4] (p 50).

Supersedeas to writs

If doubts should arise concerning the fact of the vacancy, the order for a new writ should be deferred until the House may be in possession of more certain information; and if, after the issue of a writ, it should be discovered that the House had acted upon false intelligence, the Speaker will be ordered to issue a warrant for a supersedeas to the writ.

Thus on 29 April 1765, a new writ was ordered for Devizes, in the room of Mr Willey, deceased. On 30 April it was doubted whether he was dead, and the messenger of the great seal was ordered to forbear delivering the writ until further directions. Mr Willey proved to be alive, and on 6 May a supersedeas to the writ was ordered to be made out.[5] In other cases, when the House has been misinformed, or a writ has been issued through inadvertence, or prematurely, the error has been corrected by ordering the Speaker to issue his warrant to the Clerk of the Crown to make out a supersedeas to the writ.[6]

Issue of warrants by the Speaker during adjournment or recess

When vacancies occur by death, by elevation to the peerage, or by the acceptance of office, the law provides for the issue of writs during a recess, due to a prorogation or adjournment, without the immediate authority of the House, in order that a representative may be chosen without loss of time by the place which is deprived of its Member.

---

1 HC 272 (1895). See also case of the Earl of Selborne CJ (1895) 199, 205, 223; Parl Deb (1895) 33, c 1058; HC 302 (1895).
2 HC 142 (1960–61), which refers to details of earlier cases. The House took note of the fact that on succession to a viscountcy on 17 November 1960 a Member had ceased to be a Member of the House and agreed with the Committee of Privileges in their report (CJ (1960–61) 182). A writ was then issued 'in the room of Mr Wedgwood Benn, who, by Resolution of this House on 13 April 1961, ceased to be a Member' (CJ (1960–61) 188; but see HC Deb (1960–61) 638, c 939). Mr Benn stood and was declared elected at the subsequent by-election, but a petition was brought before the Election Court and the seat was awarded to the other candidate (CJ (1960–61) 324, [1961] WLR 599).
3 Sir H Vivian, Parl Deb (1893–94) 13, c 332, 540.
4 CJ (1880) 328; ibid (1907) 308; ibid (1908) 47, 160, 238, 292. As to the grant of the Chiltern Hundreds or Manor of Northstead to a Member, who has succeeded to a peerage, see CJ (1895) 218; ibid (1911) 179; ibid (1912–13) 395, 495, 533; but see also Reports of Select Committees on House of Commons (Vacating of Seats) HC 278 (1894) and 272 (1895).
5 See 2 Hatsell 80 n, 16 Parl Hist 95, CJ (1765–66) 391, 404; see also cases of the city of Gloucester, 19 December 1702, and of Mr Vansittart, supposed to have been lost at sea, 17 Parl Hist 322; CJ (1770–72) 546.
6 CJ (1809) 48; ibid (1826) 223; ibid (1830–31) 134, 182; ibid (1851) 12 (Dungarvan writ); CJ (1880) 280, 286; Parl Deb (1880) 253, c 1918.

Death or peerage. By the Recess Elections Act 1975, on the receipt of a certificate, under the hands of two Members, that any Member has died, or has become a peer, either during the recess or previously thereto, the Speaker is required to give notice in the London Gazette; and after six days from the insertion of such notice,[1] to issue his warrant to the Clerk of the Crown to make out a new writ. The Speaker may not issue his warrant during the recess unless the return of the late Member has been brought into the office of the Clerk of the Crown fifteen days before the end of the last sitting of the House; nor unless he has received the certificate of vacancy so long before the next meeting of the House for despatch of business, that the writ can be issued before the day of meeting.[2] He may not issue a warrant in respect of any seat that has been vacated by a Member against whose election or return a petition was pending at the last prorogation or adjournment.

Acceptance of office. Under the same Act the Speaker is required, on the receipt of a certificate from two Members, together with a copy of the Gazette containing the appointment, and a notification from the Member himself, to issue his warrant for a new writ, during a recess, in the room of any Member who, since the adjournment or prorogation, has accepted any office whereby he has, either by the express provision of any Act of Parliament or by any previous determination of the House of Commons, vacated his seat (see p 47). These provisions do not apply in the case of Members who have accepted the Chiltern Hundreds or the Manor of Northstead (see also p 51).

Bankruptcy. By the Recess Elections Act 1975, similar powers are given to the Speaker in the event of a seat having become vacant by the bankruptcy of a Member, upon the issue of the certificate of the court, stating that the disqualification inflicted by section 427 of the Insolvency Act 1986 had not been removed (see p 43).

Mental illness. A new writ for the election of a Member to fill a seat which has become vacant under the procedure prescribed by the Mental Health Act 1983 (see p 41), could not apparently be issued during a recess.

Appointment of members to issue writs

At the beginning of each Parliament, pursuant to the Recess Elections Act 1975, the Speaker is required to appoint a certain number of Members, not exceeding seven and not fewer than three, to exercise the powers of the Speaker in reference to the issue of writs during a recess at any time when there is no Speaker or the Speaker is out of the United Kingdom. This appointment stands good for the entire Parliament, unless the number should be reduced to less than three; in which case the Speaker is required to appoint one or more further Members.[3] Any such appointment is ordered to

---

1 In the calculation of the six days, the day on which the notice appeared in the Gazette, and any intervening Sunday, are reckoned; ie upon notice in a Tuesday's Gazette, the writ is issued on the following Monday.
2 That is to say, the six days' provision (see note (5)) must have been complied with.
3 The Recess Elections Act 1975, s 4.

be entered in the Journals,[1] and published in the London Gazette; and the instrument is to be preserved by the Clerk of the House, and a duplicate by the Clerk of the Crown. Any one of the Members so appointed may exercise the Speaker's power; if the publisher of the Gazette receives similar notices from more than one of them, only that first received is entered in the Gazette.

Manner of issue of writs

For any place in Great Britain, the Speaker's warrant is directed to the Clerk of the Crown in Chancery: and for any place in Northern Ireland, to the Clerk of the Crown in Northern Ireland. On the receipt of the Speaker's warrant, the writ is issued by the Clerk of the Crown, and transmitted in pursuance of the provisions of the Representation of the People Act 1983.[2] Neglect or delay in the delivery of the writ, or any other violation of the Act, is an offence; and in the event of any complaint being made the House will also inquire into the circumstances.[3]

RETURN OF WRITS

Correction of error in return

If any error should appear in the return to a writ, such as a mistake in the name of the Member returned,[4] or in the date of the return,[5] or in the description of the constituency,[6] evidence is given of the nature of the error, either by a Member of the House, or by some other person who was present at the election or is otherwise able to afford information; and the Clerk of the Crown is ordered to attend and amend the return.

Failure to make return to writ

If no return be made to a writ in due course, the Clerk of the Crown is ordered to attend and explain the omission; when, if it should appear that the returning officer, or any other person, has been concerned in the delay he will be summoned to attend the House; and such other proceedings will be adopted as the House may think fit.[7]

In the course of the general election of December 1910, the writ for the borough of Portsmouth was mislaid by the returning officer, so that he was

---

1 Eg CJ (1979–80) 154.
2 Sch 1, Pt II, rr 3 and 4. Parliamentary Writs Order 1983.
3 Glasgow writ, 1837, CJ (1837–38) 410, 418. See also CJ (1840) 122, 127.
4 Newport (Hants) 1831, Mr Hope Vere, CJ (1831) 578; Kirkcaldy return 1875, Sir George Campbell, ibid (1875) 165; Perth county return, 1878, Colonel Moray, ibid (1878) 53; Poole, ibid (1884) 175; Mid Antrim, ibid (1886) 8; Longford, ibid (1887) 54; Birmingham, ibid (1889) 149; Kirkcaldy, ibid (1892) 504; Monaghan (north and south divisions), ibid (1895) 348; Buckingham (northern division), ibid (1911) 6. In the last case the Member himself directed the attention of the House to the error.
5 Carlow county, 1841, 'November' being inserted instead of 'December', CJ (1841) 3.
6 Northampton county, 1846, CJ (1846) 207; Worcester county (eastern division), 1859, CJ (1859) 74; Parl Deb (1859) 152, c 855.
7 Waterford writ, 1806, CJ (1806) 169, 175; Parl Deb (1806) 6, cc 536, 562, 751; Great Grimsby, 1831, CJ (1831) 758, 762, etc; Parl Deb (1831) 6, cc 95, 159, 294, 460.

unable to endorse the writ with the names of the Members who had been returned. The returning officer made a statutory declaration to this effect and certified the names of the Members returned. This declaration was sent by the Clerk of the Crown to the Speaker, who informed the House of its contents. An instruction was given by the House to the Clerk of the Crown to receive the names mentioned in the returning officer's statutory declaration as if they had been endorsed on the writ and to amend his certificate to the House (ie, the Return Book, see p 231) accordingly.[1]

After the general election of 1955 the Election Writ and return for Knutsford were not acted upon by the Clerk of the Crown, as, not having been received by registered post, they were not identified until some time later. Before the Member for Knutsford was sworn, the Speaker read to the House a statutory declaration by the acting Returning Officer giving the name which had been endorsed on the writ, and the Clerk of the Crown was ordered to attend the House and amend his certificate accordingly.[2]

Members returned for two places

At the commencement of each session, the House agrees to resolutions dealing with the case of Members who are returned for two or more places in any part of the United Kingdom.[3] This order regulates the manner of choosing for which place a Member will sit when he has been returned for more than one, and his withdrawal from the House, if debate arises upon the matter of his election (see p 139–140). When the time limited for presenting petitions to the court against his return has expired, and no petition has been presented, he is required to make his election within a week, in order that his constituents may no longer be deprived of a representative.[4] This election may either be made by the Member in his place[5] or by a letter addressed to the Speaker.[6]

When a petition has been presented against his return for one place only, he cannot elect to serve for either.[7] He cannot abandon the seat petitioned against, which may be proved to belong of right to another, and thus render void an election which may turn out to have been good in favour of some other candidate; neither can he abandon the other seat; because if it should be proved that he is only entitled to sit for one, he has no election to make, and cannot give up a seat without having incurred some legal disqualification, such as the acceptance of office, or bankruptcy.[8]

Double returns

Where the votes are equal a returning officer, in accordance with section 23 of the Representation of the People Act 1983 and rule 49 of the Parliamen-

---

1 CJ (1911) 6. See also HC Deb (1955–56) 542, cc 36–38, 1039–1042.
2 CJ (1955–56) 13.
3 Eg CJ (1985–86) 3.
4 CJ (1847–48) 99, 100.
5 Mr O'Connell, 1842, CJ (1842) 302; Mr Gathorne Hardy, 1866, ibid (1866) 104; ibid (1886) 28; ibid (1887) 4; ibid (1906) 6.
6 CJ (1847–48) 99; ibid (1874) 12; ibid (1880) 128; ibid (1886) 9, 26, 318; ibid (1887) 5; ibid (1892) 413; ibid (1895) 341; ibid (1896) 4; ibid (1910) 6.
7 Case of Mr O'Connell, 1841, CJ (1841) 564; Parl Deb (1841) 59, c 503; Mr Sexton, 1886, ibid (1886) 308, c 168.
8 At the general election of December 1910, Mr Hazelton was returned for North Galway and North Louth. As a Petition was presented against his return for the latter place, he did not make any election. As a result of the Petition his election for North Louth was declared to be void, CJ (1911) 51, 64.

tary Elections Rules in Schedule 1 to that Act, must forthwith decide between the candidates concerned by lot. The candidate on whom the lot falls is then considered to have received an additional vote.[1]

By an order of the House passed at the beginning of every session, all Members returned upon double returns must withdraw until their returns are determined, but it is difficult to see how such a return could now be made.

TRIAL OF CONTROVERTED ELECTIONS

Procedure under the Representation of the People Act 1983

By Part III of the Representation of the People Act 1983, the trial of controverted elections is confided to judges selected from the judiciary in the appropriate part of the United Kingdom. Provision is made in each case for constituting a rota from whom these judges are selected.[2] Petitions complaining of irregular elections and returns or of corrupt or illegal practices are presented to the Queen's Bench Division of the High Court of Justice, or, in the case of elections in Scotland or Northern Ireland, to the Court of Session and the High Court of Justice in Northern Ireland respectively, instead of to the House of Commons as formerly, and are tried by two judges of those courts within the county or borough concerned. Although a shorthand writer of the House must be present to take notes of the evidence (see p 178), the House has no cognizance of these proceedings until their determination, when the judges certify their determination, in writing, to the Speaker,[3] which is final to all intents and purposes.[4] Since the trial is not a proceeding of the House, an order of the House is not required to enable the shorthand writer who has attended such a trial to give evidence thereon elsewhere.[5] The judges are to make a report in any case where a charge has been made in the petition of corrupt and illegal practice having been committed at an election; and they may also make a special report on any matter arising which they think should be submitted to the House.[6] Provision is also made for the trial of a special case, when required, by the court itself, which

---

1 Formerly, there was no statutory provision for the contingency of an equality of votes when the returning officer himself was not on the register, or where, being on the register, he did not desire to give a casting vote. In that case a double return had to be made. A double return was made by endorsing two certificates on the writ. CJ (1866) 436, 486; *Rogers on Elections* (1928 edn) vol II, p 112. For cases see *Rogers* pp 112–113; HC 256 (1847–48) p 3; CJ (1852–53) 70, 429, 432; see also p 36.

2 Cf, as regards England, the Supreme Court of Judicature (Consolidation) Act 1925, s 67 (1), as regards Scotland, the Parliamentary Elections Act 1868, s 58 (6), and as regards Northern Ireland, the Parliamentary Elections Act 1868, s 11 (2), and the Supreme Court of Judicature (Ireland) Act 1877, s 43.

3 For recent cases see CJ (1955–56) 97 and 98, (1959–60) 193, (1960–61) 324.

4 On 1 June 1874, Mr O'Donnell (lately Member for Galway) appeared at the bar and claimed to make a statement before the certificate of the judge, by which he was unseated, was read; but the Speaker informed him that it appeared from the judge's certificate that he was disqualified from sitting, and that he therefore was not entitled to be heard. CJ (1874) 184.

5 Private ruling, 7 February 1873.

6 Representation of the People Act 1983, s 144(4)–(6). For an example of a report relating to allegations of corrupt or illegal practices see CJ (1964–65) 114 and for an example of a report of the Election Court after 1983 see CJ (1983–84) 321. For special reports presented since the Act of 1868 see CJ (1872) 258; ibid (1880) 211.

is to certify its determination to the Speaker.[1] Procedure is laid down for the withdrawal of petitions[2] and the judges are also to report the withdrawal of an election petition to the Speaker, with their opinion whether the withdrawal was the result of any corrupt arrangement.

Before 1770, controverted elections were tried and determined by the whole House of Commons, but had tended to become party questions, upon which the strength of contending factions might be tested.[3]

In order to prevent such abuses, the House consented to submit the exercise of its privilege to a tribunal constituted by law, which, though composed of its own Members, would be appointed so as to secure impartiality and the administration of justice according to the laws of the land and under the sanction of oaths. The principle of the Grenville Act, and of others which were passed at different times since 1770, was the selection by lot of committees for the trial of election petitions. Partiality and incompetence were, however, generally complained of in the constitution of committees appointed in the manner; and, in 1839, an Act was passed establishing a new system, upon different principles, increasing the responsibility of individual Members, and leaving little to the operation of chance. This principle was maintained, with partial alterations of the means by which it was carried out, until 1868, when the jurisdiction of the House in the trial of controverted elections was transferred by statute to the courts of law.

Proceedings of the House in matters of election

Section 120 of the Representation of the People Act 1983 provides that no election and no return shall be questioned except by a petition presented in accordance with the Act. This in no way supersedes the jurisdiction of the House, in determining questions affecting the seats of its own Members, not arising out of controverted elections.

The House, in fact, takes notice of any legal disabilities affecting its Members (see chapter 3), and issues writs in the room of Members adjudged to be incapable of sitting.

A petition relating to an election, but not questioning the return of the sitting Member, may properly be received.[4]

Proceedings of House upon determination of election trials

All certificates and reports of the election court are communicated to the House by the Speaker, and ordered to be entered in the Journals. It is then the duty of the House, under section 144 (7) of the Representation of the People Act 1983, to make orders for carrying the determinations of the judges into execution.

---

1 Representation of the People Act 1983, s 146.
2 Ibid ss 147–148. See also transcript of evidence of Election Court in re Parliamentary Election for North Kensington laid upon the Table by Mr Speaker, 13 April 1960.
3 Eg, Sir Robert Walpole's resignation (1741) in consequence of an adverse vote upon the Chippenham Election petition; see also 1 Cav Deb 476, 505; May *Const Hist* i 243; Porritt *The Unreformed House of Commons* vol I, pp 538–539.
4 Parl Deb (1868–69) 194, c 1185.

Where it has been determined that the sitting Member was not duly elected, and that some other candidate was duly elected, and ought to have been returned, the Clerk of the Crown is ordered to attend, and amend the return, by substituting the name of the duly elected candidate for the name of the other candidate.[1] When the election is void, a new writ is ordered.[2] In the case of a double return (see p 32), the Clerk of the Crown is ordered to attend and amend the return, by erasing the name of one of the parties, and what relates to him, in the return.[3]

Extensive corrupt practices. By the Corrupt Practices Prevention Act 1863, election committees were required to report whether corrupt practices had extensively prevailed, and consequent provision was made for the institution of prosecutions by the Attorney General. This duty is now laid upon the Director of Public Prosecutions, who, when informed that corrupt or illegal practices have prevailed in any election, shall, subject to the regulations under the Prosecution of Offences Act 1879, make such inquiries and institute such prosecutions as the circumstances of the case appear to him to require; and thus the intervention of the House, in such cases, is rendered unnecessary by the direct operation of the law.[4]

Writs suspended. When general and notorious bribery and corruption have been proved to prevail in parliamentary boroughs, the House has suspended the issue of writs, with a view to further inquiry, and proceedings for the ultimate disfranchisement of the corrupt constituencies by Act of Parliament.[5]

---

1 Eg CJ (1955–56) 97–99; ibid (1960–61) 324.
2 Eg CJ (1924) 195, 202.
3 Thetford Election, CJ (1842) 203; Montgomery Election, ibid (1847–48) 218; Dunbartonshire Election, ibid (1866) 156; Horsham Election, ibid (1868–69) 173; South Northumberland Election, ibid (1878) 333; Saint Andrews District of Burghs Election, ibid (1886) 46.
4 Representation of the People Act 1983, ss 171(1) and 181.
5 For a list of occasions when writs have been suspended, see *Erskine May* (20th edn) pp 35–36.

CHAPTER 3

Disqualification for membership of either House

In this chapter, the legal disqualifications for sitting and voting in either House of Parliament will be considered.

Any disqualifications for the Parliament of England were, at the time of the union with Scotland, made applicable to the Parliament of Great Britain.[1]

Similarly, at the time of the union with Ireland, any disqualifications for the Parliaments of Great Britain or of Ireland were by statute extended to the Parliament of the United Kingdom.[2]

DISQUALIFICATIONS FOR MEMBERSHIP OF THE HOUSE OF LORDS[3]

Aliens

Aliens are disqualified by statute for membership of the House of Lords.

By the Act of Settlement 1700–01, 'no person born out of the Kingdoms of England, Scotland or Ireland, or the Dominions thereunto belonging ... (except such as are born of English parents)' may be a member of either House (section 3). By virtue of an amendment made by the British Nationality Act 1981 (Schedule 7), this provision does not apply to Commonwealth citizens or citizens of the Republic of Ireland. Under the latter Act (section 37) 'Commonwealth citizen' means a British citizen, a British Dependent Territories citizen, a British Overseas citizen, a British subject under that Act or a citizen of an independent Commonwealth country (see also, p 40).

Persons under twenty-one

Under Standing Order No 2, made on 22 May 1685, no Lord under the age of twenty-one years shall sit in the House.

Bankruptcy[4]

A Lord of Parliament adjudged bankrupt or, in Scotland, whose estate is sequestered, is disqualified by statute for sitting and voting in the House of

1 S 29 of the Succession to the Crown Act 1707.
2 Ss 1–3 of the House of Commons (Disqualifications) Act 1801; see also s 20 of the Minors Disqualification Act (Ireland) 1797.
3 Apart from the principal restrictions on the Crown's right of summons given by 1 Anson 219–225.
4 The relevant statutory provisions are contained in the Bankruptcy Disqualification Act 1871, the Bankruptcy Act 1883, s 32, the Bankruptcy Act 1890, the Bankruptcy (Scotland) Act 1913, s 183, the Bankruptcy Act 1914, ss 106(1) and 128 and the Insolvency Act 1986, s 427.

Lords or any committee of the House. The court certifies the adjudication (or award of sequestration) to the Speaker of the House of Lords and a record thereof is entered in the Journals.[1] Disqualification ceases in accordance with the provisions of section 427 of the Insolvency Act 1986 or, where appropriate, any of the statutory provisions which that section replaced.[2] A writ of summons is not issued to any peer for the time being disqualified, and such a peer who sits and votes, or attempts to sit and vote, is guilty of a breach of privilege. A disqualified peer does not become entitled to be elected to, or to sit in, the House of Commons. Under the Insolvency Act 1986, all legislation which relates to bankruptcy or confers a power of arrest in connection with the winding up or insolvency of companies now applies to persons having privilege of Parliament or peerage as it applies to persons not having such privilege.

Treason

The Forfeiture Act 1870 abolished the old rule as to corruption of blood for treason, but (as amended) it provides that anyone convicted of treason shall be disqualified for sitting or voting as a member of the House of Lords until he has either suffered his term of imprisonment or received a pardon.[3]

In 1919, following a report by a Committee of the Privy Council appointed under the Titles Deprivation Act 1917, two peers who had adhered during the war to the King's enemies were, in accordance with that Act, deprived of their writs of summons to the House of Lords and of their privileges as peers.[4]

Mental Health Act 1983[5]

There is no statutory provision specifically applying the terms of the Mental Health Act 1983 to Members of the House of Lords, as there is to Members of the House of Commons. The Committee for Privileges of the House of Lords[6] have recommended that future legislation should provide that Members of the House of Lords are liable for detention under the mental health legislation and in such circumstances disqualified for sitting and voting in the House of Lords or for receiving a writ of summons. However, the Committee were of the opinion that, until such legislation had been enacted, there should be no change in the terms of SO No 78 (freedom from arrest).

Disqualification by sentence of the House

During the 17th century there were two cases in which the House of Lords, acting in its judicial capacity on impeachment, sentenced Lords of Parliament to permanent disqualification from sitting in Parliament. In 1725 a

---

1 For notifications of bankruptcy, see LJ (1946–47) 358; ibid (1948–49) 257; ibid (1950) 212; ibid (1953–54) 161; ibid (1968–69) 420; ibid (1974–75) 1091; ibid (1976–77) 836.
2 The House is notified in cases of discharge also; see LJ (1957–58) 324; ibid (1961–62) 186; ibid (1972–73) 778; for a case in which the certificate was rescinded, see LJ (1881) 24, 140.
3 Felony, which had been a disqualification from sitting and voting under the Forfeiture Act 1870, was abolished by the Criminal Law Act 1967.
4 LJ (1919) 107.
5 1983 c 20.
6 HL (1983–84) 254, 23 July 1984.

motion for a sentence to exclude an impeached Lord from Parliament was negatived and there have been no such proceedings since.[1] A resolution by the Lords as a legislative body could not exclude a member of that House permanently.[2]

DISQUALIFICATIONS FOR MEMBERSHIP OF THE HOUSE OF COMMONS

Aliens

An alien is disqualified both by common law and by statute for membership of either House of Parliament, but an alien who has been naturalized is not disqualified.

Before 1700, aliens (that is, persons of whatever parentage born out of the realm and the dominions) were disqualified by common law. The disqualification was not affected by denization, but could be removed by naturalization by Act of Parliament. As originally enacted, section 3 of the Act of Settlement 1700–01 declared that 'no person born out of the kingdoms of England, Scotland or Ireland, or the dominions thereunto belonging (although he be naturalized or made a denizen, except such as are born of English parents), shall be capable to be of the Privy Council or a member of either House of Parliament'.

The operation of this enactment was cut down by a series of subsequent statutes conferring on persons of British parentage born abroad, and on aliens naturalized by certificate of the Secretary of State, the same status as natural-born British subjects. By virtue of Schedule 7 to the British Nationality Act 1981 the Act of Settlement does not apply to Commonwealth citizens (ie British citizens, British Dependent Territories citizens, British Overseas citizens, British subjects or citizens of an independent Commonwealth country) or to citizens of the Republic of Ireland, and accordingly only applies to persons not falling within those categories.

Persons under twenty-one

Persons under twenty-one are disqualified by the Parliamentary Elections Act 1695, section 7, for election to the House of Commons. This disqualification was applied to Scotland by the Act of Union (Union with Scotland Act 1706), and to (Northern) Ireland by the Parliamentary Elections (Ireland) Act 1823, section 74. It was expressly excluded from the scope of the Family Law Reform Act 1969, which reduced the age of majority to eighteen.[3]

Before the passing of the Act of William III several members were notoriously under age, yet their sitting was not objected to. Sir Edward Coke held that infants were disqualified by the law of Parliament, but that several sat 'by connivency: but if questioned would be put out' (10 March

---

1 1 Anson, 228; Pike, 275; LJ (1620–28) 105–106, 383; ibid (1722–26) 558.
2 Report by the Select Committee on the powers of the House in relation to the attendance of its members, HL 67 (1955–56) pp ix, 7–9.
3 1969, c 46, Sch 2, para 2. See, however, the recommendation of the Speaker's Conference on Electoral Law 1972–74, Cmnd 5363.

1623; CJ (1547–1628) 681, and see 2 Hatsell, 6); yet on 16 December 1690, on the hearing of a controverted election, Mr Trenchard, though admitted by his counsel to be a minor, was declared upon a division to be duly elected (2 Hatsell, 9: CJ (1688–93) 508; see, however, the case of Sir Wilfred Lawson, 1717, CJ (1714–18) 672). Even after the passing of the Act some minors sat 'by connivance'. Charles James Fox was returned, sat and spoke before he was of age (Fox, Memorials, i, 51); and Lord John Russell was returned a month before he came of age (Walpole, Life of Lord John Russell, 1, 70). But there are no instances of such breaches of the law since the passing of the Reform Bill of 1832.

Mental illness

Mental illness, formerly described as lunacy or idiocy, is a disqualification at common law. There is also, under section 141 of the Mental Health Act 1983,[1] a statutory procedure for vacating the seat of a sitting Member of unsound mind.

Under this Act, if a Member is authorized to be detained on grounds of mental illness, the authority or person on whose order or application, and the medical practitioner upon whose recommendation or certificate, the Member is detained, and the person in charge of the place where the Member is detained, are to notify the Speaker; or any two Members may certify to the Speaker that they are credibly informed of the detention. The Speaker, on receipt of the notification, causes the Member so detained to be visited by two specialists in mental disorders, who are to be appointed for the purpose by the President of the Royal College of Psychiatrists. The specialists report to the Speaker whether the Member is suffering from mental illness and is authorized to be detained as such; and, if they report that that is the case, six months after the date of the report, (or as soon after that period as the House sits), the Speaker again causes the Member to be visited by two specialists. Then, if the specialists again report that the Member is suffering from mental illness and is authorized to be detained, his seat becomes vacant.

Apart from the statutory procedure described above 'the disqualification of a Member on the ground of insanity might . . . have been brought before the House in one of two ways: by petition from the constituency which is deprived of the services of its Member, if the Member is in confinement, or by a question of privilege being raised if a person certified to be of unsound mind should take part in the business of the House' (1 Anson 81–2; CJ (1810–11) 226; Parl Deb (1861) 162, c 1941).

Peers

Peers of England, Scotland, Great Britain and the United Kingdom are ineligible for the House of Commons as having the right to a seat in the

---

1 For the law on this subject between 1886 and 1959, see Lunacy (Vacating of Seats) Act 1886, Mental Deficiency Act 1913, and Police, Factories, etc (Miscellaneous Provisions) Act 1916; for the law prior to 1886, see D'Ewes 126; *Mr Perne's case*, 1566, CJ (1547–1628) 75; *Mr Alcock's case*, 1811, ibid (1810–11) 226, 265, 687. There is a curious entry in the Journal of 14 February 1609: 'Hassard—69—incurable—bed-rid—a new writ' ibid (1547–1628) 392; case of Mr A. Steuart, Parl Deb (1861) 162, c 1941; *Rogers on Elections* (19th edn) vol II, pp 5, 49.

upper House; but an Irish peer may sit for any constituency in the United Kingdom.[1]

The disqualification entailed by succession to a peerage may be avoided by making a disclaimer of the peerage under the Peerage Act 1963, provided that an instrument is lodged in accordance with the terms of the Act. The periods within which an instrument of disclaimer may be delivered under the Act are as follows:

(a) In the case of a peer who succeeds after the commencement of the Act (not being a member of the House of Commons or a candidate for election to that House), twelve months from succession or, if he is under age on his succession, twelve months from attaining the age of twenty-one (section 1 (2));[2]

(b) In the case of a member of the House of Commons who succeeds to a peerage, one month from the date of succession (section 2 (1));[3]

(c) In the case of a peer who succeeds pending an election to the House of Commons in which he is returned to that House, one month from the declaration of the result of the election (section 2 (2)).

The periods mentioned above are extended in certain cases. Under section 2(4) the period of one month does not run against a member of the House of Commons during a prorogation or when both Houses are adjourned for more than four days nor during any period when his right to the seat is in question under an election petition. Under that section and under section 1 time does not run if and so long as the successor to the peerage is prevented by illness from exercising his choice.

In the case of a dissolution of Parliament, the period prescribed by section 2 ceases to run, and any member of the House of Commons who had succeeded to a peerage within the previous month has the normal twelve months in which to disclaim under section 1 if he wishes to do so, and is not eligible for re-election unless he first disclaims.

When a Member of the House of Commons succeeds to a peerage he is not disqualified for the period of one month during which it is open to him to lodge a disclaimer, unless he applies for a writ of summons during that time; but he may not sit or vote during that time unless he has previously lodged a disclaimer. If he makes no disclaimer within the statutory period his seat is thereby vacated, and a new writ may be issued (see p 30–31).

A Member who is created a peer, on the other hand, is disqualified from the time when the letters patent conferring his dignity have passed the great seal (p 31).

The sons of English peers have been eligible since an order made by the House on 21 January 1549, but the eldest sons of Scottish peers, not having been eligible to the Scottish Parliament, were held to be ineligible to the Parliament of Great Britain.[4] Their disability was removed by the Represen-

---

1 Peerage Act 1963, s 5.
2 LJ (1962–63) 511; ibid (1963–64) 175, 200, 403; ibid (1966–67) 300; ibid (1970–71) 788; ibid (1971–72) 226, 278. A peer who succeeded before the commencement of the Act, but was then under twenty-one, can also disclaim within twelve months after attaining that age (s 1(3)).
3 CJ (1969–70) 174. See also LJ (1962–63) 511, 516; ibid (1963–64) 24.
4 2 Hatsell 12.

tation of the People (Scotland) Act 1832 (section 37). The wives of peers are not disqualified for membership of the Commons.

Bankruptcy

Under section 427 of the Insolvency Act 1986 a bankrupt is disqualified by statute for election, or, if a Member, for sitting and voting. Previously enactments applying to Scotland and Northern Ireland varied slightly, particularly in the latter case, where a bankrupt was not disqualified for election, though he became disqualified if adjudicated bankrupt while a Member.

Bankruptcy, England. By section 427 of the Insolvency Act 1986 a debtor who is adjudged bankrupt is incapable of being elected to or of sitting or voting in the House of Commons, or on any committee thereof, until the adjudication is annulled, or until he obtains from the court his discharge.

A court which adjudges a Member bankrupt shall forthwith certify the adjudication to the Speaker. Following such a certification the court shall further certify to the Speaker either that the adjudication has been annulled or that a period of six months has expired without the adjudication being annulled.[1] In the latter case, the seat of the Member thereupon becomes vacant; and, if the House be then sitting, a new writ may be issued; or if the Speaker receives the certificate during a parliamentary recess, he issues his warrant for a new writ to supply the vacancy which the bankruptcy has created.[2] As no penalty attaches to a bankrupt for sitting and voting, and as no official notice of his bankruptcy is required to be given to the Speaker for six months, a bankrupt Member may sit with impunity, unless the House takes notice that he is incapable of sitting and voting, and orders him to withdraw.[3]

So much of the 1986 Act (except section 427) as makes provision for bankruptcy or confers power of arrest in connection with bankruptcy shall apply to persons having privilege of Parliament as it applies to others.

Bankruptcy, Scotland and Northern Ireland. Although many of the provisions of the Insolvency Act 1986 and other legislation relating to Bankruptcy in England do not extend to Scotland or Northern Ireland, the provisions of section 427 of the Insolvency Act 1986 do apply to Scotland and Northern Ireland. A person adjudged bankrupt in Scotland or Northern Ireland is accordingly ineligible as a Member for any constituency.[4]

Treason

The Forfeiture Act 1870 provides that persons convicted of treason are disqualified for election or sitting or voting in either House till expiry of the sentence or receipt of a pardon.[5]

The only occasion since the passing of the Act when the House has invoked this disqualification was in *Lynch's case* in 1903, when a Member

---

1 Insolvency Act 1986, s 427.
2 Recess Elections Act 1975, s 1 which re-enacted the Bankruptcy Act 1883 provisions in this matter; and see p 32. For an example, see CJ (1928–29) 3.
3 CJ (1857–58) 229.
4 See also *Rogers on Elections* (1928 edn) vol II, p 26.
5 33 and 34 Vict, c 23, ss 2 and 7.

was convicted of treason after election to the House. The House was advised by the Attorney General on that occasion that since the provisions of the Forfeiture Act provided for disqualification for sitting, it was unnecessary for the House to have a resolution stating the effect of the judgment. No motion for expulsion was moved, but the House proceeded forthwith to consider a motion for a new writ.[1]

Other crimes

Present practice. The Representation of the People Act 1981 provides (a) for the disqualification of any person who is detained anywhere in the British Islands or the Republic of Ireland (or who is unlawfully at large at a time when he would otherwise be detained) for more than a year for any offence, (b) that the election or nomination of such persons shall be void, and (c) that the seat of a Member who becomes so disqualified shall be vacated.

Former practice. The statutory disqualification which the Forfeiture Act 1870 imposed on any person convicted of treason previously extended to any person 'convicted of . . . felony [and] sentenced to death, preventive detention or corrective training or any term of imprisonment exceeding twelve months'.[2] These words in the Act of 1870 (as amended) were, however, repealed by the Criminal Law Act 1967, which abolished the division of crimes into felonies and misdemeanours.[3]

After the passing of the Criminal Law Act, therefore, the position with regard to all criminal convictions was similar to the position with regard to misdemeanours before its passing. A person convicted of a misdemeanour (or sentenced to any lighter penalty than those described in section 2 of the Act of 1870) was not thereby disqualified for election or for sitting and voting; but when a Member was so convicted, the House might decide to expel him.[4] Expulsion, however, does not in itself create a disability, or prevent a constituency from re-electing the expelled Member (see p 113).

The following cases illustrate the procedure of the House between the passing of the Forfeiture Act 1870 and the passing of the Criminal Law Act 1967 in respect of persons returned at an election while still under sentence for felony:

> *Mitchell's case* (1875) (HC 50 (1875), CJ (1875) 49, 52, Parl Deb (1875) 222, c 493; 3 O'M & H. 37);
> *Davitt's case* (1882) (CJ (1882) 77);
> *Daly's case* (1895) (CJ (1895) 353);
> *Mitchell's case* (1955) (CJ (1955–56) 71).

The only case during that period of a Member being convicted of a felony after his election to the House was *Baker's case* in 1954–55. On that occasion, contrary to the procedure adopted in *Lynch's case* (see above), the House decided to expel the Member (CJ (1954–55) 25); HC Deb (1954–55) 535, c 1986) before subsequently ordering the issue of a new writ (CJ (1954–55) 29).

---

1 Parl Deb (1903) 118, cc 1121–25; CJ (1903) 40. For a contrary procedure, see *Baker's case*, referred to in the following section.
2 33 and 34 Vict, c 23, s 2; 1948, c 58, Sch 9.
3 1967, c 58, Sch 3, Pt III.
4 Eg CJ (1890–91) 282; ibid (1922) 319.

Corrupt practices at elections

The statutory penalties inflicted for corrupt practices at elections may have the effect of disqualification for the House of Commons. A person may, at an election, be disqualified for being elected by reason of corrupt practices committed at an election previous thereto. So also a person not disqualified before an election may, during the election, become disqualified by reason of corrupt practices being committed at such election; but the latter disqualification can only arise ex post facto upon an investigation into such election. This disqualification always existed at common law, and the statutory provisions are intended only to give fuller effect to the common law of Parliament.[1]

These provisions are now contained in sections 159 and 160 of the Representation of the People Act 1983, under which a candidate at a parliamentary election who is reported by an election court as personally guilty of a corrupt practice is incapacitated, during five years from the date of the report, from being elected for any constituency and during ten years from being elected for the constituency for which the election was held; persons convicted of corrupt practices are also, under section 173, subjected to a total incapacity to be elected for any constituency for five years. If reported by the election court as being guilty through his agents of a corrupt practice or personally guilty of an illegal practice, a candidate is incapacitated during seven years from being elected for the constituency for which the election was held; this local incapacity lasts only for the duration of the Parliament for which the election was held if the court reports that a candidate is guilty of an illegal practice by his agents. Under section 174 of the same Act there are provisions for mitigation and remission of incapacities as a result of further proceedings, where incapacity has arisen as a result of the report of an election court.

Clergy

By the House of Commons (Clergy Disqualification) Act 1801, no person who has been 'ordained to the office of priest or deacon' or who is a Minister of the Church of Scotland is capable of being elected as a Member of the House.[2] The effect of the reference to ordination is to disqualify clergy of the Church of England and of the Church of Ireland (see below), but not Ministers of Nonconformist churches.[3] Roman Catholic priests are separately disqualified by section 9 of the Roman Catholic Relief Act 1829; and holders of ecclesiastical office in the Church in Wales are expressly exempted from disqualification by section 2 (4) of the Welsh Church Act 1914.

Under the Clerical Disabilities Act of 1870 it is possible for any clergyman of the Church of England legally to relinquish the rights and privileges of his office and so to render himself eligible for election to Parliament.[4]

---

1 *Rogers on Elections* (1928 edn) vol II, pp 27–28.
2 1801, c 63, s 1. For an account of clergy disqualification before the passing of this Act, and of the events which led to its passing, see HC 120 (1940–41) pp 149–150.
3 In certain cases, however, the interpretation of this provision (which is elaborated in s 4 of the Act) may be a matter of doubt. See Report of the Select Committee on Clergy Disqualification, Session 1952–53, HC 200 (1952–53) pp iv, 5–6.
4 For instance Mr Ivor Clemitson, a priest of the Church of England, relinquished the rights and privileges of his office prior to his election in February 1974.

The disestablishment of the Church of Ireland in 1869 has not removed the disqualification imposed upon clergymen of that Church by the Act of 1801. In 1950 a select committee, appointed to consider whether the election of the Reverend J G MacManaway, a priest of that Church, was void, was unable to reach a decision,[1] and the matter was referred to the Judicial Committee of the Privy Council, who reported that Mr MacManaway was disabled from sitting and voting in the Commons.[2] The House agreed with this report on 19 October 1950. A new writ was issued on 8 November 1950 on the ground that Mr MacManaway 'was at the time of his election, and is, disabled from sitting' as a clergyman of the Church of Ireland.[3] In 1951 an Act was passed to indemnify Mr MacManaway from any penal consequences incurred under the House of Commons (Clergy Disqualification) Act 1801 by sitting or voting as a Member.

In 1953 a select committee appointed to consider whether any amendment was desirable in the law disqualifying certain clergy reported that it was undesirable to introduce legislation to deal with existing anomalies ahead of any general legislation.[4] Section 10(2) of the House of Commons Disqualification Act 1975 provides that nothing in that Act shall be construed as affecting previous enactments relating to the disqualification for membership of priests in holy orders or ministers of any religious denomination.[5]

Returning officers

A returning officer was formerly incapable of being elected for the constituency for which he made returns— a disqualification based on the nature of the duties of his office.[6] However, those duties having been statutorily transferred in England and Wales to electoral registration officers as acting returning officers, returning officers themselves are no longer so disqualified. Electoral registration officers and the chief and deputy chief electoral officer for Northern Ireland are disqualified by the House of Commons Disqualification Act 1975. Returning officers in Scotland are disqualified under the provisions of the House of Commons Disqualification Act 1975.

Petitioning candidates

At one time it was doubted whether a candidate claiming a seat in Parliament by petition was eligible for another place before the determination of his claim; but it was resolved, on 16 April 1728, 'that a person petitioning, and thereby claiming a seat for one place, is capable of being elected and returned, pending such petition.[7]

In case the petitioner should establish his claim to the disputed seat, the proper course would appear to be to allow him to choose for which place he

---

1 HC 68 (1950).
2 Cmd 8067.
3 CJ (1950–51) 13.
4 HC 200 (1952–53).
5 For the recommendation of the select committee to whom the original House of Commons Disqualification Bill of 1955–56 was referred that the position should not be altered, see HC 349 (1955–56) p vii.
6 *Rogers on Elections* (1928 edn) vol II, pp 5–7; 2 Hatsell 30–34; 4 Doug El Cas 87, 123; CJ (1667–87) 725 (*Thetford case*); *Wakefield case* Bar & Aust 295.
7 CJ (1727–32) 135; 2 Hatsell 73.

would serve, in the same manner as if he had been returned for both places at a general election (see p 34). It seems also that a person returned for one place may petition for another.[1]

DISQUALIFICATION OF CERTAIN OFFICE-HOLDERS

General

Before the passing of the House of Commons Disqualification Act 1957 (later re-enacted as the House of Commons Disqualification Act 1975), the law on disqualification for membership of the House of Commons through holding certain offices was exceedingly complicated;[2] but the position is now greatly simplified. Under section 1(4) of the Act of 1975, 'except as provided by this Act, a person shall not be disqualified for membership of the House of Commons by reason of his holding an office or place of profit under the Crown or any other office or place'. The provisions of the Act for disqualification of the holders of certain offices in fact apply to the majority of the offices which involved disqualification under the former statutory provisions before 1957, although certain anomalies have been removed, and the former provisions disqualifying pension-holders and government contractors are abolished; but the main effect of the Act has been to replace the large number of statutory and common law provisions on disqualification by a single simple code. The Act does not, however, affect the law of disqualification in respect of aliens, persons under twenty-one, persons detained under the Mental Health Act 1959, peers, bankrupts, persons convicted of treason, clergymen, or persons who are implicated in corrupt or illegal practices at elections.

1 NON-POLITICAL OFFICE

The disqualification arising from the holding of a non-political office is dealt with principally in section 1 of the Act of 1975. Disqualification is there defined partly by reference to employment in certain capacities in various branches of the public service and partly by reference to the holding of particular offices mentioned in Schedule 1 to the Act. Certain of these offices entail disqualification for membership for certain constituencies only. The Schedule is subject to amendment by Order in Council (see p 54).[3]

Public service disqualification

The Civil Service. All persons employed either whole- or part-time in the Civil Service are disqualified; and it is immaterial whether or not they are serving in an established capacity (House of Commons Disqualification Act 1975, section 1(1)(b)). This disqualification applies equally to the Home Civil Service, the Civil Service of Northern Ireland, the Northern Ireland Court Service, the Diplomatic Service, and the Overseas Civil Service

---

1 *Rogers on Elections* (1928) edn vol II, p 164.
2 An account of the law prior to 1957 may be found in the 17th and earlier editions of this work.
3 Eg Votes and Proceedings, 2 December 1986.

(section 1(3)). Colonial Governors are also disqualified under the Act insofar as they are usually members of the Diplomatic Service.

The regulations of the Civil Service contained in the Servants of the Crown (Parliamentary, European Assembly and Northern Ireland Assembly Candidature) Order 1987, regarding the requirement of resignation before becoming a candidate for Parliament, also preclude civil servants from sitting as Members.

The Armed Forces. Membership of the regular armed forces of the Crown or the Ulster Defence Regiment is a disqualification (section 1(1)(c)). The armed forces concerned are the Royal Navy, the regular forces as defined by section 225 of the Army Act 1955, the regular Air Force as defined by section 223 of the Air Force Act 1955, Queen Alexandra's Royal Naval Nursing Service, and the Women's Royal Naval Service (section 1(3)). Officers on the retired or emergency list of any of the regular armed forces and those holding emergency commissions or belonging to any reserve of officers are not, however, thereby disqualified (section 3(1)). Admirals of the Fleet, Field Marshals, and Marshals of the Royal Air Force (all of whom are always on the active list) continue to be disqualified only if they actually hold an appointment in the naval, military or air force service of the Crown (section 3(2)).

The position of recalled pensioners is safeguarded by the provision that any pensioner recalled for service for which he is liable as such shall not be disqualified as a member of the regular armed forces (section 3(1)(b)).

Members of the Royal Observer Corps who are technically civil servants rather than members of the regular armed forces are not disqualified unless they are employed on a whole-time basis (section 3(3)).

In addition members of the Armed Forces of the Crown on the active list in normal times, ie in periods not affected by emergency legislation, are prohibited from announcing themselves as candidates at a parliamentary election by their own service regulations.

The effect of these regulations is to prevent regular service personnel from being members of the House of Commons so long as they remain on the active list. The prohibition does not extend to personnel who are retired or pensioned unless recalled for active service or otherwise re-employed; in regard to Admirals of the Fleet, Field Marshals and Marshals of the RAF who are technically always on the active list, the prohibition only applies to them while holding an appointment.

Since 1963, following the report of a Select Committee and a resolution of the House, all applications for release from the armed forces to contest a parliamentary election have been examined by a special advisory Committee appointed for that purpose by the Home Secretary.[1]

Police. Persons employed as members of any police force maintained by a police authority within the meaning of the Police Act 1964 or the Police (Scotland) Act 1967, or by the Police Authority for Northern Ireland, are disqualified under the Act of 1975 (section 1(1)(d) and 1(3)).

---

1 HC Deb (1961–62) 660, c 1342; HC 111 and 262 (1962–63); CJ (1962–63) 107.

In view of the definition of 'Police authority', the effect is to disqualify members of all public police forces (eg the Metropolitan Police or a county police force); and the inclusion of the Police Authority for Northern Ireland brings the Royal Ulster Constabulary within the scope of the disqualification. Members of private police forces (eg those of transport authorities) and special constables are not included in the disqualifications under this subsection.

Members of legislatures outside the Commonwealth. Members of a legislature of any country or territory outside the Commonwealth are disqualified for membership of the House of Commons under section 1(1)(e) of the Act of 1975.

Members of all non-Commonwealth legislatures except that of the Republic of Ireland are already disqualified as aliens (p 40) unless exceptionally they have dual nationality. The effect of this provision is therefore to disqualify such persons and Members of the Seanad and the Dáil of the Republic of Ireland for membership of the House.

Disqualification by particular office

Judicial office.[1] The holders of the judicial offices specified in Part I of Schedule 1 to the Act of 1975 are disqualified for membership (section 1(1)(a)). Judges of the High Court, Court of Appeal and Court of Session are named first in the Schedule together with their counterparts in Northern Ireland. Circuit Judges and Stipendiary and Resident Magistrates are also disqualified, as are Sheriffs Principal and Sheriffs in Scotland. At the end of the list come certain Commissioners and Umpires appointed under National Insurance and National Service legislation. Justices of the Peace are not included and so are eligible for membership.

Bodies of which all members are disqualified.[2] Part II of Schedule 1 contains a list of public bodies all of whose members are disqualified (section 1(1)(f)). The Boards of the Nationalised Industries are included under this head, together with a large number of Commissions, Tribunals and other statutory bodies whose members are appointed by the Crown.

Other disqualifying offices.[3] Part III of Schedule 1 contains a long list of residual offices which disqualify either on the grounds that their holders are appointed by the Crown or that their holding is incompatible with membership of the House of Commons (section 1(1)(f)). Among those listed are Ambassadors and High Commissioners, certain directors of companies in which the state has an interest, and Election and Boundary Commissioners. No members of the Church Estates Commission are disqualified and they may therefore be represented either by a paid Commissioner, or by an unpaid Commissioner; the practice of recent years has been for an unpaid Commissioner to act as representative.

Offices disqualifying for particular constituencies.[4] Certain offices disqualify for particular constituencies (section 1(2)). Thus the Lord Lieutenant or

1 For the complete list see the certified copy (cf p 54) of Pt I of Sch 1.
2 For the complete list see the certified copy (cf p 54) of Pt II of Sch 1.
3 For the complete list see the certified copy (cf p 54) of Pt III of Sch 1.
4 For the complete list see the certified copy (cf p 54) of Pt IV of Sch 1.

sheriff of a county in England or Wales is disqualified for any constituency comprising the whole or part of the area for which he is appointed.

In regard to the limited disqualification of a High Sheriff, section 8 of the Act of 1975 provides that no member of the House of Commons or candidate for membership shall be required to accept an office which would disqualify him under the Act. Apart from the obligation to serve in the armed forces (which is expressly removed from the effect of section 8) it would appear that the office of High Sheriff is the only office under the Crown which a person may otherwise be required to accept against his wish.[1]

Offices retained for purposes of resignation or re-election.

Resignation of Members. It is a settled principle of parliamentary law that a Member, after he is duly chosen, cannot relinquish his seat;[2] and, in order to evade this restriction, a Member who wishes to retire accepts office under the Crown, which legally vacates his seat and obliges the House to order a new writ. The offices usually selected for this purpose are the office of steward or bailiff of Her Majesty's three Chiltern Hundreds of Stoke, Desborough and Burnham, or that of the steward of the Manor of Northstead, which were undoubtedly offices or places of profit in former times; and the legal fictions of their existence and of their disabling effect on Members have been carefully preserved in the various statutes relating to disqualification.[3] Under section 4 of the Act of 1975 it is provided that for the purposes of the provisions of that Act relating to the vacation of the seat of a member of the House of Commons who becomes disqualified by the Act for membership of that House, the office of steward or bailiff of Her Majesty's three Chiltern Hundreds of Stoke, Desborough and Burnham, or of the Manor of Northstead, shall be treated as included among the offices described in Part III of Schedule 1 to the Act.

These offices are today purely nominal and are ordinarily given by the Chancellor of the Exchequer to any Member who applies for them.[4] Each office is only retained until the Chancellor receives application from another Member who wishes to retire, or until the holder applies for release from it (as has happened when the holder desired to stand for election in the same, or another, constituency).

> The wording of the form of appointment makes it plain that they were once offices of profit. Thus when the new holder takes over the appointment the Chancellor 'hereby revokes and determines, together with all wages, fees, allowances and other privileges and pre-eminences whatsoever' the tenure of the previous holder. The practice is to issue the appointment to the Chiltern Hundreds and Manor of Northstead alternately, so that, if desired, two Members can vacate their seats at the same moment. All words which formerly attached honour to the appointment are omitted, in order to remove any scandal in granting these offices to persons unworthy of the favour of the Crown, who may desire to vacate their seats in Parliament; the words, 'reposing especial trust and confidence in the care and fidelity of,' etc, being first omitted in the year 1861.

1 See HC 120 (1940–41) para 36.
2 CJ (1547–1628) 724; ibid (1640–42) 201.
3 See eg Re-election of Ministers Act 1919, Sch; and HC 120 (1940–41) pp xix–xx.
4 Parl Deb (1893–94) 8, c 50; ibid (1902) 103, c 212.

According to Hatsell, the practice of applying for the Chiltern Hundreds began about 1750 (see 2 Hatsell 54 n). The offices of Steward of the Manors of East Hendred and Hempholme were at one time used for this purpose, the last occasions being in 1840 and 1865 respectively; but the titles to the manors have now passed from the Crown. See also Memorandum of Sir William Harcourt to the Select Committee on House of Commons (Vacating of Seats), HC 278 (1894) pp 57–58, which sets out the history of these offices and discusses the Chancellor of the Exchequer's power to grant or withhold an appointment.

Acceptance of Chiltern Hundreds, etc, during a recess. These offices can be granted during a recess (Parl Deb (1892) 1, c 462); but the statutory power conferred on the Speaker for the issue of a writ to fill up a vacancy caused by acceptance of office (see p 32), does not extend to vacancies caused by the acceptance of these stewardships. The acceptance of any of these offices, however, during a recess at once vacates the seat of a Member, and qualifies him to be elected elsewhere, although no new writ can be issued for the place which has become vacant by his acceptance of office until the House re-assembles.

Chiltern Hundreds applied for by disqualified Members. In the session of 1847–48, a Member having had doubts suggested whether he had not been disqualified at the time of his election, as a contractor, thought it prudent not to take his seat, in case of being sued for the penalties then applicable. He was, however, unwilling to admit his disqualification; and he accordingly applied for the Chiltern Hundreds. Doubts were raised as to the propriety of allowing him to vacate his seat by this method; but it was agreed that, as the time had expired for questioning by an election petition the validity of his return, and as the House had no cognizance of his probable disqualification, there could be no objection to his accepting the office.

Unsworn Members can avail themselves of these offices (Baron Lionel Rothschild CJ (1849) 430; ibid (1857) 343); and when Mr Bradlaugh voted, on 11 February 1884, being an unsworn Member (see p 154), the office of the Chiltern Hundreds was granted to him, whereon the new writ was issued to supply the vacancy which by his conduct had taken place (CJ (1884) 46).

Chiltern Hundreds withheld. The Chiltern Hundreds have sometimes been refused (see letter of Mr Gouldburn to Viscount Chelsea, HC 544 (1842), and see Lord Dalling *Life of Lord Palmerston* p 103). In 1775, Lord North refused to give one of these offices to Mr Bayly, who desired to stand for Abingdon in opposition to a ministerial candidate, saying, 'I have made it my constant rule to resist every application of that kind, when any gentleman entitled to my friendship would have been prejudiced by my compliance' (18 Parl Hist 418 n). 'The office of steward of the Chiltern Hundreds is an appointment under the hand and seal of the Chancellor of the Exchequer' (Colchester i, 175).

Re-election. By the law of Parliament a Member already returned for one place is ineligible for any other until his first seat is vacated. It would be necessary for a sitting Member who wished to become a candidate in another constituency first to accept the Chiltern Hundreds or Manor of Northstead; but in order to qualify himself for re-election he would need, after being appointed to the Chiltern Hundreds or Manor of Northstead, subsequently to secure his release from the appointment (if the office has not already been granted to a later applicant).

Vacation of seat for purposes of re-election. Sir Fitzroy Kelly, Solicitor General, having been returned for Harwich on 15 April 1852, immediately afterwards announced himself as a candidate for East Suffolk, the election for which county was appointed to be held on 1 May. He had been returned for Harwich without opposition, yet on 29 April a petition was lodged against his return, in the hope of preventing the Treasury from granting him the Chiltern Hundreds. But as his seat was not claimed, he at once received the required appointment, and was returned for East Suffolk, and took his seat again, before a new writ had been issued for Harwich. The entry in the votes is as follows: 'Sir Fitzroy Kelly having, since his return for the borough of Harwich, accepted the office of steward of Her Majesty's Manor of Hempholme, in the county of York, and being returned for the eastern division of the county of Suffolk, took the oaths and his seat' (Votes and Proceedings, sess. 1852, p 285).

In February 1865, The O'Donoghue, being Member for Tipperary, offered himself as a candidate for Tralee; but before the day of election, he qualified himself to be elected by accepting the Chiltern Hundreds (CJ (1865) 4, 50).

In 1878, Mr Wingfield Malcolm, Member for Boston, accepted the stewardship of the Manor of Northstead, in order to qualify himself as a candidate for the county of Argyll (CJ (1878) 402).

In 1955 Sir Richard Acland, Member for Gravesend, accepted the stewardship of the Manor of Northstead in order to present himself again at a by-election in that constituency; but a dissolution of Parliament supervened before a new writ was issued (London Gazette, 25 March 1955, No 40438, p 1780).

In 1973, Mr Taverne, Member for Lincoln, accepted the stewardship of the Manor of Northstead, and was then re-elected at the consequent by-election in that constituency (CJ (1972–73) 137, 184).

Effect and disregard of disqualification

The first subsection of section 6 of the Act of 1975 declares that if a Member of the House becomes disqualified under any of the provisions of the Act, his seat becomes vacant. In the case of a person disqualified under the Act being elected to the House while disqualified, the election is declared to be void. No special provision is made to cover the situation which arises from an election becoming void in this way; the normal procedure in the case of controverted elections will accordingly apply (pp 35–36).

But the House may itself provide relief from the effects of disqualification (section 6(2)). In any case falling or alleged to fall within section 6(1), if it appears to the House that the grounds of disqualification or alleged disqualification under the Act which subsisted or arose at the material time have been removed and that it is otherwise proper to do so, the House may by order direct that any such disqualification shall be disregarded.[1] Relief may not, however, be afforded so as to affect the proceedings on any election petition or any determination of an election court (see p 35); and under section 144(7) of the Representation of the People Act 1983, it is the duty of the House to make the appropriate orders when informed of a certificate and of any report of an election court.

Moreover this provision for relief extends only to disqualification under the Act of 1975. The House cannot therefore employ this procedure in dealing with cases of disqualification arising in any of the ways described earlier on pp 40–46.

In any case where the Speaker would otherwise be required to issue his warrant during a recess (pp 31–32) for a new writ for the election of a Member in the room of a Member becoming disqualified under the Act of 1975, he is authorized to defer the issue of a warrant if he considers that an opportunity should be given to the House of considering provision for relief (section 6(4)).

Jurisdiction of the Privy Council in disqualification

The Judicial Committee of the Privy Council has a jurisdiction to decide such matters insofar as disqualification under the Act of 1975 is concerned. Section 7 provides that anyone who claims that a person purporting to be a Member of the House is disqualified by the Act or has been so disqualified since his election may apply to Her Majesty in Council in accordance with such rules as Her Majesty in Council may prescribe[2] for a declaration to that effect; and the application is then referred to the Judicial Committee of the Privy Council in accordance with section 3 of the Judicial Committee Act 1833.

The Judicial Committee is empowered to make a declaration in such cases whether the grounds of the alleged disqualification subsisted at the time of a person's election or arose subsequently, subject to two provisos; no such declaration shall be made where an election petition is pending or has been tried unless the grounds for the alleged disqualification differ from those being tried by the election court nor in the case of disqualification incurred by any person on any grounds if an order has been made by the House of Commons directing that the disqualification shall be disregarded (see above).

The House of Commons may itself resolve that a matter should be referred to the Judicial Committee of the Privy Council under section 4 of the Judicial Committee Act 1833, as has been done on occasions in the past.[3]

Further provisions are contained in section 7(3) and (4) relating to the procedure of the Judicial Committee in hearing such cases. The applicant is required to give such security for costs not exceeding two hundred pounds as the Judicial Committee may direct; and the Judicial Committee may direct issues of fact to be tried in the High Court, the Court of Session, or the High Court in Northern Ireland where the membership of an English or Welsh, or

---

1 CJ (1974) 71.
2 No such rules have yet been made.
3 CJ (1912–13) 519; ibid (1950) 156.

of a Scottish, or of a Northern Ireland constituency respectively is concerned.

It would appear that this procedure by application to Her Majesty in Council for a declaration by the Judicial Committee provides an alternative method to procedure by election petition under Part III of the Representation of the People Act 1983 insofar as disqualifications imposed by the Act of 1975 are concerned. Furthermore, while the Representation of the People Act 1983 imposes a time limit for the presentation of petitions of 21 days after the return of the election has been made, there is no time limit fixed for an application to the Judicial Committee under the Act of 1975.

The Judicial Committee has no jurisdiction to make a declaration on disqualification arising otherwise than under the Act of 1975; they cannot therefore hear cases involving disqualifications of the types mentioned on pp 40–47.

Penalties

The Act of 1975 provides no penalties for sitting and voting when disqualified, and the former provisions for penalties to be recovered at the instance of a common informer were repealed in 1957, except in the case of penalties so recoverable under the House of Commons (Clergy Disqualification) Act 1801 and the Lunacy (Vacating of Seats) Act 1886. The latter Act, however, was repealed by the Mental Health Act 1959, and the provision for penalties was not re-enacted, so that it would appear that the penalty of five hundred pounds for each day on which a person disqualified sits and votes in the House is limited to persons disqualified by the House of Commons (Clergy Disqualification) Act 1801.

Amendment of House of Commons Disqualification Act 1975

Schedule 1 to the Act of 1975, in which the disqualifying offices are listed individually, is subject under section 5(1) of the Act to amendment by Order in Council on resolution by the House of Commons;[1] and Acts creating new offices or official bodies commonly provide for the insertion of these offices or bodies in the relevant part of the Schedule.[2]

A copy of the Act as amended from time to time by Order in Council or any other enactment is prepared and certified by the Clerk of the Parliaments and deposited with the rolls of Parliament; and the amendments, including any relating to the sections concerned with political office (see below), are incorporated in all copies of the Act printed thereafter by the Queen's printer.[3]

2 POLITICAL OFFICE

Under section 2 of the Act of 1975 not more than 95 holders of ministerial offices are entitled to sit and vote in the House of Commons at any one time. For the purposes of this provision ministerial offices are those specified in

---

1 Eg CJ (1974–75) 191; Votes and Proceedings, 2 December 1986.
2 Eg Nurses, Midwives and Health Visitors Act 1979, Sch 1, para 5.
3 House of Commons Disqualification Act 1975, s 5(2).

Schedule 2 of the Act of 1975.[1] This Schedule may be amended by Orders in Council made under s 1 of the Ministers of the Crown Act 1975 in consequence of a transfer of ministerial function or the dissolution of a Department; but the aggregate number of ministerial offices contained in the Schedule may not be increased by such an Order.

In considering the list of ministerial offices in the Schedule it should be remembered that certain of them (for example, the offices of Secretary of State and Minister of State) may be held by more than one person. Under Schedule 1 of the Ministerial and other Salaries Act 1975 the list of ministerial office-holders is sub-divided into four parts. Part I comprises the Prime Minister, the Secretaries of State and other office-holders who are members of the cabinet; Part II comprises Ministers of State and other Ministers not in the cabinet; Part III comprises the law officers; and Part IV the Parliamentary Secretaries, officers of the Royal Household and Assistant Government Whips. Not more than 21 salaries may be paid at the same time in respect of office-holders in Part I and not more than 50 in respect of office-holders in Parts I and II together; and the total number of office-holders in Parts I and II, taken together with the total number of Parliamentary Secretaries, must not exceed 83.

If at any time the number of Ministers in the House of Commons exceeds the number authorized by section 2(1) of the House of Commons Disqualification Act 1975, the Ministers appointed after the limit was reached are disqualified from sitting and voting until the numbers have been reduced by death, resignation or otherwise to the maximum permitted number (section 2(2)).

Ministers are not disqualified by reason of an office held ex officio as the holder of the Ministerial office concerned (section 2(3)).

---

1 For the complete list see the latest amended copy (cf above) of Sch 2.

CHAPTER 4

Power and jurisdiction of Parliament

EXTENT OF LEGISLATIVE AUTHORITY OF PARLIAMENT

The authority of Parliament over all matters and persons within its jurisdiction was formerly unlimited. A law might be unjust or contrary to sound principles of government; but Parliament was not controlled in its discretion, and when it erred, its errors could only be corrected by itself. In the twentieth century, however, Parliament has accepted that its unlimited legislative authority should be qualified in two important respects. First, in a series of statutes beginning with the Statute of Westminster 1931[1] Parliament formally recognised limitations on its powers over the Dominions (as they were then called); and after the war of 1939–45 it conferred independence on other countries and territories within the Commonwealth. Secondly, in 1972 it passed the European Communities Act[2] under which the authority of European institutions to adopt measures carrying the force of law in the United Kingdom was accepted. These two qualifications on Parliament's otherwise unlimited authority are considered below.

Commonwealth legislation

The preamble to the Statute of Westminster 1931 stated as the basis for its provisions the agreement of His Majesty's Governments in the United Kingdom and in the Dominions to the declarations and resolutions of the two Imperial Conferences of 1926 and 1930.[3] The Statute defined 'Dominion' as meaning Canada, Australia, New Zealand, South Africa (now the Republic of South Africa, outside the Commonwealth), the Irish Free State (now the Republic of Ireland, outside the Commonwealth) and Newfoundland.[4]

The preamble went on to declare that:

it is in accord with the established constitutional position that no law hereafter made by the Parliament of the United Kingdom shall extend to any of the said Dominions as part of the law of that Dominion otherwise than at the request and with the consent of that Dominion.

The main provisions of the Statute of Westminster were that the Colonial Laws Validity Act 1865 was not to apply to any law made in future by the

---

1 22 & 23 Geo 5, c 4.
2 1972 c 68.
3 Cmd 2768 and Cmd 3717.
4 The status of Newfoundland was placed in abeyance by the Newfoundland Act 1933 for reasons set out in the documents scheduled thereto. The British North America Act 1949 confirmed and gave effect to terms of union (agreed in 1948 between Canada and Newfoundland and approved by the Canadian Parliament and the Newfoundland Government) under which Newfoundland became a Province of Canada.

Parliament of a Dominion; and that no law made by a Dominion Parliament in future was to be void or inoperative on the ground that it is repugnant to any existing or future Act of the United Kingdom Parliament (section 2); that a Dominion Parliament has full power to legislate to make laws having extra-territorial effect (section 3); and that no Act of Parliament of the United Kingdom passed in future should extend to a Dominion as part of its law unless the Act expressly declared that the Dominion had requested and consented to the enactment (section 4). These provisions (and some others) were (by section 10) not to be applied to Australia, New Zealand or Newfoundland until those countries adopted them. Australia did so in 1942 and New Zealand in 1947 (Newfoundland becoming part of Canada in 1949). A different provision was made for Canada. Amendment of the Canadian constitution was still to require legislation by the United Kingdom Parliament (section 7). Examples of such legislation were the British North America Acts of 1951, 1960 and 1964[1] which duly recited the request and consent of the Dominion. The British North America (No 2) Act 1949 however gave legislative authority to the Parliament of Canada to amend the Constitution of Canada, though certain important matters were still reserved. Not until the passing of the Canada Act 1982, which provided that the United Kingdom should have no power thereafter to legislate for Canada, was a wholly independent constitution conferred on Canada.

Beginning with the India and Ceylon Independence Acts 1947 the United Kingdom Parliament passed a series of Acts granting independence to various Commonwealth countries without any qualifications as to request and consent; and the Burma Independence Act 1947 established Burma as an independent country outside the Commonwealth.

The legislative competence of the United Kingdom Parliament over the remaining colonies remains absolute, though it is usual for the Crown by Order in Council or letters patent to lay down the form of government for a colony and the powers conferred under the authority either of the Prerogative or of the British Settlements Acts 1887 and 1945 or in some cases of specific Acts dealing with individual territories.[2]

The European Communities Act 1972

Accession of the United Kingdom to membership of the European Communities on 1 January 1973 qualified the legislative authority of the United Kingdom. Under section 2 of the European Communities Act 1972:

> All such rights, powers, liabilities, obligations and restrictions from time to time created or arising by or under the Treaties, and all such remedies and procedures from time to time provided for by or under the Treaties, as in accordance with the Treaties are without further enactment to be given legal effect or used in the United Kingdom shall be recognised and available in law, and be enforced, allowed and followed accordingly.

---

1 14 & 15 Geo 6, c 32 (old age pensions); 9 & 10 Eliz 2, c 2 (tenure of offices of judges); 12 & 13 Eliz 2, c 73 (old age pensions).
2 Eg Anguilla Act 1971.

The primary obligations created by section 2 are, however, susceptible to amendment by Parliament, by virtue of the doctrine of the supremacy of Parliament.

The Treaties in question were those setting up the European Communities as then constructed together with those relating to the accession of the United Kingdom to the Communities. There have since been further Treaties—notably, those relating to the accession of other states and the Single European Act (Titles I, II and IV). In consequence of United Kingdom accession and the passage of the Act of 1972, certain measures adopted by the competent institution within the Communities can become law directly, without being approved by Queen, Lords and Commons. Other measures need to be implemented by domestic legislation—either primary legislation or subordinate legislation subject to parliamentary scrutiny as the particular enabling power may require. Both Houses have devised procedures intended to ensure that before the Council of Ministers adopts measures having direct or prospective legal effect in the United Kingdom under the Treaties, the participating United Kingdom Minister is made aware of the views held in Parliament (see pp 773–776).

EXTENT OF THE PREROGATIVE OF THE CROWN IN REFERENCE TO PARLIAMENT

Apart from the authority of Parliament collectively, which has been considered above, the laws and usage of the constitution have assigned peculiar powers, rights and privileges to each of its branches, in connection with their joint legislative functions.

It is by the act of the Crown alone that Parliament can be assembled. The only occasions on which the Lords and Commons have met by their own authority were before the restoration of King Charles II in 1660, and at the Revolution in 1688.

Annual meeting of Parliament

Although the Queen may determine the period for calling Parliaments, her prerogative is restrained within certain limits, as she is bound by statute[1] to issue writs within three years after the determination of a Parliament, while the practice of providing money for the public service by annual enactments renders it compulsory for her to summon Parliament to meet every year.

Summons

Parliament is summoned by the Queen's writ or letter issued out of Chancery, by advice of the Privy Council. The minimum period after the dissolution of Parliament at a general election within which a new Parliament may be appointed to meet has now been abolished.[2] The meeting of Parliament may be deferred, however, by proclamation, from the day to which it shall stand summoned to any further day, not being less than fourteen days from

---

1 16 Cha 2, c 1, and 6 & 7 Will & Mary, c 2.
2 Representation of the People Act 1985, s 28(2).

the date thereof, under the Prorogation Act 1867.[1] The writ of summons has always named the day and place of meeting,[2] without which the requisition to meet would be imperfect and nugatory.

Demise of the Crown

The demise of the Crown is the only contingency upon which Parliament is required to meet without summons in the usual form. By the Succession to the Crown Act 1707, on the demise of the Crown, Parliament, if sitting, is immediately to proceed to act; and if adjourned or prorogued is immediately to meet and sit. In such circumstances, Parliament has met on Sunday.[3] The case of a demise of the Crown after a proclamation has been given summoning a new Parliament is now governed by section 20 of the Representation of the People Act 1985.[4] This replaces provisions of the Meeting of Parliament Act 1797 (under which the old Parliament was recalled if a demise of the Crown occurred after dissolution at a general election but before polling day) with a provision postponing polling day by a fortnight. By the Representation of the People Act 1867,[5] the Parliament in being at the demise of the Crown continues as long as it would otherwise have done.

Causes of summons

As the Queen appoints the time and place of meeting, she also at the commencement of every session declares to both Houses the causes of summons, by a speech delivered to them in the House of Lords by herself in person or by Commissioners appointed by her. Until she has done this, neither House can proceed with any business; but the causes of summons, as declared from the throne, do not bind Parliament to consider them alone, or to proceed at once to the consideration of any of them (see p 233).

On two occasions, during the illness of George III, the name and authority of the Crown were used for the purpose of opening the Parliament, when the sovereign was personally incapable of exercising his constitutional functions. On the first occasion, Parliament had been prorogued till 20 November 1788, then to meet for the despatch of business. When Parliament assembled on that day, the King was under the care of his physicians, and

---

1 The power of accelerating the meeting of Parliament for despatch of business by proclamation, given by the Meeting of Parliament Act 1797, as amended (see p 223), applies only to a meeting of Parliament pursuant to a prorogation.
2 When Parliament temporarily sought other accommodation during the 1939 war (see p 166 n 4), its place of sitting was always within Westminster, and therefore within the terms of its summons.
3 Queen Anne CJ (1714–18) 3; Geo 2, ibid (1757–61) 933; Geo 3, ibid (1820) 89. For other occasions of the demise of the Crown, see ibid (1727–32) 5 (Geo 1); ibid (1830) 589 (Geo 4); ibid (1837) 490 (Will 4); ibid (1901) 5 (Queen Victoria); ibid (1910) 147 (Edw 7); ibid (1935–36) 50 (Geo 5); ibid (1936–37) 59 (Edw 8); ibid (1951–52) 88 (Geo 6).
4 1985 c 50.
5 S 51.

unable to open Parliament, and declare the causes of summons. Both Houses, however, proceeded to consider the measures necessary for a regency; and on 3 February 1789 Parliament was opened by a commission, to which the great seal had been affixed by the Lord Chancellor, without the authority of the King. Again, in 1810, Parliament stood prorogued till 1 November, and met at a time when the King was incapable of issuing a commission. His illness continued, and on 15 January, without any personal exercise of authority by the King, Parliament was formally opened, and the causes of summons were declared in virtue of a commission under the great seal, and 'in his Majesty's name'.[1] The illnesses of George V in 1928 and 1936 led (as its preamble explains) to the passing of the Regency Act in 1937, which provides for the appointment of a regent if the wife or husband of the sovereign, the Lord Chancellor, Speaker of the House of Commons, Lord Chief Justice and Master of the Rolls are satisfied, by medical and other evidence, of the sovereign's incapacity or satisfied by evidence that the sovereign is for some definite cause not available to perform the royal functions. The regent has no power to assent to a bill for changing the order of succession to the Crown or for repealing or altering the Act of the Parliament of Scotland of 1706 for securing the Protestant religion and Presbyterian Church government. The Regency Act 1937 also makes provision for less serious illness or for the sovereign's absence abroad by authorizing the appointment of Counsellors of State to whom may then be delegated such royal functions as may be specified in letters patent.[2]

Prorogation

Parliament, it has been seen, can only commence its deliberations at the time appointed by the Queen; neither can it continue them any longer than she pleases. She may prorogue Parliament by having her command signified, in her presence or by commission, by the Lord Chancellor to both Houses, or by proclamation. The prorogation of Parliament from the day to which it stood summoned or prorogued to any further day, was effected before 1867 by a writ or commission under the great seal; but by the Prorogation Act 1867 Parliament may in such circumstances be prorogued by the royal proclamation alone to a further day, being not less than fourteen days from the date thereof;[3] the Act does not, however, apply to prorogation at the close of a session.

Effect of a prorogation

The effect of a prorogation is at once to terminate all the current business of Parliament. Not only are the sittings of Parliament at an end, but all proceedings pending at the time are quashed, except impeachments by the Commons, and appeals before the House of Lords.[4] Every bill must there-

---

1 For a full statement of these proceedings, see May *Const Hist* i. 118–144.
2 Eg CJ (1968–69) 25. See also Regency Acts 1943 and 1953.
3 For instances of the exercise of powers under this Act see CJ (1887) 2; ibid (1950) 2. But see also CJ (1878–79) 2; ibid (1922) 2.
4 2 Hatsell 335. See also statute, 45 Geo 3, c 117, to continue proceedings in the House of Lords against Mr Justice Fox over the prorogation. See also an exception regarding appeals (House of Lords), p 66; proceedings in certain cases on private and provisional order bills, p 928; and on a public bill, p 526 n.

fore be renewed after a prorogation, as if it had never been introduced. As it is a rule that a bill of the same substance cannot be introduced in either House twice in the same session, a prorogation has been resorted to on three occasions to enable another bill to be brought in (see p 526).

Meeting of Parliament accelerated or deferred by proclamation

When Parliament stands prorogued to a certain day, the Queen may, by the Meeting of Parliament Act 1797, as amended by the Meeting of Parliament Act 1870 and section 34 of the Parliament (Elections and Meeting) Act 1943, issue a proclamation, giving notice of her intention that Parliament shall meet for the despatch of business on any earlier day after the date of the proclamation,[1] and Parliament then stands prorogued to that day, notwithstanding the previous prorogation.[2]

Meeting of Parliament accelerated pursuant to statute

The circumstances in which Parliament is required to be summoned to meet as a result of the proclamation of a state of emergency or the calling out of military reserves, etc, are described on p 223.

Meeting for despatch of business

When the Queen, by the advice of her Privy Council, has determined upon the prorogation of Parliament, a proclamation is issued, declaring that on a certain day Parliament will be prorogued until a day mentioned; and when it is intended that Parliament shall meet on that day for despatch of business, the proclamation states that Parliament will then 'assemble and be holden for the despatch of divers urgent and important affairs'. It was formerly customary to give forty days' notice, by proclamation, of a meeting of Parliament for a despatch of business;[3] but under the Meeting of Parliament Acts 1797 and 1870, amended (as already mentioned) in 1943, Parliament can be assembled for that purpose, in the circumstances to which those Acts apply, upon any date after the date of the proclamation.[4]

When Parliament has been dissolved and summoned for a certain day, or when it has been prorogued by commission to a certain day, it meets on that day for despatch of business, if not previously prorogued, without any proclamation for that purpose, the notice of such meeting being comprised in the proclamation relating to the dissolution and the writs then issued, or in the commission for proroguing Parliament respectively.

Adjournment

Adjournment is solely in the power of each House respectively: though the pleasure of the Crown has occasionally been signified in person, by message, commission or proclamation, that both Houses should adjourn; and in some

---

1 The 1797 Act said not less than fourteen days from the date of the proclamation; the 1870 Act substituted six days for fourteen.
2 For instances see CJ (1798–99) 745; ibid (1799–1800) 3; ibid (1900) 404; ibid (1921) 402.
3 2 Hatsell 290; 3 Chatham Corr 126 n.
4 For instance see CJ (1878) 2.

cases such adjournments have scarcely differed from prorogations.[1] But
although no instance has occurred in which either House has refused to
adjourn, the communication might be disregarded. Business has been transacted after the Crown's desire has been made known; and the question for
adjournment has afterwards been put, in the ordinary manner, and determined after debate, amendment and division.[2] The pleasure of the Crown
was last signified on 1 March 1814;[3] and it is probable that the practice will
not be revived.

A power of interfering with adjournments in certain cases has been
conceded to the Crown by statute. The Meeting of Parliament Act 1799, as
amended by the Meeting of Parliament Act 1870, enacts that when both
Houses of Parliament stand adjourned with more than fourteen days still to
run, the Queen may issue a proclamation, with the advice of her Privy
Council, declaring that the Parliament shall meet on a day not less than six
days from the date of the proclamation; and the Houses of Parliament then
stand adjourned to the day and place declared in the proclamation; and all
the orders which may have been made by either House, and appointed for
the original day of meeting, or any subsequent day, stand appointed for the
day named in the proclamation.

Dissolution

The Queen may also close the existence of Parliament by a dissolution, but is
not entirely free to define the duration of a Parliament. Before the Triennial
Act 1694 there was no constitutional limit to the continuance of a Parliament
but the will of the Crown. Under the Septennial Act 1715 it ceased to exist
after seven years from the day on which, by the writ of summons, it was
appointed to meet, a period which was reduced to five years by the Parliament Act 1911. Two great wars have made it necessary to prolong Parliaments for more than the five-year period prescribed by the Act of 1911.[4]
Before the Revolution of 1688 a Parliament was dissolved by the demise of
the Crown; but by the Act 7 & 8 Will 3, c 15, and by the Succession to the
Crown Act 1707, a Parliament was dissolved six months after the demise of
the Crown[5] (see p 59), and so the law continued until, by section 51 of the
Representation of the People Act of 1867, it was provided that the Parliament in being, at any future demise of the Crown, shall not be dissolved by

---

1 Adjournment by royal commission CJ (1547–1628) 639; Rapin ii. 205; CJ (1667–87) 158, 423,
426, 427, etc; Marvell i. 337, 343, 346, 356.
2 2 Hatsell 312, 316, 317; CJ (1547–1628) 807, 808, 809, ibid (1688–93) 694; ibid (1711–14) 26,
275; ibid (1799–1800) 49; 34 Parl Hist 1196; Colchester i 192.
3 LJ (1813–14) 747; CJ (1813–14) 132.
4 The duration of the Parliament which began on 31 January 1911 was extended to eight years
by the Parliament and Registration Act 1916, s 1(1), the Parliament and Local Elections Act
1916, s 1, and the Parliament and Local Elections Act 1918, s 1. The duration of the
Parliament which began on 26 November 1935 was extended to ten years by the Prolongation
of Parliament Acts of 1940, 1941, 1942, 1943 and 1944. See also the Parliament and Local
Elections Act 1916, s 3, for a conditional limitation of the duration of a Parliament.
5 Even the Privy Council expired at the demise of the Crown, and its members were reappointed in the new reign, and Queen Anne omitted the names of the Whig chiefs, Somers, Halifax,
and Orford. Lord Stanhope, Reign of Anne, p 44.

such demise, but shall continue as long as it would have otherwise continued, unless dissolved by the Crown.

Parliament is usually dissolved by proclamation under the great seal, after having been prorogued to a certain day, but such a proclamation has been issued at a time when both Houses stood adjourned.[1] This proclamation is issued by the Queen, with the advice of her Privy Council; and announces that the Queen has given orders to the Lord Chancellor of Great Britain and the Secretary of State for Northern Ireland to issue out writs in due form, and according to law, for calling a new Parliament; and that the writs are to be returnable in due course of law.

Since the dissolution of 28 March 1681, by Charles II, the sovereign had not dissolved Parliament in person until 10 June 1818, when it was dissolved by the Prince Regent in person. Parliament has not since been dissolved in that form, but proceedings not very dissimilar have occurred. On 22 April 1831 William IV, having come down to prorogue Parliament, said, 'I have come to meet you for the purpose of proroguing Parliament, with a view to its *immediate dissolution*'; and Parliament was dissolved by proclamation on the following day. On 17 July 1837 Parliament was prorogued and dissolved on the same day.[2] On 23 July 1847 Queen Victoria, in proroguing Parliament, announced her intention immediately to dissolve it; and it was accordingly dissolved by proclamation on the same day, and the writs were despatched by that evening's post.[3] By 1974 it had become the ordinary,[4] but not the invariable,[5] practice to proclaim the dissolution on the same day as Parliament is prorogued. More recently dissolutions have taken place when both Houses were adjourned, without recourse to prorogation.[6]

Other powers

In addition to these several powers of calling a Parliament, appointing its meeting, directing the commencement of its proceedings, determining them from time to time by prorogation, and finally of dissolving it altogether, the Crown has other parliamentary powers, which are dealt with in the relevant parts of the book in describing the functions of the two Houses.

1 CJ (1922) 330; ibid (1963–64) 340; ibid (1974–75) 2; ibid (1979–80) 2; LJ (1982–83) 353.
2 CJ (1818) 427; ibid (1830–31) 517; ibid (1837) 671; ibid (1837–38) 3.
3 CJ (1847) 960; ibid (1847–48) 3.
4 21 March 1857; 23 April 1859; 6 July 1865; 26 January 1874; 24 March 1880; 28 June 1892; 28 November 1910; 16 November 1923; 9 October 1924; 10 May 1929; 7 October 1931; 25 October 1935; 15 June 1945; 6 May 1955; 18 September 1959; 10 March 1966; 29 May 1970; 8 February 1974.
5 1859, prorogation, 19 April, proclamation, 23 April; 1886, prorogation, 25 June, proclamation, 26 June; 1895, prorogation, 6 July, proclamation, 8 July; 1900, prorogation, 8 August, proclamation, 17 September; 1905, prorogation, 11 August, further prorogations, 24 October and 11 December, proclamation, the government having resigned in the interval, 8 January 1906; 1909, prorogation, 3 December, proclamation, 10 January 1910; 1918, prorogation, 21 November, proclamation, 25 November; 1949, prorogation, 16 December, further prorogation, 21 January 1950, proclamation, 3 February 1950; 1951 prorogation, 4 October, proclamation, 5 October.
6 See p 222, n 1, for details of the practice since 1974.

RIGHTS AND FUNCTIONS OF THE HOUSE OF LORDS

Peers of the realm enjoy rights and exercise functions in four distinct capacities: first, they possess individually titles of honour which give them rank and precedence; secondly, they are individually counsellors of the Crown; thirdly, they are collectively, together with the Lords Spiritual, when assembled in Parliament, a court of judicature; and lastly, they are, conjointly with the Lords Spiritual and the Commons, in Parliament assembled, the legislative assembly of the kingdom, by whose advice, consent and authority, with the sanction of the Crown, laws are made.[1]

House of Lords as a Court of Judicature

The principal distinguishing characteristic of the Lords is their judicature, of which they exercise several kinds.

(a) Peerage claims. The House of Lords has a jurisdiction in claims of peerage and offices of honour, under references from the Crown, but not otherwise.[2] Such claims are referred by the House to the Committee for Privileges.[3]

(b) Appellate jurisdiction

Extent of jurisdiction. The House of Lords has a general judicature as a court of final appeal from other courts of justice. It has been held that this high judicial function was not at first inherent in the Lords but derived from the appellate jurisdiction in civil and criminal matters exercised, with the assent of the King, by the medieval *concilium regis ordinarium*. This body included the great officers of state and the judges and it invariably sat with the Lords Temporal and Spiritual to form the *magnum concilium in parliamento* or the *curia parliamenti*. In the course of the fourteenth century the lords took the jurisdiction into their own hands, using members of the *concilium ordinarium* only as assistants.[4] Their appellate jurisdiction appears to have received statutory confirmation from the Act, 14 Edw 3 c 5.[5] Early appeals were brought from the Court of King's Bench by way of a petition to the King or, more commonly in later years, by a writ of error issued by the Crown.[6] They also exercised an appellate jurisdiction over causes in equity on petition to themselves, without reference from the Crown, from the reign of Charles I onwards, notwithstanding the resistance of the Commons in 1675.[7] Appeals from Scotland were entertained following the Act of Union of 1707. Until an Act of 1783 conceded an appellate jurisdiction to the Irish House of Lords, the House also exercised appellate

1 1st Rep Dignity of Peer 14. But see pp 532–533.
2 See *Knowles' case* 12 State Tr 1167–1207; 1 Ld Raym 10; 2 Salk 509; Carth 297; Campbell Ch Just ii. 148; Lord Campbell's speeches 326; but see debates and proceedings upon the Wensleydale life peerage, 1856, Parl Deb (1856) 140, cc 263, 508, 591, 898, 977, 1022, 1121, 1152, 1289.
3 SO's Nos 73–77. For the composition of the committee see p 583.
4 Hale, Jurisd. Lords, c 14; Barrington on the Statutes 244; Denison and Scott xxvi–xxx.
5 Barrington on the Statutes 244.
6 Sugden 2; 27 Eliz I, c 8.
7 Sugden 3–9; 6 State Tr 711; Denison and Scott xxxvi–xlii.

jurisdiction over the Irish Courts, a jurisdiction which it resumed following the Treaty of Union in 1801.[1]

In 1873 the House's jurisdiction in respect of English appeals (but not Irish or Scottish appeals) was surrendered by the Supreme Court of Judicature Act 1873 but the operation of the Act was subsequently deferred.[2] The Appellate Jurisdiction Act 1876 repealed before they had come into operation those provisions of the 1873 Act which affected the House of Lords. The jurisdiction of the House was confirmed and defined while other provisions increased the efficiency of the House as a court of appeal.

Appeal to the House of Lords is by way of petition. Petitions may be presented in civil matters against—

(1) an order of the Court of Appeal in England and Wales, with the leave of that court or of the House;[3]
(2) an order of the Court of Appeal in Northern Ireland, with the leave of that court or of the House;[4]
(3) an order ('interlocutor') of the Court of Session in Scotland, without (but in certain cases with) the leave of that court or of the House;[5]
(4) an order of the High Court of Justice in England and Wales or in Northern Ireland, on the issue of a 'leapfrog' certificate by a judge of that court and with the leave of the House.[6]

Petitions may be presented in criminal matters against—

(1) a decision of the Court of Appeal (Criminal Division);[7]
(2) a decision of a Divisional Court of the Queen's Bench Division;[8]
(3) a decision of the Courts-Martial Appeal Court;[9]
(4) a decision of the Court of Appeal in Northern Ireland;[10]
(5) a decision of the High Court of Justice in Northern Ireland.[11]

An appeal in a criminal matter may only be brought with the leave of the court below or of the House; and such leave may not be granted unless the court below certifies that the matter involves a point of law of general public importance.[12]

Constitution of the House of Lords in its judicial capacity. An appeal may not be heard or determined by the House of Lords unless not less than three of the following persons, designated Lords of Appeal, are present: the Lord Chancellor of Great Britain, the Lords of Appeal in Ordinary, and any peer of Parliament who holds, or who has held, high judicial office, namely the office of (1) Lord Chancellor of Great Britain; (2) member of the Judicial Committee of the Privy Council; (3) Lord of Appeal in Ordinary; (4) judge

1 Denison and Scott xliv–xlviii; 23 Geo 3, c 28.
2 Supreme Court of Judicature Act (1873) Suspension Bill 1874; Supreme Court of Judicature Act (1873) Amendment Bill 1875.
3 Appellate Jurisdiction Act 1876, s 3; Administration of Justice (Appeals) Act 1934, s 1.
4 Judicature (Northern Ireland) Act 1978, s 42.
5 Appellate Jurisdiction Act 1876, s 3; Court of Session Act 1988, s 40.
6 Administration of Justice Act 1969, ss 12 and 13.
7 Criminal Appeal Act 1968, s 33.
8 Administration of Justice Act 1960, s 1.
9 Courts-Martial Appeals Act 1968, s 39.
10 Criminal Appeal (Northern Ireland) Act 1980, s 31.
11 Judicature (Northern Ireland) Act 1978, s 41.
12 In cases of habeas corpus or contempt no certificate is required.

of the Supreme Court of England or Northern Ireland or of the Court of Session in Scotland.[1] It is now established custom that none but these constitutes the Court.[2] The Lords of Appeal in Ordinary are appointed by the Crown by letters patent. Qualification for appointment is either to have held high judicial office for not less than two years, or to have been for not less than fifteen years a practising barrister in England or Northern Ireland or a practising advocate in Scotland.[3] The maximum number of Lords of Appeal in Ordinary is eleven.[4] They hold office during good behaviour subject, except in the case of those appointed to high judicial office before 1959, to a retiring age of seventy-five.[5] A Lord of Appeal in Ordinary is entitled to sit and vote on all business as a member of the House of Lords during his lifetime.[6]

Sittings. The House of Lords may meet for the transaction of judicial business on any weekday.[7] Sittings of the House to hear appeals take place when the House is not sitting for public business (usually during parliamentary recesses). Sittings of the House to give judgment take place two or three times a month during the periods when the House is sitting for public business, usually at 2 pm on Thursdays. The House may also meet during prorogation for the hearing and determining of appeals and for the introduction of Lords of Appeal in Ordinary at such time and in such manner as may be appointed by order of the House in the preceding session.[8] Moreover, notwithstanding any adjournment of the House, the House may meet for judicial business at a time earlier than that appointed if the Lord Chancellor or, in his absence, the senior Lord of Appeal in Ordinary (see below) is satisfied that it should do so.[9] During a dissolution of Parliament, the Queen may by writing under her Sign Manual authorise the Lords of Appeal in the name of the House of Lords to hear and determine appeals and to sit in the House of Lords for that purpose at such times as may be expedient.[10]

Most of the judicial business of the House is now referred to the Appellate and the Appeal Committees, sessional committees of which all Lords qualified under the Appellate Jurisdiction Acts 1876 and 1887 are members. The Lord Chancellor if present or, in his absence, the senior Lord of Appeal in Ordinary present takes the chair in these committees. Seniority is determined in accordance with the commission for the time being appointing Speakers for the purpose of hearing and determining appeals.[11]

Appellate Committees. Two Appellate Committees are appointed each session and most appeals are referred to and heard by one of these committees which then reports to the House. They may sit to hear appeals while Parliament is prorogued.[12] An Appellate Committee normally consists of

---

1 Appellate Jurisdiction Act 1876, ss 5, 6.
2 For voting by lay Lords see p 430.
3 Appellate Jurisdiction Act 1876, s 6.
4 Administration of Justice Act 1968, s 1. See p 10.
5 Appellate Jurisdiction Act 1876, s 6; Judicial Pensions Act 1959, ss 2(1), 3, Sch 1.
6 Ibid s 6; Appellate Jurisdiction Act 1887, s 2.
7 See also below p 417.
8 Appellate Jurisdiction Act 1876, s 8; Appellate Jurisdiction Act 1887, s 1.
9 SO No 14(3).
10 Appellate Jurisdiction Act 1876, s 9.
11 SO 82(1) and (4).
12 SO 82 (2)(a) and (6).

five Lords of Appeal. Judgment is given by the House following its agreement to the report of the committee which considered the appeal.

Appeal Committees. Two Appeal Committees are appointed to consider any petition for leave to appeal that may be referred to them and any matter relating thereto, or to causes depending or formerly depending in the House, and to report thereon to the House.[1] An Appeal Committee's decision is usually implemented by order of the House following its agreement to the report of the committee; but in any criminal matter, or in any matter concerning extradition, an Appeal Committee may take decisions and give directions on behalf of the House.[2]

(c) Original jurisdiction. In early times it appears that the House sometimes exercised an original jurisdiction as a court of first instance in civil and criminal matters.[3] In the seventeenth century, attempts to revive an original jurisdiction in civil matters eventually failed owing to the opposition of the Commons and of the judges.[4] The House also claimed an original jurisdiction over crimes, without impeachment by the Commons, but that too was abandoned.[5] However, a limited original jurisdiction in criminal matters continued to be exercised in relation to the privilege of peers, charged with treason or felony, to be tried by the House of Lords or, when Parliament was not sitting, the Court of the Lord High Steward. The last case of trial by peers was that of Lord de Clifford in 1935 and the practice was abolished in 1948.[6]

(d) Impeachment. The Lords have exercised a judicature in impeachments by the Commons but this has fallen into disuse.

PRINCIPAL POWER OF THE COMMONS

The dominant influence enjoyed by the House of Commons within Parliament may be ascribed principally to its status as an elected assembly, whose members serve as the chosen representatives of the people. As such the House of Commons possesses the most important power vested in any branch of the legislature, the right of imposing taxes upon the people and of voting money for the public service. The exercise of this right ensures the annual meeting of Parliament for redress of grievances, and it may also be said to give to the Commons the chief authority in the state. The financial powers and privileges of the Commons are described more fully at their

---

1 SO 82(2)(b).
2 SO 82(3).
3 Hale, Jurisd. Lords, c 15, 16 and 17.
4 *Skinner v The East India Company* and its effect on Lords jurisdiction is described in Hargreaves' preface to Hale, Jurisd. Lords pp ciii–cxxvi; see also 6 State Tr 711, 4 Parl Hist 431, 434.
5 CJ (1660–67) 38 (a precedent of dubious merit as it relates to proceedings in respect of the Regicides).
6 Criminal Justice Act 1948, s 30.

appropriate place in this work. As in the case of the Lords, the Commons'
constitutional role in passing Acts of attainder and of pains and penalties,
and in prosecuting offences before the Lords in impeachments, is now of
historical rather than current interest. But these powers have never been
formally abolished.[1]

---

1 For a full description of the procedure of impeachment, with references to the Journals and
  other authorities, see 4 Hatsell. For examples of bills of attainder see 4 Hatsell 85, 235 and
  323; for examples of bills of pains and penalties, see ibid 100, 244 and 331. For bills of
  restitution see p 1060 of the 20th edn of this work. See also pp 68 and 69 of that edition.

CHAPTER 5

The privilege of Parliament

WHAT CONSTITUTES PRIVILEGE

Parliamentary privilege is the sum of the peculiar rights enjoyed by each House collectively as a constituent part of the High Court of Parliament, and by Members of each House individually, without which they could not discharge their functions, and which exceed those possessed by other bodies or individuals. Thus privilege, though part of the law of the land, is to a certain extent an exemption from the general law. Certain rights and immunities such as freedom from arrest or freedom of speech belong primarily to individual Members of each House and exist because the House cannot perform its functions without unimpeded use of the services of its Members. Other such rights and immunities such as the power to punish for contempt and the power to regulate its own constitution belong primarily to each House as a collective body, for the protection of its Members and the vindication of its own authority and dignity.[1] Fundamentally, however, it is only as a means to the effective discharge of the collective functions of the House that the individual privileges are enjoyed by Members.[2]

When any of these rights and immunities is disregarded or attacked, the offence is called a breach of privilege and is punishable under the law of Parliament. Each House also claims the right to punish as contempts actions which, while not breaches of any specific privilege, obstruct or impede it in the performance of its functions, or are offences against its authority or dignity, such as disobedience to its legitimate commands or libels upon itself, its Members or its officers. The power to punish for contempt has been judicially considered to be inherent in each House of Parliament not as a necessary incident of the authority and functions of a legislature (as might be argued in respect of certain privileges) but by virtue of their descent from the undivided High Court of Parliament and in right of the *lex et consuetudo parliamenti*.[3] In

---

1 In this and the six following chapters, the term 'privilege' is used in the sense of fundamental right necessary for the exercise of constitutional functions. The use of the term in the context of the financial powers of the Commons, including rights both against the Crown and against the Lords, is dealt with separately in ch 21 and 30.

2 The Commons asserted in 1675 that privilege existed so that Members might 'freely attend the public affairs of the House, without disturbance or interruption' (CJ (1667–87) 342).

3 *Kielley v Carson* 4 Moore PC 63 (in 1842) overruling *Beaumont v Barrett* 1 Moore PC 59. This decision was followed by the Privy Council in *Fenton v Hampton* 1858 (Moore PC Reports), *Doyle v Falconer* (1866) (4 Moore PC Reports); by the Supreme Court of Canada in *Woodworth's case*, 1878 (2 Canada Supreme Court Rep). The doctrine is accepted that under the common law only such powers are inherent in a legislative assembly as are necessary to its existence and the proper exercise of its functions. Wider power must depend upon express grant by statute of constitutional power, as in the case of Victoria (1 Moore PC Rep (ns) 511, 512 (*Dill v Murphy* 1864), and New South Wales (LR Appeal (1908), 470–477 (*Hamitt v Crick*)).

this, the position of the UK Parliament differs from that of independent Commonwealth or colonial legislatures.[1]

LORDS: PRIVILEGES OF PARLIAMENT AND OF PEERAGE

Some privileges rest solely on the law and custom of Parliament, while others have been defined by statute. The Lords enjoy their privileges simply because of their immemorial role in Parliament as advisers of the Sovereign.

Privilege of peerage is in some respects different from privilege of Parliament; the latter is enjoyed by all members of the House of Lords, whether or not they are peers, but is denied to peers who are minors, to noblewomen, and to widows of peers; it also, in theory at least, may be interrupted during a long Prorogation or Dissolution.[2] Privilege of peerage is not liable to interruption and belongs to all peers whether or not they are members of the House of Lords. The extent of the privilege is not entirely clear, but it has been shown in recent times to confer immunity from arrest on civil process.[3] In general the privilege probably has its origin from the fact that, as major tenants-in-chief of the Sovereign, the peers were full members of his Court; they therefore could not, in ancient times, be proceeded against in the courts below, who regarded their persons as 'for ever sacred and inviolable'. It is perhaps for this reason, too, that peers have traditionally had a right of individual access to the Sovereign. By the Acts of Union of 1706 and 1800 peers of Scotland and Ireland were accorded the same privileges as peers of England.[4] If, however, a peer of Ireland is elected to the Commons he is not entitled to privilege of peerage so long as he continues to be a member of that House.[5] In 1442, by the Act 20 Hen VI c 9, the right of trial by the House of Lords was conferred upon peeresses; since that time it has been the law that peeresses by birth, creation or marriage have had the same immunity from arrest on civil process as peers.[6] A peeress by marriage forfeits her privilege of peerage if she marries a commoner.[7]

HISTORICAL DEVELOPMENT OF PRIVILEGE

At the commencement of every Parliament it has been the custom for the Speaker, in the name, and on behalf of the Commons, to lay claim by humble petition to their ancient and undoubted rights and privileges; par-

1 For an account of privilege jurisdiction in Commonwealth legislatures, see HC 34 (1967–68) p 176, and for an account of the privileges and immunities of members of national parliaments of the EEC and of the European Parliament, see Select Committee on the European Communities, 8th report, HL 105 (1985–86).
2 SO No 79; Co Litt 16 b; Bac Abr vi 542; LJ (1660–66) 298; ibid (1691–96) 241; ibid (1666–75) 714; ibid (1675–81) 67, 79, 80, 659.
3 *Stourton v Stourton* (1963) 2 WLR 397–403. See also p 39 above, and p 101 below.
4 2 Stra 990; case of Viscount Hawarden (LJ (1828) 28–34).
5 Union with Ireland Act 1800, art 4.
6 Countess of Rutland's case, 6 Co Rep 52; cases of Lady Purbeck, 1625; Lady De la Warr, 1642; Lady Dacre, 1660; Lady Petre, 1664; Countess of Huntingdon, 1676; Countess of Newport, 1699; Lady Abergavenny, 1727; LJ (1828) 28–34.
7 SO No 79.

ticularly to freedom of speech in debate, freedom from arrest, freedom of access to Her Majesty whenever occasion shall require; and that the most favourable construction should be placed upon all their proceedings.

The Lord Chancellor by virtue of a Royal Commission under letters patent replies to the Speaker's petition that, 'Her Majesty most readily confirms all the rights and privileges which have ever been granted to or conferred upon the Commons, by Her Majesty or any of her royal predecessors'.[1]

By contrast with the Lords, the acquisition and enforcement of these privileges by the Commons was both complex and prolonged. The importance of privilege today cannot be entirely divorced from its past. Each of the Speaker's petitions is briefly considered in its historical context in this chapter, together with related powers and privileges. Subsequent chapters then develop each of the themes in current procedure.

Freedom of speech

The first claim in the Speaker's petition is for freedom of speech in debate. By the latter part of the fifteenth century,[2] the Commons seems to have enjoyed an undefined right to freedom of speech, as a matter of tradition rather than by virtue of a privilege sought and obtained. Earlier Speakers made no claim for such a privilege. What they did request was permission to correct any inadvertent misrepresentation of the House's views to the King, a practice perhaps legal in origin, though with obvious political advantages.[3] Secondly, Speakers asked that if the House or the Speaker should displease

---

1   LJ (1841) 571; ibid (1847–48) 8, etc; for the form of words used at the opening of the first new Parliament after an accession to the throne, see LJ (1906) 18; ibid (1911) 9; ibid (1945–46) 22; ibid (1955–56) 13.
2   Previous editions of this work have suggested that there were earlier cases leading to the establishment of a fairly distinct privilege of freedom of speech in debate. This seems unlikely. The first such citation is *Haxey's case* (1396–97). The fact that Haxey was not a Member of the House must alter the significance of the grounds on which the House petitioned that judgment against him should be reversed, viz the 'Libertes de lez ditz Communes'. The petition of Younge (a Member) in 1455, that he should be compensated for having suffered for a speech made in the House, a punishment meted out contrary to 'the olde liberte and fredom of the Comyns of this land . . . to speke and sey in the House . . . without any maner [of] chalenge, charge or punicion', should be considered in the light of the fact that he was asking a Yorkist Parliament to compensate him for the effects of an untimely and unwelcome political proposal made to its Lancastrian predecessor. Finally, the case of Strode in 1513, who was punished in the Stannary Court for having proposed in Parliament measures to regulate Cornish tinners, is of limited significance, despite its popularity in the early seventeenth century. The statute which voided the proceedings and sanctions against Strode bore similarly, it is true, on other suits against Members of that or future Parliaments 'for any bill, speaking or declaring of any matter concerning the Parliament'. But this can hardly be a manifesto directed at the most likely source of a limitation on freedom of debate, Henry VIII; nor was it probably intended to be such. What *Strode's case* did establish was the privileged position of the Commons against inferior courts, as a full partner in Parliament. For comments on the cases mentioned, see 20th edn, pp 78–79; and see also 'The Commons Privilege of Free Speech in Parliament', Sir John Neale in *Historical Studies of the English Parliament* (ed E B Fryde and Edward Miller, 1970) vol 2 pp 147 ff, and *The Tudor Constitution* (G R Elton, 1982) pp 260 ff.
3   3 Rot Parl 216 b, 424 b, 425 b.

the King or infringe his prerogative, this should be regarded as unintentional. Neither of these requests seems consistent with the development of full freedom of speech in debate as subsequently understood.

The earliest evidence of a shift of emphasis away from reliance on traditional assumptions and attempts to avoid the visitation of royal displeasure on the Speaker, and towards a claim of privilege for the House appears to be the petition of Speaker Sir Thomas More in 1523, asking Henry VIII 'to take all in good part, interpretinge every man's words, how uncunningly soever they may be couched, to proceed yeat of a good zeale towardes the profitt of your Realme'. More's plea may or may not have been answered,[1] and what was sought in the immediately following Parliaments is not clear. By the first Parliament of Elizabeth, however, a claim for freedom of speech in debate was certainly made,[2] and in 1563 it was justified as 'according to the old antient order'.[3] Though no claim appears to have been made in 1566, by the end of the century the practice had become regular.

Such a claim, even if made Parliament after Parliament, must nevertheless be defined and defended. There were those in the Elizabethan House who, expressing the House's growing political self-awareness, made fairly advanced demands for freedom of debate. Prevailing opinion moved more slowly. Freedom of speech was important and the Crown ought not to act against a Member directly for something said in the House; but it seems to have been common ground that decorum and obedience to the Sovereign's wishes ought to be respected. Just as the House increased its ability to protect its Members from arrest and molestation, so it was frequently ready to take punitive action, without waiting for the Crown or Council, against those who overstepped the mark in debate.[4] There was much in these views with which the Crown agreed. Lord Keeper Sir Edward Coke emphasized the executive's view in 1593 when he reminded the Speaker that 'Her Majesty granteth you liberal but not licentious speech, liberty therefore but with due limitation ... To say yea or no to bills, God forbid that any man should be restrained or afraid to answer according to his best liking ... which is the very true liberty of the House; not, as some suppose, to speak there of all causes as him listeth ... No King fit for his state will suffer such absurdities'.[5]

Much of what was unresolved under Elizabeth remained debatable in the years before the civil war, though under Charles I the acuteness of successive political crises diminished the likelihood of resolution. Those who took an 'advanced' view of the basis of freedom of speech were still in evidence and argued in the Apology of 1604 that it was erroneous to believe that the House's privileges were 'of grace only, renewed every Parliament ... upon petition and so to be limited'. The view was expressed in Committee on the Commons petition in 1610 that freedom of speech 'could not well be taken from us without shaking the foundations of the liberties of Parliament'. In 1621, James I challenged these assumptions. Privileges, he said, 'were derived from the grace and permission of our ancestors and us'. To this the

1 See G R Elton *The Parliament of England, 1559–81* (1986) pp 331, 341–349.
2 CJ (1547–1628) 37.
3 D'Ewes 66.
4 Elton *The Parliament of England, 1559–81* pp 342–349.
5 Elton *Tudor Constitution* p 274.

House rejoined 'that every Member of the House of Commons hath and of right ought to have freedom of speech ... and ... like freedom from all impeachment, imprisonment and molestation (other than by censure of the House itself) for or concerning any speaking, reasoning or declaring of any matter or matters touching the Parliament or parliament business'. Without hindsight regarding the events of the next reign, the Protestation of 1621 had much in common with Elizabethan views, not least because it explicitly contemplated the reference to the king of anything questioned or complained of in Parliament, provided it was 'with the advice and assent of all the Commons'.[1]

The actions of Charles I are more difficult to fit into the same framework, particularly those of 1629 when Sir John Eliot and two other Members were charged in King's Bench for seditious words spoken in debate and for violence against the Speaker, who had been physically restrained in the Chair in order to delay the adjournment of the House. Among the Crown's arguments were the contentions that parliamentary privilege did not protect seditious comments in the Chamber, and that King's Bench could properly take note of day to day events in the High Court of Parliament, such as the assault on the Speaker.[2]

By the time of the final breakdown in the early 1640's, the House had in practice bypassed Elizabethan conventions which denied Members the initiative in debate on great matters of state, and the limits of what was unacceptable in criticism of the government had been drastically narrowed.

There was a sequel to the events of 1629. In 1641, the arrests were declared by the House to be against the law and privilege of Parliament[3] and in 1667–68 one of those arrested, now a peer, took action to secure the agreement of both Houses to the proposition that the judgment had been illegal and against the privilege of Parliament. Upon a writ of error, the judgment of King's Bench was reversed by the Lords.[4]

One of the significant elements in the decision of 1667–68 was the prevailing argument that words spoken in Parliament should be brought to account only in Parliament.[5] Such an important shift in emphasis no doubt owed much to the history of the preceding 25 years. More generally, in the years between the Restoration and the Revolution, conflict over the pre-1640 battlegrounds was, for political reasons, virtually unknown. Even James II made no direct assault on freedom of debate on the same lines as his father and grandfather.

Statutory recognition was finally accorded to the privilege by the Bill of Rights 1689.[6] In its ninth article, Crown and Parliament concluded that 'the freedom of speech and debates or proceedings in Parliament ought not to be impeached or questioned in any court or place out of Parliament'. Many tensions in the previous history of freedom of speech were resolved. The privilege was clearly and widely established, in both Houses, and was largely protected from outside interference, whether by the Crown intent on stifling political initiatives or 'indecorous' criticism, or by the courts, as in 1629. The

---

1 See J P Kenyon *The Stuart Constitution* (1986) pp 24–27, 38–42.
2 3 State Tr 309–310.
3 CJ (1640–42) 203; 3 State Tr 235; 1 Hatsell 250–280.
4 CJ (1667–87) 19, 25; LJ (1666–75) 166, 223.
5 3 State Tr 332.
6 1 William and Mary, sess 2, c 2.

exclusive jurisdiction of words spoken or acts done as proceedings in Parliament was now entrusted by law to Parliament and to no other body.

Chapter 6 will illustrate the elaboration in practice of the principles confirmed in 1689.

Freedom from arrest

The second of the Speaker's customary petitions on behalf of the Commons at the beginning of a Parliament is for freedom from arrest. The development of this privilege is in some ways linked to that of other privileges. Arrest was frequently the consequence of the unsuccessful assertion of freedom of speech, for example. At the same time, there are some distinctive features in chronology and development which mark off freedom from arrest from other such claims made by the House. Some elements which still underpin the privilege are found at a very early period. In other areas, the House has subsequently voluntarily narrowed the scope of the privilege.[1]

Whatever the origin of the privilege of freedom from arrest, whether in some recollection of the liberties attached to attendance at traditional popular assemblies or in the principle that the King's servants doing their duty in a superior court should not be impeded by litigation in a lower tribunal, the principle was clearly established at a relatively early date. The first known assertion of freedom from arrest seems to date from 1340,[2] when the King released a Member from prison during the Parliament following that in which he had been prevented, by his detention, from taking his seat. In 1404, the Commons claimed that it was privileged from arrest for debt, contract, or trespass of any kind, according to the custom of the realm.[3]

Though the principle may have been deeply engrained, its implementation was patchy and often beyond the power of the Commons alone to enforce. The delay in releasing the Member in 1340 amply illustrates this, as does the case of Mr Speaker Thorpe, a century later, in 1452. Thorpe had been imprisoned and retained in gaol by order of the House of Lords, despite advice from their assistants the judges that he was entitled to his release. In that instance, the Commons accepted the position and elected a new Speaker.[4] Indeed in two separate cases in 1472, the courts disallowed writs of *supersedeas* staying actions for debt on the grounds that Members of Parliament and their servants were protected by custom from being arrested, imprisoned or impleaded for debt during the time of Parliament: the judges upheld the plaintiff's view that there was no such custom.[5]

---

1 A claim of privilege previously made in this connection in respect of estates was omitted for the first time in 1852. Freedom from 'molestations' (for the precise meaning of which see HC 34 (1967–68) paras 109–112 and p93) was claimed until 1866. The privilege of not being impleaded (ie sued) was considerably limited by statute in the late seventeenth and eighteenth century (see p76) and the claim which afforded protection to menial servants, having been effectively extinguished by statute in 1770, was no longer made after 1892 (Parl Deb (1892) 7, c18; 2 Hatsell 225; Colchester i65) (see p76)).

2 *Bulletin of the Institute of Historical Research* vol43 (1970) pp214–215.

3 The Act 5 Hen IV, c6 (1404) provided that those who assaulted the servants of Members of Parliament should pay double damages besides a fine (3 Rot Parl 542; 1 Hatsell 15–17). The same penalty was later imposed by a general statute for assaults on Members of either House coming to Parliament (11 Hen VI, c11 (1432): 3 Rot Parl 541; 1 Hatsell 15–17).

4 5 Rot Parl 239; 1 Hatsell 28–34.

5 1 Hatsell 41–43. See also p77.

Subsequent developments, however, were to establish relatively clearly, if slowly, the basis and the limitations of the privilege. In the first place, it had always been recognized that privilege could not be pleaded against criminal offences, then adequately summed up as treason, felony, and breach of the peace. The Commons accepted this in 1429,[1] as did the judges in *Thorpe's case* in 1452.[2] A resolution of the Commons in 1675 declared that 'by the laws and usage of Parliament, privilege of Parliament belongs to every Member of the House of Commons, in all cases except treason, felony and breach of the peace'. In 1697 it was resolved 'that no Member of this House has any privilege in case of breach of the peace, or forcible entries or forcible detainers'.[3]

In connection with *John Wilkes' case*, although the Court of Common Pleas had decided otherwise, it was resolved by both Houses in 1763 that privilege of Parliament does not extend to the case of writing and publishing seditious libels, nor ought to be allowed to obstruct the ordinary course of the laws in the speedy and effectual prosecution of so heinous and dangerous an offence'.[4] 'Since that time', said the Committee of Privileges in 1831, 'it has been considered as established generally, that privilege is not claimable for any indictable offence.'[5]

The privilege as regards the Lords was explained by a resolution of 1626, 'that the privilege of this House is that no peer of Parliament, sitting the Parliament, is to be imprisoned or restrained without sentence or order of the House, unless it be for treason or felony, or for refusing to give surety of the peace'.[6] The current Standing Order of the Lords (No 78) prescribes that 'when Parliament is sitting, or within the usual times of privilege of Parliament, no Lord of Parliament is to be imprisoned or restrained without sentence or order of the House, unless upon a criminal charge or for refusing to give security for the peace.' Notification of orders for restraint must be given to the House.[7]

It was not only the criminal law against which a plea of privilege would fail. In earlier days, the privilege could not prevail against more or less arbitrary detention at the order of the Crown. The most notable case under Elizabeth was that of Strickland in 1571, who was called before the Council and inhibited from attending the House (not strictly speaking arrested) for preferring a Bill to reform the Book of Common Prayer, against the Queen's wishes.[8] In the next two reigns, however, such activities became more common. In 1615, 1621 and 1622 Members were imprisoned without trial while the House was not sitting or after a dissolution. Charles I arrested Eliot and Digges in 1626 while the House was in session, and the further

---

1 4 Rot Parl 357; 1 Hatsell 17–22.
2 5 Rot Parl 239; 1 Hatsell 28–34.
3 CJ (1667–87) 342; ibid (1693–97) 784. See also ibid (1640–42) 261.
4 LJ (1760–64) 426; CJ (1761–64) 674; 15 Parl Hist 1362–78. See also 2 Wils 150; 19 State Tr 981.
5 CJ (1831) 701. See also LJ (1709–14) 31, 34 and ibid (1741–46) 492.
6 LJ (1620–28) 562.
7 For such notifications, see LJ (1953–54) 138; ibid (1960–61) 422; ibid (1974–75) 52; ibid (1980–81) 58; ibid (1987–88) 880.
8 D'Ewes 166–168, 175–176. The cases involving Peter Wentworth involve arrests either by the House's own order or for activities out of Parliament. (Sir J E Neale *Elizabeth I and her Parliaments* vol I (1953), pp 325ff and vol II (1957) pp 157 ff and 260 ff).

action of the King in 1629 has already been mentioned[1] (see p 73). After the
Restoration, the practice effectively ceased.

From the earliest times,[2] therefore, freedom from arrest was regarded as
confined to civil suits. In its original form, the privilege was even wider than
freedom from arrest. Members were not to be 'impleaded', which was taken
to prevent civil actions being maintained against them at all, by reason of
their inability to maintain their private rights while in attendance upon
Parliament.[3] The House insisted in 1477 that the privilege had existed
'whereof tyme that mannys mynde is not the contrarie'.[4] Writs of *supersedeas* were first issued to stay such actions but from the beginning of the
seventeenth century the Speaker was ordered to stay suits by a letter to the
judges,[5] and sometimes also by a warrant to the party;[6] and the parties and
their attorneys who commenced the actions were brought by the Serjeant to
the bar of the House.[7]

In the sixteenth century, the privilege was not always allowed,[8] and
subsequently statute first eroded[9] and then extinguished it. Under the
Parliamentary Privilege Act 1770, any person may at any time commence
and prosecute an action or suit in any court of law against peers or Members
of Parliament and their servants; and no such action or process shall be
interfered with under any privilege of Parliament. It is also, however,
enacted that nothing in the Act should subject the person of any Member of
Parliament to arrest or imprisonment. Under this Act[10] a Member of Parliament may be coerced by every legal process, except attachment of his body.

1 J P Kenyon *The Stuart Constitution* (1986) p 24.
2 Exemption from distraint in time of Parliament was conceded as early as 1290, when the
   bishop of St David's was protected against a petition for leave to distrain for rent of a house
   (1 Rot Parl 61; 1 Hatsell 3) and in 1315 (1 Hatsell 12).
3 1 Hatsell 6–9, 50. For procedures with regard to the issue of writs of *supersedeas* in 1588, see
   D'Ewes 436.
4 6 Rot Parl 191, 1 Hatsell 50.
5 CJ (1547–1628) 342, 381, 525, 861.
6 CJ (1547–1628) 804.
7 D'Ewes 348, 350; CJ (1547–1628) 211, 368, 371, 655, 922, 928. For a refusal of the judges to
   obey the Speaker's letter, see Prynne, 4th Register 810; CJ (1547–1628) 861; 1 Hatsell 184,
   185. For cases in which Members waived their privilege and upon petitions from the parties
   suits were allowed to proceed, see CJ (1547–1628) 378, 421, 595, etc; ibid (1688–93) 280,
   300, 600; ibid (1693–97) 557 etc.
8 In 1585 the Lord Chancellor sitting in Chancery 'very gently and courteously' demanded
   precedents to support a claim for privilege in the case of the service of a *subpoena* on a
   Member (D'Ewes 347).
9 The Act 12 & 13 Will 3, c 3, enacted that any person might commence and prosecute actions
   against any peer, or Member of Parliament, or their servants, or others entitled to privilege,
   in the court at Westminster, and the duchy court of Lancaster, immediately after a
   dissolution or prorogation, until the next meeting of Parliament, and during any adjournment for more than fourteen days; and that during such times the court might give judgment
   and award execution. Soon afterwards it was enacted, by 2 & 3 Anne, c 12, that no action,
   suit, process, proceedings, judgment or execution, against privileged persons, employed in
   the revenue, or any office of public trust, for any forfeiture, penalty, etc., should be stayed
   or delayed by or under colour or pretence of privilege of Parliament. The Act of William III
   had extended only to the principal courts of law and equity; but by the Parliamentary
   Privileges Act 1737, all actions in relation to real and personal property were allowed to be
   commenced and prosecuted in the recess and during adjournments of more than fourteen
   days, in any court of record.
10 Cf also the Acts 45 Geo 3, c 124 and 47 Geo 3, sess 2, c 40, for further information on the
   history of privilege in relation to legal process. Both these Acts were repealed by the Statute
   Law Revision Act of 1872.

However well established the principle of freedom from arrest, practical problems remained. Where a Member of the Commons had been imprisoned in a civil suit, the House faced the difficulty of first how to secure his release, and secondly, when the Member was in execution, how to do so without damage to the rights of the plaintiff, since a Member released by pleading his privilege could not be rearrested, and the creditor lost his claim.

Initially, these problems were solved (as in 1340) with the assistance of the Crown or of the courts, when a writ of privilege would be issued by the Lord Chancellor addressed to the keeper of the prison.[1] To save the rights of plaintiffs special statutes might authorize the Lord Chancellor to issue writs for the release of Members.[2] *Ferrers' case* in 1542 is often seen as signifying an advance on previous arrangements for securing the release of an imprisoned Member. Ferrers, a Member, was arrested as surety for a debt, and the House took the novel step of sending the Serjeant, with the Mace as his only authority, to secure Ferrers' release from the City authorities. When this was resisted, the Commons laid the matter before the Lords, 'who, judging the contempt to be very great, referred the punishment thereof to the Commons House'. The Commons refused the Lord Chancellor's offer of a traditional writ of privilege. By this time, Ferrers had been released, but the House sent for and committed for contempt those who had been responsible for his detention.

Although this was in the past seen as the assumption of striking new authority by the Commons, the significance of *Ferrers' case* is probably more limited. His release may have been obtained principally because Ferrers was Henry VIII's servant, not because he was Burgess for Plymouth, against the background of the King's reported remark that he, 'being the head of Parliament and attending in his own person upon the business thereof ought in reason to have privilege for himself and all his servants attending there upon him', and 'whatsoever offence or injury . . . is offered to the meanest Member of the House is to be judged against our person and the whole court of Parliament'.[3] Moreover, the practice of seeking writs of privilege out of Chancery in order to secure the release of Members, in preference to sending the Serjeant with the Mace, continued after 1542, though no writ was obtained without a warrant previously signed by the Speaker. In particular, in *Smalley's case* in 1576, when a Member attempted to use privilege in order to avoid repaying the sum owed and not merely to escape prison for himself or his servant, the House first maintained that a writ out of Chancery was necessary, and only at the insistence of Arthur Hall, Burgess for Grantham and Smalley's master, did the House resort to enforcing the privilege by the authority of the Mace.[4] It seems clear, however, both from

---

1 For example, CJ (1547–1628) 48, 536–537; and see D'Ewes 430; 4 Rot Parl 357; 5 ibid 111 239, 374; 6 ibid 160, 191; 1 Hatsell 51.

2 'Le Roi, par advis des seigneurs espirituelx et temporelx, et a les especiales requestes des communes' 4 Rot Parl 357; also 5 ibid 374; 6 ibid 191; 5 ibid 111; 6 ibid 160; 5 ibid 239; 1 Hatsell 51.

3 See G R Elton *The Tudor Constitution* (1982) p 261 n and pp 275–277, where the reliability of the report of the King's speech is doubted. See also 1 Hatsell 53–59.

4 When Hall's fraud was discovered, he was committed by order of the House till the debt was paid and severely censured by the House (CJ (1547–1628) 107, 108, and see Sir J E Neale *Elizabeth I and her Parliaments* vol I (1953) pp 333 ff and G R Elton *The Parliament of England, 1559–81* (1986) pp 333–334.) (The fraud attempted by Hall and Smalley was not unique, cf CJ (1547–1528) 55.)

the events of Smalley's case and from incidents in 1572 when the action taken over Ferrers was quoted though not followed,[1] that at least there was a current of opinion in favour of the House's assumption of executive authority to protect and enforce freedom from arrest.[2]

The next stage in the development of the privilege in the Commons came in 1604. Sir Thomas Shirley, who had been elected to the Commons, but had been imprisoned in the Fleet in execution before the meeting of Parliament, was discharged at the demand of the Serjeant, acting on the order of the House (though not before an attempt to bring him into the House by *habeas corpus* had failed). The Warden of the Fleet was committed for contempt, having initially refused to release the Member.[3] These events were followed by the Act 1 James I c 13, which statutorily recognized the privilege of freedom from arrest, the right of either House to set a privileged person at liberty, and the right to punish those who make or procure arrests. In order to reconcile this with the reasonable rights of creditors, it was enacted that once the privilege claimed had expired with the session or the Parliament, parties might sue forth and execute a new writ. No sheriff or similar officer from whose arrest or custody persons were delivered by privilege was to be chargeable with any action.

The principal earlier cases in the Lords show an uncertainty in their practice similar to that of the Commons, privileged persons being sometimes released immediately by order and sometimes by writ.[4] During the same period, when the property of peers or of their servants was distrained, the Lords was accustomed to interfere by its direct authority,[5] but privilege did not apply to property held by a peer as a trustee only.[6] A further statute of 1700,[7] while it maintained the privilege of freedom from arrest with more distinctness than the Act 1 James I c 13, made the goods of privileged persons liable to distress infinite and sequestration, between a dissolution or prorogation and the next meeting of Parliament, and during adjournments for more than fourteen days. In suits against the King's immediate debtors, execution against Members was permitted even during the sitting of Parliament, and the privilege of freedom from arrest in such suits was not reserved to servants. By a further Act of 1703[8] executions for penalties, forfeitures, etc, against privileged persons, being employed in the revenue or any office of trust, were not to be stayed by privilege.

Freedom from arrest, however, was still maintained in such cases for the Members of both Houses but not for their servants.

---

1 T E Hartley (ed) *Proceedings in the Parliaments of Elizabeth I* (1981) pp 381, 411.
2 In the case of Fitzherbert in 1593 the House ordered that the Speaker should seek a writ of *habeas corpus* out of Chancery to secure the release of an imprisoned Member, though the alternative of following the Ferrers precedent was also argued (D'Ewes 479, 481, 502, 514, 518, 520), and the Lord Keeper himself thought it best 'in regard to the ancient liberties and privileges of the House' that the Serjeant be sent with the Mace. See also CJ (1547–1628) 807, 820; ibid (1667–87) 411; ibid (1711–14) 6; 1 Hatsell 167.
3 CJ (1547–1628) 155 ff; 5 Parl Hist 113 etc; 1 Hatsell 157.
4 LJ (1578–1614) 66, 93, 201, 205, 230, 238, 241, 270, 296, 299, 302, 588; ibid (1620–28) 30; ibid (1628–42) 654; ibid (1645–46) 577, 601, 635, 639; D'Ewes 603, 607.
5 LJ (1620–28) 776, 777; ibid (1647–48) 611.
6 LJ (1666–75) 194, 390; ibid (1685–91) 36, 78; ibid (1696–1701) 294; ibid (1722–26) 412.
7 12 & 13 William III c 3, afterwards extended by 11 Geo II, c 24.
8 2 & 3 Anne, c 12.

The freedom of a Member from arrest in civil cases having been put on a statutory footing, the means of securing a Member's release changed. Peers, peeresses and Members of the Commons were normally discharged immediately upon motion in the court from which the process issued,[1] and writs of privilege have been discontinued.

Since the enactment of section 1 of the Judgments Act 1838 and subsequent legislation, imprisonment in civil process has been practically abolished.[2] The position of Members in respect of imprisonment (or attachment) for contempt of court, bankruptcy and statutory detention is dealt with at pp 97–99, as are the related privileges of exemption from attendance as a witness and the privilege of exemption from jury service.

Chapter 7 deals more fully with freedom from arrest or molestation in modern times.

Freedom of access

The third of the Speaker's petitions is for freedom of access to Her Majesty whenever occasion shall require. This claim is medieval (probably fourteenth century) in origin, and in an earlier form seems to have been sought in respect of the Speaker himself, and to have encompassed also access to the Upper House.[3] Even when the four petitions were only hesitantly becoming standard in the mid sixteenth century, the claim for access seems to have been consistently made. The privilege of freedom of access is exercised by the Commons as a body and through their Speaker, though it is not now exercised in Parliament on the initiative of the House. The Commons attends the Queen on summons to the House of Lords, for purposes prescribed by Her Majesty. Out of Parliament, the Commons exercises its right of access for the purpose of presenting Addresses (see p 566), which may deal with any subject of public policy chosen by the House. Such an Address may be presented by the whole House or, more usually, the House will order the Address to be communicated by such Members as have access to Her Majesty as Privy Counsellors or as members of Her Majesty's Household.

The right of access to Her Majesty is a corporate privilege of the House; it is denied to individual Members,[4] so that the Queen receives only the decisions of the House as a whole and cannot take notice of matters pending

---

1 See *Colonel Pitt's case* (1734) 2 Stra 985. Even after the passing of the Act of 1700, the Commons acted to secure the release of a Member by sending the Serjeant with the Mace to the prison concerned (CJ (1705–8) 471). The House ordered the release of a Member entitled to privilege, (ibid (1807) 654; ibid (1819) 44). Action has also been taken by the Lords to punish those who caused the arrest (see LJ (1810–12) 60, 63; ibid (1828) 34; and Report of Precedents 28) by the Commons in respect of those who brought an action for a Member's escape against the keeper of a gaol who released a Member in accordance with the orders of the House (CJ (1819–20) 286).

2 See Pike *Const History of House of Lords* p 259.

3 CJ (1547–1628) 73: D'Ewes 16. Rather surprisingly, the claim for freedom of access was omitted in 1523 by Speaker Sir Thomas More, when he made his well-known request for freedom of speech (see p 72).

4 The only right claimed and exercised by individual Members in availing themselves of the privilege of access to the Queen is that of entering the presence of royalty, when accompanying the Speaker with Addresses, in their ordinary attire, the privilege entitling them to dispense with the forms and ceremonies of the court.

in the House, still less of debates or the speeches of individual Members.[1] Indeed, the Commons has long established the principle that the Sovereign may not, even as a spectator, attend its debates.

The House of Lords, like the Commons, is entitled to access to the Sovereign, as a body, and peers in addition possess the right of access as individuals, as part of the privilege of peerage (see p 70). No principle exists restricting the Sovereign's attendance at debates in the Lords.[2]

Favourable construction

The final petition which the Speaker makes is that the most favourable construction should be placed upon all the House's proceedings. As in the case of the privilege of free access, this claim was, before the reign of Elizabeth, for the benefit of the Speaker rather than the House (see p 79). Even in 1559 Speaker Sir Thomas Gargrave asked that 'if in anything himself should mistake or misreport or overslip that which should be committed unto him to declare, that it might without prejudice to the House be better declared, and that his unwilling miscarriage therein might be pardoned'; to which the Queen replied that the petition should be granted, provided that 'your diligence and carefulness be such, Mr Speaker, that the defaults in that part be as rare as may be'.[3] The request is now little more than a formal courtesy, as the proceedings of the House are guarded against any inter-ference, on the part of the Crown, not authorized by the laws and consti-tution of the country; and as by the law and custom of Parliament the Queen cannot take notice of anything said or done in the House, but by the report of the House itself.

Privilege with respect to the constitution of the House

It is a privilege of the House of Commons to provide for its own proper constitution as established by law.

The origins of this privilege are to be found in the sixteenth century. In 1515, Henry VIII transferred to the Speaker, acting for the House, the authority to license Members to depart before the end of the session.[4] Though much was to flow from the elaboration of this principle, the transfer of substantial authority was delayed. In 1536 the King authorised Thomas Cromwell to continue to sit in the Commons though he had been elevated to the peerage before the session began.[5] Thereafter, however, the House steadily advanced its claims to consider qualifications for membership. In 1571 a select committee approved returns from boroughs which had not elected Members to the previous Parliament, though only eight years before such action had required the agreement of the Lord Steward.[6] In 1576, the House determined the vexed questions of whether a Member who was also Queen's Serjeant should take his seat in the Commons or act as an official assistant in the Lords and similar issues concerning those ill, or abroad on

---

1 3 Rot Parl 456; CJ (1640–42) 345.
2 2 Hatsell 371 n.
3 D'Ewes 16.
4 6 Hen VIII, c 16.
5 G R Elton *The Tudor Constitution* (1982) p 264.
6 CJ (1547–1628) 63, 83 and G R Elton *The Parliament of England, 1559–81* (1986) pp 338–340.

official duty, or peers' sons.[1] At the same period, general rules were laid down by the House on the right to continue to sit of those who were arrested for debt, indicted for felony or even outlawed.[2] In the 1580's, Chancery began to issue writs for new elections only when notified by the House of a vacancy,[3] and for the first time the House decided the outcome of a disputed election.[4] In 1593, the scrutiny of elections and returns was entrusted to the Committee on Privileges which (leaving aside the appointment of *ad hoc* bodies in previous sessions) had first been set up in 1584–85.[5]

In the following reign, however, events were to show that much disputed ground remained, particularly as the Buckinghamshire election dispute of 1604, in which an attempt was made by Chancery to unseat a Member because of his technical outlawry, ended in a compromise. The exclusive right of the Commons to determine the legality of returns and the conduct of returning officers was not recognised by the courts till the case of *Barnardiston v Soame* 1674[6] upheld by the House of Lords in 1689[7] and by other contemporary cases.[8] The Commons' jurisdiction in determining the right of election was further acknowledged by the Act 7 & 8 Will III c 7. But in regard to the right of electors the cases of *Ashby v White* and *R v Paty*[9] led the House of Lords to draw a distinction between the right of electors and the right of the elected, the one being a freehold by common law, and the other a temporary right to a place in Parliament.[10] In the eighteenth century, however, the Commons continued to exercise the sole right of determining whether electors had the right to vote,[11] while inquiring into the conflicting claims of candidates for seats in Parliament; until, in 1868, the House delegated its judicature in controverted elections to the courts of law, retaining its jurisdiction over cases not otherwise provided for by statute.

Whenever a doubt arises as to the qualification of any of its Members the House also has the right, which it has frequently exercised, to inquire into the matter and decide whether a new writ ought to be issued. It used to be the practice, particularly in the eighteenth century, for members who held or had accepted offices of profit under the Crown which might possibly involve the vacation of their seats to bring their cases before the House itself with a view to securing its decision. In such cases the House when seized of the matter either gave its decision forthwith after debate or referred the matter to a select committee. Up to the passing of the House of Commons Disqualification Act 1957[12] (since when no case has arisen),[13] it was the practice to

---

1 CJ (1547–1628) 106; see also ibid 15, 104.
2 CJ (1547–1628) 104, 118, 122, 124.
3 CJ (1547–1628) 118; D'Ewes 283.
4 D'Ewes 244, 259–260. See also D Hirst *Elections and Privileges of the House of Commons* in *Historical Journal* (1975), vol 18, p 851.
5 M F Keeler *The Emergence of Standing Committees for Privileges and Returns* in *Parliamentary History* (1982) vol 1, pp 25–46; D'Ewes 349, 471.
6 See p 146 for a description of the case.
7 6 State Tr 1092 & 1119.
8 Onslow 1680, 2 Vent 37, 3 Lev 39; and *Prideaux v Morris* 1702, 2 Salk 502, 1 Lut 82, 7 Mod Rep 13.
9 For description see pp 148–50.
10 See 3 Hatsell, App 1.
11 Eg CJ (1766–68) 211, 229, 279, 293.
12 Since re-enacted as the House of Commons Disqualification Act 1975.
13 The House has, however, used its power to direct that a particular disqualification should be disregarded (see pp 52–53).

refer the matter in the first instance to a select committee without, as a rule, any previous debate in the House. Whichever way the House might proceed, the decision would be entirely within its hands, and there would, of course, be no question of an appeal to a court of law.

Penal jurisdiction

Without a power to commit, the privileges of Parliament would not exist in their present form, and it would hardly have been possible adequately to defend the dignity of Parliament against disrespect and affronts which could not be brought, or could be brought only by implication, under the head of any of the specific privileges.

The origin of the power seems to lie in the mediaeval concept of Parliament as primarily a court of justice, the 'High Court of Parliament'. The Lords derived its independent power to punish from their original membership of the *Curia Regis*. Immemorial constitutional antiquity was not similarly available to the Commons, and indeed its possession of penal jurisdiction was challenged on this ground as late as the nineteenth century, and has been defended by arguments which confused legislative with judicial jurisdiction.[1] The difficulties the Commons experienced in proving its case to be a court of record[2] (see p 103)—an issue never determined at law[3]—were connected with these problems. Yet whatever the legal or constitutional niceties, in practice the House on many occasions in the sixteenth and seventeenth centuries exercised its power to impose fines (see p 110) and imprison offenders. These offenders might include Members of the House itself or non-Members,[4] the latter comprising sheriffs, magistrates and even judges of the superior courts.[5]

For a full discussion of the exercise of the penal jurisdiction of Parliament, see Chapter 8.

MODERN APPLICATION OF PRIVILEGE LAW

Throughout the long history of parliamentary privilege, the need to balance two potentially conflicting principles—both first enunciated in the seventeenth century—has become clear. On the one hand, the privileges of Parliament are rights 'absolutely necessary for the due execution of its powers';[6] and on the other, the privilege of Parliament granted in regard of

---

1 Holford in *Burdett v Abbot* (14 East 1); Sir R Atkyn's argument in the case of Sir W Williams (13 State Tr 1380).
2 The House assumed this to be so in 1593, D'Ewes 502; 1 Hatsell 233; CJ (1547–1628) 604. The Apology of 1604 made the claim directly (see J R Tanner (ed) *Constitutional Documents of the Reign of James I* (1960) pp 217 ff).
3 In *Jones v Randall* in 1774, Lord Mansfield said that the House of Commons was not a court of record.
4 Among earlier cases, those of Peter Wentworth in 1576 (D'Ewes 244, 259–60), Arthur Hall in 1581 (ibid 296–298) and Dr Parry in 1584 (ibid 340–342) are particularly noticeable. See also CJ (1547–1628) 112, 113, 125, 126; ibid (1651–59) 531, 591; ibid (1667–87) 543, 645, 687; ibid (1688–93) 84; ibid (1697–99) 255, 256; D'Ewes 366.
5 Eg two judges of King's Bench in 1689 (CJ (1688–93) 227) for their decision in *Jay v Topham* (see p 148).
6 1 Hatsell 1.

public service 'must not be used for the danger of the commonwealth'[1] In consequence, it was agreed in 1704, for example, that 'neither House of Parliament hath any power, by any vote or declaration, to create to themselves any new privilege that is not warranted by the known laws and customs of Parliament'.[2] A number of privileges have been surrendered or modified over the years. A few examples may suffice. Following the Parliamentary Privilege Act 1770, the privilege of freedom from arrest previously enjoyed by Members' servants was extinguished (see p 76). The Privileges Committee concluded at the beginning of the Second World War that the detention of a Member under Emergency Powers legislation should be regarded as akin to arrest under the criminal law, so that no breach of privilege was involved.[3]

Finally, the conclusions of the Select Committee on Parliamentary Privilege of 1967–68,[4] and the recommendations of the Privileges Committee in 1976–77[5] (the latter agreed to by the House)[6] have established a new frame of reference for the House's exercise of its penal jurisdiction. In general, the House exercises such jurisdiction in any event as sparingly as possible and only when satisfied that to do so is essential in order to provide reasonable protection for the House, its Members or its officers from such improper obstruction or attempt at or threat of obstruction causing or likely to cause, substantial interference with the performance of their respective functions (see pp 135–136).

---

1 CJ (1640–42) 261. This important statement is, however, the observation of a committee rather than the conclusion of the House.
2 CJ (1702–04) 555, 560.
3 HC 164 (1939–40).
4 HC 34 (1967–68).
5 HC 417 (1976–77).
6 CJ (1977–78) 170. The House took note of the 1967–68 report (CJ (1968–69) 321).

CHAPTER 6
Privilege of freedom of speech

Following the historical development outlined on pp 71–74, final legal recognition of the privilege of freedom of speech in both Houses of Parliament is to be found in article IX of the Bill of Rights 1689,[1] which states that 'the freedom of speech and debates or proceedings in Parliament ought not to be impeached or questioned in any court or place out of Parliament'. This chapter considers in turn the practical effect of article IX on freedom of speech within Parliament itself, its application to the publication of parliamentary proceedings beyond the precincts, and the significance of the expression in article IX, 'proceedings in Parliament'.

FREEDOM OF SPEECH IN DEBATE

Subject to the rules of order in debate (see chapter 18), a Member may state whatever he thinks fit in debate, however offensive it may be to the feelings, or injurious to the character, of individuals; and he is protected by his privilege from any action for libel, as well as from any other question or molestation.[2]

At the same time, article IX preserves the authority of both Houses to restrain and even punish their Members who, by their conduct, offend the House.

In the past, Members were frequently called to account and punished by the House for offensive words spoken before the House.[3] Some have been admonished, others imprisoned, and in the Commons some have been expelled.[4] The unquestionable right of the Lords to commit a peer for words spoken in the House was recognized by the Court of King's Bench in Lord Shaftesbury's case.[5] In modern practice in the Commons, however, the disciplinary powers of privilege are not normally resorted to. It is more common for offensive words to be dealt with by the exercise of the summary

---

1 1 William and Mary, sess 2, c 2. This provision not only protects freedom of speech in Parliament from outside interference, but indicates the method by which it may be controlled, namely by each House for its own Members. The principle was earlier established by the decision of the House of Lords in 1667 in reversing the condemnation of Eliot and others in 1629 (see p 73), partly on the ground that speeches of whatever character made in Parliament could not be inquired into out of Parliament (3 State Tr 332; LJ (1666–75) 166).
2 See, for example, HC Deb (1960–61) 630, cc 385–387 and the consideration given by the Committee of Privileges (HC 365 (1986–87)) to the issue of matters of national security arising in debate. A court in 1887, having been satisfied that words spoken in the House were the cause of an action, ordered that the writ and statement should be taken off the records of the court, since it had no jurisdiction in the matter (20 LRIr 600) (*Dillon v Balfour*).
3 LJ (1628–42) 475; ibid (1642–43) 77; CJ (1667–87) 642; ibid (1693–97) 581; ibid (1882) 323, 328.
4 CJ (1547–1628) 524.
5 1 Mod 144–158.

powers conferred on the chair by Standing Orders Nos 41, 42 and 43 (see pp 394–395).

The Speaker having claimed and statutory recognition having been granted to the privilege of freedom of speech, it becomes the duty of each Member to refrain from any course of action prejudicial to the privilege which he enjoys. On 15 July 1947 the House of Commons by resolution declared that 'it is inconsistent with the dignity of the House, with the duty of a Member to his constituents, and with the maintenance of the privilege of freedom of speech, for any Member of this House to enter into any contractual agreement with an outside body, controlling or limiting the Member's complete independence and freedom of action in Parliament or stipulating that he shall act in any way as the representative of such outside body in regard to any matters to be transacted in Parliament; the duty of a Member being to his constituents and to the country as a whole, rather than to any particular section thereof'.[1]

PUBLICATION OF DEBATES OR PROCEEDINGS

The House of Commons has always claimed and enjoyed the right to exclude strangers, and to debate with closed doors (see p 170).

Closely connected with that power is the right of either House to prohibit publication of debates or proceedings. The publication of the debates of either House has in the past repeatedly been declared to be a breach of privilege, and especially false and perverted reports of them; and there is no doubt that if either House desires to withhold its proceedings from the public, it is within its power to do so, and to punish any violation of its orders.[2]

Commons

On 16 July 1971, however, the House of Commons resolved that, 'notwithstanding the Resolution of the House on 3 March 1762 and other such Resolutions, this House will not entertain any complaint of contempt of the House or breach of privilege in respect of the publication of the debates or proceedings of the House or of its committees, except when any such debates or proceedings shall have been conducted with closed doors or in private, or when such publication shall have been expressly prohibited by the House'.

The House of Commons also resolved that it would not entertain any complaint in respect of (i) the publication in advance of the relevant Division Lists or Notice Papers of a statement of how any Member voted in a division in the House or the contents of any notice of a parliamentary Question or Notice of Motion handed in, or (ii) the publication of the expressed intention of a Member to vote in a particular manner, or to refrain from voting, or

---

1 In a number of cases since 1947, the Committee of Privileges has considered the matter of a Member's freedom of speech and outside bodies with which he may be in contractual relationship and from whom he may receive payments; see HC 118 (1946–47) p xii. See also HC 85 (1943–44); HC 634 (1974–75) and HC 512 (1976–77).

2 For the provisions made in 1916 and in the 1939–45 war as to reports of debates if either House resolved to hold a 'Secret Session', see pp 252–254. In 1957, following the recommendations of the Select Committee on Broadcasting (Anticipation of Debates) the BBC suspended indefinitely its self-imposed rule prohibiting broadcast discussion and statements on issues about to be debated in Parliament within a period of 14 days.

to hand in any notice of a Parliamentary Question or Notice of Motion.[1] These resolutions followed recommendations of the Select Committee on Parliamentary Privilege[2] and were intended to bring the rules of the House into conformity with long-standing practice. A further Resolution was passed on 31 October 1980 removing the restrictions on the reporting of evidence taken at public sittings of select committees (see pp 122–124). The repeated orders made by the House forbidding the publication of the debates and proceedings of the House, or of any committee thereof, and of comments thereon, or on the conduct of Members in the House, by newspapers, newsletters, or otherwise, and directing the punishment of offenders against such rules,[3] had long since fallen into disuse.[4] Indeed, since 1909, the debates have been reported and issued by an official reporting staff under the authority of the Speaker (see p 211), and sold to the public by Her Majesty's Stationery Office.

Lords

Under Lords Standing Order No 13 the printing or publishing of anything relating to the proceedings of the Lords is subject to the privilege of the House.

Complaints of reports

When a wilful misrepresentation of the debate arises, or if it may be necessary to enforce a restriction on reporting, the House censures or otherwise punishes the offender, whether he be a Member of the House or a stranger admitted to its debates.[5]

Evidence before committees and draft reports

The privilege of freedom of speech may be invoked in certain circumstances to prevent the publication of memoranda of evidence submitted to a select committee, until it has been reported to the House, in cases where such publication has not been authorized by the select committee or by the Speaker in accordance with SO No 117;[6] but as such publication is of the nature of a contempt, it is dealt with on pp 122–124.

PUBLICATION OUTSIDE PARLIAMENT OF PROCEEDINGS AND DEBATES IN PARLIAMENT

Although the privilege of freedom of speech protects what is said in debate in either House, this privilege does not to the same degree apply to the

---

1 CJ (1970–71) 548–549.
2 HC 34 (1967–68) paras 116 ff.
3 CJ (1640–42) 501; ibid (1693–97) 193, 439; ibid (1697–99) 48, 661; ibid (1699–1702) 767; ibid (1702–04) 270; ibid (1722–27) 99; ibid (1727–32) 238; ibid (1761–64) 207; ibid (1790) 508; ibid (1819–20) 57; see also the Second Report on Sir Francis Burdett, CJ (1810) 732.
4 The Speaker has ruled that a Member cannot be required to state whether expressions alleged to have been made by him in the House were correctly reported in a newspaper, CJ (1837) 270.
5 CJ (1812) 432; ibid (1819) 537; ibid (1833) 606.
6 CJ (1831–32) 360; ibid (1837) 282.

publication of debates or proceedings outside Parliament. But the publication, whether by order of the House or not, of a fair and accurate account of a debate in either House is protected by the same principle as that which protects fair reports of proceedings in courts of justice, that the advantage to the public outweighs any disadvantage to individuals unless malice is proved. This is a matter of law, rather than of parliamentary privilege.

If a Member publishes separately from the rest of the debate a speech made by him (in either House), his printed statement becomes a separate publication, unconnected with any proceedings in Parliament, and he is responsible under the common law for any libellous matter it may contain.[1]

Nor does an order of the House for their printing and publication confer parliamentary privilege on proceedings published outside Parliament, though it may convey the protection of statute (see below). In 1837, an action (*Stockdale v Hansard*)[2] against the publisher of a report made to Parliament by a statutory body, and ordered by the House to be printed, succeeded on the ground that defamatory statements in the report were not privileged by virtue of the House's order for printing. In Lord Denman's judgment, a distinction was drawn between 'what the House may order to be printed for the use of its members', and what may be published and sold 'indiscriminately'.[3]

The Parliamentary Papers Act, which became law shortly thereafter, in 1840, provides more generally that proceedings, criminal or civil, against persons for the publication of papers printed by order of either House of Parliament, shall be immediately stayed, on the production of a certificate, verified by affidavit, to the effect that such publication is by order or under the authority of either House of Parliament. Proceedings are also to be stayed, if commenced on account of the publication of a copy of a parliamentary paper, upon the verification of the correctness of such copy; and in proceedings commenced for printing any extract from, or abstract of, a parliamentary report or paper, the defendant may give the report in evidence under the general issue, and prove that his own extract or abstract was

---

1 A speech delivered (by Lord Abingdon) in the Lords in 1795 was subsequently published separately in several newspapers at his own expense, and his Lordship was punished by the court (Esp 228). In 1813 Mr Creevey was found guilty of libel, having sent to the editor of a newspaper a corrected version of a speech made in the Commons previously incorrectly reported, with a request for publication. Upon his complaint to the House that King's Bench refused a new trial, the House came to no conclusion on whether the proceedings were a breach of privilege. (See 1 M & S 273, 277, 278; CJ (1812–13) 604; Parl Deb (1812–13) 26, c 898). See also Committee of Privileges, 2nd Report HC 246 (1974) where the Committee concluded that though following a speech outside the House a Member was threatened with proceedings in the event of future defamatory references to a certain body, no contempt occurred because there was no indication that the plaintiff acted in contemplation of a speech in the House: *Stockdale v Hansard* 3 State Tr (ns) 861, 896–898; *Wason v Walter* (1868–69) 4 QB 85; and *Cook v Alexander* [1973] 3 WLR 617 ff.
2 For fuller details, see pp 151–153.
3 9 A & E 1.

published bona fide and without malice; and if such shall be the opinion of the jury, a verdict in the defendant's favour will be entered.[1]

The Act of 1840 was subsequently amended by section 9 of the Defamation Act 1952 so as to include publication by broadcasting.[2]

Papers presented by Her Majesty's Command are not, however, printed by order of either House, and where the protection of the Parliamentary Papers Act is particularly desired, the normal practice is for an order to print to be given to a paper presented as a Return (see pp 213–214).

Comment, or publication in a form other than an extract or abstract, is not privileged.[3]

In his judgment in *Stockdale v Hansard*, Lord Denman referred to the status of matter which might be ordered to be printed by the House for the use of its Members only. Except in the case of the *Manual of Procedure in the Public Business* of the House of Commons, which is 'laid on the Table by Mr Speaker for the use of Members' and also published in printed form, no such material currently exists, but there is an analogous case on which the courts have ruled. In the case of *Lake v King* in 1667, judgment was given for a defendant who delivered printed copies of a petition containing allegations which the court found 'false and scandalous' to the members of a committee, since the committee had power to examine the truth or falsehood of the petition and it was the order and course of proceedings in Parliament to print and deliver copies whereof they ought to take judicial notice.[4]

As regards the publication of debates, the judgment in *Wason v Walter* in 1868 established that the publisher of a report of a parliamentary debate is protected from actions for defamation if the whole debate is published, and enjoys qualified privilege for the publication of extracts from debates. The decision is founded not on parliamentary privilege but on the principle that the publication of the proceedings of Parliament should be protected on the same footing as those of courts of justice: 'that the occasional inconvenience to individuals arising from it [the publication of an extract from the debates] must yield to the general good'.[5]

1 Under the provision of this statute the action of *Harlow v Hansard* was stayed on 14 July 1845 by Mr Justice Wightman in chambers, on the production of the Speaker's certificate. In the case of *Houghton and others v Plimsoll*, tried at Liverpool, 1 April 1874, Baron Amphlett directed the jury that the report of a Royal Commission, presented to Parliament in a printed form, came within the provisions of the Act, 'since it was a report which had been adopted by Parliament, and of which a distribution of copies had been ordered by Parliament'. This judgment was followed by Mr Justice Darling in *Mangena v Edward Lloyd Ltd* (1908) 89 LT 640, an action for libel brought in respect of a statement contained in an extract from a paper presented to Parliament by command of His Majesty. The decision in this case, the proceedings in which were presented to both Houses (see Cd 4403), was followed in *Mangena v Wright* [1909] 2 KB 958. See also the Committee of Privileges, 2nd Report, HC 667 (1977–78) and 2nd Report, HC 222 (1978–79) for a commentary on the protection afforded by the 1840 Act to reports of Parliamentary proceedings in criminal cases.

2 The matter of the application of the law of defamation to parliamentary broadcasts was studied by the Joint Committee on the Publication of Proceedings in Parliament (HL 26, HC 48 (1969–70)).

3 It was decided in the case of *Dingle v Associated Newspapers Ltd and others* [1961] 2 QB 162 that damages should not be reduced on the ground that a plaintiff had acquired a bad reputation by reason of the publication of a select committee's report.

4 Saund 131 (1667); 1 Lev 240; 2 Keb 361, 383, 462, 496, 659, 801. See also 2 Co Inst 228, as to evidence before a jury being privileged.

5 [1868–69] 4 QB 85 ff. Cockburn CJ explained further that, since the analogy between reports of proceedings in courts and that in Parliament was complete, the limitations on one attach to the others and 'a garbled or partial report or of detached parts of proceedings, published with intent to injure individuals, will equally be disentitled to protection' (ibid 94).

Slightly over a century later, the courts decided on appeal that the reporter who wrote a parliamentary 'sketch' was entitled to select that part of a debate which appeared to him to be of special public interest, and such a sketch would be privileged if made fairly and honestly. As a result, the sketch in question was entitled to qualified privilege and a jury's award of damages, against which the appeal had been lodged, was set aside. Lord Denning MR observed that 'fairness in this regard means a fair presentation of what took place as it impressed the hearers. It does not mean fairness in the absolute between [the plaintiff] and those who were attacking him'.[1]

In a more limited sphere, section 7 of the Defamation Act 1952 provides that a fair and accurate report in a newspaper of the proceedings of a public meeting, including those of select committees of either House, published without malice and for the public benefit, is privileged.

A study of the protection both absolute and qualified afforded to the publication of proceedings in Parliament was undertaken by the Joint Committee on that subject in 1969–70, following that of the Commons Select Committee on Parliamentary Privilege in 1966–67, and subsequently by a Joint Committee in 1977 and a Commons Select Committee in 1982,[2] as far as concerned sound recording of proceedings.

Those who participate in proceedings in Parliament, as witnesses, counsel, petitioners or otherwise, are protected from molestation, threats or legal proceedings on account of what may have been said or done before either House or a committee thereof (see pp 102, 132–134).

COPYRIGHT

The Copyright, Designs and Patents Act 1988 provides for a scheme of parliamentary copyright, including copyright in bills. Copyright in a public bill belongs in the first instance to the House in which the bill was introduced and, once the bill has reached the second House, to both Houses jointly. It subsists from the time the bill is handed in to the House in which it is introduced, and ceases on royal assent, the withdrawal or rejection of the bill, or the end of the session.[3] Work made by or under the direction of either or both Houses is subject to copyright for fifty years from the end of the year in which it was made. Such work is defined as including works made by an officer or employee in the course of duty, and sound recording, film, live broadcast or live cable programmes of proceedings of the House. The ownership of such copyright belongs to the House by or under the direction or control of which the work is made (or, as appropriate, to both Houses) and for these purposes each House is to be treated as having the legal capacities of a body corporate, which is not affected by a prorogation or

1 *Cook v Alexander* [1973] 3 WLR 617, especially 623.
2 Joint Committee on the Publication of Proceedings in Parliament, 2nd Report HL 109, HC 261 (1969–70); HC 34 (1966–67); Joint Committee on Sound Broadcasting (HL 123, HC 284 (1976–77)); and Select Committee on Sound Broadcasting, 1st Report (HC 376 (1981–82)). The matter was also dealt with by the Faulks Committee on Defamation, 1975 (Cmnd 5909) paras 203–210, 216–226.
3 Copyright in private bills belongs to both Houses jointly, subsisting from the time the bill is first deposited in either House. Copyright in personal bills belongs first to the Lords (from the time of first reading) and, when the bill reaches the Commons, jointly to both Houses. Acts and Measures are subject to Crown copyright.

dissolution. The functions of the House of Lords as owner of copyright are exercised by the Clerk of the Parliaments, and those of the Commons by the Speaker. Provisions are made for the delegation of the functions and for their discharge in vacancies of those offices and (as regards the Commons) at times of dissolution.

PROCEEDINGS IN PARLIAMENT

Right to exclusive cognisance of proceedings

The law declared in the Bill of Rights excludes all outside interference with the proceedings of either House. It encapsulates (without necessarily limiting) many historical developments sketched in chapter 5. These include the judicial pre-eminence of the High Court of Parliament, the concern that Members should not be tried or punished by any inferior court, the notion of each House as a court, and the claim to freedom of speech in the form both of the collective right of the two Houses to discuss subjects of their own desire without reference to the Monarch, and the right of the individual Member to participate freely in debate. Some of these were more readily or more widely claimed for the Lords than for the Commons. The Lords' claim to be a court could not be disputed: Commons aspirations in that direction were more difficult to achieve (see p 103). The right to trial by peers was never made by the Commons.

Nevertheless, the right of both Houses to be sole judge of the lawfulness of their own proceedings, or to settle—and depart from—their own codes of procedure is fully established. This is equally the case whether a House is dealing with a matter which is finally decided by its sole authority, such as an order or resolution, or whether, like a bill, it is the joint concern of both Houses. This holds good even where the procedure of a House or the right of its Members or officers to take part in its proceedings depends on statute.

For such purposes the House can 'practically change or practically supersede the law'.[1] This privilege is not confined to the chamber in which the House sits. For instance, it has been held to extend to the sale, within the precincts of the House, of intoxicating liquor without a licence through its employees in the Refreshment Department of the House.[2]

The case of *Bradlaugh v Gosset* in 1880 evoked an unqualified recognition by the courts of their incompetence to inquire into the internal proceedings of a House of Parliament. Question arose whether Bradlaugh had qualified himself to sit by making an affirmation instead of taking the oath. Subsequently, following re-election, he was prevented from taking the oath by order of the House. In the course of his judgment in an action seeking (inter alia) to have the order declared void, Stephen J declared that even if the House of Commons forbade a Member to do what statute required him to do and, in order to enforce the prohibition, excluded him from the House, the court had no power to interfere, because 'the House of Commons is not subject to the control of . . . [the] courts in its administration of that part of the statute law which has relation to its own internal proceedings . . . even if that interpretation should be erroneous, this court has no power to interfere

1 Coleridge CJ in *Bradlaugh v Gosset*, 12 QBD 273–274.
2 *R v Graham Campbell, ex p Herbert* [1935] 1 KB 594.

with it directly or indirectly'.[1] (Further discussion of the limits of what the courts see as internal to Parliament and what they consider lies within their own jurisdiction is to be found at pp 152, 154–156).

Almost a century later, a respondent before the House of Lords in 1973 argued that the promoters of a Private Bill had misled Parliament into granting certain rights to them. The House of Lords sitting judicially found that the appellant was not entitled to examine proceedings in Parliament to show that the promoters of a Private Bill, by allegedly fraudulently misleading Parliament, had caused him loss. It was for Parliament to lay down procedures for considering Bills, and to decide if they had been followed or to decide to depart from them. Parliament determined what documentary material or testimony might be required, and the extent to which parliamentary privilege should attach. 'It would be impracticable and undesirable for the High Court of Justice to embark upon an inquiry concerning the effect or effectiveness of the internal procedures in the High Court of Parliament, or an inquiry whether in any particular case those procedures were effectively followed'[2] (see also pp 157–158).

Members cannot be compelled to give evidence in the courts regarding proceedings in the House of Commons without the permission of the House.[3] Similarly, no Clerk or officer of the House, or shorthand writer employed to take minutes of evidence before the House, or any committee thereof, may give evidence elsewhere, in respect of any proceedings or examination had at the bar, or before any committee of the House, without the special leave of the House.[4] Parties to a suit who desire to produce such evidence, or any other document in the custody of officers of the House, accordingly petition the House, praying that the proper officer may attend and produce it (see pp 758–759), and the term 'proper officer' includes an official shorthand writer (see p 178). The motion for leave may be moved without previous notice (see p 376)[5] During the recess, however, it has been the practice for the Speaker, in order to prevent delays in the administration of justice, to allow the production of minutes of evidence and other documents, on the application of the parties to a private suit. But should the suit involve any question of privilege, especially the privilege of a witness, or should the production of the document appear, on other grounds, to be a subject for the discretion of the House itself, he will decline to grant the required authority. During a dissolution the Clerk of the House sanctions the production of documents, following the principle adopted by the Speaker.

When in 1980 the Commons gave leave for reference to be made in court proceedings to the Official Report and to the published reports and evidence of committees without the necessity for the presentation of a petition for leave to do so[6] (see pp 758–759), the resolution explicitly reaffirmed the status of proceedings in Parliament confirmed by article IX of the Bill of Rights.

---

1 12 QBD 278–286.
2 *British Railways Board v Pickin* [1974] 2 WLR 208.
3 *Chubb v Salomons* 3 Car and Kir 75.
4 CJ (1818) 389; Parl Deb (1828) 18, c 968–974.
5 CJ (1851) 212, 277; ibid (1852) 291; ibid (1967–68) 125. For a motion not preceded by a petition see, eg, HC Deb (1939–40) 365, c 135.
6 CJ (1979–80) 823: Committee of Privileges, 1st report, HC 102 (1978–79).

Meaning and scope of 'proceedings in Parliament'

The Bill of Rights 1689 and the Parliamentary Papers Act 1840 both use the word 'proceedings' without further definition, in a context where such definition is likely to be important. The primary meaning, as a technical parliamentary term, of 'proceedings' (which it had at least as early as the seventeenth century) is some formal action, usually a decision, taken by the House in its collective capacity. This is naturally extended to the forms of business in which the House takes action, and the whole process, the principal part of which is debate, by which it reaches a decision.

An individual Member takes part in a proceeding usually by speech, but also by various recognized kinds of formal action, such as voting, giving notice of a motion, etc, or presenting a petition or a report from a committee, most of such actions being time-saving substitutes for speaking. The Select Committee on the Official Secrets Act in 1938–39 argued that 'proceedings' covered both the asking of a question and the giving of written notice of such question, and includes everything said or done by a Member in the exercise of his functions as a Member in a committee of either House, as well as everything said or done in either House in the transaction of Parliamentary business.[1] Officers of the House take part in its proceedings principally by carrying out its orders, general or particular. Strangers also can take part in the proceedings of a House, eg by giving evidence before it or before one of its committees, or by securing the presentation of their petitions.

While taking part in the proceedings of a House, Members, officers and strangers are protected by the same sanction as that by which freedom of speech is protected, namely, that they cannot be called to account for their actions by any authority other than the House itself (see chapter 9).

A large description of what is comprehended by the phrase 'proceedings in Parliament' is thus not difficult to arrive at, and of course the application of any definition to a particular case will normally be a matter for the House concerned. Nevertheless, for some time there has been discussion of the advisability of attempting a closer definition, in order both to provide a more secure framework for decisions in individual cases and to help in judgments about how close to an undoubted proceeding an act done outside Parliament needs to be before it can properly benefit from the immunity conferred by privilege and declared by the Bill of Rights. The Select Committee on the Official Secrets Act gave thought to the latter problem and concluded that 'cases may easily be imagined of communications between one Member and another or between a Member and a Minister, so closely related to some matter pending in, or expected to be brought before the House, that, although they do not take place in the Chamber or a committee room, they form part of the business of the House, as, for example, where a Member sends to a Minister the draft of a question he is thinking of putting down, or shows it to another Member with a view to obtaining advice as to the propriety of putting it down or as to the manner in which it should be framed'.[2] The Committee's conclusions were agreed to by the House.[3]

---

1 HC 101 (1938–39) p v.
2 See also Committee of Privileges Report, HC 365 (1986–87) paras 36 ff, and 13 State Tr 1434–1435.
3 CJ (1938–39) 480.

On the other hand, in 1958 the House rejected the opinion of the Committee of Privileges that a particular letter written by a Member to a Minister relating to a nationalised industry was a proceeding in Parliament.[1] It had accepted however the conclusion of the Committee in 1947 that 'attendance of Members at a private party meeting held in the precincts . . . during the parliamentary session to discuss parliamentary matters . . . is attendance in their capacity of Members of Parliament', so that financial arrangements to induce a Member to disclose information from such a meeting were a breach of privilege.[2]

The Select Committee on Parliamentary Privilege in 1967 reviewed these issues once more and recommended legislation to extend and clarify the scope of both absolute and qualified privilege,[3] and the Joint Committee on the Publication of Proceedings in Parliament in its second report in 1970, in agreeing with the 1967 committee, put forward a draft definition of 'proceedings in Parliament' on essentially functional lines.[4] The Faulks Committee on the Law of Defamation reported to the same effect in 1975,[5] and two years later the Committee of Privileges repeated the recommendation for legislation 'in order to reflect the way that Parliament actually works'.[6] On the other side of the argument is the contention that a precise statutory definition of 'proceedings' would deprive the Houses of freedom of interpretation and might lead to disputes with the courts. The most recent review of the matter by a select committee simply commended the evidence received to the attention of the Commons as likely to be helpful in any future consideration of the scope of the term 'proceedings in Parliament'.[7] To date, no legislation intended to define 'proceedings' has been laid before Parliament.[8]

Proceedings, precincts and criminal acts

Even after any future definition of 'proceedings', it would no doubt remain the case, as it is now, that (for example) not everything said or done within the precincts forms part of proceedings in Parliament. The most striking example of this is the conclusion of the Privileges Committee in 1815 that the arrest of Lord Cochrane (a Member of the Commons) in the Chamber (the House not sitting) was not a breach of privilege (p 95). Particular words or acts may be entirely unrelated to any business being transacted or ordered to come before the House in due course. In the view of the Select Committee on the Official Secrets Acts 'a casual conversation in the House cannot be said to be a proceeding in Parliament, and a Member who discloses information in the course of such a conversation would not . . . be protected by privilege, though it might be a question whether the evidence necessary to

---

1 Committee of Privileges, Fifth Report HC 305 (1956–57); HC 227 (1957–58); CJ (1957–58) 260.
2 Committee of Privileges, HC 138 (1946–47) paras 17 and 21; HC 142 (1946–47); CJ (1947–48) 22.
3 HC 34 (1967–68) paras 80–92.
4 HL 109, HC 261 (1969–70) paras 12–34.
5 Cmnd 5909, paras 203–210 and p 237.
6 HC 417 (1976–77) paras 7–8.
7 Committee of Privileges Report, HC 365 (1986–87) paras 60–62.
8 A definition of 'proceedings' is however contained in s 16(2) of the Australian Parliamentary Privilege Act 1987 (No 21) (see p 159).

secure his conviction could be given without the permission of the House'.[1] The Privileges Committee concluded in 1987 that there was no precedent for the House's affording Members any privilege on the *sole* ground that their activities were within the precincts of the Palace and there were no grounds for believing that the showing of a film to Members or others under arrangements made privately by a Member, 'could of itself, be held to be a proceeding in Parliament'.[2]

Moreover, though the Bill of Rights will adequately protect a Member as regards criminal law in respect of anything said as part of proceedings in Parliament, there is more doubt whether criminal acts committed in Parliament remain within the exclusive cognizance of the House in which they are committed. In the judgment of the House of Lords in Eliot's case (see pp 73 and 84n), it was deliberately left an open question whether the assault on the Speaker might have been properly heard and determined in the King's Bench. The possibility that it might legally have been so determined was admitted by one of the managers for the Commons in the conference with the Lords which preceded the writ of error. In *Bradlaugh v Gosset*, Mr Justice Stephen said that he 'knew of no authority for the proposition that an ordinary crime committed in the House of Commons would be withdrawn from the ordinary course of criminal justice'. Since he went on immediately to refer to *Eliot's case* and accepted the proposition 'that nothing said in Parliament by a Member, as such, can be treated as an offence by the ordinary courts', it must be supposed that what the learned judge had in mind was a criminal act as distinguished from criminal speech.[3]

In such cases, it will be essential to determine where the alleged criminal act stands in relation to the proceedings of the House. An officer carrying out an order of the House is in the same position as the Members who voted the order. In *Bradlaugh v Erskine*, the Deputy Serjeant at Arms was held to be justified in committing the assault with which he was charged, since it was committed in Parliament, in pursuance of the order of the House, to exclude Bradlaugh from the House. As Lord Coleridge observed, 'The Houses cannot act by themselves as a body; they must act by officers'.[4] It would be hard to show how a criminal act committed by a Member, however, could form part of the proceedings of the House.[5] Apart from *Eliot's case* 350 years ago, no charge against a Member in respect of an allegedly criminal act in Parliament has been brought before the courts. Were such a situation to arise, it is possible that the House in which the act was committed might claim the right to decide whether to exercise its own jurisdiction. In taking this decision, it would no doubt be guided by the nature of the offence, and the adequacy or inadequacy of the penalties, somewhat lacking in flexibility, which it could inflict.

---

1 HC 101 (1938–39) p ix.
2 An interim injunction had been granted on grounds of national security against a named individual, restraining him from showing a film. A further injunction was sought and refused, which would have prevented Members from showing the film in a room within the precincts of the House of Commons. Though in the event, pursuant to an order of the Speaker, the film was not shown, the Privileges Committee considered that had the showing proceeded, it would not have enjoyed the protection of privilege (Committee of Privileges, 1st Report (1986–87) HC 365, paras 16 and 17).
3 [1884] 12 QBD 284.
4 [1884] 12 QBD 276.
5 See Report of the Select Committee on the Official Secrets Acts, HC 101 (1938–39) paras 9–10.

CHAPTER 7

Privilege of freedom from arrest or molestation

Chapter 5 has sketched the historical background to the privilege of freedom from arrest, and this chapter will illustrate the contemporary position as regards the criminal law, statutory detention, contempt of court, and bankruptcy. It will also deal with certain privileges related to that of freedom from arrest and an outline of the law of Parliament on the duration of the privilege.

CRIMINAL LAW

The privilege of freedom from arrest has never been allowed to interfere with the administration of criminal justice or emergency legislation (see p 97). Perhaps the most striking proof of this statement are the events surrounding the arrest in 1815 of Lord Cochrane, a Member of the House of Commons who, having escaped from prison where he had been committed following conviction for an indictable offence, made his way to the Chamber of the House and sat on the right hand of the Chair. No Members were present, prayers not having been read. His rearrest in the Chamber was referred to the Committee of Privileges, who reported that it was entirely of a novel nature, and that the privileges of Parliament did not appear to have been violated, so as to call for the interposition of the House, by any proceedings against the marshal of the King's Bench, who rearrested him.[1]

Both Houses have resolved in terms that parliamentary privilege does not extend to the writing and publishing of seditious libels, nor ought it 'to be allowed to obstruct the ordinary course of the law in the speedy and effectual prosecution of so heinous and dangerous an offence'.[2]

House to be informed of arrests

In all cases in which Members of either House are arrested on criminal charges, the House must be informed of the cause for which they are detained from their service in Parliament. Several Acts which have suspended for a time a Habeas Corpus Act, have contained provisions to the effect that no Member of Parliament shall be imprisoned during the sitting of Parliament, until the matter of which he stands suspected shall be *first* communicated to the House of which he shall be a Member, and the consent of the said House obtained for his commitment.[3] By the Protection of Person

---

1 CJ (1814–16) 186; Parl Deb (1814–15) 30, c 309, 336; Colchester ii, 534, 536.
2 LJ (1760–64) 426; CJ (1761–64) 689; 15 Parl Hist 1362–1378. The Court of Common Pleas had decided in a contrary sense, 2 Wils 150, 19 State Tr 981. As mentioned at p 79 arrest for civil offences is now virtually obsolete.
3 See 17 Geo II, c 6; 45 Geo III, c 4, s 2; 57 Geo III, c 3, s 4; 57 Geo III, c 55, s 4; 3 Geo IV, c 2, s 4.

and Property Act 1881, it was provided that 'if any Member of either House of Parliament be arrested under this Act, the fact shall be immediately communicated to the House of which he is a Member, if Parliament be sitting at the time, or if Parliament be not sitting, then immediately after Parliament reassembles, in like manner as if he were arrested on a criminal charge'. The arrests of Members under this Act, as long as it remained in force, were communicated to the House of Commons accordingly.[1] In cases not affected by Acts of this special character, it has been usual to communicate the cause of commitment of a Member after his arrest;[2] such communications are also made whenever Members are in custody in order to be tried by naval[3] or military[4] courts-martial, or have been committed to prison for any criminal offence by a court[5] or magistrate.[6] Although normally making an oral statement, the Speaker has notified the House of the arrest or imprisonment of a Member by laying a copy of a letter on the Table.[7] In the case of commitments for military offences, the communication is made by royal message (see p 565). In the case of naval courts-martial this communication was formerly made by the lords commissioners of the Admiralty, by whom the warrants were issued for taking the Members into custody; and copies of the warrants were, at the same time, laid before the House. Since the abolition of the commissioners, no case relating to a naval court-martial has arisen.

If a Member is detained so briefly as not to involve his being prevented from attending the House, the Speaker does not necessarily notify the House of the arrest.

House to be informed of sentences for criminal offences

The committal of a Lord or Member for high treason[8] or any criminal offence is brought before the House by a letter addressed to the Lord

---

1 Mr Dillon CJ (1881) 213, 260; Parl Deb (1881) 260, c 1744: Mr Parnell, Mr Sexton, Mr O'Kelly, and Mr Dillon, also the release of Mr Sexton CJ (1882) 8; Parl Deb (1882) 266, c 98. A motion for a committee of inquiry was negatived, ibid: arrest of Mr William O'Brien CJ (1887) 552.
2 Mrs Wise CJ (1976–77) 358.
3 CJ (1778–80) 57; ibid (1795–96) 557; ibid (1806–7) 145; ibid (1809) 214; ibid (1812) 246 etc; LJ (1809–10) 349 (Lord Gambier); and see case of Lord Torrington, ibid (1685–91) 521, 523, 525, 527.
4 CJ (1782–84) 479; ibid (1795–96) 139; ibid (1802–3) 597; ibid (1803–4) 33; ibid (1814–15) 70; ibid (1940–41) 178; LJ (1947–48) 43.
5 Mr Healy CJ (1883) 4. A motion for a committee of inquiry was negatived, ibid. Arrest of Members for offences against Defence of the Realm Regulations and sentences thereunder, see CJ (1918) 227; ibid (1919) 56, 61, 170, 320, 325, 339; ibid (1920) 61, 78, 96, 98, 390, 451, 452, 472, ibid (1921) 29, 54; under Restoration of Order in Ireland Regulations, ibid (1921) 27, 102; under an Order made pursuant to an Act of the Parliament of Northern Ireland, ibid (1922) 345; ibid (1924) 17.
6 Mr F O'Connor CJ (1852) 28; ibid (1902) 3 etc. See also ibid (1916) 227; ibid (1918) 44; ibid (1919) 16, 116, 183, 184, 209, 325, 361; ibid (1920) 88, 439; ibid (1926) 166; HC Deb (1926) 195, c 601. The communication has been made by the clerk to the court, CJ (1919) 116, 183, 325; ibid (1920) 88; ibid (1974–75) 570; Votes and Proceedings (25 January and 1 February 1988) or by the magistrate, ibid (21 October 1987 and 11 and 25 January, 1 and 25 February and 19 October 1988).
7 CJ (1975–76) 540; ibid (1977–78) 546.
8 CJ (1902) 281. See the Speaker's ruling, 12 June 1902, as to the sufficiency of a similar communication in cases of high treason as in other criminal offences, Parl Deb (1902) 109, c 480.

Chancellor or the Speaker by the committing judge or magistrate.[1] On these occasions, the first communication is made when the Lord or Member is committed to prison, bail not being allowed;[2] and subsequently, if the Member be not released from custody, or acquitted, the judge informs the Speaker of the offence for which the Member was condemned, and the sentence that has been passed upon him.[3] Where a Member is convicted but released on bail pending an appeal, the duty of the magistrate to communicate with the Speaker does not arise. No duty of informing the Speaker arises in the case of a person who while in prison under sentence of a court is elected as a Member of Parliament,[4] but when a notification has been made to the Speaker in such circumstances he has communicated it to the House.[5] On 9 May 1972 the Speaker informed the House that he had been notified by the Secretary of State for Northern Ireland that prison sentences passed on three Members had been remitted in an exercise of the Royal prerogative of mercy.[6]

STATUTORY DETENTION

The detention of a Member under Regulation 18B of the Defence (General) Regulations 1939, made under the Emergency Powers (Defence) Acts 1939 and 1940, led to the Committee of Privileges being directed to consider whether such detention constituted a breach of the privileges of the House; the Committee reported that there was no breach of privilege involved.[7] In the case of a Member deported from Northern Rhodesia for non-compliance with an order declaring him to be a prohibited immigrant, the Speaker held there was no prima facie case of breach of privilege.[8]

The detention of Members in Ireland in 1918 under the Defence of the Realm Regulations was communicated to the Speaker by a letter from the Chief Secretary to the Lord Lieutenant and read by the Speaker to the House.[9]

CONTEMPT OF COURT

A claim to the privilege of freedom from arrest made by a Member imprisoned for contempt of court may prove more difficult to determine than in the instances dealt with earlier in this chapter.

There are a few older cases, in the sixteenth and early seventeenth century, of peers and Members of the House of Commons being successfully

---

1 In the case of Lord George Gordon the communication was made by a royal message, CJ (1778–80) 903, and in the case of Mr Smith O'Brien by a letter from the Lord-Lieutenant of Ireland, ibid (1847–48) 888.
2 Parl Deb (1902) 113, c 234.
3 Marquess of Bristol, LJ (1987–88) 880; CJ (1890–91) 268; ibid (1892) 101; ibid (1903) 3; ibid (1954–55) 6; in case of misdemeanour, ibid (1922) 183; and ibid (1947–48) 19. The quashing of the last conviction was notified as a matter of courtesy by the Lord Chief Justice to the Speaker, who communicated the notification to the House, ibid (1947–48) 178.
4 HC Deb (1917–18) 93, c 1786.
5 CJ (1922) 345; ibid (1924) 17.
6 HC Deb (1971–72) 836, c 1101.
7 HC 164 (1939–40).
8 HC Deb (1958–59) 601, cc 223–227 and 454–464.
9 CJ (1918) 105; HC Deb (1918) 106, c 1235. See also CJ (1939–40) 140. For other communications in respect of preventative detention by the executive, see HC 164 (1939–40) p 3.

discharged from attachments for contempt by pleading their privilege.[1] In one such case, the Lords ordered a peer to be discharged from the attachment but declared that if at any future time cause should be shown that by the prerogative, common law or custom, statute or precedents, the persons of Lords of Parliament were attachable, the order in that case should not affect their decision in judging according to the cause shown.[2] The Commons also in the seventeenth century secured the release of Members committed for contempt by writs of *habeas corpus*.[3]

Subsequently, however, Members of the House of Commons have been fined[4] and imprisoned for contempt of court, and on examination of the circumstances of the cases, committees have not recommended that the House invoke the privilege of freedom from arrest. The Committee of Privileges in 1831 reported that the claim of privilege, made by a Member committed for contempt for having removed his daughter from the jurisdiction of the Court of Chancery, though she was a ward of court, ought not to be admitted.[5] Similarly, the Committee of Privileges reported against a claim made in 1837 by a Member who had been committed for contempt in writing a scandalous letter which also attempted to influence a decision of the Court of Chancery.[6] In 1874, the Committee of Privileges informed the House that the Lord Chief Justice had fulfilled his duty in informing the Speaker of a Member's committal for contempt of the Court of Queen's Bench and subsequent discharge, at a time when Parliament was not sitting, and reported that the matter did not demand the further attention of the House.[7] A similar report was made in 1882, when a Member had been committed for publishing certain articles calculated to prejudice the course of justice.[8] A select committee in 1902 considered the committal of a Member for refusal to enter into recognisances to be of good behaviour, and concluded that there was no difference between that case and those cited above, that the contempt was of a criminal and not civil character, and no distinction could be drawn between cases of criminal contempt and other indictable offences.[9]

---

1 Contempt of court by privileged persons was formerly punished by sequestration of their property, see the case of the Countess of Shaftesbury, 2 P Wms 110.

2 LJ (1509–77) 727; ibid (1628–42) 27; ibid (1666–75) 122; Prynne, 4th Register, 792; case of the Duchess of Sutherland, 18 April 1893. See also LJ (1620–28) 496, where Lord Vaux successfully pleaded privilege to stay proceedings on an information against him in Star Chamber, and the case of Lord Arundel, ibid 558 (Report of Precedents touching imprisonment or restraint of Lords in the time of Parliament HL 79 (1806–07)) 562 etc.

3 CJ (1547–1628) 269, 458, 466.

4 In 1873, the Court of Queen's Bench fined two Members (Mr Onslow and Mr Whalley) for a contempt of that court, and Cockburn CJ stated that the court would not have been restrained by privilege from committing them if it had thought fit.

5 CJ (1830–31) 701, and *Wellesly v Duke of Beaufort* 2 Russ and M 639 ff.

6 CJ (1837) 3 ff, and HC 45 (1837).

7 HC 77 (1874); Parl Deb (1874) 218, cc 52, 108.

8 CJ (1882) 487, 491; Parl Deb (1882) 273, cc 1978, 2049; ibid 274, c 34; HC 406 (1882); and see also CJ (1883) 4.

9 CJ (1902) 300; HC 309 (1902); see also CJ (1908) 3; Parl Deb (1908) 183, c 82; and CJ (1920) 88. As to what is criminal contempt, see 15 PD 59; 32 LR Ir 220. For further cases of Members imprisoned under attachment orders for contempt of court, see CJ (1888) 488; ibid (1902) 175; ibid (1903) 219; Parl Deb (1903) 123, c 309. Cf *In re Freston* [1883] 9 QBD 553; *In re Armstrong* [1892] 1 QB 327; *In re Hunt* [1959] 2 QB 69; and *Stourton v Stourton* [1963] 1 All ER 606. It has been held that an order for committal made following failure to attend a county court for examination as to means in connection with a judgment debt is the exercise of a disciplinary punitive power by the court (White J in Wandsworth County Court, 25 January 1989).

In 1880, it was argued, in a case for the committal of a Member for contempt in not having complied with a court order for payment of certain moneys and delivery of documents, that privilege protected Members except in cases of a gross character (as this was not). Subsequently, Parliament was dissolved but the application for commitment having been renewed within a period of forty days thereafter (see pp 101–102), the court refused to entertain it on the ground of privilege.[1] A case affecting a peer had been similarly decided by the Brompton County Court in 1878.[2]

It may therefore be generally deduced that in cases of quasi-criminal contempts Members of either House may be committed without an invasion of privilege. The extent of protection in other cases is likely to depend on the circumstances. In that connection, it may be noted that the courts will not grant an attachment against a peer or Member of the House of Commons for non-payment of money according to an award.[3]

BANKRUPTCY

The position of a Member who is adjudged bankrupt is dealt with at p 43 and in section 427 of the Insolvency Act 1986, which applies that Act and other similar legislation to persons having privilege of Parliament or of peerage as these statutes affect persons not having such privilege.

DETENTION UNDER THE MENTAL HEALTH ACT

The Committee for Privileges of the Lords has considered the effect of the powers of detention under the Mental Health Act 1983 on the privilege of freedom from arrest referred to in Standing Order No. 78 that 'no Lord of Parliament is to be imprisoned or restrained without sentence or order of the House unless upon a criminal charge or refusing to give security for the peace'.[4] The legal advice the Committee received differed on the critical issue of whether the provisions of the statute would prevail against any existing privilege of Parliament or of peerage (see p 70), and the Committee considered that, for the avoidance of doubt, the Government should, on a future occasion when cognate legislation was being introduced, consider the inclusion of a clause to provide expressly that Members of the House of Lords are liable to be detained under the Mental Health legislation and that in such circumstances they are disqualified from sitting or voting in the Lords or for receiving a writ of summons.

The Mental Health Act 1983 lays down a procedure for the detention of Members of the House of Commons suffering from mental illness (see p 41).

---

1 14 Ch D 533. See also *In re Armstrong, ex p Lindsay* 8 Morr 271, and report of proceedings in Westminster County Court on a committal order (1892) *The Times*, 10 February.

2 See also *Stourton v Stourton*, [1963] 1 All ER 606.

3 7 Term Rep 171, 448. See dicta of Lord Brougham in *Westmeath v Westmeath* (1831) 9 LJ (CH) 177.

4 Report by the Committee for Privileges on Parliamentary Privilege and the Mental Health legislation, HL 254 (1983–84). See also p 159 below.

PRIVILEGES RELATED TO FREEDOM FROM ARREST

Admissibility of Members as bail

It has been held, in civil cases, that a Member of Parliament, because of his immunity from arrest, could not be admitted as bail.[1] Under section 120(4) of the Magistrates' Courts Act 1980, however, the forfeiture of recognizances is enforced as if it were a fine, with the ultimate sanction of imprisonment. Members of both Houses have been admitted as bail on at least two occasions in recent years.[2]

Members summoned as witnesses

The service of the subpoena to attend as a witness has been treated as a breach of privilege by the House[3] and the parties responsible for service have on occasions been committed to the Serjeant for contempt. It is doubtful, however, whether under current practice the actual service would as a general rule be regarded as a breach of privilege, unless effected within the precincts of the House, *sedente domo*, on the general principle of the service of civil process.[4] But the privilege of exemption of a Member from attending as a witness has been asserted by the House upon the same principle as other personal privileges, viz, the paramount right of Parliament[5] to the attendance and service of its members; and on the matter being raised by the Member concerned the Speaker communicates with the court drawing attention to this privilege and asking that the Member should be excused because of the sitting of the House.[6] On other occasions the Commons has granted leave to its Members on the ground that their attendance as witnesses was required[7] and has admitted the same excuse for defaulters at calls of the House.[8] As regards attendance in the other House, one House will not permit one of its Members to be summoned by the other without the leave of the House and without the consent of the Member whose attendance is required (see p 677).

Exemption from jury service

The Juries Act 1974, section 9, provides that the appropriate officer shall excuse a person from attending jury service if that person can show that he is

---

1 *Graham v Sturt* (1812) 4 Taunt 249; *Burton v Atherton* (1816) 2 Marsh 232; *Duncan v Hill* (1822) 1 Dow & Ry (KB) 126; and case of Mr Feargus O'Connor, who offered himself as bail, 11 June 1848, at Bow Street. A Lord was not admitted as bail at Minehead Magistrates Court on 20 November 1978.

2 14 August 1970 at Bow Street Magistrates Court; 20 November 1978 at Minehead Magistrates Court.

3 1 Parl Hist 630; D'Ewes 347; 1 Hatsell 96–97, 169–175; LJ (1620–28) 630; CJ (1547–1628) 34, 48, 203, 205, 211, 368, 401 etc; ibid (1667–87) 339.

4 See p 125. For the special circumstances in which a military order to a Member who was a Territorial Army Officer to attend a Court of Inquiry was declared to be a breach of privilege see HC 146 (1937–38); CJ (1937–38) 351.

5 On this principle the privilege would also apply to officers of the House.

6 1 Hatsell 170, 171; CJ (1950–51) 186; ibid (1953–54) 42; HC Deb (1953–54) 521, c 957–958. And see the observations of the Court on this privilege, *Lewis v Mullally* (1953) *The Times*, 3 December.

7 CJ (1801) 122; ibid (1812–13) 218, 243, 292; ibid (1816) 110; ibid (1826–27) 306, 379; see also Parl Deb (1844) 73, c 433 (Earl of Devon).

8 CJ (1792–93) 318.

entitled to excusal. The Act specifies, in Part III of Schedule 1, amongst persons excusable as of right, peers and peeresses entitled to receive writs of summons to attend the House of Lords, Members of the House of Commons, officers of the House of Lords and officers of the House of Commons. In view of these provisions it is unlikely that either House would treat the mere summoning of a Member to serve on a jury as a breach of privilege, but this does not affect the right of the House to treat as a breach of its privileges any refusal to excuse a Member or officer of the House who is summoned as a juror from attending or serving, or any attempt to punish him for not attending or for refusing to serve as a juror.

The privilege of exemption from jury service pre-dates statutory excusal

The House of Commons in 1826 resolved that it is 'amongst the most ancient and undoubted privileges of Parliament that no Member shall be withdrawn from his attendance on his duty in Parliament to attend any other court'. This arose from a case in which two Members had been fined for non-attendance as jurymen in the Court of the Exchequer.[1] The prior claims of Parliamentary duty were recognised by Chief Justice Erle in 1861.[2]

DURATION OF THE PRIVILEGE OF FREEDOM FROM ARREST

House of Lords

The person of a peer 'is for ever sacred and inviolable' by the privilege of peerage.[3] This immunity rests upon ancient custom. It would seem to have been an ancient feudal privilege of the barons, the law assuming that there would always be, upon the demesnes of their baronies, sufficient to distrain for the satisfaction of any debt.[4]

The Lords, under Standing Order No 78, claim privilege when Parliament is sitting or 'within the usual times of privilege of Parliament'.

By the privilege of peerage, peers are privileged from arrest in civil causes not only while Parliament is sitting but at all times; this privilege is enjoyed by all peers, whether Lords of Parliament or not, and by peeresses.

Although the House has held that a Lord who had not qualified himself to sit by taking the oaths was not entitled to privilege,[5] when the matter came before a judge in chambers in 1849, the position could not be supported by authorities and the Lord in question (who, being in prison, had not taken the oaths following the death of his father) was ordered to be discharged.[6]

House of Commons

It has been the general and very long-standing opinion, allowed by the courts[7] and clearly stated by institutional authorities,[8] that the privilege of

---

1 CJ (1826) 82, 87, Parl Deb (1826) 14, c 568, 569. See also D'Ewes 560, 1 Hatsell 112; CJ (1547–1628) 898; Parl Deb (1826) 14, c 642; Parl Deb (1829) 21, c 1770.
2 *The Times*, 8 February 1861. See also West, Inq 28.
3 1 Bl Com 165.
4 1 West, Inq 27; *Stourton v Stourton* [1963] 1 All ER 302.
5 LJ (1691–96) 91; ibid (1718–21) 327.
6 *McCabe v Lord Harley* (1849) Times, 2 January.
7 *Goudy v Duncombe* (1847) 1 Exch at 435.
8 1 Bl Com 165. The right of franking letters, formerly enjoyed by Members, was by Act granted for the above-mentioned forty days. For a history of this right, see CJ (1732–37) 462.

freedom from arrest attaches to a Member of the House of Commons for forty days after every prorogation or dissolution[1] and forty days before the next appointed meeting. There may be an historical connection between such a right and the fact that in ancient custom writs of summons for a Parliament were issued at least forty days before its appointed meeting.

Cases may be cited of Members who had the benefit of privilege by obtaining release from prison upon their election, by a retrospective application of the claim.[2]

PRIVILEGE EXTENDING BEYOND MEMBERS

A privilege similar to that which protects Members from arrest and molestation in order that they may freely attend to their parliamentary duties extends to certain others, and for the same reason.[3] Those who may claim such privileges include officers of either House,[4] persons summoned to appear as witnesses before either House or a committee thereof,[5] and others in personal attendance on the service of Parliament[6] (see also pp 132–134).

---

1 *Barnard v Mordaunt* (1754) 1 Keny 125.
2 CJ (1667–87) 411; see Reports of Precedents CJ (1688–93) 401; ibid (1806–7) 642, 653, 654; 2 Hatsell 38; CJ (1819) 44; ibid (1819–20) 230.
3 CJ (1547–1628) 505; ibid (1640–42) 107; ibid (1667–87) 62; ibid (1699–1702) 521, etc.
4 Lex Parl 380; 1 Hatsell 9, 11, 172.
5 LJ (1628–42) 143, 144; CJ (1660–67) 525; ibid (1667–87) 20, 366, 472; ibid (1697–99) 364, 610; ibid (1835) 521. See also Parl Deb (1819) 39, cc 1168, 1265.
6 These have included those who had causes depending in or bills before the House LJ (1628–42) 143, 144, 262, 263, 289, 330, 477; ibid (1642–43) 476, 563, 574, 653, 680; ibid (1736–41) 625; ibid (1746–52) 19, 538; ibid (1753–56) 512; CJ (1547–1628) 702, 863, 921, 924; ibid (1640–42) 72; ibid (1699–1702) 512; ibid (1757–61) 244; ibid (1792–93) 426; and also counsel, solicitors and agents LJ (1856) 189; ibid (1860) 75, 76; CJ (1667–87) 472; ibid (1741–45) 170; ibid (1750–54) 797; ibid (1754–57) 447, 537; ibid (1792–93) 426. The Commons referred to the Committee of Privileges a complaint that an individual who was agent for a petitioner against a private bill had received adverse treatment in his employment as a consequence of his agency (HC Deb (1988–89) 153, cc 503–507).

CHAPTER 8

Penal jurisdiction of both Houses

The power of both Houses to punish Members and non-Members for disorderly and disrespectful acts has much in common with the authority inherent in the superior courts 'to prevent or punish conduct which tends to obstruct, prejudice or abuse them' while in the exercise of their responsibilities.[1] By this means the two Houses are enabled to safeguard and enforce their necessary authority without the compromise or delay to which recourse to the ordinary courts would give rise.[2] The act or omission which attracts the penal jurisdiction of either House may be committed in the face of the House or of a committee, within the Palace of Westminster[3] or outside it. Nor is it necessary that there should have been a breach of one of the privileges enjoyed, collectively or individually, by either House: anything done or omitted which may fall within the definition of contempt (see p 115), even if there is no precedent, may be punished.

COMMITTAL

The origin of the power to punish for contempt is probably to be found in the mediaeval concept of Parliament as primarily a court of justice. The power to fine or imprison for contempt belongs at common law to all courts of record. The Lords are a court of record,[4] and as such have power not only to imprison but to impose fines. They also imprison for a fixed time, and order security to be given for good conduct; and their customary form of commitment is by attachment. The Commons' claim to be a court of record has been virtually abandoned[5] (see p 90) though the consequences have not included surrender of all the concomitant powers. The power of commitment remains, exercised by the House,[6] distinctly accepted by the Lords in *Ashby*

---

1 Report of the Committee on Contempt of Court, Cmnd 5794 (1974) para 2.
2 *Burdett v Abbot* 14 East 138, 150–151: Denman CJ in *Sheriff of Middlesex* 3 State Tr (ns) 1253: Select Committee on Proceedings relating to Sir Francis Burdett, 2nd Report, CJ (1810) 732; 1 Hatsell, App 6.
3 In some cases the fact that the act is done within the precincts of the House is the essence of the offence. Thus the arrest of a Member on a criminal charge, if effected within the precincts of the House, *sedente domo*, would constitute a contempt, but not if it took place beyond the walls of Parliament, see Report from the Select Committee on the Official Secrets Acts, HC 101 (1938–39) p 23 and p 95.
4 It has been held however that the Lords, while exercising a legislative (as opposed to judicial) capacity, are not a court of record (*Flowers' case* (1799) 8 Term Rep 314).
5 In *Jones v Randall* in 1774, Lord Mansfield said the Commons were not a court of record (1 Cowp 17).
6 It has been calculated that there are over a thousand instances of its exercise up to the middle of the nineteenth century (Wynn's *Treatise on the Jurisdiction of the House of Commons* p 7). The latest case in the Commons of detention of a Member is that of Bradlaugh (CJ (1880) 235), and in respect of a non-Member, that of Grissell in the same year (CJ (1880) 77).

v White in 1704,[1] repeatedly recognised by the courts,[2] and virtually admitted by the statute 1 James I c 13, section 3, which provides that nothing therein shall 'extend to the diminishing of any punishments to be hereafter, by censure in Parliament, inflicted upon any person'. On the other hand, though the Commons formerly imprisoned offenders for a time certain,[3] it has subsequently been considered as wanting the power to commit for a period beyond the end of the session;[4] and unlike the Lords, which enjoys an undisputed status as a court of record, the Commons has not levied fines in the modern period (see p 110).[5]

Practice in committing offenders

Offenders committed by order of either House are either detained in one of HM prisons[6] or in the custody of Black Rod,[7] or the Serjeant at Arms,[8] as the case may be.

If at the time of committal the ultimate place of punishment has not been determined,[9] or when the person adjudged guilty of contempt is not already in the Serjeant's custody,[10] the Commons has first made an order for the offender to be taken into the Serjeant's custody and subsequently has committed him to one of HM prisons.

The Serjeant may also, without specific order of the House,[11] but in virtue of Standing Orders Nos 141 and 142 take into custody strangers who intrude themselves into the House or otherwise misconduct themselves (in the gallery or elsewhere).

Warrants of committal

The Lords attaches and commits persons by order, without any warrant. In the Commons, warrants are sometimes expressed in general terms, as for instance that the prisoner is committed for a 'high contempt' or a breach of

1 LJ (1701–05) 714.
2 *The Aylesbury Men, R v Paty* 2 Ld Raym 1105; 1 Wils 199; 3 ibid (1888), 19 State Tr 1137; *Burdett v Abbot* 14 East 1; 2 Chit 207, 3 B & Ald 420; *Sheriff of Middlesex* 11 Ad & El 273; Select Committee on Printed Papers, HC 305, 397; HC 39 (1847).
3 CJ (1547–1628) 269, 333, 639, 655; ibid (1651–59) 531, 591; ibid (1667–87) 543, 687, 737.
4 Per Lord Denman CJ, in *Stockdale v Hansard* 9 Ad & El 114; HC 283, 142 (1839).
5 Select committees in 1967 (HC 34 (1966–67) para 197) and 1977 (HC 417 (1976–77) para 15) have recommended legislation to give the Commons a statutory power to fine.
6 LJ (1767–70) 189; ibid 575; ibid (1779–83) 191; ibid (1783–87) 613, 647; ibid (1787–90) 338; ibid (1790) 649; ibid (1794–96) 241; ibid (1796–98) 509; ibid (1798–1800) 182; ibid (1801–02) 105; ibid (1810–12) 371, 372; ibid (1850) 367, 478; CJ (1818) 289; ibid (1826–27) 582; ibid (1835) 501; ibid (1843) 528; ibid (1865) 336; ibid (1878–79) 435; ibid (1880) 77.
7 LJ (1828) 34; ibid (1830–31) 471; ibid (1831–32) 387; ibid (1834) 743; ibid (1845) 729; ibid (1849) 135; ibid (1870) 77. See also LJ (1972–73) 56 and SO No 10.
8 CJ (1825) 455; ibid (1835) 501; ibid (1843) 523; ibid (1851) 288–9; ibid (1865) 336; ibid (1878–79) 366; ibid (1880) 235.
9 Parl Deb (1819–20) 41, c 1014.
10 CJ (1835) 501; ibid (1843) 523. This course may be most conveniently followed when the whereabouts of the offender are unknown. If his address is known, the House may make forthwith an order committing him to prison (Parl Deb (1819–20) 41, c 1016–1017).
11 CJ (1761–64) 23; ibid (1818–19) 537; ibid (1830) 461; ibid (1830–31) 323; ibid (1833) 246; ibid (1847) 99.

privilege.[1] They may also state the particular facts constituting the contempt.[2]

When the form of the warrant is general, it has been universally admitted
that it is incompetent for the courts to enquire further into the nature of the
contempt.[3] If the particular facts are stated, divergent views have been held
in the courts as to their duty of inquiry (see pp 107–108).

An order of the House of Lords to attach and commit an offender is signed
by the Clerk of the Parliaments, and is the authority under which the officers
of the House and others execute their duty. In the Commons, when an
offender is committed either to the custody of the Serjeant at Arms or to one
of Her Majesty's prisons, the Speaker is directed to issue his warrant or
warrants accordingly.

Where a person who is in the custody of the Serjeant at Arms is committed
by the House of Commons to one of Her Majesty's prisons, two warrants are
issued by the Speaker by order of the House, one to the Serjeant requiring
the Serjeant to deliver the body of the prisoner into the custody of the
keeper of the prison, and another reciting the judgment or order of the
House and requiring the keeper of the prison to receive into his custody the
body of the prisoner and safely keep him during the pleasure of the House or
until the House make further order in his case. But where the offender is not
in custody the order committing him to prison is followed up by a direction to
issue the warrants, one of them to the Serjeant at Arms reciting the judgment or order of the House and directing him to take the offender into his
custody and then forthwith deliver him over into the custody of the keeper of
the prison determined upon, and the other to the keeper of such prison
directing him to receive the offender and detain him. The warrants are
entrusted to the Serjeant at Arms as the executive officer of the House and a
refusal by the keeper of the prison to receive and detain on the delivery of
one of them would be treated by the House as a gross contempt.[4]

Warrants issued by order of the House of Commons are not vitiated by or
reversible for irregularities of form. The courts have considered it their duty
to presume that the orders of the House and their execution are according to
law.[5] Such warrants are construed on the same principles as the writs of a
superior court, and not as the warrants of a magistrate.[6]

Both Houses consider every branch of the civil government as bound to
assist when required, and have repeatedly required such assistance. By the
Speaker's warrant to the Serjeant at Arms, for taking a person into custody,
the Commons require 'all mayors, sheriffs, under sheriffs, bailiffs, constables, headboroughs and officers of the House . . . to be aiding and assist-

---

1 6 St Tr 1269, 1 Freem 153, 1 Mod Rep 144, 3 Keb 792; 1 Wills 200; CJ (1840) 25, 11 Ad & El
   273.
2 *Aylesbury Men, R v Paty* 2 Ld Raym 1105; *Brass Crosby's case* 19 St Tr 1137, 3 Wils 188;
   Burdett v Abbot (1810) 14 East 1; *Hobhouse's case* 2 Chit 207, 3 B & Ald 420.
3 *Burdett v Abbot* 14 East 150; *Sheriff of Middlesex* 3 State Tr (ns) 1254; *Gosset v Howard*
   [1847] 10 QB 453–454. See also 2 Hawkins PC (1824) b 2, c 15, s 73, and 1 Saund 74.
4 Parl Deb (1819–20) 41, c 1017.
5 *Aylesbury Men (Regina v Paty)* 2 Ld Raym 1105–1106; *Brass Crosby's case* 3 Wils 205; and
   Rex v Hobhouse 2 Chit Rep 210; *Lines v Russell* (1852) 16 JP 491, 19 LT (os) 364.
6 *Howard v Gosset* [1847] 10 QB 459, reversing [1845] 10 QB 359.

ing in the execution thereof.[1] In one instance, substantial military force was called upon, under the direction of a civil magistrate, to lodge an offender in the Tower.[2] The Lords have frequently required the assistance of the civil power in a similar manner.[3]

The power of breaking open doors when necessary to effect an arrest in pursuance of an order or warrant of committal is claimed by both Houses. The Lords has expressly conferred such a power on Black Rod,[4] and the Commons on the Serjeant at Arms.[5] In particular, the actions which arose out of the committal of Sir Francis Burdett in 1810 explained and recognized the legal consequences of a Speaker's warrant, and established the power of the Serjeant at Arms to use force for the purpose of overcoming resistance in the execution of the warrant.[6]

Protection of officers in executing warrants

Warrants of committal issued by the Speaker by order of the House of Commons provide good returns to writs of *habeas corpus*, and justify the officers acting thereunder against actions for trespass, assault, or false imprisonment, unless the causes of commitment stated in the warrants appear to be beyond the jurisdiction of the House. It is not necessary that any cause of commitment should be stated in the warrant, or that the prisoner should have been adjudged guilty of contempt before being taken into custody (see p 115). If the officer does not exceed his authority, he will be protected by the courts, even if the warrant should not be technically formal according to the rules by which the warrants of inferior courts are tested.

Resistance to the officers of either House, or others acting in execution of the orders of the House, has always been treated and punished as contempt. The Lords will not suffer any persons to be molested for executing their orders or the orders of a committee[7] and will protect them from actions. Those who brought actions against persons who had suppressed a riot in the precincts under the orders of the House, or actions of assault for refusal of admittance to Westminster Hall, have been committed;[8] the service of a doorkeeper with a process for recovery of a debt and costs for the loss of an umbrella left with the doorkeeper during a debate led to the plaintiff's being admonished by the Lords.[9] The Commons committed the sheriff of London for resisting the Serjeant at Arms with the Mace when ordered to free a

1 Cf CJ (1640–42) 29; ibid (1660–67) 586; ibid (1667–87) 193. See also ibid (1640–42) 371; ibid (1667–87) 353, 587.
2 CJ (1810) 264: Annual Register 1810, p 344 etc; Parl Deb (1810) 16, c 257, 454, 915 etc; Colchester, ii 245, 263 etc.
3 LJ (1675–81) 429; ibid (1685–91) 527, 530; ibid (1746–52) 118.
4 LJ (1685–91) 530, where Black Rod was authorised to break open the doors of any house, in the presence of a constable, in search of a peer whose arrest had been ordered.
5 CJ (1660–67) 222, where the Serjeant at Arms was empowered to break open a house in case of resistance, calling to his assistance the sheriff of Middlesex and other officers, as necessary.
6 14 East 157, 4 Taunt 401, 5 Dow 165. It was established in *Howard v Gosset* (1842) Car & M 382, that the Serjeant and his messengers are not to remain in a house if they know that the person to be arrested is away from home, in order to await his return.
7 LJ (1675–81) 104, 412; ibid (1691–96) 565; ibid (1718–21) 190; ibid (1787–90) 649; ibid (1805–06) 340, 610.
8 LJ (1767–70) 187, 197; ibid (1787–90) 249–251.
9 LJ (1826–27) 199, 206.

Member,[1] and delivered into the custody of the Serjeant at Arms judges who gave judgment against the Serjeant for executing the orders of the House to arrest certain persons.[2]

Warrants of committal and the courts

Although the Habeas Corpus Act is binding on all persons who have prisoners in their custody, and since 1704[3] it has been the practice for the Serjeant at Arms and others, by order of the House of Commons, to make returns to writs of *habeas corpus*,[4] the general rule—subject to the exception mentioned below—is that the causes of committal by warrant of the House cannot be inquired into by the courts of law.[5] Moreover, those who are committed for contempt may not be admitted to bail. The view was well stated in *Brass Crosby's case* in 1771:

> When the House of Commons adjudge any thing to be a contempt or a breach of privilege, their adjudication is a conviction, and their commitment in consequence is in execution; and no court can discharge or bail a person that is in execution by the judgment of another court. The House of Commons, therefore, having authority to commit, and that commitment being in execution . . . this court can do nothing . . . in such case this court is not a court of appeal.[6]

The position has been expressed by resolutions of the House of Commons,[7] and has been confirmed by numerous decisions of courts of law when application was made for the discharge or release on bail of persons committed by either House.[8] Lord Ellenborough observed in *Burdett v Abbot* in 1810 that 'if a commitment appeared to be for a contempt of the House of Commons generally, I would neither in the case of that court or of any other of the superior courts, inquire further'.[9]

The exception to the general rule, which was mentioned above, arises in the case of warrants stating the particular facts on which the warrant for committal was drawn. Divergent views have been held in the courts on their duty of inquiry. In the earlier cases the judges disclaimed any power to

---

1 1 Hatsell 53, citing 3 Holinshed 824–826 (see p 77).
2 CJ (1688–93) 227 (see p 148).
3 In 1675 and in 1704 the Commons endeavoured to resist the operations of a writ of *habeas corpus* by orders to the lieutenant of the Tower and to the Serjeant at Arms to make no return thereto (CJ (1667–87) 356; ibid (1702–04) 565). In 1677, two years before the passing of the Habeas Corpus Act of 31 Charles II, the Earl of Shaftesbury, who had been committed by the House of Lords 'for a high contempt', was remanded by the Court of King's Bench on the ground that it had no jurisdiction (1 Mod Rep 144).
4 *Sheriff of Middlesex* CJ (1840) 25; Parl Deb (1840) 51, c 550; *Lines v Russell* CJ (1851) 147, 148, 153.
5 CJ (1640–42) 960; ibid (1646–48) 221; 5 State Tr 365, 948; Sty 415.
6 19 State Tr 1147.
7 In 1680 4 Parl Hist 1262; CJ (1667–87) 356, 357; ibid (1697–99) 174; ibid (1702–04) 505, 599.
8 *Lord Shaftesbury's case* 6 State Tr 1269, 1 Freem 153, 1 Mod Rep 144, 3 Keb 792; *R v Paty* 2 Ld Raym 1105; *Murray's case* 1 Wils 200; *Brass Crosby's case* 19 State Tr 1137, 3 Wils 188; *Flower's case* 8 Term Rep 314; *Hobhouse's case* 2 Chit 207, 3 B & Ald 420; Sheriff of Middlesex (1840) CJ 25, 11 Ad & El 273; *Lines v Russell* CJ (1851) 147, 148, 153; ibid (1852) 64, 68, 16 JP 491, 19 LT (os) 364.
9 *Burdett v Abbot* 14 East 150. See also *Sheriff of Middlesex* 3 State Tr (ns) 1254 and *Gosset v Howard* [1847] 10 QB 453–454.

inquire,[1] but subsequently judicial opinion changed. Lord Ellenborough observed in *Burdett v Abbot* in 1810 (which was an action for assault and not on a writ of *habeas corpus*) that he could conceive a cause of committal coming collaterally before the court in the form, for example, of a justification pleaded to an action of trespass, in such a way that the court might be obliged to consider it and pronounce it defective. It would be more doubtful, however, whether a matter coming directly before the court, such as on a return to a *habeas corpus*, would lead the court to relieve the subject from the commitment of the House in any case whatever. He went on to say:

> If a commitment ... does not profess to commit for a contempt, but for some matter appearing on the return, which could by no reasonable intendment be considered as a contempt of the House committing, but a ground of commitment palpably and evidently arbitrary, unjust and contrary to every principle of positive law or natural justice; I say that, in the case of such commitment, we must look at it and act upon it as justice may require from whatever court it may profess to have proceeded.[2]

A similar view was expressed by Lord Denman in 1840: if the particular facts are stated in the warrant and do not bear out the committal, the court (in his view) should inquire into the warrant: if the warrant states a contempt in general terms, the court is bound by it.[3]

Committal without warrant

In earlier times, it was not the custom to prepare a formal warrant of the House of Commons for the execution of its orders (as is still the practice in the Lords). The Serjeant arrested persons with the Mace as his only authority.[4] At the present day, he takes into custody those who misconduct themselves in the House, without any written instructions.[5]

When accompanied by the Mace, the Speaker has ordered persons into custody for disrespect or other breaches of privilege committed in his presence, without any previous order of the House.[6] Upon information that a Member had been assaulted in the lobby, the Speaker has directed the Serjeant to take the offender into custody.[7]

Period of committal and discharge

The Lords has power to commit offenders to prison for a specified term, even beyond the duration of the session.[8] If on the other hand, no time is

---

1 See *Aylesbury Men (R v Paty)* ((1704) 2 Ld Raym 1105) though even here there was a dissenting opinion which held that the prosecuting of the action complained of (which was taken against the constables of Aylesbury for not allowing a vote) being in itself legal could not be a breach of privilege. See also Wright J in *Murray's case* 1 Wils 299, and Blackstone J, in *Brass Crosby's case* 3 Wils 188, 19 State Tr 1138.
2 14 East 147 ff. This view received the support of Lord Denman in *Stockdale v Hansard* 3 State Tr (ns) 856.
3 *Sheriff of Middlesex* 3 State Tr (ns) 154; see also *Rex v Hobhouse* 2 Chit Rep 287, 11 Ad & El 273 ff.
4 CJ (1547–1628) 109; 1 Hatsell 92; HC 397 (1854) p vi.
5 An account of the practice of the Serjeant at Arms in dealing with persons against whom complaints are made or who are adjudged to be in contempt of the House (including strangers who misconduct themselves in the Gallery of the House) is contained in the Minutes of Evidence taken before the Select Committee on Parliamentary Privilege, 1967 (HC 34 (1967–68) p 157).
6 2 Hatsell 241 *n*; D'Ewes 629; CJ (1667–87) 351, 353; Parl Deb (1812) 23, c 166.
7 CJ (1824) 483.
8 LJ (1767–70) 575; ibid (1796–98) 509; ibid (1798–1800) 182; ibid (1801–02) 105; ibid (1850) 478.

mentioned in the order of committal, it has been said that prisoners committed by the Lords could not be discharged on *habeas corpus*, even after a prorogation;[1] but in Lord Shaftesbury's case a doubt was expressed by one of the judges whether the imprisonment, which was for an uncertain time, would be concluded by the session; and another said that if the session had been determined the prisoner ought to have been discharged.[2] The latter opinion derives confirmation from the fact that on 14 January 1744, the Serjeant at Arms acquainted the House that he had kept a prisoner in his custody 'until he was discharged of course by the prorogation of Parliament, without his having made his submission'; whereupon the offender was ordered to be re-attached.[3]

The Commons abandoned its former practice of imprisoning for a time certain, and is now considered as without power to imprison beyond the session (see p 104). The more recent practice of the Commons has been not to commit offenders for any specified time, but generally or during pleasure; and to keep them in custody until they present petitions expressing proper contrition for their offences and praying for their release,[4] or until, upon motion made in the House, it is resolved that they shall be discharged.[5] A similar course has been pursued by the Lords.[6]

Persons committed by the Commons, if not sooner discharged by the House, are immediately released from their confinement on a prorogation. If they were held longer in custody, they would be discharged by the courts upon a writ of *habeas corpus*.[7]

Where, however, the House considers that an offender who has thus regained his liberty has not been sufficiently punished, he may be again committed in the next session and detained until the House is satisfied.[8]

Persons who are taken into custody of the Serjeant at Arms acting by virtue of the directions given to him by Standing Orders Nos 141 and 142 to take into custody those who misconduct themselves in the gallery or in a select or a standing committee (see pp 173, 603 and 633) are normally discharged at the rising of the House on the day in question.

---

1 Per Lord Denman CJ, in *Stockdale v Hansard* 9 Ad & El 127; HC 283 (1839) 147.
2 6 State Tr 1296; 1 Mod Rep 144.
3 LJ (1741–46) 420.
4 It has been customary to order such petitions to be printed and considered on a future day (CJ (1842) 180, 209; ibid (1851) 151; ibid (1857–58) 196; Parl Deb (1857–58) 150, c 1198; CJ (1878–79) 381). In one instance where a petition was presented from a person in the custody of the Serjeant expressing contrition for his offence and praying to be discharged from custody, the House ordered him to be brought to the bar forthwith in order to his being reprimanded and discharged (CJ (1825) 469, 470).
5 CJ (1840) 291, 337; ibid (1842) 224; ibid (1880) 241. The earlier practice current in both Houses of requiring the offender to appear at the Bar to be reprimanded (eg LJ (1850) 380, 384; ibid (1870) 77; CJ (1842) 420, ibid (1851) 289) has been dispensed with. Nor are those in custody now normally required to pay Black Rod's or the Serjeant's fees as a condition of discharge and no order for the payment of fees has been made unless called for by the nature of the offence (CJ (1857–58) 208; ibid (1859) 342; ibid (1878–79) 385).
6 LJ (1767–70) 189; ibid (1779–83) 191; ibid (1783–87) 613, 647 (1787); ibid (1787–93) 250 (1788), 338 (1789), 649 (1790); ibid (1794–96) 241; ibid (1801–02) 115, 221, 225, 230; ibid (1828) 34; ibid (1830–31) 471; ibid (1831–32) 387; ibid (1834) 745; ibid (1845) 730; ibid (1849) 135; ibid (1850) 367, 380, 384; ibid (1870) 77.
7 Per Lord Denman CJ, in *Stockdale v Hansard* 9 Ad & El 114; HC 283 (1839) p 142. This law never extended to an adjournment, even when it was in the nature of prorogation, see CJ (1688–93) 537.
8 Parl Deb (1879) 249, c 989; CJ (1750–54) 303; ibid (1860) 70, 73, 77.

PUNISHMENT OTHER THAN BY COMMITTAL

Fines

The House of Lords in its capacity as a court of record has power to inflict fines, either in substitution for, or in addition to, committal.[1] Cases are also recorded in which it has ordered security to be given for good conduct, even during the whole life of the parties.[2]

The last occasion on which the Commons imposed a fine was in 1666:[3] no fine has been levied in modern times.[4]

The Select Committee on Parliamentary Privilege in 1967 recommended that legislation should be introduced to enable the House to impose fines with statutory authority[5] and this recommendation was repeated by the Committee of Privileges in 1977, together with a proposal for the abolition of the power to imprison.[6] No action to implement these recommendations has been taken.

Reprimand or admonition

Where the offence is not so grave as to warrant the committal of the offender he is generally directed to be reprimanded[7] or admonished[8] by the Lord Chancellor[9] or the Speaker.[10]

In the Commons, when a person who is not a Member is directed to be reprimanded or admonished, the offender, if he is in attendance, is brought to the bar of the House forthwith by the Serjeant at Arms, and is there reprimanded by the Speaker in the name and by the authority of the House.[11] The offender is then discharged. If, however, he is not in attendance, he may be ordered either to be taken into the custody of the Serjeant

---

1 LJ (1620–28) 276; ibid (1660–66) 554; ibid (1666–75) 174; ibid (1685–91) 144; ibid (1760–64) 493 (Report of Precedents); ibid (1767–70) 575; ibid (1796–98) 509; ibid (1798–1800) 181; ibid (1801–02) 60, 105.
2 LJ (1660–66) 554; ibid (1790–93) 331.
3 CJ (1660–67) 690; cf ibid (1547–1628) 609, and 1 Parl Hist 1250.
4 The possession by the Commons of the power of imposing fines was denied by Lord Mansfield in *R v Pitt* and *R v Mead* 3 Burr 1335.
5 HC 34 (1966–67) para 197.
6 HC 417 (1976–77) para 15.
7 LJ (1767–70) 187; ibid (1798–1800) 646; ibid (1801–02) 60; ibid (1810–12) 341, 399; ibid (1830–31) 335; ibid (1850) 89; CJ (1826–28) 399; ibid (1837–38) 316; ibid (1839) 278; ibid (1840) 23; ibid (1887) 306; ibid (1901) 418.
8 LJ (1826–27) 206; CJ (1831–32) 294; ibid (1833) 218; ibid (1842) 143; ibid (1874) 189; ibid (1892) 166; ibid (1929–30) 503.
9 The Lords has ordered offenders to be taken into the custody of Black Rod and then to be called in and reprimanded by the Lord Chancellor and to be discharged upon payment of their fees (LJ (1805–06) 610 (1806)), or to be continued in custody until they have entered into recognizances for good behaviour (LJ (1805–06) 340 (1805)). In one instance, the Lords ordered that an offender should be discharged without any punishment but should be acquainted that if he repeated his offence he would not meet with such leniency (LJ (1767–70) 212).
10 In 1810 the Speaker said that 'the House, having voted that the person at the Bar had been guilty of a high breach of its privileges, could not pass over the offence without some degree of imprisonment' (Parl Deb (1810) 15, c 497).
11 CJ (1947–48) 22; and cf ibid (1956–57) 64, 66. The practice of making prisoners kneel at the bar to receive the judgment of the House has been discontinued (CJ (1770–72) 594), having been last insisted upon in 1750 (14 Parl Hist 894 ff and 1 Walpole's Memoirs of George II, 15). There had been one previous instance of refusal in the Commons (CJ (1750–54) 48) and others before the Lords, 3 Parl Hist 844, 880.

and brought to the bar the following or some later day, there to be reprimanded and discharged,[1] or to attend the House on a future day to be reprimanded.[2]

For the practice when the offender is a Member, see below.

What is said by the Speaker in reprimanding or admonishing offenders is always ordered to be entered in the Journals.

When an offender is brought to the bar to receive judgment of committment, or any other punishment, or to be discharged out of custody (see p 109), the Serjeant at Arms stands by him with the Mace.[3]

Prosecution of offenders

In cases of breach of privilege which are also offences at law, where the punishment which the Commons has power to inflict would not be adequate to the offence, or where for any other cause the House has thought a proceeding at law necessary, either as a substitute for, or in addition to, its own proceedings, the Attorney General has been directed to prosecute the offender.[4]

PUNISHMENTS INFLICTED ON MEMBERS

In the case of contempts committed against the House of Commons by Members, two other penalties are available in addition to those already mentioned, suspension from the service of the House,[5] and expulsion,[6] sometimes in addition to committal.[7]

A resolution by the Lords as a legislative body could not exclude a Member of that House permanently (see p 39).

Reprimand or admonition

In the Commons, a Member receives a reprimand or admonition standing in his place,[8] unless he is in the custody of the Serjeant, in which event he is reprimanded at the bar. When a Member is ordered to be reprimanded or to be admonished he may be called in to receive the reprimand or admonition forthwith,[9] or he may be ordered to attend the House in his place the following or some later day.[10]

---

1 CJ (1819) 618.
2 CJ (1887) 306.
3 2 Hatsell 144.
4 CJ (1693–97) 734; ibid (1697–99) 288; ibid (1699–1702) 230–31, 735; ibid (1741–45) 394; ibid (1750–54) 304; ibid (1778–80) 902; ibid (1841) 394, 413; ibid (1854) 159; ibid (1857) 355; ibid (1860) 258; ibid (1866) 239; ibid (1889) 363. In two recent cases the House authorities informally invited the police to consider proceeding against those responsible for gross misbehaviour in the gallery (CJ (1970–71) 68; ibid (1977–78) 438).
5 CJ (1888) 385; ibid (1890–91) 481; ibid (1911) 37.
6 CJ (1882) 62; ibid (1947–48) 22.
7 CJ (1547–1628) 917; ibid (1640–42) 158, 703; ibid (1642–44) 526; ibid (1646–48) 295; ibid (1648–51) 591; ibid (1667–87) 576, 642.
8 CJ (1790) 516; ibid (1837–38) 316; ibid (1892) 167; ibid (1929–30) 503; ibid (1947–48) 23; ibid (1967–68) 362.
9 CJ (1892) 167; ibid (1947–48) 23; ibid (1967–68) 362.
10 CJ (1790) 516; ibid (1837–38) 312.

Suspension

Although suspension from the service of the House is now prescribed under Standing Order No 43 for Members who have disregarded the authority of the Chair or abused the rules of the House (see pp 394–395), such a disciplinary power existed under ancient usage long before the making of the Standing Order in 1880.

There are a number of cases of such suspensions for varying periods in the seventeenth century,[1] though none between 1692 and 1877, at which latter date the Speaker ruled that 'any Member persistently and wilfully obstructing public business without just and reasonable cause is guilty of a contempt of this House, and is liable to punishment, whether by censure, suspension from the service of the House or commitment, according to the judgment of the House'.[2] In 1880, the procedure for suspending a Member for particular offences was laid down by Standing Order (now No 43).

Since then, most suspensions have been carried out in pursuance of that provision. Those not under Standing Order No 43 have been in respect of the terms of a letter addressed by a Member to Mr Speaker and of his conduct in the House on preceding days;[3] for publishing a letter reflecting on Mr Speaker's conduct in the Chair;[4] and for damaging the Mace (after the rising of the House) and conduct towards the Chair on a preceding day.[5]

Expulsion

The expulsion by the House of Commons of one of its Members may be regarded as an example of the House's power to regulate its own constitution, though it is, for convenience, treated here as one of the methods of punishment at the disposal of the House. Members have been expelled as being in open rebellion;[6] as having been guilty of forgery;[7] of perjury;[8] of frauds and breaches of trust;[9] of misappropriation of public money;[10] of conspiracy to defraud;[11] of fraudulent conversion of property;[12] of corruption in the administration of justice,[13] or in public offices,[14] or in the execution of their duties as Members of the House;[15] of conduct unbecoming the character of an officer and a gentleman;[16] and of contempts, libels and

---

1 CJ (1642–44) 128, 302; ibid (1648–51) 123; ibid (1660–67) 289; ibid (1667–87) 120, 156; ibid (1688–93) 846.
2 Parl Deb (1877) 235, c 1814.
3 CJ (1890–91) 481.
4 CJ (1911) 37.
5 Votes and Proceedings, 1987–88, 20 April 1988; HC Deb (1987–88) 131, cc 680–683, 929–950.
6 CJ (1714–18) 336, 467.
7 CJ (1722–27) 702; ibid (1954–55) 25.
8 CJ (1782–84) 770.
9 CJ (1718–21) 406, 412, 413; ibid (1727–32) 871; ibid (1812) 176; CJ (1892) 120; and see Colchester, ii, 373.
10 CJ (1702–04) 171; ibid (1810) 398.
11 CJ (1813–14) 433.
12 CJ (1922) 273, 276, 293, 319.
13 CJ (1547–1628) 588.
14 CJ (1711–14) 30, 97.
15 CJ (1667–87) 24; ibid (1693–97) 274, 5 Parl Hist 900–910; CJ (1693–97) 283.
16 CJ (1795–96) 661; ibid (1890–91) 268, 272, 282.

other offences committed against the House itself.[1]

Members have also been expelled who have fled from justice, without any conviction or judgment recorded against them.[2] Where Members have been legally convicted of offences which warrant expulsion, it is customary to lay the record of conviction before the House[3] In other cases the proceedings have been founded upon reports of commissions or committees of the House or other sufficient evidence.[4] It is customary to order the Member, if absent, to attend in his place before an order is made for his expulsion,[5] in order to give him an opportunity to vindicate himself;[6] but where it is apparent that no question of vindication can arise, an order for attendance has not been made.[7] Where an order has been made that a Member should attend in his place, service is made upon him of the order of the House for his attendance, or evidence furnished proving that service is impossible. If he is in prison, it has been the practice to order the governor of the prison to bring him to the House in custody, if he so desires to be brought.

Expulsion, though it vacates the seat of a Member and a new writ is immediately issued, does not create any disability to serve again in the House of Commons, if re-elected.[8] The House's attempts in the mid eighteenth century to be rid of John Wilkes, who was three times expelled and once had his return amended in favour of his defeated opponent only ended, some years later, in the expunging from the Journal as 'subversive of the rights of the whole body of electors of this kingdom' of the earlier resolution that, following his expulsion, he was incapable of being re-elected in that Parliament.[9] In 1882, when Bradlaugh was expelled and immediately re-elected, no question of the validity of his return arose.[10]

---

1 CJ (1547–1628) 917; ibid (1640–42) 301, 537; ibid (1667–87) 431; ibid (1711–14) 513; ibid (1714–18) 411; ibid (1722–27) 391; ibid (1882) 61; ibid (1947–48) 22. See also Report of Precedents touching imprisonment or restraint of Lords in the time of Parliament, HC 79 (1806–07).

2 CJ (1856) 379, Parl Deb (1856) 143, c 1386; CJ (1857) 48, Parl Deb (1857) 144, c 702. See also CJ (1890–91) 456, 469; ibid (1892) 67.

3 CJ (1782–84) 770; ibid (1812) 176; ibid (1813–14) 433; ibid (1954–55) 20, etc.

4 CJ (1693–97) 283; ibid (1722–27) 141, 391; ibid (1727–32) 870; ibid (1810) 433, etc.

5 CJ (1795–96) 661; ibid (1810) 399; ibid (1812) 176; ibid (1813–14) 433; ibid (1856) 367.

6 Parl Deb (1856) 143, c 1404; ibid (1857) 144, c 710; ibid (1891) 353, c 574.

7 In these cases, a Member who had pleaded guilty, and one who was convicted on his own confession were not ordered to attend, though a communication was sent through the Home Office of the intended motion for expulsion (CJ (1890–91) 282 and Parl Deb (1891) 353, c 574; CJ (1892) 120). In similar circumstances, when no order for attendance was made, a Member was informed of the proposed motion for expulsion and told that he might write to the Speaker; and his letter was communicated to the House before the motion was made (CJ (1954–55) 25). In one case, a letter from a convicted Member was communicated to the House on the reading of the order for his attendance (CJ (1922) 319).

8 The practice of the Commons in earlier years of creating a disability unknown to the law by adding to expulsion inability to sit again in Parliament or even to serve the State may be regarded as having lapsed (CJ (1640–42) 158, 301, 473; ibid (1660–67) 60; ibid (1711–14) 128.

9 CJ (1761–64) 721–723; ibid (1768–70) 178–179, 228–229, 385, 386, 387, 451; ibid (1780–82) 977. See also 1 Cav Deb 352.

10 CJ (1882) 62.

POWER OF BOTH HOUSES TO SECURE ATTENDANCE OF PERSONS ON MATTERS OF PRIVILEGE

The House of Commons has the power to send for persons whose conduct has been brought before the House on a matter of privilege by an order for their attendance, without specifying in the order the object or the causes whereon their attendance is required;[1] and in obedience to the order Members attend in their places, and other persons at the Bar[2] (see pp 111and 110).

Power to send for persons in custody

It has been a very ancient practice in both Houses to cause persons to be brought in custody to the Bar to answer charges of contempt[3] and in the Lords to order them to be attached and brought before the House to answer complaints of breaches of privilege, contempts and other offences.[4] This process is analogous to writs of attachment upon mesne process in the superior courts.

In *Gosset v Howard* (1847) on writ of error from the Court of Queen's Bench, the Court of Exchequer Chamber declared:

> That the privileges of the House involved in the inquiry before the Court were indisputable, because, 1st, That House, which forms the Great Inquest of the nation,[5] has a power to institute inquiries, and to order the attendance of witnesses, and in case of disobedience . . . bring them in custody to the Bar for the purpose of examination; and 2nd, If there be a charge of contempt and breach of privilege, and an order for the person charged to attend and answer it, and a wilful disobedience of that order, the House has undoubtedly the power to cause the person charged to be taken into custody, and to be brought to the Bar to answer the charge; and further, the House, and that alone, is the proper judge when these powers, or either of them, are to be exercised.[6]

---

1 See 2 Cav Deb 321 (21 February 1771), for the Speaker's suggestion that service of the order of the House by leaving a copy thereof at the usual place of abode of the person therein named should be deemed personal service.
2 CJ (1892) 157; Parl Deb (1892) 3, c 700; CJ (1897) 361; ibid (1901) 414.
3 LJ (1578–1614) 201, 256, 296; ibid (1660–66) 252 etc; CJ (1547–1628) 175, 680, 886; ibid (1667–87) 351; ibid (1727–32) 705; ibid (1774–76) 323; ibid (1825) 445; ibid (1826–27) 561; ibid (1840) 30, 56, 59; ibid (1880) 70. *Gosset v Howard* [1847] 10 QB 451, and see also Appendix IX to Second Report of committee appointed to inquire into proceedings in *Howard v Gosset*, HC 397 (1845) p 104.
4 See precedents collected in App to 2nd Report of the Select Committee on Printed Papers, HC 397 (1845) p 104.
5 4 Co Inst 11.
6 10 QB 451.

CHAPTER 9

Contempts

Generally speaking, any act or omission which obstructs or impedes either House of Parliament in the performance of its functions, or which obstructs or impedes any Member or officer of such House in the discharge of his duty, or which has a tendency, directly or indirectly, to produce such results may be treated as a contempt even though there is no precedent of the offence.[1] It is therefore impossible to list every act which might be considered to amount to a contempt, the power to punish for such an offence being of its nature discretionary (see p 103). Nevertheless, certain broad principles may be deduced from a review of the kinds of misconduct which in the past either House has punished as a contempt. It should however be borne in mind that in 1978 the House of Commons resolved to exercise its penal jurisdiction as sparingly as possible, and only when satisfied that it was essential to do so (see p 135).

MISCONDUCT IN PRESENCE OF EITHER HOUSE OR A COMMITTEE

Any disorderly, contumacious or disrespectful conduct in the presence of either House or a committee will constitute a contempt, which may be committed by strangers,[2] parties or witnesses.

Strangers

Strangers have been punished for contempt for disorderly conduct for having interrupted or disturbed the proceedings of either House[3] or a committee,[4] for remaining in the House after being directed to withdraw,[5] and for refusing to stop taking notes of proceedings when requested to do so by an officer of the House.[6]

Both Houses have passed resolutions severely condemning those who come or incite others to come in a riotous, tumultuous or disorderly manner in order to hinder or promote legislation or other matters before either House.[7] Such persons have been committed,[8] as have those who incited

---

1 See Report of the Select Committee on the Official Secrets Acts, HC 101 (1938–39) p xii.
2 A Member present at a committee, who is not of the committee or attending in accordance with Lords SO No 63, must be considered as standing, in most respects, on the same footing as a stranger.
3 LJ (1920) 405, HL Deb (1920) 41, cc 1026, 1237; CJ (1830) 461; ibid (1830–31) 323, 325.
4 CJ (1640–42) 668, 815; ibid (1842) 131, 143, Parl Deb (1842) 61, c 1003.
5 LJ (1714–18) 351, 516, 617; ibid (1718–21) 29.
6 CJ (1819) 537, Parl Deb (1819) 40, c 1182.
7 LJ (1765–67) 209; CJ (1693–97) 667; ibid (1699–1702) 230; ibid (1732–37) 115.
8 CJ (1699–1702) 230.

others against Members of the House.[1] The Commons have characterized as a high violation of privilege and a gross and notorious insult the taking possession of the lobby and approaches to the House by a large and tumultuous assembly which failed to withdraw when summoned to do so.[2]

The disruption of a meeting of a sub-committee of a select committee of the Commons sitting in public away from Westminster was considered by the Committee of Privileges to be a contempt of the House. It did not consider that the duty of the Serjeant at Arms extended to giving protection to a select committee sitting outside the precincts.[3]

Witnesses and counsel

Witnesses who have refused to be sworn or take upon themselves some corresponding obligation to speak the truth,[4] who have refused to answer questions,[5] who refused to produce or destroyed documents in their possession,[6] who have prevaricated,[7] given false evidence,[8] wilfully suppressed the truth,[9] or persistently misled a committee[10] have been considered guilty of contempt. A witness who trifled with a committee,[11] was insolent[12] or insulting,[13] or appeared in a state of intoxication[14] has been similarly punished.

In the past, counsel appearing before the Commons have been punished for reflecting upon the preceding Parliament[15] or upon Members[16] in the course of their argument.

DISOBEDIENCE TO RULES OR ORDERS OF EITHER HOUSE OR OF A COMMITTEE

General rules

An example of the general rule disobedience to which may be accounted a contempt is the presumption of the Commons that all petitions ought to be

---

 1 CJ (1699–1702) 231.
 2 CJ (1778–80) 902: see also ibid (1732–37) 115.
 3 HC 308 (1968–69).
 4 LJ (1718–21) 418, 420; ibid (1870) 77; 2 PR & D 51.
 5 LJ (1675–81) 54, 55; ibid (1691–96) 677; ibid (1718–21) 418, 420; CJ (1831–32) 360, 365; ibid (1833) 212, 218; ibid (1835) 501, 504, 514; ibid (1842) 223, 227; ibid (1852–54) 320; ibid (1897) 361, 365. See also p 681.
 6 CJ (1788–89) 173; ibid (1835) 564, 571, 575; ibid (1946–47) 320, 377. For the case of a witness who destroyed a material document after his first examination before a committee, see CJ (1818–1819) 618, 621. Refusal to answer a select committee has been condemned as a contempt in general terms, CJ (1946–47) 378.
 7 LJ (1767–70) 188, 189; ibid (1810–11) 371; CJ (1821–22) 335; ibid (1826–28) 473; ibid (1835) 601; ibid (1847–48) 258; ibid (1851–52) 147; ibid (1852–54) 699, 742; ibid (1857) 354; ibid (1865–67) 239.
 8 CJ (1806–07) 256; ibid (1826–28) 473; ibid (1828) 147; ibid (1842) 168, 198, 206. See also Committee of Privileges, 1st Report HC 336 (1982–83).
 9 CJ (1828) 122; Parl Deb (1828) 18, c 936.
10 CJ (1947–48) 22.
11 CJ (1688–93) 294.
12 CJ (1660–67) 296.
13 CJ (1640–42) 803.
14 CJ (1852–54) 389.
15 CJ (1547–1628) 488, 489.
16 1 Grey Deb 145.

signed by the petitioners by their own hands,[1] or that no person should set the name of any other to a petition to be presented to the House.[2] Contravention of the rule which forbids the publication of proceedings and debates of either House or committees of either House conducted with closed doors or in private, is dealt with elsewhere (see pp 85–86 and 122–124).

Particular rules

The most common example of this type of contempt is the refusal or neglect of a witness or other person to attend either House or a committee when summoned to do so.[3] Other examples have included neglecting to make a return,[4] refusing to withdraw when directed to do so,[5] refusing to release from custody Members or other persons entitled to the privilege of the House when required to do so,[6] refusing to refund money levied by the sale of their property to the printers to the Commons,[7] and disclosure of proceedings in Secret Session (see pp 143–144).

Orders of committees

Disobedience to the order of a committee made within its authority is a contempt of the House by which the committee was appointed. Individuals have been held to be in contempt who did not comply with orders for their attendance made by committees with the necessary powers to send for persons;[8] as have those who have disobeyed or frustrated committee orders for the production of papers.[9]

To prevent, delay, obstruct or interfere with the execution of the orders of either House or its committees is also a contempt. Among the particular actions which have been considered to fall within this definition are absconding in order to avoid being served with a summons to attend a House or a committee,[10] assisting those whose attendance is required as witnesses to avoid giving their attendance,[11] attempting illicitly to procure from a third party a document which he had been required to produce before a com-

---

1 CJ (1688–93) 285.
2 CJ (1772–74) 800.
3 LJ (1718–21) 429; ibid (1731–36) 388; ibid (1736–41) 250, 290; ibid (1767–70) 429, 575; ibid (1776–79) 692; CJ (1722–27) 92; ibid (1727–33) 705; ibid (1745–50) 308; ibid (1770–72) 208, 259; ibid (1772–74) 465, 17 Parl Hist 1021; CJ (1878–79) 366.
4 LJ (1849) 135.
5 LJ (1714–18) 331, 516, 617; ibid (1718–21) 29: CJ (1880) 235 and Parl Deb (1880) 253, c 620.
6 1 Holinshed 824; 1 Hatsell 57; CJ (1547–1628) 155 ff; LJ (1660–66) 222.
7 CJ (1840) 16, 19.
8 CJ (1688–93) 162, 180; ibid (1702–04) 551; ibid (1718–21) 143, 582, 583, 590; ibid (1722–27) 91; ibid (1780–82) 967; ibid (1790–91) 342; ibid (1803–04) 215; 2 Peck 136.
9 CJ (1714–18) 46; ibid (1732–37) 51. See also pp 627–630.
10 CJ (1774–76) 323–324, 357–358, 370; ibid (1818–19) 539; ibid (1819–20) 404; ibid (1826–28) 297; ibid (1835) 324, 330; ibid (1843) 333; ibid (1851–52) 147, 152.
11 CJ (1835) 324, 330.

mittee,[1] and assisting in the escape of someone committed by order of the House.[2]

ABUSE OF THE RIGHT OF PETITION

Any abuse of the right of petition may be treated as a contempt by either House. (See also chapter 3).

Such an offence may arise by frivolously, vexatiously or maliciously submitting a petition which contains false, scandalous or groundless allegations against any person (whether a Member of either House or not); or contriving, promoting and presenting such a petition.[3] It has been considered an abuse by the Lords to present a petition containing gross misrepresentations.[4] Other instances of contempt of this character are inducing persons to sign a petition by false representations,[5] or threatening to petition the Commons charging a Member with misconduct unless the Member conferred a benefit on the would-be petitioner.[6]

It is a contempt to present or cause to be presented to either House or to a committee forged, falsified or fabricated documents with intent to deceive, whether by forging signatures or subscribing fictitious signatures,[7] tampering with petitions,[8] fabricating documentary evidence,[9] or altering a paper ordered to be laid before the Lords after the order had been received.[10]

Conspiracy to deceive either House or any committee also constitutes a contempt.[11]

To abstract any record or other document from the custody of the Clerk or to falsify or improperly alter any records of, or documents presented to, either House or committees of either House will constitute a contempt.[12] Standing Order No 109 of the House of Commons specifically provides that no document received by the clerk of a select committee shall be withdrawn or altered without the knowledge and approval of the committee.

---

1 CJ (1806–07) 175.
2 CJ (1547–1628) 21.
3 LJ (1620–28) 462, 741; CJ (1693–97) 371; ibid (1732–37) 897; ibid (1741–45) 288; ibid (1768–70) 855; ibid (1780–82) 315.
4 LJ (1731–36) 384.
5 LJ (1862) 300, 321, 323, 331, 378, 383, 386.
6 CJ (1818–19) 158–159, Parl Deb (1819) 39, c 633.
7 LJ (1850) 367; CJ (1825–26) 445; ibid (1843) 523, 528; ibid (1851–52) 288, 289; ibid (1865) 336; ibid (1887) 306. Forging counsel's name to an appeal without their knowledge has been considered a contempt (LJ (1714–18) 345, 349, 353, 356–357, 363). The general rule against presenting false petitions extends to those who cause petitions to be presented, knowing or having good reason to believe that numerous signatures were fictitious or unauthorised (LJ (1858) 477).
8 CJ (1839) 205, 210, 235–236, 278; Parl Deb (1839) 47, c 1068.
9 CJ (1889) 311–312, 332, 346, 363; Parl Deb (1889) 338, c 410.
10 LJ (1841) 251.
11 LJ (1722–26) 406; CJ (1727–32) 568.
12 CJ (1778–80) 838.

MISCONDUCT OF MEMBERS OR OFFICERS

Members deliberately misleading the House

The Commons may treat the making of a deliberately misleading statement as a contempt. In 1963 the House resolved that in making a personal statement which contained words which he later admitted not to be true, a former Member had been guilty of a grave contempt.[1]

Corruption in the execution of a Member's duty

The acceptance by any Member of either House of a bribe to influence him in his conduct as such Member or of any fee, compensation or reward in connection with the promotion of, or opposition to any bill, resolution, matter or thing submitted or intended to be submitted to the House or any committee thereof is a breach of privilege. Members of the Commons who have been found guilty of such an offence have been expelled[2] or committed.[3] It is also a contempt for a Member to enter into an agreement with another person to advocate the claims of such person in the House, for pecuniary reward.[4]

In 1977, a select committee of the Commons was appointed to inquire into the conduct and activities of Members in connection with the affairs of an individual previously convicted for corruption, and to consider whether any such conduct or activities amounted to a contempt of the House or were inconsistent with the standards the House was entitled to expect from its Members. The committee concluded that one Member's conduct in the House in pressing certain interests was to further his own unavowed commercial interests, which amounted to a contempt of the House. The Member in question and two others were also found to have conducted themselves in a manner inconsistent with the standards the House was entitled to expect, in having been less than frank with the House regarding business relationships or in maintaining an inappropriate relationship between a Member and his employer.[5] The House took note of the report so far as it related to two Members and agreed with it so far as it related to the third, whose conduct was considered by the select committee to have amounted to a contempt.[6]

The corrupt acceptance of payment for the disclosure of information about matters to be proceeded with in Parliament obtained from other Members under the obligation of secrecy, while not held to be a breach of privilege or a contempt, has been stigmatized by the House as dishonourable conduct deserving to be severely punished.[7]

---

1 CJ (1962–63) 246.
2 CJ (1667–87) 24; ibid (1693–97) 274 (Speaker Sir John Trevor), 5 Parl Hist 900–910; CJ (1693–97) 283, 5 Parl Hist 911 (a chairman of a committee).
3 CJ (1693–97) 236; 5 Parl Hist 886.
4 CJ (1857–58) 68, 77; Parl Deb (1858) 148, c 1855: HC 115 (1857–58) p iii. See also HC5 (1940–41) and HC 63 (1944–45).
5 HC 490 (1976–77) paras 22–23, 33 and 38.
6 CJ (1976–77) 448–450.
7 CJ (1947–48) 20–23.

See also pp 384–390 on the current requirements on declaration of interest by Members; and p 128 on the offence of contempt by offering to bribe a Member.

Professional services connected with proceedings

The concern of the House of Commons extends beyond direct pecuniary corruption of Members. The House has emphasized that 'it is the personal responsibility of each Member to have regard to his public position and the good name of Parliament in any work he undertakes'.[1] The House has forbidden the acceptance of fees by its Members for professional services connected with proceedings in Parliament. Thus a Member is not permitted to practise as counsel before the House or any committee; and it is not consistent with parliamentary usage for Members to advise as counsel, upon any private bill, or other proceeding in Parliament.[2]

It has also been declared contrary to the law and usage of Parliament for any Member to be engaged, either by himself or any partner, in the management of private bills before either House of Parliament for pecuniary reward,[3] and, upon the same grounds, it was ordered on 6 November 1666 'That such Members of this House as are of the long robe shall not be of counsel on either side, in any bill depending in the Lords House, before such bill shall come down from the Lords House to this House'.[4]

The prohibition does not now extend to Members pleading at the bar of the Lords[5] and before the Committee for Privileges[6] in judicial cases.

The acceptance by a Member of either House however of a fee, compensation, gift or reward for drafting, advising upon or revising any bill, petition or other document submitted or intended to be submitted to either House or their committees is a contempt.

Advocacy by Members of matters in which they have been concerned professionally

On 22 June 1858 the House of Commons resolved, 'That it is contrary to the usage and derogatory to the dignity of this House that any of its Members should bring forward, promote or advocate in this House any proceeding or measure in which he may have acted or been concerned for or in consideration of any pecuniary fee or reward'.[7] This resolution though in wide terms was come to by the House in the context of advocacy by members of the bar.[8]

---

1 CJ (1985–86) 96. For regulations on the declaration and registration of interests, see pp 386–387.
2 The House ordered that the permission given in 1820 to certain Members to plead as counsel at the bar of the Lords in connection with the bill concerning Queen Caroline should not be drawn into a precedent (CJ (1819–20) 444; Parl Deb (1820) 2, c 400). It was also understood that, should the bill reach the Commons, the Members concerned would not be permitted to vote on it.
3 CJ (1830) 107. In 1842, leave was given to a Member to plead at the bar of the Lords in supporting a public bill (which had passed the Commons) (CJ (1842) 499), but this was not considered sufficient basis to waive the general rule to permit a Member to plead in the Lords on a private bill (CJ (1846) 627; Parl Deb (1846) 86, c 92).
4 CJ (1660–67) 646; but see ibid 322 and (1667–87) 86.
5 The last instance on which leave was specifically given is in 1710 (CJ (1708–11) 436).
6 Parl Deb (1820) 2, c 402.
7 CJ (1857–58) 247; see also ibid (1884) 167.
8 Parl Deb (1858) 151, cc 176–209.

Subsequently it was held not to preclude a Member who had been concerned in a criminal case which had been decided from taking part in a debate relating to the case.[1]

In the Lords, it is considered undesirable for a peer to advocate, promote or oppose in the House any bill or subordinate legislation in or for which he has been acting or concerned for any pecuniary fee or reward.[2]

Other misconduct by Members

Other instances of misconduct on the part of Members have included refusing to serve on a committee where attendance is, by order of the House, compulsory.[3]

Misconduct by officers

The Serjeant at Arms has been regarded as in contempt of the House of Commons for wilfully neglecting to take into his custody persons committed to him,[4] and for permitting persons committed to have liberty without any order of the House.[5] An officer of the Lords has been considered in contempt for failing duly to execute an order for the attachment of certain persons,[6] and doorkeepers have offended by admitting strangers into the Lords contrary to the order of the House.[7] The shorthandwriter gave evidence in court in relation to proceedings in the House without first obtaining leave, and the Commons agreed to a resolution stipulating that leave must be given in such circumstances.[8]

CONSTRUCTIVE CONTEMPTS

Reflections on either House

Indignities offered to the House by words spoken or writings published reflecting on its character or proceedings have been constantly punished by both the Lords and the Commons upon the principle that such acts tend to obstruct the Houses in the performance of their functions by diminishing the respect due to them.[9]

Reflections upon Members, the particular individuals not being named or otherwise indicated, are equivalent to reflections on the House. (For cases of reflections on individual Members, see p 126).

---

1 Parl Deb (1893) 8, c 1055; HC Deb (1975–76) 911, c 1429, 1730. See also Report from the Select Committee on Members' Interests (Declaration) HC 57 (1969–70) paras 20, 110.
2 LJ (1959–60) 245, 260. See also pp 432–433 below.
3 CJ (1846) 582–583, 603; Parl Deb (1846) 85, cc 1071, 1152, 1292, 1300, 1351; ibid 86, cc 966, 1198.
4 CJ (1667–87) 351; 3 Grey Deb 233–238.
5 CJ (1714–18) 436, 455–456, 458.
6 LJ (1726–31) 536.
7 LJ (1722–26) 476.
8 CJ (1818) 389; Parl Deb (1818) 18, cc 971–972. Cf SO No 22 of the House of Lords, and see pp 758–759 for procedures arising on petitions for leave to give evidence touching proceedings in Parliament.
9 In 1702 the House of Commons resolved that to print or publish any books or libels reflecting on the proceedings of that House or any Member for or relating to his service therein is a high violation of its rights and privileges (CJ (1699–1702) 767).

Such reflections have taken the form of the publication of false or scandalous libels on either House or its proceedings,[1] or the speaking of defamatory
words.[2]

Publication of false or perverted reports of debates

The Lords have a Standing Order (No 13) which declares that the printing or
publishing of anything relating to the proceedings of the House is subject to
the privilege of the House.

Among the actions treated as contempts in connection with the publication of debates are publishing a false account of the proceedings of the
House,[3] publishing a scandalous misrepresentation of the proceedings of the
House or its debates,[4] publishing a proceeding ordered to be expunged from
the Journals,[5] libelling counsel appearing before a committee under colour
of reporting the proceedings of the committee,[6] publishing a forged paper
sold as His Majesty's speech to both Houses,[7] and misrepresentation of
speeches.[8]

Before the House of Commons agreed in 1971 to rescind their ban on the
publication of their debates and proceedings, or those of any committee,[9]
misrepresentation of whatever kind[10] was regarded as an aggravation of this
offence of publication.[11] Since 1971 no complaint based on a report of a
debate has been made.

Premature publication or disclosure of committee proceedings

As early as the mid seventeenth century it was declared to be against the
custom of Parliament for any act done at a committee to be divulged before

---

1 LJ (1796–98) 506, 509; CJ (1547–1628) 125, 1 Hatsell 93 and D'Ewes 291; CJ (1547–1628)
925, 927; ibid (1790) 508, 516; ibid (1805–06) 214, 216, Parl Deb (1805) 4, cc 381, 384; CJ
(1810) 252, Parl Deb (1810) 16, cc 136, 257, 454, 14 East 1; CJ (1819–20) 55, 57, Parl Deb
(1819) 41, cc 1009–26; CJ (1947–48) 19–22.
2 LJ (1660–66) 87, 88; ibid (1714–18) 132; ibid (1722–26) 365, 367, 380; CJ (1547–1628) 60,
D'Ewes 366; CJ (1640–42) 63; ibid (1688–93) 512; ibid (1693–97) 277, 371, 651; ibid
(1699–1702) 124, 126, 735; ibid (1837–38) 306, 307, 312, 313, 316; ibid (1921) 393, HC Deb
(1921) 148, c 228; CJ (1926) 338, 340, HC Deb (1926) 199, cc 561, 709; CJ (1929–30) 477,
489, 503, HC Deb (1929–30) 242, cc 42, 309, 742; CJ (1950–51) 33, HC Deb (1950–51) 481,
cc 653–662; HC 129 (1964–65) and HC 228 (1974). A cartoon, with text, has been found by
the Committee of Privileges to constitute a contempt (HC 39 (1956–57)).
3 LJ (1765–67) 212.
4 LJ (1801–02) 57, 60.
5 LJ (1801–02) 104.
6 LJ (1798–1800) 638, 646.
7 LJ (1756–60) 16, 15 Parl Hist 779.
8 LJ (1847) 146, Parl Deb (1847) 91, c 1150.
9 CJ (1970–71) 548. For the earlier orders, see CJ (1640–42) 501; ibid (1693–97) 193, 439; ibid
(1697–99) 48; ibid (1702–04) 270; ibid (1722–27) 99; ibid (1727–32) 238; ibid (1737–41) 148;
ibid (1750–54) 754; ibid (1761–64) 207.
10 Among the categories of misrepresentation proceeded against have been scandalous misrepresentation of debates (CJ (1821–22) 327, ibid (1893–94) 324); gross or wilful misrepresentation of particular speeches (CJ (1778–80) 483, 491, 502; ibid (1812) 432 and Parl Deb
(1812) 23, c 584; CJ (1818–19) 533, 537 and Parl Deb (1819) 40, c 1163; CJ (1819–20) 436,
451); publishing as an alleged report of a Member's speech a gross libel on another Member
(CJ (1818–19) 533, 537 and Parl Deb (1819) 40 c 1163); and suppressing speeches of
particular Members (CJ (1833) 306 and Parl Deb (1833) 20, cc 6, 67; CJ (1849) 254 and Parl
Deb (1849) 104, c 1054).
11 34 Parl Hist 150.

being reported to the House.[1] Subsequently, though the House of Commons found it increasingly difficult to enforce effectively its rules against the disclosure abroad of proceedings in the Chamber, the privacy of committee proceedings and the prior right of the House itself to a committee's conclusions was upheld,[2] and punishment was inflicted on a newspaper proprietor who published the contents of a draft report laid before a select committee but not considered by it or presented to the House.[3] In 1837, the House of Commons resolved that 'according to the undoubted privileges of this House, and for the due protection of the public interest, the evidence taken by any select committee of this House and the documents presented to such committee and which have not been reported to the House ought not to be published by any Member of such committee, or by any other person'.[4] Between 1837 and the middle of the present century, there were relatively few cases of premature publication of committee proceedings or unreported evidence.[5] Subsequently, however, a number of cases have arisen, the majority involving the disclosure of the contents of draft reports,[6] though one concerned evidence taken in private.[7] Although successive Committees of Privileges have concluded that such interference with the work of select committees and contraventions of the Resolution of 1837 are a contempt of the House and damaging to the work of Parliament, in none of the recent cases involving draft reports has it been possible to identify those responsible for the original disclosure. In the absence of such information, Committees of Privileges have usually not been willing to recommend exercise of the House's penal powers against those who gave wider publicity

---

1 Clarendon (1826 edn) ii, 159.
2 CJ (1722–27) 99; ibid (1727–32) 238; ibid (1737–41) 148; ibid (1750–54) 754; ibid (1761–64) 207.
3 CJ (1831–32) 360, 365.
4 CJ (1837) 282; Parl Deb (1837) 38, c 170–171.
5 CJ (1837) 269–270, 282; Select Committee on Postal Communications between London and Paris, HC 381 (1850) p vi, Annex A; CJ (1875) 141, 148, 152 and Select Committee on Foreign Loans, HC 152 (1875); CJ (1899) 327 and Select Committee on Cottage Homes Bill, 2nd Special Report, HC 271 (1899) p x; CJ (1901) 80 and Select Committee on the Civil List, HC 87 (1901); CJ (1950–51) 257–258, HC Deb (1950–51) 489, cc 1381–1393, and Select Committee on Estimates, HC 227 (1950–51).
6 Committee of Privileges, 2nd Report, HC 180 (1971–72) (Select Committee on the Civil List); 1st Report, HC 22 (1975–76) (Select Committee on a Wealth Tax) and CJ (1975–76) 64; 1st Report, HC 376 (1977–78) (Select Committee on Race Relations and Immigration); CJ (1982–83) 324; Committee of Privileges, 1st Report, HC 308 (1984–85) (Home Affairs Committee); and 1st Report, HC 376 (1985–86) (Environment Committee).
7 Committee of Privileges, 2nd Report, HC 357 (1967–68) and CJ (1967–68) 361. Written evidence already circulated to third parties before being sent for by a committee may be referred to in the House or elsewhere before being reported, notwithstanding that it was marked confidential on reaching the committee (HC Deb (1984–85) 69, c 349–350, 351). See also Local Government (Access to Information) Act 1985, ss 1 and 2 of which oblige local authorities to make publicly available papers—which may include draft Memoranda to be submitted to select committees—under consideration at public meetings of the authority.

to the disclosure, and when they have done so the House has not been prepared to agree.[1]

The procedure for dealing with improper disclosure of select committee evidence or proceedings was altered with effect from the beginning of session 1985–86, following a report from the Committee of Privileges.[2] The committee concerned seeks to discover the source of the leak and to assess whether it constitutes (or is likely to constitute) a substantial interference with its work, with the select committee system, or with the functions of the House. If the committee considers that there has been or is likely to be such interference, it reports to the House accordingly, and a report of this character stands automatically referred to the Committee of Privileges[3] (see p 136).

The 1837 Resolution mentioned above was usually not enforced when the public were admitted to select committee meetings, and more recently this exception, together with others, has been put on a more substantial footing. Standing Order No 117 permits all select committees having power to send for persons, papers and records to authorize the publication by their witnesses or otherwise of memoranda of evidence submitted by them,[4] and Standing Order No 118 adds that the House will not entertain any complaint of contempt or breach of privilege in respect of publication of evidence given at public sittings of select committees before such evidence has been reported to the House.[5] The publication or disclosure of debates or proceedings of committees conducted with closed doors or in private, or when publication is expressly forbidden by the House, or of draft reports of committees before they have been reported to the House will, however, constitute a breach of privilege or a contempt.[6]

In the Lords, committees regularly authorize publication by witnesses of evidence, which they have submitted, in advance of the evidence being reported to the House or published by the committee.

Other indignities offered to either House

Other acts besides words spoken or writings published reflecting upon either House or its proceedings which, though they do not tend directly to obstruct

1 The Committee of Privileges recommended in 1975–76 (1st Report, HC 22 (1975–76)) that the editor of a weekly journal in which a disclosure was published and the journalist who wrote the article should be excluded from the precincts for six months. The House rejected the recommendation; nor has any legislation been enacted to enable the House to fine offenders, as the Committee believed appropriate to the case. In 1985–86, the Committee of Privileges recommended the temporary exclusion from the precincts of a journalist in similar circumstances, and the reduction for a time of the number of Lobby passes available to the newspaper (HC 376 (1985–86)). Again the House took a different view (CJ (1985–86) 374).
2 CJ (1985–86) 252; Committee of Privileges, 2nd Report, HC 555 (1984–85) paras 64–70.
3 To date, one such report has been referred under the above procedure (Environment Committee, 2nd Special Report HC 211 (1985–86); Committee of Privileges, 1st Report, HC 376 (1985–86); CJ (1985–86) 374).
4 See Report of the Select Committee on Parliamentary Privilege, HC 34 (1966–67) paras 133 ff. The Speaker authorizes publication in the case of select committees no longer in existence.
5 See Report of the Select Committee on Procedure, HC 588 (1977–78).
6 CJ (1970–71) 548.

or impede either House in the performance of its functions, yet have a tendency to produce this result indirectly by bringing such House into odium, contempt or ridicule or by lowering its authority may constitute contempts.

For example, serving or executing civil or criminal process within the precincts of either House while the House is sitting without obtaining the leave of the House is a contempt,[1] as is disorderly conduct within the precincts of either House while the House is sitting.[2] The House of Commons has considered the sending of a letter to the Speaker in very indecent and insolent terms in connection with the execution of a warrant issued by the Speaker to be a contempt,[3] and counterfeiting or altering an order or warrant,[4] or slighting an order of either House[5] has been similarly condemned. Other examples are representing oneself to be a parliamentary agent, (see pp 832–835) without possessing the necessary qualifications.[6] The Speaker has given a warning against the use of the portcullis badge and the name of the House of Commons in connection with an unofficial publication.[7]

OBSTRUCTING MEMBERS OF EITHER HOUSE IN THE DISCHARGE OF THEIR DUTY

The House will proceed against those who obstruct Members in the discharge of their responsibilities to the House or in their participation in its proceedings. Not all responsibilities currently assumed by Members fall within this definition. Correspondence with constituents or official bodies, for example, and the provision of information sought by Members on matters of public concern will very often, depending on the circumstances of the case, fall outside the scope of 'proceedings in Parliament' (see pp 92–93) against which a claim of breach of privilege will be measured (see p 69).

Arrest

An attempt to infringe the privilege of freedom from arrest in civil causes enjoyed by Members of both Houses is itself a contempt and has been punished.[8] When a Member of the House of Commons was arrested in

1 Report of the Committee of Privileges, HC 31 (1945–46) and CJ (1945–46) 198, and 1st Report of the Committee, HC 144 (1972–73). See also Report of the Select Committee on the attempted service of a summons on Mr Sheehy, CJ (1888) 503 and Parl Deb (1888) 332, cc 102–124; Report of the Committee of Privileges, HC 244 (1950–51) and CJ (1950–51) 319; 2nd Report from the Committee, HC 221 (1969–70); and also LJ (1685–91) 298, 301; and Parl Deb (1827) 17, c 34.
2 CJ (1547–1628) 259, 260; *Parliamentary Diary of Robert Bowyer* (ed D H Willson, 1931) p 8; CJ (1646–48) 232; ibid (1651–59) 410; ibid (1722–27) 185; ibid (1761–64) 843; and see Report from the Committee of Privileges, HC 36 (1946–47) and CJ (1946–47) 91.
3 CJ (1810) 260, 273 and *Memoirs of Sir Samuel Romilly* (1840) vol ii, p 312.
4 LJ (1660–66) 91; CJ (1806–07) 288, 296.
5 LJ (1660–66) 131.
6 HC Deb (1948–49) 464, c 1669.
7 HC Deb (1980–81) 3, c 789.
8 LJ (1810–11) 58, 60; ibid (1828) 15, 21, 34 ; CJ (1722–27) 504; ibid (1809) 210, 213 and Parl Deb (1809) 14, c 31.

error, the House regretted the indignity offered to him, but considering the arrest to have been a mistake, did not think it necessary to proceed further.[1]

Molestation, reflections and intimidation

It is a contempt to molest a Member of either House while attending the House, or coming to or going from it. The Commons on 12 April 1733 and the Lords on 17 May 1765, resolved 'That the assaulting, insulting or menacing any Member of this House, in his coming to or going from the House, or upon the account of his behaviour in Parliament, is an high infringement of the privilege of this House, a most outrageous and dangerous violation of the rights of Parliament and an high crime and misdemeanour';[2] and on 6 June 1780 the Commons resolved 'That it is a gross breach of the privilege of this House for any person to obstruct and insult the Members of this House in the coming to, or the going from, the House, and to endeavour to compel Members by force to declare themselves in favour of, or against any proposition then depending or expected to be brought before the House'.[3] Members and others have been punished for such molestation occurring within the precincts of the House, whether by assault[4] or insulting or abusive language,[5] or outside the precincts.[6] The Commons took no action on an incident where a stranger endeavoured to dissuade a Member from entering a room where a Standing Committee was meeting.[7]

To molest Members on account of their conduct in Parliament is also a contempt. Correspondence with Members of an insulting character in reference to their conduct in Parliament or reflecting on their conduct as Members,[8] threatening a Member with the possibility of a trial at some future time for a question asked in the House,[9] calling for his arrest as an arch traitor,[10] offering to contradict a Member from the gallery,[11] or proposing to visit a pecuniary loss on him on account of conduct in Parliament[12] have all been considered contempts. The Committee of Privileges has made the same judgment on those who incited the readers of a national newspaper to telephone a Member and complain of a question of which he had given notice.[13]

---

1 CJ (1888) 30 and Parl Deb (1888) 322, c 262.
2 LJ (1765–67) 209; CJ (1732–37) 115.
3 CJ (1778–80) 902.
4 CJ (1688–93) 348, 354, 355; ibid (1824–25) 483 and Parl Deb (1824) 11, c 1204; and CJ (1946–47) 54, 91. In the last case, it was decided that the contempt committed by the Member concerned, who struck the first blow, was greater than that of the other who retaliated (Report of the Committee of Privileges, HC 36 (1946–47)).
5 CJ (1646–48) 42; ibid (1660–67) 186; ibid (1688–93) 782; ibid (1877) 144 and Parl Deb (1877) 233, c 951; and CJ (1887) 377, 389 and Parl Deb (1887) 317, c 1167, 1631.
6 Officials of the Liberty of Westminster were committed in 1751 for having apprehended, insulted and abused a Member and refusing to discharge him except upon an assurance of his silence (CJ (1750–54) 175–176).
7 HC Deb (1948–49) 470, cc 1535–1538.
8 LJ (1830–31) 285, 335; CJ (1863–64) 80, 84; ibid (1890–91) 481 and Parl Deb (1891) 365, c 419. Challenging Members to fight on account of their behaviour in the House (CJ (1780–82) 535, 537; Parl Deb (1844) 74, c 286; CJ (1845) 589 and ibid (1862) 64) or of remarks made outside the House touching proceedings in the House (CJ (1883) 232, 238) has been considered a contempt.
9 Report of the Committee of Privileges, HC 284 (1959–60).
10 Report of the Committee of Privileges, HC 462 (1966–67) and CJ (1966–67) 415.
11 CJ (1826–28) 395, 399 and Parl Deb (1827) 17, cc 282, 343.
12 CJ (1898) 381.
13 Report of the Committee of Privileges, HC 27 (1956–57), CJ (1956–57) 31, 50.

Analogous to molestation of Members on account of their behaviour in Parliament are speeches and writings reflecting upon their conduct as Members. On 26 February 1702 the House of Commons resolved that to print or publish any libels reflecting upon any Member of the House for or relating to his service therein, was a high violation of the rights and privileges of the House.[1]

Written imputations, as affecting a Member of Parliament, may amount to breach of privilege, without, perhaps, being libels at common law, but to constitute a breach of privilege a libel upon a Member must concern the character or conduct of the Member in that capacity.[2]

Reflections which have been punished as contempts have borne on the conduct of the Lord Chancellor in the discharge of his judicial duties in the House of Lords[3] or that of the Chairman of Committees.[4] In the same way, reflections on the character of the Speaker or accusations of partiality in the discharge of his duties[5] and similar charges against the Chairman of Ways and Means[6] or Chairman of a standing committee[7] or a select committee[8] have attracted the penal powers of the Commons.

Imputations that a Member nominated to a select committee would not be able to act impartially in that service,[9] and similar reflections on Members serving on private bill committees[10] have been considered contempts. An individual who claimed that he could control the decision of a private bill committee (and offered to do so for a corrupt consideration) has been punished, along with another who assisted him.[11] More general reflections on Members accusing them of corruption in the discharge of their duties,[12] challenging their motives or veracity,[13] or describing their conduct as

---

1 CJ (1699–1702) 767.
2 See the action taken by the House, Parl Deb (1875) 222, cc 1185–1204; cf also Parl Deb (1888) 329, c 1251; ibid (1890) 341, c 43; ibid (1893) 8, c 1592. For recent cases in which this question was considered, see HC 247 (1963–64) and HC 269 (1964–65).
3 LJ (1834) 704, 737, 743; Parl Deb (1834) 24, cc 892, 941, 1006, 1065.
4 LJ (1867) 31, 33, 46, 72.
5 CJ (1772–74) 452, 456; Parl Deb (1887) 313, c 371; CJ (1888) 385 and Parl Deb (1888) 329, c 48; CJ (1890–91) 481 and Parl Deb (1890–91) 356, c 419; CJ (1893–94) 123, 408, 416 and Parl Deb (1893–94) 9, c 1866; Parl Deb (1893–94) 14, cc 820, 1094; CJ (1911) 34, 36 and HC Deb (1911) 21, cc 1435, 1553; HC Deb (1911) 29, c 34; and CJ (1937–38) 213.
6 HC Deb (1909) 8, c 31; CJ (1928–29) 50, 156, 159; and ibid (1950–51) 319 and Report of the Committee of Privileges, HC 235 (1950–51).
7 CJ (1924) 180 and Report of the Committee of Privileges, HC 98 (1924).
8 CJ (1874) 181, 189 and Parl Deb (1874) 219, cc 752, 755 and CJ (1950–51) 299. In a case in 1968–69, the Committee of Privileges considered that an assertion that a Member who was Chairman of a sub-committee of a select committee would not be able to form a sufficiently fair and dispassionate view of events when hearing evidence in her own constituency was not considered to be a contempt (HC 197 (1968–69)).
9 CJ (1900) 178.
10 CJ (1831–32) 278, 294; ibid (1857–58) 189, 196, 201 and Parl Deb (1857–58) 150, cc 1022, 1063, 1198 etc; HC Deb (1909) 7, c 235; Parl Deb (1921) 145, c 831; and CJ (1932–33) 141.
11 CJ (1878–79) 326, 366, Parl Deb (1879) 247, cc 1866 and 1956 and ibid 248 cc 602, 633, 971, 1100, and Report of the Select Committee on Privilege (Tower High Level Bridge (Metropolis) Committee, HC 294 (1878–79).
12 CJ (1667–87) 88, 95; ibid (1732–37) 245; ibid (1836) 658, 676 and Parl Deb (1836) 35, cc 167, 225; CJ (1893–94) 631 and Parl Deb (1893–94) 20, c 112; CJ (1901) 414, 418; Report of the Committee of Privileges, HC 138 (1946–47) and CJ (1947–48) 22. See also CJ (1935–36) 203 and HC Deb (1935–36) 311, c 1349–1351.
13 CJ (1901) 355; ibid (1926) 99; Report of the Committee of Privileges, HL 55 (1926); 1st Report of the Committee of Privileges, HC 302 (1974–75); and see also Report of the Committee, HC 112 (1947–48).

'inhuman' and degrading[1] have also been found objectionable and proceeded against.

To attempt to intimidate a Member in his parliamentary conduct by
threats is also a contempt, cognate to those mentioned above. Actions of this
character which have been proceeded against include impugning the conduct of Members and threatening them with further exposure if they took
part in debates;[2] threatening to communicate with Members' constituents to
the effect that, if they did not reply to a questionnaire, they should be
considered as not objecting to certain sports;[3] publishing posters containing
a threat regarding the voting of Members in a forthcoming debate;[4] informing Members that to vote for a particular bill would be regarded as treasonable by a future administration;[5] summoning a Member to a disciplinary
hearing of his trade union in consequence of a vote given in the House;[6] and
threatening to end investment by a public corporation in a Member's constituency, if the Member persisted in making speeches along lines of those in
a preceding debate.[7] When a Member stated his intention of influencing a
local authority to the detriment of other Members, a complaint was referred
to the Committee of Privileges which concluded that the words spoken
constituted a threat but recommended no further action.[8]

Improper influence

Attempts by improper means to influence Members in their parliamentary
conduct may be considered contempts. One of the methods by which such
influence may be brought to bear is bribery and in 1695 the House of
Commons resolved that 'the offer of money, or other advantage, to any
Member of Parliament for the promoting of any matter whatsoever,
depending or to be transacted in Parliament is a high crime and misdemeanour and tends to the subversion of the English constitution'.[9] In the spirit of
this resolution, the offering to a Member of either House of a bribe to
influence him in his conduct as a Member, or of any fee or reward in
connection with the promotion of, or opposition to any bill, resolution,
matter or thing submitted or intended to be submitted to the House or any
committee thereof, has been treated as a breach of privilege.[10]

It may be a contempt to offer any fee or reward to any Member or officer
of either House for drafting, advising upon or revising any bill, resolution,
matter or thing intended to be submitted to that House or any committee
thereof.[11] Although the House has expressed its grave displeasure at the

1 CJ (1880) 46, 54 and Parl Deb (1880) 250, cc 797, 1108.
2 CJ (1873) 60 and Parl Deb (1873) 214, c 733.
3 CJ (1934–35) 201 and HC Deb (1934–35) 301, c 1545.
4 Report from the Committee of Privileges, HC 181 (1945–46).
5 2nd Report of the Committee of Privileges, HC 228 (1964–65).
6 HC Deb (1974) 877, cc 466, 673. The complaint was not pursued, following a letter of
  apology.
7 Report of the Committee of Privileges, HC 214 (1980–81). Although the Committee was
  unable to establish the facts alleged, it observed that 'such an allegation, if established,
  would certainly reveal a serious affront to the privilege of freedom of speech.'
8 Report of the Committee of Privileges, HC 564 (1983–84).
9 CJ (1693–97) 331.
10 CJ (1697–99) 528; ibid (1711–14) 493; ibid (1718–21) 542. See also Report of the Committee
   of Privileges, HC 103 (1942–43).
11 CJ (1693–97) 274, 275; 5 Parl Hist 910.

offering of payment to a Member for the disclosure and publication of confidential information about matters to be proceeded with in Parliament such an action has not been held to be a breach of privilege or contempt.[1]

Conduct not amounting to a direct attempt improperly to influence Members in the discharge of their duties but having a tendency to impair their independence in the future performance of their duty may be treated as a contempt. An example of such a case is the Speaker's ruling that a letter sent by a parliamentary agent to a Member informing him that the promoters of a private bill would agree to certain amendments provided that he and other members refrained from further opposition to the bill constituted (under the procedure then in force) a *prima facie* breach of privilege.[2]

Influence by private solicitation in certain circumstances has also been found objectionable. The Lords have resolved that the private solicitation of Members on matters of claims to honours or other judicial proceedings was a breach of privilege.[3] Upon the same principle, it would be a breach of privilege when Members are acting in a judicial or quasi-judicial capacity, eg when serving on committees on private bills, to attempt, by letters, anonymous or other, to influence them in the discharge of their duties.[4]

Misrepresenting Members' proceedings

Wilful misrepresentation of the proceedings of Members is an offence of the same character as a libel.

On 22 April 1699 the Commons resolved, 'That the publishing the names of the Members of this House and reflecting upon them, and misrepresenting their proceedings in Parliament, is a breach of the privilege of this House, and destructive of the freedom of Parliament'.[5]

OBSTRUCTING OFFICERS OF EITHER HOUSE

Obstruction

It is a contempt to obstruct those employed by or entrusted with the execution of the orders of either House while in the execution of their duty. Contempts of this character have included assaults,[6] insulting and abusive behaviour[7] or threatening language,[8] resistance to those acting in execution

---

1 CJ (1947–48) 88.
2 CJ (1962–63) 251. The Member concerned, having received an apology, did not submit a motion to the House.
3 LJ (1802–03) 227.
4 LJ (1810–11) 332, 341; CJ (1884) 167 and Parl Deb (1884) 287, c 11; and HC Deb (1921) 145, c 831.
5 CJ (1697–99) 661.
6 For assaults on officers, see LJ (1718–21) 190; ibid (1805–06) 125; and CJ (1667–87) 193. For assaults on others entrusted with the execution of the House's orders, see LJ (1787–90) 649; ibid (1790–93) 665; ibid (1794–96) 241; CJ (1732–37) 308; ibid (1750–54) 900, 904; ibid (1761–64) 126, 128.
7 In the case of officers, see LJ (1805–06) 332, 340, 608, 610; ibid (1810–12) 370, 399; CJ (1722–27) 185; and of other persons, LJ (1783–87) 613, 647; ibid (1787–90) 338.
8 CJ (1693–97) 512, 514.

of the orders of either House,[1] aiding the escape of an individual from the order for his custody or committal,[2] refusal of civil officers to assist in executing the orders of either House[3] and the discharge out of custody by a magistrate of a prisoner arrested by order of either House.[4]

Both Houses will treat as breaches of their privileges, not only acts directly tending to obstruct their officers in the execution of their duty, but also any conduct which may tend to deter them from doing their duty in the future.

Molestation

Neither House will suffer any person, whether an officer of the House or not, to be molested for executing its orders or the orders of its committees or on account of anything done by them in the course of their duty.[5]

Arrest

Since officers of either House in immediate attendance on the service of Parliament enjoy a freedom from arrest similar to that of Members (see chapter 7), to arrest or to procure the arrest of such person, save on a criminal charge, is a contempt of the House whose officer he is.[6]

Legal proceedings against officers etc

Although in the past both Houses have treated as contempts the taking of proceedings (both civil[7]) and criminal[8] in a court of law against any person for his conduct in obedience to the orders of the House, according to subsequent practice the Commons has given leave to the officer to appear.

1 Resisting or hindering officers in the execution of their duty, see CJ (1660–67) 222; ibid (1667–87) 341; ibid (1930–31) 335, 338: resisting or hindering others, see CJ (1699–1702) 825; ibid (1732–37) 308, 508, 511; ibid (1761–64) 128, 130.

2 LJ (1718–21) 190; CJ (1667–87) 193.

3 LJ (1660–66) 134; CJ (1667–87) 193, 587.

4 CJ (1770–72) 263, 285, 289.

5 Assault on and abuse of a committee clerk for an act done in such capacity have been punished (CJ (1718–21) 366, 370), as has assault on a person, not being an officer, who sought the assistance of a constable in securing a delinquent whom the Commons had ordered into custody (CJ (1667–87) 678).

6 LJ (1718–21) 96; CJ (1727–32) 43.

7 Persons have been committed for bringing civil actions against officers or servants of both Houses in execution of their duty (LJ (1767–70) 185, 187, 197; (1826–27) 199, 206 and Parl Deb (1827) 17 c 34; CJ (1737–41) 620, 623; ibid (1819–20) 230, 243, 286; and ibid (1840) 11, 71, 93, 174. The Commons has even proceeded against judges for overruling the Serjeant at Arms' plea to the jurisdiction of the court (in *Jay v Topham*) (CJ (1688–93) 227) and both Houses have acted against lawyers for assisting in the conduct of actions against officers (LJ (1767–70) 185, 187, 197; CJ (1737–41) 620, 623; ibid (1819–20) 230, 243, 286; ibid (1840) 23, 66, 96. In 1840, the Commons agreed to a general resolution that persons acting as sheriffs or otherwise in the prosecuting of such actions were guilty of a breach of privilege (CJ (1840) 93, 174).

8 Actions considered in contempt in the context of criminal prosecutions have included prosecuting a constable for an assault committed in execution of an order (LJ (1787–90) 249, 250, 251); issuing a warrant for having arrested a person by order (LJ (1691–96) 565); drawing an indictment against an officer for having committed an alleged assault in the execution of an order (LJ (1691–96) 565); and signing a warrant against an officer for arresting a person in pursuance of a Speaker's warrant (CJ (1770–72) 263, 285, 289).

The Law Officers of the Crown, upon the order of the House[1] or following a direction given by a Minister have undertaken the officer's defence. Alternatively, if it seemed expedient, the Speaker would place the defence of the officer in the hands of the Government.

OBSTRUCTING WITNESSES

Arrest

On 8 March 1688 the Commons resolved, 'That it is the undoubted right of this House that all witnesses summoned to attend this House, or any committee appointed by it, have the privilege of this House in coming, staying and returning'.[2] Parties who arrest or procure the arrest on civil process of witnesses or other persons summoned to attend either House or any committee of either House while going to, attending, or returning from, such House or committee may be punished for contempt.[3]

Molestation and interference

Any conduct calculated to deter prospective witnesses from giving evidence before either House or a committee is a contempt.

It is also a contempt to molest any persons attending either House as witnesses, during their attendance in such House or committee. Assaults upon witnesses in the precincts of the House[4] and the use of threatening or abusive language within the precincts[5] have been proceeded against.

On the same principle, molestation of or threats against those who have previously given evidence before either House or a committee will be treated by the House concerned as a contempt (see p 102). Such actions have included assault or a threat of assault on witnessess,[6] insulting or abusive behaviour,[7] misuse (by a gaoler)[8] or censure by an employer.[9]

In consequence of one of the last mentioned cases, the Witnesses (Public Inquiries) Protection Act 1892 was passed; under its provisions, persons who punish, damnify, or injure witnesses before committees of either House of Parliament on account of their evidence, unless such evidence was given in bad faith, are liable on conviction to be fined or imprisoned and ordered to pay the costs of the prosecution, as well as a sum by way of compensation to the injured persons.

---

1 This course was pursued in the cases of *Burdett v Abbot* CJ (1810) 355; *Howard v Gosset* ibid (1843) 118; *Bradlaugh v Erskine*, ibid (1882) 182, 187 and *Bradlaugh v Gosset* ibid (1883) 364, 370. See also *Lines v Russell* ibid (1852) 64, 68.
2 CJ (1688–93) 45.
3 LJ (1691–96) 529; CJ (1640–42) 454, 457; ibid (1697–99) 364, 367, 368, 386.
4 LJ (1696–1701) 144; CJ (1718–21) 290; ibid (1826–28) 345, 351 and Parl Deb (1827) 16, c 1305 and ibid 17, c 7.
5 CJ (1648–51) 413; ibid (1667–87) 54; ibid (1818–19) 223 and Parl Deb (1819) 39, c 978, 986.
6 CJ (1667–87) 678; ibid (1688–93) 579; ibid (1708–11) 498, 503, 535; ibid (1818–19) 223.
7 CJ (1714–18) 371.
8 CJ (1688–93) 514, 523, 534; ibid (1727–32) 247.
9 CJ (1732–37) 146; ibid (1892) 129, 157, 166, Parl Deb (1892) 3, cc 595, 698, 883, and Special Report of the Select Committee on Railway Servants (Hours of Labour), HC 125 (1892). See also Select Committee on Nationalised Industries, 2nd Special Report (HC 237 (1974–75)) and Committee of Privileges, 3rd Report (HC 274 (1975–76)) where an individual was not considered to have been adversely affected by his employer for having been a witness in Parliament.

Tampering with witnesses

A resolution setting out that to tamper with a witness in regard to the evidence to be given before either House or any committee of either House or to endeavour, directly or indirectly, to deter or hinder any person from appearing or giving evidence is a breach of privilege has been agreed to by the Commons at the beginning of every session since 1900,[1] and there have been numerous instances of punishment for offences of this kind.[2]

Corruption or intimidation, though a usual, is not an essential ingredient in this offence. It is equally a breach of privilege to attempt by persuasion or solicitations of any kind to induce a witness not to attend, or to withhold evidence or to give false evidence.

This matter was considered in 1935 by a committee of the Commons which reported that, in its opinion, it was a breach of privilege to give any advice to a witness which took the form of pressure or of interference with his freedom to form and express his own opinions honestly in the light of all the facts known to him; and the House resolved that it agreed with the committee in its report.[3]

Legal proceedings against witnesses

Both Houses will treat the bringing of legal proceedings against any person on account of any evidence which he may have given in the course of any proceedings in the House or before one of its committees as a breach of privilege (see p 89).

The House of Commons resolved on 26 May 1818, 'That all witnesses examined before this House, or any committee thereof, are entitled to the protection of this House in respect of anything that may be said by them in their evidence'.[4] Both Houses have taken action against those who brought or as agents assisted in the bringing of actions for slander in respect of evidence given before either House or a committee.[5] More recently, the courts have refused to entertain such actions based on statements made in evidence before a committee.[6]

PROTECTION OF PETITIONERS AND OTHERS

Petitioners and other persons soliciting business before either House or its committees, eg counsel, agents and solicitors, are considered as under the protection of the High Court of Parliament, and obstruction of, or interference with such persons in the exercise of their rights or the discharge of their duties, or conduct calculated to deter them or other persons from preferring or prosecuting petitions or bills or from discharging their duties may be treated as a breach of privilege.

---

1 For example, CJ (1985–86) 3.
2 CJ (1640–42) 81; ibid (1699–1702) 400, 404; ibid (1708–11) 433, 479; ibid (1727–32) 480, 711; ibid (1809) 35 and Parl Deb (1809) 12 c 460; CJ (1835) 324, 421, 478, 508; ibid (1851–52) 147–8. See also Parl Deb (1857) 146, c 97.
3 Report of the Select Committee on Witnesses, HC 84 (1934–35) p vii; CJ (1934–35) 294.
4 CJ (1818) 389.
5 LJ (1845) 690, 712, 729 and Parl Deb (1845) 82, cc 431, 494; CJ (1693–97) 591, 613; ibid (1845) 672, 680, 696 and Parl Deb (1845) 81 c 1436.
6 *Goffin v Donnelly* 6 QBD 307, 50 LJQB 303.

Instances of this kind of contempt include causing the arrest of persons soliciting business before the House, knowing them to be such, within the period of freedom from arrest (see pp 101–102);[1] assaulting or threatening them within the precincts[2] or by reason of their approach to the House;[3] insulting them,[4] or challenging them to fight;[5] bringing an action for a libel alleged to have been contained in a petition to the House;[6] or libelling them in respect of professional conduct before a committee.[7]

Although both Houses extend their protection to witnesses and others who solicit business in Parliament, no such protection is afforded to informants, including constituents of Members of the House of Commons who voluntarily and in their personal capacity provide information to Members, the question whether such information is subsequently used in proceedings in Parliament being immaterial. But while it appears unlikely that any question of an actual or constructive breach of parliamentary privilege could arise in these cases, the special position of a person providing information to a Member for the exercise of his parliamentary duties has been regarded by the courts as enjoying qualified privilege at law.[8]

A letter from a constituent who was a clergyman was forwarded by a Member to the bishop of the diocese, and it was alleged that the clergyman was in consequence damnified. The House disagreed to a motion referring the matter to the Committee of Privileges.[9]

After a subordinate army chaplain had provided information to a Member who subsequently gave notice of a Question based on this information, it was alleged that the Deputy Assistant Chaplain General of the army district threatened his subordinate to make him persuade the Member concerned to withdraw the question. The matter was referred to the Committee of Privileges who reported that they could find no precedent where an attempt by one individual to influence another individual (not a Member of Parliament) as to the nature or content of the latter's communications with a Member of Parliament had been treated as a breach of privilege or as a contempt of the House.[10]

The application of the Official Secrets Act 1911, as amended, to persons giving information to Members was subject to the provisions of section 2(1) of the Act which provided that a person who communicated information to a person other than one to whom he was authorized to communicate it committed no offence provided that the person to whom he communicated it

---

1 CJ (1547–1628) 702, 767, 787; ibid (1644–46) 31.
2 LJ (1709–14) 752; ibid (1831–32) 384, 387 and Parl Deb (1832) 14, cc 425, 495; CJ (1667–87) 341.
3 CJ (1757–61) 264, 270.
4 LJ (1826) 128, 142, 145, ibid (1831–32) 384, 387; CJ (1547–1628) 805, 806.
5 LJ (1831–32) 388
6 CJ (1693–97) 599, 699.
7 LJ (1795–1800) 638, 646.
8 *Dickson v Lord Wilton* (1859) 1 F & F 419 NP; *R v Rule* [1937] 2 KB 375; but see also *Rivlin v Bilainkin* [1953] 1 QB 485.
9 CJ (1950–51) 148–149 and HC Deb (1950–51) 485, cc 2491–2543.
10 Report of the Committee of Privileges, HC 112 (1954–55).

was one to whom it was in the interest of the state his duty to communicate it (see also Report of the Select Committee on the Official Secrets Acts 1939).[1] The relevant section of the 1911 Act was, however, repealed in 1989 by the Official Secrets Act of that year.

Administrative action has also been taken to preserve the liberty of the electorate in communicating with Members of Parliament. After a complaint had been made by a Member that a constituent's letter forwarded by him to a government department had been disclosed by the department to a third party who had threatened proceedings for libel, the Prime Minister stated that all departments had been reminded that they must exercise greater discretion as to the circumstances in which disclosure was appropriate.[2]

As regards the forwarding of complaints by members of the armed forces to Members of Parliament, while it is the policy of service departments that the usual service channels should be used wherever possible, service regulations give an absolute right to servicemen to communicate with Members on all matters, including service matters, so long as there is no disclosure of secret information.[3]

---

1 HC 101 (1938–39). See *Regina v Ponting* ([1985] Crim LR 318), where the defendant was charged under s 2(1) of the Act of 1911 with having communicated certain official documents, which he had not been authorised to pass on, to a Member of Parliament. McGowan J held that 'the interest of the state meant what was in the interests of the state according to its recognised organs of government and the policies as expounded by the particular government of the day . . . It was not in dispute that the policy of the government was not to give the information which [the defendant] communicated'. The defendant was acquitted.
2 HC Deb (1953–54) 524, cc 1932–7 and ibid 525, cc 210–211.
3 HC Deb (1954–55) 540, c 51.

CHAPTER 10

Complaints of breach of privilege or contempt

RAISING A COMPLAINT

The current procedure of the House of Commons governing the raising by Members of complaints of breach of privilege or contempt (other than where the offence is committed in the face of the House) follows the House's approval in 1978 of recommendations made by the Committee of Privileges.[1] That Committee made their recommendations following their examination of the Report of the Select Committee on Parliamentary Privilege 1966–67, in which it was suggested that in general the House should exercise its penal jurisdiction (i) in any event as sparingly as possible, and (ii) only when satisfied that to do so was essential in order to provide reasonable protection for the House, its Members or its officers from improper obstruction or attempt at or threat of obstruction causing, or likely to cause, substantial interference with the performance of their respective functions. Accordingly, a Member who wishes to raise a privilege complaint is required to give written notice to the Speaker as soon as reasonably practicable after the Member has notice of the alleged contempt or breach of privilege. The Speaker has discretion to decide whether or not the matter should have the precedence accorded to matters of privilege (see pp 306–307). If he decides that it should not, he informs the Member by letter. If he decides to allow precedence, he informs the Member when he proposes to announce his decision to the House. When the announcement has been made, the Member is entitled to table a Motion for the following day formally calling attention to the matter, and either proposing that it be referred to the Committee of Privileges or making some other appropriate proposition.[2] A decision by the Speaker not to allow precedence in no way limits the Member's right to avail himself of other procedures for publicising his complaint. The recommendations of the 1977 Committee adopted by the House make special provisions for the Speaker's action in two particular circumstances. Thus, whereas he would normally make his decision about precedence within a day or two of receiving notice of the complaint, it is provided that he should, in appropriate cases of urgency, deal with the matter at once. Again, if, in a case which the Speaker considers not worthy

---

1 CJ (1977–78) 170 and 3rd Report of the Committee of Privileges, HC 417 (1976–77) paras 9–12. Details of the House's procedure in this regard before 1978 are to be found in previous editions of this work, eg 19th edn, pp 162 ff.

2 CJ (1977–78) 236, etc. It is not the practice for such letters to be made public (HC Deb (1984–85) 72, c 747 and ibid (1985–86) 106, c 1044). Members should not challenge the Speaker's decision in the House (ibid (1986–87) 114, c 303–304). The Speaker does not communicate an unfavourable outcome to the House or to other Members (ibid (1985–86) 87, c 1042–1043).

of precedence, he deems that a novel point of privilege ought nevertheless to be drawn to the attention of the House, he has discretion to make a statement to the House.[1]

Complaints of privilege may also be brought to the notice of the House by a communication from the Speaker,[2] by a report to the Lords from Black Rod or his Deputy or to the Commons from the Serjeant at Arms, or by a report from a committee (see pp 141–143).

A report from a select committee of the Commons to the effect that improper disclosure of its evidence of proceedings has interfered with its work stands automatically referred to the Committee of Privileges (see p 124). A matter alleged to have arisen in committee but not reported by it may not generally be brought to the attention of the House on a complaint of breach of privilege.[3]

In the past, matters affecting the privilege of the House might be raised by petition. In the Commons at least, it is unlikely that this procedure would now be followed, in view of the present practice in raising matters of privilege, which is described above. For a full account of the procedure based on a petition, see 20th edition, pp 178 ff.

When a contempt is committed in the actual view of either House, as for example by the prevarication of a witness, by his false evidence or refusal to answer, the House proceeds at once, without hearing the offender, unless by way of apology or to manifest his contrition, to punish him for his contempt. But, save sometimes where a contempt committed in the actual view of a committee is reported by the committee, neither House will punish a contempt committed out of such House or not in its actual view without hearing the party implicated in his defence.

HEARING OF COUNSEL

Persons accused of breaches of the privileges or of other contempts of either House are not, as a rule, allowed to be represented by counsel;[4] but in a few cases incriminated persons have been allowed to be heard by counsel;[5] the hearing being sometimes limited to 'such points as do not controvert the privileges of the House'.[6] Where a person has been allowed to make his defence by counsel, counsel have sometimes been heard in support of the charge;[7] and where a complaint of an alleged breach of privilege was referred to the Committee of Privileges, counsel were allowed, by leave of the House, to examine witnesses before the committee on behalf of both the Member who had made the complaint and the parties named therein.[8]

---

1 HC Deb (1980–81) 3, c 789.
2 CJ (1945–46) 38.
3 The Speaker has refused to allow a motion to have precedence as a matter of privilege for the attendance of a person who, it appeared from the minutes of the evidence taken before a Committee, had refused to answer questions and to produce certain documents which he had been ordered to produce (Parl Deb (1897) 51, c 311).
4 2 Cav Deb 428, 431; Hargrave *Jurisconsult Exercitations* i, 278.
5 CJ (1750–54) 27; ibid (1766–68) 625; ibid (1770–72) 275, 279, 280.
6 CJ (1770–72) 275, 280.
7 CJ (1750–54) 27; ibid (1766–68) 625.
8 CJ (1766–68) 540. The House gave leave for the Committee of Public Accounts to hear counsel in their investigation of the truthfulness of witnesses before them, on 14 March 1968, CJ (1967–68) 150 (see HC 192 (1967–68)).

CONSIDERATION OF REPORTS OF COMMITTEES ON COMPLAINTS

It is now the practice of the House of Commons to proceed directly to a substantive motion in connection with report of committees (whether the Committee of Privileges (see p 660) or a committee specially appointed to consider a particular issue (see p 119)) on matters of privilege.[1] The precedence afforded to such business is described at pp 306–307.

If the report is to the effect that no breach of privilege has been committed, no further proceedings are usually taken in reference to the report, though there have been a few occasions on which the Commons has agreed with such a report[2] or with a committee's conclusion that, notwithstanding that there had been a breach of privilege,[3] the House should take no further action. Other circumstances in which no further proceedings have been taken in the Commons following a Committee of Privileges recommendation to that effect include reports that an offender had explained and regretted his offence,[4] that the conduct complained of was not such a breach of privilege as called for further action,[5] that the House would best consult its dignity by taking no further notice of the libel,[6] or that no further time should be occupied in the consideration of the offence.[7]

If, however, the committee reports that a serious breach of privilege has been committed, the House will take action upon it. Sometimes the House will order the person incriminated to attend the House, in order to hear anything he may say in extenuation or mitigation, before coming to substantial judgment on the decision of the committee.[8] If the offender fails to appear, he will be ordered into custody forthwith;[9] if he attends, he will be heard and dealt with as the House thinks proper.[10] Once the House has given agreement to the committee's report,[11] it will then go on to consider the

---

1 For example, CJ (1929–30) 503; ibid (1933–34) 231; ibid (1937–38) 357. In older practice, such reports were ordered to be taken into consideration in pursuance of an order made on a previous day (CJ (1851) 265; ibid (1865) 223, 311; ibid (1878–79) 350; ibid (1887) 293; ibid (1888) 510; ibid (1889) 346): a motion that the report be now read (CJ (1826–27) 561; ibid (1839) 278; ibid (1843) 523) or a motion that the report be taken into consideration (CJ (1938–39) 38; ibid (1946–47) 377; ibid (1947–48), 19, 22).
2 CJ (1766–68) 541; ibid (1933–34) 231.
3 Report of the Committee of Privileges, HC 235 (1950–51) and CJ (1950–51) 319.
4 Report of the Committee of Privileges, HC 153 (1911) p iii; CJ (1926) 99; ibid (1932–33) 141.
5 Report of the Committee of Privileges, HC 281 (1909) p iii.
6 Report of the Committee of Privileges, HC 98 (1924) p iii.
7 Report of the Committee of Privileges, HC 31 (1953–54) p 3.
8 CJ (1765–66) 843; ibid (1839) 278; ibid (1878–79) 363; ibid (1947–48) 20; ibid (1956–57) 66.
9 CJ (1878–79) 366.
10 CJ (1839) 278; ibid (1878–79) 366.
11 In some cases the House, on taking the report of a committee into consideration, has adjudged the person incriminated guilty of a contempt or a breach of the privileges of the House, without first resolving that it agreed with the committee in their report (CJ (1825–26) 445; ibid (1826–28) 561; ibid (1865) 336; ibid (1887) 306; ibid (1947–48) 22). But it is more regular for the House to agree to the report of the committee before proceeding to act on it (Parl Deb (1835) 29, cc 1250–51).

punishment appropriate to the offence.[1] (See pp 103–104, 110–113). At this juncture also the persons named by the committee and now found guilty of a breach of privilege may be ordered (sometimes in the custody of the Serjeant[2]) to attend the House in order to be heard in extenuation or mitigation.[3]

Where, after the House had made an order for the attendance of the parties incriminated by a report, a petition was presented to the House from the offenders acknowledging their offence and expressing their contrition for the same and entreating the House to dispense with their attendance on the House and accept their submission and apology, the House resolved that in consideration of the petitioners' having acknowledged their offence and expressed their contrition for the same, the House was content to proceed no further in the matter, and the order for their attendance was discharged.[4]

In one case, after the House had considered a special report from a select committee and had resolved that the offence reported constituted a contempt of the House, a motion was made for the attendance of the incriminated party. Debate on this motion was adjourned until the next day. On the order of the day being read for resuming the adjourned debate, the Speaker announced that he had received a letter of apology from the offender, which he read; the motion for attendance was not proceeded with.[5]

The House has not always agreed with the committee that a breach of privilege has been committed,[6] and in a case where a penalty was recommended for refusal to answer questions put by the committee, the House decided that no action needed to be taken[7] (see pp 123–124).

COMPLAINTS AGAINST MEMBERS

Before making a complaint against a Member it is the practice, as a matter of courtesy, to give him notice beforehand.[8]

If a Member who makes a complaint against another Member has failed or been unable to give the Member notice of his intention to do so, or if although the latter has been given notice he neglects to attend, the more regular course is to adjourn further consideration of the matter of the

---

1 The House, after agreeing to the report, has then proceeded to adjudge the offender guilty of a breach of privilege or of a contempt (CJ (1835) 501; ibid (1843) 523; ibid (1851) 288; ibid (1929–30) 503). This step, however, is unnecessary in cases where the committee has reported that, in its opinion, the person implicated has been guilty of a breach of the privileges of the House, or of an offence which amounts on the face of it to a breach of privilege.

2 CJ (1825–26) 445, 455; ibid (1826–28) 561, 577, 581. The House has ordered the incriminated party to be taken into the custody of the Serjeant, and, when that officer reported that he had been taken into custody, adjudged him guilty of a breach of privilege and committed him to Newgate (CJ (1818) 282, 289).

3 CJ (1819–20) 243, 244; ibid (1956–57) 66. In the latter case the person attended and was heard. He then withdrew and the House resolved that he had been guilty of a serious contempt but that in view of his apology the House would proceed no further in the matter.

4 CJ (1819–20) 286.

5 CJ (1950–51) 298–299, 303.

6 Eg CJ (1957–58) 260.

7 CJ (1975–76) 64.

8 28 Parl Hist 826; Parl Deb (1844) 74, c 139; ibid (1875) 222, c 1185; ibid (1877) 236, cc 542–43; HC Deb (1924) 173, c 1349; ibid (1929–30) 242, c 42.

complaint to a future day and to order the Member whose conduct is impugned to attend the House in his place on that day.[1]

In some cases, however, a Member has been permitted to found a motion upon his complaint and the debate on this motion has been adjourned to a later day in order that the Member complained of might be present to hear the charge.[2] Sometimes the Member has been ordered to attend in his place on the day to which the debate has been adjourned.[3]

In several instances where a Member has stated that he rose to complain of the conduct of another Member, the Speaker has suggested that as the Member concerned was not in his place, the making of the complaint should be deferred until the following sitting.[4]

If a Member who has been ordered to attend in his place neglects to do so, and the Serjeant at Arms informs the House that a copy of the order has been duly served upon the Member, he may be ordered to be taken into custody of the Serjeant or even expelled.[5] But the more usual course has been to make an order for his attendance on another day[6] and not to have recourse to either of these measures until it is clear that the Member is setting the House at defiance. If the Serjeant has been unable to give the Member notice of the order[7] or the Member has written to the Speaker stating that he is unable, through indisposition, to attend[8] the House will fix another day for his attendance. In the latter instance the order for the Member's attendance may be conditional on his health permitting.[9]

Where a Member ordered to attend in his place to answer a charge has absconded, the House has sometimes proceeded with the investigation of the matter.[10]

Where the Member complained of is present when the complaint is made, or attends pursuant to the order of the House, it is the rule that he should be heard in explanation or exculpation as soon as the question on the motion founded upon the complaint is proposed from the Chair.[11] If the complaint is founded upon a written paper or other document, the Member complained of should be heard as soon as the paper on which the complaint is founded has been delivered in at the Table and read, and before the question founded upon the complaint is proposed from the Chair. The principle underlying this distinction is that all the Member complained of is entitled to know is the substance of the charge against him, and that where the complaint is found-

---

1 CJ (1770–72) 264; ibid (1883) 232; ibid (1940–41) 84, 86. See also HC Deb (1941–42) 379, cc 1216 and 1414; ibid (1943–44) 400, cc 439 and 584.
2 CJ (1887) 377; ibid (1926) 338; ibid (1928–29) 156; ibid (1929–30) 477; HC Deb (1911) 21, cc 1439 ff.
3 CJ (1887) 377.
4 Parl Deb (1907) 178, c 198.
5 CJ (1667–87) 85.
6 CJ (1697–99) 643, 645.
7 CJ (1782–84) 739; ibid (1810) 295. Cf ibid (1813–14) 427.
8 CJ (1697–99) 661; ibid (1770–72) 279.
9 CJ (1770–72) 279. The same course was followed where, though the Member himself had not communicated with the Speaker, representation was made to the House by another Member that he was unable to attend owing to the state of his health (CJ (1761–64) 709).
10 CJ (1727–32) 810, 876; ibid (1761–64) 722.
11 HC Deb (1911) 21, cc 1436, 1561; ibid (1929–30) 242, c 313; ibid (1983–84) 62, c 159 ff.

ed on a document the Member knows to what points he is to direct his exculpation.[1]

Though the older practice of the House was to require the withdrawal of the Member complained of as soon as he has been heard in exculpation or explanation, the practice was not invariable, and exceptions were permitted at the discretion of the House, according to the circumstances.[2] Modern practice has tended towards permitting Members to remain in the Chamber.[3]

In other respects the proceedings do not differ essentially from the proceedings where the person complained of is not a Member of the House.

Where the matter of complaint is a charge alleged to have been made by one Member against another in a speech outside the House, it is usual, if the Member admits the correctness of the report, and states that he is in a position to prove the charge and is willing to attempt to do so, to give him an opportunity of establishing his charge and with this object to refer the matter to a committee.[4]

When a Member has refused either to withdraw charges or to substantiate them, the House has sometimes judged him guilty of a breach of privilege and dealt with him accordingly. In similar circumstances, however, the House has been content to resolve that the imputations complained of were wholly unfounded and calumnious but did not affect the honour and character of the Members to whom they referred.[5]

Where the Member accused has made a proper apology for his offence the incriminating motion has usually been withdrawn[6] and where the Member who made the complaint has not withdrawn his motion, it has been set aside by the previous question,[7] or by an amendment that the House should proceed to the business appointed for that sitting.[8] In two instances, however, the House condemned the Member's conduct as a breach of its privileges, but resolved that in consequence of the full and ample apology he had offered to the House, or that having regard to his withdrawal of the expressions complained of, it would not proceed any further in the matter.[9]

A Member having withdrawn but not yet adjudged guilty of contempt may return to his place when debate on his conduct has been adjourned,[10] but it is otherwise if he has been adjudged guilty, even though debate on the question of the punishment to be inflicted on him has been adjourned.[11]

---

1 28 Parl Hist 833; Parl Deb (1810) 16, cc 179, 180–81, 184–85; ibid (1838) 41, cc 104–5; 2 Hatsell 171–72; CJ (1963–64) 174.
2 CJ (1883) 280 and Parl Deb (1883) 280, c 812; CJ (1887) 389 and Parl Deb (1887) 317, cc 1633–1638. See also CJ (1941–42) 129. Members who withdrew have been readmitted to make a further explanation (CJ (1790) 516; ibid (1893–94) 631; and ibid (1911) 37 and HC Deb (1911) 21, c 1553). Cf also CJ (1547–1628) 862.
3 CJ (1976–77) 448, and cf HC Deb (1983–84) 62, c 159 ff.
4 CJ (1834) 12, 17, 30; Parl Deb (1844) 74, cc 237–238; CJ (1929–30) 489. In one case this course was not followed, CJ (1926) 340 and HC Deb (1926) 199, cc 719–728.
5 CJ (1844) 239 and Parl Deb (1844) 74, c 303.
6 CJ (1873) 61; ibid (1875) 46; ibid (1887) 377; ibid (1911) 36–37; ibid (1921) 393; ibid (1928–29) 159; ibid (1935–36) 203.
7 CJ (1893–94) 631.
8 CJ (1884) 167; ibid (1907) 328.
9 CJ (1845) 589; ibid (1880) 54.
10 Parl Deb (1877) 235, cc 1815, 1833.
11 Parl Deb (1846) 85, c 1198.

A request, made through another Member, that a Member who had been adjudged guilty of a contempt, but whose punishment had not been determined upon, might be heard in his place has not been acceded to.[1] After the House had resolved that a letter written by a Member reflecting on the Speaker's conduct was a breach of privilege, the Member (who had withdrawn) was, on the Speaker's suggestion, recalled to afford him an opportunity of making an apology to the House.[2]

COMPLAINTS AGAINST MEMBERS OR OFFICERS OF THE OTHER HOUSE

Since the two Houses are wholly independent of each other, neither House can claim, much less exercise, any authority over a Member or officer of the other,[3] and thus cannot punish any breach of privilege or contempt offered to it by such Member or officer. If a complaint is made against a Member or officer of the other House, the usual mode of proceeding is to examine the facts and then lay a statement of the evidence before the House of which the person complained of is a Member or officer.[4]

In one instance after a complaint had been made in the Commons of a speech delivered (outside the House) by a Member of the House of Lords, a motion was made to refer the matter to the Committee of Privileges, but was withdrawn after the Speaker had announced that he had received a letter of apology from the peer concerned which he read to the House.[5]

When a Member, officer, or servant of either House has been guilty of any offence either against the other House or against its Members, which would be punishable by the latter if committed by one of its own Members, officers, or servants, it is the duty of the House to which such offender belongs, upon being apprised of the fact, to take appropriate measures to inquire into and punish the offence in a proper manner.

COMPLAINTS REPORTED BY COMMITTEES

In both Houses special reports from committees have been presented with reference to disorderly conduct therein, or to some contempt of the committee's authority, as where a person summoned as a witness refuses to attend or to answer questions, or prevaricates or gives false evidence, or which raise a presumption that a breach of privilege or other contempt of the House has been committed, such as a libel upon the Chairman of the committee. Such reports were formerly taken into consideration on presentation[6] or appointed for consideration on a future day by a motion made on the presentation of the report.[7]

---

1 Parl Deb (1845) 85, c 1291.
2 CJ (1893–94) 417.
3 3 Hatsell 67.
4 3 Hatsell 71. A different course was pursued where the subject of the complaint was the interference of peers in the election of Members to serve in Parliament, for reasons explained in 3 Hatsell 72 n.
5 CJ (1951–52) 201–202.
6 LJ (1810–12) 371; ibid (1845) 545; ibid (1870) 77; CJ (1874) 182; ibid (1887) 203.
7 LJ (1798–1800) 638; ibid (1862) 300.

In the Lords it is usual when a report of this description is appointed for consideration on a future day to order the parties to be summoned. When a report from a committee directing the attention of the House to what is prima facie a breach of privilege has been appointed for consideration on a day named, it is given precedence on the day so appointed over any other business appointed for that sitting.

According to present usage in the Commons, however, reports from select committees when presented are ordered as of course to lie upon the Table. Thereafter the procedure upon such reports is the same as that upon reports from the Committee of Privileges (see pp 137–138). Any Member may bring a report of this description before the House, but it is usual to leave this duty to the Chairman of the committee.[1]

Upon consideration of the report, the parties implicated may be ordered to attend the House,[2] or the report may be referred to the consideration of a select committee,[3] or referred back to the committee with an instruction to inquire into the circumstances of the case.[4]

Where, however, it is manifest that an offence has been committed, and the offence is of such a nature that no explanation the offender might offer could extenuate it, as for example, where a committee reports that a witness has been guilty of prevarication, or has given false evidence, or refused to answer questions,[5] or that a person summoned as a witness has evaded all attempts to secure his attendance before the committee,[6] or that it appears, on evidence taken before the committee that certain persons have prevented the attendance of a person summoned as a witness, and have given him money to induce him to abstain from giving evidence before the committee,[7] the House may proceed at once, without hearing the offender, to punish him for his contempt.

Where a committee on private bills reported that a Member, who had been ordered by the House to attend the committee, had not attended it, the House, after hearing the Member, adjudged him guilty of a contempt and committed him to the custody of the Serjeant.[8]

Upon consideration of a special report from a committee on a private bill respecting the forgery of signatures to a petition against the bill, the House on taking the special report into consideration, resolved that a breach of privilege had been committed, and that the parties by whom the petition had been prepared were liable to be dealt with by the House in respect thereof, but that in the circumstances it was not necessary to proceed further in the matter.[9]

On consideration of a special report from a select committee, a motion to refer the report to the Committee of Privileges was amended so as to constitute a resolution that certain conduct by a stranger was a gross libel on

1 Parl Deb (1892) 3, c 598.
2 LJ (1798–1800) 639; ibid (1862) 321; CJ (1836) 464; ibid (1842) 131; ibid (1874) 182; ibid (1892) 157; ibid (1946–47) 377.
3 CJ (1835) 421; ibid (1878–79) 327; ibid (1889) 332.
4 CJ (1887) 203.
5 LJ (1870) 77; CJ (1809) 70; ibid (1827) 473; ibid (1848) 258; ibid (1857) 354.
6 CJ (1851) 147–48.
7 CJ (1851) 147–148.
8 CJ (1846) 582, 603.
9 CJ (1878–79) 176.

the chairman of the select committee concerned, and a contempt of the House. Debate on a second motion ordering the offender to attend was adjourned and not resumed, a letter of apology from the offender having been read to the House by the Speaker.[1]

COMPLAINTS BY OFFICERS OF EITHER HOUSE

When a complaint has been made by Black Rod to the Lords or by the Serjeant at Arms to the Commons, the person complained of has been called in[2] or ordered to be brought to the bar forthwith[3] or been ordered to attend the House on a future day to answer the matter of the complaint[4] or such other action as was considered appropriate has been taken.

When the Serjeant at Arms has a communication to make directly to the House of Commons the regular course is for the Speaker to acquaint the House that the Serjeant has a communication to make to the House; whereupon the Serjeant comes to the bar and makes his communication.[5] The subject matter of the communication may be taken into consideration forthwith[6] or appointed for consideration upon a future day.[7] An alternative course is for the Serjeant at Arms to make a written report to the Speaker.

In one instance the Speaker acquainted the House that he had received a report from the Serjeant at Arms relating to the conduct of certain Members. The report stated that the messengers of the House acting under his orders had been forcibly obstructed in the execution of their duty by certain Members of the House. No immediate action was taken by the House, but the Chancellor of the Exchequer, on behalf of the Prime Minister who was absent, stated that the latter proposed to invite the attention of the House to the report and to ask that appropriate action be taken. At the next sitting the Members concerned expressed their profound regret and unreservedly apologized for their conduct, and the House accepted their apologies. The proceedings were ordered to be entered in the Journals.[8]

DISCLOSURE FOLLOWING SECRET SESSION

Arising from an alleged report of proceedings in the Commons in Secret Session, criminal proceedings were taken which led to the trial of a private individual on a charge of contravening regulation 3(2) of the Defence (General) Regulations 1939. This Regulation made it an offence to report or purport to report the proceedings of a Secret Session. As it was necessary for the prosecution to prove the resolution of the House for going into a Secret Session, leave of the House was given to a Clerk to attend the court.[9]

---

1 CJ (1950–51) 298–299, 303.
2 LJ (1805–06) 332.
3 LJ (1783–87) 613, 647; ibid (1787–90) 338; ibid (1789–90) 649; ibid (1794–96) 241; in the last instance the complaint was made by the Deputy Great Chamberlain.
4 LJ (1805–06) 332, 608.
5 CJ (1946–47) 54.
6 CJ (1840) 25; ibid (1851) 147.
7 CJ (1882) 183; ibid (1883) 365.
8 CJ (1930–31) 335.
9 CJ (1939–40) 235.

On 5 May 1942 a complaint was made in the Commons of breach of privilege by an alleged disclosure by a Member of proceedings in Secret Session. The matter of the complaint was then debated in Secret Session.[1] A report of the proceedings issued by the Speaker showed that the matter of the complaint was referred to the Committee of Privileges on a division. Later the Committee made a secret report thereon (see pp 646–647), which was not published till the end of the war.[2]

On 7 May 1942 another complaint was made by a Member that a breach of privilege had been committed by another Member by disclosing proceedings in Secret Session, and this matter was also referred to the Committee of Privileges, after being considered in open session.[3]

---

1 CJ (1941–42) 96.
2 HC 47 (1945–46). The Committee found that the charge made against the Member had not been proved.
3 CJ (1941–42) 98; Report of Committee, HC 93 (1941–42). The Committee exonerated the Member concerned of any intention to infringe the rules of the House, and recommended no further action.

CHAPTER 11

The courts and privilege

The opposing views

After some three and a half centuries, the boundary between the competence of the law courts and the jurisdiction of either House in matters of privilege is still not entirely determined. There is a wide field of agreement on the nature and principles of privilege, but the questions of jurisdiction which occasioned furious conflict in the past—usually between the Commons and the courts but at times between the two Houses—are not wholly resolved.

On the parliamentary side, both Houses claim to be exclusive judges of their own privileges, while admitting that they cannot by the simple action of either House create a new privilege any more than they could by mere declaration alter the general law.[1] It was the Commons principally which was led by this claim into disputes with the courts, and that House considered that the right to adjudicate on breaches of privilege implied in theory the right to determine the existence and extent of the privileges themselves. In other words, it claimed to be the absolute and exclusive judge of its own privileges, and that its judgments were not examinable by any other court or subject to appeal.

The courts on the other hand regarded the *lex parliamenti* not as a particular law but as part of the law of the land and therefore within their judicial notice. There might be areas of the application of privilege within which it was proper for either House exclusively to make decisions, but particularly—though not solely—where the rights of third parties were concerned, the courts considered that it was for them to form their own view of the law of Parliament and to apply it.

Origins of the conflict

The earlier views of the proper spheres of court and Commons were much influenced by political events and the constitutional changes to which they gave rise. Coke in the early seventeenth century regarded the law of Parliament as a particular law, distinct from the common law. For that reason 'judges ought not to give any opinion of a matter of Parliament, because it is not to be decided by the common laws but *secundum legem et consuetudinem parliamenti*'.[2] This line of argument was able to rely on the view taken by Fortescue CJ and his colleagues in the case of Mr Speaker Thorpe in 1452 (see p 74) that the 'determination and knowledge of that privilege [of the

1 CJ (1702–04) 555, 560, 24 Parl Hist 517.
2 4th Inst 15.

145

High Court of Parliament] belongeth to the Lords of the Parliament, and not to the justices'.[1]

A number of decisions in the latter part of the seventeenth century gave further support to the parliamentary claims.

In *Barnardiston v Soame* in 1674 a parliamentary candidate brought an action against a sheriff for a double return. The initial judgment favoured Barnardiston, the candidate,[2] but the decision was reversed on appeal, North CJ observing that the trial of elections and the functions of the sheriff were matters of privilege within the exclusive jurisdiction of the Commons. North also included in his judgment remarks about judicial ignorance of the privileges of Parliament and the right of the Houses to determine the extent and limit of their privileges. Judges 'know not what is the course of Parliament', so that North concluded that the action, and all others relating to the proceedings or privilege of Parliament, must be rejected: there was 'no other way to avoid consequences derogatory to the honour of Parliament'. An attempt to reverse the second judgment failed in the Lords.[3] In short, the outcome of *Barnardiston v Soame* seemed to put privilege outside, if not above, the general law. The issue was complicated by concern felt in the Commons about the consequences for the adequacy of the law on electoral fraud, and so it was provided by statute[4] that officers maliciously making double returns could be sued 'in any of HM courts of record at Westminster'; but it was also illegal for a returning officer to make any return which conflicted with 'the last determination in the House of Commons of the right of election'. The Commons thus attempted to have the best of both worlds—to retain the right exclusively to determine the qualifications of electors, but to provide individual Members with a remedy at law against returning officers.

When in 1677 an attempt was made to release the Earl of Shaftesbury on a writ of *habeas corpus* from the imprisonment to which the Lords had committed him for 'high contempts', it was argued for his Lordship that such a general allegation was too uncertain for the court to come to an opinion: the jurisdiction of the Lords was limited by common law and examinable in the courts. The unanimous decision of the court of King's Bench however was that they could not question the judgment of the Lords, as a superior court, on a committal order for contempt.[5]

Arguments in such terms were remarkably long-lived. Grey CJ in 1771 observed that 'we cannot judge of the laws and privileges of the House [of Commons] because we have no knowledge of these laws and privileges',[6] and in 1836–37, the Attorney General argued that the constitution supposed that the *lex parliamenti* was not known to the judges of the common law. They had no means of arriving judicially at any information. The law of

1 5 Rot Parl 240, 1 Hatsell 28–34. For judicial observations on this case, see 14 East 29, 3 State Tr (ns) 857, 914. It should be noted however that the judges were not trying the case but acting as assistants to the Lords, so that the reply cannot be construed as a disclaimer of their ability to decide any such point should it arise in their own courts. Indeed they did give their opinion on what they would hold in such a case, and the Lords adopted and acted on it.
2 6 State Tr 1063, 1110; Pollex 470.
3 LJ (1685–91) 253.
4 7 & 8 William III, c 7, made permanent by 12 Anne, stat 1, c 15.
5 6 State Tr 1271, 1296 ff.
6 19 State Tr 1149. Denman CJ in *Stockdale v Hansard* (3 State Tr (ns) 858) considered Grey's judgment unnecessarily wide at this point.

Parliament was as distinct from the common law as that administered in the equity, admiralty or ecclesiastical courts.[1]

Elements of the opposing view—that decisions of Parliament on matters of privilege can be called in question in other courts, that the *lex parliamenti* is part of the common law and known to the courts, and that resolutions of either House declaratory of privilege will not bind the courts—are found at almost as early a date, and they gained impetus as time went by.[2] In 1664, a court decided for a Member of the Commons who was sued for a debt, on the grounds that he was entitled to the benefit of an Act of Limitation (21 Jac I, c 16) notwithstanding that in the intervening period he had been secured from the creditor by his privilege as a Member. Though it was unnecessary for the court to make any direct inquiry into the questions of privilege involved,[3] Bridgeman CJ made some observations on the duty of the courts to decide such questions incidental to matters properly within their jurisdiction. He denied that decisions of the House of Commons regarding its privileges should necessarily be accepted by the courts as conclusive, and drew a distinction as regards the claim of the House to exclusive jurisdiction between matters of privilege arising *ab intra*, and (by implication) those in which persons outside were concerned.[4] The Chief Justice concluded that 'Resolutions . . . of either House of Parliament singly . . . are not so concludent in courts of law but that . . . we must give our opinion according as we conceive the law to be, though our opinions fall out to be contrary to the resolutions or votes of either House.' This train of thought, and in particular the distinction between direct and incidental raising of the issue of privilege in a cause before the courts, was to be developed in subsequent cases.[5]

Two decades later, Sir William Williams was sentenced to be fined by a court for his action some years previously, in signing, as Speaker and by order of the House, a paper which was said to have libelled James II (then Duke of York), and which was printed and published. His defence that the court lacked jurisdiction over the action on which the charge was founded was unavailing.[6] The process was however so obviously political in intention that after the Revolution the House declared the judgment to be 'illegal and subversive of the freedom of Parliament', and the Bill of Rights condemned the prosecution for having been taken in King's Bench when the matter was cognizable only in Parliament.[7] Later judgments have not relied on the case, and it seems to have been used by counsel on only one occasion.[8]

1 3 State Tr (ns) 774–775.
2 There are also several late mediaeval cases in which judges in court decided a question as to the existence of parliamentary privilege; see for example *Donne v Walsh* ((1472) 1 Hatsell 41), *Ryver v Cousins* ((1472) 1 Hatsell 43) and *Atwell's case* ((1477) 1 Hatsell 65–69).
3 See on this point the opinion of Sir John Campbell, 3 State Tr (ns) 816 and of Denman CJ, ibid 868.
4 Bridgeman 324, 124 English Reports 615.
5 The first application of the distinction did not, however, advance Bridgeman's argument. Sir T Jones J observed in 1677, following the arguments on the writ of *habeas corpus* for the release of the Earl of Shaftesbury from an order of committal made by the Lords, that 'the cases where the courts . . . have taken cognisance of privilege differ from this case. For in these it was only an incident to the case before them, which was of their cognisance: but the direct point of the matter now is the judgment of the Lords' (1 Mod Rep 157).
6 13 State Tr 1370 ff.
7 CJ (1688–93) 146, 177, 213, 215; 2 Show 471; 13 State Tr 1370 n, 1439.
8 Denman CJ (3 State Tr (ns) 863) and see Erskine's argument in *R v Wright* (8TR 294).

Perhaps more significant in the development of the courts' case against Parliament's exclusive jurisdiction is the case of *Jay v Topham*, in which (after a dissolution) judgment was given in King's Bench against the Serjeant at Arms of the Commons for having taken the plaintiff into custody and brought him to the bar for an offence committed in breach of privilege.[1] The House roundly condemned the verdict, sent for the judges, and having examined them, committed them to the Serjeant.[2] The judges claimed that they had not questioned the legality of the orders of the House, but had overruled, on technical grounds, the plea to the jurisdiction. They emphasized also that if there had been a plea in bar, the defendant would have been entitled to judgment;[3] and they admitted that where the entire matter was transacted in the House, it would have been proper to plead such a matter to be outside the jurisdiction of the court. They did, however, reassert the right of the courts to examine privilege incidentally arising.[4]

Subsequent observations in the courts have severely handled the Commons action towards the judges in *Jay v Topham*.[5] It has been pointed out in rebuttal, however, that Topham's petition to the House stated that there had in fact been a plea in bar, which had been overruled.[6]

At the same period, the Lords also collided with the increased readiness of the courts to challenge the exclusive nature of their jurisdiction. In 1694, a defendant indicted for murder as a commoner pleaded misnomer, on the ground that he was the legitimate holder of a peerage. The Crown argued that the defendant had petitioned the Lords to be tried by his peers, but that House had dismissed the petition, disallowed the peerage claim, and ordered him to be tried at common law. The court held for the defendant on the ground (among others) that the decision of the Lords was not conclusive against the peerage claim. The House had disallowed the claim neither as a court of appeal (this was an original case) nor on reference from the Crown:[7] and so their dismissal of the petition was not a judgment against the defendant's title or properly a judgment at all. Perhaps even more significantly, the court held that the law of Parliament (which according to the Attorney General justified the proceedings of the House of Lords) was to be regarded as the 'law of the realm'; but even if it were a 'particular law', this would not prevent the King's Bench deciding a matter which was properly within their jurisdiction (ie, even if it involved a question determinable by law of Parliament).[8]

There followed in the early years of the eighteenth century a series of cases in which initially dissenting judicial opinions took on a growing significance. The first such case was that of *Ashby v White and others* in 1703–4.

---

1 12 State Tr 821–834.
2 CJ (1688–93) 209, 210, 213, 227.
3 12 State Tr 826, 829.
4 See 14 East 95.
5 Ellenborough thought the judges had been punished for 'a righteous judgment' (14 East 109) and Denman considered that they had justified their judgment by unanswerable reasoning (3 State Tr (ns) 109).
6 By Sir John Campbell in 3 State Tr (ns) 769.
7 'The proper course for the trial of the right of peerage is by petition from the claimant to the King, who, thereupon, if he has any doubt upon the matter, refers it to the Lords, to examine into it and make their report of it to him; and upon their report the King determines of it' (Attorney General in *Burdett v Abbot*, assented to by Lord Ellenborough, 14 East 139 ff).
8 1 Ld Raymond 10.

Three judges (with Holt CJ dissenting) found in favour of a plaintiff who had complained that the returning officers for Aylesbury had fraudulently and maliciously refused his vote. The grounds of their conclusions were perfectly in line with the succession of cases mentioned at pp 146–147. The matter was properly cognizable only by Parliament and until the House of Commons had determined the matter, the plaintiff could not be said to have a right to vote at all.[1] The plaintiff appealed, and the Lords reversed the decision on the basis of Holt CJ's dissenting judgment in the lower court.[2] Holt had argued that the right to vote was a matter of property, an injury to which imported a damage. This was a matter determinable at common law; and the objection that the matter was cognizable in Parliament did not exclude the jurisdiction of the court, because it was determinable in Parliament only as a question incident to the trial of a controverted election.[3] The Commons made a spirited rejoinder, asserting that 'whoever shall presume to commence or prosecute any action, indictment, or information, which shall bring the right of the electors, or persons elected to serve in Parliament, to the determination of any other jurisdiction than that of the House of Commons (except in cases specially provided for by Act of Parliament) such person and persons and all attorneys, solicitors . . . prosecuting or pleading in any such case . . . are guilty of a high breach of the privilege of this House'. The House also adopted the resolution that, 'according to the known laws and usage of Parliament it is the sole right of the Commons of England . . . (except in cases otherwise provided for by Act of Parliament) to examine and determine all matters relating to the right of election of their own Members', and that Ashby in prosecuting an action at common law against White was guilty of a breach of privilege. The Lords regarded this as 'in effect to subject the laws of England to the votes of the House of Commons'.[4] The matter had not been resolved by conferences when a second action arose out of the same election, which raised very similar issues.

The House of Commons, by warrant of the Speaker, had committed a number of *Aylesbury Men* for having raised an action against the constables of Aylesbury who refused their votes, in contempt of the jurisdiction and in open breach of the known privileges of the House. Writs of *habeas corpus* were sued out, and it was argued that the warrant was informal and furthermore that it disclosed no breach of privilege since the prosecution of a suit was lawful. A majority of the court concluded that the warrant was not reversible for form (see pp 107–108) and that the court had no jurisdiction, the Commons being proper judges of their own privileges. Powell J declared that the Commons did not commit by the common law, but by the *lex parliamenti*; and that 'the Court of Parliament is a superior court to this court; and though the King's Bench have a power to prevent excesses of jurisdiction in courts, yet they cannot prevent such excesses in Parliament, because that is a superior court to them, and a prohibition was never moved for to the Parliament'. Again Holt CJ dissented. He did not deny the power of the Commons to commit for contempt, but he held that the exercise of the

---

1 2 Ld Raymond 938. Powys J said that such issues were reserved to Parliament. 'We [the judges] are not acquainted with the learning of elections, and there is a particular cunning in it not known to us, nor do we go by the same rules' (ibid 944).
2 LJ (1701–04) 369.
3 2 Ld Raymond 938.
4 CJ (1702–04) 308, LJ (1701–04) 534.

power was examinable in the courts. If there were no breach of privilege—as he found to be the case in this instance—there was no contempt, and the prisoners should be discharged.[1]

When the possibility of an appeal threatened to bring the case—and the power of the Commons to commit—under the examination of the Lords, the Commons addressed Her Majesty emphasizing its right to commit for contempt, and its exclusive jurisdiction in the matter. It was also denied that in such cases there was a possibility of appeal. For good measure, counsel and others were found 'guilty of conspiring to make a difference between Lords and Commons' by prosecuting the writs of *habeas corpus* and were committed to the Serjeant.[2] When the Commons' Address was received, it was referred to the judges for consideration whether the grant of a writ of error (on which an appeal was founded) was of right or of grace. The judges decided for the first by ten to two. The Lords then passed resolutions prohibiting the arrest of the counsel for the Aylesbury Men. It denied the power of either House to create new privileges, asserting a right to seek redress by action at law where a defendant was not in his own person entitled to privilege of Parliament, and stating that in committing the Aylesbury Men the Commons had 'claimed a jurisdiction not warranted by the constitution'.[3] Despite a series of conferences, compromise could not be reached, and the dispute between the Houses was cut short only by prorogation.[4]

The nineteenth century cases

In the nineteenth century, a series of cases forced upon the Commons and the courts a comprehensive review of the issues which divided them, from which it became clear that some of the earlier claims to jurisdiction made in the name of privilege by the House of Commons were untenable in a court of law: that the law of Parliament was part of the general law, that its principles were not beyond the judicial knowledge of the judges, and that it was the duty of the common law to define its limits could no longer be disputed. At the same time, it was established that there was a sphere in which the jurisdiction of the House of Commons was absolute and exclusive.

The facts in the case of *Burdett v Abbot* (1811) were that the plaintiff, a Member of the House of Commons, had been judged guilty of a contempt, arising from the publication of a libellous and scandalous paper. The House ordered his committal and in the course of the execution of Mr Speaker Abbot's warrant, the plaintiff's house was entered by force. He then brought an action of trespass against the Speaker. The significance of the outcome is twofold. In the first place, the House of Commons did not resort to the course of action for which earlier years provided ample precedent—committing for contempt counsel and others concerned in the prosecution of the Speaker for obeying an order of the House. The House preferred voluntarily to submit one of its privileges to the jurisdiction of the courts. Secondly, following further dispute on the old battlegrounds of whether the law of Parliament was a particular law or part of the law of the land, and whether

---

1 2 Ld Raymond 1105–1115.
2 CJ (1702–04) 549, 550, 552–553.
3 LJ (1701–04) 676, 677–678.
4 For further proceedings, see LJ (1701–04) 694–695, 698–715; CJ (1702–04) 555, 559–563, 565, 569–575.

the courts were entitled (or indeed bound) to decide questions of privilege coming incidentally before them, the Speaker's action was wholly vindicated. Lord Ellenborough CJ held that the House had acted within its power, and that the powers were no more than those enjoyed by all superior courts.[1] The court emphasized that the possession of such powers was essential for the maintenance of the dignity of both Houses, and that without them they would 'sink into utter contempt and inefficiency'.[2] At the same time, however, Lord Ellenborough contemplated the possibility of cases in which the courts would have to decide on the validity of a committal for contempt where the facts displayed could by no reasonable interpretation be construed as such (see p 108).

Events in the next case, *Stockdale v Hansard* (1836–37), proved to be more complex. Messrs Hansard, the printers of the House of Commons, had printed by order of that House a report made by an inspector of prisons against which a Mr Stockdale brought an action for libel. The court did not consider Messrs Hansard's proof of the House's order to print a sufficient defence. Lord Denman CJ observed that the House's direction to publish all parliamentary reports was no justification for Hansard or anyone else.[3] Though Hansard succeeded in a plea of justification, the Commons felt it necessary in 1837 to appoint a committee to ascertain the law and practice of Parliament in reference to the publication of papers printed by order of the House.

The result of these inquiries was the passing of resolutions by the House, declaring that the publication of parliamentary reports, votes and proceedings was an essential incident to the constitutional functions of Parliament; that the House had sole and exclusive jurisdiction to determine upon the existence and extent of its privileges; that to dispute those privileges by legal proceedings was a breach of privilege; and that for any court to assume to decide upon matters of privilege inconsistent with the determination of either House of Parliament was contrary to the law of Parliament.[4]

Despite the course of action implicit in those strong resolutions, when Stockdale commenced another suit against Hansard, the House directed the firm to plead and the Attorney General to defend them. Messrs Hansard in this case relied entirely upon the privileges of the House and its order to print. The defence was unsuccessful. The Attorney General argued the case for regarding the High Court of Parliament as a superior court of exclusive jurisdiction binding on other courts, and its law a separate law. Each House separately, it was contended, possessed the whole power of the mediaeval High Court of Parliament, and so subordinate were the courts of law to each that a writ of error ran from them to Parliament. Furthermore, were the privileges of the Commons subject to review by the courts, the Lords would be the arbiter not only of their own privileges but also of those of the Commons. Once again, an appeal was made to the principle that the constitution supposed that the *lex parliamenti*, like the law administered in equity, ecclesiastical and admiralty courts, was a system different from the

---

1 This case provides one of the principal authorities for the Commons power to commit for contempt, as does that of Lord Shaftesbury for the Lords (see p 109).
2 14 East 152, 159. The judgment was later affirmed in Exchequer Chamber and in the House of Lords, 5 Dow 199.
3 3 State Tr (ns) 723 ff.
4 CJ (1837) 418–420.

common law, the judges of which had no means of arriving judicially at knowledge of it. In such circumstances the courts must respect the general rule that they should follow the law of the court of original jurisdiction. Finally, the Attorney General cited instances of the Commons exercising its inquisitorial powers as a court by examining and committing judges.[1]

The court rebutted nearly all these contentions. It was accepted that over their own internal proceedings the jurisdiction of the Houses was exclusive: but it was (in Lord Denman's view) for the courts to determine whether or not a particular claim of privilege fell within that category. Though the Commons had claimed that the publication of certain types of papers was essential to its constitutional functions, and the Attorney General argued that the court was bound to accept such a declaration as evidence of the law, Lord Denman held that the court had a duty to inquire further. There was, in his opinion, no difference between a right to sanction all things under the name of privilege and the same right to sanction them by merely ordering them to be done. This would amount to an 'arbitrary and irresponsible' superseding of the law.[2]

As regards the difference between those matters of privilege arising directly in a cause before a court and those of indirect significance, on which a select committee had recently professed inability to discern a real distinction (which had led them to deny jurisdiction to the courts in either case)[3] the judges expressed reservations.[4] Lord Coleridge observed that 'whether directly arising or not, a court of law I conceive must take notice of the distinction between privilege and power; and where the act . . . is clearly of a nature transcending the legal limits of privilege, it will proceed against the doer as a transgressor of the law'.[5]

Lord Denman denied further that the *lex parliamenti* was a separate law, unknown to the judges of the common law courts. Either House considered individually was only a part of the High Court of Parliament, and neither could bring an issue within its exclusive jurisdiction simply by declaring it to be a matter of privilege. Any other proposition was 'abhorrent to the first principles of the constitution'. The declaration of the House based on the conclusions of the select committee (see above) was not the action of a court, legislative, judicial or inquisitorial, so that the superiority of the House of Commons over other courts had nothing to do with the question. In any case, there was, it seemed to the judges, no basis for regarding the courts of law as in principle incapable of reviewing any decision of the House of Commons. Conversely, there was no parliamentary revision of court judgments for error. The Commons was not a court of law in the sense recognized in the courts, and was unable to decide a matter judicially in litigation between parties, either originally or by appeal.[6]

---

1 3 State Tr (ns) 748 ff, 761–763, 767–770, 774–775, 785–786. See also p 148.
2 CJ (1837) 419; 3 State Tr (ns) 748 ff, 853, 876, 878.
3 CJ (1837) 352; Select Committee on Publication of Printed Papers, HC 286 (1837) paras 59, 60, 69.
4 It was argued, for example, that the courts would find themselves in an impossible situation if the two Houses fell into dispute over the extent or existence of a privilege—as they had in *Ashby v White*—and the Committee's argument took no account of the possibility of a litigant's claiming a privilege as yet undetermined by either House (3 State Tr (ns) 877, 878).
5 3 State Tr (ns) 934.
6 3 State Tr (ns) 850, 853, 916, 931–932.

Having received an unfavourable verdict, the House of Commons, again despite their strong view expressed in the resolutions referred to above, ordered to be paid the damages and costs for which Messrs Hansard were declared liable. It was however agreed that, in case of future actions, the firm should not plead and that the parties should suffer for their contempt of the resolutions and defiance of the House's authority.

When therefore a third action was commenced for another publication of the original report, judgment was given against Messrs Hansard by default. Damages were assessed and the sheriffs of Middlesex levied for the amount, though they delayed paying the money to Stockdale for as long as possible. In 1840, the Commons committed first Stockdale and then the sheriffs, who had declined to repay the money to Messrs Hansard. Proceedings for the sheriff's release on a writ of *habeas corpus* proved unsuccessful.[1] Howard, Stockdale's solicitor, was also proceeded against, but escaped with a reprimand.

While in prison, the persistent Stockdale commenced a fourth action, for which both he and Howard were committed. Messrs Hansard were again ordered not to plead, and judgment was entered against them. At this point, the situation was in part resolved by the introduction of what became the Parliamentary Papers Act 1840, affording statutory protection to papers published by order of either House (see pp 87–88).

The case of *Howard v Gosset* (1845) may be viewed however as a continuation of the conflict in some of its aspects. Howard, Stockdale's solicitor, brought an action against the Serjeant at Arms and others for having taken him into custody and committed him to prison in obedience of the House's order and the Speaker's warrant.[2] Leave to appear was given to the defendants and the Attorney General was directed to defend them.[3] The court favoured the plaintiff, on the grounds of the technical informality of the warrant. The judges proceeded on the principle that the warrant might be examined with the same strictures as if it had issued from an inferior court (see pp 107–108) while at the same time concluding that they might adjudge it to be bad in form 'without impugning the authority of the House or in any way disputing its privileges'.

A select committee roundly condemned this doctrine, but advised the House 'that every legitimate mode of asserting and defending its privileges should be exhausted before it prevented by its own authority, the further progress of the action'.[4] The House accepted the advice and an appeal was lodged.[5] In order, however, to avoid submission to any adverse judgment on appeal, the Serjeant was not authorised to give bail and execution was levied on his goods.[6] In the event, the decision of the lower court was overturned, and the court found that the privileges involved were not in the least

---

1 3 State Tr (ns) 1239. The sheriffs paid the money to Stockdale under an attachment, *Stockdale v Hansard*, 1840, 11 Ad & El 253.
2 CJ (1843) 59; 10 QB 359 and 411. The House ordered Howard to attend at the bar when he assisted in the bringing of Stockdale's fourth action against Hansard. He evaded the service of the order and the House, instead of resolving that he was in contempt, followed a precedent of 1731 (CJ (1727–32) 705) and ordered him to be sent for in custody of the Serjeant (CJ (1840) 59). This arrest was the action on which *Howard v Gosset* was founded.
3 CJ (1843) 118 and Parl Deb (1843) 67, cc 22, 945.
4 Select Committee on Printed Papers, 2nd Report, HC 397 (1845) p vi.
5 CJ (1845) 642, Parl Deb (1845) 80, c 1097 and 81, c 1208.
6 CJ (1845) 563.

doubtful. The warrant of the Speaker was valid as a protection to the officer of the House; and the warrant should be construed as if it were a writ from a superior court[1] (see p 105).

The last of the major nineteenth century cases is *Bradlaugh v Gosset* (1884).[2] The Parliamentary Oaths Act 1866 required Charles Bradlaugh, who had been elected a Member of the House of Commons, to take the oath. The House, however, had passed a resolution restraining him from doing so, and ordering the Serjeant to exclude Bradlaugh from the House until he engaged not to disturb the proceedings further (following an attempt to administer the oath to himself).[3] The plaintiff then sought a declaration from the courts that the order of the House was *ultra vires* and so void, together with an order restraining the defendant, the Serjeant at Arms, from preventing him from entering the House and taking the oath as a Member. The court decided against Bradlaugh, on the ground that the order of the House related to the internal management of its procedure over which they had no jurisdiction. The exclusive jurisdiction of the House in this instance was considered essential for the discharge of its function, and based on necessity.[4]

Modern cases

Though events have revealed no single doctrine by which all issues of privilege arising between Parliament and the courts may be resolved, many of the problems of earlier years which are dealt with above have been substantially solved.[5] Neither House is by itself entitled to claim the supremacy over the courts of law enjoyed by the undivided mediaeval High Court of Parliament. Since neither House can by its own declaration create a new privilege, privilege may be considered to be capable of being ascertained and thus judicially known to the courts. Neither House has surrendered its power to commit for contempt those whom it considers culpable of such an offence; but it seems unlikely that the power would again be exercised against Her Majesty's judges, sheriffs or counsel in order to stop actions at their source and prevent the courts from giving any judgment.[6]

Most of the modern instances of interaction between the courts and Parliament have their origin in the determination of the proper limits of proceedings in Parliament, some of them with a particular concern for what is internal to Parliament. The courts have recognised the need for an exclusive Parliamentary jurisdiction, as a necessary bulwark of the dignity

---

1 HC 39 (1847) p 164.
2 For the aspects of this case regarding the right of each House to be the sole judge of the lawfulness of its own proceedings, and the position of criminal acts in Parliament, see pp 90 and 155.
3 CJ (1883) 332.
4 12 QBD 271 ff. For other aspects of this case, see pp 90 and 94. The case was commented on recently by the Committee of Privileges, HC 365 (1986–87) para 29.
5 Speaking a century ago of the possibilities of future conflict, Lord Coleridge was willing to contemplate a declaration by the courts that a resolution of either House was illegal and unable to protect those who acted upon it, but concluded that 'such things might happen [but] it is consoling to reflect that they have scarce ever happened . . . and that in the present state of things it is but barely possible that they should ever happen again' ([1884] 12 QBD 271, 275).
6 See Report of the Judicial Committee of the Privy Council on a Question of Law concerning the Parliamentary Privilege Act 1770, Cmnd 431, 1958.

and efficiency of either House.[1] The judges have further admitted that when a matter is a proceeding of the House, beginning and terminating within its own walls, it is obviously outside the jurisdiction of the courts,[2] though there may be an exception for criminal acts so far as they may be comprehended within the term proceedings in Parliament. Equally clearly, if a proceeding of the House issues in action affecting the rights of persons exercisable outside the House, the person who published the proceedings or the servant who executed the order (for example) will be within the jurisdiction of the courts, who may inquire whether the act complained of is duly covered by the order, and whether the privilege claimed by the House does, as pleaded, justify the act of the person who executed the order.

In practice, however, a variety of views has been taken on what properly distinguishes the proceedings or the purely internal concerns of either House. In *Bradlaugh v Gosset* it was decided that even if the House of Commons wrongly interpreted a statute prescribing rights within its own walls, the courts had no power to interfere. For such purposes the House can 'practically change or practically supersede the law'.[3] In the same case, however, Stephen J limited the rights on which the Commons could interpret the statute as those such as sitting and voting. He contrasted those with 'rights to be exercised out of and independently of the House' in which the court must be arbiter.

In 1899, in a case involving the sale of liquor within the Palace of Westminster under the direction of the relevant committee of the House of Commons,[4] when it was contended that the general licensing law did not apply, the Lord Chief Justice was 'far from saying that no offence had been committed by those under whose authority the sale took place' and called for legislation 'to legalize and regulate what is going on'.

The case of *R v Graham Campbell, ex p Herbert* in 1934 did more than reverse earlier doubts that the sale of alcohol by servants of a committee of the Commons within the Palace fell within the scope of the internal affairs of that House and therefore within its privileges, so that no court of law had jurisdiction to interfere (see pp 145–146). Lord Hewart CJ took a much more liberal view of the proper extent of the internal proceedings of the House than his predecessor in 1899. In the matter complained of the House was acting collectively and 'any tribunal might well feel, on the authorities, an invincible reluctance to interfere'. Avory J added that to subject the House of Commons to the Licensing Acts would be to take away its right to regulate its own internal procedure.[5]

The select committee which reviewed the applicability of the Official Secrets Acts to Members of Parliament in 1938–39[6] (see p 92) acknowledged that the prosecution of a Member for an act which the House considered within his privilege as a Member would itself be a breach of

1 14 East 152, 159, 3 State Tr (ns) 854, [1884] 12 QBD 275, 279.
2 Lord Denman summed up this view by saying that 'all the privileges that can be required for the energetic discharge' of Members' duties must be 'conceded without a murmur or doubt'. (9 Ad & El 115, 193, 243, [1884] 12 QBD 274, [1974] 2 WLR 208 especially the judgment of Lord Simon of Glaisdale). See also p 158.
3 [1884] 12 QBD 271.
4 [1899] 1 QBD 7–15, *Williamson v Norris*.
5 [1935] 1 KBD 594 ff.
6 HC 101 (1938–39).

privilege, and that all parties concerned in the prosecution would be at risk for proceedings for contempt. The Committee commented however that 'this would not solve the difficulty', and quoted with implicit approval evidence given by the Attorney General that the courts would be likely to give a broad construction to the term 'proceedings in Parliament', 'having regard to the great fundamental purpose which freedom of speech served'.

The next important issue between the courts and Parliament arose in 1957 in a context broader than definition of the internal affairs of either House and (considered as a potential contest between Parliament and the courts) never directly came to an issue. Nevertheless, its place in any account of the modern relationship between the two is an important one. The Attorney General's opinion which the 1938–39 Select Committee cited (see above) was given in the context of the possible consideration by the courts of 'cases . . . of communications between one Member and another or between a Member and a Minister, so closely related to some matter pending in or expected to be brought before the House that, though they do not take place in the Chamber or a committee-room, they form part of the business of the House'. The House agreed with that committee's report,[1] and the Committee of Privileges in 1957 'adopted and followed' their predecessor's arguments and reasoning in considering whether a Member was protected by privilege against an action for defamation arising from a letter written to a Minister[2] (see p 93). The House, however, rejected these conclusions.[3] A further novelty arising from this case was the action of the Commons (on the advice of the Privileges Committee) in voluntarily referring to a court—the Judicial Committee of the Privy Council—the question of law 'whether the House of Commons would be acting contrary to the Parliamentary Privilege Act 1770 if it treated the issue of a writ against a Member of Parliament in respect of a speech or proceeding by him in Parliament as a breach of its privileges'.[4] Their Lordships replied to the question posed with a clear negative, concluding that the Act (and a number of preceding statutes (see p 76*n*)) apparently barring a plea of privilege of Parliament applied to proceedings against Members only in respect of their debts and acts as individuals and not in respect of their conduct in Parliament.[5]

It was held in 1960 that to impugn the validity of a report of a select committee of the House of Commons is contrary to article IX of the Bill of Rights. In an action for libel raised against a newspaper,[6] it was decided that

1 CJ (1938–39) 480.
2 Committee of Privileges, 5th Report, HC 305 (1956–57).
3 CJ (1957–58) 260.
4 CJ (1957–58) 42.
5 Cmnd 431, 1958. A dissenting judgment, which would have permitted writs for defamation in respect of speeches in Parliament to be issued, but then struck out as soon as it appeared to the court that the action was in respect of a proceeding in Parliament is set out in Public Law, Spring 1985, pp 83–92. The dissenting judge averred: 'The Bill of Rights is directed to the courts of law. It directs them not to question proceedings in Parliament. The Parliamentary Privilege Act 1770 is directed to the two Houses. . . It directs them not to seek to impeach or delay actions in the courts. If each of these two . . . obey these mandates, there will be no conflict. The right of every Englishman to seek redress in the courts of law is preserved inviolate without interference by the House of Commons. The right of Members of Parliament to freedom of speech is preserved intact because the courts will refuse to entertain an action which questions it.'
6 *Dingle v Associated Newspapers Limited* [1960] 2 QB 405.

those who published such a report *bona fide* and without malice were entitled to the protection of the Parliamentary Papers Act 1840 (see pp 87–88) and that it was not relevant to the action for the plaintiff to comment on the select committee's report or on the proceedings leading to its publication.

Of relevance to the relationship between Parliament and the courts is an observation made in the Probate, Divorce and Admiralty division in 1962. In arriving at the conclusion that parliamentary privilege protected a peer from arrest on a writ of attachment the purpose of which was to compel performance of acts required by civil process rather than to punish for contempt of a criminal court, Scarman J said that while Parliament would consider the nature of the process and all the circumstances of the case before deciding whether to regard the arrest of a Member of either House as an invasion of privilege, he, sitting in the High Court of Justice, need not take the law to be applied from the practice of the House (of Lords). 'I think that I have to look not only to the practice of the House but also to the common law as declared in judicial decisions in order to determine in this particular case whether privilege arises, and if so its scope and effect.'[1]

In 1972, in an action for damages, in which the plaintiff sought to prove malice and rebut the defendant's plea of fair comment by reading extracts from the Official Report of the Commons, the court held that the scope of parliamentary privilege was not limited to the exclusion of any cause of action in respect of what was said or done in the House, but extended to the examination of proceedings in the House for the purpose of supporting a cause of action. This was so even though the cause of action itself arose out of something done outside the House.[2]

The case of *British Railways Board v Pickin* (1973–74, see p 91)[3] demonstrated that though the courts continued to be careful not to act so as to cause conflict with Parliament, there were two views in the judiciary about where the boundary between the concerns of each should be drawn. The Court of Appeal held that the question whether a court was competent to go behind a private (but not a public) Act to investigate whether it had been properly obtained was a triable issue. If on investigation an abuse was shown to have occurred, the court might be under a duty to report the matter to Parliament. Lord Denning MR stated that 'it is the function of the court to see that the procedure of Parliament itself is not abused, and that undue advantage is not taken of it. In so doing the court is not trespassing on the jurisdiction of Parliament itself. It is acting in aid of Parliament and, I might add, in aid of justice.' The House of Lords in its judicial capacity took an entirely opposite view.[4] The function of the court was to consider and apply the enactments of Parliament. Accordingly it was not lawful to impugn the validity of the statute by seeking to establish that Parliament, in passing it, was misled by fraud or otherwise. Any investigation into the manner in

---

1 [1963] 1 All ER 606–610 (*Stourton v Stourton*).
2 *Church of Scientology of California v Johnson-Smith* [1972] 1 QB 522.
3 [1974] WLR 208. For proceedings in the Court of Appeal see 1 QB [1973] 219.
4 It was said that the case on which the Court of Appeal had in large part founded its decision (*Mackenzie v Stewart* 9 Morison's Dictionary of Decisions 7443 and 15459 (1752), and (1754) 1 Pat App 578 HL (Sc)) was not sufficient to support its conclusion, being most probably a decision on the construction of an Act. Lord Wilberforce expressed the further view that even if *Mackenzie v Stewart* had contained a clear *ratio decidendi*, it would be difficult to sustain it against the chain of explicit later decisions ([1974] WLR 216, 223).

which Parliament had exercised its function would or might result in a conflict. The Lords upheld clear authorities from the nineteenth century onwards that (for example) 'all that a court of justice can look to is the parliamentary roll. They see that an Act has passed both Houses of Parliament and that it has received the royal assent, and no court of justice can inquire into the manner in which it was introduced into Parliament, what was done previously to its being introduced, or what passed in Parliament during the various stages of its progress.'[1] Lord Reid concluded that for a century or more both Parliament and the courts had been careful not to act so as to cause conflict between them. He would support the action moved for by the respondent only if compelled to do so by clear authority: 'but it appears . . . that the whole trend of authority for over a century is clearly against permitting any such investigation'. One of the reasons given by Lord Simon of Glaisdale for concurring in the judgment was that any other conclusion would impeach proceedings in Parliament, contrary to the Bill of Rights,[2] and he instanced the *sub judice* rule as a parliamentary means of avoiding conflict, just as the courts had been careful to exclude evidence which might amount to infringement of parliamentary privilege.[3]

In the case of *R v Secretary of State for Trade and others, ex p Anderson Strathclyde plc* in 1983,[4] it was held that a report in the Official Report of the House of Commons of what had been said and done in Parliament could not be used to support a ground for relief in proceedings for judicial review in respect of something which occurred out of Parliament. Dunn LJ concluded that, were it otherwise, 'the court would have to do more than take notice of the fact that a certain statement was made in the House on a certain date. It would have to consider the statement . . . with a view to determining what was [its] true meaning . . . and what were the proper inferences to be drawn from [it]. This . . . would be contrary to article IX of the Bill of Rights. It would be doing what Blackstone[5] said was not to be done . . . Moreover, it

---

1 [1974] WLR 217. See *Edinburgh & Dalkeith Railway Co v Wauchope* [1842] 8 Cl & Fin 710, 1 Bell 252, especially per Lord Campbell 278–279. Other cases reinforcing this line of argument are *Earl of Shrewsbury v Scott* [1859] 6 CBNS 1; *Waterford, Wexford, Wicklow and Dublin Railway Co v Logan* [1850] 14 QB 672; *Lee v Bude and Torrington Junction Railway Co* [1871] LR6, CP 576; and two Privy Council cases, *Labrador Co v The Queen* [1893] AC 104 and *Hoanie Te Heuheu Tukino v Aotea District Maori Land Board* [1941] AC 308, [1941] 2 All ER 93, PC.

2 [1974] WLR 218, 228–229. Cf the reaffirmation of the authority of article IX of the Bill of Rights in the Commons resolution giving leave for reference to the Official Report to be made in court proceedings, without a preliminary petition in individual cases (pp 758–759). In the context of the desire of the courts to avoid conflict with Parliament, the observations of Pearce J in *Dingle v Associated Newspapers Ltd* [1960] 2 QB 405 may be noticed: 'The courts desire to co-operate as far as possible with the parliamentary authorities in matters where there may be some debateable ground on which a conflict may arise.'

3 See for example, *Dingle v Associated Newspapers Ltd* ([1960] 2 QB 405). See also an Australian case, *Comalco Ltd v ABC* ((1983) 50 ACTR 1, 5), where it was held that a court complied with the Bill of Rights by ensuring that the substance of what was said in Parliament was not the subject of any submission or inference. The court upheld the privileges of Parliament not by a rule as to the admissibility of evidence, but by its control over the pleadings and proceedings in court.

4 [1983] 2 All ER 233, especially 239b.

5 *Commentaries* (17th edn, 1830) vol i, p 63: 'whatever matter arises concerning either House of Parliament ought to be examined, discussed and adjudged in that House to which it relates, and not elsewhere'.

would be an invasion by the court of the right of every Member of Parliament to free speech in the House.'

The Committee for Privileges of the House of Lords received an Opinion in 1984 from the four Lords of Appeal named of the Committee that, if the matter were raised in judicial proceedings, the courts would hold that the compulsory detention powers under the Mental Health Act 1983 (see pp 39 and 99) would override any previously existing privilege of Parliament or of peerage. They added that 'the courts would not consider themselves bound by or entitled to enquire into any rulings (short of statute) made or recognised in Parliamentary proceedings'. The Attorney General, however, stated that 'the argument can be advanced that in the absence of a specific application of the [Mental Health] Act to Members of the House of Lords, it must be taken as not applying to them'; and he concluded that 'there are clearly arguments either way, and it is impossible to predict with any certainty what interpretation might be placed on the Act by the courts'.[1]

When in 1987, the Attorney General sought an injunction against a number of Members of the House of Commons with the intention of preventing them from showing a film in the House until the House had an opportunity of deciding whether or not the showing of the film should be allowed, the court refused the application, apparently on the ground (which was not set out in writing) that the matter could and should be under the control of the House authorities, even in advance of a formal decision by the House.[2]

Brief reference may be appropriate here to the events in Australia (where article IX of the Bill of Rights applies to the Federal Parliament by virtue of section 49 of the Australian constitution) connected with the case of *R v Murphy*.[3] Parties in that case were permitted to make use of evidence given (some of it in private and unpublished) to committees of the legislature and witnesses were cross-examined on the evidence they had given to such committees. The court held that the provisions of article IX should be interpreted in the (restricted) sense that the exercise of the freedom of speech given to Members and witnesses may not be challenged by way of court or similar process having legal consequences for such persons because they had exercised that freedom. In other words, article IX was restricted to preventing parliamentary proceedings from being the cause of an action: it did not inhibit proceedings from being used in support of an action. The effect of the judgment was substantially reversed by the Australian Parlia-

---

1 HL 254 (1983–84) pp xi and 9.
2 Report of the Committee of Privileges, HC 365 (1986–87). Among the conclusions of the Committee, which considered the issue partly in the context of the connection of the film with matters of national security, was that any restrictions which might be imposed on the disclosure in the House of such information should be imposed by the House and not by the courts (paras 47–48). In the event, however, the Committee found it unnecessary to recommend any changes in the privileges or procedures of the House relating to national security (para 59).
3 *R v Murphy* [1985] [1985–86] 64 ALR 498. A contrary and more traditional view of article IX was taken shortly thereafter in another Australian court (*R v Jackson et al* (1987) 8 NSWLR 116), which decided that the Bill of Rights precluded the use of the Official Report in court proceedings when it is tendered to prove more than what was said in Parliament. In *Mundey v Askin* [1982] 2 NSWLR 369, the Official Report was admitted for this limited purpose, that is, to prove as a fact that certain things had been said in the course of a debate in the Legislative Assembly.

mentary Privileges Act 1987 which in general restored on a statutory basis the previous understanding of the meaning of article IX, defined 'proceedings in Parliament' (see pp 92–93) and made certain provisions regarding the extent to which courts might concern themselves with such proceedings.

Finally, mention should be made of the position of parliamentary staff in the context of legislation, including the law on employment protection.[1] In 1974, a case was brought in an industrial tribunal against the Serjeant at Arms of the Commons alleging unfair dismissal. The respondents waived any point of privilege and submitted to the jurisdiction.[2] Subsequently section 139 of the Employment Protection (Consolidation) Act 1978 was enacted to provide, *inter alia*, that nothing in any rule of law or the law or practice of Parliament should prevent a member of the House of Commons staff from bringing a civil employment claim before the court, or from bringing before an industrial tribunal proceedings which might be brought by anyone not serving the House. The Lords agreed in 1975 that the preceding statute, the Employment Protection Act 1975, should apply to staff of the House of Lords as if they were Crown employees.[3]

---

1 The Employment Protection Act 1975 (s 122) applies s 1 of the Equal Pay Act 1970, Pts II and IV of the Sex Discrimination Act 1975 and Pts II and IV of the Race Relations Act 1976 to staff of the House of Commons. S 139 of the Employment Protection (Consolidation) Act 1978 applies certain provisions regarding terms of employment, rights arising in the course of employment, maternity, unfair dismissal and resolution of disputes.

2 *Harvey on Industrial Relations Law* vol I, pp 74–86, especially p 83, which also quotes an Australian case in which the courts adjudicated on an issue involving the legislature as an employer (*Bear v State of South Australia* 1981 48(2), South Australian Industrial Reports 604).

3 HL Deb (1975–76) 369, c 2035.

PART II

Proceedings in Parliament: Public Business

CHAPTER 12

Precincts and organisation of Parliament

Before entering upon the detailed account of the various kinds of modern procedure which is the main subject of Part II, certain preliminary matters should be described, by way of background to the way in which Parliament performs its duties. These are of a miscellaneous character. Together they may be regarded as forming the setting of parliamentary procedure; and the information which is given is intended to show briefly the environment in which Members of both Houses work, and the organisation, personal and material, which is provided to regulate the functioning of both Houses, to enable their Members to co-operate effectively and to provide them with facilities for securing the information necessary to the performance of their duties. An account is also given of the official reporting of debates and of the authorised broadcasting of proceedings.

These matters are dealt with in the following order:

(1) Palace of Westminster, the Chambers of the two Houses, and accommodation for Members and visitors.
(2) Officers of the two Houses.
(3) Other statutory officers.
(4) Party machinery in Parliament.
(5) Parliamentary Papers and publications, comprising—

    (a) papers dealing with the daily business of the two Houses;
    (b) papers presented to Parliament.

(6) Broadcasting of Parliamentary Proceedings.

1. PALACE OF WESTMINSTER

GENERAL ARRANGEMENTS

The Palace of Westminster, which comprises the present Houses of Parliament, stands on the site of the palace founded by Edward the Confessor. By the thirteenth century Westminster was the centre of royal government, and the palace became the habitual meeting place of Parliament. From at least the mid fourteenth century onwards Lords and Commons usually met for the opening of Parliament in the Painted Chamber, and after hearing the cause of summons were ordered to meet separately for deliberation. The Lords withdrew to a room known as the White Chamber at the south-east corner of the old palace; they continued to meet there until the early nineteenth century. The Commons either deliberated in the Painted Chamber or withdrew to the Chapter House of Westminster Abbey; after 1394 they often used the Abbey's refectory. They did not acquire a permanent

163

meeting place until after 1547, when they were granted the use of St Stephen's Chapel within the Palace.[1] The Palace was extensively damaged by fire in 1834, and the present Houses of Parliament were built between 1840 and 1852.

The Palace of Westminster contains accommodation in which the proceedings of the two Houses and their committees are conducted, accommodation specially set aside for royal and other important occasions, and accommodation reserved for serving the needs of the Members and officers of each House and of the Press. Besides the two Chambers with their lobbies and communicating corridors (see below), there are in the two Houses some twenty-five committee rooms of varying sizes where much of the detailed work on legislation and other committee work is done. The principal rooms used on royal and other important occasions are Westminster Hall and the Royal Gallery.[2] The remaining accommodation includes rooms for Ministers and other Members of both Houses and their staffs, office accommodation of the departments of the principal officers of both Houses and the party Whips, the Libraries of each House, interview rooms, post offices and refreshment, smoking and television rooms set aside for Members and strangers.[3]

Some of the accommodation referred to in the previous paragraph is to be found in premises close to but not forming part of the Palace itself. In particular, all the buildings to the north of the Palace between Parliament Street and the Victoria Embankment, and south of Derby Gate, with the exception of the London Underground station, now form part of the parliamentary estate. The two seven-storey red-brick buildings known after their architect as Norman Shaw (North) and (South) comprised between 1889 and 1966 New Scotland Yard, the headquarters of the Metropolitan police. They now provide offices for Members and their secretaries, and for staff of the House. Since the early 1960's a number of schemes for a major parliamentary building project on the remainder of the site have been put forward, but prior to 1983 all proved abortive. In 1983 the House approved a strategy, presently being implemented, for the development of the site in stages, beginning with the buildings in Parliament Street.[4]

The Palace of Westminster was formerly controlled on the sovereign's behalf by the Lord Great Chamberlain, an hereditary officer of state, but each House, while in occupation of the part assigned to it, had the custody

---

1 Cooper 'The Meeting Places of Parliament in the Ancient Palace of Westminster' Journal of the British Archaeological Association (1938). (See also pp 11–12).

2 In recent years Westminster Hall has been used for the presentation of addresses to Her Majesty the Queen by both Houses on the occasions of the 700th anniversary of the Parliament of Simon de Montfort, the Silver Jubilee of the accession of Her Majesty the Queen, and of the 300th anniversary of the Revolutions of 1688–89 and Bill of Rights and Claim of Rights, for the lying-in-state of Sir Winston Churchill, for an address to both Houses by the President of the French Republic, for the opening by Her Majesty the Queen of the Inter-Parliamentary Union Conferences in 1957, 1975 and 1989, the Commonwealth Parliamentary Association Conferences in 1961, 1973 and 1986, the North Atlantic Assembly in 1982, and for the presentation of a replica of Magna Carta to a delegation from the United States Congress in 1976. In the Royal Gallery formal speeches have been made to Members of both Houses by visiting Heads of State or Governments.

3 For a detailed account of the principal accommodation in the Palace of Westminster, see M H Port *The Houses of Parliament* (1976); Sir Bryan Fell, K R Mackenzie and D L Natzler *The Houses of Parliament*, (14th edn, 1988).

4 HC Deb (1983–84) 49, c 263.

and service of that part, this control being exercised in the Lords through the Gentleman Usher of the Black Rod, and in the Commons by the Serjeant at Arms. On 26 April 1965, with the consent of the Queen, control of the Palace passed to the two Houses, except that control of Westminster Hall and the Crypt Chapel became vested jointly in the Lord Great Chamberlain as representing Her Majesty and in the two Speakers on behalf of the two Houses. The Lord Great Chamberlain also retains his previous functions on royal occasions, and control of Her Majesty's Robing Room (and the staircase and ante-room adjoining) and the Royal Gallery remains in his hands.[1]

Control of the accommodation and services in that part of the Palace and its precincts occupied by or on behalf of the House of Lords is now vested in the Lord Chancellor as Speaker of the House of Lords and is exercised by the House of Lords Offices Committee and its Sub-Committees on Administration, the Library, Works of Art, and the Refreshment Department. In the House of Commons control is vested in the Speaker on behalf of the House. A select committee known as the Select Committee on House of Commons (Services) is now appointed by Standing Order (No 125) to advise the Speaker in the exercise of these functions.[2] The Committee appoints a number of special sub-committees; control of the accommodation allocated to the House of Commons is one of the matters dealt with by the Accommodation and Administration Sub-Committee.

The Secretary of State for the Environment is responsible to Parliament for the fabric of the Palace and, subject to Parliament, for its upkeep and any extension and alteration agreed upon, and for furnishings, fuel and lighting.

CHAMBERS OF THE TWO HOUSES

The chambers in which the Lords and Commons respectively meet and debate are connected by a corridor leading through the inner lobbies of the two Houses and the Central Lobby. Along this corridor, which runs south from the Commons to the Lords, pass the messages borne by Black Rod summoning the Commons to attend the Queen or Her Majesty's Commissioners in the Lords, the processions of the Commons headed by the Speaker and the mace, and the messages relative to bills and other matters borne by their Clerks from one House to the other.

The present House of Lords Chamber was first occupied by the Lords on 15 April 1847.[3] The present Chamber of the House of Commons, in which the House first met on 26 October 1950,[4] is essentially a re-construction of its

1 HL Deb (1964–65) 264, cc 524–529; HC Deb (1964–65) 709, cc 328–333.
2 Following the recommendations of the Select Committee on the Palace of Westminster, HC 285 (1964–65).
3 LJ (1847) 123–124.
4 A full description of this ceremony is given in *The New Chamber of the House of Commons in the Palace of Westminster: An Account of the Opening Ceremony, 26 of October 1950*, printed for limited circulation by HM Stationery Office.

predecessor, which was built at the same time as the Lords Chamber but which was destroyed by fire in an air raid on 10 May 1941.[1]

Though differing in size and decoration, the general arrangement of both Chambers is the same. Both are rectangular in shape, are surrounded by galleries and have at one end the seat of the presiding officer and at the other a barrier known as the bar; between these is the Table of the House. Unlike most foreign chambers, both Houses are divided lengthwise by a broad gangway with the benches on each side facing each other, an arrangement which is said to facilitate the division of Members into two main parties; and Members speak from their places and not from a special 'tribune' or 'rostrum'. In both Houses the galleries provide accommodation for strangers, the press and government officials, but in the House of Commons the side galleries are largely reserved for Members (for only 350 of whom seating is provided on the floor of the House) and a Member may speak from these galleries[2] (though he would not normally be called by the Chair unless there was no room on the floor of the House on the side on which he usually sits)[3] but not from below the bar where there is also seating. Special features of the Lords Chamber include the Throne which is at the south end and is occupied by the Queen on those occasions when she is present, the Cross Benches in the lower part of the House facing the Speaker, and the three Woolsacks which lie between the Throne and the Table of the House. It is upon one of these Woolsacks that the Lord Chancellor sits as presiding officer[4].

PLACES OF MEMBERS

(a) Lords. The arrangements for the seating of Members of the House of Lords are, in theory, governed by the House of Lords Precedence Act 1539.[5] In practice these arrangements have been modified for the sake of convenience in debate on modern party lines, with the Government and its supporters sitting on the right of the Speaker and the Opposition parties sitting on his left. Members of the House who do not wish to attach them-

---

1 For a description of the plan on which the Commons Chamber was rebuilt, see Report of Select Committee on House of Commons (Rebuilding) (HC 109 (1943–44)).
2 HC 109 (1943–44), Qs 178, 323 and 567. See also HC Deb (1967–68) 760, c 1820.
3 HC Deb (1981–82) 13, c 165, 619 and p 418; HC Deb (1986–87) 112, c 808.
4 From time to time during the war of 1939–45 the temporary place of meeting of both Houses, referred to as the Annexe, was Church House, Westminster (see for example CJ (1940–41) 3). Following the destruction of the Commons Chamber in May 1941, the Lords placed their Chamber at the disposal of the House of Commons and His Majesty the King directed that the Chamber be made available for the Commons. (CJ (1940–41) 143). During this period the House of Lords met in the King's Robing Room, although after the war they resumed occupation of their own Chamber on the occasion of the King's Speech on the opening of Parliament, when the Commons met as a temporary measure in St Stephen's Hall (CJ (1945–46) 14–16, 407). The Lords sat in the Royal Gallery from 22 July to 8 August 1980 while the ceiling of their Chamber was being repaired.
5 31 Hen 8, c 10. Ordered to be added to the Book of Standing Orders by way of Appendix, 9 February 1825. Examples of the enforcement of these arrangements can be found on the following occasions: 20 January 1640, 10 February 1640, and 1 February 1771; LJ (1736–41) 572, 593; ibid (1770–73) 47.

selves to any particular party usually sit on the Cross Benches. The bishops, however, still sit together in the upper part of the House on the right of the Speaker in accordance with the Act of 1539.

(b) Commons. In the Commons no place is allotted to any Member: but by custom the front bench, on the right hand of the chair, called the Treasury bench or government front bench, is appropriated for the members of the administration.[1] The front bench on the opposite side, though other Members occasionally sit there,[2] is reserved by convention for the leading members of the Opposition.[3] It is not uncommon for senior Members, who are constantly in the habit of attending in one place, to be allowed to occupy it as a matter of courtesy.[4]

Members who enjoy no place by usage or courtesy, except Members serving on select committees, must, pursuant to Standing Orders Nos 7 and 8, be present at prayers if they desire to secure a seat until the rising of the House. A Member's name may not be affixed to a seat in the House before the hour of prayers; attempts to secure a seat, by placing cards on the seats before prayers, have been prevented by order of the Speaker to the Serjeant.[5] A Member, however, may leave a card upon a seat, in order to indicate his intention of acquiring a right to the seat by a subsequent attendance, at prayers;[6] this 'prayer card', which is dated, may be obtained by Members personally from an attendant who is on duty in the House for that purpose from eight o'clock in the morning (or after the rising of the House, whichever is the later) until the House meets. A Member may obtain a card only for himself.[7]

Pursuant to resolutions of the House, a Member serving on a select committee[8] or a departmental committee[9] may, without being present at prayers, retain a seat in the House by affixing thereto a card (a pink card), which is delivered to him for that purpose on his application. By a ruling of the Speaker of 23 June 1933, a similar facility was granted to any Member serving on a standing committee which meets early in the afternoon. No seat can be secured by a card, paper, or gloves placed thereon, except as a matter of courtesy and not of right.[10]

---

1 On certain formal occasions the Members for the City of London have claimed the privilege of sitting on this bench. The separate constituency of the City of London was abolished by the Representation of the People Act 1948 and the right was exercised in subsequent Parliaments by the Members for the Cities of London and Westminster.
2 HC Deb (1984–85) 77, c 755–756).
3 For the allocation of seats to a party by arrangement, see Mr Speaker's remarks HC Deb (1912–13) 44, c 2267, 2507; ibid (1914) 58, c 49, 1092; see also ibid (1919) 112, c 755; ibid (1939–40) 361, c 27–28.
4 Members thanked by the House, by courtesy retain their seats, 2 Hatsell 94.
5 Parl Deb (1866) 182, c 1764.
6 HC Deb (1983–84) 55, c 21.
7 The obligation formerly imposed upon a Member to remain within the precincts of the House in order to secure his seat is no longer in force. HC Deb (1919) 113, c 1291.
8 CJ (1888) 21.
9 CJ (1927) 242. The significance of the term 'departmental committee' in the resolution referred to is to be distinguished from that given to certain select committees by SO No 130 (Select committees related to government departments).
10 Parl Deb (1842) 62, c 489; ibid. (1880) 252, c 1200.

ATTENDANCE OF MEMBERS

On ordinary occasions the attendance of Members upon their service in Parliament is not enforced by either House: but in the past, when any special business was about to be undertaken, steps were taken to secure their presence.[1] In the House of Lords, however, the name of every Lord present during the sitting of the House is taken down each day by the Clerks and entered in the Journals.

In modern times the ensuring of attendance in the Commons has become a principal function of the party machinery. The publication of the official Division Lists (see p 350), showing the number and the names of Members, provides an opportunity for a Member to place on record not only his vote but the fact of his attendance; and the Whips of the various parties (see p 202) make it their duty to secure adequate representation for all important divisions.[2] The publication of the Division Lists also affords Members an opportunity of demonstrating to their constituents their regular attendance in Parliament.

Attendance upon the service of Parliament includes the obligation to fulfil the duties imposed upon Members by the orders and regulations of the House. A Member cannot excuse himself from attending on a committee, when his attendance, as in the case of an opposed private bill committee, is made compulsory by standing or other orders.[3]

Leave of absence

(a) Lords. The procedure for leave of absence in the House of Lords is based upon Standing Order No 20.[4] The detailed supervision of the arrangements is entrusted by the House to the Leave of Absence and Lords' Expenses Committee which is appointed each Session and consists of the Chairman of Committees, the Chief Whips of the major parties and a representative of the Lords who sit on the cross benches (the 'Convenor of the Cross Benches').

Lords are to attend the sittings of the House or, if they cannot do so, obtain leave of absence. But a Lord who is unable to attend regularly is not required to apply for leave of absence, if he proposes to attend as often as he reasonably can.

Before the beginning of every Parliament the Clerk of the Parliaments in writing asks each Lord (with such exceptions as the Leave of Absence and Lords' Expenses Committee may direct) who had leave of absence at the end of the previous Parliament whether he wishes to apply for leave of absence for the new Parliament. The House grants leave to those Lords who

---

1 The 'call of the House', by which Members of both Houses were summoned to attend for urgent business and, in the Lords, on the occasion of the trial of a peer, is in abeyance (see LJ (1935–36) 33 and CJ (1836) 265 for the last occasion on which this procedure was brought into operation in each House), though the statutory prohibition on the departure without licence of Members of the Commons remains extant (6 Hen 8, c 16). More recently expulsion was considered as a penalty for persistent non-attendance (see Second Report from the Select Committee on the Rt Hon Member for Walsall North, HC (1974–75) 357).
2 In addition, daily lists of the attendance of every Member of their respective parties are kept by the Whips' offices.
3 SO 122.
4 LJ (1957–58) 204. For amendments to the Standing Order, see ibid (1974–75) 352; HL Deb (1987–88) 494, cc 429–431, 805. See also Report from the Select Committee on Leave of Absence (HL 60 (1957–58)).

so apply. At any time during a Parliament a Lord may obtain leave of absence for the rest of the Parliament by applying in writing to the Clerk of the Parliaments.

Lords who have leave of absence are expected not to attend sittings of the House except for the purpose of taking the Oath of Allegiance.

If a Lord who has been granted leave of absence wishes to attend during the period for which leave is granted, he is expected to give at least one month's written notice. His leave is terminated one month from the date of this notice, or sooner if the House so directs.

It is customary for the Lord Chancellor, as Speaker of the House, to apply for leave when he is obliged to be absent from the House in connection with official duties.[1]

(b) Commons. In the absence of any specific orders to that effect, Members are presumed to be in attendance upon their service in Parliament. Under the statutory provisions referred to, Members in the past applied to the House for 'leave of absence', for which sufficient reasons had to be given, such as urgent business, ill health, illness in their families, or domestic affliction. Upon these and other grounds leave of absence was given, though it was occasionally refused. A Member forfeited his leave of absence if he attended the service of the House before its expiration. It is not now considered necessary for a Member to be given leave of absence in the ordinary course of his business, but such leave has been frequently given to official delegations from the House, especially to those commissioned to present gifts to the Parliaments of newly independent Commonwealth Countries.[2] The Speaker has also asked the leave of the House to absent himself in order to pay official visits, to receive honorary degrees and appointments at universities, or to attend funerals of deceased Members,[3] although the usual practice is now for the Speaker to be given leave in a Motion for an Order tabled by the Government.[4]

ACCESS TO THE HOUSES OF PARLIAMENT

To facilitate the attendance of Members without interruption, both Houses, at the commencement of each session, by order, give directions that the Commissioner of the Police of the Metropolis shall keep, during the session of Parliament, the streets leading to the Houses of Parliament free and open, and that no obstruction shall be permitted to hinder the passage thereto of the Lords or Members.[5] The police accordingly give every facility to Members and officers of the two Houses to cross the streets and approach the Houses of Parliament without interruption and where necessary hold up the traffic for this purpose.[6] The Speaker has informed the House when for

1 LJ (1987–88) 366, 452, 594, 638, 732, 754, 782.
2 See for example CJ (1983–84) 56.
3 CJ (1947–48) 51; ibid (1950–51) 193; ibid (1952–53) 179; ibid (1958–59) 158; ibid (1970–71) 470.
4 Eg CJ (1981–82) 267; ibid (1982–83) 174, 278 Votes and Proceedings, 28 April 1989.
5 For interpretation of this order see Parl Deb (1903) 124, c 1494; HC Deb (1937–38) 329, cc 1390, 1417–1419; HC Deb (1950–51) 491, cc 1527–1540; HC Deb (1966–67) 727, cc 41–42; HC Deb (1978–79) 961, c 205; HC Deb (1983–84) 48, cc 809–810.
6 Parl Deb (1834) 24, c 826.

some special reason it is expected that the police will have difficulty in complying with the terms of the Sessional Order.[1]

When 'tumultuous assemblages' of people have obstructed the thorough-fares, lobby or passages, orders have been given to the authorities to disperse them.[2] With the same object, it is enacted that not more than ten persons shall repair together to the Houses of Parliament for the purpose of the presentation of a petition; and that not more than fifty persons shall meet together within the distance of one mile from the gate of Westminster Hall, save and except such parts of the parish of St Paul's, Covent Garden, as are within the said distance, to consider or prepare a petition or other Address to both Houses, or either House of Parliament, on any day on which those Houses shall meet and sit. Provided they have not gathered with the intention of preventing a petition or address, assemblies of more than fifty persons are allowed within the said distance.[3]

ADMISSION OF STRANGERS

By the ancient custom of Parliament, and by orders of both Houses, strangers used not to be admitted while the Houses were sitting.

(a) In the Lords. Standing Orders Nos 9 and 10(1) provide—

> **9.** When the House is sitting, no person shall be on the floor of the House except Lords of Parliament and such other persons as assist or attend the House. Upon an Order of the House, the persons in all or any of the galleries or in the spaces about the Throne and below the Bar are to withdraw.
> **10.** (1) The admission of strangers to the Chamber and the precincts of the House, whether or not the House is sitting, shall be subject to such orders and rules as the House may make. The Gentleman Usher of the Black Rod shall give effect to such orders and rules and shall have such powers (including the power to take into custody) as are necessary for that purpose.[4]

Provision is made for the admission to the precincts of the House of various categories of stranger. There is a public gallery. Peeresses, members of the Diplomatic Corps, and distinguished strangers are regularly admitted below the bar and in the galleries. There are places below the bar and in the galleries for Members of the Commons. The Press and government officials have their own galleries and technical facilities and access are provided for the broadcasting authorities. Instances of misconduct by strangers have occurred from time to time and the offenders have been removed.[5]

---

1 HC Deb (1966–67) 736, c 39.
2 LJ (1765–67) 206, 209, 213; ibid (1767–70) 147, 187; ibid (1779–83) 142; CJ (1693–97) 667; ibid (1699–1702) 230; ibid (1711–14) 661; ibid (1770–72) 285; ibid (1778–80) 900–901.
3 Tumultuous Petitioning Act 1661; Seditious Meetings Act 1817, s. 23; HC Deb (1983–84).
4 For the rules governing the admission of strangers, see LJ (1972–73) 56. On 25 April 1916, the Lords resolved that the sitting of that day should be secret and strangers were not admitted. A similar procedure was adopted on 20 June 1940 and on frequent occasions after those dates during the two great wars. (LJ (1916) 90; HL Deb (1916) 21, c 811; LJ (1939–40) 165). For war-time regulations relating to exclusion of strangers during secret sessions of either House, see below, pp 252–254. See also proceedings of the House of Lords with regard to a member of the Privy Council who had abused his privilege of admission to the steps of the throne during a debate, LJ (1920) 405; HL Deb (1920) 41, c 1026, 1237.
5 For example, 11 July 1957, 23 January 1985, 2 February 1988.

(b) In the Commons. Strangers are allowed into those parts of the House not appropriated to the use of Members.[1] Until 1845, the Commons by a sessional order, maintained the exclusion of strangers from every part of the House.

The admission of strangers has formed the subject of inquiry of several Select Committees.[2] More recently the House agreed to limit the number of Members' personal staff, research assistants and lobbyists who are allowed access to the House and to give a limited right of access to United Kingdom Members of the European Parliament.[3] Members are expected to take care not to introduce visitors who they have any reason to suppose will behave in a disorderly way.[4]

The galleries[5] of the Chamber comprise a Reporters' gallery, a large visitors' gallery called the Strangers' Gallery, and galleries for peers, foreign and commonwealth representatives, and distinguished strangers. There are, besides, private galleries allotted to the Speaker and the Serjeant at Arms.

The regulations for these galleries approved by the Speaker provide for the reservation of seats in these galleries until a certain hour by applications made to the Serjeant at Arms at the Admission Order Office.

Intrusion of strangers into the chamber

By Standing Orders Nos 141 and 142 the Serjeant is directed to take into custody strangers who are in any part of the House or gallery appropriated to Members, and strangers who misconduct themselves or do not withdraw when directed to do so; and Members of the House are forbidden to bring a stranger, during the sitting of the House, into any part of the House or gallery appropriated to Members. The Serjeant has taken strangers into custody who have come irregularly into the House, or have misconducted themselves there.[6] Officers of the House, and certain officials on duty, are not normally regarded as 'strangers', but are, with few exceptions, excluded from secret sessions (see p 252).

Exclusion of strangers from the galleries

According to ancient usage the exclusion of strangers from the galleries could, at any time, be enforced without an order of the House; for, on a Member taking notice of their presence, the Speaker was obliged to order them to withdraw, without putting a question.[7]

The inconvenience of the rule prompted the House to agree in May 1875 to a resolution, which provided that, if notice was taken that strangers were

---

1 There is no rule to exclude soldiers in uniform if they are unarmed.
2 HC 132 (1888); ibid 126 (1893–94); ibid 371 (1908); ibid 116 (1923).
3 HC Deb (1988–89) 146, c 139; Second Report of the Committee on House of Commons (Services) on Access to the Precincts of the House (HC (1987–88) 580); HC Deb (1988–89) 147, c 810–11.
4 Parl Deb (1895) 33, c 917.
5 For details of the galleries originally proposed when the Chamber was rebuilt and of their several uses, see HC 109 (1943–44).
6 CJ (1818–19) 537; ibid (1830–31) 323; ibid (1833) 246. In 1983 the Standing Order was extended to include misconduct by strangers present at sittings of Select or Standing Committees, having previously been interpreted in that way by the authority of a Speaker's ruling: Private ruling, HC Deb (1981–82) 19, c 385. On 13 October 1908 and 18 May 1915 persons who came irregularly into the House were removed by the Serjeant and conducted beyond the precincts.
7 Parl Deb (1810) 15, c 309; ibid (1845) 77, c 138.

present, the Speaker, or the chairman, should forthwith put the question that strangers be ordered to withdraw; reserving to the Speaker, or the chairman, the power, whenever he thought fit, to order the withdrawal of strangers from any part of the House.[1] Notice is normally taken by means of the formula 'I spy Strangers'. The Speaker has ruled that the motion that strangers do withdraw should not be accepted more than once in the same sitting.[2] An order that strangers do withdraw extends to the Press Gallery.[3]

The practice prescribed by the resolution of 31 May 1875 was followed by the Speaker in subsequent sessions,[4] and the resolution was made a Standing Order in 1888 (now No 143).[5] The Standing Order, following the resolution, also gave the Speaker the power to order the withdrawal of strangers from any part of the House, whenever he thinks fit. In session 1917–18 the Lords agreed to a resolution declaring that the privilege of being present at debates by long custom accorded by each House of Parliament to the Members of the other House should not be withdrawn on the occasion of a secret sitting, and requesting the House of Commons to make a similar order if it concurred in this proposal. The House of Commons agreed to the Lords' resolution and amended Standing Order No 143 by adding a proviso excepting Peers from its operation.[6] In the Lords there is a corresponding provision under Standing Order No 12.

By Standing Order No 143 a question that strangers do withdraw may be decided, though opposed, after the expiration of the time for opposed business (see p 242).

Many unsuccessful attempts have been made to secure the withdrawal of strangers under this standing order,[7] but on certain occasions when notice has been taken of the presence of strangers, the question for their withdrawal has been agreed to.[8]

On some occasions the House of Commons has further resolved that the remainder of the day's sitting should be a 'Secret Session'. The purpose of this was to put into operation a regulation (No 27A) made by an order in council of 22 April 1916 under the Defence of the Realm Consolidation Act 1914, by which it was provided that if either House of Parliament in pursuance of a resolution passed by that House, held a Secret Session, it should not be lawful to publish any report of, or to purport to describe or to refer to, the proceedings at such a session, excepting any report officially communicated through the Official Press Bureau.[9] A similar proceeding was made effective in the war of 1939 to 1945 by regulation 3(2) of the Defence

1 Resolution of 31 May 1875, CJ (1875) 243.
2 HC Deb (1983–84) 64, c 826.
3 HC Deb (1925) 188. c 2461, 2523: ibid 189, c 669. See also ibid (1958–59) 595, c 1118.
4 CJ (1876) 77, 79; Parl Deb (1876) 227, c 1405, 1420; CJ (1876) 348; Parl Deb (1876) 230, c 1555; CJ (1878) 186, 236; ibid (1924–25) 432.
5 CJ (1888) 85.
6 LJ (1917–18) 278; CJ (1917–18) 250, 302.
7 Eg CJ (1890) 72; ibid (1906) 414, 417; ibid (1930–31) 107; ibid (1966–67) 119, 558; ibid (1975–76) 507, 583; ibid (1976–77), 364; ibid (1978–79), 74, 104, 217; ibid (1979–80), 548; ibid (1983–84) 501, 721, 726; ibid (1985–86) 283, 386; ibid (1986–87) 183; ibid (1987–88) 38, 84, 147, 626; Votes and Proceedings (1988–89) 16 February 1989 (after the time for opposed business).
8 CJ (1916) 68; HC Deb (1916) 81, c 2463, 2486; CJ (1917–18) 94, 95, 150, 278, 291; ibid (1924–25) 432; ibid (1958–59) 32–33.
9 *London Gazette*, 1916, p 4189. For proceedings on disclosure of proceedings in Secret Session, see p 143.

(General) Regulations made under the Emergency Powers (Defence) Act 1939. (See also p 252).

Withdrawal of strangers during a division

During divisions of the House, strangers were entirely excluded from the Commons Chamber until 1853, but from 1853 until 1906 were merely directed to withdraw from below the bar. Since 1906 they have not been required to withdraw either from the seats below the bar or from those reserved for officials.

Strangers are required to withdraw from the Members' Lobby during a division.

Misconduct of strangers in the galleries

Individual instances of misconduct on the part of strangers admitted to the galleries of the House of Commons[1] have occurred from time to time, and the offenders have been removed from the galleries, or the galleries have been closed by the Speaker's directions,[2] or the Speaker has issued a warning of his intention to clear the galleries if disorderly behaviour were to continue.[3] The Speaker has suspended the sitting while the Strangers' Gallery has been cleared.[4] The Serjeant, with or without an express direction from the Speaker, has removed from the gallery of the House a stranger who was behaving in a disorderly manner[5] and when the disorder has continued, the gallery has been cleared by the Speaker's directions.[6]

2. OFFICERS AND DEPARTMENTS OF THE TWO HOUSES

OFFICERS AND DEPARTMENTS OF THE LORDS

The Lord Chancellor

The Lord Chancellor for the time being is Speaker of the House of Lords ex officio. As Speaker he sits on the Woolsack and presides over the deliberations of the House, except when it is in Committee. He puts the question on all motions which are submitted to the House, but he is not invested by virtue of his position as Speaker with powers either to maintain order or to act as the representative or mouthpiece of the House, unless the House

---

1 A select committee was appointed in December 1908 to inquire into the rules and regulations under which strangers were admitted to the House and its precincts, CJ (1908) 477. For instances of misconduct see HC Deb (1959–60) 614, c 488.
2 Parl Deb (1906) 155, c 1584; ibid (1908) 195, c 364, 368, 403; HC Deb (1920) 135, c 931; ibid (1921) 142, c 1692; ibid (1921) 144, c 1289; ibid (1921) 147, c 9.
3 HC Deb (1972–73) 850, c 1372.
4 HC Deb (1987–88) 124, c 1039. The Gallery was reopened later at the same sitting, c 1044.
5 Parl Deb (1898) 63, c 221; HC Deb (1919) 117, c 1258. For a more recent use of this power when a person was taken into custody on the authority of the Speaker, see HC Deb (1977–78) 953, c 677; ibid (1978–79) 959, c 1700.
6 Times, 24 August 1893, 13 May 1905. See also 3 December 1937.

confers the necessary authority upon him.[1] The control of the accommodation and services in that part of the Palace of Westminster and its precincts
occupied by or on behalf of the House of Lords is vested in the Lord
Chancellor as Speaker. This control is exercised by the House of Lords'
Offices Committee and its Sub-Committee on Administration whose agent
is the Gentleman Usher of the Black Rod (see pp 177–178).

The Lord Chancellor is a senior member of the Government with important ministerial and judicial functions.[2] In modern times he has invariably
been a peer or has received a peerage on appointment.[3] As Speaker he
speaks from the Woolsack. But since the Woolsack is technically outside the
House, to speak as a peer he must move to the left of the Woolsack, to his
appointed place under the Act of 1539 (see p 166).

Deputy Speakers

Standing Order No 15 states that 'it is the duty of the Lord Chancellor
ordinarily to attend the Lords' House of Parliament as Speaker of the
House'. In his absence (see p 169) his place as Speaker on the Woolsack may
be taken either by a Deputy Speaker, authorized by the Crown by commission under the Great Seal to supply that place, or by a Deputy Chairman,
appointed by the House (see below). If neither a Deputy Speaker nor a
Deputy Chairman is present, the Lords may on motion choose their own
Speaker during the vacancy.[4]

Chairman and Principal Deputy Chairman of Committees

At the beginning of every session, or whenever a vacancy occurs, Lords are
appointed by the House to fill the salaried offices of Chairman and Principal
Deputy Chairman of Committees. The Chairman of Committees takes the
Chair in Committees of the whole House, and is also Chairman ex officio of
all committees of the House of which he is a Member unless the House
otherwise directs.[5] The Chairman of Committees is also the first of the
Deputy Speakers appointed by commission. In addition to his duties in the
House, he exercises supervision and control over all provisional order
confirmation bills, private bills and certain subordinate legislation. In these
functions he is assisted by a counsel, who since 1808 has been a permanent
official of the House and for whose appointment he is responsible.[6] Since 1
August 1977 an assistant counsel has been appointed on a temporary basis.

The Principal Deputy Chairman of Committees, in addition to assisting
the Chairman in his duties, is appointed to act as Chairman of the European
Communities Committee[7] (see pp 582–583 and 774–775). A second counsel
to the Chairman of Committees is appointed for the purpose of providing
legal advice to this committee.[8]

---

1 SO Nos 15 and 16.
2 See Halsbury's Laws of England (4th edn) vol 8, pp 722 et ff.
3 For occasions when the Lord Chancellor has acted as Speaker before his patent of creation as
  a Peer has been made out, see LJ (1914–16) 163; ibid (1945–46) 15; ibid (1953–54) 305; ibid
  (1970–71) 3; ibid (1974) 3; ibid (1987–88) 1, 8.
4 LJ (1963–64) 95. Special provision is made for Deputy Speakers when the House is sitting
  judicially by a commission of 22 May 1969 (ibid (1968–69) 255).
5 SO No 59. See also p 574.
6 LJ (1808) 792.
7 LJ (1974) 75, 97.
8 LJ (1974) 181.

Deputy Chairmen of Committees

At the beginning of every session a number of Lords are, on the recommendation of the Committee of Selection, appointed Deputy Chairman
of Committees with power to perform the duties of the Chairman of Committees. If neither the Chairman nor any of the Deputy Chairmen is present,
some other Lord is appointed by the House before it goes into committee.[1]

Permanent officers of the Lords

The Clerk of the Parliaments. The Clerk of the Parliaments is the head of
the Parliament Office, consisting of the permanent staff of the House. He is
appointed by the Crown by letters patent under the great seal. He must
exercise his duties in person, and he can only be removed from office by the
Sovereign upon an address of the House of Lords for that purpose.[2]

He makes a declaration at the Table of the House upon entering office 'to
make true entries and records of the things done and passed' in the Parliaments and to 'keep secret all such matters as shall be treated therein and not
to disclose the same before they shall be published but to such as it ought to
be disclosed unto'.[3]

The Minutes of Proceedings of the House are prepared under his direction
and issued in his name, and in the House he is responsible for calling on each
item of the day's business as it is reached and keeping watch generally over
the course of business. He gives advice to members of the House on order
and procedure. He has the custody of the manuscripts and printed records
stored in the Victoria Tower. He signs all orders of the House and other
official communications. He endorses all bills sent to the Commons. In his
custody also are placed bills which have passed through both Houses and
await the Royal Assent[4] and he is responsible for the preparation of the texts
of Acts of Parliament. At the ceremony of the Royal Assent to bills by
commission, he pronounces to each Act the words by which the Royal
Assent is signified, and it is his duty by statute[5] to endorse on every Act the
date on which it received the Royal Assent.

He is Registrar of the Court in respect of the judicial business of the House
and is also Accounting Officer for the vote for the House of Lords.[6] He is
appointed to sit with the Offices Committee and all its sub-committees and
with the Leave of Absence and Lords' Expenses Committee.

The Clerk Assistant and Reading Clerk. These two officers are appointed
by the Lord Chancellor subject to the approbation of the House on their
appointments being notified and, when appointed, they cannot be suspended or removed from their offices without an order of the House. They
sit at the Table of the House on the right hand of the Clerk of the Parliaments
and in general assist him in the performance of his duties.[7]

---

1 LJ (1947–48) 244; ibid (1948) 357.
2 Clerk of Parliaments Act 1824 (s 2).
3 LJ (1974) 428; ibid (1983–84) 95.
4 With the exception in certain cases of bills of aids and supplies, see p 529.
5 Acts of Parliament (Commencement) Act 1793.
6 Clerk of Parliaments Act 1824 (s 3).
7 A fourth Clerk at the Table (Judicial) was appointed in August 1965 (see LJ (1964–65) 448;
  HL Deb (1964–65) 269, cc 395–396). Since 1971 provision has been made for other clerks to
  sit at the Table (LJ (1970–71) 406; ibid (1974–75) 122).

The Clerk Assistant keeps the Minutes of Proceedings of the House and prepares the Order Paper containing future business. The Minutes of Proceedings have been issued daily since 1825 and form the basis of the Lords Journals which are compiled from them subsequently.

The Reading Clerk records the daily attendances, reads aloud the letters patent and writs of summons of newly created peers on the occasion of their introduction and administers the oath. He also reads the commissions for Royal Assent and prorogation.

In addition to these invariable duties, the Clerk Assistant and the Reading Clerk each supervise the work of specific offices in the Parliament Office and undertake such other functions as the Clerk of the Parliaments assigns to them.

Offices under the Clerk of the Parliaments

Clerks are appointed by the Clerk of the Parliaments and are removable by him.[1]

The Department is divided into the following offices:

The Accountant's Office is concerned with the framing of the annual estimates, the repayment of travel and other expenses to peers, the payment of salaries, the collection of fees, the assessment of superannuation awards and the keeping of accounts.

The Committee Office is responsible for the conduct of the select committees of the House, principally the European Communities Committee, the Science and Technology Committee, their sub-committees, and such *ad hoc* committees as may be set up from time to time (see p 582).

The Establishment Office advises on staffing matters and is responsible for the recruitment of the staff of the Parliament Office and the Refreshment Department. It is also responsible for conditions of service of the staff, staff postings, promotion arrangements and negotiations with the staff associations.

The Journal and Information Office is responsible for the compilation and issue of the Journals of the House together with their annual and decennial indices. It is also responsible for the provision of information to the public on the work of the House.

The Judicial Office administers the judicial business of the House and supervises the preparation and arrangements for the hearing of appeals as well as the taxation of judicial costs. It is the channel for peerage claims which have been referred to the Committee for Privileges.

The Office of the Official Report is described on pp 210–211.

The Printed Paper Office is responsible for the storage and circulation of Bills, amendments and other parliamentary and European Community papers.

---

1 Clerk of Parliaments Act 1824 (s 5).

The Private Bill Office supervises the passage of private bills through the House. The Principal Clerk of Private Bills is customarily appointed one of the two Examiners of Petitions for Private Bills.[1]

The Overseas Office is responsible for relations with overseas legislatures and various international parliamentary assemblies, and receives visiting clerks from overseas parliaments.

The Public Bill Office is responsible for supervising the passage of public bills through the House, for preparing procedural briefs relating to them, for the printing of bills and amendments, for the preparation of the texts of bills that have become Acts and for the transmission to the House of Commons of all official messages.

The Record Office looks after the parliamentary and other records of both Houses including sound and video tapes.[2] It undertakes the arrangement and calendaring of the documents and their repair and preservation and it provides a public search room where they may be inspected by students and members of the public.

The Refreshment Department under the day-to-day management of the Superintendent, is responsible for the catering services of the House.

Librarian and Assistant Librarian

The Librarian is appointed by the House on the recommendation of the Offices Committee. The Assistant Librarian and other Library staff are appointed by the Clerk of the Parliaments.

The Librarian is responsible for the maintenance and growth of a library and information service supporting Lords in their legislative, deliberative and judicial capacities.

Clerk of the Crown in Chancery[3]

The Clerk of the Crown in Chancery (who is also the Permanent Secretary to the Lord Chancellor) and his Deputy are officers of the House. The Clerk of the Crown is responsible to the Lord Chancellor for the issue of Writs of Summons and for the preparation of Letters Patent creating a peerage. It is also his duty to prepare certain documents (Commissions for Royal Assent and Prorogation, Commissions for the Opening of Parliament, Deputy Speakers' Commissions) by which the Sovereign's commands are conveyed to the House. The Clerk of the Crown also takes part in the signification by Commission of Royal Assent to Acts of Parliament, and in the introduction of a Clerk of the Parliaments.

The Gentleman Usher of the Black Rod and Serjeant-at-Arms

The Gentleman Usher of the Black Rod is appointed by the Crown by letters patent under the garter seal. In addition to his parliamentary functions he

---

1 SO (Private Business) 69; for the duties of the Examiners, see pp 811 ff.
2 For these records see M F Bond *Guide to the Records of Parliament* (1971) and the continuing series of House of Lords Record Office memoranda, 1954 to date.
3 See also p 191.

has duties in connection with the Order of the Garter.[1] He, or his deputy the Yeoman Usher, is on duty when the House is sitting, and acts as the Messenger of the Sovereign whenever the attendance of the Commons is required.[2] He is the agent of the Administration Sub-Committee of the House of Lords Offices Committee (see p 583) on whose behalf he is responsible for accommodation, services and security in the House of Lords area of the Palace of Westminster.[3] He also acts as Secretary to the Lord Great Chamberlain and as such is responsible for certain ceremonial duties and arrangements. He takes part in the introduction of a new peer. By Standing Order No 10 he is responsible for giving effect to such orders and rules as the House may make for the admission of strangers to the Chamber and the precincts of the House. He employs the doorkeepers. It is his duty to execute the orders of the House in cases of contempt.[4]

Since 1971 the Gentleman Usher of the Black Rod has also held the office of Serjeant-at-Arms to which he is appointed by the Crown by letters patent under the Great Seal. In this capacity he attends the Lord Chancellor or the person acting as Speaker of the House for the time being.

The Yeoman Usher of the Black Rod and Deputy Serjeant-at-Arms acts as the Deputy of the Gentleman Usher for such of the above functions as the Gentleman Usher may assign to him. In particular he attends the Lord Chancellor in carrying the Mace in and out of the Chamber. The Lord Chancellor also appoints an assistant Serjeant-at-Arms, who is usually his Private Secretary, to attend him, primarily on judicial occasions.

Shorthand writer: Lords and Commons

The shorthand writer to the Houses of Parliament is appointed by the Clerk of the Parliaments and by the Clerk of the House of Commons, pursuant to a resolution agreed to by both Houses in 1813, 'that the Clerk of this House do appoint a shorthand writer, who shall by himself or sufficient deputy attend when called upon to take minutes of evidence at the bar of this House or in Committees of the same'.[5] The shorthand writer is assisted by a deputy shorthand writer and a staff of verbatim reporters. Under section 126 of the Representation of the People Act 1983 the shorthand writer of the House of Commons or his deputy must attend to take notes of the evidence before the judges of an election petition.

Computer Officer: Lords and Commons

The Computer Officer (see p 197) acts as adviser to both Houses of Parliament through the Sub-Committee on Computers of the House of Lords

---

1 Report of Select Committee on office of Gentleman Usher of the Black Rod (HL 140 (1906)).
2 For the Commons practice regarding the admission of Black Rod, see HC Deb (1962–63) 669, cc 409–412.
3 LJ (1969–70) 330.
4 LJ (1972–73) 55–65.
5 LJ (1812–13) 449, 482; CJ (1812–13) 497. See also HC 648 (1833) Q 973, Parl Deb (1897) 48, c 923 and HC 398 (1914–16).

Offices Committee and the Computer Sub-Committee of the Select Committee on House of Commons (Services). He is an officer of both Houses. He assists the Departments of both Houses in developing and managing all suitable computer services.

OFFICERS AND DEPARTMENTS OF THE COMMONS

The Speaker of the House of Commons

The Speaker of the House of Commons is the representative of the House itself in its powers, proceedings and dignity. His functions fall into two main categories. On the one hand he is the spokesman or representative of the House in its relations with the Crown, the House of Lords and other authorities and persons outside Parliament. On the other hand he presides over the debates of the House of Commons and enforces the observance of all rules for preserving order in its proceedings.

(1) The Speaker as representative of the House of Commons

In relation to the Queen. As stated elsewhere the Speaker is elected by the House itself, but his election is subject to the approbation of the Queen (see p 227). On submitting himself for approval he petitions the Queen for the continuance of the Commons' privileges. He leads the Commons when summoned to attend the Queen in the House of Lords. At the opening of Parliament he directs the recording of the Queen's speech in the Commons. On ceremonial occasions he presents Addresses of the Commons to the sovereign.[1] He reads written messages from the Queen and presents bills of aids and supplies for the Royal Assent. By order of the House during a session, and under statute during a recess, he issues writs to the Clerk of the Crown for the election of new Members.

In relation to the Lords. The chief function of the Speaker in relation to the House of Lords is to consider bills brought from that House and Lords amendments to Commons bills to see whether they infringe the financial privileges of the Commons, and if so to draw the attention of the House thereto, and, if necessary, to see that a special entry thereof is made in the Journal. He also certifies bills under sections 1 and 2 of the Parliament Act 1911 (see pp 534, 752–753).

In relation to outside authorities. The Speaker communicates the resolutions of the House to those to whom they are directed, conveys its thanks and expresses its censure, its reprimands, and its admonitions. He issues warrants to execute the orders of the House for the commitment of offenders, for the attendances of witnesses in custody, and for giving effect to other orders requiring the sanction of a legal form (see pp 31–32).

---

1 For example, on the occasion of the opening of the new House of Commons, 26 October 1950, CJ (1950) 244; HC Deb (1950) 478, c 2936–2937, on the occasion of the 700th anniversary of the Parliament of Simon de Montfort, CJ (1964–65) 319, and on the Tercentenary of the Revolution of 1688–89, the Bill of Rights and the Claim of Right (Votes and Proceedings, 1987–88, 20 July 1988.

Whenever it seems to him appropriate,[1] he communicates to the House letters and documents addressed to him as Speaker, such as expressions of congratulation and condolence and other messages from foreign countries and legislatures,[2] letters acknowledging a vote of the thanks of the House,[3] or relating to the rights and privileges of the House or of its Members, such as communications announcing the arrest or imprisonment of a Member[4] (see chapter 7).

When the Speaker has communicated a document to the House, it may be entered on the Votes and Proceedings of the House and on the Journal, without motion made or question put;[5] though a motion alleging a breach of privilege has been raised on the form of the document (CJ (1888) 222).

The rank of the Speaker. The Speaker's rank is defined by the Order in Council of 30 May 1919, in which it is provided that upon all occasions and in all meetings, except where otherwise provided by Act of Parliament, the Speaker shall have, hold and enjoy place, pre-eminence and precedence immediately after the Lord President of the Council.[6] Until this time the Speaker had taken precedence of all commoners, both by ancient custom and by legislative declaration.[7]

(2) The Speaker as presiding officer of the House of Commons

The chief characteristics attaching to the office of Speaker in the House of Commons are authority and impartiality. As the symbol of the powers and privileges of the House, the Royal Mace is borne before him when entering and leaving the chamber and upon state occasions by the Serjeant at Arms attending the House of Commons, and is placed upon the table when he is in the chair.[8] In debate all speeches are addressed to him and he calls upon Members to speak—a choice which is not open to dispute. When he rises to preserve order or to give a ruling on a doubtful point he must always be heard in silence and no Member may stand when the Speaker is on his feet. Reflections upon the character or actions of the Speaker may be punished as

---

1 HC Deb (1943–44) 397, c 623; CJ (1951–52) 201–2; ibid (1953–54) 42; HC Deb (1961–62) 661 c 1539.
2 CJ (1888) 142; ibid (1901) 5, 6, 7, 16, 48; ibid (1912–13) 113, 115, 138, 543, 548; ibid (1936) 50, 51, 55; ibid (1951–52) 89, 90–1, 92, 94; ibid (1964–65) 112, 116, etc; ibid (1975–76) 107, 433, ibid (1976–77) 96, ibid (1977–78) 412. See also CJ (1914) 442.
3 CJ (1844) 3.
4 Eg CJ (1970–71) 20, 209, ibid (1971–72) 276, 313, ibid (1974–75) 570, 608, ibid (1976–77) 358.
5 Parl Deb (1881) 263, c 45–49; ibid (1882) 274, c 1328. A motion, once made, that a letter communicated by the Speaker be laid upon the table (CJ (1883) 4), cannot be reckoned as a precedent.
6 *London Gazette,* 3 June 1919, p 7059.
7 The Great Seal Act 1688 (1 Will and Mary, c 21), enacts that the lords commissioners for the great seal 'not being peers, shall have and take place next after the peers of this realm, and the Speaker of the House of Commons'. See also 2 Hatsell 249 n; and regarding the precedence between the Speaker and a peer of Ireland, whilst a Member of the House of Commons, see Colchester i, 413.
8 The Mace is received by the Serjeant at Arms from the Lord Chamberlain of the Household; it is, therefore, in the first place a symbol of the Royal authority, and thence derivatively of the authority of the Speaker and the House. When the House is dissolved or prorogued it reverts to the custody of the Lord Chamberlain of the Household, but during an adjournment it remains in the control of the Serjeant at Arms. See also HC Deb (1961–62) 650, c 1544– 1552.

breaches of privilege (see p 127). His action cannot be criticised incidentally in debate or upon any form of proceeding except a substantive motion (see p 325). His authority in the chair is fortified by many special powers which are referred to below. Confidence in the impartiality of the Speaker is an indispensable condition of the successful working of procedure, and many conventions exist which have as their object not only to ensure the impartiality of the Speaker but also to ensure that his impartiality is generally recognized. He takes no part in debate either in the House or in committee. He votes only when the voices are equal, and then only in accordance with rules which preclude an expression of opinion upon the merits of a question. Until recently his seat was often uncontested at a general election and (belonging to no party) he stands as 'the Speaker seeking re-election'.[1]

Duties of the Speaker under usage. It is the duty of the Speaker to preserve the orderly conduct of debate by repressing disorder when it arises, by refusing to propose the question upon motions and amendments which are irregular, and by calling the attention of the House to bills which are out of order (and securing their withdrawal). He rules on points of order submitted to him by Members on questions either as they arise or in anticipation, but any notice of a question seeking a ruling must be notified to him privately and not placed upon the paper. The opinion of the Speaker cannot be sought in the House about any matter arising or likely to arise in a committee.[2] The Speaker is always ready to advise Members of all parties who consult him privately whether upon any action which they propose to take in the House or upon any questions of order which are likely to arise in its proceedings. Such private rulings of the Speaker generally settle the questions at issue, but they may, if necessary, be supplemented by rulings given from the chair.[3]

The Speaker's rulings, whether given in public or in private, constitute precedents by which subsequent Speakers, Members, and officers are guided. Such precedents are collected and in course of time may be formulated as principles, or rules of practice. It is largely by this method that the modern practice of the House of Commons has been developed.

A few examples may be given of motions and bills which for some irregularity the Speaker has not allowed to proceed.

Motions. A motion which would create a charge upon the people and is not recommended by the Crown (pp 691–692); a motion touching the rights of the Crown, which has not received the royal consent (pp 561–562); a motion which anticipates a matter which stands for the future consideration of the House (pp 327–328), or which raises afresh a matter already decided during the current session (p 326)—these are examples of motions upon which the Speaker refuses to propose a question.

Bills. The Speaker has ruled a private bill out of order on the ground that it should have been introduced as a public bill (p 807), and has directed the

---

1 See Report of the Select Committee on Parliamentary Elections (the Speaker's Seat), HC 98 (1938–39).
2 HC Deb (1986–87) 114, c 676; ibid (1987–88) 125, c 464.
3 For the publication of certain private rulings in the Official Report, see p 5.

withdrawal of a public bill which should have been introduced only following the passage of preliminary resolutions (pp 692–693), or which has gone beyond its title (p 467); he has also directed that a bill received from the Lords be laid aside on the ground that it infringed the privileges of the Commons (p 744). Similarly he has directed the recommittal of a bill to a standing committee when clauses affecting public money have been introduced without the necessary authority (p 606). Under Standing Order No 76(3), if he is satisfied that a Lords amendment imposes a charge upon the public revenue which has not been authorized, he shall deem the amendment to have been disagreed to.

Discretionary powers of the Speaker. By standing orders a number of discretionary powers have been vested in the Speaker. Under Standing Order No 20 he has to decide whether a proposal to move the adjournment of the House in order to discuss a specific and important matter that should have urgent consideration conforms to the provisions of the standing order. When a Member moves to introduce a bill under Standing Order No 19, he decides whether to put the question upon the motion or for the adjournment of the debate. Under Standing Order No 14(1) and Standing Order No 15, when motions relating to statutory instruments are being debated, the Speaker has the power to interrupt the business instead of putting the question at the prescribed time if he is of the opinion that the time for debate has not been adequate; the debate then stands adjourned till the next sitting (see p 316). He also decides whether a Member who has informed him of a matter of privilege should be allowed to table a motion which would take precedence over the orders of the day on the following day (see pp 310–311).

Powers to restrict debate. Various powers have been given to the Speaker to prevent obstruction in the proceedings of the House (see pp 393 ff.). He has the power to select the amendments which may be proposed on consideration of a motion or bill, and to accept and put a motion for the closure of a question when it has been adequately debated. Under Standing Order No 28, made in February 1986, he has the power to accept and put a motion 'That the Question be now proposed'. He checks irrelevance or repetition by ordering a Member to discontinue his speech, and has the power to refuse a motion for the adjournment of the House or of the debate. He prevents a division which in his opinion is unnecessarily claimed.

Powers to prevent disorder. Power is given to the Speaker to prevent disorder in the House (see pp 393 ff.).

The Speaker represses disorder in the House by calling Members to order (p 394), when the offence is committed in his presence; by putting into force Standing Order No 43(1) (the suspension of Members) (p 397); by naming a Member, under the ancient usage of the House incorporated in Standing Order No 42; and by directing him to withdraw from the precincts, under Standing Order No 44 (pp 397–399). The Speaker's powers in the event of grave disorder arising in the House are described on p 395.

Administrative duties

(1) The Speaker has the control of the accommodation and services in that part of the Palace of Westminster and precincts occupied by or on behalf

of the House of Commons. In exercising this control he is advised by the House of Commons (Services) Committee (see pp 657–658).[1]

(2) The Speaker appoints the printers of the Journals, and he is responsible, through the Clerk of the House, for the accuracy of the Votes and Proceedings, and through the Editor, whom he appoints, for the Official Report of Debates.

(3) The Speaker is by statute, a Member of the House of Commons Commission (see pp 192–193) and also has a small personal staff of his own.

Duties under statute. Various duties are laid upon the Speaker by statute, for instance by the Mental Health Act 1959 (see pp 41, 32), by the Parliament Act 1911 (pp 532–534), by the Church of England Assembly (Powers) Act 1919 (p 555), by section 2(2) of the Ministerial and other Salaries Act 1975, by section 2 of the Regency Act 1937, by section 1(4) and (5) of the Consolidation of Enactments (Procedure) Act 1949, by the Recess Elections Act 1975 (see pp 32–33), the House of Commons (Administration) Act 1978 (see p 192) and the Wellington Parliamentary Estates Acts. As a trustee under the latter Acts the Speaker has appointed the Speaker's Counsel as his attorney to act for him. Under the Parliamentary Constituencies Act 1986 he is chairman of the four permanent Boundary Commissions which keep under continuous review the distribution of seats at parliamentary elections (see p 24). It may also be his duty to transmit to the officials of the Bank of England a certificate in writing, notifying the agreement of the House to a resolution for the redemption of stock forming part of the National Debt.[2]

Functions of office after dissolution and during prorogation. By section 3(2) of the Ministerial and other Salaries Act 1972 it is provided that in the case of a dissolution the then Speaker shall be deemed to be the Speaker, for the purposes of that Act until a Speaker shall be chosen by the new Parliament. Similar provision is made in Schedules 1 and 2 of the House of Commons (Administration) Act 1978 both for the purposes of that Act and for the purposes of section 122 of the Employment Protection Act 1975.

In Session 1969–70 it was ordered by the House that during any future dissolution or prorogation of Parliament the permanent officers of the House should consult the Speaker to the same extent and in the same way as they would during a Session of Parliament (see CJ (1969–70)).

The provisions of the Recess Elections Act 1975 relating to the issue of warrants for new writs for by-elections apply during any recess of the House, whether by a prorogation or adjournment.

Speakers' Conferences on Electoral Law. Mr Speaker has also presided over the Conferences on Electoral Law following an invitation from the Prime Minister to do so. Such Conferences have examined various matters of electoral law. Mr Speaker has formally appointed the members of the Conference on receipt of party nominations. Conferences have been served

---

1 Mr Speaker has, for example, suspended the issue of a pass to a Members' research assistant; (HC Deb 1987–88) 120, cc 762–3 and he has prohibited the showing of a film subject to a High Court injunction until the House has had an opportunity to come to a decision on the matter (HC Deb (1986–87), 108, cc 1023–6).

2 National Debt (Conversion of Stock) Act 1884, s 1. This duty formerly existed also under the National Debt Act 1870, CJ (1888) 345; Parl Deb (1888) 328, c 525.

by a joint secretariat from the Clerk's Department and the Civil Service.[1] They did not enjoy the powers and privileges of Select Committees. They sat in private and did not publish their proceedings.

In Session 1982–83 the Home Affairs Committee conducted an inquiry into the Representation of the People Acts and made recommendations on a range of topics indistinguishable from the type of matters previously considered by Speakers' Conferences.[2]

Resignation of Speaker. The Speaker's decision to retire has usually been announced in a formal statement made during the course of a session, the thanks of the House for his services being expressed by resolution, and a new Speaker elected, on the two successive days thereafter;[3] but on some recent occasions his retirement has taken effect at the beginning of a new Parliament.[4] When he vacates his office he has usually been created a peer and an annuity has been settled on him (and, on his death, on his widow) by statute.[5] However, section 26 of the Parliamentary and other Pensions Act 1972 (c 48) now makes provision for a pension to be paid to any person who has ceased to be Speaker. In recent times a former Speaker has normally relinquished his membership of the House immediately after relinquishing his office (see also p 228).

Deputy Speaker in the Commons (Standing Order No 2)

In 1855, on the report of a select committee, a standing order was agreed to which enables the Chairman of Ways and Means (see p 186), as Deputy Speaker, to take the chair during the unavoidable absence or absence by leave of the House of the Speaker, and perform his duties in relation to all proceedings in the House.

The sanction of the consent of the Crown was given to the appointment of this committee, to the standing order and to its amendment.[6]

The provision of this standing order received statutory authority by the Deputy Speaker Act 1855. The standing order has since been amended by a

---

1 For recent Speakers' Conferences set up in 1972 and 1977, see HC Deb (1971–72) 842, cc 560–561; (1972–73) 560, cc 1412–1416; (1976–77) 923, c 540; (1976–77) 927, cc 619–620; (1976–77) 935–2, cc 1379–1350.
2 HC (1982–83) 32.
3 CJ (1872) 9, 22, 23; ibid (1884) 68, 72, 74; ibid (1895) 139, 147, 149; ibid (1905) 243, 247, 249; ibid (1921) 109, 113, 114; ibid (1928) 210, 213, 215 ibid (1975–76) 95, 125, 126.
4 Mr Speaker did not seek re-election in the general elections of 1951 and 1959. On 7 November 1951, in the new Parliament, a letter from the former Speaker was read to the House by his successor, and a motion thanking him for his services was moved several days thereafter, CJ (1951–52) 19, 39; in 1959, Mr Speaker announced informally, some months in advance, his intention of retiring, and his formal announcement followed by the motion of thanks was made on the last day of the session, HC Deb (1958–59) 600, cc 549–551; ibid (1958–59) 610, c 787–794. In 1970, the Speaker, having informally made known his intention to retire some months previously, made his formal announcement on 10 December, (CJ (1970–71) 165) and a new Speaker was chosen, on the first day after the Christmas recess, 12 January 1971 (ibid 184). In 1976 Mr Speaker Lloyd gave notice of his intention to retire on 20 January. He retired on 3 February after presiding over the election of his successor, HC Deb (1975–76) 963, c 1136. In 1983 Mr Speaker Thomas retired at the end of the Parliament having made an informal personal statement of his intentions on 29 January 1980, HC Deb (1979–80) 977, c 1124.
5 See, for example, Mr Speaker Morrison's Retirement Act 1959 and Mr Speaker King's Retirement Act 1971.
6 CJ (1852–53) 758, 766; ibid (1854–55) 395; ibid (1902) 65; HC 478 (1852–53).

provision for the appointment of a First and Second Deputy Chairman of Ways and Means.[1] Whenever the House has been informed by the Clerk at the Table of the unavoidable absence or absence by leave of the House both of Mr Speaker and of the Chairman of Ways and Means the First Deputy Chairman is entitled to perform the duties and exercise the authority of the Speaker in relation to all the proceedings in the House, and should the First Deputy Chairman also be thus absent, then these powers devolve upon the Second Deputy Chairman (Standing Order No 3(3)).[2]

On a number of occasions the Chairman of Ways and Means has taken the chair as deputy Speaker in the Speaker's absence.[3] The Serjeant, accompanied by the Chaplain, enters the House with the mace, which he places upon the Table. The Clerk informs the House of the Speaker's unavoidable absence or absence by leave, and if necessary of that of the Chairman of Ways and Means.[4] The Chairman of Ways and Means, or in his absence a Deputy Chairman, then proceeds to the Table, and, after prayers, takes the chair. If the House goes into committee and he takes the chair thereof, when the question for reporting progress has been agreed to, he returns to the chair of the House, and a Deputy Chairman[5] or another Member[6] makes to him the report of the committee.

The unavoidable absence of the Speaker may be announced by the Clerk at the Table at any time during a sitting;[7] but an opportunity is usually taken which interferes as little as possible with the progress of debate.

Unless the absence of the Speaker is thus formally announced the Deputy Speaker may not exercise the power of selecting amendments under Standing Order No 31, except during the consideration of estimates, nor may he perform any duties of the Speaker, such as those in connection with the issue of writs, which do not arise from the course of debate. After the unavoidable absence of the Speaker has been announced and the chair has been occupied for some time by the Deputy Speaker, the Speaker is not precluded from resuming the chair, if he wishes.[8]

Standing Order No 3(1) empowers the Speaker, without any formal communication to the House, to request the Chairman of Ways and Means or a Deputy Chairman to take the chair, either temporarily or until the adjourn-

---

1 CJ (1902) 59; ibid (1909) 337. Now SO No 2.

2 The Deputy Speaker Act 1855 does not refer to the exercise by the Deputy Speaker of any powers placed upon the Speaker by statute during his absence: such a provision is made in the House of Commons (Administration) Act 1978, Sch 2, para 2. The Recess Elections Act 1975 contains different provisions for the exercise of the Speaker's duties when there is no Speaker or he is absent from the United Kingdom (ibid s 4). Provision for absence by leave of the House in SO No 126 was made on 30 October 1980 (CJ 1979–80) 820.

3 CJ (1870) 265; ibid (1887) 306; ibid (1893–94) 414; Parl Deb (1893) 14, c 950; CJ (1933–34) 240; ibid (1946–47) 222, 229, 239, 241; ibid (1952–53) 179; ibid (1968–69) 362; ibid (1970–71) 496; ibid (1974) 170, ibid (1976–77) 109, 373, 399, 436; ibid (1979–80) 475.

4 CJ (1903) 96.

5 CJ (1950–51) 146.

6 CJ (1903) 96, 98.

7 CJ (1881) 50; see also CJ (1923) 90; HC Deb (1923) 162, c 1417. See also CJ (1886) 234, 237, 261, 263, 331, 334; ibid (1947–48) 309; ibid (1974–75) 609; ibid (1975–76) 439.

8 CJ (1903) 96; CJ (1947–48) 309.

ment of the House;[1] but before his Deputy can exercise the Speaker's powers under Standing Order No 31 the announcement of the Speaker's absence must be made (Standing Order No 3(2)).[2] Powers under Standing Order No 31 can only be exercised by a Deputy Chairman of Ways and Means in his capacity as Deputy Speaker when the absence both of the Speaker and of the Chairman of Ways and Means has been announced;[3] for their exercise by the Second Deputy Chairman, the absence of the First Deputy Chairman must also have been announced. When occupying the chair without the Speaker's absence having been announced, the Deputy Speaker may exercise all the powers of the Speaker, except for those exercisable only by the Speaker under Standing Order No 31.

When the Speaker has found that he would be unable to be present at the meeting of the House, he has requested the Chairman of Ways and Means to take the chair as Deputy Speaker, under Standing Order No 3(1), and has taken the chair himself in the course of the sitting.[4]

The Chairman of Ways and Means

In Committee the chair (at the Table) is generally taken by the Chairman of Ways and Means or in his absence by a Deputy Chairman.[5]

The Chairman of Ways and Means was formerly appointed at the beginning of a new Parliament, when the House resolved itself for the first time into the Committee of Supply, by the Leader of the House, or a Minister of the Crown in his behalf, calling upon a Member to take the chair of the committee.[6] In 1910 the Chairman of Ways and Means was appointed on a motion made by the Prime Minister as soon as the usual sessional orders had been made on the day on which the King's speech for opening Parliament was delivered.[7] This course, which has usually been followed at the beginning of subsequent parliaments,[8] has also been adopted when a vacancy has occurred in the course of a session.[9] No notice of the motion is required.[10]

> When the appointment was sought to be made in committee and a difference arose therein concerning the election of a Chairman, the matter had to be determined by the House itself. The Speaker at once resumed the chair; and a motion being made, 'That AB do take the chair of the committee', the Speaker put the question, which being agreed to, the mace was again removed from the table, and the House resolved itself into committee.[11]

---

1 CJ (1889) 393, 394; ibid (1890) 539, 580.
2 CJ (1910) 231.
3 Private Ruling, December 1912.
4 CJ (1909) 407–408, 474–475; ibid (1931–32) 150–151. HC Deb (1981–82) 21, cc 669, 685.
5 The chair may also be taken by temporary Chairman (see p 188).
6 CJ (1900) 417; ibid (1906) 36.
7 CJ (1910) 6.
8 CJ (1911) 7; ibid (1919) 16; ibid (1922) 345; ibid (1929–30) 17, etc. In session 1924 the motion was withdrawn, and the Chairman of Ways and Means was appointed by a motion made on a subsequent day, CJ (1924) 17, 35; HC Deb (1924) 169, c 49–56.
9 CJ (1911) 436; see also ibid (1942–43) 31, 59; ibid (1944–45) 140; ibid (1961–62) 85; ibid (1980–81) 173; ibid (1981–82) 380.
10 HC Deb (1961–62) 652, cc 710–718.
11 CJ (1921) 117; HC Deb (1921) 141, c 429.

The Chairman so appointed continues in office for the remainder of the Parliament.

As has already been stated he also acts as Deputy Speaker and he executes various duties in connection with private bills (see p 826 ff.). The Chairman or a Deputy Chairman is also authorised, in the event of the Speaker's inability to act, to exercise his power of recalling the House during an adjournment (Standing Order No 12(3)).

The Chairman of Ways and Means or a Deputy Chairman[1] has final authority over all points of order arising when he is in the chair and there is no appeal from his ruling to the Speaker. He has power in committee to accept a motion for the closure and a motion to propose the question (Standing Order No 28) and to select amendments, though when a Deputy Chairman exercises the power of selection he normally consults the Chairman beforehand. He has only a casting vote in committee (see also p 353). Under the terms of Standing Order No 80 he is Chairman of any business Committee that may be set up in respect of proceedings on bills.

Impartiality. The Chairman of Ways and Means during his occupation of that office follows the same tradition of abstention from party controversy as the Speaker.[2]

He no longer exercises the rights of the ordinary Member to participate in debates and divisions of the House although he has occasionally made speeches when moving motions relating to private business.[3] His independence has not the same formal guarantees as that of the Speaker, as he is appointed on the motion of a Minister of the Crown. His seat is liable to be contested and his salary is placed upon the Estimates.

As the result of a report from a select committee (CJ (1947–48) 188), the Prime Minister proposed, with the general agreement of the House, that the Chairman and Deputy Chairman should in future refrain from acting in a professional capacity on behalf of or against any Member of the House (HC Deb (1947–48) 452, c 663). For motions of censure, see p 325.

Resignation of the Chairman of Ways and Means. If the Chairman of Ways and Means resigns the chair during the sitting of Parliament, he either personally announces his retirement to the House, or addresses a letter to the Speaker making the announcement.[4] In the former case observations are made by the ministerial and opposition leaders.

Deputy Chairmen of Ways and Means

In addition to the Chairman of Ways and Means, the House has power under Standing Order No 2 to appoint two Deputy Chairmen of Ways and Means who are entitled to exercise all the powers vested in the Chairman of Ways and Means, including his powers as Deputy Speaker. The procedure for

1 HC Deb (1958–59) 597, c 1088.
2 For a recent statement of the Chairman's impartiality, see HC Deb (1983–84) 56, c 408.
3 Eg 12 February 1986 (motion to reduce the quorum of the Committee in the Felixstowe Dock and Railway Bill, HC Deb (1985–86) 81, c 1013. On that occasion the Chairman did not vote.
4 Colonel Wilson Patten, 5 April 1853, Parl Deb (1853) 125, c 591; Mr Dodson, 8 April 1872, ibid (1872) 210, c 892; Mr Lyon Playfair, 1 March 1883, ibid (1883) 276, c 1247; Sir Dennis Herbert, HC Deb (1942–43) 386, c 49. In session 1911 Mr Emmott announced his resignation by a letter addressed to the Speaker CJ (1911) 436; so also did Sir Robert Young CJ (1930–31) 406, 407, Major Milner CJ (1944–45) 139, Sir Gordon Touche CJ (1961–62) 85, and Sir Eric Fletcher CJ (1968–69) 6.

appointing the Deputy Chairmen is the same as that adopted for appointing the Chairman of Ways and Means.[1]

The office of Deputy Chairman was first created in 1902 and its occupants follow the same tradition of abstention from party controversy as the Chairman of Ways and Means, and the same procedure is followed on their resignation as on that of the Chairman.[2] Since 1971 there has also been a Second Deputy Chairman.[3]

Temporary appointment of a Member to act as Deputy Chairman. On 11 December 1928 the House resolved, the King's Consent having been signified to the motion, that during the absence of the Deputy Chairman up to and including 1 February 1929, the Member for Oxford should be entitled to exercise all the powers vested in the Deputy Chairman including his powers as Deputy Speaker (CJ (1928–29) 57). By similar resolutions in 1946 and 1947, such powers were conferred on the Member for Newton, in 1957 on the Member for Berwick and East Lothian, in 1964 on the Member for the Isle of Ely, and in 1972 on the Member for Wembley, South (CJ (1945–46) 392; ibid. (1947–48) 67; ibid (1956–57) 225; ibid (1964–65) 41; ibid (1971–72) 500). In the first three cases, no date was named for their termination.

Temporary chairmen

Under Standing Order No 4(1) it is the Speaker's duty to nominate at the commencement of every session a panel of not fewer than ten Members to act as temporary chairmen of committees when so requested by the Chairman of Ways and Means. He may add further Members to the panel, or make substitution, during the course of the session.[4] Temporary Chairmen frequently take the chair during the passage of Finance Bills or bills which require a significant amount of debating time.

From this same panel Mr Speaker appoints the chairmen of standing committees, see pp 596–597. The Chairmen's panel meets occasionally under the chairmanship of the Chairman of Ways and Means to discuss matters of procedure relating to standing committees and to report its opinion thereon to the House.[5]

Principal Permanent Officers of the Commons

Clerk of the House. The Clerk of the House is the chief permanent officer of the House of Commons. He is appointed by the Crown, for life, by letters patent, in which he is styled 'Under Clerk of the Parliaments . . . to attend

1 On going into Committee CJ (1905) 261; ibid (1910) 24; on motion in the House, ibid (1911) 7, 442; ibid (1919) 16; ibid (1922) 345; ibid (1924) 55, etc. For an occasion when a motion to appoint the Chairman and the Deputy Chairman was divided and separately decided upon, see CJ (1968–69) 6, HC Deb (1968–69) 772, c 4.
2 Eg Mr Dunnico (Deputy Chairman) CJ (1930–31) 407, Captain Beaumont (Deputy Chairman) CJ (1948–49) 3, Miss Harvie Anderson (Deputy Chairman) CJ (1972–73) 494, Mr Richard Crawshaw (Second Deputy Chairman) CJ (1980–81) 160, and Mr Bryant Godman Irvine (First Deputy Chairman) CJ (1981–82) 380.
3 CJ (1971–72) 39.
4 CJ (1945–46) 55, 278; ibid (1947–48) 43; ibid (1951–52) 147; ibid (1960–61) 127; ibid (1861–62) 105.
5 SO No 85(4).

upon the Commons'.[1] He makes a declaration, under the Promissory Oaths Act 1868, before the Lord Chancellor, on entering upon his office, 'to make true entries, remembrances, and journals of the things done and passed in the House of Commons.' He signs the addresses, votes of thanks, and orders of the House, endorses the bills sent or returned to the Lords, and reads whatever is required to be read in the House. He is addressed by Members, and puts such questions as are necessary for the adjournment of the House, when it is necessitated by the death of the Speaker during the course of a sitting (p 228), or by the absence of the Speaker and the Members competent to act as Deputy Speaker. The Clerk has the custody of all records or other documents,[2] and is responsible for the conduct of the business of the House in the offices within his department. He assists the Speaker and advises Members in regard to questions of order and the proceedings of the House. He holds the appointments of Accounting Officer for the House of Commons and Chairman of the Board of Management.

Clerks Assistant. The Clerk Assistant is appointed by the Crown, under the sign manual, on the recommendation of the Speaker, and is removable only upon an address of the House of Commons.[3] He sits at the Table of the House on the left hand of the Clerk. His duties in the House are to keep the minutes of the proceedings, to receive, and when necessary to put in order, notices of motions, questions and amendments, and to prepare the Notice Paper and Order Book for future sittings (p 207–208). He ranks third in precedence among the permanent officers of the House.

Recently only one Clerk Assistant has been appointed and the duties previously performed by the Second Clerk Assistant are now carried out by the Principal Clerk, Table Office, who as well as acting as head of the Table Office sits at the Table on the Clerk Assistant's left. Principal Clerks from the Journal Office, Committee Office and the Overseas Office also regularly sit at the Table of the House, and from time to time assistance at the Table is also given by Deputy Principal Clerks from other offices within the Department of the Clerk.

Serjeant at Arms. The appointment of the Serjeant at Arms is in the gift of the Queen,[4] under a warrant from the Lord Chamberlain, and by patent under the great seal, 'to attend upon Her Majesty's person when there is no Parliament; and at the time of every Parliament, to attend upon the Speaker of the House of Commons'; but after his appointment he is the servant of the House and may be removed for misconduct.[5] He ranks second in precedence among the permanent offices of the House. He brings to the bar persons in custody to be reprimanded by the Speaker, or persons to be examined as witnesses. He takes strangers into custody who are irregularly admitted into

---

1 2 Hatsell 255; London Gazette, 1 October 1850, 4 May 1886, 18 February 1902, 5 April 1921, 3 August 1937, 7 September 1987, etc, see also CJ (1642–44) 54, 57. For earliest grant of appointment by letters patent, 1 Edw 4, see HC 96 (1856).

2 CJ (1547–1628) 306; ibid (1648–51) 542; ibid (1711–14) 724, etc.

3 The appointment and tenure of two Clerks Assistant is provided for in the House of Commons Offices Act 1856, HC 132 (1856). First mention of the Clerk Assistant, CJ (1640–42) 12; of the second Clerk Assistant, ibid (1802–03) 7.

4 For the extent of formal and informal consultation before an appointment is made, see Prime Minister's statements (HC Deb (1962–63) 666, cc 1155–1157).

5 CJ (1675) 351; Officers and Usages of the House, MS, 1805, p 14. Thus the House places duties on the Serjeant in Standing Orders (Nos 42, 43(4) and 141) and in Resolutions passed at the beginning of each Session.

the House, or who misconduct themselves there; causes the removal of persons directed to withdraw; and gives orders to the door-keepers and others in connection with divisions. It is his duty to keep the gangway at and below the bar clear, and to desire the Members to take their places, and not to stand with their backs to the chair, nor to stand, nor remove from their places, with their hats on, when the House is sitting.[1] For the better execution of these duties he has a chair close to the bar of the House. His ceremonial duties are to attend the Speaker, with the mace, on entering and leaving the House, or going to the House of Lords, or attending Her Majesty with addresses; he introduces, with the mace, peers or judges attending within the bar, and messengers from the Lords, and attends the sheriffs of London at the bar, on presenting petitions.

Out of the House, he is entrusted with the execution of all warrants for the commitment of persons ordered into custody by the House, and for removing them to the Tower or a prison, or retaining them in his own custody. He serves, by his clerk in charge as warrant officer of the House, all orders of the House, upon those whom they concern. He also maintains order in the lobby and passages of the House[2] and may be directed by the Speaker to ascertain and report on the facts when a disturbance has occurred.[3] The police on duty in the House are under his direction. He regulates, under the Speaker, the admission of persons to the Press Gallery and lobby and has control of the arrangements for the admission of strangers. He also has the duty to give notice to all committees when the House proceeds to a division.

The Serjeant is by custom Housekeeper of the House of Commons.[4] In this capacity, acting under the directions of the Speaker, he has charge at all times of all the accommodation assigned to the House of Commons and is in attendance at meetings of the House of Commons (Services) Committee.

The House of Commons (Administration) Act 1978 gives power to the House of Commons Commission to appoint the Deputy Serjeant at Arms; but they have delegated this power to the Speaker (see p 192). The Serjeant at Arms appoints the Assistant and Deputy Assistant Serjeants at Arms.[5]

Speaker's Counsel. The Counsel to Mr Speaker was originally appointed to assist the Speaker generally in any legal questions coming before him and to discharge certain other duties in accordance with the report of the Select Committee of 1838. From 1851, as a result of another select committee of that year, he was regularly associated with the Chairman of Ways and Means to assist in the examination of private bills.[6]

He continues to assist the Chairman in the exercise and performance of his functions in relation to private bills under standing orders relating to private business (see p 827), and in relation to Scottish provisional orders under the Private Legislation Procedure (Scotland) Act 1936 (c 52) (see p 965). He is a member of the Court of Referees by which questions of *locus standi* of

---

1 Officers and Usages of the House, MS, pp 16 ff.
2 Parl Deb (1807) 9, c 1; ibid (1874) 219, c 1303; ibid (1904) 137, c 982.
3 CJ (1946–47) 53, 54; HC Deb (1946–47) 431, cc 2243–2244, 2323.
4 And was so described in s 5 of the House of Commons (Offices) Act 1812 which was repealed in 1978.
5 For a detailed description of the Serjeant at Arms' duties, see Report from the Select Committee on the Palace of Westminster, HC 285 (1964–65) pp 36–37.
6 Clifford ii, 799.

petitioners against private bills are determined[1] (see p 842). He also acts as adviser to the Standing Orders Committee[2] (see p 819) and to the Committee on Unopposed Private Bills[3] (see p 883).

Since 1943 he has advised committees having the function of scrutinizing statutory instruments, now the Joint and Select Committees on Statutory Instruments more commonly known as the 'Scrutiny Committees' (see pp 551–552). In addition he has the general duty of advising the Speaker and Officers of the House on legal questions arising in the course of public business or arising out of the administration of the affairs of the House.

Since 1974 a second Counsel has been appointed to assist the Select Committee on European Legislation (see pp 657, 774); he was formerly designated as 'Second Speaker's Counsel' but this description has now been discontinued.

Though the two Counsel to Mr Speaker generally divide their functions as described above, they are equal in status, and in the absence of one of them, his functions can be performed by the other.

The Clerk of the Crown in Chancery. The Clerk of the Crown in Chancery is appointed by Her Majesty under the Royal Sign Manual.[4] He and his deputy are officers both of the House of Lords[5] and of the House of Commons.[6] It is the responsibility of the Clerk of the Crown to issue writs for parliamentary elections, directed to the returning officers for all constituencies in Great Britain.[7] In the case of a general election the writs must be issued as soon as practicable after the issue of the proclamation summoning the new Parliament.[8] In the case of a by-election the writ is issued out of the Crown Office on a warrant from the Speaker as soon as practicable after the issue of the warrant.[9] If no return is made to a writ in due course the Clerk of the Crown is ordered to attend the House of Commons to explain the omission.[10]

It is the responsibility of the Clerk of the Crown, at the beginning of a Parliament, to enter the name of the member returned for each constituency in a book to be kept by him at the Crown Office and known as the return book.[11] He transmits what is in substance a copy of the book to the Clerk of the House of Commons.[12] In the case of a by-election the Clerk of the Crown

---

1 SO 89.
2 SO 103.
3 SO 132.
4 Great Seal (Offices) Act 1874, s 8.
5 See p 177 above.
6 Townshend *Historical Collections* (London, 1680) p 216; Hatsell ii, 252 n. And see the evidence of the Clerk of the Crown in Chancery to the Commission on the Administrative Departments of the Courts of Justice (1875) C.–1245, 7 November 1873, answers Nos 2345 and 2364.
7 Representation of the People 1983, Sch 1; Parliamentary Elections Rules, r 3. In relation to an election for a constituency in Northern Ireland 'Clerk of the Crown' means the Clerk of the Crown for Northern Ireland, who has to transmit the name of the elected candidate to the Clerk of the Crown in England: Parliamentary Elections Rules, r 51(5).
8 Parliamentary Elections Rules, r 1. And see p 28 above.
9 Parliamentary Elections Rules, r 1. And see Hatsell ii, 245–247 and 252 n, and p 28 above.
10 See p 33 above. And see also p 37 above.
11 Parliamentary Elections Rules, r 52(1).
12 *Poole Case, Hurdle v Waring* (1874) LR 9 CP 435. And see p 231 below.

sends to the Clerk of the House of Commons a certificate of the return to the writ received in the Crown Office.[1]

After an election the returning officer must forward the ballot papers and certain other documents relating to the election to the Clerk of the Crown.[2]

The House of Commons Commission

With the enactment of the House of Commons (Administration) Act in 1978[3] the structure of management of the staff in the House of Commons was altered by the abolition of the Commission for Regulating the Offices of the House of Commons, set up under the House of Commons Offices Act 1812, and the establishment of a new Commission.

Section 1 of the new Act provides that the Commission shall consist of the Speaker, the Leader of the House, a Member of the House nominated by the Leader of the Opposition and three other Members appointed by the House, none of whom may be a Minister of the Crown. Section 2 places upon the Commission the responsibility of appointing all staff in the House Departments (excluding the Clerk, any Clerk Assistant, the Serjeant at Arms and the Speaker's personal staff) and of determining their number, remuneration and other terms and conditions of service and keeping these broadly in line with those in the Home Civil Service. It also provides for staff pensions etc, to be kept in line with the provisions of the Principal Civil Service Pension Scheme. Section 3 of the Act makes financial provisions including the appointment of an Accounting Officer, and section 4 lists the Departments of the House and gives the Commission power to add to or reduce that number. In Schedule 1 the Commission is given authority to delegate to the Speaker, to Heads of Departments and to the Accounting Officer, a substantial part of their functions; but notwithstanding any such delegation, the Commission retains ultimate responsibility for considering representations by trade unions recognised as representing staff of the House and for the conduct of consultations and negotiations with those unions.

With effect from 1 January 1979 the Commission agreed to a number of instruments of delegation, as follows:

(1) The then Clerk of the House was appointed Accounting Officer.
(2) The functions of appointing (i) the Deputy Serjeant at Arms, (ii) the Librarian, (iii) the Deputy Librarian, (iv) the Head of the Administration Department, (v) the Accountant, (vi) the Head of the Establishments Office, (vii) the Editor of the Official Report, (viii) the Deputy Editor of the Official Report and (ix) the Deliverer of the Vote were

---

1 See p 299 below.
2 Parliamentary Elections Rules, r 55. And see ibid rr 56 and 57 for the power to issue orders for the production of documents and for the Clerk of the Crown's duties as to retention and disposal of documents and making certain of them available for public inspection.
3 The Act gave legislative effect to many of the recommendations of the Report to Mr Speaker by the Committee under the Chairmanship of Mr Arthur Bottomley MP, on House of Commons Administration of Session 1974–75 (HC 624).

delegated to the Speaker. The Instrument was amended in Session 1979–80 to add the General Manager of the Refreshment Department to the list of officers whose appointment is made by the Speaker.

(3) The functions of the Commission in regard to staff under section 2(1) of the 1978 Act were delegated to individual Heads of Department in regard to staff in their Departments (except for the appointments referred to above) but subject to the control of the Accounting Officer in relation to expenditure.

(4) A Board of Management was established, consisting of the Heads of the House Departments with the Clerk of the House as chairman and whose functions 'are to exercise co-ordinating authority over the separate Departments in all matters affecting more than one Department and to develop a House of Commons service in which the conditions of service of staff conform with the provisions of section 2(2) of the 1978 Act'. For these purposes the functions of the Commission in regard to staff were delegated to the Board, subject to the control of the Accounting Officer in relation to expenditure.

(5) The functions of the Commission with regard to the complementary grading, pay and pensions, of staff were delegated to the Accounting Officer, except in so far as these were limited by powers delegated to the Board of Management.

(6) The provisions of the 1978 Act, except the power to appoint them and over their tenure of office, were applied to the Speaker's personal staff.

By a further instrument, which came into effect on 30 January 1979, the Speaker's Department was abolished, and the Vote Office, including the Sale Office, was transferred to the Department of the Library. As the result of a later instrument the Refreshment Department was made a Department of the House with effect from 1 April 1980.

Under an instrument dated 21 July 1980 the functions delegated by the Commission other than to Mr Speaker are to be exercised in accordance with any direction given in writing and subject to any restrictions notified in writing by the Commission from time to time.

The Board of Management appointed an Administration Committee, consisting of the Head of the Administration Department, as chairman, and the deputy head of each of the other Departments to give first consideration to most proposals on staff matters, to conduct or oversee consultations and negotiations with the unions representing most grades of staff, and to make recommendations to the Accounting Officer or the Board of Management, as appropriate. The Board of Management and the Administration Committee together form the Official Side of the House of Commons Service Whitley Committee at meetings with the Trade Union Side at least twice a year.

The Secretary of the Commission is provided by the Department of the Clerk of the House. The total number of staff, including part-time staff, employed by the Commission in 1988 was 952, divided among the Speaker's Office and the six Departments as follows: Speaker's Office 11, Clerk's 147, Serjeant's 207, Library 175, Administration 94, Official Report 85, and Refreshment 233.

The Public Accounts Commission

The Public Accounts Commission was established by the National Audit Act 1983. It consists of the Chairman of the Committee of Public Accounts, the Leader of the House of Commons, and seven other Members of the House of Commons, none of whom shall be a Minister of the Crown.

The Commission's functions are (a) to lay before the House the estimate of the expenses of the National Audit Office prepared by the Comptroller and Auditor General, after examining it and making any modifications it thinks fit, having regard to any advice received from the Committee of Public Accounts and the Treasury; (b) to appoint the accounting officer for the National Audit Office;[1] and (c) to appoint an auditor for the National Audit Office. The Commission has power to report to the House from time to time on the exercise of its functions.[2]

By agreement with the Department of Finance and Personnel, Northern Ireland, the Commission undertakes similar duties as regards the Northern Ireland Audit Office on a non-statutory basis, the Government obtaining the Commission's views before laying the estimate or appointing an accounting officer or auditor.[3]

Departments in the House of Commons

Department of the Clerk of the House. The department of the Clerk of the House comprises several separate offices, each in charge of a Principal Clerk. The grading structure of the staff of the department follows closely that of a government department. Recruitment to the higher grades is conducted through the Civil Service Commission and normally by way of direct entry at a level comparable to that of an Administration Trainee through open competition in the same entry examination. The essential function of the Department is to provide the procedural assistance necessary for the orderly conduct of the work of the House, and its Committees, but Clerks also perform a number of administrative tasks and assist in the drafting of reports.

The *Public Bill Office* is responsible for the procedure on public bills and for financial business in the House.[4] The clerks in the Public Bill Office are the clerks to standing and grand committees. The Clerk of Public Bills is also the Clerk of Fees on Private Bills.

The principal duty of the *Journal Office,* in which is included the *Votes and Proceedings Office,* is the compilation of the annual volumes of the Journals together with the sessional and decennial indexes thereto, and the daily Votes and Proceedings.

The *Committee Office* provides the clerks for select Committees. The Clerk of Committees, has a rank equivalent to that of the Clerk Assistant.

The *Private Bill Office* assists in the conduct of private bill legislation in all its stages, supplies the clerks for private bill committees, and a clerk from the

---

1 The Comptroller and Auditor General holds the appointment.
2 Four reports have so far been made: HC (1983–84) 290, 455, (1985–86) 540, (1987–88) 604.
3 See HC (1987–88) 604, paras 15–21.
4 HC (1937) 149, Evidence Qs 65, 766–927.

Private Bill Office is attached as secretary to the Chairman of Ways and Means. The Clerk of Private Bills is an Examiner of Petitions for Private Bills.

The *Table Office* assists the Clerks at the Table in the preparation of the Order Paper, the Notice Paper and the Order Book, and has the particular function of ensuring that the parliamentary questions which appear on the Notice Paper are in compliance with the rules of the House.

The *Overseas Office* organises parliamentary courses for clerks from overseas, advises other overseas visitors and those attending courses at the Civil Service College on parliamentary practice and procedure, assists with the drafting of standing orders of Commonwealth legislatures, gives such legislatures assistance on matters of procedure, and has duties in connection with Commonwealth parliamentary conferences and seminars and international parliamentary assemblies. It supplies clerks to accompany United Kingdom delegations to the Assemblies of the Council of Europe and Western European Union and the North Atlantic Assembly (see pp 777– 785). It also provides the Clerks and other staff of the European Legislation Committee (see p 657).

There is flexibility in the arrangements made for staffing the various offices so that at times of pressure in one office, staff from other offices assist.

The names of Members voting in divisions in the House are recorded by clerks from the various offices.

There is also an *Internal Auditor*, who works directly to the Clerk of the House (see also p 197):

Department of the Serjeant at Arms. The Serjeant is assisted by a *Deputy Serjeant at Arms* who, in addition to deputizing for him, co-ordinates the work of the Department, is a member of the Administration Committee and is responsible for matters affecting the Parliamentary Press Gallery; by an *Assistant Serjeant* who has responsibility for the Chamber and Committee rooms; and by two *Deputy Assistant Serjeants* who are concerned with the housekeeping aspects of the Serjeants' duties.

Department of the Library. The Library is an information and research department for all Members of Parliament and the Librarian directs the Commons' Library in close consultation, as regards policy matters, with the Library Sub-Committee of the Select Committee on House of Commons (Services) (see p 657). The Librarian, Deputy Librarian and Deliverer of the Vote are appointed by the Speaker; all other staff in the Department are appointed by the Librarian under powers delegated by the House of Commons Commission. The Librarian is a member of the Board of Management and the Deputy Librarian is a member of the Administration Committee (see p 193). Other officers in the Department include the two Assistant Librarians in charge of the Parliamentary and Research Divisions respectively. Candidates for Library Clerkships are recruited through the Civil Service Commission by a series of open competitive interviews; all other grades of staff are recruited by House of Commons Selection Boards.

The *Parliamentary (or Library) Division* is responsible for the intake, processing and arrangement of the main collections of books, pamphlets, newspapers and periodicals; for the preservation and indexing of all British

Parliamentary Papers and of many other official publications, domestic and foreign; and for the maintenance of specialised indexing and press cuttings services. Staff provide a reference and information service to Members including, in the International Affairs Section, information on European Communities and foreign affairs. The Computer and Technical Services Section creates the database for the Library's Parliamentary On Line Information system [POLIS] and co-ordinates the Department's use of computer applications. The Public Information Office, which includes the Branch Library and is located in the Norman Shaw (North) building, answers enquiries on Parliament from outside bodies and the general public, and compiles the Weekly and Sessional Information Bulletins which are published by HM Stationery Office. The Library's Education Officer provides a parliamentary educational service for schools.

The *Research Division* is organised in five sections—Economic Affairs, Education and Social Services, Home Affairs, Science and Environment, and Statistics. Staff undertake research for individual Members; assist certain select committees and their clerks; and prepare for general use by Members annotated bibliographies (reference sheets), factual background papers and a series of shorter research notes on topics of current concern to Parliament. Specialist research staff also have access to the Treasury economic model on Members' behalf.

The Speaker has ruled that the Library should make available to Members all documents placed in the Library which relate to their work in the House, including those marked confidential.[1]

The Library also contains a category of documents known as 'deposited papers'. These are documents not published as Command or House of Commons Papers which, since 1832, have been deposited in the Library at the behest of the Speaker or of Ministers, for the use of Members. Some of these documents are confidential. Private Members may not deposit documents in the Library in this way.[2]

The *Vote Office* has formed a part of the Library Department since January 1979 and as such comes under the administrative control of the Librarian. Under the Deliverer of the Vote, it is responsible for the provision and distribution of all parliamentary and European Communities papers required by Members and Officers of the House of Commons.

During 1991 it is planned to transfer Library offices in the Norman Shaw buildings and research offices in the Palace to purpose-designed accommodation in the Derby Gate building off Parliament Street. The Members' Library will remain in its present location.

There is a separate House of Lords Library (see p 177).

Administration Department. This Department was set up on 1 January 1968. The Head of the Department is appointed by the Speaker and is responsible for making all appointments to the Department except those of Accountant and Head of the Establishments Office, both of whom are also appointed by the Speaker. He is Chairman of the Administration Committee of the Board of Management and of the General Purposes

1 HC Deb (1968–69) 780, c 491–492.
2 HC Deb (1985–86) 90, c 313–314.

Sub-Committee of the House of Commons (Services) Whitley Committee. The Department is divided into two main Offices.

The *Fees Office* is headed by the Accountant, who is assisted by the Deputy Accountant, the Senior Assistant Accountant and four Assistant Accountants. The Office is responsible for estimating, paying and accounting for the expenditure voted under the estimates for Members' salaries, allowances, pensions, etc, financial assistance to opposition parties and the Members' Fund grant in aid, and for House of Commons Commission expenditure on administration, which includes salaries and retired allowances of the staff of all Offices and Departments of the House, general expenses and police services, and receipts in respect of fees on Private Bills, etc. It also administers various facilities for individual Members and provides the secretaries of the Parliamentary Contributory Pension Fund and the Members' Fund.

The *Establishments Office* assists all Offices and Departments of the House with staff recruitment and administration and is responsible for such matters as central records, rates of pay, calculation of pensions, and consultation with staff representatives. The Head of the Office acts as Secretary to the Board of Management and adviser to the Board's Administration Committee, to which the Establishment Office provides the secretary. Together with the Deputy Head they are responsible for acting as secretaries to the House of Commons Service Whitley Committee and its sub-committees, and for conducting other consultations and negotiations with the Trade Union Side of the Whitley Committee and, where appropriate, with any of the five trade unions which together represent the great majority of the staff of the House.

The Administration Department also contains the *Computer Officer* (see p 178) and the *Welfare Officer*, both of whom provide a service to the House of Lords as well as to the House of Commons. The *Internal Auditor* and the *Staff Inspector* are located in the Department for administrative purposes but they work, respectively, to the Clerk of the House (see p 195) and to the Speaker (see p 198).

Department of the Official Report. The Official Report was established as a separate Department of the House on 1 January 1979 by section 4(2) of the House of Commons (Administration) Act 1978. The Editor and Deputy Editor are appointed by the Speaker; all other staff in the Department are appointed by the Editor. Other Officers include four Principal Assistant Editors and four Senior Assistant Editors. The Editor is responsible for producing a verbatim report of proceedings in the House and in Standing Committees and for the publication in the Official Report of written answers to parliamentary Questions. (See also pp 211–212).

Refreshment Department. In December 1979, following a recommendation by the Select Committee on House of Commons (Services) of Session 1978–79 that the Refreshment Department should become a full Department of the House with its own administrative head, the House of Commons Commission exercised its powers under section 4(3) of the House of Commons (Administration) Act 1978 to reconstitute the Department as a Department of the House responsible, through its head, to the Commission with effect from 1 April 1980. Consequently, from that day the executive functions of the Catering Sub-Committee of the Services Committee, exercised on the authority of the Speaker, ceased, though it continues in an advisory capacity, and is charged with the responsibility of considering the organisation of and services in the Refreshment Department (see p 657).

The Speaker's personal staff. The Speaker has a personal staff who are appointed by him and not by the House of Commons Commission.[1] It consists of: the *Speaker's Secretary* who is in charge of the Speaker's Office and, besides assisting the Speaker in the House, deals with his social and official relations with Members and outside bodies and persons; the two *Speaker's Counsel* (see p 190); the *Speaker's Chaplain* (an office instituted in 1659), who reads prayers at the beginning of every sitting; and two *Train-bearers* (a Trainbearer attends to the Speaker on all ceremonial occasions including entering and leaving the House). There is also a *Staff Inspector*, who advises the House authorities on staffing matters, and who works directly to the Speaker (see also p 197).

3. OTHER STATUTORY OFFICERS

The Comptroller and Auditor General

The Comptroller General of the receipt and issue of Her Majesty's Exchequer and Auditor General of Public Accounts is appointed by letters patent under the Exchequer and Audit Department Act 1866. By section 1 of the National Audit Act 1983, Her Majesty's power of appointment is exercisable on an address presented by the House of Commons, and no motion shall be made for such an address except by the Prime Minister[2] acting with the agreement of the Chairman of the Committee of Public Accounts.[3] The Comptroller and Auditor General's salary is a charge on the Consolidated Fund and he is removable from office only on an address from the two Houses.

He heads the National Audit Office (formerly the Exchequer and Audit Department) and assists the House of Commons by controlling the issue of money granted by Parliament from the Exchequer on demand of the Treasury and by auditing the accounts of government departments and a wide range of public sector bodies on behalf of the House. His reports on the Appropriation Accounts (see p 687) and his examinations of economy, effectiveness and efficiency under Part II of the National Audit Act 1983 form the basis of the work of the Committee of Public Accounts (see p 660).

Under section 1(2) of the Act, he is an officer of the House of Commons, but he, and the National Audit Office, are excluded from the control of the House of Commons Commission. The Public Accounts Commission has various duties with respect to the National Audit Office (see p 194).

There is also a Comptroller and Auditor General for Northern Ireland, who heads the Northern Ireland Audit Office, established by the Audit (Northern Ireland) Order 1987. He, too, is accorded the status of an officer of the House of Commons.[4]

---

1 See the House of Commons (Administration) Act 1978 (c 36, s 2).
2 No other Minister may act for the Prime Minister, in contrast to the usual practice.
3 See HC Deb (1987–88) 124, cc 1185–1205.
4 See Committee of Public Accounts, 2nd Report, HC (1986–87) 116, para 3.

The Parliamentary Commissioner for Administration

The Parliamentary Commissioner for Administration, an independent statutory officer, is appointed by letters patent under the Parliamentary Commissioner Act 1967, and is removable only on an address from the two Houses.

His function is to investigate complaints referred to him by Members of the House of Commons from members of the public who claim to have sustained injustice in consequence of maladministration in connection with actions taken by or on behalf of government departments or specific non-departmental public bodies under section 2 of the Parliamentary and Health Service Commissioners Act 1987. His reports to Parliament under section 10(3) and 10(4) of the Parliamentary Commissioner Act form a major part of the work of the Select Committee on the Parliamentary Commissioner for Administration (see p 659). Like the Comptroller and Auditor General, he is accorded the privileges of an officer of the House.

4. PARTY MACHINERY IN PARLIAMENT

In the same way as the seating of Members in the House of Commons is arranged on the basis of a single clear-cut division between Government and Opposition, many other matters, and in particular the arrangement and conduct of business, are based on this principle. The normal condition for the working of this arrangement is the division of the House between two major parties, but the fact that there may be several separately organized parties, supporting or opposing the Government, while it complicates the working of these arrangements, does not destroy the broad principle.

The predominant share of the Government in controlling and arranging the time and business of the House is now recognized by the standing orders of the House of Commons. But the fact that the Government is supported by a party or combination of parties and opposed by another party or combination of parties, and that the machinery evolved by these parties performs important functions in the working of procedure is still largely disregarded by the standing orders.

Changes in procedure effected by party system

The practice or ancient usage of the House of Commons was developed during a period when the relation between the Commons and the Government was that between a fairly homogeneous body with a developed corporate sense and an external and not always friendly authority.

The results of this condition, which continued to affect procedure long after the change to Cabinet government had been made, were:

(1) All Members were treated as on the same footing in respect of the business introduced by them, precedence between their orders and motions being dependent on the order in which they had been handed in or passed a particular stage, and business introduced by the Government being long refused any special priority.

(2) The principle on which time was arranged was a division of the week between motion days and order days, ie days on which new business and business which had made some progress, respectively, were taken.

(3) In order to prevent business being passed through so rapidly as to take possible opponents by surprise, Members had to rely upon their own powers of attention. The numbers of stages and questions on bills and other business were accordingly multiplied to what now seems an inordinate extent.

As government came to be associated with a party organization inside the House opposed by another party, all this changed. The control of the time of the House and the arrangement of business came to be dependent on the will of the Government and the old arrangement of notice days and order days practically disappeared. Similarly the multiplication of stages and questions on business became unnecessary, even in the interests of Members who opposed such business, and these were drastically reduced. The party organizations undertook the duty of watching the progress of business, and informed Members in advance when the taking of a decision was to be expected.

The Official Opposition

The importance of the Opposition in the system of parliamentary government has long received practical recognition in the procedure of Parliament. Even before the first Reform Act the phrase 'His Majesty's Opposition' had been coined by John Cam Hobhouse.[1] In 1937 statutory recognition was accorded through the grant of a salary to the Leader of the Opposition.[2] The prevalence (on the whole) of the two-party system has usually obviated any uncertainty as to which party has the right to be called the 'Official Opposition'; it is the largest minority party which is prepared, in the event of the resignation of the Government, to assume office.[3] The Leader of the Opposition and some of his principal colleagues in both Houses form a group, popularly known as 'the Shadow Cabinet', each member of which is given a particular range of activities on which it is his task to direct criticism of the government's policy and administration and to outline alternative policies. Since the strength of modern party discipline makes a Ministry largely invulnerable to direct attack in the House of Commons, the criticism of the Opposition is primarily directed towards the electorate, with a view to the next election, or with the aim of influencing government policy through the pressure of public opinion. The floor of the House of Commons provides the Opposition with their main instrument for this purpose. Accordingly, the Opposition has acquired the right to exercise the initiative in selecting the subject of debate on a certain number of days in each session[4] and on such occasions as the debate on the address in reply to the Queen's Speech or from time to time by putting down motions of censure. The Leader of the Opposition is by custom accorded certain peculiar rights in asking questions of Ministers (see p 297), and members of the Shadow Cabinet and other official Opposition spokesmen are also given some precedence in asking questions and in debate.

1 Porritt *The Unreformed House of Commons* vol I, p 510.
2 Ministers of the Crown Act 1937, s 5; see p 18.
3 The Speaker's decision on the identity of the Leader of the Opposition is final (Ministerial and other Salaries Act 1975, s 2(2)).
4 Of the 20 Opposition days, 17 are at the disposal of the Leader of the Opposition and 3 at the disposal of the leader of the second largest opposition party (SO No 13(2)); see also p 261.

Leader of the House of Commons

The member of the Government who is primarily responsible to the Prime Minister for the arrrangements of Government business in the House of Commons is known as the Leader of the House. He controls the arrangement of business in that House while the programme and details are settled by the Government Chief Whip (see below).

Each week after a programme of business has been arranged the Leader of the House states the business for the following week in answer to a question put to him at the end of Questions on Thursdays normally by the Leader of the Opposition, and, whenever necessary, makes further business statements from time to time. He may also move procedural motions relating to the business of the House.

In the absence of the Prime Minister the Leader expresses the sense of the House on formal occasions, such as in moving motions of thanks or congratulation; and at all times, being responsible to the House as a whole, he 'advises the House in every difficulty as it arises'.[1]

The title does not appear to have become established until about the middle of the nineteenth century[2] although the institution is much older. The Leadership of the House is not a statutory office nor is the Leader formally appointed by the Crown; for these reasons the post has usually been held together with another office. Until 1942 the Prime Minister, if a Minister of the House of Commons, generally also acted as Leader of the House, although the day-to-day duties were frequently carried out after1922 by an appointed deputy Leader. Since 1942 it has been the regular practice to have a separate Leader of the House, and there have also been instances of the appointment of a deputy Leader of the House.[3]

Under section 1 of the House of Commons (Administration) Act 1978 the Leader of the House of Commons being 'the Minister of the Crown for the time being nominated as such by the Prime Minister' is appointed a member of the House of Commons Commission.

Constitution and financing of party machinery

Inside the House of Commons each party has a fairly elaborate organisation, presided over by officials who are Members of the House and staffed by subordinate officials who are not Members. The officers or Whips of the party in office consist of the Chief Whip who holds the official position of Parliamentary or Patronage Secretary to the Treasury, three officers of the Household, and five Lords of the Treasury, with the addition of up to six Members who act as Assistant Whips; all these Whips receive salaries.[4] All Government Whips rank as Ministers of the Crown. One of the Lords of the Treasury is usually appointed Deputy Chief Whip.

The Whips of a party in opposition consist usually of the survivors of those who were Whips when it was in office together with as many other members as may be selected for the purpose. Since 1965 the Chief Opposition Whip, and since 1972 not more than two Assistant Opposition Whips, have been

---

1 W E Gladstone *Gleanings* vol I, p 241.
2 *Redlich*, vol I, p 120.
3 See, for example, HC Deb (1967–68) 763, c 77.
4 Ministerial and other Salaries Act 1975, s 1(1)(a) and Sch 1.

paid a salary out of the Consolidated Fund.[1] The Government Whips and the Whips of the official opposition and of the second opposition party (when there is more than one party in opposition) have offices as near the Chamber as may be.

Opposition parties are given financial assistance from public funds in respect of their parliamentary duties. The expenses for which assistance is claimed must have been incurred exclusively in the Party's parliamentary business. Claims are made to the Accounting Officer. Financial assistance is paid out of the House of Commons: Members' Salaries etc vote following a resolution of the House.[2]

Duties of Whips

The efficient and smooth running of the parliamentary machine depends largely upon the Whips. Certain duties are common to Whips of all parties, but by far the most important duties devolve upon the Government Chief Whip. He is concerned with mapping out the time of the session; for applying in detail the Government's programme of business; for estimating the time likely to be required for each item, and for arranging the business of the individual sitting. In drawing up the programme he is limited to a certain extent by the standing orders, which allot a modicum of time to private Members; and by statute law or standing orders, which require, or may require, certain business to be completed by specified dates; as well as by certain conventions which make it obligatory upon him to consult the Whips of opposition parties and even to put down items of their selection (see pp 259–260). In carrying out his duties, he is directly responsible to the Prime Minister and Leader of the House. It is also part of his duties to advise the Government on parliamentary business and procedure, and to maintain a close liaison with Ministers in regard to parliamentary business which affects their departments. He and the Chief Whip of the largest opposition party constitute the 'usual channels', through which consultations are held with other parties and Members about business arrangements and other matters of concern to the House.

Certain duties are common to Whips of all parties. They keep their Members supplied with information about the business of the House, secure the attendance of Members, arrange for their Members who are unable to attend divisions to 'pair' with Members of the opposite side of the House so that their votes may be neutralised and not lost, and suggest Members to serve on standing and select committees. They also act as intermediaries between the leaders and the rank and file of their parties in order to keep each informed of the views of the other.

In the Lords

As in the House of Commons the conduct of business in the House of Lords is influenced by the existence of organized Government and Opposition

---

1 Ibid s 1(1)(b) and Sch 2.
2 These payments are made at a scale of £2,550 for every seat won by each party at the preceding General Election, plus £5.10 for every 200 votes then cast for it. To qualify for such assistance a party is required either to have gained two or more seats at the General Election or, if only one seat has been won, to have received at least 150,000 votes (Votes and Proceedings 21 June 1988). For the terms of the original Resolution, see CJ (1974–75) 310.

parties. The positions of Leader of the House and Leader of the Opposition have developed for reasons which have already been described in relation to the House of Commons. The conduct of government business in the Lords is entrusted to the Leader of the House, who is appointed by the Prime Minister and is a member of the Cabinet. Because the Speaker of the Lords has no effective powers, the Leader of the House has an additional function, which is to advise the House on matters of procedure and to draw attention to transgressions of order.[1] He also expresses the sense of the House on formal occasions, such as motions of thanks or congratulation. He, and his private office, are available to assist and advise all Lords irrespective of party. It is usual for another Minister to be appointed Deputy Leader of the House. The Leader of the Opposition, who has functions similar to the corresponding figure in the House of Commons, has since 1965 enjoyed a statutory salary which is paid out of the Consolidated Fund.[2]

Whips are also appointed by the parties in the House of Lords. The Government Whips, who hold salaried offices as Members of the Royal Household, are the Captain of the Gentlemen-at-Arms (Government Chief Whip), the Captain of the Yeoman of the Guard (Deputy Government Chief Whip) and 5 Lords-in-Waiting. Since 1965 the Opposition Chief Whip has been paid a statutory salary out of the Consolidated Fund.[3]

5. PARLIAMENTARY PAPERS AND PUBLICATIONS

PAPERS DEALING WITH DAILY BUSINESS OF THE TWO HOUSES

House of Lords

Minutes of Proceedings of the House of Lords. During the course of each sitting the Clerk Assistant keeps at the Table a manuscript record of the business of the House known as the Minutes of Proceedings. These minutes are entered on a series of paper sheets which, together with certain other items such as Messages from the Commons, form a continuation of the ancient series of 'Minute Books'.

In principle the Minutes of Proceedings record what is done or deemed to be done as opposed to what is said in the House. They follow the order of business as it is taken in the House but they also include certain formal entries relating to judicial business, parliamentary papers and private bills which do not record any real occurrences in the House. Unstarred questions are briefly recorded but starred questions are not recorded.

Since the session of 1825[4] the Minutes have been circulated in printed form. The printed Minutes, which are issued over the name of the Clerk of the Parliaments, are based upon the manuscript minutes but are in some

---

1 HL Deb (1987–88) 493, c 937.
2 Ministerial and other Salaries Act 1975, s 1(1)(b) and Sch 2. S 2(1) defines the Leader of the Opposition in the Lords; s 2(3) provides that the Lord Chancellor's decision on which Lord is Leader of the Opposition is final. See p 11 above.
3 Ibid s 1(1)(b) and Sch 2. See p 11 above.
4 Following a resolution of the House of 9 June 1824 (LJ (1824) 369).

respects more detailed. The printed version also comprises what is colloquially known as the 'second half' containing notices of future business so
far as appointed, a list of motions for which no day has been named,
questions for written answer, a list of bills in progress through the House and
similar lists for General Synod Measures, instruments subject to affirmative
resolution and special procedure orders and a 'Committee Sheet' showing
the times and places of committee meetings. Amendments to bills are not
included but are issued as separate papers. This whole bundle of papers,
known ordinarily as 'the Minute', is printed on green paper. The business for
the next sitting is also separately printed as a white Order Paper.

Various supplementary papers and notices are from time to time circulated with the Minute. These include a weekly list of the meetings of select
committees (see p 574) and their sub-committees and, during recesses, a
weekly list of statutory instruments deposited under Standing Order No 67.
When necessary, notices concerning changes in business and other matters
of interest to the House are also circulated.

The Journals of the House of Lords. Journals of the proceedings of the
House of Lords are known to have been kept as early as 1461.[1] The earliest
to survive in the custody of the House record the proceedings of the session
of 1510. The series is complete from that time with the exception of some
gaps in the sixteenth century. The Journals were originally kept in manuscript. The process of printing them began in 1767[2] and since 1830 they have
been printed as soon as possible after the conclusion of the session whose
proceedings they record.

The Journals are now compiled from the Minutes of Proceedings. They
differ from the Minutes in including a daily record of the Lords present, lists
of those voting in divisions and an index.

On occasion the House orders the texts of documents which would not
otherwise be set out in full to be entered in the Journals. Such orders are
usually made in respect of communications from foreign states, received by
the Lord Chancellor and communicated by him to the House[3] although they
have been made in respect of other documents.[4]

Where entries in the Journals have been found to be incorrect, orders
have been made for them to be corrected.[5]

When the Journals are required as evidence, a party may have a copy or
extract, authenticated by the signature of the Clerk of the Parliaments, and,
if necessary, the Lords have allowed an officer of their House to attend a
trial with the original Journal. By the Evidence Act 1845, section 3 (which

---

1 See Dunham *The Fane Fragment of the 1461 Lords Journal* (1935).
2 LJ (1765–67) 509; the present practice is founded on a resolution of 1824 (LJ (1824) 369).
3 For the most recent examples, see LJ (1943–44) 20 (Chinese Mission); ibid 148 (Invitation to
 US Congress); ibid (1945–46) 48 (Unconditional Surrender of Japan; Death of President
 Roosevelt); ibid (1951–52) 82, 90 (Death of King George VI); ibid (1954–55) 157 (Austrian
 Republic); ibid (1963–64) 89 (Death of President Kennedy).
4 See Report under Special Commission Act 1888 (LJ (1890) 90).
5 LJ (1843) 107; ibid (1904) 110, 116; ibid (1905) 105; ibid (1917–18) 136.

does not extend to Scotland) it is enacted that all copies of the Journals of either House, purporting to be printed by the printers of either House of Parliament, are to be admitted as evidence by all courts, and others, without proof being given that such copies were so printed.

House of Commons

The Vote. Certain Papers known as the Vote may be delivered to Members' residences[1] in the morning of each day after that on which the House has sat. The most important of the papers which make up the Vote are set out in the following paragraphs.

The *Votes and Proceedings* is a record of the proceedings of the House on the previous day published under a sessional order first passed in 1680, and passed regularly on the first day of the session since 1689. The entries are compiled on the responsibility of the Clerk of the House by the Votes and Proceedings Office mainly from the entries in the minute books of the Clerks at the Table, and after 'being first perused by Mr Speaker', are printed and circulated. The Votes and Proceedings record all that is, or is deemed to be, *done* by the House, but they ignore everything that is *said* unless it is especially ordered to be entered (see p 208). As will be stated below there are a number of formal orders on which no question is put to the House, but as such orders have the same force as those which the House is actually asked to decide, they are recorded in the same way. It is important to bear this in mind as otherwise certain parts of the day's Votes and Proceedings will not be understood.

A typical day's Votes and Proceedings records, among the early entries, the unopposed Private Business which is actually done in the House, sometimes preceded by reports from the Examiners which are recorded as having been received at the Table.

There follows (for no reference is made to Questions, as they are not acts of the House) an entry that various papers have been presented to the House. The full list appears in an appendix at the end of the Votes and Proceedings, and most reports from select committees including those of the Committee of Selection are similarly dealt with. Since for many years reports and papers have not been presented by Members in person to the House, they can be received at any time during the sitting, but they are recorded in the Votes and Proceedings as having been received before the House entered upon the business of the day.

Messages from the Lords which are generally not noticed in the House also appear in the Votes and Proceedings at this point and any other formal business such as the reviving of a 'dropped' order, an order for considering and printing Lords amendments, or the first reading of a Lords bill. Then follow any orders made by the House 'at the commencement of public business' (see p 307).

As regards the business of the day, the record in the Votes and Proceedings is, broadly speaking, an account of what actually takes place in the House, but there are, however, a few points which may be noticed.

---

1 Delivery is undertaken by messenger within a three-mile radius of the House of Commons. For greater distances dispatch by post takes the place of delivery by hand.

If motions and the questions consequent thereon are agreed to without a division and without any other intermediate proceeding arising, only the resulting decision of the House is recorded. Amendments to bills in committee or on report which are made without a division or interruption are not set out, as the entry is merely 'Amendment(s) [an, another, or other] (No(s)—) made (to the bill).' The text of the amendments can be found on the Amendment paper to public bills set down for consideration on the current day in committee of the whole House or on report.[1] The fact that a debate has occurred is not noticed unless a motion is made for the adjournment of the debate, or the debate stands adjourned at the moment of interruption or a Member claims to move the closure of the debate. Petitions can be presented after Prayers on Fridays and before the half-hour adjournment on other days. Not all petitions are presented formally in the House and thus an entry may be made in the Votes and Proceedings while no record appears in the Official Report.

On 9 February 1961 many Members wished to challenge the record in the Votes and Proceedings of the previous evening's proceedings. To implement such a challenge a substantive motion requiring notice is necessary and for this reason nothing could be done that day. A motion to expunge certain entries from the Journal was moved and rejected on a division on 13 February.[2]

The *Private Business* paper, a blue sheet, deals with matters relating to private and provisional order bills and special procedure orders, and the standing orders relating to private business. The first part lists the stages of private bills and motions relating to them for the current day. The second part contains notices with regard to bills to be taken on future days, and memoranda of various kinds, given by the parliamentary agents acting on behalf of the promoters of, or petitioners against, private bills, etc.

The *Order Paper* (printed on white paper) lists the business to be considered by the House in the course of the day. An item which requires notice but is omitted from this paper cannot be taken. The items which this paper contains are arranged under the following headings:

(1) Private Business (the part of the private business paper (see above) which relates to the business to be taken in the House on the current day).
(2) Unopposed returns.
(3) Questions for oral answer ('Starred' Questions).
(4) A heading—'at the commencement of Public Business'—which comprises:
    (a) notices of public bills which it is intended to present to the House under Standing Order No 58(1); and
    (b) notices of certain motions to be moved either at this time or as prescribed by Standing Order No 14, such as motions moved by the Government relative to the business of the House, and motions for leave to bring in bills or nominate select committees under Standing Order No 19.

---

1 The text of an Amendment which has not been numbered (eg a manuscript Amendment) is, however, set out in full.
2 CJ (1960–61) 101–102.

(5) The 'Orders of the Day and Notices of Motions'—the heading which comprises all the items which are set down for consideration in the House on the current day. Government orders are marked with an asterisk. If there is a contingent motion to an order the contingent motion is printed immediately below it; amendments to bills which stand on the orders of the day for consideration in committees or on report, or amendments to be proposed to Lords Amendments are printed separately in the Supplement to the Votes (see below), a reference to which is placed immediately below the order concerned. In appropriate cases, an italicised note gives details of the proposed subject of debate, or of relevant documents, or of a relevant standing order, beneath the item of business concerned.[1]

(6) Notices of the various committees on public matters which are meeting that day, together with time and place of meeting. When such meetings are to take place in public the list of those due to give evidence is normally published, but it is not the practice to publish the names of witnesses who are to be examined in private.[2]

(7) Questions not for oral answer.

(8) 'Remaining Orders of the Day and Notices of Motions'. This comprises all the items which have been set down for consideration on the current day, but of which the government has not given notice of any intention to proceed with in the House on that particular day.[3] Most of these orders of the day and notices of motions are government business, so that the 'remaining orders' provide a rough guide as to the state of the government's business and of the business awaiting discussion in the House in the immediate future.

The *Supplement to the Votes* comprises amendments to public bills to be taken on the current day in committee of the whole House, in standing committees or in the House upon Report which are printed on white paper, and notices of amendments to public bills given in respect of bills to be taken on a future day in committee of the whole House, in standing committees or in the House upon report. The latter are printed on blue paper.

The *Proceedings of Standing Committees* which sat on the previous day take the form of amendment papers showing the proceedings (if any) on each amendment, new clause and new schedule, and clauses and schedules agreed to or disagreed to. This is a white paper.

Division Lists give the names of Members voting in divisions in the House. These lists are printed on white paper.

A *Notice Paper*, containing all notices of questions and motions (and amendments thereto) given the previous day, is printed daily on blue paper. The Notice Paper circulated on Saturday and during an adjournment,

---

1 It has been ruled that an italicised note drawing attention to a relevant Select Committee report does not affect the scope of debate, which continues to depend on the relevant motion (HC Deb (1987–88) 122, cc 1326–1328).
2 HC Deb (1979–80) 988, c 1769–1771.
3 Although, for the sake of convenience, the 'remaining orders' have since 1966 been printed on a sheet not consecutive with that day's proposed business, the Speaker made it clear in his statement explaining the change in printing arrangements that 'procedurally it would still be possible, as it always has been, to take a non-effective order by reading through the non-effective orders on the sheet which is published separately': HC Deb (1966–67) 734, c 41; and see CJ (1973–74) 156–157.

however, differs from those circulated on the other days of the week in arranging all notices under their respective days in a complete programme, so far as known, of future business. This paper is known as the blue Order Book.

The Order Book. The Order Book[1] is available each day during the afternoon. It serves as a programme, so far as notified, of the future business of the session, showing for each day any questions, motions, and orders (with their contingent motions) set down for that day, whether by order of the House or by notice given. It differs from the blue Order Book, to which reference is made in the preceding paragraph, in that it is printed on white paper and contains no material relating to early day motions.

The Journal. The Commons' Journal forms the permanent official record of the proceedings of the House. It is published annually, and one volume usually contains the record of one session, though if there should be two sessions comprised within one year (as in 1922 and 1948) the second session is included in the same volume.

The first extant Journal of the House of Commons records the Parliament of 1547. Thereafter—bearing in mind that no official record at all survives for the Parliaments between 1584 and 1601, and that some of the Elizabethan and Jacobean 'Journals' which do exist are probably drafts and not the finished version (if a perfected copy was ever made)—the series is nearly complete to the present day.

The Journal is compiled from the minute books of the Clerks at the Table by the Journal Office. As a result of a revision carried out in October 1969, it is almost identical in form with the Votes and Proceedings.

When the Speaker expresses on behalf of the House its censure, reprimand or admonition, his words are entered, either with or without the order of the House, in the Votes and in the Journal. Such entries have also been made on other occasions.

An Address delivered from the Chair, made on the request of the Prime Minister at the close of a personal explanation relating to the disorder which had arisen in committee on a previous day, was entered in the Journal, on the motion of the Prime Minister.[2] An order of the House for an entry in the Journal has been made in the case of the admonition of a Member, and the reprimand of a stranger and a Member.[3]

The Speaker's words addressed to the House with reference to the circumstances under which he had adjourned the House on the previous day owing to the prevalence of grave disorder, and his words acknowledging a resolution of the House thanking him for his services in presiding over the electoral reform conference, uttered as soon as the resolution was agreed to, were entered upon the Journal without an order of the House.[4]

---

1 The daily printing of this notice paper, commonly called the 'Order Book', was begun in 1856, and its weekly circulation to members dates from February 1865, Parl Deb (1865) 177, c 323.
2 CJ (1893–94) 477.
3 CJ (1929–30) 503; ibid (1947–48) 22, 23.
4 CJ (1912–13) 409; ibid (1917–18) 56, HC Deb (1917) 92, c 569.

The Speaker's words when he turned on the light in the clock tower after an interval of five and a half years of war were entered by order of the House.[1]

An extract from the records of the Assemblée Nationale of France describing its proceedings on the occasion of a visit by the Speaker of the House of Commons was ordered to be entered in the Journal.[2]

The Speaker's communication to the House, following his visit to Australia on the occasion of the presentation of a Vice-Regal Chair to the Parliament of that Commonwealth, marking the bicentenary of first European settlement and the opening of a new Parliament House, was set out in the Journal.[3]

Entries in the Journal and the Clerks' Minute Books have occasionally been ordered to be expunged.[4]

When the resolution of 17 February 1769, affirming the incapacity of Wilkes, was ordered to be expunged on 3 May 1782, 'The same was expunged by the Clerk, at the Table, accordingly'[5] and the entry was erased in the manuscript Journal of that day; but the printed Journal, though reprinted since that time, still contains the resolution.

On 16 May 1833 a motion was made by Mr Cobbett, impugning the conduct of Sir Robert Peel. Lord Althorp moved 'That the resolution which has been moved be not entered in the minutes', but the Speaker put the question thus, 'That the proceedings be expunged' on the ground that the minutes had already been entered in the Clerk's book. The question thus put was carried by 295 to 4, and no entry of the motion or other proceedings was made in the Votes and Proceedings.[6]

On 6 March 1855 a motion was made relative to the appointment of a recorder for Brighton; and on proceeding to a division the mover was left alone, the Member who had seconded his motion pro forma declining to vote with him. A Member immediately rose and moved that the motion should not be entered in the Votes and Proceedings. This was agreed to by all the Members except the mover of the original motion. Accordingly, there is no entry of either motion in the Votes and Proceedings.[7]

The House on 27 January 1891 resolved that the resolutions of 22 June 1880,[8] which debarred Mr Bradlaugh from taking the oath of affirmation, be expunged from the Journals; and accordingly the Clerk passed a red line through that resolution in the volumes preserved in the library and Journal Office of the House, and noted on the margin of the page that the paragraph was expunged pursuant to the resolution of the House.[9] The Clerk also addressed letters to the librarians of the British Library, the Universities of Oxford, Cambridge, and Dublin, and what is now the National Library of Scotland requesting them to note the proceeding on the copies of the Journal in their libraries.

---

1 CJ (1944–45) 106.
2 CJ (1947–48) 71.
3 Votes and Proceedings (1987–88) p 1127.
4 CJ (1644–46) 397, etc; ibid (1646–48) 197; ibid (1651–59) 317; ibid (1693–97) 210; ibid (1770–72) 509. In addition, some earlier entries seem to have been struck out of the Journal without any traceable order (eg CJ (1667–87) 567).
5 CJ (1780–82) 977.
6 Peel's Speeches ii, 704; Parl Deb (1833) 17, c 1324.
7 Parl Deb (1855) 137, c 202.
8 CJ (1880) 233.
9 CJ (1890–91) 45.

On 16 July 1909 the House ordered that the entry of a previous day to the effect that the Chairman had called the attention of a committee of the whole House to the disorderly conduct of a Member, and had directed him to withdraw from the House for the remainder of the sitting, and that the Member in question withdrew accordingly, should be expunged. The entry ordered to be expunged was printed in the Journal in erased type.[1]

If entries in the Journal or the Clerk's Minute Books are challenged, the proper course is to give notice of a motion to expunge the entries.[2]

A printed copy of the Journal is accepted as evidence in a court of law under section 3 of the Evidence Act 1845 (see pp 204–205). When a cause is tried in London, it is usual for an officer of the House to attend with a printed Journal, if leave is obtained (see pp 758–759); if the trial is elsewhere, a party may either obtain from the Journal Office a copy of the entries required, without the signature of any officer, and swear himself that it is a true copy; or, with the permission of the House, or, during the recess, of the Speaker, he may secure the attendance of an officer to produce the printed Journal, or extracts which he certifies to be true copies.

The Official Reports of Debates in the Lords and Commons

In the Lords and Commons the regular reporting of parliamentary debates developed gradually during the nineteenth century.[3] The name generally used to describe the reports was 'Hansard'. This was due to the fact that T C Hansard was first the printer, and later the publisher, of the official series of Parliamentary Debates covering both Houses inaugurated by William Cobbett in 1803. Grants were voted annually from 1878 to 1908 to further the publication of debates. In 1909 the present system was adopted, whereby the reports of debates are prepared by staff in the direct employment of each House and issued in separate series.[4] These reports were at first known simply as 'Parliamentary Debates, Official Report'. In 1943 the word 'Hansard' was added to the title.[5]

The Lords' Official Report. In the Lords the reporting staff, headed by an Editor of Debates, is appointed by the Clerk of the Parliaments. The reporting of debates comes within the purview of the Select Committee on House of Lords' Offices. The Official Report is published daily by the Stationery Office and later made up into bound volumes. Weekly volumes have been available since 1947. Since the introduction of questions for written answer in 1928 the answers to such questions have been printed in the Official Report.[6] The publication of additional matter, which is too lengthy or too complicated to be given orally in the House, is permitted in the case of answers to starred questions and of ministerial statements.[7] Statements may, with leave, be reproduced in the Official Report although

1 CJ (1909) 304, 311.
2 HC Deb (1960–61) 634, c 795, 938.
3 Accommodation was made available to reporters in the Galleries of the Lords on 15 October 1831 and of the Commons on 19 February 1835, 3 Walpole, Hist 287.
4 See Report of Select Committee on Parliamentary Debates, HC 239 (1907); debate on Supplementary Estimates, 14 May 1908, Parl Deb (1908) 188, c 1356; HL Deb (1915) 19, c 20.
5 LJ (1942–43) 180; HC Deb (1942–43) 391, c 2303.
6 LJ (1928–29) 56.
7 LJ (1963–64) 381.

they have not been given orally in the House.[1] Where a Commons statement is not repeated either orally or in printed form, an italic reference to the statement in question giving the appropriate reference to the Commons Hansard is included in the Lords Hansard.[2] Separate daily reports are issued for debates taking place in committees on public bills off the floor of the House.

The Commons' Official Report. The responsibility for producing the Official Report rests with the Department of the Official Report, and its head, the Editor (see p 197).

The Official Report is the record of speeches made in the House; it also contains written answers to questions. Separate daily reports are also issued of debates in standing committees. It has never been the practice of the House to allow any speech material not actually delivered in the House to be published in the Official Report. However, it has been the practice for many years to publish material in amplification of an answer to a parliamentary question or of a ministerial statement in order to save the time of the House. Successive Speakers have been vigilant in ensuring that this expedient has not been used to publish material of excessive length or dubious relevance. Thus material in amplification of ministerial speeches as opposed to ministerial answers and statements must not be included in published answers to written Questions.[3] However, in respect of the annual financial statement of the Chancellor of the Exchequer, the Speaker has ruled that, subject to prior notification having been given to him, essential material in amplification of that statement may also be published in the Official Report.[4]

The Official Report is a full report, in the first person, of all speakers alike, a full report being defined as one 'which, though not strictly verbatim, is substantially the verbatim report, with repetitions and redundancies omitted and with obvious mistakes corrected, but which on the other hand leaves out nothing that adds to the meaning of the speech or illustrates the argument'.[5] (See p 219 for the position of the Official Report *vis à vis* the taped recordings of debates.)

Verbal corrections are allowed to be made in the reports of speeches in the daily part for reproduction in the bound volume, but only if, in the opinion of the Editor, they do not alter substantially the meaning of anything that was said in the House.[6] It is not in order for a Member to obtain or quote during a current sitting the record made for the Official Report of the

1 LJ (1970–71) 596.
2 HL Deb (1987–88) 493, c939.
3 Private ruling, November 1972.
4 Private ruling, May 1975.
5 This definition was adopted in 1907 by the Select Committee on Parliamentary Debates (HC 239 (1907)).
6 See HC Deb (1914) 60, c1632; HC Deb (1942–43) 386, c217; HC Deb (1982–83) 53, cc624–627; HC Deb (1985–86) 92, cc377, 498–499 and HC Deb (1987–88) 139, c494. The Speaker has recently reaffirmed the practice of not recording interruptions from a sedentary position which are not taken up by the Member who has the floor or by the Chair (HC Deb (1983–84) 53, c626 and 60, c1260–1261; and HC Deb (1985–86) 99, c881. See also HC Deb (1986–87) 111, cc24, 161.

remarks of any other Member;[1] the Speaker, however, is not bound by this rule.[2]

A Member has sometimes been allowed, as a matter of personal explanation, to point out at a subsequent sitting an error in the report of his speech in the Official Report of Debates.[3]

No Official Report is made, or shorthand note taken, of speeches delivered in secret session, the Official Reporters being excluded as strangers.[4]

During the session the Official Report is published daily by HM Stationery Office, each Member being entitled to two copies free of charge (one copy may be sent direct from HM Stationery Office and the second copy obtained on application at the Vote Office). The daily parts for each week are also issued in the form of a Weekly Hansard and are later made up into bound volumes, each containing a fortnight's debates. These bound volumes are issued free to any Member who desires to have them.[5] Reprints of particular speeches, in leaflet form, may be obtained by Members on application to the Editor and on payment, to HM Stationery Office, of a fee based on the cost of production.

PAPERS PRESENTED TO PARLIAMENT

Papers presented to Parliament may be divided into three categories: Command Papers, Act Papers and Returns.

Command Papers

Command Papers are presented to Parliament as by command of the Queen. In practice the responsibility for presentation is that of the Minister in charge of the relevant department. In general Command Papers are those papers which are considered by the government to be of interest to Parliament but whose presentation is not required by statute. They include treaties, agreements and exchanges of notes with foreign states or give information concerning the relations of the government with international organizations. Annual reports of certain government departments and other organizations, reports of Royal Commissions and of some departmental committees and statistical reports on a wide variety of subjects are also presented as Command Papers. Statements of government policy or proposals for government legislation or administrative action are often laid

---

1 On the occasion of a printing dispute, when it was known that the Official Report would not be available the following day, the Speaker said that he would consider any application made to him for access to another Member's remarks in a current sitting, in cases where a Member was informed that he had been personally attacked by another Member (HC Deb (1979–80) 970, cc 262, 2182).

2 HC Deb (1971–72) 835, c 1276.

3 Eg HC Deb (1927) 208, c 866.

4 On occasion, however, the Speaker has issued a short 'Report of the Proceedings in Secret Session', which has been included in the Official Report, and when divisions have occurred, this Report has included the question put from the Chair and the names of the Members voting (see HC Deb (1941–42) 379, cc 1218–1220, and HC Deb (1942–43) 388, cc 200–204). The Report is also printed in the Votes and Proceedings.

5 Between 1940 and 1945 the bound volumes were charged at cost price (HC 133 (1939–40) and HC Deb (1944–45) 409, c 1153).

before Parliament in this form. In certain cases they are presented following an undertaking given in Parliament for a White Paper on a particular subject. So-called 'Green Papers', ie policy proposals issued for purposes of debate or consultation prior to final Government decision, are also normally laid before Parliament in this form.

The great majority of Command Papers are printed by the Stationery Office on the authority of the Minister presenting them and are included in a numbered series.[1] Occasionally papers are presented, by command, which do not form part of this series. Some Command Papers are presented to the House of Commons alone, for example, the annual estimates which are printed by order of the House.

Act papers

A large variety of papers are presented to Parliament pursuant to statutory requirements. Of these, statutory instruments are described separately (see pp 538–540). The remainder, which are described generically as 'Act Papers', include such documents as annual reports and accounts of statutory and other bodies, statistical reviews and statements relating to the remuneration of members of the boards of nationalised industries. Some of these papers are printed by order of the House of Commons;[2] others are published by the organizations to the activities of which they relate.[3] A few are presented in typescript and not printed.[4]

As in the case of Command Papers, the responsibility for presenting Act papers usually rests upon a Minister, though other Members, such as the Speaker, the Chairman of Ways and Means and the Chairman of the Public Accounts Commission may present papers. Where such a liability falls on someone who is not a Member of the Commons (the Lord Chancellor or the Comptroller and Auditor General, for example) the papers are laid on the Table, by practice, by the Clerk of the House.

Returns

Each House has the power to call for the production of papers by means of a motion for a return. A return from the Privy Council or from departments headed by a Secretary of State is called for by means of an Humble Address to the Queen; other information is sought direct by means of an order of the House. The power to call for papers was frequently exercised until about the middle of the nineteenth century. It is rarely resorted to in modern circumstances since much of the information previously sought in this way is now produced in the form of Command or Act Papers but the power has a continuing importance since it may be delegated to committees, thus enabling them to send for papers and records. Formerly the two Houses

1 Command Papers are numbered: No (1) in 1833 to No (4222) in 1868–69; (C1) in 1870 to (C9550) in 1899; (Cd 1) in 1900 to (Cd 9239) in 1918; (Cmd 1) in 1919 to (Cmd 9888); (Cmnd 1) in 1956 to Cmnd 9927. Cm 1 from beginning of sessions 1986–87.
2 The order for printing a paper is given in practice by the Clerk of the Journals after consultation with the presenting department, but the order and printing number are always recorded formally in the Votes and Proceedings and in the Journal.
3 For example, Reports and Accounts of most nationalised industries.
4 For example, Statements of Remuneration of members of the Boards of nationalised industries.

required the production of papers from local and other authorities not in the service of the Crown and in general such bodies may be said to be under an ill-defined obligation to produce papers to the order of either House. It cannot, however, be said that this requirement is absolute, either in the case of government departments or of public or private bodies since there are cases recorded in which obedience to an order for papers has not been insisted on.[1] There is, however, a general rule that papers should only be ordered on subjects which are of a public or official character.

If one House desires a return relating to the business or proceedings of the other it is not customary for it to be ordered. An arrangement is generally made for the necessary motion to be moved in the other House.[2]

In the Lords, although orders are still occasionally made which result in the production of specific documents[3] the usual purpose of a 'Motion for Papers' is simply to enable a subject to be ventilated (see p 425). In the Commons it is now rare for private Members to seek information by moving for papers. In certain cases, however, ministers move for the production of documents.[4] If Returns to Orders or Addresses are to be printed it is done by the House which calls for their production. Papers printed by Order of either House are numbered in the sessional series of papers of that House. These papers and Command papers printed in their numbered series, together form a category commonly known as 'Parliamentary Papers'.

Presentation of papers

The presentation of papers to the House of Lords is effected by their delivery to the Office of the Clerk of the Parliaments and to the House of Commons by their delivery to the Votes and Proceedings Office.[5] If the delivery of papers takes place at a time when Parliament is sitting, their titles are entered in the Minutes of Proceedings and the Appendix to the Votes and Proceedings for the day on which they are presented. Following presentation, papers are generally ordered by the two Houses to lie on the Table. Under Standing Order No 66 of the House of Lords and Standing Order No 137 of the House of Commons the delivery of Command Papers during periods when the House is not sitting is deemed to be for all purposes the

---

1 CJ (1884) 336.
2 See Return of Lords Attendances, LJ (1968–69) 166.
3 See LJ (1974) 440 (House of Lords furniture); ibid (1974–75) 955 (Community land policy); ibid (1976–77) 85 (Computers), 220 (Library); ibid (1981–82) 323 (Crown Agents Tribunal). The Accounts of the House of Lords Refreshment Department have since 1984 been ordered to be printed each year in this way.
4 Certain annual returns are, by custom, presented to the House of Commons in the form of returns to orders. These include the Financial Statement (Budget), returns relating to the Contingencies Fund, Offences involving Motor Vehicles, Experiments on Living Animals and statistics relating to the work of the House. Examples of other papers presented as Returns to Addresses are the Reports of the Inquiries into the appointment etc of the Queen's Police Officer (HC (1982–83) 59), into security arrangements at HM Prison, Maze (HC 1983–84) 203), into the escape of a prisoner from St Mary's Hospital Paddington (HC (1986–87) 80) and departmental handling of matters relating to Barlow Clowes (HC (1987–88) 671; and as Returns to Orders, the Report of the Advisory Committee on the Crown Agents (HC (1977–78) 50).
5 Strictly speaking papers are *presented* to each House by command, and *laid* before each House by Act. This distinction is observed in the Minutes of Proceedings of the House of Lords but not in the Votes and Proceedings of the House of Commons and for convenience has been disregarded in this account.

presentation of them to each House; and in such cases the lists of their titles are entered in the Minutes and Votes when sittings are resumed. Similar provisions enabling presentation when the Houses are not sitting extend also to Statutory Instruments (see pp 544–545), but not to other Act Papers.

When a treaty requires ratification, the Government does not usually proceed with ratification until a period of twenty-one days has elapsed from the date on which the text of such a treaty was laid before Parliament by Her Majesty's command. This practice is subject to modification, if necessary, when urgent or other important considerations arise.[1]

Following a report of the Committee of Public Accounts, when a government department wishes to give a guarantee for which there is no statutory authority, and the liability thereunder could exceed £100,000, it is the normal practice for a Minute to be laid before Parliament. Approval of the guarantee is usually withheld for fourteen days after the date of laying. If in that period a Member signifies objection by the tabling of a Question or Motion, or otherwise, final approval is not usually given, pending consideration of the objection. A similar practice is followed in the case of gifts of public stores, or property of an unusual nature or of a value exceeding £100,000.[2]

If a department which has presented a paper wishes subsequently to withdraw it, the order that the paper do lie upon the Table may be discharged, and the paper withdrawn. This has also been done on the initiative of the House, after notice was taken that the paper presented was not a correct copy.[3] It is possible to withdraw a paper even when it has been presented in a previous session.[4]

Papers are presented to Parliament in a complete form, either printed or in typescript. In exceptional circumstances and with the agreement of the Journal Office or Offices concerned papers may be presented 'in dummy', normally a sheet of paper bearing only the title of the document.

Distribution of Papers

Parliamentary papers. Copies of Parliamentary papers are made available to Members of Parliament as soon as they are issued.[5] No copies may be delivered to any department or placed on sale to the public until they have been made so available. Copies of a Command Paper may be released in

---

1 This practice, which is known as the 'Ponsonby rule', had its origin in a departmental minute dated 1 February 1924 and signed by Mr Arthur Ponsonby, then Under Secretary of State for Foreign Affairs, see HC Deb (1924) 171, cc 2001–2004. On 6 May 1981 (HC Deb (1980–81) 4, c 82w) the Lord Privy Seal announced a minor modification to the rule under which the texts of bilateral double taxation agreements would no longer be tabled in the Country Series of Command Papers but would continue to be published in the Treaty Series of Command Papers after entry into force. In the Lords the rule has been extended by analogy to the acceptance by the Government of amendments to ratified international agreements: see Sixth Report from the Joint Committee on Statutory Instruments (HL 40, HC 15–viii (1981–82) p 5).
2 Committee of Public Accounts, Tenth Report (HC 536 (1976–77)) paras 57–67.
3 CJ (1945–46) 258.
4 CJ (1945–46) 334; ibid (1952–53) 246.
5 CJ (1871) 96. For a case where an Act paper, having been presented to the House of Commons, was publicly released before being made available to Members, see HC Deb (1984–85) 83, c 884–885.

advance to the Press provided that publication does not take place until the paper is available to Members.[1]

Papers printed by order of the House are available to Members of the other House. They are also available to the public by sale through HM Stationery Office. The Commons, through the Sale Office, which is part of the Vote Office, provides printed papers to parliamentary agents and certain approved bodies, as well as to Members.[2]

The Vote Office in the Commons and the Printed Paper Office in the Lords deliver, or arrange through the Stationery Office to have delivered, printed papers to Members of their respective Houses. Members of the Lords are entitled to one copy of parliamentary papers and working papers of the House (eg Minutes of Proceedings, Notices and Hansards) by application to the Printed Paper Office, either in person or by use of printed demand forms. Demand forms are also provided for the supply of European Community papers deposited in Parliament.

Members of the Commons are entitled to receive a copy of all papers printed by order of the House; but a Member is not entitled to more than one copy.[3] All parliamentary papers of the current and preceding session are immediately available on demand from the Vote Office, either personally or by a special form provided for the purpose. Certain papers (viz Votes and Proceedings, public bills and the financial statement) and other papers which, on occasion, Ministers may order the Vote Office to deliver are distributed as a matter of course to every Member who has applied for papers on the sessional form. Parliamentary papers of sessions earlier than the previous session, if necessary to the discharge of a Member's duties, may be ordered from the Stationery Office through the Vote Office.[4]

Non-parliamentary publications. Each Member of the Lords may obtain one, and each Member of the Commons two, free copies of all non-parliamentary publications of HM Stationery Office whether presented to Parliament or not, provided that the paper is required in connection with his parliamentary duties.[5] Historical, technical, scientific, reference and similar classes of publication have been traditionally excluded from these arrangements. However, Members may, on indicating the nature of their interest, request the appropriate Minister, at present a Minister of State at the Treasury, to issue such material.[6] Special forms provided by the Vote Office[7] are used in applying for non-parliamentary publications.

European Community publications. Designated European Community publications are available at the Vote Office and Members may receive one copy either on request or by special application. European Community

---

1 HC Deb (1942–43) 385, cc 1574–1578.
2 For the early adoption of the principle of sale see Second Report of Printed Papers Committee 1835, HC 392 (1835), CJ (1835) 461–462, 543–545.
3 Up to six copies of Public Bills may be obtained by special application to the Vote Office, and, on the day of issue only, Members may receive up to five copies of the Official Report.
4 HC Deb (1965–66) 725, c 34.
5 HC Deb (1924) 171, c 1994; HC 63 (1924–25) p 108; HC Deb (1955–56) 556, c 1044.
6 HC Deb (1976–77) 758, c 253.
7 HC Deb (1927) 203, c 564, 1040; HC Deb (1945–46) 415, c 1917; ibid (1977–78) 938, c 872. When a new form was introduced the Minister of State, Civil Service Department, said that any decision to decline to make available to a Member such a publication would be made by a Minister.

documents required for debate are available in the same way as parliamentary documents.

Transmission by post. Members of both Houses are entitled to have any parliamentary paper sent to them free of postage. Members of the Commons living within three miles of the House may receive daily, by hand, a copy of the vote 'bundle', copies of public bills, and a copy of the financial statement.

BROADCASTING OF PARLIAMENTARY PROCEEDINGS

Sound

Regular sound broadcasting from both Houses began on 3 April 1978.[1]

Resolutions authorizing broadcasting and setting out the conditions on which it was to be carried out are as follows:

That, pursuant to the Resolution of the House of 16 March 1976 and certain recommendations made in the Second Report of the Joint Committee on Sound Broadcasting—

(1) the British Broadcasting Corporation and the Independent Broadcasting Authority ('the broadcasting authorities') be authorised to provide and operate singly or jointly sound signal origination equipment for the purpose of recording or broadcasting the proceedings of the House and its committees subject to the directions of the House or a committee empowered to give such directions ('the committee');

(2) the broadcasting authorities may supply signals whether direct or recorded, made pursuant to this resolution to other broadcasting organisations, and shall supply them to any other organisations whose request for such a facility shall have been granted by the committee, on such conditions as the committee may determine;

(3) no signal, whether direct or recorded, made pursuant to this resolution shall be used by the broadcasting authorities, or by any organisation supplied with such a signal, in light entertainment programmes, or programmes designed as political satire; nor shall any record, cassette or other device making use of such signal be published unless the committee shall have satisfied themselves that it is not designed for such entertainment or satire;

(4) archive tapes of all signals supplied by the broadcasting authorities shall be made, together with a selection for permanent preservation, under the direction of the committee.[2]

Both Houses have appointed select committees to give the directions referred to in the resolutions (see pp 584 and 661).

Under the resolutions, only the BBC and the IBA are authorised to record and broadcast proceedings: however, under the Broadcasting Act

---

1 In the Lords, a select committee recommended a closed circuit television experiment in 1967, later extended to include closed circuit sound broadcasting, which took place in February 1968 (LJ (1966–67) 426, 609). In the Commons, an inquiry into the possibility of sound broadcasting of proceedings was begun in 1964–65 by the Select Committee on Publications and Debates Reports and continued in subsequent sessions. An experiment in public sound broadcasting was authorised by the Commons in 1975 (CJ (1974–75) 240) which took place in June and July of that year; and permanent sound broadcasting was approved in principle by both Houses in 1976 (LJ (1975–76) 247, CJ (1975–76) 214). For a full account of the history leading up to broadcasting in the Commons see First Report of the Select Committee on Sound Broadcasting, HC 376 (1981–82).

2 LJ (1976–77) 820; CJ (1976–77) 452.

1981, the IBA operate largely through programme contractors, and one of these, Independent Radio News, under conditions supervised by the committees, takes the lead in recording and editing proceedings for use by IBA broadcasting stations.

In addition, various overseas broadcasting organisations and others have been authorised by the Committees to receive live proceedings, but only on the condition that they are prepared to supply to the Houses details of how proceedings have been used.

Three consequences flow from the resolutions. First, any public proceedings of either House or its committees may be broadcast, but broadcasting must stop in the event of an adjournment or suspension. Secondly, the only way that broadcasting can be prevented, short of rescinding the original decision, is for either House or committee to exclude strangers.[1] Finally, editorial control and responsibility rests entirely with the broadcasters. When the appointment of the Commons Sound Broadcasting Committee was debated in February 1978, amendments were moved, unsuccessfully, which would have provided for the release of the signal to be under the day-to-day control and authority of the House, in which case the editorial function would have been retained by the House.

Televising proceedings of each House

In June 1966 the House of Lords resolved in favour of televising some of its proceedings for an experimental period.[2] An experiment in closed circuit television and sound took place in February 1968. But no further broadcasting of proceedings took place until 1978 (see above). In December 1983 the House again decided in favour of the public televising of its proceedings;[3] a select committee recommended an initial six-month trial period which was extended by nine months;[4] and after further debate[5] television broadcasting began on 23 January 1985. At the end of the trial period a select committee concluded that the experiment had been useful and made suggestions for improvements;[6] and the House resolved that the public televising of its proceedings (including select committees) should continue.[7] A motion to replace the Select Committee on Sound Broadcasting by a Select Committee on Broadcasting was also agreed to.[8] This new select committee exercises the powers of the House in relation to both radio and television broadcasting.

In the Commons, though the possibility of televised proceedings was raised as early as 1959,[9] not until 1983 did the House agree to a motion for

---

1 The authorization to supply broadcasting signals is, however, subject to direction from the appropriate select committee, and in the Lords the committee directed on 23 May 1978 that judicial proceedings of the House, including the giving of judgments, should not be recorded or broadcast.
2 LJ (1965–66) 87.
3 LJ (1983–84) 210.
4 HL 299 (1983–84).
5 HL Deb (1984–85) 457, cc 764–860.
6 HL 102 (1985–86).
7 LJ (1985–86) 320, 331,
8 LJ (1985–86) 331, 431.
9 HC Deb (1959–60) 612, c 866–867.

leave to bring in a bill to make implementation possible.[1] The bill did not reach the statute book, and in 1985 the House rejected on division a proposal to approve in principle the holding of an experiment in the public broadcasting of its proceedings by television.[2] In early 1988, however, a similar motion was agreed to, and a select committee was appointed to consider its implementation.[3] The House subsequently agreed with the committee in a report which recommended that an experiment in television broadcasting of proceedings should be held,[4] with a view to its beginning in November 1989.

Retention of records

Archive tapes of all proceedings in both Houses and of such committees as are recorded by the broadcasters are preserved in the Sound Archive Unit of the House of Lords Record Office for seven years, and permanently stored thereafter in the National Sound Archive.[5] Some of the televised proceedings of the House of Lords are also preserved. The Unit also holds tapes of broadcast programmes containing parliamentary material, and film material dealing with the work of either House. Members and Officers of both Houses, and any other persons authorised by the Select Committees, have access to the Unit, which can supply tape cassettes of proceedings on the payment of a fee. The Official Report remains, subject to admissible corrections (see p 231), the authoritative record of what was said in the Commons. The Speaker has indicated that he will not accept the taped recording as in any way a check upon the Official Report.[6] For the ownership of the copyright in the tapes etc of proceedings, see pp 89–90.

1 CJ (1983–84) 155. A proposal for a television experiment was negatived in 1975, CJ (1974–75) 240.
2 CJ (1985–86) 34.
3 Votes and Proceedings (1987–88) 9 February and 29 March 1988.
4 HC 141 (1988–89) and Votes and Proceedings (1988–89) 12 June 1989.
5 HC Deb (1987–88) 139, c 575 W.
6 HC Deb (1979–80) 977, c 1578–1580; HC Deb (1987–88) 139, c 494. See also HC Deb (1979–80) 974, cc 574–581.

CHAPTER 13

A new Parliament and opening and close of session

This chapter, which is principally concerned with the arrangements for holding a session of Parliament, presents an outline of the general forms employed in summoning, dissolving and proroguing Parliament, and in the adjournment of each House; it also describes the procedure in opening a session of Parliament, stating separately the procedure peculiar to the opening of the first session of a new Parliament.

Before describing the opening of a session it is necessary to explain briefly the terms and forms employed in relation to the sitting of Parliament—how a session is begun, ended, and periodically interrupted and resumed, or, in technical language, how Parliament is summoned, dissolved, and prorogued and how each House is adjourned.

PARLIAMENTARY AND SESSIONAL PERIODS

'A Parliament' in the sense of a parliamentary period, is a period not exceeding five years which may be regarded as a cycle beginning and ending with a proclamation. Such a proclamation (which is made by the Queen on the advice of her Privy Council) on the one hand dissolves an existing Parliament, and, on the other, orders the issue of writs for the election of a new Parliament and appoints the day and place for its meeting. This period, of course, contains an interregnum between the dissolution of a Parliament and the meeting of its successor during which there is no Parliament in existence; but the principle of the unbroken continuity of Parliament is for all practical purposes secured by the fact that the same proclamation which dissolves a Parliament provides for the election and meeting of a new Parliament.

A session is the period of time between the meeting of a Parliament, whether after a prorogation or a dissolution, and its prorogation. Parliament is usually prorogued by a commission under the great seal which appoints the day and place of its meeting in the new session. The date so appointed may be deferred by a subsequent proclamation. During the course of a session either House may adjourn itself of its own motion to such date as it pleases. The period between the prorogation of Parliament and its re-assembly in a new session is termed a 'recess'; while the period between the adjournment of either House and the resumption of its sitting is properly called an 'adjournment' (although in practice the word 'recess' is generally used in this sense also).

A prorogation terminates a session; an adjournment is an interruption in the course of one and the same session.

Summons of Parliament

A new Parliament is summoned in pursuance of a proclamation issued by the Queen with the advice of the Privy Council. This proclamation, which also dissolves the old Parliament, orders the issue of writs by the Lord Chancellor and appoints a day and place for the meeting of the new Parliament.[1]

Date of meeting of Parliament

The day of meeting of a new Parliament is, as stated above, appointed in the proclamation.[2] The meeting of Parliament may be deferred, however, by a further proclamation proroguing it to a later day, not being less than fourteen days from the date of such proclamation.[3]

Dissolution of Parliament

Parliament is dissolved either by efflux of time or by proclamation (see pp 62–63). Under the Septennial Act 1715 it ceased to exist after seven years from the day on which, by writ of summons, it was appointed to meet; this period was reduced to five years by the Parliament Act 1911 (section 7). The Parliaments which assembled in 1911 and 1935 were, by annual statutes, prolonged beyond this limit (to 1919 and 1945 respectively) in the exceptional circumstances of world war. Parliament is no longer dissolved by the demise of the Crown.[4]

Parliament is usually dissolved by proclamation under the great seal. Such a proclamation has been issued after Parliament was prorogued to a certain day;[5] and when it has been proposed to dissolve Parliament at a time when both Houses stood adjourned, the provisions in their Standing Orders respecting recall (see p 224) have sometimes been put into operation, after which prorogation has taken place, followed by the issue of the proclamation of dissolution.[6] When Parliament is prorogued with a view to its dissolution, it is the usual, but not the invariable, practice to issue the proclamation the same day and dispatch the writs by that evening's post (see

1 LJ (1982–83) 353; ibid (1986–87) 383–384.
2 The provision in the Representation of the People Act 1918 (s 21(3)) that the interval between the date of proclamation and the meeting of Parliament must be not less than twenty clear days was repealed by s 28(1) of the Representation of the People Act 1985.
3 Prorogation Act 1867.
4 Representation of the People Act 1867, s 51.
5 The last such case is that of 1951 (see p 63*n*). Dissolution may also take place on the same day as prorogation, of which the last instance is that of February 1974 (see p 63*n*). In 1950, dissolution followed a proclamation which continued an earlier prorogation.
6 CJ (1950–51) 321; ibid (1958–59) 320–321; ibid (1969–70) 337.

p 63). In a number of more recent instances, dissolutions have taken place while both Houses were adjourned, without recourse to prorogation.[1]

Prorogation and adjournment

The prorogation of Parliament is a prerogative act of the Crown. Just as Parliament can commence its deliberations only at the time appointed by the Queen, so it cannot continue them any longer than she pleases. But each House exercises its right to adjourn itself independently of the Crown and of the other House.

Effect of prorogation and adjournment respectively. The effect of a prorogation is at once to suspend all business until Parliament shall be summoned again (see pp 60–61). Not only are the sittings of Parliament at an end, but all proceedings pending at the time are quashed, except impeachments by the Commons and appeals before the House of Lords.[2] Every bill must therefore be renewed after a prorogation, as if it were introduced for the first time.[3] (For the suspension or revival of private and provisional order bills, see pp 928–929.)

An adjournment has no such effect on parliamentary proceedings. Upon reassembling, each House proceeds to transact the business previously appointed, and all proceedings are resumed at the stage at which they were left before the adjournment.

Procedure of prorogation. Parliament is prorogued either by a commission (preceded by a proclamation) or by a proclamation alone.

At the close of a session, according to the usual procedure, the prorogation of Parliament is effected by an announcement of the Queen's command to that effect made before both Houses in the House of Lords by one of the commissioners by virtue of a royal commission.

---

1 See p 63n and LJ (1974–75) 2; ibid (1979–80) 2; ibid (1982–83) 353; CJ (1983–84) 2; LJ (1986–87) 383.
2 2 Hatsell 335. The statute 45 Geo III, c 117 permitted the continuation of proceedings in the House of Lords against Mr Justice Fox over the prorogation. See also an exception regarding proceedings in certain cases on private bills, pp 928–930, and on a public bill, p 526. As explained on p 612, in the House of Commons certain select committees having been appointed by standing order, are nominated by a standing order for the lifetime of a Parliament, thus enabling their proceedings and membership to be continued after a prorogation; see eg CJ (1974–75) 71–73.
3 Proposals have been made to provide, either by statute or by standing orders, for the suspension of bills from one session to another, or for resuming proceedings upon such bills, notwithstanding a prorogation. These schemes have been discussed in Parliament and considered by committees: but various considerations have restrained the legislature from disturbing the law and custom of Parliament by which parliamentary proceedings are discontinued by prorogation. See Parl Deb (1848) 98, cc 329, 981, 1255; ibid (1848) 99, c 246; ibid (1848) 100, c 131; HC 644 (1847–48); HL 95 (1861); HC 173 (1861); Parl Deb (1868–69) 194, c 588; ibid (1883) 279, c 2; HC 386 (1868–69); HC 268 (1878); HC 298 (1890) and Select Committee on Procedure, 2nd Report (HC 49—I (1984–85)). In session 1903, provision was made for resuming in the following session the proceedings on the Port of London Bill as reported from the Joint Committee. A resolution for the resumption of proceedings on the bill was agreed to in the following session, but further progress was not made with the bill, CJ (1904) 181. See also Report of Joint Committee on Suspension of Bills, HL 109 (1928–29); CJ (1931–32) 322; ibid (1932–33) 8. In session 1919 a motion for the suspension of further proceedings on the War Emergency Laws (Continuance) Bill until the following session was withdrawn, CJ (1919) 428; HC Deb (1919) 123, c 1291.

The details of this procedure are described at the end of this chapter (p 236). If Her Majesty is present at the prorogation of Parliament her command is signified by the Lord Chancellor or Speaker of the House of Lords. The last occasion of the prorogation of Parliament by a sovereign in person was in 1854.

When Parliament stands summoned (after a dissolution) or prorogued to a certain day, it may be prorogued or further prorogued to a later day, under the Prorogation Act 1867, by a proclamation made by the Queen on the advice of the Privy Council. The interval prescribed by this Act between the date of the proclamation and the day to which it prorogues Parliament is not less than fourteen days (see pp 60–61).

When it is intended that on the day to which it is so prorogued, or further prorogued, Parliament shall meet for the dispatch of business, a clause is added to the proclamation stating that Parliament will then 'assemble and be holden for the dispatch of divers urgent and important affairs'. Even when Parliament stands prorogued to a specified day 'for the dispatch of business' it may similarly by proclamation be prorogued to a later day.[1]

Meeting of Parliament accelerated during prorogation. The Queen is not only empowered to postpone the meeting of Parliament, but also to accelerate its meeting.

When Parliament stands prorogued to a certain day, the Queen may, by the Meeting of Parliament Act 1797 as amended by the Meeting of Parliament Act 1870 and the Parliament (Elections and Meeting) Act 1943, issue a proclamation, giving notice of her intention that Parliament shall meet for the dispatch of business on any day after the date of the proclamation; and Parliament then stands prorogued to that day, notwithstanding the previous prorogation.[2]

It is provided by statute[3] that whenever the Crown shall cause the reserve forces to be called out on permanent service, when Parliament stands prorogued or adjourned for more than five days, the Queen shall issue a proclamation for the meeting of Parliament within five days.[4] The Emergency Powers Act 1920 also requires that, where a proclamation declaring that a state of emergency exists has been made, the occasion thereof is communicated to Parliament,[5] and if Parliament is separated by an adjournment or prorogation which will not expire within five days, a proclamation shall be issued for the meeting of Parliament within five days.

---

1 CJ (1887) 2; ibid (1922) 2.
2 Pursuant to the first of these Acts, Parliament was assembled in September 1799 (CJ (1798–99) 745; ibid (1799–1800) 3). On 12 December 1854 Parliament assembled, having been previously prorogued to the 14th; and in 1857 in consequence of the suspension of the Bank Act of 1844, a proclamation was issued on 16 November assembling Parliament on 3 December. In 1900 the new Parliament which had been prorogued from 1 November, the day for which it had been summoned, to 10 December was summoned to meet for the dispatch of business on 3 December by a proclamation dated 26 November (CJ (1900) 404). In 1921 Parliament, which had been prorogued until 30 January 1922, was summoned to meet on 14 December by a proclamation dated 7 December (CJ (1921) 402).
3 The statutory provisions are now contained in the Reserve Forces Act 1980, s 10(2).
4 Until 1966 the interval was ten days. On 7 October 1899 Parliament, which stood prorogued till 27 October, was summoned by proclamation to meet on 17 October, CJ (1899) 428. See also CJ (1792) 1092 for proclamation under 26 Geo III, c 107, s 97, dated 1 December 1792, summoning Parliament, which stood prorogued till 3 January 1793, to meet on 13 December 1792.
5 Eg see CJ (1973–74) 28, 85, 106.

Meeting of Parliament accelerated during adjournment. When Parliament is dispersed through the adjournment of both Houses its reassembly can be effected either by proclamation or under powers specifically conferred by each House on its Speaker.

A power of interfering with adjournments in certain cases has been conceded to the Crown by statute. The Meeting of Parliament Act 1799, amended by the Meeting of Parliament Act 1870, enacts that when both Houses of Parliament stand adjourned for more than fourteen days, the Queen may issue a proclamation, with the advice of her Privy Council, declaring that the Parliament shall meet on a day not less than six days from the proclamation; and the Houses of Parliament then stand adjourned to the day and place declared in the proclamation; and all the orders which may have been made by either House, and appointed for the original day of meeting, or any subsequent day, stand appointed for the day named in the proclamation.

Further, the statutory provisions which necessitate the meeting of Parliament in the event of certain emergencies apply not only when Parliament is separated by a prorogation but also when it is separated by an adjournment of more than a certain duration.

Since 1914 it has been the practice for the House of Lords to make arrangements for its recall during a period of adjournment. From 1939 these arrangements were governed by a sessional resolution which in 1970 was incorporated in a new Standing Order, No 14. This empowers the Lord Chancellor, or in his absence the Chairman of Committees after consultation with the Government, to give notice for the meeting of the House on a day earlier than that to which it stands adjourned if he is satisfied that the public interest so requires.

In the Commons, under Standing Order No 12 the Speaker, having received representations from the Government that the House should meet at any earlier time during an adjournment, if he is satisfied that the public interest does so require, may give notice that he is so satisfied, whereupon the House meets at the time stated in the notice. The Chairman of Ways and Means, or a deputy Chairman, may act instead of the Speaker, in the event of his being unable to act owing to illness or other cause.[1]

On certain occasions when one House has already arranged a sitting for a particular day, a notice has been necessary only in respect of the other.[2]

For recall of the Lords for judicial business, see p 418.

MEETING OF A NEW PARLIAMENT

The principal proceedings which distinguish the meeting of a new Parliament from the opening of any subsequent session are the election of a

---

1 Both Houses met pursuant to such notices on 8 September 1931, 18 October 1932, 22 October 1935, 28 September 1938, 13 April, 24 August, 29 August and 1 September 1939, 27 September 1949, 12 September 1950, 4 October 1951, 12 September 1956, 18 September 1959, 17 October 1961, 26 August 1968, 22 September 1971, 9 January 1974, 3 June 1974 and 3 and 14 April 1982.
2 Thus the Commons met pursuant to notice on 30 September 1924, 16 January 1968 and 26 May 1970, and the Lords on 21 September 1931, 8 December 1941, 25 November 1963, 25 January 1965 and 22 January 1968.

Speaker, and the taking and subscription of the oath by Members of both Houses.

On the day appointed by royal proclamation for the first meeting of a new Parliament for dispatch of business (see p 221), the Members of both Houses assemble in their respective chambers. In the House of Lords, the Lord Chancellor acquaints the House, 'that it not being convenient for Her Majesty to be personally present here this day, She has been pleased to cause a commission under the great seal to be prepared, in order to the holding of this Parliament'. The five Lords Commissioners, being in their robes and seated on a form between the throne and the woolsack, then command Black Rod to let the Commons know that 'the Lords Commissioners desire their immediate attendance in this House, to hear the commission read'.

Commons attend in the House of Lords

On receiving the message from Black Rod, the Clerk and the House of Commons go up to the House of Lords. The Lord Chancellor there addresses the Members of both Houses, and acquaints them that Her Majesty has thought fit, by letters patent under the great seal, to empower several lords, therein named as Commissioners, 'to do all things in Her Majesty's name, which are to be done on Her Majesty's part in this Parliament'. The letters patent are then read, after which the Lord Chancellor, acting in obedience to these general directions, again addresses both Houses, and acquaints them:

> 'That, as soon as the Members of both Houses shall be sworn, the causes of Her Majesty calling this Parliament will be declared to you; and it being necessary a Speaker of the House of Commons should be first chosen, it is Her Majesty's pleasure that you, Members of the House of Commons, repair to the place where you are to sit, and there proceed to the choice of some proper person to be your Speaker; and that you present such person whom you shall so choose, here, tomorrow (at an hour stated), for Her Majesty's royal approbation'.[1]

On the opening of a new Parliament, the Commissioners, without express directions to that effect in the commission, direct the Commons to elect a Speaker, and afterwards signify the Queen's approbation.

Proceedings in the Lords—Oaths

The Commons withdraw immediately after the Queen's pleasure for the election of a Speaker has been signified, and return to their own House, while the House of Lords is adjourned during pleasure, to allow the Com-

---

1 HL Deb (1987–88) 488, cc 1–2.

missioners to unrobe. When the House of Lords is resumed the daily prayers are read, for the first time, by a bishop. The Lords then proceed to take the oath, beginning with the Lord Chancellor who is followed by the Archbishops, the party leaders and the occupants of the front benches (including those used by ex-Ministers nearest the Bar) and then by the remaining Lords present. The requirements in relation to the taking of the oath are the same for Members of both Houses and are fully described on pp 229–231.

Election of a Speaker by the Commons

The Commons, in the meantime, proceed to the election of their Speaker. In accordance with Standing Order No 1, the Chair is taken for this purpose by the Member, present in the House and not being a Minister of the Crown, who has served for the longest period continuously as a Member of the House. The Member taking the Chair under these circumstances is granted by the Standing Order all the powers which would be exercisable by the Speaker if, following a decision to relinquish his office during the course of a session, he were presiding over the election of his successor (see pp 228–229); he sits, however, not in the Speaker's Chair but at the Clerk's place at the Table (the Clerk sitting on his left).[1]

Having taken the Chair, the senior back-bencher calls two Members in turn[2] to move and second a motion that some other Member there present[3] 'do take the Chair of this House as Speaker', and proposes that question; other Members may then speak, but the Chair defers calling any Member who may wish to move an amendment until the candidate first proposed has been called upon to make the customary speech submitting himself to the House. At the conclusion of the debate, if no other candidate has been proposed, the Chair puts the question.

If, however, another Member is proposed, the Standing Order provides that the motions for the election to the Chair of all candidates subsequent to the first should be moved in the form of amendments to the original question. In such circumstances, the amendment having been moved,[4] the question would then be proposed 'That the Amendment be made'; the alternative candidate whose name had been put forward would then also be called upon to submit himself before the question on the amendment was put. If the first amendment were to be negatived, others could similarly be moved. Once any amendment has been agreed to, no further amendment

---

1 For the background to the making of the Standing Order, see HC 111 (1971–72).
2 It is customary for the mover and seconder to be private Members. In 1789 Mr Pitt was desirous of proposing Mr Addington himself: but Mr Hatsell, on being consulted, said, 'I think that the choice of the Speaker should not be on the motion of the minister. Indeed, an invidious use might be made of it, to represent you as the friend of the minister, rather than the choice of the House'. Mr Pitt acknowledged the force of this objection; Sidmouth, i, 78. When a Speaker is re-elected without opposition, it has been usual for the proposer and seconder to be taken from different sides of the House, as in 1852, 1859, 1866, 1868, 1874, 1880, 1886, 1892, 1895 (Sess. II), 1900 (Sess. II), 1906, 1910, 1911, 1922 (Sess. II), 1924, 1924–25, 1929–30, 1931–32, 1935–36, 1945–46, 1950, 1955, 1964–65, 1966–67, 1970–71, 1974, 1974–75, 1979–80 and 1987–88. In session 1919 two senior Members of the House chosen from the parties constituting the coalition majority acted as proposer and seconder.
3 A Member who has not taken the oath and his seat may not be nominated to the Speakership (see p 229; and Parl Hist (1800–01) 35, c 951, Court and Cabinets of Geo IV, 394, and Colchester iii, 260.)
4 It is the custom for nominations to the Speakership to be seconded.

can be moved, and the main question as amended must accordingly be decided. If every amendment is negatived, the main question is put unamended.[1]

According to usage, in the event of a division the two Members whose names have been proposed from the Chair take part in it, each Member giving his vote in favour of his rival.[2]

The Member in whose favour the House has decided stands up in his place and expresses his sense of the honour proposed to be conferred upon him and submits himself to the House; his proposer and seconder then take him out of his place and conduct him to the chair.[3]

Speaker elect returns thanks. The Speaker elect, on being conducted to the chair, stands on the upper step and expresses 'his grateful thanks', or 'his humble acknowledgments', 'for the high honour the House has been pleased to confer upon him'; and then takes his seat. The Mace, which up to this time has been under the Table, is now laid upon the Table, where it is always placed during the sitting of the House with the Speaker in the chair. The Speaker elect is then congratulated by some leading Members; he puts the question for adjournment and, when the House adjourns, leaves the House without the Mace before him.

Royal approbation of the Speaker elect. The House meets on the following day, and the Speaker elect takes the chair and awaits the arrival of Black Rod from the Lords Commissioners. When that officer has delivered his message, the Speaker elect, with the House, goes up to the House of Lords, and acquaints the Lords Commissioners:

'That in obedience to Her Majesty's command, Her Majesty's most faithful Commons have, in the exercise of their undoubted right and privileges, proceeded to the election of a Speaker', and that as the object of their choice he now presents himself at the bar of the Lords, and submits himself with all humility to Her Majesty's gracious approbation.[4]

In reply, the Lord Chancellor assures him of Her Majesty's sense of his sufficiency, and 'that Her Majesty most readily approves and confirms him as the Speaker'.[5]

Claim to privileges. When the Speaker has been approved, he lays claim, on behalf of the Commons, 'by humble petition to Her Majesty, to all their ancient and undoubted rights and privileges', (see pp 71–80) which being confirmed, the Speaker, with the Commons, retires from the bar of the House of Lords.

---

1 Since the making of SO No 1 on the election of the Speaker in 1972, there have been no contested elections to the Chair.
2 Election of Mr Abercromby, 19 February 1835, Parl Deb (1835) 26, c 56. Election of Mr Shaw Lefevre, CJ (1839) 274, Division List, 27 May 1839, No 75. Election of Mr Morrison, 31 October 1951, HC Deb (1951–52) 493, cc 18, 20. On the occasion of the election of Mr Gully, 10 April 1895, both candidates abstained from voting. In accordance with precedent, Government tellers were appointed.
3 CJ (1983–84) 3–4.
4 LJ (1987–88) 9.
5 The only instance of refusal of the royal approbation was in the case of Sir Edward Seymour in 1678, an impasse which was ended only by a prorogation. The Journal record was expunged but is to be found in *Observations, Rules and Orders*, ed W R McKay (1989) pp 33–39.

Election of Speaker in course of session. The Speaker, thus elected and approved, continues in that office during the whole Parliament, unless in the meantime he resigns or is removed by death. It will be convenient to indicate here the special forms that are observed in the election of a Speaker during the session.

If the vacancy in the Chair is caused by the Speaker's death at a time too late to enable arrangements to be made for the election of a successor at the next sitting, the Clerk announces the death of the Speaker at the earliest opportunity. Immediately after the announcement has been made, the mace is brought into the House by the Serjeant and is laid under the Table.[1] A Member then rises, and, addressing the Clerk, moves the adjournment of the House, and the Clerk puts the question, 'by the direction of the House'. If sufficient time has elapsed for arrangements to be made for the election of a new Speaker, a motion for the adjournment is not moved after the Clerk's announcement, but the House proceeds instead to the election.[2]

The Speaker, on other occasions, informs the House of the cause that compels his retirement from the chair.[3] Standing Order No 1 provides that a Speaker who has intimated his wish to relinquish his office shall continue to exercise his authority until his successor has been chosen.

The Select Committee on Procedure of 1971–72[4] recommended that wherever possible the Speaker should retire in the middle of a session, giving at least ten days' notice of his impending retirement and, if circumstances permitted, occupying the chair until his successor had been elected.

In the event of a vacancy during the session, instead of Her Majesty's desire being signified by the Lord Chancellor in the House of Lords, a Minister of the Crown, in the Commons, acquaints the House that Her Majesty 'gives leave to the House to proceed forthwith to the choice of a new Speaker'.[5] If the retiring Speaker is present, he remains in the Chair until the House has come to a decision upon his successor, at which point he leaves the Chair and the mace is placed under the Table; but in the event of the announcement of his unavoidable absence (or at an election following upon the Speaker's death) the election is conducted in the same manner as at the beginning of a session, with the Member of longest service in the Chair (see p 226).

When the Speaker has been chosen, the same Minister acquaints the House that it is Her Majesty's pleasure that the House should present their

---

1 CJ (1788–89) 45; ibid (1942–43) 57.

2 CJ (1964–65) 412.

3 Mr Speaker Manners Sutton CJ (1831–32) 534; Mr Speaker Abercromby ibid (1839) 271; Mr Speaker Shaw Lefevre ibid (1857) 89; Mr Speaker Denison ibid (1872) 9; Mr Speaker Brand ibid (1884) 68; Mr Speaker Peel ibid (1895) 139; Mr Speaker Gully ibid (1905) 243; Mr Speaker Lowther ibid (1921) 109; Mr Speaker Whitley ibid (1928) 210. A letter from Mr Speaker Clifton Brown, who did not seek re-election to Parliament after a dissolution, was read to the House by his successor, ibid (1951–52) 19. Mr Speaker Morrison and Mr Speaker Thomas informed the House of their intention to retire at the end of the Parliament (HC Deb (1958–59) 600, c 549 and CJ (1958–59) 325; and HC Deb (1982–83) 42, c 919 and CJ (1982–83) 381.) Mr Speaker Lloyd informed the House of his intention to relinquish his office on a future date (CJ (1975–76) 95); for his speech on this date see CJ (1975–76) 125.

4 HC 111 (1971–72) p xiii.

5 CJ (1839) 274; ibid (1872) 23; ibid (1884) 74; ibid (1895) 149; ibid (1905) 249; ibid (1921) 114; ibid (1928) 215; ibid (1942–43) 58; ibid (1964–65) 412. For early instances of proceedings on the death of a Speaker, see D'Ewes 95, 120; CJ (1547–1628) 116; Parl Hist (1066–1625) 1, c 811.

Speaker tomorrow (at an hour stated) in the House of Peers, for Her Majesty's royal approbation.[1] The Speaker Elect puts the question for adjournment, and, when the House adjourns, he leaves the House without the mace before him. On the following day the Speaker Elect takes the chair, after prayers have been read, and awaits the arrival of Black Rod from the royal commissioners, by whom the royal approbation is given under a commission for that purpose, with the same forms as at the meeting of a new Parliament, except that the claim of privileges is omitted.[2] On returning from the House of Lords the new Speaker reports his approbation by the Queen, and repeats his acknowledgments to the House. The appointed business for the day is then entered upon.

Oath in the Commons

The Speaker, who has been elected at the commencement of a Parliament, on returning from the Lords, reports to the House his approbation by the Queen and the confirmation of their privileges and 'repeats his most respectful acknowledgments to the House for the high honour they have done him'. He then puts the House in mind that the first thing to be done is to take and subscribe the oath required by law; and himself first, alone, standing upon the upper step of the chair, takes and subscribes the oath accordingly; in which ceremonies he is followed by the other Members who are present.

The occupants of the government front bench (see p 167) are generally the first to be sworn, and after them the occupants of the opposition front bench. When these and any privy counsellors not included among them have taken the oath the Speaker calls the other Members present bench by bench, giving precedence to the various benches at his discretion, but as a rule calling those on his right and those on his left alternately.[3]

On the following day the daily prayers are read, for the first time, by the Speaker's chaplain.

The Members normally continue to take the oath on that day and on one subsequent day, after which the greater part are sworn and qualified to sit and vote.

Oath on demise of Crown. In the event of the demise of the Crown Parliament meets immediately, pursuant to the Succession to the Crown Act 1707, and all Members of both Houses again take the oath.[4]

There appears to be some doubt whether the obligation to take the oath in these circumstances is statutory or rests merely upon the custom of Parliament. The latter opinion has been stated with authority in the House of

---

1 In 1895 and in 1905 the Speaker was elected on the day upon which the House adjourned for Easter and Whitsuntide respectively, and was presented for the sovereign's approbation on the first day on which the House met after the adjournment, CJ (1895) 149; ibid (1905) 249. See also ibid (1970–71) 184–185 for a recent instance where approbation was signified on the same day as the election of a Speaker.

2 LJ (1839) 308; CJ (1693–97) 272; ibid (1839) 274; ibid (1872) 23; ibid (1884) 74; ibid (1895) 149; ibid (1905) 249; ibid (1921) 115; ibid (1928) 215; ibid (1964–65) 412. On the election of Mr Addington, in 1789, the King himself came down to the House of Lords to signify his approbation in person, CJ (1788–89) 435.

3 HC Deb (1959–60) 612, c 20.

4 LJ (1837) 420, etc; CJ (1837) 490, etc; LJ (1901) 4, etc; CJ (1901) 5, etc; CJ (1910) 121, etc; CJ (1910) 150, etc; LJ (1935–36) 51, etc; CJ (1935–36) 50, etc; LJ (1936–37) 59, etc; CJ (1936–37) 59, etc; LJ (1951–52) 77, etc; CJ (1951–52) 88.

Commons.[1] On the death of Edward VII the House of Commons met on Saturday 7 May 1910 but, owing to the unavoidable absence of the Speaker, the Chairman of Ways and Means and the Deputy Chairman, adjourned to the following Monday, the Clerk of the House fulfilling the role which, in the now superseded procedure, he played in the election of a Speaker. The Chairman of Ways and Means, acting as Deputy Speaker, and other Members then took the oath. The Speaker took the oath at the first sitting of the House at which he was present.[2]

Manner of taking the oath. The ordinary form and manner of administering and taking the oath are prescribed by section 1 of the Oaths Act 1978. Under this section the person taking the oath holds the New Testament, or, in the case of a Jew, the Old Testament, in his uplifted hand, and says or repeats after the officer administering the oath the words, 'I swear by Almighty God that . . .' followed by the words of the oath prescribed by law.

A Member may also take the oath with uplifted hand in the form and manner in which an oath is usually administered in Scotland.[3]

Members who desire to do so may take the oath prescribed in the Promissory Oaths Act 1868 (with the necessary alteration in the sovereign's designation)[4] and kiss the book. The form of that oath is, 'I do swear that I will be faithful and bear true allegiance to Her Majesty Queen Elizabeth, her heirs and successors, according to law. So help me God.'[5]

Affirmation in lieu of oath. Members who object to be sworn may avail themselves of the power granted by section 5 of the Oaths Act 1978[6] which provides that any person who objects to being sworn shall be permitted to make his solemn affirmation instead of taking an oath.

Time for taking the oath. A definite time at the beginning of a sitting, usually immediately after Prayers, is reserved for Members returned after a general election who desire to take the oath or make the affirmation required by law on any day after the days set aside for taking the oath at the beginning of a Parliament.[7]

Penalties for omission to take the oath. By the Parliamentary Oaths Act 1866, any Peer voting by himself or his proxy, or sitting in the House of Lords without having taken the oath, is subject, for every such offence, to a penalty of £500; and any Member of the House of Commons who votes as such, or sits during any debate after the Speaker has been chosen, without having taken the oath, is subject to the same penalty, and his seat is also vacated in the same manner as if he were dead. These penalties can be

---

1 HC Deb (1937) 319, c 762.
2 CJ (1910) 147, 150,154.
3 Oaths Act 1978, s 3.
4 Oaths Act 1978, s 3.
5 Promissory Oaths Act 1868, ss 2, 8.
6 See also SO No 5. The permission to substitute for an oath a solemn affirmation was first accorded by the Oaths Act 1888, s 5.
7 CJ (1886) 5; Parl Deb (1886) 302, c 21. See also SO No 6. On 9 March 1882, the Speaker had stated that to object to any Member taking the oath except on grounds public or notorious, or within the cognizance of the House, would be simply vexatious, Parl Deb (1882) 267, c 441.

recovered upon the suit of the Crown alone.[1] When peers or Members have neglected to take the oaths from haste, accident, or inadvertence, Acts of indemnity have been passed to relieve them from the consequences of their neglect.[2] In the Commons, however, it is necessary to move a new writ immediately the omission is discovered, as the Member's seat is vacated.[3]

But although until he has taken the oath a Member may not sit and vote, he may vacate his seat by the acceptance of the Chiltern Hundreds and is entitled to all the other privileges of a Member (but not to his salary), being regarded, both by the House and by the law, as qualified to serve, until some other disqualification has been shown to exist.

Members of the Commons who have not taken the oath have been nominated to committees in exceptional circumstances.[4]

Certificate of return. At the beginning of a Parliament, the Clerk of the Crown in Chancery delivers to the Clerk of the House of Commons a Return Book of the names[5] of the Members returned to serve in the Parliament; in practice the book is received from the Clerk of the Crown by the Clerk Assistant standing below the Bar. This book is sufficient evidence of the return of a Member.

Subscription of oath and affirmation. As soon as a Member has been sworn, or has made his affirmation, he subscribes at the Table the 'test roll', which is a bound parchment volume, headed by the oath and affirmation which he has taken or made; and the Member is then introduced to the Speaker by the Clerk of the House. The rules which provide for the time and manner of taking the oath by Members returned at by-elections are stated on pp 298–300.

When the greater part of the Members of both Houses are sworn the preliminaries peculiar to the first session of a new Parliament are concluded, and Parliament is ready to hear the Queen's speech and to proceed with the initial business of the session.

OPENING OF NEW SESSION

In every session but the first of a Parliament, as there is no election of a Speaker, nor any general swearing of Members, the session is opened at once by the Queen's speech, without any preliminary proceedings in either House. Until the causes of summons are declared by the Queen, either in

---

1 [1883] *Bradlaugh v Clarke* 8 App Cas 354.
2 45 Geo 3, c5 (Lord J Thynne); 56 Geo 3, c48 (Earl Gower); 1 Will 4, c8 (Lord R. Grosvenor); 5 Vict c3 (Earl of Scarborough); Lord Plunket and Lord Byron 1880 (these are private Acts, none of them printed). Since then in the Lords, bills of indemnity have not been introduced. Four peers having sat and voted in session 1906 without having taken the oath (Parl Deb (1906) 163, c1291; ibid 164, c4), the matter was referred to the Select Committee on the Standing Orders of the House in 1907 (see LJ (1907) 105; HL (1907) 95, piv).
3 CJ (1805–06) 148; ibid (1812) 286; ibid (1813–14) 144; ibid (1816–17) 42; ibid (1924) 74. In the Bradlaugh's case, however, the Chiltern Hundreds (see pp 50–51) were accepted.
4 CJ (1714–18) 59; 6 Chandler. Deb 19; Parl Hist (1714–22) 7, c57; 2 Hatsell, 88 n, 3rd edn; CJ (1857–58) 162, 167; Parl Deb (1858) 150, c 430. In 1880, John Bright was appointed to the Parliamentary Oath Committee, on which he served and voted, though not then having made an affirmation.
5 The Committee of Privileges has recommended that a Member who has disclaimed a peerage shall appear in the official records and be addressed in the House without his previous style or courtesy title (HC Deb (1971–72) 830, cc 975–6; HC 324 (1971–72)).

person, or by commission, neither House can proceed with any public business: but the causes of summons, as declared from the Throne, do not bind Parliament to consider them alone, or to proceed at once to the consideration of any of them (see p 233).

Both Houses assemble on the day and immediately before the hour[1] appointed for the delivery of the Queen's speech. In the Commons prayers are said before the Queen's speech, but in the Lords not until their second meeting, later in the day. The Speaker, after prayers, normally suspends the sitting until Black Rod approaches the door, when he proceeds to the Chair to receive him. This practice is observed, because no business can be transacted until Parliament has been opened by the Crown.

Opening by Queen in person

When the Queen meets Parliament in person, she proceeds in state[2] to the House of Lords, where, seated on the Throne, adorned with her crown and regal ornaments, and attended by her officers of state (all the lords being in their robes, and standing until Her Majesty commands them to be seated), she commands Black Rod, through the Lord Great Chamberlain, to let the Commons know 'it is Her Majesty's pleasure they attend her immediately, in this House'. Black Rod goes at once to the door of the House of Commons, which he strikes three times with his rod; and, on being admitted, he advances up the middle of the House towards the Table, making three obeisances to the chair, and says, 'Mr Speaker, the Queen commands this honourable House to attend Her Majesty immediately in the House of Peers'. The Speaker, with the House,[3] immediately goes up to the bar of the House of Lords; upon which the Queen reads her speech to both Houses of Parliament, from a printed copy, which is delivered into her hands by the Lord Chancellor, kneeling upon one knee.[4]

When the speech has been delivered the House of Lords is adjourned during pleasure. The Commons retire and, returning to their own House, pass through it, the Mace being placed upon the Table by the Serjeant, and the House reassembles at half-past two.[5]

Opening by Commission

When the Queen is not personally present, the causes of summons are declared by the Lords Commissioners. Black Rod is sent, in the same

---

1 Before 1919 the usual hour was two o'clock; from 1919 to 1939 twelve o'clock; from 1940 to 1960 eleven o'clock; since 1961 half-past eleven.
2 Between 1917 and 1919 and between 1939 and 1948 Parliament was opened by the Sovereign with less than the customary ceremony, a course followed in special circumstances in March 1974 when the Queen interrupted a foreign tour at short notice to open Parliament in person.
3 If deemed expedient, the precedence of Members in going to the House of Lords on the opening and prorogation of Parliament by Her Majesty can be determined by ballot, in pursuance of resolutions (CJ (1851–52) 443, 445). For the arrangements made in session 1902 which have been adopted on subsequent occasions, see Report of the Joint Committee on Presence of the Sovereign in Parliament (HC 212 (1901) p x).
4 There are also precedents, followed for many years by Queen Victoria and throughout his reign by George I, for the speech to be read by the Lord Chancellor in the presence and under the personal direction of the Sovereign. See eg LJ (1509–77) 3; ibid (1578–1614) 357; ibid (1620–28) 435, 470; ibid (1714–18) 22, etc. In the absence of the Lord Chancellor in 1927 and 1936 the Speech was delivered for the King by Earl Balfour and Viscount Halifax respectively.
5 At two-fifteen in the first session of a Parliament to permit Members to be sworn before the resumption of business at half-past two.

manner, to the Commons, and acquaints the Speaker that 'the Lords Commissioners desire[1] the immediate attendance of this honourable House in the House of Peers, to hear the commission read'; and when the Speaker and the House have reached the bar of the House of Lords, the Lord Chancellor reads the royal speech to both Houses.[2]

Subsequent proceedings are as described in the case of an opening by the Queen in person.

Report of Queen's Speech

When the Houses are resumed in the afternoon, the main business is for the Lord Chancellor in the Lords, and the Speaker in the Commons, to report the Queen's speech. In the former House, the speech is read by the Lord Chancellor. In the Commons, the Speaker states that, for greater accuracy, he has obtained a copy of the speech, which he directs to be printed in the Votes and Proceedings.[3]

Business taken before consideration of Queen's Speech

Bill read pro forma. Before the Queen's speech is reported, it is the practice, in both Houses, to read some bill a first time *pro forma*, in order to assert their right of deliberating without reference to the immediate cause of summons. In the Lords this practice is governed by Standing Order No 71. In the Commons the same form is observed pursuant to ancient custom. The Select Vestries Bill is read in the Lords and the Outlawries Bill in the Commons. Debate is out of order.[4]

Sessional orders, etc. In the Commons other business is constantly entered upon before the report of the Queen's speech by the Speaker. The order of business on the first day of a session should be:

(1) Motions for the issue of new writs.
(2) Sessional orders.[5]
(3) Oral notices of introduction of bills.

---

1 On 19 May 1880, attention being drawn to the inadvertent use by Black Rod of the word 'require', the proper form was explained from the chair, Parl Deb (1880) 251, c 1221.
2 Until the end of session 1867, the Lords Commissioners' speech was framed as proceeding from themselves, and the Sovereign's name was used in the third person. On that and subsequent occasions, the speech was framed in the first person, in the name of the Sovereign, being delivered by the Lord Chancellor or one of the Commissioners by the royal command, LJ (1865) 639; ibid (1935–36) 378. At the prorogation, 10 August 1872, the Lord Chancellor's sight being impaired, the speech was read by Earl Granville, ibid (1872–73) 753.
3 Eg 25 June 1987, HC Deb (1987–88) 118, c 38.
4 HC Deb (1946–47) 430, c 3; ibid (1960–61) 629, c 3–5. The bill is recorded as having been read the first time and ordered to be read a second time, but no day is appointed for the second reading.
5 The sessional orders relating to witnesses, the police and the Votes and Proceedings, though not formally moved, have been debated and divided on (CJ (1984–85) 4).

(4) Queen's Speech.[1]

Private Notice Questions are not now accepted on the first day of a session[2] nor may an application be made for the adjournment of the House under Standing Order No 20.[3] There is no precedent for statements being made on such a day, since they can be made on the Queen's Speech.

Address in reply to Queen's Speech

When the Queen's Speech has been read, an Address in answer thereto is moved in both Houses. Two Members in each House are selected by the Government for moving and seconding the Address, which is moved in the form of a resolution expressing thanks to the Sovereign for the most gracious speech addressed to both Houses of Parliament,[4] and amendments to the Addresses are moved by way of additions to it.[5]

The debate on the Address in the Commons falls into three parts. Debate on the opening day (or days) covers the whole field of government policy, especially in relation to the contents of the Queen's Speech. Thereafter debate is usually directed to more specific areas of policy chosen by the Opposition, of which the House is informed,[6] although without prejudice to Members' right to raise other topics.[7] The final part consists of a series of amendments, which are usually moved from the front-bench of the main Opposition party. Standing Order No 32 (calling of amendments at end of debate) provides that on the final day, if an amendment to the motion for an Address has been disposed of at or after the expiration of the time for opposed business, a further amendment selected by the Speaker may be moved and disposed of forthwith; under this provision the Speaker has selected amendments tabled by opposition parties other than the official Opposition.[8] Although the scope of debate is restricted by the normal rules

---

1 Until the changes made in 1978 in the procedure for raising a complaint of privilege (see pp 135–136), matters of privilege might be brought under the notice of the House immediately before the consideration of the Gracious Speech (CJ (1840) 4; ibid (1883) 4; ibid (1890) 7; Parl Deb (1895) 30, c 54; and ibid (1905) 141, c 71. See also Parl Hist (1753–65) 15, c 1354. On one occasion, a matter of privilege was not disposed of before the moment of interruption, so that the Speaker was unable to report the Gracious Speech till the following day (Parl Deb (1890) 341, c 122).

2 Mr Speaker's Private ruling of 9 November 1965.

3 Mr Speaker's Private ruling of 3 November 1977.

4 Addresses have also contained expressions of condolence on the deaths of members of the Royal Family (LJ (1892) 7, CJ (1892) 10; LJ (1896) 16, CJ (1896) 12.) In session 1921 (II) the Gracious Speech was confined to the Articles of Agreements signed by Ministers and the Irish Delegation, and the Address of each House declared its readiness to confirm and ratify these Articles (LJ (1921) 463, 470; CJ (1921) 405, 406). The appointment of a committee to prepare the Address was discontinued in the Lords in 1861 and in the Commons in 1888, as the Address is moved in a form suitable for presentation (CJ (1890–91) 7).

5 In 1812 the Address was moved as an amendment to a question for an Address proposed by Sir F Burdett (Parl Deb (1812) 21, c 18, 33). In 1894 an amendment to the Address having been carried, the Address, as amended, was negatived, and another Address was proposed by the leader of the House and agreed to (CJ (1894) 9, 11). In 1924 an amendment to the Address having been carried, the Address, as amended, was then agreed to (CJ (1924) 32.)

6 HC Deb (1952–53) 507, c 150; ibid (1987–88) 118, c 41; ibid (1988–89) 142, c 6.

7 HC Deb (1953–54) 520, c 153; ibid (1960–61) 629, c 185; ibid (1985–86) 86, cc 255–263.

8 Second Report of Select Committee on Procedure, HC 372 (1974–75); CJ (1975–76) 15; ibid (1982–83) 19. Two amendments dealing with different subjects have been debated together on the final day, HC Deb (1975–76) 901, c 497.

once an amendment has been moved (see pp 339–40, 372–373), by practice the last two speakers are allowed some latitude in replying to the debate as a whole.[1]

The transaction of public business is carried on whilst the proceedings on the Address are in progress, bills being introduced, committees appointed, and Statutory Instruments considered. The debate on the Address is normally given precedence but it has occasionally been postponed in favour of urgent business including a motion of censure and government bills,[2] and it may be interrupted in the course of a sitting by an adjournment under Standing Order No 20 (see pp 300–302).

In the Lords the opening day's debate on the Address is brief. After the speeches of the mover and seconder, it is usual for the Leader of the Opposition to move the adjournment of the debate. On this motion he and the other party leaders congratulate the mover and seconder and comment generally on the Queen's Speech. The debate is then adjourned. The debate is resumed on the following day. Different topics (such as Foreign Affairs and Defence, Home and Social Affairs, and Economic Affairs) are taken on different days.

Presentation of Address. After the Address has been agreed to, it is ordered to be presented to Her Majesty. In the case of the Address of the House of Lords it is usual for the presentation to be ordered to be made 'by the Lords with white staves';[3] and in the case of the Address of the Commons by 'such members of the House as are of Her Majesty's most honourable Privy Council, or of Her Majesty's household'.[4]

Her Majesty's answer. Her Majesty's answer to the Address of each House is usually of a formal character, but the inclusion of unusual matter in the Address has caused variations in the reply. Thus Queen Victoria's answer to the Address, 10 June 1859, which contained a paragraph affirming that Her Majesty's then present advisers did not possess the confidence of the House of Commons, stated that Her Majesty had thereupon taken measures for the formation of a new administration.[5] On 11 August 1892, when a paragraph similar in form was added to the Address, the usual order was made for the presentation of the Address; but no answer from Her Majesty was presented to the House. On 26 January 1886, and 21 January 1924, when an amendment which occasioned a change of administration was added to the Address, the Sovereign's answer was of a wholly formal character.[6] The procedure upon the reception of the Sovereign's answer to an Address by Parliament is described on p 569.

---

1 HC Deb (1960–61) 629, c 957.
2 CJ (1884) 8, 9, 46, 66; ibid (1922) 354, 355, 357; ibid (1924–25) 27, 34. See also CJ (1928) 12.
3 I.e. the royal household.
4 The members of the household were first added to the Members ordered to present the Address in the year 1899, CJ (1899) 54.
5 CJ (1859) 219.
6 CJ (1886) 57; ibid (1924) 32.

PROCEEDINGS ON PROROGATION OF PARLIAMENT

For convenience the forms observed on the prorogation of Parliament at the close of a session are described here. Formerly Parliament was prorogued by the Sovereign in person[1] but since 1854 the royal functions on this occasion have always been exercised by certain lords acting by virtue of a commission under the great seal. If there are any bills awaiting royal assent a clause is inserted in the commission authorizing it to be signified.[2] In this case royal assent is pronounced before the reading of the Queen's Speech.[3] Otherwise the Lord Chancellor proceeds immediately to the reading of the Speech after the commission has been read by the Clerk. At the conclusion of the Speech he prorogues Parliament to the date named in the commission.[4]

On the return of the Commons to their own Chamber, the Speaker, sitting in the Clerk's place at the Table, reads to the House the terms of the commission and directs the terms of the speech to be entered in the Votes and Proceedings.[5]

---

1 For procedure when the Sovereign attends in person see 16th edn, p 294.
2 LJ (1967–68) 667. Before 1968 royal assent on prorogation was authorized by a separate commission (see also pp 527–529).
3 For cases of prorogation without a Speech, see LJ (1783–87) 383; ibid (1820) 764; ibid (1892) 422; ibid (1895) 391; 1 Creevey Papers 341; 2 ibid 5.
4 For procedure when a dissolution is contemplated, see p 221.
5 Eg, 7 November 1986 (HC Deb (1986–87) 103, c 1196.)

CHAPTER 14

A Sitting: general arrangements in the House of Commons

The purpose of this chapter is to give an account of the arrangements made for conducting a sitting of the House of Commons. This will include the rules regulating the meeting and adjournment of the House, the requirement of a quorum for divisions, and such arrangements as exist for distributing the time of the sitting between various classes of business.

DAYS AND HOURS OF SITTING

The House normally sits upon Mondays, Tuesdays, Wednesdays, Thursdays, and Fridays, rarely on Saturdays, never (except in emergency) on Sundays. The times of sitting and of other proceedings given in this and the succeeding chapter (see pp 256–257), are those laid down by Standing Orders. They were put into force under a sessional order made on 13 November 1946, which was incorporated into Standing Orders on 4 November 1947. On 17 January 1980 Standing Order No 5 (relating to Friday Sittings), now SO No 11, was amended to provide that the House should meet at half-past nine o'clock instead of at eleven o'clock.

EXTRAORDINARY SITTINGS AND ADJOURNMENTS

Under Standing Order No 11 (6) a sitting on Saturday or Sunday (except in the case of the demise of the Crown or of a recall in accordance with Standing Order No 12) can only be secured by a resolution of the House, made normally by a Minister of the Crown at the commencement of public business. As a sitting on either of these days is not subject to any rules of the House regulating the hours of meeting, interruption, and adjournment, such matters have been provided for in the resolution appointing a Saturday sitting or, when the House is recalled under Standing Order No 12, in a resolution moved at the commencement of the sitting; and such sittings have been held under the limiting conditions applying to Friday sittings,[1] or subject to special directions, such as that when government business is concluded,[2] or at a stated hour[3] the House shall adjourn without question put.

---

1 CJ (1920) 492; ibid (1921) 51, 65.
2 CJ (1889) 453; ibid (1890) 553; ibid (1893–94) 57.
3 CJ (1955–56) 429; ibid (1981–82) 286.

On the demise of the Crown,[1] and also on occasions of emergency,[2] Parliament has occasionally been assembled on a Sunday.

Prolongation of sitting till Sunday morning

The prolongation of a sitting till Sunday morning is also of infrequent occurrence, the last occasion being in 1883.[3]

Attendance of Parliament at Divine service

From time to time, on occasion of national thanksgiving, mourning or supplication, Parliament as a body has attended divine service. The Houses usually meet in their respective chambers, and the Speaker of each House, preceded by the mace, makes his way to the church appointed for the service, the House following.[4] This procedure—even when there is no preliminary meeting in the chamber—is considered as a sitting, and has been so recorded in the Journal.[5]

Attendance of Parliament at certain Royal ceremonies

Royal ceremonies which have been attended by Parliament as a body include coronations,[6] jubilees,[7] and funeral ceremonies.[8] The Houses may attend these ceremonies after a preliminary sitting,[9] or may interrupt the sitting and resume it later.[10] But a preliminary sitting is not essential.[11]

Extraordinary adjournments

One or both[12] Houses have adjourned as a mark of respect on the occasion of the death of a distinguished Member past or present,[13] or of the death of a

---

1 CJ (1699–1702) 782; ibid (1714–18) 3; ibid (1757–61) 929, 933; ibid (1819–20) 89.
2 Eg, outbreak of war, CJ (1938–39) 411, 412.
3 CJ (1883) 471.
4 LJ (1918) 186, 271; CJ (1918) 200, 235; LJ (1944–45) 112; CJ (1944–45) 121; LJ (1945–46) 31; CJ (1945–46) 16; HC Deb (1945–46) 413, cc 48–53; LJ (1964–65) 129; CJ (1964–65) 112; LJ (1966–67) 109; CJ (1966–67) 120; LJ (1967–68) 14; CJ (1967–68) 12.
5 CJ (1918) 200; CJ (1964–65) 112.
6 CJ (1837–38) 621. At coronations subsequent to this date Parliament has not attended as a body, but the Members of both Houses have attended by personal invitation; in 1911, 1937 and 1953 the Speaker, by the desire of the Sovereign and pursuant to a resolution of the House, represented the Commons, CJ (1911) 75; ibid (1936–37) 134; ibid (1952–53) 227.
7 CJ (1887) 245, 259; ibid (1897) 293, 297; ibid (1934–35) 191.
8 CJ (1910) 154; ibid (1935–36) 54; ibid (1951–52) 93.
9 CJ (1887) 259; ibid (1910) 154.
10 CJ (1935–36) 54. CJ (1976–77) 286 when the House attended at 11 am on the Queen at Westminster Hall to present an Address on the Silver Jubilee, after which the sitting was suspended till 2.30 pm that day.
11 Votes and Proceedings (1987–88) (20 July 1988).
12 LJ (1882) 139; CJ (1882) 185.
13 LJ (1861) 416; ibid (1908) 101; ibid (1946–47) 188; CJ (1914) 319; ibid (1922) 221; ibid (1937–38) 24; LJ (1944–45) 84; CJ (1944–45) 86; ibid (1947–48) 90; LJ (1951–52) 70; ibid (1962–63) 96; HC Deb (1962–63) 670, cc 40–50; LJ (1964–65) 117, 126; CJ (1964–65) 110; ibid (1976–77) 84.

Member in the precincts[1] or of a distinguished statesman of another country.[2] Parliament has also adjourned in connection with royal ceremonies.[3]

HOURS OF MEETING

On Monday, Tuesday, Wednesday, and Thursday the House meets at half-past two o'clock, while on Friday it meets at half-past nine o'clock. When the House sits on Saturday,[4] if the House has not ordered otherwise,[5] the Speaker has fixed the same hour for the meeting of the House as on Friday.[6]

> The official announcement of the hour appointed for the next meeting of the House is made by an entry placed, under the Speaker's authority, at the close of the 'Votes and Proceedings' (see p 205), as the announcement of the appointed hour of meeting in the motion which adjourns the House is an exceptional occurrence.[7]

Broken sittings

If a sitting on any day should be prolonged beyond the hour of meeting on the following day, no independent sitting can take place on that day; and the House rises when it has disposed of the business of the sitting prolonged from the previous day. The House has been prevented from meeting for this reason on twenty-three occasions in the present century. In recent Sessions it is unusual for there not to have been at least one such example.[8]

Abnormally long sittings

On several occasions the House has sat for upwards of twenty-four hours without adjourning.

> The longest sitting on record occurred on 31 January 1881 on the Coercion Bill, when the House sat for $41\frac{1}{2}$ hours. Sittings lasting over 30 hours are

---

1 CJ (1878) 264; ibid (1907) 316; ibid (1921) 334.
2 CJ (1944–45) 95; HC Deb (1963–64) 685, c 44.
3 Both Houses adjourned on the occasion of the marriages of Queen Victoria on 10 February 1840, and of the Prince of Wales on 10 March 1863, LJ (1840) 43; CJ (1840) 70; LJ (1863) 69; CJ (1863) 102; on a Friday, when the House of Lords was adjourned in the normal way, the House of Commons adjourned on the occasion of the wedding of Princess Margaret; CJ (1959–60) 212; both Houses adjourned for the wedding of the Prince of Wales on 29 July 1981; LJ (1980–81) 784; CJ (1980–81) 492. For other royal marriages Parliament has not adjourned. Parliament has adjourned for royal jubilees, eg CJ (1887) 309; ibid (1897) 301; ibid (1934–35) 188, and coronations, CJ (1911) 285.
4 CJ (1920) 495; ibid (1921) 52, 67.
5 CJ (1873) 122, ibid (1890) 222; ibid (1893–94) 234; ibid (1895) 331; ibid (1908) 386; ibid (1912–13) 533; ibid (1955–56) 429.
6 On Saturday 12 December 1936, the day after His Majesty's Declaration of Abdication Act 1936 had received the royal assent, the House met at a quarter to three o'clock for the purpose of taking the oath of allegiance to the new King.
7 CJ (1909) 547. The usual practice is for the House to vary the hours of a future meeting by a motion at the commencement of public business eg CJ (1981–82) 100.
8 Arrangements for dealing with Questions on such occasions are now laid down in SO No 17(9) (see p 284).

rare, although they have occurred on three occasions in recent Sessions on 22 May 1984, 5 March 1985 and 10 November 1987.

RULES FOR CLOSING THE SITTING

The closing of a sitting is now regulated by Standing Order No 9 (3), in the case of the first four sitting days of the week and by Standing Order No 11 on Friday. There are also provisions under Standing Order No 10 under which a sitting can be suspended on the first three days of the week until the following morning. Standing Order No 9(3), the so-called 'ten o'clock rule', provides for the interruption of business under consideration at ten o'clock, after which time only business exempted from the provisions of Standing Order No 9 whether by Standing Order No 14(1) or by a motion so exempting the business under Standing Order No 14(2), or unopposed business, may be entered upon. When such business is concluded, a motion for the adjournment of the House is necessary to enable the House to rise, and this motion can be debated until half an hour after it has been proposed. On Friday the rule is similar, with the substitution of half-past two for ten and, for the special time limits imposed by Standing Order No 14(1)(d) and by Standing Order Nos 14(1)(b) and 15, a quarter past three and four o'clock respectively. A motion may be (but rarely is) moved by a member of the Government to exempt business from the 'half-past two rule' and the same classes of business are exempt from its operation. The procedure in closing a sitting is described below in detail, first, when the 'ten (half-past two) o'clock rule' is in operation, secondly, when business is exempted from it under paragraph (1) or paragraph (2) of Standing Order No 14, and, thirdly, when the sitting is suspended in accordance with Standing Order No 10.

A. WHEN BUSINESS IS NOT EXEMPTED FROM THE TEN O'CLOCK RULE

Interruption of business

On every day of the week, except Saturday and Sunday, the sitting hours of the House are subject to the following regulations. Under Standing Order No 9, business is interrupted on Monday, Tuesday, Wednesday, and Thursday at ten o'clock, when, if the House is not engaged on business exempted under Standing Order No 14(1) (see pp 243–244), the Speaker rises from the chair and interrupts the business then under consideration; or, if the House is in committee, the chairman leaves the chair to make his report to the House. Under Standing Order No 11 the moment of interruption on Friday is half-past two o'clock. The business under consideration at the moment of interruption, if no day is named for its resumption, becomes a dropped order.

In 1972 the Select Committee on Procedure recommended that when, following a motion to resume proceedings on an unopposed bill after the moment of interruption, the question for the resumption of such proceedings is agreed to without objection, it should still be possible for proceedings to continue until objection is taken;[1] but the House has taken no action upon this recommendation.

Dilatory motions and closure. Dilatory motions, ie motions for the adjournment of the House or of the debate, or that the chairman do report progress, or do leave the chair, pending at the moment of interruption, lapse without question put[2] (see p 334). A motion for the adjournment made after the moment of interruption is therefore a new question.[3] At that moment also closure may be moved; and if closure be moved, or if proceedings under the closure rule be then in progress, the Speaker, or chairman, does not leave the chair until the questions consequent thereon, and on any further question, as provided in Standing Order No 35, have been decided. (See pp 406–407.)

Transaction of business after moment of interruption

After the business under consideration at ten o'clock, or at half-past two o'clock on Friday, has been disposed of, no opposed business can be taken. On days when private Members' business has precedence, the remaining orders of the day and notices of motions[4] as far as the first Government order or notice are called in the order in which they stand on the Paper, and proceedings on an order of the day or motion can be carried on, although debate may arise thereon, until a division be challenged upon a question proposed from the chair, or objection be taken to further proceeding, or until debate arises which, in the opinion of the Chair, constitutes opposition to the business.[5] Thus, after the moment of interruption the House has resolved itself into a Committee on a bill, a clause has been amended and agreed to, the remaining clauses have been agreed to, and the bill has been reported, considered as amended, read the third time and passed.[6] A Clause has also been disagreed to, other Clauses agreed to, some amended and agreed to, the Bill reported, considered as amended, read the third time and passed.[7] But as soon as objection is taken the business becomes opposed business; and further consideration thereof must be postponed until the next sitting at which private Members' business has precedence, or until such other sitting as the Member in charge of the business may appoint. A similar procedure is not usually followed in respect of Government business, since by a practice adopted in 1940 instructions are given for Government orders

---

1 HC (1971–72) 385.
2 On adjournment at six o'clock on Wednesday, CJ (1889) 55; interruption at midnight, ibid (1889) 134; ibid (1890) 252; ibid (1894) 7; ibid (1904) 270; progress, at midnight, ibid (1890) 370; interruption at eleven o'clock, ibid (1911) 420; ibid (1924) 39; postponed proceedings on resumption after eleven o'clock, ibid (1924) 37: at five o'clock on Friday, ibid (1912–13) 208.
3 HC Deb (1945–46) 415, c 1390.
4 On Fridays when private Members' motions have precedence it is not now the practice of the Chair to call any such motions which have not been reached by half past two o'clock unless they relate to the progress of private Members' bills then in committee (eg Notices of Motions, 30 March 1973, pp 4871–4872; HC Deb (1972–73) 853, cc 1794, 1797).
5 The expression of opposition to the question under debate has been held to constitute objection, HC Deb (1964–65) 715, c 1073. An indication that a Member would vote against the question that the clause stand part of a bill has been held to constitute objection; HC Deb (1978–79) 963, cc 1722–1723.
6 HC Deb (1957–58) 586, c 1382.
7 HC Deb (1978–79) 963, cc 856–857.

and notices of motions to continue from day to day on the Order Paper until disposed of. It is however a common practice for the Government to seek to take minor motions as unopposed business after the moment of interruption.

Business exempted under various standing orders

Standing Orders Nos 43 (Order in debate), and 61 (Committal of bills), 80 (Business committee), and 93 (Public bills relating exclusively to Scotland), 101(3)(i)(ii); (5) and (6) (Standing committees on statutory instruments etc), 55 (Contracts to be approved by Resolution), 102(4) and (5) (Standing committees on European Community documents). 134 (Petition as to present personal grievance), and 143 (Withdrawal of strangers from the House) all contain specific provision for proceedings, though opposed, to be decided after the expiration of the time for opposed business.

As during the transaction of unopposed business no division can be taken, the Speaker has disregarded a challenge to the question put on a motion for the adjournment of the House, and, treating the motion as a formal motion, has declared that the Ayes had it, and left the chair (Parl Deb (1905) 142, c 1512; HC Deb (1979–80) 990, cc 490–492).

Formal motions after interruption of business

In the case of opposed business essential to the completion of the transaction on which the House is engaged at the moment of the interruption of business, the Speaker has overruled an objection to the taking of opposed business after that hour. Thus he has not permitted opposition to formal questions, such as the addition of the words, 'upon this day six months', when the House has disagreed to the second reading of a bill; or the entry of the Speaker's reprimand or admonition upon the Journal of the House.[1] Nor can an objection that the proceeding takes place after the expiration of the time for opposed business be made to a formal motion for the purpose of carrying on the business of the House, such as a motion for the appointment of a committee to draw up reasons for disagreeing with amendments made by the Lords to a bill (although the moving of an amendment to such a motion has been held to constitute objection)[2], a motion for the discharge of an order for a return by the Member who had moved for the return;[3] or for the withdrawal of a bill by the Member in charge thereof.[4] Similarly objection cannot be taken to the announcement (which is technically a motion) by a Member in charge of an order of the day of a further day to which it is to be deferred.

Business not disposed of before the termination of a sitting

Under Standing Order No 9(5) an order of the day not disposed of before the termination of a sitting is deferred to such day as the Member in charge of that order or a Member authorized by him may appoint, and any order of

---

1 CJ (1892) 167; Parl Deb (1892) 3, c 964.
2 HC Deb (1975–76) 919, c 371–373.
3 3 June 1904, Mr Speaker's ruling (not recorded in Parliamentary Debates).
4 Parl Deb (1888) 328, c 1883.

the day not reached before the termination of a sitting, unless the Member in charge has given other instructions to the Clerk at the Table, stands over until the next sitting.

B. WHEN BUSINESS IS EXEMPTED FROM THE TEN O'CLOCK RULE

(1) Business exempted under Standing Order No 14(1)

It is provided under Standing Order No 14(1) that proceedings on a bill brought in upon a ways and means resolution, or any Consolidated Fund Bill or Appropriation Bill, proceedings in pursuance of any Act of Parliament and proceedings on European Community documents or of any Standing Order of the House which provides that proceedings though opposed may be decided after the expiration of the time for opposed business or proceedings on a motion authorizing expenditure in connection with a bill, may be entered upon at any hour, though opposed, shall not be interrupted at ten o'clock under the provision of Standing Order No 9, and if under discussion when the business is postponed under the provisions of any standing order (see pp 251–252) may be resumed and proceeded with, though opposed, after the interruption of business.[1] It is also provided under Standing Order No 20 that any proceeding postponed under that standing order (see pp 300–302 is automatically exempted from the ten o'clock rule for a period equal to the duration of the proceedings under Standing Order No 20 and may be resumed and proceeded with at or after ten o'clock. (If a motion (see below) stands on the paper to exempt the business postponed for a specified period and the motion is agreed to, the postponed business becomes exempted for the period occupied on the motion for the adjournment with the addition of the period specified in the motion (see Standing Order No 14(5)(b)). Standing Order No 14(1) also provides, however, that in the case of proceedings in pursuance of any Act of Parliament and proceedings on European Community documents save in so far as Standing Order No 15 otherwise provides (see pp 316–317), Mr Speaker shall put any questions necessary to dispose of such proceedings not later than half-past eleven o'clock or one and a half hours after the commencement of those proceedings, whichever is the later; this is subject to the proviso that, if Mr Speaker is of the opinion that, because of the importance of the subject matter of the motion, the time for debate has not been adequate, he shall, instead of putting the question as aforesaid, interrupt the business, and the debate shall stand adjourned till the next sitting other than a Friday. Standing Order No 14(1)(d) also provides that in the case of proceedings on a motion authorizing expenditure in connection with a bill (see p 263) any questions necessary to dispose of such proceedings are to be put at 10.45 or three-quarters of an hour after the business was entered upon, whichever is the later.

Proceedings under Acts of Parliament. The principal proceedings under Acts of Parliament relate to statutory instruments and drafts of statutory

---

1 However, SO No 54 (Consolidated Fund Bills) provides that on any day on which the second reading of a Consolidated Fund or an Appropriation Bill stands as first order of the day, the questions for second reading and third reading shall be put forthwith.

instruments laid before both Houses as parliamentary papers. For the conditions under which proceedings with regard to these instruments qualify to be exempted from interruption, see pp 316–317. Resolutions made under the Church of England Assembly (Powers) Act 1919 (see p 556) are exempted business; as are motions under the Statutory Orders (Special Procedure) Act 1945; CJ (1962–63) 41; and the House of Commons Disqualification Act 1975 (similar to provisions under the 1957 Act; CJ (1961–62) 44). A resolution which is not made pursuant to a statute but is necessary for the provisions of a statute to have effect is not exempted business, eg a resolution applying the Tribunals of Inquiry (Evidence) Act 1921, CJ (1922) 26, 27.

When an order of the House is in force for its adjournment without question put at, or at the end of a limited debate after, the conclusion of government business, that order overrides any exemption from the rule which Standing Order No 14 would normally afford (Parl Deb (1907) 180, c 1621; ibid (1908) 196, c 559; HC Deb (1918) 108, c 1073-4), unless special provision is made for its consideration (CJ (1914) 361; ibid (1919) 24, 325; ibid (1920) 390; ibid (1921) 291, 372; ibid (1923) 334), or facilities are afforded in individual cases by the Government (ibid (1917–18) 163; HC Deb (1917) 96, c 735).

Proceedings on European Community documents. Standing Order No 14(1) defines European Community documents as meaning draft proposals by the Commission of the European Communities for legislation and other documents published for submission to the Council of Ministers or to the European Council, whether or not such documents originate from the Commission.[1] European Community documents are generally debated in the House or in standing committee as a result of reports recommending debate from the Select Committee on European Legislation (see p 657).

(2) Exemption of specified business by order of the House

It is also provided, by Standing Order No 14(2), that at the interruption of business, a motion may be made and decided forthwith[2] 'That any specified business[3] may be proceeded with at this day's sitting though opposed (a) until any hour; (b) until a specified hour; or (c) until either a specified hour or the end of a specified period after it has been entered upon, whichever is the later, or in any form combining any or all of these effects in respect of different items of business'. Not more than one such motion may be made at the interruption of business at any one sitting.[4] To fall within the terms of the

---

1 The Chair has withdrawn documents from the consideration of the House which did not fall within the definition contained in Standing Order No 14 at the time (CJ (1977–78) 132; HC Deb (1977–78) 942, c 622).
2 If such a motion should deviate from the prescribed form it would be open to debate, Parl Deb (1905) 148, c 1144.
3 The business to be exempted is specified; though often it is specified in general terms, eg government business; CJ (1919) 110 and often thereafter, eg ibid (1962–63) 97, ibid (1968–69) 243, ibid (1970–71) 378, ibid (1974–75) 613; proceedings in any Lords Amendments to a bill, eg ibid (1922) 113, and often thereafter eg ibid (1974), 310, ibid (1976–77) 63. Also Lords Messages: eg ibid (1976–77) 461, 466. Government business other than the business of Supply, eg ibid (1973–74) 41. Her Majesty's Message (Emergency Powers): ibid (1973–74) 109.
4 SO No 14 (6).

Standing Order notice of these motions must stand upon the Order Paper in the name of a Minister of the Crown at the commencement of public business, but the motions themselves stand over until the interruption of business.[1] If the terms of a motion are other than those specified in the standing order, it must be moved at the commencement of public business and is debatable—or, it may be taken in the normal course of business on a previous sitting day. At the interruption of business, if the business interrupted is neither exempted from the operation of the 'ten o'clock rule' by Standing Order No 14(1), nor included in the terms of the motion for the exemption of business from the 'ten o'clock rule', the normal procedure for unexempted business (see pp 240–243) is followed for that item; thereafter the Speaker calls upon a Minister of the Crown to move the motion for the exemption of the business to be exempted, and, if the motion is carried, the first business covered by the motion is entered upon. If the business interrupted is itself covered by the exemption motion, the Speaker immediately (ie before a day is named for resuming the proceedings) calls upon the Minister to move the motion; and, if the House is in committee, the chairman leaves the Chair, the House resumes, and the Speaker immediately calls upon the Minister in the same way. If the business in progress at ten o'clock is itself of the class exempted from the ten o'clock rule under Standing Order No 14(1), but is followed on the Order Paper by business on which notice of an exemption motion has been given, the time for the Speaker to interrupt the business and call upon a Minister to move the exemption motion is ten o'clock, or, if the House is in process of deciding a question at ten o'clock, as soon thereafter as the question (and any other questions immediately pending on it) have been decided. The fact that any proceedings are exempted does not prevent a motion being made for the adjournment of the House in the course of those proceedings.[2] If business which has been exempted for a specified period is not concluded by the end of that period, it is then treated in every respect as if it were unexempted business which has reached the normal hour of interruption (Standing Order No 14(5)(a)). A motion taken at ten o'clock (or at half past two on a Friday) enabling certain business to be proceeded with after that hour in the terms of paragraph (2) of Standing Order No 14 is not to be construed as replacing or overriding any limitation placed upon the duration of those proceedings by other standing orders, by an allocation of time order or by any other order of the House.[3]

C. WHEN THE SITTING IS SUSPENDED PURSUANT TO STANDING ORDER NO 10

Standing Order No 10 lays down that, in order to suspend the sitting, a Minister after ten o'clock on a Monday, Tuesday or Wednesday may make a motion, 'That the proceedings of this day's sitting be suspended'. The question on this is to be decided without amendment or debate, and if it is

---

1 SO No 14 (2).
2 Speaker's Private ruling, 6 October 1931.
3 Thus an order 'That the Motion relating to Scotland Bill (Allocation of time) may be proceeded with at this sitting, though opposed, until any hour' did not affect the limitation of one hour placed upon those proceedings which had already been fixed by para 10 of the Allocation of time Order agreed to previously (HC Deb (1977–78) 953, cc 405, 461–463).

agreed to, the adjournment motion follows immediately, and is debated in
the normal fashion except that at the close of this debate or after half an
hour, the adjournment motion lapses and the Speaker suspends the sitting.
In the case of a Committee of the whole House, if the question on a motion,
That the proceedings of the Committee be suspended (Standing Order No
10(2)) is agreed to, the chairman leaves the chair and reports the decision of
the Committee to the Speaker, who then puts the question in respect of the
House. If this question is negatived, the House immediately resolves itself
again into Committee, but if it is agreed to proceedings continue as above.
The House reassembles at 10 a.m. and business is proceeded with. No
further debate is permitted on the motion for the adjournment; instead, Mr
Speaker either puts the question forthwith on a motion, that the House do
now adjourn (Standing Order No 10(3)(a)), or adjourns the House without
putting any question when business has been concluded (Standing Order No
10(3)(b)), or, if the business has not been concluded before two o'clock,
interrupts proceedings at that hour. In this case the debate, or further
consideration of the bill, stands adjourned. If the House is in Committee at
two o'clock, the chairman leaves the chair, reports progress and asks leave
to sit again, and the Speaker then adjourns the House without putting any
question.

This procedure was introduced on 12 December 1967, but has not been
used since 1969.

D. INFORMAL SUSPENSION OF A SITTING

The sitting of the House is occasionally suspended without any question
being put with the intention of resuming the transaction of business at a later
hour. Such an informal suspension of the sitting always occurs on the
opening day of a session (see p 232).[1]

A sitting may also be suspended on other occasions, as when a bill from
the Commons is under consideration by the House of Lords,[2] or whilst the
House waits for a message from the Lords Commissioners. On 17 February
1866, the Lords sent a message to the Commons, requesting them to continue sitting for some time, to which the latter agreed, the object being to
ensure the passing of the Habeas Corpus Suspension (Ireland) Bill on that
day.

If business is concluded before seven o'clock on a day when leave has been
given to move the adjournment of the House under Standing Order No 20
(see pp 300–302), or opposed private business has been set down by
direction of the Chairman of Ways and Means[3] (see pp 279–281), or when

1 Suspension of sitting 4 August 1919, on the occasion of a river pageant, HC Deb (1919) 119,
  c 36, 65; 24 November 1927, owing to failure of the lighting system, HC Deb (1927) 210,
  c 2117; 28 September 1944, for the convenience of the House, during a long speech by the
  Prime Minister, HC Deb (1943–44) 403, c 487; 1 May 1962, after the sudden collapse of a
  Member, HC Deb (1961–62) 658, c 886; 11 March 1963 (HC Deb (1962–63) 673, cc 1005,
  1008); 26 March 1968 (HC Deb 1967–68) 761, c 1442); 13 December 1973 (HC Deb (1973–74)
  866, c 707); and 10 February 1983 (HC Deb (1982–83) 36, c 1235); 30 March 1979, to
  investigate an explosion occurring in the precincts of the Palace, HC Deb (1978–79) 965,
  cc 875–876. See also p 587, n 2.
2 Parl Deb (1884–85) 298, c 1532; ibid (1907) 182, c 417; HC Deb (1914) 65, c 1832; ibid
  (1967–68) 759, c 1917; ibid (1971–72) 831, c 1454.
3 HC Deb (1956–57) 567, c 455.

private Members' motions were given precedence over Government business at seven o'clock under a former sessional order,[1] the sitting is informally
suspended until seven o'clock. On Fridays on which private Members'
notices of motions and bills have precedence under Standing Order No
13(5), if the proceedings on the private Members' motions (and the debate
on any motion for the adjournment moved under Standing Order No 9(7))
have been completed before half-past two o'clock, the sitting is suspended
and the orders of the day for the bills are not read until that hour.[2]

Occasionally, an informal suspension is granted to allow a period of
reflection following a procedural impasse.[3]

During the suspension of a sitting the Speaker, the mace being left upon
the Table, retires from the House, and returns at the appointed hour, when
business is resumed. As, technically, the House continues sitting, these
occurrences are not noted in the Journal.

DISPOSAL OF QUESTIONS PENDING AT MOMENT OF INTERRUPTION

By a convenient, and indeed necessary, elasticity of practice, the standing
orders which prescribe a limit to the time for the transaction of business are
not so strictly enforced as to prevent the House from completing, when the
fixed hour arrives, the proceeding on which a decision is in process of being
taken.[4]

Procedure thereon is extended, under this practice, beyond the hour
appointed for the interruption of business. Consequently, whenever a question is under decision, either by collecting the voices or by a division, at an
hour appointed by the standing orders for the interruption of business, the
decision of the House is announced and acted upon after that fixed hour.
Nor does the fact that the moment is passed when business should be
interrupted prevent the putting from the Chair—if necessary, after an
intervening closure motion—of the main, original or any further questions
con-
sequent upon that decision of the House, and any such contingent question
may be decided by a division.

If, however, when certain questions are proposed from the chair, a
Member objects to further proceeding, or offers to speak to the question (an
action which is construed as signifying objection)[5] his action brings into force
the provisions of Standing Order No 9(6) and converts the business then
under transaction into opposed business. The Speaker, or in Committee the

---

1 HC Deb (1961–62) 662, c 589.
2 HC 538 (1970–71) para 57.
3 HC Deb (1984–85) 77, c 762; ibid (1988–89) 144, c 212.
4 CJ (1873) 403; Parl Deb (1873) 217, cc 1230–1232; CJ (1877) 111; Parl Deb (1877) 233, c 306.
5 Care should be taken to distinguish the two cases. In the case of business arising immediately
  before the moment of interruption merely rising to speak to the question is taken to signify
  objection to proceeding with it. In the case of business *commencing after* the moment of
  interruption it is necessary for a Member to say 'I object,' or otherwise to indicate his
  opposition to the business.

Chairman, therefore proceeds to interrupt the business;[1] and its consequent disposal under the terms of Standing Order No 9(5) necessarily follows, unless thereupon closure be moved pursuant to Standing Order No 9(4) (see p 407).

The practice of completing business begun before the fixed hour by putting successively all questions pending at the moment of interruption, may be illustrated by the following examples.

Examples of procedure on business pending at moment of interruption
The following are examples of the practice of the House regarding questions put from the chair after the time prescribed for the interruption of business, or for the adjournment of the House, when closure is not moved.

(1) A division was in progress at the time fixed for the interruption of business, on an amendment to the address in answer to the Queen's speech. A division on a further amendment took place (as provided for in Standing Order No 32) and the Speaker then put the main question which was itself divided upon, there being no objection to this further proceeding.[2]

(2) A division was in progress, at the time fixed for the interruption of business, on the question that the word 'now' should stand part of the question for the second reading of a bill. The question upon the word 'now' was negatived; the words, 'upon this day six months,' were added: the main question so amended was agreed to, and the bill was put off for six months.[3]

The following are examples of the adjournment, upon objection taken, of further proceedings consequent upon a question under decision at the hour fixed for the interruption of business, the right to move closure at the moment of the interruption of business not having been exercised.

(1) When to the question that a bill be now read a second time an amendment was moved to leave out those words, and to substitute a statement urging reasons why the bill should not be read a second time, and the House had decided that the words proposed to be left out should not stand part of the question, the question for the addition of the words of the amendment was proposed from the chair; but, as the hour for interruption was passed, and objection was taken to further proceeding, the debate was immediately adjourned.[4]

(2) On the consideration of a bill on report, when a division on the second reading of a new clause was concluded after the hour fixed for the interruption of business, the Speaker announced that if no amendments were offered, he would put the question, 'That the clause be added to the bill'; but on a Member intimating that he had an amendment to offer, the Speaker adjourned further proceedings on the clause, and the consideration of the bill was appointed for the morrow.[5]

Procedure in committee on questions pending at interruption of business. Procedure in a committee of the whole House regarding questions

---

1 CJ (1887) 249; Parl Deb (1887) 315, c 488.
2 CJ (1982–83) 19.
3 CJ (1877) 111; Parl Deb (1877) 233, c 306.
4 CJ (1924–25) 186.
5 CJ (1890–91) 372; Parl Deb (1891) 354, c 877.

pending at the moment of interruption follows the procedure of the House, including the power of moving closure on the interruption of business.

ADJOURNMENT ON QUESTION

Except on occasions when the Speaker, in pursuance of a standing or other order, adjourns the House without question put, the House can only be adjourned upon a question put from the chair.[1] Such a question is debatable and affords a convenient opportunity for raising matters of administrative policy (see p 267), the discussion of which can continue for half an hour, or longer if it is proposed before ten o'clock or half-past two o'clock on Fridays.

ADJOURNMENT OF THE HOUSE, WITHOUT QUESTION PUT

Pursuant to Standing Order No 9(3) and (7) on Mondays, Tuesdays, Wednesdays, and Thursdays, the House, if not previously adjourned, sits till half an hour after a motion for the adjournment of the House has been proposed either at ten o'clock, or, if there is business exempted from the operation of the standing order (see p 243), or unopposed business, proposed at the conclusion of such business or, if the sitting is suspended at that hour, as soon as it is resumed.[2] It is then adjourned by the Speaker without question put.

On Friday (Standing Order No 11)

At a Friday sitting the same procedure is followed, half-past two o'clock being substituted for ten o'clock.

On Saturday and Sunday. The time for the adjournment of the House on Saturday and Sunday is not prescribed by standing order but the time of adjournment is usually specified in the resolution appointing a Saturday or Sunday sitting. Where the House is recalled in accordance with the provision of Standing Order No 12 on either of these days, it is necessary for a resolution to be moved, preferably at the commencement of the sitting, if it is decided to regulate its hours of sitting.

ADJOURNMENT IN CASE OF GRAVE DISORDER

Under Standing Order No 45, in the event of grave disorder arising in the House, the Speaker may adjourn the House without question put if he

---

1 CJ (1667–87) 560.
2 HC Deb (1970–71) 810, c 159.

thinks it necessary to do so[1] or he may suspend the sitting to a time to be named by him.[2]

On 13 November 1912 and 11 April 1923 the Speaker suspended the sitting for an hour. When he resumed the chair, the state of disorder continued and he adjourned the House without question put (CJ (1912–13) 409; ibid (1923) 88). On 6 December 1961, grave disorder having arisen in a Committee of the whole House, the Chairman left the chair to report the circumstances to the House; he resumed the chair as Deputy Speaker and suspended the sitting for half an hour (CJ (1961–62) 55). See also p 395.

ADJOURNMENT BEYOND THE NEXT DAY OF SITTING

When it is intended that the House should be adjourned to a day beyond the next sitting day, a motion is made, by a member of the government,[3] that the House do 'now',[4] or at its rising,[5] or at the conclusion of the sitting,[6] or at its rising on a future day,[7] adjourn until the specified day. Under Standing Order No 22, proceedings on such motions are limited to three hours. Adjournments are subject to the power given to the Speaker under Standing Order No 12 to give notice, on representations from Her Majesty's Government, for an earlier meeting of the House (see p 224).

QUORUM OF THE HOUSE

Forty Members, including the Speaker, form the quorum of the House; but the absence of a quorum does not entail the termination of a sitting, it being provided by Standing Order No 40 that the House shall not be counted at any time.

Standing Order No 40 provides, however, that if at any time it appears, on a division, that fewer than forty Members (including the occupant of the Chair and the Tellers) have taken part, the business under consideration stands over until the next sitting of the House and the next business is taken.[8] Should the division have taken place in Committee, the Chairman leaves the chair to report the fact to the House, and the Speaker declares that the Committee stands over till the next sitting, under the terms of the Standing Order.

---

1 CJ (1905) 202; ibid (1911) 351; ibid (1914) 237; ibid (1924) 178; ibid (1960–61) 98; ibid (1975–76) 360 (after he had previously suspended the sitting to a named hour, and after grave disorder had again arisen at the resumption).

2 CJ (1920) 436; HC Deb (1920) 135, c 39; CJ (1935–36) 341; HC Deb (1935–36) 315, c 838; CJ (1955–56) 428; HC Deb (1955–56) 558, c 1625; CJ (1970–71) 68, 216; ibid (1971–72) 109; ibid (1974–75) 259; ibid (1977–78) 438, when the Speaker made a statement on the suspension, HC Deb (1977–78) 953, c 677; CJ (1979–80) 851; CJ (1981–82) 27.

3 For occasions on which such motions have been made without notice, see p 324, nn 5 to 8.

4 CJ (1892) 419; ibid (1905) 151.

5 CJ (1959–60) 212.

6 CJ (1890–91) 178; ibid (1892) 182.

7 CJ (1960–61) 326, etc.

8 Eg HC Deb (1966–67) 745, cc 675–679; ibid (1983–84) 57, c 563. In a division on a closure, SO No 40 becomes effective rather than SO No 36, eg HC Deb (1982–83) 33, c 1161.

Before the passing of Standing Order No 40 in its present form in 1971, it had been possible, subject to certain restrictions, for a Member to call the attention of the Speaker to the fact that forty Members were not present; the House was then counted after a lapse of four minutes, and adjourned if less than forty Members were found to be present. For a description of the former procedure, see the 18th edition of this work, pp 298–301.

DIVISION OF THE TIME OF THE SITTING

PUBLIC AND 'OTHER' BUSINESS

The chief principle on which the time of the sitting is distributed rests on a distinction between public business and other business. 'Other business' comprises private business, questions, and a number of miscellaneous items of business which are taken before public business. Public business is composed of orders of the day and notices of motions, which is the business on which debate takes place. A full description of the arrangements for distributing the time of the sitting is given in chapter 15. The order in which the items of 'other business' are taken is set out in chapter 16 where also the nature and significance of each of these items is described in detail. Each of the classes of public business is described separately in one of the succeeding chapters.

Divisibility of sitting during public business

Public business normally continues until the moment of interruption at ten o'clock (see p 240). But it is liable to be interrupted, or, more technically, suspended and postponed at seven o'clock (see p 301) (i) by a motion for the adjournment of the House which has satisfied the conditions prescribed by Standing Order No 20 (although these motions are now more usually taken at the commencement of public business on the day following their being granted) (see p 301); or (ii) by opposed private business set down by direction of the Chairman of Ways and Means under Standing Order No 16(5) (see pp 279–281). At the conclusion of such business the business postponed on its account is resumed.

INCIDENTAL INTERRUPTIONS

Besides the interruption of business, at the moment prescribed by the standing orders (see p 240), or by a Member rising to move the closure of debate (see p 405), proceedings in Parliament may be interrupted by a matter of privilege or order, which calls for the immediate intervention of the House on a matter of recent occurrence (see p 307); by motions under Standing Order No 143 (withdrawal of strangers from House (see p 172)); by occasions of sudden disorder in the House, and by the suspension of Members, or other proceedings for the enforcement of order (see pp 394–395); by a message from the Queen or the Lords Commissioners, commanding or desiring the attendance of the House in the House of Peers;[1] by the presentation of the answer to an address to the Crown[2] (see p 569); by a message from the other House, and by proceedings taken in consequence[3] (see pp 570–571); by a report of reasons for disagreeing to Lords amendments[4] (see p 515); by the Clerk of the Crown attending by order of the House to amend a return[5] (see p 33); and by a report from the Serjeant at Arms regarding the execution of the orders of the House.[6]

When the cause of interruption has ceased, or the proceeding on it has been disposed of, the debate, or the business in hand which was interrupted, is resumed at the point where the interruption had occurred.[7] The resumption of a proceeding, subjected to an interruption, has however been sometimes delayed by further interruptions.[8]

PROCEEDINGS IN SECRET SESSION (See also p 171)

During the war of 1939–45, following the precedents of the years 1916–18, whenever it seemed that matters of value to the enemy might be revealed in debate in either House, motions were made for the House concerned to go into secret session, either to discuss a particular named subject,[9] or for the remainder of the sitting[10] without any reason being specified. It was also a frequent practice to devote part of a sitting only to secret matters, and then resume a public sitting.

Thus on Wednesday 13 November 1940 the House of Commons was moved into secret session in the usual way in order to hear a statement on

---

1 See HC Deb (1962–63) 669, cc 409–412. On 20 April 1863, the reading of a petition was so interrupted, and was resumed on the return of the Speaker from the Lords, CJ (1863) 168. On 13 November 1980 points of order were interrupted by a message to attend the Lords Commissioners, HC Deb (1979–80) 992, c 770.

2 CJ (1852–53) 438; ibid (1870) 377; ibid (1878–79) 23. This rule, however, does not apply to a message from the Crown. On 5 June 1866, a message relating to the marriage of Princess Mary of Cambridge was brought up between one motion and another; but not so as to interrupt a debate, CJ (1866) 366.

3 A message brought by the Clerk does not ordinarily interrupt the business under discussion, but there are occasions when such an interruption can arise, CJ (1871) 57; ibid (1914–16) 31; ibid (1919) 315 and on 16 July 1974 when consequential on a Message relating to corrections to a bill, the Speaker interrupted the business to announce that a Message had been received from the Lords in respect of those corrections and the question was put forthwith and agreed to, that the bill be now read the third time. HC Deb (1973–74) 877, cc 366–367.

4 CJ (1880) 431; ibid (1882) 452; HC Deb (1976–77) 919, c 669.

5 CJ (1837–38) 276, 308; HC Deb (1955–56) 545, cc 55, 57. On 31 July 1961 the Clerk of the Crown attended at the end of statements, pursuant to an Order of the House to attend forthwith, CJ (1960–61) 325.

6 Eg on 28 January 1971, the Deputy Speaker read a report he had received from the Assistant Serjeant of Arms on conduct at the doors of the 'Aye' lobby during a division on the previous proceeding, HC Deb (1970–71) 810, c 1097. The business of the House was in former times interrupted by a motion that candles be brought in: but by an order of 6 February 1717 the Serjeant was charged with the duty of having the House lighted when 'daylight be shut in', ibid (1714–18) 718. It is in pursuance of this order that the Serjeant provides emergency lanterns in the Chamber if the electricity fails (HC Deb (1986–87) 105, c 742).

7 See p 279 for an example of private business so interrupted.

8 CJ (1847–48) 550, 551, 755.

9 Eg Home Defence, LJ (1939–40) 165.

10 Eg CJ (1940–41) 5.

public business from the Prime Minister. This occurred before the commencement of public business. The motion for the secret sitting was framed as follows: 'That the proceedings in connexion with the statement on public business to be made by the Prime Minister be held in secret session.' When the statement and supplementary questions referring to it were concluded, Mr Speaker informed the House that he proposed to re-admit the public. Steps were taken informally to convey this statement to the public, and after a short pause to admit of their return, the Speaker called the Prime Minister to move the motion which stood in his name before the Orders of the Day.

On 28 November 1940, the address in reply to the King's Speech was debated partly in secret session.[1]

The considerations leading to a subject being debated in secret rather than in open session were described by the Lord Privy Seal on 9 July 1942.[2]

Also following the precedents of 1916–18,[3] when a full day's debate was in secret a report of proceedings in secret session was usually published by the Speaker. The following is an example of such a report: 'The adjournment of the House was moved, and a debate took place on Home Defence and other matters'.[4]

On 31 March 1943, in secret session, it was desired to show how Members had voted on a certain matter. The Speaker, in his published report of proceedings in secret session, indicated that a division had taken place on an amendment to a motion by the Prime Minister, and also published the form of the question and the names of Members who took part in the division.[5]

The question of communication to constituents of any general impression created on the mind of Members attending a secret session was considered on 16 July 1942, when the Speaker ruled that such communication would be irregular.[6]

Other points arising from the necessity of holding secret sessions which the House of Commons considered, or on which rulings were given, were:

Arrangements for Commons' Members attending secret sitting in the Lords (HC Deb (1939–40) 361, c 1148).

Divisions (ibid (1940–41) 374, c 1912).

Method of ensuring administrative action on suggestions made in secret (ibid (1939–40) 362, c 595).

Mr Speaker's ruling on disclosure by Members and penalties (ibid (1939–40) 355, c 1031; CJ (1941–42) 96, 129).

Mr Speaker's ruling on disclosure by Members to Lords (HC Deb (1939–40) 355, c 1210).

Reporting of, by Mr Speaker (ibid (1941–42) 376, c 2246).

Subsequent discussion on, with other Members not present (ibid (1941–42) 376, cc 2246–2250).

Ruling on raising again in open session a matter which has been decided in secret session (HC Deb (1943–44) 402, cc 1608–1609).

---

1 CJ (1940–41) 12.
2 HC Deb (1941–42) 381, c 951–955.
3 Eg HC Deb (1916) 81, c 2463.
4 HC Deb (1939–40) 362, c 270.
5 HC Deb (1942–43) 388, cc 200–204.
6 HC Deb (1941–42) 381, cc 1363–1368.

On 19 December 1945, it was resolved that no proceedings during the last Parliament held in secret session be any longer secret.[1]

---

1 CJ (1945–46) 120.

CHAPTER 15

The control and distribution of time in the House of Commons

INTRODUCTION

The preceding two chapters described the general procedure and arrangements relating to Parliaments, Sessions of Parliament and Sittings of the House of Commons. This chapter considers the time available to the Commons in the course of a session and the manner of distributing that time between the various types of business. At the end of the chapter is a table analyzing the time spent on the floor of the House of Commons on the main varieties of public business between 1978 and 1988.

THE TIME AVAILABLE TO THE HOUSE IN A SESSION

THE LENGTH OF A SESSION

Chapter 13 describes how the period of a Parliament, between two general elections, is divided into sessions. The ends of sessions are marked either by dissolution or prorogation, which are prerogative acts of the Crown. In other words, the duration of a session is determined by the Government. The Government's freedom of choice in this matter is, however, circumscribed both by convention and by the necessity of passing certain items of business in accordance with the procedures set out in standing orders and elsewhere. In recent times, there have been, on average, four sessions in each Parliament.[1] A session usually begins in November and continues until the following October, although this pattern is not infrequently interrupted by a dissolution. In a Parliament elected in a month other than October, the first session commonly continues until late October or early November of the year following, after which the normal pattern is resumed. Until the middle of this century, however, it was not uncommon for new sessions to begin after Christmas.[2] Normally the House adjourns in the week before Christmas for a period of between two and four weeks and again for periods of between one and two weeks at Easter and around the date of the Spring Bank Holiday; then again from the end of July until mid October when it resumes sitting for a period of between two and four weeks. The period after the summer adjournment is colloquially known as the 'spillover' and is used principally to complete the remaining stages of public bills which had not been completed before August. The House is then prorogued for a few days and the new session is opened in November.

---

1 From 1945 to 1987 there were 12 Parliaments totalling 44 sessions.
2 See, for example, the 14th edn of this work, pp 294–296.

In recent normal sessions the number of days on which the House has sat has varied between 160 and 180. The shortest session since 1945 was 1948 (8 days) and the longest that of 1966–67 (246 days).

TIMES OF SITTING

Times at which the House normally sits

Standing Orders Nos 9 to No 16 are those principally concerned with regulating Sittings of the House and the distribution of its time.

Under the terms of Standing Orders Nos 9 and 11 the House normally sits on Monday, Tuesday, Wednesday, Thursday and Friday. Saturday and Sunday sittings, which have been found necessary in times of emergency, can only be secured by a resolution of the House or by the recall of the House under Standing Order No 12. Standing Order No 9 lays down that on the first four sitting days of the week the House should meet in the afternoon at half-past two and adjourn (subject to certain qualifications) not more than half an hour after the moment of interruption at ten o'clock. Standing Order No 11 lays down that on Fridays the House should meet at half-past nine o'clock in the morning and normally adjourn, similarly half an hour after the moment of interruption at half-past two o'clock in the afternoon.

Methods of prolonging Sittings

The amount of time provided under the terms of Standing Orders No 9 and No 11 is invariably insufficient to enable the House to deal with all the business which falls to be considered during a session. This is despite the frequent use of standing committees to consider bills, the increased use of delegated legislation, and regular recourse to allocation of time orders (known as 'guillotines') to limit the time for the discussion of Government Bills on the floor of the House. The standing orders therefore provide the Government with methods for prolonging, with the agreement of the House, the amount of time which can be made available to the House.

By far the most important of these is Standing Order No 14, which provides that certain categories of business should automatically be exempted from the provisions of Standing Order No 9, thus enabling the House to discuss them after the moment of interruption at ten (or, on Fridays, half-past two) o'clock. The standing order further provides that a Minister of the Crown may, after having given due notice upon the Order Paper move to suspend from the operation of the ten o'clock rule[1] any business, even though opposed, for a specified or unlimited period of time. Widespread use has been made of the provisions of this standing order by all governments in recent times.

Standing Order No 10 provides for the sitting to be suspended on Mondays, Tuesdays and Wednesdays after ten o'clock upon the passage of a motion moved without notice by a Minister of the Crown. Under this procedure the half-hour adjournment debate follows immediately upon the House agreeing to the Government motion to suspend the sitting. The suspended sitting is resumed at ten o'clock the following morning (or the

---

1 The Standing Order is applied to Friday sittings by SO No 11.

same morning, if the suspension takes place after midnight), and the interrupted business and the remaining business set down for consideration may then be proceeded with. However, no use has been made of this provision in recent sessions.

ARRANGEMENT OF SITTINGS

The daily arrangement of business is discussed in detail in the succeeding chapter. The principal standing orders applying to the order in which business is taken are Nos 16, 17(2) and (3), and 19 to 25. Of these, the most significant is No 24 which allows the Government to arrange its business on any day in the order of precedence of its choosing.

Division of Sittings between public and other business

The sitting is divided between public business and other business. 'Other business' comprises unopposed private business, questions and a number of miscellaneous items of business which are taken before public business (see chapter 16). Public business is composed of orders of the day and notices of motions, which is the business on which, in general terms, debate takes place, and with which this chapter is principally concerned. As far as 'other' business is concerned there is a marked distinction between the first four days of the week and Fridays. No opportunity is provided on Friday under standing orders for taking certain items under this heading, for example oral questions. Nor are the time limits and the arrangements for dividing the sitting referred to below applicable to Friday sittings. Details are given in chapter 16.

Time available for business other than public business

Business taken before the commencement of public business. In general terms, 'other' business occupies the first hour of each sitting day other than Friday. Unopposed private business is taken immediately after prayers and, under the terms of Standing Order No 16, may continue until not later than a quarter to three o'clock, though normally it occupies much less time. Oral questions follow until half-past three. Public business may then commence unless certain other classes of business such as Private Notice Questions, government statements or applications for debate under Standing Order No 20 require to be disposed of. It has become increasingly common in recent Sessions for the commencement of public business to be delayed regularly by such other business, often until half-past four o'clock or later.

A full description of business taken between prayers and the commencement of public business is given in chapter 16.

Opposed Private Business. Under Standing Order No 16 Private Business, when opposed, may be set down by the Chairman of Ways and Means for consideration at seven o'clock. Details of this procedure are given in chapter 16. This is the only type of business other than public business which may be taken during the time for public business.

MAIN VARIETIES OF PUBLIC BUSINESS

Public business may be classified in various ways. By the standing and sessional orders regulating the time of the House it is divided into Government business, Opposition business and private Members' business. Some knowledge of the overall classification of business within these categories is necessary to make sense of the analysis which follows of how time is apportioned by the House. In procedural terms public business can be divided into:

(i) Substantive motions. A substantive motion is a self-contained proposal submitted for the approval of the House and drafted in such a way as to be capable of expressing a decision of the House. The special uses of the substantive motion for the adjournment of the House are described later in this chapter. A full procedural description of motions is given in chapter 17.

(ii) Bills. A bill is a draft legislative proposal which, when it has passed through its various stages and received Royal Assent, becomes an Act of Parliament. Bills can be further subdivided into Public Bills which deal with matters of public general interest; Private Bills which are for the particular interest or benefit of any person or body; and Hybrid Bills which are public bills which may in certain respects affect private rights. A full description of the procedure relating to public and hybrid bills is given in chapter 21 and that relating to private bills in chapters 33–39. Public bills, the type with which this chapter is principally concerned, may be introduced by any Member of the House: those introduced by a Minister are known as Government Bills, those introduced by other Members as Private Members' Bills.

(iii) Delegated legislation. Many public and general Acts of Parliament include provisions giving powers to Ministers to make certain types of subordinate legislation by means of statutory instruments, subject to various forms of parliamentary procedure. These are more fully described in chapter 22.

(iv) Financial business. Financial business may be defined as the business of the House which relates directly either to expenditure or taxation, and it is transacted under specially devised forms and procedures which are described in chapters 26 to 29.

CONTROL OF TIME IN THE HOUSE

In the first section of this chapter a description was given of the time available to the House in the course of a session. In principle the control of the distribution of this time rests with the House itself. In practice the House has by standing orders delegated this control, with some exceptions for opposition and private Members' business and other minor reservations, to the Government. This control is the result of a process which has continued over more than a century whereby an increasing proportion of the time of each Session has been appointed to the Government.

BASIS AND NATURE OF THE GOVERNMENT'S CONTROL

The real basis of the Government's control over the business of the House lies in Standing Order No 13, which gives the Government's business precedence at every sitting, except on 20 Fridays and 4 other half-days where precedence is given to private Members, 20 other days at the disposal of the opposition parties, and three days allotted for the consideration of Estimates recommended by the Liaison Committee. This, coupled with the provision in Standing Order No 24 allowing the Government to arrange its business, whether orders of the day or notices of motions, in any order it thinks fit, gives the Government virtually complete control over the time of the House (except in respect of certain carefully defined business, mostly of an urgent character, which under standing order or practice is given priority whenever it is brought forward). This far-reaching control can be further extended by the government, if the need arises, by inviting the House to agree to a motion suspending the relevant standing or sessional orders under which certain time is allotted to private Members or by making a special order for the purpose.

It should, however, be stressed before going on to describe the formal arrangement for allocating time that the actual time spent in debating a particular matter, or one particular aspect of a matter, is frequently determined by the wishes of the Opposition, and on other occasions by the wishes of groups of private Members or even of a single private Member. While certain days are specifically allotted to the opposition parties, there are a wide variety of other ways in which the official opposition, and to a lesser extent the minority parties, are able to influence the amount of time spent by the House on particular matters. For example, the opposition parties can expect to debate subjects of their own choice during the debate on the Address in reply to the Queen's Speech. By the conventions of the House the official opposition may also seek to ensure that the House considers any Government statutory instrument subject to the negative resolution procedure which it believes should be debated.

In a sense therefore all Government time is equally Opposition time, and the opposition parties' use of the multifarious opportunities available for influencing the way in which the proceedings of the House in Government time are conducted is thus of the first importance in the distribution of the time available for business in any session.

The same is true of private Members' time. Although, as described below, specific time is allotted to private Members in every session, and although numerous instances occur in government time in which the matter under debate is in practice raised by a private Member, private Members also retain the right to intervene at any juncture during the discussion of public business. This right is exercised daily by private Members in all parts of the

House, and in that sense the Speaker plays an important role in the use of parliamentary time by the use of his discretion in calling representatives of majority and minority views in all quarters of the House.

THE ALLOCATION OF TIME TO OPPOSITION AND PRIVATE MEMBERS' BUSINESS

The House is informed by the weekly Business Statement which items of government business (and in what order of precedence) it is intended to take on Government days, and which days or half-days have been allocated to Opposition and private Members' business, opposed Private Business or for consideration of estimates. The Business Statement is made every Thursday, after Question time, normally by the Leader of the House in reply to a private notice question by the Leader of the Opposition or the 'shadow' Leader of the House. In recent times it has been the practice of the Chair to allow supplementary questions on the Business Statement to continue for about half an hour. The order of business thus notified is seldom varied, save for the addition of minor items of business, without a supplementary statement being made.

PRIVATE MEMBERS' TIME

Bill days and motion days

Standing Order No 13 provides for 20 Fridays on which private Members' business has precedence over Government business, and for a further 4 days other than Fridays on which private Members' business has precedence until seven o'clock at which hour such proceedings lapse. The terms of the standing order provide that on 10 of these Fridays private Members' bills only shall have precedence, and that on the other 10 Fridays private Members' motions and private Members' bills shall have precedence (in that order). On the four half-days other than Fridays private Members' motions only have precedence.

The distribution of the 20 private Members' Fridays into 10 on which bills have precedence and 10 on which motions have precedence continued from Session 1950–51 until Session 1966–67, although it was not incorporated into standing orders until the end of Session 1962–63.

There are several examples of sessions in which this division has been varied. In recent sessions the standing order has been varied so as to provide for 21 Fridays, 12 for bills and 9 for motions. In Sessions 1983–84 and 1987–88 (both unusually long) the sessional order provided for 12 bill days and 10 motion days.

The sessional orders specify the days on which private Members' business is to have precedence, and the dates of the ballots for motions.

The provision for the allocation of four days other than Fridays for the discussion of private Members' motions until 7 pm has not been varied by sessional orders.

Order of precedence of Private Members' Bills and Motions

Unless varied by a sessional order, on the first six Fridays allotted to private Members' bills, precedence is given in accordance with the results of a ballot; on subsequent Fridays bills are arranged upon the paper in the following order: consideration of Lords amendments, third readings, consideration of reports not already entered upon, adjourned proceedings on consideration, bills in progress in committee, bills appointed for committee, and second readings.

The order of precedence of motions on private Members' Fridays and the four half-days is also determined by ballot, three names being drawn for each such occasion. The procedure for the ballot is more fully described on pp 303–304.

OPPOSITION TIME

Standing Order No 13 provides that on 20 days in each session, proceedings on business chosen by the opposition parties shall have precedence over government business.[1] It also provides that two Friday sittings should be deemed the equivalent of a single day for the purposes of this calculation.

Seventeen of the days so allocated are at the disposal of the Leader of the Opposition, and three at the disposal of the leader of the second largest opposition party.[2] This is defined in the Standing Order as the party of those Members not represented in the Government which has the second largest number of Members *elected* to the House as members of that party.[3]

The Standing Order provides that not more than two of the days at the disposal of the Leader of the Opposition, and not more than one of the three remaining days, might be taken in the form of half-days on any day other than a Friday.

The allocation under this standing order of Opposition days, dating from the decision of the House of 19 July 1982, replaced the long-established practice whereby the Opposition chose subjects for debate on 'Supply Days'. The provision of the facility for taking half-days has its origin in the decision of the House of 14 November 1967, arising from a report of the Select Committee on Procedure, to make such a facility available to the Opposition to raise urgent matters at short notice.[4]

---

1 HC Deb (1981–82) 28, cc 125–126 for statements on the timing of Opposition days.
2 The allocation of the three days to the second largest Opposition party was pursuant to a decision of the House of 23 May 1985, CJ (1984–85) 460.
3 In Session 1987–88, following the dissolution of the Liberal Party and the formation of the Social and Liberal Democrats, for the purposes of the Standing Order the disposal of these three days fell to the leader of the Official Ulster Unionist Party.
4 See HC Deb (1967–68) 754, c 259 and CJ (1967–68) 22; see also HC Deb (1971–72) 829, c 994 and HC Deb (1984–85) 68, c 406.

It has been the practice in recent Sessions for the leader of the second largest opposition party to put a portion of the three days at his disposal informally at the disposal of other opposition parties.[1]

BUSINESS TAKEN IN GOVERNMENT TIME

THE GOVERNMENT PROGRAMME

A Government's programme as outlined in the Queen's Speech is mainly implemented, so far as proceedings in Parliament are concerned, by the passing of Government bills and the necessary ancillary motions, and by the passing of motions for approving instruments made by Ministers under powers delegated by statute. There are certain items of business in these categories which the Government is virtually obliged to bring forward as a matter of routine, the main example being those parts of the Finance Bill without the passage of which the levying of taxation could not be continued. By convention too, one of the Ways and Means resolutions upon which the Finance Bill is introduced (that for the amendment of the law) gives scope for the Opposition and private Members to table amendments relating to taxation. The most important parts of the Government's programme are contained in the remainder of the legislation introduced by Ministers.

Address in reply to the Queen's Speech

A description of the Opening of Parliament and the delivery of the Queen's Speech was given in chapter 13. The speech sets out the main items of the Government's programme for the Session. By the practice of the House, at the opening of a session the Address in reply to the Queen's Speech is moved on the first day. In recent sessions, the House has devoted five or six days to the debate on the Address, covering the main areas of the proposed programme. A fuller description is given on pp 234–235.

Other forms of Addresses to the Queen. The other most common form of motions for an Address to the Queen relate to delegated legislation subject to certain parliamentary procedures and is dealt with in the section below on delegated legislation.

Other examples of Addresses to the Queen, which do not occur with any regularity, are dealt with in chapter 23.

Government bills

The amount of time spent on the floor of the House on bills varies greatly from session to session, depending on the amount of legislation introduced and the amount of controversy which that legislation attracts. This is particularly true of the amount of time spent in Committee of the Whole House. The committee stages of bills are in the large majority debated in standing committees, except where they are of constitutional or other special import-

---

1 A full account of the former procedure can be found on pp 285 and 286 and 728–733 of the 19th edn, and p 295 of the 20th edn of this work.

ance. For example, in Session 1971–72, the session in which the European Communities Bill was introduced, about 250 hours were taken up debating committee stages of bills, but this figure was unusually large.

Consolidated Fund Bills. Legislative sanction to expenditure is given by annual Consolidated Fund and Consolidated Fund (Appropriation) Bills. The procedures relating to such bills are described in chapter 27. There are at least three Consolidated Fund Bills in every full session. Under the provisions of Standing Order No 54 no debate may take place on any stage of a Consolidated Fund Bill if it stands as first order of the day. Arrangements relating to adjournment motions following Consolidated Fund Bills are described below.

Financial business

In general terms, financial business relates to expenditure and taxation, and is transacted under special procedures described below. In addition there are certain regular items of business which are closely related to public expenditure which are debated on motions moved by the Government.

Consideration of Estimates. Ordinary annual expenditure falls mainly within special arrangements made for the Consideration of Estimates set out in chapter 27. Under the terms of Standing Order No 52 three days, other than Fridays, before 5 August are allotted in each session to the consideration on the floor of the House of Estimates recommended for such debate by the Liaison Committee subject to endorsement by the House. Not more than one of these days may be taken in the form of two half-days.

Money resolutions and Ways and Means business. Expenditure for new purposes contained in legislation for which there is no authority is authorized by the House agreeing to money resolutions. Under Standing Order No 14(1)(d) proceedings on motions authorizing expenditure under a bill must end at a quarter to eleven o'clock or three-quarters of an hour after they are entered upon, whichever is the later, though in many cases there is no debate at all.

Some Government bills, of which the annual Finance Bill is the most notable example, are brought in only after the House has passed enabling resolutions, known as Ways and Means resolutions. Motions for such resolutions may be made in the House without notice on any day after the Address in reply to the Queen's Speech has been agreed. Debate on the Budget resolutions normally continues for four or five days (excluding the Friday) following the Chancellor's Budget Statement in March. Proceedings upon bills brought in upon Ways and Means resolutions are, under Standing Order No 14(1)(a), exempt from interruption at ten o'clock and may continue until any hour, but this exemption does not apply to debate on such resolutions themselves.

Other business related to financial matters. In addition to debate under the special procedures relating to financial business the Government has in recent years provided a day for debate on the Chancellor of the Exchequer's Autumn Statement and a day for debate on the annual public expenditure

White Paper. One or two days in each session are also set aside for general debate on the Defence Estimates and a day for discussion of reports from the Committee of Public Accounts.

Delegated legislation, etc, and European Community documents

Statutory instruments etc, made and laid pursuant to Acts of Parliament, are recorded in an Appendix to the Votes and Proceedings of the day on which they are laid. The Appendix indicates the form of parliamentary procedure to which, under the parent Act, they may be subject. Certain other legislative instruments, while not strictly statutory instruments, are subject to cognate procedures. Examples of these are Statutory Rules of Northern Ireland, Church of England Measures and Statements of Changes in Immigration Rules.

Instruments subject to affirmative resolution procedure. For those instruments which are subject to affirmative resolution procedure, it is necessary for the Government to secure the approval of the House either before, or within a specified time after, the instrument comes into effect (for a detailed account of this procedure see pp 545–547). Proceedings under the affirmative procedure are most frequently taken after ten o'clock, in which case under the provisions of Standing Order No 14(1)(b) debate may continue for one and a half hours. The majority of such instruments are now debated in Standing Committee and not on the floor of the House (see pp 594–595).

Instruments subject to negative resolution procedure. A larger number of government instruments laid before the House are subject to what is known as the negative resolution procedure. Under this procedure the Government may give time to the debate of a motion for an Address praying that the instrument be annulled (for a detailed account see p 547). Such motions are most frequently moved by a member of the official Opposition, but many are also moved by private Members or spokesmen of other opposition parties. Proceedings under the negative procedure do not normally take place until after 10 o'clock and under the provisions of Standing Order No 15 are required to end by 11.30 p.m. Again, many orders which would formerly have been debated under this procedure are now referred for consideration to a Standing Committee on Statutory Instruments, &c.

Instruments subject to cognate procedures. The Government always provides time for the discussion of Church of England Measures and provision is made in standing orders for their reference to standing committees, and for their treatment in this regard as if they were statutory instruments, although this provision has not in practice been much used. Standing Order No 15 also provides for its application to documents other than statutory instruments which are dealt with by methods analogous to the annulment procedure.

European Community Documents. Draft proposals by the Commission of the European Communities for legislation and other documents published by the Commission for submission to the Council of Ministers or the European Council are also frequently debated on the recommendation of the

Select Committee on European Legislation (see chapter 32, pp 775–776). Proceedings on motions relating to such documents are usually taken after ten o'clock and debate is limited to one and a half hours under the provisions of Standing Order No 14. Again, provision is made for the reference of such documents to standing committees in the same way as statutory instruments. The majority are, however, debated on the floor of the House. Complex motions which refer both to European Community Documents and to other publications (eg White Papers) cannot be so referred.[1]

OTHER GOVERNMENT BUSINESS

Apart from legislation, both primary and delegated, and financial business, Government business is brought before the House for debate on other days on motions moved by Ministers. Such motions may be in the form of a self-contained proposal or a motion for the adjournment, described below. In practice many of the forms of adjournment motion provide opportunities for private Members' to initiate debate.

Government motions

This category of business covers a wide variety of the matters which come before the House. Among the most important are motions to take note or approve of reports, including, for example, the reports of Select Committees, and of the Government's own White and Green Papers. Changes in the procedure of the House are generally brought about through the passing of resolutions moved by the Government. Also classified under this heading are the motions regularly brought forward by the Government for regulating the length of the Christmas, Easter, Spring and Summer adjournments of the House. A maximum of three hours' debate on such a motion is provided by Standing Order No 22. Another important example is that of allocation of time or 'guillotine' orders, which the Government moves in order to hasten progress on one or more of its bills (see pp 408–416). On these debate is also limited to three hours under Standing Order No 81. Gifts by the House to overseas Parliaments are usually agreed to following the moving of motions by the Government.

Substantive motions for the adjournment

The substantive motion for the adjournment 'That this House do now adjourn' may be moved to provide a vehicle for discussing many subjects other than the termination of a Sitting. Once such a motion has been agreed to, a Sitting is necessarily terminated but it frequently happens that an adjournment motion is moved without any intention of pressing it to a conclusion, and it is consequently withdrawn. The substantive motion for the adjournment is in fact a technical form devised for the purpose of enabling the House to discuss matters without recording a decision in terms. It is, therefore, not subject to amendment.[2] It is a general rule applicable to

---

1 CJ (1983–84) 683, HC Deb (1983–84) 63, cc 890 ff and CJ (1984–85) 504, HC Deb (1984–85) 81, cc 464 ff.
2 Parl Deb (1893) 440, c 449, HC Deb (1974–75) 897, c 1719.

all substantive motions for the adjournment that the subject to be discussed must not involve legislation, except incidentally.[1]

Adjournment motions moved by a Minister. With the exception of motions under Standing Order No 20 (see below), motions for the adjournment are moved either before or between the Orders of the Day, and can therefore, in accordance with the custom of the House, be moved only by a Minister (see pp 319–320).

Adjournment motions moved to provide for general debate. If no decision by the House is required, or if for some reason it is not desired to formulate a motion in express terms, a matter for which the Government has allotted time may be discussed on a motion for the adjournment of the House. Such motions are often the form used for, for example, a general foreign affairs debate, or for a wide-ranging debate on a topic such as the protection of the environment, or for debate of a report from a Select Committee. The Government may move such a motion to provide for discussion of a topic at the instance of the Opposition. The proposed subject for debate is indicated on the Order Paper but the Journal records only the substantive motion 'That this House do now adjourn'. Such motions are commonly withdrawn with the leave of the House at the conclusion of the debate, although occasionally a division is forced to indicate dissent from Government policy, in which case the Government will vote against the motion.

Occasional uses of the Adjournment Motion in Government time. Adjournment motions have occasionally been made when a Minister wishes to interpose a statement of Government policy between two orders of the day (see pp 298–299) or, when a statement is made at the normal time, to provide a question on which immediate debate can take place.[2]

Extraordinary Adjournments. The moving of the adjournment in Government time is also used for the expression of the respect or condolence of the House (see pp 238–239). Adjournments of this nature (known as Extraordinary Adjournments) are moved by the Government either at the commencement of public business or, should the occasion arise, without notice during the course of a sitting. Discussion is restricted to the occasion of the motion, and the motion is never withdrawn, the premature termination of the sitting being in itself the sign of the respect of the House.[3]

Holiday Adjournments. Whenever the House adjourns for one of its customary holidays, the whole day is normally devoted to the discussion, on a motion for the adjournment, of topics selected by private Members. It is customary for the day to be divided into convenient periods, and the Speaker selects the matter for discussion during each period, either by ballot or other means. Times are allocated to these periods, and notice of them appears on the Order Paper, but the times are provisional only.[4] Holiday Adjournments have been preceded by other Government business on

---

1 See chapter 16, pp 319–320.
2 See for example, CJ (1974–75) 500, HC Deb (1974–75) 984, cc 163–168.
3 See for example CJ (1964–65) 110.
4 HC Deb (1962–63) 669, c 1681.

several occasions[1] and in 1957 one such debate took place on the day before the House adjourned.[2]

Daily Adjournments. The conclusion of public business at each sitting is followed by the moving of an adjournment motion by a member of the Government. Standing Order No 9 allows an interval of half an hour between the moving of this motion and the compulsory adjournment of the House without question put (see p 318) and the right to choose the subject of, and initiate, the discussion during this period falls to a private Member, chosen by the method detailed in chapter 16 (see pp 318–319). The subject of debate chosen by the Member is given on the Order Paper.

Such debates are normally conducted exclusively between the Member who has the debate and the Minister replying on behalf of the Government. The Chair will permit other Members to intervene only if it is satisfied that this is with the agreement of both the Member who has the debate and the Minister.[3]

Should all the business for the day be concluded before the hour of interruption, an adjournment motion is immediately moved by a member of the Government, and the Member who has his name down for that day, may then initiate the discussion of the topic to be debated. Should the debate continue until the hour of interruption, the adjournment motion lapses, and another adjournment motion is moved, which may be debated for not more than half an hour, on which the subject under discussion at the moment of interruption may be further debated.

Occasionally when the business for the day and the daily adjournment debate have been concluded before the hour of interruption, a private Member raises another subject on the motion for the adjournment.[4]

On occasion, with or without the consent of the private Member successful in the ballot, the whole or part of the adjournment debate has been taken up by Government statements on important matters and by business statements (see p 319).

Adjournment Motions pursuant to Consolidated Fund Bills. As stated earlier, there are, in a normal Session, at least three Consolidated Fund Bills. Standing Order No 54 provides that on any day on which the second reading of a Consolidated Fund or an Appropriation Bill stands as first order of the day, all stages of the bill are to be taken formally, without debate. At the conclusion of the proceedings on the bill, it is further provided that a member of the Government may move the motion 'That this House do now adjourn'. This motion does not lapse at ten o'clock but may continue until nine o'clock on the following morning (or eight o'clock on a Friday morning). The standing order is intended to provide time to private Members for raising matters of their choice similar to that which was formerly afforded by the second reading debates on such bills. The order in which Members are called to initiate debate is determined by ballot for these occasions, and a list of names with the topic proposed to be raised is printed on the Order Paper.

1 CJ (1951–52) 354; CJ (1968–69) 363; CJ (1980–81) 500–501 and HC Deb (1980–81) 9, c 1402 ff.
2 CJ (1957–58) 61 and 62; HC Deb (1957–58) 580, cc 617–731 and 739 ff.
3 HC Deb (1983–84) 50, cc 136 and 138.
4 See ch 16, p 319.

The Speaker normally allots informal time limits of either one and a half or three hours to each topic.[1]

ADJOURNMENT MOTIONS UNDER STANDING ORDER NO 20

Under the terms of Standing Order No 20 a motion for the adjournment of the House may be moved by a private Member 'for the purpose of discussing a specific and important matter that should have urgent consideration'. Debate can only take place with the leave of the House given after Mr Speaker has stated that he is satisifed that the matter is proper to be discussed under the terms of the standing order. The standing order is designed to give the discussion of some recently occurring matter of emergency precedence over the programme of business previously arranged. In recent Sessions only between one and three such applications have been successful.

PRIVATE MEMBERS' BUSINESS TAKEN IN GOVERNMENT TIME

From time to time business proposed by private Members is taken in Government time. Such business can be usefully divided into that on which time is given as of right (on matters of privilege and for motions under Standing Order No 19), business for which time is by tradition invariably given (motions from the Committee of Selection and relating to Church of England Measures), and miscellaneous business for which time may in exceptional circumstances be made available.

Matters of privilege

If the Speaker decides to allow a motion which raises a matter of privilege to have precedence over the orders of the day (see p 135), the motion tabled by the Member concerned relating to that matter has precedence over the orders of the day at the next sitting.

Motions under Standing Order No 19 (The Ten Minute Rule)

Under the terms of Standing Order No 19, on Tuesdays and Wednesdays one private Member is able to set down a notice of motion for consideration at the commencement of public business for leave to bring in a bill. The Member who makes the motion and a Member who opposes it are each allowed to make a brief explanatory statement. Such bills are therefore known colloquially as 'Ten Minute Rule Bills'. In recent years full use has been made of this facility by private Members. Bills which are successfully introduced by this means may then have precedence over Government business on private Members' Fridays, as described above. However, since the ballotted private Members' bills have precedence over Standing Order

---

1 For the decision of the Speaker on the organisation of the first debate under the new procedure, see HC Deb (1982–83) 36, c 19.

No 19 bills, the latter rarely obtain a second reading, unless they are uncontroversial.

Under the Standing Order, motions for the nomination of Select Committees may also be made under the same procedure, but this facility has rarely been used in recent times.[1]

Committee of Selection

Under Standing Order No 104, nomination of departmental Select Committees is made on behalf of the Committee of Selection by the chairman or another member of the committee, all of whom are private Members. Such motions are placed on the effective Order Paper on the authority of the Government and on the instruction of the Chairman of the Committee and are debatable. It has proved necessary for the Government to provide time for the debate of the motions relating to the establishment of these committees in the first Session of each of the last two Parliaments, but subsequent changes in membership have normally passed without debate.

Church of England Measures

Church of England Measures are treated for procedural purposes like delegated legislation, as has been described above. Motions for an Address requesting that the Measure be made in the form in which it has been laid before Parliament are traditionally moved by the Second Church Estates Commissioner, a private Member, but are treated as if they were Government business.

Miscellaneous private Members' business taken in Government time

On rare occasions the Government provides some of its own time for the discussion of a private Member's bill. The reason for such provision may be that the Government considers that the House should be given an opportunity which at certain stages of the session may not be readily available in private Members' time, to come to a decision on a bill to which the Government is not itself committed in principle. It is more common for the Government to provide time for the discussion of Lords Amendments to private Members' bills received at a later stage of the session. In all cases, the bill in question is treated as a government order of the day on the occasion on which it is set down for consideration, since under Standing Order No 13 (1) only Government business can have precedence at such sittings. This is denoted on the order paper by distinguishing the name of the bill with an asterisk, as is done with all government orders of the day on the Order Paper.

It is rare for the Government to provide some of its own time for the discussion of a private Member's motion, but in recent sessions this has been done occasionally.[2]

Other examples of private Members' motions being moved in Government time include the reference of a matter of procedure to a Select

---

1 See Votes and Proceedings, 27 January 1988.
2 A private Member's motion authorizing an experiment in the television broadcasting of the proceedings of the House was debated in government time on 9 February 1988.

Tabular analysis of time spent on the main varieties of public business on the floor of the House of Commons, 1978–88

(All times in hours are rounded to the nearest quarter hour)

Session		1978–79	1979–80	1980–81	1981–82	1982–83	1983–84	1984–85	1985–86	1986–87	1987–88	Total 1978–88
Length of session	(days)	86	244	163	174	115	213	172	172	109	218	1666
	(hours)	738½	2177	1485¼	1534¼	984¾	1914½	1566¼	1536¼	931½	1978½	14846¾
Average sitting length	(hh.mm)	8.35	8.55	9.07	8.49	8.34	8.59	9.06	8.56	8.33	9.05	8.55
Additional time secured under SO No 14	(hours)	97¼	376¼	272¼	245	126¼	342	285½	249½	123	371½	2488½
	(% of total)	**13.17**	**17.28**	**18.33**	**15.97**	**12.82**	**17.86**	**18.23**	**16.24**	**13.20**	**18.78**	**16.76**
Debate on Addresses to the Queen	(hours)	48	40¾	36½	39	37	37½	38	37	35¾	40	389½
	(% of total)	**6.50**	**1.87**	**2.46**	**2.54**	**3.76**	**1.96**	**2.43**	**2.41**	**3.84**	**2.02**	**2.62**
Debate on Govt motions	(number)	9	48	17	14	13	24	17	21	7	23	193
	(hours)	54½	145	69¼	64¾	57¼	77	87¾	74	28¾	78¾	737
	(% of total)	**7.38**	**6.66**	**4.66**	**4.22**	**5.81**	**4.02**	**5.60**	**4.82**	**3.09**	**3.98**	**4.96**
Debate on Govt Adjournments	(number)	4	21	7	18	12	28	17	19	12	25	163
	(hours)	20¾	103	41½	91	63½	144½	82	96	60½	117½	820¼
	(% of total)	**2.81**	**4.73**	**2.79**	**5.93**	**6.45**	**7.55**	**5.24**	**6.25**	**6.49**	**5.94**	**5.52**
Holiday Adjournments	(hours)	9¼	55½	33¾	33½	8½	23	18¾	18	8¾	15¼	224¼
	(% of total)	**1.25**	**2.55**	**2.27**	**2.18**	**0.86**	**1.20**	**1.20**	**1.17**	**0.94**	**0.77**	**1.51**
SO No 20 applications	Number made	59	89	48	61	50	84	60	84	48	88	671
	Number successful	3	2	1	2	2	3	1	1	2	1	18
	(hours)	9½	3½	3¼	6¼	6¼	9½	3¼	3	6½	3¼	54¼
Government Bills: stages taken on the floor of the House												
(1) 2nd Reading (hours)		136¾	230	196	154¾	107	173½	162¼	151	92½	178½	1582¼
(2) Committee (hours)		19¾	101¼	57½	115¾	40	90½	81½	34¼	66¼	59	665¾
(3) Consideration (hours)		40	294¾	196¼	150¼	74½	175¾	139	164¼	69	266¾	1570½
(4) 3rd Reading (hours)		4¼	32	21	27	11¼	40¼	26½	26½	0½	27¾	217
(5) Lords Amendments (hours)		2¼	40¾	25¾	32¾	0½	67¾	26½	41¼	8½	74½	320½
Total (hours)		203	698¾	496½	480½	233¼	547¾	435¾	417¼	236¾	606½	4356
	(% of total)	**27.49**	**32.10**	**33.43**	**31.32**	**23.69**	**28.61**	**27.82**	**27.16**	**25.42**	**30.65**	**29.34**

Ways and Means Resolutions*											
(hours)	0	42¾	38½	21½	22½	23¾	23¾	22¼	24½	21	240½
(% of total)	**0.00**	**1.96**	**2.59**	**1.40**	**2.28**	**1.24**	**1.52**	**1.45**	**2.63**	**1.06**	**1.62**
Debates on SIs subject to affirmative resolution											
Number of occasions	32	98	61	57	44	83	66	45	39	81	606
(hours)	49½	144½	89	108	81½	164	128	87¼	51¼	130¾	1033¾
(% of total)	**6.70**	**6.64**	**5.99**	**7.04**	**8.28**	**8.57**	**8.17**	**5.68**	**5.50**	**6.61**	**6.96**
Debates on SIs subject to negative resolution											
Number of occasions	3	11	15	16	8	26	14	10	6	18	127
(hours)	4½	16¼	19¾	35¾	16	31½	28½	18¾	9	26	206
(% of total)	**0.61**	**0.75**	**1.33**	**2.33**	**1.62**	**1.65**	**1.82**	**1.22**	**0.97**	**1.31**	**1.39**
Debates on EC Documents											
Number of occasions	10	26	21	6	7	21	12	21	14	25	163
(hours)	22¾	75½	43	17¼	14½	51¼	22	42¼	29¾	47¼	365½
(% of total)	**3.08**	**3.47**	**2.90**	**1.12**	**1.47**	**2.68**	**1.40**	**2.75**	**3.19**	**2.39**	**2.46**
Debate on Motions under SO No 19											
Number of occasions	22	77	51	59	35	72	56	58	31	67	528
(hours)	6¾	16½	14¾	11½	6½	15	11¼	13	6¾	14¼	116¼
(% of total)	**0.91**	**0.76**	**0.99**	**0.75**	**0.66**	**0.78**	**0.72**	**0.85**	**0.72**	**0.72**	**0.78**
Debate on Opposed Private Business											
Number of occasions	14	19	5	10	4	14	14	15	3	28	126
(hours)	10¾	36½	11¼	23¾	6¾	33	19	42¼	3½	67½	254¼
(% of total)	**1.46**	**1.68**	**0.76**	**1.55**	**0.69**	**1.72**	**1.21**	**2.75**	**0.38**	**3.41**	**1.71**
Censure Motions (number)	1	2	2	1	0	0	1	1	0	0	8
(hours)	6¾	13	13½	6	0	0	6¾	6¾	0	0	52¾
Time taken by statements											
(hours)	25¼	73¼	38¾	55¾	31¾	75¼	66¼	69½	35½	77¼	548½
(% of total)	**3.42**	**3.36**	**2.61**	**3.63**	**3.22**	**3.93**	**4.23**	**4.52**	**3.81**	**3.90**	**3.69**
Number of Private Notice Questions granted	29	40	8	9	7	48	26	43	19	39	268
Average per day	0.34	0.16	0.05	0.05	0.06	0.23	0.15	0.25	0.17	0.18	0.16

The Table does not show times for Opposition Days or Private Members' business as these are fixed by standing order (see above). For the same reason, Estimates Days since Session 1982–83 are not shown.

* Includes Budget Debate.

Committee on Procedure.[1] Time has also been given to motions in the names of private Members critical of the conduct of the Chair.[2]

CENSURE MOTIONS

From time to time the Opposition put down a motion on the paper expressing lack of confidence in the Government—a 'vote of censure' as it is called. By established convention the Government always accedes to the demand from the Leader of the Opposition to allot a day for the discussion of such a motion. In allotting a day for this purpose the Government is entitled to have regard to the exigencies of its own business, but a reasonably early day is invariably found. This convention is founded on the recognized position of the Opposition as a potential Government, which guarantees the legitimacy of such an interruption of the normal course of business. For its part, the Government has everything to gain by meeting such a direct challenge to its authority at the earliest possible moment.

After a period of decline, the numbers of censure motions debated tended to increase during the late 1970's when Government majorities were small, although they were still infrequent. The Government was defeated on a motion of no confidence on 28 March 1979 and subsequently resigned.

TIME SPENT ON THE MAIN VARIETIES OF PUBLIC BUSINESS

On pp 270–271 is a table showing the proportion of time spent on the floor of the House on each of the main varieties of public business described in this chapter. Figures are given for each of the last ten sessions and for the period 1978 to 1988 as a whole.

---

1 CJ (1967–68) 249.
2 For example, see CJ (1956–57) 283, CJ (1960–61) 109, CJ (1975–76) 511.

CHAPTER 16

Outline of items of business in programme of sitting of the House of Commons

The purpose of this chapter is in the first place to describe each of the minor items of business, other than public business, in the House of Commons, stating the order of sequence in which they are normally taken; and, secondly, with regard to the various classes of public business, while leaving their detailed description to subsequent chapters, to set out the rules and conditions which apply to such items by virtue of their being brought before Parliament either as orders of the day or as notices of motions. Corresponding information in regard to the House of Lords is given in chapter 20 (see pp 416–438).

1. DIFFERENCE IN ORDER OF BUSINESS BETWEEN FRIDAY AND OTHER DAYS

When the House meets at half-past two, as it does ordinarily on the first four days of the week, the programme of business appointed for the day is disposed of in the order set out below. The items of the programme appear in this order in the private and public business notice papers circulated to Members on the morning of each day on which the House sits (see pp 206–207). But the programme is not absolutely rigid. The Government may, for example, choose to supersede the printed Order Paper by moving the Adjournment of the House, and any Member may seek to raise, under the Standing Order No 20 procedure, a specific and important matter which should have urgent consideration (see pp 300–302).

When the House meets at half past nine o'clock, as it regularly does on Friday, no provision is made for those of the items taken before public business on other days which require an appreciable amount of time for consideration—such as oral questions, applications for adjournment motions under Standing Order No 20, opposed private business, and the presentation of public bills under Standing Order No 19. The items which may be taken on Friday are taken in the same order as on other days, except that, in view of the early hour at which Friday sittings begin, provision is made in Standing Order No 11 for the interruption of business at eleven o'clock for private notice questions, ministerial statements or personal explanations by Members. Public petitions, which on weekdays are presented after the conclusion of public business, are presented on Fridays immediately after Prayers (see pp 317–318).

2. ORDER OF BUSINESS

The following table of business is given not as representing the programme of a typical sitting, but as indicating the order of relative precedence between any two of the various classes of business, items of which may happen to come up for disposal on the same day. The order given is not absolutely invariable, but is the one which on the whole has been found to be the most convenient in modern practice. Certain classes—for instance, matters relating to privilege requiring immediate intervention—may be taken either in the places indicated below or between orders of the day, or may even interrupt debate on an order of the day.

A. *Prayers*

B. *Business taken immediately after prayers*

    (1) Reports of Queen's answers to addresses.
    (2) Formal communications by Mr Speaker.
    (3) Motions for new writs.
    (4) Private business.
    (5) Motions for unopposed returns.

C. *Questions*

    (1) Questions for oral answer and answers to oral and written questions.
    (2) Private notice questions.

D. *Business taken after Questions*

    (1) Ministerial statements (and statements by the Speaker including decisions and statements on matters of privilege).
    (2) Introduction of new Members.
    (3) Proposals to move the adjournment under Standing Order No 20.
    (4) Ceremonial speeches.
    (5) Giving notice of motions and holding of ballots.
    (6) Personal statements.
    (7) Consideration of Lords amendments (if not of substance) or message.
    (8) Matters relating to privilege.

E. *Business taken 'at the commencement of Public Business'*

    (1) Presentation of public bills.[1]
    (2) Government motions relating to Committees.
    (3) Government motions regulating the business and sittings of the House.
    (4) Motions for leave to bring in Bills or nomination of select committees.[2]

F. *Privilege motions admitting of notice*

G. *Orders of the Day and Notices of Motions*

Orders of the Day and Notices of Motions to be proceeded with in the order in which they appear.

---

1 See SO No 58.
2 See SO No 19.

Private business set down under Standing Order No 16 and certain particularly urgent motions for the adjournment under Standing Order No 20 start at 7 p.m., any business then under discussion being postponed until such proceedings are over.

H. *Business motions under Standing Order No 14(2)*

I. *Business exempted under Standing Order Nos 14(1) and 15*

Proceedings on statutory instruments etc.

J. *Presentation of public petitions (except on Fridays)*

K. *Adjournment motions under Standing Order No 9(7)*

A. PRAYERS

When entering the Chamber, Mr Speaker is accompanied by the Serjeant at Arms and the Speaker's Chaplain. The Serjeant at Arms places the Mace upon the Table, bows, and retires; Mr Speaker and the Chaplain then proceed to the west and east sides of the Table respectively, bow to the empty Chair, and take their places at the Table. Upon the words 'Let us pray', Mr Speaker and the Chaplain kneel on stools placed at the Table for the purpose; the Members present remain standing, but turn towards their places. At the conclusion of Prayers the Speaker takes the Chair.[1] No strangers are admitted into the galleries until Prayers are over.[2]

Should the Speaker be unavoidably absent, or absent with leave, an announcement to that effect is made by the Clerk as soon as the Mace has been placed on the Table and before Prayers are read; the Speaker's place at the Table is then taken by the Deputy Speaker.[3]

A Member may secure for himself a place at Prayers by the use of a 'prayer card' (see p 167).

B. BUSINESS TAKEN IMMEDIATELY AFTER PRAYERS

(1) Report of Queen's answers to addresses

When an address has been presented in the ordinary way (ie by a privy councillor or member of the Household) Her Majesty's answer is reported

---

1 For a case of disorder during Prayers, see p 395.
2 This rule was relaxed on 26 October 1950, at the opening of the new Commons Chamber, when certain visiting Speakers and Presiding Officers of Legislatures within the Commonwealth (see p 568), some Members of war-time Parliaments, the architect of the new Chamber and certain workmen who had helped to build it, were admitted to the gallery before Prayers, HC Deb (1950) 478, cc 2929–2930. Another departure from precedent was made on the same occasion by the reading of a special Prayer by the Dean of Westminster (a former Chaplain to Mr Speaker), ibid c 2929. Strangers were also admitted, and a special Prayer read, on 22 June 1965, when the House met before proceeding to Westminster Hall in connection with the 700th Anniversary of Simon de Montfort's Parliament, HC Deb (1964–65) 714, c 1433.
3 However, in the case of a temporary absence, the Speaker may request the Chairman of Ways and Means or a Deputy Chairman to take the Chair under SO No 3(1) (see pp 185–186). No announcement is made by the Clerk in such cases.

to the House by a member of her Household, usually the Vice-Chamberlain, who acts in the House as one of the Government Whips. This officer presents himself at the bar immediately after Prayers, and on being called by the Speaker, announces 'Her Majesty's answer to a loyal and dutiful address', proceeds to the Table with the customary three bows, and having read the terms of the royal answer to the House, presents the document containing them to the Clerk for the purpose of entry in the records of the House and proceeds to make his exit in the same formal manner. (For the general subject of communications between the Crown and Parliament, see Chapter 23).

(2) Formal communications by the Speaker

Immediately after Prayers, or after any item of the kind described above, the Speaker, when occasion has arisen, communicates to the House at his discretion the purport, or reads the contents, of any letters he may have received from or sent to external authorities. These may include replies to communications of condolence or congratulation made by the House to members of the royal family (see p 566) or messages of the same kind sent by or to foreign legislative bodies (see p 180). They may also include such matters as a letter from a judge communicating the cause of commitment of a Member arrested upon a criminal charge or the sentence passed upon him after trial (see pp 96–97). It is at this time also that the Speaker announces the death of any Member which has been officially notified since the last sitting of the House.[1] He may also at this point ask for leave of absence for himself to attend official functions,[2] although the current practice is for leave to be given by means of an order moved for by a member of the Government after notice.[3]

(3) Motions for new writs

The next item to be taken after any such communication is any motion for an order of the House to the Speaker to make out his warrant for the issue of a writ for the election of a new Member to fill a vacancy arising in the course of a session. Such motions are moved normally, but not necessarily, by the Chief Whip of the party to which the Member vacating the seat belonged.[4] As such a motion is technically a matter of privilege it is made without notice[5] and having, accordingly, precedence over other business can be taken at any time. The order of precedence here assigned to it is that which is

---

1 HC Deb (1936–37) 326, c 3100. An announcement is made whether the Member has taken his seat or not, HC Deb (1980–81) 4, c 1.
2 Eg HC Deb (1966–67) 729, c 891; ibid (1972–73) 818, c 833; ibid (1974) 874, c 1799; ibid (1976–77) 924, c 935; 934, c 855; 935–I, c 1117, etc.
3 CJ (1981–82) 267, 444; ibid (1982–83) 174.
4 In 1973 the Speakers Conference on Electoral Law recommended that the motion should normally be moved within three months of a vacancy arising (Cmnd 5500).
5 A private Member wishing to move for a new writ should nevertheless give notice of his intention to the Speaker's Secretary, in order that he may obtain the right form of Motion. HC Deb (1956–57) 569, c 1146–1147.

generally found to be most convenient.[1] In cases where such a motion moved at this time is opposed, the Speaker has ruled that the debate should be suspended until the conclusion of question time to the time for taking matters of privilege.[2] The same position in the order of business is assigned to announcements by the Speaker of the fact that he has, during a recess due to adjournment or prorogation, issued his warrant, as by law provided, for the election of a Member without the immediate authority of the House.

For the conditions which have to be fulfilled before the issue of a warrant for a new writ, see pp 29–33.

(4) Private business

After any of the above items have occurred, or, if none has occurred, immediately after Prayers, the Speaker calls upon the Clerk at the Table to read the titles of the private bills set down for consideration that day. The Chairman of Ways and Means makes the motions necessary to dispose of the stages of the bills so appointed or states the day to which he desires them to be postponed (see p 278), and also makes any motions standing in his name; and the Speaker calls on Members to make the motions relating to private business of which they have given notice, according to the order in which the motions are arranged on the paper.

(a) Notice paper of private business. The notice paper, containing the orders of the day and notices of motions relating to private business and to provisional order bills, is prepared by the Private Bill Office, in pursuance of the provisions of Standing Orders 174, 190, and 218 and of the orders of the House, under instructions received from the Chairman of Ways and Means and from notices given by the parliamentary agents. The private business is set down upon the paper in the following order:

(1) Stages of private bills

    (a) Consideration of Lords amendments.
    (b) Third readings.
    (c) Consideration of bills ordered to lie upon the table.

---

1 For instances of new writs moved after the interruption of business, see CJ (1896) 133; ibid (1902) 74; ibid (1905) 300; at the end of the orders of the day on a Friday before the adjournment of the House under SO No 5, CJ (1913) 141; between items of business, so as to enable the Clerk of the Crown to seal the writ on that day, CJ (1983–84) 486; and as one of the final items taken during a prolonged sitting, CJ (1976–77) 468. A new writ has also been moved as a matter of privilege at the conclusion of government business, although an order was in force directing the Speaker to adjourn the House without question put at the conclusion of government business each day, CJ (1895) 389; Parl Deb (1895) 36, cc 766–768; on the motion of a private member, CJ (1907) 448.

2 For procedure when the issue of a new writ is opposed see HC Deb (1943–44) 395, cc 1515–16, 1566; ibid 396, cc 655–8; ibid (1956–57) 569, c 1146, 1182–1185; ibid (1961–62) 654, cc 177 and 219–223; ibid (1972–73) 859, cc 1231 and 1260–1274, on which occasion the Government succeeded in setting aside the motion for a new writ, which had been moved by a private Member, by means of an amendment proposing that the House should pass to the orders of the day; ibid (1980–81) 9, c 966; ibid (1985–86), 102, cc 1311–1325; ibid (1988–89), 145, cc 591–660, on which occasion the Government succeeded in setting aside the motion for a new writ which had been moved by a private Member by moving the previous Question; ibid (1988–89) 146, cc 277, 297–336. For an occasion when a motion was amended so as to specify a future day for the issue of the writ, see HC Deb (1982–83) 41, cc 164–171. Encroachment on time for questions by prolongation of proceedings on the issue of a new writ is contrary to SO No 17 (HC Deb (1942–43) 387, cc 1011, 1779).

(d) Second readings.

(2) Notices of motions relating to private business other than stages of bills appointed for that day.

(3) Stages of bills for confirming provisional orders and orders under the Private Legislation Procedure (Scotland) Act 1936 arranged in the same order as for private bills, ending with notices of the presentation of such bills.

Within each of these categories, business set down for the first time is placed on the paper before business deferred from a previous sitting and set down by order of the House.[1] The latter business is distinguished by the addition in brackets of the words 'By Order'. This distinction is occasioned by the fact that an item of private business differs from an item of public business in being set down for the first time on the paper not by order of the House but by the notification of a parliamentary agent. Provisional order bills, though always set down by order of the House, conform to private bill practice in this respect.

(b) Time for taking unopposed private business. On the first four days of the week, when the House meets normally at half-past two o'clock, the time during which private business can be taken amounts at the most to ten minutes, allowance being made for the time taken by Prayers.[2] Business still under discussion at a quarter to three o'clock stands adjourned.[3] Any private business not reached by a quarter to three o'clock, or in respect of which, when it is called, no motion is made, stands over to the next sitting at the time of unopposed private business. A motion which is contingent on a bill not reached by a quarter to three o'clock follows the bill and is similarly set down for the next sitting. But a motion which is not contingent on a bill and is not reached lapses unless fresh notice is given by the Member in whose name it stands. Any item of private business to which, when the order for its consideration is read by the Clerk (or, if it is a notice of motion, when the name of the mover is called by the Speaker), a Member signifies objection, becomes opposed and cannot be taken at this time. Opposed business also includes any proceedings on a private bill or a confirming bill which have already been deferred to which notice of an amendment stands on the notice paper in the form of a notice of motion on second reading, consideration or third reading of the bill. Such motions do not remain on the paper for more than seven days unless renewed.[4]

Such an item of opposed business is accordingly postponed (by implication by order of the House) to another day. The Chairman of Ways and Means, with whom the discretion rests, may appoint a future day for its consideration without stating the time at which it is to be taken. In that event, it is taken at the commencement of the appointed sitting under the procedure laid down by Standing Orders 190 and 218, as described above. Alternatively the Chairman may appoint it, under Standing Order No 16 and Standing Order 174, for consideration on a stated day at seven o'clock. Whichever course is adopted, the item of private business objected to becomes an entry 'By Order' in the notice paper of private business.

---

1 SO 190(2).
2 SO No 16(1).
3 CJ (1941–42) 29 and HC Deb (1991–92) 376, cc 2045–2048.
4 SO 174(2).

When the order for the consideration of an item of private business has been read by the Clerk, the Chairman, instead of moving it, may appoint a future day for its consideration. In this case also the item becomes an entry 'By Order' on the notice paper of private business, since this postponement is also by implication by order of the House.

When the consideration of private business had been interrupted, or had not been commenced, owing to a message requiring the attendance of the House in the House of Peers, and the House had not returned until after the time during which such business could be taken, the private business that could not be considered owing to the attendance of the House in the House of Peers was set down for the following day, CJ (1905) 249, Private Business (1905) 567, 577; CJ (1921) 115, Private Business (1921) 183, 187.

Similarly the private business of which notice had been given for Friday 12 March 1954 was set down again for Monday 15 March when the sitting of 11 March was prolonged beyond 11 a.m. on 12 March, and on 5 August 1980 private business set down for a Tuesday was set down for the following day because of a prolonged sitting.[1]

(c) Time for taking opposed private business. Under Standing Order No 16 and Standing Order 174 the Chairman of Ways and Means, in dealing with an item of private business which has been postponed owing to objection having been taken, may appoint it for consideration on some future day (or occasionally on the same day)[2] at seven o'clock. The resulting procedure will for the sake of convenience be described here.

Private business so appointed for seven o'clock is taken after any motion for the adjournment of the House under Standing Order No 20 has been disposed of (see p 301), and is set down in such order as the Chairman of Ways and Means directs. Opposed private business may be proceeded with subject to the provisions of the ten o'clock rule (see pp 240–241), and any business not concluded or not entered upon at that hour is postponed to a day which the Chairman of Ways and Means appoints.

If the Member in whose name a motion contingent upon opposed private business stands fails to move it immediately after the business upon which it is contingent is decided, it lapses unless set down again at the time of unopposed private business, when, if it is again opposed, the Chairman of Ways and Means may, notwithstanding that a previous opportunity for moving it was neglected, appoint a day for its consideration at the time of opposed private business (HC Deb (1928–29) 225, c 514). Instructions to a committee on a private bill are not directly contingent upon the second reading, and may be moved independently of that stage (see p 873).

A motion set down for seven o'clock which is not contingent upon a stage of a bill set down for the same hour, if entered upon but not disposed of by the time at which business is interrupted, may be postponed to such time as the Chairman of Ways and Means may appoint. If such a motion has not been entered upon before the interruption of business, then when the

---

1 Private Business (1953–54) 93, 95; ibid (1979–80) 544–545.
2 Parl Deb (1905) 151, c 779; CJ (1910) 307; ibid (1917–18) 71; ibid (1921) 334; ibid (1924) 364, 366; ibid (1926) 282; ibid (1927) 299; ibid (1929–30) 353; ibid (1952–53) 158; ibid (1961–62) 109; ibid (1979–80) 392.

Speaker interrupts business under Standing Order No 9, he calls the Member in whose name it stands in order to give an opportunity for the announcement of a day to which the motion is to be postponed. If, upon its title being read, no motion relative to a private bill is made, the proceedings upon it are postponed till the next sitting at the time for unopposed private business.

No opposed private business may be set down for, or deferred to, a Friday sitting.

Bills for confirming provisional orders, like private bills, may be set down by the Chairman of Ways and Means for seven o'clock in any order which he directs; they may even be set down before private bills (Standing Orders 174 and 218). Motions relating to such bills are treated in the same way as motions relating to private bills.

To suit the convenience of the House or to forward government business orders have been made varying the time at which opposed private business may be taken. It has been ordered to be taken immediately after government business, if that business should be disposed of before the hour for opposed private business,[1] or at a Saturday sitting at the end of government business.[2] On one occasion it was ordered to be taken on the last two days allotted to the business of supply at the conclusion of that business, instead of at the hour for opposed private business, and was allowed to be proceeded with, though opposed, and was exempted from interruption under the former Standing Order No 1.[3] On other occasions on days when the questions on all outstanding votes were to be put from the Chair at half-past nine under the former Standing Order No 18, the questions have instead been ordered to be put at seven o'clock.[4] A similar arrangement has been made to enable it to be taken at the end of government business;[5] and at the end of the proceedings ordered to be concluded at a certain time under an order of the House prescribing the method and times for bringing certain business to a conclusion.[6] In 1972 the Select Committee on Procedure considered the proposal that opposed private business should normally be taken at ten o'clock.[7] The Committee concluded by recommending that there should be no change in the time for debating opposed private business. Since then, however, orders have occasionally been made providing for private business to be taken at a time later than seven o'clock.[8] On a day on which opposed private business is to be taken at seven the sitting may, if other business has been prematurely concluded, be suspended till that hour. But if the House should have adjourned before that hour, private business not reached on that account is set down at the time of unopposed private business at the next sitting of the House.[9] Private business is sometimes included along

1 CJ (1914–16) 40; ibid (1916) 13; ibid (1917–18) 11; ibid (1918) 6; ibid (1919) 24, 325; ibid (1920) 390; ibid (1940–41) 193.
2 CJ (1908) 512.
3 CJ (1911) 403, 409.
4 CJ (1958–59) 140; ibid (1961–62) 150.
5 CJ (1914) 418; ibid (1920) 52; ibid (1971–72) 520.
6 CJ (1906) 255; ibid (1971–72) 466; ibid (1979–80) 515, 775.
7 HC 512 (1971–72).
8 Eg CJ (1972–73) 387 and 488; ibid (1977–78) 229; ibid (1981–82) 294, 351.
9 Taf Fechan Water Supply Bill (Lords), CJ (1921) 329, 334; Buckhaven and Leven Gas Commission Order Confirmation Bill, ibid (1922) 213, 221.

with items of public business in motions permitting proceedings after ten o'clock.[1]

(5) Motions for unopposed returns (see also pp 213–214)

Immediately after private business or on a Friday immediately after the presentation of any public petitions is the proper time for moving motions for returns (of accounts and other documents) of which notice stands upon the notice paper for the day, and which the Minister responsible for the government department concerned has signified his readiness to render. Such motions arc also made by Ministers, and in that case may be made either at this time or at any other convenient opportunity. A Member may, if duly authorized, make such a motion on behalf of another Member, in his absence. Before an unopposed return can be moved, the Speaker should be assured that the department which furnishes the return has notified its consent; and if an order for a return is obtained as unopposed, without such consent, the order may be struck out of the minute books by the Speaker's direction, or on a subsequent day the order may be read and discharged.

To such an extent is the conventional rule accepted, namely, that a motion for a return which is proposed by the Minister responsible for the department concerned ought not to be opposed by any other Member, that such opposition has been overruled by the Speaker (Parl Deb (1889) 338, c 1232; ibid (1895) 33, c 895; ibid (1898) 53, c 466; ibid (1905) 142, c 1037–1038; ibid (1906) 154, c 197; HC Deb (1909) 5, c 1162; ibid (1922) 157, c 1231–1232). In refusing to accept an objection to a motion for an unopposed return, the Speaker has suggested that the Member who objected should bring pressure upon the department with a view to the order being rescinded (HC Deb (1915–16) 77, c 588).

C. QUESTIONS

(1) Questions for oral answer and answers to oral and written questions

(a) Time for asking questions. After private business and motions for unopposed returns have been disposed of, and not later than a quarter to three on Mondays, Tuesdays, Wednesdays, and Thursdays, the Speaker calls on the Members who have given notices of questions to which oral answers are desired. No questions are taken when a Royal Commission is expected to summon the House to attend the Lords for prorogation[2] and no questions may be taken after half-past three o'clock even when interrupted.[3] On several occasions, to meet the general wish of the House (no objection being expressed) to proceed immediately to the orders of the day, questions have not been taken but have instead been deferred en bloc.[4] On Fridays questions for oral answer have been asked, but Ministers are under no

---

1 Eg CJ (1969–70) 201.
2 HC Deb (1977–78) 955, c 1047.
3 Eg by a Royal Commission: HC Deb (1935–36) 310, c 2948.
4 13 February 1893, Parl Deb (1893) 8, c 1241; 20 May 1898, ibid (1898) 58, c 118; 7 and 14 December 1916, HC Deb (1916) 88, cc 792, 795.

obligation to be present to answer them,[1] and as Standing Order No 11 provides no place for questions on Fridays, the practice, except for private notice questions (see pp 296–297), is now held to be irregular. As the House stands adjourned from Friday to Monday under Standing Order No 11, no questions can be put down for any Saturday.

The time limit for questions was waived by general consent on 27 August 1914;[2] but on subsequent occasions the Speaker has refused to allow the time to be extended without an order of the House.[3]

When the House meets at half-past nine o'clock on days other than a Friday, it is usually provided by resolution that questions can be taken up till half-past ten o'clock.[4]

Questions which have not been answered in consequence of the absence of the Minister to whom they are addressed may be answered after half-past three, if the Minister is then present.[5] Although formerly a question upon the paper which was not reached by the time-limit for questions was allowed to be asked, if it was urgent and of sufficient importance[6] or because it was urgent and related to an order of the day,[7] urgency is not now accepted as a sufficient reason for permitting a question to be so asked, and an answer may not be given unless the Speaker has been so requested by the Minister concerned;[8] on a request by a Minister being made a question upon the paper for written answer has been answered orally at half-past three.[9] The motion for the adjournment of the House at the conclusion of business cannot be used for the purpose of asking a question not reached by half-past three.[10]

(b) Notice of questions. Notice of a question to a Minister or other Member is placed upon the notice paper, unless the question relates to a matter of urgency or to the course of public business. Notice of a question is given by delivering its terms in writing to the clerks at the Table or in the Table Office. A Member's name must appear on the copy so delivered. Notices of questions may be transmitted by post. A question submitted otherwise than in person must bear the Member's full signature[11] unless the question is signed or brought in by another Member on his behalf.[12] A Member tabling a question on behalf of another must have the latter's specific authority.[13] No notice of a question may be accepted over the telephone, but questions may

---

1 Parl Deb (1901) 91, cc 994, 995, 1440; HC Deb (1917–18) 94, c 1204; ibid (1924) 169, c 389.
2 HC Deb (1914) 66, c 166.
3 HC Deb (1919) 116, c 575; ibid (1919) 121, c 628; ibid (1924) 169, c 531; see also ibid (1942–43) 387, cc 1779–80.
4 Eg CJ (1985–86) 275.
5 The practice of calling a second round of questions, comprising those unanswered on the first occasion owing to the absence of the Members concerned, was discontinued in 1942; see HC Deb (1942–43) 385, cc 1436–1437; ibid (1962–63) 677, c 673.
6 HC Deb (1929–30) 231, c 1248.
7 Parl Deb (1908) 188, c 738.
8 HC Deb (1958–59) 595, c 1014, etc. For such a request made orally, see HC Deb (1983–84) 63, c 19.
9 HC Deb (1952–53) 509, c 35, etc.
10 Parl Deb (1905) 143, c 1310.
11 HC Deb (1930–31) 249, c 36.
12 HC Deb (1975–76) 901, cc 179–80, ibid (1977–78) 951, cc 998–999.
13 HC Deb (1975–76) 901, cc 179–80.

be accepted if sent by telex or datapost by Members who are members of the European Parliament.[1]

(c) Questions for oral answer. A Member who desires an oral answer to his question must distinguish it by an asterisk, and the notice of any such question must appear at latest on the notice paper circulated two days (excluding any Sunday) before that on which an answer is desired; except that questions received before half-past two on Mondays and Tuesdays, may, if so desired, be put down for oral answer on the following Wednesdays and Thursdays respectively.[2] Questions for Monday must be received before 10.30 p.m. on the preceding Thursday (Standing Order No 17).

If the House is adjourned for more than one day, notices of questions received at any time not later than half-past four (1) on a day before the last day but one of adjournment, are treated as if they had been received after half-past two on the last day but one, and (2) on either of the two last days of adjournment (excluding any Saturday or Sunday), are treated as if the House were then sitting, and the notices had been received after half-past two (Standing Order No 17(8)).

By an amendment made to Standing Order No 17 in 1971, notice of a question for oral answer cannot be given for more than ten sitting days ahead. Following the recommendations of the Select Committee on Procedure in 1964–65, as re-defined in the Second Report from the Select Committee on Procedure in the session 1969–70,[3] it has been the practice to exclude, for the purpose of calculating this period, any days upon which the House is anticipated to stand adjourned. From the moment when the Leader of the House announces to the House the intention of the Government to adjourn for a specific period, the Table Office accepts notices of oral questions on the assumption that the House will stand adjourned for that period.[4]

The order in which Ministers and other Members answer oral questions is decided by the Government.[5] The list, known as the question rota, in which this order is set out is prepared by the Table Office on the instructions of the Secretary to the Chief Whip. Most Ministers appear on the list for one day each week, rotating to the top of the list in a four-week cycle. Some Ministers, for example the Leader of the House, and those private Members answering (see p 286 below), answer at fixed points of time at fixed intervals; the Prime Minister answers on two days each week at 3.15 p.m.

(d) Questions for written answer. Under a new procedure for written questions recommended by the Select Committee on Parliamentary Questions of Session 1971–72,[6] a Member who wishes to receive a written answer

---

1 Private Ruling, 27 May 1977.
2 This rule does not apply to notices of questions received on a day when the House meets under the provisions of SO No 12 or on the first day of a session, under the terms of SO No 17(5).
3 HC 198 p ix, para 13; the Report was approved by the House on 7 April 1971. CJ (1970–71) 380.
4 On 23 July 1981 the Speaker ruled that if the intended dates of adjournment were not announced in the House, the day upon which the Motion relating to the adjournment appeared on the Order Paper was the first day on which oral questions, anticipating the period of adjournment, could be accepted. (HC Deb (1980–81) 9, c 510.)
5 HC Deb (1975–76) 898, c 1592.
6 HC 393 (1971–72) p xiii; CJ (1972–73) 84.

on a named day may indicate this by marking the question with the letter W, to indicate priority and the specified date, subject to the same minimum amount of notice as is required for an oral question. Under Standing Order No 17, the Minister must cause the answer to be printed in the Official Report on the day for which notice has been given.

In the absence of this indication, written questions are put down for answer on the second sitting day after the day on which they are handed in, unless the Member gives a special instruction that a question be put down for the following day. The answer will not necessarily be given on that date; the House has, however, endorsed the view that Ministers should endeavour to answer unmarked questions within a working week of their being tabled.[1]

(e) Withdrawal of questions. The notice of a question may be withdrawn at any time before the question is due to be asked; and if the notice is withdrawn before the day on which the question is to be asked, the text is reprinted in a memorandum, as being withdrawn, at the end of the next issue of the notice paper.

(f) Deferral of questions etc. Questions may also be deferred for answer on a later day, or brought forward to an earlier day, subject to the general rules on notice. By an amendment made to Standing Order No 17 on 27 February 1986, questions tabled for written answer on a day on which the House does not sit as a result of the continuance of a previous sitting (see p 239) are deemed to be questions for written answer on the next sitting day.

(g) Speaker's control of questions. The Speaker is the final authority as to the admissibility of questions. Irregularities in a notice of a question are dealt with in the manner adopted regarding notices of motions (see pp 328–330) and are corrected in the Table Office or at the Table, or reserved for consideration. The Speaker has refused to permit a question to be asked although it stood upon the paper, on his attention being drawn to an irregularity.[2]

The Speaker's responsibility in regard to questions is limited to their compliance with the rules of the House. Responsibility in other respects rests with the Member who proposes to ask the question.[3] On many occasions the Speaker has stopped a Member asking by private notice a question that had been refused at the Table, or asking the parts of questions struck out at the Table[4] or taking the opportunity when raising a point of order to read out a question which has been refused at the Table,[5] or by the Speaker as a private notice question.[6] The refusal of a question at the Table cannot be raised incidentally in the course of a debate.[7] When a question has been refused and the Member concerned wishes to make representations to the Speaker on the matter, the practice is for these to be made privately to the Speaker and not raised by way of a point of order in the House.[8]

---

1 HC 393 (1971–72) p xiii; CJ (1972–73) 84.
2 HC Deb (1956–57) 569, cc 340–341; ibid (1957–58) 580, c 389.
3 Parl Deb (1880) 252, c 1903; ibid (1897) 47, c 1310; HC Deb (1961–62) 660, c 413.
4 Parl Deb (1881) 265, c 879; ibid (1900) 82, c 432; HC Deb (1940–41) 368, cc 1227–1228.
5 HC Deb (1928) 225, c 785; ibid (1984–85) 73, c 733.
6 HC Deb (1954–55) 536, cc 425–426; ibid (1959–60) 617, cc 676–677.
7 Parl Deb (1903) 127, c 711.
8 HC Deb (1970–71) 803, c 1366; ibid (1971–72) 827, c 1298; ibid (1986–87) 112, c 935.

The Clerks at the Table have full power to sub-edit questions,[1] and the Speaker also has called the attention of the House to an alteration made by his direction in a question.[2]

(h) *Limitation of number of oral questions*. The number of oral questions which may be asked by any one Member is limited to eight during any period of ten sitting days; within this period there is a further limitation to two questions in any one day, of which not more than one may be addressed to any one Minister.[3]

The number, formerly unlimited, was first fixed at eight, and then successively at four, three, and two per day (HC Deb (1909) 1, c 1108, etc.; ibid (1919) 112, c 1384; ibid (1920) 125, cc 1050–1051, 1225–1275; ibid (1959–60) 617, cc 245–246).

The limitation is formally applied at the time of a notice being handed in. When the Notice Paper is received each day, the previous day's notices are checked by the Table Office, and, if the allowance of any Member is found to have been inadvertently exceeded, the surplus questions are put down as ordinary written questions for the second sitting day which follows. In the event of more than one question being tabled by a Member to the same Minister for the same day, priority is given to that which is the lowest in the order of priority established by the random 'shuffle' carried out in the Upper Table Office at 4 p.m. In the event of the ration of eight being exceeded, or of two for any one day, priority is given to the questions in the order in which they are handed in with, however, priority accorded to questions to the Prime Minister over those to other Ministers.[4]

There is no limit to the number of questions for written answer (whether or not marked with a W) which a Member may ask on the same day.

(i) *Persons to whom questions may be addressed*.

(i) Questions to the Speaker. Questions dealing with matters within the jurisdiction of the Speaker should be addressed to the Speaker by private notice; no written or public notice of questions addressed to the Speaker is permissible. Questions cannot be addressed to the Speaker on matters of order or privilege;[5] such matters must be raised as points of order or under the procedure laid down for raising matters of privilege (see pp 135–136). A question can, however, be addressed to him on a matter which urgently concerns the proceedings of the House for which he is responsible.

(ii) Questions to Ministers. Questions addressed to Ministers should relate to the public affairs with which they are officially connected, to proceedings pending in Parliament, or to matters of administration for which they are responsible.[6] A question should be addressed to the Minister who is primar-

---

1 Parl Deb (1906) 158, cc 1123–1124; HC Deb (1920) 128, c 409; ibid (1970–71) 819, cc 1771–1772.
2 Parl Deb (1861) 161, c 342.
3 HC 393 (1971–72) p x; CJ (1972–73) 84.
4 HC Deb (1985–86) 87, cc 275–276, and Select Committee on Parliamentary Questions, HC 393 (1971–72).
5 Parl Deb (1901) 91, c 103.
6 HC Deb (1958–59) 599, c 1181–1182.

ily responsible, and misdirected questions are transferred by the clerks in the Table Office on the notification of the departments concerned.[1] The Speaker has ruled that it is out of order to ask a Minister for his reasons for transferring a question.[2] It is a long established principle that decisions on the transfer of questions rest with Ministers and it is not a matter in which the Chair seeks to intervene.[3]

(iii) Questions to private Members. Questions addressed to private Members relating to a bill, motion, or other matter connected with the business of the House for which such Members are responsible, have been allowed.[4] The Speaker has, however, expressed doubt whether it would be in accordance with modern parliamentary practice for questions to be addressed to private Members except in the case of the Second Church Estates Commissioner and chairmen of certain select committees[5]; questions are also sometimes addressed to the chairmen of committees directly concerned with the working of the House. The Leader of the House regularly answers questions not only in this capacity, but as Chairman of the House of Commons (Services) Committee, and in exercising this function private Members who are members of the Committee have answered questions on his behalf including, on catering matters, the Chairman of the Catering Sub-Committee. Since the establishment of the House of Commons Commission, questions, on their behalf, have been regularly answered by a private Member who is a member of the Commission. Questions may be similarly addressed to the Chairman of the Public Accounts Commission. It is currently the practice of the Government to provide a place on the rota of oral questions for Members answering on behalf of the Church Commissioners, the House of Commons Commission and the Public Accounts Commission. A question addressed to a Member, the leader of the Opposition, inquiring the course he intended to adopt regarding a motion by the Government, was not allowed.[6] Questions may not be asked regarding statements made by Members outside the House,[7] nor may questions be addressed to private Members about matters with which they are concerned as members of commissions or authorities outside the House;[8] and a question to an ex-minister with regard to transactions during his term of office has been ruled out of order.[9] On 17 March 1944

---

1 HC Deb (1929) 231, c613; ibid (1941–42) 382, c859.
2 HC Deb (1963–64) 698, c1032; ibid. (1963–64) 699, cc49–53. The Select Committee on Procedure of Session 1966–67 recommended that Ministers should, as a general rule, not later than two sitting days after the appearance of a question on the Notice Paper inform the Member of a proposed transfer (HC 410 of 1967, para 13) and the 1969–70 Procedure Committee requested the Leader of the House to acquaint Departments of the importance which they attached to notice of transfers being given within two sitting days. (HC 198 of 1970.) The Speaker has said that he regards it as a discourtesy and unfair when Ministers do not, within two days, notify the Member concerned that they intend to transfer a question (HC Deb (1979–80) 986, c566).
3 Eg HC Deb (1983–84) 54, c570.
4 HC Deb (1941–42) 381, c215.
5 Private ruling, 24 May 1962.
6 Parl Deb (1880) 253, c974. A question relating to the views of the Leader of the Opposition has also not been allowed (HC Deb (1972–73) 855, cc504–505).
7 Parl Deb (1872) 209, c141, etc.
8 Parl Deb (1889) 334, c712; HC Deb (1911) 22, c1200; ibid (1916) 88, c35; ibid (1917–18) 95, c1322.
9 Parl Deb (1906) 160, c217.

Mr Speaker ruled privately that a Member may not seek by means of a question to the chairman to interfere in the proceedings of a select committee by suggesting a particular subject for inquiry (although such subject fell within its order of reference).

(j) Rules of order regarding form and contents of questions. The purpose of a question is to obtain information[1] or press for action; it should not be framed primarily so as to convey information, or so as to suggest its own answer or convey a particular point of view, and it should not be in effect a short speech. Questions of excessive length have not been permitted.[2]

The content of a question must comply with the general rules which apply to the content of speeches (see pp 372–384), and is subject to the more detailed limitations set out below.

The Select Committee on Parliamentary Questions of Session 1971–72 expressed its concern that the cumulative effect of previous decisions relating to the orderliness of questions should not be allowed to become unduly restrictive. It therefore recommended that, while the Speaker should continue to have regard to the basic rules concerning the form and content of questions which are set forth in the pages which follow, he should not consider himself bound, when interpreting these rules, to disallow a question solely on the ground that it conflicted with any previous individual ruling.[3]

(i) Argument and disorderly expressions. Questions which seek an expression of an opinion,[4] or which contain arguments, expressions of opinion, inferences or imputations,[5] unnecessary epithets,[6] or rhetorical, controversial, ironical[7] or offensive expressions, are not in order.

(ii) Factual basis. The facts on which a question is based may be set out as briefly as practicable within the framework of a question, provided that the Member asking it makes himself responsible for their accuracy,[8] but extracts from newspapers or books, and paraphrases of or quotations from speeches, etc, are not admissible.[9] Where the facts are of sufficient moment the Speaker has required prima facie proof of their authenticity.

(iii) Personal reflections. It is not in order in a question to reflect on the character or conduct of those persons whose conduct may only be chal-

---

1 Parl Deb (1893–94) 9, c 1620, etc.
2 Parl Deb (1887) 318, c 42; HC Deb (1942–43) 388, c 472; ibid (1967–68) 757, c 1344–1345.
3 HC 393 (1971–72) p vii; CJ (1972–73) 84.
4 Parl Deb (1870) 269, c 242; ibid (1871) 270, c 1764; HC Deb (1961–62) 651, c 424. Questions are also disorderly which ask a Minister to convey an opinion; HC Deb (1958–59) 599, cc 1182–1184.
5 Parl Deb (1864) 175, c 100, etc.
6 HC Deb (1920) 130, c 1255; ibid (1920) 132, c 226.
7 Parl Deb (1860) 160, c 1827, etc; HC Deb (1957–58) 583, cc 376–377.
8 Parl Deb (1882) 270, c 1132; HC Deb (1915) 75, c 330; ibid (1961–62) 660, c 413.
9 Parl Deb (1907) 172, c 225; HC Deb (1957–58) 583, c 822; ibid (1963–64) 694, c 198; ibid. (1975–76) 912, c 16; ibid (1986–87) 106, c 21.

lenged on a substantive motion[1] (see pp 325–326), nor is it permissible to reflect on the conduct of other persons otherwise than in their official or public capacity. Moreover, a question introducing names (whether of persons or of bodies) invidiously or for advertisement or in any way not strictly necessary to render the question intelligible is not in order.[2] The Speaker has ruled that questions referring to communications between an individual Member (other than the Member asking the question) and a Minister should not be allowed on the notice paper[3] and that discourteous references to a friendly foreign country, or the head of State of such a country, are inadmissible.[4]

(iv) Royal Family. No question can be put which brings the name of the Sovereign or the influence of the Crown directly before Parliament, or which casts reflections upon the Sovereign[5] or the royal family. A question has been altered by the Speaker's direction on the ground that the name of the Sovereign should not be introduced to affect the views of the House.[6]

(v) Royal Prerogative. Questions may be asked of the Ministers who are the confidential advisers of the Crown regarding matters relating to those public duties for which the sovereign is responsible. It has been ruled that the Prime Minister cannot be interrogated as to the advice that he may have given to the sovereign with regard to the grant of honours,[7] or the ecclesiastical patronage of the Crown[8] or the appointment and dismissal of Privy Councillors[9] or the dissolution of Parliament.[10]

In any case involving a capital sentence the circumstances on which the exercise of the prerogative of mercy depends should not be made the subject of a question while the sentence is pending[11] nor may the sentence itself be raised in a question while it is pending.[12]

This rule applies to sentences imposed by courts in Colonies as well as those in the United Kingdom. However, the Speaker has allowed a question about the exercise of the Prerogative in the case of death sentences imposed in a Colony whose authorities were in revolt.[13]

(vi) Statements outside Parliament. The Prime Minister may be asked whether statements made outside Parliament by Ministers of Cabinet rank

---

1 Parl Deb (1872) 210, c39; ibid (1906) 157, c487; HC Deb (1913) 55, cc2024, 2057; ibid (1920) 128, c408; ibid (1955–56) 557, cc921–924; ibid (1979–80) 977, cc923–924, but see ibid (1960–61) 629, cc651–654 for references to Members of the House of Lords otherwise than in their capacity as Members of that House.
2 Parl Deb (1880) 253, c1631; HC Deb (1912–13) 46, c1005. For commendation of the practice of supplying a Minister privately with the name of an individual, see HC Deb (1985–86) 94, c26.
3 Parl Deb (1896) 40, c1561.
4 Private ruling of 24 June 1924. HC Deb (1911) 30, c1283.
5 Parl Deb (1867–68) 192, c711; ibid (1887) 318, c1372–1374.
6 Notices of Motions, 1912, pp3891, 3944.
7 Parl Deb (1907) 178, c61; ibid (1908) 190, c1338; HC Deb (1922) 155, c1842.
8 Private ruling, 9 March 1923.
9 Private ruling, 24 June 1926.
10 HC Deb (1964–65) 716, c1340.
11 CJ (1960–61) 109; HC Deb (1960–61) 634, cc1773–1838. See also Parl Deb (1887) 319, cc253, 1103; ibid (1889) 340, c128; HC Deb (1921) 139, c845; ibid (1921) 142, c1523; ibid (1946–47) 434, cc37–41, 485–489, and 958–961.
12 HC Deb (1946–47) 436, cc2179–2182.
13 HC Deb (1967–68) 760, cc35–39.

or Ministers with specific responsibilities on public occasions represent the policy of the Government, but questions about statements so made by other Ministers are not in order.[1] Questions about proposals or statements made by Ministers or Departmental Representatives attending conferences or negotiations on behalf of the Government should, however, be addressed to the Minister in charge of the Department concerned.[2] Recently, questions have occasionally been allowed when Ministers have made statements elaborating new policies in public speeches outside the House, or in a broadcast[3] or on the texts of such speeches when these have been officially distributed.[4] When the Prime Minister has made a speech on a public occasion outside the House, a question may be asked in the form of asking for a copy of that speech to be placed in the Library;[5] it has been ruled that questions in this particular form are *sui generis* and not capable of being 'blocked' by an answer of the sort which would normally be interpreted as a refusal to answer further questions.[6]

(vii) Ministerial responsibility. Questions to Ministers must relate to matters for which those Ministers are officially responsible. They may be asked for statements of their policy or intentions on such matters, or for administrative or legislative action. A number of decisions from the Chair have closely defined the interpretation of this rule of Ministerial responsibility. Among them are the following:

(1) Questions asking whether statements in the Press, or of private individuals, or unofficial bodies are accurate[7] or asking for comment on statements made by persons in other countries (unless the statement is a message from another government to Her Majesty's Government) are not in order.[8]

(2) Questions are not admissible which seek information about the internal affairs of foreign countries or an independent Commonwealth country.[9] However, questions are allowed seeking information about the internal affairs of such countries if the information can be obtained by the Government from international organizations of which they are members.[10] The Speaker has ordered the removal from the paper of a question referring to the speech of a Commonwealth Minister.[11] Questions which ask Ministers to assist United Kingdom citizens coming before the courts or being sub-

---

1 HC Deb (1918) 104, c 484; ibid (1924) 170, cc 45, 473.
2 Private ruling, 20 December 1963; HC Deb (1972–73) 852, cc 1496 and 853, cc 919–290, 1098–1099.
3 Eg HC Deb (1979–80) 973, c 251.
4 Eg HC Deb (1981–82) 13, c 346.
5 Private ruling, 18 June 1969; HC Deb (1971–72) 840, cc 32–33.
6 HC Deb (1971–72) 839, cc 1695 and 840, cc 32–33.
7 Parl Deb (1882) 270, c 1132; ibid (1893–94) 10, c 674; ibid (1948–49) 470, cc 204–206; ibid (1956–57) 560, c 1541; ibid (1962–63) 666, c 956; ibid (1963–64) 684, cc 1192–1193.
8 HC Deb (1914–16) 75, c 330; ibid (1956–57) 560, c 1541.
9 Parl Deb (1908) 190, c 61; ibid (1922) 153, cc 1522, 1526, 1534–1536; private ruling, 15 March 1928; HC Deb (1929) 232, c 1932. See also HC 198 (1969–70) p xiii.
10 An extension of this principle is comprised in questions relating to mutual commitments made by signatory nations to the Final Act of the Conference on Security and Co-operation in Europe, Helsinki, 1975 (Cmnd 6198) particularly those relating to human rights, eg HC Deb (1980–81) 1000, c 236; HC Deb (1981–82) 25, cc 191, 198.
11 Notices of Motions, 1928–29, p 686.

jected to arrest in foreign countries, or to protect United Kingdom citizens or companies who are being discriminated against by foreign authorities are allowed; but questions about the actions of independent states in refusing entry to United Kingdom citizens have not been allowed.[1]

(3) It is not in order in a question to ask for action to deal with matters under the control of local or other statutory authorities, or of bodies or persons not responsible to the Government such as banks, the Stock Exchange, companies (except where there is a Government shareholding in such companies), employers' organizations and trades unions;[2] or to ask for action regarding or information about the activities of such persons or bodies which Ministers have no power to perform or obtain.

(4) Questions relating to nationalised industries, ie, industries or services placed by Parliament under the control of statutory bodies, are restricted to those matters for which a Minister is made responsible by the Statute concerned[3] or by other legislation and to those matters in which Ministers are known to be involved. In general Ministers have powers, under the statutes, to make regulations concerning (or otherwise deal with) certain specific matters such as safety and to give directions to the industry, or part of it. They can therefore be asked about the use of these powers.

The statutes also confer on Ministers power to obtain information from the Boards or governing bodies concerned, but successive governments have refused, on grounds of public policy, to answer questions seeking information on the day to day administration of the industries or on administrative matters contained in the annual reports of the industries.[4] Since the refusal to answer a class of questions prevents further questions dealing with that class of matters (see para ix on p 292) most questions asking for information on the working of the Boards are in practice inadmissible.[5] There are however two general exceptions. Ministers have undertaken to answer questions asking for statistical information on a national basis; such questions are therefore in order.[6] The Speaker has also undertaken to allow questions on what might otherwise be called day to day administration provided that they raised matters of urgent public importance such as might in other circumstances fall within the meaning of Standing Order No 20.[7]

(5) Questions are inadmissible which refer to the evidence of witnesses or other matters before a royal commission[8] or a parliamentary committee, or deal with matters within the jurisdiction of the chair-

---

1 HC Deb (1958–59) 597, cc 1315–1318.
2 HC Deb (1929–30) 233, c 246; HC Deb (1914) 66, cc 162, 939; ibid (1924) 169, c 838.
3 HC Deb (1947–48) 449, cc 1630–1634. This matter was debated by the House on a motion for the adjournment on 3 March 1948, HC Deb (1947–48) 448, c 391.
4 HC Deb (1950–51) 482, cc 524–526; HC Deb (1980–81) 1000, c 163.
5 HC Deb (1947–48) 449, cc 1630–1634; see also ibid (1947–48) 445, cc 565–572; ibid (1947–48) 451, cc 1633–1643; ibid (1950–51) 481, cc 781–783; ibid (1958–59) 599, cc 205–207.
6 HC Deb (1962–63) 682, c 450.
7 Mr Speaker's ruling, HC Deb (1947–48) 451, cc 1635–1637; ibid (1951–52) 493, c 648; ibid (1976–77) 935–I, cc 220–224.
8 Private ruling, 25 May 1936.

man of a select committee or the authorities of the House.[1] No question can be asked regarding proceedings in a committee which have not been placed before the House by a report from the committee.[2] However, questions are regularly asked about the administrative decisions of the Select Committee on House of Commons (Services).

(6) Questions addressed to a court official or referring to the action of a court official are inadmissible.[3]

(7) A question may not be asked which deals with the action of a Minister for which he is not responsible to Parliament.[4] For example, in 1924 a question asking the Attorney General whether he had communicated with certain Members before deciding to withdraw a prosecution was disallowed privately by the Speaker.

(8) Questions seeking an expression of opinion on a question of law, such as the interpretation of a statute, or of an international document, a Minister's own powers, etc, are not in order[5] since the courts rather than Ministers are competent in such matters. Moreover, questions requiring information set forth in accessible documents (such as statutes, treaties, etc.)[6] have not been allowed when the Member concerned could obtain the information of his own accord without difficulty. Ministers may however be asked by what statutory authority they have acted in a particular instance, and the Prime Minister may be asked to define a Minister's responsibilities.

(9) It is not in order to put to a Minister a question for which another Minister is more directly responsible, or ask one Minister to influence the action of another.[7]

(10) Questions are out of order which seek legislation to deal with circumstances of a very restricted or particular character presently outside ministerial powers or responsibilities, and thus evade the rule that questions must relate to matters for which Ministers are officially responsible, as are those which cite individual incidents in relation to which the Minister has no administrative power or responsibilities when asking for general legislation.[8]

(11) Questions which suggest amendments to bills before the House or in committee are inadmissible unless such amendments would only be in order if a financial resolution were first moved by a Minister.[9]

(viii) Parliamentary business. Limitations have been placed on the sort of question which may be asked about the conduct of public business in Parliament for which Ministers are responsible. The Speaker has refused to allow questions as to whether the government proposed by resolution to put

1 Parl Deb (1897) 46, c784.
2 Parl Deb (1883) 280, c1147; HC Deb (1929–30) 237, c1926; ibid (1968–69) 778, c1271.
3 Private ruling, 23 July 1934.
4 Private ruling, 4 August 1924.
5 Parl Deb (1897) 47, c1184; ibid (1901) 89, c1056; ibid (1905) 143, c36; ibid (1955–56) 543, c960–964.
6 Parl Deb (1896) 39, c1156; ibid (1901) 90, c207; HC Deb (1927) 204, c2074.
7 HC Deb (1947–48) 453, c985.
8 HC 198 (1969–70) pxiii.
9 HC 198 (1969–70) pxii.

a close to a stage of a bill,[1] and as to the time at which a Minister would move the closure;[2] and a question asking a Minister about a motion on the paper when under standing orders that motion must be decided without amendment or debate has been ruled out.[3] Questions anticipating discussion upon an order of the day have also been disallowed.[4] Questions about the day to day progress of the business of the House are not placed on the notice paper; such questions are asked as supplementaries to the weekly private notice question on business which the Leader of the Opposition customarily asks of the Leader of the House (see p 296).

(ix) Questions already answered, or to which an answer has been refused, or on secret matters. Questions are not in order which renew or repeat in substance questions already answered[5] or to which an answer has been refused or which fall within a class of question which a Minister has refused to answer.[6] Where, however, a Minister has refused to take the action or give the information asked for in a particular question, he may be asked the same question again after an interval of three months; and where successive administrations have consistently refused to answer certain classes of questions, Ministers may be asked once a session whether they will now answer such questions.[7] Similarly, where a Minister answers a question on a matter previously blocked, questions may be asked on that matter.[8] Among the subjects on which successive administrations have refused to answer questions upon grounds of public policy are discussions between Ministers[9] or between Ministers and their official advisers[10] or the proceedings of Cabinet or Cabinet committees;[11] security matters including the operation of the security services[12]; operational defence matters including the location of particular units;[13] and details of arms sales to particular countries.[14] In addition to such classes of questions there are certain matters, of their nature secret, relating to the secret services and to security, and questions on these matters are not in order.[15] A question which one Minister has refused to answer cannot be addressed to another Minister[16] and a question answered by one Minister may not be put to another.[17]

---

1 Parl Deb (1893–94) 15, c 1782.
2 Parl Deb (1901) 89, c 1061; ibid (1905) 141, c 781.
3 Parl Deb (1896) 40, c 1152; ibid (1901) 93, c 1196.
4 Parl Deb (1876) 228, c 1557.
5 Private ruling, 8 August 1907 [Decision 1685]; see also Parl Deb (1875) 225, cc 792, 952, 1142; ibid (1884) 285, c 877; HC Deb (1918) 108, c 1979.
6 Parl Deb (1898) 55, c 770.
7 HC 393 (1971–72) p vi; CJ (1972–73) 84. A fuller list of matters on which there has been consistent ministerial refusal to answer is given in App 9 to the Evidence of the Select Committee on Parliamentary Questions, HC 393 (1971–72) p 114. See also, HC Deb (1979–80) 973, cc 322, 323, 324, 335, 338, 339, 342, 343, 348, 349, 350, 356, 362, 365, 368, 373, 374, 382, 451.
8 HC Deb (1986–87) 106, cc 135–140.
9 Eg HC Deb (1954–55) 537, c 1268.
10 Eg HC Deb (1972–73) 847, cc 1685–1687.
11 HC Deb (1967–68) 763, cc 999–1001.
12 Eg HC Deb (1979–80) 973, c 373; ibid (1977–78) 949, c 41.
13 Eg HC Deb (1979–80) 973, c 322; ibid (1977–78) 949, c 109.
14 Eg HC Deb (1979–80) 973, c 322.
15 Private ruling, 31 March 1953; HC Deb (1988–89) 147, c 327. For relationship of this rule to that on questions to which an answer has been refused, see First Report from the Committee of Privileges, Session 1986–87 (HC 365) pp 7, 9–10.
16 Parl Deb (1895) 34, c 1547.
17 HC Deb (1968–69) 783, c 283.

An answer to a question cannot be insisted upon, if the answer be refused by a Minister,[1] and the Speaker has refused to allow supplementary questions in these circumstances.[2] The refusal of a Minister to answer a question on the ground of public interest cannot be raised as a matter of privilege,[3] nor should leave be sought to move the adjournment of the House under Standing Order No 20 for this reason.[4]

(x) Decisions of either House. Questions which criticize the decisions of either House of Parliament are inadmissible;[5] nor is it in order to refer to debates or questions and answers of the current session[6] other than for the purpose of seeking further clarification of a previous answer. The Speaker has also ruled that questions referring to the time taken by individual speeches may not be asked.[7]

(xi) Matters sub judice. By a resolution of the House[8] matters awaiting or under adjudication in a criminal court or a court martial, and matters set down for trial or otherwise brought before a civil court may not be referred to in any debate or question (see pp 377–379); though the House has further resolved to give the Chair some discretion to allow reference to be made to matters awaiting or under jurisdiction in all civil courts in certain specified circumstances, provided that there is no real and substantial danger of prejudice to the proceedings.[9] The 'sub-judice rule' as it is often called, also applies to matters before a coroner's court.[10] If the subject matter of the question is found to be, or becomes, sub judice after notice of the question has been given, the Member is asked to withdraw it, or the Speaker may direct it to be removed from the notice paper or refuse to allow it to be asked if it is on the Order paper.

The rule does not apply to matters which are sub judice in courts of law outside Great Britain and Northern Ireland,[11] nor to matters which are the subject of administrative enquiry.[12]

Questions which reflect on the decision of a court of law are not in order. The Speaker has ruled privately that questions relating to a sentence passed by a judge, and to the circumstances under which rules of court were made and issued by the Lord Chancellor, were inadmissible.[13]

(xii) Miscellaneous. Questions are also inadmissible which seek the solution of hypothetical propositions;[14] raise questions of policy too large to be

---

1 Parl Deb (1897) 47, c 60. Refused in public interest, Parl Deb (1907) 178, c 529; HC Deb (1915) 73, c 1488.
2 HC Deb (1960–61) 635, c 1580.
3 Parl Deb (1901) 89, c 322.
4 HC Deb (1909) 2, c 200; ibid (1955–56) 552, c 1222–1223.
5 Parl Deb (1906) 167, c 1863.
6 Parl Deb (1871) 207, c 1883, etc.
7 Private ruling, 23 June 1904.
8 CJ (1962–63) 297; see also First Report from Select Committee on Procedure, Session 1962–63 (HC 156).
9 CJ (1971–72), 407–408.
10 Private rulings, 12 June 1978, and 20 March 1980, HC Deb (1979–80) 981, c 940.
11 HC Deb (1950) 476, c 868; ibid (1986–87) 105, cc 436–440, 565–566.
12 HC Deb (1952–53) 511, c 413–414.
13 Decisions 1596 and 1597.
14 Parl Deb (1898) 63, c 705.

dealt with in an answer to a question; seek information on matters of past history for the purposes of argument;[1] are multiplied with slight variations on the same point;[2] or are trivial, vague or meaningless.

(k) Manner of asking questions. As each Member is called, he rises to ask the question standing in his name by reading its number on the question paper; a Member may not rise to ask a question which stands on the order paper in the name of another Member.[3] If the Member responsible for a question does not answer to the Speaker's call, a Minister may make such statement upon the question as the public interest demands,[4] but it has been ruled that such a statement ought to be made at the end of questions.[5] When a Member stated that it was not his intention to ask a question standing in his name, as the subject of it had been discussed in debate on a previous day, the Speaker refused to allow the Minister concerned to answer it.[6]

A Member, other than the Member in whose name a question stands, which contains allegations affecting personal character or conduct and requires therefore prompt reply, may ask for an answer to the question[7] or a statement may be made thereon, although the question is not asked.[8] An attempt to raise a point of order on a question which has not been called has been ruled out of order.[9] When a Minister in answering a question has referred to the answer to be given to a question which had not been asked, he has been allowed to give the answer to that question in spite of the absence of the Member in whose name it stood.[10] A Member need not disclose any personal interest he might have in the subject-matter of his question.[11]

(l) Printed answers. If a Member does not distinguish his question by an asterisk, or if he is not present to ask it, or if it is not reached by half-past three, the Minister to whom it is addressed causes an answer to be printed in the Official Report, unless the Member has signified his desire to postpone or withdraw the question[12] before the interruption of questions at half-past three or by midday on a Friday.[13]

Printing in the Official Report was substituted for printing and circulation with the Votes by an amendment of Standing Order No 17 (then No 7) on 28 September 1915.[14] Until that date the answers had been printed in the Official Report since its institution in 1909 as well as being circulated with the Votes. Since October 1945 written replies to questions have been

1 Private ruling, 31 January 1961. For the purposes of this rule, the passage of 30 years or more is generally deemed to constitute past history (Private Ruling, 5 July 1983).
2 HC Deb (1953–54) 524, c 1905–1906; private rulings, 2 April 1899 and 8 March 1957.
3 Parl Deb (1883) 279, c 1756; HC Deb (1924) 172, c 1834.
4 Parl Deb (1900) 84, c 286; HC Deb (1946–47) 437, c 2187–2188.
5 HC Deb (1971–72) 834, cc 430, 433.
6 HC Deb (1910) 17, c 20.
7 Parl Deb (1886) 304, c 437; HC Deb (1924) 172, c 1360.
8 HC Deb (1914–16) 72, c 1624.
9 HC Deb (1946–47) 441, c 27.
10 HC Deb (1923) 163, c 1609; ibid (1964–65) 701, c 840.
11 HC Deb (1954–55) 536, c 415; ibid (1962–63) 666, c 968; CJ (1974–75) 480.
12 But a question which has been answered together with another question cannot be postponed (HC Deb (1955–56) 554, c 1238).
13 For this reason, it is not proper for an answer to be released before those times (HC Deb (1981–82) 15, c 625; ibid (1984–85) 80, c 306.
14 CJ (1914–16) 246.

printed at the end of the Official Report.[1] Oral questions to the Prime Minister seeking a list of engagements and not reached have not, since July 1984, received a written reply unless specifically requested.[2] Since November 1987, answers to the effect that the Minister will reply as soon as possible, known as 'holding answers', have not been printed; the date of any such holding answer is given at the time of publication in the Official Report of a substantive answer.[3] The Speaker has deprecated long statements being circulated in the Official Report as answers to questions.[4] In the event of a discrepancy between the texts of the answers sent to the Member and the Official Report, the text sent to the Member must be considered to be the authentic reply; any alteration must be made orally in the House by the Minister.[5]

If a Member, having placed notices of questions upon the paper, ceases to be a Member of the House or becomes a member of the Goverment, answers to his questions should not be printed.[6]

(m) Oral answers and supplementary questions. An answer should be confined to the points contained in the question, with such explanation only as renders the answer intelligible, though a certain latitude is permitted to Ministers of the Crown;[7] and supplementary questions, without debate or comment, may, within due limits, be addressed to them, which are necessary for the elucidation of the answers that they have given.[8] The Speaker has called the attention of the House to the inconvenience that arises from an excessive demand for further replies,[9] and, to hinder the practice, he has frequently felt it necessary to call upon the Member, in whose name the next question stands upon the notice paper, to put his question,[10] and has for the same reason asked Members not to ask supplementary questions[11] and has suggested that lengthy answers should be circulated with the Official Report instead of being given orally.[12] In accordance with the recommendation of the Select Committee on Parliamentary Questions, the Speaker has indicated that he would not necessarily call for a supplementary question every Member who had placed an identical question on the order paper.[13] When an answer has been refused on security grounds, the Speaker has not allowed further supplementary questions.[14] A supplementary question may

---

1 HC Deb (1945–46) 414, c 1372.
2 HC Deb (1983–84) 63, c 357 w.
3 See eg HC Deb (1987–88) 121, c 613 w.
4 HC Deb (1958–59) 595, cc 34–35.
5 HC Deb (1956–57) 563, cc 853–862; ibid (1984–85) 78, cc 594–595, 655–656.
6 HC Deb (1912–13) 42, c 2552.
7 Parl Deb (1861) 161, c 497; HC Deb (1983–84) 57, cc 647–649. For example, the rules governing the reading out of material and quotations from speeches at question time do not apply to Ministerial replies. Eg HC Deb (1979–80) 986, c 1026.
8 Parl Deb (1872) 211, c 1994; ibid (1901) 96, c 264; HC Deb (1914–16) 73, c 41; ibid (1921) 142, c 1055.
9 Parl Deb (1884) 290, c 686; ibid (1892) 5, c 551; HC Deb (1924) 169, c 1507; ibid (1948–49) 461, c 1580.
10 Parl Deb (1888) 323, c 374; ibid (1905) 142, c 937; HC Deb (1920) 125, c 1023; ibid (1951–52) 493, c 1170–1171.
11 HC Deb (1920) 130, c 886.
12 HC Deb (1924) 172, c 1980.
13 HC Deb (1972–73) 860, c 258.
14 HC Deb (1960–61) 635, c 1580; ibid (1961–62) 652, c 1263.

refer only to the answer out of which it immediately arises,[1] must not be read or be too long,[2] must not refer to an earlier answer or be addressed to another Minister[3] and is governed by the general rules of order affecting all questions.[4] As a consequence of the rule of anticipation (see pp 327–328), when a Member gives oral notice in the House of his intention to seek to raise on the adjournment a matter arising out of oral answers, further supplementary questions thereon are not permitted.[5] The Speaker has also refused to call Members to ask a supplementary question to Ministers (other than the Prime Minister) when their original question was of so general a character as to provide a wide area for supplementaries; this has been interpreted as applying particularly to questions about meetings or visits.[6]

(2) Private notice questions

Questions which have not appeared on the paper, but which are of an urgent character and relate either to matters of public importance,[7] or to the arrangement of business, may be taken after half-past three or at eleven o'clock on a Friday provided that they have been submitted to the Speaker[8] before noon on the day on which they are to be asked[9] (or, on a day on which the House meets at half-past nine o'clock, before ten o'clock)[10] and have been accepted by him as satisfying the conditions imposed by Standing Order No 17(3), and provided that notice has been given to the Minister concerned.

For many years a weekly private notice question on the business for the following week has been asked on Thursdays, normally by the Leader of the Opposition, after any other private notice questions have been disposed of and supplementary questions covering a wide field are subsequently allowed. On other days only business questions relating to the business of the day, or to any change in the business for the week already announced, are permitted.[11]

A question cannot be asked by private notice in order to anticipate a question for oral answer of which notice has been given and which in the Speaker's opinion is likely to be answered orally on a reasonably early date.[12] The latter must first be withdrawn; such withdrawal becoming effective on the publication of an Order Paper no longer containing the question. Questions which are asked without appearing on the paper are governed by the same rules of order as questions of which notice has been given.[13] Neither the submission of a private notice question nor its subsequent

1 Parl Deb (1900) 82, c 12.
2 HC Deb (1935–36) 313, c 995; ibid (1947–48) 452, c 2203; ibid (1952–53) 518, c 22; ibid (1956–57) 560, cc 731–732.
3 Parl Deb (1901) 91, c 103; HC Deb (1958–59) 599, cc 987–988.
4 Parl Deb (1907) 172, c 225; HC Deb (1935–36) 307, c 1381; ibid (1948–49) 463, c 1843; ibid (1960–61) 639, cc 1601–1602. HC Deb (1979–80) 986, cc 1358, 1568.
5 HC Deb (1984–85) 74, c 14; ibid (1987–88) 133, c 7.
6 HC Deb (1983–84) 54, c 130; ibid (1983–84) 56, c 706; ibid (1988–89) 152, cc 361–362.
7 HC Deb (1935–36) 309, c 42.
8 HC Deb (1917–18) 94, c 595; ibid (1920) 132, cc 942, 1636; ibid (1948–49) 462, c 37.
9 HC Deb (1958–59) 595, c 196.
10 HC Deb (1979–80) 977, c 440.
11 HC Deb (1958–59) 595, c 36.
12 HC Deb (1918) 106, c 1125; ibid (1924) 169, c 266; ibid (1943–44) 399, cc 1203–1204; ibid (1966–67) 747, cc 812–813.
13 Parl Deb (1892) 3, c 861; HC Deb (1921) 147, c 1028; ibid (1928–29) 224, c 1777.

rejection by the Speaker should therefore be publicly referred to.[1] The Speaker has ruled privately that a Member may ask a question by private notice even though he has already the maximum number of questions for oral answer on the paper, and that a Member may not ask more than one question by private notice on any day, though a Member has been permitted to submit more than one. The Leader of the Opposition never puts a question on the paper for oral answer, but asks it by private notice and the factor of urgency has not been insisted on.[2]

When a private notice question (other than one relating to business) is allowed by the Speaker, a notice is put up in the Members' Lobby and is also displayed on the annunciator.[3] It is not the practice to inform Members whose constituencies are particularly affected by a private notice question.[4]

D. BUSINESS TAKEN AFTER QUESTIONS

(1) Ministerial statements

Explanations are made in the House by Ministers on behalf of the Government regarding their domestic and foreign policy; stating the advice they have tendered to the Sovereign regarding their retention of office or the dissolution of Parliament; announcing the legislative proposals they intend to submit to Parliament; or the course they intend to adopt in the transaction and arrangement of public business.[5] These explanations are sometimes elicited by arrangement in reply to a question. But the older practice under which they were volunteered spontaneously is also often followed.[6] Prior notice to the Speaker is necessary,[7] but neither his permission[8] nor the leave of the House[9] is required. Since 1964[10] notice has whenever possible been given to Members of impending ministerial statements by means of notices placed in the Members' Lobby and displayed on the annunciator. As no question is before the House, debate on such statements is irregular,[11] but questions arising from the statement are frequently raised and replies given by the Minister. It is not the normal practice for questions on more than one

---

1 HC Deb (1974–75) 892, cc 28–30; ibid (1983–84) 50, c 611; ibid (1984–85) 71, cc 861–865, 881.
2 HC Deb (1957–58) 580, c 431; ibid (1972–73) 857, cc 1700–1703; ibid (1987–88) 140, cc 21–27; ibid (1988–89) 149, cc 289–316, 909–917.
3 On a Friday the subject matter of the question is shown on the annunciator screen at 10.15 a.m., 10.30 a.m. and 10.45 a.m. for three-minute periods (HC Deb (1979–1980) 977, c 440).
4 HC Deb (1975–76) 918, c 1203.
5 Although the Leader of the House usually announces the business for the following week each Thursday at about half-past three in reply to a question made without notice by the Leader of the Opposition, he occasionally makes such an announcement by way of ministerial statement, and subsequent changes to the arrangements announced at that time are normally announced in this manner. The Speaker has ruled that when a narrow business statement is made, changing only one item of business, supplementary questions are confined to that item. HC Deb (1979–80) 985, cc 1070–1071; ibid (1984–85) 72, cc 28–29.
6 HC Deb (1938–39) 350, cc 2174–2176; ibid 352, cc 173–174; ibid (1941–42) 380, cc 1982–1983, etc.
7 HC Deb (1942–43) 392, c 394; ibid (1984–85) 69, cc 173–174. For an example of such notice being given orally in the House, see HC Deb (1983–84) 46, cc 789, 797.
8 HC Deb (1963–64) 698, c 414; ibid (1985–86) 91, c 306.
9 HC Deb (1942–43) 390, c 2267; ibid (1983–84) 62, cc 490–491.
10 HC Deb (1963–64) 698, cc 222–223; see also HC Deb (1966–67) 740, cc 1563–1564.
11 HC Deb (1939–40) 361, cc 796–797; ibid (1941–42) 376, cc 1698–1699; but see HC Deb (1948–49) 464, cc 373–374.

statement to be taken at the same time.[1] Debate on a ministerial statement has been raised upon a motion for adjournment, moved for that purpose.[2] A statement relating to an adjourned debate, which was shortly to be resumed, has been allowed.[3]

Exceptionally, statements, including statements on future business, have been permitted by the Speaker, in urgent circumstances and with the leave of the House, at other times, including:

—after the disposal of motions at the commencement of public business;[4]
—at seven o'clock, on the lapsing of private Members' motions accorded precedence under Standing Order No 13(8);[5]
—during the course of consideration of an order of the day;[6]
—between orders of the day;[7]
—following the moment of interruption.[8]

Substantive interventions on points of order made by Ministers may be treated by the Speaker as statements, so that questions may be raised thereon and replies given.[9]

The Speaker may also make statements to the House. He does so regularly on matters connected with arrangements for ballots for debates following the passage of Consolidated Fund Bills (see p 267) and on the holiday adjournment Motions (see p 266)[10] and on matters of procedure or practice.[11] The Speaker also makes statements in connection with arrangements for ceremonial occasions,[12] the retirement of senior Officers of the House,[13] etc. (For the Speaker's rulings on matters of privilege, see p 135.)

For explanations made by Members of the circumstances which have caused their resignation of an office in the Government, see p 306.

(2) Introduction of new Members

A Member who has been returned at a by-election is normally introduced immediately after questions[14] in order that he may be in a position to take part in public business as early as possible.

It is usual for Members who have not yet taken the oath to sit below the bar;[15] and care must be taken that they do not, inadvertently, take a seat

---

1 HC Deb (1979–80) 985, c 1047.
2 Parl Deb (1884) 290, c 696; ibid (1905) 150, c 70; HC Deb (1914) 65, c 1833; ibid (1948–49) 458, c 1415.
3 HC Deb (1962–63) 675, cc 1097–1104.
4 HC Deb (1916) 84, c 573.
5 HC Deb (1986–87) 110, c 70.
6 HC Deb (1981–82) 23, c 120. For the use of a dilatory motion moved to permit a statement, see HC Deb (1987–88) 122, c 465; also Parl Deb (1867) 185, c 1339.
7 HC Deb (1979–80) 980, c 1664.
8 Parl Deb (1908) 185, c 1067; HC Deb (1981–82) 21, cc 619–621; ibid (1984–85) 72, c 244; ibid (1985–86) 100, cc 1265, 1370, ibid (1985–86) 102, c 1504; ibid (1987–88) 120, c 1093.
9 HC Deb (1985–86) 91, cc 958–965.
10 Eg HC Deb (1987–88) 123, c 1135; ibid (1987–88) 124, c 596.
11 Eg HC Deb (1983–84) 54, c 130; ibid (1985–86) 87, c 275; ibid (1986–87) 116, c 261; ibid (1987–88) 140, c 511.
12 Eg HC Deb (1985–86) 94, c 19; ibid (1987–88) 137, c 533.
13 Eg HC Deb (1986–87) 116, c 177.
14 A Member has taken his seat on a Friday, there being no oral questions, at the commencement of public business, CJ (1943–44) 24.
15 When on 18 May 1849 notice was taken that strangers were present, Baron Rothschild retained his seat below the bar, although he had not taken the oath; and Mr Bradlaugh was present below the bar during many divisions, while forbidden to take the oath.

within the bar, by which they would render themselves liable to the penalties and disqualifications imposed by statute (see p 230).

If a Member is elected at a by-election, the Clerk of the Crown sends to the Clerk of the House a certificate of the return received in the Crown Office; and the Member must obtain a certificate from the Public Bill Office of the receipt of that certificate for production at the Table, before the Clerk of the House will administer the oath.

In the case of a Member who was sworn at the Table before his return was received by the Clerk of the Crown, it was questioned whether the oath which he had taken before the receipt of the return had been duly taken. A committee which was appointed to inquire into the matter reported that the non-return of the indenture to the Crown Office cannot affect the validity of the election or the right of a person duly elected to be held a Member of the House, but recommended a strict adherence to the practice of requiring the production of the usual certificate, or, in cases in which that may be from accidental circumstances impossible, of requiring satisfactory proof of the person's title to be admitted as a Member.[1]

For a delay in delivery of a return to the Crown Office, see Parl Deb (1889) 334, cc 52–53; HC Deb (1955–56) 542, cc 36–38, 1039–1042.

Members returned upon new writs issued after the general election take the oath or make their affirmation in the same manner as those returned at a general election (see p 229). By Standing Order No 6, Members may take and subscribe the oath at any time during the sitting before the orders of the day and notices of motions have been entered on (the usual time), or after they have been disposed of, so long as no debate or business is interrupted.[2] The oath must be taken in English,[3] but the Speaker has allowed Members to recite Welsh and Gaelic forms of oath in addition.

On the occasion of a Member coming to the table to be sworn, on 26 July 1858, a Member rose to speak on a point of order, but the Speaker maintained 'that the taking of his seat by a Member is a matter of privilege, and ought not to be interrupted by any discussion whatever' (Parl Deb (1857–58) 151, c 2106).

Under the resolution of 23 February 1688, 'in compliance with an ancient order and custom, they are introduced to the Table between two Members, making their obeisances as they go up, that they may be the better known to the House':[4] but this practice is not observed in regard to Members who, having been chosen at a general election, have established their claim to a seat by an election petition;[5] for they are supposed to have been returned at the beginning of the Parliament, when no such introduction is customary.

---

1 HC 256 (1847–48), case of Mr Hawes.
2 Parl Deb (1907) 169, cc 159 and 315.
3 HC Deb (1966–67) 732, cc 879–880.
4 CJ (1688–93) 34.
5 2 Hatsell 85, n.

On 13 February 1875, Dr Kenealy, a new Member, came to the Table to be sworn, without the introduction of two Members. The Speaker acquainted him with the order of the House, and, refusing to hear any comments from him, directed him to withdraw; whereupon the House resolved that the order be dispensed with, on this occasion (CJ (1875) 52; Parl Deb (1875) 222, c 486). On a similar occasion, however, in the case of Mr McIntyre on 17 April 1945 the House, on a division, refused to dispense with the order, and on the following day the new Member was introduced in the customary way (HC Deb (1944–45) 410, cc 34 and 222).

The Select Committee on Procedure in 1972–73 considered the question of the introduction of new Members after by-elections, and recommended that there should be no change in the order and custom laid down by the resolution of 1688.[1]

(3) Proposals to move the adjournment of the House under Standing Order No 20

Standing Order No 20, which took its present shape on 14 November 1967,[2] gives private Members an opportunity to move the adjournment of the House for discussing a specific and important matter which should have urgent consideration, if the Speaker agrees that the matter in question warrants this. Such motions may not by the Standing Order be made on Friday or Saturday.

The Member wishing to move such a motion must inform the Speaker of his intention before twelve o'clock if the urgency of the matter is then known, and if not as soon thereafter as it becomes known.[3] The Speaker has declined to accept an indication of intention given by a Member in the House on the previous day, and unsupported by any subsequent written application, as sufficient notice.[4] He rises in his place after all questions to Members have been disposed of and before[5] the commencement of public business, and asks leave to move the adjournment of the House. Standing Order No 20 was amended on 27 February 1986 so as to limit to three minutes the time permitted for such an application; the limit is strictly enforced.[6] It is not in order for another Member to make a further submission while an application is being made;[7] nor are points of order normally taken. A further application on the same subject on the same day from another Member will not normally be accepted by the Chair.[8] A notice of the specific and important matter which it is proposed shall be discussed must be supplied to Mr Speaker. In coming to his decision (which he may defer till a stated time) the Speaker is expected to have regard to the extent to which the matter concerns the administrative responsibilities of Ministers of the

---

1 HC 336 (1972–73).
2 The new Standing Order was passed following a recommendation from the Select Committee on Procedure (HC 282 (1966–67)). For a description of the procedure under the standing order in its previous form, see May (17th edn) pp 360–369.
3 Eg HC Deb (1977–78) 951, c 1194, ibid (1977–78) 954, c 1146; ibid (1983–84) 45, c 157.
4 HC Deb (1979–80) 979, cc 1372–1374.
5 HC Deb (1969–70) 801, cc 825–826.
6 HC Deb (1986–87) 106, c 24; eg ibid (1986–87) 121, cc 651–652.
7 HC Deb (1967–68) 763, c 1306; ibid (1985–86) 91, c 307.
8 HC Deb (1979–80) 986, cc 36–37.

Crown or could come within the scope of ministerial action, and the probability of the matter being brought before the House in time by other means.
Under the terms of the Standing Order the Speaker has to state whether or
not he is satisfied that the matter is proper to be discussed without giving the
reasons for his decision to the House. If he decides that the matter should
not be made the subject of an emergency debate under Standing Order
No 20, further debate on the submission is out of order.[1] If he considers that
the terms of the motion are in order, he asks whether the Member has the
leave of the House, and if such leave is not unanimously given, calls on those
Members who support the motion to rise in their places. If 40 or more
Members then rise to support the motion, the question as to whether it
should be proceeded with is decided in the affirmative. If, however, fewer
than 40 Members, but more than 10 so rise, the question is decided on a
division.[2] Once the leave of the House has been signified, the motion usually
stands over until the commencement of public business the next day (when
proceedings on it are interrupted after three hours), or, on a Thursday, until
the following Monday.[3] If the Speaker considers the matter sufficiently
urgent, it may stand over until seven o'clock the same evening,[4] when it has
precedence over all other business; in this case any business postponed at
seven o'clock is not (except as provided in Standing Order No 14(2)) interrupted at ten o'clock and may be resumed and proceeded with at or after that
hour for a period of time equal to the duration of proceedings on the motion
for the adjournment. The Speaker has declined to hear any further applications for a debate under Standing Order No 20 when leave has been
granted by the House for a debate, when he took the view that all other
subjects which were proposed to be raised at that time could be debated
within the terms of the motion which he had granted.[5]

Members raising matters in the House under the Standing Order No 20
procedure are frequently called to order by the Chair, and the Speaker has
reminded the House that applications must be directed solely to seeking to
prove that an issue is sufficiently important, specific and urgent to change
the business of the House so as to provide for an emergency debate, and is
not an occasion to debate the issue itself.[6] The House rejected a recent
recommendation from a Select Committee on Procedure that motions
should only be allowed in the House if, after having first been submitted to
the Speaker, he considered them proper to be raised.[7] The joint submission
of an application under Standing Order No 20 and of a private notice
question is contrary to the practice of the House.[8]

Under the terms of the Standing Order debate on motions for the
adjournment of the House under Standing Order No 20 may include refer-

1 HC Deb (1969–70) 798, cc 214–215.
2 CJ (1961–62) 235; ibid (1975–76) 379.
3 CJ (1969–70) 117, 120; ibid (1982–83) 274, 282.
4 CJ (1968–69) 98; ibid, (1974–75) 171; ibid (1978–79) 110, 143–144.
5 HC Deb (1978–79) 961, c 57.
6 HC Deb (1978–79) 964, c 1101. A SO No 20 application, deprecated by the Speaker, was not
  proceeded with, HC Deb (1982–83) 32, c 864. For a refusal by the Speaker to submit an
  application relating to the exercise of the Royal Prerogative of Mercy, see HC Deb (1977–78)
  940, c 747.
7 CJ (1979–80), 202.
8 HC Deb (1984–85) 83, c 738.

ence to any matter that would be in order on a motion to take note of the subject under discussion.

(4) Ceremonial speeches

At this time ceremonial speeches have been allowed. Originally confined to commemorating on their deaths the public services of distinguished statesmen who were or had been members of the House, in recent times the practice has been extended to other occasions of mourning and certain occasions of rejoicing.[1] For example, at this time the Speaker has paid tribute to a former Speaker who died on the previous day.[2] However, in the case of tributes to a Member, the Speaker has called on Members to pay tributes immediately after questions and before ministerial statements.[3] Motions on matters of this kind, and amendments thereto, have been allowed to be moved without notice.[4] Such speeches are usually made by the Leader of the House and supported by brief speeches from leaders of parties not in office. Speeches have also been made at this point by Members given leave of absence to present gifts on behalf of the House to Commonwealth legislatures.[5] When a Member has reported that the legislature passed a resolution on the occasion of the presentation, the resolution has been entered in the Journal.[6]

(5) Giving notice of motions and holding of ballot

If oral notice is given of the intention to move a motion, the proper time for this is after any application for moving the adjournment of the House under Standing Order No 20 has been disposed of. But such notice is now seldom given orally in the House because, by a practice dating from the beginning of the last century, the terms of a substantive motion should be printed on the notice paper and such printed notice is ordinarily sufficient.[7] Accordingly the usual method of giving notice of a motion is to deliver its terms in writing at any time during the sitting of the House to the Table Office.

A substantive motion, as a rule, must be moved by the Member in whose name the notice stands (see p 314).

A notice orally given holds good for the day on which it is given and cannot be withdrawn. It must be supplemented by a written notice handed in at the Table during the same sitting, if it is to continue effective.[8] A written

---

1 HC Deb (1941–42) 376, cc 320–324; ibid (1942–43) 386, cc 48, 1059–1063; ibid 390, cc 1946–1950; ibid (1947–48) 448, c 1245; ibid (1962–63) 666, cc 801–804; ibid (1964–65) 718, cc 165–171; ibid (1970–71) 806, cc 211–216; ibid (1971–72) 838, cc 37–49; ibid (1972–73) 846, cc 914–921; ibid (1986–87) 108, cc 21–31.
2 HC Deb (1977–78) 950, c 774.
3 HC Deb (1981–82) 13, cc 2, 19–21.
4 HC Deb (1971–72) 838, cc 37, 49.
5 Eg HC Deb (1948–49) 460, cc 752–754; ibid (1961–62) 652, cc 904–906.
6 Eg CJ (1961–62) 87.
7 3 and 27 February 1806, Colchester ii, 35, 41; Parl Deb (1806) 6, c 229; see also 2 March 1836, Parl Deb (1836) 31, c 1154; 9 July 1861, ibid (1861) 164, c 630. For earlier cases, see 21 Parl Hist 147, 622, 885, 888.
8 As notices of motions are effective only when given on a sitting day before the rising of the House, any notices received after the rising of the House or on days other than sitting days are held over to the next sitting day for printing, and consequently appear on the paper on the day after the next sitting day.

notice becomes effective for purposes of the rule of anticipation only when it appears on the notice paper on the day following that on which it was handed in at the Table and continues effective as long as it remains on the paper (HC Deb (1912) 40, cc 980, 1151). A notice cannot be withdrawn from the notice paper of the day or the current issue of the order book in the course of a sitting (Parl Deb (1892) 4, cc 189–190; HC Deb (1929–30) 230, c 1494); but by an intimation to the Clerks at the Table it can be withdrawn from a future issue of the Order Book. A Member may not keep the same notice standing in the Order Book for two different days; nor may more than six names appear in the Order Book in connection with one notice (Mr Speaker's rulings (private) 5 April 1905; 18 July 1917).

Ballots

In view of the limited time available for private Members' business (see pp 260–261), precedence between Members who desire to move motions or introduce bills is conferred by means of the ballot.[1]

(i) Ballot for notices of Motions. Ballots are held in the House for private Members' motions on such Wednesdays as the House may appoint in pursuance of Standing Order No 13(7) for the Fridays allotted to private Members' motions, and on such days as the House may appoint under the same paragraph for the four half-days allotted to private Members' motions. A sessional order providing for such dates is agreed to early in the session.

Any Member who desires to ballot signs his name on the ballot paper, which is placed in the 'No' division lobby for that purpose, on the day on which a ballot for notices of motion is to be taken. Notice may be given on behalf of a Member at that moment absent from the House; in that case, the Member who gives the notice enters upon the paper the name of the Member for whom he acts, may answer for him when his name is called, and may deliver at the Table the written notice in his behalf but he cannot when so acting sign his own name on the ballot paper.[2] The name or signature of a Member must not appear more than once upon the ballot paper. Numbers are assigned by the ballot paper to the names or signatures of the Members intending to give notice, and slips of paper bearing the corresponding numbers are folded up and placed in a ballot box.

When the Speaker orders the ballot to be taken, the Clerk Assistant draws out of the ballot box numbered slips of paper one by one (three slips are usually drawn). He calls each number that has been drawn out, and the Speaker thereupon announces the name of the Member to whose signature that number is attached upon the ballot paper. No confirmation by the successful Members is needed on the day of the ballot, and future editions of the Order Book contain the fact that on the private Members' motion day in

---

1 The precedence so conferred has been overruled on one occasion (in favour of a Member who had surrendered his right of priority on an earlier day in deference to the general desire of the House) by an order made by the House at the commencement of public business (CJ (1924–25) 180; HC Deb (1924–25) 181, c 2081; ibid (1924–25) 182, cc 1094, 1224, 2226). The motion thus preferred was printed in italics at the head of the notices of motions. (Notices of Motions (1924–25) 1522.)

2 Parl Deb (1843) 68, c 1002; ibid (1901) 92, cc 92, 589; ibid (1902) 102, c 1271. A Member may not move a motion on behalf of another Member.

question such Members will each draw attention to a subject and move a resolution. Each Member hands in notice of his subject at the Table or the Table Office not later than the ninth day preceding the day on which it is to have precedence (Standing Order No 13(7)), when it is entered in the Order Book. Failure to hand in the notice of subject in time results in removal of the Member's name from the Order Book. When the terms of the motion are taken to the Table or the Table Office they are scrutinized to ensure that they are within the scope of the subject and otherwise in order.

It is possible[1] for Members still to follow the procedure prevailing before January 1968. Under this, a successful Member or another Member authorized by him[2] rises and states the notice of the subject[3] he has chosen. The written notice should not be wider in scope than the oral notice. When the written notice has been more limited in its scope than the oral notice, the former has been ruled to be the effective notice. When a Member wishes to change a subject of which he has given oral notice, notice of the new subject must also be given orally in the House.[4]

Names of supporters may not be added to ballot notices, as the ballot gives precedence solely to the Member who has secured a place.

(ii) Ballot for private Members' bills. The ballot for private Members' bills is taken on the second Thursday on which the House shall sit during the session[5] at a time and place fixed by the Speaker, and is conducted by the Chairman of Ways and Means. The same method as for private Members' notices of motions is adopted, save that the ballot paper is in the 'No' division lobby on the two days immediately prior to the day of the ballot, and that the ballot is held in a committee room.

(6) Personal statements

In regard to the explanation of personal matters, the House is usually indulgent, and will permit a statement of that character—also referred to as personal explanations—to be made without any question being before the House provided that the Speaker has been informed of what the Member proposes to say,[6] and has given leave.[7] Because the practice of the House is not to permit such statements to be subject to intervention or debate, the

---

1 HC Deb (1967–68) 757, c 221–222; ibid (1982–83) 40, c 357.
2 HC Deb (1911) 23, c 2010; ibid (1922) 152, c 1349; ibid (1924) 171, c 245; ibid (1924) 172, cc 1370, 1559, 1672; ibid (1924–25) 179, c 1218; ibid (1924–25) 180, c 186; ibid (1927) 202, c 762.
3 A Member cannot give alternative notices, HC Deb (1927) 202, c 763.
4 HC Deb (1986–87) 106, c 778.
5 SO No 13(6).
6 HC Deb (1960–61) 629, c 368; ibid (1968–69) 777, c 1584.
7 HC Deb (1946–47) 431, c 2191; ibid (1974–75) 898, cc 46–52. Such information is not required from a former Minister wishing to explain the circumstances in which he has resigned, ibid (1974–75) 893, c 670. The Speaker has no control over statements made by Ministers in a ministerial, as opposed to a personal, capacity, even if they are concerned with matters which might appropriately have been dealt with by means of a personal statement, ibid (1974) 872, cc 33, 41–42. Objection has however been taken to a Minister correcting a previous ministerial statement by means of a personal explanation, ibid (1962–63) 681, c 338.

precise contents of the proposed statement are submitted in advance to the Speaker to ensure that they are appropriate. The Member granted the privilege of making such a statement may not therefore depart from the agreed text.[1] Such statements are made in the order indicated on p 274 before the commencement of public business;[2] no debate should ensue thereon, but if another Member is involved in the personal statement, he is generally allowed to give his own view of the matter and to say whether he accepts it or not.[3] Personal statements may not be made when the House is in Committee.[4] For the case of a personal statement which was subsequently admitted not to be true, see HC Deb (1962–63) 674, c 809; ibid 679, c 655; CJ (1962–63) 246. For the case of a personal statement withdrawing allegations which were subsequently found to be justified and a resolution of the House thereon, see HC Deb (1962–63) 681, c 682; CJ (1962–63) 288.

The indulgence of a personal statement is granted with caution; for, unless discreetly used, it is apt to lead to irregular debates.[5] General arguments or observations beyond the fair bounds of explanation or too distinct a reference to previous debates are out of order;[6] though a Member has been permitted by the Speaker to make, at a subsequent sitting, a statement regarding alleged misrepresentation in debate[7] or in a question to a Minister.[8] A personal statement has been allowed by a Member on his reasons for applying for the Manor of Northstead.[9]

On 30 November 1915 a Minister at the close of a personal statement moved the adjournment of the House in order to afford an opportunity for debate.[10] On 4 August 1947 a Member made a personal statement relative to a matter then before the Committee of Privileges; he was directed to withdraw, and his statement was referred to the Committee of Privileges on a motion by the Leader of the House.[11] On 26 July 1977 when the report from a Select Committee appointed to consider the conduct of certain Members was considered, two of the Members, according to custom, addressed the House first, after which they withdrew from the Chamber.[12] The third Member, having applied for the Chiltern Hundreds, had made a statement on an earlier occasion. Subsequently three separate Motions, each relating to the conduct of a Member, were moved, and the two Members were permitted to return to the Chamber.

---

1 HC Deb (1974–75) 898, c 47; ibid (1987–88) 131, cc 675–676, 681.
2 Parl Deb (1905) 146, c 302; HC Deb (1912) 45, cc 1486, 1532.
3 HC Deb (1954–55) 535, 2609–2610; ibid (1968–69) 777, c 1584.
4 HC Deb (1964–65) 713, c 241.
5 Parl Deb (1859) 153, cc 334–336; ibid (1864) 174, c 191–211; ibid (1864) 174, c 1203–1218; ibid (1865) 178, cc 372–378; ibid (1882) 269, cc 106–132; HC Deb (1968–69) 784, c 239. See also motion to express regret that imputations made against a Member had not been withdrawn on the occasion of a personal statement, ibid (1864) 174, c 305. For further examples of past rulings on personal statements, see *May* (20th edn) p 356.
6 Lord C Paget, Parl Deb (1864) 173, c 1911–1914.
7 Parl Deb (1846) 87, c 480; HC Deb (1911) 21, c 1066.
8 HC Deb (1912) 45, c 1532.
9 HC Deb (1981–82) 23, c 38.
10 CJ (1914–16) 296; HC Deb (1915) 76, c 549.
11 CJ (1946–47) 354; HC Deb (1946–47) 441, c 991–996.
12 HC Deb (1976–77) 936, cc 332–343; ibid 935, c 2047; CJ (1976–77) 448.

The Speaker himself has made personal statements,[1] and on 22 March 1948 the Chairman of Ways and Means made a personal statement to inquire into which the House appointed a select committee the next day.[2]

Explanation by a Member of the circumstances which have caused his resignation of an office in the Government may be made immediately before the commencement of public business.[3]

Though debate must not arise upon such explanation, statements pertinent thereto on behalf of the Government have been permitted.

(7) Consideration of Lords amendments or message

Lords amendments to public bills are normally included among the orders of the day, at any point of the Government's choosing. When Lords amendments to bills have been verbal or, if more than verbal, not of material importance or numerous or contentious, and accordingly have not been printed (see pp 510–511), they have been taken before the commencement of public business. Such amendments have also been taken before questions or after the conclusion of public business, when such a course has been more convenient.

Similarly, a Lords message relative to the destruction of the Commons chamber by enemy action was considered forthwith (HC Deb (1940–41) 371, c 1268).

(8) Matters relating to privilege

By custom this position in the order of business has long been assigned to matters of privilege, and for many years until the procedure was changed (see ch 10) in 1978 this time was regarded as the most appropriate for Members to raise complaints of breach of privilege or of contempt. But matters which fall under the designation of privilege in the widest sense occupy a different position in the order of business. For instance, the moving of a new writ to fill a casual vacancy (which is one of the means by which the House exercises the privilege of making provision with respect to its own proper constitution) is taken at the very beginning of a sitting (see p 276) though if the moving of a new writ is opposed it is taken at this point. Other privileges, the enforcement of which is regulated in part by standing orders, are dealt with as so provided. For instance, breaches of order in the House are dealt with and punished, if necessary, as they arise; and the right to exclude strangers may be exercised at any time under the procedure laid down by Standing Order No 143 (see p 171). A motion to rescind an order for the suspension of a Member is not treated as a matter of privilege, and consequently is not entitled to the priority which would enable it to be taken at this place in the order of business.[4] A breach of the financial privileges of the Commons by the House of Lords, if, as is usually the case, it occurs in relation to a bill, is raised in the course of proceedings on the bill.[5]

---

1 HC Deb (1947–48) 445, cc 1205–1206; ibid (1964–65) 713, c 1033; ibid (1966–67) 728, c 1570; ibid (1969–70) 796, c 1405.
2 HC Deb (1947–48) 448, cc 2584–2586.
3 For examples of such statements, see *May* (20th edn) p 357.
4 Parl Deb (1887) 313, c 1124.
5 For example of the raising of alleged cases of breach of the financial privilege of the Commons, see 20th edn, p 358.

Matters requiring immediate intervention of the House. Urgent matters which require the immediate intervention of the House, if they should occur during a sitting of the House, may be raised at once in spite of the interruption of the debate or other proceedings (except a division in progress). A complaint on such a matter is entertained by the House as soon as it is raised, but if complaint is made in committee the chairman reports progress and the Speaker resumes the Chair. If the matter does not require the immediate intervention of the House, however, leave will be refused.

> Proceedings have been interrupted to allow the raising of a communication to a newspaper of a memorandum explanatory of a bill which was to be introduced the next day, after the memorandum had been presented but before it was available for Members (HC Deb (1909) 9, c 2423). Proceedings have also been interrupted by a report from the Serjeant at Arms on the facts of an incident which had been reported by a Member to the House as a breach of privilege earlier in the day; a letter from a stranger concerned in this incident was then communicated to the House by the Speaker (CJ (1946–47) 54; HC Deb (1946–47) 431, cc 2323–2325). But where immediate action by the House was not needed, the Speaker has refused to allow the interruption of business (HC Deb (1913) 51, c 720; and see also ibid (1951–52) 499, c 880). The chairman has refused to interrupt committee proceedings in a case where he considered the complaint did not so obviously concern privilege as to justify suspending the work of the committee and sending for the Speaker (HC Deb (1909) 9, c 2370; ibid (1970–71) 810, cc. 1031–1034).

E. BUSINESS TAKEN 'AT THE COMMENCEMENT OF PUBLIC BUSINESS'

Public business commences when the Speaker has called the first Member who has given notice to present a bill, or to make a motion at the commencement of public business, or upon the Member in charge of the first motion standing at the head of the orders of the day, or upon the Clerk to read the orders of the day. Consequently, after the Speaker's call no motion can be made for the adjournment of the House by a private Member[1] or for adjournment under Standing Order No 20; nor, until the business set down for that sitting is concluded, can a notice be given, nor, save with the indulgence of the House, can a question be asked.

Before the House enters on the main business of the sitting, ie Orders of the Day and notices of motions standing on the Order Paper of public business, an opportunity is afforded for the consideration of certain items of a more formal character or dealing with the business of the House, which require notice and are placed together on the Order Paper under a general title 'at the commencement of public business'. These items fall into the following sub-divisions:

---

1 HC Deb (1929–30) 237, c 903.

(a) The presentation of public bills under Standing Order No 58.
(b) Government motions relating to committees.
(c) Government motions regulating the business of the House.
(d) Motions under Standing Order No 19 for bringing in public bills or nominating select committees.

(1) Presentation of public bills under Standing Order No 58

The presentation of public bills is a subject belonging to another chapter (see pp 461 ff). All that need be said here is that it is a form of procedure *sui generis*. It is not a motion and no question is put upon it. Any Member, by placing on the paper notice of the short and long titles of a bill, can secure its first reading (which is deemed to be given by the House when the Clerk has read the title) and an order for printing it, and also secure the appointment of a date for its second reading. In view of the small amount of information about a bill required in the notice of presentation, objection that a bill is not in order is seldom raised at this stage. When, however, the purpose of a bill, as defined in the title, is obviously unfit for legislation, notice may be taken and the presentation disallowed.

Objection on the following grounds has been upheld in the past:

(i) When the purpose of a bill, being to allocate time for certain bills before the House, was a matter for the decision of the House alone and not for legislation (Parl Deb (1908) 190, c 879).

(ii) When the purpose was to oblige the Government to introduce certain legislation (HC Deb (1914) 60, cc 1196–1200).

(iii) A notice of the presentation of a bill has been removed from the Notice Paper by the Speaker's instructions because it had the same title as a bill for the introduction of which leave had been refused by the House earlier in the session (Private Ruling, 4 June 1931).

Under Standing Order No 13 no notice of a presentation of a Bill may be given by a private Member in pursuance of Standing Order No 58 until after the fifth Wednesday in a session on which the House sits.

(2) Government motions relating to Committees

Motions to refer to appropriate standing committees, statutory instruments, European Community Documents, estimates, matters and, in some cases, bills are normally made with notice by a Minister at the commencement of public business; for details, see pp 591–596.

(3) Government motions regulating the business and sittings of the House

Such motions, which do not have precedence unless moved by a Minister,[1] are normally moved by the Leader of the House and invariably require notice (see p 322).

Motions regulating the business of the House are of two kinds; those which are referred to specifically in Standing Order No 14 (Exempted business), which are moved at the interruption of business (see pp 244–245), and

---

1 Parl Deb (1883) 279, c 419.

general motions not contemplated by the standing orders. In the case of the latter, questions on them may be debated and amendments moved, but such amendments must be strictly relevant to the terms and purpose of the motion; and amendments stating, as an argument against the motion, that the House had no confidence in the Government, or that motions giving precedence to government business might be rendered unnecessary by altering the procedure of the House, have therefore been ruled to be out of order.[1]

Such motions may also be moved in the ordinary course of the day's business, in which case notice is given as for any other notice of motion. For example, although in the past it was not always considered necessary to give previous notice in the case of motions for the adjournment of the House over Christmas, Easter, or the Spring bank holiday,[2] notice is now given, and the motions relating to such adjournments are generally set down among the orders of the day, including those providing for the meeting of the House and the taking of questions at a different hour from that appointed by the standing orders.

Motions not contemplated by the standing orders and which may be moved at the commencement of public business are for such purposes as the following:

—To give precedence to Government business over private Members' business either on a particular day or days or for a period, for example, until the end of the financial year (CJ (1928–29) 10).
—To give precedence to specified business either on a particular day or at all sittings until concluded. The business is usually a Government bill, but precedence has been given to a private Member's motion over other private Members' business (CJ (1924) 57; ibid (1924–25) 180).
—To provide for morning sittings on a particular bill (CJ (1964–65) 180–181).
—To provide for a Saturday sitting (CJ (1948–49) 350;
—To provide for adjournment at a stated hour on a Saturday sitting (CJ (1981–82) 282).

A motion for a vote of thanks, when moved by a Minister of the Crown,[3] is placed among these motions.

(4) Motions for leave to bring in bills or for nomination of select committees under Standing Order No 19

Motions for leave to bring in bills and for the nomination of select committees[4] may be set down at the commencement of public business after the foregoing motions on Mondays, Tuesdays, Wednesdays and Thursdays by members of the Government[5] and on Tuesdays and Wednesdays by

---

1 Parl Deb (1890–91) 335, c 1433; Notices of Motions (1894) 1080; Parl Deb (1894) 25, c 49; ibid (1895) 33, c 53; Notices of Motions (1895) 1215; Parl Deb (1895) 31, c 78; Notices of Motions (1910) 118; HC Deb (1910) 14, c 594; Notices of Motions (1892) 1593; ibid (1893–94) 1980, 3656; Parl Deb (1893) 16, cc 532, 654; CJ (1893–94) 513; Parl Deb (1896) 40, c 1263.
2 Eg CJ (1868–69) 206; ibid (1886) 178; ibid (1896) 243.
3 CJ (1849) 231; ibid (1854–55) 9; ibid (1857–58) 35; ibid (1878–79) 397; ibid (1882) 492; ibid (1942–43) 108; ibid (1945–46) 62, etc; Parl Deb (1884) 288, c 434.
4 HC Deb (1974–75) 887, c 504.
5 Parl Deb (1898) 53, c 1383; ibid (1899) 68, c 42.

private Members. But notice of presentation of a bill under this Standing Order may not be given by a private Member until after the fifth Wednesday in a session on which the House sits (Standing Order No 13(6)). This Standing Order is in practice now used for the presentation of bills only by private Members.

The rules which apply to private Members' motions for leave to bring in bills are set out on pp 463–464.

Motions for the nomination of select committees (CJ (1974–75) 248), for the discharge of a Member from a select committee (CJ (1918) 141), and for the discharge of Members, and the addition of other Members (CJ (1903) 118; ibid (1912–13), 151, 178; ibid (1914–16) 279; ibid (1919) 283; ibid (1967–68) 203) may also be set down at this place, but not motions for the appointment of select committees.

When such motions are opposed the Speaker, after permitting, if he thinks fit, a brief[1] explanatory statement from the Member who moves,[2] and from a Member who opposes the motion,[3] puts the question thereon without further debate,[4] or else the question that the debate be now adjourned.[5] The Speaker, pursuant to the standing order, reserves to himself the power of proposing the question for an adjournment of the debate.[6] It has been ruled that interventions by other Members are out of order whether or not the Member who is speaking is willing to give way;[7] an intervention has however been permitted following criticism of another Member in a speech under this Standing Order.[8] A motion to adjourn the debate cannot be moved by a Member.[9]

F. PRIVILEGE MOTIONS ADMITTING OF NOTICE

The priority of a notice of motion or order of the day relating to a matter of privilege is not prejudiced by the fact that the day on which it is to be raised is a day on which, under an order of the House, government business has precedence.[10] When a Member is informed by the Speaker, following a written complaint, that he is entitled to table a motion relating to that

---

1 This has been defined by the Speaker (who in doing so referred to the procedure by its colloquial description 'the Ten-minute Rule'), see HC Deb (1930–31) 252, c 1785; see also HC Deb (1987–88) 114, c 682.
2 Parl Deb (1890) 346, c 1615.
3 A Member who rises after the question has been proposed can only speak if he opposes the motion, Parl Deb (1894) 23, c 225; ibid (1905) 150, c 362; ibid (1907) 171, cc 687, 882; HC Deb (1910) 14, c 1489; ibid (1938–39) 349, c 1120; but he need not divide the House, HC Deb (1910) 18, cc 200, 364; ibid (1922) 151, c 391 (but see HC Deb (1953–54) 523, c 1191).
4 CJ (1905) 358; ibid (1906) 165. An amendment cannot be moved to the question, Parl Deb (1902) 113, c 249; ibid (1908) 190, c 1736; ibid (1938–39) 349, c 1120.
5 CJ (1890–91) 81; ibid (1899) 167; ibid (1905) 339; ibid (1906) 166; ibid (1911) 351; ibid (1929–30) 188. See also the Speaker's remarks in refusing to put the question for the adjournment of the debate on the motion for leave to introduce a government bill, Parl Deb (1901) 97, c 868.
6 Parl Deb (1899) 67, c 1375; ibid (1905) 148, c 388; HC Deb (1933–34) 280, c 2601; ibid (1961–62) 654, c 430; ibid (1974–75) 887, c 509. In the latter instance the question that the debate be now adjourned was negatived on a division, and the debate therefore continued.
7 HC Deb (1961–62) 654, c 422–428; ibid (1981–82) 28 c 224; ibid (1969–70) 795, cc 1459–1460.
8 HC Deb (1968–69) 787, c 417–418.
9 HC Deb (1932–33) 278, c 361.
10 Parl Deb (1906) 167, c 1051.

complaint (a procedure which is more fully described on pp 135–136), such a motion is given precedence over other business and notice of such a motion is given by the Member on the previous day. Priority is also accorded a matter of privilege if, through the adjournment of the debate on the motion in which it is embodied, it becomes an order of the day.[1]

A motion that the report of a committee on a matter of privilege[2] be now taken into consideration or a substantive motion expressing the agreement or disagreement of the House with the report has been accorded the priority assigned to a matter of privilege unless there has been undue delay in bringing it forward;[3] such a motion is either placed at the head of the Paper immediately after any 'notices of motions at the commencement of public business'[4] (see p 307), or if placed lower in the list, may be taken as if it stood first.[5] A Member was not held to have delayed unduly if he waited until the report of, and the minutes of the evidence taken before, the committee had been printed and circulated.[6] When a report has been appointed for consideration on a future day, it will be given priority as a matter of privilege on the day so appointed.[7]

G. ORDERS OF THE DAY AND NOTICES OF MOTIONS

The ordinary public business of the House consists of orders of the day, ie a stage of a bill or other matter which the House has ordered to be taken into consideration on a particular day (including orders for the resumption of adjourned debates on bills and motions, see p 313); and notices of motions.

(1) Reading of the orders of the day

When the orders of the day are reached, the Speaker, pursuant to Standing Order No 23, directs the Clerk at the Table to read the orders of the day, without any question being put; and the orders are thereupon disposed of in accordance with Standing Order No 24, following the order in which they stand upon the notice paper, although this order has been varied by a motion moved by a Minister of the Crown at the commencement of public business with the agreement of the House,[8] or by the assignment of priority to a later

---

1 Case of the printers, CJ (1837) 450; Parl Deb (1837) 38, c 1249; CJ (1840) 13, 15, 19, 23, 70; Parl Deb (1840) 51, cc 196, 251, 358, 422; ibid 52, c 7; case of Azeem Jah CJ (1865) 252; *Mr Plimsoll's case* Parl Deb (1875) 226, c 178; Public Petitions Committee (Special Report) CJ (1878) 130; Parl Deb (1878) 238, c 1741; case of Mr Wedgwood CJ (1911) 36; case of North Galway writ, ibid (1914) 329; case of Kilkenny city writ, Notices of Motions, sess. 1917–18, p 3278; case of county of Surrey, Reigate division writ, CJ (1918) 236, 252; Notices of Motions, sess. 1918, pp 3170, 3225, 3360; *Dr Salter's case* CJ (1926) 340; *Miss Wilkinson's case* CJ (1928–29) 159; *Mr Sandham's case* CJ (1929–30) 489.
2 For the general procedure on reports of committees on questions of privilege, see pp 137–141.
3 But see HC Deb (1946–47) 439, cc 2437–2439; ibid (1950) 476, c 223–224.
4 Notices of Motions (1929–30) 4643, (1933–34) 2005, (1937–38) 3511, (1940–41) 259, (1967–68) 9389, etc.
5 Parl Deb (1889) 338, c 1089; although this ruling was occasioned by the position of an order of the day, its terms apply both to orders of the day and notices of motions.
6 Parl Deb (1892) 3, c 597.
7 Parl Deb (1888) 331, c 1613; ibid (1889) 338, c 1089.
8 CJ (1894) 394; Parl Deb (1894) 29, c 178; HC Deb (1963–64) 687, cc 40, 178.

order as a matter of privilege.[1] The reading of the orders of the day is also subject to incidental interruptions of the proceedings of the House (see pp 251–2), and the postponement of business in certain circumstances at seven o'clock (see p 251).

Notices of motions standing among the orders of the day are similarly taken in the order in which they stand upon the paper, and Standing Order No 24 is held to apply to them in the same way as to orders of the day.

Accordingly, whilst the Clerk is reading the orders of the day, the proceedings thereon may not be interrupted by any other business or debate which Members may endeavour to interpose.[2] A motion for the adjournment of the House cannot be made, therefore, whilst the orders of the day are being read, either upon an order of the day being read or in the interval between reading one order and another, unless by a member of the Government[3] with a view to the adjournment of the House forthwith[4] or in order that an opportunity may be provided for debating a subject that could not otherwise be raised.[5]

There is no standing order authority for this concession to members of the Government, but it is now well established. The practice grew up and was accepted, probably because it was felt that the main purpose of Standing Orders Nos 23 and 24 was to protect the programme of government business from interruption, and that this programme did not need to be protected from members of the Government.

(2) Procedure upon orders of the day

When an order of the day has been read, it must thereupon be proceeded with, appointed for a future day, or discharged. It cannot be postponed till after another order except as the result of a motion moved by a Minister of the Crown at the commencement of public business.[6] The Speaker, therefore, calls upon the Member in charge of the order, no other Member being allowed to interpose, unless with his consent;[7] or, in the case of an adjourned debate, upon the Member who moved the adjournment, or was speaking when the debate was interrupted if he rises to address the Chair (see p 368). The Speaker, therefore, will not permit any question to be asked of a Minister or other Member when an order of the day has been read, unless it relates thereto.

> Because the right to move an order of the day belongs to some extent to the House at large, rather than being vested solely in the Member in charge of the order, a motion thereon may, in his absence, be made by another Member.[8] The Speaker has however declined to accept a motion deferring an order to a remote future date in order to defeat a bill;[9] nor may a motion be made in contradiction to any information regarding an

1 Parl Deb (1889) 338, c 1089.
2 Parl Deb (1872) 213, c 644.
3 HC Deb (1943–44) 402, cc 1251–1252, etc.
4 CJ (1905) 346; ibid (1923) 87; ibid (1935–36) 158.
5 CJ (1914) 408; ibid (1935–36) 140; ibid (1947–48) 180.
6 CJ (1947–48) 77.
7 Parl Deb (1860) 157, c 1301; ibid (1860) 160, c 349.
8 Parl Deb (1886) 305, c 353; ibid (1908) 191, c 1107.
9 Mr Speaker's ruling (private), 13 May 1886; see also HC Deb (1936–37) 324, cc 276–277.

order of the day which the member in charge thereof has made at the Table. Private Members' Bills may only be deferred with the authority of the Member in charge.[1] The revival of an order of the day (see p 315) is, according to the habitual practice of the House, also reserved for the Member in charge of the order.

(3) Deferment of orders and motions

If, after the interruption of business, the orders of the day which were not reached before ten o'clock, or before half-past two o'clock on a Friday, are read at the table (see p 241), a Member in charge of an order has the opportunity, by saying 'Now' when the title of his bill is called, to secure its passing the stage at which it stands, if no objection is raised by another Member, and also, similarly, if no objection is raised, of its passage through further stages. A single objection, however, stops proceedings (see p 247), and it then only remains for a Member in charge of an order to name a day to which he desires it to be deferred (Standing Order No 9(5)). This action is in theory a motion but no question is put on it, the Speaker merely announcing the day proposed by the Member. In the absence of the Member in charge and of any other Member acting on his behalf, or of written instructions to the Table by or on behalf of the Member in charge, that a bill should be deferred to a certain day, the bill concerned automatically becomes a 'dropped order' until such time as the Member in charge gives instructions that it should be revived.[2] The announcement of a day by the Speaker secures its entry in the Votes and Proceedings and in the Order Book (see pp 205 and 208).

The procedure with regard to notices of motions is similar, except that the Speaker calls the name of the mover without the title being read. If it is deferred a date is announced in the same manner as for an order, except that it is entered in the Order Book only and not in the Votes and Proceedings.

(4) Orders of the day not to be brought forward to an earlier date.

When the House has appointed a day for the consideration of a bill or other matter, no earlier day can afterwards be substituted.

> This rule was enforced, even when a day had been named by mistake, and though no objection was raised to the appointment of an earlier day.[3] If, however, an error has arisen in the postponement of an order of the day, whilst the orders are being read, the transfer of the order of the day to an earlier day than that originally named has been allowed, on an appeal to the Speaker.[4]

---

1 Report from the Select Committee on Procedure, HC 348 (1972–73); CJ (1973–74) 42. For instances of the Chair deprecating attempts to discharge or postpone consideration of an order in the absence of the Member in charge, see Parl Deb (1873) 216, c 276; ibid (1875) 224, c 1236; ibid (1878) 240, c 1675.
2 HC 348 (1972–73) pp vi–vii; HC Deb (1973–74) 867, cc 2048–2049.
3 London, Chatham and Dover Railway Bill, 6 July 1863. In this case the standing orders were suspended in order to accelerate the next stage of the bill, CJ (1863) 337; Parl Deb (1863) 172, c 246. See also ibid (1886) 305, c 379.
4 Vehicles' Lights (No 2) Bill, 31 July 1893, Parl Deb (1893) 15, c 871; certain government orders of the day, 16 April 1907, Parl Deb (1907) 172, c 1012.

A motion moved by the government to bring forward the consideration of a private Member's bill in order to ensure its passage before a dissolution contained the words 'that, notwithstanding the practice of the House which forbids the bringing forward of an Order of the Day, the said day (ie the day originally appointed for consideration) having been appointed before the intention to prorogue Parliament had been announced, the Bill . . . be considered Tomorrow'.[1]

(5) Orders of the day not reached before the adjournment of the House.

Orders of the day which, owing to the suspension of a sitting, or to an adjournment of the House, or to the prolongation of the previous sitting, have not been read at the Table, are set down upon the notice paper after the orders of the day appointed for the next sitting of the House, subject to the right of Government to arrange the order of its business, whenever such business has priority.[2]

(6) Discharge of orders of the day.

On the order of the day being read for any stage of a bill, an order may, on the motion of the Member in charge of the bill, be made that the order be discharged and the bill be withdrawn.

A bill other than a Lords bill may also be withdrawn by notice given at the Table before the day on which the bill stands as an order of the day (see also p 472).

(7) Procedure on notices of motions

A motion, notice of which stands upon the order paper of public business, is brought before the House by the Speaker calling the name of the mover according to the order in which it stands upon the paper; and if a Member does not rise when his name is called, he cannot subsequently ask that his name should be called again, for the purpose of moving the motion of which he had given notice. A member of the Government may act on behalf of a colleague in all cases, including the proposal of new clauses on the report stage of a bill.[3] In the case of motions in the name of the chairman or a member of the Committee of Selection relating to the composition of committees any member of the select committee may move the motion. With these two exceptions no motion can be moved save by a Member in whose name the notice stands.[4] The power of moving a motion in terms that differ from the notice standing upon the paper is defined on p 324.

(8) Unexpected ending of business and dropped orders

An order under consideration when the House is adjourned owing to grave disorder[5] becomes a 'dropped order'. A dropped order may be replaced on

---

1 Public Service Vehicles (Travel Concessions) Bill, 25 April 1955, CJ (1954–55) 134. See also ibid (1936–37) 268.
2 Parl Deb (1888) 323, c 1538.
3 Parl Deb (1864) 176, c 2034; ibid (1881) 258, c 1664.
4 HC Deb (1945–46) 419, c 339. A Member who has given notice of a motion may move it even if his name does not appear on the Order Paper among the first six signatures (see also p 330).
5 Or, in earlier days, owing to the unexpected adjournment of the House when lacking a quorum (see p 251). A number of the instances which follow relate to orders which have been dropped in such circumstances.

the order paper by a motion taken at the commencement or after the close of public business to appoint the order for a subsequent day.[1] Such a motion is moved without notice and is usually entered by the Clerks in their books without the attention of the House being drawn to it.[2] A dropped Government order may be reinstated for the day following that on which the unexpected adjournment takes place by means of a motion to that effect appearing on that day's order paper in the name of a Minister of the Crown at the commencement of public business. The dropped order itself appears printed in italics either at the head of the list of orders of the day[3] or at the place where the Government wishes it to be taken.[4]

If on such an order of the day procedure has been commenced and interrupted, the proceeding thus revived is set down for resumption at the position indicated by the last decision of the House entered upon the Votes and Proceedings.[5] If the interruption occurs after the adjournment of the debate has been moved, the motion for the revival of the order of the day relates to the order itself, the motion for the adjournment of the debate being treated as a lapsed motion.[6] If the interruption occurs after proceedings upon an order of the day have been postponed and before their resumption, the order of the day is not treated as a dropped order.[7]

For orders of the day not reached because of an unexpected adjournment, see p 314.

(9) Superseded orders

An order of the day may be superseded by the vote of the House, as, for instance, when an amendment embodying an abstract proposition is substituted for the question that the bill be now read a second time. For the effect of superseding orders in this way, see p 475.

(10) Renewal of notices of motions

A notice of motion standing upon the notice paper for the day's sitting, which is not brought on before the adjournment of the House, disappears from the paper, unless the Member in whose name the notice stands, or a Member on his behalf, gives a direction at the Table for the replacement of the notice upon the notice paper for a future day.

---

1 CJ (1864–65) 348, 351; ibid (1865) 225, 230, 352, 355; ibid (1867) 377, 404.
2 If debate occurs on such a motion, it must be strictly limited to the precise object of the motion, HC Deb (1917) 99, c 237; ibid (1923) 162, cc 1221, 1251.
3 CJ (1876) 282, 283; Parl Deb (1876) 230, c 431; CJ (1877) 294, 296; Parl Deb (1877) 235, c 203; CJ (1878) 212, 213; ibid (1884–85) 239, 240; ibid (1889) 112, 115; ibid (1890) 81, 83; Parl Deb (1890) 342, c 347; CJ (1895) 162, 164; Notices of Motions (1912) 5026; Notices of Motions (1919) p 1247. The Parliamentary Elections (Soldiers) Bill was proceeded with after such a motion in 1919, with the general consent of the House, CJ (1919) 93–95. Debate on a motion, CJ (1917–18) 238. Notices of Motions (1917–18) 4336. For objection taken to such a proceeding, see HC Deb (1952–53) 508, cc 455–457; Notices of Motions (1952–53) 541. See also HC Deb (1966–67) 740, cc 798–805. On the latter occasions, because the motion was controversial, the Speaker advised that it be not proceeded with.
4 CJ (1877) 326, 328; ibid (1919) 92, 93.
5 Sale of Intoxicating Liquor (Ireland) Bill, CJ (1878) 419, 424; Redistribution of Seats Bill, ibid (1884) 208, 209; Rivers (Prevention of Pollution) Bill, ibid (1960–61) 251.
6 CJ (1878–79) 122, 124; ibid (1911) 351, 388.
7 Trades Disputes and Trade Unions Bill 1927, CJ (1927) 144, 145; Notices of Motions (1927) 1336.

(11) Transaction of business as a matter of course

Certain formal motions necessary for the transaction of business are sometimes entered as a matter of course as agreed to by the House in the Clerks'
books without the questions thereon being put from the Chair. Examples
are motions for the first reading of bills received from the House of Lords;
for the consideration of Lords amendments on a future day; for the postponement or discharge of an order of the day or an order for a future day by
the Member in charge; for the revival of a dropped order; for returns or
papers to be presented forthwith; and for the reference of papers to a select
committee.

H. BUSINESS MOTIONS UNDER STANDING ORDER NO 14(2)

On the interruption of business under Standing Order No 9, motions may be
moved under Standing Order No 14 to exempt the business interrupted or
other business or both[1] from the provisions of Standing Order No 9 (see
pp 244–245), either indefinitely or for a specified period.

I. BUSINESS EXEMPTED UNDER STANDING ORDERS NOS 14(1) AND 15 (PROCEEDINGS ON STATUTORY INSTRUMENTS ETC)

The various kinds of business exempted from the operation of the ten
o'clock rule under Standing Order No 14(1) have been mentioned above
(pp 243–244). All the items composing such business may be taken before
ten o'clock; and many of them generally are so taken and accordingly do not
require special notice in this chapter. However proceedings on subordinate
legislation, mainly consisting of statutory instruments and European Community documents, are usually debated after ten o'clock when they are not
debated in standing committee. In the case of statutory instruments, only
proceedings for the purpose of approving or disapproving such subordinate
legislation explicitly required or permitted in each case by the parent statute, are exempted from the operation of the ten o'clock rule.[2]

When the motion before the House is one to approve a statutory instrument, the Speaker is directed by Standing Order No 14(1)(b) to put the
question at half-past eleven o'clock or one and a half hours after the
commencement of the proceedings, whichever is the later. If he considers
that the matter has been insufficiently debated he may instead interrupt the
proceedings at the prescribed hour, in which case the debate stands
adjourned until the next sitting day other than a Friday.[3] Motions to disapprove subordinate legislation ('Prayers') are governed by Standing Order
No 15 which lays down that proceedings on such motions may not be entered
upon at or after half-past eleven o'clock, at which hour Mr Speaker is

1 The Speaker has on occasion agreed to divide a motion exempting two different bills (CJ (1920) 292).
2 Parl Deb (1899) 71, c 222; ibid (1901) 96, c 1009; ibid (1904) 135, c 807; HC Deb (1935–36) 313, cc 1908, 1910.
3 Eg CJ (1982–83) 181.

directed to put the question forthwith,[1] unless he considers that insufficient debate has taken place, in which case he interrupts the proceedings and the debate stands adjourned until the conclusion of Government business on the next sitting day other than a Friday.[2] If proceedings are not then resumed before eleven o'clock, the debate stands further adjourned. For exemption motions on 'out-of-time' prayers, see p 549.

There is no general statute which requires Statutory Instruments to be laid before Parliament or which exposes them to annulment on an adverse motion or stipulates that they be confirmed by an affirmative resolution. It is necessary to look in each case at the parent statute in order to ascertain what degree or method of parliamentary control (if any) is prescribed. The different types of control are described in a later chapter (p 542).

J. PRESENTATION OF PUBLIC PETITIONS

Standing Order No 133 provides for the presentation of public petitions, on every day except Friday, before the House enters upon the Motion for the Adjournment under Standing Order No 9(7). On Fridays, however, public petitions continue under the earlier practice to be presented between private business and the presentation of unopposed returns (see p 762). A consequence of the Standing Order is that Petitions may also be presented on days, not being Fridays, immediately before the series of adjournment debates on the last day before a holiday adjournment.[3] At the appropriate time, the Speaker calls on those Members to present petitions who have intimated their desire to do so by entering their names on a list headed 'Public Petitions' which is kept in the Table Office. The Member so called upon may not address the House (nor may any other Member speak except to raise a point of order) but must confine himself to a statement of the parties from whom it comes, the number of its signatures and its material allegations; and to reading the prayer.[4] The Member then leaves his place and deposits the petition in the bag behind the Chair. A petition may be read by the Clerk at the Table if required (Standing Order No 133).[5]

Any Member wishing to present a petition in his place first consults the Clerk of Public Petitions who examines the petition and advises the Member whether or not it is in order and can be received. He then enters his name on the list in the Table Office not later than twelve o'clock on the day on which he wishes to present it, or, if presentation is on a Friday, before the rising of the House on the previous day. This procedure has been devised to avoid the reading to the House and entering in the Votes and Proceedings of petitions which are out of order.[6]

Although this formal procedure is frequently employed—doubtless for the sake of the prominence which it confers— the presentation of a petition may be effected by simply depositing it at any time during the sitting of the House in a bag placed behind the chair for the purpose. In whichever way it is presented a petition which is prima facie in order is recorded in the Votes

---

1 HC Deb (1953–54) 527, c 2052.
2 HC Deb (1954–55) 537, cc 343, 511; ibid (1972–73) 848, cc 1528–1529.
3 HC Deb (1983–84) 51, cc 574–575.
4 HC Deb (1985–86) 88, cc 1187–1189.
5 HC Deb (1948–49) 458, c 1814, etc.
6 HC Deb (1946) 427, c 1325.

and Proceedings. Standing Order No 135 requires that all petitions other than those proceeded with under Standing Order No 134 are to be printed and transmitted by the Clerk of the House to Ministers, whose observations in reply are also printed and circulated with the Vote. If a petition is presented which is obviously irregular, the words 'an informal Petition is not noticed' appear at the foot of a page of the Votes and Proceedings.

The rules governing the preparation of public petitions and other matters connected therewith are stated in chapter 31.

K. ADJOURNMENT MOTIONS UNDER STANDING ORDER NO 9(7)

(1) Rules on adjournment motions under Standing Order No 9(7)

Until the time at which the House is adjourned without question put under Standing Order No 9(7) is reached, the House can only be adjourned on motion (unless it is adjourned in pursuance of Standing Order No 45), and this motion is debatable, thus affording private Members an opportunity of raising various matters (see p 267).

On 18 January 1944, Mr Speaker instituted a system of informal notice[1] of the subject of debate to be raised (HC Deb (1943–44) 396, c 42). The following arrangements are now in force:[2]

(a) The ballot is held on Thursdays. Applications in writing must be in the Speaker's Office by 10.00 p.m. Wednesday.

(b) The subjects for the Adjournment on Monday, Tuesday, Wednesday and Friday are balloted, while that on Thursday is selected by the Speaker.

(c) Members successful in the ballot may not enter their names for the next succeeding week.

(d) A Member desiring to raise a matter on the adjournment should write to the Speaker stating the subject of his proposed adjournment.

(e) An oral notice to raise a matter on the adjournment is not considered by the Speaker unless it is confirmed in writing.

(f) Forty-eight hours' notice is required for a change of subject of a balloted adjournment motion, and the change of subject is notified in the notice paper.

(g) When a Member does not wish to pursue the subject of a balloted

1 This system of informal notice is not binding, but individual Members who have secured the adjournment and then raised a subject other than that of which they had given notice, although within their rights, cause other Members inconvenience. (See Mr Speaker's statements HC Deb (1943–44) 396, cc 1916–17; ibid 401, cc 977–978; and ibid (1961–62) c 1678).

2 HC Deb (1966–7) 740, c 1354–1355.

adjournment motion and cannot give forty-eight hours' notice, his right to the adjournment lapses.
(h) On Thursday, as selection relates to the subject and not the Member, no alteration of the subject is permissible without the Speaker's consent.
(i) No Member's name will be carried forward from one ballot to another. A fresh application must be made.
(j) A Member who has the adjournment for a certain day and is unable to take it cannot exchange dates with another Member.
(k) A Member may not have more than one entry current at the same time; accordingly, if a letter is received from a Member whose name is already in the book, the original entry will be expunged.

On occasion it happens that there is time for a second or subsequent adjournment debate. For many years successive Speakers have deprecated the introduction of subjects in such debates unless due notice had been given to the Minister concerned; and on occasion the Chair has expressed this view in forceful terms.[1] The Speaker has also ruled that it is unreasonable, after eight o'clock in the evening, or after 12 noon on Fridays, to call on Ministers and their advisers to be ready to answer an adjournment debate that day of which no prior notice had been given to the House.[2] On 7 March 1980, the Speaker ruled that, in respect of applications for second adjournment debates, he would give preference to the first applicant with an orderly subject to have secured the agreement of a Minister in the course of the day before it was time for the second debate to take place.[3] The agreement both of the Member originating a debate and of the Minister responding to it is required before other Members can take part in adjournment debates under Standing Order No 9(7).[4]

Motions for the adjournment of the House moved under Standing Order No 9(7) have been used as vehicles for ministerial statements. On occasions when this has been done before the completion of the business expected to be transacted, the motions for the adjournment have been withdrawn before the expiry of the half-hour provided for by the Standing Order, and the House has then proceeded with the remaining business;[5] but when such a statement has been made after all expected business has been completed, it has had the effect of supplanting the debate initiated by a private Member which would otherwise then have taken place[6] (see p 267).

(2) General restrictions on motions for the adjournment of the House

As has been stated above (see p 266), a motion for the adjournment of the House, moved by a Minister, may be moved either before or between the orders of the day, and is not, like a motion for the adjournment when offered

1 Eg HC Deb (1963–64) 689, c 681; ibid (1974–75) 884, c 161; ibid (1976–77) 932, cc 1493, 1496; ibid (1986–87) 110, cc 742–750, 776–780.
2 Eg HC Deb (1979–80) 973 c 1661; ibid (1981–82) 14, cc 211–216, 267. Private Ruling, 9 December 1981, HC Deb (1981–82) 14, c 970.
3 HC Deb (1979–80) 980, cc 924–925.
4 HC Deb (1984–85) 77, cc 239–241; ibid (1985–86) 98, c 155.
5 HC Deb (1971–72) 826, cc 1085–1086; ibid (1974–75) 894, cc 163–168.
6 HC Deb (1968–69) 773, cc 1790–1805; ibid 775, cc 828–842; ibid 786, cc 1919–1928.

by a private Member, confined to this particular place in the programme of
the business of the sitting. Still, it is convenient to deal with the general
restrictions upon such motions at this point since they apply equally to all
adjournment motions except those moved following a successful application
by a private Member under Standing Order No 20 (see pp 300–302).

The general restrictions are as follows:

(a) Members are precluded, under the rule of *anticipation* (see pp 327–328),
    from discussing on an adjournment motion a notice of motion[1] or an
    order of the day[2] which already stands upon the notice paper or order
    book.

    On a motion for the adjournment of the House, the Speaker has
    refused to allow a Member to discuss the merits of a bill standing upon
    the notice paper for that sitting.[3] Members have also been forbidden to
    raise on a motion for the adjournment for the recess a matter that could
    properly be raised on the report of the vote on account which stood on
    that day's order paper,[4] and on a motion for the adjournment a matter
    which was similar to the main purpose of a Private Member's bill which
    he had previously presented and which was ordered to be read a second
    time upon the following day.[5]

    For debates upon the effect of notices of motions standing on the
    order book upon debates on motions for the adjournment of the House,
    see Parl Deb (1900) 81, c 1414; ibid (1904) 135, c 379; ibid (1907) 171,
    c 1883.

    In determining whether a discussion is out of order on the ground of
    anticipation, the probability of the matter anticipated being discussed
    within a reasonable time must be considered (Standing Order No 26).

(b) *In general, matters which would entail legislation* must not be discussed
    on a motion for the adjournment;[6] but under Standing Order No 29 Mr
    Speaker may permit such incidental reference to legislative action as he
    may consider relevant to any matter of administration under debate on a
    motion for the adjournment when enforcement of the prohibition
    would, in his opinion, unduly restrict the discussion of the matter.[7]

(c) Matters for which the government has *no administrative responsibility*
    may not be raised.[8]

(d) Matters which may only be debated on a *substantive motion expressed in
    specific terms* (see p 325) are inadmissible on an adjournment motion.

(e) Matters which *have already been discussed on the same day* in debate,[9]
    including the debate on the Address[10] may not be raised on the motion
    for the adjournment after the hour of interruption that evening.

---

1 Parl Deb (1860) 157, c 1166; ibid (1901) 94, c 1011; HC Deb (1910) 14, c 1054.
2 Parl Deb (1860) 157, c 1804; ibid (1901) 94, cc 995, 999; HC Deb (1910) 15, c 1013, ibid
   (1987–88) 121, c 1230.
3 Parl Deb (1901) 92, c 301.
4 Parl Deb (1896) 39, c 403.
5 HC Deb (1978–79) 962, c 1440.
6 Parl Deb (1899) 71, c 1034; ibid (1903) 123, c 204; ibid (1904) 132, c 1043; HC Deb (1948)
   456, cc 218–219; ibid (1948–49) 470, cc 2304–2308, etc. Upon the motion for the adjournment of the House, moved when the orders of the day have been disposed of, HC Deb
   (1924) 170, cc 844, 2728; ibid (1924) 171, cc 903, 1088; ibid (1961–62) 649, cc 1677–1682.
7 This discretion is not usually exercised in respect of adjournment motions under SO No 9(7)
   (HC Deb (1974–75) 885, c 956).
8 HC Deb (1939–40) 356, c 1228; ibid (1943–44) 399, cc 1161, 1166; ibid (1945–46) 427, c 752;
   ibid (1948–49) 465, cc 850, 1059–1060; the conduct of nationalised industries may, however,
   be discussed on the adjournment, HC Deb (1948–49) 465, c 1063.
9 HC Deb (1941–42) 383, c 114.
10 HC Deb (1944–45) 406, c 59.

CHAPTER 17

The process of debate in the House of Commons by Motion, Question and Decision

A matter requiring the decision of the House of Commons is decided by means of a question put from the Chair upon a motion made by a Member. The essential stages in obtaining a decision of the House are the moving of a motion; the proposing of a question by the Chair; and the putting of the question and collection of voices by the Chair.

At the conclusion of the speech (if any) made by the Member moving a motion the Chair proposes the Question (which repeats the terms of the Motion)[1] and debate may then take place. At the conclusion of debate the Chair puts the question (except when it has been withdrawn) and collects the voices, after which the Chair announces that in its opinion either the ayes or the noes are in the majority. If the opinion of the Chair is challenged, the House proceeds to a division to determine which side has the majority of votes. Between the proposing and putting of a main motion, subsidiary questions on amendments may be proposed and decided in the same way. The moving, proposing and putting of questions are often proceeded with formally, that is without debate. Many questions before the House are decided in this way. Standing Orders require that certain types of question are put forthwith without debate, for example motions to approve statutory instruments reported by a Standing Committee under Standing Order No 101(5) and business of the House motions under Standing Order No 14.[2]

The process of debate is described below under the following headings:

(1) Motions
(2) Questions
(3) Amendments
(4) Decisions and Divisions.
(5) Reversal of Decisions

1. MOTIONS

SUBSTANTIVE AND SUBSIDIARY MOTIONS

A motion is a proposal made for the purpose of eliciting a decision of the House. Motions may be classified either as substantive, or as subsidiary. Substantive motions are self-contained; subsidiary motions may be (1) ancillary motions dependent on an order of the day, such as the motion that a bill be now read a second time, or that the House agrees with the

---

1 Two recognized exceptions to this rule are given on p 330.
2 See chapter 19, pp 400–402.

report of a committee; (2) motions made for the purpose of superseding questions, such as motions for the adjournment of a debate (see pp 332–334); (3) motions dependent on other motions such as amendments. Substantive motions for the adjournment of the House (ie when moved as the main Question and not as a dilatory motion) form a separate and distinct class. The general purpose of such motions, which is to enable the House to conduct a debate without coming to a decision in terms, is more fully described on pp 265–266. The rules governing matters which may be raised on motions for the adjournment are given on pp 319–320.

RULES REGULATING NOTICE OF MOTIONS

Manner of giving notice

Motions are tabled by being handed in either at the Table of the House or (more usually) to the Clerks in the Table Office. Notice of a motion can be given in a variety of ways. It may appear for the first time on the Order Paper for the day on which it is proposed to be taken. It may (as is the normal practice with government motions) be placed on the 'Remaining Orders of the Day' and motions frequently reappear daily on the Remaining Orders for long periods before they are placed on the 'effective' Orders.[1] Notice may be given for a specific future day, in which case the motion is printed in the daily blue list of notices of motions and questions and in the Order Book for the specified day. Finally, motions may be tabled for which 'no day has been fixed'. These are known as 'Early Day Motions'. They appear in the blue list on the day after tabling and are reprinted on any subsequent day on which new Members have added their names in support either of any such Motion or of any amendments proposed thereto.[2] If a list of names in support of a motion is handed in it must be authorised by the signature of a Member.[3]

Period of notice

In general substantive motions require notice, whilst subsidiary motions do not. The rules regulating the requirement of notice, however, depend more upon practical than upon logical considerations, and are set out below. When notice is required, the terms in which a motion is moved should be the same as the terms of the notice, or should at any rate be covered by them, without the importation of any fresh matter.[4] Except where the length of notice required is laid down in Standing Orders, there is no rule regulating the amount of notice required.[5] Notices of motions to which opposition seems unlikely to arise are frequently given during the day before the sitting on which the motions are submitted to the House although the Speaker has deprecated the delaying of notice so as to deprive Members of an oppor-

---

1 Remaining Orders of the Day standing in the name of a Minister are reprinted each day. By extension, this applies to motions relating to Church of England Measures in the name of the second Church Estates Commissioner and motions from the Committee of Selection. Other remaining orders must be re-tabled each day.
2 Pursuant to a resolution of the House of Commons (Services) Committee of 13 June 1989, early day motions (with certain specified exceptions) which were tabled more than approximately a week previously appear on the Notice Paper only once a week (on Thursdays) with a consolidated list of names added in the previous week.
3 HC Deb (1947–48) 495, c 215; ibid (1960–61) 642, c 1477.
4 Parl Deb (1907) 171, c 680.
5 Parl Deb (1871) 207, c 143.

tunity of learning the terms of a debate.[1] Notice is required for motions under Standing Order No 14 exempting business from the operation of Standing Order No 9 (see pp 244–245); notice is required of a motion under Standing Order No 19 for leave to bring in a bill (see pp 268, 463–465); under Standing Order No 58, notice must be given of the presentation of a bill without an order of the House (see pp 465–466); under Standing Order No 68, of new clauses on the report of a bill (see pp 503–504); and under Standing Order No 90 at least ten days notice must be given of motions to refer a bill to a second reading committee. Under Standing Order No 104 notice must be given of a motion or an amendment relating to the nomination of Members for service on select committees.

Under Standing Order No 18, notice of a question to a Member or of an amendment to a motion for which no day has been fixed, or of the addition of a name in support of such a motion or amendment, if given after half-past ten o'clock in the evening, is treated as if it were a notice handed in after the rising of the House on that day.

Change of day for a motion

A Member who wishes to change the day for which he has given notice must defer the notice to a more distant day, or, if an earlier day is sought, must withdraw his notice and give a fresh one;[2] the new notice must conform to any requirements laid down in Standing Orders as to length of notice. The same notice of motion may not be given for two or more different days.

Motions made without notice

Certain procedural motions relating to the transaction of business may be made without notice. These include motions made immediately after second reading, that a bill be committed to a Committee of the whole House, a Select Committee, a joint committee or a special standing committee under Standing Order No 61; motions for giving provisional statutory effect to any proposals in pursuance of section 5 of the Provisional Collection of Taxes Act 1968 (under Standing Order No 50) and motions for the consideration of Lords amendments forthwith (see pp 510–511).

Motions arising out of a matter of privilege, including motions for an order of the House to Mr Speaker to make out his warrant for the issue of a writ for the election of a new Member (see pp 276–277), are also moved without notice. A motion for a message to the Lords requesting the return of a bill which was incorrect, due to irregularities in divisions, has also been allowed to be moved without notice as a matter of privilege.[3] A motion granting special powers to a chairman of a standing committee has similarly been moved without notice as a matter of privilege, following a report of disorder in the Committee made in the House by the chairman concerned.[4]

On the presentation of a petition seeking leave for a Member or officer to attend a court as a witness, the motion for leave of the House to be granted may be moved without notice, unless objection is taken before the motion is

1 HC Deb (1985–86) 93, c 568.
2 HC Deb (1928) 214, c 362.
3 HC Deb (1974) 877, c 259.
4 HC Deb (1972–73) 849, c 667; Votes and Proceedings, 14 March 1989.

moved.[1] If objection is not voiced to a Member's request for leave to move such a motion, subsequent objection is not sufficient to prevent the question being debated and put.[2] Notice is not customarily given of motions to appoint the Chairman or Deputy Chairmen of Ways and Means.[3]

With the exceptions stated above, it is the almost invariable practice of the House that notice should be given of substantive motions.

Waiver of the requirement for notice

The House can waive the requirement of notice for a substantive motion if the motion is moved under the sanction of the Chair and with the concurrence of the House.[4]

Motions have been made without notice to provide for a Saturday sitting,[5] to alter the time for the next sitting of the House,[6] to delay the moment of interruption,[7] or to regulate the adjournment of the House.[8] A motion to give immediate effect to a resolution of the House has also been moved without notice; for example, after the House had rescinded and discharged the order for the appointment of a select committee, an order was made immediately for the reappointment of the committee with altered terms of reference.[9] A motion to rescind the committal of a bill to a standing committee has been made in a similar way.[10] A message from the House of Lords communicating the desirability of appointing a joint committee has been considered without notice and a resolution for concurring with the Lords, agreed to.[11]

The objection of any Member is enough to prevent the waiver of notice,[12] although a motion to compensate for time taken by a Government statement has been allowed to be moved without notice despite objection.[13]

Change of terms of notice of motion. Modification of the terms of a notice of motion standing upon the notice paper is permitted, if the amended notice does not exceed the scope of the original notice,[14] and the Speaker decides that it is proper for the motion to be moved in the altered form.[15] If a motion is proposed which differs materially from the terms of the one of which

---

1 HC Deb (1978–79) 974, cc 739–740; ibid (1981–82) 18, c 492.
2 HC Deb (1974–75) 896, cc 220–222.
3 CJ (1979–80) 17; ibid (1981–82) 380.
4 CJ (1924–25) 409; HC Deb (1963–64) 685, c 35. See also Address in the case of Emergency Regulations, 30 August 1926, HC Deb (1926) 199, c 6.
5 CJ (1914) 435; ibid (1955–56) 429.
6 CJ (1878) 355, 396; ibid (1890–91) 410; ibid (1892) 137; ibid (1909) 106; HC Deb (1909) 3, c 1119; CJ (1917–18) 202; HC Deb (1917) 97, cc 1186, 1301, 1344; ibid (1926) 199, c 6.
7 CJ (1970–71) 68.
8 CJ (1920) 379; HC Deb (1920) 133, c 543; CJ (1924) 386; HC Deb (1924) 177, cc 319, 473; CJ (1923) 92; HC Deb (1923) 162, c 1639; see also CJ (1893–94) 57; Parl Deb (1893) 8, c 1153; CJ (1896) 243; Parl Deb (1896) 41, c 210.
9 CJ (1870) 169; Parl Deb (1870) 201, c 79.
10 Employers' Liability Bill, 4 May 1893, CJ (1893–94) 249; Beer Bill, 26 July 1901, CJ (1901) 347.
11 CJ (1895) 127, 131; ibid (1911) 27, 28; HC Deb (1911) 21, c 1245.
12 HC Deb (1926) 199, c 254.
13 HC Deb (1981–82) 25, cc 701–702. The motion was subsequently withdrawn. See also Mr Speaker's ruling on the Gold Standard (Amendment) Bill, HC Deb (1930–31) 256, cc 1289–1290.
14 Parl Deb (1907) 171, c 680; HC Deb (1962–63) 682, c 243; ibid (1976–77) 934, cc 1571–1575. Where motion exceeded scope of oral notice see HC Deb (1957–58) 586, cc 1293–1295.
15 HC Deb (1979–80) 977, cc 1687–95.

notice has been given, it can be made only with the consent of the House, or after a new notice has been given.[1]

Withdrawal of notice. A Member whose name stands first on the notice of a motion or an amendment to a motion may withdraw the motion or amendment even though other names have been added to it. A Member who has added his name to a notice of motion may subsequently withdraw his name if the motion has not been moved or withdrawn. Both forms of withdrawal are indicated by a memorandum at the end of the Notices of Motions.[2]

Amendments to motions

Amendments to motions may be tabled as soon as the motions have been tabled. It is not necessary to wait until a motion has been published.[3]

RULES GOVERNING THE FORM AND SUBJECT-MATTER OF MOTIONS

Length of motions

On 22 July 1983 the Speaker ruled that private Members' motions tabled by Members successful in the ballot for precedence on private Members days (see p 260) should not generally exceed 250 words in length.[4] On 23 February 1984 the Speaker extended the scope of this ruling to include early day motions.[5] This rule has been interpreted to require that any amendment tabled, if added to the original motion, would not bring its total length above this limit.

Matters which may be raised only on a substantive motion

Certain matters cannot be debated, except on a substantive motion which allows a distinct decision of the House. Amongst these (see pp 375–384) are the conduct of the sovereign, the heir to the throne or other members of the Royal Family, a Governor-General of an independent territory, the Lord Chancellor, the Speaker,[6] the Chairman of Ways and Means,[7] Members of either House of Parliament and judges of the superior courts of the United Kingdom, including persons holding the position of a judge, such as a judge in a court of bankruptcy and a county court, or a recorder.[8] Such matters

---

1 Parl Deb (1857–58) 148, c 719; ibid (1861) 161, c 854; ibid (1872) 212, c 219; ibid (1895) 33, c 961.
2 Eg Notices of Motions (1989–90) pp 4239, 4528.
3 HC Deb (1977–78) 939, c 206.
4 HC Deb (1983–84) 46, c 692.
5 HC Deb (1983–84) 54, c 977.
6 Parl Deb (1902) 107, cc 1020–1050; HC Deb (1924–25) 184, cc 1390, 1591–1612; ibid (1951–52) 500, cc 397–417; ibid (1956–57) 574, cc 878–909; ibid (1960–61) 634, cc 1773–1838.
7 HC Deb (1948–49) 463, cc 2859–2880; ibid (1950–51) 489, c 721–746; ibid (1952–53) 509, cc 43–105; ibid (1960–61) 634, cc 1026–1070; ibid (1961–62) 656, cc 1026–1080; ibid (1966–67) 731, cc 441–492; ibid (1976–77) 926, cc 655–660. Temporary chairman, Parl Deb (1901) 98, c 245.
8 On 6 November 1986 Mr Speaker ruled that Masters of the Supreme Court did not fall within this category, HC Deb (1985–86) 103, c 1103.

cannot, therefore, be raised by way of amendment, or an adjournment motion.[1] For the same reason, no charge of a personal character can be raised, except on a direct and substantive motion.[2] No statement of that kind can be incorporated in a broader motion,[3] nor, for example, included in a reply to a question.[4]

Matters awaiting judicial decision

The House has resolved that no matter awaiting or under adjudication by a court of law should be brought before it by a motion or otherwise (see pp 377–379). This rule may be waived at the discretion of the Chair. Exceptions have, for example, been made on matters before civil courts which relate to Ministerial decisions or concern issues of national importance,[5] matters which have no likelihood of coming before the courts in the reasonably foreseeable future, and matters which, though touching upon issues which are *sub judice*, are unlikely to affect any judgment.[6] The general rule also applies to motions for leave to bring in bills[7] but the House has expressly resolved that the *sub judice* rule is qualified by the right of the House to legislate on any matter.[8]

Matters already decided during the same session

A motion or an amendment which is the same, in substance, as a question which has been decided during a session may not be brought forward again during that same session.[9] The question has been raised, as to whether this rule would apply as between a motion and a bill but so far no case for the application of the rule has been made out.[10] Attempts have been made to evade this rule by raising again, with verbal alterations, the essential portions of motions which have been negatived. Whether the second motion is substantially the same as the first is finally a matter for the judgment of the

---

1 Parl Deb (1882) 268, c 1140; ibid 271, c 1290; CJ (1884–85) 78; Parl Deb (1884–85) 294, cc 1912–1917; HC Deb (1913) 55, cc 39, 242; ibid (1924) 175, cc 940–942.
2 Parl Deb (1848) 96, c 1206.
3 Parl Deb (1883) 227, c 1500 and private rulings of 10 June 1969 and 27 January 1978.
4 HC Deb (1985–86) 103, c 1103.
5 See p 378, n.
6 HC Deb (1971–72) 836, c 1705; ibid (1975–76) 918, c 1621; ibid (1976–77) 935–2, c 1850; ibid (1979–80) 975, c 1056; ibid (1986–87) 102, c 1315.
7 HC Deb (1977–78) 960, c 665.
8 Resolution of the House of 23 July 1963, CJ (1962–63) 297 and Resolution of 28 June 1972, CJ (1971–72) 408; see also HC Deb (1971–72) 836, c 389–90. A notice of motion relating to a matter which had been the subject of a conviction was withdrawn from the paper when an appeal against the conviction was lodged and subsequently re-inserted when the appeal had been determined, Notice of Motions, 1969–70, pp 3141, 3277, 3404. Signatures may not be added to motions relating to matter which are sub judice until the cases have been disposed of, HC Deb (1976–77) 933, cc 733–4; ibid (1981–82) 13, c 163; ibid (1984–85) 83, c 28; see also Notices of Motions, 1988–89, pp 1871, 1901; ibid 2612, 2619.
9 CJ (1547–1628) 162, 306, 434. Cases when the Speaker has intervened to enforce this rule, CJ (1840) 495; Parl Deb (1844) 76, c 1021; ibid (1860) 158, c 1348; ibid (1870) 201, c 824; ibid (1873) 214, c 287; CJ (1900) 139; ibid (1902) 236; Parl Deb (1906) 160, c 364; CJ (1908) 225; HC Deb (1912) 38, c 1754; CJ (1920) 167; HC Deb (1920) 129, c 931. For application of rule to a notice of motion which raised a question discussed on an amendment to the address in the same session, see HC Deb (1912) 35, c 1043. The rule also prevents a matter which has been decided in Secret Session being reopened in Open Session, HC Deb (1943–44) 402, cc 1608–1609.
10 For application of the rule to bills see p 374. For occasions (in the last century) on which the question was raised see *Erskine May* (19th edn, 1976) p 369.

Chair. In some cases the second motion has been ruled to be substantially the same as an earlier motion.[1] The same rule has been applied to an amendment renewing a motion which had been already negatived.[2] Some motions, however, have been framed with sufficient ingenuity to avoid the rule.[3]

However, a question which has not been definitely decided may be raised again. Thus a motion or amendment which has been withdrawn,[4] or on which the Chair has declared the question not decided when it appeared that fewer than forty Members had taken part in a division,[5] or for some other reason,[6] may be repeated. In such cases a Member may speak for a second time in the resumed debate.[7] Where a certain course in relation to the procedure of the House has been rejected on a particular day, it may be revived on a subsequent day.[8]

The rule of anticipation

A motion must not anticipate a matter already appointed for consideration by the House,[9] whether it be a bill or an adjourned debate upon a motion.[10] The fact that a bill has not been printed does not withdraw it from the operation of this rule.[11]

Stated generally, the rule against anticipation (which applies to other proceedings as well as motions) is that a matter must not be anticipated if it is contained in a more effective form of proceeding than the proceeding by which it is sought to be anticipated,[12] but it may be anticipated if it is contained in an equally or less effective form. A bill or other order of the day is more effective than a motion; a substantive motion more effective than a motion for the adjournment of the House or an amendment, and a motion

---

1 Parl Deb (1870) 201, c 824; ibid (1864) 176, c 497; ibid (1882) 269, c 340. See also Parliamentary Affirmation, ibid (1880) 253, c 1266; Mr O'Donnell's suspension, ibid (1881) 261, c 1985, Railway Servants (Hours of Labour) ibid (1890–91) 349, c 1176.
2 Parl Deb (1844) 76, c 1021.
3 CJ (1780–82) 814, 861; ibid (1833) 195, 317; ibid (1845) 59, 69, 81; ibid (1845) 42, 54, 185, 199, 214.
4 Parl Deb (1845) 80, cc 432, 798; CJ (1977–78) 152, 168, 169.
5 CJ (1972–73) 269, 273; ibid (1977–78) 405. Formerly, before the making of SO No 40, motions were frequently interrupted by an adjournment as the result of a count of the House, and were repeated on a later day. See, eg CJ (1966–67) 338, 343.
6 CJ (1972–73) 414–415, 435.
7 HC Deb (1983–84) 57, c 1266.
8 HC Deb (1912) 42, c 367.
9 Parl Deb (1874) 219, c 1054; ibid (1875) 224, c. 915; ibid (1890) 344, c 307; ibid (1891) 352, c 1636; ibid (1907) 171, c 1525; ibid 176, c 631; ibid (1908) 192, c 228; HC Deb (1911) 29, c 1362; ibid 32, c 2706; ibid (1914) 61, c 172; ibid (1924–25) 180, c 1231; ibid (1981–82) 12, c 672.
10 A motion to give time for the remaining stages of a bill was privately ruled out of order as anticipating the adjourned debate on the motion for committing the bill to a standing committee (Notices of Motions, Session 1904, p 946) as was a motion for a select committee to consider the question of women's franchise, as anticipating a bill upon the order book on 21 February 1895. The Speaker restricted the debate on a motion for a select committee to matters outside the scope of bills on the order book dealing with the same subject. (Parl Deb (1903) 118, c 1437). See also the Speaker's opinion regarding a proposed amendment, mentioned by Mr Chamberlain in debate, with reference to Mr Parnell's amendment on the address after notice had been given of the Protection of Person and Property (Ireland) Bill. (CJ (1881) 11; Parl Deb (1893–94) 8, c 294).
11 Parl Deb (1890) 341, c 762; ibid (1902) 102, c 379.
12 But see HC Deb (1945–46) 417, c 629.

for the adjournment is more effective than a supplementary question.[1] Thus for a Member to declare his or her intention of raising a matter on the adjournment during question time precludes further supplementary questions even where the Member has not yet been allowed a specific opportunity for an adjournment debate.[2] A motion (other than another motion for leave to bring in a bill) is out of order if it anticipates a notice of motion for leave to bring in a bill[3] that includes the subject proposed to be dealt with by the motion. A matter already appointed for consideration by the House cannot be anticipated by a motion[4] or an amendment.[5] It has been ruled that while a notice of motion whether for a specified day or not, remains on the order paper, its subject-matter cannot be discussed by means of an amendment to a motion[6] or of a motion for the adjournment of the House[7] (see p 320), including a motion under Standing Order No 20, although in practice the existence of the notice of an early day motion would not be taken into account since, in determining whether a discussion would be out of order on the ground of anticipation, Standing Order No 26 requires that the Speaker must have regard to the probability of the matter anticipated being brought before the House within a reasonable time.[8] A private Member has, for example, been allowed to bring forward on a motion for which he was won precedence in a ballot substantially the same matters covered by private Members' bills standing upon the notice paper in his name which had little prospect of being reached on a future day.[9] The reference of a matter to a select committee does not stop the House considering the same matter.[10] The House has resolved that to put a motion upon the paper or to introduce a bill to prevent the discussion of notices of motions for which precedence had been gained in the ballot, or the moving of the adjournment of the House under Standing Order No 20, was hurtful to the usefulness of the House and an infringement of the rights of Members, and a select committee was appointed to consider the procedure of the House in relation to anticipatory motions and bills.[11] The House has also ordered that debate on a motion for an holiday adjournment be not restricted by the rule against anticipation.[12]

Manner of dealing with irregular notices of Motions

A notice of motion which contains unbecoming expressions, infringes the House's rules, or is otherwise irregular, may, under the Speaker's authority,

1 HC Deb (1945–46) 420, c 1081.
2 HC Deb (1984–85) 74, c 14.
3 Parl Deb (1871) 207, c 500.
4 Parl Deb (1908) 192, c 228 ff.
5 Parl Deb (1886) 308, c 1755. See also HC Deb (1963–64) 684, c 629.
6 Parl Deb (1882) 271, c 1290; ibid (1887) 310, c 1830; ibid (1889) 333, c 851; ibid (1899) 66, c 922; HC Deb (1913) 50, c 588.
7 For motions waiving this rule for a particular debate, see HC Deb (1941–42) 377, c 1552; CJ (1911) 256.
8 HC Deb (1941–42) 383, c 533–534; ibid (1968–69) 782, c 1039.
9 Votes and Proceedings, 13 June 1988 (coal mining subsidence); ibid 16 June 1989.
10 Parl Deb (1891) 351, c 933; HC Deb (1918) 107, c 430.
11 CJ (1907) 96, 302; HC 264 (1907). For debates upon the effect of notices of motions standing upon the Order Book upon debates on motions for the adjournment of the House and upon the power of moving the adjournment of the House under Standing Order No 20, see Parl Deb (1897) 46, c 1349; ibid (1900) 81, c 1414; ibid (1904) 135, c 379; ibid (1907) 171, c 1883.
12 CJ (1911) 256.

be corrected by the Clerks at the Table.[1] The alterations, if necessary, are submitted to the Speaker, or to the Member who gave the notice. A notice which is wholly out of order, by, for instance, reflecting on a vote of the House,[2] may be withheld from publication on the notice paper.[3] If the irregularity is not extreme, the notice may be printed, and reserved for future consideration.[4] If the Clerk at the Table decides that a motion should be withheld, he informs the Member concerned. If the Member does not accept that view, he should ask for the matter to be referred to Mr Speaker. If Mr Speaker decides to uphold the view of the Clerk the Member is informed, and if the Member is still dissatisfied he can see the Speaker to argue his case further. If, at the end of this process, he is still dissatisfied, he can raise the matter in the House, and if he disagrees with the Speaker's ruling he can challenge it by a motion. The object of this procedure is to save the time of the House.[5]

The precedence to which a notice, if in order, would have been entitled cannot be claimed for it when it appears for the first time in an orderly form on a subsequent day.[6] It is not the duty of the Clerks at the Table to inform the Member who gave the notice of any informality that it may contain,[7] but communication regarding an irregular notice is made to Members if the pressure of business permits. When a notice publicly given is obviously irregular or unbecoming, the Speaker has intervened, and the notice has not been received in that form.[8] He has also directed that a notice of motion should not be printed, because it was irregular or obviously not a proper subject for debate, being tendered in a spirit of mockery, or being designed merely to give annoyance.[9] The Speaker has also ruled against the excessive use of quotation in motions in an attempt to write statements or speeches made by persons outside the House into its record.[10] On the same principles, he has directed that certain titles given to their motions by Members should be changed before the motions were printed. If an objection is raised to a

1 Parl Deb (1867) 188, c 1065; ibid (1871) 206, c 468; ibid (1871) 207, c 1881; ibid (1872) 212, c 700; HC Deb (1919) 113, c 604; ibid (1921) 147, c 211; ibid (1977–78) 950, cc 1359–1361.
2 Parl Deb (1888) 329, c 157.
3 Parl Deb (1881) 263, c 1012; ibid (1887) 313, c 232; ibid (1898) 55, c 770; ibid (1947–48) 454, cc 39–40; ibid (1952–53) 510, c 845; Private Rulings, 22 May 1978, 10 June 1981.
4 See, for example, a motion published on 28 April 1953 which, because it appeared to infringe the rule against reflecting on a vote of the House, was withdrawn; a new motion was then set down in its place (Notices of Motions (1952–53) pp 2718, 2754).
5 HC Deb (1974) 872, c 452.
6 Parl Deb (1884) 288, c 684.
7 Parl Deb (1892) 3, c 964; ibid (1882) 270, c 1409; ibid (1906) 158, c 1163; HC Deb (1920) 134, c 2100; ibid (1926) 200, c 547.
8 Parl Deb (1861) 161, c 342; ibid (1907) 170, c 1451; HC Deb (1927) 205, c 1630; ibid (1928) 222, c 1090.
9 Among private rulings by the Speaker are the following: 9 February 1951 (motion imputing insobriety to a section of the Opposition); 11 December 1952 (motion reflecting on a Member's mental and physical condition); 9 February 1961 (motion advocating a memorial to mark the completion of the Suez operation); 11 July 1964 (motion containing copious quotations from private correspondence); 17 November 1965 (motion containing a reference to an obscene expression); 3 February 1971 (motion quoting the entire text of a newspaper article); 23 January 1978 (motion tendered in spirit of mockery); 2 June 1981 (motion containing references to the Bible). See also HC Deb (1967–68) 756, cc 647–650; ibid (1974) 872, c 452; ibid (1984–85) 72, c 286–287; and ibid (1986–87) 110, c 1083–1084.
10 HC Deb (1988–89) 151, cc 806, 969.

notice of motion upon the notice paper, it is for the Speaker to decide upon its regularity; and, if the objection is sustained, the notice must be amended or withdrawn.[1] The House has also, by order, directed that a notice of motion be taken off the notice paper.[2]

Alterations in the terms of question from terms of motion

The general rule that the question proposed and put from the Chair should repeat the terms of the motion on which it is based admits of certain recognized exceptions. Thus on the stages of bills the form of motion for the rejection of a bill, ie that this House declines to give the bill a second or third reading for various stated reasons, is translated by the Speaker into an amendment to the question 'That the bill be now read a second (or the third) time', expressed in the terms 'to leave out all the words after "That" and add the words "[embodying the reasons for rejection]"'.

On proposing the question, an opportunity may be taken to rectify any irregularities in a motion which has been moved without notice, or any irregularities which, although notice has been given, have previously been overlooked. Any such necessary change is within the discretion of the Chair (see also pp 324–325).[3]

MOVING OF MOTIONS

Proposal of motions

A motion of which notice has been given may be moved only by one of the Members in whose names it stands,[4] although it may arise that a Member's name does not stand on the Order Paper for the day on which the Motion is set down as, in accordance with practice, only the first six names appended to the motion and those added the previous day are actually printed.[5] But a motion standing in the name of a Minister may be moved by any other Minister in accordance with the constitutional practice which permits Ministers to act for each other on the grounds of the collective nature of the Government.[6]

A Member called to move a motion may speak in its favour before he actually proposes it, on the understanding, first, that he speaks to the motion, and, secondly, that he concludes by proposing his motion formally. Even when notice of a motion is not required (see pp 323–324), the motion should be placed, in written form, in the Speaker's hands; as, except where any informality in the form of the motion necessitates the Speaker's intervention, or compels him to decline to propose the question from the chair, the Speaker proposes the question in the words of the mover.

If the mover of a motion or an amendment has not finished his speech when business is interrupted or postponed, or if the Speaker has not proposed the question on a motion or an amendment, no entry appears in the Journal, as the House is not put in possession of it.

1 Parl Deb (1876) 228, c 1183; ibid (1880) 250, c 1313; ibid (1882) 267, c 388.
2 CJ (1835) 435.
3 Parl Deb (1858) 148, c 719.
4 HC Deb (1945–46) 419, c 339; ibid (1967–68) 762, cc 962–963.
5 See, for example, Order Paper for 6 March 1986 (p 2103); Notices of Motions for 27 February 1986 (p 5640); CJ (1985–86) 226.
6 Parl Deb (1881) 258, c 1664; HC Deb (1981–82) 27, c 398; Notices of Motion (1981–82) 3300; HC Deb (1985–86) 98, c 458.

Under a new standing order agreed by the House on 27 February 1986 (Standing Order No 28 (Powers of the Chair to propose question)), when a Member is in the course of making a motion or moving an amendment at any stage of proceedings on a bill, a Member rising in his place may claim the move 'That the question be now proposed' and, unless it appears to the Chair that the motion is an abuse of the rules of the House, that question shall be put forthwith by the Chair. It is not debatable (see also p 408).

Motions debated together

Where the content of two or more motions is cognate (for example, certain orders or regulations subject to affirmative procedure) or where a number of complex motions relate to a single subject of debate (for example Members' salaries and allowances),[1] it is common practice for them to be debated together. A single dissentient voice given at the beginning of the debate is enough to prevent motions from being debated together.[2] But if the House agrees at that time to proceed in this way, after the joint debate each motion is moved separately, and the question on the second and subsequent motions has to be put from the Chair without further debate.[3]

The practice of debating motions together is analogous to that on amendments (see p 405).

Seconding of motions

Standing Order No 27 provides that no motion or amendment shall require to be seconded before the question thereon is proposed from the Chair. It is, however, the practice for the Speaker on formal occasions, such as the debate on the address in reply to the Queen's speech, before proposing the question, to call on another Member after the motion has been moved, so giving an opportunity for seconding. It is also the practice to second the motion that a Member 'do take the Chair of this House as Speaker'.

2. QUESTIONS

PROPOSAL OF QUESTION UPON A MOTION

When the question has been proposed by the Speaker, and read to the House, the House is in possession of the question, debate begins and the

1 HC Deb (1982–83) 46, c 265.
2 HC Deb (1974–75) 889, c 820; ibid (1981–82) 26, c 941; ibid 28, c 843.
3 HC Deb (1978–79) 964, c 583–588; ibid (1981–82) 13, cc 843, 856; ibid (1982–83) 38, cc 566, 641.

House must dispose of the question in one way or another before it can proceed with any other business. Standing Order No 52, however, provides for the questions on Estimates proposed for debate by the Liaison Committee on an Estimates Day to be deferred, at the conclusion of debate, until ten o'clock on the same day.

WITHDRAWAL OF MOTIONS

A Member who has made a motion can withdraw it only by leave of the House, granted without any negative voice. This leave is signified, not upon question but by the Speaker taking the pleasure of the House. He asks, 'Is it your pleasure that the motion be withdrawn?' If no one dissents, the Speaker says, 'Motion by leave withdrawn'. However, if there is any objection, or if a Member rises to continue the debate, the Speaker must put the question at the end of the debate as, even if a dissentient Member no longer objects, the motion can no longer be withdrawn.[1] An amendment can be withdrawn in the same way, but neither a motion nor an amendment can be withdrawn except by the Member who moved it.[2] It is, however, the practice for a member of the Government to withdraw a motion in the absence of the Member (also a member of the Government), who moved it.[3] Occasionally a motion[4] or amendment[5] is, by leave, withdrawn, and another motion or amendment substituted, in order to meet the views of the House, as expressed in debate. This course can be taken only with the general assent of the House. Where an amendment has been proposed to a question, the original motion cannot be withdrawn until the amendment has been first disposed of by being agreed to, withdrawn, or negatived,[6] since the question on the amendment stands before the main question.

SUPERSEDING THE QUESTION

Use of motion for adjournment of House or of debate. During debate upon a question any Member may move, 'That this House do now adjourn,' or 'That the debate be now adjourned,' or, where applicable, 'that further consideration of the bill [or of the Lords amendments to a bill] be now adjourned'. He does so not by way of amendment to the original question, but as a distinct question, which interrupts and supersedes that already under consideration. The use of the motion for the adjournment of the House to supersede another question must be distinguished from its use as a

---

1　Parl Deb (1867) 186, c 887; ibid (1879) 247, c 841; ibid (1882) 274, c 1360.
2　Parl Deb (1860) 159, c 1309; HC Deb (1915) 73, c 1792. On 8 December 1943 (when practice required the seconding of some motions), during the absence through illness of the mover, the seconder was permitted to withdraw an amendment, HC Deb (1943–44) 395, c 1074.
3　See eg HC Deb (1962–63) 667, cc 1574, 1675.
4　Parl Deb (1872) 212, c 219; CJ (1877) 301; ibid (1895) 48; ibid (1916) 199; HC Deb (1916) 85, c 2647.
5　Parl Deb (1847) 91, c 1236; CJ (1893–94) 360; ibid (1895) 48. An amendment has been withdrawn after the words proposed to be left out of the original question have been negatived and the question for adding the words of the amendment has been proposed, CJ (1882) 172.
6　CJ (1830–31) 912; Parl Deb (1876) 227, c 787; ibid 230, c 1026; CJ (1870) 270.

substantive motion, ie before or between the orders of the day, when it can be moved only by a member of the Government (see p 312).[1] A dilatory motion cannot therefore be proposed before the Orders of the Day have been entered upon as a means of superseding debate.[2] Nor can a dilatory motion be made while another Member is speaking; and it can be offered only by a Member who, on being called by the Speaker in the course of the debate, is in possession of the House. If the question for the adjournment is agreed to, the original question is superseded; and (if the motion was for the adjournment of the debate) the next order or notice of motion is proceeded with, or (if the motion was for the adjournment of the House) all the business for the day ends and the House must immediately adjourn.[3]

In order to supersede a question, the motion for the adjournment must be simply that the House do *now* adjourn (or that the debate be *now* adjourned) and cannot be coupled with any prefatory words.[4] Nor is it in order to move that the House do adjourn (or that the debate be adjourned) to any future specified time, or to move an amendment to that effect to the question for adjournment.[5] A motion may not be made for the adjournment of the debate, if a question for the adjournment of the House is being debated;[6] nor can a motion for the adjournment of the House be made while a question for the adjournment of the debate is under discussion.[7]

If a motion is superseded by the adjournment of the House, notice of the motion must be renewed before the matter can be brought before the House again (see p 315); if an order of the day is so superseded, the order of the day must be revived (see pp 314–315).

Restrictions on motions for adjournment of House or of debate. When a motion for the adjournment of the House or the debate has been negatived, it may not be proposed again without some intermediate proceeding.[8] Furthermore, the Speaker has power under Standing Order No 34, if he believes that any dilatory motion is an abuse of the rules of the House, to decline to propose the question on it to the House or to put the question thereon forthwith (see also p 404).

A Member who has already spoken to the main question is not permitted to move either form of dilatory motion;[9] nor, having moved a dilatory motion, may he later speak to the main question if his motion is negatived.[10]

---

1 For an occasion when the adjournment of the House was moved by a member of the Government during a debate to enable an urgent statement to be made, see HC Deb (1967–68) 760, c 1855; for an occasion in committee when the Chairman left the Chair, a motion for the adjournment of the House was moved and withdrawn, and the committee stage was resumed, see HC Deb (1978–79) 965, cc 663–675.
2 HC Deb (1986–87) 108, c 603.
3 CJ (1854–55) 367; ibid (1860) 393.
4 Parl Deb (1891) 353, c 1246.
5 2 Hatsell 113.
6 Parl Deb (1857) 144, c 1906; ibid (1905) 146, c 1071; HC Deb (1914–16) 75, c 1294.
7 Parl Deb (1881) 260, c 1617.
8 2 Hatsell 109 n; Colchester ii, 129. Hence arose the practice of moving the two forms of motion alternately; see proceedings, 23 November 1819, Parl Deb (1819–20) 41, c 136; CJ (1851–52) 216; ibid (1857) 263; ibid (1862–63) 388; ibid (1881) 49–50.
9 HC Deb (1963–64) 690, c 1472.
10 HC Deb (1928) 215, c 593.

Similarly, a Member who has moved a dilatory motion is not entitled to move another in the course of debate on the same question.[1]

A motion for the adjournment of the debate, if carried, merely defers the decision of the House (an opportunity being given for fixing a day for the resumption of the debate when the decision to adjourn it is announced from the Chair), while a motion for the adjournment of the House supersedes the question altogether; and therefore Members who desire only to postpone the debate to another day should refrain from voting for an adjournment of the House, as that motion, if carried, would supersede the question which they may be prepared to support.[2] If, at the moment for the interruption of business under the standing orders (see p 241), a motion for the adjournment of the House or of the debate has been proposed from the Chair, such motion lapses without question put, pursuant to the provision in Standing Order No 9.

Use of the previous question

A method occasionally employed in order to withhold from the decision of the House a motion that has been proposed from the Chair is to move the previous question. The form in which the previous question is put to the House is 'That the question be *not now* put'.[3] The House is thus compelled to decide in the first instance whether the original motion shall or shall not be submitted to the House. If the previous question is agreed to, the Speaker is prevented from putting the original question, as the House has refused to allow it to be put. The original motion, however, may be brought forward again on another day, as the decision of the House only binds the Chair not to put the question on that motion at that time. If the previous question is negatived, the original question on which it was moved must be put forthwith. No amendment, debate or motion for adjournment is allowed, because the House has negatived the proposal, 'That the question be *not now* put,' and the question must therefore be put at once to the vote.

The motion for the previous question, unlike a motion for closure, is debatable; nor may it be moved, as may a motion for closure, while another Member is speaking. The Chair has declined to accept an attempt to move the previous question by a Member who had already exhausted his right to speak in a debate.[4]

The previous question has been moved upon the various stages of a bill,[5] but it cannot be moved upon an amendment,[6] although, after an amendment has been disposed of, the previous question can be moved on the main

---

1 Parl Deb (1866) 184, c 1450. SO No 33.
2 An instance of this occurred on 23 March 1848, on a motion relative to the game laws, Parl Deb (1848) 97, c 963; and again on 2 March 1875, on a motion relating to education in rural districts, ibid (1875) 222, c 1122.
3 The Speaker, with the concurrence of the House, first put the previous question in this form, 20 March 1888, CJ (1888) 112, because the earlier form, 'That the question be now put,' was akin to the closure motion, see p 405.
4 HC Deb (1985–86) 100, c 133.
5 CJ (1547–1628) 226, 825; ibid (1660–67) 421; ibid (1765–66) 418; ibid (1844) 504; ibid (1857–58) 220; ibid (1861) 103, 135, 177; ibid (1875) 356; ibid (1880) 261, etc.
6 2 Hatsell 116; Parl Deb (1872) 212, c 926.

question (as amended).[1] The previous question cannot be moved upon a motion relating to the transaction of public business or the meeting of the House,[2] or in committee (see p 587).[3] It has been moved on a motion for the issue of a writ for a by-election[4] and on a motion for the appointment of a Chairman and Deputy Chairman of Ways and Means.[5] The motion for the previous question cannot be amended, but may be withdrawn.[6] It may also be superseded by a motion for adjournment,[7] and it may be subject to a closure motion.[8]

The motion, 'That the orders of the day be read,' is obsolete as a substantive motion, though it survives in the form of an amendment, 'That this House do pass to the orders of the day', moved upon a motion, such as a privilege motion, including a motion for a new writ for electing a Member, made before the ordinary business of the day. This amendment, when agreed to, supersedes all business before the first Order of the Day, which term includes notices of motions where these stand first on the Order Paper.[9]

Consideration of questions interrupted. Consideration of a question is also liable to casual interruption and postponement from other causes (see pp 251–252).

COMPLICATED QUESTIONS

The old rule that when a complicated question is proposed to the House, the House may order such question to be divided, has been variously interpreted at different periods. Originally the division of such a question appears to have required an order of the House.[10] As late as 1883 it was generally held that an individual Member had no right to insist upon the division of a complicated question. In 1888, however, the Speaker ruled that two propositions which were then before the House in one motion could be taken separately if any Member objected to their being taken together.[11] Although this ruling does not appear to have been based on any previous

---

1 Previous question moved, after amendments proposed and negatived, CJ (1862–63) 129; ibid (1863) 268. Previous question moved to main question, as amended, ibid (1839) 496. See also ibid (1864) 45, 179; Parl Deb (1864) 174, c 1376; CJ (1865) 117.
2 Speaker's private ruling, 30 May 1892.
3 The report of the Committee on Privilege (Mr Gray), 1882, was recommitted on account of an oversight in its proceedings in regard to this rule, CJ (1882) 509.
4 Votes and Proceedings, 20 January 1989; ibid 3 May 1989.
5 HC Deb (1942–43) 386, c 252.
6 HC Deb (1942–43) 386, cc 252–264.
7 CJ (1876) 45, etc.
8 Votes and Proceedings, 20 January 1989.
9 CJ (1878) 196; ibid (1887) 358; CJ (1972–73) 415–416; HC Deb (1984–85) 80, c 578; CJ (1984–85) 475–476.
10 CJ (1768–70) 710.
11 Parl Deb (1888) 324, c 1828. See also Mr Speaker's remarks, ibid (1905) 149, c 897; HC Deb (1912) 43, c 1994.

decision, it has since remained unchallenged.[1] A complicated question, however, can only be divided if each part is capable of standing on its own.[2]

The House does not recognize the right of individual Members to insist on the division of motions giving special facilities for the transaction of public business, although such motions have sometimes been divided following the appeal of an individual Member. In particular, motions which under a Standing Order must be decided without amendment or debate, eg business motions under Standing Order No 14, have been divided when a request has been made (see p 316, n 1).

CONCLUSION OF DEBATE

At the conclusion of debate (or, when there is no debate, immediately after proposing the question) the Chair proceeds to seek the opinion of the House. This process is described below (see pp 342–343).

3. AMENDMENTS

As indicated earlier (p 321), an amendment is a subsidiary motion moved in the course of debate upon another motion which interposes a new cycle of debate and decision between the proposal and decision of the main motion and question. In its turn the debate on an amendment may be similarly intercepted by the proposal of and decision upon a further subsidiary amendment (amendment to an amendment), or it may be superseded by a dilatory motion (pp 332–333).

OBJECT OF AN AMENDMENT AND EFFECT ON DEBATE

The object of an amendment may be either to modify a question in such a way as to increase its acceptability or to present to the House a different proposition as an alternative to the original question.

Amendments superseding a question

The latter purpose may be effected by moving to omit all or most of the words of the question after the first word 'That' and to substitute an alternative proposition which must, however, be relevant to the subject of the question. The debate that follows is not restricted to the amendment, but includes also the content of the motion, both matters being under the consideration of the House as alternative propositions.

With amendments of this type, the proposal of the question 'That the amendment be made' effectively places before the House two alternative propositions, contained in the motion and in the amendment respectively, between which the House has to make a preliminary choice before deciding

---

1　Eg HC Deb (1968–69) 772, c 4 (Motion); ibid (1968–69) 785, c 1014 and ibid (1971–72) 834, c 1313 (Amendments to bills).
2　HC Deb (1962–63) 667, cc 390, 523; ibid (1979–80) 979, cc 1743–1748, 1787–1788; ibid (1985–86) 98, c 1198.

finally whether to agree to either of them. Consequently, if the question 'That the amendment be made' is agreed to, this vote does not by itself express a decision against the motion, but only a preference for taking a decision upon the alternative proposition contained in the amendment. When, however, the main question, as amended, is agreed to, the original motion may be regarded as having been negatived by implication. This depends both upon the fact that the amendment has been agreed to and upon the fact that its terms are such as to imply disagreement with the motion. A motion which has been superseded by a temporizing or non-committal amendment[1] has not strictly been decided and in substance may be submitted again to the decision of the House; and so may a motion which has been superseded by a conditional prohibition, as soon as that condition has ceased to operate. But a motion which has been superseded by a hostile amendment, ie one which contains a conflicting or incompatible proposition, cannot be repeated in the same session (see pp 326–327). It is, therefore, important to recognize that the question whether the proposition contained in a superseded motion has been decided depends, not upon the fact that its words have been omitted, but rather upon the nature of the amendment by which the motion has been superseded.

Where it is sought to supersede a question, by leaving out the words after 'That' and adding other words, the proposed amendment should not be confined to a mere negation of the terms of the motion, as the proper method of expressing a contrary opinion is by voting against a motion without seeking to amend it.

Amendments modifying a question

If it is intended only to modify the question by leaving out or adding words, debate should be restricted to the desirability of the omission or the addition of those words. Similarly, if it is intended to leave out certain words only and to substitute other words, then although both the original and the proposed words may be discussed, debate should not range over the other words of the motion to which the amendment is not directed.

SELECTION OF AMENDMENTS

Since 1919, the Speaker has had the power, under Standing Order No 31, to select amendments for debate. Thus, although an amendment may be in order, it may not necessarily be moved if the Chair has declined to select it. Further details are given in chapter 19 (see pp 404–405).

NOTICE OF AMENDMENTS TO MOTIONS

Notice of amendments is normally given; and only on rare occasions does the Speaker select amendments of which no notice has been given, for example when notice of the main motion has been given only on the previous sitting day.[2] The Speaker has held that it would be unfair to give advantage

---

1 HC Deb (1912) 42, c 367; CJ (1837–38) 418, 541.
2 See for example a manuscript amendment to refer the matter of a Speaker's ruling to the Committee of Privileges which was passed; HC Deb (1986–87) 109, cc 211–213, 221, 275.

to a Member seeking to move a manuscript amendment which would be taken before amendments of which longer notice had been given.[1] An amendment which appears on the paper can be moved by any Member, if the Member who gave notice of the amendment does not rise to move it. When, however, notice of an amendment is specifically required as, for instance, of the names of Members to be nominated, by way of amendment, to Select Committees (pp 613–614), and, under certain conditions, of an amendment to an instruction (p 485), the amendment can be moved only by the Member or by one of the Members in whose name it stands upon the notice paper.[2]

ORDER IN MOVING AMENDMENTS

The time for moving an amendment is after a question has been proposed by the Speaker, and before it has been put. A Member who has given notice of an amendment is not entitled to precedence on that account or to be heard before a Member who rises to speak to the main question.[3] According to the rules of debate, the Member who first rises and is called by the Speaker, being in possession of the House, is entitled to conclude with any motion which may properly be made at that time. When a series of amendments are to be proposed to a motion, Members must rise at the appropriate time, if they are to be called to move their amendments. Amendments to motions are in any case subject to selection by the Speaker under Standing Order No 31 (see pp 404–405), and it is customary for him to announce at the commencement of a debate which, if any, of the amendments standing on the paper he is prepared to call.

QUESTIONS PROPOSED ON AMENDMENTS

Amendments may be classified into three types: (1) to leave out certain words; (2) to leave out certain words in order to insert or add others; and (3) to insert or add certain words.

Under the terms of Standing Order No 30, the question proposed on amendments is, with two exceptions, 'That the amendment be made'.[4] The exceptions are (i) when an amendment to leave out the word 'now' has been moved to a question that a bill be now read a second or third time (see p 330), when the question proposed from the Chair is 'That the word "now" stand part of the question', and (ii) on an Opposition day, allotted under Standing Order No 13, when an amendment to leave out words and insert (or add) others has been moved to a substantive motion by a Minister of the Crown, when the questions proposed are 'That the original words stand part of the question', and, if that question is negatived, 'That the proposed words be there inserted (or added)'.[5]

---

1 For examples, see HC Deb (1963–64) 691, c 1604; ibid (1967–68) 756, c 1165; ibid (1979–80) 977, cc 1694–1697); ibid (1986–87) 109, c 213; for an exception see ibid (1982–83) 46, c 321.
2 Parl Deb (1893–94) 9, c 1663.
3 Parl Deb (1846) 84, c 641; ibid (1861) 163, cc 1424, 1486; ibid (1878–79) 246, c 265; ibid (1880) 250, c 80; ibid (1883) 282, c 1869.
4 For the passing of the Standing Order, see HC Deb (1967–68) 754, cc 356–370; Sixth Report of Select Committee on Procedure, 1966–67, HC 539, paras 33–37. For the procedure before the passing of this Standing Order, see *Erskine May* (17th edn, 1964) pp 415–416.
5 HC Deb (1979–80) 973, c 435.

Rejection both of amendment and original question

The rejection of an amendment (even an amendment to substitute a complete alternative proposition) does not constitute a final decision upon the original motion, but a further question has to be put upon this expressly for the purpose of securing such a decision. A Member who is adverse both to the main question and to the proposed amendment is not expressing an opinion favourable to the question by voting against the question 'That the amendment be made', for after the amendment has been disposed of, the question itself remains to be put, and a Member may thus vote with the 'noes' on both the amendment and the main question.

Under Standing Order No 30, however, when an amendment which involves leaving out all the effective words of a motion and adding other words has been disposed of, the Speaker forthwith declares the main question (as amended) to be agreed to.

RULES WITH RESPECT TO FORM AND CONTENT OF AMENDMENTS

Amendments to be relevant

The fundamental rule that debate must be relevant to a question (see pp 372–373) also means that every amendment must be relevant to the question to which it is proposed.[1]

Stated generally, no matter ought to be raised in debate on a question which would be irrelevant if moved as an amendment, and no amendment should be used for importing arguments which would be irrelevant to the main question. Thus the Speaker has ruled that on the third reading of a bill, when debate is limited to the contents of the bill, a reasoned amendment should not urge the rejection of the bill because of what it omits (see p 509).[2]

The effect of moving an amendment is to restrict the field of debate which would otherwise be open on a question. This is not obvious if an amendment proposes to leave out all the words of a question and substitute a different (but of course relevant) proposition. Even that kind of amendment, however, by concentrating debate on the main question and the amendment as alternative propositions, does tend to exclude the consideration of other relevant alternatives.

It would be impracticable to attempt to classify here all the grounds on which amendments have been held to be irrelevant to a question. Some examples are given elsewhere in connection with specialised forms of pro-

---

1 Parl Deb (1903) 120, c 806; ibid 121, c 505; ibid (1905) 144, c 1497. This principle was asserted for the first time in the 9th edn (1883) p 325. See also Parl Deb (1843) 70, c 213; ibid (1882) 266, c 1846; ibid 269, c 461.
2 The Speaker has ruled that an amendment to add another subject for inquiry to a question declaring the expediency of establishing a tribunal for the purpose of inquiring into a definite matter of urgent public importance, under the Tribunals of Inquiry (Evidence) Act 1921, would not be relevant, HC Deb (1922) 150, c 1676. See also ibid (1957–58) 577, c 1147; ibid (1962–63) 667, c 385; but an amendment relating to the constitution of a tribunal of inquiry has been allowed; CJ (1928) 181.

cedure such as bills, particularly in committee (pp 491–493) and business motions (p 309).

Amendments to be intelligible

Every amendment proposed to be made, either to a question or to a proposed amendment, should be so framed that, if agreed to by the House, the question or amendment, as amended, would be intelligible and internally consistent.

Other restrictions on contents of amendments

Various considerations that render amendments out of order have been described earlier. An amendment is also out of order if it is inconsistent with an amendment already agreed to, or if it is substantially the same as an amendment to the same motion which has already been negatived.[1] It is not in order to move to leave out all the words of a question without proposing the insertion of other words, and the Speaker has also ruled that an amendment that was merely an expanded negative,[2] or otherwise irregular in form,[3] could not be proposed from the Chair. An Amendment on a motion to approve changes in Immigration Rules which although a direct negative of the main question was so drafted as to follow the terms of section 3(2) of the Immigration Act 1971, has, however, been allowed.[4] The Speaker has declined, on the ground of informality revealed during debate, to put the question upon an amendment which had been proposed.[5]

Amendment to words added to, or inserted in, question, out of order

Once the House has agreed to add or insert words in a question, those words may not be amended. If it is desired to alter the words of a proposed amendment, an amendment should be moved to the proposed amendment before it has been decided upon by the House (see p 342).

Certain stock forms of questions not amendable

Amendments to motions for the adjournment of the House or of the debate are out of order.[6] To certain other forms of motion, only recognised forms of amendment are in order. For example, no amendment may be moved to a motion that the House at its rising do adjourn till a future day, unless it relates to the term of an adjournment. Thus a reasoned amendment relating to such a motion, even where it includes alteration of the dates of sitting, has not been selected by the Speaker[7] but the qualification has embraced

---

1 Parl Deb (1893–94) 18, c 955.
2 Parl Deb (1893–94) 9, c 456; ibid (1905) 146, c 991; ibid (1906) 167, c 475; HC Deb (1938–39) 343, c 906.
3 CJ (1881) 26.
4 CJ (1984–85) 596.
5 Parl Deb (1881) 257, c 1039; CJ (1922) 196.
6 Parl Deb (1893) 18, c 449; HC Deb (1974–75) 897, c 1719.
7 HC Deb (1984–85) 83, c 1084.

amendments to alter the hour of meeting on the day proposed for reassembly[1] and to provide that, pursuant to Standing Order No 12, should the public interest so require, representation should be made to the Speaker that the House ought to meet earlier.[2] No amendment is possible to a motion to approve or to annul a statutory instrument pursuant to an Act of Parliament, when the relevant Act makes no such provision (see pp 546–547).

ORDER OF AMENDMENTS

Order in which amendments are considered

Each amendment should be proposed in the order in which, if agreed to, it would stand in the amended question.[3] When more than one Member rises to move an amendment, the Speaker will give priority to the Member whose amendment is offered at the earliest place.[4] If the question has already been proposed upon an amendment, no other amendment to the main question can be moved until the amendment under consideration has been disposed of by being agreed to, negatived or withdrawn. If the amendment is agreed to, no amendment affecting the main question at an earlier point may be moved. If, however, the amendment is rejected or withdrawn, the main question is open to amendment as far back as the last point at which a decision was made on an amendment or, in committee on a Bill, to the last decision that a clause stand part of the bill (if no decisions have subsequently been made on amendments). The withdrawal of an amendment is not a decision. Thus if the last decision was that the amendment be made, the main question would be open to amendment as far back as the point immediately after any words inserted by that amendment, or, in the case of an amendment to leave out words without inserting other words, as far back as the point immediately after the last word left out. If the last decision was against an amendment, the main question would be open to amendment as far back as the point at which the defeated amendment proposed to insert words or, in the case of an amendment to leave out words (with or without the insertion of other words) as far back as the point immediately before the first of the words proposed to be left out.

Special arrangements on taking amendments

For greater freedom of discussion and amendment, the rule that no Member may speak twice to the same question, except in committee (see p 369), has

---

1 CJ (1914) 132. Cf Parl Deb (1856) 141, c 1541; ibid (1878) 242, c 2076.
2 CJ (1981–82) 373.
3 2 Hatsell 123.
4 Parl Deb (1887) 319, c 1475; ibid (1892) 4, c 1961. When two Members who proposed to move amendments rose almost simultaneously, although his call had been given to the other Member, the Speaker gave priority of speech to the mover of the prior amendment, notice having been given thereof, ibid (1893–94) 14, c 483. See also HC Deb (1982–83) 40, cc 321–322.

been relaxed on the consideration of the rules of procedure,[1] and of motions for ensuring the completion at a prescribed time of the outstanding stages of a bill or other business (see pp 408–415),[2] to enable Members to speak first on the main question, and subsequently to move amendments thereto.[3]

AMENDMENTS TO PROPOSED AMENDMENTS

Before an amendment is put to the House in its original form, an amendment may be proposed to it. In that event the question on the original amendment is first proposed as a distinct question, and then another question on the amendment to the amendment; at that point the question on the original amendment is temporarily laid aside. If that were not done, there would be three matters under consideration at once, viz. the question, the proposed amendment and the amendment to that amendment. An amendment to a proposed amendment is moved after the question 'That the amendment be made' has been proposed from the Chair. The question on this subsidiary amendment, namely, 'That the amendment to the proposed amendment be made,' must be disposed of before the question on the original amendment is put to the House. Not infrequently the Speaker permits discussion on the original amendment to range also over the subsidiary amendments proposed to it, without those subsidiary amendments being moved or the questions on them being proposed to the House. The Speaker may then put separately the subsidiary amendments for the purposes of a division.[4]

4. DECISIONS AND DIVISIONS

PUTTING OF QUESTION AT CLOSE OF DEBATE

When debate on a question is concluded, the question must be put. This is done by the Speaker rising from the Chair,[5] and putting to the House 'The

---

1 Parl Deb (1880) 250, c 1450; ibid (1887) 311, cc 204, 207; ibid (1888) 322, c 1252; ibid (1899) 67, c 309; ibid (1907) 171, c 888. Members were allowed to move several amendments to the motions implementing the First Report of the Select Committee on Procedure on 15 November 1945, HC Deb (1945–46) 415, c 2414. See also HC Deb (1947–48) 443, c 1637; ibid (1966–67) 738, c 470; CJ (1979–80) 200, 816.
2 Parl Deb (1887) 315, c 1616; ibid (1893–94) 14, c 366; HC Deb (1921) 144, cc 459, 465, 521, 541, 556; ibid (1967–68) 760, c 1647. An amendment to limit the duration of speeches on the bill dealt with by the proposed motion has been ruled out of order, HC Deb (1911) 32, c 849.
3 In session 1902 a general discussion of the proposed new rules of procedure was taken on a motion, 'That the proposals of the Government on the order paper relating to the procedure of the House be now considered' (Parl Deb (1902) 102, c 548). A similar course was followed in session 1919 (HC Deb (1919) 112, c 815). The consideration of a sessional order is not exempted from the ordinary rules of debate (Parl Deb (1901) 89, c 1317; ibid 98, c 1550); but in session 1929–30 on a sessional order containing a series of paragraphs laying down a special form of procedure for private bills contributing to the relief of unemployment, a general discussion was allowed without prejudice to the subsequent moving of amendments (HC Deb (1929–30) 233, c 564). See also HC Deb (1983–84) 55, c 613.
4 HC Deb (1967–68) 765, cc 663, 676; ibid (1968–69) 783, cc 848, 884; ibid (1974) 876, cc 1692, 1716.
5 On 9 April 1866 the Speaker, on returning to the House after an illness, said that he should claim the indulgence of sitting while putting the questions, CJ (1865–67) 197.

question is, That . . .'. This form of putting the question is always observed, and precedes every vote of the House except in cases where a vote is a formal direction in virtue of previous orders.[1] The Speaker takes the sense of the House by desiring that 'As many as are of that opinion say, "aye,"' and 'As many as are of the contrary opinion say, "no."' When each party has responded, the Speaker endeavours to judge from the loudness and general character of the opposing exclamations, or from a consideration of the probabilities of the case,[2] which party has the majority. As his judgment is not final, he expresses his opinion by saying: 'I think the "ayes" (or "noes") have it'. If the House acquiesces in this decision, the question is said to be 'agreed to' or 'negatived' as the case may be, but if those declared to be the minority dispute the fact, they respond with further exclamations of 'aye' (or 'no'). The Speaker will then say, 'Clear the lobby,' in order to start the process of counting the numbers on each side, which is termed a division.

Voice and vote

The opinions of Members are collected from their voices in the House, and not merely by a division. If their voices and their votes should be at variance, the voice will bind the vote. A Member therefore who gives his voice with the 'ayes' or 'noes' when the Speaker takes the voices, is bound if he votes to vote with them;[3] although a Member has been permitted to correct his voice at the second call.[4] Mr Speaker has condemned the practice of forcing a division by voice contrary to vote as 'irregular and unparliamentary'.[5] A Member who gives his voice with the 'ayes' or 'noes' cannot, however, be obliged to go into the division lobby to cast a vote.[6]

The objection that a Member's vote was contrary to his voice should be taken either before the numbers are reported by the tellers or immediately afterwards; it will not be entertained after the declaration of the numbers from the Chair (see p 350).[7]

A Member who makes a motion is entitled to vote against it, provided that he gives his voice with the 'noes' when the question is put from the Chair.[8] Similarly, a Member whose name appears on the Notice Paper in support of an amendment is not precluded from voting against it.[9]

PROCEDURE ON A DIVISION

The method of taking divisions is the same in Committees of the whole House as in the House itself.[10]

---

1 CJ (1979–80) 774; CJ (1981–82) 360, 362.
2 HC Deb (1955–56) 547, c 602.
3 CJ (1854) 373; ibid (1864) 359; Parl Deb (1864) 176, c 235; ibid (1906) 158, c 1052; CJ (1912–13) 378; HC Deb (1912) 42, c 2133.
4 HC Deb (1946–47) 436, c 710.
5 Parl Deb (1866) 183, c 1919; HC Deb (1970–71) 808, cc 1119, 1376.
6 SO No 38 (2). See also HC Deb (1981–82) 21, c 322.
7 Parl Deb (1856) 141, c 1103; HC Deb (1936–37) 326, c 2811.
8 Parl Deb (1876) 227, c 473; 25 July 1879, Sir H Selwin Ibbetson, Votes (1878–79) 697.
9 HC Deb (1962–63) 679, cc 1685–1686.
10 The present method of taking divisions was introduced experimentally in session 1906, after the Whitsuntide adjournment (Parl Deb (1906) 158, c 445), and the amendments in the standing orders necessitated by the change were made at the end of that session (CJ (1906) 494; Parl Deb (1906) 167, c 472).

On a division being called the Speaker or the Chairman, as the case may be, gives the order 'clear the lobby,'[1] the tellers' doors in both lobbies are locked, and the division bells are rung. After the lapse of two minutes from this direction the Speaker or Chairman again puts the question, and the ayes and noes must again declare themselves. If at this stage the opinion of the Chair is not again challenged, the division is called off and the decision is declared as so decided. If his opinion is again challenged, the Speaker or Chairman directs the ayes to go into the lobby on his right, and the noes into the lobby on his left, and then appoints two tellers for each side of the question. One teller for the ayes and one for the noes go to each lobby, to check each other in the telling.

A Member is bound to act as teller for that side of the question with which he has declared himself, when appointed by the Speaker, and his refusal to do so would be reported to the House.[2] A Member cannot act as a teller on a question for his own suspension.[3]

If two tellers cannot be found for either side of the question, the division cannot take place; and the Speaker forthwith announces the decision of the House. For instance, if it appears that there are no tellers, or only one teller, for the ayes, the Speaker declares 'that the noes have it', and *vice versa*.[4] When there are two tellers for each side of the question, they proceed at once to the doors leading from the lobbies into the House, which are then unlocked and the counting begins. Where the tellers, after nomination, fail to go and tell, they have been instructed by the Chair to do so.[5] In each division lobby, clerks are stationed at desks, on which there are alphabetical lists of Members. As the Members pass by, the clerks place a mark against their names; and, at the way out from the lobby into the House, the tellers count the numbers. If any Members who are disabled by infirmity from passing through the lobby are present in the precincts of the House and wish to vote, their names are communicated to the clerks and to the tellers, and are included in the numbers counted. At the expiration of at least six minutes (now in practice eight minutes) from the time at which the lobby was ordered to be cleared, the Speaker or Chairman directs the doors leading from the House into the division lobbies to be locked and they remain locked until the announcement of the numbers from the Chair.[6] The Chair has discretion to vary the period which must elapse before the doors are locked.[7]

1 Ie the Members' lobby. The Speaker's order derives from an earlier procedure for taking divisions (before division lobbies had been built) under which the ayes (or noes, as directed by the Speaker) went out into the lobby and were told on re-entering the chamber. Accordingly the lobby had first to be cleared. See Notebook of John Clementson, Deputy Serjeant at Arms 1770–1804, annexed to *Ceremonial and the Mace in the House of Commons* (1980) by Sir Peter Thorne, Serjeant at Arms, 1976–82.
2 Private Mem. 7 July 1859.
3 Parl Deb (1882) 268, c 1017; ibid (1882) 271, c 1128; ibid (1901) 98, c 505; Private Ruling, 12 February 1981.
4 CJ (1842) 183, 354; ibid (1960–61) 203; ibid (1979/80) 532, etc; HC Deb (1987–88) 122, c 372.
5 HC Deb (1983–84) 58, cc 338 and 343.
6 See SO No 37. In 1975 the Speaker extended this period to eight minutes to enable Members to reach the chamber from outlying offices, HC Deb (1974–75) 888, c 535.
7 HC Deb (1974–75) 894, cc 1205, 1480; ibid (1979–80) 978, cc 1976–1986; ibid 979, cc 27–28. Timing devices with flashing lights are used at the Table for regulating divisions and other timed business.

In 1906 the House agreed to a new Standing Order (now No 38) which provided that a Member might vote in a division although he had not heard the question put; and also established that no Member was obliged to vote. At the same time the provisions of Standing Orders requiring strangers to withdraw during divisions were repealed.

Declaration of numbers

Until a Member has passed the tellers his vote is not counted.[1] When the tellers have concluded their count, they return to the House and inform a Clerk at the Table of the numbers voting on each side of the question; these are entered upon the division paper. The tellers then stand in line in the centre of the Chamber in front of the Table (those for the majority being on the right), bow to the Chair, take a pace forward and bow again. One of the tellers for the majority then reports the numbers. The division paper is handed by the Clerk to the Speaker or Chairman, who declares the numbers, and states the determination of the House.

A division in which fewer than than 35 Members have voted in both lobbies is invalid, since Standing Order No 40 provides that if it appears that fewer than 40 Members have taken part in a division, the business under consideration stands over (see p 250). In reckoning the figure of 40 Members, the occupant of the Chair and the four tellers are included.

It is the duty of the tellers to remain in the House until the numbers have been declared,[2] but when one of the tellers, having counted, has failed to come to the Table, the report of the remaining tellers has been accepted.[3]

Divisions unnecessarily claimed

Under Standing Order No 39, if the Speaker or the Chairman considers that a division is unnecessarily claimed, he may, after the lapse of two minutes, take the vote of the House or committee by calling upon the Members who support and those who challenge his decision successively to rise in their places; and he thereupon, as he may think fit, either declares the determination of the House or the committee[4] or names tellers for a division.[5]

---

1 HC Deb (1981–82) 13, c 376; ibid (1982–83) 31, c 761.
2 See Parl Deb (1895) 36, c 1060; HC Deb (1912–13) 47, c 245.
3 Parl Deb (1895) 36, cc 877, 1059; HC Deb (1912–13) 47, c 91.
4 CJ (1920) 55; HC Deb (1920) 126, c 1463; CJ (1960–61) 203; ibid (1970–71) 299 (five successive divisions), etc; Votes and Proceedings, 25 May 1988 (47 divisions).
5 CJ (1897) 299; ibid (1918) 56. Formerly any two Members could compel the House to divide when a question was put from the Chair. Experience showed the need to place this power under some restraint; and in 1882 a standing order gave the Chair for the first time power to call on Members to rise in their place, though only in respect of a vote on dilatory motions, such as a motion to adjourn a debate. In 1888 that standing order was repealed, and the present standing order (No 39) was passed, though until 1919 the power of the Chair was restricted to divisions 'frivolously or vexatiously' claimed. In that year, too, the House repealed (CJ (1919) 35. See also Sir T Erskine May's pamphlet on 'Public Business in Parliament' (1849, 2nd edn) p 29, and the Report of the Select Committee on Public Business, HC 268 (1878)) a provision that, where there was not a division, the number of Members who had risen should be declared from the Chair and their names taken down in the House and printed with the division lists (CJ (1890) 580; ibid (1890–91) 476; ibid (1892) 102, etc). Neither names nor numbers of the minority are now announced, though the numbers appear in the Journal (HC Deb (1936–37) 326, c 2814; CJ (1970–71) 299; ibid (1974–75) 521).

Irregularities discovered at the time of a division

When, in the course of a division, the Speaker has been apprised of a breach of order which, although reflecting upon the conduct or votes of individual Members, is not of such a nature as to cast doubts upon the validity of the division as a whole, he has directed that the division should proceed and has dealt with the matter when it was completed.[1] When, however, a major irregularity occurs in the conduct of a division, the usual practice is for the Chair to interrupt the process of division as soon as the irregularity is discovered, put the question again and proceed to take the division *de novo*.[2] The following are examples of major irregularities.

Division bells not rung, or not rung correctly. On complaint being made that the division bells had not rung, the Speaker has put the question again and the House has proceeded again to a division.[3] The Speaker has, however, ruled in advance that as it was known that a division would take place at ten o'clock, he would be unlikely to order a division to be held again if the division bells or even the lifts failed.[4]

Confusion over question. When a Member claimed that Members were confused about whether they were voting on the Closure or the main question, the Deputy Speaker put the question again.[5]

Failure of teller to attend in lobby. When it appeared to the Chairman that there was delay in completing a division, he asked the tellers to come to the Table; one of the tellers then stated that a teller for the noes had not appeared at the door of the No lobby, and that therefore the doors had not been opened. The Chairman ruled that in these circumstances the question must again be put from the Chair.[6] But when the tellers for the ayes in a division reported that the two Members appointed tellers for the noes had failed to act as such, the Speaker declared that the ayes had it, and on one occasion when one of the tellers for the ayes failed to act, the Chairman declared that the noes had it.[7]

Absence of tellers during part of a division. A division was taken again when several Members were counted by only one teller[8] as well as when the tellers left the doors before the direction 'lock the doors' had been given by the Chair.[9] On an occasion when the tellers were not present when the door of a division lobby was unlocked and Members entered the House untold, the division was taken again.[10] Upon a Member complaining, before the result of the division had been reported, that he had

---

1 CJ (1881) 56; Parl Deb (1881) 258, cc 74–77; CJ (1886) 347; Parl Deb (1886) 308, c 1165; HC Deb (1948–49) 458, cc 499–500; ibid (1950–51) 488, cc 1177, 1232.
2 CJ (1926) 116–117; ibid (1938–39) 337; ibid (1951–52) 189; ibid (1956–57) 150, 222; ibid (1962–63) 51. See also HC Deb (1981–82) 29, cc 905–906.
3 HC Deb (1937–38) 337, c 1092; CJ (1956–57) 222; CJ (1966–67) 611; HC Deb (1966–67) 751, cc 1593–1594; see also CJ (1974–75) 261; HC Deb (1974–75) 887, c 1348.
4 HC Deb (1978–79) 965, c 461.
5 HC Deb (1979–80) 970, c 980, 1806–1808; and ibid (1985–86) 87, c 361.
6 CJ (1928–29) 83; HC Deb (1929) 224, c 69. See also CJ (1931–32) 151; ibid (1938–39) 361.
7 CJ (1945–46) 193; ibid (1924) 121.
8 CJ (1946–47) 51.
9 CJ (1950–51) 94.
10 CJ (1900) 125.

gone into the lobby to vote but that the tellers had left the door before he reached it, the Chairman ordered the division to be taken again.[1] For similar complaints made after the declaration of the result of a division, see p 348.

Failure of tellers to return to the chamber. After a delay in the progress of a division in committee, it was alleged that several Members were refusing to pass the tellers. The Chairman called for a report from the Serjeant at Arms and then directed the tellers to bring the figures to the Chair leaving some Members still in the lobby untold.[2]

Member tells though not nominated. When the tellers came to the Table following a division and it became apparent that a Member who had not been nominated had told during the whole or part of the division, the Chair ruled that the division must be regarded as void, and that the question must again be put.[3]

Irregularity in locking the doors. Divisions have been taken again when the doors were locked before the expiration of the prescribed time;[4] they have also been taken again when one door remained unlocked after the direction 'lock the doors' had been given.[5] The doors have been re-opened and additional time allowed when it had been discovered that the order to lock the doors had been given early as a result of a malfunctioning clock.[6]

Members not allowed to vote. When several Members complained, before the result of the division had been declared, that they had been impeded from reaching the doors before they were locked, the Deputy Speaker ordered the division to be taken again.[7] For similar complaints made after the declaration of the result of a division, see pp 348–349.

Members enter lobby after order given to lock the doors. When complaint was made that certain unnamed Members had interfered with the door-keeper on duty at the door of the Aye lobby, the Assistant Serjeant at Arms reported that one or two Members had got through the door after the direction 'lock the doors' had been given; the Speaker thereupon ruled that the question must again be put.[8] Similar action was taken by the Deputy Speaker on 21 April 1953.[9] But when a similar complaint was made regarding a particular Member, the division was not vitiated, the Member's vote being disallowed.[10]

Disagreement between tellers. If two tellers differ as to the numbers on the side told by them, or if a mistake regarding the numbers is discovered,

---

1 CJ (1968–69) 161.
2 CJ (1977–78) 146; see also CJ (1926) 117; HC Deb (1979–80) 969, cc 763, 765; ibid (1987–88) 122, cc 340, 351 and 371.
3 HC Deb (1932) 262, c 1840; See also CJ (1924–25) 434; HC Deb (1925) 188, c 2641; CJ (1924–25) 95; HC Deb (1925) 181, c 397; CJ (1954–55) 55; ibid (1956–57) 222; ibid (1959–60) 69; ibid (1962–63) 51; ibid (1966–67) 463; HC Deb (1969–70) 796, c 944.
4 CJ (1938–39) 337; ibid (1956–57) 150; ibid (1964–65) 94; ibid (1970–71) 230, 338, 512.
5 CJ (1953–54) 148.
6 HC Deb (1987–88) 131, c 798.
7 CJ (1961–62) 275.
8 HC Deb (1951–52) 498, cc 2808–2810, 2813–2816.
9 HC Deb (1952–53) 514, c 852.
10 HC Deb (1948–49) 458, cc 499–500.

unless the tellers agree thereon, a second division must take place.[1] In 1860 a question was raised privately, whether a Member who had voted with the ayes in the first division could afterwards vote with the noes; but it was held that, as the first division had become null and void, the House could only deal with the Member's voice and vote in the last and valid division.

Tellers' miscount. On 6 July 1971 the tellers came to the Table and reported that the numbers in the Aye lobby had been miscounted. The Speaker thereupon directed the House to proceed again to a division.[2]

Tellers voting. On one occasion one of the tellers voted in the No lobby before acting as teller: he reported the fact after the numbers had been reported by the tellers but before the result of the division had been declared. The Speaker directed his name to be struck from the noes and declared the correct numbers.[3] On another occasion, on the tellers being called to the Table and before they had stated the numbers, a Member reported that one of the tellers had voted in the lobby before acting as a teller. The Chairman thereupon directed the House to proceed again to a division.[4]

Errors discovered after a division

If a mistake is subsequently discovered, it will be ordered to be corrected in the Journal.[5] Where an error in the numbers has been discovered before the end of a sitting, the tellers being agreed on the correct figures have come to the Table and stated the corrected numbers and the Speaker has reported the numbers accordingly.[6] When an error in the numbers reported by the tellers in a committee of the whole House has been discovered before the Chairman has left the chair, the Chairman has ordered the numbers to be corrected accordingly.[7] An error in the report of the numbers taken at a division is brought before the House by both the tellers of the lobby in which the error arose; though a statement made by one of the tellers has been accepted,[8] as has the statement of the Member concerned.[9]

Members not counted by tellers, or prevented from voting. When Members have complained immediately after the declaration of the numbers in a division from the Chair that the tellers had left the door of a lobby before they had reached it, the Speaker or the Chairman has directed the tellers of

---

1 CJ (1810) 253; ibid (1860) 332; ibid (1872) 140; ibid (1960–61) 117; HC Deb (1981–82) 23, c 682; ibid (1979–80) 969, cc 761–762.
2 CJ (1970–71) 525; HC Deb (1975–76) 905, cc 519–522.
3 CJ (1911) 400.
4 CJ (1968–69) 185.
5 CJ (1847) 131; ibid (1860) 216; ibid (1863) 111; ibid (1882) 98; ibid (1886) 57, 103; ibid (1887) 506; ibid (1893–94) 496; ibid (1896) 187; ibid (1897) 221; ibid (1899) 146, 349; ibid (1901) 240; ibid (1908) 49; ibid (1929–30) 448; ibid (1946–47) 219; ibid (1953–54) 143; ibid (1956–57) 81, 231; ibid (1962–63) 85; proceedings declared null and void as result of error by tellers, ibid. (1938–39) 95, 96; ibid (1962–63) 196; ibid (1974) 256.
6 CJ (1847–48) 102; ibid (1930–31) 430; ibid (1945–46) 360; ibid (1971–72) 444.
7 CJ (1867–68) 16; ibid (1873) 223; ibid (1936–37) 243.
8 CJ (1946–47) 101; when after the tellers in both lobbies had been in error a statement from one teller for the ayes and one teller for the noes was accepted, CJ (1962–63) 196.
9 CJ (1974) 256.

that lobby to come to the Table, and having heard their explanation, has directed the Clerk to alter the numbers by adding the names of the Members and then again declared the numbers as so corrected.[1] Where a Member has made such a complaint the Chair has undertaken to inquire into the matter and on the following day directed the record of the division to be amended accordingly.[2] Both the tellers in the lobby through which the Member has passed must agree that he should be counted.[3] Such an error may be drawn to the attention of the House by a teller although no complaint has been made by the Member concerned.[4]

The Chair has on occasion accepted the complaints of Members about such errors without requiring the agreement of the tellers, and has directed that the numbers should be corrected.[5]

When a Member complained that he had been impeded from reaching the doors before they were locked, the Deputy Speaker directed the Journal to be altered on the following day.[6]

Member wrongly counted as having voted. On 16 July 1974 a Member acquainted the House that his name had been included among those voting in two divisions on 11 July as being a Member disabled by infirmity but present in the precincts of the House (in accordance with the practice stated on p 344); but that he had not in fact been in the precincts. The Speaker thereupon directed that the numbers in those divisions should be corrected and certain subsequent proceedings were ordered to be null and void.[7]

Members voting in the wrong lobby. If a Member goes into the wrong lobby, through inadvertence, he is bound by the vote he has actually given[8] (but see also below).

Members voting in both lobbies. Members who have voted in both lobbies in the same division have been allowed on the following day to state as a matter of personal explanation (see pp 304–306) in which lobby they intended to vote, and the numbers of the division have been directed to be corrected accordingly.[9] A correction has been directed to be made at the end of government business on the same day after an explanation by a member of the Government on his own and a colleague's behalf.[10] The Speaker has deprecated as 'unparliamentary' the practice of voting in both lobbies as a demonstration of a 'third' position, but intentionally voting in both lobbies is

---

1 CJ (1895) 186; Parl Deb (1895) 33, c 658; CJ (1912–13) 424; HC Deb (1912) 44, c 1151; CJ (1912–13) 457; HC Deb (1912) 45, c 939; CJ (1920) 493; HC Deb (1920) 136, c 1043.
2 HC Deb (1984–85) 80, cc 845 and 892; CJ (1984–85) 483, 486–487.
3 Parl Deb (1901) 98, c 1189. See also Parl Deb (1899) 67, c 1200.
4 Parl Deb (1861) 164, c 210; CJ (1946–47) 101.
5 CJ (1970–71) 327, 344.
6 CJ (1950–51) 230.
7 HC Deb (1974) 877, cc 248–265; CJ (1974) 256.
8 Parl Deb (1864) 176, c 31. For similar cases, see CJ (1856) 129; ibid (1860) 229; ibid (1864–65) 359; ibid (1865–67) 136. See also CJ (1882) 172 and also HC Deb (1912) 43, c 1716. See also ibid (1918) 105, c 2031; ibid (1919) 122, c 1327; ibid (1932–33) 188, c 2239; ibid (1950) 481, c 1071–1072.
9 CJ (1906) 257; Parl Deb (1906) 159, c 58. For Mr Speaker's statement on voting in both lobbies as a demonstration rather than a mistake, see HC Deb (1977–78) 939, c 1530–1531.
10 CJ (1917–18) 233; HC Deb (1917) 98, c 2116.

an accepted way of cancelling out the effect of inadvertently voting in the wrong lobby.[1]

Member voting twice in the same lobby. A Member who voted twice in the same lobby in one division was allowed to make a personal explanation to that effect, and the Clerk was accordingly directed by Mr Speaker to correct the number of Members voting in that lobby.[2]

Time and manner of dealing with errors in a division. As has been mentioned (see p 343), the objection that a Member's vote in a division was contrary to the way in which he had given his voice in the House must be made before the declaration of the division numbers from the Chair.[3]

Publication of division lists. Division lists are circulated with the Votes and Proceedings of the House and are also printed in the Official Report.[4] If an error occurs in marking the name of a Member on the division list or in the printing, the error is corrected, upon application made at the Table of the House or to the Public Bill Office, by a memorandum published at the earliest opportunity at the end of a subsequent division list or daily part of the Official Report. A Member has been permitted on a subsequent day to request the correction of the accidental omission or inclusion of his name in the official division list.[5]

Pairing. A system, known as 'pairing', enables a Member to absent himself, and to agree with another Member that he also will be absent at the same time. By this mutual agreement, a vote is neutralized on each side of a question, and the actual size of the majority is not affected. The practice of pairing is not officially recognised in the procedures of the House; it is therefore conducted privately by individual Members, or arranged by the Whips of the respective parties.[6] The Speaker has ruled that agreements to pair are private arrangements between Members and in no sense matters in which either he or the House can intervene.[7]

CASTING VOTE OF SPEAKER

If the numbers in a division are equal, the Speaker, who otherwise does not vote, must give the casting vote.[8]

---

1 HC Deb (1977–78) 939, cc 1752–1753.
2 CJ (1947–48) 89.
3 HC Deb (1936–37) 326, c 2811.
4 The issue of the printed lists of the divisions began on Monday, 22 February 1836.
5 HC Deb (1947–48) 452, c 1141; ibid (1979–80) 975, c 423; ibid (1980–81) 997, c 924.
6 A motion condemning this practice, 6 March 1743, was negatived, on division CJ (1741–45) 602.
7 HC Deb (1953–54) 552, cc 1750–1752; ibid (1975–76) 912, c 769.
8 A casting vote was not given when, on correction of an error reported by the tellers on a day subsequent to that on which the division took place, the numbers were found to be equal, but the proceedings subsequent to the division were declared null and void (CJ (1938–39) 95, 96).
    When two casting votes had been given but it subsequently appeared that on both occasions a Member had been incorrectly counted with the noes and that there was accordingly a majority of one for the ayes the Speaker directed that the numbers should be corrected accordingly and the casting votes were declared null and void by notice in the Journal (HC Deb (1974) 877, cc 258–259; CJ (1974) 256).

In the performance of this duty to give a casting vote, the Speaker is at liberty to vote like any other Member, according to his conscience, without assigning a reason;[1] but, in order to avoid any imputation upon his impartiality, it is usual for him, when practicable, to vote in such a manner as not to make the decision of the House final, and to explain his reasons, which are entered in the Journal.[2]

Principles on which Speaker gives casting vote

The occasions on which a Speaker is required to give a casting vote are usually rare, and in seeking to deduce principles upon which a vote is given, the precedents of the last two centuries are relevant. These are recorded in the pages which follow. Although the decisions of successive Speakers have not invariably been consistent, three principles have emerged:

(1) that the Speaker should always vote for further discussion, where this is possible, eg Mr Speaker Addington's decision of 1796;[3]
(2) that, where no further discussion is possible, decisions should not be taken except by a majority, eg Mr Speaker Denison's decision of 1867;[4] and
(3) that a casting vote on an amendment to a bill should leave the bill in its existing form.

Mr Speaker Addington's decision of 1796

The first principle which guides a Speaker in giving his casting vote was explained by Mr Speaker Addington in 1796. On the third reading of the Succession Duty on Real Estates Bill, there having been a majority against 'now' reading the bill the third time, and also reading it that day three months, there was an equality of votes on a third question, that the bill be read the third time to-morrow, when the Speaker gave his casting vote with the ayes, saying 'that upon all occasions when the question was for or against giving to any measure a further opportunity of discussion, he should always vote for the further discussion, more especially when it had advanced so far as a third reading; and that when the question turned upon the measure itself—for instance, that a bill do or do not pass—he should then vote for or against it, according to his best judgment of its merits, assigning the reasons on which such judgment would be founded'.[5] Similarly, the voices being equal on 24 February 1797 on the question for going into committee on the Quakers Bill, Mr Speaker Addington gave his vote with the ayes.[6]

In the proceedings taken against Lord Melville, 8 April 1805, which resulted in his impeachment, the numbers were equal upon the previous question (moved in the form 'That the question be now put')—that question being the motion on which Lord Melville's impeachment was based. Mr Speaker Abbot gave his casting vote in favour of the previous question, on

1 CJ (1837–38) 587.
2 CJ (1837–38) 631; ibid (1843) 163; ibid (1847) 872; ibid (1851–52) 205; ibid (1887) 397; Parl Deb (1887) 317, c 2015; CJ (1897) 219; ibid (1905) 105; ibid (1979–80) 351, etc.
3 Colchester i, 57, CJ (1795–96) 764.
4 CJ (1867) 395; ibid (1975–76) 359.
5 Colchester i, 57, CJ (1795–96) 764.
6 Sidmouth i, 187, Colchester i, 85; CJ (1796–97) 335.

the ground that 'the original question was now fit to be submitted to the judgment of the House'.[1]

On 1 May 1828, the numbers being equal on an amendment proposed to the question that a bill be read a second time, Mr Speaker Manners-Sutton stated that as the Bill had been entertained by the House, although they were now undecided as to whether it should proceed or not, he considered that he should best discharge his duty by leaving the Bill open to further consideration and accordingly gave his vote against the amendment.[2]

The numbers being equal on the division on the third reading of the Tests Abolition (Oxford) Bill, 1 July 1864, Mr Speaker Denison said that he would afford the House another opportunity of deciding upon the merits of the bill, by declaring himself with the ayes; the subsequent question that the bill do pass was negatived by a majority of two.[3]

On 3 April 1905, the numbers being equal upon an instruction to the committee on the London County Council (Tramways) Bill to omit certain tramways, Mr Speaker Gully stated that in order that the matter might be considered by the committee and that the House might have a further opportunity of coming to a more decisive conclusion he gave his voice with the noes.[4]

On 12 April 1938, the numbers being equal upon the question of leave to bring in a bill under Standing Order No 19 (at that time No 10) to extend Palestinian nationality, Mr Speaker FitzRoy stated that he thought he ought to vote for the introduction of the bill so that the House could deal with it as the House thought fit.[5] On two similar occasions the Deputy Speaker has taken the same course.[6]

Mr Speaker Denison's decision of 1867

The next principle which guides the Speaker in giving his casting vote was explained by Mr Speaker Denison in 1867. The numbers being equal on a proposed resolution relating to Trinity College Dublin, Mr Speaker Denison stated 'that this was an abstract resolution, which, if agreed to by the House, would not even form the basis of legislation; but undoubtedly the principle involved in it was one of great importance; and, if affirmed by a majority of the House, it would have much force. It should, however, be affirmed by a majority of the House, and not merely by the casting vote of its presiding officer. For these reasons he declared himself with the noes'.[7]

The numbers being equal on the third reading of the Church Rates Abolition Bill, 19 June 1861, Mr Speaker Denison gave his casting vote against the bill stating that it appeared to him that a prevailing opinion existed in favour of a settlement of the question different, in some degree,

1 CJ (1805–06) 201, Colchester i, 548.
2 CJ (1828) 292.
3 CJ (1864) 388; Denison 167.
4 CJ (1905) 105. See also HC Deb (1975–76) 912, cc 761–762.
5 HC Deb (1937–38) 334, c 947.
6 (Licensing of Airports) HC Deb (1951–52) 502, c 2057; (Televising of Parliament) HC Deb (1979–80) 977, cc 1369–1371.
7 CJ (1867) 395. See also ibid (1975–76) 359. On two occasions Mr Speaker has voted for the postponement of a proceeding to a future day, ibid (1878) 423; ibid (1837) 397. For examples (1846 and earlier) of a casting vote being given on grounds of merits rather than procedure, see *Erskine May* (19th edn, 1976) p 405.

from that contained in the bill; and that he thought he should best discharge his duty by leaving to the future judgment of the House to decide what change in the law should be made, rather than take the responsibility for the change on his single vote.[1]

Mr Speaker Denison's decision of 1860

The third principle which guides the Speaker in giving his casting vote was explained by Mr Speaker Denison in 1860. The numbers being equal on an amendment proposed to a bill, Mr Speaker Denison stated that as the House was unable to form a judgment on the propriety of the proposed amendment, he should best perform his duty by leaving this bill in the form in which the Committee had reported it to the House; accordingly he gave his voice against the amendment.[2]

> The numbers being equal on an amendment proposed to be inserted in the Regency Bill, on consideration as amended, on 22 July 1910, the effect of which was to replace words which had been in the bill as introduced but had been left out in committee, the Speaker stated that he thought that he ought to vote for the bill in the form in which it was originally introduced into the House, and accordingly he gave his voice with the ayes.[3]
>
> On 12 March 1958 after the Government had been defeated on the question that a new clause be read a second time on consideration of the Maintenance Orders Bill, the numbers were equal on the question that the clause be added to the Bill; the Deputy Speaker stated that it was his duty to vote for the Bill as it emerged from the Committee, and accordingly he gave his casting vote against the question that the new clause should be added to the Bill.[4]
>
> The numbers being equal on an amendment proposed to be inserted in the Trade Union and Labour Relations Bill, on consideration as amended, Mr Speaker stated that he must vote for the Bill as it came from Committee and accordingly he cast his vote against the amendment[5] (but see also p 351).
>
> On 24 July 1862 the numbers being equal on a question for disagreeing to a Lords amendment, Mr Speaker Denison said he should support the Bill, as passed by the House of Commons. This precedent has been followed on other occasions.[6]

Casting vote of Chairman in Committee of whole House

When the voices are equal in a Committee of the whole House the Chairman, who does not otherwise vote, gives his casting vote, and in doing so is guided by the same principles as the Speaker in the House.[7] Thus, the numbers being equal upon the reduction of a vote, the Chairman declared

---

1 CJ (1861) 282; Denison 94. See also CJ (1821–22) 229.
2 CJ (1860) 235.
3 CJ (1910) 265; HC Deb (1910) 19, c 1717.
4 CJ (1957–58) 122; HC Deb (1957–58) 584, cc 521 and 555–557.
5 HC Deb (1974) 876, c 1691. See also ibid cc 1719–1720; ibid 877, cc 258–259.
6 CJ (1862–63) 365; Parl Deb (1862) 168, c 785; Denison 124; CJ (1975–76) 620, 628; ibid (1977–78) 463.
7 For cases in which the chairman has given his casting vote without assigning a reason, see CJ (1834) 430; ibid (1847–48) 661; ibid (1859) 333; ibid (1860) 256.

himself with the noes, as the committee would have an opportunity of voting upon any other reduction of the proposed vote,[1] and in committee on a bill, on an amendment to leave out words, the Chairman gave his casting vote for their retention in the bill, as the House would have another opportunity of considering the same question on consideration of the bill, as amended.[2]

VOTES ON MATTERS AFFECTED BY PERSONAL PECUNI-ARY INTEREST

No Member who has a direct pecuniary interest in a question is allowed to vote upon it; but, in order to operate as a disqualification, this interest must be immediate and personal, and not merely of a general or remote character. On 17 July 1811 the rule was explained thus by Mr Speaker Abbot: 'This interest must be a direct pecuniary interest, and separately belonging to the persons whose votes were questioned, and not in common with the rest of his Majesty's subjects, or on a matter of state policy'.[3] 'State policy' may be equated with 'public policy' and is not confined to public bills introduced by the Government, but is also the subject-matter of private Members' bills.[4]

Objections overruled by the Chair

On occasions when the objection of personal interest in a vote has been raised, which came obviously within the exemption from the application of the rule, defined by Mr Speaker Abbot, the Speaker or the Chairman has overruled the objection, or has decided that a motion to disallow the vote would be out of order.[5]

Personal interest in votes on questions of public policy

The only instance to be found in the Journals in which the votes of Members have been disallowed upon a question of public policy is the case of the votes

---

1 CJ (1868–69) 371; Parl Deb (1868–69) 198, c 950.
2 CJ (1876) 398; Parl Deb (1876) 231, c 772; HC Deb (1964–65) 713, cc 1867–1868.
3 Parl Deb (1811) 20, cc 1001–1012 (Votes of bank directors on the gold coin bill). See also HC Deb (1932) 261, c 193 (Order made under the Abnormal Importations (Customs Duties) Act 1931); ibid (1946–47) 431, cc 1614–1615 (Transport Bill). On 20 July 1984 the Speaker ruled that the question of the Lord Chancellor's salary was a matter of public policy upon which a Member who was his son was entitled to vote (HC Deb (1983–84) 64, cc 669–70).
4 See the Speaker's statement HC Deb (1983–84) 50, c 679.
5 The following are examples of Speaker's rulings to this effect: Parl Deb (1889) 334, c 732 (minister voting against reduction of his official salary); ibid (1898) 61, c 826 (owners of land in Ireland on clause providing for payment out of public money of landlord's share of rates, Local Government (Ireland) Bill); HC Deb (1917) 92, c 2429 (Members who were land-owners or farmers, Corn Production Bill); ibid (1953–54) 522, c 206 (Members having interest in advertising and the manufacture of wireless apparatus, on a motion to approve the government's policy on television development).
   Chairmen's rulings: Parl Deb (1871) 206, c 1742 (votes of officers on full pay in committee on Army Regulation Bill on clause giving compensation to officers holding saleable commissions); ibid (1890) 345, c 1232; ibid (1904) 137, c 910, 1305 (votes of Members interested in licensed property on proposals for giving compensation for extinction of licences); ibid (1906) 156, c 505 (votes of Members who were solicitors on amendment to clause of Justices of the Peace (No 2) Bill making solicitors eligible to the commission of the peace); HC Deb (1911) 29, c 1679 (voting of salaries of Members); ibid (1912–13) 48, c 609, 745 (vote of Member, professionally retained by a private client in an inquiry, on the vote which included a provision for the cost of the inquiry); ibid (1926) 197, c 554. St Co Deb (1951–52), Co C 2214–2220 (vote of Member with brewing interest).

of three Members given in session 1892 in favour of the grant in aid of a preliminary survey for a railway from the coast to Lake Victoria Nyanza, which had been undertaken on behalf of the Government by the British East Africa Company, of which two of the Members in question were directors and shareholders and the third was a shareholder.[1]

On 1 June 1797, however, Mr Manning submitted to the Speaker whether he might vote, consistently with the rules of the House, upon the proposition of Mr Pitt for granting compensation to the subscribers to the Loyalty Loan, he being himself a subscriber. The Speaker explained generally the rule of the House and Mr Manning declined to vote.[2] After the division the votes of two other Members were objected to as being subscribers: but one stated that he had parted with his subscription, and the other that he had determined not to derive any advantage to himself; upon which questions for disallowing their votes were negatived.[3]

On 3 June 1824, a division took place on a 'Bill for repealing so much of an Act 6 Geo. I as restrains any other corporations than those in the Act named, and any societies or partnerships, from effecting marine insurances, and lending money on bottomry'. An entry in the Journal in the form of a memorandum states that an objection was made on the numbers declared by the tellers, that certain Members who voted with the ayes were personally interested in the passing of the bill, as being concerned in the Alliance Insurance Company; but it was decided that they were not so interested as to preclude their voting for the repeal of a public act.[4]

On 10 July 1844, on the question for hearing counsel against a bill for suspending certain actions for penalties under the gaming laws, objections were taken to the votes of Members who were defendants, but one stated that it was not his intention to take advantage of the provisions of the bill and plead the same in bar of such action, and the other that he had not been served with any process. Motions for disallowing their votes were, therefore, withdrawn.[5]

On 11 July 1844 the vote of a Member upon the second reading of a public bill relating to railways was objected to upon the ground that he had a direct pecuniary interest as the proprietor of railroad shares, but a motion for disallowing his vote was withdrawn.[6]

On 25 May 1982, in the Standing Committee on the Finance Bill, the votes of four Members in favour of a clause relating to retirement annuity relief for Lloyds underwriters, were objected to on the ground that they were members of Lloyds. A motion was made that their votes be disallowed but, after explanations were given by two of the Members, the motion was withdrawn.[7]

---

1 CJ (1892) 98. See also Report of Select Committee on Members of Parliament (Personal Interest), HC 274 (1896).
2 Parl Hist (1797–98) 33, c 791. For a general ruling, see HC Deb (1932) 261, c 192; ibid (1936–37) 323, c 363.
3 CJ (1796–97) 632.
4 CJ (1824) 455.
5 CJ (1844) 486.
6 CJ (1844) 491.
7 Parl Deb Stg Co A (1981–82) cc 388–395.

On 14 January 1986 the Speaker ruled that members of Lloyds could vote on an amendment seeking to bring Lloyds within the terms of the Financial Services Bill, since the bill itself was a matter of public policy and any amendment designed to extend its scope was thus also a matter of public policy.[1]

Personal interest in votes on private bills

The votes of Members, who were subscribers to undertakings proposed to be sanctioned by a private bill,[2] or who were otherwise interested in a private bill, have frequently been disallowed.

In 1800 the votes of three Members were disallowed, as having a direct interest in a bill for incorporating a company for the manufacture of flour, wheat and bread.[3] On 20 May 1825 notice was taken that a Member, who had voted with the ayes on the report of the Leith Docks Bill, had a direct pecuniary interest in passing the bill: he was heard in his place and stated that on that account he had not voted in the committee on the bill, and that he had voted, in this instance, through inadvertence. His vote was ordered to be disallowed.[4] Motions to disallow the votes of shareholders in the company which was promoting the bill on which the division was taken, have been negatived.[5]

On the second reading of the Birmingham and Gloucester Railway Bill, 15 May 1845, objection was taken to one of the tellers for the noes, as being a landholder whose property would be injured by the proposed line; while on the second reading of the London and North Western Railway Bill, 14 April 1896, objection was taken to the vote of a Member on the ground that he was a director of the company. In both cases the motion for disallowing the vote was withdrawn.[6]

On 15 July 1872 objection was made to two of the tellers in a division, which had been taken on 18 June against the Birmingham Sewerage Bill, on the ground of personal pecuniary interest; but the Speaker stated that they had no such pecuniary interest in the bill as would disqualify them from voting against it.[7]

Personal interest in votes on competing bills

The extent to which the rule about personal interest applies to a vote given by a Member against a private bill, which would create a project intended to compete with an undertaking in which he has a pecuniary interest, is as yet undecided. As the Speaker stated on 12 May 1885, there is no rule of the House on the subject. He recommended that each Member should be guided by his own feelings in the matter and should vote, or abstain from voting, as he thought fit; though he added that Members should be aware

---

1 HC Deb (1985–86) 89, c 1013.
2 CJ (1825–26) 110; ibid (1836) 271.
3 Parl Hist (1800–01) 35, c 463, Perceval i, 76.
4 CJ (1825–26) 443; see also ibid (1825–26) 110; ibid (1836) 271.
5 CJ (1883) 189; ibid (1884) 103.
6 CJ (1845) 436; ibid (1896) 143.
7 Parl Deb (1872) 212, c 1136.

that they ran the risk of having their votes disallowed by the subsequent action of the House.[1]

On 22 February 1825 a Member voted against a bill establishing the London and Westminster Oil Gas Company and notice was taken that he was a proprietor in the Imperial Gas Light and Coke Company, and thereby had a pecuniary interest in opposing the bill. A motion was made that his vote be disallowed: but, after he had been heard in his place, it was withdrawn.[2]

On 16 June 1846 objection was taken to the vote of a Member who had voted with the noes, because, as director and shareholder in the Caledonian Railway Company, he had a direct pecuniary interest in the rejection of the Glasgow, Dumfries and Carlisle Railway Bill. The Member stated that the sole direct interest that he had in the Caledonian Railway was as holder of twenty shares to qualify him to be a director in that undertaking; and that he voted against the bill, conceiving the proposed railway to be in direct competition with the Caledonian Railway, as decided by the legislature in the last session. A question for disallowing his vote on the ground of direct pecuniary interest was negatived.[3]

On 9 March 1886 objection was taken to the votes of two Members given in favour of committing the Manchester Ship Canal Bill to a select committee on the ground that, as directors of the London and North Western Railway Company, the receipts and dividends of which might be affected by the construction of the canal, they were pecuniarily interested in the matter. The motion for disallowing their votes was negatived.[4]

On 24 March 1981 a Member raised a point of order on whether the 53 Members who were also members of Lloyds were permitted to vote on the Lloyds Bill. The Member who was steering the Bill through the House advised Members who were also members of Lloyds to refrain from voting. In the division on second reading only two members of Lloyds were recorded as voting or telling. Their votes were not challenged.[5]

Procedural Motions: no interest involved

As no financial interest is involved in procedural motions such as closure, Members have been allowed to vote for the closure on bills in which they may have a financial interest.[6]

Time and manner for making motions to disallow votes

An objection to a vote on the ground of personal interest can only be raised on a substantive motion; it cannot be brought forward as a point of order.[7] The motion must be made as soon as the division is completed and cannot be

1 Parl Deb (1884–85) 298, c 342.
2 CJ (1825–26) 110.
3 CJ (1846–47) 873.
4 CJ (1886) 83.
5 HC Deb (1980–81) 1, cc 811–812, 893–894.
6 HC Deb (1980–81) 1, c 859.
7 Parl Deb (1884) 285, c 1222; ibid (1892) 2, c 90; HC Deb (1912–13) 48, c 607. But see Parl Deb (1872) 212, cc 1134–1137; CJ (1872) 276. A motion for a committee to inquire into the legality of votes given in a division has also been held to be out of order, Parl Deb (1901) 92, c 419.

heard at a later stage.[1] Such an objection on the same ground against a vote in committee of the whole House must be determined by the committee on a motion made in committee that the vote be disallowed,[2] and a motion to report progress, in order to bring such an objection before the House, has not been permitted.[3] The Chair then rules on whether the motion objecting to a vote is in order, and if the motion is allowed the Member whose vote is under consideration is heard in his place, and then withdraws immediately, before the question founded on the objection has been proposed.[4]

Personal interest in votes in private bill committees

Under Standing Order 120 relating to Private Business, Members locally or personally interested are excluded from committees on opposed private bills; Standing Order 133 provides that no such Member shall be entitled to vote in committees on unopposed bills. A member of a committee on an opposed private bill, or group of bills, will be discharged from further attendance, if it is discovered, after his appointment, that he has a direct pecuniary interest in one or more of the bills[5] (see also p 892). Recent practice has established that the holding by a member of the Committee of some debenture or ordinary stock on a railway company petitioning against a private bill does not constitute a direct pecuniary interest.[6]

Personal interest other than pecuniary

Disallowance of a vote on the score of personal interest is restricted to cases of pecuniary interest and has not been extended to those occasions when the dictates of self-respect and of respect due to the House might demand that a Member should refrain from taking part in a division.[7]

---

1 HC Deb (1912–13) 48, c 747; ibid (1926) 191, c 1937.
2 HC Deb (1912–13) 48, cc 607, 609, 745–747.
3 Parl Deb (1890) 345, cc 1232–1235. Owing to the interruption of business at ten minutes to seven o'clock, a motion, that certain votes given in the Committee of Supply on 4 March 1892 be disallowed, was made in the committee on 11 March. On 14 August 1911, being the last allotted day for Committee of Supply, objection was taken to a Member's vote after ten o'clock notwithstanding the Standing Order, and the Chairman ruled upon the objection; CJ (1892) 98; HC Deb (1911) 29, c 1679.
4 CJ (1825–26) 110; ibid (1836) 271. See also CJ (1883) 189; ibid (1886) 83.
5 Special Report from Committee on Group A of Private Bills relative to Kent Electric Power Bill, 28 May 1941.
6 Before 1844 the contrary practice obtained, although it was not brought directly under the notice of the House until 21 June 1844, when the Middle Level Drainage Bill Committee instructed their chairman to report that a Member 'had received an intimation that he ought not to vote on questions arising thereon, by reason of his interest in the said bill'; and desired the decision of the House upon the following question: 'Whether a Member, having property within the limits of an improvement bill, which property may be affected by the passing of the bill, has such an interest as disqualifies him from voting thereon'. The reply the House made to the application from the committee was an instruction thereto, 'That the rule of this House relating to the vote, upon any question in the House, of a Member having an interest in the matter upon which the vote is given, applies likewise to any vote of a Member so interested, in a committee'. Parl Deb (1844) 76, c 16.
7 See Statement by the Speaker, 18 March 1864, Parl Deb (1864) 174, c 340. For cases of Members who voted against the motion for their suspension, see Mr Bradlaugh's votes, 22 February 1882, CJ (1882) 61; 11 February 1884, ibid (1884) 41. On the first occasion, the Speaker stated that it was for the House to consider what should be done with regard to Mr Bradlaugh's vote; on the second occasion, his vote was disallowed, because he was not a Member of the House. See also division lists, sess. 1887, Nos 91, 481, 483; sess. 1890, No 16. For the usage regarding the vote of rival candidates for the Speakership, see p 227.

Member interested may propose motion and amendment

Although a Member with a pecuniary interest may be disqualified from voting, he is not restrained by any existing rule of the House from proposing a motion or amendment. (For advocacy by Members of matters in which they have been concerned, see pp 120–121).

On 26 July 1859 Mr Whalley moved an amendment to a clause added by the Lords to a railway bill, in which he admitted that he was personally interested. In the debate exception was taken to such an amendment having been proposed by a Member with a pecuniary interest. But the Speaker ruled that, though it was a well-known rule of the House that a Member under such circumstances could not be permitted to vote, and though the course adopted was certainly most unusual, there was no rule by which the right of a Member to make a motion was restrained, and he had been given to understand that Mr Whalley did not intend to vote.[1]

On 15 June 1904 Mr Kerr formally moved the committal to a joint committee of the Leith Corporation Tramways Order Confirmation Bill without objection being taken to his action, although his personal interest in the bill was stated in the House. He did not vote in the subsequent division.[2]

Objections that a Member alleged to be personally interested could not give notice of opposition to a bill, and that a Member, who moved an instruction to a committee on a private bill, was a member of a corporation which petitioned against the bill, were overruled by the Speaker.[3]

ORDERS AND RESOLUTIONS

Every question, when agreed to, becomes either an order or a resolution of the House. By its orders the House directs its committees, its Members, its officers, the order of its own proceedings and the acts of all persons whom they concern; by its resolutions the House declares its own opinions and purposes.

Orders and resolutions agreed to *nemine contradicente*

Orders and resolutions are sometimes declared to have been agreed to *nemine contradicente*. Entries to this effect are made in the case of addresses of congratulation or condolence to the reigning Sovereign[4] and of messages of a similar character to other members of the royal family.[5] They have also been used for resolutions condemning a breach of privilege and the consequential order for the attendance of the offenders.[6] Votes of thanks,[7] an address for a monument to a deceased public servant,[8] a resolution of the

1 Parl Deb (1859) 155, c 459. See also HC Deb (1926) 199, c 1172.
2 Parl Deb (1904) 136, c 212.
3 Parl Deb (1881) 263, c 1477; ibid (1884) 287, c 875.
4 CJ (1901) 6; ibid (1963–64) 150; ibid (1964–65) 200; ibid (1981–82) 426.
5 CJ (1837) 493; ibid (1910) 153; ibid (1951–52) 93; HC Deb (1979–80) 789, cc 1757–1766.
6 CJ (1901) 414, 418, etc.
7 CJ (1856) 186; ibid (1919) 285, 286; ibid (1963–64) 329; ibid (1979–80) 156, etc.
8 CJ (1920) 378, etc.

House,[1] the grant of a vote of credit[2] and the third reading of a bill have been similarly recorded.[3] The addition of these words is made on the direction of the Speaker or chairman, who does not direct their use if a single dissentient voice is raised.[4]

5. REVERSAL OF DECISIONS BY DISCHARGE, REPEAL, ANNULMENT AND RESCISSION

The present procedures by which the House reverses its previously expressed opinions, directions or proceedings vary, according to the object to be attained. The forms of procedure are: discharge of an order; repeal of a standing order; an order that proceedings be null and void; and rescission of a resolution.

DISCHARGE OF AN ORDER

The discharge of an order is the indispensable preliminary to the making of a different order on the same subject (see also p 361). If it is wished for any reason to withdraw a bill from the consideration of the House, it is necessary first to discharge the order for the current stage of the bill.[5] Similarly, before a paper presented to the House can be withdrawn, the order that the paper do lie upon the Table must first be discharged.[6]

On occasions an order may be discharged without further action being taken, for example an order for printing a paper or for a return.[7] An Order of 19 April 1983 for the issue of a writ for a by-election caused by the death of a Member was discharged on 10 May as a dissolution had subsequently been announced which would have overtaken the by-election.[8] Part of an order has also been discharged.[9] A motion that an order be discharged has been made so as to afford an opportunity for discussion of the order, which had previously been agreed to without debate; after discussion the motion for discharge was withdrawn.[10]

Addresses to the Crown. There is a difficulty in discharging an order for an address to the Crown, after it has been presented to the Sovereign; a second address qualifying the opinions embodied in the first address is agreed to.[11]

REPEAL OF A STANDING ORDER

The House regularly repeals certain of its standing orders when it has resolved to alter its own procedures, often following a recommendation of a

---

1 CJ (1921) 390; ibid (1966–67) 468, etc; in 1905 a resolution was agreed to *nemine contra-dicente* after an amendment had been negatived, ibid (1905) 95.
2 CJ (1914) 426.
3 CJ (1688–93) 280; ibid (1857) 110; ibid (1884) 321.
4 Parl Deb (1884) 289, c 1561; ibid (1907) 178, c 463.
5 Eg CJ (1921) 191; ibid (1959–60) 161; ibid (1966–67) 371, 503; ibid (1980–81) 18 March 1981.
6 Eg CJ (1966–67) 340; ibid (1980–81) 20 November 1980, etc. In this case discharge is effected by notice in the Appendix to the Journal and no motion is moved in the House.
7 CJ (1921) 96; ibid (1922) 147; ibid (1926) 418; ibid (1962–63) 261.
8 HC Deb (1982–83) 42, c 727; CJ (1982–83) 365.
9 CJ (1909) 211; ibid (1920) 58.
10 HC Deb (1967–68) 763, c 921.
11 CJ (1850) 383, 509; Parl Deb (1850) 111, c 1404; CJ (1856) 272, 289, 298.

Select Committee on Procedure. Such repeals are normally made as part of an order creating a new standing order to embody the new procedure.[1]

PROCEEDINGS NULL AND VOID

An order declaring proceedings to be null and void is employed where there has been some form of irregularity in procedure.[2] It is used either where there is no resolution which can be rescinded or order which can be discharged,[3] or where the *status quo ante* cannot be restored merely by rescinding the resolution or discharging the order, as where a resolution is irregularly reported from a committee. If, however, the *status quo* could be restored merely by discharging an order, there would be no question of annulling and voiding the proceedings.

> On 11 July 1974 divisions took place on two amendments to a bill on consideration. The numbers of ayes and noes were equal in each case, and Mr Speaker and Mr Deputy Speaker respectively gave their casting votes against the amendments. On 16 July the House was acquainted that as the result of an irregularity a Member had been incorrectly recorded as voting with the noes. The Speaker directed that the numbers should be corrected accordingly and it therefore appeared that there had been a majority for each amendment. The proceedings relating to the Speaker's and the Deputy Speaker's casting votes were declared null and void by notice in the Journal, no motion being made in the House. The proceedings in relation to the third reading of the bill were ordered to be null and void on a motion moved in the House without notice. It was further ordered that a message should be sent to the Lords requesting them to return the bill (which had been sent to them on 11 July), and that when the bill had been returned by the Lords and corrected, it should be read the third time.[4] On Friday 31 January 1986, the Protection of Military Remains Bill passed through all stages up to and including its third reading without debate. It was immediately discovered that no money resolution had been passed after second reading to cover two italicized clauses contained in the Bill. A Motion was tabled forthwith to nullify the irregular proceedings (ie Committee and third reading) which was passed without objection on the next sitting day. It was held that since the motion to nullify the proceedings had been tabled immediately, the Bill should not be sent to the Lords and there was therefore no requirement to send a message requesting its return.[5]

RESCISSION OF RESOLUTIONS

There is nothing in the practice of the House to prevent the rescission of a resolution or discharge of an order of a previous session, where such is held to be of continuing force and validity, or of a standing order.

1 Eg CJ (1970–71) 308; ibid (1971–72) 29 and 31; ibid (1979–80) 79; ibid (1982–83) 291–292.
2 CJ (1956–57) 201; ibid (1962–63) 196, etc.
3 CJ (1938–39) 95, 96, etc.
4 CJ (1974) 245, 256, 257; HC Deb (1974) 877, cc 248–265.
5 CJ (1985–86) 152, 155, 158 and 166.

Technically, indeed, the rescinding of a vote is a new question, the form being to read the resolution of the House and to move that it be rescinded[1] and thus the question which has been agreed to is not again offered, although its effect is annulled.

Restrictions on power of rescission

When Parliament was regarded as a court of law rather than a legislative body, the rescission of a resolution or discharge of an order of the current session was very difficult. The rule was urged (2 April 1604), 'That a question, being once made and carried in the affirmative or negative, cannot be questioned again, but must stand as a judgment of the House'.[2] Also, by a rule formerly in force, a second bill, at variance with the provisions of a bill passed during the same session, could not be introduced (see pp 468–469). Further rescission is opposed to the spirit of the existing rule that no question shall be offered which is substantially the same as one on which judgment has been expressed during the current session (see pp 326–327). But the practical inconvenience of a rigid rule, especially where the House as a whole wishes to change its opinion, has proved too great for a body confronted with the ever-changing problems of government; and the rule prohibiting reconsideration of a decided question has come to be interpreted strictly so as not to prevent open rescission when it is decided that that is desirable.

The power of rescission has only been exercised in the case of a resolution resulting from a substantive motion, and even then sparingly.[3] It cannot be exercised merely to override a vote of the House, such as a negative vote. Proposing a negatived question a second time for the decision of the House, would be, as stated earlier, contrary to the established practice of Parliament. Sufficient variation would have to be made, not only from the form but also from the substance of the rejected question, to make the second question a new question.

Similarly the House of Commons has shown strong objection to rescinding a vote by which the House has made an amendment to a resolution.[4]

Notice necessary to rescind a resolution

Notice is required of a motion to rescind a resolution,[5] or to expunge or alter an entry in the Votes and Proceedings or the Journal,[6] and in no circum-

---

1 CJ (1867–68) 132, 145; see also ibid (1882) 346.
2 CJ (1547–1628) 162.
3 CJ (1834) 59; ibid (1864–65) 463; ibid (1867–68) 145. See also Colchester ii, 9, 12.
4 On 11 November 1912 an amendment was made to a resolution authorizing the financial provisions embodied in a bill. Subsequently the Government desired to rescind this amendment before the consideration of the resolution, as amended, was resumed. Objection was taken to this, but the Speaker stated that the House could not reconsider its decision on the further consideration of the resolution. An amendment was proposed to the motion for rescission affirming the principle that a question should not be again proposed or questioned in the same session. The Speaker had to adjourn the House in consequence of grave disorder arising during debate on the amendment. On the following day, the amendment was not proceeded with. The resolution, as amended, was subsequently disagreed to and a new resolution differing from the original resolution was proposed in a committee of the whole House and agreed to, and the necessary amendments were made in due course. CJ (1912–13) 404, 408, 409, 410, 414, 416; HC Deb (1912) 43, cc 1993, 2090; ibid 44, cc 36, 121. See also ibid (1918) 105, c 1956.
5 Parl Deb (1887) 313, c 1124.
6 Parl Deb (1882) 271, c 1268; ibid (1884–85) 294, c 1423; HC Deb (1909) 7, c 2303.

stances may the House rescind a resolution during the sitting in which the resolution was agreed to.[1] However, notice is not required of motions brought forward as matters of privilege.[2]

Modification of resolution

A motion modifying a resolution of the same session, by omitting or altering subsidiary portions of it, is in order so long as no attempt is made to reverse the substance of the motion. A motion reversing the effect of a previous decision on the ground of its inapplicability to changed circumstances has been allowed.

> Thus, a resolution having been agreed to which condemned an official appointment, the House by a subsequent resolution withdrew the censure which the previous resolution had conveyed.[3] Under the Government of India Act 1919, section 44, rules might be laid before both Houses by direction of the Secretary of State for India, and in that case the rules could not be made unless they had been approved by both Houses, either without modification or only with modifications and additions to which both Houses agreed. In session 1920 the House of Lords approved of the rules, as laid, but the approval of the House of Commons was given subject to certain modifications. The approval of the House of Lords was not rescinded, but that House passed a resolution agreeing to the modifications, subject to which the draft rules had been approved by the House of Commons, and approving the draft rules as so modified.[4] A similar course was followed in the case of the London and Home Counties Electricity District Order 1925.[5] The effect of a resolution, by which the House determined that no legislation should be entertained, during the session, regarding traffic in intoxicating liquor, until provisions dealing with that subject had been placed before the House by the Government, was modified by a subsequent resolution which declared that, as the House was made aware that the Government did not intend to undertake legislation regarding the liquor traffic, the House was free to deal therewith.[6]

REVERSAL OF DECISION

Attempts to reverse or override resolutions or orders by proposing new questions which seek to nullify previous decisions may, without actually proposing the same question, amount to an indirect form of rescission. The

1 Parl Deb (1855) 138, c 1307.
2 Notice was not required of a motion which affected the seat of a Member, Parl Deb (1880) 253, c 644. On 27 June 1884 a motion to omit '*Nem. Con.*' (see pp 359–360) from the entry in the Votes of the third reading of the Representation of the People Bill was brought forward without notice as privilege, CJ (1884) 324. On 16 July 1974 a motion to declare certain proceedings null and void was moved without notice as a matter of privilege, HC Deb (1974) 877, c 259.
3 CJ (1877) 345, 367.
4 LJ (1920) 319, 343; CJ (1920) 316; HL Deb (1920) 41, c 542.
5 LJ (1924–25) 287, 327; CJ (1924–25) 349; HL Deb (1924–25) 62, c 505.
6 CJ (1890) 214, 257; Parl Deb (1890) 343, c 1170.

rejection of a bill by a decision on a reasoned amendment directed against certain of its provisions has been held to prevent the insertion in another bill of the provisions objected to by the reasoned amendment, even though the words of the reasoned amendment had not been added to the question on the rejected bill,[1] but after a reasoned amendment on second reading had been negatived, an instruction on similar lines was allowed.[2]

The reason why motions for open rescission are so rare and the rules of procedure carefully guard against the indirect rescission of votes, is that both Houses instinctively realise that parliamentary government requires the majority to abide by a decision regularly come to, however unexpected, and that it is unfair to resort to methods, whether direct or indirect, to reverse such a decision.[3] The practice, resulting from this feeling, is essentially a safeguard for the rights of the minority, and a contrary practice is not normally resorted to, unless in the circumstances of a particular case those rights are in no way threatened.

1 CJ (1924) 128–129; HC Deb (1924) 173, c 67.
2 HC Deb (1925) 182, c 517.
3 HC Deb (1975–76) 905, cc 1133–1134.

CHAPTER 18

Maintenance of order during debate in the House of Commons

This chapter describes the rules, based upon ancient practice, somewhat modified by standing orders, which lay down a standard of correct behaviour for Members of the House of Commons both in speaking and in listening to the speeches of other Members, and which check and punish lapses from this standard. The chapter is divided into the following sections:

(1) Rules governing the manner and time of speaking.
(2) Rules governing the contents of speeches.
(3) Rules of behaviour for Members not speaking.
(4) Powers of the Chair to enforce order.

There is some similarity between the content of the first two sections of this chapter and that of the previous chapter on 'The Process of Debate', but in general the contents are fairly clearly distinguished, as the previous chapter deals with procedures through which a decision of the House may be obtained, while this chapter is concerned principally with the rules which govern the orderliness of parliamentary behaviour during debate.

1. RULES GOVERNING THE MANNER AND TIME OF SPEAKING

MANNER OF SPEAKING

A Member must address the Speaker and not direct his speech to the House or to any party on either side of the House.

Speeches must be made in English,[1] but quotation in another language has been allowed on occasion, though a translation should be provided.[2]

Reading speeches

A Member is not permitted to read his speech,[3] but he may refresh his memory by reference to notes. A Member may read extracts from documents,[4] but such extracts and quotations should be reasonably short.[5] The

---

1 Parl Deb (1901) 89, c 546; HC Deb (1957–58) 583, c 1146; ibid (1981–82) 18, c 290.
2 HC Deb (1957–58) 583, c 1146; ibid (1977–78) 945, cc 692–693; ibid (1979–80) 979, c 136; ibid (1987–88) 119, c 400.
3 CJ (1547–1628) 272, 494; Parl Deb (1806) 7, c 208; ibid (1833) 17, c 1281; ibid (1846) 83, c 1169; ibid (1875) 223, c 178; ibid (1877) 235, c 773; ibid (1903) 122, c 554; ibid (1908) 192, c 742; HC Deb (1916) 80, c 391; ibid (1981–82) 18, c 754; ibid (1983–84) 64, c 178.
4 Parl Deb (1873) 217, c 841; HC Deb (1953–54) 523, cc 1582–1586.
5 HC Deb (1981–82) 17, c 376.

purpose of this rule is to maintain the cut and thrust[1] of debate, which depends upon successive speakers meeting in their speeches to some extent the arguments of earlier speeches; debate is more than a series of set speeches prepared beforehand without reference to each other. For the same reason the Speaker has urged Members to remain in their places after they have spoken and to return to the House for the concluding speeches of a debate.[2]

Unless appealed to, the Chair does not normally intervene to enforce the rule against reading a speech; and, unless there is good ground in the interests of the debate for intervening, the matter is usually passed off with a remark to the effect that the notes used by the honourable Member appear to be unusually full, or that the honourable Member has provided himself with rather copious notes.[3]

The rule against reading speeches is, in any case, relaxed for opening speeches or whenever there is special reason for precision, as in important ministerial statements, notably on foreign affairs, in matters involving agreements with outside bodies or in highly technical bills. Even at a later stage of a debate, prepared statements on such subjects may be read without objection being taken, though they should not constitute an entire speech. The reading of speeches is even less suited to a committee than to the House itself.

Place of speaking

Members must speak standing and uncovered.[4] In cases of sickness or infirmity, however, speaking while seated may be allowed, at the suggestion of a Member and with the general acquiescence of the House.[5] A Minister answering a series of questions has been permitted, on grounds of infirmity, to remain leaning on the dispatch box without resuming his seat while questions were being asked.[6] Only when a question of order arises during a division may a Member speak seated and covered.[7]

A Member may speak from the side galleries appropriated to Members (though this is inconvenient and rarely resorted to), but he will not be called by the Chair to speak from a gallery unless there is no room on the floor of the House on the side on which he normally sits.[8] A Member may not speak when standing before the Table[9] or in the aisle,[10] or from below the bar.[11] The Chair has declined to intervene when a 'back bench' Member chose to

1 See Mr Speaker's remarks, HC Deb (1935–36) 307, c 7.
2 HC Deb (1981–82) 18, c 754.
3 HC Deb (1935–36) 307, c 385; ibid (1937–38) 330, c 1494 etc.
4 Lady Members are permitted to wear hats when speaking.
5 Mr Wynn, Parl Deb (1843) 67, c 658; HC Deb (1919) 112, c 456; ibid (1969–70) 799, c 1681. Question proposed by the Speaker sitting owing to illness, CJ (1866) 197.
6 HC Deb (1952–53) 510, c 1999; ibid (1958–59) 596, c 1158.
7 Parl Deb (1883) 278, c 854; ibid (1886) 308, c 1164; ibid (1904) 135, c 1024; ibid (1945–46) 416, c 343. See also 2nd Report from the Sessional Committee on Procedure, HC 152 (1976–77), HC Deb (1979–80) 972, c 1617 and ibid (1983–84) 64, cc 1349, 1353.
8 HC Deb (1920) 128, c 31, 41; ibid (1967–68) 760, c 1820; ibid (1981–82) 13, cc 165, 619.
9 HC Deb (1968–69) 765, c 893.
10 HC Deb (1975–76) 918, c 1101.
11 Parl Deb (1879) 246, c 1362; HC Deb (1919) 112, c 1962; ibid (1919) 116, c 105; ibid (1960–61) 642, c 324.

speak at a dispatch box.[1] A Member should not move his place while speaking.[2] For a Member to place his foot on the seat while speaking has been described by the Chair as 'ungainly'.[3]

Time of speaking

Debate arises when a question has been proposed by the Speaker and before it has been fully put. No Member may speak to any question after the same has been fully put by the Speaker; and a question is fully put when he has taken the voices both of the ayes and of the noes.[4] Mr Speaker has, however, called Members to speak despite having fully put the question, after points of order revealed that some Members had not heard the motion being made or the question being put.[5]

Precedence in speaking

When two or more Members rise to speak the Speaker has complete discretion over whom to call[6] though he will generally call alternately backbench Members from either side of the House (or, when the subject of debate is not a matter of party politics, from those whom he adjudges to be supporters or opponents of the question). Although it is customary for a Privy Councillor to be called when he rises, this is not a matter of right,[7] and of recent years the Chair has declined to call two consecutive Privy Councillors from the same side of the House.[8] Members of the front benches are normally given precedence over those on the backbenches.[9]

It is often the practice for Members who wish to speak in a particular debate to submit their names in advance to the Speaker. This practice, while not fettering the discretion of the Speaker, affords to Members who avail themselves of it a better opportunity of 'catching the Speaker's eye', and to the Speaker a means of distributing the available time as equitably as possible between the various sections of opinion[10] and assists him in deciding whether to impose a time-limit on speeches (see pp 371–372). However, the Speaker has strongly deprecated the practice of submitting in advance requests to be called to ask supplementary questions.[11]

In debates on bills and motions to which a series of amendments stands upon the paper, Members are called in the order in which their amendments stand (see p 338). But a Member who, having been called by the Speaker, is

---

1 HC Deb (1971–72) 831, c 377.
2 HC Deb (1942–43) 391, cc 2001–2002; ibid (1983–84) 57, c 1172; ibid (1984–85) 79, c 1257.
3 HC Deb (1953–54) 520, c 2113.
4 17 May 1606, 'Any man may speak after the affirmative question and before the negative:' CJ (1547–1628) 310; Parl Deb (1819) 40, c 79, Colchester iii, 74; HC Deb (1913) 50, cc 1673, 1859; ibid (1922) 152, c 111; ibid (1979–80) 983, cc 645–646.
5 HC Deb (1976–77) 930, cc 1375–1377; ibid (1977–78) 951, cc 524–525.
6 HC Deb (1976–77) 928, c 1463–1464; ibid (1980–81) 7, c 167.
7 HC Deb (1954–55) 536, c 2106; see also Report of Select Committee on Procedure, HC 108 (1958–59), para 29.
8 HC Deb (1978–79) 972, c 1264; ibid (1979–80) 982, c 271.
9 HC Deb (1967–68) 770, c 1245.
10 See Speaker's remarks, HC Deb (1935–36) 307, c 301; ibid (1980–81) 7, c 168. For earlier observations about a 'Speaker's List' see *Erskine May* (19th edn, 1976) p 416.
11 HC Deb (1977–78) 945, c 662.

'in possession of the House' cannot be interrupted by a Member who desires to gain priority in moving an amendment or to move a dilatory motion.[1]

New Members. A new Member, who has not previously spoken, is generally called before other Members rising at the same time to make his 'maiden' speech; but this privilege is not conceded unless claimed within the Parliament to which the Member was first returned.[2] A Member subsequently returned for a different constituency cannot claim the privilege for a second time.[3]

Precedence on resuming an adjourned debate

When a debate has been adjourned while a Member was speaking, as a consequence of the interruption of business prescribed by the standing orders, he is entitled, on the next occasion, to resume the adjourned debate, and continue his speech.[4]

Similarly when a debate has been adjourned on motion, the Member who moved its adjournment is, by courtesy, entitled to speak first on the resumption of the debate, though he must rise in his place at that time to avail himself of that entitlement, and unless he rises it is not the duty of the Chair to call him.[5] If however he does not rise, he is not debarred from taking part later in the debate.[6] A Member who moves the adjournment in order to resume his speech on the main question on a future day must, to gain this entitlement, confine himself to that formal motion.[7] A Member who has moved a motion for the adjournment of a debate, which has been negatived, is not entitled to speak again to the main question;[8] and the Member whose subsequent motion for adjournment has been agreed to is, therefore, entitled to be called upon on resuming the debate.[9] If a motion for adjournment to secure the power of first speech on the resumption of the debate is discussed until the business of the House is interrupted and adjourned pursuant to the standing orders, the mover of the motion, although his motion has lapsed (see p 312), does not on that account lose the entitlement which he sought by making the motion for adjournment.[10] In practice, as a motion to adjourn a debate is usually moved by a Whip, the question of entitlement to speak when the debate is resumed does not often arise.

RESTRICTION OF SPEECHES

Members to speak only once to a question

Subject to a number of exceptions mentioned below, it is the rule that a Member shall not speak more than once to the same question. Accordingly,

---

1 HC Deb (1943–44) 398, c 1693.
2 Parl Deb (1859) 153, c 839.
3 See, eg, HC Deb (1979–80) 982, cc 254–259.
4 HC Deb (1937–38) 329, c 165, 243; ibid (1970–71) 803, c 201.
5 Parl Deb (1853) 126, c 1243; ibid (1858) 148, c 979.
6 Parl Deb (1886) 308, c 614; HC Deb (1912) 38, c 624.
7 HC Deb (1909) 5, c 1552.
8 Parl Deb (1868–69) 194, cc 1451, 1467; ibid (1876) 227; c 1098; ibid (1905) 141, c 330; HC Deb (1923) 162, c 1029; ibid (1928) 215, cc 592, 593.
9 Parl Deb (1872) 213, c 760. See also ibid (1874) 220, cc 1183–1185, 1527.
10 Parl Deb (1892) 7, cc 300, 333.

when a Member speaks to a motion and resumes his seat without moving an amendment that he intended to propose, he cannot subsequently rise to move the amendment, having already spoken to the question before the House.[1] The House has, however, relaxed this application of the rule in respect of certain classes of business to obtain a greater freedom of discussion and amendment (see pp 341–342).

A second speech has been allowed to a private Member under special circumstances following an explanation from the Speaker and with the pleasure of the House having been signified.[2] A Minister who has spoken early in a debate (but not being the mover of a motion) is usually allowed to speak again, though the objection of a single Member is enough to stop him.[3]

Practice in committee

In a Committee of the whole House the restriction upon speaking more than once is altogether removed (see p 587).

Relaxation of rule on consideration of bill reported from a standing committee

On the consideration by the House of a bill committed to a standing committee, or that portion of a bill so committed, Standing Order No 74 provides that the rule against speaking more than once does not apply to the Member in charge of the bill or to the mover of any amendment or new clause in respect of that amendment or new clause.

Interventions

A Member who has been called by the Speaker cannot be interrupted by a Member seeking to move a dilatory motion, although he may be interrupted by a motion for the closure. Members have the right to decide whether to accept interventions, but once they have given way, the Member intervening has the right to speak.[4] Maiden speakers are usually heard without interruption.[5] Interventions in interventions are not allowed.[6] (For personal statements see pp 304–305).

Right of reply

A right of reply is allowed to a Member who has moved a substantive motion in the House or a substantive motion for the adjournment of the House.[7] A Member who moves an order of the day, such as a motion that a bill be read a

1 Parl Deb (1867–68) 191, c 1083.
2 Parl Deb (1864) 173, c 1549; ibid (1870) 201, cc 530, 534.
3 HC Deb (1974) 878, cc 233–237.
4 HC Deb (1978–79) 557, c 958; ibid (1986–87) 114, c 46.
5 HC Deb (1987–88) 119, c 236.
6 HC Deb (1963–64) 689, c 494; ibid (1984–85) 73, c 963. See also ibid (1977–78) 955, c 645.
7 Parl Deb (1858) 148, c 762, 770; ibid (1859) 153, c 1301, 1342; ibid (1867) 186, c 1505; ibid (1871) 207, c 1350; ibid (1872) 210, c 1846; HC Deb (1976–77) 929, c 1360; ibid (1976–77) 930, c 158; ibid (1983–84) 53, c 951.

second time,[1] or an amendment,[2] a new clause,[3] the previous question,[4] an adjournment of a debate,[5] a motion on the consideration of Lords amendments,[6] or an instruction to any committee,[7] can only reply with the unanimous agreement of the House. In the spirit of this rule, a Member moving an order of the day may do so formally, without rising to address the Chair, and reserve his speech for a later period in the debate.[8] In moving an amendment or a motion for the adjournment, a Member cannot avail himself of this privilege,[9] as he must rise in his place to make the motion, and thus cannot avoid addressing the House, however briefly. A Member who moves an amendment cannot speak again upon the main question after the amendment has been withdrawn or otherwise disposed of, since he has already spoken while the main question was before the House and before the amendment had been proposed from the Chair.[10] For the same reason, a Member who has addressed the House in moving the second reading of a bill cannot subsequently move the adjournment of the debate, unless an amendment has been since proposed,[11] nor can a Member who has spoken upon an amendment proposed on the report stage of a bill move the adjournment of the debate, or, until the amendment has been disposed of, move the adjournment of further consideration of the bill.[12] A Member who has unsuccessfully moved the adjournment of a debate (or of the House) may not subsequently speak upon the question upon which he has moved that motion.[13]

Power to speak again when new question is proposed

Apart from the Member who moved the adjournment (see above, p 369), Members may not make a second speech when debate is resumed, even if this occurs after a considerable interval.[14] Once a new question has been proposed, however, as for example 'that the Amendment be made' or 'that the debate be now adjourned', they may speak to that question. If a Member has already moved a motion for the adjournment of the House or of the debate, he may not subsequently move a similar motion unless the Chair declined, under Standing Order No 34, to propose the question to the House,[15] while a Member who has moved an amendment to a question may

1 HC Deb (1981–82) 17, cc 684–685.
2 Parl Deb (1864) 174, c 2022; ibid (1878) 240, c 1527.
3 HC Deb (1953–54) 530, cc 134–135.
4 8 February 1858 (Operations in India, Mr Disraeli), Parl Deb (1858) 148, c 890.
5 Parl Deb (1867) 186, c 1505.
6 HC Deb (1970–71) 822, cc 696, 859.
7 Parl Deb (1867) 186, c 1443; Conventual and Monastic Institutions, etc, 10 May 1870 (Mr Matthews), ibid (1870) 201, cc 530, 534.
8 Parl Deb (1872) 210, c 304; HC Deb (1922) 155, cc 1626, 2501.
9 Parl Deb (1851) 118, cc 1147, 1163; ibid (1855) 138, cc 1300, 1756; ibid (1892) 5, c 1744; HC Deb (1923) 163, c 2100.
10 Parl Deb (1878) 237, c 1532; ibid (1878) 240, c 123; ibid (1878) 241, c 1311; ibid (1901) 89, cc 1077, 1128.
11 Parl Deb (1876) 227, c 1659.
12 HC Deb (1919) 117, c 1346.
13 HC Deb (1928) 215, cc 592, 593. See also pp 341–342 for relaxation of this rule in special cases, eg debate on rules of procedure and guillotine orders.
14 CJ (1547–1628) 245 (1604).
15 HC Deb (1954–55) 536, cc 1297, 1311.

not subsequently move an unrelated amendment thereto.[1] However, a Member may speak to such questions when proposed by other Members.

The subsequent consideration of business upon which a question has been put, but not decided because of the lack of a quorum in the division (see pp 250 and 345), does not constitute an adjourned debate. When the business is considered again, the motion or order of the day concerned must be moved afresh, and Members who have spoken in the earlier debate may speak again.[2]

On 27 October 1884 an amendment to add words to the address in answer to the Queen's speech was amended, without opposition, by leaving out the earlier portion of it. A query was raised as to whether the amendment so amended had become a new question, upon which Members who had already spoken might again address the House. After consideration, it was ruled that it was still the same question.[3]

Speech on point of order

A Member who has already spoken, may rise and speak again upon a point of order or privilege, if he confines himself to that subject, and does not refer to the general tenor of the debate.[4]

LENGTH OF SPEECHES

When it is known to the Chair that a large number of Members wish to speak in a debate, the Speaker has frequently appealed for brief speeches to be made.

Successive Select Committees on Procedure from Session 1966–67 onwards considered the problem of the length of speeches and on several occasions recommended the introduction of time limits.[5] In Session 1979–80 an experiment was conducted restricting speeches at certain hours during debates on the second reading of bills to ten minutes. Further experiments, which extended the practice to full day debates on Opposition Days and on Government motions, were conducted on a sessional basis in Sessions 1984–85 and 1985–86.

On 13 July 1988, following further recommendations from the Select Committee on Procedure,[6] the House agreed to the making of a new Standing Order No 45A. Under this, the Speaker may announce at the commencement of public business on the relevant day that, on Mondays to Thursdays either between six o'clock and ten minutes to eight o'clock or between seven o'clock and ten minutes to nine o'clock and on Fridays

---

1 Parl Deb (1867–68) 190, c 674; ibid (1872) 211, c 87.
2 See, eg, Proceedings on the Calf Subsidies (United Kingdom) (Variation) Scheme 1975 on which the question was not decided owing to the lack of a quorum in the division (HC Deb (1974–75) 888, cc 714–741); the motion was subsequently moved afresh and Members who had spoken in the earlier debate spoke again (ibid (1974–75) 889, cc 319–407).
3 CJ (1884–85) 10; Parl Deb (1884–85) 293, c 298.
4 Parl Deb (1868–69) 195, c 2008.
5 HC (1966–67) 153; ibid (1977–78) 588; ibid (1984–85) 623.
6 HC (1985–86) 592; CJ (1987–88) 1042–1043.

between half-past eleven o'clock and one o'clock, he will call Members to speak for not more than ten minutes.[1] The Standing Order applies only to debates on the second reading of public bills, on allotted opposition days, on motions in the name of a Minister of the Crown and on motions for an address in answer to the Queen's Speech. Whenever the Speaker has made such an announcement, the occupant of the Chair may between the specified hours direct any Members who has spoken for ten minutes to resume his seat forthwith.

The power exercised by the Chair is purely discretionary. If it appears subsequently that there is no need for a limit, the rule can be relaxed.[2]

2. RULES GOVERNING THE CONTENTS OF SPEECHES

RELEVANCE IN DEBATE

A Member must direct his speech to the question under discussion or to the motion or amendment he intends to move,[3] or to a point of order. The precise relevance of an argument may not always be perceptible[4] but a Member who wanders from the subject will be reminded by the Speaker that he must speak to the question. Debate must not anticipate a matter appointed for the consideration of the House,[5] or of which notice has been given.[6] Reference to prior debates of the current session is discouraged (see p 374).[7]

For instance, upon a motion for the appointment of a committee on the game laws, a Member was restrained from criticizing the provisions of certain bills before the House for the amendment of those laws;[8] though when bills, in the charge of the Government, dealing with subjects bound together by a common principle, stand in a series upon the Notice Paper, debate on the first bill may include a discussion of the bills of a cognate character.[9] An example of irrelevance which frequently arises is in debate on motions for Money Resolutions following the second reading of public bills. The matters covered by such motions are often fairly restricted in their scope and the occupant of the Chair has to remind Members that debate should be confined to what is contained in the motion.[10] On a

---

1 Speeches which begin before the designated starting hour must not continue for more than ten minutes after that hour.
2 HC Deb (1979–80) 984, c 612; ibid (1988–89) 154 c 421.
3 Parl Deb (1902) 112, c 404; ibid (1906) 167, c 839; HC Deb (1915) 75, c 720; ibid (1916) 85, c 1510.
4 See the celebrated debate, 6 May 1791, on the Quebec Government Bill, in which Mr Burke insisted upon the relevancy of Paine's Rights of Man and the recent events of the French Revolution, Lord John Russell's *Life of Fox*, ii, 253.
5 Parl Deb (1856) 140, c 2037; ibid (1862) 167, c 1140; ibid (1865) 176, c 1797; ibid (1867) 189, cc 91, 96; ibid (1872) 210, c 1815; ibid (1872) 212, c 1430; ibid (1878) 241, c 807; ibid (1907) 171, c 1740 See also p 327.
6 Parl Deb (1857) 146, c 1702; ibid (1859) 153, c 331; ibid (1906) 165, c 662; ibid (1907) 180, c 1621.
7 Parl Deb (1908) 197, c 161.
8 Parl Deb (1868–69) 195, c 1718; see also ibid (1881) 257, c 812.
9 Parl Deb (1988) 324, c 1066; ibid (1889) 336, c 1594. See also ibid (1896) 39, c 5; HC Deb (1921) 140, c 566; ibid (1921) 147, cc 18, 23; ibid (1924) 174, c 1597; ibid (1928) 214, c 42; ibid 219, c 2543.
10 HC Deb (1988–89) 143, c 278, 1059–1060.

motion for the appointment of a select committee[1] or for determining the number of its members,[2] the merits of the matter referred to the committee have not been allowed to be debated. Nor on a motion prescribing procedure for concluding the consideration of stages of a bill or other business, can the bill or the business itself be discussed.[3] In debating delegated legislation, the House often has to be reminded that a wide debate is not possible within the terms of a motion to approve or annul an instrument with a single narrow purpose. For example, on a motion to approve an order granting immunities and privileges for members of a Council of Europe Committee set up to examine the treatment of persons deprived of their liberty, the occupant of the Chair ruled that the debate should be confined to the granting of the privileges and should not extend to the citing of examples in different countries of the kind of practices which the Committee might wish to investigate.[4]

Again, upon a motion to disapprove consolidated regulations (the National Health Insurance (Medical Benefit Consolidated) Regulations 1928) the Speaker refused to allow the discussion of a regulation which was already in force, because the disapproval of the consolidated regulations would have no effect on the validity of any regulations already in force.[5]

A remark which has been ruled to be out of order cannot be the subject of a debate.[6]

Under Standing Order No 41, the Chair has power to deal both with irrelevance and the tedious repetition of a Member's own arguments or of those of other Members (see pp 393–394).

DEBATE ON DILATORY MOTIONS

Formerly, there was considerable laxity in debate upon motions of adjournment,[7] and though efforts were made to enforce a stricter practice, it was not until 27 November 1882 that a Standing Order was passed which restricted debate on all dilatory motions, such as motions for the adjournment of a debate, or of the House during any debate, or in committee that the Chairman do report progress, or do leave the Chair, to the matter of such motion.[8] A Member who moves such a motion is forbidden by the Standing Order from moving a similar motion during the same debate (Standing Order No 33). In March 1971 the Standing Order was extended to motions that further consideration of a bill, or of Lords amendments to a bill, be adjourned. Under the terms of Standing Order No 34, which was also passed in November 1882, the Speaker, or the Chairman, if he be of opinion that such dilatory motions are an abuse of the rules of the House, is empowered

---

1 Parl Deb (1905) 146, c 993; HC Deb (1937–8) 337, c 2157.
2 HC Deb (1909) 3, c 997.
3 Parl Deb (1904) 137, cc 349, 678; ibid (1905) 143, cc 81, 86; ibid (1906) 167, c 173; HC Deb (1912) 44, c 1671; ibid (1913) 54, c 898; ibid (1921) 144, c 485.
4 HC Deb (1987–88) 133, cc 566–570.
5 HC Deb (1929) 224, c 1097.
6 Parl Deb (1886) 308, c 738.
7 Parl Deb (1848) 99, cc 1147, 1196; ibid (1848) 101, c 508; ibid (1849) 102; cc 226, 1100; ibid (1877) 232, c 1733.
8 See Mr Speaker's remarks, HC Deb (1935) 299, c 913; ibid (1938–39) 352, c 1127.

to put forthwith the question thereon from the Chair[1] or to decline to propose the question thereon to the House or committee.[2]

MOTIONS FOR ADJOURNMENT OF THE HOUSE

Motions for the adjournment of the House, made when there is no question under discussion, must be clearly distinguished from similar motions made during a debate (see pp 332–333). The former are used to discuss extraneous subjects; the latter have reference only to the adjournment of the question then before the House. The discussion of the former is governed, however, by the established rules of debate and the restrictions which apply (see pp 319–320).

On a motion that the House at its rising do adjourn to a day beyond the next ordinary sitting day (see p 250) it has been frequently ruled that in raising particular matters Members should refer to the need for them to be debated in greater detail before the proposed date of adjournment.[3] The same kind of ruling has been applied on a motion to secure a sitting of the House on the following day when the House would not have sat otherwise.[4]

REFERENCE TO PRIOR DEBATES OF CURRENT SESSION

Reference to prior debates of the current session whether in the House or in a Committee of the whole House,[5] which would tend to re-open matters already decided, has been discouraged even where such reference would not be irrelevant. This rule has not always been strictly enforced: particular circumstances may make reference to speeches made in past debates justifiable, and it is for the Speaker to judge in each case how far the rule may properly be relaxed.[6] The rule does not apply to debates upon different stages of a bill.

Reference to a speech made in a previous debate is permitted when a Member wishes to complain of something said[7] or to clear up alleged misrepresentation[8] or to make a personal explanation[9] but only so much of a previous speech as is necessary for such purposes should be referred to.[10] Where a motion practically rescinded a resolution of the House, reference was permitted to the debate upon that resolution.[11]

---

1 CJ (1888) 414; ibid (1902) 326; ibid (1905) 269; ibid (1977–78) 152; HC Deb (1985–86) 95, c 55.
2 Parl Deb (1887) 311, c 1648; ibid (1888) 328, c 1887; ibid (1888) 329, c 1095; ibid (1889) 338, c 887; ibid (1889) 339, c 1733; ibid (1895) 36, c 355; ibid (1901) 98, c 1213; ibid (1905) 150, c 199; CJ (1975–76) 336. See also the Speaker's remarks in refusing to put a motion for the adjournment of the debate for the purpose of bringing on a subsequent order of the day, Parl Deb (1894) 24, c 1661.
3 Parl Deb (1902) 116, c 1030; HC Deb (1921) 149, c 363; ibid (1939–40) 364, c 1343; ibid (1943–44) 401, cc 939–940; ibid (1979–80) 982, c 487.
4 HC Deb (1917) 97, c 1579; ibid (1955–56) 558, c 1852.
5 Parl Deb (1859) 154, c 985.
6 Parl Deb (1876) 231, c 749; ibid (1878) 238, c 1403; HC Deb (1933) 283, c 1258; ibid (1942–43) 385, cc 1319–1321; ibid (1962–63) 679, c 1865.
7 Parl Deb (1841) 59, c 485; see also ibid (1842) 65, c 642.
8 Parl Deb (1850) 109, c 462; see also ibid (1846) 85, c 300.
9 HC Deb (1981–82) 19, c 21.
10 Parl Deb (1856) 140, c 1708; ibid (1858) 149, cc 10–14; ibid (1877) 235, c 1192; ibid (1877) 236, cc 36, 172; ibid (1893) 10, c 523; ibid (1907) 172, c 1520.
11 Parl Deb (1871) 235, c 1703.

REFERENCE TO PROCEEDINGS IN STANDING AND SELECT COMMITTEES

No appeal can be made to the Speaker from the decisions of the chairman of a standing committee (see p 602). References in the House to the proceedings on a bill in standing committee, particularly if such references attempt to deal with the content of the debate in the committee, are out of order,[1] although references to the progress of business in standing committees have been permitted in certain circumstances.[2]

The proceedings in, and report of, a select committee may not be referred to in debate before they have been laid upon the Table,[3] but this restriction does not apply to evidence taken in public.[4]

REFLECTING UPON VOTES OF HOUSE

The objections to the practice of referring to past debates apply with greater force to reflections upon votes of the House, unless made for the purpose of justifying a motion that the vote be rescinded. Such reflections not only revive discussion upon questions already decided, but are irregular, because the Member is himself included in, and bound by, a vote agreed to by a majority.[5] Reflections on the action taken by the Speaker, the Chairman of Ways and Means and the House upon a closure motion are not permitted.[6]

REFERENCES TO DEBATES IN HOUSE OF LORDS

The content of a speech made in the House of Lords in the current session may be summarised, but it is out of order to quote from it unless it is a speech of or a statement by a Minister in relation to Government policy.[7] It is considered undesirable that any Member of the House of Lords should be mentioned by name, or otherwise identified, for the purpose of criticism of a personal nature.[8]

The same rule has been applied to restrain the discussion of a bill which has been passed and sent to the Lords, upon a motion for an address to the Crown.[9] Members are restrained by the Speaker from commenting upon the proceedings of the House of Lords. When a Member raised the question of

---

1 HC Deb (1976–77) 934, c 1424; ibid (1985–86) 93, c 941.
2 HC Deb (1974–75) 890, cc 442–5; ibid (1974–75) 891, c 1626; ibid (1979–80) 980, cc 660–661, 666–667.
3 HC Deb (1940–41) 373, c 1325.
4 HC Deb (1980–81) 995, cc 275–276.
5 2 Hatsell 233 n; see also Parl Deb (1867) 186, c 885.
6 Parl Deb (1888) 328, c 1899; ibid (1888) 329, c 58; ibid (1891) 354, c 431; ibid (1896) 39, c 867; ibid (1896) 40, c 1731.
7 Speaker's Private Ruling, 29 November 1933; also HC Deb (1931) 304, cc 1579–1581; ibid (1935–36) 314, c 507; ibid (1936–37) 326, c 2315; ibid (1942–43) 390, c 373; ibid (1962–63) 672, c 1476; ibid (1977–78) 953, c 1931; ibid (1979–80) 992, c 372; ibid (1983–84) 53, c 363. See also the Speaker's rulings concerning the power of quotation from a speech in the House of Lords, ibid (1891) 351, c 1500; ibid (1907) 180, c 1884; or reference to a ministerial statement made in the House of Lords, HC Deb (1922) 151, c 2207.
8 HC Deb (1977–78) 941, cc 511–512.
9 Parl Deb (1876) 228, c 1183.

the handling by the Government of a bill which had been sent to the Lords, he was advised that the business of the House of Lords was their concern and not a matter for the Speaker.[1]

The rule that references to debates of the current session in the other House are out of order prevents fruitless arguments between Members of two distinct bodies who are unable to reply to each other, and guards against recrimination and offensive language in the absence of the other party.[2]

The rule has been held not to apply to reports of committees of the other House, even though they have not been communicated to the Commons,[3] nor is it extended to the votes or proceedings of either House, as they are recorded and printed by authority.[4] Indeed, since 1860 the Lords' Minutes have been placed upon the Table of the House of Commons for reference.[5]

REFERENCES TO QUEEN IN DEBATE

Disloyal or disrespectful reference to Queen

Treasonable or seditious language or a disrespectful use of Her Majesty's name are not permitted. Members have not only been called to order for such offences, but have been reprimanded, committed to the custody of the Serjeant or even sent to the Tower.[6]

Use of Queen's name to influence debate

The irregular use of the Queen's name to influence a decision of the House is unconstitutional in principle and inconsistent with the independence of Parliament. Where the Crown has a distinct interest in a measure, there is an authorized mode of communicating Her Majesty's recommendation or consent, through one of her Ministers (see p 560); but Her Majesty cannot be supposed to have a private opinion, apart from that of her responsible advisers; and any attempt to use her name in debate to influence the judgment of Parliament is immediately checked and censured.[7] This rule extends also to other members of the Royal Family,[8] but it is not strictly applied in cases where one of its members has made a public statement on a matter of current interest so long as comment is made in appropriate terms.[9]

---

1 HC Deb (1976–77) 927, cc 923–925.
2 See Mr Speaker's declaration that it was a very wholesome rule of the House not to allude to statements or debates of the current session in the other House, as to do so might bring the two houses into collision, Parl Deb (1893) 15, c 1781; ibid (1867–68) 191, c 1786; ibid (1867–68) 192, c 1077; ibid (1871) 208, c 1682; ibid (1876) 229, c 1630; ibid (1878) 237, c 1262; ibi (1878) 242, c 228; ibid (1902) 116, c 1354; ibid (1907) 176, c 344; ibid (1908) 193, c 214; H('eb (1915) 75, c 2147; ibid (1922) 157, c 1828.
3 Parl Deb (1848) 99, c 631.
4 Parl Deb (1902) 105, c 732.
5 Parl Deb (1860) 159, c 856. But see Parl Deb (1902) 105, c 732.
6 CJ (1547–1628) 50, 51, 104, 333, 335, 866; ibid (1667–87) 760; ibid (1693–97) 581; ibid (1705–08) 70; ibid (1714–18) 49, 54, 653; Parl Hist (1660–88) 4, c 1385; ibid (1714–22) 7, cc 51, 511; D'Ewes, 241–44.
7 CJ (1547–1628) 697; ibid (1640–41) 27, 344; ibid (1782–84) 842; Parl Deb (1808) 10, c 577; ibid (1812) 22, c 51; HC Deb (1936–37) 317, c 71.
8 HC Deb (1948–49) 464, c 1924; ibid (1985–86) 88, c 26.
9 HC Deb (1988–89) 142, c 32.

A Minister is, however, permitted to make a statement of facts in which the Sovereign's name may be concerned.[1]

WORDS AGAINST PARLIAMENT, OR EITHER HOUSE

Offensive expressions against the character and conduct of Parliament itself are not permitted; for they are not only a contempt of that high court, but are calculated to degrade the legislature in the public estimation. If directed against the other House, and passed over without censure, they would appear to implicate one House in discourtesy to the other though criticism of the role and functions of the other House is in order;[2] if against the House in which the words are spoken, it would be impossible to overlook the disrespect of one of its own Members. If, when called to order, a Member fails to retract or explain his words or make a satisfactory apology, he may be punished by reprimand, commitment[3] or under the powers given by Standing Orders Nos 41, 42 or 43 (see pp 394–395). It is most important that the use of offensive words should be immediately reproved in order to avoid complaints and dissensions between the two Houses.

Against a statute

At one time it was considered that disrespectful or abusive mention of a statute was partly open to the same objection as improper language applied to Parliament itself, on the ground that it imputed discredit to the legislature that passed the statute. However, the Speaker has ruled that any Act of Parliament may be criticized as strongly as Members desire.[4] The Speaker has refused to intervene when a Member claimed that the enactment of a law might justify an appeal to force.[5]

MATTERS AWAITING JUDICIAL DECISION

Subject to the discretion of the Chair and to the right of the House to legislate on any matter[6] or to discuss any matters of delegated legislation,[7] matters awaiting the adjudication of a court of law should not be brought forward in debate (see p 326).

Following the First Report of the Select Committee on Procedure, 1962–63,[8] the House passed a resolution (23 July 1963) which set out the rule in

---

1 7 Chandler, Deb 61, 64; Parl Deb (1843) 69, cc 24, 574; ibid (1876) 228, c 2037. See also HC Deb (1914–16) 71, c 227; ibid (1981–82) 27, c 645.
2 Parl Deb (1887) 313, c 101; ibid (1887) 319, c 303; ibid (1889) 337, c 1104; ibid (1892) 5, c 1842; ibid (1893) 8, c 1780; ibid (1906) 167, c 1771; HC Deb (1977–78) 944, c 1313. The Speaker has condemned the use by a Member of improper language directed against the House of Lords, in giving notice of a motion, ibid (1884) 290, c 691. See also questions to ministers, p 293.
3 CJ (1693–97) 581. See also *Mr Duffy's case*, ibid (1852–53) 461.
4 HC Deb (1973–74) 865, c 1092.
5 Parl Deb (1886) 308, c 1108.
6 See eg HC Deb (1984–85) 83, c 28.
7 See eg HC Deb (1984–85) 74, cc 22–23.
8 HC 156 (1962–63).

detail.[1] This resolution bars references in debate (as well as in motions, including motions for leave to bring in bills, and questions, including supplementary questions) to matters awaiting or under adjudication in all courts exercising a criminal jurisdiction from the moment the law is set in motion by a charge being made[2] to the time when verdict and sentence have been announced, and again when formal notice of appeal is lodged until the appeal is decided;[3] and in courts martial from when the charge is made until the sentence of the court has been confirmed and promulgated, and again when the convicted man petitions the Army Council, the Air Council, or the Board of Admiralty.

The resolution of 23 July 1963 also applies to the civil courts, and in general bars reference to matters awaiting or under adjudication in a civil court from the time that the case has been set down for trial or otherwise brought before the court, as for example by notice of motion for injunction;[4] such matters may be referred to before such date unless it appears to the Chair that there is a real and substantial danger of prejudice to the trial of the case. The ban again applies from when formal notice of appeal is lodged until judgment is given.

On 28 June 1972 the House came to a further resolution, that notwithstanding the Resolution of 23 July 1963 and subject to the discretion of the Chair, reference may be made in questions, motions or debate to matters awaiting or under adjudication in all civil courts, in so far as such matters relate to a ministerial decision which cannot be challenged in court except on grounds of misdirection or bad faith, or concern issues of national importance such as the national economy, public order or the essentials of life; and that in exercising its discretion the Chair should not allow reference to such matters if it appears that there is a real and substantial danger of prejudice to the proceedings; and should have regard to the considerations set out in paragraphs 25 to 28 of the Fourth Report from the Select Committee on Procedure of session 1971–72.[5] The restriction on reference in debate also applies in the case of any judicial body to which the House has expressly referred a specific matter for decision and report, from the time when the resolution of the House is passed, but ceases to have effect as soon as the report is laid before the House. It does not apply to matters referred to a departmental inquiry.[6]

Successive Speakers have exercised their discretion to allow matters to be discussed, on which (although they fall within the strict terms of the sub-judice rule) they have considered that no substantial risk of prejudicing proceedings would arise.[7] The Speaker has also exercised his discretion to allow a debate under Standing Order No 20 to proceed when it seemed possible that civil proceedings in relation to the subject might be instituted.[8]

1 CJ (1962–63) 246, 297.
2 The law can be set in motion by other means; for example, by a law officer applying to commence contempt of court proceedings (HC Deb (1986–87) 115, c68).
3 HC Deb (1968–69) 775, cc1384–1385; ibid (1976–77) 932, cc1188–1189, 1425–1429; ibid (1976–77) 933, c877; ibid (1976–77) 934, cc568–569.
4 HC Deb (1970–71) 807, cc1083–1085; ibid (1978–79) 960, cc1238–1239.
5 HC 298 (1971–72). See also HC Deb (1975–76) 916, cc649–653, 882–884; ibid (1980–81) 4, c742.
6 HC Deb (1983–84) 62, cc807–809.
7 HC Deb (1971–72) 836, c1705; ibid (1975–76) 918, c1621; ibid (1976–77) 935, c1849; ibid (1978–79) 975, cc1085–1086; ibid (1986–87) 102, c1314–1315; ibid (1988–89) 152, cc 859.
8 HC Deb (1975–76) 918, c1621.

Deliberations of non-domestic courts, including the courts of the European community, are not subject to the sub judice rule.[1]

Discussion of a capital sentence

A capital sentence cannot be raised in debate while the sentence is pending.[2] After the sentence has been carried out, the Minister responsible may be criticized in appropriate terms either on a substantive motion or on a substantive motion for the adjournment[3] (see also 288).

REFLECTIONS ON SOVEREIGN, ETC

Unless the discussion is based upon a substantive motion, drawn in proper terms (see p 325), reflections must not be cast in debate upon the conduct of the Sovereign, the heir to the throne, or other members of the royal family,[4] the Lord Chancellor,[5] the Governor-General of an independent territory,[6] the Speaker,[7] the Chairman of Ways and Means,[8] Members of either House of Parliament,[9] or judges of the superior courts of the United

---

1 HC Deb (1976–77) 932, cc 1194–1195; ibid (1985–86) 91, c 41.
2 This rule was partially relaxed on the occasion of a statement in the House by the Foreign Secretary explaining the legal processes available to a British serviceman condemned to death in a Crown Colony court (see HC Deb (1966–67) 740, c 1114). See also HC Deb (1976–77) 940, c 747.
3 CJ (1960–61) 109; HC Deb (1960–61) 634, cc 1773–1838. See also ibid (1946–47) 436, c 2179–82.
4 Parl Deb (1887) 312, c 1061; ibid (1889) 338, c 1338; ibid (1895) 33, c 896; ibid (1901) 93, c 1362; ibid (1901) 97, c 1164; ibid (1901) 99, c 471; HC Deb (1927) 202, c 1231; ibid (1969–70) 791, c 195; ibid (1971–72) 831, c 436; ibid (1977–78) 946, c 1728.
5 Parl Deb (1898) 56, c 859; ibid (1899) 75, c 890; ibid (1906) 156, c 597; ex-Lord Chancellor; ibid (1906) 167, c 1367.
6 HC Deb (1910) 15, c 894; ibid (1913) 55, c 243; ibid 56, c 809.
7 CJ (1884–85) 78; Parl Deb (1887) 311, c 954; ibid (1887) 313, c 371, 472; ibid (1902) 107, c 1020; ibid (1905) 142, c 1507; HC Deb (1924–25) 184, cc 1390, 1591; ibid (1951–52) 500, c 397; ibid (1971–72) 832, c 1039; ibid (1981–82) 16, c 751.
8 Parl Deb (1886) 302, c 1710; ibid (1901) 95, c 235; HC Deb (1917) 100, c 1892; ibid (1966–67) 731, c 441; ibid (1976–77) 926, cc 655–660.
9 A peer, HC Deb (1914) 60, c 279; ibid (1985–86) 98, c 797; a Member, ibid (1964–65) 714, cc 242–246; ibid (1986–87) 114, cc 164–172; a Minister, ibid (1920) 131, c 1205; chairman of a standing committee, ibid (1924) 170, c 2769; ibid (1924) 173, cc 1348–1350. See Speaker's ruling, that the explicit statement of the Prime Minister must be accepted, Parl Deb (1883) 280, c 116. Discussion of the conduct of the chairman of a joint committee on a bill has been ruled out of order in committee on the re-committed bill, ibid (1902) 111, cc 19, 27, 707; ibid (1908) 196, cc 363, 568. Privy Councillors are not protected by this rule, HC Deb (1933) 277, cc 1222–1226. Criticism of a Member of the other House has been permitted for his activities in another capacity, eg as a newspaper proprietor, HC Deb (1948–49) 467, c 2668; see also ibid (1971–72) 832, c 1451.

Kingdom,[1] including persons holding the position of a judge, such as circuit judges and their deputies, as well as recorders.[2] Opprobrious reflections must not be cast in debate on heads of state[3] or governments of[4] independent Commonwealth territories or countries in amity with Her Majesty, or their representatives in this country.[5]

PERSONAL ALLUSIONS AND UNPARLIAMENTARY EXPRESSIONS

In order to guard against all appearance of personality in debate, no Member should refer to another by name. Each Member must be distinguished by the office he holds, by the place he represents or by other designations, as 'the noble Lord the secretary of state for foreign affairs', 'the honourable' or 'right honourable gentleman the Member for York', or 'the honourable and learned Member who has just sat down' or, when speaking of a member of the same party, 'my (right) honourable friend the Member for . . .'.[6]

Allegations against Members

Good temper and moderation are the characteristics of parliamentary language. Parliamentary language is never more desirable than when a Member is canvassing the opinions and conduct of his opponents in debate.[7] It is

1 Parl Deb (1877) 234, c 1558; ibid (1878) 238, c 1953; ibid (1884) 286, c 1732; ibid (1887) 312, c 736; ibid (1887) 313, c 637; ibid (1887) 315, c 1530; ibid (1888) 322, c 463; ibid (1893–94) 12, c 1807; ibid (1893–94) 14, c 1090; ibid (1895) 36, c 201; ibid (1897) 52, c 23; ibid (1899) 75, c 891; ibid (1901) 96, c 306; ibid (1904) 132, cc 683, 696; ibid (1906) 163, c 507; ibid (1908) 183, c 807; HC Deb (1911) 30, c 1170; ibid (1912) 41, c 2779. Reflections against the judges generally are equally out of order, ibid (1911) 26, c 1082; ibid (1917) 91, cc 664, 667. The Speaker has also intimated that the same rule should be applied to the case of judges in dependent territories, ibid (1912) 40, c 622; ibid (1955–56) 557, cc 921–929. The rule also applies to Tribunals of Inquiry under the Tribunals of Inquiry (Evidence) Act 1921, ibid (1971–72) 833, cc 1239–1266. On 4 December 1973 Mr Speaker ruled that it can be argued that a judge has made a mistake, that he was wrong, and the reasons for those contentions can be given, within certain limits; but reflections on a judge's character or motives cannot be made except on a motion, nor can any charge of a personal nature be made except on a motion (see also HC Deb (1987–88) 118, c 641. Any suggestion that a judge should be dismissed can only be made on a motion, HC Deb (1973–74) 865, cc 1092, 1144, 1199. See also ibid (1982–83) 34, cc 285–286.
2 Parl Deb (1887) 312, c 1110; ibid (1887) 320, cc 1024, 1031; ibid (1906) 164, c 1572; HC Deb (1951–52) 493, c 591. The Speaker has also ruled out of order language disrespectful to persons administering justice, such as resident magistrates in Ireland, ibid (1902) 103, c 462; and criticism of sentences imposed by magistrates, HC Deb (1926) 196, c 2498, including Justices of the Peace, ibid (1926) 200, c 855. The Speaker has held that masters of the Supreme Court do not fall within this category, HC Deb (1985–86) 103, c 1103.
3 Parl Deb (1878) 237, c 1639; ibid (1878) 238, c 799; ibid (1897) 46, c 892; ibid (1908) 190, c 254; HC Deb (1909) 6, c 806; ibid (1916) 88, c 116; ibid (1980–81) 10, cc 989–990.
4 HC Deb (1940–41) 371, c 1294.
5 HC Deb (1936–37) 317, c 260.
6 *Diary of Thomas Burton, Member in the Parliaments of Oliver and Richard Cromwell* vol iii, p 141. Mr Berkeley was called to order, 20 March 1860, for referring to Members by name, as having spoken, in former sessions, against the ballot, Parl Deb (1860) 157, c 939. The same rule applies to standing committees, HC Deb (1919) 118, c 1823.
7 For earlier practices with regard to words of heat and challenges see *Erskine May*, (19th edn, 1976) pp 430–431.

not out of order, however, to cast aspersions on former-Members of the House, even if they are Privy Councillors.[1]

Reference in debate to either House of Parliament must be courteous, and abusive language, and imputations of falsehood, uttered by Members of the House of Commons against Members of the House of Lords have usually been met by the immediate intervention of the Chair to compel the withdrawal of the offensive words,[2] or, in default, by the punishment of suspension.[3] However, criticism of a Member of the House of Lords for his acts in another capacity has been permitted.[4]

Expressions which are unparliamentary and call for prompt interference include:

(1) The imputation of false or unavowed motives:

See Parl Deb (1864) 176, c 1005; ibid (1867–68) 193, c 1741; ibid (1903) 125, c 1530; ibid (1904) 133, c 748; ibid (1906) 155, c 261; HC Deb (1961–62) 663, c 1485, ibid (1967–68) 757, cc 1740–1742; ibid (1975–76) 916, cc 2293–2294; ibid (1983–84) 58, c 213; ibid (1985–86) 101, c 290.

(2) The misrepresentation of the language of another and the accusation of misrepresentation:

See 2 Cav Deb 118, 120; Parl Deb (1848) 96, c 1206; ibid (1871) 205, c 1743; ibid (1907) 171, c 376; HC Deb (1930–31) 256, c 1596; ibid (1962–63) 681, c 190; it has been held that the accusation must be of deliberate misrepresentation (St Co Deb (1959–60) St Co C Public Bodies (Admission of the Press) Bill cc 92, 113); cf HC Deb (1959–60) 620, cc 893–894.

(3) Charges of uttering a deliberate falsehood:

See Parl Deb (1867) 187, c 953; ibid (1875) 223, c 1015; ibid (1887) 314, c 258; ibid (1901) 92, c 159; HC Deb (1909) 9, c 215; ibid (1915) 74, c 1050; ibid (1921) 140, c 333; ibid (1921) 141, c 492; ibid (1930–31) 244, c 1520; ibid (1935–36) 315, cc 836, 845–846; ibid (1948–49) 467, cc 439–440; ibid (1953–54) 532, c 1445; ibid (1961–62) 656, c 206; ibid (1963–64) 696, c 1637; ibid (1963–64) 698, c 1204; ibid (1967–68) 759, c 964; ibid (1973–74) 866, c 786; ibid (1974–75) 884, c 457; ibid (1977–78) 952, cc 1562–1563; ibid (1979–80) 984, cc 1789–1792; ibid (1983–84) 61, cc 473, 523. See in particular the Speaker's ruling on 16 April 1973, HC Deb (1972–73) 854, c 1525 and ibid (1972–73) 855, cc 28–30. The suggestion that a Member is deliberately misleading the House is not parliamentary, ibid (1972–73) 859, c 186.

(4) Abusive and insulting language of a nature likely to create disorder. The Speaker has said in this connection that whether a word should be regarded as unparliamentary depends on the context in which it is used.[5]

---

1 HC Deb (1933) 277, cc 1222–1226; ibid (1983–84) 53, c 75.
2 Parl Deb (1884–85) 298, c 101; ibid (1884–85) 299, c 1792; ibid (1886) 302, c 230; ibid (1886) 308, c 937; HC Deb (1960–61) 629, c 358; ibid (1977–78) 944, c 1313; ibid (1979–80) 922, c 241.
3 CJ (1890) 72; Parl Deb (1890) 341, c 1570.
4 HC Deb (1948–49) 467, c 2668. But see HC Deb (1977–78) 951, cc 1182–1186; ibid (1977–78) 952, cc 29–30; ibid (1977–78) 954, cc 797–798.
5 HC Deb (1983–84) 61, cc 307–308.

For example, expressions which are unparliamentary when applied to individuals are not always so considered when applied to a whole party.[1]

A charge that a Member has obstructed the business of the House or that a speech is an abuse of the rules of the House is not out of order.[2]

A Member is not allowed to use unparliamentary words by the device of putting them in somebody else's mouth.[3]

CITING DOCUMENTS NOT BEFORE HOUSE

A Minister of the Crown may not read or quote from a despatch or other state paper not before the House, unless he is prepared to lay it upon the Table. Similarly, it has been accepted that a document which has been cited by a Minister ought to be laid upon the Table of the House, if it can be done without injury to the public interests.[4] A Minister who summarizes a correspondence, but does not actually quote from it, is not bound to lay it upon the Table.[5] The rule for the laying of cited documents does not apply to private letters or memoranda.

On 18 May 1865 the Attorney General on being asked by Mr Ferrand if he would lay upon the Table a written statement and a letter to which he had referred on a previous day, in answering a question relative to the Leeds Bankruptcy Court, replied that he had made a statement to the House upon his own responsibility, and that the documents he had referred to being private, he could not lay them upon the Table. Lord Robert Cecil contended that the papers, having been cited, should be produced; but the Speaker declared that this rule applied to public documents only.[6] On 10 August 1893 the Speaker ruled that confidential documents or documents of a private nature passing between officers of a department, cited in debate, are not necessarily laid on the Table of the House, especially if the Minister declares that they are of a confidential nature.[7] On 20 June 1974 the Deputy Speaker ruled that a letter from a department to a private

---

1 HC Deb (1945–46) 414, c 794; ibid (1962–63) 672, c 284; ibid (1978–79) 965, cc 56–57, 68.
2 See Parl Deb (1886) 308, c 1170; ibid (1903) 125, c 945; HC Deb (1909) 6, c 2046.
3 HC Deb (1948–49) 469, c 72; ibid (1975–76) 902, c 345; ibid (1986–87) 113, c 895.
4 See motion of Mr Adam, 4 March 1808, to censure Mr Canning for having read to the House despatches and parts of despatches, none of which had then been communicated to the House, and some of which the House had determined should not be produced, Parl Deb (1808) 10, c 898, Colchester ii, 141. Mr Canning and Mr Tierney, 11 February 1818, ibid (1818) 37, c 393. Debate in committee of supply, 17 July 1857 (Sir C Wood), Parl Deb (1857) 146, c 1759. See debate, 23 May 1862, on the Longford Election, in which Sir Robert Peel referred to information received by the Government without citing documents; and comments made upon this course, and precedents cited, ibid (1862) 166, c 2128–2131. Also statement of rule by Viscount Palmerston, 12 May 1863, ibid (1863) 170, c 1585, and ibid (1864) 176, c 962; ibid (1865) 179, c 489; ibid (1877) 235, c 935; ibid (1887) 319, cc 1859, 1869; ibid (1889) 336, c 651; HC Deb (1913) 54, c 2345; ibid (1944–45) 407, c 409; ibid (1962–63) 668, cc 31–42. See also debate, 11 March 1903, when a Minister quoted the evidence given before a military court of inquiry, and the Speaker's statement, 16 March, that the rule of debate had been complied with by laying upon the Table the evidence of the witness quoted, Parl Deb (1903) 119, cc 501, 570, 858. A minister quoting a document in committee of the whole House ought to lay that document on the Table, HC Deb (1947–48) 449, cc 1635–1637. Lapse of time removes the necessity to lay a document, HC Deb (1982–83) 34, c 969.
5 Parl Deb (1905) 151, c 814; HC Deb (1944–45) 407, c 1797; ibid (1951–52) 498, cc 1356–1357; ibid (1982–83) 36, cc 32, 34; ibid (1984–85) 89, c 1212.
6 Parl Deb (1865) 179, c 489; see also ibid (1883) 282, c 2108; HC Deb (1941–42) 376, c 2194.
7 Parl Deb (1893) 15, c 1778; HC Deb (1957–58) 579, cc 1266–1267.

individual did not come within the category of having to be laid.[1] However, in exceptional circumstances and because they had become matters of acute political controversy, the Secretary of State for Defence on 18 February 1985 laid on the Table documents on the advice given to Ministers by an individual civil servant.[2] As the House deals only with public documents in its proceedings, it could not incidentally require the production of papers which, if moved for separately, would be refused as beyond its jurisdiction.

In relation to the rule requiring papers being cited to be laid on the Table of the House, special conditions attach to European Community documents. These documents though clearly of a public nature and regularly debated and cited in the House are never formally laid upon the Table. They are however made available to Members by being supplied to the Vote Office, and no question has been raised about the propriety of this procedure.[3] A recommendation by the Select Committee on Procedure that they should be presented as Command Papers has not been adopted.[4] Accordingly, in spite of their general availability, no record of their presentation appears in the Journal.

There is no rule to prevent Members not connected with the Government from citing documents in their possession, both public and private,[5] which are not before the House, even though the House will not be able to form a correct judgment from partial extracts.

Law officers' opinions

The opinions of the law officers of the Crown, being confidential, are not usually laid before Parliament, cited in debate or provided in evidence before a Select Committee,[6] and their production has frequently been refused; but if a Minister deems it expedient that such opinions should be made known for the information of the House, he is entitled to cite them in debate.[7]

Responsibility for the laying of documents

It is the responsibility of the Government and not of the Chair to see that documents which may be relevant to debates are laid before the House and are available to Members.[8] It is not for the Chair to decide what documents are relevant.[9] Only when the Speaker himself has control of a document can he be involved in making it available to the House or a committee.[10] However, the Speaker has accepted the recommendation of the House of

---

1 HC Deb (1974) 875, cc 712–5 and 720–21.
2 CJ (1984–85) 246.
3 For Mr Speaker's Ruling, see HC Deb (1979–80) 986, c 301.
4 First Report from the Select Committee on Procedure, Session 1974–75, HC 294, pv.
5 Parl Deb (1855) 137, c 261; ibid (1883) 280, c 250. A private Member's action in handing a document to a Minister in support of arguments was ruled to be 'very irregular', HC Deb (1946–47) 433, c 1566.
6 HC Deb (1985–86) 92, c 279 w.
7 Parl Deb (1865) 177, cc 354, 355. See for example HC Deb (1981–82) 16, c 423.
8 HC Deb (1964–65) 718, cc 407–408, 963; ibid (1971–72) 832, cc 571, 575.
9 HC Deb (1965–66) 720, c 321.
10 HC Deb (1968–69) 780, cc 491–493.

Commons (Services) Committee that a department should supply to the library in advance a list of all older papers which appear relevant to a forthcoming debate,[1] and has accepted a motion for the adjournment of the debate where this did not appear to have been done.[2]

DISPLAY OF ARTICLES TO ILLUSTRATE SPEECHES

The rules of the House of Commons forbid bringing certain articles, notably weapons, into the Chamber.[3] Members have been permitted to display articles (but not weapons) to illustrate an argument in a speech.[4]

REFERENCE TO STRANGERS

It is not in order to refer to persons in the Galleries (except generally for the purpose of an order for their withdrawal).[5]

DISCLOSURE AND REGISTRATION OF PERSONAL PECUNIARY INTEREST

On 22 May 1974 the House of Commons agreed to two resolutions relating to the declaration of interests by Members—

> 'That, in any debate or proceeding of the House or its committees or transactions or communications which a Member may have with other Members or with Ministers or servants of the Crown, he shall disclose any relevant pecuniary interest or benefit of whatever nature, whether direct or indirect, that he may have had, may have or may be expecting to have.[6]
>
> 'That every Member of the House of Commons shall furnish to a Registrar of Members' Interests such particulars of his registrable interests as shall be required, and shall notify to the Registrar any alterations which may occur therein, and the Registrar shall cause these particulars to be entered in a Register of Members' Interests which shall be available for inspection by the public.'

At the same time the House agreed to the appointment of a Select Committee to consider the arrangements to be made relative to the declaration of Members' interests and the way in which the register of such interests should be compiled.[7]

The Select Committee reported to the House on 12 December 1974. The report[8] was debated on 12 June 1975, when the House broadly accepted the conclusions and recommendations of the Committee.[9] The present practice

---

1 HC Deb (1965–66), 725, c 34.
2 HC Deb (1977–78) 950, cc 1458–1460; ibid (1978–79) 972, cc 1581–1586.
3 See HC Deb (1951–52) 498, c 2750; ibid (1981–82) 15, c 170.
4 See HC Deb (1951–52) 517, c 1963; ibid (1955–56) 555, c 1061; ibid (1969–70) 792, c 1193; ibid (1971–72) 842, c 564; ibid (1983–84) 54, c 1020.
5 See HC Deb (1972–73) 847, c 454; ibid (1985–86) 92, c 954.
6 See also HC (1969–70) 57, para. 114.
7 CJ (1974) 143–144.
8 HC (1974–75) 102.
9 HC Deb (1974–75) 893, cc 735–804.

of the House with regard to both declaration and registration of interests is described below.

DECLARATION OF INTERESTS IN DEBATE

So far as debates are concerned, it is now a rule of the House, rather than a convention as was previously the case, for every Member to declare 'any relevant pecuniary interest or benefit of whatever nature, whether direct or indirect, that he may have had, may have or may be expecting to have'.[1] The definition of relevance is left to the discretion of the Member concerned. The extent to which details of the relevant interest are disclosed is also a matter for the Member; in certain cases, if the interest is recorded in the Register of Members' Interests (see below, p 388), it may be sufficient simply to draw attention to this. A Member will normally declare his interest at the beginning of his remarks. This rule applies not only to debates in the House, but to almost all proceedings of the House or its committees in which Members have an opportunity to speak, such as debates in standing committees,[2] presentation of a public petition, and meetings of a select committee at which evidence is heard. It does not, however, apply to the asking of supplementary questions or to answers.[3]

DECLARATION IN OTHER PROCEEDINGS OF THE HOUSE OR ITS COMMITTEES

The resolution of the House of 22 May 1974 extended the rule regarding declaration of interests to all proceedings of the House or its committees. The Select Committee on Members' Interests (Declaration) drew attention in its report of December 1974[4] to the difficulties involved in proceedings when Members do not speak. They devised certain procedures, some involving the use of symbols, to cover proceedings such as questions, the giving notice of a motion or amendment, and voting. The administrative difficulties involved in these procedures were great, however, and accordingly the House resolved that the term 'proceedings' (as used on 22 May 1974) 'shall be deemed not to include the giving of any written notice, or the asking of a supplementary question'. As a result, the tabling of a question, a motion or an amendment (whether to a motion or a bill) does not require to be accompanied by any declaration of a relevant interest, and the same applies to the adding of a Member's name to a motion or amendment already on the Order Paper.

A Member is required to declare his interest when putting a question to a witness before a select committee, whether the meeting is in public or private. He is also required to declare his interest at deliberative meetings of select committees; any such declarations are recorded and published in the minutes of proceedings of the committee. In practice a single declaration made by a Member at the start of an inquiry and duly minuted is considered

1 CJ (1974) 143.
2 Standing Committee A, Proceedings on Local Government Bill, Session 1986–87, c 4.
3 HC Deb (1983–84) 53, c 24. See, however, HC Deb (1983–84) 56, cc 9–10 w.
4 HC (1974–75) 102 pp xiii–xv.

sufficient to cover all the subsequent deliberations of the committee during that inquiry.

So far as voting in the House or a committee is concerned, and for this purpose only, the recording of an interest in the Register of Members' Interests is by itself regarded as sufficient disclosure, since the House on 12 June 1975 resolved:

> 'That, for the purposes of the Resolution of the House of 22 May 1974 in relation to disclosures of interests in any proceeding of the House or its Committees, any interest disclosed in a copy of the Register of Members' Interests shall be regarded as sufficient disclosure for the purpose of taking part in any division in the House or in any of its Committees.'[1]

The Speaker has made it clear that the right of Members to vote on matters of public policy remains the same during the period which occurs at the beginning of each Parliament before a new Register is published.[2]

OTHER DECLARATIONS

There is also a requirement to disclose any relevant interest in any 'transactions or communications which a Member may have with other Members or with Ministers or servants of the Crown'.[3]

CLASSES OF INTEREST TO BE REGISTERED

The report of the Select Committee on Members' Interests (Declaration), which was endorsed by the House on 12 June 1975, defined the purpose of the Register in the following terms:

> 'to provide information of any pecuniary interest or other material benefit which a Member of Parliament may receive which might be thought to affect his conduct as a Member of Parliament or influence his actions, speeches or vote in Parliament'.

Within that general purpose, the Select Committee identified nine classes of pecuniary interest or other benefit which were to be disclosed in the Register. They are:

(1) remunerated directorships of companies, public or private;
(2) remunerated employments or offices;
(3) remunerated trades, professions or vocations;
(4) the names of clients when the interests referred to above include personal services by the Member which arise out of or are related in any manner to his membership of the House;
(5) financial sponsorships, (a) as a parliamentary candidate where to the knowledge of the Member the sponsorship in any case exceeds 25 per cent. of the candidate's election expenses, or (b) as a Member of Parliament, by any person or organization, stating whether any such sponsorship includes any payment to the Member or any material benefit or advantage direct or indirect;

---

1 CJ (1974–75) 480.
2 HC Deb (1987–88) 119, cc 195–197.
3 CJ (1974) 143.

(6) overseas visits relating to or arising out of membership of the House where the cost of any such visit has not been wholly borne by the Member or by public funds;

(7) any payments or any material benefits or advantages received from or on behalf of foreign Governments, organizations or persons;

(8) land and property of substantial value or from which a substantial income is derived;

(9) the names of companies or other bodies in which the Member has, to his knowledge, either himself or with or on behalf of his spouse or infant children, a beneficial interest in shareholdings of a nominal value greater than one-hundredth of the issued share capital.

A Member is only required to enter the source of the remuneration or benefit and not the amount received.

The Select Committee on Members' Interests (see below) has from time to time provided interpretations of these rules in order to assist Members: Ministerial office, membership of the European Parliament, the Council of Europe, the Western European Union and the North Atlantic Assembly do not need to be registered (HC (1974–75) 677); a Member is 'clearly required' to register the name of a client where he has no doubt that his personal services to the client arise out of or are related in any manner to his membership of the House, but the provision relating to registration does not in any way release a Member from the obligation to declare his interest in any proceedings of the House which involves his private practice (ibid); a Member need not register the fact that he is supported at an election by his local constituency party (ibid); visits undertaken on behalf of the Inter Parliamentary Union, the Commonwealth Parliamentary Association, the Council of Europe, the Western European Union and the North Atlantic Assembly, or any Select Committee of the House, and any visit paid for by Her Majesty's Government or by any institution of the European Community need not be registered (ibid); in registering an overseas visit a Member should disclose the sponsor of the visit (ibid); the words 'any pecuniary interest or other material benefit' used in the definition of the purpose of the Register may include pensions and annuities, but state pensions, a pension stemming from the former occupation of a Member, or a pension being received prior to 10 October 1974, or pensions and annuities paid in respect of interests which have themselves been registered, are not registered (ibid); any Member who sponsors a function in the Palace of Westminster from which sponsorship he derives a taxable benefit should declare the source of that benefit (HC (1979–80) 337). Receipt of gifts in relation to a Member's parliamentary duties, other than from overseas (to which Category 7 applies) should be registered under subsection (b) of Category 5, Financial Sponsorship (ibid). When a Member is provided by an external organisation with the full or part-time services of a research assistant or secretary that interest should be registered (HC (1987–88) 314.)

On 17 December 1985 the House confirmed by Resolution the recommendations of the Committee HC (1984–85) 408, that the scope of the requirement to register remunerated trades, professions or vocations includes any remunerated activity in the field of public relations and political and parliamentary advice and consultancy; and that in regard to the registration and declaring of clients the services which require such registration and, where appropriate, declaration include as well as any action connected with any proceedings in the House or its Committees, the sponsoring of functions in the Palace, making representations to Ministers, Civil Servants and other Members, accompanying delegations to Ministers and the like (CJ (1985–86) 96).

REGISTER OF MEMBERS' INTERESTS

The Register of Members' Interests is compiled on the basis of the returns made by Members of their registrable interests under the nine headings set out above. The task of collating the returns is that of the Registrar of Members' Interests, a senior member of the department of the Clerk of the House. It is his duty to send out the appropriate form for Members to complete at the beginning of each Parliament; a form is similarly sent to every Member returned at a by-election after he has taken his seat. It is the responsibility of Members to return the completed form within four weeks; it is also their responsibility to notify the Registrar of any changes in their registrable interests within four weeks of the changes occurring.

When the Register is complete the Registrar, after securing the authorisation of the Select Committee on Members' Interests[1] (see below), arranges for its publication by Her Majesty's Stationery Office as a House of Commons paper. He also arranges for a revised Register, recording changes which have occurred, to be published from time to time. In the period before such changes are published, they may be viewed in the Registry by the general public under conditions laid down from time to time by the Select Committee, and by Members at any time during sitting days or by appointment in the recess. An up-to-date version of the Register is available for Members to see in the Library.

Select Committee on Members' Interests

The Select Committee on Members' Interests (Declaration) recommended the appointment of a Select Committee to 'examine the arrangements made for the compilation, maintenance and accessibility of the Register of Members' Interests; to consider any proposals made by Members or others as to the form and contents of the Register; to consider any specific complaints made in relation to the registering or declaring of interests; and to report on these and any other matters relating to Members' interests'.[2] Such a Select Committee with an almost identical order of reference (see p 658) was first appointed on 2 February 1976.

The Committee also recommended that the Registrar would act as clerk of the new Committee. The new Committee would be appointed for the duration of a Parliament, and have two separate functions. It would exercise a general oversight of the new procedures for the registering and declaring of interests and make recommendations for changes therein; it would also be required to consider any specific complaints or disputes which may arise over particular interests. The House has laid down the procedures which must be followed in such cases.

---

1 HC Deb (1983–84) 47, c 875.
2 In Session 1974–75 this task was undertaken by the Select Committee on Members' Interests (Declaration) itself.

In consonance with the first function, the Committee has from time to time reported to the House its interpretation of the scope of various of the nine classes of pecuniary interest.

Under the terms of the recommendations of the Select Committee on Members' Interests (Declaration) as agreed to by the House,[1] at the request of a Member or the Registrar, a difference of opinion between them about the inclusion of any item on the Register may be referred for solution to the Select Committee. Such a reference must, however, be in general terms, without mentioning the Member by name, except with his consent. If the Committee decides that the interest should be registered, the Member is so informed; if he is not satisfied, the Committee makes a report to the House together with a recommendation as to what action should be taken; such a report is still, however, in general terms. The final decision rests with the House itself.

Where one Member makes an allegation against another Member, he is required to do so in writing to the Registrar, who refers the allegation to the Committee and informs the Member concerned. The Committee may then hear both Members together with such other evidence as it thinks fit, and may make a report to the House together with a recommendation as to what action is to be taken. Again it is for the House to make the final decision.

Where a member of the public wishes to allege that a Member is in breach of the resolutions of the House relating to registration or disclosure of interests, he must make a complaint in writing to the Registrar. The Registrar is required to inform any member of the public who wishes to complain that before taking any further action he should know that any communication between them is not covered by parliamentary privilege or privileged at law. The Registrar is empowered to determine whether prima facie evidence exists of the accuracy of the allegation; if it does not in his opinion, he has discretion to refuse to consider the matter further. If in his opinion the possibility of a failure to comply with the resolutions of the House has been established, the Registrar must report the matter to the Select Committee. It may call for an explanation from the Member concerned, and may hear evidence from such persons as it thinks fit, including the Member and his witnesses. A report with an appropriate recommendation is made to the House, with which, as in other cases, the final decision rests[2].

Enforcement of requirements to register

The procedure outlined in the preceding paragraphs is designed to ensure that, so far as possible, the House is not faced with the need to consider what may be inadvertent or minor breaches of the rules relating to registration and disclosure of interests. But as was pointed out in the report of the Select Committee on Members' Interests (Declaration), endorsing the evidence of the Clerk of the House: 'The ultimate sanction behind the obligation upon Members to register would be the fact that it was imposed by resolution of the House . . . There can be no doubt that the House might consider either a refusal to register as required by its resolutions or the wilful furnishing of

1 CJ (1974–75) 480.
2 HC 428 (1988–89).

misleading or false information to be a contempt. The sanction of possible penal jurisdiction by the House should be sufficient'.[1]

OTHER REGISTERS

Following appropriate recommendations from the Select Committee on Members' Interests,[2] the House resolved on 17 December 1985, that:

(1) those holding permanent passes as lobby journalists, as journalists accredited to the Parliamentary Press Gallery or for parliamentary broadcasting be required to register not only the employment for which they had received their pass, but also any other paid occupation or employment where their privileged access to Parliament is relevant;

(2) holders of permanent passes as Members' secretaries or Members' research assistants be required to register any relevant occupation which they may pursue other than for which the pass is issued; and

(3) Commons officers of All Party and Registered Groups be required to register the names of the officers of the Group, the source and extent of any benefits financial or in kind from outside sources which they may enjoy, together with any other relevant occupation of any staff which they may have. Where a public relations agency provides the assistance, the ultimate client should be named.[3]

In conformity with this resolution, these registers are now placed in the Library for the use of Members. They are not open for inspection by other persons.

3. RULES OF BEHAVIOUR FOR MEMBERS NOT SPEAKING

MEMBERS TO KEEP THEIR PLACES

By the resolutions of 10 February 1698 and 16 February 1720 Members are ordered to keep their places.[4] If, after a call to order, Members who are standing at the bar or elsewhere do not disperse, the Speaker will order them to take their places.[5] It is the duty of the Serjeant at Arms to clear the gangway and to enforce the order of the Speaker, by desiring those Members who still obstruct the passage immediately to take their places (see p 190). If they refuse or neglect to comply, or oppose the Serjeant in the execution of his duty, he may report their names to the Speaker. Members who enter or leave the House during a debate must be uncovered and should make an obeisance to the Chair while passing to or from their places.[6]

Crossing before Members speaking

Members must not cross between the Chair and a Member who is speaking from either of the two lower benches, or between the Chair and the Table, or

---

1 HC (1974–75) 102 p xii.
2 HC (1984–85) 408.
3 CJ (1985–86) 97.
4 CJ (1697–99) 496; ibid (1718–21) 425.
5 HC Deb (1976–77) 929, c 1041.
6 D'Ewes 282; 2 Hatsell 232 n.

between the Chair and the mace, when the mace is taken off the Table by the Serjeant.[1] When they cross the House, or otherwise leave their places, they should make obeisance to the Chair.

READING OF BOOKS, ETC

Members must not read any book, newspaper or letter in their places except in connection with the business of the debate.[2]

SILENCE

All Members should maintain silence, or should converse only in undertones. Whenever the conversation is so loud as to make it difficult to hear the debate, the occupant of the Chair calls the House to order.[3]

> On 5 May 1641 it was resolved: 'That if any man shall whisper or stir out of his place to the disturbance of the House at any message or business of importance, Mr Speaker is ordered to *present his name* to the House, for the House to proceed against him as they shall think fit.'[4]

Hissing or interruption

Members must not disturb a Member who is speaking, by hissing, chanting, clapping, booing, exclamations or other interruption. On 22 January 1693, it was resolved 'that Mr Speaker do call upon the Member by name, making such disturbance, and that every such person shall incur the displeasure and censure of the House'.[5] A considerable volume of noise, however, frequently arises from the fullness of the House, when five or six hundred Members are impatiently waiting for a division, which it is scarcely possible to repress. The conduct of Members in the Chamber, and appropriate penalties for misbehaviour, were considered in a Report from the Select Committee on Procedure in 1989.[6]

> On 19 March 1872, while strangers were excluded, notice was taken of the crowing of cocks, and other disorderly noises, proceeding from Members, principally behind the Chair; and the Speaker condemned them as gross violations of the orders of the House and expressed the pain with which he had heard them.[7]

Cries of 'hear, hear', etc.

There are words of interruption which, if used in moderation, are not unparliamentary, but when frequent and loud, cause serious disorder. These include the cries of 'question', 'order, order', 'hear, hear', or 'divide,

---

1 HC Deb (1977–78) 944, c 1212.
2 CJ (1644–46) 51; HC Deb (1984–85) 73, c 959; Stg Co Deb (1953–54) Co A, Cotton Bill, c 398; ibid (1955–56) Co E, (Pensions (Increase) Bill) 21 March 1956.
3 HC Deb (1988–89) 143, cc 1014, 1031, 1040.
4 CJ (1640–42) 135.
5 CJ (1547–1628) 152, 473; see also motions against hissing, etc, ibid (1604) 243, 935; ibid (1693–97) 66; booing, HC Deb (1952–53) 508, cc 1565–1566.
6 HC (1988–89) 290.
7 Parl Deb (1872) 210, c 307.

divide', which have been sanctioned by long parliamentary usage. When intended to denote approbation of the sentiments expressed, and not uttered till the end of a sentence, the cry of 'hear, hear', offers no interruption of the speech. The same words may be used for very different purposes, and instead of implying approbation, they may express dissent, derision or contempt. Whenever exclamations of this kind are obviously intended to interrupt a speech, the Speaker calls the House to order, and, if the cries are persisted in, he may direct the disorderly Members to withdraw from the House or name them (see pp 394–395). If the interruption should be so continuous and prolonged as to constitute a state of grave disorder[1] the Speaker may use the powers given him by Standing Order No 45 (see p 395).

Cry of 'shame'

A gross form of interruption by loud cries of 'shame', has been strongly condemned by the Speaker, who declared his intention to take notice of the committal of the offence.[2]

MEMBERS' DRESS

Members are not permitted to wear decorations in the House.[3] The wearing of military insignia or uniform inside the Chamber is not in accordance with the long-established custom of the House. The Speaker has also stated that it is the custom for Members to wear jackets and ties.[4]

SMOKING AND REFRESHMENTS

The practice of smoking during any of the proceedings of the House is forbidden.[5] Nor may refreshment be brought into, or consumed in, the Chamber.[6]

4. POWERS OF THE CHAIR TO ENFORCE ORDER

In so large and active an assembly as the House of Commons, it is absolutely necessary that the Speaker should be invested with authority to repress disorder and to give effect promptly and decisively to the rules and orders of the House. The ultimate authority on all these matters is the House itself; but the Speaker is the executive officer by whom its rules are enforced.

---

1 HC Deb (1912) 43, c 2054; ibid 44, c 33; ibid (1923) 162, c 1265.
2 Parl Deb (1887) 310, c 166; ibid (1893) 12, cc 731, 790; ibid (1893) 14, c 469.
3 HC Deb (1951–52) 498, c 2750; ibid (1979–80) 984, c 986.
4 HC Deb (1981–82) 27, c 468; ibid (1987–88) 119, c 194.
5 For the order 'That no Member do presume to take tobacco in the gallery of the House or at a committee table', see CJ (1693–97) 137; HC Deb (1919) 117, c 846; in the lobbies and corridors, ibid (1928) 215, c 348; in the division lobbies, ibid (1927) 209, c 1469; ibid (1979–80) 978, c 1882; in Standing Committees, see Stg Co Deb (1955–56) Co A (Agriculture (Safety) Bill) 6 March 1956. The rule is not enforced in Select Committees when a Committee is deliberating.
6 HC Deb (1970–71) 803, c 1006; ibid (1978–79) 960, c 690; in Standing Committee, see Stg Co Deb (1955–56), Scottish Co (Food and Drugs (Scotland) Bill) 24 November 1955.

In most cases the breach of order is obvious and is immediately checked by the Speaker. In other cases if his attention is directed to a breach of order at the proper time, namely, the moment when it occurs,[1] he at once gives his decision and if he fails to secure the compliance of the Member at fault directs him to withdraw or names him and leaves it to the House to inflict the appropriate penalty (see p 398).

The power to punish disorder derives from the ancient usages of the House in proceeding against a Member; but in modern times the Speaker has been armed by standing orders,[2] with precisely defined summary powers, which largely supersede those exercised under ancient usage. Nevertheless, one of these orders (Standing Order No 43) expressly saves the power of the House to proceed against a Member under ancient usage. (For a full description of the disciplinary powers of the Speaker under ancient usage, including the procedure for words taken down, see 20th edition of this work, pp 442–444.)

DISCIPLINARY POWERS UNDER STANDING ORDER

Under Standing Orders Nos 41 to 45 the Chair is entrusted with summary and expeditious powers of dealing with disorder.[3] Standing Orders Nos 41 to 44 were passed in the 1880s, and Standing Order No 45 in 1902. With subsequent amendments, and as interpreted in practice, they provide a graduated code of punishments for infringements of the rules for the conduct of debate and for breaches of order and decorum, which has been found adequate to deal with all the cases which ordinarily arise. Offences and the appropriate methods of dealing with them may be classified as follows:

(1) irrelevance or tedious repetition;
(2) minor breaches of order;
(3) the use of disorderly or unparliamentary expressions;
(4) grossly disorderly conduct;
(5) grave disorder, and
(6) obstruction of the business of the House otherwise than by disorderly conduct or persistence in irrelevance or tedious repetition.

(1) Irrelevance and tedious repetition

If any Member wanders from the question under discussion, the Speaker will interrupt him and remind him that he must speak to the question. If a Member persists in irrelevance or tedious repetition either of his own arguments, or of the arguments used by other Members in debate, Standing Order No 41 empowers the Speaker, after calling the attention of the House to the Member's conduct, to direct him to discontinue his speech.[4] If he refuses to obey the direction of the Chair, the Speaker, acting under Standing Order No 42, may either direct him to withdraw from the House for the

---

1 Parl Deb (1872) 210, c 534; ibid (1878–79) 247, c 325; HC Deb (1972–73) 854, c 1525; ibid (1972–73) 855, cc 28–30. See also Denison 42.
2 SO Nos 41 to 45.
3 HC Deb (1975–76) 919, cc 1565–1566.
4 Eg CJ (1933–34) 334; ibid (1967–68) 340; ibid (1970–71) 280; ibid (1975–76) 279; ibid (1985–86) 94, c 885.

remainder of the sitting,[1] or name him for disregarding the authority of the Chair.[2]

(2) Minor breaches of order

When any Member transgresses the rules of debate, otherwise than by using disorderly or unparliamentary expressions, or makes any noise or disturbance whilst another Member is speaking, or commits any other breach of order or decorum not amounting to grossly disorderly conduct (see below), it is the duty of the Speaker, if in his judgment the occasion demands it, to intervene and call the Member to order, or direct him to resume his seat.[3] If he persists in his disorderly conduct it becomes the duty of the Speaker to take the action set forth in Standing Order No 42 in respect of grossly disorderly conduct. The Speaker has also directed Members to withdraw from the Chamber without invoking the powers of Standing Order No 42 (see paragraph (4) below).[4]

(3) The use of disorderly or unparliamentary expressions

Where any disorderly or unparliamentary words are used, whether by a Member who is addressing the House or by a Member who is present during a debate, the Speaker will intervene and call upon the offending Member to withdraw the words. If the Member does not explain the sense in which he used the words so as to remove the objection of their being disorderly, or retract the offensive expressions, or make a sufficient apology for using them, the Speaker will repeat his call for the words to be withdrawn, and inform the Member that if he does not immediately respond to it, it will be the duty of the Chair to take action in pursuance of Standing Order No 42.[5]

(4) Grossly disorderly conduct

To prevent any Member being taken unawares it is usual for the Speaker or the Chairman repeatedly to warn any Member who may be transgressing the rules of debate or otherwise conducting himself in a disorderly manner, before ordering him to withdraw from the House or naming him. When, however, a Member persists in disorderly conduct or conducts himself in a grossly disorderly manner the Speaker is enjoined by Standing Order No 42 either (i) forthwith to order him to withdraw from the House for the remainder of the sitting,[6] or (ii) if he thinks the authority and dignity of the House would not be sufficiently vindicated by excluding the offender from the House for the remainder of the sitting, to name him.[7] If a Member who has been ordered to withdraw from the House does not immediately obey,

1 CJ (1897) 265; ibid (1898) 96; ibid (1975–76) 279.
2 CJ (1897) 264.
3 HC Deb (1975–76) 918, c 1409.
4 HC Deb (1981–82) 18, c 251; ibid (1981–82) 19, cc 296, 367; ibid (1984–85) 73, c 1217.
5 CJ (1950–51) 224; HC Deb (1977–78) 954, cc 417–419.
6 CJ (1932–33) 68; ibid (1946–47) 373; ibid (1950–51) 252; HC Deb (1977–78) 954, cc 416–417; ibid (1982–83) 31, c 88.
7 CJ (1935–36) 341, 342; HC Deb (1980–81) 2, c 950.

the Speaker or Chairman may either direct the Serjeant at Arms to remove him,[1] or name the Member to the House.[2]

When a Member behaved in a grossly disorderly fashion by attempting to make a speech during Prayers, the Speaker directed him to withdraw. When the Member declined to comply with the Speaker's direction, he was named for disregarding the authority of the Chair.[3]

When attention was drawn to the fact that a Member who had been directed to withdraw from the House had not withdrawn, the Chair reminded the Member of the direction that had been given him, and on the Member's refusing to withdraw, named him for disregarding the authority of the Chair.[4]

After the Prime Minister had replied to a question, a Member left his seat below the gangway, and, walking to the end of the ministerial bench above the gangway, addressed the Prime Minister in grossly discourteous terms; whereupon the Speaker at once ordered him to withdraw from the House.[5]

A Member who used insulting language to the Chairman during the progress of a division was ordered to withdraw.[6]

Again, a Member who used insulting language to the Speaker from beyond the bar, and a Member who seized the mace and carried it away from the Table, have been named for grossly disorderly conduct.[7]

(5) Grave disorder

In the event of grave disorder arising in the House, the Speaker is empowered by Standing Order No 45, if he thinks it necessary, to adjourn the House without question put,[8] or to suspend the sitting for a time to be named by him.[9] (See also pp 249–250).

(6) Obstruction of the business of the House otherwise than by disorderly conduct or persistence in irrelevance or tedious repetition

A Member who 'abuses the rules of the House by persistently and wilfully obstructing the business of the House', that is to say, who, without actually transgressing any of the rules of debate, uses his right of speech for the purpose of obstructing the business of the House, or obstructs the business

---

1 CJ (1896) 242; ibid (1897) 265; ibid (1900) 380; Parl Deb (1900) 87, cc 523–526; HC Deb (1979–80) 987, cc 216–218.
2 CJ (1923) 156, 237; ibid (1924–25) 102; ibid (1926) 60, 327; ibid (1927) 218, 340–341.
3 Votes and Proceedings (1987–88) 11 January 1988. It was necessary for the Speaker to take the Chair for this proceeding, and a division took place. Mr Speaker then left the Chair and Prayers were said.
4 CJ (1913) 37; HC Deb (1913) 50, c 1695.
5 HC Deb (1912–13) 40, cc 217–218.
6 CJ (1900) 380.
7 HC Deb (1937–38) 328, c 1773; ibid (1929–30) 241, c 1465. See also HC Deb (1975–76) 912, c 769.
8 CJ (1905) 202; ibid (1911) 351; ibid (1914) 237; ibid (1924) 178; ibid (1926) 232; ibid (1960–61) 98; ibid (1984–85) 41.
9 CJ (1920) 436, HC Deb (1920) 135, c 39; CJ (1935–36) 341, HC Deb (1935–36) 315, c 838; CJ (1955–56) 428; HC Deb (1955–56) 558 c 1625; CJ (1961–62) 55; CJ (1974–75) 259; HC Deb (1974–75) 887, c 1275; CJ (1979–80) 851.

of the House by misusing the forms of the House, is technically not guilty of disorderly conduct.[1] It would seem, therefore, that a Member so obstructing the business of the House cannot be required under Standing Order No 42 to withdraw from the House for the remainder of the sitting. He may be, however, guilty of a contempt of the House,[2] and may be named. Comparatively little use has been made of this power by the Chair.[3]

(7) Member suspended other than by standing order procedure

A Member, who damaged the mace immediately after the House had adjourned and who on the next day declined to make a personal statement in the form previously agreed with the Speaker, was on the following day suspended from the service of the House for twenty days and held responsible for the damage he had caused, following the House's agreement to a motion to that effect moved by the Leader of the House.[4]

Effective restraints upon other forms of obstruction are provided by the powers of the Chair to accept a motion that the question be now proposed (Standing Order No 28) or for the closure of the debate (Standing Order No 35), to put the question upon a dilatory motion forthwith or to decline to propose the question on such a motion (Standing Order No 34), to select the amendments to be proposed to any bill or motion (Standing Order No 31), and, where a division is unnecessarily claimed, to take the vote of the House or committee by calling upon the Members who support, and who challenge his decision, successively to rise in their places (Standing Order No 39). (See also chapter 19.)

RIGHT OF MEMBERS TO DIRECT THE ATTENTION OF THE CHAIR TO SUPPOSED BREACHES OF ORDER

It is the duty of the Speaker to intervene to preserve order, though he may refrain from intervening if he thinks it unnecessary to do so. If he does not intervene, however, whether for the above reason or because he has not perceived that a breach of order has been committed, it is the right of any Member who thinks that such a breach has been committed to rise in his place, interrupting any Member who may be speaking, and direct the attention of the Chair to the matter.[5] A Member speaking to order must simply direct attention to the point complained of, and submit it to the decision of the Speaker. If the Speaker is of the opinion that the words or conduct complained of are disorderly, he will call upon the Member to conform to the rules of the House.

Speakers have exercised discretion over the taking of points of order[6] and have indicated at what point in the proceedings they are prepared to hear them.[7]

---

1 Mr Speaker Brand's evidence, Select Committee on Public Business, HC 268, p 142, Q 1381 (1878); Parl Deb (1881) 257, c 1944.
2 CJ (1877) 375–376.
3 For instances of the exercise of the power, see CJ (1882) 322, 324; ibid (1901) 62; ibid (1926) 117.
4 Votes and Proceedings (1987–88) 20 April 1988.
5 Parl Deb (1872) 210, c 534; ibid (1878–79) 247, c 325. See also Denison 42.
6 HC Deb (1979–80) 971, cc 103–104 etc.
7 HC Deb (1986–87) 110, cc 459–460.

Doubtful cases may arise upon which the rules of the House are indistinct or obsolete or do not apply directly to the point at issue. The Speaker will then usually give a ruling to cover the new circumstances, although he has on occasion referred the matter to the judgment of the House.[1]

The Speaker has deprecated the practice of Members raising points of order on political issues which have nothing to do with the Chair,[2] and has expressed the hope that points of order will not be used as an extension of Question time.[3]

On 1 July 1952 the Deputy Speaker deprecated a growing practice of interruptions of debate by Members who, 'when the hon. Member who is speaking refuses to give way, think that the only way that they can get their word in is by raising a point of order'. He stated that in his opinion such interruptions constituted fraudulent points of order, and should be stopped.[4]

PROCEDURE WHEN THE SPEAKER RISES

Whenever the Speaker rises to intervene in a debate, he should be heard in silence,[5] and any Member who is speaking or offering to speak should immediately sit down.[6] Members should not leave their seats while the Speaker is addressing the House. Members who do not maintain silence, or who attempt to address the Speaker, are called to order by the majority of the House with loud cries of 'order' and 'Chair'. A Member who persists in standing after the Speaker has risen and refuses to resume his seat when directed by the Chair to do so may be either directed to withdraw from the House for the remainder of the sitting or named for disregarding the authority of the Chair.[7]

PROCEEDINGS ON THE NAMING OF A MEMBER

When a Member is named by the Speaker for grossly disorderly conduct (Standing Order No 42) or for disregarding the authority of the Chair or for persistently or wilfully obstructing the business of the House by abusing the rules of the House, or otherwise (Standing Order No 43), a motion may be made 'That Mr . . . [the offending Member] be suspended from the service of the House'; and the question on that motion must be put forthwith (Standing Order No 43).

When a Member is named by the Chairman to a Committee of the whole House, the Chairman forthwith suspends the proceedings of the Committee and reports the circumstances to the House; and the Speaker, on a motion being made for the suspension of the offending Member from the service of the House, forthwith puts the question, as if the offence had been committed in the House itself.

---

1 Parl Deb (1806) 6, c 847; ibid (1807) 7, c 208.
2 HC Deb (1986–87) 106, cc 271–272.
3 HC Deb (1983–84) 57, c 1109–1110.
4 HC Deb (1951–52) 503, c 277.
5 CJ (1604) 244.
6 Parl Deb (1897) 49, c 122; HC Deb (1976–77) 931, c 213.
7 HC Deb (1923) 165, c 2395; ibid (1981–82) 13, cc 999–1000.

Proceedings on a motion for the suspension of a Member under Standing Order No 43 are exempt from interruption under Standing Order No 9. They may be taken after the moment of interruption.[1]

Not more than one Member may be named at a time unless several Members present together have jointly disregarded the authority of the Chair.[2]

Suspension continues on the first occasion for five sitting days,[3] and on the second occasion for twenty sitting days,[4] including in either case the day on which the Member was suspended, and on any subsequent occasion until the House orders that the Member's suspension shall terminate or, in default of such order, for the remainder of the session. The first (or subsequent) occasion has been interpreted to mean the first (or subsequent) occasion in the same session.

A Member who is suspended from the service of the House under this order is required by Standing Order No 44 to withdraw from the House forthwith. If he does not withdraw, he will be directed to do so by the Speaker. If the Member does not comply with the direction, the Speaker will order the Serjeant at Arms to summon him to obey the Speaker's direction.[5] If he still refuses to obey, the Speaker will call the attention of the House to the fact that recourse to force is necessary in order to compel obedience to his direction, and will direct the Serjeant to remove the refractory Member. The standing order provides that in such a case the Member shall thereupon, without any further question being put, be suspended from the service of the House for the remainder of the session.

Where the Speaker has directed the Serjeant to cause a Member who had been suspended but refused to leave the House to be removed from the House, he has suspended the sitting until the Member had been removed.[6]

On 2 July 1931 a Member persisted in disregarding the authority of the Chair, whereupon the Speaker named him and he was suspended on the motion of the Prime Minister. The Speaker then directed the Member to withdraw, but he refused to comply. Accordingly the Speaker directed the Serjeant at Arms to remove him. The Serjeant at Arms, finding that force was necessary, brought in his officers, who in their attempts to remove the Member were resisted not only by that Member but by certain other Members. The Member who had been suspended was eventually removed. While this was taking place, the Speaker announced that grave disorder had arisen and suspended the sitting. After an interval of a quarter of an hour the Speaker resumed the Chair, and informed the

---

1 HC Deb (1987–88) 123, c 232.
2 For instances of several Members being named at the same time, see CJ (1926) 117; HC Deb (1981–82) 13, cc 24–25.
3 SO No 43(2). Between 1902 and 1926 no period was assigned by the Standing Order, and suspension therefore continued until the end of the session unless sooner terminated by the House. CJ (1902) 130, ibid (1912–13) 349; ibid (1913) 75; ibid (1916) 211; ibid (1920) 395; ibid (1923) 176, 321. Although a motion to rescind or terminate the suspension of a Member is not entitled to priority as a question of privilege, the Speaker has accorded priority to such a motion when it appeared that the Member had been named in error for disregarding the authority of the Chair, Parl Deb (1901) 90, cc 699, 831.
4 HC Deb (1980–81) 8, c 1159.
5 HC Deb (1967–68) 765, c 895; ibid (1981–82) 13, c 25; ibid (1987–88) 123, cc 232–233.
6 CJ (1916) 155; HC Deb (1916) 84, c 1861; CJ (1917–18) 171; ibid (1918) 141; HC Deb (1918) 107, c 1410; CJ (1930–31) 333.

House that, resort to force having been necessary to remove the Member, he was therefore suspended from the service of the House for the remainder of the session.

The next day, the Speaker read to the House a report which he had received from the Serjeant at Arms to the effect that his officers, when carrying out the Speaker's instructions, had been obstructed by certain Members. The Chancellor of the Exchequer, on behalf of the Prime Minister who was absent, stated that the Prime Minister proposed to draw the attention of the House to the report and to ask that appropriate action be taken.

On 6 July after the conclusion of questions, the Members concerned expressed deep regret for the incident, and the Prime Minister acknowledged the expressions of regret and suggested that they should be accepted by the House. The House ordered that the proceedings be entered in the Journals.[1]

Suspension, withdrawal and exclusion from precincts

Members ordered to withdraw from the House under Standing Order No 42 or suspended from the service of the House under Standing Order No 43 must withdraw forthwith from the precincts of the House.[2] A Member suspended from the service of the House on a motion not made pursuant to Standing Order No 43 is not excluded from the precincts of the House unless the order for his suspension expressly provides therefor.[3]

Suspension from the service of the House does not, however, exempt a Member from serving on any committee for the consideration of a private bill to which he has been appointed before his suspension.

Notices standing in the name of a suspended Member are removed from the Notice Paper for as long as his suspension lasts.[4] No motion can be made that a suspended Member be heard at the bar.[5]

Misbehaviour in the lobbies

A Member cannot be named unless the offence is committed in the House, or a Committee of the whole House, in the actual view of the Chair and is dealt with at once. Misbehaviour in the lobbies, such as the use of offensive expressions[6] or insulting words[7] or threats,[8] is accordingly left to the House to be dealt with under the ancient practice as a contempt. But action in a division lobby which obstructs the proceedings of the House, such as the indefinite prolongation of a division by the refusal of certain Members to pass the tellers, has been punished under Standing Order No 43 by naming, after the Chairman had directed the Serjeant to ascertain the names of the Members concerned.[9]

---

1 CJ (1930–31) 333, 335, 338.
2 For definition of precincts see Select Committee on Privilege (Service of a Summons on a Member in the Outer Lobby), HC 411, p 64, Q 1164 (1888); HC Deb (1916) 85, c 1426.
3 CJ (1890–91) 481.
4 Parl Deb (1901) 90, c 1048.
5 Parl Deb (1887) 313, cc 1126–1128.
6 CJ (1877) 144, Parl Deb (1877) 233, c 951.
7 CJ (1887) 377, 389; Parl Deb (1887) 317, c 1167.
8 Parl Deb (1881) 263, c 50.
9 CJ (1926) 117. See also HC Deb (1979–80) 969, cc 765, 779–781, 915–916.

CHAPTER 19

Methods of curtailing debate

There exist as part of the general practice and procedure of the House a number of methods of curtailing or avoiding debate, providing for questions to be put forthwith, or for time limits on debate. The principal methods are:

(1) By standing orders or occasional orders.
(2) Selection.
(3) Closure.
(4) Allocation of time orders (guillotines).

All these were originally designed to counteract the use of the ordinary forms of procedure to prolong debate and so obstruct the progress of business. Although probably a permanent feature of modern procedure, the last two methods—closure and guillotine—are felt to be an unfortunate necessity and to be justified only by the pressure of business or to counteract obstruction.[1]

1. STANDING ORDERS AND OCCASIONAL ORDERS

A. QUESTIONS PUT FORTHWITH

A number of standing orders require the Speaker to put forthwith various questions.

(1) Referral to committees

Motions to refer to committees bills, matters, estimates, statutory instruments and European Community Documents under Standing Orders Nos 90, 92, 93, 96, 97, 98, 99, 100, 101 and 102 are put forthwith. Under the same Standing Orders, substantive motions following such committees reporting back to the House are also put forthwith including in the case of motions

---

1 See, however, Second Report from the Select Committee on Procedure on Public Bill Procedure HC 49 (1984–85), and Second Report from the Select Committee on Procedure on Allocation of Time to Government Bills in Standing Committee HC 324 (1985–86).

relating to European Community Documents, the question on any amendment selected by the Chair.

Similarly, questions on motions to commit bills to a committee of the whole House, a special standing committee, select or joint committee, if made immediately after second reading, are put forthwith, under Standing Order No 61.

(2) Business of the House

Certain classes of motions which regulate the proceedings of the House and its committees are put forthwith by standing order. Debate on those business motions which are not covered by such standing orders may, however, be lengthy.

Questions put forthwith are:

—That the report of a Business Committee be considered, *and, if agreed,* that the House agrees with the Committee in its resolution: Standing Order No 80(b);

—That the House agree with the report of the Liaison Committee on the consideration of estimates on an Estimates Day: Standing Order No 131(2);

—That the proceedings of a day's sitting be suspended *and, when a suspended sitting is resumed,* That this House do now adjourn: Standing Order No 10;

—That the House adjourn till seven o'clock: Standing Order No 21(b);

—That the question be now proposed: Standing Order No 28;

—That the question be now put, *and, if agreed,* any question so claimed: Standing Order No 35;

—That the Scottish Grand Committee may meet in Edinburgh: Standing Order No 94(3);

—That strangers do withdraw: Standing Order No 143;

—That a Member be suspended from the service of the House: Standing Order No 43;

—[After the interruption of business] That specified business may be proceeded with until a specified hour or until any hour or until either a specified hour or the end of a specified period after it has been entered upon, whichever is the later: Standing Order No 14.

(3) Financial procedure

A number of questions relating to financial procedure are put forthwith:

—on second and third reading of a Consolidated Fund or an Appropriation Bill, if first order of the day: Standing Order No 54;

—on a motion for giving provisional statutory effect to any proposals in pursuance of section 5 of the Provisional Collection of Taxes Act 1968: Standing Order No 50(2);

—on all but the first of several Ways and Means motions upon which a bill is to be brought in: Standing Order No 50(3).

(4) Other

When an amendment on second or third reading of a bill to leave out all the words after 'That' has been negatived, the main question is put forthwith: Standing Order No 60.

B. TIME LIMITS

Standing orders in a number of circumstances provide for the putting of the question, or for the termination of debate, *either* (a) after the elapse of a specified period of time, *or* (b) by a particular time of day, *or* (c) both.

(a) Elapse of period

—An application to move the adjournment of the House for the purpose of discussing a specific and important matter that should have urgent consideration may not last more than *three minutes*: Standing Order No 20;

—The House is adjourned by Mr Speaker *half an hour* after a motion for the adjournment has been made at or after ten o'clock, without putting any question: Standing Order No 9(7);

—The Question 'That this House do now adjourn' in order to facilitate the business of select or standing committees is put *half an hour* after it has been proposed: Standing Order No 21(a);

—Questions necessary to dispose of proceedings on a motion for the adjournment of the House for a specified period or periods must be put *three hours* after they have been entered upon, if not previously concluded: Standing Order No 22;

—Questions necessary to dispose of proceedings on a motion providing for the allocation of time to any proceedings on a bill must be put not more than *three hours* after the commencement of those proceedings: Standing Order No 81;

—Proceedings on a motion for the adjournment of the House standing over from an application previously made under Standing Order No 20 are interrupted by the Speaker after *three hours*, without a requirement to put the question: Standing Order No 20(2).

(b) Time of day

—No opposed business can be taken after *ten o'clock* on Mondays to Thursdays, and *half-past two o'clock* on Fridays, unless otherwise provided for: Standing Orders Nos 9(3) and 11(2);

—Motions for the adjournment of the House moved at the conclusion of proceedings on a Consolidated Fund or an Appropriation Bill lapse at *nine o'clock in the morning*, or at eight o'clock on a Friday, if not previously concluded: Standing Order No 54.

—Motions to annul statutory instruments must be brought to a conclusion *at half-past eleven o'clock*, with a discretion for the Speaker to adjourn the debate if he considers the time allowed has not been adequate: Standing Order No 15.

(c) Elapse of period or time
—Questions necessary to dispose of proceedings on a money resolution must be put at *a quarter to eleven o'clock or three quarters of an hour* after the commencement of those proceedings, whichever is the later: Standing Order No 14(1)(d);
—Questions necessary to dispose of proceedings in pursuance of any Act of Parliament or on European Community documents must be put not later than *half-past eleven o'clock or one and a half hours* after the commencement of those proceedings, whichever is the later, but with discretion for the Speaker to adjourn the debate if he considers that the time allowed has not been adequate: Standing Order No 14(1)(b);

C. BRIEF DEBATE

Standing Order No 19 allows a brief explanatory statement from the Member who makes and from a Member who opposes a motion for leave to introduce a bill or for the nomination of Select Committees, but then requires the Speaker to put either the question thereon or the question 'That the debate be now adjourned' (see p 310). The practice of the House is to permit a maximum of 10 minutes on each such statement (see p 310). Similarly, under Standing Order No 61, if a motion to commit a bill to a standing committee in respect of some of its provisions and to a Committee of the whole House in respect of other provisions, or under Standing Order No 72, a motion to re-commit a bill, is opposed, the Speaker may permit a brief explanatory statement from the Member who makes and from a Member who opposes the motion, and is then required to put the question thereon. Such statements are also by practice limited to 10 minutes.

D. DISCRETION OF CHAIR

Standing orders also allow for some discretion for the Chair to curtail debate.

If, during the consideration of a bill in a Committee of the whole House, the chairman is of opinion that the principle of a clause or schedule and any matters arising thereon have been adequately discussed in the course of debate on the amendments, he is authorized by Standing Order No 67 to state this to be his opinion and forthwith to put the question that the clause or schedule stand part.

Under Standing Order No 34, when a dilatory motion has been moved, the Speaker has the option of putting the question forthwith, rather than declining to put the question thereon or allowing a debate.

For the Speaker's powers to limit the length of speeches under Standing Order No 45A, see pp 371–372.

E. ORDERS FOR PARTICULAR OCCASIONS

Business of the House motions which provide for time limits for particular items of business are frequently moved to meet particular circumstances often on a day before that on which they are to have effect. Such motions are debatable and cannot be proceeded with, if opposed, after the expiry of the time for unopposed business. For debate on several related motions, for example, the House has ordered that if not disposed of by a stated hour, the question is to be put successively on each motion and on any amendments selected thereto which may be moved. On other occasions, the House has ordered that questions necessary to dispose of proceedings on a bill or a motion be put at a given time, or after the elapse of a given period, or both.[1]

2. SELECTION OF AMENDMENTS

The power to select amendments was conferred upon the Chair in 1919. By Standing Order No 31 the Speaker is given power to select the amendments, new clauses or new schedules to be proposed in respect of any motion, or any bill under consideration on report or any Lords amendment to a bill; the Chairman of Ways and Means and either Deputy Chairman has the same power in committee of the whole House.[2]

By paragraph (4) of Standing Order No 31 an instruction to a committee on a bill, a motion to commit or re-commit a bill and motions relating to the proceedings on bills are treated as if they were amendments proposed in respect of that bill.

Under paragraph (3) of Standing Order No 31 the Chair may ask any Member who has given notice of an amendment to give such explanation of his amendment as may be necessary to form a judgment upon it.[3] Unless shortage of time forbids, however, it is the practice for the Speaker (or in Committee of the whole House, the Chairman of Ways and Means) to post an advance notice indicating which amendments, new clauses, and new schedules he has provisionally decided to select.[4]

The power to select amendments includes the power to select amendments proposed to be moved to an amendment,[5] and to reject a sole

1 See eg Votes and Proceedings (1986–87) 12 December 1986, 30 March 1987; ibid (1987–88) 27 November 1987, 20 May 1988.
2 CJ (1919) 37. Between 1909 and 1919 the standing orders authorized the moving of motions to empower the Chair to select amendments offered to motions, clauses and schedules.
3 HC Deb (1921) 147, c 1109.
4 HC Deb (1964–65) 703, c 37.
5 HC Deb (1909) 9, c 808.

amendment.[1] It is a common practice to allow several amendments to be discussed together, although they have not all been selected to be moved.[2] The Speaker or chairman may at his discretion call for division one or more of those amendments selected for debate with another or other amendments, if requested to do so.[3]

The Speaker's power of selection may be exercised in the House by the Deputy Speaker only during consideration of the estimates, under paragraph (5) of Standing Order No 31; or if the House has been informed by the Clerk at the Table of the absence of the Speaker.

Selection is made by the Chair in such a way as to bring out the salient points of criticism, to prevent repetition and overlapping (including repetition, without good cause, of debates at a previous stage of a bill), and where several amendments deal with the same point, to choose the more effective and the better drafted. Experience has shown that in most cases the discretion conferred on the Chair to select the amendments which may be moved is the best method of securing reasonable opportunities for all varieties of opinions. Under modern practice the Chair does not give reasons for not selecting an amendment.[4]

3. CLOSURE OF DEBATE

The conditions governing the application for, and granting of, the closure are laid down in Standing Orders Nos. 35 and 36. The closure has two principal forms: (1) the ordinary closure, with the extension known as 'closure upon contingent questions' to secure an immediate decision on any question already proposed from the Chair; and (2) the power of the Chair to accept a motion 'That the question be now proposed', under Standing Order No 28.

A. THE ORDINARY CLOSURE

After a question has been proposed, a Member may rise in his place and move 'That the question be now put'. That question must be put forthwith, without amendment or debate, unless it appears to the Chair that the motion is an abuse of the rules of the House or an infringement of the rights of the minority. The discretionary power of the Chair to protect the rights of the minority by refusing the closure is frequently exercised.

The powers of the Chair in regard to closure may be exercised by the Speaker or any Deputy Speaker, or by the Chairman of Ways and Means or either Deputy Chairman in a Committee of the whole House. No motion for the closure can be accepted by a temporary Chairman of a Committee of the whole House acting in that capacity at the request of the Chairman of Ways and Means.

---

1 HC Deb (1964–65) 708, cc 1492–1493.
2 See HC Deb (1962–63) 678, c 325.
3 HC Deb (1981–82) 25, c 214.
4 In a Memorandum to the Procedure Committee (HC 539, Session 1966–67) the Speaker explained the principles by which selection of amendments at report stage of bills was governed. For instances where reasons for selection were given, under previous practice, see 20th edn, pp 466–467.

The question for closure may be agreed to without a division.[1] If, on a division being taken, it appears from the numbers declared from the Chair that not fewer than a hundred Members voted in the majority in support of the motion, it is decided in the affirmative.[2] The two tellers are not included in reckoning the prescribed majority.[3] If fewer than a hundred Members vote in the affirmative majority, the motion fails.[4] As soon as the question for closure has been agreed to, the question originally proposed from the Chair must be put.[5]

(1) When closure is movable

Closure may be moved by a Member at the conclusion of his speech,[6] at the conclusion of a speech made by another Member,[7] or while a Member is addressing the House. The intervention of the Chair regarding closure is restricted to occasions when the motion is made in abuse of the rules of the House, or infringes the rights of the minority. A closure motion may therefore be sanctioned by the Chair, either immediately upon, or within a few minutes of, the proposal of a question to the House. In deciding whether, given the importance of the subject, the amount of time already occupied by the debate is adequate, the Chair is guided by a number of considerations. For instance, when a private Member's bill or motion has been debated during the sitting on a Friday, or half-sitting on a Monday, which the standing orders allot for such proceedings, it is reasonable that the Member in charge should be entitled to obtain the decision of the House on his proposal; and accordingly in such a case the Speaker would withhold his assent to a motion for the closure only if the subject proposed by the private Member was manifestly of too far-reaching or controversial a character to be adequately debated in the time provided by the standing order. The discretion of the Chair is absolute and not open to dispute.[8]

(2) Closure on contingent questions

Without some further provision, the House might, even with the help of the closure, be unable to complete the matter then immediately in hand. As

---

1 Closure motions were carried (with or without a division) 499 times between sessions 1920–21 and 1929–30, 119 times between sessions 1930–31 and 1939–40, 110 times between sessions 1940–41 and 1950, 177 times between sessions 1950–51 and 1959–60, 221 times between sessions 1960–61 and 1969–70, 325 times between sessions 1970–71 and 1979–80 and 106 times between sessions 1980–81 and 1986–87.
2 CJ (1979–80) 750, 763, etc.
3 CJ (1964–65) 407; HC Deb (1975–76) 917, c 784.
4 Not decided in the affirmative, insufficient majority, CJ (1887) 506; ibid (1920) 109; ibid (1959–60) 132, ibid (1979–80) 248, etc; negatived, ibid (1888) 232; ibid (1924) 42, 58; ibid (1959–60) 159, ibid (1979–80) 454, etc; less than 40 voting, ibid (1982–83) 86.
5 For closure in standing committees see p 601.
6 Parl Deb (1893) 12, c 790.
7 HC Deb (1975–76) 919, c 1376, etc.
8 Parl Deb (1887) 313, c 177; ibid (1888) 329, c 57; HC Deb (1921) 146, c 1595; ibid (1935–36) 309, c 823; ibid (1971–72) 832, c 1376; ibid (1977–78) 955, c 712; ibid (1979–80) 971, cc 94–101; ibid (1984–85) 74, cc 875–878. For cases in which the Chair has explained the acceptance or refusal of a motion for closure after a short debate, see Parl Deb (1892) 3, c 1640; ibid (1901) 89, c 1390; HC Deb (1911) 29, c 1268; ibid (1956–57) 570, c 1540; ibid (1958–59) 595, c 1608; ibid (1981–82) 17, c 701. A question to a Minister as to the time at which the closure will be moved is irregular, Parl Deb (1901) 89, c 1061; ibid (1905) 141, c 781.

soon therefore as the motion, 'That the question be now put,' has been carried, and the question consequent thereon has been decided, the right is given under Standing Order No 35 (2) to claim, subject to the discretion of the Chair, *and without having recourse to any further closure motion*, that any further question be put which may be requisite to bring to a decision any question already proposed from the Chair.[1] The utility of this power is specially proved by its application at the moment when, pursuant to standing order, an interruption of business would otherwise immediately take place.

(3) Closure at moment of interruption

Under Standing Order No 9(4) closure may be moved at the moment for the interruption of business. Under ordinary circumstances, on the appointed hour being reached, the Speaker or chairman says, 'Order, order,' and proceeds to interrupt the business. The Speaker announces that the debate stands adjourned, or the chairman proceeds to leave the Chair to make his report to the House. These proceedings on the part of the Speaker or the Chairman create the moment of the interruption of business, when closure may be moved. But if at that time a division is in progress, the moment of interruption is projected beyond the hour laid down in the standing orders. The Speaker, or the Chairman if the House is in committee, after the question upon which the division is being taken has been decided, continues the proposal of such further questions as are necessary to complete the proceedings, until a Member rises to speak or says, 'I object to further proceedings'. It is then that the moment for the interruption of business arrives and that the closure motion may be moved.[2]

(4) Closure claimed on contingent questions at or after moment of interruption

As explained above, after a closure motion has been moved and acted upon, any Member may claim that such further questions be put forthwith as are requisite to bring to a decision the question already proposed from the Chair, no second closure motion being necessary.[3] The same practice applies if the closure is moved and acted on at or after the moment of interruption: unless the assent of the Chair is withheld, such further questions are successively put forthwith, regardless of the fact that the time fixed for the interruption of business has passed.

> When a closure motion had been carried which disposed of an amendment to a motion, the question on the motion was forthwith claimed and decided by the House.[4]

---

1 Parl Deb (1892) 3, c 138; CJ (1963–64) 298; ibid (1975–76) 488; ibid (1979–80) 149; HC Deb (1979–80) 971, cc 91–94. Contingent questions, which have not actually been proposed from the Chair—such as the question that the House agrees with the report of a Committee after an amendment has been disposed of under the closure—fall within the scope of this provision.
2 CJ (1888) 242, 246, 268, 470; ibid (1896) 304; ibid (1902) 342; ibid (1907) 289; Parl Deb (1907) 177, c 266; CJ (1908) 477; Parl Deb (1908) 197, c 1843; CJ (1914) 251; ibid (1971–72) 228; ibid (1980–81) 379; ibid (1985–86) 386.
3 CJ (1888) 504, Parl Deb (1888) 331, c 1703; CJ (1889) 53, Parl Deb (1889) 333, c 1101; CJ (1892) 249; ibid (1904) 51, Parl Deb (1904) 130, c 869.
4 CJ (1975–76) 488; ibid (1976–77) 451.

When a closure motion had been carried which disposed of an amendment to an amendment, first the question on the amendment itself, and then on the main question, were forthwith claimed and decided by the House.[1]

When in committee closure had been moved on a motion to report progress and the latter motion had been negatived, the question on the amendment under consideration when progress was moved was claimed and put from the Chair.[2]

B. CLOSURE ON MOVING OF MOTION OR AMENDMENT

Under Standing Order No 28, agreed to on 27 February 1986, a Member may rise in his place and move 'That the question be now proposed', when a Member is in the course of making a motion or moving an amendment at any stage of proceedings on a bill. The question 'That the question be now proposed', must be put forthwith, unless it appears to the Chair that the motion is an abuse of the rules of the House. Under Standing Order No 36, if a division is held, not fewer than one hundred Members must vote in the majority in support of the motion for it to be decided in the affirmative. The exercise of the power by the Chair is subject to the same restrictions as apply to the ordinary closure (see p 405 above).[3]

C OTHER

(1) Closure upon words of clause or schedule

Until the repeal of the standing order on 27 February 1986, a motion could be made to the effect that part or all of a clause or schedule under consideration stand part of the bill, or that a new clause or schedule be added to the bill. For details of how this form of closure—known as 'kangaroo' closure—was used, see *May* 19th edn (1976) pp 450–451.

(2) Previous question

The 'previous question' may be used to produce the same effect as the closure. It is put in the form 'That the question be not now put' and, if negatived, the original question must be put immediately. If it is agreed to, the Speaker is prevented from putting the original question, as the House has thus refused to allow it to be put (see p 334).

4. ALLOCATION OF TIME ORDERS (GUILLOTINES)

In many sessions in order to secure the passage of particularly important and controversial legislation, Governments have been confronted with the choice, unless special powers are taken, of cutting down their normal programme to an undesirable extent, or of prolonging the sittings of Parlia-

---

1 CJ (1892) 166, 196.
2 CJ (1902) 408; ibid (1923) 221.
3 For examples of the operation of this form of closure, see Stg Co Deb (1987–88) Co C (Protection of Animals (Amendment) Bill), c 14; ibid (1987–88) Co D (Immigration Bill), c 439.

ment, or else of acknowledging the impotence of the majority of the House in the face of the resistance of the minority. In such circumstances resort is had sooner or later to the most drastic method of curtailing debate known to procedure, namely, the setting of a date by which a committee must report, or the allocation of a specified number of days to the various stages of a bill and of limited amounts of time to particular portions of a bill. Orders made under this procedure are known as 'allocation of time' orders, and colloquially as 'guillotine' motions. They may be regarded as the extreme limit to which procedure goes in affirming the rights of the majority at the expense of the minorities of the House, and it cannot be denied that they are capable of being used in such a way as to upset the balance, generally so carefully preserved, between the claims of business and the rights of debate. But the harshness of this procedure is to some extent mitigated either by consultations between the party leaders or in the Business Committee (see p 410) in order to establish the greatest possible measure of agreement as to the most satisfactory disposal of the time available.

The allocation of limited amounts of time to the stages of bills, and occasionally other kinds of business, forms no part of the general procedure of the House, but is applied in each case to a particular bill (or several bills jointly)[1] or other specified business by a special order.

Provision for a financial resolution in connection with a bill has sometimes been included in an order allotting time to the stages of a bill, and in such a case the Queen's recommendation is signified to the motion for allotting time.[2]

A. PROCEDURE ON ALLOCATION OF TIME ORDERS

A motion for the allocation of time to a bill (or bills) sets out in detail some or all of the provisions which are to be made for further proceedings on the bill. Under Standing Order No 81 the Speaker is required to put any question necessary to dispose of an allocation of time motion not more than three hours after the motion has been entered upon. Such motions generally provide for motions (with a more restricted time limit) varying or supplementing their provisions (see p 413). A motion under Standing Order No 14 (2) to allow proceedings on a motion for allocation of time to take place after ten o'clock cannot extend the three hours allowed for the latter motion.[3]

If a bill before a standing committee is the subject of an allocation of time order, Standing Order No 103 (Business sub-committees) applies and a detailed timetable is recommended to the standing committee by the Business Sub-Committee (see pp 609–610). If a bill is not before a standing committee, some or all of the details of the timetable may either be prescribed in the allocation of time order itself[4] or they may be left to the Business Committee to recommend; the participation of the Business Committee is excluded in cases where the order lays down a full timetable.[5] Time

---

1 Two bills, CJ (1908) 42; ibid (1961–62) 81, ibid (1975–76) 470, 473, Votes and Proceedings (1987–88) 11 November 1988; three bills, CJ (1913) 193; ibid (1914) 204.
2 CJ (1908) 39; ibid (1910) 102; see also ibid (1938–39) 402, 405; ibid (1939–40) 139.
3 HC Deb (1977–78) 939, c 576.
4 CJ (1951–52) 199, 326; ibid (1981–82) 417.
5 See eg CJ (1985–86) 459.

limits by which the reports of the Business Committee have to be made are usually prescribed in the order.[1] The order may also provide for the variation of any report by a further report, whether or not within the above time limit, and whether or not the resolutions in the report have been agreed to by the House.[2]

B. BUSINESS COMMITTEE

The Business Committee, set up under Standing Order No 80, consists of the Chairman of Ways and Means, who acts as chairman, and not more than eight other Members nominated by Mr Speaker in respect of each bill. The quorum is four. The duty of the Committee is to divide the bill into such parts as it sees fit and allot to each part such time as it considers appropriate within the allocation laid down by the order of the House.[3]

In the House, the question on the motion to consider the Business Committee's report has to be put forthwith; if that question is agreed to, the question which immediately follows, 'That the House doth agree with the committee in its resolution (or resolutions)' must also be put forthwith. Both these questions, even if opposed, may be decided after the expiration of the time for opposed business.

C. USUAL PROVISIONS MADE UNDER ALLOCATION OF TIME ORDERS

(1) Stages of bills

An allocation of time order is not usually moved until after the second reading of a bill, and usually not until the rate of progress in committee has provided an argument for its necessity. The order provides that a certain number of days or parts of days are allotted in the form of a timetable to each of the remaining stages of the bill; on allotted days time limits may be laid down by which proceedings on specified portions of the bill are to be concluded.

> The second reading of a bill has been taken immediately after the order allocating time to it has been made, and has been ordered to be brought to a conclusion at eleven o'clock that day or at the expiration of four hours from the commencement of the proceedings thereon, whichever might be the later.[4]
>
> One day has been allotted to the report stage and third reading of a bill;[5] and one day has been allotted to all the stages after second reading.[6] The time at which the third reading of a bill should be brought to a conclusion

---

1 CJ (1952–53) 33; ibid (1953–54) 101.
2 For examples of reports varied by further reports see CJ (1979–80) 369, 375; 559, 576; ibid (1985–86) 343, 363. For a meeting of the Business Committee during an informal suspension of the House in order to vary its resolution agreed to by the House earlier that day, see HC Deb (1988–89) 147, cc 1004–1019 and Votes and Proceedings (1988–89) 22 February 1989.
3 HC Deb (1948–49) 463, cc 2854–2855.
4 CJ (1920) 362.
5 Eg CJ (1981–82) 417.
6 CJ (1920) 362.

has been changed by order of the House;[1] and similar changes have been made in respect of the committee stage[2] and the report stage[3] of bills.

In a number of instances an allocation of time order has been supplemented by a later order, so that the consideration of Lords amendments to the bill should be concluded at a stated time.[4] Since 1978 supplemental orders have made specific provision for deciding forthwith questions relating to the appointment of committees to draw up reasons for disagreeing to Lords amendments.[5] Allocation of time orders have been made in respect of consideration of Lords amendments to bills, earlier proceedings on which had not been the subject of such an order.[6]

(2) Definition of allotted day

Another provision usually defines an allotted day as 'any day (other than a Friday) on which the bill is put down as the first Government order of the day'.

The day on which an allocation of time order has been passed has been used as the first allotted day of the bill to which it related.[7] Orders have also been made providing for the completion of proceedings on a bill a specified number of hours after the commencement of proceedings on the motion for such an order.[8]

If required, provision may be made for setting out the changes in the timetable which will be necessary in the case of an 'allotted day' falling on a Friday.

(3) Application of Ten o'clock rule

It is provided that proceedings which are to be brought to a conclusion on an allotted day shall not be interrupted under the provisions of Standing Order No 9. Provision has frequently been made applying the provisions of Standing Order No 14(1) for a specified period of time after ten o'clock.[9]

Provision has also been made to compensate for time lost to the consideration of the bill on an allotted day because of private notice questions, Government statements, or other proceedings, before the commencement of public business. This was done either by adding to the times specified in the timetable the equivalent of the time so lost,[10] or by the substitution of references to half-past ten o'clock for references to ten o'clock in Standing

1 CJ (1921) 332.
2 CJ (1938–39) 232.
3 CJ (1961–62) 194.
4 Eg CJ (1952–53) 198; ibid (1962–63) 300; ibid (1979–80) 504, 768; ibid (1980–81) 489, 530.
5 CJ (1977–78) 431.
6 Votes and Proceedings (1987–88) 14 March, 11 November 1988.
7 CJ (1938–39) 223–225.
8 Votes and Proceedings (1987–88) 14 March, 25 May, 2 November 1988. For such an order relating to two bills, see ibid (1987–88) 11 November 1988.
9 See eg Industry Bill (Allocation of Time) Order, CJ (1974–75) 430.
10 CJ (1951–52) 324; ibid (1968–69) 328.

Order No 9 (with consequential amendments to the new arrangements for business under Standing Orders Nos. 16 (5) and 20).[1]

(4) Adjournment motions

An allocation of time order normally provides that any proceedings on the bill due to be concluded on a day on which a motion for the adjournment of the House has been obtained under Standing Order No 20 (adjournment on specific and important matter that should have urgent consideration) shall be postponed for a period equal to that taken by the motion.

Standing Order No 20 (7) allots to proceedings on the bill a period of time equal to that taken by the adjournment motion, and provides that they shall not be interrupted at ten o'clock. The allocation of time order provides that the time given to compensate for that taken by the motion is in addition to any time after ten o'clock allotted to proceedings on the bill by the order. The order further provides that the adjournment motion shall not be moved until any proceedings due to be concluded at or before seven o'clock have been so concluded. It also provides that any proceedings due to be concluded after that time shall be postponed for a period equal to that taken by the adjournment motion.

(5) Opposed private business

A provision is made in case any opposed private business should be set down under Standing Order No 16 (5) on an allotted day. Such business is deferred until the proceedings on the bill have been concluded, and may then continue for as long a period as it could have done had it commenced at 7 o'clock.[2]

The setting down of private business on an allotted day has sometimes been forbidden.[3]

(6) 'Ten Minute Rule' bills

It has in the past been specified that Standing Order No 19 (Motions for leave to bring in bills and nomination of select committees at commencement of public business) shall not apply to any allotted day.[4] The Speaker has accordingly passed over a notice of motion appearing on the paper on an allotted day.[5] But this provision was omitted by an amendment made to a motion for an allocation of time order,[6] and no such provision has been included in an order since then.

(7) Dilatory motions etc

It is provided that on days on which proceedings under the order are to be brought to a conclusion, or in some cases on any allotted day, dilatory motions on the bill are forbidden unless moved by a member of the Govern-

---

1 CJ (1953–54) 196.
2 CJ (1953–54) 101.
3 CJ (1907) 167; ibid (1967–68) 291.
4 CJ (1953–54) 196.
5 HC Deb (1969–70) 800, cc 1252–1253.
6 CJ (1974–75) 261.

ment, when the question thereon is to be put without amendment or debate.[1] The postponement of clauses, schedules, new clauses or new schedules is also forbidden; but where there is a Business Committee on the bill, it may recommend an alteration in the order in which such clauses or schedules are to be taken in committee or on consideration. It has also been provided that on committee and report stages, on any day on which proceedings are to be brought to a conclusion, no motions relating to the sittings of the committee or of the House should be moved except by a member of the Government and that the question on any such motion should be put forthwith without debate[2] or after a brief explanatory statement from the Member who moved it and a Member who opposes it.[3]

(8) Machinery for bringing proceedings to a conclusion

Provision is also made for the purpose of bringing to a conclusion any proceedings which are to be brought to a conclusion at a time appointed by the order or by a resolution of the Business Committee, and which have not previously been brought to a conclusion. The Speaker or the Chairman has first to put forthwith the question on any amendment or motion already proposed from the Chair (and if a new clause has been read a second time, also the question 'That the clause be added to the bill').[4] Thereafter questions are put forthwith, and only on those amendments, new clauses or new schedules moved by a member of the Government, and such other questions as are necessary to dispose of that part or stage of the bill to be concluded at the time appointed, including (in committee) 'That the clause stand part of the bill'. With a view to reducing the number of divisions to be taken it is laid down that the only question to be put from the Chair on a new clause or new schedule is 'that such clause (or schedule) be added to the bill'. No points of order may be taken while these questions are being put.[5]

Another small saving of time is achieved by the provision that at the end of the proceedings in any committee on the bill (including one to which the bill has been recommitted), the Chairman is to report the bill to the House without putting any question.[6]

(9) Provision for subsequent supplemental orders

A provision may specify that if a member of the Government should later move a motion for varying or supplementing either the order itself or a resolution of the Business Committee which has been previously agreed to by the House, debate on the motion should be concluded after a certain time. One hour is the time generally specified, and allowance is made for any

---

1 A motion to re-commit a bill is not a dilatory motion and may be made unless it is specifically forbidden, CJ (1906) 362. It is therefore generally provided that on an allotted day no debate should be permitted on any motion to re-commit the bill (whether as a whole or otherwise) and that the question necessary to dispose of the motion, including the question on any amendment selected under SO No 31, should be put forthwith, eg CJ (1961–62) 132.
2 CJ (1948–49) 41.
3 CJ (1961–62) 131; ibid (1967–68) 256.
4 CJ (1928–29) 101.
5 HC Deb (1970–71) 814, cc 700–701.
6 CJ (1953–54) 196; ibid (1967–68) 256.

interruption of the debate under Standing Order No 20 (Adjournment on specific and important matter that should have urgent consideration).[1]

This provision has been invoked later in order to pass a supplementary order imposing a time limit on the consideration of the Lords amendments to the bill in question.[2] Supplemental orders generally contain provision for the questions on Lords amendments to be put en bloc when the guillotine falls, with an exemption for Lords amendments involving privilege. Where a time-limit for debate on any supplemental order has been provided under the original order, this time-limit has been held to supersede the time-limit specified in Standing Order No 81.[3]

(10) Savings

It is regularly provided that nothing in the order, or in a resolution of the Business Committee or the Business Sub-Committee, shall prevent any proceedings to which the order or resolution applies from being entered upon or completed earlier than the order or resolution requires or prevent any business (whether on the bill or not) from being proceeded with on any day, after the proceedings under the order or resolution on that day have been already completed.

(11) Other powers conferred by orders

In addition to these normal provisions and to suit special circumstances other provisions have occasionally been made.

(a) Motion to leave out clauses, etc before discussion thereon. Provision has been made to enable the government to move to leave out a part of the bill or any clause or schedule or consecutive clauses or schedules of the bill before consideration of any amendments thereto in committee, and the question on any such motion has been ordered to be put forthwith by the chairman, without amendment or debate,[4] or after a brief explanatory statement from the Minister in charge and from any one Member who rises to criticize the statement.[5] When a part of a bill was committed under one of these orders to a standing committee, this power was extended to the standing committee during its consideration of this part of the bill.

(b) Provision for one question on a series of clauses. The chairman has been directed in the case of a series of clauses to which no notice of amendment has been given by the Government to put the question that those clauses stand part of the bill instead of putting a question on each clause separately.[6]

(c) Committal of part of a bill to a standing committee. By one of these orders in the case of a bill which had been read a second time and

---

1 CJ (1980–81) 489; for variation of an order, see eg Votes and Proceedings (1987–88) 17 February 1988.
2 CJ (1952–53) 198; ibid (1962–63) 300; ibid (1979–80) 504, 768; ibid (1980–81) 530 etc.
3 HC Deb (1977–78) 953, cc 462–463.
4 CJ (1906) 255; ibid (1908) 338, 464; ibid (1909) 229; ibid (1910) 305.
5 CJ (1911) 439; ibid (1912–13) 366; ibid (1921) 196, 248, 344.
6 CJ (1921) 196, 259.

committed to a Committee of the whole House, the House ordered that one part of the bill (including the schedules therein referred to, and any new clauses dealing with the subject-matter of that part of the bill) should stand committed to a standing committee, as if the bill on being read a second time had as respects those provisions been so committed.[1] On another occasion a bill which had been committed to a standing committee and allocated by the Speaker was ordered to be allocated to another standing committee in respect of certain portions of the bill.[2] The remaining provisions of the bill continued committed to the original committee in each case, and the House ordered that when the provisions committed to each committee should have been reported to the House, the report stage of the bill should be proceeded with as if the bill had been reported as a whole to the House.[3]

(d) Precedence over private Members' business. Provision has been made for giving precedence to proceedings under the order on days allotted by Standing Order No 13 to private Members' business.[4]

(e) Money bills. In the case of money bills based on a charging resolution, provision has also been made to enable the order to have effect notwithstanding the practice of the House relating to the interval between the stages of any bill.

(f) Provision as to Saturday sitting. Power has been taken to obtain a sitting of the House on a Saturday at a specified hour or to change the hour of meeting on a Friday,[5] for the purposes of the bill dealt with in the order, while notices of questions for oral answer on a Friday or Saturday, which was an allotted day under the order, were ordered to be treated as notices for the following Monday.[6]

D. ORDERS IN CASE OF BILLS REJECTED BY LORDS

Special provisions have been made in allocation of time orders dealing with bills rejected by the House of Lords.

In the case of bills which have been re-introduced into the House of Commons, in the session subsequent to that in which they did not pass the House of Lords, with only such alterations as are contemplated by section 2(4) of the Parliament Act 1911 (see p 533), the chairman has been ordered on the committee stage of a bill to put forthwith the question that he do report the bill, without amendment, to the House, without putting any other question. The question so put has been ordered to be decided without amendment or debate.[7] In some cases the Speaker has been directed, when the order of the day is read for the House to resolve itself into committee on the bill, to leave the chair without putting any question, notwithstanding

1 CJ (1911) 439.
2 CJ (1921) 247.
3 CJ (1911) 439; ibid (1921) 247, 273, 281.
4 CJ (1938–39) 224.
5 CJ (1908) 465; ibid (1912–13) 506.
6 CJ (1908) 465.
7 CJ (1913) 192; ibid (1914) 204; ibid (1948) 410; ibid (1976–77) 19.

that notice of an instruction has been given.[1] The chairman has been directed to put forthwith the question that he do report the bill without amendment to the House.[2] Alternatively, the chairman has been directed at the
close of a specified period to bring to a conclusion the committee stage of any
financial resolution relating to the bill, and on the report stage of the
financial resolution the Speaker has been directed to put forthwith the
question that the House doth agree with the committee in the resolution
without putting any other question, the question so put being decided
without amendment or debate.[3]

In the case of a bill which the Examiners of Petitions for Private Bills had
been ordered to examine, the order was discharged and special provisions
were made for the committal and report of the bill after second reading.[4] For
proceedings on the order relating to the Finance (1909–10) Bill, see 20th
edn, pp 461–462.

E. VOLUNTARY ARRANGEMENTS IN PLACE OF ALLOCATION OF TIME ORDERS

Instead of the compulsory provisions of an allocation of time order, an
agreement between parties in the House for the purpose of securing the
completion of business within a limited time is not infrequently arrived at;
for instances where the details of such an agreement have been communicated to the House, see 20th edn, p 462.

F. USE OF ALLOCATION OF TIME ORDERS

From the inception of allocation of time orders in 1887 with the Criminal
Law Amendment (Ireland) Bill,[5] regular use has been made of them, and
since the 1939–45 war few sessions have passed without one or more bills
being subjected to them (in 1975–76 five bills were the subject of three
orders passed on one day).[6] The orders are not, however, always identical in
form; for a list of examples of some of the principal variations, see 20th edn,
pp 462–463.

---

1 CJ (1914) 204; ibid (1948) 410; ibid (1976–77) 19.
2 CJ (1976–77) 19.
3 CJ (1913) 192; ibid (1914) 204. These orders were made under the former procedure which
required preliminary consideration of financial resolutions in Committee.
4 CJ (1976–77) 19.
5 CJ (1887) 284, 332.
6 CJ (1975–76) 468. For a list of allocation of time orders between 1979–80 and 1987–88, see
HC Deb (1987–88) 130, cc 595–598w. Five bills were subject to orders in the 1970–74
Parliament, 11 in the 1974–79 Parliament, 12 in the 1979–83 Parliament and 10 in the 1983–87
Parliament.

CHAPTER 20

Organisation and conduct of business in the House of Lords

ARRANGEMENT OF BUSINESS

Arrangement of the Session

In general the House of Lords sits during the same weeks of the year as the House of Commons. But the fact that most major bills are introduced first into the House of Commons means that the programme of business in the Lords is much heavier at the end of the session than at the beginning. In recent years the Lords have returned after the summer recess earlier than the Commons in order to deal with business which has already passed the Commons. The House of Lords does not always meet on Mondays, and meets regularly on Fridays only after Easter. As a result the House sits for fewer days a year than the Commons—192 days in session 1987–88, compared with 218 days in the Commons.

Days and times of sitting

(1) Public business. The House meets for public business on Mondays, Tuesdays, Wednesdays and Thursdays. It sometimes meets on Fridays.[1] The normal hour of meeting on Mondays, Tuesdays and Wednesdays is 2.30 p.m.; on Thursdays, 3 p.m.; and on Fridays, 11 a.m. The House often meets at 11 a.m. on the last day before a recess. In exceptional circumstances the order of adjournment may prescribe any other time for the meeting of the House[2].

(2) Judicial business. The House may meet for the transaction of judicial business on any weekday. During the periods when the House is meeting for public business judicial sittings take place two or three times a month, usually at 2 p.m. on Thursdays. The principal purpose of these sittings is the delivery of judgments, since the hearing of appeals is normally undertaken not in the House but by the Appellate Committees sitting in a committee room (see pp 66–67). At the end of judicial business the House is 'adjourned during pleasure' until the commencement of public business later in the afternoon.

During parliamentary recesses the House may meet both to hear appeals and to deliver judgments. When the House meets for judicial business during recesses the sittings usually begin at 10.30 a.m. and end at 4 p.m.

Adjournment

There is no fixed time for the adjournment of the House. The motion 'That the House do now adjourn' is proposed at the end of business from the

---

1 Very rarely it has sat on Saturday (eg 3 April 1982) and Sunday (eg 3 September 1939).
2 Eg the House met at 9.30 am on 7 April 1989 to accommodate a debate on three consultation papers on proposals for reform of the legal profession.

417

Government front bench, usually by a junior whip. The Lord Chancellor puts the question but does not collect the voices because it is not the practice to debate this question.[1] If any Lord wishes to speak on the motion he should inform the Lord Chancellor beforehand. There is no special procedure for long adjournments over recesses, the dates of which are announced by the Chief Whip some weeks in advance. In 1947 the House did not accept the adjournment proposed by the Government on the eve of the summer recess and varied it by amendment.[2]

Where arrangements have been made for judicial sittings at a time earlier than that fixed for the next sitting for public business, the recent custom has been to adjourn the House until one date and time for judicial business and another date and time for public business. But where the time of the next judicial sitting has not been precisely known, the House has on occasion been adjourned to the next sitting for public business 'except for judicial business'.

Under Standing Order No 14(3), notwithstanding any adjournment of the House, the House may meet for judicial business at a time earlier than that appointed if the Lord Chancellor or, in his absence, the senior Lord of Appeal in Ordinary, is satisfied that it should do so and has signified that he is so satisfied and has given notice to such Lords as he thinks fit.[3]

For the recall of the House for public business under Standing Order No 14(1), see p 224.

Order of business

In general, items of business are taken each day in the order in which they are entered on the order paper. No distinction is made between government business and other business. On all sitting days except Wednesdays, public bills, measures, affirmative instruments and reports from Select Committees have precedence over most other notices (Standing Order No 38 (4)). On Wednesdays, motions have precedence over public bills, measures and delegated legislation (Standing Order No 38(4A)). But the House retains a considerable degree of flexibility in the arrangement of business, and when occasion arises the standing order may be suspended. In particular, towards the end of the session, when there may be congestion of Government business originating in the House of Commons, the standing order is often suspended to give the Government power to control the order of business.

Standing Order No 37 provides that the House shall proceed with the Notices and Orders of the Day in the order in which they stand on the Order Paper. But the House has resolved that, notwithstanding the terms of Standing Order No 37, business may with the unanimous leave of the House be postponed without notice. The resolution is in force until further order.[4]

---

1 Brief debate may take place on motions for the adjournment before a recess; see for example, HL Deb (1987–88) 500, c 564. For examples of debate at other times, see LJ (1958–59) 131; ibid (1960–61) 356, 414.
2 LJ (1946–47) 493.
3 LJ (1979–80) 508.
4 LJ (1984–85) 291. See also HL Deb (1987–88) 494, c 431.

Business may also be adjourned for a period for dinner; and other business may be taken during the dinner adjournment.

The following list gives a general indication of the order in which business may be taken at a sitting, though variations may be made in certain cases to suit the convenience of the House.

(1) Prayers.
(2) Introductions.
(3) Oaths of Allegiance.
(4) Messages from the Crown.
(5) Royal Assent (or at any convenient time during the sitting).
(6) Addresses of congratulation or sympathy to the Crown.
(7) Obituary tributes.
(8) Personal statements.
(9) Starred questions.
(10) Private notice questions.
(11) Presentation of public petitions.
(12) Questions of privilege.
(13) Statements on business.
(14) Ministerial statements.
(15) Presentation and first reading of public bills.
(16) Messages from the Commons.
(17) Private bills.
(18) Business of the House motions.
(19) Motions relating to the Chairman of Committees' business.
(20) Motions for the appointment of select committees.
(21) Public bills, measures, affirmative instruments and reports from Select Committees.
(22) Other motions.
(23) Unstarred questions.

Each of these proceedings is described below, with references to other parts of the book where appropriate.

(1) Prayers

Prayers are read at the beginning of each day's sitting. When the House sits in its judicial capacity, Prayers are read before judicial business but not again when the House resumes for public business. Ordinarily they are read by one of the bishops (except the two archbishops and the bishops of London, Durham and Winchester) who take a week each in turn. In the absence of a bishop a Lord who is a clergyman of the Church of England, if present, reads Prayers. If no such Lord is present Prayers are read by the Lord Chancellor or Deputy Speaker. A Lord who intends to take the Oath may be present at Prayers. During Prayers the doors and galleries of the House are closed and strangers are excluded.

(2) Introductions

Under Standing Order No 3 all peers by descent, who are at least twenty-one years of age, may take their seats in the House of Lords without introduction.

Ceremonial introduction is necessary in the case of a newly created hereditary or life peer, or an hereditary peer if no previous holder of the title has been introduced, a peer advanced to a higher degree or the eldest son of a peer called up in his father's barony during his father's lifetime,[1] a newly-appointed Lord of Appeal in Ordinary who is not already a member of the House, and an archbishop on appointment or translation or bishop on first receiving a writ of summons, or if already a member of the House on translation to another see. If a newly created hereditary peer dies before taking his seat, his successor is introduced.[2]

The ceremony of introduction usually takes place on a Tuesday or Wednesday after Prayers. A peer is introduced between two other peers of his own degree, all wearing parliamentary robes. Preceded by the Gentleman Usher of the Black Rod, Garter King of Arms (or another herald) who carries the patent, and on occasion by the Earl Marshal and the Lord Great Chamberlain, they enter the House from the bar and advance to the Woolsack. The new peer, kneeling, presents his patent, which he receives from Garter, and his writ of summons to the Lord Chancellor, after which he returns with his supporters to the Table. The patent and writ are read by the Reading Clerk, who has received them from the Lord Chancellor. The peer takes the oath and signs the Test Roll. He and his supporters are conducted to his place on the bench of their degree, from where they bow three times to the Lord Chancellor, rising and removing their hats on each occasion. The new peer is then conducted to the Woolsack where he shakes hands with the Lord Chancellor. When the Lord Chancellor is introduced the ceremony is substantially the same except that, since the Woolsack is unoccupied, he places his patent and writ on the Throne before handing them to the Reading Clerk.[3]

When the Prince of Wales is introduced a more elaborate procession is formed and his coronet is carried by a member of his household. His patent is read by the Clerk of the Parliaments and he is conducted to his chair on the right of the Throne.[4] A Royal duke, having special precedence under the House of Lords Precedence Act 1539, is conducted to a chair placed on the left of the Throne.[5]

In the case of a peer called up in his father's barony, no patent is produced or read.

By Standing Order No 6 a bishop is introduced on first receiving a writ of summons or on translation to another see. The ceremony is similar to that observed in the case of a temporal Lord, but no heralds or officers of state attend and no patent is read. The bishop is conducted by two other bishops to the appropriate bench.

(3) Oaths of Allegiance

The Oath of Allegiance must be taken, or affirmation made, by every Lord before he can sit and vote in the House:

(1) in every new Parliament;
(2) on succession or introduction;

---

1 LJ (1940–41) 29, 30; ibid (1950–51) 70.
2 LJ (1941–42) 169, ibid (1944–45) 147.
3 LJ (1945–46) 21; ibid (1951–52) 220; ibid (1953–54) 305; ibid (1961–62) 341; ibid (1974) 12; ibid (1987–88) 13.
4 LJ (1863) 6; ibid (1918) 14; ibid (1969–70) 140.
5 LJ (1928) 93; ibid (1933–34) 353; ibid (1986–87) 142.

(3) after a demise of the Crown.

The form of the Oath is prescribed by section 2 of the Promissory Oaths Act 1868 and section 1 of the Oaths Act 1978. Lords who conscientiously object to the taking of an Oath may make a solemn affirmation.[1]

The Oath is usually taken after Prayers, but it may be taken at the end of business before the adjournment (Standing Order No 38(5)). The Oath may also be taken at a judicial sitting.

(4) Messages from the Crown

A Message from the Crown may be delivered without notice at the beginning of a sitting or at any time during a sitting and may, upon motion, be taken into consideration forthwith (Standing Order No 39(1)). Sometimes, however, a Message is set down for consideration on a subsequent date when a Humble Address is moved, usually by the Leader of the House, thanking the Queen for her most gracious Message and assuring her that the House will adopt such measures as are necessary to comply with her wishes (see p 564).

In modern times, however, the great majority of Messages from the Crown are in response to Addresses, so that no action need be taken upon them.

(5) Royal Assent

Royal Assent may be notified at any convenient break between two items of business. When Royal Assent is given by Commission a fixed hour is usually appointed, business being interrupted if necessary (see pp 528–529).

(6) Addresses of congratulation or sympathy to the Crown

Addresses of congratulation or sympathy to the Crown are customarily moved at this point (see chapter 23).

(7) Obituary tributes

By private arrangement, conducted through the party whips, tributes may be paid, before other business commences, on the occasion of the death of distinguished Members of the House or of public servants. It is usual to honour in this way peers who were Cabinet Ministers while members of the House. The House may also show its respect to the memory of a deceased statesman by an extraordinary adjournment.[2]

(8) Personal statements

A personal statement may be made to explain passages in a previous speech which have given rise to misconception, or to correct information given in a speech, or to justify conduct which has been criticized in the House. Personal statements are usually taken at the beginning of Public Business and are not debatable.

---

1 Lords may take the Oath in Welsh, in addition to—but not instead of—the Oath in English: HL Deb (1982–83) 439 c 224.
2 LJ (1861–62) 416; ibid (1882) 139; ibid (1908) 101; ibid (1946–47) 188; ibid (1964–65) 117, 126.

(9) Starred questions

Starred questions (marked * on the Order Paper) are asked for information
only. They may be put on the Order Paper for any day on which the House is
sitting for public business. No starred question may be tabled less than
24 hours before it is due to be asked. Starred questions are addressed to Her
Majesty's Government and not to a particular Minister; they may also be
addressed to Lords who hold certain official positions, such as the Leader of
the House and the Chairman of Committees. If a Lord is unable to be
present to ask a starred question on the Order Paper, he may authorize
another Lord to ask it on his behalf. The Lord who is in fact to ask the
question informs the Table in advance. The Table then informs the Government.[1]

The number of starred questions for any one day is limited to four, and to
two for any individual Lord. The number of starred questions permitted on
the Order Paper at any one time is limited to two per Lord.[2]

No debate may take place on starred questions. Supplementary questions
may be asked but they should be short, raise not more than two points and be
confined to the subject of the original question. Ministers should not answer
irrelevant supplementary questions and, if several points are raised in supplementary questions, need answer only two of the points. By custom, the
Lord who asks a starred question is permitted to ask the first supplementary
question, but has no automatic right to ask a final question.[3]

Question time is expected not to last more than 20 minutes and should not
exceed half an hour.

(10) Private notice questions

A Lord who wishes to give the Government private notice of his intention to
ask a question on a matter of urgency should submit his question in writing to
the Leader of the House by noon on the day on which he proposes to ask the
question (by 10 a.m. on a day when the House sits before 1 p.m.). The
decision whether the question is of sufficient urgency to justify an immediate
reply rests in the first place with the Leader and ultimately with the general
sense of the House. If a Lord wishes to challenge the Leader's preliminary
decision he must give notice to the Leader of his intention; and he must not
seek to raise the issue of his question on any motion on the day of the
question.[4] Private notice questions may be used to elicit from the Government the time at which they propose to make a statement (see below).
Private notice questions asked in the House of Commons are now sometimes repeated in the House of Lords in the form of a statement.[5] Supplementary questions may be asked, but private notice questions should not
be made the occasion for immediate debate (Standing Order No 33).

---

1 HL Deb (1984–85) 465, c 1187.
2 HL Deb (1987–88) 493, c 938.
3 Ibid.
4 LJ (1959–60) 206; HL Deb (1965–66) 272, c 1148; ibid (1981–82) 427, c 1289.
5 HL Deb (1984–85) 465, c 1188.

(11) Presentation of public petitions

Public petitions are customarily presented at this point (see p 754).

(12) Questions of privilege and (13) Statements on business

Items 12 and 13 are taken at this point.

(14) Ministerial statements

A statement by a Minister on a matter of national importance may be made by leave of the House without notice. Such statements are commonly synchronized in the two Houses, and it is normal for the House of Lords to be informed after Starred Questions, by a Government announcement, of the time when the statement will be made. If the responsible Minister sits in the House of Lords, the statement is made in that House after Questions. If the responsible Minister sits in the House of Commons, the statement may be repeated in the Lords at a convenient moment after 3.30 p.m. (ie after the statement has been started in the Commons), if the Leader, after consulting the Opposition parties, considers it to be a matter of national importance.[1] Questions may be asked and brief comments made upon ministerial statements, but they should not be made the occasion for immediate debate (Standing Order No 33).[2] Discussion on ministerial statements should not exceed twenty minutes.[3] If debate on a statement is desired, notice should be given on the Order Paper.

If the Lords are not sitting on a day on which a statement is made in the House of Commons, it is not the practice to repeat it when the Lords next sit, except in the case of an unusually important statement. A statement may, however, with the leave of the House, be included in the Lords Hansard without being given orally, if this is for the convenience of the House. If a statement made in the House of Commons is neither repeated in the Lords nor printed in the Lords Hansard, an italic reference to the statement giving the appropriate reference in the Commons Hansard is inserted in the Lords Hansard.[4]

(15) Presentation and first reading of new public bills

New bills may be presented either at the beginning or (much less usually) at the end of public business. Bills brought from the House of Commons may

1 HL Deb (1987–88) 493, c 939.
2 HL Deb (1984–85) 465, c 1187.
3 HL Deb (1987–88) 493, c 940.
4 Ibid c 939.

be read the first time at any convenient moment during public business (Standing Order No 39(3)) (see pp 443, 445).

(16) Messages from the Commons

Messages from the House of Commons may be received at any time during a sitting without interruption of business (Standing Order No 39(2)) (see p 570).

(17) Private bills

Private bills are taken at this point. If, however, it appears that a private bill is likely to be debated, the Chairman of Committees has discretion to propose the postponement or adjournment of that stage of the Bill either to a later time on the same day or to another day. Lords intending to debate a private bill should accordingly give notice of their intention to the Chairman of Committees.[1] Where a Lord wishes to move the rejection of the Bill, notice of his intention should appear on the Order Paper.

Private bills may also be entered later in the Order Paper at the discretion of the Chairman of Committees (Standing Order No 38(2)).

(18) Business of the House motions

Standing Order No 82 provides that no motion shall be agreed to for making any new standing order or for dispensing with a standing order unless notice shall have been given on the Order Paper. Consequently, when it is desired that a standing order be suspended for a period, or dispensed with for a specified purpose, notice of a motion, in the name of the Leader of the House, is inserted in the Order Paper under the heading 'Business of the House'. Such motions are disposed of before other notices relating to Public Business (Standing Order No 38(3)).

The suspension of Standing Orders Nos 38 and 44, which is often agreed to when pressure of business increases before a recess, enables the Government to arrange the priority of business and to take more than one stage of a bill at a sitting.

(19) Motions relating to the Chairman of Committees' business

Such motions may be taken at this point if the Chairman of Committees so desires.

(20) Motions for the appointment of select committees

Such motions may be taken at this point.

(21) Public bills, measures, affirmative instruments and select committee reports

Standing Order No 38 provides that, except for notices already mentioned and unstarred questions (see below), notices shall be entered on the Order

---

1 LJ (1958–59) 344.

Paper in the order in which they are received at the Table. Such notices relate principally to proceedings on public bills, measures, affirmative instruments, select committee reports and motions of a general character. On all sitting days except Wednesdays notices relating to public bills, measures, affirmative instruments and select committee reports have precedence over other notices. On Wednesdays notices of motions have precedence over notices relating to public bills, measures and delegated legislation.

Once a notice (except a starred or unstarred question) has been placed on the Order Paper for a particular day it may not be advanced to an earlier day unless a motion to that effect has been agreed to by the House (Standing Order No 40(1)). Nor can the order of business for a particular day be disturbed except with the consent of the Lords in whose names the relevant notices appear and then only if notice has been given in the Order Paper. A notice may, however, be postponed at the request of the Lord concerned.

If at the close of the speech of any Lord it is moved that the business then in hand be adjourned, or, the House being in Committee, that the House be resumed, and it is so ordered, the House may thereupon without notice make further order that the business in question shall be taken first, either at some later hour of the evening or on some future sitting day to be then fixed (Standing Order No 43).

(22) Other motions

(a) Motions for papers. It is a common practice to add at the end of a notice giving a subject for debate the words 'and to move for papers'. This is usually done in order that there may be a motion before the House, thus giving the mover a right of reply to the debate. The wording of such motions is expected to be so far as possible short and couched in neutral terms avoiding provocative or tendentious phraseology, though the character of such motions is not understood to inhibit Lords from advancing controversial points of view in the course of debate. A Lord tabling a motion for papers who wishes to highlight in the text of the motion a particular aspect of a subject may do so provided that the text does not amount to a statement of opinion or the demonstration of a point of view. It is recognized that such a motion should be withdrawn and not pressed to a division, since it is treated as a neutral motion and there is neither advantage nor significance in pressing it.[1]

(b) Motions for resolutions. Where it is desired that the House should reach a definite decision on a matter, if necessary on a vote, a Lord may table a motion for a resolution. Such a motion can with propriety incorporate statements of opinion or the demonstration of a point of view.[2] Motions have been tabled with the addition of the words 'and to move a resolution', notice being given later, before the motion is debated, of the actual words of the resolution.

(c) Motions 'To take note'. Debate may also take place on the Motion 'To take note'. This formula enables the House to debate a situation or a

---

1 LJ (1966–67) 50; HL Deb (1984–85) 465, cc 1186–1198; ibid (1985–86) 471, c 41.
2 HL Deb (1985–86) 471, c 411.

document without coming to any positive decision. The formula is regularly used on select committee reports. It is also appropriate for use by a Minister when he wishes to put down a neutral motion; a motion for papers would be inappropriate in this case, since papers can be laid only by the Government. The 'take note' formula makes withdrawal of the motion unnecessary.

(d) Short debates. One day a month, normally a Wednesday, is set aside each session during the period up to the Whitsun Recess for two short debates, each of a maximum duration of $2\frac{1}{2}$ hours. The right to propose subjects for these debates is reserved to backbenchers and crossbenchers. In order to establish which Lords are so eligible, the political parties prepare lists of those who have full front bench status and who cannot therefore initiate short debates. The debates are intended to provide a forum for discussion rather than to raise questions on which the House is required to come to a decision. Motions for short debates are therefore phrased in such a way as to avoid the risk of a division.[1] The choice of the two subjects is made by ballot, which is carried out by the Clerk of the Parliaments some weeks before the debates are due to take place.[2] In view of the time limit, Lords taking part in short debates are expected to keep their speeches short. To facilitate this, the amount of time each speech should not exceed is announced to the House before the debates begin. Pursuant to Standing Order No 35, if a short debate is still continuing at the end of the time allotted to it, the Lord Speaker brings it to an end by inquiring whether the mover of the motion wishes to withdraw it, or by putting the question. Standing Order No 35 is often applied, by order of the House, to motions other than those chosen by ballot,[3] and also to limit certain other debates to five hours.[4]

(e) Motions to annul negative instruments. Unlike motions to approve affirmative instruments, motions for the annulment of negative statutory instruments (see p 547) and of special procedure orders (see p 959) do not have precedence over other motions.

(23) Unstarred questions

A question to Her Majesty's Government which may give rise to debate is known as an unstarred question. It may be put down on the order paper for any day on which the House is sitting. Such a question is entered last (Standing Order No 38(6)). Speeches may be made upon it, but the Lord asking it (since he moves no motion) has no right of reply. It is the practice for the Minister who is to reply on behalf of the Government to wait until he is satisfied that no other Lord wishes to speak before he rises. It is considered undesirable for Lords to continue the debate after the Government's reply has been given, save for questions to the Minister before he sits down. It is considered undesirable, as a general rule, for a second unstarred question to be taken after 8 p.m. unless there are special circumstances.[5]

---

1 HL Deb (1985–86) 471, c 410.
2 LJ (1971–72) 275–276.
3 Eg HL Deb (1988–89) 508, c 725.
4 HL Deb (1988–89) 507, cc 750–751.
5 LJ (1968–69) 174.

Tabling of motions and questions

No motion or question, except motions relating to bills and subordinate legislation, may be tabled for a date more than one month ahead. The period of one month does not include any time during which the House is in recess, except in the case of Starred Questions (Standing Order No 41).[1]

If a Lord wishes to give notice of a question or motion without fixing a definite date, he may put it down in the Order Paper under the heading 'No Day Named'. In the earlier part of each session motions under 'No Day Named' are sorted into two Parts. Motions in Part II are those which are to be entered in the ballot for short debates (see p 426). After the last such ballot has taken place the division into two Parts ceases.

PROCESS OF DEBATE

The process of debate, by motion, question and decision, has already been described in chapter 17. The procedure of the House of Lords, which is elaborated here, is fundamentally the same as that of the House of Commons; but the number of standing orders and rules governing Lords practice is much smaller.

Moving of motions

A notice of motion may be tabled in the name of one Lord only. When a motion on the Order Paper is reached, the Clerk at the Table calls on the Lord in whose name it stands, who then rises to move the motion. In his absence the motion may be moved by another Lord who has been authorised by him to take his place, but otherwise the motion cannot be proceeded with until notice of it has been renewed (Standing Order No 40(2)). Motions are not seconded except in the case of the motion for an address in answer to the Queen's Speech. The mover of a motion has a right of reply. Other Lords may speak only once to each motion (Standing Order No 28).

It is not consistent with the practice of the House to move the same motion twice in the same session of Parliament.

Proposal of question upon a motion

After a motion has been moved the Lord Speaker (or in Committee of the whole House the Lord Chairman) proposes the question (Standing Order No 26). This usually takes the form 'That this motion be agreed to' without the terms of the motion being elaborated; but on the stages of bills and on some other occasions the full terms of the motion are put. Once the question has been proposed, debate on it may arise.

Adjournment of debate on motions

See below, p 431.

Withdrawal of motions

Once the question on a motion has been proposed, the motion can be withdrawn only by the unanimous leave of the House (Standing Order No

1 HL Deb (1983–84) 447, c 241.

29). If the mover seeks leave to withdraw his motion the Lord Speaker asks the House: 'Is it your Lordships' pleasure that this motion be withdrawn?'. A single dissenting voice prevents withdrawal, but it is rare for any objection to be taken.

Putting of question at end of debate

When debate on a question has ended and after the Lord moving the motion has (if he wishes) replied, the question is put for the second time. The Lord Speaker stands and states the question to the House, beginning with 'The question is, That . . .'. He then collects the voices by saying 'As many as are of that opinion will say "Content". The contrary, "Not-content"'; and the opposing sides call 'Content' or 'Not-content'. If there is a response from only one side the Lord Speaker says 'The Contents [or Not-contents] have it', and the question is resolved accordingly. If there is a response from both sides he judges which is the more numerous and says 'I think the Contents [or Not-contents] have it'. If this expression of opinion is not challenged he says 'The Contents [or Not-contents] have it' and the question is decided accordingly. If it is challenged he may repeat his expression of opinion. When, however, it is apparent that a division must be called, he says 'Clear the bar'.

Divisions

The procedure on a division is governed by Standing Order Nos 51–58. On the order being given to clear the bar, the bar and the division lobbies are cleared of strangers, but not the galleries, the space within the rails of the Throne, nor the seats below the bar, unless the House so orders. The doors at the exits from the division lobbies are locked.

As soon as the order for clearing the bar has been given the Clerk at the Table turns a three-minute sandglass[1] and two tellers, are appointed for each side. Where no tellers, or only one teller, can be found for one side, the question is resolved in favour of the side which has appointed two tellers, without a division taking place.[2] If neither side appoints two tellers the question is resolved in the same way as if there had been an equality of votes (see below).[3] After the lapse of three minutes the doors at the exits from the division lobbies are unlocked and the Lord Speaker or Lord Chairman again puts the question and collects the voices. If one side no longer persists in its challenge, he resolves the question without resort to a division. If both sides persist he directs that the division take place. Thereupon the Clerk turns the three-minute sandglass for the second time. The Contents go by the door to the right of the Throne through the lobby on the spiritual side and re-enter the House through the door beyond the Bar. The Not-contents go through the door beyond the Bar on the temporal side and re-enter the House through the door to the left of the Throne. One teller for the Contents and one for the Not-contents, and two Clerks, attend in each lobby to record the numbers and names of those voting.

A Lord may vote in a division although he was not in the House to hear the question put. The vote of the Lord Speaker or Lord Chairman is taken in the

---

1 LJ (1956–57) 38, 72.
2 LJ (1967–68) 487; ibid (1986–87) 71, 189, 264, 295; ibid (1987–88) 74, 170, 777, 924.
3 HL Deb (1981–82) 428, c 97.

House by the Clerk but they do not have a casting vote. Any Lord may on the ground of infirmity be told in his seat and his vote notified by the Clerk to the tellers on their return from the division lobbies (Standing Order No 52).

After the lapse of the second three-minute period the Lord Speaker or Lord Chairman repeats for the information of the House or the Committee the question which is the subject of the division. The doors of the Chamber are then locked and only Lords who are already in the lobbies or in the House may vote. When the tellers are satisfied that all Lords who wish to vote in their respective lobbies have done so, they return to the Table and communicate the numbers (including their own votes) to the Clerk, who adds the votes of the Lord Speaker or Lord Chairman and any Lord voting in his place. The Clerk writes down the result on a paper and hands it to one of the tellers for the winning side who presents it to the Lord Speaker or Lord Chairman. He reads the result of the division to the House and resolves the question as follows: 'So the Contents [or Not-contents] have it'.

Correction of numbers voting. The responsibility for counting the votes rests with the tellers but, if a discrepancy is discovered between their figures and the number of names recorded by the Clerks, and the tellers agree that a correction is necessary, an announcement to this effect is made by the Lord Speaker or the Lord Chairman at the earliest possible moment.[1] If the correction involves the reversal of a decision of the House, any further proceedings that may have been taken on the basis of that decision are, unless irreversible, vacated.[2]

Publication of division lists. Alphabetical lists of those who have voted are printed in the Official Report and are also entered in the Journals.[3]

Correction of wrong vote. If a Lord goes into the wrong lobby, he may, pursuant to Standing Order No 53, correct his error. After informing the tellers of his mistake he accompanies them to the Table after the other votes have been counted and there declares the vote that he intended to give, which is recorded by them accordingly.[4] If any Lord votes in both lobbies in a division, his name is struck off the lists of Lords voting in that division, and his vote is disregarded.[5]

Quorum. Standing Order No 55 provides: 'If, on a division upon a Bill, or upon a question for the approving or disapproving of subordinate legislation, less than thirty Lords have voted, the Lord Speaker shall declare the question not decided, and the debate thereon shall stand adjourned to a subsequent sitting; and, if such division take place when the House is in Committee, the Chairman shall declare the question not decided, where-

---

1 HL Deb (1979–80) 400, cc 782, 800; LJ (1979–80) 64.
2 LJ (1966–67) 48, 58. When tellers were appointed only for the Not-contents, and it was erroneously announced that tellers had been appointed only for the Contents, a statement was made by one of the tellers concerned, and the proceedings vacated and the Minutes amended by a subsequent order of the House: HL Deb (1970–71) 318, cc 1305, 1519; LJ (1970–71) 467, 508, 548.
3 LJ (1856–57) 535, 548.
4 LJ (1862–63) 230; Parl Deb (1862) 166, c 1608; LJ (1884) 254; ibid (1906) 488.
5 HL Deb (1981–82) 434, c 408.

upon the House shall resume, and shall be again in Committee at a subsequent sitting.'[1] There is no quorum for divisions on other questions, other
than the quorum of the House, which is three.

Equality of voices. If the Contents and Not-contents are equal, the question was, until 1951, decided according to the ancient rule, *'semper præsum-
itur pro negante'*, but the matter is now governed by Standing Order No 54:

(1) In relation to bills and subordinate legislation, the practice of the House
    is governed by the principle that no proposal to reject or amend a bill or
    instrument in the form in which it is then before the House shall be
    agreed to unless there is a majority in favour of such rejection or
    amendment.
(2) Similarly no proposal to reject or amend any motion relating to the
    stages of a bill shall be agreed to unless there is a majority in favour of
    such rejection or amendment.
(3) In relation to all other matters, the practice of the House is governed by
    the principle that the question before the House shall be decided in the
    negative unless there is a majority in its favour.
(4) In this Standing Order 'stages of a bill' means First Reading, Second
    Reading, Committee of the whole House, Report, Third Reading,
    Consideration of Commons Amendments and Consideration of Com-
    mons Reasons.

When the House is sitting judicially, the question is put first for reversing,
and not for affirming the judgment of the court below; and consequently, if
the numbers are equal, the House refuses to reverse the judgment and an
order is made that the judgment of the court below be affirmed.[2]

Votes of lay Lords in judicial cases. Although all Lords are theoretically
entitled to take part in the sittings of the House of Lords for judicial
business, the constitution of the Court has in effect been established by the
Appellate Jurisdiction Act 1876, which lays down that an appeal shall not be
heard and determined by the House of Lords unless there are present not
less than three of the following persons, namely, the Lord Chancellor, the
Lords of Appeal in Ordinary and such Peers as hold or have held certain
specified high judicial offices. It is now established practice that other Lords
do not take part.

Proxies

At one time Lords who were not present might vote in a division. Absent
Lords were entitled to vote by proxy.[3] The use of proxies was discontinued

---

1 For example, see LJ (1981–82) 237; ibid (1983–84) 158; ibid (1985–86) 311; ibid (1987–88)
  569.
2 LJ (1883) 461; ibid (1890–91) 278; ibid (1970–71) 243.
3 During the king's illness, in 1811, it was doubtful whether proxies were admissible; see Parl
  Deb (1810–11) 18, c 976.

by standing order in 1868. Two days notice is required of any proposal to suspend the standing order (Standing Order No 58). No attempt has since been made to revive proxies.

Methods of postponing or superseding the question

(a) Adjournment of debate. A motion for the adjournment of a debate may be moved at any time during the debate without notice and may be debated. But when it has been arranged in advance for a debate to be adjourned, it is usual for its adjournment to be moved formally by the Lord who will speak first when the debate is resumed.

The House may make an order, without notice, for adjourned business to be taken later the same day, or taken first on some future day (Standing Order No 43). Alternatively, the motion for the adjournment of the debate may specify the day to which it is to be adjourned.[1]

(b) Amendment to motion. After a motion has been moved and the question put on it, an amendment to the motion may be moved. At the end of the speech of the Lord proposing the amendment, the question is put on the amendment. In principle subsequent debate takes place only on the amendment. In practice the amendment and the original motion are usually debated together, so that only the mover of the amendment and of the original motion speak more than once. When the amendment has been disposed of, the original motion (as amended) is again put, and is decided usually without further debate.

Amendments to amendments are dealt with similarly.

(c) 'Next business' motion. A Lord who considers it undesirable that the House should record an opinion on a motion that has been moved may move 'That the House do proceed to the next business'. Notice should, if possible, be given. A 'next business' motion supersedes the original motion before the House and, if it is agreed to, the question on the original motion is not put, and the debate ends. If it is disagreed to, the debate on the original motion may be resumed and the question is put in the usual way. The 'next business' motion is not admitted on an amendment; though, after an amendment has been agreed to, it may be moved on an original motion as amended. It may not be moved in any committee of the House.[2]

The 'next business' motion is debatable and, since it cannot be debated without reference to the original motion, the subject matter of both motions may be debated together. It should be distinguished from the closure—'That the question be now put'—which, if carried, compels the House at once to come to a decision on the original motion (see below).

The 'next business' motion has replaced the older procedure known as the 'previous question'.

1 LJ (1881) 72.
2 LJ (1971–72) 128.

The closure

The closure (that is, the motion 'That the question be now put') is a most exceptional procedure.[1] When a Lord seeks to move the closure the Lord Speaker or Lord Chairman brings the attention of the House to its exceptional nature and gives the Lord concerned the opportunity of reconsidering his action by reading the following paragraph before the question is put:

> I am instructed by order of the House to say that the motion 'That the question be now put' is considered to be a most exceptional procedure and the House will not accept it save in circumstances where it is felt to be the only means of ensuring the proper conduct of the business of the House; further, if a Lord who seeks to move it persists in his intention the practice of the House is that the question on the motion is put without debate.

If, nevertheless, the Lord who is seeking to move the closure persists in his intention, the Lord Speaker or Lord Chairman puts and completes the question forthwith without debate.

If the closure is carried the Lord Speaker or Lord Chairman immediately puts and completes the original question without further debate; the original question cannot be withdrawn, because the House has decided that the question be now put; and no other question can be put until the original question has been disposed of.

Protests

A Lord has the right without leave to enter a 'protest' against any decision of the House, and may append his reasons.[2] Pursuant to Standing Order No 57 the entry of a protest in the Clerk's book must be made not later than the end of business on the next sitting day,[3] but leave has sometimes been given to enter a protest after the period limited by the standing order.[4] When a protest has been entered, other Lords may sign it without remark, if they agree with all the reasons assigned in it, or they may signify the particular reasons which have led them to attach their signatures. By usage, the right to enter a protest is restricted to Lords who were present and (in the case of a division) voted on the question to which they wish to express their dissent.

Leave has been given to Lords to sign the protest of another Lord, although they were not present when the question was put.[5]

Personal pecuniary interest

Votes. In 1796, a general resolution was proposed 'That no Peers shall vote who are interested in a question': but it was not adopted.[6] It is presumed, however, that such a resolution was deemed unnecessary; for it is held that the personal honour of a Lord will prevent him from forwarding his own

---

1 LJ (1960–61) 359; ibid (1970–71) 467, 508; HL Deb (1984–85) 464, c 718; ibid (1987–88) 496, c 428.
2 For the most recent protests, see LJ (1950) 90; ibid (1953–54) 404.
3 As to dissents in judicial cases, see Macqueen 28, 29.
4 LJ (1868–69) 257, 480; ibid (1890) 216.
5 LJ (1868–69) 493.
6 LJ (1794–96) 640, 650.

pecuniary interest by his votes in Parliament.[1] By Private Bill Standing Order No 96, Lords are 'exempted from serving on the committee on any private bill wherein they have an interest'.

Debate. The House has agreed that 'if a Peer decides that it is proper for him to take part in a debate on a subject in which he has a direct pecuniary interest he should declare it'.[2] Subject to this there is no reason why a Lord with an interest should not take part in debate or vote in a division.[3] It is however considered undesirable for a Lord to advocate, promote or oppose in the House any bill or subordinate legislation in which he is concerned for any pecuniary fee or reward.

CONDUCT OF BUSINESS

Quorum

The quorum of the House of Lords is three, of whom one may be a Lord attending to take the oath. Standing Order No 55 provides, however, that if fewer than thirty Lords have voted in a division upon a bill or subordinate legislation, the question is to be declared not decided and the matter adjourned to a subsequent sitting.

Preservation of order

The preservation of order in the House and the maintenance of the rules of debate are the responsibility of the House itself, and therefore of all Lords who are present. All Lords have a duty to call attention to breaches of order or procedure. The Lord Speaker has no controlling powers (Standing Order No 16). The Leader of the House has a special part to play in expressing the sense of the House and in drawing attention to transgressions of order. In his absence the Deputy Leader, Chief Whip or other senior whips assume these responsibilities. But the Leader is not invested with any special powers. The House's system of self-regulation means that the orderly conduct of business depends on all members of the House.[4]

Precedence in speaking

Lords are not called on to speak by the Lord Speaker. The order in which Lords may speak depends upon the will of the House. When two Lords rise at the same time, unless one immediately gives way, the House calls upon one of them to speak; and if each be supported by a party, there is no alternative but a division. Thus, on 7 February 1775, the Earl of Dartmouth and the Marquess of Rockingham both rising to speak, it was resolved, upon question, that the former 'shall now be heard'.[5] If the Leader of the House or

---

1 HL Deb (1981–82) 428, cc 966–967.
2 LJ (1969–70) 212–213, 301; see also HL Deb (1968–69) 302, c 523.
3 For the position in the House of Commons, see pp 384–386.
4 HL Deb (1987–88) 493, c 937.
5 LJ (1774–76) 305; see also Parl Deb (1810–11) 18, c 719 n; LJ (1884) 325; HL Deb (1911) 9, c 1059.

the Lord Chancellor rises to address the House, it is customary to give him precedence over other Lords who may rise at the same time.[1]

For most debates a list of Lords intending to take part is issued by the Government Whips Office. This list is the responsibility of the Leader of the House, and is drawn up after consultation with the Chief Whips of the main parties and the mover of the motion or the Lord asking the unstarred question. The Private Secretary to the Leader of the House acts as editor of the list. However, the list is for guidance only and may be varied. A Lord whose name is not on the list is not debarred from speaking but is expected to wait until just before the winding-up speeches.[2]

Place of speaking

Pursuant to Standing Order No 24, Lords must speak standing and uncovered, except by permission of the House.[3] However, disabled peers may sit, and women peers may wear a hat, without seeking permission.[4] A spiritual Lord must speak from the bishops' benches. No temporal Lord may speak from either of the two bishops' benches. Lords are not permitted to speak from the gangways in the House. Because the Woolsack is deemed to be outside the House, when the Lord Chancellor speaks other than as Lord Speaker he moves to the left of the Woolsack to the upper end of the Earls' bench, his appointed place under the House of Lords Precedence Act 1539 (see p 166); in Committee of the whole House, however, he speaks from the Government despatch box.

Manner of speaking

Pursuant to Standing Order No 25, a Lord addresses his speech 'to the rest of the Lords in general'.

Lords speak for themselves and not on behalf of outside interests. While they may indicate that an outside body agrees with the substance of the views that they are expressing, they should avoid creating an impression that they are speaking on behalf of outside interests.[5] The reading of speeches is alien to the custom of the House. It is recognized, however, that in certain circumstances, such as when a Ministerial Statement is being made, it is necessary for a Lord to read from a prepared text. In practice speakers often have recourse to 'extended notes', but it is considered contrary to the interests of good debate that they should follow them too closely.[6]

Restrictions on speeches

Under Standing Order No 26, debate must be relevant to the question before the House, and, where more than one question has been put, the debate must be relevant to the last question so proposed until it has been disposed of.

---

1 Debate on Roman Catholic Relief Bill, 3 April 1829, when the Lord Chancellor and Lord Kenyon rose together, Parl Deb (1829) 21, c 187.
2 LJ (1966–67) 49; ibid (1970–71) 759; ibid (1971–72) 69; HL Deb (1981–82), 427, cc 1289–1290.
3 See the case of Lord Wynford LJ (1831–32) 167.
4 LJ (1965–66) 59.
5 LJ (1969–70) 213, 301.
6 LJ (1935–36) 241; ibid (1969–70) 212.

Standing Order No 28 provides that no Lord is to speak more than once to any motion, subject to the following exceptions. The prohibition does not apply when the House is in Committee. The mover of a motion may always speak again in reply. Otherwise leave to speak again must be sought from the House, and this may be granted only to:

(a) a Lord to explain himself in some material point of his speech (no new matter being introduced);
(b) the Chairman of Committees, or in his absence a Deputy Chairman;
(c) the Chairman of a select committee on the report of such a committee; and
(d) a Minister of the Crown.

No Lord may speak more than once to any unstarred question (see p. 426), except with the leave of the House for the purpose of explaining himself in some material point of his speech (no new matter being introduced).

Standing Order No 27 provides that when at the end of debate the question has been put no Lord is to speak save on a point of order.

The content of a speech made in the House of Commons or in a Committee of that House in the current session may be summarized, but it is out of order to quote from such a speech unless it is a speech of a Minister in relation to government policy. It is considered undesirable that any Member of the House of Commons should be mentioned by name, or otherwise identified, for the purpose of criticism of a personal nature.[1]

It is undesirable to refer to strangers whether in the public gallery or in any other precincts of the chamber (except for the purpose of an order for their general withdrawal).[2]

Words of heat etc.

Standing Order No 30 directs 'that all personal, sharp, or taxing speeches be forborn' in the House; and that if any offence be given of that kind, the House 'will sharply censure the offender'.[3] When heat is engendered in debate, it is open to any Lord to move that the standing order be read by the Clerk.[4] The motion is debatable.

In order to prevent quarrels in debate between members,[5] Standing Order No 31 provides that a Lord who conceives himself to have received an affront or injury from another Member within the precincts of the House shall appeal to the Lords in Parliament for his reparation; or shall, if he declines the justice of the House, undergo their severe censure. The House has extended this principle sometimes to the prevention of quarrels which have arisen outside the House.[6]

If in a speech a Lord is thought to be seriously transgressing the accepted practice of the House, it is open to another Lord to move 'That the noble Lord be no longer heard'.[7] This motion is rare and is moved only in

---

1 HL Deb (1958–59) 216, cc 65–68; HL Deb (1985–86) 475, c 37. See also HL Deb (1987–88) 500, c 173.
2 HL Deb (1980–81) 417, c 132; HL Deb (1987–88) 493, c 726.
3 Mirror of Parliament, 1833, vol III, p 2855. See also LJ (1666–75) 31.
4 HL Deb (1979–80) 410, c 511.
5 Earls of Peterborough and Orford and Earl Rivers, 8 and 9 February 1698, LJ (1696–1701) 378.
6 LJ (1779–83) 188–191.
7 HL Deb (1981–82) 428, c 1070; ibid (1987–88) 496, c 428.

exceptional circumstances. It is debatable. The effect of agreeing to it is to prohibit the Lord in question from speaking further on the substantive motion, but not on any subsequent motion.

Length of speeches

The House has resolved 'That speeches in this House should be shorter'[1]. Since 1972 clocks have been installed in the Chamber to show how long a Lord has been speaking or how long a particular class of business has taken. Clocks are used (a) for timing speeches in those debates for which lists of speakers are issued; (b) for timing speeches on the second reading, third reading and passing of public bills and on motions to approve or annul delegated legislation; and (c) to measure the total time taken for starred questions, for ministerial statements and discussion on such statements, and for individual amendments and consideration of clauses (or schedules) in public bills. In 1988 the House approved guidelines for the length of speeches in debates not formally time-limited. These are up to twenty minutes for Lords from either side opening or winding-up a debate, and up to fifteen minutes for others.[2]

Attendance at debate

A Lord who is taking part in a debate is expected to attend the greater part of that debate. It is considered discourteous for him not to be present for the opening speeches, for at least the speech before and that following his own, and for the winding-up speeches.[3]

Lords are expected to remain in their seats when a maiden speech is being made and not leave the chamber.[4]

Conduct of Lords not speaking

By Standing Order No 17 Lords are directed to keep their dignity and order in sitting, and not to move out of their places without just cause; and when they cross the House, they are not to pass between the Woolsack and the Table, nor between the Woolsack and the Lord who is speaking; and on entering the House they are to make obeisance to the cloth of estate.

Standing Order No 19 provides:

> If any Lord has occasion to speak with another Lord while the House is sitting, they are to retire to the Prince's Chamber, and not converse in the space behind the Woolsack, or else the Lord Speaker is to call them to order, and, if necessary, to stop the business in agitation.

It is contrary to the custom of the House for books and newspapers (except for purposes specifically related to the debate), briefcases and ministerial boxes to be brought into the Chamber.[5]

Wording of questions and motions

There is no Lord or officer in whom authority is vested to refuse questions or motions on the ground of irregularity. The House has agreed to guidelines

---

1 LJ (1964) 386.
2 LJ (1971–72) 69, 275; (1976–77) 821; (1977–78) 23, 893; (1978–79) 41; HL Deb (1979–80) 414, c 1484; ibid (1982–83) 439, c 224; ibid (1987–88) 494, c 430.
3 LJ (1969–70) 212.
4 LJ (1977–78) 386.
5 LJ (1969–70) 213.

for motions for papers (see p 425). But in general the wording of questions and motions is the responsibility of the Lord who hands them in, and it is his discretion which governs the form in which they appear on the Order Paper. The Clerks at the Table are available to give help to any Lord in the drafting of a question or motion; they act in an advisory capacity only, but the House has agreed that Lords should accept the advice tendered by the Clerks on the wording of questions and motions.[1] The decision whether or not a question is 'in order' and may properly be asked is in the last resort one for the House itself. Although the House allows considerably more latitude than the House of Commons does, there are certain categories of question which are generally regarded as not being in accordance with the traditions of the House, ie are considered inadmissible.[2]

Such questions are:

(a) those casting reflections on the Sovereign or Royal Family;
(b) those relating to matters sub judice (see below);
(c) those relating to Church of England matters;[3]
(d) those phrased offensively.

The tabling of questions on nationalized industries is considered undesirable save for those asking for statistical information on a national basis or which raise matters of urgent public importance.[4] In some privatized industries the Government retains an interest, either through a power to give directions (whether directly or through a regulatory body) or through a shareholding. Questions may be tabled on those matters for which the Government has retained responsibility. Questions about the day-to-day administration of either nationalized or privatized industries do not fall within Government responsibility and are considered undesirable.[5]

It is considered undesirable to incorporate statements of opinion or the demonstration of a point of view in the text of any questions, starred, unstarred or written. Words in the text of motions or questions should not be italicized or underlined in order to give them emphasis.[6]

It is open to any Lord to call attention to a question or motion which has appeared on the Order Paper and to move that leave to ask the question (or move the motion) be not given or that it be removed from the Order Paper. This motion, which is debatable, is then decided by the vote or opinion of the House,[7] but it is moved only in exceptional circumstances.

Matters *sub judice*

A matter awaiting or under adjudication in any court exercising a criminal jurisdiction or in a court-martial should not be referred to in any motion or debate on a motion or in any question, including a supplementary question. A case which has been decided by a court, but is still open to appeal, is not considered *sub judice* until notice of appeal has been given.

Matters awaiting or under adjudication in a civil court should not be referred to in any motion or debate on a motion or in any question, including

---

1 HL Deb (1982–83) 439, c 223.
2 LJ (1966–67) 49.
3 LJ (1976–77) 167.
4 LJ (1977–78) 385.
5 HL Deb (1987–88) 494, c 429.
6 LJ (1970–71) 710.
7 LJ (1960–61) 140; HL Deb (1982–83) 437, cc 1407–1411.

a supplementary question, from the time that the case has been set down for trial or otherwise brought before the court, as for example by notice of motion for an injunction: such matters may be referred to before such date unless it appears to the House that there is a real and substantial danger of prejudice to the trial of the case.

These rules do not apply to bills or delegated legislation nor to matters being considered by departmental inquiries and the like. The House has recognized that the practice governing motions and questions relating to matters *sub judice* should be similar in both Houses of Parliament.[1]

---

1 LJ (1963–64) 43.

CHAPTER 21

Proceedings of Parliament in passing public bills

In this chapter the current procedures for passing bills through both Houses of Parliament are described. The practice of the Lords is in the main similar to that of the Commons. In both Houses the principal stages of bills are: first and second reading, committee, consideration on report from committee, and third reading. For the sake of clarity, however, the passage of a bill through the House of Lords is described in a separate section, with the exception of the final stages, which are common to both Houses and are treated in detail in the section dealing with the House of Commons.

Public and private bills

Bills are divided into the two classes of public and private bills. The former relate to matters of public policy and are introduced directly by members of the House. Private bills are bills for the particular interest or benefit of any person or persons, public company or corporation, or local authority, and are solicited by the parties themselves who are interested in their promotion, being founded upon petitions deposited in accordance with the standing orders relating to private business.

In spite of this general distinction, however, it is sometimes difficult to determine to which category particular bills belong, and the question may arise whether a public bill, in that it affects certain private interests, ought not more properly to have been introduced as a private bill, or whether a bill, introduced as a private bill, should be prevented from proceeding on the ground that its scope is so wide that it affects public policy. If it is found that certain of the standing orders relating to private business are applicable to a public bill, it is then treated as a hybrid, and its passage through Parliament is governed by a special procedure which is elaborated later in this chapter (p 519).

The process of enacting private bills is the same in its essential elements as that for enacting public bills. The details, however, differ widely and private bill procedure is subject to a different set of standing orders. For that reason the procedures for passing private bills are described in a separate section (chapters 36 to 39).

Where bills originate

As a general rule bills may originate in either House. Government bills which are likely to arouse major controversy are generally introduced into the House of Commons, and because of the exclusive right of that House to grant supplies and to impose and appropriate all charges upon the people, bills of aids and supplies must be introduced into the House of Commons (cf p 461). Standing Order No 78 however makes it possible for a bill having as its main object the imposition of a charge on the people or on public funds to originate in the House of Lords, and, subject to the use of the usual devices for avoiding privilege (see p 460), for such a bill to be taken charge of in the House of Commons by a Minister of the Crown;[1] nevertheless, by far the greater proportion of bills whose main object is the imposition of a charge are introduced in the House of Commons. Consolidation bills and bills dealing with legal and judicial topics are normally introduced in the House of Lords.

Bills concerning privileges of one House. It was formerly held that a bill which concerns the privileges or proceedings of either House should, in courtesy, commence in the House to which it relates.[2] However, while bills have occasionally been withdrawn or not proceeded with both in the first House[3] and in the second House[4] in deference to this principle, bills which have affected the composition or powers of the Lords have been introduced and proceeded with in the Commons.[5] Provisions of bills which related to the composition, powers, privileges and administration of one House have frequently been debated and amended in the other.[6]

The Lords claim that bills for the restitution of honours and in blood should be first introduced in the Lords. Such bills, as well as bills of attainder and bills for a general pardon, are now mainly of historical interest.

Form of a bill. A public bill is in the form of a draft statute, and contains some, but not necessarily all, of the following elements:

(1) Citation and short titles. The citation title, under which the Act is cited amongst the statutes, is usually set out in the last clause—'This Act may be cited as the ... Act 19 ..'.[7] Occasionally the short title at the head of the bill, and the title set out in the citation or short title clause, are not identical, as in the case of the Consolidated Fund (Appropriation) Bill, which is always enacted as the Appropriation Act. When the short title of a bill would otherwise be the same as that of a bill already introduced in the same session in either House the identifying description '(No 2)' is inserted. Such an identifying description will be removed by the Lords Public Bill Office at Royal Assent if no previous Act with the same short title has been passed

---

1 CJ (1972–73) 154.
2 3 Hatsell 69; 1 Bl Com 168.
3 LJ (1832) 294, 333; Parl Deb (1832) 13, cc 611, 1086.
4 LJ (1920) 251; HC Deb (1920) 40, cc 992–998.
5 Representative Peers (Scotland and Ireland) Bill 1869, Parl Deb (1869) 194, c 984. Bill subsequently withdrawn. Bishops in Parliament (motion for leave to bring in a bill) 1834. Irish Church Act 1869. Lords Spiritual (motion for leave to bring in a bill) 1870. Welsh Church Act 1914. Peeresses Bill 1924. Peerage Bill 1962–63, which concerned both Houses (introduced in the House of Commons). The Parliament (No 2) Bill 1969, which dealt comprehensively with the composition and powers of the House of Lords, was introduced into the House of Commons.
6 Eg Court of Chancery Improvement Bill, Parl Deb (1851) 117, c 1069; Parliament (Qualification of Women) Bill 1918, LJ (1918) 288, CJ (1918) 232; Life Peerages Bill [Lords] 1957–58, CJ (1957–58) 90.
7 The citation clause is sometimes the first clause of the bill, eg Government of India Bill 1934, European Communities Bill 1972.

during that calendar year. Similarly an identifying description will be inserted at Royal Assent if an Act of the same title has been passed in the same calendar year (though not in the same session). Thus, for example, in session 1987–88 the Consolidated Fund Bill became the Consolidated Fund (No 2) Act 1987, and the Consolidated Fund (No 3) Bill became the Consolidated Fund Act 1988. By the Short Titles Act 1896 short titles were given to many public general Acts, passed between 1707 and 1896, which did not already possess them, and groups of Acts were given collective titles.[1] Further short titles extending from 1236 to 1860 were conferred by the Second Schedule to the Statute Law Revision Act 1948.

While a bill is before Parliament, if it originates in the Lords it is distinguished in that House by the letters HL in square brackets, as for example the 'Landlord and Tenant Bill [HL]'. While in the Commons it is distinguished by the word Lords in square brackets—the 'Landlord and Tenant Bill [*Lords*]'. Bills originating in the Commons carry no corresponding suffix. The suffix does not appear in the citation clause and it is not retained when the bill is published as an Act after Royal Assent.

(2) Long title. The long title sets out in general terms the purposes of the bill, and should cover everything in the bill. When the term 'title' is used without qualification it usually refers to the long title.

Both the long title and the short title may be amended, if amendments to the bill make that course appropriate. The long title has also been amended where a bill as drafted has been found to be narrower than its title.

(3) Preamble. The purpose of a preamble is to state the reasons for and the intended effects of the proposed legislation. Though a preamble is not often incorporated now in a public bill, one still appears in a bill of great constitutional importance or in a bill to give effect to international conventions.[2] In the case of the Abnormal Importations (Customs Duties) Bill 1931, the Import Duties Bill 1932 and the Ottawa Agreements Bill 1932, an expression of the aims of the legislation was incorporated with the enacting words.[3] In the case of the Legal Aid Bill [Lords] 1987 a 'purpose' clause stating the purpose of the bill was inserted at third reading before the other clauses in the bill.[4]

(4) Enacting Formula. The enacting formula is a short paragraph which precedes the clauses of the bill. This formula, which was developed in the

---

1 Ilbert, *Legislative Methods and Forms* (1901) p 272.
2 Eg Parliament Bill 1911 and Parliament (No 2) Bill 1969 (but not the Parliament Bills of 1947–49); Government of India Bill 1919; Statute of Westminster 1931; His Majesty's Declaration of Abdication Bill 1936; British North America Bill 1949; Geneva Convention Bills 1911 and 1936; Patents, etc (International Conventions) Bill [Lords] 1938; Canada Bill 1982; Foreign Nuclear Chemical and Biological Bases (Prohibition) Bill [Lords] 1983; Australia Bill [Lords] 1985; Brunei (Appeals) Bill [Lords] 1989. The Government of India Bill 1934 had no preamble, as the preamble of the Act of 1919 was regarded as covering the policy of the later bill; neither did the Indian and Burmese Independence Bills of 1947 nor the European Communities Bill 1972. Preambles have been incorporated in private Members' bills as presented to Parliament, eg Minimum Wages etc Bill 1984–85, European Communities Amendment Bill 1987–88.
3 For preambles to hybrid bills see Report of the Select Committee on Hybrid Bills (Procedure in Committee), HC (1947–48) 191, paras 6–17 and Minutes of Evidence p 2.
4 HL Deb (1987–88) 494, c 10. See also The Preparation of Legislation (1975), Cmnd 6053, paras 11.6–11.8.

fifteenth century, now runs as follows: 'Be it enacted by the Queen's most Excellent Majesty, by and with the advice and consent of the Lords Spiritual and Temporal, and Commons, in this present Parliament assembled, and by the authority of the same, as follows.' In Consolidated Fund and Finance Bills, the usual formula is preceded by certain words which define the sole responsibility of the Commons for the grant of money or duties:[1] 'Most Gracious Sovereign, We, Your Majesty's most dutiful and loyal subjects, the Commons of the United Kingdom in Parliament assembled (*in a Consolidated Fund Bill*) [towards making good the supply which we have cheerfully granted to Your Majesty in this Session of Parliament, have resolved to grant unto Your Majesty the sum hereinafter mentioned] (*or in a Finance Bill*) [towards raising the necessary supplies to defray Your Majesty's public expenses, and making an addition to the public revenue, have freely and voluntarily resolved to give and grant unto Your Majesty the several duties hereinafter mentioned];[2] and do therefore most humbly beseech Your Majesty that it may be enacted, and be it enacted, etc.' For bills presented for Royal Assent under the Parliament Acts 1911 and 1949 (see p 534) the Acts prescribe the formula 'Be it enacted by the [Queen's] most Excellent Majesty, by and with the advice and consent of the Commons in this present Parliament assembled, in accordance with the provisions of the Parliament Acts 1911 and 1949, and by the authority of the same, as follows'.

(5) Clauses. The text of a bill is divided into a series of numbered clauses, each with a descriptive title (known as a 'side-note') printed in the margin. Clauses may be divided into subsections '(1),' '(2)' etc, subsections into paragraphs, and paragraphs into sub-paragraphs. Long and complicated bills may have their clauses grouped in 'parts' distinguished by Roman numerals and titles in capitals, and these may again be broken up into 'chapters' or into small groups of clauses with a group title in italics. A table of clauses (and schedules), known as the 'arrangement of clauses', may be prefixed to a bill, showing the numbered titles of the clauses and schedules, and also any grouping into parts.[3] On enactment, 'clauses' become 'sections' of Acts.

(6) Schedules. At the end of a bill there may be one or more schedules which contain matters of detail dependent on the provisions of the bill. A schedule is part of the bill and is dependent on one or more of the preceding clauses, by means of which the provisions of the schedule are carried into effect.

(7) Explanatory memorandum. An explanatory memorandum, though not technically part of the bill, is often attached to the first print of a bill in each House, together with a financial memorandum if the bill is a Government bill which involves expenditure. For rules governing these memoranda, see p 470.

---

1 Maitland *Constitutional History of England* (1926 edn) p 185; Anson *Law and Custom of the Constitution* (5th edn, 1922) vol I, *Parliament* p 298.
2 See also the enacting formula in the Abnormal Importations (Customs Duties) Bill 1931; Import Duties Bill and Ottawa Agreements Bill 1932; Armed Forces (Housing Loans) Bill 1949.
3 Such a table is customarily affixed to a bill (and consequently to the Act) when it consists of more than four pages or more than twelve clauses.

1. PROCEEDINGS IN THE HOUSE OF LORDS

INTRODUCTION AND FIRST READING

In the House of Lords it is the privilege of any Member of the House to present a bill without notice and without moving for leave to bring it in.[1] Occasionally, however, notice is given. In both cases the first reading of the bill is moved immediately after introduction and the question is put thereon from the Woolsack. An order is then made for the bill to be printed. In contrast with the practice in the House of Commons, a bill is always printed immediately after it has been introduced. The bill is endorsed with the name of the Lord who has introduced it. It is not the practice to add other names. When a day is appointed for the second reading, notice is given in the 'second half' of the Minutes of Proceedings (see p 204); meanwhile the bill is entered in the order paper in the list of bills in progress as 'waiting for second reading.'

Introduction without notice

A Lord who wishes to present a bill rises in his place at the beginning of public business before the notices and orders of the day are called on, or at the end of public business immediately before the adjournment of the House (Standing Order No 39(3)). He reads out the long title of the bill and moves the first reading formally. It is usual for the text of the bill to be submitted in advance to the Public Bill Office. Otherwise, as soon as the question has been put and decided he hands in a draft to the Table. The proceedings on the first reading of a bill presented in this manner are usually formal and there is seldom any discussion on the bill at this stage.[2]

Introduction after notice

Occasionally notice is given of the introduction of a bill.[3] The usual method by which this is done is for the Lord to hand in to the Table a notice for a particular date stating that he will call attention to the subject and present a bill. The notice is then inserted in the order paper for that day and takes its place among the notices in the ordinary manner (see p 424). When on the day appointed the notice is called on, the Lord in whose name it stands explains his motives in presenting the bill and moves the first reading. A debate may then take place, not so much on the merits of the bill, the

---

1 8 Parl Hist 1179; Parl Deb (1805) 3, c 42.
2 The reason for introducing a bill similar to one already introduced in the same session may be explained; eg HL Deb (1966–67) 278, c 2064; ibid (1967–68) 289, c 101.
3 Instances of the introduction of bills by notice are the Authorised Companies (Liquor) Bill by the Bishop of Chester on 2 March 1893, (LJ (1893–94) 70), the Motor Vehicles Compulsory Insurance Bill by the Earl Russell on 15 July 1925, (LJ (1924–25) 289), and the Parliament (Reform) Bill by the Marquess of Salisbury on 19 December 1933 (LJ (1933–34) 39).

contents of which are not yet available to the House, but rather on the question whether legislation on the subject, as outlined in the introductory speech, is desirable.

First reading

In virtually every case the first reading of a bill in the House of Lords is agreed to without discussion or dissent. Very occasionally the mover of a bill has made a short speech before a bill is read a first time when he proposes to withdraw another bill in favour of the bill in question.[1] However there have been occasions when the first reading was debated (this has always been so when notice of the introduction of a bill has been given), and on four occasions the first reading has been opposed.[2]

Reference of certain bills to Examiners. A bill is examined by the Public Bill Office to see whether it may affect any private interests to which protection is given by the standing orders. If, prima facie, this is found to be so, an order is made referring the bill to the Examiners, and the second reading of the bill cannot be moved until the report of the Examiners has been received, although notice of second reading of the bill may be entered in the Order Paper. In the case of a Commons bill, an order is usually made for it to be referred to the Examiners if it was so referred by that House (but see p 445n2). If the Examiners find that the standing orders relating to private bills are applicable, the bill is a hybrid bill (see p 519), and after second reading, if it is petitioned against it follows the procedure of a private bill until reported from the committee to which it is committed. If, however, the Examiners report that no standing orders are applicable, the bill may proceed on its ordinary course.

The National Gallery (Lane Collection) Bill 1926, the object of which was to enable the Trustees of the National Gallery to transfer or lend the Lane Collection to the Trustees of the National Gallery of Ireland, was referred to the Examiners[3] and, on a report from them that the standing orders were applicable and had not been complied with, the bill was dropped. The Commons Registration Bill 1964–65 was referred to the Examiners and, on a report from them that the standing orders were not applicable,[4] a date was appointed for the second reading. The London Government Bill 1962–63 was found by the Public Bill Office not to affect private interests, but the opposition nevertheless divided the House on the motion that the Bill be referred to the Examiners on the day of the second

1 HL Deb (1966–67) 278, c 2064.
2 The first reading of the Local Government (England and Wales) Act 1988 Repeal Bill 1988 was negatived twice (4 December, 20 December 1988); a reasoned amendment to the motion for the first reading of the Parliament (Reform) Bill 1933 was defeated on a division (19 December 1933); the first reading of the Statute of Westminster 1931 (Amendment) Bill 1943 was negatived (4 November 1943); and the Parliament (No 6) Bill 1969 was read a first time after a division (21 April 1969).
3 LJ (1926) 109, 161.
4 LJ (1964–65) 109, 134.

reading.[1] The Aircraft and Shipbuilding Industries Bill 1977, a Government bill, was found by the Examiners to be hybrid. The Government then announced its intention of proposing amendments to delete the offending provisions of the bill, and on that basis the House agreed to a motion which enabled the bill to proceed as if it had not been hybrid.[2]

Bills brought from the Commons. Bills which have been initiated in the House of Commons and passed through all their stages in that House are brought to the House of Lords by a House of Commons Clerk with a message stating that the Commons have passed the bills. The message is read by the Clerk at the Table as soon as the item of business in progress has ended, and the first reading of each bill is moved forthwith by the Chief Whip or in his absence by another Government Whip. An order is made for the bill to be printed and the Lord who is to take charge of the bill in the House of Lords may give notice of a date for the second reading,[3] and the bill is entered in the order paper.

Bills from the House of Commons may be carried up to the Office of the Clerk of the Parliaments when the House of Lords is not sitting. Under Standing Order No 48 they are deemed to have been brought from the Commons and may be printed before first reading if it is for the convenience of the House.

The first reading of bills received from the Commons is almost invariably agreed to without discussion. There are, however, instances of a departure from this practice.[4]

Money Bills under the Parliament Act. Bills which have been certified by the Speaker of the House of Commons as Money Bills under the Parliament

---

1 LJ (1962–63) 226.
2 LJ (1976–77) 182, 223; HL Deb (1976–77) 380, c 641. A similar bill had been ruled to be prima facie hybrid in the Commons in the previous session, but that House resolved to dispense with standing orders relating to private business and with any consideration of their application, and so exempted the Bill from the hybrid procedure.
3 In 1885 a dispute arose as to who should move the second reading of the Medical Relief Disqualification Removal Bill, two peers claiming the right to do so. The House decided in favour of the peer who first gave notice to the Clerk of the Parliaments, LJ (1884–85) 414; Parl Deb (1885) 300, c 27.
4 The first reading of the Corn Importation Bill in 1846 was opposed, (LJ (1846) 418) and debates took place upon the first reading of the Customs Duties Bill in 1846, (LJ (1846) 441) the Copper and Lead Duties Bill in 1848, (LJ (1847–48) 847) the Irish Free State (Agreement) Bill in 1922 (LJ (1922) 77), the Government of India Bill in 1935 (LJ (1934–35) 214) and the Licensing Bill in 1961 (HL Deb (1960–61) 232, c 720). On the occasion of the first reading of the Representation of the People Bill on 11 December 1917, an explanatory statement was made by Viscount Peel, who was in charge of the bill. (LJ (1917–18) 293; HL Deb (1917–18) 27, c 86).

Act 1911 bear an endorsement to that effect on the title page and are so recorded in the Minutes of Proceedings of the House of Lords at the time of their receipt from the Commons.

Commons Bills not taken up within twelve sitting days. Standing Order No 47 provides that when a bill received from the Commons shall have remained on the Table for twelve sitting days without any Lord giving notice of the second reading, such bill shall not be further proceeded with in the same session, except after eight days' notice of the second reading.

In the case of the Public Worship Facilities Bill on 20 May 1873, this standing order was considered and dispensed with.[1] A similar motion to dispense with the standing order in respect of the Copyhold Enfranchisement Bill in 1886 was, however, objected to and negatived, it being stated on this occasion that there was no precedent for the motion except that of 1873.[2] The standing order was again dispensed with on 6 July 1895, when a motion was moved that it be considered and dispensed with and that the Local Government Act 1894 (Stock Transfer) (No 2) Bill be read the second time,[3] and since then similar motions have been agreed to on occasions, LJ (1933–34) 274; ibid (1934–35) 238; ibid (1935–36) 346; ibid (1938–39) 341; HL Deb (1979–80) 412, c 1193.

Withdrawal of bills. By an old parliamentary rule, a bill from the other House may not be withdrawn at any stage. A bill originating in the House of Lords may (with the leave of the House, granted without a dissenting voice) be withdrawn by the Lord who presented it at any time after first reading.[4]

Successive stages of a bill to be taken on different days. No two stages of a bill may be taken on one day.

Standing Order No 44 provides that 'No Bill shall be read twice the same day; no Committee of the whole House shall proceed on any Bill the same day as the Bill has been read the Second time; no report shall be received from any Committee of the whole House the same day such Committee goes through the Bill, when any amendments are made to such Bill; and no Bill shall be read the Third time the same day that the Bill is reported from the Committee, or the order of commitment is discharged.' Consequently, if it is desired to take more than one stage of a bill on one day, this standing order must be suspended and notice of the proposed suspension must be given

---

1 LJ (1873) 375.
2 LJ (1886) 261.
3 LJ (1895) 267.
4 In the case of the Meteorites Bill, leave to withdraw the bill was refused on the 24 March 1971 as there were dissenting voices, and the bill was read a second time on 30 March 1971. LJ (1970–71) 332, 342.

(Standing Order No 83). The passage of a bill with unusual expedition, both in the House of Lords and the House of Commons, is described below on pp 529–532.

Recommended minimum intervals between the stages of a bill. Following a recommendation of the Procedure Committee in 1977,[1] notice is given whenever certain recommended minimum intervals between stages of public bills are departed from, except when Standing Order No 44 has been suspended. Such notice is normally given by means of a § against the bill in the order paper.

The recommended minimum intervals are as follows:

(a) two week-ends between the introduction of a bill, or of a bill as brought from the Commons, and the debate on second reading;
(b) fourteen days between second reading and the start of the committee stage;
(c) on all bills of considerable length and complexity, fourteen days between the end of the committee stage and the start of the report stage;
(d) three sitting days between the end of the report stage and third reading.

Reasonable notice should when possible be given for consideration of commons amendments.[2]

SECOND READING

The second reading is the stage at which the general principles of a bill are considered. As soon as the Clerk has read the notice for the second reading, the Lord in charge of the bill moves, and explains the bill's purpose. At the end of his speech the question 'That this bill be now read a second time' is proposed from the Woolsack and the debate follows. Discussion of the bill's details should be left to the committee stage. But a Lord may indicate the points on which he thinks the bill needs amendment and the general nature of amendments which he will propose.

Methods of opposing second reading

A bill may be opposed on second reading in three ways.

Opposing without moving amendment. The first method of opposition is by opposing the question for the second reading. If the motion is disagreed to,[3] the second reading is in theory only negatived for that particular day but in practice the bill is treated as having been rejected and is removed from the list of bills in progress.

Delaying amendment. The second method is by an amendment to the motion for second reading to leave out the word 'now' and insert at the end

---

1 Second Report from the Procedure Committee 1976–77; LJ (1976–77) 821; ibid (1977–78) 23. The recommendation derived from the 1st Report from the Select Committee on Practice and Procedure 1976–77 (HL 141).
2 HL Deb (1987–88) 493, c 938.
3 LJ (1981–82) 43, 56, 192, 220; ibid (1984–85) 361, 591.

of the motion 'this day six months'. The intention of such a motion is to deny
the bill a second reading during the current session. Notice is generally given
in the order paper of this amendment and the mover of it usually, though not
invariably, speaks after the mover of the motion for the second reading. An
amendment of this kind has, however, been moved without previous
notice.[1] As soon as the amendment has been moved it is proposed from the
Woolsack, and the question then before the House is that the amendment be
agreed to. If the amendment is withdrawn or defeated on a division, the
original question is put 'That this bill be now read a second time'. If,
however, the amendment is agreed to, the bill is treated as having been
rejected; the original question, as amended, is not put; and the bill is
removed from the list of bills in progress.[2]

Reasoned amendment. The third method of opposing a bill on second
reading is by moving a reasoned amendment, notice of which is always
given. The main question being 'That this bill be now read a second time',
the usual form of the amendment is to leave out all the words after 'That' and
to insert words to the effect that the House declines to proceed with the bill
for certain specified reasons, or until further information upon the subject
matter of the bill from specified sources has been made available.[3] If the
amendment is agreed to, no further question is put.

Several amendments moved on second reading. When notice has been
given of several amendments to the second reading of a bill, they are dealt
with in the order in which they relate to the motion for the second reading,
or, if they relate to the same place in the motion, in the order in which they
are tabled. In such cases it is usual for the whole debate to take place upon
the first amendment. The Lords in whose names the subsequent amendments stand speak to this first amendment and indicate the reasons why they
prefer their own amendments. When the debate is concluded the question is
put on each amendment in turn or upon so many of them as must be disposed
of before a positive decision is reached. If none is agreed to, the original
question is put.

Motion for rejection of bill. A form of opposition to the second reading of
a bill which was once common but which would now be treated as obsolete is
by a motion that the bill be rejected. This is considered to be a more
summary manner of registering disapproval of a bill than the methods
mentioned above, and the most recent instances of its use were cases of an
unusual character.[4]

---

1 LJ (1924) 240.
2 LJ (1982–83) 57, 171, 223; ibid (1983–84) 137; ibid (1985–86) 67; ibid (1987–88) 589.
3 LJ (1977–78) 288, 350; ibid (1980–81) 53; ibid (1982–83) 272; ibid (1985–86) 245.
4 LJ (1887) 19, 435, 449; ibid (1902) 160.

Other motions on second reading

In addition to reasoned amendments in opposition to the second reading of a bill, it is also in order to move reasoned amendments in support of, or without seeking to negative, the second reading, where it is desired to invite the House to put on record a particular point of view in assenting to the bill.[1]

Motion for adjournment of second reading debate

It is also possible to move that the second reading be adjourned *sine die*[2] or more usually for a particular purpose[3] with or without notice or reasons but such a motion, if passed, does not prevent the motion for the second reading being put down for a subsequent day.

Resolution on the same day as second reading

A resolution deprecating or enlarging on certain provisions of a bill has been moved on the same day as the second reading.[4]

Any such motion must be sufficiently different from the bill so as not to attract the rule against offering the same question to the House as one on which its judgment has already been expressed in the same session.

Instructions

An instruction to the committee on a bill may be moved after second reading. The motion for an instruction may be moved at the end of the second reading or when the notice is read for the House to resolve itself into a committee; or as a Business of the House motion in the interval.

Instructions are of two kinds, permissive and mandatory.

Permissive instructions. The object of a permissive instruction is to confer on the committee authority to do something which, without the instruction,

---

1 LJ (1979–80) 344; ibid (1980–81) 614; ibid (1983–84) 465, 582; ibid (1984–85) 185, 261; ibid (1985–86) 45.
2 LJ (1948) 106, 294.
3 LJ (1971–72) 474, 490, 493; ibid (1974) 322; ibid (1977–78) 288; ibid (1987–88) 508.
4 Immigration Bill, LJ (1970–71) 597; British Nationality Bill, ibid (1980–81) 614.

they would have no power to do, for example, to divide a bill into two bills,[1] to consolidate two bills into one,[2] or to extend the scope of a bill.[3] Instructions of this kind merely confer on the committee the power to take the course of action specified, leaving it to the discretion of the committee whether they exercise the power.

In this century permissive instructions have been moved three times; on 25 May 1906, to extend the scope of the Colonial Marriages Bill; on 29 July 1919 to divide the Ministry of Ways and Communications Bill; and on 13 May 1936, to commit the Malta (Letters Patent) Bill to a select committee and to divide it into two.

Mandatory instructions. The object of mandatory instructions is to define the course which the committee on a bill must follow.

The most common of these instruct the committee to consider the schedules to the bill immediately after the related clause, or the clauses and schedules in an order other than that of the bill. An instruction was moved on the Coal Bill 1939 to leave out certain parts of the bill.[4]

COMMITMENT

As soon as a bill has been read a second time it is ordinarily committed to a Committee of the whole House without question put, under Standing Order No 45. The exceptions, for which the House orders otherwise, are given below.

Committee negatived

In the case of supply bills, such as the Finance Bill and Consolidated Fund Bills, the committee stage is usually dispensed with. In order to effect this, the question is put after the second reading 'That this bill be not committed' and, if this is agreed to, the bill then awaits third reading. This practice is applied to other bills, and particularly to 'money' bills under the Parliament Act (see p 752), with a view to saving time when by general consent there is no desire from any quarter of the House to propose amendments.

Order of commitment discharged

If, at the time appointed for the House to go into committee upon a bill, no amendment has been set down, and it appears that no Lord wishes to speak on the bill or to table a manuscript amendment,[5] the Lord in charge of the

---

1 LJ (1852-53) 289. Only one attempt has been made to divide a bill brought from the Commons (LJ (1919) 310) and this was defeated. But the instruction was objected to on its merits as well as on its unprecedented nature and the technical difficulties it would create, so that the propriety of dividing a Commons bill has not been decided. The Government of India Act 1935 was divided, between the date of Royal Assent and the date of coming into operation, by a separate Act (the Government of India (Reprinting) Act 1935).
2 LJ (1890-91) 158.
3 LJ (1899) 304.
4 LJ (1937-38) 204.
5 Ie an amendment of which notice has not been given (see p 453).

bill may move 'That the order of commitment be discharged'.[1] This motion may be moved only on the day appointed for the committee stage and notice must be given. If the motion is agreed to, the next stage is the third reading. In accordance with Standing Order No 44, the bill may not be read a third time on the same day as the order of commitment is discharged.

The question cannot be put on the motion 'That the order of commitment be discharged' if any Lord objects. In such a case, the Lord in charge of the bill moves in the usual way 'That the House do now resolve itself into a committee upon the bill' (see p 452).

Bill committed to select or joint committee

A public bill may be committed to a select committee or a joint committee of both Houses at any stage between the second and third readings when a more minute investigation of its provisions than is possible in a Committee of the whole House is required or when the hearing of evidence is considered necessary.[2] To achieve this a motion 'That this bill be committed to a select committee' is required, or 'That it is desirable that a joint committee of both Houses be appointed to consider the bill'. If the bill is referred to a joint committee a message is sent to the House of Commons informing them and desiring their agreement.[3]

The Bill of Rights Bill 1976–77 was not referred to a select committee, but the House agreed to an amendment to the motion for second reading providing that the bill should not proceed further until a select committee had reported on the question whether a Bill of Rights was desirable and if so what form it should take, and that a select committee be appointed for that purpose. A select committee was appointed in due course, but no order of commitment was made on second reading.[4]

The order committing a bill to a Committee of the whole House may be discharged and an order made to commit the bill instead to a joint[5] or to a select[6] committee. A bill may be committed to a select committee on another bill.[7]

Public bill committees

Under a procedure introduced in 1968, when the House faces acute pressures of time, public bills of a technical and non-controversial nature may be committed after second reading to committees off the floor of the House known as public bill committees.[8] The committees have consisted of either twelve or fourteen named Lords together with the Chairman of Committees. In the committees all other Lords are free to speak and move

---

1 SO No 45(2). See HL Deb (1970–71) 311, c 1077.
2 LJ (1977–78) 182; ibid (1979–80) 305; ibid (1982–83) 334; ibid (1983–84) 41; ibid (1986–87) 143; ibid (1987–88) 86. The London Bridge Bill was referred to a select committee after the third reading had been moved, LJ (1878-79) 273.
3 LJ (1958–59) 97.
4 LJ (1976–77) 137.
5 LJ (1974–75) 247.
6 LJ (1986–87) 143.
7 LJ (1983–84) 58.
8 HL Deb (1987–88) 493, c 938. For a recent public bill committee, see LJ (1986–87) 45, 392–395.

amendments,[1] but not to vote (Standing Order No 63). The committees are instructed to follow the procedure of a Committee of the whole House as closely as possible.[2] Initially it was the practice for bills which had been committed to public bill committees to be re-committed to a Committee of the whole House, but in May 1975 it was provided that, unless the House ordered otherwise, such bills should proceed directly from the public bill committee to report stage on the floor of the House.[3] The bill considered by the House on report is the bill as reported from the public bill committee. The verbatim report of proceedings of public bill committees is published separately by the Official Report. The minutes are published as an annex to the Minutes of Proceedings and, ultimately, as an appendix to the Journals.

Consolidation bills

Consolidation bills are referred automatically after second reading to the Joint Committee on Consolidation Bills (Standing Order No 49 [HL]; Standing Order No 123 [HC]). The bill is subsequently recommitted to a Committee of the whole House. If the Joint Committee amend a bill, it is the amended bill which is then considered (see pp 667–669 below).

COMMITTEE STAGE (COMMITTEE OF THE WHOLE HOUSE)[4]

When the notice has been read for the House to be in committee on a bill, the Lord in charge of the bill moves 'That the House do now resolve itself into a committee upon the bill'. This motion is sometimes used as an opportunity to question the relevance of certain amendments[5] or to raise general points relating to the amendments.[6] When the committee stage lasts more than one day, the motion 'That the House do now again resolve itself into a Committee upon the bill' may provide an opportunity to raise matters relating to the progress of the bill.[7]

The motion may be opposed by reasoned amendment[8] or by an amendment to postpone the committee stage[9] or to discharge the order of commitment and to commit the bill instead to a select committee,[10] though opposition to the motion seldom occurs.[11]

---

1 Ibid 392–395, when amendments were moved by various Lords who had not been named members of the Committee.
2 LJ (1986–87) 45.
3 LJ (1974–75) 587, 610.
4 See also pp 572–573.
5 Administration of Justice Bill 1968 (HL Deb (1967–68) 288, cc 1075–1086); Rent (Agriculture) Bill 1976 (HL Deb (1975–76) 375, cc 1281–1283).
6 HL Deb (1983–84) 445, c 120; ibid (1987–88) 495, cc 920–923.
7 HL Deb (1987–88) 491, cc 313–314; ibid 495, cc 685–686.
8 Royal Titles Bill, LJ (1876) 110; Agricultural Labourers' Holidays (Scotland) Bill, ibid (1887) 419.
9 Marriages (Prohibited Degrees of Relationship) Bill, LJ (1928) 266; Trade Union Bill, HL Deb (1983–84) 453, cc 85, 135.
10 HL Deb (1987–88) 488, c 350.
11 When the order of the day was read for the House to resolve itself into a committee on the Housing (Financial Provisions) Bill 1924, a resolution was moved that the House, before going into committee, desired the setting up of an immediate inquiry into the possibility of achieving the objects of the bill by the use of building materials other than brick. The resolution was agreed to and the House then went into committee on the bill; LJ (1924) 334.

Amendments

Amendments handed in are printed overnight and published the next working day. Shortly before the day appointed for the committee, the various amendments are arranged in the order in which they relate to the bill (except where the order is altered by an instruction), and they are numbered and published as a marshalled list. When the committee stage is not completed in one day, a further marshalled list is published for each subsequent day.

Rules as to amendments. Amendments may be handed in at any time[1] after second reading.[2] Where more than one amendment is handed in relating to the same place in the bill, precedence is given to the Lord in charge of the bill. Otherwise the order is that in which notices of the amendments were received. Amendments may appear in the names of up to four Lords, or five if the Lord in charge of the bill wishes to add his name.[3] Amendments may, at the wish of the proposer and with the agreement of any Lords who may have added their names to his, be removed from the list of amendments at any time. An amendment which has been tabled need not be moved. If an amendment is not moved by any of the named Lords, any other Lord may move it[4].

Amendments must be relevant to the subject matter of the bill[5] and to the clause to which they are proposed; and they must not be inconsistent with a previous decision of the committee on the same question. The clerks draw attention to any amendment which appears to be inadmissible. The admissibility of an amendment, however, can only be decided by the House itself, there being no authority which can in advance rule an amendment out of order.

An amendment to leave out words, where it occurs at the same place in a bill as an amendment to leave out the same words and insert others, takes precedence. All amendments to a clause, including amendments to leave out the clause and substitute another,[6] are considered before the question that the clause stand part of the bill (see pp 454–455). An amendment to insert a new clause is considered at the place in the bill where the new clause is proposed to be inserted. Amendments to an amendment may be moved, and they are considered before the question on the original amendment is finally put. Once an amendment has been moved, it can be withdrawn only by leave, which must be unanimous. If there is no such unanimity the question is put on the amendment. The question on all amendments is 'That this amendment be agreed to'.

Manuscript amendments. Manuscript amendments are amendments of which notice has not been given. These may be moved in committee, but the practice has great disadvantages in that other Members of the House may not have had an opportunity of considering the terms of such amendments

---

1 By practice a Lord has always been able to hand in notices during a recess.
2 In those exceptional cases where the second reading and committee stages are expected to take place on the same day, amendments have been accepted before second reading, eg Southern Rhodesia Bill 1979, Sporting Events (Control of Alcohol etc) Bill 1985.
3 LJ (1974–75) 142.
4 HL Deb (1983–84) 449, c 1325.
5 See HL Deb (1967–68) 288, cc 1075–1086.
6 Amendments to leave out a clause and substitute another come after amendments to leave out the clause on report and third reading.

and may be deprived of the opportunity of moving amendments to them. Whenever possible, therefore, notice should be given of any amendments. Occasionally a manuscript amendment is justified, for instance, to correct an amendment already tabled, or when an amendment under consideration is objected to and it is clear that with slight alteration of language it would become acceptable to the committee. While any Lord may move a manuscript amendment, it is for the general convenience of the House that it should seldom be done.[1] When a manuscript amendment is moved, the text of the amendment should, unless the committee otherwise directs, be read out to the committee, both by the mover and by the Chairman when putting the question.

Proceedings in committee

As soon as the motion that the House do now resolve itself into committee has been agreed to, the Lord Chancellor leaves the Woolsack and the Lord Chairman takes his place at the Table and presides over the committee. Standing Order No 28, which forbids a Lord to speak more than once to any motion, does not apply when the House is in committee. The procedure of a Committee of the whole House is described on pp 572–573.

Postponement of title and preamble. The first question put by the Lord Chairman is that the title of the bill be postponed, and this is followed, if there is a preamble, by the question that the preamble be postponed.[2] The title and preamble of the bill are thus considered after the clauses and schedules have been disposed of, and any amendment to them which is consequential upon changes which have been made to the bill can then be made.

Preambles have been omitted in committee[3] and also amended,[4] and it has been held that it is in order to insert a preamble in a bill where none exists.[5]

Clauses. The clauses of the bill are then considered in order. The Lord Chairman first calls the amendments to each clause. When those have been disposed of, he puts the question that the clause, or the clause as amended,

---

1 LJ (1970-71) 240.
2 The motion to postpone the preamble, in cases where the bill contains one, is ordinarily agreed to without discussion; on 29 June 1869, however, the motion to postpone the preamble to the Irish Church Bill was opposed by Earl Grey, who stated that it was competent and sometimes convenient to consider the preamble before the clauses. Lord Cairns replied that if the committee agreed to a preamble in the expectation of clauses that were to follow and then decided upon the clauses in a contrary sense, there would be a preamble inconsistent with the clauses, which seemed a sufficient reason for adhering to the usual practice, and the motion for postponement was agreed to. LJ (1868-69) 408; Parl Deb (1869) 197, cc 689–743.
3 Petroleum (Amendment) Bill, LJ (1928) 141.
4 Expiring Laws Continuance Bill, LJ (1930–31) 66; Judiciary (Safeguarding) Bill, ibid (1933–34) 107.
5 HL Deb (1971–72) 324, cc 207–209. (See also Government of India Bill, 10 July 1935, HL Deb (1934–35) 98, cc 233–237.)

stand part of the bill.[1] Because the question on clause stand part must be put on each clause and schedule, an amendment to leave out a clause or schedule is not technically an amendment, but a statement of intention to oppose the question that the clause or schedule stand part of the bill. Notice is usually given of an intention to oppose this question. Such notices are printed in italics and are unnumbered in the marshalled list.[2]

In order to avoid repetition at several points during the committee (or other) stage, related amendments are often grouped and debated together. Lists of such amendments are prepared and made available by the government whips office; but groupings are informal and not binding. A Lord may ask leave to speak to a group of amendments (not necessarily consecutive or in his own name) when the first amendment in the group is called. Debate takes place on the first amendment in the group, even though it may be a minor or paving amendment. But the question must be put separately on each amendment in the group when the amendment is called according to its place in the marshalled list. Proceedings on later amendments in a group are often formal but further debate may take place. Amendments may also be moved en bloc provided that they appear consecutively on the marshalled list, that they all relate to the same clause or schedule, that they are consequential on an amendment already agreed to, and that no Lord objects. A division cannot take place on amendments en bloc. The first amendment is moved and the question on it resolved separately. If the amendment is withdrawn or disagreed to, the other amendments are not normally moved. If the first amendment is agreed to, the other amendments may be moved formally en bloc, without further debate.[3]

Where there are several consecutive clauses to which no amendment has been set down, it is the practice to put the question on all of them, or on groups of them, together.

Postponement of clauses. Clauses[4] or Parts[5] may be postponed on a motion made to that effect of which notice has been given and are also postponed as the result of an instruction. A clause has been postponed without notice after consideration of it has begun[6] but it may not be postponed if it has already been amended.

Division of clauses. A clause may be divided by amendment. Such an amendment is taken after the clause has been stood part of the bill[7]

Transposition of clauses. A clause or clauses may be transposed to another place in the bill by amendment.[8] An amendment to transpose a clause is taken after the question 'That clause . . . stand part of the bill'.

---

1 The marginal notes to clauses in the bill, and the headings placed above parts of the bill or above groups of clauses, are not technically part of the bill and are not open to amendment. See Parl Deb (1906) 166, c 1085. The punctuation is also technically not part of the bill.
2 HL Deb (1983–84) 443, c 1251.
3 HL Deb (1982–83) 440, c 1234.
4 LJ (1967–68) 85: cl 11 of Consumer Protection Bill 1967.
5 LJ (1967–68) 201: Pt III of Agriculture (Miscellaneous Provisions) Bill 1968; Pt IX of Consumer Credit Bill: ibid (1974) 104.
6 LJ (1937–38) 226: cl 12 of Coal Bill 1938; HL Deb (1985–86) 469, cc 573–583: cl 1 of the Shops Bill 1985.
7 HL Deb (1980–81), c 752: Countryside (Scotland) Bill.
8 Eg LJ (1971-72) 634.

Schedules. The schedules to the bill are considered in order after the clauses and may be postponed, divided or transposed in the same manner as clauses. A notice to leave out a schedule may be tabled but the question is put in the form 'That this be Schedule . . . to the bill.' Amendments to a schedule are out of order if they go outside the scope of, or are contrary to, the relevant clause which the committee has passed.

Preamble and title. As soon as the clauses and schedules have been disposed of, the Lord Chairman puts the questions 'That this be the preamble of the bill' (if there is one) and 'That this be the title of the bill.' Amendments to the preamble and title may be moved before each of these questions is put.

House resumed. The Lord Chairman then puts the questions that he report the bill to the House with or without amendment, and that the House be resumed. He then leaves his seat at the Table and either he (now acting as Deputy Speaker) or the Lord Chancellor or another Deputy Speaker takes his place on the Woolsack.

If the committee stage is not completed at one sitting, it is necessary for a Lord (usually a Government Whip) to move 'That the House be resumed'. When this motion has been agreed to, the Lord Chairman leaves the Chair and the Lord Chancellor or a Deputy Speaker takes his seat on the Woolsack. The House goes into committee again either later on the same day (on occasions when the House has been resumed in order to take other business) or on a future day.

When it is agreed that there should be a break for dinner during a committee stage, and there is no other business to be taken, it is the practice not to resume the House and adjourn formally but simply to break off the committee stage without question put until a time announced by a government whip.

When the House is resumed at the end of the committee stage, the Lord Chairman reports the bill to the House with or without amendment. If the bill has been amended, it is ordered that the bill be printed as amended. It used to be the practice that, if no amendment had been made to a bill in committee, the Lord in charge of the bill moved forthwith 'That this report be now received'. The next stage was then third reading. Since 1957 however the report stage may be taken on a later date even when the bill has not been amended in committee.[1] This ensures that there is still an opportunity to amend the bill before third reading. This procedure is now frequently used, especially with regard to government bills.[2]

Following the recommendation of the Select Committee on Procedure in April 1968, several bills may be considered in committee without the House being resumed between each, provided that no amendments have been put down and it is unlikely that the bills will be debated. When the House is resumed after consideration of the last of the bills, each bill is separately reported.[3] In practice, and provided that notice has been given, the order of commitment is now discharged in cases where no amendments have

---

1 LJ (1956–57) 38.
2 Petroleum Bill 1987, HL Deb (1986–87) 486, cc 139–140. Official Secrets Bill 1989, HL Deb (1988–89) 505, c 1087; ibid 506, c 698. See also HL Deb (1983–84) 452, cc 839–840.
3 There have only been three instances of this procedure since it was introduced—4 March 1970, 13 March 1975 and 26 January 1978. All the bills were consolidation bills in committee on recommitment.

been tabled to a bill and no Lord has indicated a wish to move a manuscript amendment or to speak in committee.

RECOMMITMENT

A bill which has been referred to a select or joint committee is, after being reported by that committee, recommitted to a Committee of the whole House unless the select or joint committee has reported that the bill should not proceed.[1] Consolidation bills (which are frequent) and hybrid bills (infrequent) are the most common examples of bills being recommitted.

Other bills may on motion of which notice is required be recommitted to a Committee of the whole House[2] at any time between committee and third reading, or may be recommitted in respect of certain clauses or schedules.[3] This course is adopted when it is desirable that there should be the freedom of debate possible on a committee stage to give further detailed consideration to the bill or certain parts of it; for instance when substantial amendments are tabled too late in the committee stage to enable them to be properly considered; or after the committee stage;[4] or where there is extensive redrafting.[5] This procedure reserves to the report stage its proper function as an opportunity to review and perfect the bill as amended in committee. Standing Order No 45(2) provides for the order of recommitment to be discharged on the same conditions as apply in the case of the discharge of the order of commitment (see pp 450–451).

Procedure on recommitment is the same as in Committee of the Whole House.

REPORT

If a bill has been amended in committee, the report stage cannot be taken until a subsequent day (unless Standing Order No 44 has been dispensed with). On the appointed day, when the notice for the report stage has been read, the Lord in charge of the bill moves 'That this report be now received'. The motion may be objected to and debated;[6] an amendment may be moved to postpone the report, or a reasoned amendment may be moved in opposition to the motion.[7]

Amendments on report

When the motion 'That this report be now received' has been agreed to, amendments may be moved to the bill. Notice of these is given in the same

---

1 A bill referred to a public bill committee is not recommitted to a Committee of the whole House. For a case of a bill which had been considered by a Committee of the whole House referred on report to a select committee, see LJ (1894) 181.
2 Consumer Protection Bill, LJ (1967-68) 81.
3 Water Bill: HL Deb (1982–83) 441, cc 101, 230; Insolvency Bill: ibid (1984–85) 459, cc 637, 833; Transport Bill: ibid 467, c 345; Public Order Bill: ibid (1985–86) 480, c 357; Criminal Justice (Scotland) Bill: ibid (1986–87) 484, c 1211.
4 Airports Authority Bill 1965, HL Deb (1964–65) 264, c 438; Companies Bill 1989, ibid (1988–89) 505, c 1016.
5 Abortion Bill 1966, HL Deb (1965–66) 273, cc 92–93.
6 LJ (1963–64) 400: Refreshment Houses Bill; ibid (1980–81) 429: Marriage (Enabling) Bill; ibid (1987–88) 220: Sunday Sports Bill.
7 LJ (1886) 309: Shop Hours Regulation Bill: LJ (1985–86) 279: Patents, Designs and Marks Bill.

way as for committee. Proceedings on report are confined to dealing with amendments, either in the order in which they relate to the bill or in a particular sequence agreed to in advance by order of the House. The bill is not considered clause by clause and schedule by schedule as in Committee of the whole House and the question on clause and schedule stand part is not put. Thus an amendment to leave out a clause or schedule is shown and numbered as an amendment in the marshalled list, whereas in committee it appears merely as notice of the Lord's intention to speak against the clause or schedule when the question is put (see p 455). Such an amendment is not desirable if its purpose is to probe rather than a genuine desire to leave out the clause or schedule.[1]

The amendments moved on the report stage relate principally but not exclusively to matters which have been discussed in committee and which the committee agreed to defer to the report stage with a view to allowing time in the interval between the two stages to reach a settlement or to enable passages of the bill to be redrafted.[2] Arguments fully deployed in committee of the whole House should not be repeated at length on report.[3] Except for the mover of an amendment who has a right of reply a Lord may speak only once on report; and only the mover of an amendment should speak after the Minister, except for short questions of elucidation or when a Minister has spoken early to assist the House in debate[4]

Manuscript amendments are not out of order on report, but the disadvantages and inconvenience attaching to the moving of manuscript amendments in committee are even greater on report than at the committee stage.[5]

If amendments have been made on report, it is ordered that the bill be reprinted as amended.

THIRD READING

Except when amendments are to be moved, the third reading of a bill is the stage of final consideration. In the case of a non-controversial bill the proceedings are usually brief and confined to the formal moving of the motion 'That this bill be now read a third time' and the putting of the question thereon from the Woolsack. This is followed by the motion 'That this bill do now pass'.

Queen's and Prince of Wales's consent

When a bill requires the Queen's or Prince of Wales's consent to be signified (see p 561), such signification is normally given before third reading. If,

---

1 LJ (1970–71) 710.
2 Thus, for example, on the Education Reform Bill (21–23, 27–28 June 1988), 26 new clauses were added, 4 clauses left out, a clause left out and a new clause substituted for it, and another clause divided into two clauses.
3 LJ (1976–77) 821; ibid (1977–78) 23.
4 HL Deb (1987–88) 493, c 938.
5 LJ (1970-71) 241.

however, the interests involved are fundamental to the bill then signification is normally given before the second reading.

Opposition to third reading

In the case of bills which have given rise to considerable discussion on the previous stages, a debate may take place on the third reading, in which the bill in the form in which is has emerged[1] is finally reviewed. The motion for the third reading may be opposed and reasoned or delaying amendments may be moved to it in the same way as on the second reading.[2]

Amendments on third reading

No amendment, other than a privilege amendment (see p 460), may be moved on third reading without notice; and notice must be given in sufficient time for the amendment to be printed and circulated in the form in which it is to be moved (Standing Order No 46). The principal purposes of amendments on third reading are to clarify any remaining uncertainties, to improve the drafting and to enable the Government to fulfil undertakings given at earlier stages of the bill.[3] It is considered undesirable that an issue which has been fully debated and decided upon at a previous stage of a bill should be re-opened on third reading.[4]

Further proceedings after third reading

If the amendments are not disposed of on the same day as the third reading the 'further proceedings after third reading' are appointed for a subsequent date, when the debate on the amendments is resumed.[5]

Passing of bill

If no amendments have been moved on third reading, the motion 'That this bill do now pass' is almost invariably treated as a formality, although instances have occurred where it has been opposed.[6]

If, however, amendments have been tabled on third reading, the motion for the third reading is agreed to formally and the final debate on the bill takes place on the motion 'That this bill do now pass' rather than on third

1 HL Deb (1987–88) 493, c 938.
2 Temperance Scotland Bill: LJ (1913) 254; European Communities Bill; LJ (1971–72) 621; Dock Work Regulation Bill: LJ (1975–76) 907; Aircraft and Shipbuilding Industries Bill: HL Deb (1975–76) 377, c 188; Education Bill: ibid (1985–86) 475, c 547.
3 HL Deb (1980–81) 417, c 132.
4 LJ (1960-61) 358; ibid (1976–77) 821. For recent applications of the rule, see HL Deb (1983–84) 450, cc 376, 387, 398; ibid (1985–86) 474, c 200; ibid, 479, c 25; ibid (1987–88) 499, c 855.
5 Tenants Compensation Bill, LJ (1890) 555; Education Reform Bill, HL Deb (1987–88) 499, cc 512, 522.
6 LJ (1847-48) 99; LJ (1866) 352; LJ (1906) 451; LJ (1908) 463.

reading. The motion 'That this bill do now pass' may be opposed[1] and reasoned or delaying amendments may be moved to it[2].

Privilege amendments

On the third reading of a bill originating in the House of Lords the provisions of which may infringe the privileges of the House of Commons with regard to the control of public money, a 'privilege amendment' is made formally. The motion is made 'That the privilege amendment be agreed to', without notice, without the amendment being circulated and without stating its nature. The amendment consists of a new subsection, inserted at the end of the final clause of the bill, in the following form: 'Nothing in this Act shall impose any charge on the people or on public funds, or vary the amount or incidence of or otherwise alter any such charge in any manner, or affect the assessment, levying, administration or application of any money raised by any such charge'. When the bill is printed for the House of Commons these words are marked by a thick black line in the margin, and the subsection is struck out by amendment in the House of Commons.

It was formerly the practice to insert the privilege amendment in the above form only when it was difficult to identify the precise passages which might infringe the privileges of the Commons. Otherwise, the privilege amendment or amendments consisted of the omission of the offending words, which were then enclosed in brackets and underlined when the bill was printed for the House of Commons. They were reinserted as amendments by the House of Commons. The simpler procedure described above is, however, now invariably adopted. The subject of privilege amendments is more fully dealt with on pp 745 ff.

Bill sent to the Commons

When a bill which originated in the House of Lords has completed all its stages in that House, a fair print of it, known as the 'House Bill', is endorsed by the Clerk of the Parliaments and sent down to the House of Commons with a message desiring their agreement (see pp 510, 526–527).

CONSIDERATION OF COMMONS AMENDMENTS, ETC

The further history of bills after passing through both Houses, the consideration by one House of the amendments made by the other, the insistence or

---

1 Sexual Offences Bill 1966, LJ (1966–67) 90; Marriage (Enabling) Bill 1981, LJ (1980–81) 479; Chronically Sick and Disabled Persons (No 2) Bill 1984, LJ (1983–84) 451; Local Government Bill 1986, LJ (1985–86) 216.
2 London Government Bill 1963, LJ (1962–63) 422; Scotland Bill 1978, LJ (1977–78) 741; Teachers Pay and Conditions Bill 1987, HL Deb (1986–87) 484, c 888.

non-insistence by one House on amendments to which the other has disagreed, and the final stages of agreement upon bills are fully explained in the portion of this chapter dealing with the House of Commons, and since the proceedings of both Houses with regard to them are similar, need not be further enlarged upon here (see pp 510–519).

2. PROCEEDINGS IN THE HOUSE OF COMMONS

INTRODUCTION AND FIRST READING

In the House of Commons there are three ways in which a bill may be introduced:

(a) It may be brought in upon an order of the House.
(b) It may be presented without an order under the provisions of Standing Order No 58(1).
(c) It may be brought down from the House of Lords.

Bills brought in upon an order of the House

In former times the normal method of presenting bills was upon an order of the House; and such an order was made upon resolutions,[1] or in response to messages from the Sovereign,[2] or after ordering to be read parts of speeches from the House, Acts of Parliament, entries in the Journal, resolutions of a former session, reports of committees or other documents in the possession of the House. But this procedure is now almost entirely confined to bills founded upon Supply or Ways and Means resolutions, and to bills introduced under Standing Order No 19 (Motions for leave to bring in bills etc).

Bills founded upon financial resolutions

The procedure for the introduction of bills upon financial resolutions[3] is now most commonly exemplified by Consolidated Fund Bills (see p 707), which are founded upon Supply resolutions, and by Finance Bills and other taxing bills, which are founded upon Ways and Means resolutions (see pp 736–737). Before 1938 any bill the main object of which was the creation of a public charge whether by way of taxation or expenditure was required to be founded upon a resolution; but since the passage of Standing Order No 48 in that year a bill of which the main object is to create a charge by way of expenditure may, if presented by a Minister of the Crown, be proceeded with in the same manner as a bill which involves a charge subsidiary to its main purpose; and this procedure is almost invariably

---

1 Eg Resolutions for annuities for Speakers of the House on their retirement. (Provision is now made under the Parliamentary and Other Pensions Act 1972.)
2 Eg Regency Bill 1910, CJ (1910) 171, 174.
3 Until 14 December 1966 all such resolutions were required to originate in a Committee of the whole House, and bills were ordered to be brought in after the resolutions had been reported and agreed to by the House.

employed.[1] As a result of a further change made in 1972, under Standing Order No 78 a bill the main object of which is the imposition or alteration of a charge, other than a bill of aids and supplies, may be brought from the Lords and taken charge of by a Minister of the Crown in the House of Commons.[2]

In addition to resolutions, a bill may also be founded upon orders of the House which further define its content.[3] When resolutions have been agreed to, a bill may be ordered in upon some of the resolutions and another bill upon other resolutions,[4] and two bills have been ordered in upon the same resolution.[5] When a bill which has been brought in on resolutions is withdrawn, and it is desired to bring in another bill of the same nature, the resolutions on which the first bill was founded are again read, and another bill is ordered on these and, if necessary, further resolutions.[6] Similarly when a bill founded on resolutions has received the Royal Assent, and it is desired to introduce another bill on the same subject, one of the original resolutions has been again read, and the second bill ordered in.[7]

Civil list bills, when designed to make provision for the honour and dignity of the Crown and the Royal Family for an entire reign, are brought in on resolution, following a message from the Sovereign and a report of a Select Committee on the message, see p 628.

Motion for leave to bring in a bill

In the absence of any preliminary proceedings, a motion may be made that leave be given to bring in a bill.[8] Before the passing in 1902 of Standing Order No 58(1), under which any Member may present a bill without an order for its introduction, a motion for leave was the usual method of introducing bills which were not founded on resolutions in committee or of the House.

This form of procedure is rare and survives almost exclusively in the modified form under Standing Order No 19 (see p 463) so far as that Order relates to motions moved by private Members. In the case of government bills, with the exception of the Parliament Bill 1911, it has been resorted to principally on grounds of extreme urgency.[9] The practice of the House ordinarily requires notice of a motion for leave to bring in a bill, but notice has been dispensed with in some urgent cases.[10]

In moving for leave to introduce a bill a Member may explain the object of the bill and give reasons for its introduction, but, normally, this is not the

---

1 Eg CJ (1985–86) 433. Bills introduced under this SO bear the words 'This Bill was presented under SO No 48' at the top of the first page of the text of the bill (see also p 721).
2 CJ (1972-73) 154.
3 A procedure most commonly adopted in the case of Finance Bills, eg CJ (1985–86) 261–270.
4 CJ (1825) 471, 476; ibid (1847–48) 981; ibid (1924–25) 45; ibid (1974–75) 68, 69.
5 CJ (1873) 249.
6 CJ (1856) 126; ibid (1857) 185; ibid (1884–85) 264, 306; ibid (1944–45) 117, 138; ibid (1967–68) 65, 93, 95.
7 Telephone Transfer and Telephone Transfer Amendment Bills, CJ (1911) 292, 523.
8 For a discussion of the procedure in moving for leave to bring in a bill and for cases in which a motion was made 'to bring up a bill,' see 8 Parl Hist 1178.
9 See also National Service Bill 1950, which was introduced on an order immediately after the House had agreed to a resolution approving proposals for legislation contained in two White Papers (CJ (1950) 221).
10 CJ (1914) 407, 422, 427, 435, etc ; ibid (1914–16) 137, 257; ibid (1918) 45; ibid (1930–31) 423–424; ibid (1938–39) 405–406; ibid (1971–72) 171; ibid (1973–74) 156.

proper time for any lengthened debate upon its merits. If the motion is opposed, or if there is a likelihood of its being negatived and no further occasion arising for discussion, or if there are grounds of urgency, this opportunity may be taken for a full exposition of the character and objects of the bill; but, except under such circumstances, a prolonged debate on the introduction of a bill can rarely serve any useful purpose, and cannot fail to anticipate the discussion of the principle of the bill proper to the second reading.[1]

Amendments have been made or proposed to a question for leave to bring in a bill, either hostile to the motion[2] or designed to alter it.[3] An amendment to postpone proceedings on the motion to that day three months is out of order.[4]

A motion for leave to bring in a bill, the objects of which are substantially the same as those of a bill upon which the House has come to a decision in the current session, is out of order.[5]

Proceedings under Standing Order No 19 ('ten minute rule bills' and Select Committee nominations)

Under the provisions of this Standing Order notices of motions may be given by private Members[6] for leave to bring in bills (often referred to as 'ten minute rule bills'). The notices may be set down for consideration at the commencement of public business[7] on Tuesdays and Wednesdays.[8] They are not part of the orders of the day and notices of motions (see p 311) which form the main business of the day, and accordingly are not subject to the rule (see Standing Order No 13(i)) that Government business has precedence on those days. Under paragraph (2) of the Standing Order, the following rules apply to private Members' motions for leave to bring in bills under the Order—

(a) notices shall be given in the Public Bill Office, by the Member in person or by another Member on his behalf, but on any one day not more than one notice shall be accepted from any one Member;

(b) no notice shall be given for a day on which a notice of motion under this order already stands on the paper;

(c) no notice shall be given for a day earlier than the fifth or later than the fifteenth sitting day after the day on which it is given;

1 A debate at this stage of the Protection of Life and Property (Ireland) Bill continued over five sittings (24 January–2 February 1881) before it was closed by Mr Speaker Brand. The introduction of the Government of Ireland Bill occupied four sittings in 1886 and four sittings in 1893; that of the Criminal Law and Procedure (Ireland) Bill 1886, occupied five sittings, and four further sittings were taken on the motion to give precedence to procedure on the bill.

2 CJ (1852–54) 516; ibid (1861–62) 65; ibid (1881) 49; ibid (1909) 115.

3 CJ (1814–16) 62; ibid (1816–17) 430; ibid (1851–52) 205.

4 Parl Deb (1858) 151, c 1242.

5 CJ (1840) 495; Parl Deb (1840) 55, c 553; HC Deb (1912) 38, c 1754.

6 Ministers of the Crown are permitted under the Standing Order to give notices for any day except Friday and such notices are not subject to the restrictions which apply to notices given by private Members.

7 Other times have been prescribed by sessional orders, namely immediately before the motion for the adjournment of the House (CJ (1964–65) 422) and at morning sittings (CJ (1966–67) 290).

8 Exceptionally, the House has given leave for a private Member to give notice for a Thursday, see CJ (1975–76) 122, 132.

(d) not more than one such notice shall stand on the paper in the name of
any one Member for a day within any period of fifteen sitting days.

In addition under Standing Order No 13(10) no private Member may give
notice of a motion under Standing Order No 19 until after the fifth Wednesday on which the House sits during the session. Since private Members' bills
introduced under the ballot (see p 304) are presented and read the first time
on that Wednesday, it is those bills which have the first opportunity to be put
down for second reading on the Fridays on which private Members' bills
have precedence.

The normal rules as to what bills may contain apply (see pp 467–471), so
that, for example, a private Member may not move for leave to bring in a bill
of which the main object is to create a charge by way of taxation or
expenditure (see p 468),[1] or of which the objects are substantially the same
as those of a bill upon which the House has come to a decision in the current
session (see ibid).[2] It has been ruled by the Speaker that no names may be
added to a motion for leave to bring in a bill, and that no one else may move
it should the Member who tabled it be absent.[3]

After a brief explanatory statement[4] of the objects of the bill[5] by the
mover, the Speaker proposes the question. If any Members wish to oppose
the motion he then calls on one of them[6] to make a brief explanatory
statement of opposition. This statement must oppose the motion,[7] though it
need not necessarily lead to a division.[8] In neither statement should matters
awaiting adjudication in a court be referred to,[9] and interventions by other
Members are normally ruled out of order, whether or not the Member
speaking is willing to give way.[10]

Under the Standing Order there is no provision for further debate,[11] or for
any motion to adjourn the debate[12] or for amendments[13] to be moved. The
Speaker thus normally at once puts the question on the motion for leave to
introduce the bill, though he may in exceptional circumstances put instead
the question that the debate be now adjourned,[14] and in one case he has
invited the mover to withdraw his motion.[15]

---

1 See eg, HC Deb (1928–29) 226, cc 216–219. Even the use of the word 'Finance' in the short
   title has been refused: private rulings 1985. For the use of the Social Security Fund and
   similar funds see p 717; HC Deb (1957–58) 579, cc 1270–1279; ibid 580, cc 207–210. See also
   HC Deb (1985–86) 99, c 1078; ibid (1987–88) 124 cc 1109–1112.
2 CJ (1840) 495; Parl Deb (1840) 55, c 553; HC Deb (1912) 38, c 1754.
3 Private Ruling 5 May 1967.
4 The Speaker defined this as a maximum of ten minutes, see HC Deb (1930–31) 252, c 1785.
5 The mover should explain what the bill will do, HC Deb (1987–88) 124, c 1109–1112.
6 It is within the Speaker's discretion to call whom he wishes, HC Deb (1964–65) 713, c 618.
7 See HC Deb (1966–67) 740, c 1568, (1985–86) 99, c 1080, (1987–88) 124, c 929.
8 HC Deb (1985–86) 97 c 565, (1986–87) 115, c 318.
9 See paras (1) and (2) of the Resolution of the House of 23 July 1963 and pp 377–379. See also
   HC Deb (1978–79) 960, c 665.
10 HC Deb (1984–85) 77, c 277. But see HC Deb (1968–69) 787, cc 417–418 where an inter-
    vention was permitted when the mover directly criticized another Member. See also HC
    Deb (1987–88) 133, c 322.
11 See HC Deb (1983–84) 50, c 165.
12 HC Deb (1932–33) 278, c 361.
13 Parl Deb (1902) 113, c 249, (1908) 190, c 1736; HC Deb (1938–39) 349, c 1120.
14 Parl Deb (1901) 97, c 868, (1905) 148, c 388; ibid (1905) 149, cc 1195–1196; ibid (1929–30)
    235, cc 225–226; HC Deb (1932–33) 280, c 2601, (1961–62) 654, c 430. If the debate is
    adjourned it must take its place among the orders of the day.
15 HC Deb (1957–58) 579, cc 1279–1280.

Standing Order No 19 also permits notices of motions to be given for nominations (but not the appointment) of select committees. As in the case of bills, such notices if given by private Members[1] must be for Tuesdays and Wednesdays. The other restrictions (see p 463) apply only to notices in respect of bills; hence notices for nominations of Select Committees may be given for days for which notices for leave to bring in bills have already been given.[2] As with bills, only one speech for and one speech against the motion is permitted.

Method of presentation of bills upon order

When the order of leave to bring in a bill has been made, or when a bill has been ordered to be brought in upon a resolution or resolutions, it is presented forthwith, though formerly it might be presented at a subsequent sitting whilst the House was not engaged in the transaction of business.[3] The bill must be presented by one of the Members who have been ordered to prepare and bring it in.[4] The Speaker asks 'who will prepare and bring in the bill?' Thereupon the Member in charge reads the names of the Members, concluding with his own name (see also p 470), and, having in his hand a dummy bill which he has previously obtained from the Public Bill Office, goes from his place, in pursuance of the order of 10 December 1692, to the bar.[5] On his name being called by the Speaker, he proceeds to the Table, with the customary three bows, and hands the dummy bill to the Clerk of the House, who reads the short title aloud. This constitutes the first reading of the bill (see p 466). The Speaker then calls upon the Member to name a day for second reading in the manner described below.

Bills presented without an order (under Standing Order No 58(1))

The large majority of bills introduced by Ministers of the Crown, and many of those introduced by private Members, are presented, after notice, under the provisions of Standing Order No 58(1). Under Standing Order No 13(10) no notice of a presentation of a Bill may be given by a private Member in pursuance of Standing Order No 58 until after the fifth Wednesday in a session on which the House sits (see p 467).

Notices of the presentation of bills without an order of the House for their introduction are set down on the notice paper at the commencement of public business, immediately before the notices of motions that may be taken at that time.

When the name of a private Member, who has given notice of presentation of a bill, is called by the Speaker, he brings the dummy bill, which he

---

1 Ministers of the Crown are permitted to give notice for any day except Friday. For notice by a Minister for the discharge of one Minister from a Select Committee and the addition of another see CJ (1967–68) 203.

2 For proceedings on a motion to nominate Members to a Select Committee on the same day as a motion for leave to bring in a bill see CJ (1974–75) 248.

3 CJ (1865) 373, 376. For modern instances of a bill presented at a subsequent sitting, see CJ (1968–69) 357, 360 and HC Deb (1974) 883, c 1830.

4 CJ (1770–72) 255. The order is ordinarily formal; but on 20 February 1852, Lord Palmerston having carried an amendment to the motion for leave to bring in Lord John Russell's Militia Bill, discussion arose upon the question by whom the bill should be brought in, Parl Deb (1852) 119, c 876. See further CJ (1852) 68, 131.

5 CJ (1688–93) 740 (1692).

has obtained from the Public Bill Office, to the Clerk of the House from behind the Chair; and the Clerk then reads the short title aloud. When the bill is presented under the procedure of the ballot for private Members' bills (see p 304), the Member who has given notice of presentation may, by notice in writing to the Clerks at the Table, name another Member to present the bill on his behalf (Standing Order No 13(6)). In the case of government bills, the Public Bill Office will have previously provided the Clerk with the dummy bill, and the Minister in charge, or any other Minister on his behalf (see p 330), when called by the Speaker, formally moves the presentation, whereupon the Clerk reads the short title. As no question is put on a bill presented without an order of leave, the House has no power to object to its presentation,[1] but notices of presentation may be ruled out of order on the same grounds as notices of motion for leave to bring in bills (see p 464).

Bills brought from the Lords

A bill brought down from the House of Lords is not proceeded with in the Commons unless a Member takes charge of it, in which case he signifies his intention to do so at the Table (see p 467).

Under Standing Order No 48(2) any bill brought from the House of Lords the main object of which is a public charge may proceed to second reading without the authorisation of a money resolution only if it is taken charge of by a Minister of the Crown.

First reading and printing of bills

The first reading of a bill, the order for printing, and the appointment of a day for second reading, are taken together as one formal stage, which is recorded in the Journal.

(a) Bills originating in the Commons. Whether a bill is brought in upon an Order of the House or presented under Standing Order No 58(1), Standing Order No 58(2) provides that it shall be read the first time without any question being put, shall be ordered to be read a second time on such day as the Member presenting it shall appoint, and shall be ordered to be printed.

As soon as a bill has been presented, therefore, its short title, as entered upon the notice paper and set out on the dummy of the bill, is read by the Clerk. This is taken to be a sufficient compliance with Standing Order No 58(2). Attempts to secure that a bill should be read to the House clause by clause have been overruled by the Speaker.[2]

After the short title has been read, the Speaker calls upon the Member presenting the bill to name a day[3] for second reading. The Speaker repeats the day so named and the bill is then entered in the Journal as having been

---

1 Parl Deb (1907) 171, c 1525; HC Deb (1911) 32, c 2706; ibid (1914) 60, c 1198; ibid (1916) 84, c 1696.
2 Parl Deb (1865) 178, c 181; ibid (1868) 192, c 322.
3 The day named must be a specific date, see HC Deb (1978–79) 959, c 450.

read the first time and ordered to be read a second time on that day,[1] and to be printed.

Presentation of bills after the ballot. Standing Order No 13(6) provides that private Members' bills presented under the ballot (see p 304) shall be presented on the fifth Wednesday of a session on which the House sits. Members may hand in at the Table, not later than the rising of the House on the day before that day, the titles of the bills that they propose to present. The notices of the bills to be presented are arranged upon the notice paper in the order determined by the ballot. On the day appointed for that purpose the bills are presented at the commencement of public business in the order in which the Members concerned were drawn in the ballot; they must be presented in person by the Member successful in the ballot or by another Member named by him in writing to the Clerks at the Table.[2] After he has presented his bill, the Member is called upon to name a day for second reading in the way described above.

(b) Bills brought from the Lords. In accordance with Standing Order No 58(3) if a Member informs the Clerks at the Table of his intention to take charge of a bill brought from the Lords, the bill is deemed to have been read the first time on that day and to have been ordered to be read a second time on the day he appoints, and is recorded in the Journal as having been read the first time and ordered to be read a second time on the day so appointed, and is ordered to be printed.

Examination of a bill

The Member in charge of a bill takes the draft to the clerks in the Public Bill Office, who, before the bill is printed, are responsible for its examination, to see whether it has been prepared in conformity with the rules of the House. The following are the chief questions which have to be considered, and which should be borne in mind by Members in drafting bills.

(a) Provisions to be within the order of leave or notice of presentation. In preparing a bill, care must be taken that it does not contain provisions which are not authorized by the notice of presentation or the order of leave; or, when it is founded upon resolutions, by the resolutions upon which it was ordered to be brought in. The title of the bill must correspond with the notice of presentation,[3] or the order of leave,[4] and the bill itself must be prepared

1 For occasions on which the second reading of a bill has been taken immediately after its first reading, see CJ (1914) 407; ibid (1914–16) 173; ibid (1919) 42; ibid (1939–40) 25, 140; ibid (1971–72) 171; ibid (1973–74) 155; ibid (1978–79) 272; ibid (1979–80) 806. For a motion allowing the second reading of a Consolidated Fund bill to be taken immediately after the first reading, see CJ (1966–67) 176, 192. See also pp 531–532.
2 CJ (1969–70) 54.
3 House Letting (Scotland) Bill and Coal Mines (Check-weighers) Bill, CJ (1908) 188, 225; Parl Deb (1908) 188, c 1439; ibid 189, c 1437. The title of a bill as presented must not contain any alterations not covered by the notice on the paper, HC Deb (1909) 9, c 2313. For the withdrawal of a bill when the title referred to objects not referred to in the clauses of the bill, see HC Deb (1931) 247, c 345.
4 New Zealand Bill, CJ (1847) 832; Elective Franchise and Registration of Electors (Ireland) Bill, CJ (1847–48) 522.

pursuant to the order of leave[1] or resolution[2] and in proper form. If it should appear that these rules have not been observed, the bill cannot be proceeded with,[3] if the irregularity is in any way substantial.[4]

Such objections, however, should be taken before the second reading;[5] for it is not the practice to order bills to be withdrawn, after they are committed, on account of any irregularity which can be cured while the bill is in committee,[6] or on re-committal.

(b) Financial provisions in bills. As explained on p 461, some bills must be brought in upon financial resolutions. Consequently, if on examination a bill is found to be of this kind and has not been so brought in, it is not allowed to proceed.[7] If, on the other hand, a bill is of the kind which does not require to be brought in on financial resolutions, any financial provisions which it may contain must be authorized by a resolution of the House before they can be considered by the committee on the bill. Any clause or part of a clause, which on examination of the draft bill directly imposes a charge, must be printed in italics.[8] Where, however, expenditure provisions are dispersed through a bill, and are authorized by an 'expenses' clause, normally only the latter is italicized. In the case of a bill brought from the House of Lords, the subsection inserted by the 'privilege' amendment is marked by a black line in the margin (see p 460), an explanatory note being placed at the head of the bill. It should be noted that provisions in Lords bills which impose a charge are not, in addition, printed in italics.

(c) Bills which are prima facie hybrid. If it appears that the standing orders relating to private business may be applicable to a public bill, notice of this circumstance is sent from the Public Bill Office to the Member in charge of the bill and the words 'to be reported upon by the Examiners' appear on the Order Paper after the order for second reading. (For an account of proceedings on hybrid bills, see pp 519–24).

(d) Bills with the same purpose as other bills of the same session. There is no rule or custom which restrains the *presentation* of two or more bills relating to the same subject, and containing similar provisions.[9] But if a decision of the House has already been taken on one such bill, for example, if the bill has been given or refused a second reading, the other is not

---

1 Poor Removal (Ireland) Bill, CJ (1883) 161; Speaker's Ruling, Registration of Electors Bill, Parl Deb (1893) 10, c 938.
2 Parl Deb (1894) 24, c 1201; HC Deb (1914) 63, c 1569.
3 CJ (1825) 329; ibid (1826–27) 325; ibid (1829) 261; ibid (1837) 254; ibid (1937–38) 220, 221.
4 HC Deb (1919) 120, c 548. Cf HC Deb (1913) 52, c 1221; ibid (1955–56) 548, c 1217.
5 A bill has been withdrawn on recommittal when notice was taken of an irregularity in the drafting and it appeared that the second reading had been agreed to under a misapprehension of its contents, Parl Deb (1871) 206, cc 577, 631.
6 Parl Deb (1843) 71, c 403; ibid (1894) 27, cc 1091–96; HC Deb (1911) 32, c 215.
7 Eg private ruling, 19 April 1977.
8 See also the chairman's remarks in respect of italicized words in the Finance Bill, where italics were found not to be necessary, HC Deb (1931) 254, cc 289–291.
9 Parl Deb (1882) 268, c 1656; ibid (1883) 278, c 92; HC Deb (1975) 885, cc 411–413. However the Speaker has ruled out of order the notice of presentation of a bill under Standing Order No 58 when leave had been refused to introduce a bill of the same long title under Standing Order No 19. Notices of presentation of bills to regulate proceedings in the House on other bills (Parl Deb (1908) 190, c 879) and to require the Government to introduce other bills (HC Deb (1914) 60, c 1198) have also been ruled out of order.

proceeded with if it contains substantially the same provisions;[1] nor could such a bill be introduced on a motion for leave (see p 463). The Speaker has declined to propose the question for the second reading of a bill which would have had the same effect as a clause of a bill which had already received a second reading.[2] Similarly a new clause offered at the consideration stage of one bill was ruled out of order when it substantially repeated the provisions of another bill of the same session, the consideration stage of which had been adjourned.[3] But if a bill is withdrawn, after having made progress, another bill with the same objects may be proceeded with.[4] Objection to a bill related to, but not identical with, another bill being considered by the House of Lords, has been overruled.[5]

The following examples illustrate the application of the rule laid down by the Commons on 1 June 1610, that 'no bill of the same substance be brought in in the same session.'[6]

On 7 July 1840 Mr Speaker called attention to a motion for a bill to relieve dissenters from the payment of church rates, before he proposed the question from the Chair.[7] Its form and words were different from those of a previous motion, but the object was substantially the same; and the House agreed that it was irregular and ought not to be proposed from the Chair (see pp 326–327). On 16 May 1860 the order for the second reading of the Charity Trustees Bill was withdrawn, as it was discovered to be substantially the same as the Endowed Schools Bill, which the House had already put off for six months.[8]

On 4 May 1951 the Speaker ruled that the National Insurance (Amendment) Bill, set down for second reading that day, could not be proceeded with since the subject-matter of all its provisions was dealt with in the National Insurance Bill, which had been read a second time on 26 April. The Member in charge of the bill was, however, permitted to make a brief explanatory statement before withdrawing it.[9]

In session 1976–77 the Reduction of Redundancy Rebates Bill provided for a reduction expressed in percentage terms in the rebate payable under previous Acts; but the question 'That the bill be now read a second time' was negatived on division. A second bill was drafted, but the Speaker ruled privately that it could not be presented since it contained provisions which would achieve the same object as that of the original bill. The Redundancy Rebates Bill, which gave power to vary the rebates within wide limits by order, was then introduced, and proceeded without objection.

---

1 CJ (1920) 167; ibid (1929–30) 242; HC Deb (1950–51) 487, c 1513.
2 HC Deb (1987–88) 125, c 638.
3 HC Deb (1987–88) 134, c 734.
4 Ministers of the Crown (Fisheries) Bills, CJ (1953–54) 254, 275, and Speaker's ruling, HC Deb (1953–54) 529, c 2349.
5 HC Deb (1979–80) 983, c 219; see also ibid (1977–78) 942, c 67.
6 CJ (1547–1628) 434. For the reasons leading the Commons on one occasion to disregard this rule, see CJ (1806–07) 61. By Mr Speaker's instructions the notice of presentation of the Hospital Lotteries Bill was removed from the Paper on the ground that leave had on 19 May 1931 been refused to bring in the same bill under SO No 19 (private ruling, 4 June 1931).
7 CJ (1840) 495; Parl Deb (1840) 55, c 553.
8 CJ (1860) 249; Denison 45.
9 HC Deb (1950–51) 487, cc 1513, 1553–1555.

Objection on these grounds has been overruled, however, where the question previously decided has related to an amendment on second reading;[1] to a rejected instruction on a previous bill;[2] to a new clause offered to an earlier bill;[3] to an earlier bill which only partly overlapped a second bill;[4] to allowing a clause which reproduced a bill rejected on second reading;[5] and to a reasoned amendment to an earlier bill which was not directed against the provisions of the second bill.[6] When a bill was withdrawn by the Government after an amendment had been carried against them in committee, a fresh bill to the same effect as the original bill was introduced and ultimately passed.[7]

There is now no rule against the amendment or repeal of an Act of the same session. Formerly it was expressly disallowed,[8] but it has been permissible since 1850.[9]

(e) Members 'backing' a bill. The names of Members ordered to bring in a bill may not exceed twelve in number:[10] This limit applies equally to bills presented under Standing Order No 58.[11] If a Member acts as teller against a motion for leave to introduce a bill, his name is not permitted to appear among the names on the back of the bill.[12]

(f) Explanatory or financial memorandum. A memorandum explanatory of the contents and objects of a bill may appear on the front of the bill. The memorandum should be framed in non-technical language and should contain nothing of an argumentative character.[13] The same considerations apply to a financial memorandum which the Treasury[14] require to be prefixed to all government bills involving expenditure. The memorandum sets out briefly the financial effect of the bill and contains estimates, where possible, of the amount of money involved. Frequently, in such cases, the

---

1 Representation of the People Bill 1859, and CJ (1859) 145, 170.
2 Parliamentary Elections (Redistribution) Bill and Medical Relief Disqualification Removal Bill, 1884–85; see CJ (1884–85) 78, 317 and Parl Deb (1884–85) 294, cc 1938–1943.
3 National Insurance (Widowed Mothers) Bill and Family Allowances and National Insurance Bill (1961–62); see HC Deb (1961–62) 653, c 876 and ibid 651, cc 487–518.
4 Game Laws Abolition Bill 1870, see Parl Deb (1870) 203, c 563. For the application of the principle where Lords amendments have overlapped a bill rejected in the same session see p 525.
5 Profiteering Bill 1919, see HC Deb (1919) 119, c 1178.
6 Rent and Mortgage Interest Restrictions Bill 1924 and Prevention of Eviction Bill 1924. See CJ (1924) 128, 129 and HC Deb (1924) 172, c 138 and 173, c 67. But a clause offered to the second bill which repeated the matter covered by the reasoned amendment was ruled out of order.
7 Factories Bill and Factories (No 2) Bill 1844, CJ (1844) 181, 225.
8 In 1721 a prorogation for two days was resorted to in order to enable Acts relating to the South Sea Company to be passed, contradictory to clauses contained in another Act of the same session, CJ (1718–21) 640 (1721).
9 See Interpretation Act 1978, s 2. The British Nationality Act 1981 included in sch 9 (which was to come into force on an appointed day) the repeal of s 49 (which came into force on the passing of the Act).
10 Private ruling, 1 February 1873. See also HC Deb (1979–80) 975, c 442.
11 Parl Deb (1902) 104, c 1292.
12 HC Deb (1970–71) 808, cc 1119–1120 and 1372–1377; ibid (1986–87) 99, c 1081; ibid (1987–88) 124, c 930.
13 Mr Speaker's instruction to the Public Bill Office, 9 March 1882, Parl Deb (1881) 260, c 423; ibid (1884) 289, c 1513.
14 This requirement arose from a recommendation of the Estimates Committee, HC 81, (1927) p xiv; HC 76, (1961–62) p 3.

memorandum is both explanatory and financial. Explanatory memoranda accompanying government bills also include forecasts of any changes in the non-industrial and industrial staff of government departments, or in manpower requirements in the public sector as a whole, expected to result from the passing of the bill.[1]

(g) Temporary laws. Under Standing Order No 79 the precise duration of every temporary law or enactment must be expressed in a distinct clause or subsection of the bill containing it.

Printing of a bill before second reading

After the draft of a bill has been examined, it is sent, in accordance with the order already made by the House, to be printed, in order that its contents may be published and made available to every Member before the second reading.[2] A serial number is given to each bill by the Public Bill Office and appears on its face. When a bill is reprinted at any subsequent stage another number in the series is assigned to it. Lords amendments are also numbered in the same series. A fresh series is begun each session.

If a bill has not been printed when it is called for second reading it is the practice for Mr Speaker to decline to propose the question that the bill be read a second time.[3]

Alterations in a bill

After a bill has been printed and circulated, it is only permissible to correct a clerical or printing error. If such an error is serious, a corrected copy of the bill may be circulated in substitution for the first print with a note on the front of the bill showing how it differs from the previous version.[4] If the error is more suitably dealt with by a corrigendum a separate slip is circulated (and is issued with any copies of the bill issued after the error is discovered).[5] In minor cases the Speaker calls attention to errors before second reading[6] or at other stages, as appropriate.[7]

Bills withdrawn and other bills presented

If for any reason the Member in charge of a bill wishes to make alterations to its text before second reading, he can do so only by withdrawing the bill and presenting another one. The same course is followed if a change in the title is required.[8] In the case of bills ordered upon resolution, a bill has been

1 HC Deb (1968–69) 773, c 1546. For examples see Explanatory and Financial Memoranda to the Post Office Bill 1968 and to the Education Reform Bill 1987.
2 In earlier times copies of annual Indemnity Bills, in accordance with a resolution of the House, were not circulated, but were obtainable by Members, CJ (1863–64) 134. Consolidated Fund Bills which were included in the same resolution have been circulated to Members since 1910.
3 CJ (1920) 167; HC Deb (1920) 129, c 933; CJ (1966–67) 165; HC Deb (1967–68) 762, c 834; ibid (1975–76) 915, c 1237; ibid (1987–88) 136, cc 1365–1370.
4 See eg Bill 22, 1987–88, as re-issued.
5 See eg HC Deb (1976–77) 934, c 73; ibid (1982–83) 32, c 863.
6 See HC Deb (1962–63) 666, c 1314.
7 Eg HC Deb (1979–80) 987, c 647.
8 Eg CJ (1966–67) 468, 503, 507.

withdrawn and another bill ordered, after reading the resolution upon which the first bill was founded.[1]

Withdrawal of bills

A bill which stands as an order of the day may be withdrawn before the order is read by notice given to the Clerk at the Table by the Member in charge,[2] as may a bill which has been set down for a future day.[3] On the order of the day being read for any stage of a bill, an order may, on the motion of the Member in charge of the bill, be made that the order be discharged and the bill be withdrawn.[4]

A bill may be withdrawn by the Member in charge after the question for its second reading (or other stage) has been proposed, provided that the question itself is first withdrawn.[5] If, however, there is objection to its withdrawal, the question for the stage concerned must be put.[6] A Member other than the Member in charge of the bill, if he has made the motion for second reading, can withdraw that motion but not the bill itself.[7] A bill may also be withdrawn during its committee stage if the committee is first discharged from (further) consideration of the bill.[8] See also pp 480, 486, 536.

By an old parliamentary rule, which has not been invariably observed in the House of Commons, a bill, whether public or private, brought from the other House, should not be withdrawn.

SECOND READING

Second reading moved

Once a day has been appointed for second reading, the bill stands upon the notice paper amongst the other orders of the day, and when the day arrives, is called in its proper turn. The second reading is the most important stage through which the bill is required to pass; its whole principle is then at issue, and is affirmed or denied by the House.[9] If matters affecting the royal prerogative or interests form a fundamental part of a bill, Queen's consent is signified on the order for second reading being read (see p 561).

It has been ruled that on the second reading of a consolidation bill the only question that can be discussed is whether the law should be consolidated by

---

1 CJ (1856) 126; ibid (1857) 185. Cf also CJ (1884–85) 264, 306; ibid (1967–68) 93, 96.
2 CJ (1981–82) 87.
3 Eg CJ (1985–86) 381.
4 CJ (1968–69) 130; Votes and Proceedings (1986–87), 8 May 1987.
5 CJ (1968–69) 170.
6 HC Deb (1953–54) 529, c 832.
7 HC Deb (1966–67) 730, cc 1105, 1139.
8 CJ (1974) 299.
9 Instances of protracted debate on the second reading of bills: 1851, Ecclesiastical Titles Assumption Bill, seven sittings; 1881, Land Law (Ireland) Bill, eight sittings; 1884, Representation of the People Bill, six sittings; 1886, Government of Ireland Bill, twelve sittings; 1887, Criminal Law (Amendment) Ireland Bill, seven sittings; 1888, Local Government (England and Wales) Bill, six sittings; 1890, Purchase of Land and Congested Districts (Ireland) Bill, five sittings; 1893, Government of Ireland Bill, twelve sittings; 1927, Trade Disputes and Trade Unions Bill, four sittings; 1935, Government of India Bill, four sittings; 1976, Scotland and Wales Bill, four sittings.

the bill in question, or should be left expressed in a number of different statutes.[1] This rule applies equally to bills only to consolidate and bills to consolidate with corrections and improvements under the Consolidation of Enactments (Procedure) Act 1949 (see p 494)[2] and to motions to approve Orders in Council made under the Northern Ireland Act 1974 consolidating the law in Northern Ireland.[3] On second reading of a bill to consolidate enactments with amendments to give effect to Law Commission recommendations, it is permissible to refer to those recommendations.[4]

When the order for second reading is read, the Member in charge of the bill (or any other Member acting on his behalf)[5] moves 'That the bill be now read a second time'. Debate at this stage is not strictly limited to the bill's contents; other methods of attaining the bill's object may be considered, and the inclusion of cognate objects may be recommended. But debate should not be extended, for example, to a general criticism of the administration,[6] or of the provisions of other bills before the House.[7] Debate on second reading should not extend to the details of the clauses.[8] Opponents of a bill may, and commonly do, vote against the question for second reading, but the traditional way of opposing second reading is by moving an amendment to the question (see p 474). Defeat on second[9] (or third[10]) reading is fatal to a bill since no future day is appointed for that stage, and the introduction of a fresh bill in substantially the same terms has been ruled out of order.[11] Other courses open to members opposed to a bill at the second reading stage are described below.

A motion that a bill be rejected, formerly not uncommon,[12] is not now consistent with established practice. In more ancient times bills were treated with even greater ignominy. On 23 January 1562 a bill was rejected and ordered to be torn; so, also, on 17 March 1620 Sir Edward Coke moved 'to have the bill torn in the House'; and it is entered that the bill was accordingly 'rejected and torn, without one negative'.[13] Even so late as 3 June 1772 the Lords having amended a money clause in the Corn Bill, Governor Pownall moved that the bill be rejected, which motion being seconded, the Speaker said 'that he would do his part of the business, and toss the bill over the Table.' The bill was rejected, and the Speaker, according to his promise,

---

1 HC Deb (1953–54) 532, c732; ibid (1979–80) 977, c1282.
2 HC Deb (1950) 478, c393; ibid (1952–53) 503, c2053; ibid (1959–60) 619, cc1057–1063.
3 HC Deb (1977–78) 940, c1830.
4 HC Deb (1966–67) 751, cc1508–1519; ibid (1968–69) 787, c1408.
5 HC Deb (1967–68) 759, cc893–894.
6 HC Deb (1935–36) 307, cc1456–1457; ibid (1941–2) 379, c987.
7 HC Deb (1941–42) 379, c996. But when four cognate consolidation bills were before the House on the same day the Chair permitted a single debate to cover all four bills, HC Deb (1984–85) 74, c557.
8 Parl Deb (1875) 224, c1297; ibid 225, c684; ibid (1878) 237, c1593; HC Deb (1959–60) 627, cc1032–1033.
9 Eg Votes and Proceedings (1987–88), 15 January 1988.
10 CJ (1976–77) 406.
11 CJ (1976–77) 125 (see also pp 468–470).
12 CJ (1778–80) 444; ibid (1825) 425.
13 CJ (1547–1628) 63 (1563); ibid 252 (1604); ibid 311 (1606); ibid 560 (1620).

threw it over the Table, 'several Members on both sides of the question kicking it as they went out'.[1]

Amendments to question for second (or third) reading

The two types of amendments to the question for the second reading of a bill, which are described in the following paragraphs, are also applicable to the question for third reading.[2]

'Six (or three) months' amendment. A traditional[3] way of opposing the second reading of a bill is to move an amendment to the question, by leaving out the word 'now' and adding the words 'upon this day six (or three) months.' The amendment 'upon this day three months' is usually employed in a normal session after the Spring Bank Holiday. The question proposed upon such an amendment is, that the word 'now' stand part of the question (Standing Order No 30(1)). The acceptance by the House of such an amendment being tantamount to the rejection of the bill, if the session extends beyond the period of postponement, a bill which has been ordered to be read a second time upon that day 'six (or three) months' is not replaced upon the notice paper of the House.[4]

'Reasoned amendment'. A Member who desires to place on record any special reasons for not agreeing to the second reading of a bill, may move what is known as a 'reasoned amendment'. Such an amendment is to leave out all the words in the main question after the word 'that' and to add other words; and the question proposed upon it is, that the amendment be made. A reasoned amendment is placed on the paper in the form of a motion and may fall into one of several categories.

(1) It may be declaratory of some principle adverse to, or differing from, the principles, policy or provisions of the bill.[5]
(2) It may express opinions as to any circumstances connected with the introduction or prosecution of the bill,[6] or otherwise opposed to its progress.[7]

---

1 17 Parl Hist 512–515.
2 The illustrations cited below also include amendments moved on other, now obsolete, stages of bills.
3 Under former practice, if the question that a bill be *now* read a second (or the third) time was negatived, the bill was held to be still before the House and a future day was named for the stage. Hence the naming of a remote day was regarded as a more effective form of defeating a bill. Parliamentary Electors' Bill, CJ (1847) 822, 837, 872, 901; Church Rates Redemption Bill, CJ (1863) 206, 222; Parochial Boards (Scotland) Bill and Crofters' Holdings (Scotland) Act (1886) Amendment Bill, CJ (1888) 58, 74, 78, Parl Deb (1888) 322, c1496. See also Dublin, Wicklow, etc, Railway Bill (on consideration), CJ (1887) 394, 402.
4 CJ (1952–53) 108; ibid (1956–57) 140.
5 Eg Gas Bill, CJ (1985–86) 76.
6 Conspiracy to Murder Bill, CJ (1857–58) 65; Paper Duty Repeal Bill, ibid (1860) 126; Intoxicating Liquor, etc (Ireland) Bill, ibid (1890) 214; Newfoundland Fisheries Bill, ibid (1890–91) 313; Government of India Bill, ibid (1934–35) 66; Guyana Independence Bill, ibid (1966–67) 31. Cf also CJ (1851) 321; ibid (1854) 90.
7 Australian Colonies Government Bill, CJ (1850) 334; Government of India Bill, ibid (1852–53) 609; Representation of the People Bill, ibid (1866) 213; Elementary Education Bill, ibid (1876) 262; Valuation of Property Bill, ibid (1877) 86; Customs and Inland Revenue Bill, ibid (1878) 282.

(3) It may seek further information in relation to the bill by committees,[1] commissioners,[2] the production of papers or other evidence.[3]

Such amendments have tended in modern times to become rather stereotyped and are confined generally to the first two categories; and amendments selected by the Speaker for discussion have commonly included the words, 'this House declines to give a second reading', or similar words.

The following rules govern the contents of reasoned amendments:

(1) The principle of relevancy in an amendment (see pp 339–340) governs every such motion. The amendment must 'strictly relate to the bill which the House, by its order, has resolved upon considering',[4] and must not include in its scope other bills then standing for consideration by the House.
(2) The amendment must not be concerned in detail with the provisions of the bill upon which it is moved, nor anticipate amendments thereto which may be moved in committee;[5] nor is it permissible to propose merely the addition of words to the question, that the bill be now read a second time, as such words must, by implication, attach conditions to the second reading.
(3) An amendment which amounts to no more than a direct negation of the principle of the bill is open to objection.

Effect of carrying a 'reasoned amendment'. According to modern practice, after a reasoned amendment has been carried on the second or third reading of a bill, no order is made for second (or third) reading on a future day.[6]

Questions on amendments proposed on second (or third) reading

When an amendment to leave out the word 'now' has been moved to the question that a bill be now read a second or the third time, the question proposed by the Chair is that the word 'now' stand part of the question (Standing Order No 30(1); p 474). If this question is decided in the affirmative, Mr Speaker has forthwith to declare the bill to be read a second or the third time, as the case may be (Standing Order No 60(1)).

On all other amendments to the motion for second or third reading of a bill, the question proposed from the Chair is that the amendment be made. If this question is negatived, the main question is put forthwith under Standing Order No 60(2).[7] An opponent of a bill who does not support the terms of the particular reasoned amendment that has been moved thus has

---

1 CJ (1840) 476; ibid (1844) 31; ibid (1849) 384; ibid (1850) 105; ibid (1855) 238; ibid (1870) 90; ibid (1875) 98. Cf also CJ (1843) 354.
2 CJ (1845) 719. Cf also CJ (1840) 469. (Amendment for an Address.)
3 CJ (1882) 77. Cf also CJ (1847) 865; ibid (1851) 382; ibid (1852) 186.
4 HC 517 (1837) p 5; Parl Deb (1856) 143, c 643; ibid (1882) 269, c 961; ibid (1900) 86, c 506; HC Deb (1917) 97, c 523.
5 Parl Deb (1905) 145, c 1149; ibid (1908) 188, c 76. Cf also Parl Deb (1868) 192, c 1571.
6 CJ (1957–58) 138. See also HC Deb (1976–77) 922, c 1736. Cf p 474, note 3.
7 Eg CJ (1967–68) 101–102. There have been two cases when this Standing Order (in an earlier form) was not applied. Both, however, occurred shortly after the Standing Order was first passed in 1919, and should not be regarded as precedents: CJ (1919) 149, 159, HC Deb (1919) 116, c 338; CJ (1920) 107, 108; HC Deb (1920) 127, c 1981.

an opportunity to vote against the bill on the main question; and similarly it is open to a Member to vote in favour of a reasoned amendment and nevertheless support the bill when the main question is put.[1]

When both a 'six (three) months' amendment and a reasoned amendment are put down on the second or third reading of a bill, it is for the Speaker to decide, in accordance with his powers under Standing Order No 31, which, if either, he will select.

Bills dropped

If, when the order of the day is read at the Table, no motion is made for the second reading or other stage of a bill, and no proposal is made for its postponement, it becomes a dropped order, and does not appear again upon the notice paper, unless another day is subsequently appointed for its consideration (see pp 314–315).

Deferment of private Members' bills after the interruption of business

As already described on p 260, ten[2] Fridays are set aside under Standing Order No 13(4) for private Members' bills. If the proceedings on the bill under consideration at the moment of interruption of business are not completed, the Member in charge may name a future day for consideration of the bill. In his absence, either another Member, publicly stating that he is acting on behalf of the Member in charge, may name a day or the Clerk at the Table, if he has received written instructions from the Member in charge, or another Member on his behalf, specifically authorized for that occasion, will advise the Chair of the day to which the bill should be deferred. No other Member may name a day for further consideration of the bill. Failing an instruction by any of these means the bill becomes a dropped order. The same procedure applies to subsequent bills where proceedings are objected to on the reading of the relevant order of the day.[3]

Proceedings on bill null and void

If a bill has been read a second (or the third) time by mistake or inadvertence, the proceedings have been declared null and void, and another day has been appointed for the second or third reading.[4]

Counsel ordered

The second reading is the stage at which counsel have been heard, when the House has been of opinion that a public bill was of so peculiar a character as

---

1 Sixth Report of the Select Committee on Procedure, 1966–67, HC 539 (1966–67) para 37.
2 This number has been varied by sessional order, eg to twelve in Session 1987–88, see Votes and Proceedings (1987–88) 30 June 1987.
3 HC Deb (1973–74) 867, cc 2048–2049.
4 CJ (1859) 139; Parl Deb (1859) 153, c 816; CJ (1893–94) 244, 249, 252 (motion for committal of a bill to a standing committee rescinded); ibid (1896) 134; ibid (1914–16) 271; HC Deb (1915) 75, c 46; CJ (1926) 217 (second reading and committal); ibid (1937–38) 360; ibid (1948–49) 323: ibid (1956–57) 201 (third reading); ibid (1985–86) 155 (committee and third reading).

to justify the hearing of parties whose interests, as distinct from the general interests of the country, were directly affected by it.[1] Under modern practice a bill of such a character as to justify the hearing of parties will be likely to come within the scope of the established procedure for hybrid bills (see pp 519–24).

Bills referred to a second reading committee

Under the provisions of Standing Order No 90 a public bill, instead of being debated on second reading in the House, may be referred to a Second Reading Committee on motion made by a Minister of the Crown at the commencement of public business.[2] At least ten days' notice must be given of any such motion, and no motion can be made until the bill to which it relates has been printed. The question on the motion is put forthwith and must be decided without amendment or debate; but if not fewer than twenty Members signify their objection by rising in their places, the Speaker must declare that the noes have it.[3]

The Standing Order also enables private Members to move motions to refer their bills to Second Reading Committees subject to the following conditions: (i) the Member must give at least 10 days' notice; (ii) the bill must have been printed before the notice is given; (iii) the notice must be for a day on which private Members' bills or notices have precedence; (iv) it must be for a day not earlier than the seventh Friday on which such bills have precedence; and (v) it can be moved only with the leave of the House, with the result that a single objection nullifies the motion.[4] If all these conditions are met, the motion is moved at the commencement of public business and the question on it is put forthwith. If the question is agreed to, the order for second reading (whether for that day or a future day) is treated as discharged.

When a Second Reading Committee (see p 593) has reported to the House whether or not it recommends that the bill ought to be read a second time, a note of its recommendation is appended to the order for the second reading of the bill among the remaining orders of the day; and when the bill subsequently comes before the House, the question for its second reading is decided without amendment or debate.[5]

Since its first introduction this procedure has been generally regarded as suitable only for bills 'which are not measures involving large questions of policy nor likely to give rise to differences on party lines'.[6]

---

1 Mr Buckingham's Compensation Bill, CJ (1835) 589; Lower Canada Government Bill, CJ (1837–38) 233; Jamaica Government Bill, CJ (1839) 208, 213; Jamaica Laws Bill, ibid (1839) 318; Newfoundland Fisheries Bill, CJ (1890–91) 308, 313; Parl Deb (1891) 352, c 1131. For explanations of the principle upon which Parliament has permitted counsel to be heard against public bills and precedents cited, see Lords' Debate on Australian Colonies Bill, Parl Deb (1850) 111, c 943.
2 This Standing Order was made in November 1967, following sessional orders in the two previous sessions.
3 Eg CJ (1966–67) 178; ibid (1968–69) 62.
4 See HC Deb (1979–80) 975, c 919; ibid (1988–89) 153, c 589.
5 Eg Insurance Companies Bill [Lords], CJ (1979–80) 376, 397, 403. No Second Reading Committee has ever recommended that a bill ought not to be read a second time. Proceedings on the question are not exempted business for the purposes of Standing Order No 14, see Votes and Proceedings 1988–89, 4, 5, 6 and 10 April 1989.
6 First Report of the Select Committee on Procedure, 1964–65, HC 149 (1964–65) para 3. See also HC Deb (1964–65) 718, c 172.

Scottish bills referred or committed on order for second reading

If, after any public bill has been printed, the Speaker is of the opinion that its provisions relate exclusively to Scotland,[1] he is directed by Standing Order No 93 to give a certificate to that effect. Bills which related mainly[2] but not exclusively to Scotland have been ordered to be proceeded with as if they had been certified by the Speaker as relating exclusively to Scotland. (See also p 480.) When the order for second reading of such a bill is read, a motion, to be decided without amendment or debate, may be made by a Minister of the Crown to refer the bill to the Scottish Grand Committee, which consists of all the Members for Scottish constituencies.[3] If, when the question is put, not fewer than ten Members by rising in their places signify their objection thereto, the Speaker must declare that the noes have it.[4]

When a bill is thus referred, the Committee considers it in relation to its principle and reports that fact to the House, whereupon the bill is ordered to be read a second time upon a future day. When subsequently the order for second reading is read, a motion, to be decided without amendment or debate, may be made by a Minister of the Crown to commit the bill to a Scottish standing committee, but this procedure is not applicable if notice of an amendment has been given by not fewer than six Members.[5] If the motion is agreed to, the bill is deemed to have been read a second time and is committed to a Scottish standing committee,[6] proceeding thereafter in the ordinary course.[7]

Second reading and remaining stages of Consolidated Fund and Appropriation Bills

Under Standing Order No 54 if the second reading of a Consolidated Fund or Appropriation Bill stands as first order of the day, the question for second reading is put forthwith when the order is read. The bill then proceeds immediately to third reading with no order for committal; and the question for third reading is also put forthwith.

COMMITTAL

The committal of a bill in the Commons is regulated by the provisions of Standing Order No 61 under which a bill which has been read a second time stands committed to a standing committee[8] (see chapter 24). There are,

---

1 This SO was originally passed in 1948.
2 Amendments to Sch 1 of the House of Commons Disqualification Act 1975 or Sch 1 to the Northern Ireland Assembly Disqualification Act 1975 have been specifically excluded from consideration by a proviso to SO No 93(1).
3 SO No 94(1). See also p 591.
4 For a bill which was ordered to be proceeded with as though it had been certified under SO No 93 but was nevertheless refused referral to the Scottish Grand Committee see CJ (1974–75) 172.
5 Eg CJ (1960–61) 147.
6 For orders varying the application of the Standing Order by providing for motions to commit Bills to a Committee of the whole House, see CJ (1979–80) 423; Votes and Proceedings (1987–88) 29 June 1988.
7 Eg National Heritage (Scotland) Bill, CJ (1984–85) 29, 36, 56.
8 Before 1907 a bill was committed to a Committee of the whole House, unless a motion for committal to a standing or select committee was carried.

however, exceptions to this practice, which are provided for in the standing order.

Exceptions to general practice

(1) Consolidated Fund or Appropriation Bills (see p 709) are expressly exempted from the operation of Standing Order No 61.[1]

(2) Bills for confirming provisional orders are likewise exempted, and, after committal, stand referred, under Standing Order 217, to the Committee of Selection, and are dealt with by that committee in the same way as private bills. (For bills read a second time in pursuance of section 9 of the Private Legislation Procedure (Scotland) Act 1936 see p 974.)

(3) In the case of any other public bill which receives a second reading,[2] Standing Order No 61(2) provides that a motion may be made by any Member that the bill be committed to a Committee of the whole House, or to a select committee,[3] or to a special standing committee,[4] or that it is expedient that the bill be committed to a joint committee;[5] but only one such motion may be made.[6] Such a motion, if made immediately after the bill has been read a second time, does not require notice[7] and must be decided without amendment or debate. It may be made and, if opposed, decided after the expiration of the time for opposed business, or after seven o'clock, when other business has been set down for that hour.[8] If the motion is negatived, the bill stands committed to a standing committee.[9] If a motion to commit a bill to a Committee of the whole House is agreed to, the usual practice is to make an order for the committee on a future day. If it is desired that the committee stage should follow immediately, and objection is taken, the Member in charge of the bill must move that 'This House will immediately resolve itself into the said Committee'. (See also pp 531–532.)

It is the regular practice for Government bills of first class constitutional importance to be committed to a Committee of the whole House.[10]

Standing Order No 61(3) provides that the Member in charge of a bill may move that the bill be committed to a standing committee in respect of some of its provisions and to a Committee of the whole House in respect of other

---

1 Before SO No 61 was amended in December 1967 (CJ (1967–68) 47) this exemption extended also to bills for imposing taxes; all such bills were automatically committed to a Committee of the whole House.

2 Bills presented pursuant to s 7 of the Private Legislation Procedure (Scotland) Act 1936 and bills to confirm orders pursuant to s 6 of the Statutory Orders (Special Procedure Act) 1945 by statute omit the second reading stage.

3 Eg CJ (1972–73) 145. Bills have sometimes been committed to a select committee to which other bills have been committed, CJ (1851) 243; ibid (1861–62) 146, etc; or to a select committee appointed to inquire into a related matter (see p 618).

4 See p 594.

5 Wills and Intestacies (Family Maintenance) Bill, CJ (1930–31) 135, 156, 176; Customs and Excise Bill, CJ (1951–52) 98, 103, 108.

6 HC Deb (1914) 61, c 2079; ibid (1924) 170, c 1885.

7 Notice is, however, often given, eg Local Government Finance Bill, 16 December 1987, see Order Paper (1987–88) p 2167.

8 Cf HC Deb (1909) 3, c 417.

9 Eg CJ (1985–86) 136–137.

10 Eg CJ (1971–72) 160; ibid (1977–78) 28; ibid (1984–85) 511; Votes and Proceedings (1987–88) 11 July 1988. See also First Report from Select Committee on Procedure (HC 9–1 (1945–46) p xi and CJ (1945–46) 81.

provisions. Notice is not obligatory, but is normally given. When such a motion is opposed, the Speaker, after permitting, if he thinks fit, a brief explanatory statement from the Member who makes and from a Member who opposes the motion, is directed to put the question thereon without further debate[1]; and the motion may be decided after the expiration of time for opposed business. If the motion, however, has other matter attached to it, as for example is customary in the case of hybrid bills, it is debatable.[2]

Bills withdrawn after committal

Bills other than Lords Bills have been withdrawn by notice given at the Table by the Member in charge, after committal to standing committees, following an order that the standing committee concerned be discharged from considering the Bill;[3] and after committal to a Committee of the whole House, following an order that the order for the Committee be discharged.[4]

Distribution of bills committed to standing committees

The bills committed to a standing committee are distributed among the committees by the Speaker,[5] who may change his allocation of them from time to time if so requested by the Member in charge.[6] Bills which have been certified by the Speaker under Standing Order No 93 as relating exclusively to Scotland, if committed to a standing committee, are allocated to one of the two Scottish standing committees.[7] Bills which have not been certified as relating exclusively to Scotland have, on motion, been ordered to be considered by a Scottish standing committee.[8] The House has also ordered that certain sections of a bill be considered by a Scottish standing committee, the remainder being allocated to another standing committee in the normal way;[9] and motions to this effect have been made after consideration of the bill has been entered upon in standing committee.[10] But a motion to commit part of a bill to a standing committee consisting of all Members for constituencies in Wales has been ruled privately not to come within the terms of Standing Orders.[11]

---

1 HC Deb (1962–63) 669, c 343. CJ (1968–69) 240 (Notice of the motion was given in these cases). This practice is now followed in the case of the majority of Finance Bills.
2 CJ (1956–57) 214; HC Deb (1957) 571, cc 673–683.
3 CJ (1953–54) 254, and Speaker's ruling HC Deb (1953–54) 529, cc 2349–2350; CJ (1959–60) 226; ibid (1963–64) 112; ibid (1964–65) 200, 248; ibid (1976–77) 299; ibid (1984–85) 428 and HC Deb (1984–85) 78, c 911.
4 CJ (1976–77) 353, 465.
5 SO No 84(2).
6 Eg CJ (1979–80) 198, 255. See also Speaker's ruling, HC Deb (1984–85) 74, c 493.
7 SO Nos 93(5) and 95.
8 Legal Aid and Solicitors (Scotland) Bill, CJ (1948–49) 70; Mental Health (Scotland) Bill, ibid (1959–60) 104; Criminal Justice (Scotland) Bill [Lords], CJ (1962–63) 112; Social Work (Scotland) Bill [Lords], CJ (1967–68) 231. The more usual practice is for the House before second reading to order bills relating mainly but not exclusively to Scotland to be proceeded with as if they had been certified as relating exclusively to Scotland (see p 478). See also Votes and Proceedings (1988–89) 13 January 1989.
9 CJ (1947–48) 62, 66. Cf SO No 86(2)(i).
10 CJ (1955–56) 177; ibid (1963–64) 91. See also ibid (1921) 247, where an allocation of time order provided for the reallocation of part of a bill to a different standing committee.
11 Notices of Motions (1960–61) p 494.

Transfer of bill from standing committee to Committee of the whole House or select committee, and vice versa

If it should be desired that a bill which stands committed to a standing committee should be considered in a Committee of the whole House or by a select committee, a motion is made for committing it to a Committee of the whole House[1] or a select committee,[2] as the case may be. If a bill has already been allocated to a particular standing committee, the motion begins with a proposal that that standing committee be discharged from considering the bill.[3] Such a motion may be made after consideration of the bill has been entered upon in standing committee, in which case the wording of the motion is 'discharged from *further* considering the bill'.[4]

With the exceptions stated above (p 479), bills stand committed to a standing committee, unless the House otherwise orders. Hence a motion to transfer a bill which has been specially committed to a Committee of the whole House, to a standing or select committee is a most unusual occurrence. It is possible, however, to move to discharge the order and commit the bill to a standing or select committee.[5] An amendment to such a motion, whereby only parts of such a bill would have been committed to a standing committee, was ruled privately not to come within the terms of Standing Order No 42(3) (now 61(3)).[6]

Motions for the committal of a bill to a committee other than that first ordered by the House are debatable, but debate should be confined to the effect or expediency of referring the bill to the proposed committee, and general debate upon the merits or clauses of the bill is not permitted.[7]

FINANCIAL RESOLUTION

When a bill is brought in upon a financial resolution the whole principle of the bill (so far as it can be inferred from the resolution) is open for discussion during the prior debate on the resolution. Money resolutions in respect of a bill introduced under Standing Order No 48, or involving a charge subsidiary to its main purpose, or brought from the Lords under Standing Order No 78, are customarily debated after the second reading of the bill to which they relate, and on this occasion the financial implications of the measure alone are the proper subject for consideration (see pp 461, 720). It is possible,

---

1 Eg CJ (1953–54) 46; ibid (1964–65) 238.
2 CJ (1909) 179.
3 Eg Votes and Proceedings (1987–88) 4 March 1988.
4 CJ (1964–65) 161; ibid (1966–67) 193; ibid (1969–70) 341. See also CJ (1933–34) 256, 336. For orders discharging standing committees from considering such provisions of bills as they had not yet considered and for the chairman to report the provisions which had been considered, and providing for further proceedings on the bills in Committee of the whole House and on report, see Votes and Proceedings (1986–87) 12 May 1987.
5 CJ (1917–18) 19, 26; ibid (1951–52) 288; ibid (1966–67) 494 (standing committees); CJ (1854–55) 143; ibid (1856) 207; ibid (1857) 337; ibid (1955–56) 195–196 (Select Committees).
6 See Notices of Motions (1951–52) p 3032.
7 Parl Deb (1883) 278, cc 335, 341; ibid (1884) 287, c 1870; ibid (1892) 4, cc 305, 1310; HC Deb (1951–52) 502, c 2667.

however, for such a money resolution to be taken before the second reading of a bill.[1]

INSTRUCTIONS

Before the committee to which a bill has been committed begins its consideration of the bill, an instruction may be given, the purpose of which is either to empower it to do something which it could not otherwise do, or to define the course of action which it must follow. The first type of instruction, which is called permissive, may be given to a Committee of the whole House, or to any other committee. The second type, which is called mandatory, may be given only to a select committee or to a committee on a private bill. (For instructions to joint committees, see p 665.)

Instructions are much less common than in former times,[2] but occasions continue to arise when an instruction from the House enables a committee to consider amendments of wider scope than would otherwise be permissible under Standing Order No 63, which provides that amendments must be relevant to the subject matter of the bill. Even an instruction, however, cannot authorize consideration of an amendment that is not cognate to the purposes of the bill, so the area within which an instruction can be effective is closely circumscribed, as the following examples of admissible and inadmissible instructions illustrate.

Admissible instructions

(i) Extension of objects. An instruction is necessary to authorize the introduction of amendments into a bill, which extend its provisions to objects not strictly covered by the subject matter of the bill as disclosed on the second reading. But for such an instruction to be in order the objects must be cognate to the general purposes of the bill.

The Public Bodies (Admission of the Press to Meetings) Bill 1959–60 was limited to the single purpose of admitting the Press to meetings. An instruction was necessary to extend the bill to the general public.[3]

The Employment Agencies (Regulation) Bill 1966–67 was limited to fee-charging agencies. An instruction was necessary to extend the bill to non-fee-charging agencies and to undertakings which supply persons in their own employ.[4]

The Road Traffic (Amendment) Bill 1966–67 was 'to make provision for securing compliance with' certain requirements. An instruction was necessary to permit exemption from the consequences of conviction in certain circumstances.[5]

The Passenger Vehicles (Experimental Areas) Bill [Lords] 1976–77 permitted the modification of statutory requirements applying to public

---

1 CJ (1974–75) 97.
2 Particularly before 1854, when SO No 63 was first passed (as SO No 47). See *May* 20th edn, for fuller treatment of this subject, and see also pp 726 and 740 for instructions relating to Finance Bills.
3 HC Deb (1959–60) 619, c 927.
4 HC Deb (1966–67) 734, c 359.
5 HC Deb (1966–67) 743, c 178.

service vehicles operating in experimental areas to be designated under the Bill. An instruction was necessary to permit the modification to apply to vehicles used on journeys partly in and partly outside the areas.[1]

The Football Spectators Bill [Lords] 1988–89 proposed a national membership scheme for spectators at designated football matches. An instruction was necessary to permit provision as to the safety of spectators there.[2]

(ii) Extension of area. An instruction is necessary to render applicable to the whole of the United Kingdom the provisions of a bill (or part of a bill) which is limited *by its title* to a part of the United Kingdom, or otherwise to extend its operation beyond the limits defined in the title.[3] A committee can, without an instruction, extend the operation of a bill to Scotland or Northern Ireland, if the bill is not by the title restricted to England, or limit the area to which the bill is to apply.

In default of such an instruction, the chairman has declined to propose, or, having proposed, has declined to put the question on an amendment[4] or on a new clause.[5] When such a clause was inserted in a bill in committee without an instruction, the Speaker stated, on consideration of the bill, as amended, that the proper course would be to recommit the bill, but in the circumstances the bill was allowed to proceed on the understanding that the clause in question would be struck out.[6]

(iii) Division of bill. An instruction is required to enable a committee to divide a bill into two or more bills,[7] but such an instruction is in order only if the bill is drafted in two or more distinct parts, or otherwise lends itself to such division into parts.[8]

(iv) Consolidation of bills. An instruction is required to empower a committee to consolidate two bills into one bill.[9]

(v) Priority to portion of bill. An instruction must be moved, if it is desired to give priority to the consideration of a portion of a bill, with power to report the same separately to the House.[10]

(vi) Power to hear counsel. Instructions have been given to committees of the whole House, on the presentation of a petition, empowering the committee to hear counsel and examine witnesses.[11]

---

1 CJ (1976–77) 282. For other cases where an instruction was necessary to empower a committee to consider the amendments proposed by the instruction, see Established Church (Wales) Bill, HC Deb (1912) 44, c 1829; Petroleum (Amendment) Bill, ibid (1928) 215; Coal Mines Bill, ibid (1932) 266, c 1167; Gas Undertakings Bill [Lords], ibid (1932) 266, c 2077; Control of Liquid Fuel Bill, ibid (1966–67) 750, c 734; European Assembly Elections Bill; ibid (1977–78) 943, c 723; Corneal Tissue Bill, ibid (1985–86) 121.
2 Votes and Proceedings (1988–89) 27 June 1989.
3 Criminal Justice (Scotland) Bill [Lords], CJ (1948–49) 373; Deer (Scotland) Bill, ibid (1958–59) 169; General Rate Act 1967 (Exemption from Constant Attendance Allowances (Amendment)) Bill, ibid (1972–73) 241; Avoidance of Liability (England and Wales) Bill, ibid (1976–77) 150; Local Government Act 1974 (Amendment) Bill, ibid (1977–78) 194.
4 HC Deb (1914) 68, c 739; ibid (1918) 110, c 1424.
5 HC Deb (1914) 68, c 745; CJ (1887) 333; ibid (1888) 500 (clause withdrawn).
6 HC Deb (1914) 65, c 1938.
7 CJ (1861) 376; ibid (1868–69) 192; ibid (1871) 114; ibid (1893–94) 592; ibid (1905) 333; ibid (1909) 103; ibid (1911) 310; ibid (1912–13) 199, 435, 508; ibid (1913) 214, 218; ibid (1916) 75; ibid (1917–18) 112; ibid (1979–80) 562.
8 Parl Deb (1894) 27, c 1028; HC Deb (1917) 94, c 162; HC Deb (1987–88) 124, c 1113.
9 CJ (1866) 344. For similar instructions to a standing committee, see CJ (1883) 141; ibid (1890) 418; ibid (1890–91) 254; ibid (1901) 324; ibid (1903) 280; ibid (1929–30) 203.
10 CJ (1890–91) 30; ibid (1895) 182; ibid (1911) 124.
11 CJ (1828) 122; ibid (1831–32) 461; Parl Deb (1867) 186, c 982.

(vii) To consider certain amendments. A mandatory instruction has been given to a select committee on a bill to consider certain amendments.[1]

(viii) To insert provisions in a bill with like effect to a clause previously disagreed to. On recommittal of a bill to the former standing committee, a permissive instruction has been given to the committee allowing it to insert in the bill provisions with a like effect to a clause to which it had previously disagreed.[2]

Inadmissible instructions

Instructions are out of order if they attempt to embody in a bill principles that are foreign or not cognate to it; if their objects are inconsistent with the decision of the House on second reading or seek to replace that decision by means of an alternative scheme or postponement; or if they propose to amend Acts which are not cognate to the bill, or attempt to introduce into a bill a subject which should properly constitute a distinct measure. They are out of order if they seek to authorize the committee to go beyond any Money Resolution or Ways and Means resolution passed in connection with the bill.[3] They are also out of order if they seek to confer powers on a committee which it already has,[4] or are otherwise superfluous, if they propose an impracticable division of the bill into two or more bills[5] or generally are not clear and specific.

The following are examples of instructions that have been ruled inadmissible.

> On the Representation of the People Bill 1947–48 an instruction was put down to give the committee power to provide for the suspension of the issue of writs for the return of Members in Northern Ireland during such times as in the opinion of Parliament free elections were impossible in Northern Ireland. The Speaker ruled the instruction out of order on the ground that it was outside the scope of the bill and raised a matter of such magnitude that it could only be introduced by a separate statute.[6]

> An instruction put down to the Scotland and Wales Bill 1976–77 sought to provide for alterations to the structure and functions of Government in any or all parts of the United Kingdom. As the Bill was to provide for changes in the Government of Scotland and Wales this object was ruled not to be cognate to the Bill, and the instruction was ruled out of order.[7]

Application of instruction to recommitted bill

The powers conferred by an instruction moved when a bill is committed for the first time continue operative, if the bill is recommitted.[8]

---

1 CJ (1955–56) 196.
2 CJ (1969–70) 281; HC Deb (1969–70) 800, c 424.
3 HC Deb (1929–30) 234, c 1721.
4 Eg HC Deb (1955–56) 551, c 1789.
5 Parl Deb (1901) 97, c 453.
6 HC Deb (1947–48) 448, c 1892. For cases of similar instructions ruled out of order, see Demise of the Crown Bill, ibid (1901) 93, c 1259; London Water (recommitted) Bill, ibid (1902) 111, c 9; Education (Provision of Meals) (recommitted) Bill, ibid (1906) 166, c 1273; Parliament Bill, HC Deb (1911) 23, cc 1815, 1849; Solicitors (Examination) Bill [Lords], ibid (1917) 97, c 1339; Trade Disputes and Trade Unions Bill, ibid (1927) 206, cc 401, 402; Local Government Finance Bill, ibid (1987–88) 124, c 1113.
7 HC Deb (1976–77) 941, c 1663.
8 National Education (Ireland) Bill 1892, see CJ (1892) 358, 369.

Procedure

Notice, selection, etc. Notice is required of instructions and is also required of any amendment which would widen their terms.[1] Under Standing Order No 31(4) the Speaker has the same power to select motions for instructions to committees on bills as he has to select amendments. Any amendment moved to an instruction must be strictly relevant thereto and must be drawn in such a way that, if accepted, the question as amended would retain the form and effect of an instruction.

Time for moving instructions. An instruction to a committee of the whole House upon a bill is usually moved when the order of the day for the first sitting of the committee has been read and before the Speaker has left the Chair, except an instruction founded on a resolution or order which is given when the resolution or order in question has been agreed to by the House.[2] In the case of bills referred to standing or select committees, an instruction can be moved as soon as the bill has been committed,[3] or subsequently.[4] Instructions have, with the leave of the House, been debated together with the question for second reading,[5] but proceedings on instructions are not exempted from interruption under Standing Order No 9, unless a motion to exempt them under Standing Order No 14(2) has been agreed to.

Member to move one instruction only. Pursuant to the established practice of the House, a Member cannot move more than one instruction to a committee in respect of the same bill, whether public or private.[6]

Debate on motion for instruction. Debate on a motion for an instruction must be strictly relevant thereto, and must not be directed towards the general objects of the bill to which the instruction relates,[7] or anticipate the discussion of a clause of a bill. In accordance with the general practice of the House regarding motions and debates (see pp 326–327), matters which have already been decided during the current session, or have been appointed for the future consideration of the House, cannot be brought forward by an instruction. The mover of an instruction has no right of reply.[8]

PROCEEDINGS IN COMMITTEE OF THE WHOLE HOUSE

A bill is committed to a Committee of the whole House as described on p 479 above.

Whenever an order of the day is read for the House to resolve itself into a Committee on a bill the Speaker is directed by Standing Order No 64 to leave the Chair without putting any question unless there is an instruction to be disposed of first.

The mace is then placed under the Table, the Chairman of Ways and Means, or one of his deputies, takes his seat at the Table and, the Clerk

---

1 HC Deb (1909) 2, c 286. Notice is not required for an instruction founded on a resolution of the House.
2 CJ (1957–58) 290; ibid (1966–67) 510, etc.
3 CJ (1955–56) 196; CJ (1979–80) 278 (a private Member's bill).
4 CJ (1959–60) 143; ibid (1979–80) 657.
5 Eg HC Deb (1986–87) 106, c 667.
6 Parl Deb (1896) 39, c 1708 (a private bill); ibid (1896) 41, c 866 (a public bill).
7 HC Deb (1969–70) 800, c 433; ibid (1988–89) 155, cc 842, 936.
8 HC Deb (1969–70) 800, c 433.

having read the short title, the Committee begins the consideration of the bill.

Functions of a committee on a bill

The function of a committee on a bill is to consider the bill clause by clause and, if necessary, word by word, and to approve the text or to modify it to reflect the committee's legislative intentions. The rules as to the admissibility of amendments are explained in detail on pp 490–495 below, but the general powers of a committee and the limitations by which it is bound should be clearly borne in mind.

(1) A committee is bound by the decision of the House, given on second reading, in favour of the principle of the bill, and should not, therefore, amend the bill in a manner destructive of its principle.
(2) The objects of a bill are stated in its long title, which should cover everything contained in the bill, as introduced (see p 467). Amendments, however, are not necessarily limited by the title of the bill, since a committee is empowered by Standing Order No 63 to make amendments 'relevant to the subject-matter of the bill', provided that, where such amendments are outside the title, the committee extends the title so as to cover them.
(3) An amendment which is outside the 'scope' (as described on p 491) of the bill is out of order and cannot be entertained, unless an instruction has been given by the House to the committee.

It will be seen, however, that in spite of these limitations a committee has, in practice, considerable power over a bill. John Moore, a Member of the Long Parliament, states in his unpublished diary[1] that 'no committee can destroy a bill, but they may lay it down'. Thus, while a bill cannot be withdrawn in committee, for this requires the leave of the House, a Committee of the whole House can indirectly achieve this object by reporting progress, without asking leave to sit again, and so putting an end to its existence or by agreeing to a motion 'That the Chairman do now leave the Chair' (see pp 587–588). This course is equivalent to refusing to proceed with the bill. Again, notwithstanding the rule which forbids the moving of an *amendment* which is destructive of the principle of the bill, there is nothing to prevent a Committee from negativing a clause or clauses, the omission of which may nullify or destroy the bill, and reporting the bill, as amended, to the House; a Committee may also negative every clause of which the bill is composed, and substitute for those clauses new clauses, if relevant to the bill as read a second time, and otherwise in order.[2] But when bills have been very extensively amended they have on occasion been withdrawn so that a new bill incorporating the amendments could be introduced.[3]

Order in which bill is considered

Unless the Committee otherwise order, the text of a bill is considered in committee in the following order:

---

1 Brit Mus Harl 476, f 450 (14 April 1641).
2 Coroners in Boroughs Bill, CJ (1892) 259; Rehabilitation of Offenders Bill, Stg Co Deb (1974), Co C, cc 8, 30, 56, etc; see also Parliamentary Control of Expenditure (Reform) Bill (changed to National Audit Bill) Stg Co C, Proceedings (1982–83).
3 Parl Deb (1856) 140, c 2200; ibid (1889) 339, c 1487; CJ (1913) 510; HC Deb (1913) 47, c 1019; see also ibid cc 643, 878.

(1) Clauses.
(2) New Clauses.
(3) Schedules.
(4) New Schedules.
(5) Preamble (if any).
(6) Title (if amendment thereto is required).

Motions are however frequently proposed to consider a bill in a different order, most commonly to enable schedules to be considered after the clauses to which they are related.[1] Under Standing Order No 31(4) such motions are subject to the Chair's power of selection, and will normally be selected only if moved by the Member in charge of the bill. They may be moved at any stage during the proceedings, and do not require notice.[2]

Division of clauses

The committee has power to divide one clause into two,[3] or decide that the first part of a clause, or the first part of a clause with a schedule, shall be considered as an entire clause.[4] A motion to divide a clause must be taken before the clause is ordered to stand part of the bill.[5]

Transfer of clauses

A clause (or subsection) or series of clauses (or subsections) may be transferred, on motion, from one place in a bill to another place specified in the motion.[6]

Postponement of consideration of clauses

Consideration of a clause may be postponed, upon motion,[7] provided that no amendment has been agreed to[8] or negatived, and provided that the question for its standing part of the bill has not been proposed.[9] If, however, an amendment has been proposed and withdrawn consideration of the clause may be postponed.[10] Consideration of part of a bill,[11] or of a consecutive group of clauses en bloc, may also be postponed. As to the postponement of consideration of a preamble, see p 498.

A proposal to postpone consideration of the only effective clause of a bill until the subordinate clauses have been considered,[12] or to postpone consideration of part of a clause,[13] is out of order.

---

1 Eg Stg Co B, Proceedings (1985–86), Social Security Bill, 3.
2 Stg Co E, Proceedings (1987–88), Local Government Finance Bill p 9.
3 CJ (1834) 409; ibid (1868–69) 384; HC Deb (1920) 132, c 2689.
4 CJ (1830–31) 728; ibid (1831–32) 80.
5 Stg Co Deb (1968–69), First Scottish Stg Co, 17 June 1969, c 327.
6 Suppl to Votes (1937–38) p 1924; CJ (1937–38) 379; Suppl to Votes (1953–54) pp 990–991; ibid (1967–68) p 4836 (subsection).
7 Parl Deb (1871) 207, c 74; CJ (1934–35) 84; ibid (1947–48) 140; Stg Co D, Proceedings (1980–81), 11 June 1981, 262.
8 Parl Deb (1871) 207, c 721.
9 HC Deb (1935–36) 313, c 161.
10 CJ (1873) 340; ibid (1917) 200; HC Deb (1917) 97, c 1251; CJ (1917) 216; HC Deb (1917) 98, c 344.
11 CJ (1929–30) 177; Stg Co D, Proceedings (1980–81), 4 June 1981, 255.
12 Parl Deb (1899) 74, c 325; ibid (1904) 139, c 1221; HC Deb (1912) 39, c 744; ibid (1916) 82, c 472; ibid (1918) 110, c 1503.
13 Parl Deb (1901) 97, c 453; ibid (1904) 139, c 1220.

Upon a question for the postponement of consideration of a clause, the debate is limited to the simple question of postponement, and may not be extended to the merits of the bill[1] or the clause.[2] Postponed clauses, unless provision to the contrary is made in the motion, are considered after the other clauses of the bill have been disposed of, and before any new clauses are brought up, but they may also be considered, in special circumstances, at any other appropriate place, eg after all[3] or certain[4] new clauses or other clauses[5] or schedules,[6] and they may be further postponed.[7]

Notice of amendments in committee

It is usual, though not obligatory, to give notice of an amendment to a bill in committee. Notice should be given whenever possible of every amendment, as the moving of any amendment without notice causes obvious difficulty and inconvenience to the committee. Amendments of which notice has been given only on the previous day are marked on the notice paper with a star, and chairmen regularly decline to select such amendments; amendments of which no notice has been given until the day itself (manuscript amendments) are rarely selected.

Notices of amendments to a bill in committee are not normally received until the bill has been read a second time. When a bill has required to be passed with unusual expedition, however, the House has authorized the acceptance of amendments before second reading,[8] and the same procedure is sometimes followed in the case of consolidation or other bills when it is intended that the committee stage should be taken on the same day as second reading. For the remainder of the day on which a bill has received a second reading amendments may be handed in only to the Clerks at the Table, and not to the Table Office or the Public Bill Office.

Under Standing Order No 62, whenever the House is adjourned for more than one day, notices of amendments, new clauses or new schedules received in the Public Bill Office at any time not later than 4.30 pm on the last day on which the House is not sitting may be accepted as if the House were sitting, but Saturdays, Sundays, bank holidays and public holidays in England are excluded from being regarded as the 'last day'.[9]

The notices of amendments are printed and circulated with the Votes and Proceedings. On the day upon which a bill is to be considered in committee, the amendments appear marshalled on the notice paper in the order in which the text of the bill is to be considered.[10] An amendment to leave out words in order to insert other words takes precedence over an amendment merely to leave out words. Otherwise, amendments are marshalled, if relating to the

---

1 Parl Deb (1871) 207, c 1378; ibid (1887) 318, c 145; ibid (1896) 41, c 870.
2 HC Deb (1909) 6, c 1376; ibid (1916) 81, c 1884; ibid (1918) 110, c 1504.
3 CJ (1877) 235; ibid (1887) 206, 210; ibid (1893–94) 455; ibid (1906) 407; ibid (1929–30) 387.
4 CJ (1867) 141, 149; ibid (1909) 461; ibid (1917–18) 177.
5 Stg Co D, Proceedings (1980–81), 4 June 1981, 255.
6 CJ (1875) 328, 425; ibid (1917–18) 216, 223; ibid (1951–52) 226.
7 CJ (1920) 273.
8 Eg CJ (1974) 82; HC Deb (1974–75) 882, c 570; ibid (1974–75) 986, c 702; Votes and Proceedings (1987–88) 29 April 1988.
9 No notice of motion, eg to recommit a bill or to vary the order in which a bill is considered, may be received under this SO.
10 HC Deb (1987–88) 132, c 1143. The Speaker has the power to direct that amendments relating to the same point in a bill be marshalled in the order that he thinks most appropriate.

same point in the bill, in the order in which they were first handed in, except that amendments by the Member in charge of the bill take precedence over all others offered at the same place in a clause.[1] When notice has been given by the Member in charge of the bill of a motion to vary the order in which clauses are considered, the amendments will be marshalled in accordance with the order to be proposed, with an explanatory note to that effect. When a great number of amendments has been handed in, a marshalled list of amendments is often printed and circulated for the convenience of Members, on one or more days before the day for which the committee stage of the bill is set down.

To avoid the repetition of identical amendments on the notice paper, the names of the Members who have handed in an identical amendment are printed together at the head of the amendment. After the first appearance of an amendment on the notice paper, the names of Members attached to it are limited to six, and the names of additional Members who support it are printed below[2] and to the right-hand side of those six names on one occasion only.[3]

Amendments of which notice has been given

If notice has been given of any amendments, the chairman calls on the Member who has given notice of the first amendment which he has decided to select. If the Member called does not move an amendment, any other Member may do so.[4]

After an amendment has been moved, the chairman reads its terms, stating the page and line in the bill in which the alteration is to be made, and proposes the question, that the amendment be made (Standing Order No 30).[5]

The normal practice is for the chairman to make known his provisional selection and proposed grouping of amendments for debate in advance, by means of a typed list issued on his authority.

Amendments of which no notice has been given

Amendments of which notice does not appear on the notice paper ('manuscript amendments', see p 488), may be moved if the chairman allows this course to be adopted. When it is desired to propose an amendment without notice, the chairman should be informed beforehand of its terms and of the

---

1 Parl Deb (1893) 18, c 1162.
2 If the Member in charge of the bill adds his name to an amendment his name appears at the top.
3 This arrangement began in 1911 and applies equally at report stage.
4 HC Deb (1971–72) 832, c 599.
5 Cf p 338. On request the chairman (or, on consideration stage, the Speaker) may consent to the question on an amendment to leave out words and substitute others being put to the House in two parts, HC Deb (1968–69) 785, c 1014.

exact place in the clause where it would occur, in order that, if he thinks fit to select it, he may call on the proposer to move it when that place is reached.

Withdrawal of amendments

When once the question on an amendment has been proposed from the Chair, it can be withdrawn only at the request of the Member who moved it and by the unanimous leave of the committee.[1] If a Member rises to continue the debate when the mover of an amendment has formally asked leave to withdraw it, leave is treated as withheld, and may not subsequently be sought again.

Order in which amendments are taken

The chairman normally calls amendments in the order in which they appear upon the paper, though he may decide to exercise his powers of selection under Standing Order No 31.[2] It is also within his discretion to decide that an amendment is being offered at a wrong place in the bill and to advise the Member concerned accordingly, or that an amendment should be moved as a new clause. As in the House, if an amendment is withdrawn or negatived, it is open to the committee, subject to the chairman's selection, to entertain amendments back to the point at which it last came to a decision (see p 341).

For the convenience of the committee, the chairman frequently permits debate to range over several amendments which are linked or raise different aspects of the proposal in the actual amendment under consideration. This grouping of amendments for debate is designed to prevent repetition; it thus operates to prevent any further debate whatever on the subsequent amendments in a group once a decision has been taken on the first amendment in the group. The chairman may at his discretion allow separate divisions on one or more of the subsequent amendments.[3] New clauses and new schedules may be grouped with amendments for debate in the same way (see p 497).[4]

Admissible amendments

Amendments may be made in every part of the bill, whether in the clauses or the schedules. Clauses and schedules may be left out and new clauses and schedules added. Amendments to the preamble and title are also admissible where amendments have been made to the bill which render them necessary (see p 499).

The marginal notes or short titles of clauses and the headings of parts of a bill, however, do not form part of the bill and are not open to amendment.[5]

---

1 HC Deb (1928) 219, c 185.
2 See also p 489.
3 For the practice of the Chair in selecting amendments for division in such cases, see HC Deb (1963–64) 692, c 54; ibid (1967–68) 766, c 52 (consideration).
4 Whole clauses have occasionally been grouped together for debate, though the question that each clause stand part of the bill must be put separately, except with the leave of the committee when no divisions are required: HC Deb (1987–88) 132, c 754.
5 Parl Deb (1896) 41, c 873; ibid (1906) 166, c 1085 (ruling in the Lords); HC Deb (1917) 95, c 1761; ibid (1918) 105, c 1995.

Amendments cannot be moved to the granting or enacting words of bills for granting aids or supplies to the Crown, or to the enacting words of other bills. These words are part of the framework of the bill and are not submitted to the committee.[1]

Inadmissible amendments

The special rules of order respecting amendments to a bill in committee are classified below.[2] These rules relate primarily to amendments to clauses, but will be found applicable for the most part to amendments to schedules. Amendments which are out of order are normally included in the printed list of amendments, although in exceptional circumstances the Speaker has ordered that a grossly disorderly amendment should not be printed.

The question on an amendment which is out of order on any of the following grounds cannot be proposed from the Chair:

(1) An amendment is out of order if it is irrelevant to the subject matter[3] or beyond the scope of the bill,[4] or if it is irrelevant to the subject matter[5] or beyond the scope of the clause under consideration.[6] Amendments which are irrelevant to the clause under consideration should, as a general rule, if they are within the scope of the bill, be moved as new clauses.

(2) An amendment cannot be admitted if it is governed by or dependent upon amendments which have already been negatived.[7]

(3) An amendment must not be inconsistent with, or contrary to, the bill as so far agreed to by the committee,[8] nor must it be inconsistent with a decision of the committee upon a former amendment.[9]

1 HC Deb (1912) 41, c 2518; ibid (1920) 132, c 649; ibid (1960–61) 635, c 805. See also ibid (1932) 261, cc 1871–1873.
2 See p 336 ff for general rules for amendments. Most of the rules cited here apply equally to amendments offered to bills at the report stage (cf p 503).
3 CJ (1856) 213; Parl Deb (1865) 179, c 521; ibid (1881) 258, c 1451; ibid (1893) 14, c 918; ibid (1896) 41, cc 12, 1702 (consideration), 1704 (consideration); ibid (1902) 114, c 912; ibid (1902) 116, c 1043; HC Deb (1919) 120, c 359.
4 Parl Deb (1905) 147, c 311; ibid (1906) 158, c 355; HC Deb (1912) 41, c 2859; ibid (1914) 61, cc 128, 1069; ibid (1914) 68, c 745; ibid (1916) 78, c 661; ibid (1917) 99, c 526; ibid (1918) 105, c 1070; ibid (1918) 108, c 2045; ibid (1919) 121, c 1985; ibid (1923) 165, c 1357; ibid (1924) 169, c 1593; ibid (1926) 196, c 1627; ibid (1930) 234, cc 2123–2129; ibid (1932) 264, c 595; ibid (1960–61) 630, cc 976–982.
5 Parl Deb (1857) 147, cc 1189, 1190, 1198; ibid (1877) 232, c 1242; ibid (1877) 233, c 359; HC Deb (1959–60) 616, c 282.
6 HC Deb (1914) 68, c 739; ibid (1917) 95, c 1048.
7 Parl Deb (1862) 167, c 112; ibid (1872) 211, cc 137, 2026; ibid (1881) 258, c 1333; ibid (1885) 296, c 800; ibid (1886) 305, c 83; ibid (1889) 74, c 851; ibid (1902) 111, cc 962–965; HC Deb (1910) 18, c 647; ibid (1914) 61, c 128; ibid (1919) 117, c 1739.
8 Parl Deb (1881) 258, cc 1239, 1455; ibid (1896) 41, c 360; ibid (1902) 113, c 493; ibid (1908) 198, c 883 (consideration); HC Deb (1911) 30, c 449; ibid (1912) 44, c 2199.
9 HC Deb (1911) 22, c 1666; ibid (1915) 75, c 927; ibid (1916) 83, c 1738; CJ (1920) 303; HC Deb (1920) 132, c 319.

(4) Amendments are inadmissible if they refer to, or are not intelligible without, subsequent amendments or schedules, of which notice has not been given,[1] or if they are otherwise incomplete.[2]

(5) An amendment which is equivalent to a negative of the bill, or which would reverse the principle of the bill as agreed to on the second reading, is not admissible.[3] Where the scope of a bill is very restricted, the extent to which it may be amended at all may thus be severely limited.[4]

(6) An amendment to leave out a clause is not in order, as the proper course is to vote against the clause standing part of the bill. Consequently it is out of order to propose to leave out the only effective words of a clause, or the words upon which the rest of the clause is dependent, or to offer any other amendment which is equivalent to a direct negative of the clause.[5] Amendments to leave out a clause often appear upon the notice paper. While such amendments are never called, they provide an indication to the Chair that certain Members wish to speak, or to vote, on the question that the clause stand part of the bill.

Furthermore, an amendment may not be moved to insert words at the beginning of a clause with a view to bringing forward an alternative scheme to that contained in the clause,[6] or to leave out the whole substance of a clause in order to insert different provisions,[7] or to substitute in effect a new draft for an existing clause.[8] In all such cases the question that the clause stand part of the bill should be negatived and a new clause brought up at the proper time.

(7) If an amendment would make the clause which it is proposed to amend unintelligible or ungrammatical, or if it is incoherent and inconsistent with the context of the bill, it is out of order.

---

1 Tithe Rent-Charge Recovery Bill, 29 January 1891, private ruling: Parl Deb (1899) 70, c449; ibid (1902) 112, c203; HC Deb (1909) 7, c496; ibid (1911) 23, c2251; ibid (1917) 97, c1284; ibid (1917) 98, c96; ibid (1919) 119, c1499; ibid (1921) 143, c2205; ibid (1939–40) 357, cc2293–2295.

2 HC Deb (1918) 106, c1703. This rule is sometimes relaxed in minor cases, and was held not to apply to the Canada Bill 1982, which contained both an English and French text, insofar as the tabling of consequential amendments to the French text was concerned (HC Deb (1981–82) 18, c290).

3 HC Deb (1910) 19, c2398; ibid (1917) 92, cc790, 823, 824, 1679; ibid (1917) 100, c1875; ibid (1918) 107, c136; ibid (1943–44) 400, c1809.

4 Parl Deb (1880) 251, cc1134–1137; ibid (1903) 122, cc1886, 1897; cf also the Speaker's ruling on a proposed amendment to the second schedule to the Air Force Bill, HC Deb (1917) 99, c817; ibid (1981–82) 18, c762.

5 Parl Deb (1869) 196, c74; HC Deb (1915) 72, c1961; ibid (1915) 74, c1648; ibid (1916) 82, c473; ibid (1917) 95, c1048; ibid (1920) 129, c92; ibid (1920) 131, c2421.

6 Parl Deb (1896) 41, cc873–875; ibid (1899) 74, c326; ibid (1908) 197, c1107. But see also Parl Deb (1870) 200, c1058.

7 Parl Deb (1851) 116, c666; ibid (1870) 200, c1057; cf HC Deb (1911) 30, c1938, where the same ruling was applied in the case of an amendment to leave out part of the first subsection of a clause in order to insert an alternative scheme. Cf also the Chairman's ruling on the Ottawa Agreements Bill, HC Deb (1932) 269, cc1330–1338.

8 HC Deb (1916) 85, c2163.

(8) Amendments which are vague,[1] trifling,[2] or tendered in a spirit of mockery,[3] are held to be out of order.

(9) An amendment is out of order if it is offered at a wrong place in the bill.[4]

(10) An amendment is irrelevant and cannot be admitted if it seeks to delay the coming into force of a bill relating to England only, until a similar bill should have been passed for Scotland.[5]

(11) Amendments or new clauses creating public charges cannot be proposed, if no money resolution or Ways and Means resolution has been passed, or if the amendment or clause is not covered by the terms of such a resolution. This rule, which is of fundamental importance, is fully explained in chapter 26 and on p 722.

It is to be noted that amendments affecting the interests of the Crown (see p 561) or which may make a bill hybrid (see p 521) are admissible.[6]

Amendments to particular types of bill

The rules (and particularly the first rule) set out above, when applied to certain classes of bill, have the following consequences:

(i) Bills to confirm agreements. When a bill is introduced to give effect to an agreement or to confirm a scheme, the text of which is contained in a schedule to the bill, and the independent origin and status of which is described in an introductory provision in the bill, amendments cannot be made to the schedule,[7] but the contents of the schedule can be modified or qualified by amendment to the clauses of the bill.[8]

In the past such introductory provisions were often contained in the preamble to the bill,[9] but modern practice is to include them in one of the early clauses.[10]

---

1 Parl Deb (1908) 195, c 551; HC Deb (1915) 73, c 558; ibid (1915) 75, c 887; ibid (1916) 78, c 235; ibid (1917) 92, c 1713. In the case of a new clause on consideration, HC Deb (1913) 53, c 1195.

2 HC Deb (1914) 61, c 189.

3 Parl Deb (1882) 270, c 862; ibid (1898) 58, c 461; HC Deb (1910) 19, c 1718 (consideration); ibid (1915) 71, c 2172 (consideration); ibid (1976–77) 926, c 1670.

4 Parl Deb (1898) 57, c 54; ibid (1898) 60, c 651; ibid (1899) 74, c 326.

5 Parl Deb (1896) 41, c 1702 (consideration).

6 In accordance with the latter rule amendments were made to the Park Lane Improvement Bill 1957–58 (already a hybrid bill), which, if it had been a private bill would have required a petition for additional provision. The bill was referred to the Examiners of Petitions for Private Bills on motion at report stage (CJ (1957–58) 147; see also p 920).

7 HC Deb (1917) 98, c 2408; ibid (1922) 159, cc 537–538.

8 HC Deb (1922) 159, c 538; ibid (1982) 18, c 762.

9 Eg Coal Mines Control Agreement (Confirmation) Act 1918 and Ottawa Agreements Act 1932.

10 Eg Carriage by Air and Road Act 1979; Civil Jurisdiction and Judgments Act 1982. In the case of the Canada Bill 1982, the Chairman ruled that the preamble, as well as the clause introducing the schedule, was evidence of the origin and status of the Constitution Act 1982, which formed the contents of that schedule; but he also stated that his ruling arose from the way in which that particular bill was drafted, and that no general conclusions were to be drawn, HC Deb (1981–82) 19, cc 289–290.

(ii) Statute Law Revision Bills. An amendment cannot be moved to a Statute Law Revision bill to deal with an Act still in force, as such a bill deals solely with statutes no longer in force.[1]

(iii) Statute Law (Repeals) Bills. Though it has become the practice in both Houses not to move amendments to these bills but to rely on the Joint Committee's report, there is no formal restriction on the amendments which may be moved.

(iv) Consolidation Bills. Where the title of a bill is only *to consolidate* the law on a particular subject, it is out of order to amend the provisions of the statutes which by the bill are to be consolidated and fused together,[2] as any such amendments are regarded as outside the scope of the bill, and were not contemplated when the House gave it a second reading.[3] If they are justified by the circumstances, the following amendments may be excepted from this rule and be moved to such a Consolidation bill:

An amendment to change the date on which the bill is to come into operation if, owing to the date when the bill is being considered, it would be inconvenient to bring it into operation on the date laid down in the bill, or if it is desired that 'the appointed day' for the bill coming into operation should be not earlier than a certain date.[4]

An amendment which would make the words of the bill express more clearly the law as it stands.[5]

An amendment which seeks to bring the bill into conformity with the existing law, if the Chairman is satisfied that the bill, as reported from the Joint Committee, would nevertheless effect an alteration of the law.[6]

Where the title of the bill is *to consolidate with corrections and improvements made under the Consolidation of Enactments (Procedure) Act* 1949, amendments in Committee of the whole House are further restricted by the terms of the Act (section 1(7)).[7] The corrections and minor improvements as defined in the Act (section 2) are laid before Parliament by the Lord Chancellor or, where the bill is purely Scottish, by the Lord Advocate, in a memorandum which is printed by both Houses[8] and must be approved by the Joint Committee on Consolidation Bills, and the Lord Chancellor and the Speaker must concur in such approval. When the bill has been reported by the committee, the authorized corrections and minor improvements are deemed to have become law and cannot be amended when the bill subsequently comes before a Committee of the whole House, nor can new ones be proposed.[9]

Where the title of the bill is *to consolidate with amendments to give effect to recommendations of the Law Commissions,* the only amendments permiss-

---

1 Parl Deb (1890) 346, c 1618.
2 HC Deb (1921) 146, c 1140.
3 See HC Deb (1922) 156, c 465 (ruling by the Speaker).
4 HC Deb (1921) 146, c 1142.
5 HC Deb (1921) 146, c 806.
6 HC Deb (1921) 146, c 1143; ibid (1948–49) 468, cc 1728, 1729; ibid (1987–88) 137, c 157.
7 For an example of an amendment accepted as in order by the Chairman, see HC Deb (1966–67) 736, cc 570–574.
8 Eg LJ (1966–67) 42; CJ (1966–67) 46.
9 For Speaker's rulings on the scope of the Act, see HC Deb (1950) 478, c 390; ibid (1951–52) 503, cc 2050, 2053.

ible are, first, amendments which would have been permissible if the bill had been a pure consolidation bill and, secondly, amendments relating directly to the recommendations of the Law Commissions. [1] These recommendations are contained in a report made to the Lord Chancellor and (when applicable) to the Lord Advocate, and are published as a White Paper.

Where the title of the bill is *to consolidate and amend,* or *to consolidate with amendments,* the law, amendments may be moved to the statutes which are to be consolidated.[2]

Amendment to leave out subsection of a clause

When a clause contains two or more subsections which are not mutually dependent, an amendment to leave out each subsection is in order.[3] When the subsequent subsections are dependent upon or ancillary to the first subsection, an amendment to the clause to leave out that subsection is out of order, as the effect of such an amendment being carried would be to destroy the clause. The decision that should be reached, and the discussion that should properly arise, on the question of the clause standing part of the bill would thus be anticipated.[4]

Amendment ruled out of order after debate begun

If it should appear in the course of debate that an amendment or new clause which has been allowed to be moved is out of order, the chairman directs the committee's attention to the fact and withdraws the amendment or clause from the consideration of the committee.[5]

Proceedings upon italicized words and privilege amendments

It has already been explained (see p 468) that in bills introduced in the Commons any clause or part of a clause which imposes a charge is either printed in italics or authorized by an 'expenses' clause which is itself italicized. Italicized words or clauses governed by them cannot be considered by the committee unless a money resolution authorizing them has been agreed to by the House.[6] By Standing Order No 66 no question is put for inserting words already printed in italics,[7] and accordingly, if no alteration has been made in such words (and no amendment has been made elsewhere), the bill is reported without amendment. If it is desired to alter the italicized words, an amendment can be moved in the ordinary manner, provided that it falls within the limits of the money resolution;[8] but any increase or extension of

---

1 HC Deb (1966–67) 749, cc 23–24; ibid 751, cc 1638, 1643.
2 Supreme Court Bill [Lords], CJ (1980–81) 389, 438.
3 HC Deb (1915) 75, c 116; ibid (1916) 84, c 1954; ibid (1917) 94, c 1633.
4 HC Deb (1909) 7, c 493; ibid (1912) 39, c 748; ibid (1913) 54, c 1757; ibid (1915) 75, cc 105, 200; ibid (1917) 95, c 2054; ibid (1918) 107, c 1577.
5 CJ (1914) 155, HC Deb (1914) 61, cc 1021, 1069; CJ (1917–18) 153; ibid (1918) 152; HC Deb (1941–42) 380, c 583; Stg Co Deb (1959–60) Co A, 24 November 1959, cc 5–9; CJ (1975–76) 641.
6 Chronically Sick and Disabled Persons Bill 1969,Stg Co Deb (1969–70) Co C, c 145; Alkali Inspectorate Bill, Stg Co Deb (1972–73) Co C, c 3; Dogs Bill, Stg Co Deb (1974–75) Co C, c 3.
7 Until this SO was made in 1854 words in italics did not form part of the bill until agreed to by the committee.
8 Stg Co Deb (1934–35) Sc Co, c 805, Housing (Scotland) Bill.

the charge authorized by the italicized words is only in order to the extent to which the limits of the money resolution exceed the effect of the italicized words (see p 468). (The same rule applies to charges imposed by bills brought from the Lords, although it is not the practice to print the relevant words in italics in Lords bills.)

In bills brought from the Lords where words have been inserted in that House to avoid questions of privilege (see p 460) and are printed in the bill with a black line in the margin, the leaving out of these words in committee in the Commons must be moved as an amendment. Notice is usually given of such amendments by the Member in charge of the bill.

Clauses received pursuant to instruction

When instructions have been given by the House for the purpose, the committee may receive clauses or make provision in the bills committed to them which they could not otherwise have considered.[1]

Question for clause standing part of a bill

When the amendments, if any, to a clause have been disposed of, the question put from the Chair is, 'That the clause [as amended] stand part of the bill'; and no other amendment can be proposed to a clause after this question has been proposed from the Chair.[2] Debate upon this question must be confined to the clause as amended (or not amended), and must not extend to a discussion of the circumstances under which particular amendments were made or to a review in detail of the proceedings on the clause.[3] It has been ruled that when the question, 'That the clause (as amended) stand part of the bill', has been proposed from the Chair, it must be agreed to or negatived, as it necessarily follows upon the consideration of the clause and is not a motion made by any Member which he could ask leave to withdraw.[4] While, strictly, a separate question is necessary on each clause, in the case of non-contentious bills, in order to save time, the question has sometimes been put on groups of clauses.[5] This practice is almost invariably resorted to in the case of Consolidation Bills.

Standing Order No 67 provides that if the chairman is of opinion that the principle of a clause, and any matters arising out of it, have been adequately discussed in the course of debate on the amendments which have been proposed to it, he may state that he is of that opinion and shall then forthwith put the question 'That the clause [as amended] stand part of the Bill.'

Occasionally chairmen, with the agreement of a committee, allow debate on an amendment or on the question that a clause stand part of a bill to cover the merits of other related clauses (cf p 490). In such a case the questions that

---

1 For the extent to which the rejection of an instruction affects the power of a committee in considering amendments which trench upon the purport of the rejected instruction, see the chairman's ruling on the Tithe Rent Charge Recovery Bill, Parl Deb (1889) 339, cc 1185, 1228.
2 Parl Deb (1857) 147, c 1191.
3 Parl Deb (1893) 12, c 1180; ibid (1894) 20, cc 503, 696; HC Deb (1918) 106, cc 2069, 2073; ibid (1919) 122, c 491; ibid (1921) 147, c 954; ibid (1935) 300, c 1356.
4 Hypothec Abolition (Scotland) Bill, 1 April 1879 (private ruling).
5 HC Deb (1939) 349, c 2201. See also the order on the Government of India Bill, CJ (1934–35) 82; HC Deb (1935) 298, c 146.

the clauses concerned stand part of the bill are put (without debate) as soon as they are reached.[1]

New clauses

New clauses are considered after the clauses of the bill have been disposed of, unless the committee has ordered otherwise. The decision on where in the bill a new clause is to be inserted is not a decision for the committee, but is left to be settled between the Member in charge of the bill and the Public Bill Office, which is responsible for reprinting the bill as amended. New clauses, subject to any motion for considering them in a different order (see p 487), are considered in the order in which they stand on the notice paper, that is, the order in which they have been handed in, except that clauses offered by the Member in charge of the bill are placed first[2] and may be arranged in any order he wishes.

The procedure on a new clause gives an opportunity for a debate on its principle and then for the proposal of amendments before its incorporation in the bill. The Member in whose name it stands, or another Member in his stead, on being called by the chairman, 'brings up' the clause in a speech, explaining its merits. Under the provisions of Standing Order No 68 a new clause is read the first time without question put, and the reading of the marginal note by the clerk is taken as complying with the standing order. The question, that the clause be read a second time, is then proposed, and, if this is agreed to, amendments may be moved in the ordinary manner. Finally, the question is put that the clause, or the clause as amended, be added to the bill. This question is often not debated, particularly if the clause is unamended (in which case the scope of debate is virtually identical to that on the question for second reading).

At the chairman's discretion new clauses and schedules may be grouped together for discussion in the same way as amendments (see p 490).

A new clause may be ruled to be out of order for many of the same reasons as an amendment (see pp 491 ff).[3]

Withdrawal and postponement of new clauses. A new clause may be withdrawn even after its second reading so long as no decision has been taken upon it after that stage. Its consideration may be postponed if the question for reading it a second time has not yet been proposed[4] but cannot be postponed after second reading has been agreed to.[5]

Schedules and new schedules

Schedules to a bill are considered after the new clauses have been disposed of, unless the committee has ordered otherwise. A schedule can be amended

---

1 Eg HC Deb (1987–88) 133, cc 102, 114.
2 Such Member does not forfeit precedence for his clauses, if he has taken them off the Paper by agreement with the Chair for technical reasons. Private ruling, 17 June 1941 (Decision 2176). See Supplement to the Votes (1940–41) 740, 747, 772.
3 Parl Deb (1907) 175, c 985 (on consideration, as amended); HC Deb (1916) 85, cc 2195, 2428; ibid (1919) 114, c 2074 (on consideration, as amended); ibid (1919) 120, c 392; ibid (1925) 181, c 2135 (on consideration, as amended).
4 CJ (1947–48) 140.
5 Parl Deb (1901) 95, c 1549.

and is treated in the same manner as a clause. The final question on a schedule is, 'That this schedule (as amended) be the (first) schedule to the bill'. Under Standing Order No 67 this question, like the question that a clause stand part of the bill (p 496), may be put forthwith by the chairman if he considers that the principle of the schedule and any matters arising from it have already been adequately discussed during debate on the amendments proposed to it.

New schedules may be offered in the same way as new clauses; they are normally considered after any existing schedules. A new schedule is brought up, read the first time and second time, amended, if need be, and added to the bill.[1]

Bills which propose to amend or apply by reference an existing enactment sometimes contain a schedule showing how the enactment will read if the bill becomes an Act, the proposed amendments being printed in heavy type.[2] In such a schedule only consequential amendments which are required to give effect to amendments already inserted in the bill are in order,[3] and these may be made consequentially on the direction of the chairman.[4]

Consolidation of bills

When, pursuant to an instruction, two bills are to be consolidated, the preambles (if any) of the two bills are severally postponed, and the clauses of each are successively proceeded with.[5]

Division of bills

When an instruction has been given to the committee that a bill may be divided into two or more bills, those clauses which are to form a separate bill have been postponed[6] or considered in the position assigned to them by the bill.[7] When they have been considered, preambles (if necessary), enacting words and titles have been annexed to them, and the separate bills have then been separately reported.[8]

Preamble

By Standing Order No 65, the preamble (if any) stands postponed without question put until after the consideration of the clauses and schedules. This practice is adopted because the House has already affirmed the principle of the bill on the second reading, and it is therefore the province of the committee to settle the clause first, and then to consider the preamble in reference to the clauses only. Accordingly when all the clauses and sched-

---

1 CJ (1914–16) 71; ibid (1917–18) 179; CJ (1980–81) 496 (on consideration, as amended).
2 See eg Rating and Valuation (Amendment) (Scotland) Bill 1983. Such schedules are sometimes known as 'Keeling Schedules', following their introduction in response to a memorandum by Mr (later Sir Edward) Keeling to the Prime Minister, see HC Deb (1937–38) 338, cc 2919–2920.
3 HC Deb (1947–48) 446, cc 1873–1875.
4 HC Deb (1983–84) 57, c 504.
5 CJ (1889) 297, 333, 339. See also ibid (1929–30) 203; Stg Co C, Proceedings (1929–30), Road Traffic Bill [Lords], 122–125.
6 CJ (1861–62) 376; ibid (1871) 114.
7 Local Government, Planning and Land (No 2) Bill, Stg Co Deb (1979–80) Co D c 929.
8 CJ (1861–62) 385; ibid (1871) 120; ibid (1979–80) 562.

ules have been considered, and any new clauses or schedules added, the preamble (if any) is considered, and amendments may be moved to it. Normally amendments are admissible only if rendered necessary by amendments made to the bill.[1] Occasionally a preamble has not only rehearsed the reasons for and intended effects of a bill, but has in addition recorded certain proposals which might have been but were not included in the bill itself. On such occasions amendments to that additional part of the preamble have not been ruled out of order although unrelated to any amendments made to the body of the bill.[2]

The question put by the chairman is 'That this be the preamble of the bill'. Where the bill, as introduced, does not contain a preamble, it is not competent for the committee to introduce one.[3]

Title

Except in the circumstances described below, the title can be amended only if the bill has been so altered as to necessitate such an amendment;[4] but any amendment to the title that may be necessary is made.[5] No question is put that the title, or that the title as amended, stand part of the bill; and debate on an amendment must be limited to the question of whether the alteration is necessary to bring the title into conformity with the bill.[6]

Where a bill has been divided in committee and it is necessary to provide the new bill with a title, the question 'That the Title be the Title to the Bill' is put after notice of the title has been given.[7]

Where a title has referred to a proposal not contained in a bill as introduced, an amendment to the title not consequential on any amendment to the bill has been permitted to be made.[8]

When committee makes no report

The proceedings in committee of the whole House on a bill may be brought abruptly to a close by an order, 'That the chairman do now leave the Chair';[9] or by a division revealing that a quorum is not present (see p 250). The chairman in such cases, being without instructions from the committee, makes no report to the House. If the proceedings are so terminated for want of forty Members taking part in a division, under Standing Order No 40 the business under consideration stands over until the next sitting of the House; but when the chairman has been ordered to leave the Chair, the order for committee is 'dropped', and can be revived only by a further order (see pp 314–315),[10] when it is resumed at the point where it was discontinued.

---

1 HC Deb (1932) 264, c598; ibid (1939–40) 363, c899.
2 Parliament Bill 1911, preamble, second and third paras, CJ (1911) 190; Parliament (No 2) Bill 1968–69, preamble, second para, HC Deb (1968–69) 778, c219.
3 HC Deb (1913) 55, c455; ibid (1935) 300, c1359.
4 HC Deb (1930) 246, c996; ibid (1976–77) 923, c1679.
5 CJ (1854–55) 223; ibid (1933–34) 150, 161; ibid (1934–35) 208 (on recommittal).
6 HC Deb (1913) 55, cc457–458, 465.
7 Local Government, Planning and Land (No 2) Bill, Stg Co Deb (1979–80) Co D, c932.
8 New Streets Bill, St Co Deb (1950–51) Co B, c718; Local Government (Miscellaneous Provisions) Bill, ibid (1952–53) Co B, c1059; Parliamentary Control of Expenditure (Reform) Bill (changed to National Audit Bill), Stg Co Deb (1982–83) Co C, c254. See also p 509, note 3 for corresponding amendments moved on Third Reading.
9 CJ (1835) 497, 562; ibid (1857) 310; ibid (1865) 201; ibid (1871) 339; ibid (1955–56) 128.
10 CJ (1955–56) 130.

Proceedings of committee not known until reported

The House is not formally aware of the detailed proceedings of any committee until the bill has been reported; and attempts to refer in the House to proceedings on a bill during its consideration in committee are consequently irregular.

REPORT OF BILL

Close of committee proceedings and report of bill

When consideration of the bill has been completed the chairman proposes the final question, 'That I do report the bill without amendment (or, as amended) to the House'.[1] This question having been agreed to, he leaves the Chair. Under Standing Order No 82, the Chairman of a Committee of the whole House does this without any further question being put and the Speaker resumes the chair. The Chairman, as directed by Standing Order No 69, then reports the bill forthwith to the House. If the bill has not been amended the Chairman states, 'I beg to report that the committee has gone through the bill and directed me to report the same without amendment'. If the bill has been amended the formula is, 'I beg to report that the committee has gone through the bill and made amendments thereunto'. If the title of the bill has been amended, it is laid down in Standing Order No 63 that such amendment must be specially reported.[2]

If the citation clause of a bill has been amended, it is necessary, in consequence, to change the short title by which the bill is known. The entry in the Votes and Proceedings and the Journal describes the bill as '. . . Bill (changed to . . . Bill)'. When the next stage is put down on the order paper the new title is put first, eg '. . . Bill (changed from . . . Bill),' but in all subsequent proceedings the new title only is employed.[3] Lords bills, however, continue to be referred to as '. . . Bill [*Lords*] (changed to . . . Bill [*Lords*])' until the relevant amendment has been agreed to by the Lords.[4]

If the short title has been changed by an amendment made by the Lords, on its return to the Commons, the bill is described as '. . . Bill (changed to . . . Bill)'.[5]

Proceedings on report

Bills reported from a Committee of the whole House. If the bill has been reported from a Committee of the whole House without amendment, it is ordered to be read the third time forthwith, or a future day is appointed for the third reading.

If amendments have been made to the bill in committee the Member in charge, in reponse to the Speaker's request, names a day on which the bill, as

---

1 This is now regarded as a formal question and the chairman has deprecated debate on it, HC Deb (1934–35) 301, cc 1852, 1856; ibid (1978–79) 960, c 1893, and ruled debate out of order, ibid (1978–79) 996, c 799.
2 CJ (1860) 343; ibid (1865) 95; ibid (1933–34) 150, 161; ibid (1934–35) 208 (on recommittal); ibid (1966–67) 559; ibid (1979–80) 130, etc See also HC Deb (1914) 64, c 2117.
3 Eg CJ (1933–34) 254; ibid (1985–86) 287, 310, 341.
4 Eg Merchant Shipping Bill [Lords] 1983–84.
5 Eg CJ (1981–82) 452, 458.

amended, is to be taken into consideration. This is the normal practice, but (see p 532) the bill may be considered immediately after it has been reported provided that a question for its consideration has been put and agreed to.

According to the usual practice of the House a bill introduced on a Ways and Means resolution may not go through more than one stage on the same day (see pp 688–689, 692);[1] however, orders are frequently agreed to by the House waiving this practice in the case of particular bills.[2] In the case of Consolidated Fund and Appropriation Bills under Standing Order No 54, if the second reading stands as the first order of the day, the questions for second and third readings are successively put forthwith, with no order being made for the committal of the Bill.

Bills reported from standing committees. Under the provisions of Standing Order No 71 a bill reported from a standing committee, whether amended or not, must be considered on report by the House, except where it is referred under Standing Order No 92 (see p 505) for consideration on report to a standing committee. No formal proceeding takes place upon the report, but the House is deemed to have ordered the bill to be considered on a day fixed by the Member in charge and an entry to that effect is made in the Votes and Proceedings.

Bills reported from select or joint committees. A Commons bill reported from a select or joint committee is normally recommitted to a Committee of the whole House, and the House is deemed to have ordered the recommittal of the bill for the day fixed by the Member in charge, the requisite entry being made in the Votes and Proceedings.[3] In the case of hybrid bills (see p 524), this order is often subsequently discharged and the bill is re-committed to a standing committee.[4]

Reprinting of bills

When a bill has been amended in Committee, unless the amendments are of a very limited and simple nature,[5] it will be reprinted, time permitting, before the consideration stage. The order is made formally as a book entry in the Votes and Proceedings when the bill is reported to the House. Occasionally, while a bill has been in progress, amended clauses, so far as they have been agreed to,[6] or certain specified clauses[7] have been ordered to be printed. When a bill, already reprinted when reported from a standing committee, was further amended on re-committal by the addition of new clauses and a new schedule, the new clauses and new schedule were ordered to be printed.[8]

---

1 Eg HC Deb (1956–57) 570, cc 1041–1042. In this case proceedings on third reading taken on the same day as committee were declared null and void.
2 Eg CJ (1985–86) 476.
3 Eg Votes and Proceedings (1987–88) 15 December 1987 (select); CJ (1951–52) 166 (joint).
4 See eg Votes and Proceedings (1986–87) 31 March and 29 April. Orders committing hybrid bills to select committees usually provide that if the committal order stands discharged because no petitions are presented against the bill, the bill is to stand committed to a standing committee.
5 Votes and Proceedings (1987–88) 12 April 1988, Farmland and Rural Development Bill. If the only amendment made has been the striking out of the 'privilege amendment' (see p 745) it is not the practice to reprint the bill.
6 CJ (1917–18) 130; ibid (1927) 174; ibid (1934–35) 168.
7 CJ (1914–16) 281; ibid (1917–18) 152, 164, 174.
8 CJ (1982–83) 347.

Formerly, amended clauses were sometimes printed by direction of the Speaker and circulated with the Votes,[1] but an order of the House is now the normal practice.

A bill, or part of a bill, has been ordered to be printed so as to show the effect of the amendments to be proposed by the Government,[2] or has been so presented as a command paper.[3] For general convenience the first three or four parts of a bill have been reprinted before the conclusion of the committee stage of the bill.[4]

A bill may also be reprinted after it has been amended on the consideration stage, if time permits, before the third reading is proceeded with.[5]

CONSIDERATION OF BILL

The consideration of a bill, commonly called the report stage, is an opportunity for the House to consider afresh the text of the bill. The rules of debate and procedure differ somewhat from those for the committee stage: in particular no question is put for the successive clauses and schedules to stand part of the bill (cf pp 486–487). Also, a Member may speak only once to the same question, though, in the case of a bill reported from a standing committee, this rule, under the provisions of Standing Order No 74, is relaxed in favour of the Member in charge of the bill or of the mover of any amendment or new clause in respect of that amendment or clause. The same arrangements for the notice of amendments, new clauses, etc, apply as for the committee stage (see pp 488–489), except that Standing Order No 68 provides specifically that notice must be given of new clauses. The provisions of Standing Order No 62 with regard to notices handed in during an adjournment apply to amendments, new clauses or new schedules to be moved on consideration (see p 488). While amendments which were rejected or withdrawn in committee may be moved again, and attempts may be made by amendments to restore the original text of the bill, the power of selection of amendments, conferred upon the Speaker by Standing Order No 31 (see pp 404–405), is a check upon excessive repetition of debates which have already taken place in committee. The power of selection is usually exercised more rigorously by the Speaker on consideration than in committee by the chairman.[6] The normal practice is for the Speaker to make known his provisional selection and proposed grouping of amendments in advance (cf p 489).

Order for consideration read

Under Standing Order No 70, when the order of the day for the consideration of a bill, as amended in Committee of the whole House, has been read, the House proceeds to consider the bill without question put, unless the Member in charge of it nominates a future day for its consideration, or a motion is made to recommit the bill (see p 506). By Standing Order No 71,

1 Representation of the People Bill 1867; Irish Church Bill 1869; Irish Land Bill 1870; Land Law (Ireland) Bill 1881; Land Purchase (Ireland) Bill 1891, etc.
2 CJ (1909) 360, 370, 482; ibid (1916) 329; ibid (1917–18) 162, 237, 261.
3 CJ (1910) 301.
4 CJ (1964–65) 298; HC Deb (1964–65) 713, c 2124; CJ (1971–72) 397.
5 Eg CJ (1962–63) 257; ibid (1979–80) 684; Votes and Proceedings (1988–89) 14 June 1989.
6 HC Deb (1967–68) 767, c 297.

the same practice is followed in the case of a bill which has been considered in a standing committee, whether amended or not. If no Member moves a new clause, of which notice stands upon the notice paper, or an amendment to the bill, no question arises on this stage; and the Speaker calls upon the Member in charge of the bill to name a day for the third reading (cf p 505).

Order in which bill is considered

At the consideration stage the entire bill is open to review, new clauses and schedules may be added, and amendments made to the bill. The order in which the bill is proceeded with differs from the order in committee, and is as follows:

(1) New clauses.
(2) Amendments to the bill.
(3) New schedules.
(4) Amendments to the schedules to the bill.

The House has frequently ordered a bill to be considered in a different order.[1]

Notice of new clauses, new schedules or amendments may not be given until the bill has been reported from committee.[2] This rule has, however, been waived on occasions by order of the House.[3]

Rules regarding amendments

The moving of amendments to a bill on the consideration stage is governed by Standing Order No 73, which prohibits the proposal of any amendment which could not have been moved in committee without an instruction from the House,[4] unless it has been authorised by a resolution of the House. Consequently the rules of order respecting the admissibility of amendments in committee, which are set out on pp 490–493 above, are generally applicable to amendments moved on consideration, and many of the instances quoted there are in fact drawn from the later stage.

New clauses. Under the provisions of Standing Order No 68, no new clause may be offered at the consideration stage without notice.[5]

Except in the case where one Minister acts for another (cf p 330), a Member is not permitted to move a clause unless he has put his name to it.[6] New clauses are considered in the order in which they stand upon the paper,[7] that is, the order in which they have been handed in, except that priority is

---

1 CJ (1968–69) 335; ibid (1972–73) 364; ibid (1981–82) 250.
2 Notice can be given before the bill, as amended in committee, has been published, HC Deb (1967–68) 765, c 538.
3 CJ (1964–65) 302; ibid (1969–70) 341.
4 HC Deb (1928) 216, c 142. See also HC Deb (1924) 175, cc 1726–1728.
5 Notice of an amendment has been treated as notice of a new clause, CJ (1898) 365; Supplement to the Votes, p 2547.
6 Parl Deb (1876) 231, c 662; ibid (1883) 282, c 1995; HC Deb (1916) 85, c 1962; HC Deb (1979–80) 984, c 1765; ibid (1985–86) 90, c 317.
7 For orders of the House varying the usual procedure see eg CJ (1947–48) 215, 216; ibid (1979–80) 662.

given to clauses offered by the Member in charge of the bill, who may arrange his clauses in any order he wishes.

On being called by the Speaker, the mover of the new clause brings it up, and may speak in support of it; thereupon, the clause is read the first time without question put. As in committee, the reading of the marginal note of the clause by the clerk is held to comply with the provisions of Standing Order No 68.

The question is then proposed from the Chair, 'That the clause be read a second time.' This is the proper time for opposing the clause, and the proposer may again address the House in its favour.[1]

If so desired, the clause may, by leave of the House, be withdrawn.[2]

When the clause has been read a second time amendments may be made to it. The last question proposed by the Speaker is, 'That the clause (or the clause as amended) be added to the bill' and on this question a further debate may arise.[3]

Amendments to bill

When the new clauses on the notice paper have been disposed of, the Speaker calls on the Members who have given notice of amendments to the bill. Notice of an amendment is not obligatory, and, if called by the Speaker, a Member may propose an amendment of which he has not previously given notice; but the desirability of giving notice of important amendments is even greater on report than in committee, and it is rare for manuscript, or even starred, amendments to be called (cf pp 489–490.) Amendments are offered, as in committee, in the order in which, if agreed to, they will stand in the amended bill, but, as the bill is not considered clause by clause, they are referred to by page and line and marshalled by pages instead of by clauses, though the number of the clause is, for convenience, added in brackets. If a proposed amendment is withdrawn or negatived, an amendment at a prior place in the bill may be moved,[4] provided that it does not extend beyond the last point at which the House has already made a decision (see p 341).

Amendments are moved to the bill, not to a particular clause, and amendments to leave out a clause, a series of clauses or the preamble,[5] are moved as amendments to the bill; and no question is put for each clause standing part of the bill. A motion to divide a clause[6] or to transfer a clause or subsection or series of clauses or subsections from one part of the bill to another[7] is in order.

New schedules and schedules

After the amendments to the clauses of the bill have been considered, new schedules may be proposed and amended in the same way as new clauses.[8]

---

1 Parl Deb (1863) 171, c 189.
2 See eg CJ (1985–86) 570.
3 For the limitations on debate at this stage see HC Deb (1984–85) 77, cc 443–444.
4 Parl Deb (1872) 213, cc 672–673; CJ (1959–60) 221.
5 Debate on amendment to leave out the preamble may not extend to the whole question of the merits of the bill; Parl Deb (1893) 16, c 293; ibid (1907) 180, c 1428.
6 CJ (1963–64) 135; ibid (1968–69) 131, 243, 311; ibid (1985–86) 542.
7 CJ (1952–53) 281; ibid (1985–86) 542.
8 Eg CJ (1985–86) 510.

Amendments may then be made to any schedules to the bill as reported by the committee.

Amendment of title

When all the new clauses, amendments, new schedules, and schedules have been disposed of, the title of the bill is, if necessary, amended.[1]

Irregularities in committee noticed on report

Notice may be taken at the consideration stage of any irregularities which have occurred in committee which have not been noticed or corrected in that committee. In such cases the bill is usually recommitted (see p 506).

In Session 1948–49 an instruction was given to the Scottish Standing Committee empowering it to extend the Criminal Justice (Scotland) Bill [Lords] to England for the purpose of certain reciprocal arrangements between the two countries.[2] By a new clause and a new schedule the committee inadvertently further extended the bill to the Isle of Man and Channel Islands. On consideration the Speaker called the attention of the House to the fact that the committee had thus inadvertently further extended the bill and it was recommitted to the committee in respect of the clause and schedule in question.[3] Another instruction was subsequently given to the committee empowering it further to extend the bill to the Isle of Man and Channel Islands. The bill was then considered by the committee in respect of the clause and schedule and reported without amendment.[4]

Conclusion of consideration stage

When all the amendments to the bill have been disposed of, the Speaker calls upon the Member in charge to name a day for the third reading. (See p 501 for the rule with regard to bills introduced on a Ways and Means resolution of the House.) The Member usually responds with the words 'Now, Sir' and proceedings on third reading follow. If a future day is named for third reading, the bill may be ordered to be reprinted as amended (cf p 502).

Consideration stage taken in standing committee

Under Standing Order No 92 a bill which has been considered by a second reading committee or by the Scottish Grand Committee in relation to its principle (see pp 477–478), may be referred for consideration on report to a standing committee or to the Scottish Grand Committee as the case may be.[5] A bill can only be referred in this way by motion made after notice by a Minister of the Crown at the commencement of public business. The ques-

---

1 Eg CJ (1985–86) 374.
2 CJ (1948–49) 373.
3 CJ (1948–49) 400; HC Deb (1948–49) 469, cc 1939–1940.
4 CJ (1948–49) 401, 402. See also CJ (1864) 172; ibid (1929–30) 387, 399, 411.
5 The SO was made in November 1967, following a recommendation from the Procedure Committee of the previous session, HC 539 (1966–67), para 26; HC Deb (1967–68) 754, c 248. Only one reference has been made under the SO (CJ (1967–68) 225).

tion on such a motion is put forthwith and must be decided without amendment or debate; but if not fewer than twenty Members signify their objection by rising in their places, the Speaker must declare that the noes have it.

After completion of the consideration stage in the standing committee (see pp 593–594), the bill is reported to the House with or without amendment and an entry is made in the Votes and Proceedings ordering the bill to be read the third time on a day determined by the Member in charge.[1]

RECOMMITTAL OF BILL

A bill may be recommitted, if desired, to a Committee of the whole House, a standing committee (see p 606) or a Select Committee. A motion for this purpose may be made immediately after the bill has been reported from a Committee of the whole House.[2] Where consideration of a bill has been set down as an order of the day, a motion may be moved as soon as the order has been read.[3] A motion may also be moved immediately after the consideration stage,[4] but not during proceedings on consideration.[5] In the case of a bill set down for third reading, the order of the day may be discharged and the motion moved thereupon,[6] or the motion may be moved as an amendment to the question that the bill be now read the third time.[7]

A motion for recommittal may be made in respect of the whole bill, in which case the provisions of Standing Order No 72 (see p 507) will apply. Where a motion in respect of certain clauses or amendments only is made, the debate on the motion is restricted to the purpose and extent of the proposed recommittal of the bill.[8] Any Member may move to recommit or partially to recommit a bill but priority is given to any such motion which stands in the name of the Member in charge of the bill[9] and in the case of a partial recommittal the other motions may, if selected by the Speaker,[10] then be moved by way of amendments to the motion of the Member in charge.[11]

Although it has not been the practice for the Member in charge of the bill to resist such amendments[12] the Speaker exercises his power of selection on them since Chairmen have considered themselves obliged to select all amendments in respect of which the House has recommitted a bill. The Speaker, therefore, has sometimes selected motions for recommittal only if they were moved in a particular form[13] or has refused to call them at all.[14]

---

1 CJ (1967–68) 235.
2 CJ (1933–34) 167; ibid (1978–79) 104.
3 CJ (1960–61) 214; Votes and Proceedings (1987–88), 23 May 1988.
4 CJ (1974) 278.
5 HC Deb (1976–77) 935, c 1628.
6 CJ (1950–51) 244.
7 CJ (1922) 255.
8 Parl Deb (1872) 212, c 1278; ibid (1899) 72, c 1079; ibid (1906) 161, c 757; ibid (1907) 175, c 969; ibid (1907) 179, cc 296, 502; HC Deb (1909) 6, c 662; ibid (1911) 28, c 1907; ibid (1924) 176, cc 1562, 1598.
9 Parl Deb (1865) 179, c 800.
10 HC Deb (1951–52) 502, cc 49–51; see also ibid (1946–47) 438, cc 207–209; ibid (1947–48) 447, cc 1171–1172.
11 For a private Member's motion to recommit a government bill accepted together with amendments to it by other private Members, see CJ (1960–61) 214.
12 CJ (1946–47) 195, 220.
13 HC Deb (1951–52) 503, c 2041.
14 HC Deb (1920) 132, c 1359; ibid (1987–88) 134, c 994.

Nowadays a bill is seldom recommitted except partially, for one of the following purposes:

(a) to enable a new clause to be added to the bill when the House, on report, has passed the stage at which new clauses are taken;[1]
(b) to enable the committee to take advantage of an instruction from the House to make amendments which would otherwise be outside the scope of the bill;[2]
(c) to enable the committee to reconsider amendments it had previously made (see p 606);
(d) to enable the committee to consider in a regular manner a clause improperly agreed to before a money resolution had been passed (see pp 495–496).

If the bill is recommitted without limitation, the entire bill is again considered in committee and reported with 'other' or 'further' amendments. Sometimes, also, a bill is recommitted with an instruction to the committee that it has power to make some particular or additional provision.[3]

Procedure under Standing Order No 72

If a motion to recommit a bill as a whole is opposed, the Speaker is directed by Standing Order No 72 to permit a brief explanatory statement of the reasons for recommittal from the Member who moves and from a Member who opposes the motion, after which he must put the question without further debate.[4] The limitation of the motion to a partial recommittal of the bill, or the inclusion of any matter other than that necessary for recommittal[5] removes the motion from the scope of the Standing Order and the restriction on the number of speakers is not enforced;[6] nor does the Standing Order apply where recommittal is sought to be obtained by an amendment to the question for third reading. Motions have been made to recommit bills to a select committee. Standing Order No 72 has been applied to a motion confined to recommittal,[7] but not to a motion specifying the composition of the proposed select committee.[8]

The Standing Order was first made in 1919, with the intention of preventing the use of recommittal motions for purposes of obstruction.[9]

Partial recommittal

A bill may be recommitted in respect of a clause or clauses or schedules in the bill,[10] or in respect of new clauses, schedules or amendments which are to be proposed to the bill.[11]

---

1 CJ (1974) 278.
2 CJ (1974–75) 474; ibid (1981–82) 503.
3 CJ (1837–38) 605; ibid (1839) 318; ibid (1921) 259; ibid (1969–70) 281; see also ibid (1809) 370; ibid (1810) 184. In 1960 a motion to recommit the Finance Bill to a Select Committee was not selected by the Speaker (HC Deb (1959–60) 626, cc 861–865).
4 CJ (1919) 198, 378; ibid (1922) 241; ibid (1923) 197; HC Deb (1969–70) 800, cc 431–432, 456–462.
5 HC Deb (1920) 135, c 331.
6 HC Deb (1924) 176, cc 1562, 1598.
7 CJ (1928) 256.
8 CJ (1929–30) 336.
9 See evidence given before Select Committee on House of Commons (Procedure), HC 378 (1914), Questions 2410, 2621–2626, 2591.
10 CJ (1918) 122; ibid (1919) 161; ibid (1933–34) 167.
11 CJ (1920) 446; ibid (1921) 259; ibid (1924) 334; ibid (1934–35) 207, 228, 271; ibid (1945–46) 206; HC Deb (1945–46) 421, cc 41, 42; CJ (1961–62) 99.

Only so much of the bill as is specified in the order for recommittal is considered in the committee.[1] If a bill is recommitted in respect of specified amendments to a clause, only those amendments and amendments relevant to them may be moved, and not other amendments.[2] When the amendments have been disposed of in respect of any clause, the question for the clause standing part of the bill has to be put.[3]

Further recommittal

A bill may be recommitted as often as the House thinks fit. Bills have been recommitted twice,[4] and even four and five times.[5]

Report of recommitted bill

The proceedings on the report of a recommitted bill are similar to those already explained; after a partial recommittal (made after a full consideration stage or where a bill has not been amended in Committee of the whole House) amendments can only be made on the report stage if they are consequential on the amendments made in the committee on the partially recommitted bill.[6] On report the bill, as amended, is taken into consideration forthwith[7] and is read the third time, or further proceedings thereon are appointed for a future day.

THIRD READING

It has already been explained (p 500) that, when a bill is reported from a committee of the whole House without amendment, or when the consideration of a bill, as amended, is concluded, the Member in charge may move the third reading of the bill forthwith, or name a future day for that stage. The former course is now frequently followed, and may be regarded as the usual procedure, except where the bill is one of great importance or has been extensively amended on consideration; in such cases an interval before the third reading may be thought desirable.[8] The rule with regard to bills introduced on a Ways and Means resolution has been mentioned on p 501. The passing of bills with unusual expedition, through all or several stages in one day, is described on p 531.

On the reading of the order for third reading the Queen's consent is signified to bills affecting the Crown's interests or prerogative if it has not already been signified (see p 561).

Debate on third reading

Procedure on the third reading of a bill is similar to that on second reading, and the amendments that may be moved to the question for third reading

---

1 Parl Deb (1865) 179, c 826.
2 HC Deb (1917) 100, cc 273, 280, 285, 677, etc.
3 CJ (1917–18) 271; ibid (1918) 216; ibid (1920) 441.
4 CJ (1828) 218, 265, 354; ibid (1834) 157, 178, 277, 286; ibid (1914–16) 327, 330.
5 CJ (1810) 384, 396, 420; ibid (1813–14) 420, 444, 460.
6 Private ruling, 2 March 1943.
7 In the case of a bill founded on a Ways and Means resolution (see p 736) an order of the House has been regarded as necessary to permit more than one stage of a bill to be taken on the same day, CJ (1953–54) 266, etc.
8 Eg CJ (1979–80) 684.

follow the same pattern. The provisions of Standing Order No 60 concerning the questions to be proposed on such amendments apply equally to second and third reading (see pp 474–476). Debate on third reading, however, is more restricted than at the earlier stage, being limited to the contents of the bill;[1] and reasoned amendments which raise matters not included in the provisions of the bill are not permissible.[2]

Amendments on third reading

By Standing Order No 75, only verbal amendments may be made to a bill on the third reading.[3] If material amendments are desired the order for the third reading of the bill should be discharged, and the bill recommitted to allow the introduction of the amendments in committee. In such cases, which are very rare, the bill has been considered, as amended on recommittal, and read the third time immediately.[4]

Bill passed

The question 'That this bill do pass' is no longer put in the House of Commons,[5] and, according to established usage, a bill, when read the third time, has passed. The form, however, is preserved in the Votes and Proceedings and Journal, where the bill is recorded as having been read the third time and passed, and, in addition, in the case of bills brought from the Lords, with or without amendment. An entry is occasionally made in the Journal, at the discretion of the House, that a bill was read the third time and passed, *nemine contradicente*.[6]

Bill not to be altered otherwise than by amendment

Throughout all these stages and proceedings the bill itself continues in the custody of the Public Bill Office, and, with the exceptions mentioned below, no alteration whatever is permitted to be made in it, without the express authority of the House or a committee, in the form of an amendment regularly put from the Chair, and recorded by the Clerks at the Table or by the clerks from the Public Bill Office in standing committee.[7]

Any alterations in a bill which are necessitated by the renumbering of clauses or by a change in the date of the citation title, and in marginal notes and headings, which are not technically part of the bill, and any printing corrections which are not of substance, are made by the Public Bill Office

---

1 HC Deb (1918) 108, cc 974, 976; ibid (1920) 127, cc 347, 1982; ibid (1924) 169, c 1594; ibid (1966–67) 749, cc 1506, 1507, 1508; ibid (1976–77) 934, c 83; ibid (1977–78) 945, c 403. For a consolidation bill see HC Deb (1950) 477, c 820.
2 HC Deb (1935–36) 314, c 718.
3 CJ (1905) 401; ibid (1960–61) 117. For amendments made to the title on third reading, see CJ (1916) 234. See also Votes and Proceedings (1988–89) 14 April 1989; HC Deb (1988–89) 150, cc 1160–1209.
4 CJ (1857) 384; ibid (1860) 174; ibid (1922) 255.
5 Parl Deb (1881) 258, c 1832; ibid (1884) 289, c 1583.
6 CJ (1688–93) 280; ibid (1857) 110, Mr Speaker's Retirement Bill, on which occasion the Speaker expressed his acknowledgments to the House. See also debate and motion regarding this entry in the case of the Representation of the People Bill, CJ (1884) 321, 324; Parl Deb (1884) 289, c 1560, etc.
7 See eg 23 Parl Hist 989.

before the bill is reprinted at any stage.[1] As to amendments made consequentially to a 'Keeling' schedule, see p 498 and footnote 2.

Communication between the two Houses

From Lords to Commons. The next step is to communicate the bill to the other House. The Lords ordinarily send their bills to the Commons by the Clerk of the Parliaments, or by a clerk deputed for the purpose. When the bill has originated in the Lords a message is sent to the Commons desiring their agreement. If the bill has been sent up by the Commons, and has been agreed to without amendment, the Lords send a message to acquaint the Commons that they have agreed to the bill without amendment; but they do not return the bill unless it is a bill for granting aids or supplies and the Royal Assent to it is to be pronounced by Commission (see p 527). If they have made amendments, they return the bill to the Commons with a message that they have agreed to the bill with amendments, to which they desire the agreement of the Commons. The amendments are marked in the bill, which is also endorsed by the Clerk of the Parliaments (see p 527).

From Commons to Lords. The Commons send up their bills to the Lords by their Clerk, or by one of the clerks deputed for the purpose. The form of message adopted by the Commons in sending bills to the upper House is similar, *mutatis mutandis*, to that used by the House of Lords (see also pp 527 and 569–571).

Bills sent by mistake. If a bill is carried to the other House by mistake, or if any other error is discovered, a message is sent to have the bill returned or the error otherwise rectified.[2]

CONSIDERATION OF LORDS AMENDMENTS

The following sections describe the further proceedings on a bill which has originated in the House of Commons and is returned with amendments from the House of Lords. Certain restrictions on the Lords' right to amend bills are considered below (pp 746–750).

In the case of a bill which has originated in the Lords and is returned amended by the Commons, the roles of the two Houses will, of course, be reversed: Lords Amendments will be Commons Amendments, and Commons Reasons will be Lords Reasons.

Time for considering Lords Amendments

A Lords message is ordinarily received without communication being made to the House, and the message and the order appointing a day for the consideration of the amendments is entered in the Votes and Proceedings,

---

1 See HC Deb (1947–48) 446, cc 1873–1875.
2 CJ (1945–46) 166; ibid (1950) 102; ibid (1969–70) 358; LJ (1971–72) 493; ibid (1974) 322; ibid (1979–80) 1139; ibid (1983–84) 381; ibid (1984–85) 190; ibid (1984–85) 644 (a private bill); Votes and Proceedings (1987–88), 26 February 1988. See also CJ (1844) 637, 638, 644; Parl Deb (1844) 76, cc 1994–1995 (refusal of Commons to consider accidentally omitted Lords Amendments).

the Member in charge of the bill informing the Clerks at the Table of the day which he wishes to select. The amendments are normally ordered to be printed at the same time.[1]

Although Lords Amendments are normally appointed to be considered on a future day, the House may order that the amendments be considered forthwith (Standing Order No 76(1)), in which case the Speaker first reads the text of the Lords message concerning them. An order to consider Lords Amendments forthwith results in their being considered without being set down as an order of the day, whether the order is made immediately following the communication of the Lords message to the House or later on the day on which the message is received[2] or on a subsequent day.[3] A motion that the Lords Amendments be considered forthwith is moved by the Member in charge of the bill, after notifying the Speaker, before the commencement or at the end of the orders of the day. As this practice involves the consideration of the amendments without notice and without their having been printed, it is generally reserved for amendments which are not material.

In the case of amendments which are material, provided there is any need for urgency owing to the state of business, the Lords message may be communicated to the House, and the motion for considering the Lords Amendments forthwith may be made between any two orders of the day,[4] or by interrupting the business under discussion.[5]

A motion for the consideration forthwith of Lords Amendments is debatable, but debate on such a motion must not extend to the provisions of the bill.[6]

Proceedings on consideration of Lords Amendments

When the consideration of Lords Amendments has been put down as an order of the day the House proceeds immediately to consider the amendments without any question being put, unless the Member in charge nominates a future day for their consideration or withdraws the bill.[7] The Speaker calls the amendments one by one, and unless it is proposed to divide, postpone or amend the amendment, a motion is made, normally by the Member in charge of the bill, 'That this House doth agree (or disagree) with the Lords in the said amendment'. Notice may be given of motions to disagree with Lords Amendments.[8] For the convenience of the House a list of provisional groupings for debate (which may include amendments to Lords Amendments etc,) is now commonly circulated in advance (cf p 489)

1 Bills, as amended by the Lords, have been ordered to be printed *in extenso*. CJ (1856) 312, 324; ibid (1876) 365.
2 CJ (1933–34) 46, 47, 241, 243; ibid (1934–35) 40, 43; ibid (1944–45) 167.
3 CJ (1931–32) 276, 283; ibid (1933–34) 199, 200.
4 CJ (1890–91) 340; ibid (1906) 505; ibid (1917–18) 76; ibid (1919) 316; HC Deb (1919) 119, c 1861; CJ (1920) 382; ibid (1921) 362; HC Deb (1968–69) 775, c 1329.
5 CJ (1914–16) 31; HC Deb (1914) 68, c 1595; CJ (1919) 315; HC Deb (1919) 119, cc 1822–1823; CJ (1933–34) 259; ibid (1938–39) 383.
6 Parl Deb (1894) 28, c 1489; ibid (1900) 87, c 825; HC Deb (1915) 74, cc 2059 ff.
7 SO No 76 (2). HC 539 (1966–67), para 28.
8 For an example of notice given of a motion to agree with a Lords Amendment, see Supplement to Votes (1968–69) 7013.

and the Speaker accordingly permits debate to range over several amendments which raise matters related to the subject of the amendment actually under consideration; but no debate on any amendment may extend to the general merits of the bill.[1] No reply or second speech is permitted[2] and an amendment to insert the word 'not' in the question is inadmissible.[3] Motions both for agreeing and disagreeing with Lords Amendments have been negatived;[4] but if the question for disagreeing with an amendment is negatived the amendment is thereby agreed to.[5]

On two occasions the question for agreeing or disagreeing with Lords Amendments has been put by order of the House with respect to the amendments as a whole.[6] Under modern practice an allocation of time order for a bill will enable a supplemental order or orders to be made for time limits to be applied to Lords Amendments and subsequent proceedings (see pp 413–414).

Postponement of Lords Amendments. A Lords Amendment may be read and postponed and subsequent amendments may be taken into consideration,[7] but a motion for the postponement of an amendment cannot be made after the question for agreeing or disagreeing with it has been proposed.[8] The House can order that amendments should be taken in a different order,[9] and a supplemental allocation of time order may provide for Lords Amendments to be disposed of in some particular order.[10] Lords Amendments to the title are normally printed after the other amendments and taken last.[11]

Lords Amendments agreed to. If the Lords Amendments are agreed to by the Commons a message is sent acquainting the Lords accordingly, and the bill is returned to await the Royal Assent.

Privilege amendments. The Commons may agree to Lords Amendments which infringe their financial privileges; but where such amendments involve a charge upon the public revenue not sanctioned by any money resolution already agreed to in respect of the bill, a (further) money resolution must be agreed to by the House before the amendments are considered[12] (see also p 749). If no such money resolution is agreed to, the Speaker[13] is required under Standing Order No 76(3) to declare that he is satisfied that an amendment imposes a charge on the public revenue. Thereupon the amendment is deemed to have been disagreed to and is so recorded

---

1 Parl Deb (1878) 241, cc 846, 1059; ibid (1906) 167, c 1879; ibid (1907) 181, c 1201; HC Deb (1911) 29, c 1104.
2 Parl Deb (1869) 197, c 1949.
3 Parl Deb (1876) 231, c 1176.
4 CJ (1908) 511; ibid (1914–16) 88; ibid (1916) 259; ibid (1919) 318; ibid (1921) 351; ibid (1937–38) 343–347.
5 CJ (1908) 511; ibid (1916) 260; HC Deb (1918) 101, c 2171; ibid (1975–76) 620.
6 CJ (1906) 491; ibid (1909) 529; HC Deb (1909) 12, c 2179.
7 CJ (1835) 624; ibid (1887) 456. Consideration of Lords reasons for disagreeing to Commons amendments may also be postponed, CJ (1887) 456; ibid (1917–18) 315.
8 HC Deb (1919) 119, c 1869. See also Parl Deb (1891) 351, c 1470.
9 CJ (1972–73) 480.
10 See eg CJ (1985–86) 527.
11 HC Deb (1966–67) 737, c 1495.
12 See eg CJ (1968–69) 360–361; ibid (1980–81) 485.
13 For a declaration by the Deputy Speaker see Votes and Proceedings (1987–88) 19 July 1988.

in the Journal. When a Lords Amendment has involved a charge upon the people not sanctioned by a Ways and Means resolution he has called upon the Member in charge of the bill forthwith to move to disagree to the Lords Amendment.[1]

Consideration of Commons Amendments in the Lords. In the Lords a Message relating to Commons Amendments is read out to the House and a day is appointed for considering the amendments which are printed and circulated. Reasonable notice of consideration of Commons Amendments is given when possible.[2] The amendments may, however, be considered forthwith without notice (Standing Order No 39(4)) at any convenient time during public business. Commons Amendments may with the leave of the House be moved in groups provided that the amendments are all consecutive in the list and consequential on an amendment already agreed to.

Stages in process of securing agreement between the two Houses. When amendments made to a bill by the Lords are disagreed to by the Commons, or where amendments are made by the Commons to a Lords Amendment, the process of securing agreement between the two Houses could in theory be carried on indefinitely. It is proposed here to review the successive stages and their complications only up to the point beyond which it would normally be impossible to proceed.

Relevance of amendments to Lords Amendments, and of consequential amendments to the bill. Before describing the proceedings in the Commons when that House desires to disagree to amendments which have been made by the Lords, or to make further amendments thereto, the general rules of practice with regard to such amendments must be noticed.

   (1) An amendment made to a Lords Amendment must be relevant to the same subject-matter. If an amendment is proposed to a Lords Amendment which is not consequent on or relevant to it, the question will not be put from the Chair.[3]

   (2) No objection can be taken to a Lords Amendment on the ground of being outside the scope of the bill,[4] or otherwise as to its orderliness (except so far as sanction by way of a financial resolution is concerned, see above).

   (3) According to a long-established rule, the Commons, when considering Lords Amendments, may not leave out or otherwise amend anything which they have already passed themselves, unless such amendment be immediately consequent upon the acceptance or rejection of an amendment made by the Lords. In 1678 it was stated by the Commons 'that it is contrary to the constant method and proceedings in Parliament to strike out anything in a bill which hath been fully agreed and passed by both Houses';[5] and in

---

1 HC Deb (1984–85) 78, c 220.
2 HL Deb (1987–88) 493, c 938.
3 CJ (1860) 494; see also LJ (1839) 643.
4 Parl Deb (1898) 64, c 241; ibid (1902) 116, c 1403; HC Deb (1916) 81, c 2690; ibid (1916) 85, c 2695; ibid (1919) 119, c 2105; ibid (1921) 146, c 1057.
5 CJ (1667–87) 547 (1678); cf CJ (1547–1628) 388 (1607).

allowing consequential amendments either in the body of the bill or in the amendments, the spirit of this rule is maintained.[1]

The Commons disagreed to a clause inserted by the Lords in the Poor Law Boards (Payment of Debts) Bill 1859, on the ground of privilege, but inadvertently agreed to a subsequent amendment, which was consequent on that clause. The Lords did not insist upon their clause, and corrected the latter part of the bill by a consequential amendment to which the Commons agreed.[2]

In 1920 the Lords left out a clause in the Derwent Valley Water Board Bill but had not left out the passages of the preamble referring to it. The Commons agreed to the Lords Amendment and made the amendment necessary to bring the preamble into conformity with the bill as a consequential amendment.[3]

Lords Amendments disagreed to, or amended, by the Commons. Several alternatives are open to the Commons, when that House desires to disagree to amendments which have been made by the Lords.

(1) The Commons may simply disagree with the amendment, either by agreeing to the question 'That this House doth disagree with the Lords in the said amendment', or by negativing the question, 'That this House doth agree with the Lords in the said amendment'.

(2) The Commons may amend the Lords Amendment—

(a) by leaving out words in the amendment;[4]
(b) by leaving out words in the amendment and inserting or adding words instead thereof;[5]
(c) by inserting words in[6] or adding words to the amendment.[7]

Notice is customarily given of amendments proposed to be moved to Lords Amendments. The Speaker's powers of selection extend to amendments to Lords Amendments (and to consequential amendments to the bill and to amendments in lieu of Lords Amendments).[8] He will ordinarily make his selection known in advance in the same way as he does at the report stage (see p 511). Any amendments to a Lords Amendment which have been selected will be called in sequence when the Lords Amendment concerned is selected, and before the question is proposed for agreeing (or disagreeing) to the Lords Amendment. Once that question has been proposed no amendment (or further amendment) may be moved to the Lords Amendment concerned.[9]

(3) While agreeing to the amendment, the Commons may make consequential amendments to the bill;[10] or, where the Lords Amendment proposes to leave out words of the bill, amendments may be made to the bill

1 Parl Deb (1854) 135, cc 827–828; HC Deb (1918) 101, cc 2204–2206; ibid (1968–69) 780, cc 1823–1824.
2 CJ (1859) 375.
3 CJ (1920) 430; HC Deb (1920) 134, c 1839.
4 Eg CJ (1984–85) 544.
5 Ibid.
6 Eg CJ (1985–86) 596.
7 Eg CJ (1984–85) 543.
8 HC Deb (1952–53) 514, cc 821–822; ibid (1964–65) 714, c 181; ibid (1967–68) 770, cc 740, 742.
9 Parl Deb (1907) 181, c 312; HC Deb (1918) 101, c 2171.
10 Eg CJ (1985–86) 531.

instead of the words left out.[1] Any consequential amendment to the bill which has been selected will be called immediately after agreement with the Lords Amendment to which it is consequential even though it is out of sequence with the subsequent amendments.[2] Consequential amendments which involve the insertion of new clauses are treated as amendments.

The title of a bill can be amended to make it conform with the Lords Amendments,[3] and the short title of a bill may be changed in consequence of the House agreeing to Lords Amendments[4] (see also p 500).

(4) While disagreeing to the amendment, the Commons may make amendments to the bill in lieu of the Lords Amendment to which they have disagreed;[5] or, where the Lords Amendment proposes to leave out words or to leave out words and insert other words,[6] amendments may be made to the words so restored to the bill.[7] In both these cases consequential amendments may also be made to the bill.

(5) A Lords Amendment may be divided into two or more parts so that separate decisions can be taken. Thus, for example, both parts of a Lords Amendment may be agreed to,[8] part of it may be agreed to and part disagreed to,[9] two or more parts may be disagreed to,[10] or one part may be agreed to and the other amended and agreed to.[11]

(6) A Lords Amendment may be agreed to, but the words proposed to be inserted may be transferred to another place in the bill.[12]

Committee to draw up reasons. If any Lords Amendments have been disagreed to by the Commons without any alternative proposal being offered (see also p 748), it is necessary to appoint a committee to draw up a reason for each such disagreement. Motions for the nomination of such a committee are amendable and debatable.[13] The committee is appointed at the conclusion of the consideration of the Lords Amendments, withdraws immediately and normally reports its reasons at the same sitting.[14] These reasons, normally very brief, are taken as agreed to by the House and communicated by message to the Lords.[15] If, a Lords Amendment is amended or if an amendment has been made to the bill in lieu of the amendment which has been disagreed to, or if words restored to the bill are amended, no reason for disagreement is offered and a committee is not appointed.[16]

---

1 CJ (1919) 246.
2 CJ (1934–35) 324; ibid (1947–48) 359; ibid (1956–57) 253; ibid (1967–68) 340.
3 Eg CJ (1985–86) 593, 604.
4 CJ (1981–82) 458.
5 Eg CJ (1985–86) 529, 530.
6 Eg CJ (1984–85) 543.
7 CJ (1881) 445, 448, 449, 452, 453; ibid (1917–18) 310; ibid (1920) 509, 512, 513; ibid (1930–31) 382, 383; ibid (1966–67) 591; ibid (1972–73) 482.
8 CJ (1937–38) 346; ibid (1966–67) 522, 541.
9 CJ (1930–31) 384; ibid (1937–38) 346.
10 CJ (1930–31) 382.
11 CJ (1920) 512, 514.
12 CJ (1890–91) 510; ibid (1937–38) 343.
13 Eg CJ (1984–85) 512. For an order which restricted debate on all such motions for the remainder of a session, see CJ (1975–76) 619.
14 For instances when the committee reported its reasons to the House at a subsequent sitting, see CJ (1967–68) 313; ibid (1975–76) 626.
15 CJ (1852–53) 808, 809; ibid (1932–33) 277, 278; ibid (1937–38) 348; ibid (1953–54) 213; ibid (1955–56) 373.
16 Eg CJ (1985–86) 596–597.

Message to the Lords. In the case where a Lords Amendment has been disagreed to with no alternative proposal, a message is sent to the Lords to communicate the reason for disagreement, together with the bill and the Amendment. If any amendments have been made in respect of other Lords Amendments to the bill, or if consequential amendments or amendments in lieu of amendments disagreed to have also been made to the bill, they are sent with the message communicating the reason and the bill. In the case where amendments of these types are put forward and no original amendment is disagreed to, the bill is returned to the Lords with the fresh proposals accompanied only by a message desiring concurrence.

Bill returned to Lords. The bill having been returned to the Lords, that House has now to consider—

(1) any Commons reason for disagreeing to a Lords Amendment;
(2) any Commons Amendments to or in lieu of a Lords Amendment;
(3) any consequential amendments made to the bill by the Commons.

In regard to (1) the Lords may—[1]

(a) not insist on their amendment, in which case agreement is reached;
(b) not insist on their amendment but propose an amendment in lieu;[2]
(c) insist on their amendment and give a reason.[3]

In regard to (2), the Lords may—[4]

(a) agree to the Commons Amendment, in which case agreement is reached;
(b) disagree to the Commons Amendments and give a reason;[5]
(c) propose further amendments[6] to or in lieu of the Commons Amendment or make a consequential amendment to the bill.[7]

The same courses are open to the Lords in (3) as in (2).

The bill is then returned to the Commons with a message, in the case of disagreement communicating the reason or in the case of alternative proposals once more desiring concurrence.

When the Lords do not insist on their amendment or agree without amendment to the amendments now proposed by the Commons, a message is sent to that effect and the bill proceeds to Royal Assent.[8]

Further proceedings in Commons. On a message being received in the Commons which shows that agreement has not been reached, an order is made according to the facts of the case for the consideration of (for example):

(1) the Lords reason for insisting upon their amendment;[9]

---

1 See eg Education Reform Bill 1988 and Local Government Finance Bill 1988, HL Deb (1987–88) 500, cc 10–50; ibid cc 153–191; Health and Medicines Bill 1988, ibid 501, cc 541–590.
2 Eg CJ (1985–86) 587.
3 Eg CJ (1985–86) 599.
4 See fn 1 above.
5 Eg CJ (1983–84) 550.
6 Ibid.
7 See fn 2 above.
8 Eg CJ (1985–86) 534.
9 CJ (1881) 459; ibid (1917–18) 314; ibid (1919) 167.

(2) the Lords reason for disagreeing to the Commons Amendment to the Lords Amendment;[1]
(3) the Lords Amendment to the Commons Amendment to the Lords Amendment,[2] or to the Commons Amendment proposed in lieu of the Lords Amendment;[3]
(4) the amendment which the Lords have made to the bill in lieu of their amendment disagreed to by the Commons.[4]

The consideration may be taken forthwith[5] or appointed for a future day, in which case the reasons and/or amendments are normally ordered to be printed.[6]

(1) Lords reason for insisting upon their Amendment. Upon consideration of the Lords reason for insisting upon their amendment disagreed to by the Commons, the latter may not insist upon their disagreement to the Lords Amendment, and thus agreement between the Houses is reached.[7] If, however, the Commons insist upon their disagreement, without offering alternative proposals, the bill would normally be lost.[8]

(2) Lords reason for disagreeing to Commons Amendment to Lords Amendment. On considering the Lords reason for disagreeing to an amendment which the Commons have made to a Lords Amendment, the Commons can amend the bill in lieu of their amendment to the Lords Amendment disagreed to by the Lords[9] or may insist upon their amendment,[10] or not insist upon it.[11]

(3) Lords Amendment to Commons Amendment to Lords Amendment or to Commons Amendment in lieu. The Commons may further amend the Lords Amendment,[12] or may disagree thereto and communicate a reason, or may agree to it.[13]

(4) Lords Amendment to the bill in lieu of Lords Amendment disagreed to by the Commons. In the same way as in (3) above, the Commons may amend the Lords Amendment, or may disagree thereto and communicate a reason,[14] or may agree to it.[15]

In order to secure agreement and save the bill, every effort at compromise is usually made, and this interchange of amendments, as has been already stated, can be carried still further. Usually, however, the proceedings do not go beyond this stage, and one House or the other waives its disagreement, or takes a step which results in the bill being lost.

---

1 CJ (1920) 514; ibid (1975–76) 636.
2 CJ (1881) 459; ibid (1917–18) 314; ibid (1920) 514.
3 CJ (1983–84) 609.
4 CJ (1917–18) 314; ibid (1937–38) 361; ibid (1975–76) 549, 636, 640, 651.
5 CJ (1917–18) 314.
6 CJ (1985–86) 599.
7 CJ (1919) 172, 422; ibid (1930–31) 392; ibid (1947–48) 373.
8 CJ (1906) 509; ibid (1912–13) 553.
9 CJ (1929–30) 504.
10 CJ (1917–18) 315; ibid (1983–84) 610.
11 CJ (1929–30) 504; ibid (1975–76) 652.
12 CJ (1917–18) 316.
13 CJ (1985–86) 600.
14 CJ (1929–30) 504; ibid (1975–76) 652–653.
15 CJ (1985–86) 600.

The chain of events by which a bill originating in the Commons and amended by the Lords would normally be lost may be shown as follows:

the Commons disagree to the amendment with a reason; and
the Lords insist on their amendment with a reason, and
the Commons insist on their disagreement to the amendment, or take no action.

Thus each House has one opportunity of drawing back from the position which it has taken up, unless it offers alternative proposals. It must be remembered, however, that there is no binding rule of order which governs these proceedings in either House, and, if there is a desire to save a bill, some variation in the proceedings may be devised in order to effect this object.[1]

Bill originating in the Lords

It is not necessary to describe at length the further stages of a bill originating in the Lords, which has been amended by the Commons; for, as has been observed above, the proceedings match those of a Commons bill amended in the Lords. In the Lords a committee to draw up reasons is appointed in the same circumstances, *mutatis mutandis*, as in the Commons. The motion for the appointment of the committee is not however formally moved in the House but is recorded in the Minutes of Proceedings. The committee ordinarily consists of the proposer of the disagreement and one of his supporters, together with the Lord Chancellor or the Lord in charge of the bill. The committee immediately withdraws and agrees upon the reasons, which are reported to the House by means of an entry in the Minutes.

The Lords may—

(1) agree to the Commons Amendments;[2]
(2) agree to the Commons Amendments with amendments,[3] and make consequential amendments to the bill;[4]
(3) disagree to the Commons Amendments, with a reason;[5]
(4) disagree to the Commons Amendments but propose amendments in lieu thereof.[6]

When the bill is returned to the Commons the latter may—

(1) insist on their amendments with a reason, or not insist;[7] or
(2) agree to any further amendments which the Lords have made;[8] or
(3) amend the bill in lieu of their amendment disagreed to by the Lords.[9]

1 See eg CJ (1907) 453; ibid (1948–49) 401–410; ibid (1983–84) 508, 550, 609, 625.
2 CJ (1985–86) 186 etc; sometimes with consequential amendments to the bill, CJ (1928) 286; ibid (1952–53) 291; LJ (1979–80) 803; CJ (1985–86) 591; LJ (1985–86) 720.
3 CJ (1922) 324; ibid (1933–34) 299; ibid (1950) 229; LJ (1972–73) 664; CJ (1980–81) 503; LJ (1980–81) 881.
4 CJ (1906) 475; ibid (1933–34) 299; LJ (1972–73) 502; CJ (1980–81) 520; LJ (1980–81) 881.
5 CJ (1906) 475; ibid (1922) 324; LJ (1972–73) 502; CJ (1980–81) 503; LJ (1980–81) 847.
6 CJ (1906) 475; ibid (1922) 324; ibid (1931–32) 162; LJ (1972–73) 664; CJ (1984–85) 610; LJ (1984–85) 575.
7 Eg CJ (1980–81) 524.
8 Eg CJ (1984–85) 640.
9 CJ (1922) 325.

To this last amendment the Lords may agree.[1]

3. GENERAL MATTER RELATING TO THE PASSING OF PUBLIC BILLS

PROCEEDINGS ON HYBRID BILLS

Public bills to which the Standing Orders relating to private business apply[2] are subject in the House of Commons to certain proceedings additional to the normal stages in the passing of public bills. The initial examination of such bills in the House of Lords has already been described on p 444.

The Speaker has defined a hybrid bill as 'a public bill which affects a particular private interest in a manner different from the private interest of other persons or bodies of the same category or class'.[3] It is rare for public bills to be objected to on the ground that they ought to have been private bills (see pp 807–808), but it is not uncommon for objection to be taken that they ought to be treated as hybrid bills and ought to be referred accordingly to the Examiners under the procedure described below.

As such objections of their nature arise from particular cases it is not easy to describe generally the ground on which such objections have been sustained or over-ruled. A bill has not been regarded as hybrid if all the persons or bodies affected by it, and no others, belong to a category or class germane to the subject matter of the bill[4] and it is not the practice to treat as hybrid, bills dealing with matters of public policy whereby private rights over large areas or of a whole class are affected. Thus the Railways Bill in 1921[5] (which amalgamated the main existing railways companies with larger companies), the Electricity (Supply) Bills of 1926 and 1934–35[6] and the Iron and Steel Bill of 1948–49[7] were all ruled to be matters of public policy and to treat alike the various classes of interests affected by the bills. A bill which sought to transfer compulsorily only certain canals to a central canal trust[8] and a bill in which one company was not proposed to be nationalised although it fulfilled the qualifying conditions[9] have been ruled to be hybrid.

A class must be defined by reference to criteria germane to the subject matter of the bill.[10] The subject of legislation may form a class of its own without necessarily rendering a bill *prima facie* hybrid. Thus bills providing, for example, either separately or exclusively for London or for the Port of

---

1 CJ (1922) 327.
2 For a consideration of the difference between public and private bills, see pp 793–808.
3 HC Deb (1962–63) 669, c 45.
4 HC Deb (1966–67) 732, cc 1221–1223; Certificate from the Examiners relating to the Aircraft and Shipbuilding Industries and Statement of Reasons therefor, HL 71 (1976–77) pp 11–12.
5 HC Deb (1921) 142, cc 42–44.
6 HC Deb (1926) 193, cc 1683–1689; HC Deb (1934) 295, cc 1021–1027.
7 HC Deb (1948–49) 458, cc 47–51. See also London Government Bill 1962–63 (HC Deb (1962–63) 669, cc 45–48); certain clauses of the Finance Bill 1966–67 (HC Deb (1966–67) 729, cc 297–301).
8 CJ (1905) 201, 210, 214–216. Another bill was similarly introduced but with somewhat different provisions and to this standing orders were held not to apply. CJ (1905) 289, 327.
9 HC Deb (1975–76) 912, cc 299–305, 445.
10 HC Deb (1966–67) 732, cc 1215–1223; HC Deb (1987–88) 123, c 770

London Authority or for the City of London have, depending on their subject matter, been ruled not to be *prima facie* hybrid[1] (cf pp 795–796).

Reference to Examiners of Petitions for Private Bills

(a) Before second reading. If on examination in the Public Bill Office it appears that the Standing Orders relating to private business may be applicable to a public bill[2] notice of this circumstance is sent from the Public Bill Office to the Member in charge of the bill, and the Examiners of Petitions for Private Bills (see pp 811–812) are ordered by the House to examine the bill with respect to the applicability thereto of those Standing Orders (Standing Order No 59). The order for examination does not supersede the order for the second reading of the bill, which remains on the notice paper, with a memorandum 'to be reported upon by the Examiners' in brackets after the title of the bill; but the second reading cannot be moved until the report of the Examiners has been received.[3] Pending that report the bill is described as *'prima facie* hybrid'.[4] An order for the examination of a bill before second reading has been discharged in the case of a bill which was reintroduced under the Parliament Acts 1911 and 1949, following its rejection by the Lords in the previous Session.[5]

In the case of a bill referred to them as *prima facie* hybrid the Examiners examine the bill as a whole, including the possible application of the 'Wharncliffe Orders' (see pp 865–866 and Standing Order 224).[6]

Bills to which the standing orders do not apply. If the Examiners report that none of the standing orders, compliance with which, in the case of a private bill, would have to be proved before them, is applicable to the bill, the note 'to be reported upon by the Examiners' is removed from the notice paper and the bill proceeds on its course as an ordinary public bill.

Bills which have not complied with the standing orders. If the Examiners report that the standing orders applicable to the bill have not been complied with, the report is referred to the Standing Orders Committee (see p 819); the order of the day relating to the bill remains on the paper, with a note that the bill is to be reported on by the Standing Orders Committee. No further action can be taken on the bill in the House until the report is received.[7] If the Standing Orders Committee reports that the standing orders ought not

---

1 See eg London Government Bill 1962–63 and the special exceptions therein for the City; HC Deb (1983–84) 60, cc 1150–1151; ibid (1986–87) 108, c 37.
2 Eg Museum of London Bill, CJ (1985–86) 10; Channel Tunnel Bill; ibid 310.
3 Parl Deb (1886) 306, c 425; HC Deb (1985–86) 94, c 584. When the Examiners have reported compliance with Standing Orders on the day on which second reading was proceeded with, the fact that they had so reported was announced to the House from the Chair, HC Deb (1986–87) 106, c 667.
4 When a bill was ruled to be *prima facie* hybrid only after it passed its committee stage, a motion to dispense with Standing Orders was agreed to and a subsequent motion to refer the bill to a Select Committee was negatived, HC Deb (1975–76) 912, c 445; CJ (1975–76) 355, 359, 416.
5 CJ (1976–77) 19.
6 Cf CJ (1945–46) 55 (Bank of England Bill).
7 For the reference to the Standing Orders Committee of a petition against dispensing with Standing Orders, notwithstanding that the petitioners had not presented a memorial to the Examiners as required by SO 107A, see CJ (1985–86) 345.

to be dispensed with, the order of the day for the second reading of the bill is read and discharged, after which the bill is usually withdrawn.[1]

Bills in respect of which the standing orders have been dispensed with. If the Standing Orders Committee reports that the standing orders should be dispensed with, the note 'to be reported upon by the Standing Orders Committee' is removed from the notice paper, and the second reading of the bill may be moved in the ordinary way.

(b) After committee stage. The Examiners of Petitions for Private Bills may be ordered by the House to examine public bills to determine whether the standing orders relating to private business are applicable to them at other stages as well as before second reading. Thus when a hybrid bill was amended in a standing committee to an extent which, if it had been a private bill, would have required a petition for additional provision, the bill was referred to the Examiners on a motion moved by a member of the Government.[2] When the Lords (as second House) similarly widened the scope of a hybrid bill, they communicated to the Commons that they had referred the amendments concerned to the Examiners;[3] and on a motion moved by a member of the Government the amendments set out in the Lords message were referred to the Examiners.[4]

Hybrid bills originating in House of Lords. Certain preliminary proceedings on a hybrid bill which originates and is pending in the House of Lords are regulated, so far as the House of Commons is concerned, by Standing Order 224, under which the Examiners are directed to report to the House of Commons whether any of the standing orders of that House relating to private business are applicable to the bill, and, if so, whether or not they have been complied with.[5] If the Examiners report that the standing orders are applicable and have not been complied with, notwithstanding that the bill has not yet been introduced into the House of Commons, the report is forthwith referred to the Standing Orders Committee, which is empowered to report to the House whether such standing orders ought or ought not to be dispensed with (see Standing Order 104).

Committal of hybrid bills. A hybrid bill, after being read a second time, is committed to a select committee (see p 501). The committal motion usually provides for the members of the Committee to be nominated partly by the House and partly by the Committee of Selection.[6] But hybrid bills have been committed to committees of three[7] members and of nine[8] members

---

1 SO No 59. Military Manoeuvres Bill 1900; Canals Bill 1905; Bank of England (Nationalisation) Bill 1926 (this bill was not withdrawn, CJ (1926) 77). For a case where the Standing Orders Committee reported that they declined to reach a decision, and the House ordered Standing Orders to be dispensed with, see CJ (1985–86) 371, 386. For a case where (at a later stage of a bill) the House ordered dispensation with Standing Orders notwithstanding that the Committee had recommended that they be not dispensed with, see Votes and Proceedings (1987–88) 21 July 1987.
2 CJ (1957–58) 147.
3 Votes and Proceedings (1986–87) 7 May 1987.
4 Votes and Proceedings (1987–88) 8 July 1987.
5 CJ (1934–35) 67; ibid (1936–37) 70; ibid (1963–64) 61; ibid (1937–38) 163, 193, 241; ibid (1983–84) 193.
6 Eg CJ (1985–86) 37.
7 Dean Forest Bill 1904, CJ (1904) 220.
8 Channel Tunnel Bill, CJ (1985–86) 397. When the proceedings on the Bill were suspended at the end of the session, the House ordered that the Bill should be committed to a committee consisting of the same Members in the following session, ibid 600.

nominated entirely by the Committee of Selection. Nominations to the Select Committee are usually made only after petitions have been deposited against the Bill.

Hybrid bills have also been committed to joint committees,[1] the Commons' Members being nominated, as a rule, by the Committee of Selection. Hybrid bills have also been committed to select committees on private bills,[2] or a joint committee on private bills.[3] The House has occasionally committed to select committees bills on which the Examiners have reported that no standing orders are applicable[4] and bills which have not even been referred to the Examiners,[5] and referred petitions to the select committees as though the bills had been hybrid.

An order is made by the House that any petitions praying to be heard against the bill deposited in the Private Bill Office not later than a certain number of days after the day the order is made are to stand referred to the committee, but that if no such petitions are deposited, or if all such petitions are withdrawn before the meeting of the committee, the order for the committal of the bill to a select committee is to be discharged and the bill committed to a Committee of the whole House or, more usually, to a standing committee; that any petitioner is, subject to certain conditions, to be entitled to be heard by himself, his counsel or agents upon his petition, and the Member in charge of the bill is to be entitled to be heard by his counsel or agents in favour of the bill against such petition.[6]

Unless the order expressly provides that petitions against the bill may be deposited in the Private Bill Office they must be presented to the House as public petitions and must comply with the rules and orders of the House relating to public petitions (see p 754).

Petitions against alterations in a hybrid bill are regularly referred by the House to the committee,[7] and a public petition relating to a bill has been so referred.[8]

---

1 London Water Bill 1902; Port of London Bills 1903 and 1908 (Members nominated by the House); Ouse Drainage Bill 1927; Doncaster Area Drainage Bills 1929 and 1933; Public Offices (Sites) Amendment Bill 1931; London Passenger Transport Bill 1931; Roosevelt Memorial Bill 1946.

2 Metropolis Water Supply Bill and Metropolitan Water Companies (Charges) Bill 1891, to the Committee on the London Water Commission Bill. See also CJ (1860) 176, 187, 231.

3 Doncaster Area Drainage Bill 1929, to the Joint Committee on Railways (Air Transport) Bills.

4 Dublin Barracks Bill 1892; Osborne Estate Bill 1902.

5 Brine Pumping (Compensation for Subsidence) Bill 1891; Barge Owners, etc. Liability Bill 1892; Merchant Shipping (Tonnage Deduction for Propelling Power) Bill 1907.

6 This order follows the recommendations of the Select Committee on Hybrid Bills (Procedure in Committee) (HC 191 (1947–48)), which was agreed to by the House subject to the modification that the bill could also, if unopposed, be committed to a Standing Committee. See Sugar Bill 1955, CJ (1955–56) 120, 125, for a bill committed to a standing committee. For a bill committed to a Committee of the whole House, see Commonwealth Telegraphs Bill, CJ (1948–49) 165, 174. Cf also Milford Haven Conservancy Bill, CJ (1957–58) 39, 41. For examples of earlier orders see those on North Killingholme (Admiralty Pier) Bill 1931; Bethlem Hospital (Amendment) Bill [Lords] 1931; Doncaster Area Drainage Bill 1933; Welsh Church (Amendment) Bill [Lords] 1938; Bank of England Bill 1945, etc.

7 Eg CJ (1985–86) 398.

8 CJ (1960–61) 122.

If no petitions are deposited or if all deposited petitions are withdrawn, at the end of the period specified in the order for committal a further order is made as a matter of course to discharge the committal, and the bill stands committed to a Committee of the whole House or to a standing committee accordingly.[1] When committees have determined that none of the petitioners should be heard since they had no *locus standi* (see below) they have made Special Reports to the effect that they have not considered the provisions of the bills concerned and the bills have been recommitted to a Committee of the whole House[2] or to a standing committee.[3]

Proceedings in committee. The proceedings in a select committee on a hybrid bill are conducted in the main in the same manner as those in a committee on a private bill (see pp 892 ff) and not those in a select committee on a public bill (see p 653). Substantial modifications were, however, recommended by the Select Committee on Hybrid Bills (Procedure in Committee) and were approved by the House on 14 February 1949.[4] As a result, unless the House has given any instruction or indication to the contrary, the second reading is considered to remove from the promoters the onus of proving the expediency of the bill. The petitioner, therefore, opens to the committee, calling such evidence as he wishes. If the committee determines that there is a case to answer, the promoters then answer the petitioner's case, and if they call evidence this entitles the petitioner to a right of reply. The procedure is, however, subject to the will of the committee and the requirements imposed by each bill.[5] This procedure is not affected by the presence or absence of a preamble to the bill.

Chairmen of select committees on hybrid bills have exercised only a casting vote (and not, as in a private bill committee, an original vote).[6]

All opponents who have presented petitions within the time allowed by the order of the House,[7] and who have a *locus standi* according to the rules and usage of Parliament, are entitled to be heard, but may not argue on matters which cannot give them a *locus standi*. If the *locus standi* of a petitioner is objected to, it is decided by the committee, upon whom the decisions of the Court of Referees (see chapter 35) are binding.[8] The committee also decides the limits of the *locus standi* of each petitioner.[9]

Witnesses before a committee on a hybrid bill are usually, though not always,[10] examined on oath.

When the case for the petitioners has been concluded and the promoters heard in reply, the committee goes through the clauses of the bill and reports it with or without amendments.[11]

---

1 Eg CJ (1985–86) 52.
2 Charlwood and Horley Bill, CJ (1973–74) 67.
3 Park Lane Improvement Bill, CJ (1957–58) 121, 135; Transport (London) Bill, CJ (1968–69) 148, 152.
4 HC Deb (1948–49) 461, cc 791–835.
5 HC 191 (1947–48), para 34.
6 HC 34, (1986–87) p clviii.
7 If an opponent fails to present a petition in due time, he cannot be heard unless the order of the House is suspended in his favour by the House (CJ (1912–13) 238.)
8 See eg Proc. of Select Committee on the Festival Pleasure Gardens Bill 1951–52 (HC 64 (1951–52)).
9 HC 191 (1947–48), paras 20–25.
10 See proceedings of the Select Committee on the Mercantile Marine (Memorial) Bill, HC 57 (1927) p iv.
11 Parliament Square (Improvements) Bill, CJ (1948–49) 420; in this case the committee obtained leave to report minutes of speeches delivered by counsel.

If the House passes a suitable instruction, amendments may be made in committee which, if the bill were a private bill, would require a petition for additional provision.[1] Such amendments make necessary, before the consideration stage of the bill, further reference to the Examiners of Petitions for Private Bills (see pp 493 and 920–921).

When a joint committee has not considered it expedient to proceed further with a hybrid bill, it has reported the bill without amendment to the House and made a special report to that effect.[2]

If the committee wishes to express its views upon the matters dealt with in the bill, it makes a special report to the House.

Similarly, if a committee on a hybrid bill is informed that it is not intended to proceed with the bill, it reports the fact to the House.[3]

Fees are charged to opponents of a hybrid bill as if it were a private bill.[4] Fees are also charged in like manner to promoters, except in the case of bills introduced by the Government, but these fees are only payable in respect of those proceedings which are of a character analogous to those on a private bill.

The minutes of the evidence taken before a committee on a hybrid bill are printed by order, and at the expense, of the House. A shorthand note is taken, and half the cost is borne by the promoters and the other half by the House. Transcripts of the note may be obtained from the promoters' agents, who are entitled to charge for their provision to persons other than Members. Committees are normally given power to report the minutes of evidence from day to day, and on occasion the minutes have been printed from day to day[5] before being reissued as a single publication with the committee's report.

Report of bill and remaining stages. A hybrid bill reported from a select committee or a joint committee is customarily re-committed to a Committee of the whole House, but the order is frequently discharged and the bill is then re-committed to a standing committee.[6] Thenceforward proceedings upon it are the same as upon other public bills.

PRACTICE WITH REGARD TO BILLS REJECTED

When a bill has been rejected, or lost through disagreement, it should not, according to the practice of Parliament, be reintroduced in the same session (see also pp 61, 326, 468–470). This follows from the general rule that the same question should not be twice offered.

---

1 For instructions empowering committees to consider such amendments, see CJ (1957–58) 91, and (1985–86) 512.
2 CJ (1927) 321.
3 CJ (1890–91) 398.
4 See Table of Fees in Standing Orders (Private Business) and p 835.
5 Channel Tunnel Bill (CJ (1985–86) 444 and subsequent days).
6 Eg Votes and Proceedings (1987–88) 15 December 1987 and 12 January 1988.

In the case of bills which have passed one House and been rejected by the other the rule is not applied so rigidly as to prevent a portion at any rate of a rejected bill being introduced again as a new bill.

The principle was stated by the Lords on 17 May 1606, on the occasion of a second Purveyors Bill being brought from the Commons after the Lords had rejected the first: 'When a bill hath been brought into the House, proceeded withall, and rejected, another bill of the same argument and matter may not be renewed and begun again in the same House, and in the same session, where the former bill was begun; but if a bill begun in one of the Houses, and there allowed and passed, be sent unto the other House, although it be there, upon reading thereof, disliked and refused; nevertheless if the matter be thought fit to be proceeded withall, and that it may be done better by a new bill, it is holden agreeable to the order of the Parliament, that a new bill of the same matter may be drawn and begun again in that House, whereunto it was sent as aforesaid; and if a bill begun in either of the Houses, and committed, be brought in by the committees, and thought fit, before the Third Reading, to be renewed, in respect that the matter may better proceed by a new bill, it is likewise holden agreeable to good order, in such case, to draw a new bill, and to bring it unto the House'.[1]

It was also declared in a protest, signed by seven Lords on 23 February 1692 in reference to the Poll Bill, in which a proviso contained the substance of a bill which had dropped in the same session, that a bill 'having not passed through the two Houses, by reason of their disagreement upon some amendments offered by the Lords to the said bill, ought not, by the known and constant methods of proceedings, to be brought in again in the same session'. The Lords, nevertheless, agreed to that bill, but with a special entry, declaring that they would not hereafter admit, upon any occasion whatsoever, of a proceeding so contrary to the rules and methods of Parliament.[2]

In the Commons it was agreed for a rule on 1 June 1610 that 'no bill of the same substance be brought in the same session'.[3]

Application of principle. If in the second House the second or third reading of a bill is deferred for three or six months, or if a bill is rejected, it cannot be brought from the first House a second time in the same session. However, when part of a bill has been omitted by the Lords, and the Commons have agreed to such amendment, the part so omitted has been renewed in the same session in the form of a separate bill,[4] and a bill deferred for six months by the Lords has nevertheless been incorporated by way of amendment into another bill sent from the Commons.[5]

Proceedings in Lords with regard to bill laid aside by Commons. If a bill has been postponed or laid aside in the House of Commons, the Lords have sometimes appointed a committee to search the Journals of the Commons,

---

1 LJ (1578–1614) 435.
2 LJ (1691–96) 90.
3 CJ (1547–1628) 434.
4 CJ (1884–85) 317; Parl Deb (1884–85) 298, c 1590; CJ (1908) 384, 514.
5 CJ (1899) 386; ibid (1908) 500.

and may, if they think fit, introduce another bill and send it to the Commons.[1]

In more recent times, when bills have been laid aside in the Commons because they infringe the Commons' financial privilege, the Lords have introduced second bills without searching the Journals. The second bills, identical in wording with the first, have then to be taken formally through all their stages and sent to the Commons with the appropriate privilege amendments made.[2]

Prorogation to revive bills. Parliament has occasionally been prematurely prorogued to give an opportunity to revive bills whose passage was blocked by disageement between the two Houses. Thus Parliament was prorogued from 21 to 23 October 1689 in order to revive the Bill of Rights, concerning which a difference had arisen between the two Houses that was fatal to its progress;[3] in 1707, for a week, in order to permit the revival of a bill dealing with fraudulent commerce with Scotland, which had been rejected by the Lords;[4] and in 1831, from 20 October to 6 December, in order to bring in the third Reform Bill.[5]

Proposals for suspending or resuming bills

Proposals have been made for a provision, either by statute or by standing orders, for the suspension of public bills from one session to another, or for resuming proceedings upon such bills, notwithstanding a prorogation. These schemes have been discussed in Parliament and carefully considered by committees; but various considerations have restrained the legislature from departing from the rule that parliamentary proceedings are discontinued by a prorogation.[6] For the suspension of hybrid, private and provisional order bills, see p 928.

ENDORSEMENT OF BILLS

The official record of the decision of one House with respect to a bill passed, or to amendments made, by the other House is by endorsement of the bill in

1 LJ (1843) 590; ibid (1845) 505.
2 Guardianship and Maintenance of Infants (No 2) Bill, LJ (1950–51) 243; Trade Descriptions (No 2) Bill, LJ (1967–68) 147.
3 CJ (1688–93) 272.
4 Burnet ii, 467; 2 Coxe's Walpole 8; 2 Hatsell 127.
5 CJ (1830–31) 935.
6 Earl of Derby's Parliamentary Proceedings Adjournment Bill 1848, Parl Deb (1847–48) 98, c329, 981, 1255; ibid 99, c246; ibid 100, c131; Report of Commons Committee on Public Business, HC 644 (1847–48); Report of Lords Committee on Public Business, HL 95 (1861); Report of Commons Committee on Business of the House, HC 173 (1861); Marquess of Salisbury's Parliamentary Proceedings Bill 1869, Parl Deb (1868–69) 194, c588; ibid (1883) 279, c2; Report of Joint Committee on Despatch of Business in Parliament, HC 386 (1868–69); Reports of Commons Committees on Public Business, HC 268 (1878), and on Abridged Procedure on Partly Considered Bills, HC 298 (1890); Report of Joint Committee on Suspension of Bills, HC 105 (1928–29). The abortive Parliament (No 2) Bill 1969 proposed that a bill on which there was disagreement between the Houses could be carried over a prorogation or dissolution in order to secure its passage, HC Deb (1968–69) 777, c50. In Session 1919, a motion for the suspension of further proceedings on the War Emergency Laws (Continuance) Bill until the following session was withdrawn, CJ (1919) 428; HC Deb (1919) 123, c1291.

Norman French. Every bill is authenticated upon leaving the first House by the signature of the Clerk of that House. Thus, when a bill is passed by the Commons, the Clerk of the House[1] writes at the top of the first page 'Soit baillé aux Seigneurs', and signs the bill on the last page. When the Lords make amendments the bill is returned with the endorsement of the Clerk of the Parliaments 'A ceste bille avecque des amendemens les Seigneurs sont assentus'. When it is sent back with these amendments agreed to, the Clerk of the House of Commons writes, 'A ces amendemens les Communes sont assentus'. When amendments are disagreed to, a message is sent to the Lords stating the fact and communicating the reasons agreed to by the House for their disagreement and the bill is endorsed 'Ceste bille est remise aux Seigneurs avecque des raisons'.

Bills are communicated by the Lords to the Commons with similar endorsements, *mutatis mutandis*. If amendments made by the Lords are agreed to by the Commons, the latter return the bill with the message signifying their agreement. If amendments made by the Commons are agreed to by the Lords, the Lords send a message[2] but retain the bill for the Royal Assent (see below).

ROYAL ASSENT

When bills, either public or private, or measures, have been finally agreed to by both Houses, they only await the Royal Assent to be declared to Parliament to give them, as Lord Hale says, 'the complement and perfection of a law',[3] and from that sanction they cannot be legally withheld.[4]

When Royal Assent is wanted, the Lord Chancellor submits to the Sovereign a list of those bills which are ready for Royal Assent or which are likely to have passed by the time Royal Assent is to be declared. The list is prepared by the Clerk of the Parliaments.[5] An advance copy is sent to the Clerk of the Crown so that he may include those bills in the Letters Patent[6] by which the Sovereign is to signify the Royal Assent. Bills for granting aids and supplies to the Crown are placed first in the list, and are followed by public bills, provisional order bills, private bills and personal bills. Measures submitted for Royal Assent in pursuance of the provisions of the Church of England Assembly (Powers) Act 1919 are placed last.

Care is taken that all bills which are expected to have passed are included in the Letters Patent. Nevertheless a bill not named in the Letters Patent may unexpectedly pass during the period after the submission to the Sovereign and before the Royal Assent is declared to Parliament. Since there is no authority for withholding from inclusion in the Letters Patent any bill which

---

1 In his absence, the Clerk Assistant is authorized to endorse bills.
2 This message has been received by the Commons after the Royal Assent has been given to the bill, 2 Hatsell 339.
3 Hale, Jurisd. of Lords c 2.
4 See 2 Hatsell 339; LJ (1675–81) 756 (1681); Burnet ii, 274; Campbell, Lives iii, 354.
5 Bills awaiting Royal Assent remain in the custody of the Clerk of the Parliaments, with the exception that, when the Royal Assent is to be pronounced by commission (see below), bills for granting aids and supplies to the Crown are kept in the custody of the Clerk of the House of Commons and brought up by him at the reading of the commission.
6 The forms of Letters Patent to be used for signifying the Royal Assent are prescribed by rules made by Order in Council pursuant to the Crown Office Act 1887. These Letters Patent now have the wafer great seal embossed instead of the pendent wax seal.

has passed all its stages, a further submission by the Lord Chancellor to the Sovereign must then be made for the Royal Assent to be given to the additional bill and for its inclusion in the Letters Patent. Similarly, any bill which unexpectedly fails to pass before the declaration of Royal Assent is struck out of the Letters Patent. When the list of bills for Royal Assent is finally settled, the Clerk of the Parliaments signs it to certify the passage of the bills through both Houses, and sends it to the Lord Chancellor.

To avoid untimely submissions to the Sovereign, proceedings on third reading and on Lords Amendments have been postponed.

It is usual for the Royal Assent to be notified to each House sitting separately, by the Speaker of that House, in accordance with the Royal Assent Act 1967. But at the end of each session the five Lords who are appointed Commissioners by Letter Patent to prorogue Parliament are commanded by the same Letters Patent to declare the Royal Assent to both Houses together in the House of Lords.[1] The Sovereign retains the power to declare the Royal Assent in person in Parliament (see p 529).

Proceedings on Royal Assent

Royal Assent notified by the Speaker. Royal Assent is notified to each House, sitting separately, at a time convenient to each House during the course of the day's business by the Speaker of that House or, in his absence, by the person acting as Speaker. In the Commons Royal Assent may be notified by a Deputy Speaker, notwithstanding that the House has not been informed of the unavoidable absence of the Speaker.[2] The Speaker uses these words: 'I have to notify the House, in accordance with the Royal Assent Act 1967, that the Queen has signified her Royal Assent to the following Acts [and Measures]' (which he then lists). The Clerk of the Parliaments subsequently endorses the Acts with the customary Norman French formulae (see p 529); they are not spoken in either House.

In the Lords Royal Assent may be notified at any convenient break between two items of business or at the end of business, if necessary after an adjournment. The words used are the same as in the Commons.

In the Commons Royal Assent must be notified to the House itself, and not to a Committee of the whole House. It has been notified immediately after prayers, at the commencement of public business, between orders of the day, between speeches in a debate[3] and between amendments on the consideration stage of a bill.[4] The House on occasion[5] agrees to orders providing that the Speaker shall not adjourn the House until he has notified the Royal Assent to a bill or bills; and acting under such an order the Speaker has suspended a sitting after the completion of business until a relevant bill has been passed by the Lords.[6]

Royal Assent by Commission. Three or more of the Lords Commissioners, seated on a form between the Throne and the Woolsack in the House of Lords, command Black Rod to summon the Commons to hear the

1 When the Royal Assent is given by commission at times other than prorogation, three Lords Commissioners are appointed for this purpose.
2 Eg CJ (1975–76) 484.
3 HC Deb (1967–68) 765, c 2263.
4 CJ (1968–69) 261.
5 Eg CJ (1967–68) 133; ibid (1984–85) 340.
6 HC Deb (1967–68) 759, cc 1767, 1917; ibid (1971–72) 841, c 1454.

commission read. The Commons, with their Speaker, then come to the Bar of the Lords. The commission is read by the Reading Clerk. The short titles of the bills are read by the Clerk of the Crown and the Royal Assent to each in turn is pronounced by the Clerk of the Parliaments in Norman French.

A bill for granting aids and supplies to the Crown (see p 689), being carried up by the Clerk of the House of Commons, is handed to the Clerk of the Parliaments by the Speaker and receives the Royal Assent before all other bills. The Assent to such a bill is declared in the words 'La Reyne remercie ses bons sujets, accepte leur benevolence, et ainsi le veult'. For all other public, as also for private, Acts the formula is 'La Reyne le veult', and for personal Acts 'Soit fait comme il est désiré'.

The right to refuse the Royal Assent has not been exercised since 1707–08, when Queen Anne refused her Assent to a bill for settling the militia in Scotland. The form of words used to express this refusal was 'La Reyne se avisera'.[1]

Assent given by the Sovereign in person.   The Royal Assent has not been given in person since 12 August 1854.

When the Queen comes in person, the Clerk of the Parliaments waits upon Her Majesty in the robing room, before she enters the House, reads a list of the bills and receives her commands upon them.[2] After the Queen is seated on the Throne, the Clerk of the Crown reads the titles of the bills, and the Clerk of the Parliaments bows to the Throne, and then signifies Her Majesty's assent in the usual manner. The Queen, who has already given her commands, nods her assent.

Assent given in the Sovereign's absence from the realm.   In pursuance of the Regency Acts 1937, 1943 and 1953, Letters Patent for Royal Assent may now be signed by Counsellors of State appointed under these Acts.[3]

Report of Royal Assent in the House of Commons.   When the Commons have returned from the House of Lords to their own chamber, the Speaker reports that the Royal Assent has been given to certain Acts, and this is recorded in the Votes and Proceedings and Journal.

BILLS PASSED WITH UNUSUAL EXPEDITION

(1) In the House of Lords

The time required for the successive stages of a bill is regulated in part by Standing Order No 44, which provides that no two stages be taken in one day, and in part by the minimum recommended intervals between stages (see p 447).[4]

---

1 LJ (1705–09) 506. Cf LJ (1509–77) 162 (1540); ibid (1675–81) 394 (1678).
2 Mr Birch's evidence, HC 413 (1843) p 10.
3 LJ (1938–39) 227; ibid (1943–44) 173.
4 LJ (1976–77) 821.

Standing Order No 44 dispensed with. It frequently happens, however, that it is necessary for a bill to be passed with greater expedition than the observance of Standing Order No 44 would permit. It is then necessary for notice to be put on the order paper, usually in the name of the Leader of the House, of a motion to dispense with Standing Order No 44 for the purpose of taking the bill through its remaining stages on one day. Consolidated Fund bills are commonly taken through all their stages in one day. It is essential that notice of the proposed suspension of the standing order be given, since Standing Order No 83 provides that no motion shall be granted for dispensing with a standing order unless notice shall have been given in the order paper to consider the said motion.

Standing Order No 44 suspended. Frequently towards the close of a session or before a recess when the press of legislation is heavy, a motion is moved to suspend Standing Order No 44 for the remainder of the session,[1] or until the adjournment for the recess,[2] or for the remainder of the week[3] or for the next day[4].

Emergency bill passed through all stages in one day. On occasions of national emergency, a bill has been passed through all its stages in both Houses in a single day. In such cases, since notice of the suspension of Standing Order No 44 cannot be given, a special procedure, laid down by Standing Order No 83, is observed. Standing Orders Nos 44 and 83 are read at the Table by the Clerk of the Parliaments and a resolution is moved that it is essential for reasons of national security that the bill (or bills) should immediately be proceeded with and that the provisions of Standing Order No 44 should be dispensed with to enable the House to proceed that day with every stage of the bill (or bills) which it thinks necessary. Upon this motion being agreed to, any such bill may be passed through all its stages.

This procedure was adopted for a bill to suspend the Habeas Corpus Act in Ireland on 17 February 1866;[5] for the Explosive Substances Bill on 9 April 1883;[6] for the Postponement of Payments Bill on 3 August 1914;[7] for the Gold Standard (Amendment) Bill on 21 September 1931,[8] for a number of bills on 1 September 1939,[9] and for the Northern Ireland Bill on 23 February 1972.[10]

When a bill is to be taken through all its stages in one day in the Lords, on a day later than that on which it was introduced into the Commons, notice may be given of a motion to dispense with Standing Order No 44 'in the event of the bill being brought from the Commons'.[11]

---

1 LJ (1986–87) 369.
2 LJ (1985–86) 502.
3 LJ (1914–16) 18; ibid (1918) 230, 276; HL Deb (1918) 32, c 1.
4 LJ (1985–86) 84.
5 LJ (1866) 41.
6 LJ (1883) 76.
7 LJ (1914) 355.
8 LJ (1930–31) 365.
9 LJ (1938–39) 376, 377.
10 LJ (1971–72) 159.
11 Southern Rhodesia Bill, LJ (1965–66) 12; Commonwealth Immigrants Bill, LJ (1967–68) 170, when the motion was divided upon; Imprisonment (Temporary Provisions) Bill, LJ (1979–80) 1641.

Other procedural devices. On occasion a (No 2) bill, in identical form to a
bill before the Commons, has been introduced in the Lords.[1] Consideration
of such a bill has, by general agreement, enabled the proceedings on the
Commons bill to be abbreviated. Similar expedients, such as the presentation of the text of a Commons bill as a return to an order of the House,
have also been adopted.[2]

(2) In the House of Commons

In the ordinary progress of a bill the proceedings either follow from day to
day, or some days are allowed to intervene between each stage subsequent
to the first reading. It has already been observed that, in the House of
Commons, the report and third reading of a bill are usually taken on the
same day, and there are no rules in that House which forbid the taking of
several or all the stages of a bill at one sitting. Such a course is only an
occasional departure from the usage of Parliament, justified by the circumstances of the particular case. Acts of indemnity, for example, protecting
persons against the consequence of any breach of the law are often passed
through second reading and subsequent stages as being an urgent matter.[3]
On the other hand the Chair regularly deprecates the passing of a private
Member's bill through second reading and all remaining stages on a Friday.[4]
   When bills are considered in a Committee of the whole House immediately after the second reading, normally no question is proposed from the
Chair. But if objection to this course is signified, the Chair will propose the
question 'That the House will immediately resolve itself into a Committee
on the Bill'.[5] Bills committed immediately after second reading, and reported without amendment, have been read the third time,[6] or, if amended in
committee, have been considered forthwith and read the third time.[7] A bill
has been considered in committee immediately after the second reading,
and on being reported with amendments, has been ordered for consideration on a subsequent day,[8] or on being reported without amendment has
been ordered to be read the third time on the same[9] or a future[10] day.
Similarly a bill reported with amendments from a standing committee has
been considered on the same day.[11] Sometimes, where a bill has been
considered in committee immediately after the second reading, progress has
been reported, usually in response to objections to completing the com-

---

1 Commonwealth Immigrants Bill 1968 (LJ (1967–68) 164); Northern Ireland (Temporary
   Provisions) Bill 1972 (LJ (1971–72) 205); Community Land Bill 1975 (LJ (1974–75) 863).
2 Prices and Incomes Bill 1966 (LJ (1966–67) 165); Prices and Incomes (No 2) Bill 1967 (LJ
   (1966–67) 615); Community Land Bill 1975 (LJ (1974–75) 955).
3 Eg Niall Macpherson Indemnity Bill, CJ (1953–54) 197; Validation of Elections (No 3) Bill,
   ibid (1955–56) 129.
4 Eg HC Deb (1971–72) 835, c 1015; ibid (1987–88) 131, c 520.
5 CJ (1952–53) 126; HC Deb (1984–85) 82, c 423. For such a motion withdrawn and a future
   day named for a committee see CJ (1955–56) 88.
6 CJ (1908) 512; ibid (1914) 439, 446; ibid (1930–31) 74, 189; ibid (1931–32) 214; ibid (1967–68)
   332; ibid (1968–69) 378, 381; ibid (1973–74) 88; ibid (1976–77) 122; ibid (1983–84) 319–320.
7 Eg CJ (1914) 438, 446, 457, 460. See also HC Deb (1982–83) 42, cc 737, 766–768.
8 CJ (1914) 458; ibid (1919) 29; ibid (1920) 19.
9 Eg HC Deb (1984–85) 73, c 1386.
10 CJ (1958–59) 127; Votes and Proceedings (1987–88) 13 May 1988.
11 CJ (1982–83) 364, 366.

mittee stage in one sitting.[1] If it is desired to take on the same day the second reading and remaining stages of a bill for which a money resolution is necessary, a special procedure motion is required;[2] while on occasions the House has agreed to a motion dispensing with the requirement for a financial resolution in respect of a bill.[3] (For the rule with regard to bills imposing a financial charge introduced upon resolution, and the exceptions to it, see p 501.)

When it is desired to take forthwith the report stage of a bill which has been reported with amendments from a Committee of the whole House,[4] and objection is taken to that proceeding, a question for the consideration of the bill, as amended, has to be proposed.[5]

When a pressing emergency arises bills are passed through all their stages on the same day.[6] Normally the leave of the House is sought for such bills to be brought in.[7] Exceptionally, a bill has been presented under Standing Order No 58 after the House had agreed to a procedural motion enabling all stages of the bill (as well as a money resolution) to be proceeded with forthwith in the event of the bill being presented.[8] A bill was on occasion ordered to be brought in upon a resolution reported pursuant to an order of the House on the same day as that on which it was considered in committee, and was passed through all its stages at the one sitting.[9]

Again, a bill has been brought from the Lords, passed through all stages, and returned to the Lords on the same day.[10] Bills have also been passed through both Houses,[11] and received the Royal Assent,[12] on the same day. Leave has been given to bring in a bill, which has then passed through all its stages in both Houses and received the Royal Assent on the same day.[13]

PROCEDURE UNDER THE PARLIAMENT ACTS 1911 AND 1949

Conditions are laid down by the Parliament Act 1911, as amended by the Parliament Act 1949, under which bills which have passed the House of

---

1 HC Deb (1917) 90, c 752, 764; ibid (1918) 101, c 950; ibid (1918) 108, c 276; ibid (1919) 114, c 187; ibid (1919) 117, cc 1261, 2142; ibid (1970–71) 811, cc 1158–1159; Decisions: 2637.
2 Eg CJ (1955–56) 43; ibid (1964–65) 423; ibid (1979–80) 806. See also p 535.
3 CJ (1938–39) 402, 405; ibid (1965–66) 11.
4 Or as amended in the standing committee, with further amendments on recommittal, CJ (1982–83) 347.
5 Motions have been withdrawn, CJ (1918) 181; HC Deb (1918) 108, c 2091; CJ (1955–56) 58; HC Deb (1955–56) 543, cc 1360–1363; CJ (1959–60) 84; HC Deb (1959–60) 616, cc 285–288; or agreed to after closure, CJ (1968–69) 59.
6 CJ (1843) 491, 492; ibid (1847–48) 770; ibid (1852–53) 21, 251, 823, 836; ibid (1914) 427, 435, 437, 461; ibid (1914–16) 137, 257; ibid (1920) 504; ibid (1931–32) 164; ibid (1938–39) 402, 405; ibid (1939–40) 138.
7 CJ (1971–72) 171; ibid (1973–74) 156.
8 CJ (1979–80) 806.
9 CJ (1919) 422; the reference is to a bill founded according to the practice of the time on a Money Resolution of a Committee of the whole House (cf p 461).
10 CJ (1849) 475, 477.
11 CJ (1802–03) 645, 646, 647; ibid (1883) 126, 128; LJ (1883) 76; CJ (1914) 427; LJ (1914) 377; CJ (1914) 464; LJ (1914) 420.
12 CJ (1741–45) 636–639; ibid (1796–97) 555, 557, 558; ibid (1866) 87, 88, 89; ibid (1914) 407, etc; ibid (1930–31) 423, 424, 425; ibid (1936–37) 57, 58; ibid (1938–39) 410; ibid (1965–66) 11, 12 (the latter two bills were presented in the House of Commons on the previous sitting day); LJ (1971–72) 159.
13 CJ (1971–72) 171; LJ (1971–72) 159.

Commons may acquire the force of law without passing the House of Lords. The Parliament Acts do not apply to (a) bills originating in the House of Lords; (b) bills to extend the maximum duration of Parliament beyond five years; (c) provisional order bills; (d) private bills; (e) delegated legislation. Public bills are divided for the purposes of the Act into 'money bills' as defined by the Act, and other public bills. The procedure with regard to 'money bills' is described in chapter 30.

Bills other than money bills

Proceedings on the bill. In the case of public bills, other than money bills within the meaning of section 1 of the Act of 1911, it is provided that a bill which is passed by the House of Commons in two successive sessions (whether of the same Parliament or not), and which, having been sent up to the House of Lords at least one month before the end of the session, is rejected by the House of Lords in each of those sessions, shall, on its rejection for the second time by the House of Lords, unless the House of Commons direct to the contrary, be presented to Her Majesty and become an Act of Parliament on the Royal Assent being signified to it.[1] One year must elapse between the second reading of the bill in the House of Commons in the first of these sessions and its passing in the House of Commons in the second session. No Act has been passed under the Parliament Act procedure since the 1949 Act itself, but two bills have been introduced in a second session with a view to it.[2]

By section 2 (3) of the Act of 1911 a bill is deemed to be rejected by the House of Lords if it is not passed by that House either without amendment or with such amendments only as may be agreed to by both Houses.

Limits of changes of bill in succeeding session. A bill is deemed to be the same bill as the bill sent up to the House of Lords in the preceding session if, when it is sent up to the House of Lords, it is identical with the former bill or contains only such alterations as are certified by the Speaker to be necessary owing to the time which has elapsed since the date of the former bill,[3] or to represent any amendments which have been made by the House of Lords in the former bill in the preceding session.[4] Commons amendments made in lieu of Lords amendments and Commons amendments made to Lords amendments, if agreed to by the Lords in the preceding session, have been held to represent amendments made by the Lords for the purposes of the

---

1 Government of Ireland Act 1914, and Welsh Church Act 1914, LJ (1914) 423; CJ (1914) 466; Parliament Act 1949, LJ (1948–49) 518; CJ (1948–49) 445. For a conference on the Parliament Bill 1947, see Cmd 7380 (1948).
2 Both bills were eventually agreed to by the Lords in the second session, see Trade Union and Labour Relations Bill (1975–76); Aircraft and Shipbuilding Industries Bill (1976–77). With the exceptions of the Government of Ireland Act 1914 and the Welsh Church Act 1914, the only other instance since 1911 of a bill introduced in a second session with a view to using the Parliament Act procedure was the Temperance (Scotland) Bill 1913. Since this bill was agreed to by the Lords in the second session, there was no need to resort to the Parliament Act.
3 CJ (1913) 235; ibid (1914) 226, 244, 264; ibid (1947–48) 410.
4 CJ (1913) 244; ibid (1975–76) 114, 118; ibid (1976–77) 34.

Parliament Acts and certified accordingly.[1] If any of the amendments made by the Lords in the second session are agreed to by the Commons they are inserted in the bill as presented for the Royal Assent and are certified by the Speaker as having been so made and agreed to.

Suggestion of amendments by the Commons.   Provision is also made by which the House of Commons may, on the passage of such a bill through that House in the second session, suggest further amendments without inserting them in the bill.[2] Such amendments must be suggested before the third reading of the bill, each suggested amendment being moved as a separate resolution. The Speaker has ruled that suggested amendments cannot be moved without notice.[3] If agreed to, they are sent to the House of Lords with the bill after it has passed the House of Commons.[4] Any such suggested amendments are to be considered by the House of Lords, and, if agreed to by that House, are to be treated as amendments made by the House of Lords and agreed to by the House of Commons.[5] It is also provided that the exercise of this power by the House of Commons shall not prejudice the position of the bill in the event of its rejection by the House of Lords.

Enacting words.   Under section 4 of the Act of 1911, as amended by the Act of 1949, a form of enacting words is prescribed for use in the case of a bill passed under the provisions of the Acts.[6]

Speaker's certificate.   A bill other than a money bill when presented to Her Majesty for assent pursuant to section 2 of the Act of 1911 must be endorsed with the certificate of the Speaker signed by him that the provisions of the section have been duly complied with.[7] When the Royal Assent has been signified by commission (see p 528) to such bills at the same time as to bills which have been agreed upon by both Houses, a separate commission has been issued for the purpose.[8]

SUBSIDIARY POINTS IN CONNECTION WITH LEGISLATIVE PROCEDURE

Printing and promulgation of statutes

As soon as a public bill has received the Royal Assent a print of the Act in the form in which it was finally passed is prepared in the Public Bill Office of the House of Lords. The date on which the Royal Assent was signified is

1 CJ (1976–77) 34; HC Deb (1976–77) 922, c 453.
2 CJ (1913) 243; HC Deb (1913) 55, c 469; CJ (1975–76) 102; ibid (1976–77) 33.
3 HC Deb (1948) 456, c 713.
4 HC Deb (1914) 61, c 1348; ibid (1914) 62, c 931; CJ (1975–76) 114.
5 In 1976 the Lords considered the Commons suggested amendments to the Trade Union and Labour Relations (Amendment) Bill, but moved them as amendments to the bill in identical form and agreed to them in this manner. They also made one further amendment to the bill before returning it to the Commons on 9 March. The Commons disagreed to the additional amendment, but accepted the remaining amendments. The Lords did not insist on the additional amendment to which the Commons had disagreed, and the bill subsequently received the Royal Assent in the normal way.
6 See eg 4 & 5 Geo 5, c 90, 91; 12, 13 & 14 Geo 6, c 103; cf p 442.
7 CJ (1914) 466; ibid (1948–49) 445.
8 LJ (1914) 423; CJ (1914) 466; ibid (1948–49) 445.

inserted after the title (see below) and the Act is given a chapter number. Acts are numbered serially throughout each calendar year in the order in which they receive the Royal Assent.[1] Public General Acts form one series and are numbered in Arabic characters; Provisional Order Confirmation Acts and Local Acts[2] form a second series and are numbered in small Roman characters; Personal Acts[3] form a third series and are numbered in italicized Arabic figures; and General Synod Measures form a fourth series, numbered in Arabic characters.

After examination of the text to ensure that it is correct, a proof copy of every public Act and Measure is certified by the Clerk of Public Bills in the House of Lords and sent to the Queen's Printer,[4] and a request is sent to the Controller of the Stationery Office to issue instructions for its immediate publication.

Two prints are prepared on durable vellum. One of these is sent for custody to the Public Record Office; the other, having been endorsed with the words by which the Royal Assent was signified, is signed by the Clerk of the Parliaments and becomes the official copy of the Act; and is lodged in the House of Lords Record Office.

Paper prints of the Act are placed on sale to the public, and such printed copies, known as Queen's Printer's copies, are accepted as evidence in courts of law.

Commencement of Act

All Acts of Parliament, of which the date of commencement was not specifically enacted, were formerly held, in law, to take effect from the first day of the session; but the Clerk of the Parliaments is now required by the Acts of Parliament (Commencement) Act 1793 to endorse, in English, on every Act of Parliament, immediately after the title, the day, month, and year when the same received the Royal Assent. This endorsement, which is taken to be a part of the Act, is the date of its commencement, when no other date is enacted. Every Act is in force for the whole of the day of its commencement.[5]

Informalities in bills

Forms not binding in progress of bills. Although the forms of passing bills which have been explained are commonly observed by both Houses, it must be understood that they are not absolutely binding. Though founded upon long parliamentary usage, either House may vary its own peculiar forms, without question elsewhere, and without affecting the validity of any Act which has received, in proper form, the ultimate sanction of the three

---

1 Acts of Parliament Numbering and Citation Act 1962. Before 1963 Acts were numbered serially by sessions, and the regnal year or years of the session were printed at the top. The session during which a bill was presented is now indicated by the number of the current Parliament and session thereof in the bottom right-hand corner of the title page. This is omitted in the Act copy.
2 The printing of these Acts is dealt with by the Private Bill Office in the House of Lords.
3 The printing of these Acts is dealt with by the Private Bill Office in the House of Lords.
4 See question relating to a printer's error in the Elementary Education Act 1891, Parl Deb (1892) 1, c 687.
5 See Interpretation Act 1978, s 4.

branches of the legislature. If an informality is discovered during the progress of a bill through the House in which it originated, that House will either order the bill to be withdrawn, or will annul the informal proceeding itself, and all subsequent proceedings;[1] but if irregularities escape detection until the bill has passed, no subsequent notice can be taken of them by the other House, as it is the business of each House to enforce compliance with its own orders and practice.

Informalities in the agreement of both Houses. Although a departure from the usage of Parliament during the progress of a bill will not vitiate a statute, informalities in the final agreement of both Houses have on occasion been treated as if they might affect its validity. If a bill should receive the Royal Assent without the amendments made by one House having been communicated to the other and agreed to, serious doubts naturally arise concerning the effect of this omission; since the assent of the Queen, Lords, and Commons is essential to the validity of an Act, except where the provisions of the Parliament Acts 1911 and 1949 are enforced in relation thereto. It is necessary to consider whether the Royal Assent will cure all prior irregularities, in the same way as the passing of a bill in the Lords would preclude inquiry as to informalities in any previous stage; whether the endorsement on the bill, recording the assent of Queen, Lords, and Commons, is conclusive evidence of that fact; or whether the Journals of either House should be permitted to contradict it. The point has never been directly determined in a court of law, but judgments delivered in modern cases have maintained that no attack should be permitted in the courts upon the validity of the enacting provisions of an Act of Parliament.[2] On occasion informalities[3] have been noticed and have been rectified by legislation.

Accidental omission from endorsement. In case of any accidental omission in the endorsement the bill should be returned to the House whence it was received; as, on 8 March 1580 (23 Elizabeth I), when a schedule was returned to the Commons and the endorsement amended there, because 'soit baillé aux Seigneurs' had been omitted and the Lords had therefore no warrant to proceed.[4]

Informalities in the Royal Assent

The consequence of any defect or informality in the commission or Royal Assent is illustrated in the following case.

---

1 CJ (1851) 82, 209; ibid (1852–53) 412, 578; ibid (1854) 96; ibid (1859) 138; ibid (1878–79) 300; ibid (1926) 217; ibid (1927) 270; ibid (1937–38) 360; ibid (1948–49) 323; ibid (1956–57) 201; ibid (1974) 256; ibid (1985–86) 155; LJ (1969–70) 278; ibid (1983–84) 381, 383; ibid (1984–85) 190, 193.

2 *Pickin v British Railways Board* [1974] App Cas 789; see also other cases cited in that appeal.

3 In the cases of the Cotton Factories Regulation Bill 1829 and the Schoolmasters' Widows Fund (Scotland) Bill 1843, amendments made in the second House were included in the Acts concerned without being approved by the first House; in the cases of the Local Government Bill 1972 and the Rent (Agriculture) Bill 1976, amendments made in the second House were not submitted to the first House, and were omitted from the Acts concerned. In the latter cases subsequent legislation enacted the missing amendments, but did not expressly validate the original Acts.

4 D'Ewes 303; CJ (1547–1628) 132 (1580); Order and Course of Passing Bills in Parliament, 4to, 1641.

In 1546, when Henry VIII was dying, the Royal Assent was not formally given in Parliament to the Act of Attainder against the Duke of Norfolk. The Duke was saved, owing to the King's death. Some years later the Act of Attainder was declared void by statute[1] because, after reciting certain informalities in the commission, no record existed showing that the commissioners did give the King's Royal Assent to the bill, which therefore 'remayneth in verie dede as no Acte of Parlyament, but as a bill onelie exhibited in the saide Parlyament, *and onelie assented unto by the saide lordes and comons*, and not by the saide late king.'

Transposition of titles. In 1809 the titles of two bills relating to the town of Worthing were transposed, and the Royal Assent signified to both, so incorrectly endorsed, without further notice. In 1821 the titles of two local Acts were, by a similar error, transposed in the endorsement when the bills received the Royal Assent. Each Act, consequently, had been passed with the title belonging to the other; and the mistake was corrected by Act of Parliament.[2]

Royal Assent given by mistake. In 1844 there were two Eastern Counties Railway Bills in Parliament. One had passed through all its stages, and the other was still pending in the House of Lords, when on 10 May the Royal Assent was given, by mistake, to the latter, instead of to the former. On the discovery of the error an Act was passed by which it was enacted that when the former Act 'shall have received the Royal Assent it shall be as valid and effectual from 10 May as if it had been properly inserted in the commission, and had received the Royal Assent on that day; and that the other bill shall be in the same state as if its title had not been inserted in the commission, and shall not be deemed to have received the Royal Assent'.[3]

---

1 1 Mary, No 27; Stat. of the Realm i, p lxxv.
2 1 & 2 Geo 4, c xcv (local and personal).
3 7 Vict c xix (local and personal), CJ (1844) 328.

Delegated legislation

Over the last half-century or more Parliament has passed an increasing volume of legislation, extending the activities of government into a great number of fields and often involving provisions of considerable complexity. At the same time, it has been recognized that the greater the number of details of an essentially subsidiary or procedural character which can be withdrawn from the floors of both Houses, the more time will be available for the discussion of major matters of public concern. Consequently, legislative power is often conferred upon the executive by statute, and various arrangements are made for parliamentary scrutiny of its exercise.[1]

The most frequent criticism of delegated legislation is that since it is made by delegated authority and not by Parliament, it avoids the normal scrutiny to which Parliament-made law is subjected, and, in particular, the possibility of being amended.[2] The volume of delegated legislation was greatest in war-time or in periods of national emergency.[3] Most recently, it has been argued that there has been a tendency for secondary legislation both to increase in quantity and to have been used more frequently than before to change rather than to adapt policy.[4] The justification and advantages of delegated legislation arise from its speed, flexibility and adaptability. Once Parliament has by statute laid down (often in some detail) the principles of a new law, the executive may by means of delegated legislation work out the application of the law in greater detail within these principles, adapting it to fit changing circumstances; and power may even be conferred to amend the statute itself by delegated legislation (see p 539). A principle enacted in a statute may be extended by delegated legislation in a cognate direction. The commencement of a statute may more conveniently be provided for by delegated legislation.

Delegated legislation is often extremely complex in its terms, by reason of the involved nature of the matter with which it is dealing, and because it is often necessary to set forth its provisions at length and in detail. For this

---

1 The actual use made of delegated legislation was subject to periodical review in the special reports of the Commons Statutory Instruments Committee. There have been three general reviews of the subject, namely that of the Committee on Ministers' Powers in 1932 (Cmd 4060), that of the Select Committee on Delegated Legislation in 1953 (HC 301 (1952–53)) and that of the Joint Committee on Delegated Legislation in 1972 (HL 184 (1971–72), HC 475 (1971–72)) and in 1973 (HL 188 and 204 (1972–73), HC 407 and 468 (1972–73)).
2 For exceptional cases of amendable instruments, see p 546n.
3 Defence of the Realm Acts 1914 and 1915; Emergency Powers Act 1920; Statutory Rules and Orders 1926, pp 541, 546; Emergency Powers (Defence) Act 1939.
4 Joint Committee on Statutory Instruments, Special Report, HL 216, HC 31–xxxvii (1985–86).

reason, brief explanatory notes[1]—first adopted in relation to Defence Regulations—are added to most statutory instruments. Every such note is prefaced by the warning that the note is not part of the instrument. In addition the 'scrutiny committees', that is the Joint Committee on Statutory Instruments and the Commons Select Committee on Statutory Instruments (see pp 551–553) may draw the attention of both Houses or of the Commons only, as the case may be, to a statutory instrument where the committee considers that its form or content requires further elucidation, that its drafting is defective or that there is doubt whether its provisions are intra vires.[2]

If the exercise of power by delegated legislation should be ultra vires, ie beyond the powers authorized by the enabling Act, the validity of that delegated legislation can be contested in the law courts.[3]

The scrutiny committees may also draw attention to provisions in statutory instruments made in pursuance of enactments specifically excluding them from challenge in the courts.[4] Modern statutes frequently confer power on the executive to make delegated legislation which amends the statutes themselves. This is done by what is known as the 'Henry VIII Clause', which is used, broadly speaking, to confer power to alter financial limits, to bring lists up to date, to make exceptions to the operation of a statute, or to make alterations of detail within a narrowly defined field.[5]

Statutory Instruments etc

The Statutory Instruments Act 1946, which was brought into force on 1 January 1948, gave the comprehensive name of 'Statutory Instruments' to most, but not all, delegated legislation. In cases where the parent statute was passed in or after 1948, every Order in Council is a statutory instrument and every instrument made by a Minister of the Crown[6] is a statutory instrument if the parent statute so provides. In cases where the parent statute was passed before 1948 the old provisions of the Rules Publication Act 1893 were substantially re-enacted and, with a few exceptions,[7] every document, being

---

1 See Report of Committee on Ministers' Powers, Cmd 4060 (1932), p 66, and observations of the scrutiny committees (pp 551–553) on such notes (Joint Committee on Statutory Instruments, Sixth Report, HL 40, HC 15–viii (1981–82), and Special Report, HL 216, HC 31–xxxvii (1985–86); and Government observations, Cmnd 8600 (July 1982). Since 1980, it has been the practice to add to a second or subsequent commencement order a note as to any earlier commencement order.
2 For example, see Eighteenth Report from the Joint Committee on Statutory Instruments (HL 127, HC 29–xxi (1986–87)).
3 It has been ruled in the House of Commons that doubts concerning the vires of delegated legislation did not prevent the House from discussing the orders in question, HC Deb (1954–55) 535, cc 1914–1916; ibid (1966–67) 734, cc 842–844.
4 Sixth Report from the Select Committee on Procedure, HC 539 (1966–67) Evidence, Q 150 n. Most provisions conferring power to make delegated legislation which should have as much force as the original Act (or cognate terminology) were repealed by the Statute Law (Repeals) Act 1986, Sch 1, Pt XII.
5 See Committee on Ministers' Powers, Cmd 4060 (1932) pp 36–37 and p 123, Annex II. For examples of such clauses, see Building Societies Act 1986, s 27(6); Banking Act 1987, s 4(3); Social Security Act 1986, s 64(2); and Finance (No 2) Act 1987, Sch 6, para 8.
6 See s 11(1) of the Statutory Instruments Act 1946. Certain statutes (eg Solicitors Act 1974, s 46 and Dentists Act 1984, s 45) confer on documents issued by non-governmental bodies the status of statutory instruments.
7 See Statutory Instruments (Amendment) Regulations, 1982/1728.

of a legislative and not of an executive character, made after the commencement of the Act of 1946 by a rule-making authority as defined in the Rules Publication Act 1893[1] in the exercise of a statutory power conferred on that authority by or under any Act of Parliament passed before the commencement of the Act of 1946 is a statutory instrument.[2] The Act of 1946 extends the ambit of 'statutory instruments' to cover, if the parent statute so provides, instruments which confirm or approve subordinate legislation made by another authority.[3]

It should be noted that by no means all delegated legislation falls within the terms of the Statutory Instruments Act. Certain other documents such as Immigration Rules, alterations to the Highway Code, draft Codes of Practice on Industrial Relations, and Recommendations for the Welfare of Livestock[4] although technically not statutory instruments are by virtue of their parent Acts required to be laid before Parliament and are subject to approval or disapproval by either House. In addition, the various classes of bye-laws made under statutory powers by local authorities or public corporations, even though they may require confirmation by a Minister, are neither made nor confirmed by statutory instrument and are not required to be laid before Parliament. It may also be the case that statutes under which other delegated legislation not subject to the terms of the 1946 Act is made prescribe a different period during which parliamentary control may be exercised, which may be longer or shorter than the 40 days prescribed by the 1946 Act and may even be calculated in a different manner.[5]

By the Act of 1946, immediately after a statutory instrument has been made, it must be sent to the Queen's printer of Acts of Parliament (the Controller of HM Stationery Office) and, with certain exceptions, printed and put on sale. Ministers when sending instruments to the Queen's printer are required to classify them as local or general, according to their subject-matter.[6] Those printed and sold are, broadly speaking, 'general' instruments, analogous to public and general Acts.[7] Local instruments are exempt from printing and sale unless the Minister concerned requests otherwise. Other instruments are so exempt if the Minister gives the appropriate certificate.[8]

---

1 That is, Her Majesty in Council, all government departments, and any person or body authorized to make rules of court.
2 S 1(2) of the Act of 1946. The Minister for the Civil Service, with the concurrence of the Lord Chancellor and the Speaker, is empowered to make regulations determining the classes of cases in which the exercise of power by a rule-making authority does or does not constitute the making of a statutory instrument (s 8(1)(d) of the Act of 1946 and Statutory Instruments Regulations 1947 (SI 1948/1)).
3 A corresponding extension has been applied in cases where the parent statute was passed before 1948. See Statutory Instruments Act 1946, s 9(1); Statutory Instruments Regulations 1947 (SI 1948/1); Statutory Instruments (Confirmatory Powers) Order 1947 (SI 1948/2).
4 See, for instance, Immigration Act 1971, s 3, CJ (1972–73) 41 and ibid (1982–83) 105; Road Traffic Act 1972, s 37 (as substituted by the Transport Act 1982, s 60); and CJ (1977–78) 61; Employment Act 1980, s 3 and CJ (1979–80) 851; Agriculture (Miscellaneous Provisions) Act 1968, s 3.
5 See College Charter Act 1871, s 2; Universities and Colleges (Trusts) Act 1943, s 3.
6 Statutory Instruments Regulations 1947 (SI 1948/1).
7 It is usual to include under 'general' those instruments which refer to London.
8 See Statutory Instruments Regulations 1947 (SI 1948/1). Such certificates may relate to general instruments regularly printed and made available to persons affected thereby; temporary instruments; related schedules or other bulky documents; and confidential instruments.

The Statutory Publications Office is responsible for allocating statutory instruments to the series of the calendar year in which they are made. They are numbered consecutively in that series as nearly as may be in the order in which they are received by that Office.

Instruments may be cited by the year and number in the series, as well as by the short title assigned to each.

Statutory Instruments Reference Committee. The Statutory Instruments Reference Committee decides questions arising in connection with the numbering, classification and printing of instruments. The Committee is nominated by the Lord Chancellor and the Speaker. It consists of the Lord Chairman of Committees, the Chairman of Ways and Means, and six senior officers of both Houses. The Reference Committee may override certificates by Ministers for exemption from printing and sale of instruments (except confidential instruments). It may also consider such matters as the numbering, classification, printing and publication of statutory instruments, and whether an instrument made under an Act passed before 1948 is to be regarded as a statutory instrument.[1]

Sub-delegation. If an order or regulation made under a statute be regarded as a second 'tier' of legislation, power may exist to create further tiers. During the war of 1939–45 the phenomenon of a three-tier system appeared—first the enabling statute, secondly Orders in Council or regulations made under that statute, often in very wide language, and thirdly orders or other instruments made under the Orders in Council or regulations. This sub-delegation was expressly authorized by the Emergency Powers (Defence) Act 1939 (section 1(3)).[2] By section 4(1) of the Supplies and Services (Transitional Powers) Act 1945, the orders or other instruments made under Defence Regulations were exposed to annulment by resolution of either House. The departmental directions resulting from sub-delegation have been judicially criticized as escaping the system of official publicity.[3] The Joint Committee on Statutory Instruments has drawn attention to the need for Departments to take care not to include in instruments provisions amounting to sub-delegation where the parent statute did not so provide.[4]

---

1 See Statutory Instruments Act 1946, s 8(1); Statutory Instruments Regulations 1947 (SI 1948/1); and the Reports of the Statutory Instruments Reference Committee, No 1, 1 January 1948 to 31 December 1950 (HMSO 1951). The Lord Chancellor and the Speaker lay the Reports of the Reference Committee on the Table of their respective Houses, eg LJ (1984–85) 112; CJ (1984–85) 182.
2 There was no such express authorization in the similar Defence of the Realm Acts in the First World War. The Select Committee on Statutory Rules and Orders commented on instances of five-tier legislation, 3rd Special Report, HC 187 (1945–46). See also Civil Aviation Act 1949, s 57(1); Air Navigation Order 1980 (SI 1980/1965), arts 61 and 66; and regulations made thereunder.
3 Per Scott LJ, *Blackpool Corporation v Locker* [1948] 1 KB at 367–370.
4 First Special Report (HL 51, HC 169 (1977–78)). See also Special Reports of the Commons Select Committee, HC 187 (1945–46); HC 201 (1947–48); HC 301 (1952–53); HC 266 (1966–67). Recent criticism by the scrutiny committees has been levelled at attempts to make an instrument operate by reference to primary or to other secondary legislation which includes not only amendments previously made thereto but any amendment which may be made in future (Joint Committee on Statutory Instruments Special Report (HL 216, HC 31–xxxvii (1985–86), para 31–37).

Each year over 2,200 statutory instruments are registered under the 1946 Act, of which about 1,200 are of a general character.[1] The necessity for effective parliamentary scrutiny has not therefore diminished since the Committee on Ministers' Powers in 1932 drew attention to the then current danger that without such scrutiny and control the servant might be transformed into the master.[2]

PARLIAMENTARY CONTROL AND SCRUTINY

The conditions of the making of statutory instruments and the degree of parliamentary control over them will depend in each case upon the particular statute which authorizes them, though there is at present no consistent pattern or direct connection between the subject matter of any particular instrument and the procedure to which it may be subjected.[3] It should also be remembered that a great many statutory instruments are local and not subject to any parliamentary control.

Under one type of procedure the resultant instrument has no effect, or no continuing effect, until Parliament has expressly approved it. Under another type it can be annulled if, within a time-limit, either House records its disapproval; the Address to Her Majesty praying that an instrument be annulled is colloquially termed a 'prayer'. The two procedures may be spoken of as the *affirmative* and the *negative* types; in either case they are 'exempted business' in the House of Commons, being 'proceedings in pursuance of any Act of Parliament' within the meaning of Standing Order No 14(1)(a) or motions within the terms of Standing Order No 15. Details of the exemptions in these cases are set out on pp 243–244. In many cases the purport of the instrument is not deemed important enough to need any form of control and though they fall (if they are general) within the orders of reference of the scrutiny committees (see pp 552–553), such instruments may not even be laid before Parliament. If the enabling Act seeks the maximum of parliamentary supervision, it will probably direct that the document be laid as a draft and that it be not made unless approved. If the subject be taxation, the required resolution will be that of the House of Commons only. Thus draft Orders in Council affording relief from double taxation are not submitted to Her Majesty unless an Address is presented by the Commons, praying that such an Order be made,[4] and orders under section 17(4) of the Customs and Excise Duties (General Reliefs) Act 1979, which restrict relief from customs or excise duty or value added tax, lapse within twenty-eight days unless approved by that House. Orders in Council defining certain treaties as Community Treaties within the meaning of the European Communities Act 1972 are subject to affirmative procedure in both Houses even if a charge arises from an obligation under such a treaty.[5]

---

1 The total for 1987 was 2,278, of which some 1,200 were general in character.
2 Cmd 4060 (1932), the Report of the Donoughmore Committee.
3 See Joint Committee on Delegated Legislation, Second Report (HL 204 (1972–73), HC 468 (1972–73)).
4 Income and Corporation Taxes Act 1988, s 788(10).
5 European Communities Act 1972, ss 1(3) and 2(3); HC Deb (1978–79) 964, cc 49–51.

Certain instruments made under the European Communities Act 1972 (Schedule 2, paragraph 2(2)) may be subject to either affirmative or negative procedure, at the option of the executive.[1]

Exceptionally a parent Act may contemplate the making of an instrument part of which requires affirmative approval and part is exposed to annulment on a negative 'prayer'.[2] It has, however, been ruled that the House of Commons cannot accept the type of composite document in which regulations already accepted by the House are joined with regulations subject to annulment,[3] and the scrutiny committees have adversely commented on instruments which embodied in one document the exercise of powers subject to proceedings in Parliament under the 'negative' procedure and also of provisions not subject to any parliamentary procedure.[4]

Laying before Parliament

The first step in parliamentary control is the requirement that the document be laid before Parliament, though, if its contents be of minor significance only, the enabling Act may not insist upon this step or may require nothing more.

Documents laid before the House of Lords must include at least one which is suitable for permanent preservation with the records of Parliament; it must therefore be in a durable form, printed, typewritten, lithographed or handwritten in ink on good quality paper.[5] Statutory instruments and other documents which require to be laid must be complete and in full,[6] and correct.[7] The laying copies must be certified by the responsible Department as true copies of the original document retained by the Department. If a mistake in the laid copy is more than an obvious printer's error it must be considered a matter of substance.[8] Where the laid copy is a true copy of the

---

1 The manner in which this choice should be exercised has been commented on by the scrutiny committees (Joint Committee on Statutory Instruments, First Special Report (HL 57, HC 69 (1977–78)), Second Special Report (HL 236, HC 579 (1977–78)), Sixth Report (HL 40, HC 15–viii (1981–82)) and by the Government (Cmnd 8600, July 1982). A cognate power is available under Sch 1(4) to the Northern Ireland Act 1974, where Orders in Council may be approved in draft or, in cases of urgency, continued in force within forty days of having been made.

2 For example, Orders in Council under s 1(2) of the Census Act 1920. In this case, the provisions which are subject to the affirmative procedure have been identified by being printed in italics in the order as laid. In the House of Commons, motions relating to both parts of the order have been tabled so that the scope of debate on the order was not restricted to those parts which required affirmative resolution (CJ (1959–60) 209; ibid (1964–65) 181; ibid (1969–70) 165. See also HC Deb (1964–65) 708, cc 1617, 1643–1644; ibid (1969–70) 796, c 329; and ibid (1974–75) 889, c 407). For the position regarding the operation of SO No 14 and SO No 15 in such cases, see ibid (1969–70) 796, c 329.

3 HC Deb (1950–51) 480, c 1797–9.

4 Joint Committee on Statutory Instruments, Thirty-second Report (HL 249, HC 31–xli (1985–86)) and Eleventh Report (HL 78, HC 29–xiv (1986–87)).

5 Statutory Instrument Practice, 1987, para 4.12.

6 HC Deb (1950–51) 486, c 660. See also Parl Deb (1899) 69, cc 625, 647; ibid (1901) 96, c 1007; HC Deb (1909) 6, cc 712, 1372; ibid (1910) 17, c 1315; ibid (1950–51) 486, c 205.

7 HC Deb (1945–46) 422, c 1881 and ibid (1985–86) 98, c 459–460. See also Special Report of the Statutory Instruments Committee, HC 324 (1948–49), p 12.

8 HC Deb (1945–46) 422, c 1881, and 423, c 998; ibid (1954–55) 535, cc 2704–2720; ibid (1978–79) 965, cc 1182–1184. See also HC Deb (1934) 296, cc 918, 967 and the Speaker's comment at c 969.

original instrument, but the original is found to be defective, it is normally revoked by another instrument.[1]

Breach of a statutory duty to lay an instrument before Parliament will not of itself invalidate the instrument. The resulting situation has been dealt with both by statute and by statutory instrument.[2]

Under section 4 of the Statutory Instruments Act 1946, if an enabling statute requires a statutory instrument to be laid before Parliament, a copy must be laid before each House and 'shall be so laid before the instrument comes into operation'. If, however, it is essential that an instrument should come into operation before copies can be laid, the instrument may be made so as to come into operation before laying; in this event, the Lord Chancellor and the Speaker of the House of Commons must forthwith be notified that copies have yet to be laid, with an explanation why there has been no laying before operation.[3] By Standing Order No 68 (HL) and Standing Order No 139 (HC) the Lord Chancellor and the Speaker are directed to lay the notification on the Table. Section 4 of the Act of 1946 further requires that, where instruments have to be laid, every copy must bear on the face of it a statement of the date on which it came or will come into operation, and either a statement of the date on which copies were laid or a statement that copies are to be laid. By practice, instruments laid before Parliament other than draft instruments usually bear also the date on which they were made.

What constitutes laying must be a matter for the decision of each House. In 1948, however, the Laying of Documents before Parliament (Interpretation) Act was passed 'for the removal of doubt'. It declared that statutory references to the laying of instruments or other documents before either House are (unless the contrary intention appears) to be construed as references to the taking, during the existence of a Parliament, of such action as, under the Standing or Sessional Orders or other directions of that House, or under the practice of that House, constitutes laying, notwithstanding that the action can be taken at a time when that House is not sitting. By Standing Order No 138 the House of Commons has directed that the delivery of a copy of a statutory instrument (but not a draft instrument) to the Votes and Proceedings Office on any day during the existence of a Parliament shall be deemed to be a laying. As a matter of practice, instruments are not normally laid on Saturdays, Sundays, bank holidays, Good Friday, Christmas Day or after 3.30 pm on Fridays, unless the House is still sitting. The Standing

---

1 See eg Education (Publication of School Proposals) (No 2) Regulations, SI 1980/658. For an instance of a failure to follow this prescription, see Joint Committee on Statutory Instruments, Eighteenth Report (HL 125, HC 31–xxiii (1985–86)).

2 The National Fire Services (Regulations) Indemnity Act 1944 and the Town and Country Planning Regulations (London) Indemnity Act 1970 (now repealed) declared that instruments not laid should be deemed to have been laid. SI 1984/887 and 1984/1213 revoked and re-enacted instruments not laid which ought to have been laid. Older statutes (eg Court of Chancery Acts 1841 and 1850) had expressly stipulated that instruments made thereunder, if not laid, should be of no effect. In the absence of such stipulation, the requirement has been deemed to be merely directory, see *Stacey v Graham* [1899] 1 QB 406, especially per Channell J, at 412, and *Bailey v Williamson* LR 8 QB 118. See also HC Deb (1969–70) 797, cc 269–272. In *R v Department of Health & Social Security ex p London Borough of Camden and Another (The Times*, 6 March 1986) it was decided, in the case of regulations which were not to be made until a draft had been approved by Parliament, that express approval was required before the regulations could come into force.

3 The Scrutiny Committees (see pp 551–553) are empowered to draw special attention to any case of unjustifiable delay in sending this notification.

Order does not apply to special procedure orders (see chapter 38) or to any other instruments, including those subject to the affirmative resolution procedure, which are required to be laid before Parliament or before the Commons only before coming into operation. These can be laid only on sitting days. By Standing Order No 67 the House of Lords similarly accepts as laying the deposit of a copy in the Office of the Clerk of the Parliaments during the existence of a Parliament when that House is not sitting for public business except Sundays, bank holidays, Christmas Day or Good Friday; laying is permitted by the Standing Order between eleven and one o'clock on Saturdays and between eleven and five o'clock on other weekdays.

The laying of statutory instruments on the Table of the House of Commons means in practice that the paper, having been delivered to the Votes and Proceedings Office, is placed in the Library of the House. The document is usually (though not always) laid in duplicate in accordance with a direction of the Speaker.

Copies are also made available to Members of the House of Commons in the Vote Office. In 1954 the Government undertook to ensure that at least fifty copies of instruments and drafts subject to negative resolution should normally be made available in the Vote Office when such drafts or instruments were laid. When in exceptional and urgent cases this was not possible, a supply of copies would be made available as soon as possible after laying.[1] It has subsequently become general practice to treat all statutory instruments and drafts as if they were covered by the undertaking. Copies are also invariably supplied to the House of Lords.

The arrangements for notifying Members of what has been laid are as follows. In the House of Lords notice appears in the Minutes of Proceedings, and the papers themselves are available for inspection in the Printed Paper Office. When papers are laid in the House of Commons, notice appears in the daily Votes and Proceedings. A list of statutory instruments etc, is published weekly in the House of Commons, showing all the instruments and draft instruments against which motions to annul can be moved within the statutory period, the date from which that period began to run and the number of days unexpired.

The affirmative procedure

The affirmative procedure on statutory instruments takes one of three forms, according to the formula of the enabling Act. An instrument or Order in Council may be made by the appropriate authority, and have immediate effect, subject to the requirement that its effect shall not continue beyond a specified period (usually 28 or 40 days) unless one or both Houses within that period agree to the appropriate resolutions approving the document.[2] Secondly, an Order or an instrument may be required to be laid in draft before one or both Houses, and not to be made and to have effect unless one or both Houses present Addresses to the Crown praying for the Order to be made, or have agreed to resolutions approving the draft instru-

---

1 HC Deb (1953–54) 526, cc 119–120 w; ibid (1973–74) 868, c 465 w.
2 Finance Act 1972, s 52(6); Town and Country Planning (Scotland) Act 1972, s 273(7); Customs and Excise Duties (General Reliefs) Act 1979, s 17(4).

ment.[1] In the third case, a Minister may make and lay an instrument, but it will have effect only after a resolution has been passed approving it.[2] The first type is frequently resorted to when delegated legislation must come into force immediately on being made, and without any prior consultation— usually but by no means always in the field of taxation. There is no substantial difference between the second and third types, and the government have agreed in normal circumstances to avoid the use of the third type in future enactments.[3] All three are used principally for substantial and important portions of delegated legislation, on which a high degree of scrutiny is sought.

Regulations made under the Emergency Powers Act 1920 must be presented to Parliament as soon as may be after they are made, but do not continue in force after the expiration of seven days from the time when they are so laid, unless a resolution is passed by both Houses providing for their continuance; the resolution may add to, alter or revoke regulations.[4] The duration of such regulations is in any event limited to one month. (See also p 564.)

Power has occasionally been given to both Houses to approve a draft Order in Council or draft departmental order with modifications,[5] and in such cases the orders could only be made with such modifications as have been agreed to by both Houses. If the two Houses differ in their amendments, machinery must be improvised for reconciling the differences.[6] Though they may be moved as independent motions, motions which propose to treat delegated legislation, or other matters subject to proceedings in pursuance of an Act of Parliament, in a manner which would be outside the provisions of the parent statute, such as motions to refer instruments to select committees, or motions not to approve instruments or to approve them upon conditions, may not be moved in the House of Commons as

1 Northern Ireland Constitution Act 1973, s 2; Rehabilitation of Offenders Act 1974, s 10(2). Use of the exceptional statutory formula whereby resolutions of the two Houses authorize the making of an Order in Council but no draft need be laid (for example, in s 8(3) of the Statutory Orders (Special Procedure) Act 1945) was deprecated by the Commons Select Committee on Statutory Instruments (Special Report, HC 281 (1948–49) para 6). For an occasion when the House of Commons approved an Order, and the relevant motion was subsequently defeated in the House of Lords, see CJ (1967–68) 296, 343; LJ (1967–68) 381, 487. For an instance of the agreement of the House of Commons to a motion that an instrument 'be not approved', see CJ (1969–70) 31.
2 Valuation for Rating (Scotland) Act 1970, s 1(2); Legal Advice and Assistance Act 1972, s 11(2).
3 Joint Committee on Delegated Legislation, Second Report (HL 204 (1972–73), HC 468 (1972–73) p 49).
4 Emergency Powers Act 1920, s 2(2), (4); LJ (1921) 97, 99, 146, 184; CJ (1921) 81, 131, 176.
5 CJ (1920) 314. An amendment to the question approving an order suggesting a modification in the order must be drafted in such a way as to specify the amendment which it is sought to make, HC Deb (1920) 132, c 829. A list of Acts which confer on Parliament the power to amend, modify or adapt delegated legislation is to be found in the Report of the Joint Committee on Delegated Legislation (HL 184, HC 475 (1971–72) p 181).
6 To meet such a difficulty in the case of motions for Addresses to approve orders under the Government of India Act 1935, it was informally agreed that debate on the motion for the Address under the Act should be adjourned in the Commons until the relevant select committee had reported to the House of Lords. If thereafter the latter House amended the order, similar amendments could then be moved in the Commons, LJ (1935–36) 329; CJ (1935–36) 324, 344.

amendments to questions which arise in the normal way out of proceedings under the parent Act.[1]

It has been ruled that the question cannot be put on a motion to approve a draft instrument which depends on a bill which has not yet received Royal Assent.[2]

For the limits imposed on the duration of debate on motions under the affirmative or the negative procedures, see pp 243–244.

The negative procedure

As already mentioned, the commonest type of parliamentary control is a provision in the parent Act that the instruments made thereunder, though taking effect forthwith or on some named future date, shall be subject to annulment in pursuance of a resolution of either House of Parliament adopted within a named time limit. In pre-1948 Acts there was necessarily a specific provision that the instrument, when made, should be laid before Parliament; after 1947 this stage is universally required by the standardized procedure prescribed by the Statutory Instruments Act 1946. If the parent Act stipulates that a statutory instrument made thereunder 'shall be subject to annulment in pursuance of a resolution of either House of Parliament', this formula attracts the requirement of laying and the conditions of annulment contained in section 5(1) of that Act.[3] Under the same section, a resolution to annul does not prejudice the making of a new instrument of similar effect or the validity of anything previously done under the instrument.[4]

Though its incidence has become more infrequent in recent years, the negative method is sometimes prescribed in a different form. A draft of the document is required to be laid before Parliament; if, within a time-limit, either House resolves that the statutory instrument be not made (or, in the case of an Order in Council, that the draft be not submitted to Her Majesty), then no further proceedings are to be taken thereon, though this procedure does not prevent a fresh draft being laid before Parliament.[5] Power has occasionally been given to both Houses to resolve against part of an instrument subject to annulment.[6]

---

1 See Parl Deb (1889) 339, c 1742; HC Deb (1966–67) 741, cc 483, 487; ibid (1974) 872, c 1051; ibid (1975–76) 902, c 1531; ibid (1976–77) 925, c 1368. See also Notices of Motions (1963–64) p 6126. For an instance of the moving of such an amendment where it was possible for the House to amend the order, see CJ (1932–33) 241: and cf the case of amendments to a motion to approve a statutory report (HC Deb (1983–84) 52, c 637).

2 HC Deb (1979–80) 971, cc 605–607.

3 Examples of annulments: CJ (1945–46) 119, 121; ibid (1950–51) 273, 278; ibid (1969–70) 220, 230; ibid (1978–79) 45; ibid (1979–80) 188. For an instance of regulations made in the form of a statutory instrument and laid before Parliament subject to the negative procedure, which in the event were shown to be neither of such a character nor subject to such procedure, see Joint Committee on Statutory Instruments, Eleventh Report, HL 75, HC 29–xiv (1986–87).

4 HC Deb (1950) 478, c 466. See, for example, the Fats, Cheese and Tea (Rationing) (Amendment No 2) Order 1951, No 470, revoked by SI 1951/1040, and HC Deb (1974–75) 885, cc 1107–1108, and 887, cc 506–507 w.

5 See the Second Report from the Joint Committee on Delegated Legislation (HL 204 (1972–73), HC 468 (1972–73) p 49) for the Government's agreement in normal circumstances to avoid the use of this type of procedure in future enactments. For a resolution that a draft instrument be not made and the laying of a fresh draft, see CJ (1978–79) 45, 48.

6 For example, Census Act 1920, s 1(2).

Scope of debate

Where the instrument merely consolidates previous instruments without altering the law, debate will, by analogy with the procedure on consolidation bills (see pp 472–473) be restricted.[1]

On a motion to annul an instrument which substantially amended a previous instrument, it was ruled that discussion must be confined to the amending order.[2]

Debate on any statutory instrument, whether subject to the affirmative or the negative procedure, is confined to the contents of the instrument, and discussion of alternative methods of achieving its object is not in order.[3] Where the effects of an instrument are confined to a particular geographical area or areas, discussion of other areas is out of order.[4] Nor is criticism of the provisions of the parent Act permitted.[5] An attempt which was made, on a motion for the annulment of an order which had already ceased to operate although the forty day period had not expired, to discuss the method by which that order had been made, was held to be out of order; the debate being accordingly confined to the effect of the instrument, the Chair expressed the opinion that it was a waste of parliamentary time to discuss the annulment of an order which was already dead.[6]

Time limits

When a limit is put on proceedings in Parliament in relation to delegated legislation to which the affirmative procedure applies, the parent statute itself lays down details. Since 1 January 1948 the period during which a negative resolution in relation to a statutory instrument may be moved has been standardized at forty days in respect of either the negative procedure for annulment, or the negative procedure for preventing further proceedings in the case of a draft instrument.[7] In the case of documents which are statutory instruments, the period begins for each House when a copy is laid before it. If, however, the document is a draft of a statutory instrument and is laid before each House on a different day, the period begins with the later of these days. In reckoning this period of forty days, no account is to be taken of any time during which Parliament is dissolved or prorogued or during which both Houses are adjourned for more than four days.[8]

---

1 HC Deb (1946–47) 433, c 2012; ibid (1960–61) 631, c 335; ibid (1977–78) 940, cc 1830–1831.
2 HC Deb (1945–46) 421, cc 499–500.
3 HC Deb (1950–51) 484, c 1537; ibid (1963–64) 691, c 174; ibid (1977–78) 940, c 30.
4 HC Deb (1948–49) 463, c 1343; ibid (1952–53) 511, c 2221.
5 HC Deb (1950–51) 484, c 1537–1539. In the case of an instrument made necessary by the provisions of an Act of the Parliament of Northern Ireland, criticism of that Act was not permitted, HC Deb (1961–62) 663, cc 1639–1641. See also ibid (1953–54) 531, c 1459.
6 HC Deb (1951–52) 497, cc 1508–1514.
7 Statutory Instruments Act 1946, ss 5, 6: for the position of delegated legislation other than statutory instruments, see p 540.
8 Statutory Instruments Act 1946, s 7. Practical difficulties and questions of calculation which arise in the operation of this section were discussed by the Joint Committee on Delegated Legislation (HL 184, HC 475 (1971–72); and HL 188, HC 407 (1972–73)). In addition to the above requirements, account may also have to be taken, for example, of days over which the Commons has adjourned but on which the Lords sits for judicial business; and of days on which both Houses meet in a new Parliament before the State Opening, the 'swearing in' days (HC Deb (1951–52) 497, c 1515). Unless the parent Act otherwise provides (see Customs and Excise Duties (General Reliefs) Act 1979, s 17(4)) calculations based on the sitting days of the Lords will affect praying time for instruments laid before the Commons only.

The number of 'prayers' moved in the House of Lords used to be relatively small, since debate on instruments subject to the negative procedure may be raised by way of motion or of unstarred question. 'Prayers' are now more common. Almost half the 62 'prayers' tabled since 1950 were tabled since the start of the 1979–80 session.

In the House of Commons, it became increasingly difficult in the mid-1960s to ensure that all 'prayers' were debated, despite long standing undertakings that special measures could be taken to deal with exceptional cases where a debate could not be arranged within the statutory period.[1] Two solutions were devised. The first was the practice of debating motions taking note of an instrument, calling for its withdrawal, or otherwise disapproving of it, notwithstanding the elapse of praying time.[2] In such cases the provision of the Statutory Instruments Act to the effect that no further proceedings may be taken under an instrument after the date of any resolution does not apply.[3] Motions in the terms referred to are not exempted business under Standing Order No 15 and if they are to be entered on and proceeded with at or after ten o'clock, a specific motion is required.[4]

The second solution, which is currently more common, is that of consideration of delegated legislation (including 'prayers') by Standing Committees on Statutory Instruments. The procedure for the reference of instruments by the House to such committees, and for their proceedings and report is considered on pp 594–595.

A further informal time limit in parliamentary scrutiny and control of delegated legislation is the '21 day rule' operated by the Joint and Select Committees on Statutory Instruments. This rule is the embodiment of an undertaking that, wherever possible, an instrument subject to the negative procedure will be laid at least 21 days before it is to come into effect.[5] Scrutiny of the instrument is thus usually ensured before its provisions come into force.

Following comment by the scrutiny committees, the Government has agreed that where an international agreement is made or amended and, though it is not subject to ratification, a statutory instrument needs to be made before implementation, the text of the agreement or amendment will be made available to Parliament, preferably when the instrument is made

1 HC Deb (1951–52) 497, c 1522; ibid (1953–54) 525, c 2170; ibid (1953–54) 526, c 119 w; ibid (1963–64) 691, c 665–668.
2 See, for example, CJ (1966–67) 81, 333, 336; ibid (1970–71) 208; ibid (1985–86) 42; and also ibid (1963–64) 203 and HC Deb (1963–64) 693, c 1017 ff. The House had in fact before 1964 occasionally considered prayers after praying time had expired, eg CJ (1951–52) 166, 167, and HC Deb (1951–52) 498, c 339–40. Such motions are amendable (CJ (1974–75) 245). For a case where debate was resumed on a motion praying that an instrument be annulled, notwithstanding the elapse of praying time between the adjournment and resumption of the debate, see CJ (1965–66) 35, 49. For a motion that an instrument which the parent statute did not require to be laid be withdrawn, see CJ (1966–67) 406; ibid (1968–69) 145.
3 HC Deb (1951–52) 498, cc 340, 1413–1415.
4 This motion may or may not specify an overall time limit analogous to that in SO No 15; see CJ (1967–68) 57, 210 and ibid (1985–86) 40. When a time limit is set for such proceedings, unless the motion setting out the limit so provides, the Speaker has no powers such as he has under SO No 15 to put forthwith the necessary question, or to interrupt proceedings so that the debate stands adjourned (HC Deb (1967–68) 769, cc 203–205, 1125).
5 The Joint Committee on Statutory Instruments commented on this rule in their First Special Report in 1973 (HC 76, HL 184 (1972–73)). The scrutiny committees are normally informed of the reasons for non-compliance with the rule in any case where the reasons are such as fall within their orders of reference.

and normally before it comes into force. This procedure is an adaptation of the Ponsonby rule (see p215*n*) as it applies to ratification of treaties.[1]

Hybrid instruments (House of Lords)

In the House of Lords but not in the House of Commons, there is a procedure for the consideration of hybrid instruments. House of Lords Private Business Standing Order 216 provides that, where in the opinion of the Chairman of Committees, an affirmative instrument, as defined by Lords Public Business Standing Order No 69, is such that, apart from the provisions of the Act authorising it to be made, it would require to be enacted by a private or hybrid bill, he shall report his opinion to the House and to the Minister or other person responsible for it. An instrument upon which such a report has been made is known as a hybrid instrument[2] and is subject to petitioning procedure.

A petition to the House not to affirm a hybrid instrument must be deposited in the office of the Clerk of the Parliaments within fourteen days following the day on which the Chairman's report is laid before the House. If no petition is received, or any petition so received is withdrawn within this period, the Chairman reports accordingly to the House. Any petition received during the period and not withdrawn, together with the instrument petitioned against, stands referred to the Hybrid Instruments Committee.[3] This Committee is appointed each session with the Chairman of Committees in the Chair.

The Hybrid Instruments Committee, after considering any representations in writing by the parties to the proceedings and after hearing, if it thinks fit, the parties in person or by counsel or agents, decides whether the petitioner has a locus standi. If it so decides, the Committee reports to the House, in accordance with the criteria specified in Standing Order 216, whether there ought to be a further inquiry by a select committee into all or any of the matters complained of.

Where the Hybrid Instruments Committee has reported that there ought to be a further inquiry, the House may refer all or any of the matters on which the Committee has reported to a select committee consisting of five Lords, named by the House on the proposal of the Committee of Selection, with orders of reference specified by the House.[4]

Where the proceedings under Standing Order 216 have not been completed in respect of an instrument which has expired or lapsed, a further

---

1 Joint Committee on Statutory Instruments, Sixth Report, HL 40, HC 15–viii (1981–82) and Cmnd 8600 (July 1982).
2 The Standing Order provides that Orders made under s 1 of the Manoeuvres Act 1958 shall not be the subject of a Report. Instruments made under para 1 of Sch 3 to the Local Government Act 1972 are excluded from the operation of the Standing Order.
3 Before 1973 all affirmative instruments in the Lords were referred to the sessional Special Orders Committee. From 1973 all except hybrid instruments were referred instead to the Joint Committee on Statutory Instruments, and in 1975 the Special Orders Committee was replaced by the Hybrid Instruments Committee.
4 For examples of select committees on hybrid instruments see London Docklands Development Corporation (Area and Constitution) Order 1980, LJ (1980–81) 123, 638; Cardiff Bay Development Corporation (Area and Constitution) Order 1987, ibid (1986–87) 202, 292; and Bristol Development Corporation (Area and Constitution) Order 1988, ibid (1987–88) 842, 953. In all three cases the House agreed that the proceedings should be conducted 'as if they were a committee on an opposed Private Bill'.

instrument may be substituted for the purposes of those proceedings. Under Public Business Standing Order 69 no motion to approve an affirmative instrument may be moved until the proceedings under Standing Order 216 have been terminated.[1]

The procedure is modified in the case of an expedited hybrid instrument which is defined in Standing Order 216A as an instrument which, by virtue of the Act authorising it to be made, is, after the expiry of a period prescribed by that Act (the 'prescribed period'), to proceed in Parliament as if its provisions would, apart from that Act, require to be enacted by a public bill that is not hybrid.[2] The procedure in this case is governed by Private Bill Standing Order 216A and differs from that applicable to other hybrid instruments in several respects. A petition not to affirm an expedited hybrid instrument must be deposited within ten days following the day on which it is laid. No preliminary report is made by the Chairman. If the Hybrid Instruments Committee is of the opinion that there ought to be a further inquiry it conducts that inquiry itself forthwith. Under Public Business Standing Order No 68 a motion for the approval of an expedited hybrid instrument may be moved at the end of the prescribed period, whether or not the proceedings under Private Bill Standing Order 216A have been completed.[3]

Scrutiny Committees

Joint Committee on Statutory Instruments. In 1972 the Joint Committee on Delegated Legislation recommended that the technical scrutiny of statutory instruments be undertaken by a joint committee, since it was considered that the separate systems which had developed in both Houses had produced defects and anomalies in overall parliamentary control. The Joint Committee on Statutory Instruments is now constituted by sessional order of the House of Lords and by Commons Standing Order No 124.[4] The Committee consists of seven members of each House, of whom two are a quorum. The Chairman has been a Commons Member from the Opposition side of the House.

The Joint Committee considers instruments laid before each House and upon which proceedings may be, or might have been, taken—that is, statutory instruments and draft statutory instruments; schemes (including amendments of schemes and draft schemes) requiring approval by statutory instrument; other instruments where, pursuant to statute, the proceedings are by way of an affirmative resolution; and special procedure orders (see chapter 38); but Orders in Council and draft Orders in Council under paragraph 1 of Schedule 1 to the Northern Ireland Act 1974 are excluded.[5] General statutory instruments laid before both Houses not within the preceding categories, excluding Church of England Measures and instruments made thereunder (see p 554), are also considered by the Committee.

---

1 See SO 216(7).
2 Expedited hybrid instruments may be made under s 1(7) of the Offshore Petroleum Development (Scotland) Act 1975.
3 There have been no instances of expedited hybrid instruments since SO 216A was made (27 March 1975, LJ (1974–75) 437).
4 The Committee was initially appointed by sessional order (LJ (1972–73) 161; CJ (1972–73) 141). The Commons Standing Order was first made in 1983.
5 LJ (1976–77) 586; CJ (1976–77) 355. See pp 553–554.

The grounds upon which the Committee may draw an instrument to the special attention of Parliament are very similar to those in the order of reference of the Statutory Instruments Committee appointed by the Commons between 1944 and 1972. The Committee may draw the attention of Parliament to an instrument on any of a series of specified grounds, or on any other ground not impinging on the merits of or policy behind the instrument. The particular grounds on which the Committee may act are that an instrument imposes or prescribes a charge on the public revenues or requires payments to be made for any licence or consent or other service from a public body; is made under an enactment excluding it from challenge in the courts (see p 539*n*); purports to have retrospective effect where the parent statute does not so provide; has been unjustifiably delayed in publication or being laid before Parliament; has not been notified in proper time to the Lord Chancellor and the Speaker where it comes into effect before being presented to Parliament; gives rise to doubts whether it is intra vires, or appears to make an unusual or unexpected use of the powers conferred by the parent statute; requires elucidation as to its form or purport; or is defective in drafting.

Before drawing the special attention of Parliament to an instrument, the Committee must give to the Department concerned an opportunity of making explanations orally or in writing. The Committee is also empowered to take evidence from Her Majesty's Stationery Office concerning the printing and publication of an instrument. It is not expressly permitted to take evidence from any other person.[1]

The Committee has power to appoint sub-committees to consider any of the matters within its order of reference. The House of Commons has conferred on the Commons Members of the Committee and any sub-committee the power to sit notwithstanding the adjournment of the House, which is already possessed by the Lords (see pp 576 and 625). The Joint Committee has the assistance of the Counsel to the Lord Chairman of Committees and of the Counsel to the Speaker.

Commons Select Committee on Statutory Instruments. When the House of Commons nominates Members to join with the committee appointed by the Lords on statutory instruments as the Joint Committee, an instruction is given to those Commons Members nominated not to join with the Lords for the consideration of certain instruments. The excluded instruments are those which are directed by Act of Parliament to be laid before and subject to proceedings in the House of Commons only, being statutory instruments, schemes requiring approval by statutory instrument, and other instruments where, pursuant to statute, the proceedings are by way of affirmative resolution. Instruments not subject to any parliamentary proceeding but laid before the Commons only are not within the Select Committee's orders of reference. The Commons Members enjoy the same powers in the consideration of such instruments as they do when joined with the Lords as a

---

1 The House of Commons has conferred on the Commons Members the power to send for persons, papers and records at a particular meeting and to report the minutes of evidence taken at that meeting (CJ (1977–78) 372). A similar power is vested in the Lords Members by custom.

Joint Committee to consider instruments laid before both Houses. Though the membership so far as the Commons is concerned is the same, the reports and proceedings of the Joint and Select Committees are distinct.

Scrutiny Committee reports. Under Lords Public Business Standing Order No 69, no motion for an affirmative resolution of the House of Lords in connection with any instrument[1] may be moved until the report of the Joint Committee on Statutory Instruments has been laid before the House. The House of Commons is not similarly prevented from taking proceedings on any instrument, notwithstanding that the Committee has not concluded its consideration of it.[2] The scrutiny committees have expressed concern, however, that the timing of debate in the Commons on an instrument within their order of reference should not precede the completion of their work. The Government has agreed that, where possible, such a situation should be avoided. Such cases will be kept to a minimum but, in the Government's view, circumstances may arise where the pressure of business necessitates an occasional breach of the general rule.[3] When a notice of motion relating to an instrument (other than a notice given for 'an early day') appears first on the Order Paper, if a scrutiny committee has not begun its consideration of the instrument, or having begun its consideration, has not concluded it, an italicized note is printed below the notice of motion, drawing the attention of the House to the fact. When a notice stands on the Order Paper in respect of an instrument to which a scrutiny committee has drawn special attention, this fact too is noticed.

When a scrutiny committee has drawn special attention to an instrument, no procedure in either House necessarily follows.

DELEGATED LEGISLATION AFFECTING NORTHERN IRELAND

The Parliament of Northern Ireland was prorogued by the Northern Ireland (Temporary Provisions) Act 1972, which made provision also for the consideration in the United Kingdom Parliament of legislation which previously came before the Parliament of Northern Ireland. The following year, the Parliament of Northern Ireland was abolished, and the Northern Ireland Assembly Act 1973 set up a single-Chamber Assembly. It was envisaged in the Northern Ireland Constitution Act 1973 that the Assembly would make laws for Northern Ireland, with a number of specified topics excepted from the Assembly's competence. The Northern Ireland Act 1974, however, effectively suspended the Assembly from the exercise of its functions,[4] and for an interim period (since extended at intervals) made provision for the consideration of Northern Ireland legislation very similar to the scheme laid down in 1972.

---

1 SO No 69 exempts from this requirement regulations under the Emergency Powers Act 1920, Measures under the Church of England Assembly (Powers) Act 1919, and Orders in Council under the Northern Ireland Act 1974.

2 See for example HC Deb (1963–64) 696, c 1487, and ibid (1974) 872, cc 379–380.

3 Joint Committee on Statutory Instruments, First Special Report (HL 57, HC 169 (1977–78)), Sixth Report (HL 40, HC 15–viii (1981–82) and Cmnd 8600 (July 1982).

4 The Northern Ireland Act 1982 empowered a new Assembly to make proposals for (inter alia) the resumption of its legislative functions. No such proposal was made, and the Assembly was dissolved by the Northern Ireland Assembly (Dissolution) Order 1986.

Her Majesty is empowered by Order in Council to make laws for Northern Ireland, and in particular for any matter which the Constitution Act of 1973 authorized or required provision to be made by the Assembly. No recommendation may be made to Her Majesty to exercise such a power unless a draft of the Order in Council has been approved by resolution of each House. In cases of urgency, an alternative procedure is laid down by which an Order in Council may be made and come into force, though its continuing validity will depend on the agreement of both Houses given within forty days of the date of the making of the Order in Council. In calculating such a period, no account is taken of days on which Parliament is dissolved or prorogued, or both Houses are adjourned for more than four days.[1]

By reason of their character as effectively primary legislation such Orders in Council are excepted from the order of reference of the scrutiny committees[2] (see pp 551–552). Motions to approve such Orders in Council or draft Orders, being proceedings in pursuance of an Act, enjoy the exemption from interruption at ten o'clock provided by Standing Order No 14 and may be proceeded with until half past eleven o'clock (half-past two and four o'clock respectively on Fridays) or for one and a half hours after commencement of the proceedings, whichever is the later. They may also be referred to a Standing Committee under Standing Order No 101. Subordinate legislation for Northern Ireland, where subject to affirmative procedure in the Parliament of Northern Ireland or in the Assembly, is by the Northern Ireland Act 1974 subject to annulment in pursuance of a resolution of either House of Parliament, and analogous provisions of the Statutory Instruments Act 1946, as to time limits etc, apply to it (see p 548). Such instruments are scrutinised by the Joint Committee on Statutory Instruments, may be prayed against in either House, and in the Commons may be referred to a Standing Committee on Statutory Instruments under Standing Order No 101.

DELEGATION IN CHURCH OF ENGLAND MATTERS

Delegated legislation in matters concerning the Church of England is dealt with by a system which is quite distinct from that referred to above, being governed by the provisions of the Church of England (Assembly) Powers Act 1919, as amended by the Synodical Government Measure 1969. Measures under that Act are framed by the General Synod of the Church of England, and are presented to Her Majesty for the Royal Assent in pursuance of resolutions of both Houses of Parliament.

Measures. Measures are defined by the Act of 1919 as legislative measures touching matters concerning the Church of England, intended to receive the Royal Assent and to have effect as Acts of Parliament in accordance with the

---

1 Northern Ireland Act 1974, Sch 1.
2 For the same reason, the statute does not require these Orders in Council to be bound up with the annual collected editions of Statutory Instruments. SO No 123 in the Commons brings within the order of reference of the Joint Committee on Consolidation etc Bills such Orders in Council or drafts thereof which but for the Northern Ireland Act 1974 would, in the opinion of that Committee, have been enacted by a consolidation bill (public or private) or by a Statute Law Reform Bill.

provisions of that Act. They have express authority to amend or repeal Acts of Parliament, including the Act of 1919, with the exception of those provisions which relate to the composition, powers or duties of the Ecclesiastical Committee (see below) or the procedure in Parliament prescribed by section 4 of that Act. Measures have dealt with a broad range of subjects, from the liturgy used in the Church of England to arrangements for the pensions of its clergy and the powers of its parochial church councils. If a Measure does not in terms apply to the Isle of Man, it may provide for its extension thereto, with or without modifications, by Act of Tynwald. Measures which do not expressly extend to the Channel Islands may contain provisions for such an extension by the special procedures of the Channel Islands (Church Legislation) Measures 1931 and 1957.

Ecclesiastical Committee. Measures agreed to by the General Synod are submitted by its Legislative Committee to the Ecclesiastical Committee of Members of both Houses set up under the 1919 Act. The Ecclesiastical Committee is different in form from the usual joint committee (see p 662) since it is a statutory body and its proceedings are not proceedings in Parliament; but the Committee has power by statute to regulate its own procedure except as otherwise provided by section 2 of the 1919 Act, and has in fact done so in terms of a resolution (22 March 1921) to adopt the procedure of joint committees.

The Committee is appointed for the duration of a Parliament and consists of fifteen Members of the House of Lords nominated by the Lord Chancellor, and a like number of Members of the House of Commons nominated by the Speaker.[1] Casual vacancies are filled by nominations by the Lord Chancellor or the Speaker, as the case may be.[2] The quorum of the Ecclesiastical Committee is twelve of its members, and the Committee may sit whether Parliament is sitting or not, and notwithstanding a vacancy in its membership.

When a Measure is submitted to the Ecclesiastical Committee (along with such comments or explanations as the Legislative Committee may deem it expedient or be directed by the General Synod to add), it is considered with a view to the presentation to Parliament of a report dealing with its nature and legal effect. The report contains also the Committee's views on the Measure's expediency 'especially with relation to the constitutional rights of all Her Majesty's subjects'. The Ecclesiastical Committee may not amend a Measure. Witnesses are not heard; but representatives of the Synod assist the Committee in its consideration of a Measure. A conference concerning a Measure may be arranged at the instance of the Legislative Committee or the Ecclesiastical Committee[3] and the latter is bound, before presenting its report to Parliament, to communicate it in draft to the Legislative Committee, and not to present its report to Parliament until the Legislative Committee signifies its desire that it shall be so presented (see below). If the Legislative Committee signifies such a desire, the Measure and report are presented forthwith to both Houses and printed as parliamentary papers. If at that time Parliament is not sitting, the presentation is made immediately

---

1 See, for example, LJ (1987–88) 301; Votes and Proceedings (1987–88) 17 November 1987.
2 See, for example, LJ (1982–83) 57; ibid (1986–87) 12; CJ (1970–71) 261; ibid (1985–86) 340.
3 Eg 19 March 1964, Clergy (Ordination and Miscellaneous Provisions) Measure; 13 February 1989, Clergy (Ordination) Measure.

after the next meeting of Parliament. In addition the Legislative Committee may, at any time before the presentation of the Ecclesiastical Committee's report to Parliament, withdraw a Measure from the further consideration of that Committee and has invariably done so in the face of an unfavourable draft report.

Proceedings in both Houses. When a Measure and report have been laid before Parliament and ordered to be printed, a motion may be tabled in both Houses that the Measure be presented to Her Majesty for her Royal Assent in the form in which it was laid before Parliament. In the House of Commons neither the motion itself nor the Measure is open to amendment,[1] and such motions, being in pursuance of an Act of Parliament, are exempt from interruption at ten o'clock, and proceedings thereon may continue until half-past eleven, or for an hour and a half after their commencement, whichever is the later (Standing Order No 14(1)(a)) (see pp 243 and 269). The Speaker has declined to propose the question that a Measure be presented to Her Majesty when it appeared that the Legislative Committee had not formally signified its desire that the Ecclesiastical Committee's report on the Measure should be presented to Parliament, along with the Measure.[2] Where proceedings in relation to a Measure have not been completed in one session of Parliament, that Measure is not required to be laid again in the following session nor is the Ecclesiastical Committee of a new Parliament required to consider again a Measure reported on in the previous Parliament.[3]

Motions for the submission of a Measure have sometimes been agreed to by one House, and disagreed to by the other.[4] The most notable example of the use of the powers conferred on Parliament to reject a Measure is the rejection by the House of Commons of a Prayer Book Measure in 1927 and 1928.[5]

The Queen's consent must be signified to Measures affecting the prerogative or interest of the Crown before the Question is proposed on motions for the presentation of such Measures to Her Majesty.[6]

---

1 HC Deb (1926) 200, c 1531; ibid (1957–58) 581, c 1129; ibid (1968–69) 772, c 315. A motion (set down for an early day) has been tabled in the House of Commons asking the House to decline to approve a measure until certain action had been taken by the Church Assembly (Notices of Motion (1962–63) p 4828).
2 Reference was made in this connection to the practice of the Legislative Committee in authorizing its secretary to signify its desire that the Measure should be presented to Parliament in the event of a favourable draft report being received. The Measure in question was withdrawn and relaid (HC Deb (1967–68) 768, c 1676–1677; ibid 769, c 1000–1001; ibid (1968–69) 772, c 311; CJ (1967–68) 373, 378; ibid (1968–69) 9, 61).
3 See, for example, the Church of England (Legal Aid and Miscellaneous Provisions) Measure 1987, laid and reported on in session 1986–87 and considered by both Houses in session 1987–88 (new Parliament): LJ (1986–87) 352; ibid (1987–88) 135: Votes and Proceedings (1986–87) p 498 and ibid (1987–88) p 449.
4 LJ (1926) 55, 244; CJ (1926) 49, 378. When the Commons rejected the Appointment of Bishops Measure 1984, on 16 July 1984, (CJ (1983–84) 697) the motion to approve the Measure was withdrawn from the Lords Order Paper.
5 CJ (1927) 378; ibid (1928) 204.
6 For example, LJ (1967–68) 306; CJ (1971–72) 93; ibid (1974–75) 112; ibid (1979–80) 628; ibid (1983–84) 697; ibid (1985–86) 197, 417. The Government have made clear that the signification of Queen's Consent to a Measure does not necessarily imply government support for the proposal (HC Deb (1983–84) 64, cc 126–127).

When a Measure has been laid before Parliament the Lord Chairman of Committees and the Chairman of Ways and Means may, if they are of the opinion that it deals with two or more subjects which might more properly be divided, divide the Measure into two or more other Measures.[1]

Sub-delegation. It is often the case that Measures contain provisions enabling schemes, regulations or orders to be made under them, so that these documents stand in the same general relationship to Measures as statutory instruments to their parent Act. These schemes, etc, are not invariably subject in terms of the Measure to parliamentary scrutiny, and unless the Statutory Instruments Act 1946 is applicable, any expression of parliamentary disapproval would have no necessary effect. The matter of sub-delegation was considered by a sub-committee of the Ecclesiastical Committee in 1930, when it was concluded that sub-delegation should be restricted within the closest limits, and the subjects upon which such schemes or regulations might be made should be clearly defined. It recommended that such powers should be carefully scrutinised by the Ecclesiastical Committee.[2]

Measures may provide in terms for forms of parliamentary control over schemes or other documents made under them.[3] A number of Measures provide that once the General Synod has agreed to a scheme or other document under those Measures, the Statutory Instruments Act 1946 shall apply to that scheme or other document as if they were statutory instruments and as if the Measure were an Act providing that the scheme or document should be subject to annulment in pursuance of a resolution of either House of Parliament.[4]

---

1 LJ (1963–64) 224; CJ (1963–64) 200.
2 Ecclesiastical Committee: Minutes of Proceedings I, 379–382.
3 See Second Special Report from the Commons Statutory Instruments Committee, HC 7–v (1953–54).
4 For example, Faculty Jurisdiction Measure 1964; Clergy Pensions (Amendment) Measure 1972. Certain schemes made under the Ecclesiastical Fees Measure 1962 may amend private, personal or local Acts, but before coming into effect, they are to be laid by the Church Commissioners before Parliament, and only part of the Statutory Instruments Act is to apply to them.

CHAPTER 23

Formal communications between Crown and Parliament and between Lords and Commons

1. COMMUNICATIONS BETWEEN CROWN AND PARLIAMENT

The contents of this section are concerned only with the formal communications made by the Crown to Parliament as a whole, or to each House separately, and the replies returned by the House; and also with the methods by which each House, on its own initiative, communicates with the Crown and the manner in which such communications are acknowledged. These formal communications take place only on special occasions. The Crown and Parliament are in constant communication through the presence of Ministers of the Crown in both Houses of Parliament.

The Queen's presence in Parliament

The Queen is supposed to be present in the High Court of Parliament, by the same constitutional principle which recognizes her presence in other courts.[1]

The functions which the Queen, as one of the constituent parts of Parliament, performs in summoning and dissolving Parliament, in opening and closing the session, and in giving her assent to Acts of both Houses, have been described in earlier chapters (see pp 58 and 528). According to modern practice, it is only for the purpose of reading her speech from the Throne at the opening of the session that the Queen is personally present in Parliament. The other royal functions in Parliament, which might constitutionally be performed in person, are now performed by a commission appointed under the great seal.[2]

COMMUNICATIONS FROM THE CROWN TO PARLIAMENT

Communications by messages under the sign manual

On certain important occasions, such as those mentioned in the next paragraph, communication is by a written message under the royal sign manual, to either House singly,[3] or to both Houses separately.[4] The message is brought by a Member of the House, being a Minister of the Crown or one of

---

1 See Hale, Jurisd, Lords, c 1; Fortescue, c 8 (by Amons), with n B; and 2 Co Inst 186.
2 Since the Lords and Commons deliberate as separate Houses, the presence of the Crown would be inconsistent with the freedom of debate. In mediaeval times, the personal presence of the Sovereign in the House of Lords—the 'King's Great Council'—was essential; but by the time of Charles II, who revived the practice, the presence of the Crown at debates of the House of Lords had become unusual, and it has never been revived since the death of Queen Anne (Anson I, 330, 331).
3 CJ (1830–31) 488.
4 LJ (1834) 958; CJ (1834) 574.

the royal household.[1] In the House of Lords, the Lord who is charged with the message acquaints the House from the Government Front Bench, that he has a message under the royal sign manual, which Her Majesty has commanded him to deliver to their lordships. He then reads it and hands it to the Lord Chancellor. In the House of Commons, the Member who is charged with the message appears at the bar, where he informs the Speaker that he has a message from the Queen to this House signed by Her Majesty. He brings the message up to the Table, where he reads it before handing it to the Clerk of the House. The same procedure is followed in respect of a message signed on Her Majesty's behalf by the Counsellors of State.[2] A message from the Crown under the sign manual is always received by Members uncovered;[3] but this custom does not apply to an answer to an address, or to the speech from the Throne when read to the House from the Chair.[4]

These messages are usually communications in regard to important public events which require the attention of Parliament;[5] the declaration of a state of emergency[6] or revocation of a previous declaration of a state of emergency;[7] the making of provisions for the exercise of the royal authority;[8] the prerogatives, or property of the Crown;[9] provision for the royal family, and other occasions which compel the executive to seek for pecuniary aid from Parliament (see p 703). They may be regarded, in short, as additions to the royal speech, at the commencement of the session, submitting other matters to the deliberation of Parliament, besides the causes of summonses previously declared.

All messages under the sign manual should be sent, if practicable, to both Houses; but when they are accompanied by original papers, they have occasionally been sent to one House only. The more proper and regular course is to deliver messages on the same day; but from the circumstances of both Houses not sitting on the same day, or other particular reasons, it has frequently happened that messages have been delivered on different days.[10]

Other messages

Another form of communication from the Crown to either House of Parliament is in the nature of a verbal message delivered, by command, by a Minister of the Crown to the House of which he is a member. Verbal messages are most frequently of certain recognized types, adapted to special forms of procedure to which the names 'Queen's pleasure', 'Queen's rec-

---

1 If brought by one of the household, in the Lords, where he wears morning dress, he appears in his place; in the Commons, where morning dress is optional, he appears at the bar.
2 CJ (1971–72) 145; ibid (1973–74) 155.
3 All the Members present uncovered on the announcement of the death of the German Emperor Frederick, 15 June 1888.
4 Parl Deb (1882) 267, c 1443; ibid (1884–85) 293, c 260; HC Deb (1914) 58, c 1958.
5 LJ (1794–96) 186; ibid (1802–04) 74; CJ (1826–28) 111.
6 LJ (1921) 95, 174; ibid (1973–74) 119; CJ (1921) 77, 164; ibid (1926) 151, etc; ibid (1966–67) 76, 109; ibid (1970–71) 51.
7 CJ (1970–71) 180.
8 LJ (1953–54) 6; CJ (1830) 466; ibid (1840) 520; ibid (1910) 171; ibid (1942–43) 169; ibid (1953–54) 7.
9 CJ (1834) 189, 574.
10 2 Hatsell 366; LJ (1834) 958; CJ (1834) 574; LJ (1850) 368; CJ (1850) 539.

ommendation' and 'Queen's consent' are given. These are explained below. But verbal messages may also be sent for other purposes.[1]

Queen's pleasure. The signification of the Queen's pleasure is the form employed for communicating to Parliament the Queen's wishes with regard to certain matters which are mostly of a formal and regularly recurrent nature and connected with the procedure of Parliament. Thus the Queen's pleasure is signified at the commencement of each Parliament, by the Lord Chancellor, that the Commons should elect a Speaker (see pp 225–227); and when a vacancy in the office of Speaker occurs in the middle of a Parliament, a communication of the same nature is made by a Minister in the House (see p 228). Her Majesty's pleasure is also signified for the attendance of the Commons in the House of Peers; in regard to the times at which she appoints to be attended with addresses; and concerning matters personally affecting the interests of the royal family.[2] At the end of a session, also, the royal pleasure is signified, by the Lord Chancellor, that Parliament should be prorogued. Under this head may likewise be included the royal approbation of the Speaker elect, signified by the Lord Chancellor.

Queen's recommendation. The Queen's recommendation is a technical form of great importance in financial procedure, as it is required to sanction the proposal of a charge and thus reserves the initiation of expenditure to the Crown. The Queen's recommendation is given to motions which involve any public expenditure or grant of money not included in the annual estimates, or which would have the effect of releasing or compounding any sum of money owing to the Crown. Before 1966[3] the Queen's recommendation was signified to the Commons by a Minister of the Crown in person (that is, a Minister of Cabinet rank who was head of a department). Certain changes in practice were made in 1966, so that the Queen's recommendation to the type of motion mentioned is now normally notified in writing to the Clerk of the House by the Financial Secretary to the Treasury, and the fact that it has been signified is entered on the Order Paper on which appears the notice of motion to which it relates.[4] No petition for any sum relating to the public service and having the Queen's recommendation has been presented since 1963.

The forms and rules observed in connection with the signifying of the Queen's recommendation are stated fully in chapter 29, p 713.

The Civil List Bills of 1936, 1937 and 1952 were, through a Minister of the Crown, recommended to the consideration of the House of Commons in

---

1 Arrest of a Member to be tried by a military court martial, CJ (1782–84) 479; ibid (1940–41) 178; attendance of the Speaker as representing the House, at Thanksgiving Service at St Paul's Cathedral, ibid (1872) 61; at Westminster Abbey, ibid (1887) 293; at the Coronation, ibid (1911) 75; ibid (1936–37) 134; ibid (1952–53) 227. For the royal consent to the appointment of a select committee affecting the sovereign, see CJ (1901) 102. In 1964, the Speaker informed the House of Commons of the terms of a letter Her Majesty had received from the President of the United States, in reply to a communication from Her Majesty to the President, in respect of which the House had addressed Her Majesty, CJ (1963–64) 75.
2 CJ (1830–31) 460.
3 See Report from Select Committee on Procedure, HC 122, para 19 (1965–66); HC Deb (1966–67) 738, c 484.
4 For example, CJ (1966–67) 389, 612. Until 1966, the Queen's recommendation might also be given to certain motions for the appointment of Committees of the whole House.

respect of provisions enabling the Sovereign to assent to arrangements for the payment of certain sums out of the revenues of the Duchy of Cornwall.[1]

Queen's consent on bills. Bills affecting the prerogative, hereditary revenues, personal property or interests of the Crown, the Duchy of Lancaster or the Duchy of Cornwall[2] require the signification of Queen's consent before they are passed. When the Prince of Wales is of age, his own consent as Duke of Cornwall is given.[3]

The Queen's consent has been given in respect of motions for leave to bring in bills,[4] amendments to bills,[5] bills in any of their stages,[6] instructions to committees on bills,[7] Lords (or Commons) amendments to bills,[8] or to motions directing that Measures under the Church of England Assembly (Powers) Act 1919 be presented for the Royal Assent.[9] In the case of bills it is now usual to defer signification until the third reading unless the interests involved, particularly those of the royal prerogative, are fundamental to the bill. This distinction is, to a great extent at least, one of convenience. In ordinary cases the communication is deferred to the latest stage in order that account may be taken of any amendment of the bill before the Queen's consent in respect of the whole bill is given. But if the matters affecting the royal interests form the main or a very important part of a bill, it would be courting waste of time if the permission of the Crown to proceed with the bill were not ascertained at the outset. In such cases, accordingly, the communication from the Queen is signified at the earliest stage of debate—usually the second reading.[10]

The Queen's consent is expressed in terms to the effect that Her Majesty, having been informed of the purport of the bill, has consented to place her prerogative or interest, or both, at the disposal of Parliament for the purposes of the bill. The Queen's consent is signified by a Privy Counsellor, who in the Lords must be a Minister. In the Commons, when the Queen's consent is signified on third reading it is indicated formally by a Privy Counsellor; the communication on second reading of the fact that the Queen has placed her prerogative and interest at the disposal of Parliament is made orally in full, generally by a Minister of the Crown. In the absence of the Queen from the United Kingdom, the communication refers instead to Counsellors of State, acting on Her Majesty's behalf.[11] The Queen's consent is signified in the

1 CJ (1935–36) 212; ibid (1936–37) 264; ibid (1951–52) 312.
2 On rare occasions the Queen, or Prince of Wales when of age, gives consent as Prince and Steward of Scotland, CJ (1847) 551; ibid (1969–70) 321.
3 CJ (1922) 313; ibid (1970–71) 34; LJ (1986–87) 220; Votes and Proceedings (1986–87), 9 April 1987.
4 CJ (1851–52) 232; ibid (1852) 142; the Queen's consent and recommendation were signified to the Lands Revenues Bill, CJ (1852–54) 625.
5 CJ (1846–47) 843; CJ (1852) 321.
6 CJ (1964–65) 47, 109; ibid (1912–13) 442–443; ibid (1913) 218–9; LJ (1967–68) 648. The Prince of Wales' consent as well as that of the King was signified on the third reading of the Duchy of Lancaster (Application of Capital Moneys) Bill, CJ (1921) 345.
7 Civil List Bill 1837, CJ (1837–38) 204.
8 CJ (1919) 246; ibid (1935–36) 348; ibid (1966–67) 608; ibid (1979–80) 780.
9 CJ (1924) 222; ibid (1945–46) 257; ibid (1948–49) 266; ibid (1967–68) 238; ibid (1969–70) 220; LJ (1967–68) 306.
10 Eg Ireland Bill 1949; Park Lane Improvement Bill 1957–58; Life Peerages Bill 1957; Human Rights Bill 1987.
11 CJ (1973–74) 146.

Lords immediately before the motion for second or third reading is made, in the Commons on the order for second or third reading being read.

In 1935 the Speaker intimated that he was not prepared to propose the question for the second reading of the Peace Bill unless the requisite communication in respect of the King's interests therein had been made; and in subsequent sessions the printing of the same bill was by the Speaker's direction delayed until an intimation that such a communication would be made had been received. In 1937 the King's consent, as far as his prerogative was concerned, was signified on the reading of the order for second reading.[1]

When the principle of a bill wholly concerns a matter within the royal prerogative, it is usual in the House of Lords for an address for the Queen's consent to be moved before the bill is introduced. This has been done by the Opposition and by private members, particularly where the proposed bill concerns the composition of the House of Lords or other constitutional change.[2] This convention does not apply to Government bills, whether mentioned in the Speech from the Throne or not.[3]

The fact that a bill affecting the interests of the Crown has been mentioned in the Speech from the Throne does not exempt it from the need for Queen's consent.[4]

Where a bill affecting the interests of the Crown has been allowed, through inadvertence, to be read the third time and passed without the Queen's consent being signified, the proceedings have been declared null and void.[5]

Amendments in committee affecting the Crown. As it is for the House, and not for a committee, which cannot receive any communication from the Sovereign, to guard the interests of the Crown, no question can arise upon an amendment in committee as to whether the Queen's consent should be signified before the question is proposed. Many precedents exist of amendments, which affected the interests of the Crown, being made in committees on bills, and the Queen's consent being signified at a later stage.[6]

Amendments at later stages affecting the Crown. On 29 June 1951 in the Commons, amendments to the Mineral Workings Bill were made both on recommittal and on consideration which affected the Crown's interests in the Duchy of Lancaster and in the Duchy of Cornwall. The King's consent, which had not previously been required, had to be given on third reading the same day, and a notice to this effect was placed on the order paper in anticipation of the amendments being made. The consent was signified separately in respect of each Duchy.[7] The Queen's or Prince of Wales's consent may also be signified to a Lords Amendment affecting their interests.[8]

---

1 CJ (1937–38) 61.
2 LJ (1952–53) 31; Life Peers Bill 1952.
3 LJ (1957–58) 4, 22: Life Peerages Bill 1957; ibid (1966–67) 15, 431: Royal Assent Bill 1967.
4 Parl Deb (1833) 17, cc 966–970; CJ (1833) 381.
5 CJ (1852) 157; ibid (1911) 388; ibid (1948–49) 323.
6 Validation of War Time Leases Bill [Lords] CJ (1943–44) 171; Lancaster Palatine Court (No. 2) Bill, CJ (1951–52) 290. See also Valuation of Property Bill, Parl Deb (1874) 220, c 631, when in committee the chairman decided that he was bound by precedent to put the question on an amendment to make Crown property rateable, though the consent of the Crown had not been signified. See also Stg Co Deb (1954–55) Co A (Oil in Navigable Waters Bill) c 94.
7 CJ (1950–51) 262; Notices of Motions (1950–51) p 3283.
8 CJ (1974–75) 399; ibid (1979–80) 780.

Withholding of Queen's consent. The withholding of the Queen's consent
to a bill which requires it results in the withdrawal of the bill as the relevant
question cannot be proposed thereon. Similarly, if the Queen's consent is
necessary for a motion to introduce a bill under the 'ten-minute' rule
procedure and that consent is not given, the motion cannot be moved.[1]

On the third reading of the St. Asaph and Bangor Dioceses Bill 1844 in the
House of Lords the question was raised whether the bill could pass without
the Queen's consent having been signified. A select committee reported that
the bill was of that class to which it was usual to signify the consent of the
Crown. Since the Government opposed the bill and the Queen's consent was
withheld, the Lord in charge of the bill withdrew it.[2] In 1866, on the third
reading of the Blackwater Bridge Bill, in the House of Commons, notice
being taken that the Queen's consent had not been signified, the Speaker
declined to put the question.[3] In 1868 the Peerage (Ireland) Bill was withdrawn on second reading, when it was intimated that ministers would not
advise Her Majesty to give her consent to the bill at a later stage.[4] In 1964 the
Home Secretary declined to recommend that the Queen's consent be given
in respect of the Titles (Abolition) Bill, on the grounds that the bill was
unlikely to be debated, and that whether he made a recommendation was
entirely at his discretion.[5]

Queen's consent on motions. Her Majesty may give her consent also to
certain types of motion, such as that to appoint a temporary additional
Deputy Chairman of Ways and Means.[6]

Constitutional character of these communications. These several forms
of communication are recognized as constitutional declarations of the
Crown, made on the advice of its responsible ministers, by whom they are
announced to Parliament in compliance with established usage. They cannot
be misconstrued into any interference with the proceedings of Parliament,
as some of them are rendered necessary by resolutions of the House of
Commons, and all are founded upon parliamentary usage, which both
Houses have agreed to observe. This usage is not binding upon Parliament;
but if, without the Queen's consent previously signified, Parliament should
dispose of the interests or affect the prerogative of the Crown, the Crown
could still protect itself, in a constitutional manner, by the refusal of the
Royal Assent to the bill. It is one of the advantages of this usage, that it
obviates the necessity of resorting to the exercise of that prerogative.

The fact that the Crown gives its consent in respect of a bill should not be
taken to mean that the Crown, through its advisers, approves of the pro-

---

1 HC Deb (1927) 208, c 218.
2 LJ (1844) 453, 478; Parl Deb (1844) 76, cc 122, 294, 591.
3 CJ (1866) 423.
4 Parl Deb (1868) 191, c 1564. In the same year the Government being unwilling to advise the
   Queen to place her interest in the temporalities of the bishoprics and benefices in Ireland at
   the disposal of Parliament, the House of Commons voted an address to Her Majesty, praying
   that such interest should be placed at their disposal. In reply, the Queen desired that her
   interest should not stand in the way of consideration of any measure relating to the Irish
   Church and the bill for suspending appointments to bishoprics and benefices in Ireland was
   proceeded with and passed by the Commons in opposition to the Ministers of the Crown. A
   similar course was adopted by the Lords in 1875 in regard to Irish peerages.
5 HC Deb (1963–64) 690, c 619; see also Rhodesia Independence Bill, CJ (1969–70) 337 and
   HC Deb (1969–70) 801, c 1694.
6 CJ (1945–46) 392; ibid (1947–48) 67; ibid (1956–57) 225; ibid (1964–65) 41.

visions which require its consent, but only that the Crown does not intend that, for lack of its consent, Parliament should be debarred from debating such provisions.[1] If the refusal of the Royal Assent to a bill were still resorted to, there would be nothing inconsistent in such refusal in the case of a bill to which the Queen's consent had previously been signified. Still less could ministers be charged with inconsistency for speaking and voting against a bill in respect of which they had signified the Queen's consent.[2]

Acknowledgment of messages from the Crown

Written messages. The forms observed on the meeting and prorogation of Parliament, and the proceedings connected with the address in answer to the royal speech (see p 234), and the Royal Assent to bills (see p 529) have been already described. Messages under the royal sign manual are generally acknowledged by addresses in both Houses, which are presented from one House by the 'Lords with white staves', ie the Lord Steward and the Lord Chamberlain; or sometimes by other Lords specially named; and from the other by privy councillors, or members of the royal household, in the same manner as addresses in answer to royal speeches at the opening of Parliament (see p 234).[3] In the Commons, however, it is not always necessary to reply to messages under the sign manual by address; as a prompt provision made by that House (see p 203) is itself a sufficient acknowledgment of royal communications for pecuniary aid.[4] Messages, other than messages touching pecuniary aid, such as messages relating to important public events,[5] or matters connected with the prerogatives, interests, or property of the Crown,[6] or calling for general legislative measures,[7] are answered by an address.[8]

In 1926 messages declaring the existence of a state of emergency within the meaning of the Emergency Powers Act 1920 were answered in both Houses in certain cases by addresses[9] of thanks, and in others merely by resolving that the regulations made as a result of the emergency should continue in force.[10] In 1966, 1970 and 1974, on the other hand, the two Houses both answered Her Majesty's messages by addresses of thanks and resolved that the regulations should continue in force.[11]

---

1 HC Deb (1966–67) 743, c 891.
2 See Lord Hailsham's statement on Life Peerages Bill [HL] 1935, HL Deb (1935) 96, c 34; see also ibid (1911) 7, c 773, and Established Church (Ireland) Bill 1868, p 563n4 above.
3 CJ (1854) 169; Parl Deb (1854) 132, c 307.
4 In 1931 the reply of the House of Commons to a message under the sign manual expressing the need for additional taxation was to set up the Committee of Ways and Means, CJ (1930–31) 407.
5 CJ (1826–28) 114, etc, calling out the reserve force; ibid (1882) 399; ibid (1964–65) 110 (Sir Winston Churchill's Funeral and Lying-in-State).
6 CJ (1830) 466; ibid (1834) 574; ibid (1840) 520; ibid (1910) 171.
7 CJ (1830) 214.
8 CJ (1921) 337, 346.
9 LJ (1926) 116, 140, 193, 260; CJ (1926) 151, 186, 244.
10 LJ (1926) 288, 291, 297, 330, 370; CJ (1926) 313, 327, 335, 340, 380. The failure to acknowledge by means of an address has occasioned protest in the House, HC Deb (1926) 198, c 2112.
11 LJ (1966–67) 74, 106; ibid (1970–71) 60; LJ (1873–74) 122; CJ (1966–67) 83, 118; ibid (1970–71) 56.

Orders for taking a message into consideration, and for resuming an adjourned debate on a motion for an address in answer to a message, have been discharged.

Verbal messages. When the House has been informed, by command of the Crown, of the arrest of a Member to be tried by a military court martial (see p 96), it has immediately resolved upon an address of thanks to the Sovereign 'for his tender regard to the privileges of this House'.[1]

An address was also voted in reply to the communication of Lord George Gordon's arrest in 1780.[2] As the arrest of a Member to be tried by a naval court martial did not proceed immediately from the Crown, and the communication was only made from the Lords of the Admiralty (see p 96), no address was necessary in answer to this indirect form of message.

On royal pleasure etc. being signified. The matters upon which the royal pleasure is usually signified need no address in answer, as immediate compliance is given by the House; and the recommendation and consent of the Crown, as already explained, are only signified as introductory to proceedings in Parliament, or essential to their progress.

COMMUNICATIONS TO THE CROWN ORIGINATING IN PARLIAMENT

Addresses to the Crown

An address to Her Majesty[3] is the form ordinarily employed by both Houses of Parliament for making their desires and opinions known to the Crown as well as for the purpose of acknowledging communications proceeding from the Crown.

Joint addresses. Addresses are sometimes agreed upon by both Houses, and jointly presented to the Crown, but are more generally confined to each House singly. When some event of unusual importance[4] makes it desirable to present a joint address, the Lords or Commons, as the case may be, agree to a form of address, and, having left a blank for the insertion of the title of the other House, communicate it (formerly at a conference, but now by message),[5] and desire their concurrence. The blank is filled up by the other House, and a message is returned, acquainting the House with their concurrence, and that the blank has been filled up. Such addresses are presented either by both Houses in a body,[6] or by two Lords and four Members of the House of Commons;[7] and they have been presented also by com-

---

1 CJ (1814–16) 70; ibid (1940–41) 178.
2 CJ (1778–80) 903.
3 Addresses have also been made to Their Majesties, CJ (1918) 150, etc.
4 CJ (1831–32) 421; ibid (1834) 232; ibid (1840) 442; ibid (1842) 324.
5 CJ (1882) 88; ibid (1906) 276.
6 CJ (1831–32) 424; LJ (1840) 393; ibid (1842) 279.
7 CJ (1830) 652; ibid (1882) 94; a joint address having been agreed to, 2 September 1880, when the Queen was at Balmoral, Her Majesty dispensed with its formal presentation, see LJ (1880) 391.

mittees of both Houses;[1] by a joint committee of Lords and Commons,[2] and by the Lord Chancellor and the Speaker of the House of Commons.[3] The Lords always learn Her Majesty's pleasure, and communicate to the Commons, by message, the time at which she has appointed to be attended.

Separate addresses. In the House of Commons the procedure upon a motion for an address is the same as upon an ordinary substantive motion. It requires notice and admits of debate, amendment and division. Usually, the motion for an address is made in the form 'That an humble address be presented to Her Majesty to . . .' and the necessary prefatory words are inserted when the actual copy of the address is prepared. An amendment to leave out the word 'humble' is not in order.[4] In both Houses addresses or resolutions are ordered to be presented by the whole House;[5] or by privy councillors,[6] or members of the royal household,[7] or, in the Lords, by the Lords with white staves;[8] and, in some cases, by Members specially nominated.[9]

Subjects of addresses. Addresses have comprised every matter of foreign[10] or domestic policy;[11] the administration of justice;[12] the expression of congratulation or condolence (which is agreed to *nemine dissentiente* by the

---

1 CJ (1547–1628) 877.
2 CJ (1640–42) 462.
3 CJ (1708–11) 54.
4 HC Deb (1918) 103, c 112.
5 CJ (1857–58) 31; ibid (1861) 16; LJ (1897) 255; CJ (1918) 250; ibid (1944–45) 131; ibid (1945–46) 18. See also CJ (1950) 241 and ibid (1964–65) 309, 317, 319 for occasions on which the House of Commons was accompanied in the presentation of an address by invited representatives of Commonwealth Parliaments.
6 LJ (1948–49) 20.
7 CJ (1904) 226.
8 LJ (1946–47) 217.
9 CJ (1688–93) 295; ibid (1812) 391 (after motion for presentation by whole House withdrawn, and for presentation by privy councillors negatived); LJ (1947–48) 224; ibid (1972–73) 33.
10 CJ (1823) 278; ibid (1826–28) 114; ibid (1833) 471; assassination of President Lincoln, 1865, CJ (1865) 229; invasion of Belgium, 1914, LJ (1914) 402; CJ (1914) 449.
11 CJ (1830) 472, 653; appointment of a royal commission with power to examine witnesses on oath, CJ (1888) 46 (as to the administration of an oath by a royal commission, see 2 Todd 99; Parl Deb (1905) 147, c 1341, and by a tribunal of inquiry appointed at the instance of both Houses of Parliament, see Tribunals of Inquiry (Evidence) Act 1921; CJ (1921) 55; LJ (1922) 46; CJ (1922) 27); reference of questions of law relating to the alleged disqualification of a Member to the judicial committee of the privy council, CJ (1912–13) 519.
12 CJ (1830) 472 (an address to remove a judge from office).

Lords and *nemine contradicente* by the Commons);[1] and, in short, representations upon all points connected with the government and welfare of the country; but they ought not to be presented in relation to any bill depending in either House of Parliament.[2] Addresses have been frequently presented in recent years praying that Her Majesty will give directions for the presentation, on behalf of the House of Commons, of gifts such as ceremonial maces or parliamentary libraries to legislatures of new member states of the Commonwealth.[3] Frequent occasion for moving addresses is afforded by provisions, of the same general type, contained in many recent statutes, which prescribe the methods by which parliamentary control is exercised over orders or regulations made under authority of the respective statutes by the Privy Council, Ministers or other authorities (see pp 545–547).

Mode of presentation of addresses

Joint addresses. When a joint address is to be presented by both Houses, the Lord Chancellor and the House of Lords, and the Speaker and the House of Commons, proceed in state to the palace at the time appointed. On reaching the palace, the two Houses assemble in a chamber adjoining the throne room, and when Her Majesty is prepared to receive them, the doors

1 On the birth of royal children, see, for example, LJ (1948–49) 20; CJ (1948–49) 27; LJ (1959–60) 131; CJ (1959–60) 117; LJ (1963–64) 172; CJ (1963–64) 150; Votes & Proceedings (1981–82) 24 June 1982. On the deaths of sovereigns and on succession to the throne, LJ (1901) 8; CJ (1901) 6; LJ (1910) 128; CJ (1910) 153; LJ (1935–36) 61; CJ (1935–36) 54; LJ (1951–52) 85; CJ (1951–52) 93. On succession to the throne, LJ (1936–37) 63; CJ (1936–37) 60. On the deaths of members of the royal family, see, for example, LJ (1923)173; CJ (1923) 204; LJ (1924–25) 389; CJ (1924–25) 409; LJ (1930–31) 83; CJ (1930–31) 83; LJ (1935–36) 24; ibid (1939–40) 11; CJ (1939–40) 10; LJ (1941–42) 37, 186; CJ (1941–42) 35, 164; ibid (1943–44) 207; LJ (1951–52) 85; CJ (1951–52) 93; LJ (1952–53) 134; CJ (1952–53) 158; LJ (1964–65) 229; CJ (1964–65) 200. On royal marriages, LJ (1893–94) 325; CJ (1893–94) 434; LJ (1947–48) 9; CJ (1947–48) 9; CJ (1980) 450. On royal anniversaries, LJ (1897) 255; CJ (1897) 299; LJ (1918) 165; CJ (1918) 250; LJ (1934–35) 161; CJ (1934–35) 190; LJ (1947–48) 233; CJ (1947–48) 246. CJ (1972–73) 36; CJ (1976–77) 284. On the deaths of foreign royal personages or heads of state, see, for example, LJ (1914) 247; CJ (1914) 303; LJ (1927) 22; CJ (1927) 12; LJ (1931–32) 176; CJ (1931–32) 192; LJ (1933–34) 74; CJ (1933–34) 79; LJ (1935–36) 181; CJ (1935–36) 203; LJ (1944–45) 97; CJ (1944–45) 96; LJ (1950–51) 251; CJ (1950–51) 298; LJ (1963–64) 28; CJ (1963–64) 22. In respect of other public events: conclusion of the armistice, LJ (1918) 291; CJ (1918) 250; victory in Europe, LJ (1944–45) 114; CJ (1944–45) 128; victorious conclusion of the war, LJ (1945–46) 31; CJ (1945–46) 17; departure of Queen Elizabeth on Commonwealth tour and return therefrom, LJ (1953–54) 19, 187; CJ (1953–54) 26, 204; return of Queen Elizabeth from Nigerian visit, LJ (1955–56) 217; return of Queen Elizabeth from West African tour, LJ (1961–62) 50; death of Sir W Churchill, CJ (1964–65) 110. The sympathy of the legislature on the occasion of royal deaths has been expressed in the address in reply to the Gracious Speech, LJ (1862) 6; CJ (1862) 7; LJ (1892) 7; CJ (1892) 10; LJ (1896) 16; CJ (1896) 13. The House of Commons has instructed the Speaker to send a message of sympathy to the President of the Chamber of Deputies in Paris on the occasion of an explosion there, CJ (1893–94) 621, Parl Deb (1893–94) 19, cc 1050, 1178, 1617. For a division on such a motion, see CJ (1897) 299.

2 LJ (1666–75) 72, 81, 88; CJ (1660–67); 1 Grey Deb 5. For the application of this rule to legislation by the Tynwald, see HC Deb (1959–60) 620, c 678.

3 See, for example, CJ (1967–68) 254, 263. Votes and Proceedings 18 January 1988. An address to Her Majesty from a recipient legislature relating to such a gift has been ordered to be entered in the Journal of the House of Commons, CJ (1967–68) 396.

are thrown open, and the Lord Chancellor and the Speaker[1] advance side by side, followed by the Members of the two Houses respectively, and are conducted towards the Throne by the Lord Chamberlain. The Lord Chancellor reads the address, and on his knee presents it, Her Majesty returns an answer, and both Houses retire from the royal presence.

Separate addresses. When addresses are presented separately, by either House, the forms observed are similar to those already described, except that the addresses of the Commons are read by their Speaker.

In November 1918 the King appointed the Royal Gallery of the Palace of Westminster as the place in which he would be attended with the addresses of both Houses with regard to the armistice with Germany. The Houses proceeded there at the appointed time and awaited the arrival of His Majesty, who after the addresses had been presented in the usual manner made a speech in answer thereto.[2] The same procedure was followed in May and August 1945 in answering addresses regarding the victory in Europe and the victorious conclusion of the war.[3]

A similar procedure was followed in 1950, on the opening of the new House of Commons, when arrangements were made for the House of Commons to be accompanied while presenting the address by the Speakers or other Presiding Officers of the lower Houses of the Legislatures of Commonwealth countries, Northern Ireland, the Isle of Man and the Channel Islands, and of colonial legislatures with unofficial majorities.[4] On the occasion of the seven hundredth anniversary of Simon de Montfort's Parliament, the House of Commons sought and obtained Her Majesty's leave to present her with an address in reply to a reference to the anniversary in the Gracious Speech, accompanied by invited representatives of Commonwealth parliaments.[5] In 1988 a similar ceremony was held to mark the Revolution of 1688–89 and the Bill of Rights and the Claim of Right.[6]

When the Lord Chancellor or Speaker has read the address, he presents it to Her Majesty upon one knee.

According to modern practice, Members of both Houses may attend Her Majesty in their ordinary attire.[7] When in the temporary absence of the Sovereign certain royal functions are by letters patent delegated to Counsellors of State, and addresses are in that period ordered by the House of Commons to be presented to the Sovereign, the addresses are presented to and the replies made by the Counsellors of State on behalf of the Sovereign.[8]

---

1 The Speaker is always on the left hand of the Chancellor.
2 LJ (1918) 291, 293; CJ (1918) 251; HL Deb (1918) 32, cc 167, 199; HC Deb (1918) 110, c 3228.
3 LJ (1944–45) 119; CJ (1944–45) 131, 132; LJ (1945–46) 32, 38; CJ (1945–46) 24, 26.
4 CJ (1950) 241, 244; HC Deb (1950) 475, c 2240–2241; ibid 478, cc 2703–2710, 2793–2797, 2929–2936.
5 CJ (1964–65) 309, 317, 319. On the occasion of the Silver Jubilee of King George V, each House resolved to present an address of congratulation, the terms of which were conveyed in speeches made by the Speakers of each House to His Majesty in Westminster Hall, the Speakers' words being afterwards entered in the Journals: LJ (1934–35) 161, 163–164; CJ (1934–35) 190, 191.
6 Votes and Proceedings, 20 July 1988.
7 They are not permitted to enter the royal presence with sticks or umbrellas, see 2 Hatsell 390 n; Colchester iii, 604–607.
8 CJ (1946–47) 92, 161; ibid (1953–54) 40; ibid (1962–63) 103, etc.

Answers to addresses

When addresses have been presented by the whole House, the Lord Chancellor in one House, and the Speaker in the other, report the answer of Her Majesty; but when they have been presented in the ordinary way, the answer is reported, in the Lords, generally by the Lord Chamberlain; and in the Commons, by one of the royal household, who appears at the bar and, on being called by the Speaker, reads Her Majesty's answer.[1]

Communications with the royal family

It is to the reigning Sovereign, or regent, alone that addresses are presented by Parliament; but messages have frequently been sent by both Houses to members of the royal family, to congratulate them upon their marriage or other auspicious events;[2] or to offer condolences on family bereavements.[3] Resolutions have also been ordered to be laid before members of the royal family. Certain Members are always nominated by the House to present the messages or resolutions; one of whom afterwards acquaints the House (in the Lords, in his place or at the Table, and, in the Commons, at the bar) with the answers which were returned.[4]

Communications have also been made to both Houses by members of the royal family, which are either delivered by Members in their places,[5] or are conveyed to the House by letters addressed to the Speaker.[6]

2. COMMUNICATIONS BETWEEN THE LORDS AND THE COMMONS

The two Houses of Parliament have frequent occasion to communicate with each other, not only in regard to bills which require the assent of both Houses, but with reference to other matters connected with the proceedings of Parliament. Representatives of the Government sit in both Houses, so that every public question is presented by the executive to both Houses from a single point of view. When, however, the Government cannot rely upon a majority in the House of Lords, disagreement between the Houses may arise. In the past, such disagreements have touched on fundamental consti-

---

1 The proceedings of the House have sometimes been interrupted to receive the Sovereign's answer, CJ (1852–53) 438; ibid (1878–79) 23. On 19 November 1914, the King's answer was reported by a privy counsellor who appeared at the bar in uniform, CJ (1914–16) 15.
2 LJ (1794–96) 584; ibid (1840) 53; ibid (1842) 6; CJ (1818) 424; ibid (1840) 88; ibid (1893–94) 434; ibid (1979–80) 754.
3 LJ (1820) 367; CJ (1819–20) 480; ibid (1837) 493 (the Queen Dowager); ibid (1850) 508. To the Duke of Connaught, LJ (1917–18) 63; CJ (1917–18) 45; to Queen Mary, CJ (1935–36) 54, etc.
4 LJ (1820) 369; ibid (1840) 53; ibid (1910–11) 144; CJ (1840) 95; ibid (1917–18) 48. In the case of the messages of condolence to the German Empress in 1888 and to the Duchess of Saxe-Coburg and Gotha, Duchess of Edinburgh, in 1900, the Speaker was directed to communicate the messages to Her Majesty's ministers resident at their courts for presentation, CJ (1888) 293; LJ (1900) 398; CJ (1900) 380.
5 CJ (1802–03) 211; ibid (1819–20) 288.
6 CJ (1809) 86; ibid (1812–13) 253; ibid (1813–14) 324, 433.

tutional points, as in 1831–32 and 1909–11,[1] but disputes have also arisen over what may be regarded as more or less short-lived political matters.[2]

The modes of communication are: by message; by joint committees; and by select committees of both Houses communicating with each other (see p 669). Only communication by message is considered in this section, as communication by joint committees and by select committees communicating with each other is more conveniently dealt with in the chapter on committees (chapter 24). Conferences between the Houses are now obsolete, since their main function, that of providing an occasion for communicating reasons for disagreement to amendments to bills, has been taken over by the modern practice of sending messages. The last free conference (at which discussion was permitted) was in 1836, and its immediate predecessor in 1740. The last ordinary conference, when written communications were handed over without debate, was in 1860. Under resolutions of 1851, it remains theoretically possible for either House to request a conference with reference to amendments to bills disagreed to.[3]

Messages

A message is the most simple mode of communication; it is frequently resorted to, for sending bills from one House to another, and for the interchange of reports and other documents. Messages are carried from one House to the other by one of the Clerks of the House which sends the message.[4] The reception of a message need not interrupt the business then proceeding; though it may do so.[5]

In the Lords a message from the Commons is recorded in the Minutes of Proceedings and the Journal. The message may, if desired, be taken into consideration forthwith without notice (Standing Order No 39). In the Commons the reception of a message from the Lords is recorded in the Votes and Proceedings and the Journal, and any action required to be taken is normally set down for a subsequent day. Notice is generally given of the proceedings to be taken. In that case, if the matter of the Lords' message concerns a bill, these proceedings are set down as an order of the day (see p 311). Proceedings on other matters are set down as notices of motions.

If it is necessary to proceed upon a Lords' message on the day of its reception, the Speaker informs the House between the orders of the day (or may even interrupt the business under discussion) of the receipt of a message from the Lords, whereupon, the House having ordered the Lords' message

---

1 See J R M Butler *The Passing of the Great Reform Bill* (1914); R C K Ensor *England 1870–1914* (1963) and LJ (1909) 451; ibid (1911) 381; CJ (1909) 546; ibid (1911) 388.
2 For example, on the form of the Palestine mandate, LJ (1922) 242; HL Deb (1922) 50, c 994; CJ (1922) 246; HC Deb (1922) 156, cc 292, 340: on the Singapore naval base, HL Deb (1924) 56, cc 759, 817; CJ (1924) 106; HC Deb (1924) 171, c 1181: on Rhodesian policy, LJ (1967–68) 381, 487; CJ (1967–68) 296, 343.
3 Hatsell iv, 1 ff, CJ (1836) 783; ibid (1851) 210, 217, 223; ibid (1858) 182; ibid (1860) 125, 126.
4 LJ (1854–55) 159; CJ (1854–55) 254. But in 1950 the leaders of the three political parties in the Commons, the Leader of that House, and the Father of the House delivered to the Lord Chancellor at the bar of the House of Lords a message from the Commons thanking the Lords for placing their Chamber at the disposal of the Commons from 1941 to 1950. The message was considered forthwith and the reply handed by the Lord Chancellor to the bearers of the Commons message, who had remained in attendance: HC Deb (1950) 478, c 2716; HL Deb (1950) 168, cc 1289–1291.
5 CJ (1854–55) 254; ibid (1871) 57.

to be read and considered forthwith, motions are made and questions put from the Chair which arise upon its consideration (see pp 510–511).

CHAPTER 24

The system of committees

In both Houses of Parliament the practice of delegating to small bodies of Members, regarded as representing the House itself, the consideration of detailed or technical questions, is as old as any part of their settled procedure. In the course of time the various functions of these bodies were differentiated into a few fixed types; and a standard of size appropriate to each of these functions was also arrived at by experiment. While for certain functions of a quasi-judicial character four or five Members were deemed sufficient, at the other end of the scale for matters of general interest the notion of a committee was extended to include the whole House.

Each House accordingly now possesses an organized system of committees which comprises committees of the whole House; select committees and committees on private bills; in the House of Lords, public bill committees; and, in the House of Commons, standing committees on public bills and other matters. The functions of these committees include the consideration and amendment of public and private bills, inquiries (sometimes of a quasi-judicial character) into matters which the House refers to them for investigation, and (for domestic purposes) functions of an administrative character. In addition, the two Houses sometimes collaborate in joint committees, which consist of select committees of both Houses sitting and voting together. In this chapter the procedure of these committees will be described in the following order:

(1) Committees in the House of Lords; (2) Committees in the House of Commons; (3) Joint Committees.

Private bill committees are dealt with in Part III (see pp 892–919 and 935–941).

1. COMMITTEES IN THE HOUSE OF LORDS

COMMITTEES OF THE WHOLE HOUSE

A Committee of the whole House consists, as its name implies, of all the Members of the House. It is, in fact, the House itself in a less formal guise, presided over by a Chairman instead of by the Lord Speaker and conducting its business according to more flexible rules of procedure. Standing Order No 60 states: 'To have more freedom of debate, and that arguments may be used (pro and contra), Committees of the whole House are appointed, sometimes for Bills, sometimes to discuss matters of great moment'. The provisions of public bills are usually considered in a Committee of the whole House;[1] and occasionally other questions have been dealt with in this way.[2]

On a day appointed for the consideration by a Committee of the whole House of a bill or other matter committed to it, it is moved 'that the House do now resolve itself into a Committee upon the Bill (or other matter)'. When the question has been agreed to, the Lord Speaker leaves the Woolsack and the Chairman of Committees, unless the House otherwise directs, takes the Chair (at the Table).[3] If the Chairman of Committees is absent, one of the Deputy Chairmen takes his place; if none of the deputies is present, the House appoints another Lord to act as Chairman.

The powers and duties of the Chairman are the same as those of the Lord Speaker when the House is sitting. They are generally confined to the calling on of clauses and amendments in bills referred to the committee, and putting the question thereon. The Chairman also makes the committee's report to the House. Like any other Lord, he may vote if he wishes to do so; he does not (as in the Commons) have a casting vote.

Procedure in the committee is similar to that when the House is sitting except that Standing Order No 28 does not apply.[4] Lords, therefore, have greater freedom of debate because they may speak more than once on the same question. A next business motion (see p 431) is not admitted.

A Committee of the whole House can only consider those matters which have been referred to it, including any instruction to the committee agreed to by the House. If a bill has been committed to the committee, the whole bill is the committee's order of reference.

A Committee of the whole House has no power to adjourn its own sitting or to adjourn its consideration of any matter to a future sitting.[5] If consideration of the matter is not completed, or if all the matters referred to the committee have not been considered, the House is resumed on motion and can again go into committee on a future day. If on a division in committee on a bill, less than thirty Lords have voted, the Chairman declares the question not decided and the House resumes without question put. It goes into committee again on the matter at a subsequent sitting.[6]

The procedure in Committees of the whole House in respect of bills is fully described elsewhere (pp 452–457).

PUBLIC BILL COMMITTEES

For an account of these committees see pp 451–452.

---

1 Bills referred to a public bill committee are not (unless the House otherwise orders) recommitted to a Committee of the whole House (see pp 451–452).
2 For example, Standing Orders, LJ (1953–54) 180; Leave of Absence, LJ (1957–58) 202; Procedure of the House, LJ (1971–72) 138.
3 SO No 60.
4 SO No 60.
5 Committees of the whole House frequently break their consideration of a bill without question put for a dinner interval.
6 SO No 55.

SELECT COMMITTEES

Select committees, that is, committees composed of a number of Lords specially named, are appointed to consider particular matters or bills. Like a Committee of the whole House, a select committee possesses no authority except that which it derives by delegation from the House. The scope of its inquiry is therefore defined by the order appointing the committee, known as its order of reference, and the committee must confine its deliberations within those limits. When a bill is referred to a select committee, the bill itself is the order of reference and the committee must confine its deliberations to the bill and amendments relevant to it. Interpretation of the order of reference is a matter for the committee.

A select committee may be appointed by the House to examine any matter which, in the opinion of the House, requires investigation.

Appointment and membership

The manner of appointment may be in the form of two separate motions, the first appointing the committee's order of reference and the second nominating the members,[1] or in a single motion combining the order of reference and nomination of members.[2] The latter procedure is normal for the appointment of committees which recur every session. When there is a separate motion appointing the order of reference, this is generally moved by the Leader of the House. Otherwise the motion is moved by the Chairman of Committees.

Under Standing Order No 61 the Committee of Selection selects and proposes to the House the names of the members of each select committee except (a) the Committee of Selection itself, and (b) unless the Chairman of Committees or two members of the Committee of Selection decide otherwise, select committees concerned with private business. There is no limit to the number of members who may be named except for a committee on a private bill, a personal bill or a provisional order confirmation bill.[3] The quorum, unless otherwise ordered in the motion of appointment, is three. The size of the committee may be enlarged by the addition of members appointed in the same way as those originally nominated. If, however, a vacancy occurs in the membership, this may be filled without reference to the Committee of Selection (see p 584). The Chairman of Committees has discretion to propose the names of Lords to fill casual vacancies, and he moves a motion to give effect to his proposal.

The chairman of a select committee may be appointed by the House on the proposal of the Committee of Selection. Alternatively, the select committee may be given power to appoint its own chairman as part of the order appointing the members of the committee. Unless the House otherwise directs, the Chairman of Committees takes the chair in any committee of the House. In the absence of the duly appointed chairman a committee may appoint its own chairman.

---

1 LJ (1983–84) 705, 745; ibid (1984–85) 18, 23; HL Deb (1987–88) 499, c 1491; ibid 500, c 388.
2 LJ (1987–88) 30, 43.
3 Private Bill SO 104, 161, 185.

The order of appointment of most select committees[1] does not lapse with the prorogation of Parliament but continues into the next session, in accordance with Standing Order No 62, until such time as the House makes further orders of appointment in the new session. Such 'sessional committees' however cannot sit during prorogation or dissolution, being periods when they cease to exist. All committees not exempted by Standing Order No 62 automatically die at the end of a session.

A committee may be given power to co-opt additional Lords to serve on the committee or one of its sub-committees (see p 577) without such Lords being nominated by the House as members of the committee. Furthermore, under Standing Order No 63, any Lord, although not a member of the committee, may attend a meeting of the committee and speak, but he must not attend a meeting while the committee deliberates unless invited by the committee to do so,[2] and must not vote. This privilege does not extend to a secret committee.[3]

Instructions. If it is thought desirable that a committee should extend its inquiry beyond the limits laid down by its order of reference, the House may amend the order[4] or may give the committee authority for the same purpose by an instruction. This instruction may be mandatory[5] or permissive.[6] An enlargement of the order of reference may also be achieved by committing a bill, or additional bill, to the committee[7] or by referring a paper to it.

On the other hand an instruction may be given at any time to restrict the scope of the enquiry, to limit the committee's powers, to report by a certain date[8] or to comply with whatever procedural requirement is contained in the instruction.[9] See pp 449–450 for instructions to committees on bills.

Reference of papers to select committees. Reports of previous committees, or the minutes of evidence taken before them, and other papers which have been laid upon the Table of the House are sometimes referred to committees.[10] Such a reference serves to direct the particular attention of the committee to documents relating to the subject of their inquiry, or to explain or enlarge the original terms of reference.

Any Lord can move to refer to a select committee any document within the scope of its inquiry. If a committee wishes to have recourse to documents in the custody of the officers of the other House, the House will, at the request of the committee, send a message to the other House requesting them to communicate a copy of the document. The document, when communicated, will be referred to the committee.

---

1 Ie the following committees: Broadcasting, Consolidation Bills, European Communities, House of Lords Offices, Hybrid Instruments, Leave of Absence and Lords' Expenses, Personal Bills, Privileges, Procedure, Science and Technology, Standing Orders (Private Bills) and Statutory Instruments.
2 The European Communities Committee has issued a general invitation to Lords to attend all meetings, deliberative or otherwise.
3 The last such committee in the Lords was appointed in 1847.
4 LJ (1888) 367; ibid (1907) 105.
5 LJ (1884) 200.
6 LJ (1906) 208.
7 LJ (1896) 116; ibid (1932–33) 224, ibid (1983–84) 58.
8 LJ (1975–76) 89.
9 LJ (1987–88) 49.
10 LJ (1969–70) 31; ibid (1987–88) 154.

Petitions relating to the subject of inquiry have been referred to a committee.[1]

A committee of the House of Lords may send for persons and papers without being given special powers by the House. In this respect the House differs from the Commons, where such power must be specifically given. Ordinarily witnesses attend and documents are produced at the request of the committee, but if necessary an order of the House for the attendance of witnesses or the production of documents may be made.[2] Members and officers of the House of Commons, foreign diplomats and witnesses from overseas may give evidence to select committees but cannot be compelled to do so (see chapter 25). A committee has no power to send for any paper which, if required by the House itself, would be sought by address or to require an officer of a public department to produce a paper which the House would not usually order to be laid before it (see pp 213–214).

Proceedings in select committees

Select committees are governed for the most part in their proceedings by the same rules as those which apply in the whole House, and where the rules of procedure in a Committee of the whole House differ from those in the House, the former are generally followed in a select committee. Thus the 'next business' motion cannot be moved in any committee. In certain respects however select committee proceedings differ from those in the whole House.

Lords speak sitting in select committees and the rule against smoking is relaxed when the committee deliberates.

A select committee may sit at any time when the House is adjourned, including recesses, without special leave. It may be adjourned from one sitting to another, or it may be reconvened at the discretion of the chairman.

A select committee usually sits in one of the committee rooms of the House. If however it has been given the power to adjourn from place to place, it may sit and hear evidence outside the precincts of the House, both in the United Kingdom and overseas.

The names of the members present each day at a sitting are entered in the minutes of proceedings of the committee.[3]

Questions are decided in the same way as in the whole House, but when a division is taken the names of the members are called in alphabetical order by the Clerk and each member replies 'content' or 'not content', or indicates that he abstains. The chairman has a vote but not a casting vote. If the votes are equal, the question is decided as in the whole House (see p 430). The question proposed, the name of the proposer and the votes of each member are entered in the minutes of proceedings of the committee (see p 577).[4]

A select committee must not hear witnesses by counsel unless so authorised by order of the House.[5]

Evidence. Meetings at which evidence is being taken are, by custom, held in public and strangers are admitted. A committee may at any time, how-

1 LJ (1889) 62; ibid (1904–5) 227.
2 LJ (1883) 114; ibid (1919) 315.
3 Pursuant to a Resolution of 25 June 1852, LJ (1852) 344.
4 Pursuant to a Resolution of 7 December 1852, LJ (1852–3) 44.
5 SO No 64.

ever, order that a meeting or part of a meeting be held in private, and strangers are then required to withdraw. Meetings at which committees deliberate are invariably held in private. For a description of the examination of witnesses and methods of obtaining their attendance, see chapter 25. For the privilege and protection of witnesses and the punishment of contumacious witnesses, see Part I.

The evidence of witnesses under examination is taken down verbatim by a shorthand writer and is usually printed and published in pursuance of an order of the House. The order of reference may include an order that the minutes of evidence taken before the committee from time to time be printed and, if the committee think fit, be delivered out; this power enables the committee to publish such of its evidence as it chooses without reporting it to the House and without waiting for the completion of the inquiry.

Past practice placed a general restriction on the publication of oral and written evidence before it had been reported to the House. This restriction no longer applies in most cases. Provided that the committee's order of reference allows evidence to be delivered out, all oral and written evidence may, subject to the committee's agreement, become publicly available from the time when it is submitted to the committee.

The names of the Lords present at the sitting are entered in the minutes of evidence, and to every question or series of questions there must be prefixed the name of the Lord putting the question or questions.[1] Questions and answers may be struck out of the minutes by order of the committee.

A copy of each witness's examination is sent to him for his correction, with an instruction that the corrections must be confined to inaccuracies in the transcript, punctuation and minor changes of wording to clarify the sense. If the witness wishes to add to or modify an answer, he may suggest a footnote. The corrected copy should be returned to the clerk within seven days of its receipt; otherwise it may be printed in its original form.

Sub-committees. A select committee, having only a delegated authority, cannot, without the leave of the House, divide itself into sub-committees or delegate to a sub-committee any of the authority delegated to it by the House. By custom this rule does not apply to the House of Lords Offices Committee or to the Procedure Committee (see pp 583–584) which appoint sub-committees without specific authority from the House. Committees with powers to appoint sub-committees may confer on those sub-committees no powers in excess of their own.

Sub-committees report to the committee by which they were appointed and not to the House. In the European Communities Committee, however, the chairman may, in cases of urgency, present the report of a sub-committee to the House on behalf of the main committee[2] (see pp 582–583).

The powers and procedures of a sub-committee follow that of its parent committee, unless otherwise ordered.

Specialist advisers and expert assistance. Committees are now frequently given powers to secure the assistance of professional or technical advisers who are paid a daily fee for their assistance. Such advisers normally attend

1 Pursuant to a Resolution of 25 June 1852, LJ (1852) 344.
2 LJ (1973–74) 172; eg seventh Report (1986–87), HL 121 (8 April 1987).

both public and private sessions of the committee. They do not examine witnesses or take part in voting. Since 1988 the European Communities Committee and the Science and Technology Committee have each had authority to appoint for a period of two years a temporary committee specialist assistant.[1]

On occasions committees may invite expert individuals, such as civil servants or members and officials of the European Commission, to assist them in their deliberations. Such individuals, who are not paid advisers, may take part in private meetings for informal discussion, with or without a verbatim record.

Certain other persons attend sittings of committees but are not witnesses. These include the two Counsel to the Chairman of Committees, who assist the Joint Committee on Statutory Instruments, the Hybrid Instruments Committee, the Personal Bills Committee and the European Communities Committee, and other officials who attend the House of Lords Offices Committee and its sub-committees.

Reports of select committees. Select committees can be divided into two categories. On the one hand there are committees appointed to undertake particular inquiries. The culmination of the work of such an ad hoc committee is the report which it makes to the House and, unless the committee has been given leave to report from time to time, the report brings the committee's existence to an end. On the other hand there are sessional committees appointed regularly to consider and report upon the same subject or class of subjects from session to session. These committees may make frequent reports without special leave from the House since authority to do so is included in their order of reference. What follows concerns primarily the first category.

Form of report. The report of a select committee on a public matter usually takes the form of a document giving an account of what the committee has done, reviewing the evidence which it has received, and offering the committee's opinions and conclusions. With a select committee on a public bill, the procedure is somewhat different since it is the bill itself which is reported to the House. Such a select committee may report the bill without amendment, or report the bill with amendment,[2] or report that the bill should not proceed.[3] In each case the committee may add its reasons in a form similar to the report on a public matter.

Preparation of draft report. When the examination of witnesses has been concluded, the chairman prepares a draft report for circulation to the committee's members. Preparation of the draft is often preceded by one or more meetings to discuss the general approach to be adopted. An alternative method of proceeding is for the committee to come to resolutions on the subject of its reference on the basis of which the chairman or some other member proceeds to draft a report.

Every member of a committee is entitled to submit a draft report for the consideration of the committee. If, after the chairman has submitted his

1 HL Debs (1987–88) 495, cc 869–870.
2 Eg Foreign Boycotts Bill [HL], LJ (1977–78) 903; Laboratory Animals Protection Bill, LJ (1979–80) 895.
3 Parochial Charities (Neighbourhood Trusts) Bill [HL] and Small Charities Bill [HL], LJ (1983–84) 735; Infant Life (Preservation) Bill [HL], LJ (1987–88) 346.

draft report, any member who has not already submitted an alternative draft report wishes to do so, the committee may adjourn in order to afford him time to prepare it. No alternative draft report can be submitted once a draft report has been ordered to be taken into consideration, unless the final question for agreeing to the draft report (as amended) is negatived (see below).

Consideration of draft report. If only one draft report is submitted for consideration, the chairman proposes the question 'That the draft report be now considered'. If however more than one draft report is submitted, a motion must be made that one of them (usually that submitted by the chairman) be now considered. To this question an amendment may be moved, to leave out the name of the member by whom the report is prepared and substitute that of another member, with the object of substituting the alternative (or, if more than two draft reports have been submitted, another) draft report, as the basis of the committee's report. Amendments that each of the draft reports be considered instead of that submitted by the chairman may be moved seriatim to the question for considering the latter. Any draft report on which a division takes place is entered in full in the minutes of proceedings.

Each paragraph of the draft report adopted as the basis for the committee's report is then separately considered and may be amended according to the ordinary rules which govern amendments. After a decision has been taken on an amendment to any part of a paragraph, it is not out of order for an earlier part to be amended; and further consideration of a paragraph may be postponed after a decision has been reached on an amendment to the paragraph.[1] If no amendment is offered to a paragraph, or when all amendments proposed have been disposed of, the question is put that the paragraph, or the paragraph as amended, stand part of the report. After this question has been agreed to, no further amendment can be made to the paragraph. An amendment consisting of a new paragraph may be moved when the committee reaches the place in the draft report where the paragraph is proposed to be inserted.

An amendment to leave out a whole Part of a draft report and insert an alternative Part may be moved before the individual paragraphs of that Part are considered. If this is disagreed to, portions of the alternative Part may be offered as amendments to the individual paragraphs, provided that they are relevant thereto. Portions of any alternative draft reports may be offered as amendments to the draft report the committee has chosen for consideration provided that they are relevant thereto.

When every paragraph and proposed new paragraph has been considered and disposed of, the question is put 'That the report (as amended) be agreed to'. Once this question has been agreed to, the report cannot be further amended. If the question is negatived, the committee may either proceed with the consideration of one of the other draft reports, if any, or of any further draft which may be submitted by any member of the committee, or make a special report to the effect that it is unable to agree a report.

---

1 Indian Constitutional Reform (Joint) Committee, HL 6 (1934–35) pp 312, 538; Select Committee on Unemployment HL 142 (1981–82) II p xxxiii.

Consideration by select committee of reports from sub-committees. Where a committee works through sub-committees it is usually content to report the sub-committee's report with or without amendment as its own report to the House.[1] The committee is free to refer a report back to the sub-committee in whole or in part or to adopt a further report on the basis of that submitted by the sub-committee.

Minority reports. It is the opinion of the committee as a committee, not that of individual members, which is required by the House, and failing unanimity the conclusions agreed to by the majority are the conclusions of the committee.[2] No signatures may, therefore, be attached to a report for the purpose of showing any difference of opinion in the committee or the absence thereof; nor may the report be accompanied by any counter-statement, memorandum of dissent, or protest from any dissenting or non-assenting Lord or Lords. If a Lord disagrees to certain paragraphs in the report, or to the entire report, he can record his disapproval by dividing the committee against those paragraphs to which he objects, or against the entire report, as the circumstances of the case require; and can put on record his observations and conclusions, as opposed to those of the majority, by proposing an alternative draft report or moving amendments to the draft. Any alternative draft or amendment on which a division takes place is entered in full in the minutes of proceedings of the committee.[3]

Procedure where a committee is unable to agree upon a report. Where a committee is unable to agree on a report, it may make a special report to that effect, together with the minutes of the evidence taken before it, or merely report the minutes of the evidence taken before it to the House without observations or expression of opinion.[4]

Leave to report from time to time. Where a committee is authorised to report from time to time, it is at liberty to make as many reports as it thinks proper.

Presentation of report to the House. When a select committee has agreed upon its report, the chairman or some other member is directed to make the report to the House. By Standing Order No 65 the report is laid on the Table and ordered to be printed.

Special reports. Besides the report, properly so called, on the subject-matter referred to the committee it may be necessary for a committee to make a 'special report' on some incidental matter relating to the powers,

---

1 This is regular practice in the European Communities Committee and the Science and Technology Committee.
2 HL Deb (1981–82) 431, cc 632, 709–712.
3 HL Deb (1981–82) 434, c 362; ibid (1982–83) 439, c 223.
4 The Select Committee on a Bill of Rights, being unable to agree whether such a bill was desirable, summarised the arguments of witnesses for and against without reaching any conclusion on the arguments. HL (1977–87) 176 pp 30–34. The Select Committee on Televising the Proceedings of the House agreed to present their report on the experiment of televising the House in as neutral a way as would be consistent with a proper evaluation of the experiment. They therefore made no recommendation as to whether television should be allowed to continue, but presented the facts and left it to the House to decide (HL (1985–86) 102; HL Deb (1985–86) 474, cc 963–977).

functions or proceedings of the committee. Such reports are similar in form to, and are subject to the same procedure as, the main report of the committee.

Unfinished inquiries. When a committee, whose appointment is terminated by the end of the session (see p 575) lacks sufficient time to conclude an inquiry, it may report the fact to the House with its minutes of proceedings and evidence and recommend the appointment of a committee in the next session to continue the inquiry.[1] If a committee is reappointed the evidence taken in the previous session may be referred to the new committee.[2] Since the making of Standing Order No 62 in 1975 to continue the appointment of sessional committees over the prorogation of Parliament, the practice of referring evidence to the reappointed sessional committee has been discontinued; the new sessional committee takes cognizance of evidence submitted in the previous session.

Publication of report. A report of a select committee may not be made publicly available until it has been presented to the House and is available to members of the House. Select committees, however, have power to supply advance copies of their reports to such officers of government departments, witnesses, lobby journalists and other press representatives as the committee think fit. Such copies are supplied in strictest confidence until publication of the report.

Government replies to reports. When a select committee has made a report touching on the responsibilities of a government department, Her Majesty's Government commonly replies to the committee's recommendations and observations. The reply may be given in debate, in reply to a question for written answer in the Official Report (Hansard), in a memorandum to the committee or as a command paper.[3] Replies are expected by all committees which are scrutinising Government activities. Following a reply a committee may invite a minister to give evidence on the progress made in implementing recommendations or take further evidence and make a further report.[4]

Consideration of reports. When it is proposed to take the report of a select committee into consideration in the House, notice must be given on the order paper (Standing Order No 65). The usual form of the motion is 'to take note' of the report (see pp 425–426). Sometimes the report is the subject of a motion for papers (see p 425). Motions have been made expressing the agreement[5] or disagreement[6] of the House with the report as a whole or with certain paragraphs thereof,[7] or for agreeing to the recommendations contained in the report generally or with certain exceptions.[8] The House has

---

1 LJ (1979–80) 1704; ibid (1983–84) 793.
2 HL Deb (1987–88) 489, c 1206.
3 LJ (1982–83) 21; ibid (1985–86) 85; HL Deb (1985–86) 468, cc 1201–1202.
4 Science and Technology Committee, Third and Fourth Reports (1981–82); First Report (1987–88).
5 LJ (1894) 250; ibid (1933–34) 309.
6 LJ (1904–05) 348.
7 LJ (1904–05) 347, 348; ibid (1978–79) 75.
8 LJ (1875) 318.

resolved itself into a committee to consider a report[1] and has referred back a report to the committee which made it for further consideration, the committee being enlarged by the appointment of additional members.[2]

Procedure in select committees on public bills

The procedure in public bill committees, and in hybrid bill committees, private bills and provisional order bills is dealt with on pp 450–451, 523–524, 936–939, 954–956. This section concerns select committees to consider public bills when the hearing of evidence or other minute investigation is thought necessary.

After the evidence, if any, has been concluded, the clauses of the bill are considered. Clauses and amendments are considered in the same manner and subject to the same rules of relevance as in Committee of the whole House.

The select committee to which a bill has been committed has no power to put an end to the bill. A report recommending that the bill should not proceed is normally acquiesced in by the House;[3] but the bill may proceed[4] and a bill has been recommitted to a committee after the latter had reported that it was not expedient to proceed further therewith.[5]

If a committee is unable to complete its consideration of the bill, it makes a special report to that effect and reports the bill without amendment.[6]

Sessional Committees

There are now seventeen sessional committees in the Lords, ie those regularly appointed from session to session. The constitution and functions of ten of these are described elsewhere, viz the two Appeal Committees, the two Appellate Committees (see pp 66–67), the Leave of Absence and Lords' expenses Committee (see pp 168–169), the Personal Bills Committee (see pp 943–944), the Hybrid Instruments Committee (see p 550) the Standing Orders (Private Bills) Committee (see p 933) and joint select committees on Consolidation, etc Bills (see pp 667–669) and on Statutory Instruments (see pp 551–552). The remaining committees are described below.

Most sessional committees are subject to a rotation rule whereby all members, save those in certain exempted categories, are obliged to retire from the committee after serving for three sessions. After one session they are again eligible for selection.[7] In the European Communities Committee and the Science and Technology Committee, members retire after five sessions' service. Chairmen of sub-committees are exempted from the rotation rule for three sessions after assuming the chairmanship.[8]

European Communities Committee. The committee was first appointed in 1974 on the recommendation of the Select Committee on Procedures for

1 LJ (1889) 47; ibid (1953–54) 180.
2 LJ (1889) 47.
3 LJ (1975–76) 361; ibid (1977–78) 903; HL Deb (1987–88) 495, c 384.
4 LJ (1865) 420.
5 LJ (1854–55) 277, 334.
6 LJ (1886) 306; ibid (1971–72) 693. A committee has reported that it had considered a bill up to cl 53 and had ordered the bill to be reported with some amendments; LJ (1888) 434.
7 LJ (1971–72) 23–25, 70; ibid (1974–5) 142; ibid (1976–77) 167; ibid (1979–80) 206.
8 HL 128 (1984–85).

the Scrutiny of Proposals for European Instruments.[1] The Principal Deputy Chairman of Committees for the time being acts as chairman (see p 174). The order of reference of the committee is to consider Community proposals, whether in draft or otherwise, to obtain all necessary information about them, and to make reports on those which, in the opinion of the committee, raise important questions of policy or principle, and on other questions to which the committee consider that the special attention of the House should be drawn. The committee has power to appoint sub-committees and to refer to them any of the matters within its order of reference. The quorum of a sub-committee is two. At present there are six sub-committees covering defined policy areas. These sub-committees consider the proposals referred to them by the chairman of the select committee, who distinguishes between those proposals not requiring parliamentary scrutiny (known as A Proposals) and those thought to require examination (known as B proposals). The committee may co-opt any Lord to serve on the sub-committees. It also has power to appoint specialist advisers, a legal assistant and since 1988 a committee specialist assistant. Second Counsel to the Chairman of Committees acts as its legal adviser (see p 174). It has power to confer with the Commons Select Committee on European Legislation.

House of Lords Offices Committee. This committee considers and reports on all domestic affairs of the House including the staffs of the Departments of the Clerk of the Parliaments and the Gentleman Usher of the Black Rod, their duties, salaries, retirements and superannuation. The committee delegates the supervision of the details of certain of its responsibilities to sub-committees which are appointed each session and of which the quorum is two. At present sub-committees are appointed on Administration, Computers, Finance, the Library, the Refreshment Department, Staff of the House and Works of Art.[2] The Chairman of Committees is ex officio chairman of certain of the sub-committees; the chairmen of the others are appointed by the committee.

Committee for Privileges. This committee is appointed under Standing Order No 73. It consists of sixteen Lords together with any four Lords of Appeal. It considers such questions of privilege as may be referred to it by the House.[3] It also considers claims of peerage and precedence (Standing

---

1 HL (1972–73) 194; HL (1974) 62 and 139.
2 HL Deb (1987–88) 488, c 741.
3 For example, LJ (1983–84) 600: the privilege of peerage, freedom from arrest and detention of persons suffering from mental disorder.

Order Nos 74, 76(3) and 77). In any claim of peerage the committee may not sit unless three Lords of Appeal are present.[1]

Procedure Committee. The function of this committee is to consider proposals for alterations in the procedure of the House and whether the Standing Orders require to be altered to give effect to such alterations.

Science and Technology Committee. The committee was first appointed in 1979 following the discontinuance of a similar committee in the House of Commons. Its terms of reference are 'to consider science and technology' and accordingly it has a wide choice of subject. Subjects are chosen which concern areas where Parliament can help and stimulate the advancement and application of science and technology in the United Kingdom, aspects of science and technology in which the Government or statutory bodies are involved, or issues of science and technology over which there is public concern. The committee consists of fourteen members with the power to co-opt others. It divides into two sub-committees to conduct its inquiries and co-opts Lords to these sub-committees for the duration of particular inquiries. It appoints a third sub-committee for general purposes, whose main function is to recommend topics for inquiry and to follow-up past inquiries. It regularly exercises its power to appoint specialist advisers and since 1988 a committee specialist assistant.

Committee of Selection. This committee is appointed under Standing Order No 61. Its function is to select and propose to the House the names of the Lords to form each select committee of the House (except the Committee of Selection itself, any committee otherwise provided for by statute or by order of the House[2] and, unless the Chairman of Committees or two members of the committee think otherwise, select committees on private business) (see p 574). It may propose the names of the Lords who will be the chairmen of such committees. The committee also selects and proposes to the House the panel of Lords to act as Deputy Chairmen of Committees for each session (see p 175).

Committee on Broadcasting. This committee, with the Chairman of Committees in the chair, has responsibility for supervising the arrangements for, and dealing with problems or complaints arising out of, both the televising and the sound broadcasting of the proceedings of the House and its com-

---

1 The most recent claims of Peerage to be considered by the committee were in relation to the barony of Ampthill (LJ (1975–76) 326), the viscounty of Oxfuird (LJ (1976–77) 523), the earldom of Annandale and Hartfell (LJ (1984–85) 522), the barony of Strange (LJ (1985–86) 388) and the barony of Grey of Codnor (1988–89) 20 June 1989. The committee has reported on matters relating to Peers of Scotland (LJ (1963–64) 66, 80), on the petition of the Irish Peers (LJ (1966–67) 31, 118) and on peerages in abeyance (LJ (1986–87) 64).

2 The committee does not select the Lords members of the Joint Committee on Consolidation Bills who are appointed by the House on the recommendation of the Lord Chancellor (Standing Order No 49). For membership of the Appellate and Appeal Committees, see pp 66–67.

mittees. The televising and sound broadcasting of proceedings are governed by resolutions of 15 May 1986 and 28 July 1977 respectively (see pp 217–218).[1]

2. COMMITTEES IN THE HOUSE OF COMMONS

COMMITTEES OF THE WHOLE HOUSE

The manner in which bills are considered by Committees of the whole House has been dealt with in chapter 21. Although Standing Orders prescribing that a broad range of the financial business in the House of Commons should be proceeded with in Committees of the whole House were repealed in 1966, the House is not precluded from considering any business other than bills in Committee; indeed, express provision is made by Standing Orders Nos 25, 82 and 83 for the consideration of such business in a Committee of the whole House (see pp 589–590) and for the reporting of any resolutions. It is difficult, however, to envisage any circumstances in which the House would wish to avail itself of such a procedure in future.

Appointment

A Committee of the whole House is appointed by a resolution that the House shall immediately or on a future day resolve itself into a Committee of the whole House. Whenever an order of the day is read for the House to resolve itself into a Committee on a bill, the Speaker is directed by Standing Order No 64 to leave the Chair without putting any question. When the Speaker has left the Chair, the mace is removed from the Table and placed under it, and the Committee commences its sitting.

Chairmen of Committees of the whole House

The chair (at the Table) is generally taken by the Chairman of Ways and Means (see p 186), or in his absence by one of the Deputy Chairmen. In the absence of the Chairman of Ways and Means and the Deputy Chairmen, the Chair of a Committee of the whole House is usually taken by one of those ten or more Members whom, in pursuance of the provision contained in Standing Order No 4, the Speaker nominates at the commencement of every session to act as temporary chairmen of committees when requested to do so by the Chairman of Ways and Means. In the course of a sitting of a Committee of the whole House it is customary for the chairman when he so desires to withdraw and to be replaced by another Member without any question. In a Committee of the whole House it is customary for the Clerk Assistant to officiate as the Clerk of the Committee.

Power and duties of Chairman. Order in debate in a Committee is enforced by the chairman, as he is responsible for the conduct of business

---

1 LJ (1976–77) 820–821; ibid (1985–86) 331.

therein, and from his decision no appeal should be made to the Speaker.[1] Nor should an appeal from a decision given by a Deputy Chairman[2] or a temporary chairman[3] be made to the Chairman of Ways and Means on his resuming the Chair. The rules observed by the House regarding order in debate are followed in committee. For example, the rule that a Member who has used objectionable words must explain or retract them, or offer an apology (see p 394), is as operative in committee as it is in the House. As reference to debate in committee is not permitted in the House (except on the later stages of a bill; see p 374), reference in committee to the conduct of the Speaker is not allowed;[4] nor can the enforcement of closure at a previous sitting of the committee be discussed.[5]

In addition, the Chairman of Ways and Means and the Deputy Chairmen have the following powers under Standing Orders:

(1) Under Standing Order No 35 they may administer the rules for regulating the closure of debate.
(2) Under Standing Order No 31 they may select the amendments, new clauses and schedules to be proposed to bills.

Any chairman of a Committee of the whole House has the following powers under standing orders:

(1) Under Standing Order No 41 he may direct a Member to discontinue his speech for persistent irrelevance or tedious repetition.[6]
(2) Under Standing Order No 42 he has the power to order a Member whose conduct is grossly disorderly to withdraw immediately,[7] or, if he deems such power to be inadequate, he may name the Member for disregarding the authority of the Chair[8] or for persistently and wilfully obstructing the business of the House.[9] In the latter event, as the suspension of a Member from the service of the House or other serious forms of punishment such as committal are only inflicted by the House with the Speaker in the Chair, he is directed under Standing Order No 43 to suspend the proceedings of the committee and to report the circumstances to the House. A similar course is followed in the event of grave disorder arising in committee of the whole House.[10]
(3) Under Standing Order No 34 he may put forthwith or decline to propose the question on a dilatory motion.
(4) Under Standing Order No 37, if he considers a division unnecessarily claimed he may take the vote of the committee by calling on Members

---

1 Parl Deb (1893) 9, c 975; ibid (1901) 98, c 978; ibid 99, c 365; ibid (1904) 135, c 722; HC Deb (1912–13) 48, c 749; ibid (1960–61) 634, cc 644–645. In this connection, see also CJ (1836) 104; ibid (1854–55) 352; Parl Deb (1852–53) 126, c 1245; ibid (1855) 139, c 486; HC Deb (1912) 40, c 1275, 1338.
2 Parl Deb (1906) 157, c 731.
3 Parl Deb (1893–94) 18, c 1883.
4 HC Deb (1964–65) 708, c 429.
5 Parl Deb (1888) 323, c 1446.
6 For example, CJ (1965–66) 38.
7 CJ (1893–94) 424.
8 CJ (1881) 111; ibid (1890) 72; ibid (1901) 62; Parl Deb (1901) 90, c 691; CJ (1908) 404; ibid (1923) 156, 237; ibid (1930–31) 22; ibid (1936–37) 125; ibid (1951–52) 54.
9 CJ (1882) 322; ibid (1926) 117.
10 CJ (1961–62) 55.

who support and who challenge his decision successively to rise in their places.

(5) Under Standing Order No 143 he has the same powers as the Speaker with regard to the withdrawal of strangers.[1]

Procedure on bills

Proceedings in committee are conducted for the most part in the same manner as when the House is sitting. Members address the chairman, who performs in the committee all the duties which devolve on the Speaker in the House, including the giving of a casting vote when the voices are equal.[2] Members must speak standing and uncovered as when the House is sitting. The main difference between the proceedings of the committee and those of the House is that in the former a Member is entitled to speak more than once to the same question in order that the details of the bill may have the most minute examination.

Notice is normally required of amendments which it is proposed to move to bills in Committees of the whole House, although the Chairman may allow an amendment to be moved without notice. A motion for the previous question cannot be moved in Committee (pp 334–335).

Motions to report progress, etc

A Committee of the whole House has no power either to adjourn its own sitting or to adjourn its consideration of any matter for a future sitting.[3] A Member who desires to close the sitting of a committee may move that 'the chairman do report progress and ask leave to sit again'[4] in order to put an end to the proceedings of the committee on that day. This motion may be made either in order to provide further time for the consideration of the bill in committee on a future day, or as a form of dilatory motion analogous to that used in the House (see pp 332–333). If the motion is agreed to, the chairman leaves the Chair and, when the House has resumed, reports to the Speaker that the committee has made progress in the bill, and that he has been directed to move that the committee may have leave to sit again. The Member in charge, in response to the Speaker's invitation, thereupon names a day for the further consideration of the bill in committee.

If proceedings in committee are interrupted for the purpose of moving a motion under Standing Order No 14(2) and are either specified in the motion or exempted under Standing Order No 14(1), the proceedings in committee are resumed (Standing Order No 14(3)) after the motion has been agreed to.[5]

1 For example, CJ (1966–67) 558.
2 For example, CJ (1964–65) 298.
3 Parl Deb (1902) 108, c 392. At the general desire of the Committee, the sitting of a Committee of the whole House was suspended for a certain time on the following occasions: Parl Deb (1848) 101, c 90; HC Deb (1909) 4, c 520; ibid (1920) 129, c 1950; see also CJ (1667–87) 68.
4 It is usual for the chairman to accept such a motion from the Member in charge of a bill, even if no proceedings have taken place upon the bill (HC Deb (1961–62) 651, c 1162).
5 The Chairman has ruled that if the Member speaking at the moment of interruption rises to speak again on the resumption of proceedings it would be proper to call him in preference to other Members (HC Deb (1976–77), 941, cc 116–117).

On 21 January 1913, when progress had been reported at the conclusion
of the portion of a bill which had to be completed at seven o'clock under
an order of the House, the House resolved that on the disposal of the
report of a money resolution, which had to be agreed to before the next
clauses of the bill could be considered, it would resolve itself again into the
committee on the bill.[1]

A motion may also be moved 'that the chairman do now leave the chair',
but this motion, if carried, supersedes the order of the day for the committee
and converts it into a dropped order; in that case, when the Speaker resumes
the Chair, no report whatever is made from the committee.[2] The same result
is obtained if, when the chairman reports progress in the matter referred to
the committee, he refrains, upon a direction given by the Member who had
obtained the appointment of the committee, from asking leave to sit again.[3]
A motion to report progress having been negatived, it cannot be repeated
while the same question is before the House being subject to the same rules
as that observed in the House itself, which will not admit of a motion for the
adjournment of a debate to be repeated without some intermediate proceeding (see p 333). In the circumstances the motion for reporting progress
may be alternated with a motion 'that the chairman do now leave the chair'.[4]

At the moment of interruption (pp 240–243) the chairman leaves the
Chair, reports progress, and asks leave to sit again, pursuant to Standing
Order No 9(3). If a motion that the chairman do leave the Chair or do report
progress is at that time under consideration, the motion lapses.

Other interruptions of proceedings

If a motion made by a Minister of the Crown under Standing Order No 10
that the proceedings of the committee be suspended (see p 245) is agreed to,
the chairman leaves the chair and reports to that effect to the House. If the
question which the Speaker thereafter puts, that the proceedings of that
day's sitting be suspended, is negatived, the House immediately again
resolves itself into a committee.

If an occasion of public business arises with which the House is concerned,
as, for example, if the Usher of the Black Rod arrives to summon the House
to attend Her Majesty or the lords commissioners in the House of Peers, the
Speaker resumes the chair at once without any report from the committee.

If complaint is made in Committee of the whole House of a breach of
privilege which has been recently committed and requires instant attention,
the chairman leaves the Chair on an order to report progress[5] (see p 587).

1 CJ (1912–13) 499.
2 CJ (1830–31) 403; ibid (1908) 478; ibid (1924) 197; ibid (1955–56) 128.
3 CJ (1890–91) 501.
4 CJ (1877) 312; ibid (1929–30) 364. But see HC Deb (1937–38) 336, cc 1001–1002. On 7 June
  1858, in committee on the Government of India, the question for reporting progress having
  been negatived, the committee some time afterwards was prepared to assent to such a
  motion; but, in order to adhere to the rule, the chairman put the question upon a formal part
  of an amendment which had been proposed, before he proceeded to put the question for
  reporting progress (CJ (1857–58) 214; see also CJ (1860) 323).
5 CJ (1888) 483.

Motions for resolutions

Procedure on motions for resolutions. Under Standing Order No 25, whenever an order of the day is read for the House to resolve itself into a Committee, other than a Committee on a bill, the Speaker leaves the Chair without putting any question, and the House thereupon resolves itself into Committee.

It is not necessary to give notice of the express terms of the resolution (or an amendment) to be proposed in a Committee; though such resolutions must be within the terms of the order under which the Committee was appointed, and notice is usually given, for the convenience of the Committee. Questions embodying several distinct propositions are not divided by the chairman (see pp 335–336).[1] The mover has discretion regarding the order of resolutions to be proposed in Committee; but a motion may not be postponed after the question thereon has been proposed.[2] By an ancient practice, 'when there comes a question between the greater and lesser sum, or the longer or shorter time, the least sum and the longest time ought first to be put to the question' in order that the charge may be made as easy upon the people as possible.[3]

Report of resolutions. When a Committee has agreed to certain resolutions but is unable to conclude the discussion of other resolutions, the chairman is directed to report the former, and to report progress upon the resolution under consideration when the proceedings of the Committee were brought to a close. It is not necessary for the Committee in such circumstances to enter again at its first sitting thereafter on the motion upon which progress was reported.[4] When a Committee enters upon consideration of a motion on which progress has previously been reported, the chairman proposes the question thereon disengaged from any amendment which might have been proposed.[5] Accordingly a Member cannot claim to speak first on the renewal of a debate in Committee, on the ground that he was in possession of the Committee when the chairman reported progress.[6]

When a Committee has completed its proceedings, the chairman proposes the question, 'That I do report this resolution (or resolutions) to the House', and upon this question being agreed to (if necessary on a division)[7] he leaves the chair for the purpose, without question put, pursuant to Standing Order No 82.

Consideration of reports of resolutions. By Standing Order No 82 reports from Committees of the whole House are brought up without any question being put. In the case of resolutions creating a charge upon the people the House orders the report to be received on a future day: but the report of resolutions upon other matters may be received immediately.[8] The reading of the resolution by the Clerk at the Table is taken to be the second reading

---

1 HC Deb (1909) 4, c 1467, 1737; ibid (1912) 43, c 1483; ibid (1922) 159, c 1385.
2 Parl Deb (1858) 149, c 2066.
3 CJ (1667–87) 367.
4 For example, CJ (1851–52) 57, 104, 145; ibid (1852–53) 442, 446.
5 Parl Deb (1887) 319, c 1629; ibid (1904) 133, c 1530.
6 Parl Deb (1858) 150, c 1615; HC Deb (1915) 69, c 600; ibid (1920) 128, c 431; ibid (1920) 131, c 709; ibid (1943–44) 400, c 955.
7 CJ (1960–61) 107.
8 Established Church (Ireland) Report, CJ (1867–68) 160. See *Erskine May* (17 edn) p 800.

of the resolution. When several resolutions are reported, each resolution is read and either postponed, or considered and disposed of by the House, before the next is taken. Amendments may be moved immediately after the Clerk has read the resolution; and after such amendment has been disposed of, or if no amendments are moved, the Speaker proposes the question 'That this House doth agree with the Committee in the said resolution', and upon this question debate may take place, but once it has been proposed, no amendment (or further amendment) may be moved.[1] Amendment or debate, arising upon the consideration of the report of a resolution, must be strictly relevant thereto.[2]

Records of Committees of the whole House. Proceedings of Committees of the whole House have been entered in the Journal since 1829.[3]

STANDING COMMITTEES

Appointment of standing committees

Standing committees, as they exist today, have developed from those introduced in the 1880s to meet the demand made upon the time of the House by the consideration of bills in Committee of the whole House. Their most important function is still to consider bills committed to them. In addition, provision is now made for standing committees, where appropriate, to consider the principle of bills awaiting second reading, and any bills so referred again on report, Scottish estimates, matters relating exclusively to Scotland, Wales and Northern Ireland or to regional affairs in England, statutory instruments, measures under the Church of England Assembly (Powers) Act 1919, and European Community documents. Provision is made by Standing Order No 84 for the appointment of as many standing committees as may be necessary for the consideration of public bills and other business committed or referred to a standing committee, although Standing Order No 95 limits to two the number of Scottish standing committees (for the consideration of Scottish bills).

With the exceptions mentioned below, a standing committee consists of a chairman appointed by the Speaker and between sixteen and fifty members, nominated by the Committee of Selection to serve on the committee during the consideration of each bill or other business allocated to it. In nominating those members the Committee of Selection is directed to have regard to their qualifications and to the composition of the House. It is also provided that for the consideration of a public bill relating exclusively to Wales committed to a standing committee, the committee shall be so constituted as to include all the Members sitting for constituencies in Wales (Standing Order No 86(2)(ii)).

Standing committees on bills. The procedure by which (with certain exceptions) bills, when they have been read a second time, stand committed to a standing committee is provided for by Standing Order No 61, and bills so

---

1 Parl Deb (1908) 195, c 516.
2 Parl Deb (1864) 174, c 1551; ibid (1907) 174, c 1698; ibid (1908) 195, c 516; HC Deb (1915) 73, c 205; ibid (1923) 164, c 2544.
3 CJ (1829) 78.

committed are allocated by the Speaker to particular standing committees under Standing Order No 84.

The committees to which they are allocated by the Speaker are designated 'A', 'B', 'C' and so on, except that bills certified by the Speaker as relating exclusively to Scotland are committed to a Scottish standing committee (Standing Order No 95) and allocated by him to one of them. Bills not so certified, but predominantly relating to Scotland, have also been ordered to be considered by a Scottish standing committee,[1] or have been proceeded with by order of the House as if they had been so certified.[2]

Once a bill has been allocated, the Speaker may, at the request of the Member in charge, transfer it from one standing committee to another.[3] In all but one of the standing committees thus alphabetically designated precedence is given to government bills (Standing Order No 84(3)). The Committee of Selection traditionally designates Standing Committee C as the committee in which precedence is given to private Members' bills. If certified as relating exclusively to Scotland, however, private Members' bills are considered by one of the Scottish standing committees, Government bills having precedence in the other.

Bills allocated to standing committees, other than to those in which private Members' bills have precedence, are considered in such order as the Government from time to time determine. Bills allocated to the standing committees in which private Members' bills have precedence are considered in the order of their allocation, unless the Members in charge of the bills which stand above any particular bill on the list agree to give it precedence over their bills. When the precedence to which a bill is entitled is thus waived in favour of another bill, the first bill continues to take precedence over the remaining bills on the list.[4] By arrangement with the Ministers in charge of government bills, private Members' bills have occasionally been allowed to take precedence over Governments bills in standing committees where Government bills were entitled to precedence.[5]

Scottish Grand Committee. For the consideration of bills referred to it in relation to their principle (see p 478) or on report (see p 505), of matters relating exclusively to Scotland (see p 592), and of estimates referred to it (see p 592), Standing Order No 94 provides that the Scottish Grand Committee shall consist of all the Members representing Scottish constituencies.

When a bill has been referred to the Scottish Grand Committee under Standing Order No 93, the debate follows the lines of a Second Reading debate in the House[6] and takes place on a motion 'That the Chairman do

---

1 See p 478 and fn 4.
2 See p 480 and fn 8.
3 If, however, a transfer is intended after Members have been nominated to a particular committee in respect of the bill, the first standing committee is discharged from consideration of the bill, and another standing committee (frequently comprising the same members) nominated. (CJ (1966–67) 57, 63, 70; ibid (1967–68) 82; ibid (1968–69) 114, 124, 129, 178; ibid (1981–82) 221.)
4 Standing Committee E, Law Reform (Miscellaneous Provisions) Bill, 1948–49.
5 Standing Committee B, Superannuation (Ecclesiastical Commission and Queen Anne's Bounty) Bill 1914; Scottish Standing Committee, Slaughter of Animals (Scotland) Bill 1948–49.
6 Stg Co Deb (1948–49) vol III, c 1584, Education (Scotland) Bill.

now report to the House that the bill has been considered in relation to its principle'. The bill is reported as having been so considered and is ordered to be read a second time upon a future day (see p 478).

Under Standing Order No 97, the Scottish Grand Committee, on not more than six days in a session, considers such matter or matters relating exclusively to Scotland as have been referred to it by the House on the motion of a Minister of the Crown, decided without amendment or debate. Such a motion is negatived if, on the question being put, not fewer than ten Members in their places signify their objection.[1] In considering such matters the only question before the committee is 'That the Chairman do now report to the House that the committee has considered' the said matter or matters.

The House may also, on the motion of a Minister of the Crown under Standing Order No 96, refer estimates for which the Secretary of State for Scotland is responsible, or any part of them, to the Scottish Grand Committee for its consideration on not less than six days in any session.[2] Debate in the committee takes place on the motion 'That the Chairman do now report to the House that the committee has considered' the relevant Vote in its Class. The Scottish Grand Committee thus does not in its consideration of this question assume the functions of the House in its consideration of the estimates.[3] If agreed to, the estimate or estimates concerned must be reported to the House the same day. It is customary, however, for the motion to be 'talked out' on every day but the last, when the question is put on the estimate under discussion and on the remaining estimates referred to the committee. Only then is a report made to the House. The selection of estimates for discussion is arranged by the government at the request of the opposition.

For the functions of the Scottish Grand Committee in regard to the consideration of bills on report, see p 505; and for its sittings in Edinburgh, see p 597.

The Welsh Grand Committee. The Welsh Grand Committee is appointed by Standing Order No 98[4] to consider bills and such specified matters relating exclusively to Wales as may be referred to it. The Committee consists of all Members sitting for constituencies in Wales, together with not more than five other Members, nominated and discharged from time to time as appropriate by the Committee of Selection.[5] Bills are referred to the Committee in the same manner and subject to the same conditions[6] as to second reading committees (see below); and the committee reports to the House whether or

---

1 CJ (1967–68) 335.
2 The number of days set aside for discussion of Scottish estimates has sometimes been varied by sessional order, CJ (1960–61) 284; ibid (1961–62) 266; ibid (1962–63) 263; ibid (1963–64) 287; ibid (1966–67) 516. In sessions 1954–55, 1965–66, 1978–79 and 1986–87, no estimates were considered.
3 In 1919 an experimental sessional order was made under which nearly all estimates were referred to standing committees. They were allocated among the committees by Mr Speaker, and when considered, were reported to the House. The House then proceeded as if the estimates had been reported by the Committee of Supply. Provision was made for consideration of estimates in that Committee rather than in a standing committee, notice of such proceedings having been given (CJ (1919) 39).
4 In sessions from 1959–60 to 1967–68 such a committee was constituted by sessional order.
5 As to previous practice see Stg Co Deb (1987–88) Welsh Gr Co, effect of Government legislation on the people of Wales, cc 9–10, when Members participated who had not, due to an oversight, been formally nominated.
6 Except that a Private Member may not move to have his bill referred, as may be done under Standing Order No 90(2).

not it recommends that a bill ought to be read a second time. If it recommends that a bill ought not to be read a second time, it may state its reasons. Upon a motion being made for the second reading of a bill reported from the committee, the question is put forthwith (Standing Order No 98 (4)). Matters are referred to the committee on the motion of a Minister of the Crown, decided without amendment or debate; the committee reports only that it has considered the said matter or matters.

The House has by order specified the days on which the committee should sit to consider matters.[1]

Northern Ireland Committee. The Northern Ireland Committee is appointed by Standing Order No 99 to consider such matters relating exclusively to Northern Ireland as may be referred to it. The committee consists of all Members sitting for constituencies in Northern Ireland together with not more than twenty-five Members nominated by the Committee of Selection. Matters may be referred to the committee on a motion made by a Minister of the Crown at the commencement of public business, decided without amendment or debate. The committee may report[2] only that it has considered the matter or matters referred to it.

The committee last met on 26 June 1985.

Standing Committee on Regional Affairs. Standing Order No 100[3] provides for the appointment of a standing committee, known as the Standing Committee on Regional Affairs, to consider any matter relating to regional affairs in England which is referred to it. The committee consists of all Members sitting for English constituencies, together with not more than five others appointed by the Committee of Selection.

Questions to refer matters to the committee are decided without amendment or debate on motions made by Ministers of the Crown. If twenty or more Members rise in their places to signify objection, the question is negatived. Any matter referred is considered by the committee on a motion 'That the Committee has considered' the matter(s) for a period of not more than two and a half hours, after which the committee must report to the House.

The committee last met on 26 July 1978.

Second reading committees. Under Standing Order No 90 second reading committees are declared to be standing committees, and the method of appointment relating to the latter applies (see p 590). Committees consider the bills referred to them (see p 477) and report to the House whether or not they recommend that the bill ought to be read a second time. When such a motion is under discussion, it is not in order to move an amendment to the motion; but if a committee recommends that a bill ought not to be read a second time, it may state its reasons for so recommending. (In fact, no Second Reading Committee has exercised this power.) The rules governing a second reading debate in the House apply in second reading committees, so that, in particular, no Member may speak more than once except by leave of the committee.[4]

Standing committees for the consideration of bills on report. Under Standing Order No 92 bills which have been considered by a second reading

---

1 CJ (1974–75) 92.
2 No report is made if the motion is negatived. For a subsequent order to lay minutes of proceedings see CJ (1985–86) 372.
3 SO No 100 (then SO No 72B) was made on 2 December 1975; a sessional order was first made on 9 June 1975.
4 Stg Co Deb (1965–66) Second Reading Co, Misrepresentation Bill, c3.

committee or by the Scottish Grand Committee in relation to their principle may, after their committee stage, be referred for consideration on report to standing committees of not fewer than twenty nor more than eighty Members or to the Scottish Grand Committee, as the case may be; and in the case of a bill relating exclusively to Wales the committee is to include all Members sitting for constituencies in Wales (Standing Order No 92(2)).

Questions to refer bills under the Standing Order are decided without amendment or debate on motions made by Ministers of the Crown. If twenty or more Members rise in their places to sign objection, the question is negatived.[1]

Only one bill has been referred to a Standing Committee under Standing Order No 92.[2]

Special standing committees. Standing Order No 91[3] provides for the appointment of special standing committees to which bills may be committed after second reading under Standing Order No 61(2). Such committees have power under Standing Order No 91(1) for 28 days[4] after committal (excluding periods when the House was adjourned for more than two days) to send for persons, paper and records, to hold one morning sitting in private and to hold up to three morning sittings in public, each of not more than three hours' length, for the purpose of taking oral evidence. Unless the committee otherwise orders, evidence is given in public. It is printed in the Official Report of the committees' debates, together with any written evidence ordered by the committee to be printed.

For these sittings any Member other than a Minister can be appointed chairman; the chairman so appointed has been[5] counted for the purpose of calculating the quorum. The chairman so appointed is in each case the chairman of the select committee relevant to the subject matter of the bill committed to the committee. After the sittings to take evidence have been concluded, a special standing committee proceeds to consider the bill in the same way as any other standing committee appointed to consider a bill. For these latter proceedings the chair is taken by a chairman nominated by the Speaker from the Chairmen's Panel (cf p 597).

Standing committees on statutory instruments, etc. Standing Order No 101 provides for the appointment of one or more standing committees to consider statutory instruments or draft statutory instruments or measures under the Church of England Assembly (Powers) Act 1919 or instruments made under such measures, referred to them. A motion for such a reference can be made only by a Minister of the Crown. Where the motion is for the reference of an instrument subject to the affirmative procedure (see p 545) notice of a motion appropriate to that procedure must first have been given by a Minister; where the motion is for the reference of a measure or a related instrument an appropriate notice must first have been given by any Member;

1 CJ (1977–78) 355.
2 CJ (1967–68) 225.
3 Passed on 27 February 1986, and replacing sessional orders first made on 28 October 1980 and 17 March 1982.
4 Under SO No 91(4) the period of 28 days may be extended on a motion made by a Minister.
5 Three bills were referred to such committees in 1980–81 and one each in 1981–82 and 1983–84, CJ (1980–81) 89, 115, 299; ibid (1981–82) 256; ibid (1983–84) 356. Since then there has been no further such referral.

but in the case of a motion for the reference of an instrument subject to the negative procedure (see p 547) the equivalent notice may be either the notice appropriate to that procedure or a notice that the House takes note of the instrument; and the notice may be given by any Member. If such a motion to refer is made at the commencement of public business, the question is decided without amendment or debate, but if twenty or more Members rise in their places to signify their objection, the question is negatived.[1]

In addition to the Members nominated to a committee on statutory instruments etc, by the Committee of Selection, any Member of the House may attend and address the committee, but is not counted in the quorum, may not make any motion and may not vote.

The committee to which instruments are referred is required to consider them only on a motion, 'That the committee has considered the instrument [or draft instrument]'. The chairman customarily accepts such a motion, in the case of instruments subject to affirmative procedure from a Minister in charge of the instrument, or in the case of instruments subject to the negative procedure from one of the Members who have given notice of a motion relating to the order. If the proceedings have not been previously concluded, the chairman is required to put any question necessary to dispose of them when the committee has sat for one and a half hours after the commencement of those proceedings, except that when orders relating exclusively to Northern Ireland are being considered proceedings must be concluded after two and a half hours.

The committee may divide on the question, but whether it is agreed to or not the chairman is required to report the instrument without putting any further question.[2]

If a motion is made in the House under either the affirmative or the negative procedure, or to take note, in respect of any instrument reported from a standing committee, it is exempted business (see p 242) and the question is put forthwith.

Standing committees on European Community documents. Standing Order No 102 provides for the appointment of one or more[3] standing committees for the consideration of European Community documents referred to them; European Community documents are defined under Standing Order No 14(1) as draft proposals by the Commission of the European Communities for legislation and other documents published for submission to the Council of Ministers or to the European Council whether or not such documents originate from the Commission.[4] A motion for such a reference can be made only by a Minister of the Crown, and only in respect of a document in relation to which notice of a motion has been given. If such a motion to refer is made at the commencement of public business, the question is decided without amendment or debate, but if twenty or more Members rise in their places to signify objection, the question is negatived.

---

1 Eg CJ (1977–78) 35; Votes and Proceedings (1987–88) 8 July 1987; ibid (1988–89) 8 February 1989.
2 First Stg Co on SIs, Proceedings (Civil Aviation (Navigation Services Charges) (Fifth Amendment) Regulations 1975) HC 240 (1974–75).
3 On 26 July 1988 three such committees sat concurrently.
4 Other documents have in specific cases been treated as if they were such documents.

In addition to the Members nominated to a standing committee on European Community documents by the Committee of Selection, any Member of the House may attend and address the committee, but is not counted in the quorum and may not vote.

A committee considers each document, or each group of documents, referred to it on a motion made by a Minister of the Crown. The chairman may select amendments to the motion. The chairman is required after two and a half hours to interrupt the proceedings, if they have not been previously concluded, and to put successively the questions on any amendment proposed from the chair, on any further amendments selected by him and on the main question or the main question as amended. (Because of the requirement of the standing order, these questions may be decided after 1 p.m.) When all the questions have been disposed of, the document or documents, together with any resolution to which the committee has come, is reported to the House without any further question being put.[1]

Thereafter, if a motion is made in the House in relation to any document or documents reported from a committee, the Speaker puts forthwith the question on any amendment selected by him which may be moved and the main question or the main question as amended; proceedings on such a motion are exempted business.[2]

Discharge of members of standing committees. The Committee of Selection is also empowered to discharge members appointed to serve on standing committees from time to time (in the case of the Welsh Grand Committee, the Northern Ireland Committee and the Standing Committee on Regional Affairs this applies only to the members nominated by the Committee of Selection), and to appoint other members in substitution for them (Standing Orders Nos 98, 99 and 100).

In accordance with a resolution of the Committee of Selection regularly renewed at the commencement of each session, no application for a change in the composition of a standing committee in respect of a particular bill will be entertained by the Committee of Selection while the bill is under consideration by the standing committee unless a Member is incapacitated from attendance by illness or has been appointed, or ceased to be, a member of the Government, or has changed his office for another or has acquired other duties or ceased to hold or changed such duties.[3] The Speaker has deprecated criticism in the House of the appointments made by the Committee of Selection[4] and has ruled that he cannot interfere with that committee and that it would be inappropriate for the House to do so.[5]

Chairmen of standing committees. The chairman or chairmen of each standing committee are appointed by the Speaker[6] from a panel consisting of

1 Eg CJ (1985–86) 220.
2 Eg CJ (1985–86) 226.
3 CJ (1919) 45; ibid (1920) 30, etc; the exception for illness was added in 1952, ibid (1952–53) 23, and the exceptions relating to members of the Government in 1956, ibid (1956–57) 32; the reference to 'other duties' is interpreted to cover Members who speak officially on particular subjects on behalf of opposition parties, and was added in 1981 (ibid (1980–81) 79).
4 Parl Deb (1906) 159, c 953; HC Deb (1921) 144, c 785; ibid (1924) 171, c 451; cf ibid (1961–62) 655, cc 201–205.
5 HC Deb (1924) 171, cc 451–452; ibid (1972–73) 849, cc 45–46; ibid (1974–75) 886, cc 1743–1744.
6 For validation of an irregular appointment see Votes and Proceedings (1988–89) 13 January 1989.

not less than ten Members nominated by him at the commencement[1] of every session to act as temporary chairmen of Committees of the whole House when requested by the Chairman of Ways and Means (see p 485), together with the Chairman of Ways and Means and the Deputy Chairmen (Standing Orders Nos 4 and 85(1)). The Speaker is given power to change the chairmen so appointed from time to time (Standing Order No 85(2)). Any member of a standing committee may act as temporary chairman, at the request of a chairman of the committee, for not more than a quarter of an hour on any one occasion, but without the powers granted by Standing Order No 89(3) (Standing Order No 85(5)).

The Chairmen's Panel, of whom three are a quorum, considers points of procedure which are not covered by the rules of the House, and is empowered to report to the House from time to time any resolutions it may come to on matters of procedure relating to standing committees (Standing Order No 85(4)). Certain resolutions relating to standing committee procedure are customarily reported each session.[2]

Sittings of standing committees

Every standing committee for the committee stage of bills continues to exist, once appointed, for the remainder of the session. However a separate chairman (or chairmen) and a separate membership are nominated for each bill allocated to a standing committee, even on the rare occasions[3] when more than one bill has been considered by the same committee on the same day. The day on which, and hour at which, a committee is to begin the consideration of each bill are appointed by the Member who has been appointed chairman of the committee in respect of that bill, acting so far as possible on the request of the Member in charge of the bill. 10.30 a.m. is the time usually appointed for a sitting to begin, but other times may be chosen, in the afternoon as well as in the morning.[4]

Except in the case of the Scottish Grand Committee, standing committees have no power to adjourn from place to place,[5] except by leave of the House, and accordingly are bound to meet only at Westminster. For the Scottish Grand Committee, Standing Order No 94(3) provides that a Minister of the Crown may move that the committee may meet in Edinburgh on any specified Monday at 10.30 a.m. to debate any bill, estimate or matter referred to it; that the question on the motion should be put forthwith; and

1 CJ (1947–48) 41; ibid (1985–86) 10, etc, but sometimes later.
2 For example, CJ (1937–38) 19; ibid (1985–86) 47. For Special Standing Committees, see p 594.
3 Standing Committee on Scottish Bills, Proceedings (Circuit Courts and Criminal Procedure (Scotland) Bill [Lords] and Roads and Streets in Police Burghs (Scotland) Bill) HC 176, 177 (1925); Stg Co B Proc (Imperial War Museum Bill and Trustee Savings Bank (Pensions) Bill) HC 65 (1954–55); Stg Co C, Proceedings (Road Traffic (Driving of Motor Cycles and Mopeds) Bill and Road Traffic (Amendment) Bill) HC 215, 230 (1959–60); ibid (Pharmacy and Poisons (Amendment) Bill and Dangerous Drugs Bill) HC 145, 146 (1963–64); Sc Stg Co A, Proceedings (Local Government (Scotland) Act 1947 (Amendment) (No 2) Bill, Criminal Procedure (Scotland) Bill and Solicitors (Scotland) Bill) HC 257–259 (1964–65); Stg Co E, Proceedings (Adoption Bill and Friendly and Industrial and Provident Societies Bill) HC 255, 256 (1967–68); Stg Co C, Carriage of Passengers by Road Bill, Mines (Working Facilities and Support) (Amendment) Bill, Town and Country Amenities Bill, CJ (1974) 202–203; Stg Co A, Proceedings (Reverter of Sites Bill [Lords], Minors' Contracts Bill [Lords] and Recognition of Trusts Bill [Lords], HC 266 (1986–87).
4 Eg the standing committee on the Finance Bill regularly sits in the afternoon.
5 Stg Co Deb (1947–48) Sc Stg Co (Scottish Estimates), cc 1161–1163, 1213–1214.

that if twenty or more Members rise to signify objection the question is
negatived.[1]

Standing committees, like select committees, may sit on any day on which
the house is sitting, before, during and after the conclusion of the sitting of
the House (Standing Order No 106);[2] accordingly, standing committees
have regularly met after the rising of the House on days when the House's
sitting of the previous day has continued beyond the usual hour of its
meeting on the day concerned.[3]

When a division is called in the House or in a Committee of the whole
House, the chairman of a standing committee must suspend its proceedings
for such time as will, in his opinion, enable members to vote in the division
and return to the committee. If a division is in progress at the hour appointed
for the sitting of a standing committee, the chairman will delay the start of
the sitting accordingly.

The dates and times of the subsequent sittings (after the first) for the
further consideration of each bill are determined by the committee itself.[4] If,
however, the committee has not agreed to a sittings motion at the end of the
first day's sitting, it is for the chairman to appoint a day and time for the next
sitting.[5] Under Standing Order No 88 a standing committee must meet on
such days at half-past ten unless the committee otherwise determines.

At one o'clock, unless it has been previously adjourned, the chairman
must adjourn a standing committee without putting any question; except
that if proceedings under Standing Order No 35 (closure of debate) are in
progress at one o'clock the chairman must not adjourn the committee until
the question on the closure, and any question or questions consequent
thereon and on any further motion necessary to decide any question already
proposed from the chair, are disposed of.[6] If, however, in the chairman's
opinion the proceedings on a bill or other business could be finally[7] concluded by an extension of the sitting until a quarter-past one he may defer
adjourning the committee until that time.[8] Under the same standing order
no committee may sit between one o'clock and half-past three, except as
stated above.

Where it seems likely that the consideration of a bill will not be concluded
at a single sitting, it is usual for the committee, before entering on the

1 This provision, added to the SO in 1983, followed ad hoc orders to similar effect first made in
   1981–82 (see CJ (1981–82) 9), and is now quite frequently invoked. Provision has been made
   for a sitting in Edinburgh to continue till 3.30 p.m. (Eg CJ (1985–86) 422).
2 HC Deb (1921) 144, c 43; Stg Co Deb (1919) i, Local Government (Ireland) Bill, 14.
3 Standing Committee A (Finance Bill) 22 June 1977; First Scottish Standing Committee
   (Education (Scotland) (No 2) Bill) 2 April 1981, etc.
4 Stg Co Deb (1922) Co A (Trade Union Act (1913) Amendment Bill), cc 250, 296; ibid
   (1932–33) Scottish Stg Co (Trout (Scotland) Bill), c 1023.
5 Stg Co Deb (1937–38) Co C (Administration of Justice (Miscellaneous Provisions) Bill)
   c 981; Stg Co D, Proceedings, Iron and Steel Bill, HC 281 (1966–67) p 4; Stg Co A,
   Proceedings, Finance Bill, HC 283 (1967–68) p 5.
6 In the case of standing committees on European Community Documents the question must
   also be put on any amendment to a motion selected by the chair (SO No 102(4)(b)).
7 This SO accordingly does not enable sittings on Scottish Estimates, other than the final one of
   a series, to be extended beyond one o'clock, Stg Co Deb (1952–53) Scottish Stg Co c 2696.
8 On 18 February 1988 a sitting of Standing Committee F was extended to complete consideration of a specific clause. The resultant division was declared invalid at the next sitting and the
   decision was taken again; St Co Deb (1987–88) Co F (Firearms (Amendment) Bill) cc 170–
   173.

consideration of the bill, to determine, by resolution, on what days in each week it will sit and at what hour it will meet for the purpose of considering the bill. (Resolutions covering successive sittings have also been passed by the Scottish Grand Committee for a series of sittings to consider Scottish Estimates and by the Welsh Grand Committee for further sittings on matters relating exclusively to Wales.) The days of sitting, or any of them, or the hour of meeting may be altered upon motion at a subsequent sitting, and the committee may adjourn over a day on which it has previously resolved to sit, or to a day other than that appointed for its next sitting, or to an hour other than that fixed for its next meeting (see below). Motions for fixing or altering the dates of sittings of standing committees, or the hour of meeting, may be made only at the beginning of a sitting or after further proceedings on the bill before the committee have been adjourned and may be amended only in respect of the days of sitting or the hour of meeting.

Adjournment of standing committees. The chairman of a standing committee has no power under the Standing Orders[1] to adjourn the committee except at the end of a morning's sitting pursuant to Standing Order No 88 or when a quorum is not present (see p 603). Any member may at any time during the consideration of a bill, (except while another member is speaking), move the adjournment of the debate, or of further consideration of the bill, as the case may require. In certain circumstances, chairmen of standing committees have accepted motions in the form, 'That the committee do now adjourn'.[2] If the motion is accepted by the chairman (see p 373) and agreed to by the committee, the debate, further consideration of the bill, or the committee, as the case may be, is adjourned to the day, if any, previously appointed for the next sitting of the committee; or, if the committee has previously decided to sit in the afternoon (see below) of the same day, until the hour decided upon. If, however, no day has been so appointed, or it is desired to alter the date or time of the next meeting, the committee must appoint a day and hour (or either as the case may be) for resuming the debate or taking the bill into further consideration. After a day and hour have, if necessary, been fixed for resuming further proceedings on the bill, and any motions which may be made respecting the dates or times of future sittings have been disposed of, the chairman adjourns the committee to the day and hour appointed for the next meeting, or for resuming further proceedings on the bill, as the case may be. If a dilatory motion is under

---

1 On 19 January 1988 the Chairman adjourned the First Scottish Standing Committee without question put when a Member who had not been nominated to serve on the committee persistently intervened and refused to withdraw (Stg Co Deb (1987–88) first Sc Co (Housing (Scotland) Bill, cc 3–7).
2 The reasons for such adjournments have included marks of respect for deceased members (Stg Co on Trade, Proceedings (Locomotives on Highways Bill) HC 233 (1898) p 7); absence of shorthand writers (Stg Co B, Proceedings (Race Relations Bill) HC 262 (1964–65) p 8); member in charge not ready or unwilling to proceed (Stg Co Deb (1959–60) Co C (Road Traffic (Driving of Motorcycles and Mopeds) Bill) c 5; ibid (1963–64) Co C (Representation of the People Act, 1949 (Amendment) Bill) cc 3–8; ibid (1968–69) Co C (Insurance (Employers' Liability) Bill) cc 3–20); questions having arisen concerning the availability or circulation of relevant papers (Stg Co Deb (1963–64) Co C (Protection of Birds Act 1954 (Amendment) Bill) cc 3–10; ibid (1988–89) First EC Docs (Health and Safety) cc 3–14); to facilitate the progress of the bill under consideration (Stg Co Deb (1950–51) Co B (New Streets Bill) c 683).

discussion at one o'clock, when the chairman is directed to adjourn the committee without putting any question, such motion lapses.[1]

If it is desired further to adjourn a standing committee to a day later than that appointed for its next sitting, the House will, on the motion of the chairman, make the necessary order.[2]

A standing committee ought to be adjourned to a specified day.[3] A committee has, however, sometimes adjourned, with the general concurrence of the members, to a day to be subsequently fixed by the chairman.[4] For a committee to endeavour to dispose of a bill which has been committed to it by adjourning *sine die*, or to some distant day, would be inconsistent with the duty imposed on the committee by the order of the House committing the bill to the committee.[5] Nor can a committee relieve itself from the obligation of considering the bills allotted to it and reporting them to the House by adjourning further proceedings on a particular bill *sine die*, or to some distant day, for once a committee has met to consider a particular bill, it cannot, except in the circumstances described in the following paragraph, or those mentioned on p 606, enter upon the consideration of another bill before it has completed the consideration of the first.[6]

Postponement of further consideration of a bill. In order to avoid the inconvenience which sometimes arises from this rule, the Chairmen's Panel has regularly since 1933 resolved that further consideration of a bill might, on the motion of the Member in charge of the bill, be postponed until after the next bill on the list had been disposed of, if it appeared to the chairman[7] that the business of the committee would be thereby expedited. For the Panel's resolution on bills failing to obtain a quorum see p 604.

Suspension of sitting of standing committee. The sitting of a standing committee may at any time be suspended *informally* by the chairman, in which case he will announce to the committee that the sitting is suspended and that he will resume the chair at a certain hour. It should be noted, however (as stated on p 598), that when a division is called in the House or in a Committee of the whole House, the chairman *must* suspend the proceedings for such time as will, in his opinion, enable Members to vote in the

---

1 Stg Co E, Proceedings (Companies Bill) HC 519 (1966–67) p 31; Stg Co A, Proceedings (Countryside Bill) HC 150 (1967–68) p 41.
2 For example, CJ (1937–38) 323; ibid (1967–68) 69.
3 A standing committee has adjourned to 'the first Tuesday or Thursday' on which the House should sit after an adjournment. Stg Co A, Proceedings (Countryside Bill) HC 150 (1967–68) p 11; Stg Co B, Proceedings (Agriculture (Miscellaneous Provisions) Bill) HC 118 (1967–68) p 12.
4 Standing Committee D, Proceedings, Betting and Lotteries Bill [Lords], HC 125 (1933–34) p 16; Standing Committee A, Proceedings, Marriage Bill, HC 40 (1936–37) p 9; Welsh Grand Committee, Proceedings, HC 167 (1960–61) p 3; Northern Ireland Committee, Proceedings, HC 357 (1981–82) p 3; Stg Co F, Proceedings, Civil Aviation Bill HC 384 (1984–85) p 3.
5 But see Standing Committee F, Proceedings, Civil Aviation Bill, HC 384 (1984–85) p 3.
6 The Scottish Grand Committee may consider a different class of business while debate respectively on a matter, estimates or a bill in relation to its principle stands adjourned, but may not proceed eg to a debate on a different matter while debate on a matter stands adjourned, see Scottish Gr Co Proceedings, 9 December 1980 and 14 July 1981. For action to overcome such a difficulty see Votes and Proceedings (1988–89) 10 March 1989.
7 CJ (1933–34) 30, etc, Stg Co Deb (1967–68) Co C (National Lottery Bill) c 22; ibid (1980–81) Co C (Industrial Diseases (Notification) Bill) c 34. For an earlier and similar procedure, see Chairmen's Panel Proceedings, HC 112 (1908), CJ (1919) 263.

division and return to the committee.[1] In accordance with Standing Order No 107 as applied to standing committees by Standing Order No 89, if at any time during the sitting a quorum is not present the chairman must suspend the proceedings until a quorum is present, or adjourn the committee until some future day (see p 604).

Afternoon and evening sittings. If it is desired that a committee should sit in the afternoon or evening as well as in the morning a motion to that effect must be agreed to by the committee.[2] Such a motion cannot be moved on the *same* day as it is proposed that there should be an afternoon (or evening) sitting unless oral notice of the intention to move such a motion has been given on a previous day.[3] Other courses are for the House to give the committee the leave it requires, eg if it wishes to meet twice on the day on which it first sits,[4] or for the committee to move and agree to the requisite motion on a *previous* day, and it is for the general convenience, though this is not essential, that notice should be given that a such a motion will be moved. Afternoon or evening sittings are treated and recorded as separate sittings.

Under Standing Order No 88 afternoon sittings cannot begin until half-past three o'clock, but can continue thereafter till one o'clock pm the following day, and have sometimes done so.[5] To conclude proceedings before that hour the committee must agree to a motion either 'That the debate be now adjourned' (if there is a question before the committee) or 'That further consideration of the bill be now adjourned' (if there is no question before the committee).

Procedure in standing committees

A standing committee has no power to frame regulations for its own procedure.[6] By Standing Order No 89(3) the powers of the chairman of a standing committee are assimilated to those exercised by a chairman in a Committee of the whole House in relation to dilatory motions in abuse of the rules of the House (Standing Order No 34), irrelevance or repetition (Standing Order No 41) and debate on clause or schedule standing part (Standing Order No 67); and to those reserved to the Chairman of Ways and Means or the Deputy Chairman in relation to the powers of the chair to propose the question (Standing Order No 28), the selection of amendments (Standing Order No 31) and the closure of debate (Standing Order No 35). Where appropriate, the chairman has such powers as Mr Speaker has under Standing Order No 31 in the selection of amendments to any bill under consideration on report. Standing Order No 89(3)(d) provides that certain standing orders relating to quorum and minutes of proceedings, which govern the procedure in a select committee (Standing Orders Nos 107, 108 and 111) shall apply to a standing committee. In Standing Order No 36, as applied by Standing Order No 89(3)(b) to proceedings in a standing committee, the number prescribed as the quorum of the committee (see p 603) is substituted

---

1 SO No 89(4).
2 Stg Co Deb (1936) Co B, c 732.
3 Stg Co Deb (1919) Scot, cc 868, 906; ibid (1969–70) Scottish Grand Co (Report of Royal Commission on Local Government) c 59.
4 Eg CJ (1985–86) 42, 230.
5 Eg Stg Co E, Housing Finance Bill, 8 February 1972.
6 Parl Deb (1883) 276, c 413.

for one hundred as the number necessary to make the majority effective for the closure.[1] In other respects procedure in a standing committee has, in practice, been assimilated as closely as possible to procedure in a Committee of the whole House.

The rules which govern the admissibility of amendments in a Committee of the whole House apply to proceedings in a standing committee,[2] and the chairman of a standing committee regularly makes known his provisional list of selected amendments and proposed groupings in the same way as the Chairman of Ways and Means does for a Committee of the whole House (see p 489). Following the principle which governs procedure in Committees of the whole House, no appeal can be made to the Speaker regarding the decisions and rulings of a chairman of a standing committee.[3] Equally, reference to the proceedings of a committee before it has reported, which might prejudice the proceedings of the committee, is not allowed, but a limited reference, germane to a question before the House, has been permitted.[4]

Rules of debate. The rules observed by the House regarding order in debate are followed in a standing committee, as also are the rules relating to the preservation of order and standards of behaviour of Members. Accordingly, members of a standing committee address the Chair standing, and may not refer to other members by name,[5] may not smoke[6] or read newspapers, books, etc, unless relevant to the bill before the committee[7] or attempt the solution of crossword puzzles[8] or listen to radios[9] or distribute propaganda literature[10] or bring refreshment into the room.[11] The rule prohibiting the citing of documents not before the House (see p 382) applies in standing committees.[12]

Disorder in standing committees. A standing committee has no power to punish one of its members for disorderly words, contemptuous conduct, or any other offence committed against it, but can only report the offence to the House.[13] The provisions of Standing Orders Nos 42 (disorderly conduct) and 43 (order in debate) have not been extended to standing committees, and

---

1 When a closure was mistakenly declared carried although an insufficient number had voted with the majority and the bill was reported without rectifying the error, the bill was recommitted to the same committee in respect of the amendment, CJ (1945–46) 206, 213; HC Deb (1945–46) 421, cc 41, 42.
2 Parl Deb (1889) 339, c 1226.
3 Parl Deb (1889) 339, cc 1222 ff; HC Deb (1920) 128, c 579; ibid (1928) 219, cc 851 ff; ibid (1987–88) 119, cc 1142–1144.
4 HC Deb (1946–47) 434, cc 1145–1146.
5 Stg Co Deb (1919) Co A (Restoration of Pre-war Practices (No 3) Bill) c 20; HC Deb (1919) 118, c 1823.
6 Stg Co Deb (1919) Supply, c 1; ibid (1935–36), Co A (Unemployment Insurance (Agriculture) Bill), cc 351, 352; ibid (1955–56) Co A (Agriculture (Safety) Bill) c 1.
7 Stg Co Deb (1955–56) Co E (Pensions (Increase) Bill) c 99.
8 Stg Co Deb (1979–80) Co H (Transport Bill) c 1154.
9 Stg Co Deb (1980–81) Co E (Finance Bill) c 46.
10 Stg Co Deb (1955–56) Co D (Criminal Justice Administration Bill [Lords]) c 50.
11 Stg Co Deb (1955–56) Scot Stg Co (Food and Drugs (Scotland) Bill) c 578; and Stg Co Deb (1967–68) Co C (Divorce Reform Bill) cc 305–306.
12 See Stg Co Deb (1966–67) Co D (Iron and Steel Bill) cc 547–549; ibid (1969–70) Co D (Ports Bill) c 1115.
13 Stg Co D, Proceedings (Unemployment Insurance Bill) HC 149 (1924–25) p 16; Stg Co Deb (1924–25) Co C (Unemployment Insurance Bill) c 634; CJ (1924–25) 337; HC Deb (1924–25) 186, c 2012.

the chairman has, therefore, not the power with which the Speaker and the chairman of a Committee of the whole House are invested to order a Member who is guilty of grossly disorderly conduct to withdraw, or to name a Member for disregarding the authority of the Chair or abusing the rules of the House by persistently and wilfully obstructing the business of the House or otherwise.

When Members who were not nominated to a standing committee have insisted on sitting in the part of the room reserved for nominated members, they have on occasion been reported to the House,[1] and the committee has on one occasion adjourned.[2] On two such occasions the House made an order empowering the Chairman of the Committee to order any Member not a member of the Committee to withdraw, and directing the Serjeant at Arms to act on any consequent orders received from the Chairman.[3]

Admission of strangers. Members have the right of access, as in the case of select committees (see p 632), to the room occupied by a standing committee, but under modern practice[4] a Member of the House who is not a member of the committee is not allowed to sit with or to address the committee, subject to the following exceptions:

(1) The four law officers, if Members of the House of Commons though not members of a standing committee, may under Standing Order No 87(1) address the committee but may not vote, move any motion or amendment or be counted in the quorum.

(2) Ministers of the Crown, being Members of the House but not of the standing committee, may, under the same restrictions, take part in the deliberations of a standing committee appointed to consider a bill brought in upon a Ways and Means resolution (Standing Order No 87(2)).

(3) Any Member may, under the same restrictions, take part in the deliberations of a standing committee on statutory instruments, &c (Standing Order No 101).

(4) Any Member may take part in the deliberations of a standing committee on European Community Documents but may not vote or be counted in the quorum (Standing Order No 102(2)).

Strangers are admitted, except when the committee orders them to withdraw (Standing Order No 89(2)). Under Standing Order No 141 the Serjeant at Arms may take into custody strangers misconducting themselves at a sitting of a standing committee if the chairman so directs.[5]

Quorum. The quorum of all standing committees except the Scottish Grand Committee is seventeen or one third of the number of its members, excluding the chairman, whichever is the less (Standing Order No 89(1)); the quorum of the Scottish Grand Committee is ten (Standing Order No 94). Until a quorum is present the committee cannot proceed to business, nor can

1 Stg Co Deb (1972–73) First Sc Co (Local Government (Scotland) Bill) cc 25–68; ibid (1987–88) Co E (Local Government Finance Bill) cc 6–7; Votes and Proceedings (1987–88) 21 January 1988.
2 Stg Co Deb (1987–88) First Sc Co (Housing (Scotland) Bill) cc 3–7.
3 CJ (1972–73) 109; HC Deb (1972–73) 849, cc 666–678; Votes and Proceedings (1988–89) 14 March 1989.
4 On two occasions before the relevant standing orders were made Ministers of the Crown were allowed to address standing committees to which they had not been nominated.
5 Eg Welsh Gr Co, Proceedings (effect of Government Legislation) HC 615 (1987–88) p 3.

any business be proceeded with when the members present are reduced below the quorum.[1] It is the duty of the clerk attending the committee, as in a select committee (see Standing Order No 107), to call the attention of the chairman to the fact when the number of members present falls below a quorum, whereupon the chairman must suspend the proceedings until a quorum is present or adjourn the committee (see also 'Divisions in standing committees', p 605). The chairman is included in the quorum, but is not taken into account when calculating the quorum under Standing Order No 89.

No time-limit within which a quorum must be present is prescribed by standing order, but if a quorum is not present within twenty minutes from the time at which a standing committee is appointed to meet, it is customary[2] for the chairman to adjourn the committee to a future day unless there are any special circumstances which, in his opinion, make it advisable to allow a longer period of grace.[3] Similarly in cases where in the course of a sitting the members present become less than a quorum it is not usual for chairmen to allow more than twenty minutes for the re-assembling of a quorum.

If a committee has to be adjourned for want of a quorum, and a day has already been appointed for the next meeting of the committee, the chairman adjourns the committee to that day; and if the failure of a quorum to assemble or to continue in attendance occurs on a day on which, pursuant to a previous resolution of the committee, there is to be an afternoon sitting (see p 601), the chairman suspends the sitting until the hour appointed for the beginning of that sitting.[4]

In order to deal with the delays caused to the consideration of other bills allotted to a standing committee by the repeated failure of a quorum to attend in the case of a particular bill, since 1959 the Chairmen's Panel has resolved that if at any two sittings of a standing committee called for the consideration of a bill the committee is adjourned by reason of the absence of a quorum before twelve noon, the committee should not consider that bill again until any other bills committed to the committee have been considered.[5]

---

1 Stg Co Deb (1919) Supply, c 4. See also Parl Deb (1907) 177, cc 715–720; CJ (1907) 356.
2 This follows a decision made by the Chairmen's Panel in 1929.
3 For the case of a chairman waiting thirty minutes for a standing committee to assemble, see Stg Co Deb (1968–69) Co B (Divorce Reform Bill) cc 471–473.
4 Stg Co Deb (1920) Co B (Ministry of Mines Bill) c 455; Stg Co C, Proceedings (Cinematograph Films Bill) HC 92 (1927) p 108. Stg Co B, Proceedings (Divorce Reform Bill) HC 212 (1968–69) p 20.
5 CJ (1959–60) 41, etc. For examples of such procedure, see Stg Co Deb (1930–31) Co A (Rabbits Bill) cc 37–38; ibid (1937–38) Co B (Public Meeting Act (1908) Amendment Bill) cc 1438–1440. In cases of failure of a quorum to attend at two sittings to consider a bill which was the last bill on the list of those referred to the standing committee, the standing committee concerned has adjourned to a day on which it was expected the House would not sit. Stg Co Deb (1928) Co B (Dog Racing Bill), cc 2001–2002; Stg Co C, Proceedings (Sale of Milk Bill) HC 4 (1957–58), p 4; ibid (Representation of the People Act 1949 (Amendment) Bill), HC 14 (1963–64) p 7. In another case, when the bill concerned was the last on the list, and a quorum had failed to attend at two successive meetings, the Committee nevertheless went on to consider the bill (Stg Co C, Proceedings, Merchandise Marks Acts (1887–1911) (Amendment) Bill, HC 173 (1924–25)). See also Stg Co D, Proceedings, Coroners (Amendment) Bill, HC 157, (1926) pp 4–5, where the consideration of the bill was interrupted by consideration of two other bills referred to the committee, after a quorum had failed to attend at meetings to consider the bill.

Divisions in standing committees. Divisions in a standing committee are taken in the same manner as in a select committee (see p 623).

The question is put only once, and if the chairman's opinion as to the decision of a question is challenged, the committee must proceed to a division.[1] It is the practice to allow a short interval to elapse before directing the doors of the committee room to be locked in order to give members, who were not in the room when the question was put, time to come in.[2] The length of the interval has been varied by chairmen to meet the circumstances of particular cases.[3]

Following the rule adopted by the House in 1906 (see p 345) a member may vote although he did not hear the question put, and is not compelled to vote although he is present when the question is put.[4] A member who voted when outside that part of the committee room reserved for members has had his vote disallowed.[5] When the numbers voting in a division are less than the number required (in addition to the chairman) to constitute a quorum, the fact that other members were present who completed the quorum, but did not vote, is recorded in the minutes.[6] If, however, through inadvertence a division is called while less than a quorum is present and this fact is established when the numbers are announced after the division, the chairman should either suspend the proceedings until a quorum is present or adjourn the committee to a future day or, if there is to be an afternoon sitting, to the hour appointed for that sitting (see Standing Order No 107 and pp 599–600). When a quorum is again present the question must be put again. A member who has voted under a misapprehension will be allowed to alter his vote provided that he makes his request before the numbers have been declared from the chair, but cannot alter his vote after the numbers have been so declared.[7] A member's vote in a standing committee must agree with his voice,[8] and if the chairman is satisfied that a member has deliberately voted in a sense contrary to his voice, or has failed to vote after declaring himself with the 'Ayes' or the 'Noes', he can direct that the vote be recorded in accordance with the voice.[9] A standing committee has the power of deter-

---

1 Stg Co Deb (1921) Co A (Railways Bill) c 1539; Stg Co Deb (1946–47) Sc Stg Co (National Health Service (Scotland) Bill) cc 952–953.
2 Stg Co Deb (1921) Co B (Railways Bill) c 1009; ibid (1929–30) Co B (Industrial and Provident Societies (Amendment) Bill) cc 1762, 1855.
3 Stg Co Deb (1966–67) Co A (Prices and Incomes (No 2) Bill) cc 150–151, 197–200; ibid (1968–69) Co B (Divorce Reform Bill) cc 190–191; ibid (1987–88) Co A (Finance (No 2) Bill) c 4.
4 Standing Committee on Law, Proceedings, Marriage with a Deceased Wife's Sister Bill, HC 87 (1907) p 10.
5 Standing Committee D, Proceedings, New Towns Bill, HC 212 (1958–59) p 4; Stg Co Deb (1966–67) Co B (Prices and Incomes Bill) c 751.
6 Standing Committee B, Proceedings, Local Government (Miscellaneous Provisions) Bill, HC 168 (1952–53) p 10; see also ibid Companies Bill, HC 84 (1928) p 30.
7 Stg Co Deb (1919) Co A (Ministry of Ways & Communications Bill) c 918; ibid (1920) Co B (Dyestuffs (Import Regulations) Bill) c 688; ibid (1923) Co A (Rent (Notices of Increase) Bill) c 5; ibid (1945–46) Co B (Civil Aviation Bill) c 566.
8 Stg Co Deb (1945–46) Co A (National Insurance (Industrial Injuries) Bill) c 121; ibid (1959–60) Co B (Cinematograph Films Bill) cc 176–177. See also ibid (1967–68) Co F (Transport Bill) c 852.
9 Standing Committee B, Proceedings (Local Authority Social Services Bill) HC 250 (1969–70) p 6; Stg Co Deb (1979–80) Co A, Companies Bill [*Lords*] c 653.

mining the question of a personal interest in a vote.[1]

The chairman in a standing committee, as in a select committee (see p 623), can vote only when there is an equality of votes. In giving a casting vote the chairman is guided by the same principles as the Speaker in the House or the chairman in a committee of the whole House (see pp 350–354). When the chairman states his reasons for his vote they are entered in the minutes of the proceedings.[2]

Recommittal of bills to standing committees. Bills have been committed to the former committee in respect of certain amendments made by a standing committee to a bill[3] or in respect of a part of the bill.[4] The House has also recommitted to a standing committee a bill so far as amended by the committee, at the same time giving a permissive instruction to the committee to the effect that it had power to insert in the bill provisions with a like effect to a clause to which it had disagreed.[5] In such cases, the chairmen and members of the committee are the same as before.

Power of standing committees with regard to provisions imposing charges. A standing committee cannot proceed to the consideration of provisions imposing a charge on the public or on public funds unless a resolution of the House authorizing such a charge has been agreed to (see p 495).[6] It is, however, the duty of a standing committee to proceed with the consideration of a bill containing such provisions (if necessary by postponing the clause which imposes a charge), although the necessary resolution has not been agreed to by the House, in the hope that a resolution will have been passed by the time the committee reaches those provisions, or that the bill will have been so amended as to avoid the imposition of such a charge.[7] When the first and only effective clause of a bill created a charge not covered

---

1 Standing Committee B, Proceedings, Industrial and Provident Societies (Amendment) Bill, HC 72 (1929–30) p 9; Stg Co Deb (1929–30) Co B (Industrial and Provident Societies (Amendment) Bill) cc 1828 ff; ibid (1933–34) Co D (Betting and Lotteries Bill) cc 386, 425; ibid (1951–52) Co C (Licensed Premises in New Towns Bill) c 2215; ibid (1961–62) Co A (South Africa Bill) cc 197–198; ibid (1979–80) Co A (Companies Bill [Lords]) c 653; ibid (1981–82) Co A (Finance Bill) c 393 (Motion withdrawn).
2 See, for example, First Scottish Standing Committee Proceedings HC 273 (1972–73) p 43.
3 CJ (1948–49) 400.
4 CJ (1950–51) 245.
5 CJ (1969–70) 281; see also HC Deb (1969–70) 800, cc 424–498.
6 Stg Co E, Proceedings, Analgesia in Childbirth Bill, HC 198 (1948–49) p 6; Stg Co Deb (1963–64) Co C (Trading Stamps Bill) c 3; ibid Co C (Representation of the People Act, 1949 (Amendment) Bill), cc 3–8; ibid (1969–70) Co C (Chronically Sick and Disabled Persons Bill) cc 178–179; ibid (1979–80) Co C (Affiliation Orders and Aliments (Annual Up-dating) Bill) cc 3, 33. In cases where the government indicated before the first sitting of a standing committee to consider private Member' bills that no such resolution would be forthcoming, the chairman of the committee with the consent of the member in charge has refrained from appointing a day for consideration of the bill in question and the committee has been convened to consider the next bill on the list (Empire Settlement Bill, 1928; Children (Provision of Footwear) Bill, 1928–29).
7 Stg Co Deb (1950–51) Co B (New Streets Bill) c 589; ibid (1969–70) Co C (Chronically Sick and Disabled Persons Bill) cc 178–179; Stg Co C, Proceedings, Official Information Bill, HC 238 (1978–79), p 4. A chairman has also permitted a private member in charge of a bill for which no money resolution was to be provided to move at the beginning of the proceedings on the bill that the committee do not proceed with the consideration of the bill (Stg Co A, Proceedings (Housing of the Working Classes Bill) HC 108 (1913) p 6); ibid HC 268 (1914) p 6.

by a money resolution, a standing committee adjourned in the hope that a resolution would be provided.[1] When a standing committee considered such provisions before the necessary resolution was agreed to, Mr Speaker drew the attention of the House to the fact on consideration of the bill, and it was recommitted to the committee in respect of the clause improperly considered by it.[2]

Reference to standing committees of notices of amendments. Notices of amendments to a bill committed to a standing committee are printed and circulated with the Votes, and automatically stand referred to the committee. Such amendments may be tabled by any member of the House but can only be considered if they are moved by a member of the committee. Notices of amendments to motions to be considered by standing committees on European Community Documents are treated in the same manner. Petitions are not received by a standing committee.[3]

Instructions to standing committees. If appropriate instructions are given to them by the House (see p 482), standing committees may consolidate bills committed to them into one bill,[4] extend the provisions of a bill to other parts of the United Kingdom[5] or to other classes of persons,[6] divide a bill into two bills (see p 498) or consider a clause similar to one they have previously rejected.[7]

Division of bills between standing committees. By order of the House made before or after consideration of the bill has been entered upon in standing committee, bills committed to such committees may be divided between two standing committees.[8] Bills have been divided between a Scottish Standing Committee and another committee,[9] or between standing committees and committees of the whole House.[10]

Reporting of bills before consideration has been completed. It is the duty of a standing committee, as of all committees, to give the matters referred to it due and sufficient consideration. The chairman of a standing committee will not therefore normally accept motions in pursuance of which the committee would conclude its deliberations before it has gone through the bill committed to it.

On the other hand, circumstances have arisen which, in the opinion of the Member in charge of the bill, have rendered it inexpedient to proceed further with consideration of the bill, and on these occasions that Member has been permitted to move, 'That the committee do not proceed (or

---

1 Stg Co Deb (1963–64) Co C (Representation of the People Act 1949 (Amendment) Bill) cc 3–8.
2 CJ (1907) 196; Parl Deb (1907) 174, c 1068; ibid 177, c 716. CJ (1927) 105; ibid (1929–30) 387; ibid (1950–51) 245.
3 Stg Co on Law, etc, Proceedings (Aliens Bill), HC 242 (1904) p 18.
4 CJ (1890) 465; ibid (1890–91) 254; ibid (1901) 351; ibid (1903) 296; ibid (1929–30) 203.
5 CJ (1903) 120; ibid (1976–77) 150.
6 CJ (1959–60) 143.
7 CJ (1969–70) 281.
8 CJ (1921) 247, 252.
9 CJ (1947–48) 62, 66; ibid (1955–56) 177; ibid (1963–64) 91.
10 This is now the usual practice in regard to Finance Bills.

proceed further) with the bill'.[1] The circumstances in which such motions
have been moved have varied considerably[2] but their general nature may be
indicated by a few examples. Such motions have been made when there
seemed no prospect of the bill being reported to the House in sufficient time
to allow it to be considered by the House;[3] when the government had
declined to move a resolution in the House sanctioning the charge on the
public or on public funds proposed in a private Member's bill;[4] when the
government had indicated that it would take action, whether by legislation
or otherwise, in connection with the subject-matter with which a private
Member's bill proposed to deal;[5] when the committee had disagreed to the
effective provisions in the bill,[6] or had amended the bill in such a way that the
Member in charge was not willing to proceed.[7]

It has been ruled by the Speaker that such a motion can normally be
moved only by the Member in charge of the bill.[8] Other Members have,
however, been permitted in particular circumstances to make such a motion.
A member of the government has made an analogous motion on informing a
committee of the government's intention to bring in a bill similar in intention
to that under consideration, which was a private Member's bill.[9] A Member

1 See HC Deb (1920) 128, cc 576–579. Such a motion has been negatived, Stg Co on Law, etc,
   Proceedings, HC 154 (1905) p 20.
2 See for example, Stg Co Proceedings, Stg Co on Trade, etc (Plumbers Registration Bill) HC
   347 (1893–94), pp 8–9; ibid Co A (Education Acts (Single School Areas) (Amendment) Bill)
   HC 105 (1912–13), p 14; ibid Co A (Market Gardeners' Compensation (No 2) Bill) HC 390
   (1912–13) p 7; ibid Co D (Representation of the People Bill) HC 113 (1920) p 20; Stg Co Deb
   (1924) Co A (Rent Restrictions Bill) c 444; Stg Co Proceedings, Sc Stg Co (Law Agents
   (Scotland) Bill) HC 143 (1924–25) p 11, ibid Co A (Wild Birds Protection Bill) HC 84 (1927)
   p 10; Stg Co Deb (1933–34) Co B (Employers' Liability Bill) c 1207; ibid (1958–59) Co C
   (Baking Industry (Small Establishments and Seasonal Resorts) Bill) c 92.
3 Eg Stg Co Deb (1954–55) Co B (Non-Industrial Employment Bill) c 40. In such circumstances, a committee has negatived all the remaining clauses in a bill, and made a Special
   Report to the House when the bill was reported, as amended, Stg Co Proceedings, Co B
   (Mental Deficiency Bill) HC 385 (1912–13) p 56.
4 Stg Co Proceedings, Co A (Housing of the Working Classes Bill) HC 108 (1913) p 6; ibid Co
   A (Housing of the Working Classes Bill) HC 268 (1914) p 6. See also Stg Co Deb (1963–64)
   Co C (Representation of the People Act 1949 (Amendment) Bill) cc 3–8.
5 Stg Co Proceedings, Stg Co on Trade, etc (Coal Mines (Eight Hours) Bill) HC 123 (1907) p 4;
   Stg Co Deb (1931–32) Co B (Sunday Performances (Regulation) Bill) cc 1697–1701; ibid
   (1950–51) Co B (Matrimonial Causes Bill) c 902; ibid (1967–68) Co C (National Lottery Bill)
   cc 46–48.
6 Stg Co Proceedings, Co A (Dogs (Protection) Bill) HC 223 (1913) p 14; ibid Co A (Dogs Bill)
   HC 313 (1914) p 10; ibid Co D (Rating Returns Bill) HC 104 (1923) p 3; Stg Co Deb (1929–30)
   Co B (Playing Fields (Exemption from Rating) Bill) c 2259; ibid (1929–30) Co B (Mock
   Auctions Bill) c 2207; ibid (1969–70) Co A (Education Bill) c 338 (a Government bill).
   Committees have also disagreed to all the clauses of a bill, and made a special report to that
   effect to the House, Stg Co Proceedings, Co E (Trade Disputes (No 2) Bill) HC 137 (1919)
   p 5; Stg Co Deb (1950–51) Co B (Transport (Amendment) Bill) cc 875–878.
7 Stg Co Proceedings, Stg Co on Trade, etc (Labourers (Ireland) Bill) HC 284 (1904) p 15; Stg
   Co Deb (1929–30) Co B (Industrial and Provident Societies (Amendment) Bill) c 1899; ibid
   (1929–30) Co C (Blasphemy Laws (Amendment) Bill) c 1936; ibid (1930–31) Co C (Trade
   Disputes and Trade Unions (Amendment) Bill) c 419; ibid (1931–32) Co C (Juries (Exemption of Firemen) Bill) c 1946; ibid (1936–37) Co A (Annual Holiday Bill) c 442.
8 Times, 24 July 1913; see also Times, 24 May 1892; Parl Deb (1907) 173, c 273; Stg Co Deb
   (1919) Co E (Compensation for Subsidence Bill) c 316; ibid (1924) Co A (Rent Restrictions
   Bill) c 444; ibid (1958–59) Co C (Baking Industry (Small Establishments and Seasonal
   Resorts) Bill) cc 59–60. But see Stg Co Proceedings, Co C (Representation of the People Bill)
   HC 113, (1920) p 12.
9 Stg Co Proceedings, Stg Co on Trade, etc (Coal Mines (Eight Hours) Bill) HC 123 (1907) p 4.
   For Mr Speaker's observations on the procedure, see Parl Deb (1907) 173, c 273.

of the government made such a motion when the only effective clause had been negatived but the Member in charge of the bill declined to do so.[1]

A motion, that the committee do not proceed (or proceed further) with the consideration of a bill, is debatable, but may not be amended. If the motion is agreed to, the chairman is then ordered to report the bill to the House without amendment or with such amendments as the committee has made. The committee should then agree to a special report setting out the facts of the case.

Committees have also, on the motion of the Member in charge of the bill, been discharged by the House from further consideration thereof (see p 480).

Allocation of time orders

As explained on p 408 an allocation of time order is sometimes made by the House, on the motion of the government, in relation to a particular bill or bills.[2] The part of this procedure which governs standing committees is now prescribed by Standing Order No 103.[3]

The allocation of time order gives general instructions to the standing committee and fixes a date on or before which the bill must be reported. A sub-committee, designated the business sub-committee, consisting of the chairman or one of the chairmen of the standing committee in respect of the bill in question and seven other members, is nominated by the Speaker, four being the quorum.[4] The chairman then calls a meeting of the sub-committee, whose proceedings are analogous to those of a select committee though less formal. The minutes are not printed. A draft recommendation, usually circulated in advance of the meeting, is submitted to the sub-committee by the Member in charge of the bill. This recommendation, which comprises a detailed time-table showing the number of sittings to be allotted to the consideration of the bill, the business to be taken at each sitting and the hour at which proceedings must be concluded, is considered by the sub-committee and may be amended. The agreed resolution is then printed forthwith and made known to the members of the standing committee. At the commencement of the proceedings at the next sitting the resolution is reported and the Member in charge of the bill moves that the resolution of the business sub-committee be agreed to by the standing committee. This question must be decided without amendment or debate. The resolution is entered in the minutes of proceedings of the standing committee.[5]

If the resolution is agreed to by the standing committee it operates as if it had formed part of the allocation of time order made by the House, the rule that a standing committee may not frame regulations for its own procedure[6] thus being preserved. But if it is disagreed to, it must be recommitted to the business sub-committee. Apart from this, further meetings of the business sub-committee may be called at the discretion of the chairman, to amend the original resolution where it is found that a rearrangement of the time-table is

1 Stg Co Deb (1929–30) Co B (Playing Fields (Exemption from Rating) Bill) c 2259.
2 Eg CJ (1985–86) 181, 300.
3 This Standing Order was made in November 1947, replacing sessional orders made in the two previous sessions.
4 Eg CJ (1985–86) 185.
5 Eg Standing Committee J, Proceedings, Education Reform Bill, HC 364 (1987–88) pp 47–48.
6 Parl Deb (1883) 276, c 413.

desired[1] or to consider further motions where the original resolution did not cover the whole of the bill.

The provisions of Standing Order No 81 (see p 409) apply to bills which are being considered by a standing committee.

When the time specified in an allocation of time order for bringing to a conclusion any proceedings falls during the suspension of a committee for the purpose of allowing Members to vote in the House, the chairman puts any question necessary to dispose of the business to be concluded by that time as soon as the committee is resumed.[2]

Records of proceedings in standing committees

Minutes of proceedings. All standing committees have leave to print and circulate their proceedings with the Vote (Standing Order No 89(5)). The proceedings of individual sittings of standing committees are circulated[3] from day to day in the form of a reprinted amendment paper (see p 207) showing how each amendment, and each clause or schedule, was disposed of at the sitting concerned, together with any procedural resolutions considered.[4] The minutes of proceedings in respect of all the sittings on a particular bill are reported to the House at the conclusion of the proceedings, and are ordered to be printed. They are then published in their complete form, setting out the terms of any amendments moved but not made, any amendments made on a division, and any resolutions come to, with the names of those voting for and aginst. Amendments made otherwise than on a division are listed by number, referring to the notice papers of the Committee, except in the case of manuscript amendments (see p 489) which are set out in full, whether made or not.

If a committee has begun the consideration of a bill, but has not reported it to the House, as, for instance, where further consideration of a bill is postponed owing to the repeated failure of a quorum to attend (see p 604), where the announcement of a General Election results in a dissolution or where the committee has been discharged from further consideration of the bill, the House will order the minutes to be laid before it, and, when presented, will order them to be printed.[5]

Official reports of debates. A shorthand note or mechanical recording of the debates in standing committees is taken by the official reporters (see p 197), and the reports of the debates are published in separate issues.[6] Standing committees have on occasion decided to proceed with the con-

---

1 Standing Committee C, Proceedings, Iron and Steel Bill, HC 110 (1948–49) p 12; Standing Committee C, Proceedings, Housing Repairs and Rents Bill, HC 123 (1953–54) pp 26, 30, 40; Standing Committee A, Proceedings, Rent Bill, HC 109 (1956–57) pp 31, 42; Standing Committee J, Proceedings, Education Reform Bill, HC 364 (1987–88) p 79.
2 Stg Co Deb (1967–68) Co F (Transport Bill) c 2395.
3 This practice was introduced in Session 1966–67.
4 See Select Committee on House of Commons (Services) Second Report, HC 94 (1966–67) para 6.
5 CJ (1937–38) 288, 289; ibid (1957–58) 10, 11; ibid (1964–65) 172, 173; ibid (1978–79) 276.
6 Before 1979–80, the reports of the debates of Second Reading Committees were issued as part of the Official Report of the House for the day concerned.

sideration of bills in the absence of shorthand writers, when these were not available.[1]

SELECT COMMITTEES

Function of select committees in the Commons

Select committees, that is committees composed of a number of Members specially named, are regularly appointed to consider, inquire into, or deal with particular matters or bills. Successive Parliaments have found in them a flexible means of accomplishing a wide variety of different purposes. Select committees may be given different powers to meet different circumstances. They may be appointed once only to meet a particular requirement or be reappointed from session to session or from Parliament to Parliament to carry out a more continuous function.

The idea that it should be in part through select committees that the House should play an active part in informed criticism and scrutiny of the aims and actions of the executive is one which is central to the select committee system. The related problem of adapting that system to meet this need is one which the House has always to solve afresh as the nature and scope of the executive's activity alters. Committees specializing over a period in areas of governmental activity rather than specific actions or events were suggested as long ago as 1918.[2] From 1966 to 1979 several committees were appointed specializing in certain subjects or departments of state. Examples of 'subject' select committees were the Select Committees on Science and Technology, and Race Relations and Immigration. Examples of departmental select committees were the Select Committees on Agriculture, Education and Science, and Overseas Aid.[3] Meanwhile the main thrust of select committee activity in the House was maintained by the Estimates Committee and its sub-committees. First set up in 1912 this committee was appointed in every session apart from the war years (when it was replaced by a National Expenditure Committee) until 1970. In 1971 it was replaced by the Expenditure Committee with wider terms of reference to examine public expenditure.[4] Following recommendations made by the Select Committee on Procedure in 1978[5] the Expenditure Committee and

---

1 Stg Co Deb (1947–48) Co D (Gas Bill) cc 1590, 1593–1594; Stg Co B, Proceedings, Race Relations Bill, HC 262 (1964–65) p 8. See also Stg Co Deb (1967–68) Co C (Divorce Reform Bill) cc 233–238 and ibid (1967–68) Co E (Administration of Justice Bill) c 6.
2 Report on the Machinery of Government, 1918, Cd 9230 (the Haldane Report). See eg also Procedure Committee HC 161 (1930–31) pp 153–170; Procedure Committee, HC 91–I, (1958–59) p xxiv; Science and Technology Committee, Second Report, HC 213 (1968–69) para 183. Fuller details of such proposals since the 1930s will be found in the Hansard Society's 'Parliamentary Reform: A Survey of Recent Proposals' (2nd edn, 1967) pp 45–60.
3 For further details of these committees, see *Erskine May* (18th edn) pp 656–658.
4 Procedure Committee, Fourth Report, HC 303 (1964–65) pp vi–ix. For a description of the development of the Estimates Committee, the Expenditure Committee and other specialist committees, see *Erskine May* (19th edn) pp 671–672, 674, 676.
5 Procedure Committee, First Report, HC 588–I (1977–78).

other existing committees were replaced by a new system of select committees relating to government departments. Established for the first time in the 1979–83 Parliament the departmental committees have been reappointed in the two successive Parliaments. They constitute the largest part of the select committee structure at the present time.

Other regularly appointed committees deal with matters as diverse as public accounts (see p 660), advising the Speaker on the accommodation and services in that part of the Palace of Westminster and its precincts occupied by the House of Commons (see p 657), exercising certain functions in connection with the Register of Members' Interests (see p 658) and examining the reports of the Parliamentary Commissioner for Administration, the Health Service Commissioners and the Parliamentary Commissioner for Northern Ireland (see p 659). The consequences arising from the application of European Community legislation to the United Kingdom were also partly met by the House through the appointment of a select committee. A select committee to consider European Community Legislation (see pp 774–776) was first appointed in 1974 shortly after the entry of the United Kingdom into the Community and a committee with broadly similar powers is now set up regularly in each Parliament (see p 657).

Apart from the committees which are regularly re-appointed, other occasional ad hoc committees play an important part in the work of the House. Procedure or aspects of procedure, taxation or financial matters, social questions, matters of immediate public concern, and matters dealing with the Palace of Westminster or the working conditions of Members are frequently considered by committees appointed specifically for the purpose.

Appointment and Nomination

Procedures for appointment. There are three different procedures in current use for the appointment of select committees and the nomination of their members:

(1) The orders of reference of some committees, together with the number of members and the quorum, and the powers with which the committee is invested, are contained in the standing orders.[1] Such standing orders normally contain the provision that members of the committee are nominated for the remainder of the Parliament.[2]

(2) On occasion, the orders of reference of proposed committees, together with the proposed number of members and the number to be proposed as the quorum, and the powers with which it is proposed the committee should be invested, have been moved for in the House in the form of temporary standing orders valid until the end of the Parliament. Members of such committees can then be nominated on motion for the remainder of the Parliament by the use of a similar procedure. Select committees were set up and nominated in this fashion for the first time in Session 1974–75.[3]

(3) In each session, other committees may be set up upon motions in which are laid down their orders of reference, the number to be proposed as

---

1 Eg SO Nos 121, 122, 125 to 131.
2 Eg SO Nos 121 to 131.
3 Eg CJ (1974–75) 72, 73; ibid (1979–80) 58, 87, 94–95; ibid (1983–84) 423, Votes and Proceedings (1987–88), 29 March 1988.

the quorum and the powers with which it is proposed that the committee should be invested. The members are usually nominated at the same time.[1] Such committees cease to exist at prorogation or (if they have not been given power to report from time to time) after they have made their report to the House.

Committees have also been appointed by the passing of an amendment to a question,[2] and following the agreement of the House to a motion moved by a private Member.[3]

Unless, as is sometimes the case;[4] the House makes specific provisions to the contrary in respect of a particular committee, the appointment of a select committee and the nomination of members must be the subject of separate motions[5] and it is not in order, on the motion for the appointment of a select committee, to discuss the names of the Members who, it is proposed, shall compose it.[6]

The committees by which opposed private bills and provisional order bills are usually considered are appointed, not by the House, but by the Committee of Selection under the standing orders relating to private business (see pp 825, 826, 954, 960) and are not designated select committees. Hybrid bill committees are nominated either by the House and the Committee of Selection or by the Committee of Selection alone (see pp 825, 521–522 and fn 11 on p 615).

It used to be the case that under a standing order no select committee could, without leave of the House, consist of more than fifteen members.[7] The standing order, however, was repealed in 1983.[8]

Nomination of members. Unless the House otherwise orders, the members of a select committee are named by the House upon the motion of a Member.

Many of the regular select committees of the House are now appointed by virtue of a particular standing order containing their terms of reference and their powers. They thus require no motion of appointment, but only a motion or motions to nominate their membership in order to function.

Standing Order No 104 requires previous notice to be given of the names of Members intended to be proposed as members of select committees. In

---

1 Eg CJ (1980–81) 71.
2 CJ (1878) 376; ibid (1884) 98; ibid (1884–85) 238; ibid (1922) 118; ibid (1924) 387. A select committee has been appointed to consider the subject-matter of a bill by means of an amendment to the question for the second reading of the bill, CJ (1854–55) 238; ibid, (1870) 90.
3 CJ (1957–58) 78.
4 Eg Votes and Proceedings (1987–88) 25 and 29 March 1988, 25 May 1988.
5 Parl Deb (1873) 216, c 59; for scope of debate on motion for appointing, see HC Deb (1937–38) 337, c 2157; ibid (1938–39) 342, c 906; see also Parl Deb (1905) 146, c 993.
6 Parl Deb (1880) 252, c 489.
7 Examples of large committees include the Select Committee on Agriculture which had 25 members, CJ (1967–68) 69, the Select Committee on Televising the House which had 20 members, Votes and Proceedings (1987–88) 29 March 1988, the Expenditure Committee which was appointed from 1970–71 until 1979 and had 49 members, CJ (1970–71) 207, etc (this Committee conducted its work through sub-committees), the Select Committee on the Wealth Tax which in Session 1974–75 had 21 members, CJ (1974–75) 136 (this is a common feature of committees on tax matters) and the Liaison Committee which has 20 members, Votes and Proceedings (1987–88) 17 December 1987. A recent example of a small committee is the Select Committee on Sound Broadcasting which has had as few as 5 members, CJ (1979–80) 139, etc.
8 CJ (1982–83) 291.

those cases where a select committee is appointed on motion, it may be nominated immediately upon its appointment only if previous notice has been given both of the motion for the appointment of the committee and of the names of the proposed members. This rule does not, however, apply to committees upon matters of privilege,[1] committees appointed to draw up reasons to be assigned to the other House for disagreeing to amendments made by that House to a bill, or committees appointed in fulfilment of the orders of the House.[2]

As a general rule a motion for the nomination of a select committee is tabled and moved by a member of the Government, even where the committee was moved for by a private Member. A major exception to this is motions in respect of select committees relating to Government departments appointed under Standing Order No 130. Under Standing Order No 104(2) no motion may be made for the nomination of members of these committees or for their discharge, unless notice of the motion has been given at least two sitting days previously, and the motion is made on behalf of the Committee of Selection by the chairman or another member of that committee.[3] Additionally, private Members very occasionally nominate select committees by using the provisions of Standing Order No 19 (motions for leave to bring in bills and nomination of select committees at commencement of public business)[4] (See also pp 309–310, 463–465.)

A Member intending to move for the nomination, addition or substitution of members of a select committee must endeavour to ascertain previously whether each Member proposed to be named by him to serve on such committee will give his attendance thereupon and must endeavour to give notice to any Member whom he proposes to be discharged from a select committee (Standing Order No 104).[5]

In strictness a motion ought to be made, and a question put, in respect of each Member proposed as a member of a committee, that he be a member (or another member) of the committee. In practice, however, the Speaker puts a single question in respect of all the proposed Members, and, if no objection is taken to any of the proposed names, they are considered to have been accepted by the House.[6] If, however, objection is taken to any particular name, or notice has been given of an amendment proposing the substitution of another Member for one of those proposed, the Speaker proposes a question upon the name to which objection is taken for the determination of the House.

When a Member wished to make observations on the general composition of a select committee, the Deputy Speaker read out the first name on the

---

1 Eg Parl Deb (1857) 146, cc 97 ff; ibid (1857–58) 148, cc 1855–1867; HC Deb (1947–48) 448, cc 2781–2782; CJ (1970–71) 59.
2 Eg Members Interests (Declaration), CJ (1974–75) 53; Violence in the Family, ibid (1975–76) 167; Direct Elections to the European Assembly, ibid (1975–76) 323.
3 Since 1983 the Committee of Selection has resolved early in each session that no motion to alter the membership of these select committees may be tabled on behalf of the Committee unless previously approved at a meeting of the Committee of Selection, eg CJ (1983–84) 49.
4 Eg CJ (1974–75) 248–9.
5 CJ (1714–18) 59; Chandler, Deb 19; 7 Parl Hist 58. On three occasions on each of which there were special circumstances, a Member has been nominated to serve on a committee before taking the oath; see p 231n3.
6 Parl Deb (1857) 147, c 1011.

list, and suggested that he should make his observations on the motion relative to that name. This the Member accordingly did. Another Member was subsequently ruled out of order when he sought to object to the nominations on the ground that a decision of the committee of the previous session was wrong.[1]

An amendment proposing the substitution of an alternative name for one of those on the list of proposed members cannot be moved without notice.[2]

Amendments have also been moved to the question that a particular Member be a member of a committee, that the committee be chosen by ballot;[3] that it be nominated wholly[4] or partially[5] by the Committee of Selection, that, (where the committee is not nominated immediately on its appointment) the order for the appointment of the committee be discharged[6] or that the nomination of the committee be put off for six months,[7] or that the order that the committee do consist of a certain number of members be discharged.[8]

The Committee of Selection is often entrusted by the House with the task of proposing for nomination members of other select committees. As previously mentioned, under Standing Order No 104 the fourteen committees appointed to monitor the expenditure, administration and policy of government departments are nominated by the House on the proposal of that committee—though the motion nominating members to such a committee is amendable. Where an inquiry of a quasi-judicial character is referred to a select committee it is usual for the nomination of the members of the committee,[9] or some of them,[10] to be delegated to the committee (see pp 825, 886–887). A similar course is followed in the case of select committees on hybrid bills, provisional order bills, and special procedure orders (see pp 825, 521–522, 954).[11] Committees on private bills are also nominated by the Committee of Selection (see p 960).

In the nomination of Members to serve on select committees neither the House, nor, where the nomination is entrusted to that committee, the Committee of Selection, is bound to consider whether Members are personally interested in the matter or bill referred to the committee, and no objection can be raised in this respect to the composition of the committee. But it is not the practice for a member of a select committee to take part in any enquiry while the affairs of any body in which he has a direct personal

---

1 HC Deb (1944–45) 406, c 1304–1306; see also Parl Deb (1881) 259, c 884 and HC Deb (1967–68) 754, c 394.
2 Parl Deb (1860) 158, c 1176; ibid (1864) 174, cc 500, 1569; ibid (1876) 227, c 1496; ibid (1881) 262, c 222; ibid (1882) 274, c 284; HC Deb (1917–18) 95, c 226.
3 CJ (1805–6) 214; ibid (1833) 512.
4 CJ (1860) 294, 304; cf ibid (1864) 275, 281.
5 CJ (1873) 307.
6 CJ (1844) 300; ibid (1870) 223.
7 CJ (1854) 166, 251; ibid (1867) 261.
8 CJ (1868–69) 278.
9 CJ (1857) 43; ibid (1860) 304; ibid (1883) 143; ibid (1887) 108.
10 CJ (1868–69) 85; ibid (1878–79) 263; ibid (1880) 47. Committees on public bills, CJ (1890–91) 96; ibid (1892) 134; ibid (1907) 204.
11 The committees on the New Forest Bill 1949, and the New Forest Bill [Lords] 1964, both hybrid bills, were appointed partly by the House and partly by the Committee of Selection, CJ (1948–49) 365; ibid (1963–64) 229. The committee on the Channel Tunnel Bill, also a hybrid bill, was wholly appointed by the Committee of Selection, HC Deb (1985–86) 98, cc 1195–1276; CJ (1985–86) 398.

interest are under investigation.[1] The practice relating to declaration of interest in a select committee and the circumstances in which such a declaration should be made are set out on p 620.

> In 1979 when the House was debating the first motions from the Committee of Selection for the select committees relating to government departments, the chairman of the Committee of Selection stated that in proposing members of such committees the Committee enjoyed full discretion and was under no obligation to consult, to take advice or to indicate any criteria of choice. To assist the House he indicated that the committee would not for the time being propose members of the Government, Parliamentary Private Secretaries and regular Opposition Frontbench spokesmen.[2] This has remained the practice,[3] so far as circumstances permit.[4]

Lists of Members serving on select committees. By Standing Order No 105, lists are to be affixed in some conspicuous place in the Committee Office and in the lobby of the House of all Members serving on each select committee.

Addition of Members to, and discharge of Members from, select committees. Once nominated a select committee may subsequently be enlarged by the addition of other members appointed in the same manner. Members cannot be added so as to increase the size of the committee beyond such number as the House may have agreed upon, unless a motion that the committee shall consist of the larger number be first agreed to by the House.[5] Such a motion requires notice.

Members have been added to a select committee for the purpose of their consideration of a particular matter within the committee's order of reference.[6] Members have also been nominated by the House to sub-committees without being nominated to the main committee (see p 640).

Although, as has been noted above, any Member nominating another to membership of a committee is required (under Standing Order No 104(i)) to endeavour to ascertain previously whether that Member will attend, a Member cannot relieve himself from his obligation to obey the commands of the House by declining to serve on a committee.[7] Members originally nominated to serve on committees are, however, particularly in the case of committees of long duration, often discharged from that committee, and members added to committees in the place of members who have been so discharged, or have died or have otherwise ceased to be Members of the House. Members are also frequently discharged from a committee when

---

1 See eg HC Deb (1943–44) 395, c 1402. A Member has disclosed an interest which was so direct that he decided to take no further part in the Committee's inquiry; Industry and Trade Committee Proceedings (1981–82) 535, p ix.
2 HC Deb (1979–80) 974, c 3 w and 1029–1036.
3 HC Deb (1983–84) 50, cc 1129–1132; HC Deb (1987–88) 123 c 1042–1043.
4 The Scottish Affairs Committee, prior to the dissolution of Parliament in 1987, included three Parliamentary Private Secretaries within its membership.
5 CJ (1857) 157; Parl Deb (1857) 145, c 539.
6 CJ (1967–68) 123.
7 As the Speaker has recently reminded the House, it could order a Member to attend: HC Deb (1988–89) 144, c 297.

they become ministers or accept an official position which is incompatible for one reason or another with continued membership of the committee concerned. However, once nominated, a Member cannot resign from a committee unless and until a motion discharging him from membership is agreed to by the House.

In the case of committees set up under a standing order which itself requires that membership should continue for the remainder of a Parliament (eg Standing Order No 121), a single motion is often used to discharge one member and add another.[1] A similar motion may also be used in the case of a change in the membership of a sessional select committee.

In the case of select committees set up under a standing order, but nominated for the duration of a Parliament by means of a different standing order, changes in membership are effected by amending the latter order.[2]

Reference of papers to select committees. Reports of previous committees, or the minutes of the evidence taken before them, and other papers which have been laid upon the Table of the House are sometimes referred to committees.[3] Such a reference may serve to direct the particular attention of the committee to documents relating to the subject of its inquiry, or, in particular cases, to explain or enlarge the original terms of reference. Reports or minutes of evidence of previous committees which have lapsed are frequently referred to later committees which are to continue inquiries left uncompleted (see p 648). Any Member of the House can move to refer to a select committee any document within the scope of its inquiry.[4]

By an instruction given to the Commons committee ordered to join with a Lords committee on a matter, all papers submitted to it were first to be examined by the chairman. He would determine, if necessary after consultation with the other Members, which papers should be seen by the committee, which should be shown to witnesses etc, and which should be reported or referred to in a report.[5] The Lords did not however concur in the establishment of the joint committee, which accordingly never met.

If a committee wishes to use documents in the custody of the officers of the other House, the House will, at the request of the committee, send a message to the other House requesting it to communicate a copy of the document. The document, when communicated, will be referred to the committee.

Notwithstanding the practice described above, there is no rule which prevents a committee from using previously published reports or evidence or other papers without such material being specifically referred to them,

---

1 Eg CJ (1974–75) 105; ibid (1985–86) 361
2 Eg CJ (1979–80) 101, 285.
3 Report of a previous committee, eg CJ (1936–37) 100; ibid (1945–46) 160; evidence given before a previous committee, eg CJ (1974–75) 73; memoranda received by a previous committee, CJ (1969–70) 14, 16, 41, 43; evidence given before and memoranda received by a previous committee, eg CJ (1981–82) 44; minutes of evidence taken before a committee appointed by a government department, CJ (1931–32) 276; reports of, and evidence given before, a commissioner, CJ (1898) 188. Petitions have occasionally been referred to committees eg, CJ (1875) 75; ibid (1881) 293; ibid (1888) 196; see too Parl Deb (1867) 189, c 1047.
4 Parl Deb (1900) 82, c 1066–1068.
5 CJ (1978–79) 140 (Special Commission on Oil Sanctions Joint Committee).

particularly when the use of such material is supplementary or incidental to the inquiry in progress and, indeed, it is common practice to do so.

Discharge of orders for the appointment of select committees. Orders for the appointment of select committees have occasionally been discharged.[1] When the order for the appointment of a committee has been so discharged, a committee for a similar purpose but with a different order of reference may be appointed.[2]

Scope of deliberations or inquiries

Orders of reference. A select committee, like a Committee of the whole House, possesses no authority except that which it derives by delegation from the House by which it is appointed. When a select committee is appointed to consider or inquire into a matter, the scope of its deliberations or inquiries is defined by the order by which the committee is appointed (termed the order of reference), and the deliberation or inquiries of the committee must be confined within the limits so imposed. But when a bill is committed, or referred, to a select committee, the bill itself is the order of reference, and the inquiries and deliberations of the committee must be confined to the bill and amendments relevant to its subject-matter.

The interpretation of the order of reference of a select committee is, however, a matter for the committee. Thus on 21 July 1981 the Welsh Affairs Committee resolved 'That in the opinion of the Committee, the Boundary Commission for Wales may be regarded for the purposes of this Order of Reference as an associated public body of the Welsh Office'[3]

Instructions. If it is thought desirable that a committee should extend its inquiries beyond the limits laid down in the order of reference, the House may give the committee authority for that purpose by means of an instruction.[4] Such an instruction may be either mandatory,[5] or merely permissive.[6]

---

1 CJ (1837–38) 265; ibid (1844) 300; ibid (1854) 251; ibid (1892) 223. For instances of the discharge of the order for the committal of a bill to a select committee, see CJ (1861) 400; ibid (1895) 213.

2 CJ (1852–53) 487; ibid (1870) 169.

3 On 2 April 1906 the Select Committee on Post Office Servants divided on the question 'That (a certain subject) is within the terms of reference of the committee', Evidence, HC 226 (1906), Qs. 677–678. The Speaker having been consulted as to the regularity of this proceeding gave it as his view that the chairman had been right in leaving the matter for the decision of the committee. For other instances of committees coming to resolutions as to the scope of their orders of reference, see Proceedings of Committees on Ministers' Money (Ireland), HC 559 (1847–48) pp x–xi; Income and Property Tax, HC 570 (1852) pp xi–xii; Indian Territories, HC 768 (1852–53) pp iv–v; Land Transport Corps, HC 401 (1857–58) p viii; Contagious Diseases Acts, HC 351 (1881) p x; Privilege (Mr Gray), HC 406 (1882) pp xix–xx; and Aged Deserving Poor, HC 296 (1899) p xv, HC 494 (1980–81) p xxii. The Speaker has upheld this practice in a particular case, HC Deb (1982–83) 40, c 183.

4 The same result has been achieved by an amendment made to the order of reference on a subsequent day, CJ (1945–46) 72, 263; ibid (1947–48) 95. A select committee on a bill may be instructed to inquire into a matter also, CJ (1922) 258.

5 Eg CJ (1836) 215; ibid (1882) 36; ibid (1936–37) 103; ibid (1961–62) 106.

6 Eg CJ (1880) 48; ibid (1884) 388; ibid (1902) 119.

The order of reference may also be enlarged, in the case of a committee on a matter, by the committal of a bill to the committee[1] and, in the case of a committee on a bill, by the committal of an additional bill to the committee,[2] or by the reference of a paper to the committee.[3]

If, on the other hand, it is deemed advisable to restrict the scope of the inquiry, or to limit the committee's powers, an instruction may be given to the committee requiring it to refrain from considering the matter,[4] or doing the act[5] which forms the subject of the instruction; and, if so desired, instructions may also be given to committees prescribing or affecting their course of proceedings.[6] An example of this is the instruction given respectively to the Lords and Commons members of the Joint Committee on Statutory Instruments, that before reporting that the special attention of the House be drawn to any instrument they must afford to any government department concerned an opportunity of furnishing oral or written evidence.[7]

Instructions may be given to committees at the time of their appointment, or at any time thereafter before they have presented their final report.

Where an instruction is proposed to be given to a committee on its appointment, it may be moved immediately after the committee has been appointed; but it is more convenient to move it after the members have been

---

1 CJ (1908) 239; ibid (1909) 44, 179. For the committal of private bills and provisional order bills to a select committee on a matter, see CJ (1867) 65; ibid (1873) 176.

2 CJ (1867) 65; ibid (1906) 83.

3 Parl Reg xxii 258; Parl Deb (1876) 230, cc 1679–1680.

4 CJ (1819–20) 259; ibid (1835) 522; ibid (1864) 147. The same result may be achieved by an order discharging so much of the order appointing the committee as refers to a particular subject, CJ (1833) 286, or discharging the committee from the further consideration of a portion of the matters referred to it, CJ (1835) 504.

5 CJ (1844) 284. By an instruction the House has ordered a proposed joint committee that all papers submitted to it should be dealt with in a certain manner, CJ (1978–79) 140.

6 Eg to make a special report upon certain matters, CJ (1882) 98; to omit particular clauses from a bill, CJ (1890) 194; to report, in the first place, the result of their inquiries into certain matters referred to their consideration, CJ (1945–46) 33; ibid (1964–65) 94; ibid (1966–67) 61; to inquire, in the first place, into a particular portion of the matter referred to their consideration, and to report specially thereon, CJ (1847) 24; to consider certain amendments standing on the Notice Paper CJ (1955–56) 196; to sit and proceed forthwith and to sit from day to day, CJ (1868–69) 87; to take evidence on oath, CJ (1887) 97; to consider the subject-matter of the bill to them committed and to report thereon, CJ (1888) 211; to report only the evidence already taken (the committee not having completed its inquiry, and a dissolution of Parliament being imminent), CJ (1837) 621; to inquire into and report upon a certain matter before going through the bill committed to the committee, CJ (1904) 147; to report as soon as possible upon a certain matter and, during the consideration of such matter, to report, day by day, the minutes of evidence relating thereto and, if the House was not sitting, to send such minutes to the Clerk of the House, CJ (1945–46) 33; to report by certain dates, CJ (1968–69) 31; to hear petitioners praying to be heard by themselves, their counsel, or agents, CJ (1867–68) 263; to report the minutes of the proceedings on a particular day, CJ (1940–41) 200. The same result may be achieved by an order differing from a mandatory instruction only in the omission therefrom of the words 'that it be an instruction to the committee', eg to report from time to time the evidence taken, ibid (1798–99) 482; to sit *de die in diem* notwithstanding any adjournment of the House, ibid (1867–68) 183; to report any evidence taken by the committee or any sub-committee thereof, CJ (1936–37) 20; to report by a certain date, CJ (1968–69) 17, 29, 31; cf committee to report by a certain date in its order of reference, CJ (1975–76) 86; to report their recommendations on certain matters within the shortest reasonable period, CJ (1974) 144.

7 SO No 124(9).

nominated, the quorum has been fixed, and the committee given power to send for persons, papers and records.

Notice of an instruction can be placed upon the notice paper to be moved after the appointment of a select committee, after the nomination of the members, or as an independent motion.

For rules relating to instructions to committees on bills, see pp 449–450, 482–485.

Proceedings in select committees

Select committees are regarded as extensions of the House, limited in their inquiries by the extent of the authority given them, but governed for the most part in their proceedings by the same rules as those which prevail in the House.[1]

Where the rules of proceedings in a Committee of the whole House differ from those in the House, the former are generally followed in a select committee. Thus the previous question cannot be moved upon any question in a select committee.[2] In certain respects, however, the practice in select committees differs both from the practice of the House and from that in Committees of the whole House. Members invariably speak when sitting, and the rule against smoking, which is strictly observed when witnesses are under examination, is not enforced when the committee is deliberating.

In any proceeding of a select committee a Member must disclose any relevant pecuniary interest or benefit of whatever nature, whether direct or indirect, that he may have had, may have or may be expecting to have. Any such declaration is entered in the minutes of proceedings of the committee (see pp 385). It is additional to the requirement to declare interests in the Register of Members' Interests (see pp 386–387).

Time of first meeting. The day and hour of the first meeting of a select committee are fixed by the senior member of the committee, that is, the person who has been a Member of the House for the longest period, irrespective of continuity of service.[3] The meeting cannot be held on a day on which the House is not sitting unless, as is now a common practice, the committee has been empowered to sit notwithstanding any adjournment of the House. Nor may a select committee hold its first meeting on the day on which it is appointed, unless the House has given it leave to sit and proceed forthwith.[4]

Chairman of a select committee. The chairman of a select committee is chosen by the committee itself except in rare cases when the House other-

---

1 Parl Deb (1836) 32, c505.
2 2 Hatsell 116; Parl Deb (1882) 274, cc1485, 1700–1701.
3 Mr Speaker's private ruling, 13 December 1934. If the committee has the same terms of reference as one which lapsed in the previous session (a general election not having intervened in the meanwhile), the day and hour of meeting are fixed by the member who was chairman of the committee in the preceding session unless he is no longer a member of the committee.
4 The last occasion on which such power was given was in the case of the Select Committee on Mr Gladstone's Funeral, CJ (1898) 224. It is the general practice for committees appointed to draw up reasons for disagreeing to Lords amendments to be given the power to sit forthwith, eg CJ (1985–86) 530.

wise orders.[1] The first proceeding of a committee is therefore to choose a chairman. The chairman is ordinarily called to the chair by the general voice of the members present, but if there is a difference of opinion as to who shall be called to the chair, the practice is that the clerk of the committee puts the question that the member first proposed 'do take the chair of the committee'. If the majority is in favour that member thereupon takes the chair; but if not, a similar question is put in relation to the second member proposed. This process has to be repeated until a member has secured a majority. When a vote on this question has resulted in a tie, a committee has called a member to the chair for a single sitting only (it confirmed his appointment on a more permanent basis at a subsequent meeting).[2]

In July 1987, at the first meeting of the Select Committee on European Legislation, the clerk invited the normal proposition that a Member do take the chair. No Member present was willing to make such a motion. A motion was instead agreed to that a Member take the chair for the sitting. This procedure was repeated at the second and third meetings of the committee. At the fourth meeting of the committee a motion was made that a Member do take the chair and an amendment to restrict the appointment to that sitting was lost on a division. The main question was then agreed without a division.[3]

A member has been chosen chairman in his absence,[4] in which case it is necessary to call another member to the chair for that meeting.

If at any sitting the chairman is absent, or has to leave before the sitting is concluded, the members present choose one of their number to be chairman for that sitting, or the remainder thereof, as the case may be; but the member who has been thus called to the chair vacates it on the chairman's arrival or return and the chairman takes or resumes the chair.[5] A similar course is followed if the chairman leaves the chair to give evidence.

In the case of a contested temporary chairmanship the same procedure is adopted as for the election of the chairman.[6]

A select committee has resolved that in the absence of the chairman a particular member shall take the chair,[7] or has ordered a particular member to take the chair whenever the committee is informed by the clerk of the unavoidable absence of the chairman.[8] Upon a strict construction, however, such a resolution debars the committee from proceeding in the event of both the chairman and the other member being absent.[9] Occasionally a member

---

1 See also CJ (1847–48) 555; ibid (1852–53) 518.
2 First Report from the Home Affairs Committee, HC 434 (1979–80) p ix.
3 Select Committee on European Legislation, Proceedings, HC 43–i (1987–88) p xxx; HC 43–ii, p xlviii; HC 43–iii, p xl; HC–iv, p xxviii.
4 Clergy Disqualification, HC 200 (1952–53) p vii; Select Committee on Statutory Instruments, First Report, HC 10–i (1969–70) p 5.
5 Select Committee on Welsh Affairs, HC 546 (1981–82) p iii.
6 Education Science and Arts Committee Proceedings, HC 646 (1984–85) p x.
7 National Expenditure Committee Proceedings, HC 133 (1942–43) p 9; ibid, HC 125 (1943–44) p 5; ibid, HC 104 (1944–45) p 5; Estimates Committee Proceedings, HC 149 (1946–47) p ccxxviii; ibid, HC 205 (1947–48) p iv; Defence Committee Proceedings, HC 842 (1979–80) p 3.
8 Estimates Committee Proceedings, HC 293 (1953–54) p 5; ibid, HC 130 (1954–55) p xii; ibid, HC 427 (1955–56) p 5; ibid, HC 308 (1956–57) p 4.
9 But see Select Committee on National Expenditure Proceedings, HC 133 (1942–43) p 11.

of the committee has regularly taken the chair in the place of the usual chairman when evidence is being taken on a particular matter.[1]

Another member is sometimes appointed chairman in place of the one first chosen, at the request of the latter, or otherwise.[2]

In 1863 in the Select Committee on the Inland Revenue and Customs Establishments Mr Horsfall, the chairman, proposed a draft report which was rejected by a majority of one. Mr Cardwell then proposed a draft report embodying the opinions of the majority. At the next meeting of the committee Mr Horsfall declined to take the chair, stating that he had resigned the chair, and proposed that Mr Cardwell should take the chair. On this the clerk attending the committee objected that there was no one authorized to put the question. The committee decided to refer the matter to the Speaker for an opinion. The Speaker gave it as his opinion that the chairman, having been elected into the chair, and having accepted the post with a full knowledge of its duties and liabilities, ought to go through with the duties. Reasons of a personal nature, failing health, or a feeling that he was unequal to the task, might afford sufficient reasons for wishing to be released. But after having exercised all the power and influence which belonged to the chair, then to vacate it in order to have the privilege of giving a vote, and altering the balance of opinions, seemed to him (the Speaker) contrary to the spirit of parliamentary proceedings. Mr Horsfall went back to the committee room and took the chair.[3]

The chairman of a select committee has, and exercises, within the more limited authority conferred on the committee, substantially the same formal duties and powers as the chairman of a Committee of the whole House. Standing Orders Nos 31, 34, 35, 41 and 42, however, do not apply to proceedings in a select committee and the chairman has consequently not the power of accepting a motion for the closure of a debate, the power to deal with dilatory motions (though a dilatory motion may be moved[4]) and with irrelevance and repetition in debate, or if the select committee is considering a bill the power of selecting which new clauses or amendments shall be proposed, powers which are exercised by the Chairman of Ways and Means and the Deputy Chairmen in Committees of the whole House, and by the chairmen of standing committees (see p 404). There is nevertheless an inherent right in the chairman of a select committee, if he sees that the transaction of business is becoming impossible, to attempt to secure the progress of business.[5]

Unlike the chairman of a Committee of the whole House or the chairman of a standing committee, the chairman of a select committee takes a full part

---

1 Eg Defence Committee, Proceedings in respect of the inquiry on 'The Physical Security of Military Installations in the United Kingdom', HC 387 (1983–84).

2 Proceedings of Committees on Open Spaces (Metropolis), HC 178 (1865) p iv; Married Women's Property Bill, HC 210 (1868–69) p iv; Apothecaries Licences Bill, HC 310 (1874) p v; Butter Substitutes Bill, HC 208 (1887) p vi; Town Holdings, HC 260 (1887) pp iv, v; Procedure, HC 153 (1966–67) p xiii; First Report from the Home Affairs Committee, HC 434 (1979–80) p xv; Committee on Scottish Affairs, Proceedings, HC 539 (1981–82) p 6; Transport Committee, Proceedings, HC 618 (1984–85) 12.

3 Denison 145.

4 Eg Energy Committee, First Report, HC 165 (1986–87) p lxxxi.

5 Parl Deb (1893) 10, c 913.

in the proceedings of the committee, and, in practice, normally exercises a substantial measure of authority in the conduct of the committee's affairs.

Divisions in select committees. Questions are determined in select committees in the same manner as in the House, except that when a division is taken, the names of the members are called over in alphabetical order by the clerk, and each member, as his name is called, answers aye or no, or states that he declines to vote.[1]

As in the House, the occupant of the chair can only vote when there is an equality of voices.[2] When a division is being taken, the doors of the committee room are deemed to be locked, and a member's vote has been disallowed, as he was not in the room when the question was put.[3] A member who has voted by mistake may be allowed to correct the error.[4]

By Standing Order No 110, in the event of a division taking place, the question proposed, the name of the proposer of the motion or amendment, the question put, and the respective votes thereon of each member must be entered on the minutes of the proceedings of the committee.

In a select committee, unlike a standing committee, the chairman is not obliged to suspend the sitting to enable members to vote in a division in the House, though it is the frequent practice to do so.

Rescission of resolutions of select committees. It is a rule of the House of Commons that 'every question by voice in committee bindeth, and cannot be altered by themselves'.[5] In practice, this rule is sometimes disregarded, and resolutions or other decisions of committees are rescinded.[6] Previous notice must, however, be given to all the members of any motion for rescinding a resolution.

Quorum. The quorum of a select committee is fixed by the House having regard to its purpose and any other relevant consideration. The size of the quorum is most usually set out in terms of reference of a committee when first appointed, or in the standing order relating to its appointment. If no quorum has been fixed, the committee cannot transact business unless all the members are present.

The quorum is usually fixed at three when the committee consists of eleven members or less, though committees of eleven or twelve members have had a quorum of four or even five.[7] On the other hand, a quorum of three has been fixed for a committee of as many as fifteen members.[8] Most committees of thirteen to eighteen members have had a quorum of four or

---

1 Formerly, a member who had heard the question put could not abstain from giving his vote, but this rule is now no longer enforced. Such 'absentions' are not recorded.
2 Parl Deb (1836) 32, cc 501–504; CJ (1836) 214 etc. This rule does not apply to a joint committee where the practice of the Lords prevails (see p 667), nor to a private bill committee (see p 895).
3 Railways (Rates and Fares) Committee, Proceedings, HC 317 (1882) p lxiii.
4 Ibid p 1.
5 CJ (1547–1628) 379 (1607).
6 Proceedings of Committees on Imprisonment for Debt, HC 348 (1873) p xx; Railways, HC 374 (1881) p xvi; Tuberculosis (Animals) Compensation Bill, HC 272 (1904) p ix; House of Commons Members' Fund, HC 110 (1946–47) p xv; Scottish Affairs, HC 539 (1981–82) pp 3–4; Transport, HC 733 (1987–88) p 11.
7 Eg CJ (1963–64) 13, 128; ibid (1966–67) 489; ibid (1967–68) 33; ibid (1974) 91.
8 CJ (1963–64) 17, etc; ibid (1968–69) 28; ibid (1975–76) 137.

five, though here again there are significant exceptions. The Committee of Privileges, with its membership of seventeen, has a quorum of six.[1] Among larger committees the relationships are similarly diverse. A committee of twenty-five members has had a quorum of only six[2] and a committee of thirty-three a quorum of only seven.[3] Conversely, a committee of nineteen has had a quorum of nine,[4] two committees of sixteen a quorum of eight[5] and a committee of fourteen a quorum of six.[6] An example of diversity is the Select Committee on Sound Broadcasting which consists of six members and has a quorum of two (Standing Order No 129). Standing Order No 123 relating to the Joint Committee on Consolidation etc Bills provides for a membership of twelve (although for some years only eleven Commons members have been appointed) and a quorum of two.

In the past, when an inquiry undertaken by a select committee was of a quasi-judicial character, the quorum was proportionately large; or else, if the committee membership was small, no quorum was fixed. In addition to fixing a quorum in the case of such inquiries, the House has also ordered the committee to report the absence of any member on two consecutive days.[7]

A select committee or a sub-committee cannot proceed to business unless a quorum is present, and if, after a committee has proceeded to business, the number of members present should be reduced below the quorum, the clerk of the committee is required to call the attention of the chairman to the fact, and the chairman must thereupon either suspend the proceedings till a quorum is present, or adjourn the committee to a future day[8] (Standing Order No 107).

Pursuant to Standing Order No 107, in determining whether a quorum of a select committee is present, the chairman is to be counted.

Occasionally the quorum of a committee or a sub-committee is reduced, usually towards the end of a session.[9] Where the quorum is prescribed by a standing order, the change is made by motion to amend the order.[10] These motions require notice.

Matters sub judice. The statement of the House's practice with regard to matters that are awaiting judgement (see pp 377–378) makes no mention of proceedings in select committees. Nevertheless the principle that such matters should not be prejudiced by public comment holds good in select committees.[11] The bar does not however operate when evidence is being taken in private and, since there is no restriction on the right of the House to

---

1 SO No 121.
2 CJ (1967–68) 69; ibid (1968–69) 31.
3 CJ (1968–69) 26.
4 CJ (1923) 128.
5 CJ (1968–69) 135, 222.
6 CJ (1970–71) 427; ibid (1971–72), 49.
7 CJ (1847–48) 555; ibid (1854) 75; ibid (1854–55) 87; ibid (1857–58) 68. For such committees where no quorum was fixed, see CJ (1852–53) 158, 428, 583; ibid (1854) 182; ibid (1857) 192; ibid (1864) 281; ibid (1865) 313; ibid (1887) 108. For orders regarding the absence of Members, see CJ (1835) 457, 504; ibid (1861–62) 305.
8 HC 571 (1849) p vii; HC 775 (1852–53) p v, etc. For procedure when the chairman also is absent, see HC 426 (1955–56) p 6 and CJ (1955–56) 348.
9 CJ 1894) 223; ibid (1899) 364; ibid (1919) 303; ibid (1945–46) 58; ibid (1972–73) 437.
10 CJ (1929–30) 400; ibid (1974–75) 112; ibid (1979–80) 94.
11 Science and Technology Committee, Genetic Engineering Sub-Committee, HC 355 (1978–79) p 19; Energy Committee, HC 307 (1987–88) p 110.

legislate, the proceedings of a select committee on a bill need not be affected by it.

Minutes of proceedings. By Standing Order No 111 the minutes of proceedings of a select committee must be laid upon the Table of the House during the session to which they relate, unless the committee proposes to bring them up with a report in a following session of the same Parliament. They are usually ordered to be printed (there is no such reference in the standing order to the minutes of proceedings of sub-committees). When a committee has made no report, the minutes of its proceedings have been ordered to be laid before the House.[1]

By Standing Order No 110 the names of the members present at each sitting of a select committee are entered on the minutes of the proceedings. For the recording of divisions in the minutes of proceedings, see p 623; for the entry of draft reports in the minutes of the proceedings, see p 642.

Sittings and adjournment of select committees. Formerly, without leave of the House, no committee could sit whilst the House was sitting,[2] but now, by Standing Order No 106, all committees have leave to sit during the sitting of the House and, notwithstanding any adjournment of the House, on any day on which the House has sat.

Standing Order No 106 applies to select committees so that a select committee not empowered in its order of reference to sit notwithstanding any adjournment of the House may do so only with the leave of the House. A motion for such leave may not be moved without notice. However, it is now usual for select committees to be given leave on appointment to sit notwithstanding the adjournment of the House; and this power is customarily given to those committees appointed by standing order. When this power has been given to a committee it has been extended in most cases to its sub-committees. Leave has also been granted to select committees without this power to sit on a particular day on which the House is not sitting,[3] and leave to sit notwithstanding any adjournment of the House for the remainder of the session, or for some specified period, has sometimes been given to particular committees,[4] or to all committees.[5]

A select committee is regularly adjourned from one sitting to another, but the reassembling of the committee is sometimes left to be arranged afterwards by the chairman, by whose direction members are summoned for a future day.

In 1871 complaint was made that, a day having been fixed for the next meeting of the committee by the chairman, he had subsequently, after consulting certain members of the committee, appointed an earlier day. The chairman stated that he had acted for the general convenience of the committee and in accordance with the desire of such members as he had

---

1 CJ (1936–37) 252; ibid (1955–56) 429; ibid (1985–86) 81.
2 CJ (1693–97) 126, 494.
3 CJ (1896) 425; ibid (1898) 414.
4 CJ (1914–16) 22, 132, 189; ibid (1917–18) 197; ibid (1918) 208; ibid (1919) 177, 303; ibid (1920) 350; ibid (1921) 229; ibid (1922) 35, 315; ibid (1923) 26, etc.
5 For the remainder of the session, CJ (1892) 390; ibid (1895) 304; during a specified period, ibid (1908) 142; ibid (1910) 153; ibid (1914–16) 87.

been able to consult; and the Speaker expressed the opinion that in these circumstances the proceeding was not irregular.[1]

When it has been necessary further to adjourn a committee beyond the date fixed for its next meeting, the House, on the application of the chairman, has made the necessary order.[2] For the most part, however, such arrangements are made informally on the instruction of the chairman, with the general concurrence of members of the committee and for their convenience.

In respect of those committees which have no power to sit notwithstanding the adjournment of the House, if such an adjournment takes place suddenly, over a day on which the House ordinarily sits or over several such days, and without any order being made in reference to the sittings of committees in the meantime, all such committees which stand adjourned to any time during the interval will be without day and cannot sit until revived by order of the House.[3] When the House has resolved that it will, at its rising, adjourn over the following day, an order has in the past been made, 'That all committees have leave to sit [tomorrow] notwithstanding the adjournment of the House'.[4]

Sittings outside the precincts of the House. A select committee usually sits in one of the committee rooms of the House, arrangements being made by the officers of the House for accommodating particular committees in different rooms. In recent years, there has been an increasing tendency for committees to sit and hear evidence outside the precincts of the House[5] and the majority of select committees now are given leave on appointment 'to adjourn from place to place'. If such provision is not made in its order of reference, a committee must obtain the leave of the House to meet outside the precincts.[6]

It is also the regular practice for select committees having the power to adjourn from place to place, especially those concerned with investigations into aspects of government policy or more general issues, to make informal visits outside the precincts of the House for a variety of purposes relevant to their inquiries.

A committee has also been given power to travel to and hold sittings in a particular place[7] or within the United Kingdom only.[8]

Sittings outside the United Kingdom. Doubts expressed in the 1950s about the constitutional propriety of select committees travelling and meeting

---

1 Parl Deb (1871) 205, cc 685–689.
2 CJ (1934–35) 48; ibid (1955–56) 300; ibid (1956–57) 67; ibid (1957–58) 67; ibid (1969–70) 194, 262.
3 CJ (1817) 201.
4 CJ (1818) 218; ibid (1818–19) 500, etc.
5 In this connection, see Committee of Privileges, Second Report, HC 308 (1968–69).
6 CJ (1864) 255; ibid (1881) 336; ibid (1914–16) 22; ibid (1983–84) 451 (when a sub-committee, having power to adjourn from place to place within the United Kingdom was given, for the remainder of the session, power to visit Canada and the USA); see too HC Deb (1983–84) cc 1143–1152.
7 CJ (1928) 203; see also ibid (1834) 69; ibid (1835) 39.
8 Eg CJ (1975–76) 122; ibid (1979–80) 58.

abroad[1] were resolved in 1966, when the House agreed that the cost of such travel, if undertaken with the leave of the House, should be borne on the House of Commons Vote.[2] Two years later in 1968, following a recommendation of the Services Committee, motions for leave of absence for select committees travelling overseas were discontinued. In substitution a practice was established under which an informal liaison committee, composed of certain select committee chairmen, gave or withheld approval of the expenditure involved in any proposed visits by committees overseas.[3]

In July 1980 the House agreed to the appointment of a formal Liaison Committee (see p 658), which at the behest of the House of Commons Commission has continued to examine applications for overseas travel by select committees. Guidelines for the submission of applications were originally issued by the Commission and applied by the Liaison Committee, but now the Commission is largely content to leave the decisions to the Liaison Committee with a limit fixed each year by the Commission on the total expenditure which may be incurred by select committees on overseas travel.

Oral evidence (or memoranda containing transcripts of discussions) is sometimes taken from British nationals whilst a committee is engaged on a visit overseas,[4] and oral evidence has also been given voluntarily by foreign nationals overseas.[5] Sometimes agreed minutes of discussions held abroad between committees or sub-committees and foreign nationals have been published by select committees.[6] (For the position of foreign nationals coming as witnesses to give evidence before select committees sitting in the United Kingdom, see pp 630–631.)

For the most part, however, select committees travelling overseas now do so for the purpose of gathering information through informal visits and private discussions with representatives of official and other organisations in the countries visited. In such cases, no formal evidence is heard, nor are the meetings recorded in the official minutes of the proceedings of the committee concerned though it is common practice for the staff of the committee to prepare a memorandum recording impressions received during a visit, and this may be published as an appendix to the minutes of evidence[7].

Sending for persons, papers and records

In the ensuing paragraphs are described the general powers of select committees in the Commons regarding the attendance of witnesses and the

---

1 Estimates Committee, Seventh Report, HC 242 (1950–51) pp xxix, 167–175, 283–284; Estimates Committee, Third Special Report, HC 149 (1953–54) pp iv, 1–11; Estimates Committee, Seventh Report, HC 290 (1953–54) pp iv–vii. These doubts culminated in a statement by the government of the day that it would be improper for a committee of the House to act as such in a foreign country, see HC Deb (1953–54) 527, c 1437; ibid (1953–54) 528, c 1090.
2 House of Commons (Services), First Report, HC 70 (1965–66); CJ (1965–66) 81.
3 House of Commons (Services), Fifth Report, HC 232 (1967–68); CJ (1967–68) 244. See also Cmnd 4507. For leave given for a specific visit to a committee otherwise without power to travel, see Votes and Proceedings, 28th June 1989.
4 See Estimates Committee, Seventh Report, HC 442 (1967–68) p v and Fourteenth Report, HC 666 (1966–67) p vii; Foreign Affairs Committee, Minutes of Evidence, HC 31–viii, xii (1982–83).
5 HC 463–ii (1972–73) pp 217–247, 264–271 (European Secondary Legislation); HC 405 (1984–85) pp 27–51 (Treasury and Civil Service Committee).
6 Report from the Nationalised Industries Committee, HC 340 (1966–67) pp 10, 219–229; Report from the Science and Technology Committee, HC 381–xvii (1966–67) pp viii–ix, liii–lxv; Report from the Education and Science Committee, HC 449–i (1968–69) p 8; Estimates Committee, Fourth Report, HC 473–iii (1968–69) pp 968–981.
7 Environment Committee, Second Report, HC 22 (1988–89) Appendix I.

production of papers. The methods of obtaining or compelling the attendance of witnesses are dealt with more fully in chapter 25, where a description of the proceedings of select committees in regard to the examination of witnesses, and other matters relating to witnesses, including the privilege and protection accorded to witnesses, the punishment of contumacious witnesses, and the provision made for witnesses' expenses, are also found.[1]

A select committee cannot require the attendance of witnesses or the production of documents without express authority from the House. Thus it is usual, in the appropriate standing order, or in the order relating to its appointment, or subsequently on the motion of the chairman,[2] to give a select committee the power to send for persons, papers, and records.[3]

By virtue of this authority (but subject to certain qualifications: see below) witnesses may be summoned, by an order signed by the chairman, to attend the committee and to bring with them all such documents as they are informed will be required for the use of the committee. If a witness fails to appear, when summoned in this manner, his conduct is reported to the House, which has usually ordered the offender to attend at the bar.[4] If in the meantime the witness appears before the committee, the order for his attendance is usually discharged;[5] but if he still neglects to appear, he will be dealt with as in other cases of disobedience to the order of the House (see chapter 8). A committee which has not been given power to send for persons may not, without leave of the House, request persons to attend as witnesses or examine persons who tender themselves as witnesses.[6]

Sometimes select committees are given narrower powers. In 1947 the Committee on the Civil List was given power to examine all witnesses who voluntarily appeared before it.[7] Similar powers were conferred on the committees on the same subject in 1952 and 1971.[8] The Joint Committee on Statutory Instruments is given power to require any government department concerned to submit a memorandum explaining any instrument or other documents which may be under its consideration or to depute a representative to appear before it for the purpose of explaining any such instrument or other document.[9]

---

1 A comprehensive description of the powers of select committees to send for persons, papers and records, is contained in the memorandum by the Clerk of the House in the First Report of the Select Committee on Procedure in 1977–78, HC 588–I, pp 15–37.
2 CJ (1894) 236; ibid (1946–47) 45.
3 The Committee on Fisheries (Ireland) was given power to send for papers and records only, CJ (1849) 75. The Committee on the Boundaries of Boroughs was given leave only to receive and call for maps, memorials, reports, papers and records concerning the boroughs in question, CJ (1867–68) 183.
4 A witness who has been reported to the House by a committee for his failure to attend has been merely ordered to attend the committee, CJ (1920) 263. But as obedience is as much due to the summons of a committee which has been invested with power to send for persons, papers and records as to the order of the House, a person who fails to obey such a summons is guilty of contempt, and the more regular course would, therefore, seem to be to order him to attend at the bar.
5 CJ (1836) 352.
6 Civil List Committee, Report, HC 22 (1837–38) p 4; Committee of Selection, Special Report, CJ (1841) 118. Where parties are given a right to be heard before a committee, the committee may examine any witnesses called by such parties notwithstanding that power to send for persons has not been conferred upon the committee.
7 CJ (1947–48) 53.
8 CJ (1951–52) 239–240; ibid (1970–71) 448.
9 CJ (1948–49) 9; ibid (1968–69) 17, etc.

The general practice of select committees is to request witnesses to give evidence to them by means of an informal invitation issued through their clerks or the chairman of the committee. Select committees seldom use their formal powers to summon individuals, preferring to keep them in reserve. Nevertheless, when a select committee has the power to send for persons, that power is unqualified,[1] except to the extent that it conflicts with the privileges of the Crown and of Members of the House of Lords, or with the rights of Members of the House of Commons.

Civil servants frequently give evidence to select committees and in extending invitations to government departments it is usual to rely on departmental co-operation in selecting witnesses and not to summon individual officers. Successive Governments have taken the view that officials giving evidence before select committees do so on behalf of their ministers and it is therefore customary for ministers to decide which official should represent them for that purpose. A memorandum exists within the Civil Service to give guidance to officials appearing as witnesses before select committees.[2] In 1986 the Government of the day proposed to amend the memorandum in the light of the opinion that a select committee 'was not a suitable instrument for inquiring into or passing judgement upon the actions or conduct of an individual civil servant'. The point was explored in an interchange of correspondence between ministers and committees. The Government gave an undertaking that if a civil servant was unable to answer a question asked by a departmental committee because he was inhibited in his duty to, or by instructions of, ministers, the relevant departmental minister would himself be prepared to attend the committee. Secondly, if the conduct of a civil servant was called into question the Government argued that the committee should take this up with the minister concerned who would look into the matter and inform the committee of the result. Suitable words to this purpose were added to the memorandum of guidance.[3] No change has been made by the House to its practice, nor have the powers regularly given to committees been changed.

The effect of the qualification to the powers of committees referred to above is that Members of the Commons, including of course many ministers, are not summoned to a select committee but can be invited to attend. Only an order of the House itself can require a Member to attend a committee. In the case of Peers Standing Order No 22 [HL] provides that any Lord requested by a Commons committee to attend before it or any of its sub-committees shall have the leave of the House to attend if he think fit. No messages are exchanged. In the case of officers of the House of Lords appearing before a Commons committee, a message must first be sent requesting their lordships to give leave to the witness concerned to attend (see chapter 25).

1 A select committee has expressed surprise that certain departments seemed unaware of the powers of select committees in this respect (Science and Technology Committee, HC 421–I (1967–68) p xlix). This aspect of the power was reaffirmed by the Select Committee on the Parliamentary Commissioner for Administration, which recognized at the same time its responsibility for maintaining a balance between the exercise of its functions and the protection of ministerial responsibility, Second Report, HC 350 (1967–68) p xii.

2 HC Deb (1985–86) 93 c 10 w. From time to time Governments have taken the view that it would not be appropriate for certain officials to appear before select committees, eg HC Deb (1984–85) 76, c 13 w (the Director General of the Security Service or members of his staff). See too HC Deb (1983–84) 92, cc 895–896.

3 Cm 78, pp 4–5; HC 100 (1986–87); Cmnd 9916, para 44; HC 519 (1985–86); HC 62 (1986–87).

A select committee has no power to send for any papers which, if required by the House itself, would be sought by address (see pp 212–214). Consequently a select committee is not capable of taking the formal step of ordering a Secretary of State to produce papers. If a Government were at any time to rest upon this formal position[1] it would be open to the chairman of the committee to seek to move an address in the House, or communicate with the Secretary of State to whose department the papers relate, who would lay them before Parliament, if he thought it proper, 'by command of Her Majesty'.[2] The papers, when received, would then be referred to the committee by the House. Nor can a committee require an officer of a public department to produce any paper which, according to the rules and practice of the House, it is not usual for the House itself to order to be laid before it (see pp 212–214).[3]

There is no restriction on the power of committees to require the production of papers by private bodies or individuals, provided that such papers are relevant to the committee's work as defined by its order of reference. A select committee has formally ordered the chairman of a nationalised industry to produce certain papers.[4]

As when sending for persons, select committees generally hold in reserve their power formally to send for papers and records and proceed by informal invitation.

Arrangements exist for reimbursing witnesses' expenses (see pp 682–683).

Witnesses from overseas. Committees sitting abroad cannot exercise a power to send for persons, papers and records. Nor are witnesses summoned from overseas to give evidence in the United Kingdom,[5] but foreign or Commonwealth nationals are often invited to attend to give evidence before committees.[6] There have, for example, been a number of occasions in recent years when Commissioners or officials of the European Commission, irrespective of nationality, have given evidence.[7] Travel costs and subsistence allowances may be paid to witnesses from abroad under arrangements made by the House of Commons Commission. (For the position regarding select committees and foreign nationals outside the United Kingdom, see p 627). Witnesses from foreign or Commonwealth countries are presumed not to be subject to the same constraints and obligations as those who are

---

1 In February 1985 the then Leader of the House informed the Liaison Committee by letter that the Government did not intend to take any advantage of a select committee's inability to order papers from a Secretary of State.
2 For example, a case laid before the law officers, see Select Committee on the Thames Embankment, Proceedings, HC 411 (1871) pp iv–v; see also HC 390 (1865) p xviii.
3 This would include papers on security matters, HC Deb (1984–85) 76, c 13 w.
4 CJ (1977–78) 126.
5 For instances where the Secretary of State for the Colonies was requested to secure the attendance of witnesses from British Colonies, see Ceylon Committee, First Report, HC 66 (1850) p 4; British South Africa Committee, Second Report, HC 311 (1897) p iii.
6 For cases prior to 1939, see *Erskine May* (20th edn) p 698 fn 9. Recent cases where foreign nationals have been invited to give evidence include the Energy Committee, the Foreign Affairs Committee and the Employment Committee, HC 397-iii (1979–80); HC 843 (1979–80); HC 98 (1984–85).
7 Eg HC 248 (1987–88) pp 9–12 (Treasury and Civil Service Committee); HC 303-iii (1987–88) pp 51–64 (Transport Committee); HC 461-ii (1987–88) pp 170–178 (Transport Committee); HC 22–II (1988–89) pp 253–265 (Environment Committee).

United Kingdom citizens.[1] Select committees now frequently obtain written information from overseas persons or representative bodies, either direct or through government departments, about matters within the committee's order of reference.

There is no record of foreign or Commonwealth nationals resident (temporarily or permanently) in the United Kingdom being summoned, but on the analogy of the process in courts of law, there would appear to be no bar to their being summoned if they are present within the jurisidiction of Parliament.

Hearing of parties before select committees

By leave of the House, parties whose conduct forms the subject, or one of the subjects, of an investigation by a select committee, or whose rights and interests, as distinct from those of the general public, are directly affected by a public bill or other matter which has been referred to the consideration of such a committee, are sometimes allowed to be heard in person or by counsel before the committee.

The order for the hearing of the party or parties concerned is made either on the appointment of the committee,[2] or subsequently as a result of a special report from the committee,[3] or merely on the motion of the chairman.[4] Orders for the hearing of parties have also been made upon the petition of the party interested, praying to be heard.[5]

Orders may specify the hearing of particular persons[6] or of all such persons as shall, within a time limited by the order, have presented petitions praying to be heard.[7]

Orders specifying the forms of representation open to parties before select committees have varied. The most modern type of order is that giving the committee leave to hear counsel to such extent as it shall see fit;[8] or to hear parties by themselves, their counsel[9] or agents.[10] Orders have added witnesses to or included witnesses within those categories of persons a

---

1 See HC 2–ii (1973–74) p 892. For the position with regard to obtaining evidence from multi-national companies, see the memorandum of the Clerk of the House to the Procedure Committee 1977–78, HC 588–1 (1977–78) p 24.
2 CJ (1913) 18; ibid (1918) 65; ibid (1931–32) 178; ibid (1932–33) 26; ibid (1934–35) 103; ibid (1935–36) 289; ibid (1966–67) 163.
3 CJ (1864) 188, 193; ibid (1888) 234; ibid (1912–13) 384, 388, 430; ibid (1939–40) 247–248.
4 CJ (1861–62) 307; ibid (1890) 458; ibid (1893–94) 344; ibid (1898) 146; ibid (1967–68) 150.
5 CJ (1806–07) 110, 228; ibid (1822–23) 405; ibid (1833) 568; ibid (1857) 43; ibid (1857–58) 150; ibid (1860) 314; ibid (1867–68) 268, 272, 273; ibid (1868–69) 51.
6 CJ (1868–69) 51; ibid (1877) 258; ibid (1880) 188.
7 CJ (1890–91) 96; ibid (1892) 134, 244; ibid (1907) 204.
8 CJ (1888) 234; ibid (1897) 29; ibid (1900) 178; ibid (1912–13) 384, 388, 430; ibid (1913) 18; ibid (1918) 65; ibid (1931–32) 178; ibid (1932–33) 26; ibid (1934–35) 103; ibid (1967–68) 150; ibid (1975–76) 590; ibid (1978–79) 140. Leave has also been given 'to hear counsel upon the matters referred to' a select committee, CJ (1861–62) 307; ibid (1890) 458.
9 See 10 Chandler Deb, 68. For instances of leave given to hear parties by counsel and agents, see CJ (1854–55) 367; ibid (1864) 193.
10 CJ (1880) 188; ibid (1935–36) 289; ibid (1936–37) 33; ibid 1938–39) 59; ibid (1966–67) 163. Committees have also been given power to hear parties by themselves or their counsel, no mention being made of agents, CJ (1868–69) 51; ibid (1939–40) 247–248; ibid (1940–41) 8. In the last two cases, the Committee was empowered to hear the Member whose conduct was the subject of the inquiry by himself or his counsel, and to hear counsel on behalf of any other persons.

committee is empowered to hear.[1] Where a select committee is to consider a bill, orders have given leave for parties appearing on petitions against the bill to be heard by themselves, their counsel or agents, and for counsel to be heard in support of the bill.[2] More infrequently, orders of a more restrictive character have been made.[3]

When orders are made for the hearing of parties, orders are at the same time sometimes made for the hearing of parties on the other side.[4] In some instances parties have been given leave to examine witnesses before committees through their counsel or agents.[5]

Where a party is given the right to be heard he may adduce evidence; but he may not do so where the hearing is at the discretion of the committee.

Admission of strangers

Unless the House otherwise orders, a select committee (and any of its sub-committees, except as the committee otherwise orders) has the power to admit strangers during the examination of witnesses, if it so orders (Standing Order No 108). The effect of this standing order is that, unless a resolution is passed to allow the admittance of strangers, evidence has to be held in private. Many committees make a practice of passing such a resolution, so as to ensure that their evidence is held in public.[6]

When committees are deliberating, it is the practice to exclude all strangers; this rule does not apply to appropriate officers or staff of the House, or to specialist advisers (see p 641).

Presence of Members at sittings of select committees. Members of the House are entitled to be present at the sittings of committees, as well during the deliberations of the committee as while witnesses are being examined;[7] and though, if requested to retire, they rarely make any objection, and ought, on the grounds of established usage and courtesy to the committee, immediately to retire when the committee is about to deliberate, the committee, in case of their refusal, has no power to order them to withdraw.[8] As

---

1　CJ (1806–07) 228; ibid (1833) 568; ibid (1877) 258; ibid (1893–94) 344; ibid (1898) 146; ibid (1912–13) 393–394.
2　CJ (1877) 258; ibid (1890–91) 96; ibid (1892) 134, 244; ibid (1907) 204.
3　Party alone without agent or counsel, CJ (1737–41) 249; ibid (1892) 124. A committee has been given power in its discretion to hear counsel on behalf of such persons as it decides should appear before it, CJ (1889) 253. The House has directed Mr Attorney General to attend a committee to present to the committee evidence in the possession of the government relative to the subject-matter of the inquiry; and has given him leave to examine witnesses, CJ (1939–40) 248; ibid (1940–41) 8.
4　Committees on matters, CJ (1822–23) 405; ibid (1868–69) 51; committees on public bills, CJ (1890–91) 96; ibid (1892) 134, 244; ibid (1907) 204.
5　CJ (1833) 167, 169, 558.
6　Sittings in public were not uncommon in the nineteenth and early twentieth centuries, but they were rare in the twenty years after 1945. Strangers are from time to time excluded by resolution during the examination of particular witnesses, eg Foreign Affairs Committee, Evidence (Famine in the Horn of Africa), HC 297 (1987–88) pp 24, 70, 83; Defence Committee, Evidence (Future size and role of the Royal Navy's Surface Fleet), HC 309 (1987–88) pp 20, 39, 56.
7　For a full discussion of this subject, see Third Report from the Procedure Committee, HC 270 (1971–72). The House took no action following this report.
8　Parl Deb (1842) 64, cc 755 ff; ibid (1849) 102, c 1182; ibid (1855) 137, c 18; ibid (1857) 146, c 137; ibid (1861) 162, c 2095; ibid (1879) 247, c 1957; HC 68 (1950) p 16; HC Deb (1979–80) 988, cc 1769–1775; ibid (1983–84) 53, c 895.

Members cannot be excluded from a committee room by the authority of the committee, the committee, if it desires that other Members should not be present at its proceedings, and such Members refuse to withdraw, should adjourn and, if they persist in attending at subsequent meetings, should apply to the House for power to effect their exclusion.[1]

A Member of the House, who is not a member of a committee, may not address the committee, put questions to witnesses, or interfere in any manner whatever in the proceedings;[2] nor has a Member (not being a member of the committee) who is under examination at a committee any right to be present during any deliberation upon the answers given by him.[3]

Disorder in select committees. When the public are admitted the rules which govern their conduct when present at sittings of the House (see pp 170–173) and at sittings of standing committees (see p 603) apply.[4] Under Standing Order No 141 the power granted to the Serjeant at Arms to take into his custody any stranger who, having been admitted into the gallery of the House, misconducts himself or does not withdraw when ordered to do so, may, if the chairman so directs, be exercised in respect of strangers so misconducting themselves at meetings of select committees sitting within the precincts of the House.[5]

Secret committees. Formerly both Houses appointed secret committees when in their opinion the nature of the inquiry appeared to require such a course. In these committees the proceedings were conducted thoughout with closed doors and it was the invariable practice for all Members who were not members of the committee to be excluded from the room. The last such committee was appointed in the Commons in 1857.[6] However, in 1976 the House ordered that no persons other than members of a particular committee should be present during any of the committee's proceedings unless so required by the committee.[7]

Minutes of evidence

The evidence of the witnesses examined before a select committee is taken down in shorthand or tape-recorded for later transcription, and, after each day's sitting, a typescript version is usually produced for the use of the members of the committee under the authority of Mr Speaker.[8] Every select committee now has leave under Standing Order No 115 to report the minutes of evidence taken before it. Formerly such power was given either on

---

1 Parl Deb (1849) 102, c 1183.
2 4 Hatsell 135; Parl Deb (1844) 73, cc 725–726.
3 CJ (1780–82) 870.
4 Eg thus a member of the public may not make an unauthorized tape recording of committee proceedings; Minutes of Evidence of the Energy Committee, HC 76–II (1985–86) pp 307–308.
5 The standing order was based on a private ruling by Mr Speaker published in HC Deb (1981–82) 19, c 385.
6 CJ (1857) 24, 38. See also Colchester i, 91.
7 CJ (1975–76) 590. See also CJ (1978–79) 140.
8 Parl Deb (1837) 38, c 196. Evidence has been given in Welsh, the published official record being in English (Welsh Affairs Committee, HC 448–I (1980–81) p xciv).

appointment[1] or subsequently on the application of the chairman.[2] Power to report the minutes of the evidence taken before sub-committees from time to time may be conferred at the time the committee is appointed or in the standing order setting out the terms of reference and powers of the committee. Once the evidence is reported, the House will normally order it to be printed (see p 636).[3] Such powers make possible the intermediate publication of evidence without waiting for the completion of the enquiry and the preparation and presentation of the report. Committees have discretion over the best division of their evidence for the purpose of reporting it to the House.[4] Evidence taken in private is frequently not reported until the report to which it relates is made to the House.

Select committees, when given power to sit notwithstanding the adjournment of the House and to report the minutes of evidence taken before them from time to time or otherwise, have also been authorized, when the House was not sitting, to send the minutes of evidence (or minutes of proceedings or other papers) to the Clerk of the House; and the delivery of such minutes or papers has been deemed to be the reporting of them to the House. In such cases either the Clerk has been authorized to give directions for their printing and circulation and to lay them on the Table of the House at its next sitting,[5] or the committee has been given power to direct the printing of such minutes or papers, such printing being deemed to be by order of the House[6] (see also pp 645–647).

By Standing Orders Nos 112 and 113, the names of the members present at the sitting must be entered on the minutes of evidence, and to every question or series of questions asked of a witness under examination in the proceedings of a select committee, and at the beginning of each page of the minutes of evidence, there must be prefixed the name of the inquiring member.

If a question, which, on being objected to, is decided to be improper or inadmissible, has already been inserted in the minutes, the question is expunged. Other matters which have been expunged by the order of the committee have included answers which, properly speaking, were not evidence and ought not to have been received as such; part of, or certain words in, a witness's evidence; questions and answers relating to a case of which the witness subsequently admitted he had no personal knowledge;

1 CJ (1833) 548; &c; ibid (1968–69) 31, &c.
2 CJ (1847) 126; ibid (1857) 282; ibid (1934–35) 235, 317. For instances of leave given (on a date subsequent to the appointment of the committee) to report Minutes of Evidence taken before a sub-committee, see CJ (1945–46) 303, 340, 405. Such an application has been refused, CJ (1846) 787.
3 In practice the clerk, acting on behalf of the chairman of the committee, delivers the appropriate entry to the Journal Office both for reporting the evidence and, if desired, for printing it.
4 Parl Deb (1837) 38, c 185, 190; Committee on Army and Navy Estimates, HC 216 (1887) p vi; CJ (1939–40) 58; ibid (1945–46) 110.
5 CJ (1932–33) 184, 322; ibid (1933–34) 12; ibid (1937–38) 395; ibid (1945–46) 33, 36.
6 CJ (1974) 297; ibid (1974–75) 606; ibid (1979–80) 784, 805.

and even the whole of the evidence given by a witness.[1] (For the procedure on objection to a question see p 680.)

A copy of the text of his examination is sent to each witness for his
revision, with an instruction that alterations should be confined to the
correction of inaccuracies in the reporting or printing of evidence, or to the
correction of matters of fact which do not materially alter the sense of the
answer, and should be in the handwriting of the witness himself, unless he is
disabled by accident or infirmity, in which case they may be written by
another person at his dictation. The corrected copy should be returned
without delay to the committee clerk, who is required to examine the
corrections, and if any appear to be irregular, to submit them to the chairman. Should the evidence not be returned with corrections within ten days,
or some other reasonable time, according to the circumstances, it is printed
in its original form.[2] Minutes of evidence taken at sittings of select committees sitting in public have sometimes been published without correction,
but prefaced by a note indicating that they were subject to correction. The
corrected minutes of evidence were subsequently published with the committees' reports.[3]

In recent years, some committees have also deposited copies of the
uncorrected typescript of evidence taken in public in the Library of the
House or in the Vote Office for the use of Members, particularly when the
evidence relates to matters which are likely to be subject to debate in the
House or in other committees before a printed text of the evidence is
available. Occasionally, too, it has been the recent practice to place copies of
corrected transcripts of the evidence in the Vote Office in circumstances
where a debate in the House is imminent upon a matter pertaining to a
report to which that evidence relates and where there is insufficient time to
make available a printed copy of the evidence.

Where evidence has been taken upon oath, all corrections, except corrections of printer's errors, must be made by the witness personally to the
committee.

> Where it appeared that a witness had corrected his evidence more exten-
> sively than the rules of the House permitted, and that his corrections had
> consequently not been reported by the committee, the report, together
> with the minutes of the evidence taken before the committee, was re-
> committed to the committee with an instruction to re-examine the witness
> 'touching his former evidence'.[4]

Where a witness considers that the publication of his evidence given in
private to a select committee or part of it would be prejudicial to the public
interest or injurious to character, or would disclose matters of commercial
confidentiality, or would be undesirable on similar grounds, he may request
that the evidence in question should not be published; and the committee at

---

1 Proceedings of Committees on East India Finance, HC 363 (1871) p xiii; Railway Servants
  (Hours of Labour), HC 342 (1890–91) pp v, vi; Game Laws, HC 337 (1872) p ix; and Cattle
  Plague and Importation of Live Stock, HC 362 (1877) p xvii.
2 Instructions by the Speaker, 16 April 1861; and see Parl Deb (1867) 189, c 1223.
3 Eg, the Select Committee on Science and Technology in 1966–67, and Sub-Committee B of
  the Estimates Committee in 1967–68 published uncorrected evidence in this way. See also
  Minutes of Proceedings of the Foreign Affairs Committee, HC 395 (1986–87) pp ix, x.
4 CJ (1849) 525.

its discretion may refrain from reporting that evidence to the House or may report such summary of the evidence as appears necessary in order to present the grounds of its conclusions to the House.[1] If part of the evidence given to a committee is not reported to the House, the committee will indicate in the evidence as printed the places in the text where material has been omitted.

Occasionally the House orders unreported evidence to be laid before it.[2] When the evidence is presented in pursuance of such an order, it is usually ordered to be printed[3] (see above).

A committee which has heard counsel but not witnesses has been given leave to report to the House minutes of speeches delivered by counsel.[4]

Documentary evidence received by a select committee is frequently printed and published with the report, or with the oral evidence, or by itself. It is increasingly the practice, particularly when the written evidence received by a committee is extensive, for a proportion of such written evidence not to be printed but to be made available to Members in the Library and to the public in the House of Lords Record Office or in the Committee Office. When this is done it is usual to mention the fact in any report which is published to which that evidence relates.

Publication of evidence taken before select committees before it is reported to the House. It is a contempt of the House to publish or disclose any portion of the evidence given before, or any document presented to, a select committee after such evidence or document has been reported to the House but before it has been published.[5] (For the procedure recommended by the Privileges Committee in cases of premature disclosure see p 649). For the historic development of the treatment of premature publication and disclosure of Committee proceedings, see pp 122–124.

The increasing practice of committees taking evidence in public has led to a relaxation of these rules in certain circumstances. In 1980, the House agreed to waive its privileges by resolving that it would not entertain any complaint of contempt or breach of privilege in respect of the publication of reports of evidence given by witnesses before select committees meeting in public before such evidence had been reported to the House.[6] The House's waiver is now set out in Standing Order No 118. It is in any case the practice for a committee to report to the House, on the day in question, the evidence given to it in public.

1 Parl Deb (1837) 38, c 191; HC Deb (1948–49) 466, cc 456–458. The practice by which witnesses indicate their request that certain evidence should not be published is known as 'side-lining'.
2 Parl Deb (1837) 38, c 191; CJ (1821–22) 438; ibid (1830–31) 168; ibid (1833) 671; ibid (1850) 637; ibid (1895) 325; ibid (1896) 406. Evidence taken before a committee in the preceding session has similarly been ordered to be laid before the House, CJ (1837–38) 703, 707; ibid (1947–48) 24, 37; ibid (1952–53) 6, 8; ibid (1962–63) 13, 15.
3 See HC Deb (1969–70) 791, cc 624–625. Evidence of a previous session ordered to be printed, eg Votes and Proceedings 7 December 1987. The House has also discharged an order made in the previous session for printing minutes of evidence, eg Votes and Proceedings, 13 December 1987.
4 CJ (1934–35) 214.
5 CJ (1837) 282; ibid (1875) 141. See also Parl Deb (1894) 28, c 1257, and Privileges Committee, Second Report, HC 357 (1967–68). However, under the Local Government (Access to Information) Act 1985 local authorities are obliged to make available to the press and public papers that are being considered at meetings held in public. Thus from time to time memoranda are, in pursuance of this Act, made available before being submitted to, or reported by, a select committee.
6 HC Deb (1980) 991, c 992; ibid 995, c 418.

Furthermore, under Standing Order No 117, all select committees having power to send for persons, papers and records have power to authorize the publication of the names of persons who have appeared as witnesses before them, and to authorize the publication by the witnesses concerned or otherwise of memoranda of evidence submitted by them. Under the same standing order the Speaker has the power to authorize publication in similar circumstances in the case of any select committee which is no longer in existence.

The transcript of evidence is produced for the use of the members of the committee; consequently neither they nor witnesses to whom copies are entrusted for correction are at liberty to communicate them to any other persons.[1] The Speaker, has, however, authorized select committees, if they think fit, to supply prospective witnesses with copies of the evidence taken before them, or part of it. If they wish to supply any other persons with copies of the evidence, they must obtain the Speaker's permission.

> Where parties are admitted to be heard by counsel, leave has been given to such parties to print the evidence from the committee clerk's copy from day to day.[2]

Charges made against Members in committees

On 16 March 1688, the Commons resolved, 'That if any information came before any committee that chargeth any Member of the House, the committee ought only to direct that the House be acquainted with the matter of such information, without proceeding further thereupon'.[3]

> Where a committee reported that a Member was mentioned to be concerned in the matters directed by the House to be inquired into, the House ordered, 'That the said committee has power to inquire into the matters to it referred, notwithstanding any Members of this House may be concerned therein; and that it does report the same to the House'.[4]

Documents presented to select committees

No document received by the clerk of any select committee of the House may be withdrawn or altered without the knowledge and approval of the committee (Standing Order No 109).[5]

> Documents submitted to one committee are not available for the use of other committees unless reported to the House, except that under Standing Order No 130 (select committees related to government departments) any committee appointed under that order has power to communicate to any other such committee documents (or any other evidence) received by it which relate to matters of common interest.

Sub-committees

A select committee, having only a delegated authority, cannot, without the leave of the House, divide itself into sub-committees and apportion its

---

1 Parl Deb (1837) 38, c 196.
2 CJ (1880) 209; ibid (1900) 188.
3 CJ (1688–93) 51.
4 CJ (1688–93) 647 (1691); Parl Deb (1897) 49, c 1273.
5 For examples of leave being formally given, see Welsh Affairs Committee, Proceedings, HC 840 (1979–80) p xi; Overseas Aid, CJ (1969–70) 41.

functions among such sub-committees, or delegate to a sub-committee any of the authority delegated to it by the House.[1] A committee may, however, avail itself of the service of its members individually or in the form of sub-committees for purposes connected with the business of the committee, such as drafting,[2] or visits outside the precincts of the House which do not involve a delegation of authority.

Where a committee is empowered to appoint sub-committees the House usually makes an order prescribing the quorum of such sub-committees[3] and investing them with power to send for persons, papers and records and such other powers as may be considered necessary.[4]

Committees have been empowered to divide themselves into sub-committees consisting of seven members at the least;[5] to appoint one or more sub-committees and to apportion the subjects referred to the committee between such sub-committees;[6] to appoint one or more sub-committees to take evidence or to consider any matter that may be referred to them by the committee;[7] to appoint sub-committees and to refer to such sub-committees any of the matters referred to the committee;[8] to appoint sub-committees for any purpose within their order of reference;[9] or one sub-committee with no specified purpose,[10] or to appoint sub-committees and to delegate to such sub-committees any of the powers which had been conferred on the committee.[11] Committees have also been empowered to appoint a sub-committee for a specified purpose.[12]

The House has limited the number of sub-committees which may be appointed and the number of members to be nominated to each.[13]

On one occasion the House, having authorized a committee to appoint a sub-committee for a specified purpose, instructed any sub-committee so appointed to inquire specially into a certain matter.[14]

A select committee which had been given power to appoint a sub-committee to review, co-ordinate and direct the work of the investigating sub-

---

1 Parl Deb (1819) 39, cc 776–777.
2 Select Committee on the Official Secrets Act, HC 173 (1937–38) p xlvi. For a recent example of such a sub-committee, see Welsh Affairs Committee, Proceedings, HC 840 (1979–80) pp v–vi, viii.
3 Estimates, CJ (1921) 229; ibid (1922) 35, etc; National Expenditure, CJ (1939–40) 17; ibid (1940–41) 9, etc. For orders varying the means of determining the quorum of a sub-committee in different circumstances, see CJ (1941–42) 45.
4 CJ (1967–68) 95, 220; ibid (1968–69) 37, 278, etc. It has been provided that sub-committees shall have the full powers of the undivided committee, CJ (1921) 229; ibid (1938–39) 24.
5 Petitions for Private Bills, CJ (1836) 743; ibid (1837) 636.
6 Estimates, CJ (1921) 229; ibid (1922) 35, etc.
7 CJ (1932–33) 266; ibid (1933–34) 12.
8 See, eg CJ (1972–73) 27, etc; ibid (1973–74) 20, etc; ibid (1974) 57, etc.
9 Procedure, CJ (1945–46) 33.
10 SO No 130(3).
11 Kitchen and Refreshment Rooms (House of Commons), CJ (1953–54) 10–11; ibid (1954–55) 11, etc.
12 Eg to confer with a sub-committee appointed by a committee of the House of Lords, CJ (1944–45) 79; to review, co-ordinate and direct the work of any investigating sub-committees appointed by the committee (the committee having been empowered to refer to sub-committees any of the matters referred to its examination) and to refer to such sub-committees any of the matters referred to the committee, CJ (1941–42) 45; ibid (1942–43) 9 etc; to hear evidence abroad, CJ (1969–70) 41.
13 CJ (1969–70) 19, 21, 41; ibid (1970–71) 427; ibid (1971–72) 49.
14 CJ (1946–47) 368.

committees which it was authorized to appoint, was given power to delegate to this sub-committee its power of appointing such sub-committees as might seem to it desirable and referring to such sub-committees any of the matters referred to the committee, and to confer on it power to alter sub-committees' orders of reference, to direct sub-committees to hold joint sittings, to nominate the members and appoint the chairmen of sub-committees, and to discharge members from sub-committees and appoint other members in substitution. Any action taken by the sub-committee in the exercise of these powers was to be invalid unless approved by the committee within twenty-one days.[1]

Though committees with power to appoint sub-committees cannot confer on such sub-committees powers in excess of those which the House has authorized, they may nevertheless make orders regulating the transaction of business by their sub-committees. Thus committees may appoint chairmen of sub-committees;[2] and have ordered that no sub-committee shall sit during the sitting of the committee without leave specially granted.[3] Two or more sub-committees have been empowered to sit together for the purpose of hearing evidence;[4] and a sub-committee has been authorized to direct other sub-committees to hold joint sittings.[5] Power to discharge members from sub-committees and to appoint others, or to add to another sub-committee members added to the committee, has been entrusted to a sub-committee.[6] A committee has also ordered that if a member is appointed to the committee in place of another, he shall take the place of the member discharged on the sub-committee on which the latter served; and if two or more members are simultaneously replaced, the chairman of the committee is to allocate them to the vacant sub-committee places.[7] Sub-committees have been authorized to admit certain strangers.[8]

A sub-committee may not report directly to the House, but only to the committee by which it has been appointed.

Under Standing Order No 130(4) provision is made for setting up from time to time a sub-committee, drawn from the membership of two or more of the Energy, Environment, Trade and Industry, Scottish Affairs, Transport, and Treasury and Civil Service Committees, to consider any matter affecting two or more nationalized industries. The order does not identify the select committee to which the sub-committee should report and no joint sub-committee has yet been established.

---

1 National Expenditure, CJ (1942–43) 9; ibid (1943–44) 13; ibid (1944–45) 30.
2 See, for example, Select Committee on Science and Technology, First Special Report, HC 28 (1969–70) and First Special Report, HC 57 (1974–75). Co-ordinating sub-committees may appoint chairmen of other sub-committees, CJ (1942–43) 10. Provision may also be made for the absence of the chairman of a sub-committee by specifying by resolution of the committee that a certain member should take the chair, or that the sub-committee should choose a member to take the chair, Estimates Committee, Proceedings, HC 149 (1946–47) p cxxviii; idem HC 308 (1956–57) pp 3, 4.
3 Estimates Committee, Proceedings, HC 149 (1946–47), pp ccxxvii–ccxxviii etc.
4 Estimates Committee, Proceedings, HC 149 (1946–47), p ccxxvii, ccxxxi etc.
5 CJ (1942–43) 9; ibid (1943–44) 13; ibid (1944–45) 30.
6 See preceding footnote and Estimates Committee, Proceedings, HC 149 (1946–47) p ccxxix; ibid HC 262 (1950–51) p 4.
7 Estimates Committee, Proceedings, HC 444 (1967–68) p 4.
8 Estimates Committee, Proceedings, HC 130 (1954–55) p xii; ibid HC 427 (1955–56) p 5.

On giving power to select committees to appoint sub-committees, the House has also ordered that every such sub-committee must report any evidence taken to the select committee.[1] It is customary for the select committee then to report the evidence to the House. But when, as is now generally the case, the committee has been given power to report from time to time the evidence taken before its sub-committees, it is usual for the chairman of the committee to report the evidence to the House without a prior meeting of the main committee for that purpose.

Nomination of non-members of committee. Committees have recommended to the House the nomination by the House of additional members to serve on sub-committees appointed by them.[2] This procedure has been mentioned in a committee's order of reference.[3] Committees have also been authorized to appoint persons not being Members of the House to serve on sub-committees.[4] On rare occasions and, more recently, a committee has been given power to invite such persons as it might select to attend any of its meetings, and to take part in the deliberations of the committee and its sub-committees. In this latter case the power was not used.[5]

Expert assistance and consultation

In the past, select committees have been given unusual powers to secure assistance when it appeared necessary for them to consider and evaluate complex technical or professional evidence. These sometimes took the form of powers to employ qualified individuals who should conduct their own investigations and report to the committee.[6] More frequently, orders made by the House of Commons have envisaged the committee's consultation with persons of professional capacity and expertise.[7] Following the development of this practice in the 1960s[8] committees are now regularly empowered to appoint specialist advisers either to supply information which is not readily available or to elucidate matters of complexity either within the

---

1 For example, CJ (1939–40) 17; ibid (1940–41) 9, etc.
2 CJ (1966–67) 479, 507; see also Science and Technology Committee, Fifth Special Report, HC 463 (1966–67). In one case, a committee recommended such nominations but the House took no action, Education and Science Committee, Second Special Report, HC 231 (1967–68).
3 CJ (1965–66) 44, 52; ibid (1966–67) 69, 80. See also Select Committee on House of Commons (Services), Special Report, HC 27 (1965–66); ibid Special Report, HC 64 (1966–67).
4 CJ (1917–18) 170; ibid (1918) 13, 72, 204; ibid (1919) 98; ibid (1920) 94. For objection to such a course see Notes of Debates and Procedures at the Parliament, B M Harl Mss 1058; Commons Debates 1621 (ed W Notestein, F H Relf and H Simpson) vol vi, p 348; Committee on Controverted Elections, Report HC 496 (1836) p 5; Committee on Referees on Private Bills, Report, HC 108, pp iv, 9–10, 17, 20 (1876).
5 Procedure, CJ (1975–76) 371.
6 CJ (1887) 399, 407, 413; ibid (1912–13) 124; ibid (1913) 18; ibid (1914) 252. See also Select Committee on the National Land Company, Sixth Report, HC 577 (1847–48) pp vii, ix; Select Committee on Army and Navy Estimates, Fifth Report, HC 259 (1887) p iii. There were twenty-five extraordinary payments to individuals for services performed on behalf of committees of the House of Commons between 1872 and 1914.
7 CJ (1921) 50; ibid (1922) 25; ibid (1943–44) 29. In these cases the individuals concerned attended meetings at which the committees deliberated.
8 Select Committee on Procedure, Fourth Report, HC 303 (1964–65) p ix; Estimates Committee, Fifth Special Report, HC 161 (1964–65); Select Committee on House of Commons (Services), First Report, HC 70 (1965–66).

committee's order of reference,[1] or in connection with the matter referred to it, as appropriate.[2] In modern practice, such advisers normally attend not only meetings of the committee at which oral evidence is taken but also meetings at which the committee deliberates. They do not examine witnesses or take part in voting. They are normally paid a daily fee at rates broadly in line with payments made for similar work done by members of academic institutions for government departments.[3]

Other persons,[4] being in most cases officers of the House with special responsibility in the matter concerned, attend sittings of committees (including their deliberations) without being witnesses. For example, Counsel to Mr Speaker is appointed to assist the Joint Committee on Statutory Instruments (see pp 551–552) as is Counsel to the Lord Chairman of the House of Lords, and other committees receive assistance of a similar kind.[5]

It has also recently been the practice of some select committees, in particular the Foreign Affairs Committee,[6] to hold, either occasionally or on a regular basis, informal meetings attended by persons whom they believe can assist them in fulfilling their duties to the House. Such persons are not treated as witnesses: the information they give is not evidence and may not be regarded as enjoying the protection of privilege which surrounds a proceeding in Parliament (see pp 92–93).

Committees have been specially empowered to consult with certain individuals officially concerned with the matters of their inquiry.[7] Committees on the Army, Air Force, and Naval Discipline Acts have sometimes been given authority to communicate with governmental drafting committees.[8]

Reports of select committees

Power of committees to report their opinion. By Standing Order No 115 every select committee may report its opinion and observations upon the matters referred to its consideration, even though it is not expressly directed to do so by its order of reference.

Consideration of resolutions recommending public expenditure. Select committees may consider and report to the House resolutions recommending an outlay of public money for the specified purposes without the previous signification of the royal recommendation (see p 560) because such a resolution is regarded as analogous to those abstract resolutions by the

---

1 Eg SO No 130.
2 Eg SO No 129.
3 HC Deb (1981–82) 21, c*331*.
4 The general practice is however stated by a Speaker's private ruling (Mr Speaker FitzRoy, 1930) that the rule that the deliberations of a committee should be conducted in private ought to be observed strictly. See Estimates Committee, First Report, HC 59 (1926); Estimates Committee, Proceedings, HC 145, (1939) pp lviii ff. See also Estimates Committee, Twentieth Report, HC 316 (1948–49) p 4; Estimates Committee, Proceedings, HC 427 (1955–56) p 5; Estimates Committee, Sixteenth Report, HC 306 (1948–49) p 102.
5 CJ (1972–73) 142, etc. See p 657 (European Legislation, and House of Commons (Services) Committees). See also pp 659 and 660 (Parliamentary Commissioner for Administration, and Public Accounts Committees).
6 First Report from the Liaison Committee, HC 383 (1984–85) pp xli, xlii (Report to the Liaison Committee by the then Chairman of the Foreign Affairs Committee).
7 CJ (1867–68) 182–183; ibid (1932–33) 136; ibid (1933–34) 12. These persons were not present at the deliberations of the committees.
8 CJ (1951–52) 245; ibid (1952–53) 10; ibid (1953–54) 9; ibid (1955–56) 194.

House in favour of public expenditure which are in the nature of suggestions, and are not in themselves effective.[1]

Preparation of draft report. When the examination of witnesses has been
concluded in a committee on a matter, the chairman normally prepares a
draft report or, less frequently, resolutions, copies of which it is customary
to circulate to the members before consideration by the committee.

Sometimes a meeting is held for the purpose of discussing the conclusions
to which the evidence leads and the general line to be adopted in the
recommendations before a draft report is prepared. Another method of
proceeding is for the committee to come to resolutions on the subject of its
reference on which the chairman or some other member proceeds to draft a
report.

Every member of a committee is entitled to submit a draft report for the
consideration of the committee. Any draft report brought up before the
committee but not forming the basis of an agreed report is entered in full in
the minutes of the proceedings of the committee.

If, after the chairman has submitted his draft report, any member who has
not already submitted an alternative draft report wishes to do so, the
committee may adjourn in order to afford him time to prepare it. No
alternative draft report can be submitted once a draft report has been
ordered to be taken into consideration, or to be read a second time, paragraph by paragraph, unless the final question for agreeing to the draft report
(as amended) is negatived (see below).

Consideration of draft report. It is common practice for committees to
consider a draft report informally before proceeding to formal consideration. The procedure for formal consideration is as follows. If only one draft
report is submitted for consideration, the report is taken as read the first
time. The chairman then proposes the question, 'That the draft report be
read a second time, paragraph by paragraph'. If, however, more than one
draft report is submitted, a motion must be made, that one of them (usually
that submitted by the chairman) be read a second time, paragraph by
paragraph. To this question an amendment may be moved, to leave out the
name of the member by whom the report is prepared and substitute that of
another member, with the object of substituting the alternative (or, if more
than two draft reports have been submitted, another) draft report, as the
basis of the committee's report. If the decision is against the amendment,
further amendments having for their object the substitution of other draft
reports can be moved in turn.

Each paragraph of the draft report adopted as the basis for the committee's report is then separately considered and becomes liable to amendment according to the ordinary rules which govern amendments.

After a decision has been given on an amendment to any part of a
paragraph, an earlier part cannot be amended, nor can the further consideration of a paragraph be postponed after a decision has been come to upon an
amendment proposed thereto. It is common practice for a committee to
agree that substantive amendments to a draft report should be submitted to

1 East India Finance Committee, Second Report, HC 194 (1873) p 4; House of Commons
(Ventilation) Committee, Second Report, HC 173 (1886) p ix (I); but see CJ (1837) 478 for an
instance where the House re-committed such a recommendation to the committee.

the clerk in writing, to agree on a time limit for the submission of such amendments, and to instruct the clerk to prepare a marshalled list of amendments to a draft report. Although the chairman of a select committee, unlike the chairman of a standing committee, has no power to select or to group amendments for the consideration of his committee, such informal agreements have proved useful in ensuring the orderly consideration of the draft reports presented to select committees.

If no amendment is offered to a paragraph, or when all amendments proposed thereto have been disposed of, a question is put, that the paragraph, or the paragraph, as amended, stand part of the report. After this question has been agreed to, no further amendment can be made to the paragraph. An amendment consisting of a new paragraph or paragraphs may be moved when the committee reaches the place in the draft report where it is proposed to insert the new paragraph or paragraphs.

Portions of a draft report other than that adopted as the basis of the committee's report may be offered as amendments to the latter provided they are relevant to it.

When every paragraph and proposed new paragraph has been considered and disposed of, the question is put, 'That the report (as amended) be the report of the committee to the House'. Once this question has been agreed to, the report cannot be further amended. If the question is negatived, the committee may either proceed with the consideration of one of the other draft reports, if any, or of any further draft which may be submitted by any member of the committee,[1] or make a special report to the effect that it is unable to agree upon a report.[2]

A committee, finding itself prevented by the impending dissolution of Parliament from completing the consideration of a draft report, postponed the consideration of the remaining paragraphs, agreed to a new paragraph setting out the facts, and resolved that so much of the proposed report as had been agreed to should be the report of the committee to the House.[3] In similar circumstances committees have appended a draft report to a special report, explaining the circumstances, to the House.[4] Such a course is to be resorted to with caution, since the publication of a draft report fails to give an indication of the balance of opinion within a committee.

Consideration of draft resolutions. Where, instead of a draft report, resolutions are submitted, each proposed resolution is moved as a substantive motion to which amendments may be proposed, subject to the same rules as in a Committee of the whole House. No resolution or amendment may be proposed which is not within the order of reference (see p 618); and if any such resolution or amendment is proposed, the chairman will decline to put it from the chair. When a resolution has been agreed to, the committee cannot review and amend it. When more than one series of resolutions is submitted, each set is entered in full in the minutes as read, after which it is

---

1 Workmen's Trains Committee, HC 270 (1905) pp xix ff.
2 CJ (1919) 426; ibid (1923) 297; see also Select Committee on Wealth Tax, HC 696 (1974–75).
3 Contracts (Public Departments) Committee, Fifth Report, HC 438 (1857–58) p xix; Betting Duty Committee, HC 139 (1923) p lviii.
4 Treasury Committee, HC 385 (1982–83), Second Special Report, Appendix A; Agriculture Committee, HC 379 (1986–87), Second Special Report, Appendix A.

usual to move that those proposed by Mr A (generally the chairman), be now taken into consideration; which question may be amended by leaving out 'Mr A', and inserting 'Mr B', and, the opinion of the committee being ascertained, the consideration of the resolutions preferred by the majority is proceeded with.

Any one of the draft resolutions submitted by other members may be moved as an amendment to any resolution to which it is relevant, and, after all the proposed resolutions have been disposed of, other resolutions may be proposed, provided that they are within the order of reference and not inconsistent with any previous decision of the committee.

Consideration of reports from sub-committees. Where a committee works through sub-committees it is, in the majority of cases, content to report the sub-committee's report to the House with or without amendment as its own report.[1] On occasion a committee has substantially amended a report[2] or referred it back to the sub-committee in whole or in part;[3] or, having considered the sub-committee's report, has adopted it as the basis of a report and ordered the chairman to prepare a draft report accordingly.[4] Occasionally sub-committees have considered separate aspects of the same subject and their reports have constituted parts of the committee's report.[5] or have been published as an appendix to a committee's report.[6]

Minority reports. It is the opinion of the committee, as a committee, not that of the individual members, which is required by the House, and, failing unanimity, the conclusions agreed to by the majority are the conclusions of the committee. No signatures may, therefore, be attached to the report for the purpose of showing any difference of opinion in the committee or the absence thereof; nor may the report be accompanied by any counter-statement, memorandum of dissent, or protest from any dissenting or non-assenting member or members; nor ought the committee to include in its report any observations which the minority or any individual member desires to offer, but which are not subscribed to by the majority;[7] nor may a draft report which has been submitted to the committee, but has not been entertained by it, be printed as an appendix to the report.[8] If a member disagrees to certain paragraphs in the report, or to the entire report, he can record his disapproval by dividing the committee against those paragraphs to which he objects, or against the entire report, as the circumstances of the case require; and can put on record his observations and conclusions, as opposed to those of the majority, by proposing an alternative draft report or

---

1 Eg Expenditure Committee, Proceedings, HC 170 (1973–74); Select Committee on Science and Technology, Proceedings, HC 160 (1973–74); Select Committee on House of Commons (Services), Second Report, HC 120 (1978–79).

2 Eg Third Report of the House of Commons (Services) Committee, HC 437 (1984–85).

3 National Expenditure Committee, Proceedings, HC 133 (1942–43) p 9; idem, HC 125 (1943–44) p 12.

4 National Expenditure Committee, Proceedings, HC 133 (1942–43) p 7; Estimates Committee, Proceedings, HC 296 (1952–53) p vii.

5 Select Committee on Scottish Affairs, HC 267 (1969–70); ibid, HC 511 (1971–72).

6 Nationalized Industries Committee, First Report, HC 340 (1966–67) App; Procedure Committee, First Report, HC 588 (1977–78) Apps A and B.

7 Opinion expressed by Mr Speaker FitzRoy in reference to the proceedings of the Shop Assistants Committee (1930–31).

8 Select Committee on the Select Committee on Railways, CJ (1847) 682–683; HC Deb, 16 June 1847. Evidence, HC 236, Qs. 106, 108 (1847).

moving an amendment to the question for reading the draft report a second time.[1] For the entry of an alternative draft report in the minutes of proceedings, see p 644.

Procedure where a committee is unable to agree upon a report. Where a committee is unable to agree upon a report, it may make a special report to that effect, together with the minutes of the evidence taken before it,[2] it may lay its minutes of proceedings before the House, thereby making public the text of any draft report which it may have considered and rejected, or merely report the minutes of the evidence taken before it to the House without any observations or expression of opinion.[3] This latter course has been followed by committees in other circumstances.[4]

Presentation of more than one report. Where, as is now generally the case for the majority of committees, a committee is authorized to report from time to time, it is at liberty to make as many reports as it thinks proper, and at convenient intervals as it makes progress in the business referred to its consideration. This authority gives power to the committee to report, not only upon the subject originally referred to it or upon the general subject of its appointment, but also upon matters occasionally referred to it.[5] When the matter referred to the consideration of a select committee has been one which either could be or requires to be reported upon in parts, the necessary power has been conferred upon the committee at the time of its appointment,[6] or the House has given leave subsequently to the committee, on the application of the chairman, to report, or to report its opinion (or observations), from time to time.[7]

If a committee, not having power to report from time to time, makes a report to the House, the committee is dissolved, and if further proceedings were desired, it would be necessary to revive the committee.[8]

Presentation of reports to the House. When a select committee has agreed to a report, or come to resolutions, the chairman or some other member is directed to make the report to the House, or to report the resolutions to the House as the circumstances of the case require. The clerk, acting on behalf of the chairman or other member of the committee charged with the duty of presenting the report to the House, delivers the appropriate entry to the Journal Office. The report is deemed to have been, and is entered in the

---

1 Denison 68–70. Select Committee on House of Commons (Procedure), First Report, HC 89 (1906) p ix; Select Committee on the Radio-telegraphic Convention, HC 246 (1907) p lii; Select Committee on Members' Interest (Declaration), HC 57 (1969) p xxxi.
2 Nationality of Married Women (Joint) Committee, HC 115 (1923) pp vi, xxiv–xxv; CJ (1923) 297; Wealth Tax Committee, HC 696 (1974–75).
3 Inland Revenue and Customs Establishment, HC 424 (1863) p xxiv; Scottish Affairs, HC 133 (1985–86); CJ (1985–86) 81.
4 See, for instance, Callan Schools, HC 255 (1873) pp iii, vi; Water Resources and Supplies (Joint) Committee, HC 121 (1934–35) p viii; CJ (1934–35) 317.
5 East India Finance Committee, First Report, HC 179 (1873) pp iii; Publications and Debates Reports Committee, HC 127 (1936–37). In the Commons a Procedure Committee has occasionally in the past been appointed and nominated early in the session and later given specific tasks on which it has reported, see eg Items referred CJ (1962–63) 35, 147, 246; Reports, ibid 128, 179, 269.
6 CJ (1847–48) 139; ibid (1906) 45; ibid (1920) 94.
7 CJ (1893–94) 517; ibid (1917–18) 215; ibid (1918) 200; ibid (1921) 104.
8 CJ (1801) 273; Parl Reg xv 50; CJ (1955–56) 68.

Votes and Proceedings and the Journal as having been, received and ordered to lie upon the Table and to be printed, and no other order can be made in reference to it the same day.[1] Committees frequently come to resolutions of their intentions, or the methods they propose to use to fulfil the requirements placed upon them by the House. These are often reported to the House and set out in full in the Votes and Proceedings and the Journal.[2] The reports regularly made by the Liaison Committee recommending the consideration of certain Estimates are also set out in full (see pp 704–705, 658).[3]

Under Standing Order No 119, whenever the House stands adjourned for more than two days, and any select committee having power to sit notwithstanding any adjournment of the House has agreed to a report, or has resolved that its minutes of proceedings should be printed or that the minutes of the evidence taken before it or before any sub-committee appointed by it or any papers laid before it should be reported to the House and printed, the committee has power to direct the printing of such report, minutes or papers, and such printing is done under the authority of the House. Any such reports, minutes or papers are deemed to have been reported to the House and are laid upon the Table when the House next sits.[4] Similar powers have been given to individual committees on occasions in the past.[5]

In some cases the House has ordered that only such number of copies of the report of a committee, with the appendix to it, be printed as shall be sufficient for the use of the Members of the House;[6] or that the report be printed, together with the minutes of the proceedings, but without the minutes of the evidence.[7]

In Session 1941–42 the House ordered that the report from the Committee of Privileges on a certain matter and the minutes of the evidence taken before the committee should be printed for the use of Members only and that not more than 615 copies should be printed. The order provided that any Member or any other person who disclosed, or purported to disclose, the contents of the reports, or the proceedings of, or the evidence taken before, the committee, or any portion or the substance thereof, except in a secret session and thereafter as the House might in secret session determine, should be guilty of a breach of privilege. The order provided further that the printed copies of the report were to be delivered to the Vote Office in sealed envelopes and could be obtained by Members only on applying personally to that Office. When the report had been considered by the House, Members were to return their copies to the Vote Office under cover. The Clerk of the House was to preserve two

---

1 Parl Deb (1810) 17, c318.
2 Eg CJ (1985–86) 21; Votes and Proceedings, 23 November 1988.
3 Eg CJ (1985–86) 75, etc.
4 CJ (1979–80) 805.
5 A committee which had received leave to sit during a prolonged adjournment of the House was given leave to send its report, if it thought fit and the House was not sitting, to the Clerk of the House, who was in that event to give directions for the printing of the report and its circulation, and to lay the report upon the Table at the next sitting of the House, CJ (1914–16) 22; ibid (1937–38) 395.
6 CJ (1801–02) 413; see also ibid (1835) 544.
7 CJ (1874) 204.

copies of the report and cause the rest to be destroyed.[1] On 19 December 1945 so much of the order as related to the disclosure or purported disclosure of the contents of the report or of any proceedings of, or evidence taken before, the committee was discharged, and the report was ordered to be reprinted without the minutes of evidence.[2]

In Session 1939–40, on the recommendation of the Select Committee on National Expenditure, a sub-committee which had been appointed by that committee to co-ordinate the work of the sub-committees appointed to examine the current expenditure of certain departments was given power, in cases where considerations of national security precluded the publishing of certain recommendations and of the arguments on which they were based, to address a memorandum to the Prime Minister for the consideration of the war cabinet. Whenever this power was exercised, however, the committee was to report the fact as soon as possible to the House.[3] A similar order was made in the next session.[4] In the four following sessions, however, power to address such memoranda to the Prime Minister was conferred on the committee itself, and not on a sub-committee.[5]

Special reports. Besides the report properly so called, relating to the subject-matter referred to the committee, it is sometimes necessary for a committee to make what is termed a special report in reference to some matter incidentally arising relating to the powers, functions or proceedings of the committee. Such reports are similar in point of form to, and are proceeded upon in the same manner as, the principal reports of the committee.[6]

A report from a committee desiring the instructions of the House as to the authority of the committee or the proper course for it to pursue,[7] or a report that a witness has failed to obey a summons to attend[8] or has refused to answer questions addressed to him by the committee,[9] are examples of such special reports. It is common practice for committees to make a special report incorporating government replies to their reports when such replies are made in the form of a memorandum to the relevant committee (see pp 648–650).

Any select committee may make a special report of any matters which it may think fit to bring to the notice of the House without obtaining the leave of the House (Standing Order No 115); prior to 30 March 1983 a select committee could make a special report, without leave, only if it had power to send for persons, papers and records.

---

1 CJ (1941–42) 123.
2 CJ (1945–46) 121.
3 CJ (1939–40) 146.
4 CJ (1940–41) 9.
5 CJ (1941–42) 10; ibid (1942–43) 9; ibid(1943–44) 14; ibid (1944–45) 31.
6 On 5 November 1940 a special report from a committee was read by the Clerk at the Table, after which a motion founded on the report was moved by the chairman of the committee, HC Deb (1939–40) 365, c 1205.
7 Parl Deb (1812) 23, c 883.
8 CJ (1920) 263.
9 CJ (1897) 361; ibid (1912–13) 543; ibid (1985–86) 282; the following day the committee made another Special Report to the effect that the witness had now answered the questions which he had previously refused to answer.

Unfinished inquiries. Committees appointed by standing order for a Parliament are terminated by a dissolution. In the case of committees appointed on a sessional basis, orders appointing them cease to have effect at prorogation.[1] When a committee finds that it lacks sufficient time to complete an inquiry, it reports the fact, together with any evidence which it may have taken, to the House.[2] Such evidence may or may not be ordered to be printed.[3] Occasionally a committee has made a special report explaining the circumstances to the House.[4] On occasions, a committee may recommend the appointment of a committee in the next session of Parliament to continue the inquiry. If a committee is re-appointed the evidence taken in the previous session is referred to the new committee.[5] When that committee reports, the House orders the printing of that evidence, together with any evidence taken in the current session of Parliament.[6]

A committee has been appointed to inquire into that portion of the reference to the original committee on which that committee had been precluded by lack of time from reporting in the preceding session.[7]

Where for any reason the evidence taken before the committee of the previous session has not been reported, the House has ordered the evidence to be laid before it, and when the evidence was presented has referred it to the committee.[8] When the latter presented its report the House ordered the evidence taken in the previous session to be printed.[9]

Where a committee is not expected to sit before the anticipated date of prorogation, and has not reported the minutes of the evidence taken before it, the House has ordered the minutes of the evidence to be laid before it, and when presented has ordered them to be printed.[10]

Publication of reports of committees. Any publication of a draft report which has been submitted to a committee, before such report has been agreed to by the committee and presented to the House,[11] may be treated as a contempt; and when the report of a committee, which had been presented to the House, but was not yet available to Members in printed or photocopied form, was communicated to the press, the Speaker stated that the more regular practice was that the Members of the House should be the first to be

---

1 HC Deb (1921) 148, c 177.
2 See, for instance, CJ (1929–30) 495; ibid (1930–31) 446; ibid (1932–33) 338; ibid (1969–70) 350.
3 CJ (1960–61) 338; ibid (1962–63) 313; ibid (1965–66) 113.
4 CJ (1969–70) 349 (Estimates Committee, Second Special Report, Education and Science Committee, Second Special Report; Overseas Aid, Fifth Special Report); ibid 350 (Race Relations Committee, Second Special Report; Procedure Committee, Second Special Report; Votes and Proceedings 13 May 1987 (Transport Committee, Second Special Report).
5 CJ (1930–31) 33; ibid (1931–32) 107; ibid (1933–34) 12; ibid (1958–59) 12, 13; ibid (1961–62) 13; ibid (1963–64) 14, 15; ibid (1966–67) 46; ibid (1969–70) 21.
6 CJ (1961-62) 70; ibid (1963–64) 62; ibid (1965–66) 113; ibid (1966–67) 177, 199; ibid (1975–76) 122; ibid (1981–82) 172.
7 CJ (1890–91) 139.
8 CJ (1857) 326, 339; ibid (1859) 321; ibid (1940–41) 23, 24; ibid (1950) 39, 42; ibid (1952–53) 6, 10; ibid (1962–63) 15; ibid (1969–70) 14, 41.
9 CJ (1940–41) 24; ibid (1950) 119; ibid (1952–53) 240. Cf CJ (1953–54) 40.
10 CJ (1934–35) 349, 350.
11 CJ (1831–32) 360.

put in possession of the results of the deliberations of a select committee.[1] The practice was modified in 1967–68 by the terms of Standing Order No 116 which provides that all select committees should have power to authorize the Clerk of the House to supply copies of their reports to officers of government departments, to those witnesses who have given evidence to committees or their sub-committees as these committees consider appropriate, to lobby journalists and to such other press representatives as the committee thinks fit. Copies are to be supplied after they have been laid on the Table, but not more than forty-eight hours before the intended time of publication of the report; and they are to be regarded as strictly confidential until such publication.[2]

In its report on Premature Disclosure of Proceedings in Select Committees,[3] the Privileges Committee recommended that in the event of premature disclosure of the content of a report which a committee has under consideration, or which it has agreed but not yet published, certain procedures should be followed. With the subsequent addition of references to the Liaison Committee,[4] those procedures are:

(1) The committee should carry out its own investigation to try to discover the source of a leak, in particular by formally asking all members of the committee and the committee's staff if they can explain how the leak came about;

(2) the committee should decide whether or not the leak constitutes a substantial interference, or the likelihood of such, with the work of the committee, with the select committee system or the functions of the House;

(3) it should inform the Liaison Committee, so that it may take a view;

(4) in the light of the views of the Liaison Committee it should make a special report to the House to that effect, outlining the action it has taken and the conclusions it has reached;

(5) such a special report would automatically be referred to the Privileges Committee without a debate in the House: it is then for that committee to consider the matter and make a report to the House, whereupon the House would consider its recommendations.

The committee also made recommendations in respect of procedures select committees should adopt to lessen the risks of premature disclosure taking place. The House agreed to the committee's report in March 1986.[5]

Government replies to reports. It is now the regular practice that where a select committee has made a report relating to government administration or policy, the government will reply to the committee's recommendations

---

1 Parl Deb (1893–94) 14, c 812; HC Deb (1947–48) 454, cc 1125–1126; HC Deb (1968–69) 780, cc 1042–1046.

2 Procedure Committee, Second Report, HC 295 (1963–64); CJ (1966–67) 45; ibid (1967–68) 18, 365, 403–4.

3 Privileges Committee, Second Report, HC 555 (1984–85). A fuller description of the practices which the Privileges Committee recommended that a committee should adopt when a leak of its confidential proceedings comes to light and the guidelines to which it should have regard in determining whether the leak is of sufficient seriousness as to constitute substantial interference, is contained in the Report (paras 51 to 54 and 63 to 70 and the final paragraph of the summary of conclusions and recommendations).

4 Liaison Committee Proceedings, HC (1985–86) 618, p vi.

5 CJ (1985–86) 252. For an example of the procedure, see Second Special Report of the Environment Committee, HC (1985–86) 211; First Report from the Privileges Committee (1985–86) 376.

and observations. Such a reply may be published as a command paper[1] or submitted by the department most directly concerned as a memorandum to the committee. In the latter case the usual practice is for the committee to publish the observations appended to a special report[2] which may, or may not, express the views of the committee on the reply. Reply by memorandum was the almost invariable practice between 1945 and the mid-1960s.[3] Thereafter reply by command paper came to be more used.[4] Since the establishment in 1979 of the committees related to government departments, replies have generally been made by command paper or by memorandum. Occasionally the reply has been given in the House in debate[5] and on one occasion in debate in standing committee.[6] In some cases, chairmen of committees have received a letter from a minister replying to a report, and the committee has subsequently published the letter as a special report.[7] Occasionally a reply to a report has also been given in a written answer to a parliamentary question.[8] In other cases a memorandum submitted by a department together with oral evidence given by a minister upon it constituted the reply.[9]

In the case of the Committee of Public Accounts, treasury minutes are laid before the House each session embodying the Government's views on previous committee reports.[10] The treasury minute co-ordinates the replies of all government departments. Likewise, in the case of Northern Ireland, a Northern Ireland Department of Finance memorandum, corresponding to a treasury minute, has been laid.[11]

In whatever form they are made, replies are normally expected by all committees engaged in scrutinizing government activity and are requested if they are not forthcoming. Following recommendations made by the Select Committee on Procedure in 1978,[12] it was agreed by government departments that replies should if possible be made within two months of the publication of a report. In some circumstances a longer delay may be considered permissible when those circumstances have been explained to

1 Eg replies to the reports on the Foreign Affairs Committee in session 1987–88, Cm 432 (Famine in the Horn of Africa), Cm 505 (Current UK Policy towards the Iran–Iraq conflict), Cm 476 (Political Impact of the Process of Arms Control and Disarmament), etc.
2 Eg Overseas Development Committee, HC 318 (1974), HC 233 (1974–75), etc; Expenditure Committee, HC 30 (1973–74), Second Special Report; Welsh Affairs Committee, HC 122 (1980–81), First Special Report; Home Affairs Committee, HC 737 (1987–88), Second Special Report; Treasury and Civil Service Committee, HC 675 (1987–88) Fourth Special Report.
3 There were exceptions, CJ (1954–55) 55; Nationalised Industries Committee, HC 166 (1961–62) pp 13 ff. Before the second world war departmental observations to committee reports were presented as treasury minutes or command papers.
4 See HC Deb (1969–70) 791, c 406.
5 HC Deb (1979–80) 984, c 289–292.
6 Sixth Standing Committee on Statutory Instruments, etc, 20 February 1980.
7 Third Special Report from the Select Committee on Science and Technology, HC 40 (1968–69); Third Special Report from the Expenditure Committee, HC 262 (1974–75).
8 Eg HC Deb (1968–69) 787, c 24; ibid (1979–80) 988, cc 359–60; ibid (1980–81) 992, cc 150–152. In one case where a report dealt with a Statutory Instrument which was the subject of a motion for a negative resolution the minister's reply to the debate on the motion constituted the Government's reply to the report, HC Deb (1987–88) 129, cc 477–80.
9 Science and Technology Committee, HC 63 (1972–73) and HC 473 (1971–72).
10 CJ (1969–70); ibid (1970–71) 100; ibid (1968–69) 10; ibid (1967–68) 15; ibid (1978–79) 43.
11 CJ (1978–79) 43; ibid (1982–83) 101.
12 First Report from the Select Committee on Procedure, HC 588–I (1977–78) pp lxxii–lxxiv.

the committee concerned. Following a published reply a committee has invited a minister to give evidence on the progress made in implementing recommendations,[1] or has taken further evidence and made a further report.[2] The Committee of Public Accounts frequently asks the accounting officers from government departments to report on actions taken on reports in preceding sessions. Some committees have also asked departments for progress reports on recommendations previously made by them.[3]

Consideration of reports of select committees. The report of a select committee may be taken into consideration in pursuance either of an order made upon a previous day,[4] or of a motion that the report be now read,[5] or be now taken into consideration.[6] According to present practice a motion for appointing the report of a committee for consideration on a future day requires notice, and cannot be made on the presentation of the report.

On the consideration of a report, motions may be made expressing the agreement,[7] or the disagreement of the House with the report as a whole or with certain paragraphs thereof,[8] or for agreeing to the recommendations contained in the report generally or with certain exceptions;[9] or motions may be made which are founded upon, or enforce, the resolutions of the committee,[10] or are otherwise relevant to the subject-matter of the report, or the business of the committee. Motions may also be made upon consideration of the report of a select committee for the recommittal of the report.[11]

Debates on select committee reports now usually take place upon motions to take note of a report.[12] Such motions often refer also to any document setting out government observations on the report (see above).[13]

Under arrangements introduced in 1960[14] for giving the House additional opportunities for reviewing the control of public expenditure, reports of

1 Science and Technology Committee, Minutes of Evidence, HC 63–i (1972–73). See too, Science and Technology First Special Report, HC 181 (1971–72), letters exchanged between the Prime Minister and the Chairman of the Committee.
2 Expenditure Committee, Sixth Report, HC 167 (1973–74); Industry and Trade Committee, Second Report, HC 192 (1981–82), and Fourth Report, HC 308 (1981–82); Environment Committee, Fourth Report, HC 446 (1983–84), First Special Report, HC 51 (1985–86), and First Report, HC 270 (1987–88).
3 Eg Energy Committee, Minutes of Evidence, HC 513 (1987–88), App; Transport Committee, Minutes of Evidence, HC 398 (1987–88).
4 CJ (1801–02) 413, 481; ibid (1806) 147, 152; ibid (1876) 405; ibid (1888) 510; special reports, ibid (1830–31) 168; ibid (1875) 134; ibid (1887) 399.
5 CJ (1834) 471; ibid (1854) 188; ibid (1859) 175.
6 CJ (1857–58) 348; ibid (1862–63) 377; ibid (1905) 359; ibid (1907) 449; ibid (1908) 505; ibid (1910) 207; ibid (1916) 215; ibid (1917–18) 303; ibid (1960–61) 181.
7 CJ (1705–08) 597; ibid (1772–74) 649, 740; ibid (1834) 471; ibid (1854) 188; ibid (1888) 511; ibid (1934–35) 31; ibid (1967–68) 219.
8 CJ (1809) 413; ibid (1854) 188.
9 CJ (1948–49) 112; ibid (1950) 170.
10 CJ (1839) 352; ibid (1845) 642; ibid (1852–53) 766, 770; ibid (1857–58) 348; ibid (1887) 306; ibid (1889) 363; ibid (1892) 157; ibid (1966–67) 288; ibid (1968–69) 291.
11 CJ (1865) 252.
12 For recent examples see CJ (1978–79) 63, 91; ibid (1979–80) 200; ibid (1985–86) 96.
13 Eg CJ (1977–78) 401; ibid (1978–79) 63. In 1986 the Trade and Industry Committee's report on the Tin Industry was debated on a motion to debate the Government's response, CJ (1985–86) 475.
14 HC Deb (1959–60) 627, cc 1292–1293.

the Committee of Public Accounts of the previous session and the related treasury minutes have been debated early in the new session (see also pp 660–661).

When the House debates a matter to which a select committee report is relevant, the Order Paper often includes, with the agreement of the Member in charge of the particular item of business, an italicized reference to the report in question.

Recommittal of reports. The report of a select committee, may be recommitted in whole[1] or in part[2] to the committee, or it may be recommitted and the order of reference amended.[3]

A motion for the recommittal of a report may be made upon the consideration of the report or as a substantive motion.

The effect of recommitting a report is to undo all that has previously been done in the House with reference to the report, and to throw back the subject into the hands of the committee for revision or completion, or for whatever other purpose the recommittal may be ordered; though, of course, it does not impose upon the committee any obligation to go again over the whole matter, or to re-examine the witnesses already fully and properly examined. A recommittal generally takes place for some cause which sufficiently indicates to the committee what it is expected to do, and, hence, it is not usual for instructions to be given on recommittal; but the committee is to gather from the sense of the House in such proceedings what method it is to pursue.[4] When a report is thus recommitted, the committee, with all its powers, is thereby revived.

For the recommittal of reports to the Standing Orders Committee see p 822.

Select committee returns

Each session the House calls for the production of a paper giving statistics 'relating to the membership, work, costs and staff of select committees with so much of the same information as is relevant to the Chairmen's Panel and the Court of Referees'.[5] The return lists every select committee which met in the previous session, its members and staff, the number of meetings held and the number each member attended, the specialist advice it received, the visits (if any) it made both in the United Kingdom and abroad and their cost. It also gives information on the categories of witnesses who appeared before it, the number of meetings at which evidence was taken, any divisions which occurred in the committee, reports made, and the Government replies it received to those reports. Itemized information on Committee expenditure for the most recent financial year and the costs to HMSO of printing and publishing are also included. Entries relating to each committee are prefaced by an alphabetical list of the names of Members approached to serve on select committees and tables summarising expenditure and staffing infor-

---

1 CJ (1826–27) 318; ibid (1833) 583; ibid (1837) 478; ibid (1865) 252.
2 CJ (1772–74) 260.
3 CJ (1814–16) 430.
4 Parl Deb (1805) 5, c 163.
5 Eg Votes and Proceedings (1988–89) 56.

mation appear at the end. Returns relating to select committees have been made for each session since 1848.[1]

A substantial revision in the form of the return was made in session 1980–81 with further additions from session 1985–86 onwards. The return is published by Her Majesty's Stationery Office as a House of Commons paper.

Procedure in select committees on public bills

The procedure in select committees on public bills only is described below, the procedure in select committees on hybrid bills, private bills and provisional order bills being dealt with elsewhere (see pp 519–524, 886–887). The procedure in special standing committees on public bills is described on pp 935–939, 954–955.

In a select committee on a public bill, when the evidence, if any, has been concluded, the clauses of the bill are considered. The rules which govern the admissibility of amendments in a Committee of the whole House apply equally to proceedings in a select committee, but the chairman has not the power of selecting which amendments or new clauses shall be proposed, or of putting the question 'That the clause (as amended) stand part of the bill' forthwith.

In dealing with clauses or amendments which involve charges on public funds a select committee is subject to precisely the same restrictions as a Committee of the whole House (see pp 495–496).

On 17 July 1843, the Speaker drew the attention of the House to a clause inserted in a bill by a select committee which, unsanctioned by a financial resolution, charged the payment of certain salaries upon the Consolidated Fund, and the bill was consequently recommitted to the committee.[2] In the session of 1924–25 the Select Committee on the Sandwich Port and Haven Bill inserted in one of the clauses of the bill a new subsection which in terms imposed an obligation on the Secretary of State to pay £5,000 towards the construction of a certain bridge, though it was intended that the obligation should fall on the purchasers of the undertaking. When the bill was considered in a Committee of the whole House, this subsection was omitted, and a new clause substituted making it clear upon whom the obligation was to fall.[3]

A select committee may, if so empowered or directed by an instruction, consolidate two or more bills into one bill,[4] or divide a bill into two or more bills,[5] or extend the operation of a bill which is, by its title, limited to a part only of the United Kingdom to another part, or to the whole of the Kingdom.[6] When two or more bills of the same subject-matter are committed to a select committee, the committee adopts one bill as a basis for its proceed-

1 CJ (1848) 986; ibid (1853) 327.
2 CJ (1843) 487.
3 HC Deb (1925) 186, cc 1759 ff.
4 CJ (1906) 374.
5 CJ (1868–69) 192.
6 CJ (1870) 113; ibid (1882) 17.

ings, and reports the other bill or bills without amendment, with a special report explaining the course it has followed.[1]

If, in addition to reporting the bill with or without amendments, the committee desires to inform the House of any matters relating to the bill, it makes a special report.[2]

If a committee is unable to complete its inquiry, or to complete the consideration of the bill, it makes a special report to that effect, and reports the bill without amendment.[3]

> A committee, thinking it inexpedient, the session being well advanced, to complete the consideration of the bill, has negatived such clauses as it had been unable to consider, and the schedules to the bill, and reported the bill, so amended, to the House with a special report setting forth its reasons for so doing.[4]
>
> A committee has reported a private Member's bill without amendment at the same time making a special report of conclusions and recommendations for inclusion in forthcoming legislation by the Government.[5]

Inability of select committees to decide against bills. A select committee to which a bill has been committed has no power to put an end to the bill,[6] though a committee has negatived all the clauses and the preamble of a bill, and made a special report to that effect to the House.[7] Where a committee has been of opinion that a bill should not be further proceeded with, it has made a special report to that effect, and reported the bill, without amendment, to the House.[8]

A report from a select committee that it is not expedient to proceed further with a bill is usually acquiesced in by the House, the bill being ordered to lie upon the Table.

> In the case of the Architects (Registration) Bill 1927, where the committee, after going through the bill, negatived the question, 'That the chairman do report the bill, as amended, to the House', and made a special report to that effect to the House, further action was not taken by the House.[9]
>
> On 16 June 1871, the Select Committee of the Commons on the Benefices Resignation Bill [Lords], to whom the Sequestration of Benefices Bill had been committed, having gone through the latter and disagreed to several clauses and to the preamble thereof, negatived the question, 'That the chairman do report the bill, as amended, to the House'. Upon consideration this was agreed to be irregular, and at the next sitting the committee resolved, on the motion of the chairman, that the decision should be rescinded, and reported the bill, as amended, to the House,

1 CJ (1892) 277; ibid (1893–94) 396.
2 Eg Select Committee on the Armed Forces Bill, HC 253 (1980–81).
3 CJ (1895) 312, 317; ibid (1908) 482; Fourth Special Report of the Select Committee on the Abortion Bill, HC 692–II (1974–75) p viii.
4 Petit Juries (Ireland) Bill Committee, Proceedings, HC 390 (1867–68) pp 3, 4.
5 HC 333 (1972–73) p iv (Anti-Discrimination (No 2) Bill).
6 Parl Deb (1864) 176, c 99.
7 CJ (1867–68) 305.
8 CJ (1919) 413; ibid (1929–30) 424.
9 HC 105 (1927) pp iii, xi.

with a special report stating that they did not consider it expedient to proceed any further with the bill.[1]

Reference of bills as documents to select committees. When a bill which has not been read a second time is referred to the consideration of a committee, the committee does not go through the bill clause by clause, but simply inquires into the merits of the bill, or takes the proposals contained in the bill into consideration in the same manner as proposals embodied in any other document. No report or recommendation of the committee with regard to the bill can have any effect whatever by way of advancing the bill a stage in the House.[2]

Select committees regularly appointed

With the exception of the Standing Orders Committee, which is appointed under a Standing Order relating to Private Business (see p 819), short descriptions of those select committees regularly appointed are set out below.[3]

Select Committees related to government departments. In 1978 a report of the Select Committee on Procedure recommended the setting up of a new select committee structure based on the areas of responsibility of the principal departments of state.[4] The principle of the recommendation was accepted by the House in the following year and embodied in standing orders.[5]

Standing Order No 130 provides for the appointment of select committees to examine the expenditure, administration and policy of government departments and their associated public bodies, and similar matters within the responsibilities of the Secretary of State for Northern Ireland. The committees appointed under this order, the departments of government with which they are concerned, the maximum numbers of each committee and the quorum in each case are currently as follows:

Name of committee	Principal government departments concerned	Maximum number of members	Quorum
Agriculture	Ministry of Agriculture, Fisheries and Food	11	3
Defence	Ministry of Defence	11	3

1 HC 266 (1871) pp iv, ix, x.
2 Parl Deb (1899) 70, cc 406–407. For recent examples of a committee commenting on current legislation see eg Fourth Report from the Transport Committee, HC 344 (1980–81); Second Report from the Transport Committee, HC 38 (1984–85).
3 While no permanent standing order covers the appointment of a Select Committee on Procedure, such a committee has been appointed in some form in most recent Parliaments either with general or narrow orders of reference eg Select Committee on Procedure, 1976–79; Sessional Committee on Procedure, 1975–76 to 1977–78; Select Committee on Procedure (Supply), 1980–81; Select Committee on Procedure (Finance), 1981–83; Select Committee on Procedure, 1981–83; Select Committee on Procedure, 1988.
4 First Report from the Select Committee on Procedure, HC 588–I (1977–78) p cxxv.
5 HC Deb (1979–80) 969, cc 33–252.

Education, Science and Arts	Department of Education and Science	11	3
Employment	Department of Employment	11	3
Energy	Department of Energy	11	3
Environment	Department of the Environment	11	3
Foreign Affairs	Foreign and Commonwealth Office	11	3
Home Affairs	Home Office	11	3
Scottish Affairs	Scottish Office	13	5
Social Services	Department of Health and Social Security	11	3
Trade and Industry	Department of Trade and Industry	11	3
Transport	Department of Transport	11	3
Treasury and Civil Service	Treasury, Management and Personnel Office, Board of Inland Revenue, Board of Customs and Excise	11	3
Welsh Affairs	Welsh Office	11	3

The standing order also provides for the appointment of one sub-committee each by the Foreign Affairs Committee, the Home Affairs Committee and the Treasury and Civil Service Committee and for the appointment of a sub-committee on nationalised industries. All the committees have power to appoint specialist advisers, and, unless the House otherwise orders, their members are nominated for the remainder of the Parliament (see p 612). Amendments to the standing order in December 1983 increased the maximum number of members of several committees from nine to eleven and, in order to help facilitate further co-ordination of their work, gave the committees power in cases of common interest to communicate their evidence to each other and to meet concurrently for certain purposes.[1]

Nomination and discharge of the members of committees appointed under Standing Order No 130 are functions of the Committee of Selection. Notice of the relevant motions must be given at least two sitting days previously and must be made on behalf of the Committee of Selection either by the chairman or by a member of the Committee (Standing Order No 104(2)).

In the first session of the present Parliament the Committee of Selection twice reported to the House its inability to nominate the Scottish Affairs Committee,[2] and the House subsequently agreed to a Resolution acquiescing to this state of affairs.[3]

---

1 SO No 130(5); HC Deb 14 December 1983, c 1112. The first power has been used extensively; the second has not yet been used.
2 Special Reports, Votes and Proceedings (1987–88) 9 December, 29 June; HC Deb (1987–88) c 397.
3 HC Deb (1988–89) 144, cc 326–396.

Select Committee on European Legislation. A Select Committee on European Legislation[1] was first appointed in Session 1974 following the recommendations of the Select Committee on European Community Secondary Legislation. The committee's functions, as set out in Standing Order No 127, are to consider draft proposals by the Commission of the European Communities for legislation and other documents published for submission to the Council of Ministers or to the European Council, whether or not such documents originate from the Commission, to report its opinion as to whether such proposals or other documents raise questions of legal or political importance, to give its reasons for its opinion, to report what matters of principle or policy may be affected thereby, and to what extent they may affect the law of the United Kingdom, and to make recommendations for the further consideration of such documents by the House. The committee is appointed and nominated for the whole of the Parliament, consists of sixteen members (with a quorum of five) and is empowered to appoint sub-committees and to draw upon the assistance of specialist advisers; it also has leave to confer with the equivalent committee in the Lords (see p 670). The committee is assisted by one of the Speaker's Counsel.[2] The committee's practice is to make regular reports to the House. It hears evidence from time to time, usually in public. The procedures for the scrutiny of Community legislation are more fully described on pp 773–776.

Select Committee on House of Commons (Services). As a result of the passing of control of that part of the Palace of Westminster and its precincts occupied by or on behalf of the House of Commons into the hands of the Speaker on behalf of the House, and in the light of a select committee report,[3] the House since 1965–66 has regularly appointed a select committee to advise Mr Speaker on the control of that accommodation and the services therein.[4] The committee is now appointed under Standing Order No 125 and nominated for the duration of the Parliament.

Most of the detailed work of the Services Committee is conducted through sub-committees with specified areas of responsibility. These have regularly included sub-committees on Accommodation and Administration (which considers all aspects of accommodation for Members and their staff, and general services and facilities for Members); Catering (which considers the organisation of, and services provided by, the Refreshment Department) and the Library (which considers the organisation of, and services provided by, the House of Commons Library). In recent Parliaments the Committee has also appointed sub-committees on Computers (which makes recommendations on computer developments in the House) and on New Building (which considers the future accommodation needs of the House, and in particular the provision and design of new Parliamentary buildings). The

---

1 HC 463–I (1972–73). Until December 1976 the Committee was known as the Select Committee on European Secondary Legislation, etc; and had terms of reference which only covered documents submitted by the Commission to the Council of Ministers, CJ (1976–77) 26. In 1976 it became the Select Committee on European Legislation, etc; with wider terms of reference. A further slight change took place in March 1983 when the Committee's title became the Select Committee on European Legislation.
2 HC Deb (1974) 872, c 524 w; SO No 127(3).
3 Select Committee on the Palace of Westminster, HC 285 (1964–65).
4 CJ (1965–66) 44; ibid (1983–84) 54.

sub-committees have the assistance of the appropriate officers of the House, who regularly attend their meetings in an advisory capacity.

In respect of minor matters, when no new service or policy is involved, sub-committees have a limited degree of delegated authority to make recommendations directly to the Speaker or to the relevant officers of the House. In most cases, however, the Resolutions of sub-committees are considered by the full committee before being reported to the Speaker for his approval; and where important matters of general interest to Members or significant expenditure of public funds are involved, the committee usually makes reports to the House, setting out its recommendations. The minutes of the proceedings of the committee, which detail not only the Resolutions come to but also include an indication of other matters considered, are laid on the Table and printed after each meeting, for the information of Members.

Following the approval by the House of its Report on Access to the Precincts of the House[1], the Committee has since April 1989 been empowered to vary in individual cases the limit of three photo-identity passes for the Palace of Westminster which may be held by each Member's personal staff, and to regulate the allocation of passes to other individuals and organisations. The Committee also compiles a register (known as the 'approved list') of groups of Members which meet the minimum criteria laid down by the House, on the Committee's recommendation, for the membership, election of officers, and organisation of meetings of unofficial all-party and parliamentary groups.[2]

In 1989 the Select Committee and its sub-committees (subject to the approval of the committee) were given power to adjourn from place to place.[3]

Liaison Committee. In 1979 the House set up a select committee called the Liaison Committee to consider general matters relating to the work of select committees,[4] and to give such advice on their work as was sought by the House of Commons Commission. The committee has been nominated to include the chairmen of most select committees and a representative of the smaller parties. This has given it a membership of about 20, of whom six comprise a quorum. The committee has the usual powers to send for persons, papers and records, to sit notwithstanding any adjournment of the House, and to report from time to time (Standing Order No 131).

The committee brings together the collective experience of select committees, and enables their joint views to be expressed when necessary. It has taken steps to reduce the possibility of two or more committees inquiring into the same subject. For its work in overseeing expenditure on foreign travel on behalf of the House of Commons Commission, see p 627.

On 19 July 1982 the House placed on the committee the additional duty of recommending how the time for debate in the House should be allocated on any day or half day allotted for the consideration of estimates (see p 705).

---

1 HC 580 (1987–88); Votes and Proceedings (1988–89) 30 January 1989.
2 Votes and Proceedings (1987–88) 9 November 1988.
3 Votes and Proceedings (1988–89) 26 May 1989.
4 An unofficial chairmen's liaison committee had existed in the period 1967–1979. For a description of its activities, see First Report from the Procedure Committee, HC 588–I (1977–78) paras 6.54 ff.

Select Committee on Members' Interests. The House resolved on 12 June 1975 (see p 386) that a Register of Members' Interests (see p 388) be established as soon as possible in accordance with the proposals made in the Report of the Select Committee on Members' Interests (Declaration).[1] A first edition of the Register was published in November of that year. In the next session a select committee was appointed 'to examine the arrangements made for the compilation, maintenance and accessibility of the Register of Members' Interests; to consider any proposals made by Members or others as to the form and contents of the Register; to consider any specific complaints made in relation to the registering or declaring of interests; to consider what classes of person (if any) other than Members ought to be required to register; and to make recommendations upon these and any other matters which are relevant'. The committee consisted of thirteen Members and was appointed for the remainder of that Parliament. A like committee of thirteen Members with the same order of reference was appointed on 18 July 1979 for the remainder of the Parliament, and is now the subject of Standing Order No 128.

The report of the Select Committee on Members' Interests (Declaration) whose recommendations relating to the arrangements for the registration of interests were agreed to by the House in 1975 (see above) requires the Registrar of Members' Interests, when he has compiled a Register at the beginning of each Parliament, to put it before the committee; and it is the committee's duty to direct when it and subsequent periodic editions shall be laid before the House and printed.

The committee and its predecessors have made various reports to the House setting out their interpretation of the scope of various registrable interests and have drawn the attention of the House to the failure of certain Members to register their interests. In 1985 following an inquiry into parliamentary lobbying the committee recommended the establishment of three new registers in respect of certain classes of persons other than Members and these were established by the House later that year.[2] A description of these registers is given on p 390.

It has been the general practice of the committee to sit in private. However, in Session 1987–88, the committee decided to admit the public, as a general rule, when taking evidence in respect of its inquiry into parliamentary lobbying.

Select Committee on Parliamentary Commissioner for Administration. Under the Parliamentary Commissioner Act 1967 the Commissioner is to lay an annual report on the performance of his functions before each House of Parliament. He may also make other reports with respect to his functions or special reports under section 10(3) of the Act. From Session 1966–67, the House of Commons has appointed a committee to examine the reports and matters in connection therewith.[3] The committee has stated that it is not its function to re-try cases reported by the Commissioner or to review his findings by going over ground already covered by his investigations.[4] The committee has considered in its reports general

1 HC 102 (1974–75).
2 First Report, HC 408 (1984–85); CJ (1985–86) 97.
3 Eg CJ (1966–67) 447, 489; ibid CJ (1974–75) 89; ibid (1983–84) 252.
4 Second Report, HC 350 (1967–68) p xii; First Report, HC 49 (1969–70) p iv.

topics of Members' use of the Commissioner and the Commissioner's functions; and has reported its comments on the significance to the scope and functions of the Commissioner of an individual case on which he reported.[1] The committee has the help of the Parliamentary Commissioner; in session 1975–76 it was given the power to appoint specialist advisers, and from session 1979–80 this power has been included in the appointing order. The committee is now appointed and nominated for the whole of a Parliament.[2] The committee usually sits in public when taking evidence except where publicity might be against the interests of a particular complainant.

By the National Health Service (Scotland) Act 1972 and the National Health Service Reorganisation Act 1973 a Health Service Commissioner for England, for Scotland and for Wales, was appointed, and the Parliamentary Commissioner has been appointed to this office. He makes an annual report on his work as Health Service Commissioner to the appropriate Secretary of State, who lays it before each House of Parliament. From session 1973–74 the order of reference of the committee has been extended to enable it also to examine these reports, and such other reports to the Secretary of State as the latter may lay before Parliament. In 1980 the order of reference of the committee was extended to enable it to consider reports from the Parliamentary Commissioner for Northern Ireland.

Committee of Privileges. It has been the practice of the House of Commons from the seventeenth century to appoint a Committee of Privileges.[3] It was until recently customary to appoint the committee by means of one of the sessional orders at the opening of every session, and to nominate it at an early date in the session instead of waiting until some matter had been referred to its consideration.[4] Since 1974–75, however, the appointment of the committee has been extended to last for the duration of the Parliament by standing order, and its seventeen members have been nominated for the duration of the Parliament; these requirements were then incorporated in Standing Order No 121. The quorum is six. The scope of any inquiry comprises all matters relevant to the complaint (see also, pp 135–136).[5] The committee does not sit in public.[6]

Committee of Public Accounts. The Committee of Public Accounts was first appointed in 1861.[7] Standing Order No 122 now provides for its examination of the appropriation accounts and of 'such other accounts laid before Parliament as the committee may think fit'. The number of members of the committee is fixed by the same standing order at not more than fifteen. By tradition its chairman is chosen from the Opposition. He is also *ex officio* a

---

1 First Report, HC 258 (1967–68).
2 SO No 126.
3 The appointment of the committee was discontinued in 1833, but was revived in 1837 and has been continued since that year.
4 During the period comprising the years 1841 to 1903 inclusive it was not the practice to nominate the committee unless some matter had arisen which had been referred to its consideration. Since then, however, it has regularly been so nominated, except in 1910, 1913–18 inclusive, 1920–22 inclusive and most recently in session 1987–88 when, no matters having been referred to the committee, it was not nominated.
5 CJ (1947–48) 23.
6 On 10 February 1987 a motion to admit strangers at certain sittings was negatived on the casting vote of the chairman, First Report, HC 365 (1986–87) p xii.
7 CJ (1861) 130.

member of the Public Accounts Commission (see p 194). The committee does not seek to concern itself with policy; its interest is in whether policy is carried out efficiently, effectively and economically. Its main functions are to see that public moneys are applied for the purposes prescribed by Parliament, that extravagance and waste are minimised and that sound financial practices are encouraged in estimating and contracting, and in administration generally. The committee also has a particular duty to look at excess votes, the questions on which cannot be put under the provisions of Standing Order No 53 unless the committee has reported that it sees 'no objection to the sums necessary being provided by excess vote'.[1]

The committee bases its work on reports by the Comptroller and Auditor General, namely those presented to Parliament under section 9 of the National Audit Act 1983, together with those on the appropriation and other accounts laid before Parliament. The committee also considers memoranda submitted to it by the Comptroller and Auditor General (either on his own initiative or in response to requests made by the committee, and treasury minutes containing the Government's observations on previous committee reports. The Comptroller and Auditor General is required to take into account any proposals made by the committee in determining his programme of economy, efficiency and effectiveness examinations.[2] The committee also reports on the Northern Ireland Accounts, with the assistance of the Comptroller and Auditor General (Northern Ireland). The Comptroller and Auditor General (see p 198) attends all meetings, and regularly appears (as does the Treasury Officer of Accounts) as a witness. Other witnesses are normally the permanent secretaries of government departments, who (as accounting officers) have a direct and personal responsibility for their departments' expenditure.

In recent years the committee has begun to hold many of its meetings in public. It has also been given power to travel. At least one day each session is provided for debate in the House of its reports and the Government's replies to them (see pp 651–652).

The chairman of the committee has to give his agreement to any motion for an address to appoint a new Comptroller and Auditor General (see p 198)[3].

Committee of Selection. Though much of the work of the Committee of Selection is related to the consideration of nominations to committees on public bills and other business committed or referred to a standing committee, the Committee of Selection itself is appointed under a standing order relating to Private Business.[4] The committee consists of nine members of whom three are a quorum. Members who are Whips of their political parties have usually been among those nominated. For the functions of the committee so far as they relate to public bills and other business committed to a standing committee, see pp 590–596; so far as they relate to select committees, see p 612, p 615; so far as they relate to hybrid bills and private business, see pp 521–522 and 882–887.

---

1 CJ (1981–82) 479.
2 National Audit Act 1983, s 1(3).
3 CJ (1976–77) 118. For other aspects of the chairman's functions see HC Deb (1986–87) 109, cc 245–249.
4 SO 109.

Select Committee on Sound Broadcasting. The Select Committee on Sound Broadcasting was first appointed in 1978.[1] Its terms of reference, now set out in Standing Order No 129, are 'to give directions and perform other duties in accordance with the provisions of the Resolution of the House of 26 July 1977 in relation to Sound Broadcasting and to make recommendations thereon to the House'. It consists of six members, of whom two constitute a quorum, and it has power to join with the Lords committee on the same subject (see pp 670, 584–585). Its principal function is to oversee, on behalf of the House, the use to which the recordings and live broadcasts of Commons proceedings are put. The committee was not nominated in session 1987–88 or in session 1988–89. In 1989 the House resolved, that; 'notwithstanding the provisions of Standing Order No 129 (Select Committee on Sound Broadcasting), the Select Committee on Televising of Proceedings of the House' (a select committee appointed persuant to the decision of the House to permit an experiment in televising the proceedings) 'should have power to give directions and perform other duties in accordance with the provisions of the Resolution of the House of 26th July 1977, in relation to sound broadcasting, and to make recommendations thereon to the House'.

Select Committee on Statutory Instruments. This committee was first appointed in session 1943–44. It has now been subsumed in the Joint Committee on Statutory Instruments whose powers and terms of reference are set out in Standing Order No 124. It retains a separate existence in connection with statutory instruments laid before the Commons only (see pp 552–553).

3. JOINT COMMITTEES OF LORDS AND COMMONS

Appointment

Joint committees composed of an equal number of Members of each House[2] are appointed from time to time at the instance of one House or the other.

A joint committee may be appointed to consider a particular matter or bill, or to consider a number of bills, or to consider all matters of a particular class arising during the course of the session or such of them as are referred to the committee by either House. The proposal for the appointment of a joint committee on a matter, or of a standing joint committee, may originate with either House, but a proposal for the committal of a bill to a joint committee can regularly originate only with the House in which the bill is pending.

If either House considers it expedient that a joint committee should be appointed to consider some matter, or that a bill should be committed to a

---

1 CJ (1977–78) 169. At the beginning of session 1979–80 it was appointed and nominated for the duration of the Parliament, CJ (1979–80) 139.

2 In the case of the Joint Committee on House of Lords Reform (1961–62 and 1962–63) the membership was unequal. The Lords appointed twelve members and the Commons eleven, CJ (1961–62) 209, 212; ibid (1962–63) 17, 18. The proposal put forward by the Commons to appoint a joint committee entitled the Special Commission on Oil Sanctions provided for five Members of the Commons and a motion to appoint four Members of the Lords was negatived, CJ (1978–79) 138; LJ (1978–79) 199; see too pp 667–668 (Joint Committee on Consolidation, etc, Bills).

joint committee, it passes a resolution to that effect, and sends a message to the other House to inform it of the resolution and to desire its agreement. If the other House concurs in the resolution, it sends a message to that effect to the first House, which then appoints a committee of a certain number of Members, and sends a message to the other House informing it that it has done so, and requesting the other House to appoint an equal number of its Members to join with the committee appointed by the first House. The other House complies with this request, and sends a message to the first House to inform it that it has done so. The House which originally desired the appointment of a joint committee finally sends a message to propose a time and place of meeting.[1]

A reasoned amendment has been proposed to a motion for taking into consideration a Lords message communicating such a resolution.[2] Resolutions communicated by one House or the other, proposing that a certain bill, or that certain bills, should be committed to a joint committee, have been disagreed to by the second House,[3] or no action has been taken thereon.[4] On three occasions a resolution communicated by the Lords as to the expediency of appointing a joint committee has been concurred in by the Commons without further action being taken by either House.[5]

Sometimes the second House has appointed a committee of a larger number than the committee appointed by the first House, and has sent a message to the latter requesting it to add another member, or a certain number of members, to its committee, with which request the first House has complied.[6] On two occasions, however, when the Commons had appointed a committee of eleven members, the Lords appointed a committee of twelve members, but did not request the Commons to appoint an additional member.[7]

The circumstances and manner in which certain bills under the Private Legislation Procedure (Scotland) Act 1936 or special procedure orders under the Statutory Orders (Special Procedure) Act 1945 are committed to joint committees are described in chapters 38 and 39.

---

1 LJ (1986–87) 91, 109; ibid (1987–88) 117, 120. On two occasions, after the Commons had concurred with the Lords in a resolution as to the expediency of committing certain bills to a joint committee, but before the bills had been so committed, the Lords communicated a further resolution affirming the expediency of committing another bill to the committee to which the bills were to be committed, to which the Commons agreed, CJ (1908) 170, 180, 198, 245; ibid (1920) 83, 207, 215, 230. In the House of Commons a motion for concurring with a resolution communicated by the Lords as to the expediency of appointing a joint committee has been made without notice, HC Deb (1911) 21, c 1245. The Lords did not concur with the Commons in the appointment of a joint committee to be entitled the Special Commission on Oil Sanctions, CJ (1978–79) 138, 155; LJ (1978–79) 199 (see fn 1).
2 CJ (1918) 165. See also Notices of Motions (1966–67) p 11977.
3 LJ (1928–29) 161; ibid (1930–31) 260; CJ (1908) 79, 102; ibid (1928–29) 150, 168; ibid (1930–31) 285, 294.
4 No action taken by the Lords upon a proposal of the Commons, Housing of the Working Classes 1901; no action taken by the Commons upon proposals of the Lords, Town Improvements (Betterment) 1893; Declaration against Transubstantiation 1901; Professional Accountants Bill and Rights of Way Bill 1911.
5 Motor Omnibuses and Trolley Vehicles Traffic, CJ (1914) 394, 403; Indian Affairs, CJ (1929–30) 117, 143; Publication of Proceedings in Parliament, CJ (1967–68) 361, 367.
6 CJ (1893–94) 581, 593, 597; ibid (1908) 261, 280, 293; ibid (1918) 169, 179, 197; ibid (1922) 246, 265, 271; ibid (1928) 203, 208, 231.
7 CJ (1961–62) 209, 212; ibid (1962–63) 17, 18.

Committal of additional bills to joint committees. A bill has sometimes been committed to a joint committee on another bill,[1] or to a joint committee on a matter.[2] This step is preceded by the passing, by the House in which the bill is pending, of a resolution, which is communicated to, and concurred in by, the other House, affirming the expediency of this course.[3]

In some instances the Lords, in reply to a proposal on the part of the Commons that a bill should be committed to a joint committee, have made a counter-proposition that it should be committed to a joint committee already appointed to consider another bill or bills, to which the Commons have agreed.[4]

Nomination of members of joint committees

The Lords members of joint committees are selected and proposed to the House in the same way as members of select committees, that is by the Committee of Selection or in certain cases by the Chairman of Committees (Standing Order No 60, see pp 574, 584). The Lords members of the Joint Committee on Consolidation, etc, Bills however are appointed on the recommendation of the Lord Chancellor (Standing Order No 49). In the Commons the nomination of the members of joint committees on private bills, provisional order bills or hybrid bills is usually, though not invariably, entrusted by the House to the Committee of Selection,[5] and in special cases the nomination of members to serve on a joint committee on a public matter has also been referred by the House to the Committee of Selection.[6]

When the nomination of the members of a joint committee has been referred to the Committee of Selection, it reports the selected names to the House.

The names of the members nominated to serve on a joint committee are not communicated to the other House.

Alterations in the composition of joint committees. Members appointed to serve on joint committees are sometimes discharged and others appointed in their place; and members are sometimes added to fill vacancies caused by death or otherwise. The names of members thus discharged from further attendance on, or added to, joint committees are not communicated to the other House any more than the names of the original members.

One or other House has sometimes added one or more members to its committee, and sent a message to the other House informing it of the fact, and requesting it to make a corresponding addition to its committee, with

---

1 CJ (1924–25) 209; ibid (1928) 67; LJ (1974–75) 247; ibid (1984–85) 27, 357; ibid (1987–88) 645.
2 CJ (1892) 248, 341.
3 CJ (1924–25) 193, 203; ibid (1928) 62, 65; ibid (1968–69) 267, 271; ibid (1974–75) 213; ibid (1984–85) 47, 457.
4 CJ (1894) 66, 67; ibid (1928–29), 181, 195; LJ (1928–29) 189, 202, 208.
5 In the following instances the Commons' members were named by the House: Railways, etc (Transfer and Amalgamation) Bills, CJ (1873) 179; Port of London Bill, CJ (1908) 184; Ministry of Health Provisional Order (Birkenhead Extension) and (Widnes Extension) Bills, CJ (1920) 224; Ouse Drainage Bill, CJ (1927) 219; Roosevelt Memorial Bill, CJ (1945–46) 386.
6 Channel Tunnel, CJ (1883) 143; Electric Powers (Protective Clauses), CJ (1893–94) 288; Municipal Trading, CJ (1900) 142.

which request the other House has complied.[1] In some instances members have been added to joint committees on statute law revision or consolidation bills for the consideration of particular bills.[2]

Where the Commons' members originally appointed to serve on a joint committee were nominated by the Committee of Selection, that committee has sometimes assumed the power of discharging members so nominated and appointing others in substitution.[3]

Powers of joint committees

Any of the powers which are given to select committees to enable them to discharge the duties of their appointment may be given to a joint committee. Generally speaking, each House gives identical powers to the members appointed by it to serve on a joint committee. A joint committee has only such authority, and can exercise only such powers, as have been conferred upon it by the two Houses concurrently, nor can the powers of a joint committee be enlarged by an order of one House alone. This rule is, however, subject to an exception in cases where the power conferred is one which is related to select committees of the one House, but not to committees of the other, as, for example, power to appoint their own chairmen, or to sit notwithstanding the adjournment of the House. For a joint committee to act on an authority which had been delegated to it by one House only would be ultra vires.

A joint committee has the same power to administer an oath to witnesses examined before it as a select committee.[4]

Power to send for persons, papers and records was conferred upon the joint committees on House of Lords Reform in sessions 1961–62 and 1962–63 by both Houses, although it is not the normal practice of the Lords to invest their committees specifically with this power (see p 576).[5] In sessions 1986–87 and 1987–88 the Joint Committee on Private Bill Procedure was given power by both Houses to appoint specialist advisers.[6] Committees on Special Procedure Orders have occasionally been given power to inspect sites.[7]

All orders made by either House on the appointment of a select committee to join with a committee of the other House are communicated to the latter House, irrespective of whether the proposal for the appointment of the committee originated with the Commons or with the Lords, and if after a joint committee has been appointed, either House confers any additional powers on its committee, a message is sent to the other House to inform it of the fact.

---

1 LJ (1896) 295, 299, CJ (1896) 341, 347; LJ (1928) 157, 169, CJ (1928) 196, 202; LJ (1928–29) 79, CJ (1928–29) 93; LJ (1964–65) 324, CJ (1964–65) 314.
2 LJ (1894) 62, 67, 181, 193; CJ (1894) 96, 101, 240, 247; LJ (1896) 127, 161; CJ (1896) 167, 197; LJ (1896) 276, 289; CJ (1897) 326, 337.
3 CJ (1893–94) 329; ibid (1900) 173; ibid (1928) 145, 156.
4 See proceedings of the Joint Committee on Railway, etc (Transfer and Amalgamation) Bills 1873, etc.
5 LJ (1961–62) 216; ibid (1962–63) 21.
6 Votes and Proceedings 2 March 1987, 23 July 1987; LJ (1986–87) 212, 216; ibid (1987–88) 115.
7 Eg CJ (1985–86) 170; ibid (1984–85) 339.

Instructions to joint committees. A mandatory instruction can be given to a joint committee only with the concurrence of both Houses. If either House gives a mandatory instruction to a select committee appointed to join with a committee of the other House, but no corresponding instruction is given by the other House to its committee, the instruction, though binding upon the members appointed to serve on the joint committee by the first House, is not binding on the joint committee, as a committee. Permissive instructions stand on the same footing as other orders investing select committees appointed to join with committees of the other House with particular powers (see pp 618–620); they can be implemented or not, as the committee thinks fit.

Reference of papers to joint committees. Reports of or evidence taken before former committees,[1] petitions relating to the subject of inquiry,[2] and other papers[3] may be referred by either House to a joint committee.

Sittings and procedure of joint committees

Time and place of meeting. It is the custom that the Lords should propose the time and place of meeting, whether the proposal for the appointment of the committee originated with the Lords or with the Commons; and the Commons, if they concur in these proposals, direct their committee to meet the Lords' committee accordingly and send a message to that effect to the Lords.

In 1955, the time proposed by the Lords for the meeting of a joint committee being inconvenient to the Commons' members, the Commons took no action upon the proposal and the Lords subsequently sent a further message to the Commons proposing another time for the meeting.[4]

Where the proposal for the appointment of a joint committee originated with the Lords, it is usual for them to defer communicating their proposals as to the time and place of meeting until they have been informed by message that the Commons have appointed a committee to join with the committee appointed by the Lords. In 1979 and 1983 the Lords communicated their proposals as to the time and place of meeting before the Commons members had been appointed; and the Commons requested that the proposed meeting be postponed. When the Lords received the Commons message that their members had been appointed, they proposed a new time and place of meeting.[5]

Where the proposal for the appointment of the committee was made by the Commons, the Lords communicate their proposal as to the time and place of meeting when they inform the Commons that they have complied with the latter's request for the appointment of an equal number of Lords to join with the committee appointed by the Commons, or subsequently, as they think proper.

---

1 LJ (1906) 117; CJ (1873) 178; ibid (1903) 232; Minutes of Evidence, CJ (1944–45) 20; ibid (1954–55) 47.
2 CJ (1864) 77; ibid (1934–35) 103; ibid (1945–46) 386.
3 CJ (1872) 375; ibid (1883) 116; Memoranda, CJ (1962–63) 18; ibid (1969–70) 43.
4 CJ (1955–56) 61, 77.
5 CJ (1979–80) 55, 73, 75, 105, 108, 112; LJ (1979–80) 63, 107, 170, 174; CJ (1983–84) 130, 138, 139, 262, 265, 275; LJ (1983–84) 131, 136, 225, 229.

The date of the meeting may be advanced,[1] or the meeting put off to a later day,[2] by the same method as that by which the time of the meeting was originally fixed.[3]

Quorum of a joint committee. A joint committee cannot transact business unless a quorum of the Members appointed by each House to serve on the committee is present.[4]

The quorum of the Lords' members of a joint committee is fixed by usage at three. However, in two instances the Lords have appointed a committee of twelve members and fixed the quorum at five and a committee of three members and fixed the quorum at two.[5] In the case of the Joint Committee on Consolidation, etc, Bills, Standing Order No 123 specifies that twelve Commons members be appointed with a quorum of two. However the quorum is usually fixed as a higher proportion of the total membership. The quorum of the Commons' members is fixed by the standing order in respect of those committees regularly appointed or in respect of other committees by the order of the House on the appointment of the committee or subsequently.[6] When four or five members are appointed to join with a similar number of lords, the quorum of the Commons' members is often fixed at three though, in a number of instances it has been fixed at two.[7] If no quorum has been fixed by the House of Commons, the committee cannot transact business unless all the Commons' members are present.[8]

Procedure in joint committees. The first proceeding of a joint committee is to elect a chairman who may be chosen from among the members appointed to serve on the committee by either House.

Power to agree with the Commons' committee in the appointment of a chairman is expressly given by the Lords to a select committee appointed to join with a committee of the Commons, but the Commons' committee agrees in the appointment of a chairman without specifically receiving such a power from its House.

The procedure of a joint committee follows the procedure of select committees of the House of Lords when such procedure differs from that of select committees of the House of Commons, whether the chairman is a member of the Commons or the Lords. For example, the practice of the House of Lords according to which the chairman of a committee votes like the other members, but has no casting vote, and the Lords' method of

---

1 CJ (1910) 90, 96.
2 CJ (1928–29) 151.
3 In 1881 a joint committee on the Stationery Office was appointed and nominated, and the time and place of the meeting of the committee were fixed, but the committee did not meet, CJ (1881) 281, 315, 318, 320.
4 Proceedings of joint committees on the Law of Libel Amendment Bills, HC 125 (1927) p vii; the Suspension of Bills, HC 105 (1928–29) p xix and the Publication of Proceedings in Parliament, HC 48 (1969–70) pp 14, 15.
5 LJ (1961–62) 215–216; ibid (1968–69) 39.
6 CJ (1892) 111.
7 Eg CJ (1898) 102; ibid (1969–70) 36; ibid (1979–80) 82.
8 Late in the session the quorum of the Commons' members of a joint committee has been reduced. Eg (1919) 303.

deciding the question if the votes are equal (see p 430), are followed by a joint committee.[1]

Report of a joint committee

The report of a joint committee is presented to both Houses. It is ordered to be presented by the chairman to the House to which he belongs, and by a member, selected for the purpose by the committee, to the other House. When the consideration of a bill by a joint committee has been concluded, the bill is reported to the House in which it originated. In addition to reporting the bill to the House in which it originated, a joint committee frequently makes a report to both Houses upon the bill. Where no such report is made, the committee, after ordering the bill to be reported to the House in which it originated, directs one of the members appointed to serve on the committee by the other House to report 'accordingly' to that House.[2] Since 1935 it has been the practice, when both Houses order the report of a joint committee to be printed, to publish the report as both House of Lords and a House of Commons paper.

Joint committees regularly appointed

Consolidation, etc, Bills. A joint committee was first appointed in 1894 to consider consolidation bills. The committee has been appointed in most sessions since then and its terms of reference have from time to time been widened to include other analogous classes of bills.[3] The committee is now appointed each session pursuant to a Standing Order of each House (Standing Order No 49 [HL]; Standing Order No 123 [HC]). The committee consists of twelve members from each House,[4] the Lords members being appointed on the recommendation of the Lord Chancellor and the Commons members being appointed on a motion moved by a minister. Consolidation bills are invariably introduced in the House of Lords. The following classes of bills are referred without motion to the committee pursuant to the standing order:

(1) Consolidation bills, whether public or private;
(2) Statute law revision bills;
(3) Bills prepared pursuant to the Consolidation of Enactments (Procedure) Act 1949, together with any memoranda laid pursuant to that Act and any representations made with respect thereto;
(4) Bills to consolidate any enactments with amendments to give effect to recommendations made by one or both of the Law Commissions together with any report containing such recommendations;
(5) Bills prepared by one or both of the Law Commissions to promote the reform of the Statute Law by the repeal, in accordance with Law

---

1 Joint Committees on Channel Tunnel, Proceedings, HC 248 (1883) p xliv; on Railway Rates, etc, Provisional Order Bill, Proceedings, HC 394 (1890–91) p xxv, etc.
2 London Passenger Transport Bill, HL 90 (1930–31) p xlix; Consolidation Bills, HC 38 (1934–35) p xiv, (Unemployment Insurance Bill [Lords]).
3 CJ (1894) 33, 52, etc. In sessions from 1899 to 1911 no such committee was appointed. In 1893–94, only Statute Law Revision bills were so referred, CJ (1893–94) 92, 111. See also Report of the Joint Committee on Statute Law Revision, HC 258 (1892); Joint Committee on Consolidation, etc, Bills, Sixth Report, HC 341–I (1966–67) pp 12–29.
4 But see p 662, fn 1.

Commission recommendations, of certain enactments which (except insofar as their effect is preserved) are no longer of practical utility, whether or not they make other provision in connection with the repeal of those enactments, together with any Law Commission report on any such bill.[1]

(6) Since October 1980 the joint committee has also considered Orders in Council subject to affirmative resolution which, but for the provisions of the Northern Ireland Act 1974, would have been enacted by a consolidation bill, whether public or private, or a statute law revision bill.[2]

Bills which are not consolidation bills but which contain ancillary provisions normally found in a consolidation bill, and which are part of a consolidation, may be referred to the joint committee. The ancillary provisions are placed in a separate bill when the rest of the consolidation consists of two or more bills and the ancillary provisions relate to all of the bills rather than to a single bill. It is convenient for such consequential provisions bills to be considered by the joint committee at the same time as the related consolidation bills. In the case of such bills, a motion is moved after the second reading of the bill to refer the bill to the joint committee and a message is sent to the Commons asking for their agreement to this proceeding.[3]

The joint committee takes evidence from the parliamentary draftsman responsible for the bill and from any departmental or other witnesses; the bill is then reported to the House of Lords with or without amendment. Where amendments are made by the joint committee, the bill is usually reprinted as amended. The bill is recommitted to a Committee of the whole House and thereafter follows the same course as other public bills.

Much of the joint committee's work has been in the field of pure consolidation. The Consolidation of Enactments (Procedure) Act goes further in allowing minor amendments to be made in Acts to be consolidated, without departure from the expeditious and non-controversial consolidation procedure.[4] Under that Act corrections and minor improvements in a bill which has been reported by such a joint committee are deemed, for the purpose of future proceedings in Parliament relating to the bill, to have become law as if they had been made by an Act. Pursuant to section 3(1)(d) of the Law Commissions Act 1965, a comprehensive programme of consolidation and statute law revision is being undertaken, giving effect to Law Commission recommendations. In considering such recommendations, the joint committee has expressed the view that amendments to the law in a consolidation bill, 'should be for the following purposes: to tidy up errors of the past, to

---

1 In 1947 and again in 1959 and 1973 the joint committee was empowered to consider 'Bills for re-enacting, in the form in which they apply to Scotland, the provisions of an existing statute', LJ (1946–47) 200; CJ (1958–59) 265, 267; LJ (1972–73) 383.

2 CJ (1979–80) 821.

3 LJ (1974–75) 247; LJ (1984–85) 27, 357; LJ (1987–88) 645.

4 The joint committee is precluded from approving any corrections or minor improvements under the Act of 1949 if they effect changes in the existing law of such importance that they ought, in the opinion of the committee, to be separately enacted by Parliament (s 1(5)). Corrections and minor improvements are defined in the Act of 1949 as those amendments the effect of which is confined to resolving ambiguities, removing doubts, bringing obsolete provisions into conformity with modern practice, removing unnecessary provisions or anomalies not of substantial importance, or facilitating improvement in the form or manner in which the law is stated. Necessarily consequential transitional provisions are included (s 2).

remove ambiguities, and generally to introduce common sense on points where the form of drafting in the past appeared to lead to a result which departed from common sense; though not to introduce any substantial change in the law or one that might be controversial—indeed, nothing that Parliament as a whole would wish to reserve for its consideration'.[1] The joint committee has also approved a procedure for dealing with amendments which do not fall within these guidelines but are desirable to achieve a satisfactory consolidation.[2] Proposed amendments of this kind are to be examined by the joint committee together with Law Commission recommendations but the committee, instead of being asked to make the amendments, is to be invited to report to both Houses that the amendments change the law no more than is necessary to achieve a satisfactory consolidation. The amendments, supported by such a report, would then be moved on the floor of the House of Lords on recommitment.

Statutory instruments. Since 1973 a joint committee has existed to consider all statutory instruments. A description of the committee is given on pp 551–552.

Communications between committees of both Houses

As an alternative to the appointment of a joint committee, a select committee of either House may be given power to receive any communication which may be made to it from time to time by a committee of the other House upon the same or a cognate subject,[3] or to communicate from time to time or confer with a committee of the other House.[4]

Select committees of the two Houses which possess similar functions are now regularly given power to confer and meet concurrently for the purpose of deliberating and examining witnesses.[5] At such meetings a chairman is appointed but no decisions may be taken and no reports may be made. Select committees and sub-committees are now often empowered to join with the corresponding committee or sub-committee of the other House from time to time and to meet jointly.[6]

---

1 LJ (1976–77) 514.
2 First Report (1981–82), HL 46–I, HC 103–I.
3 Corresponding Societies, LJ (1794–96) 202; CJ (1794) 619.
4 Corresponding Societies, CJ (1794) 620; State of Ireland, CJ (1801) 287, LJ (1801–02) 105; Business of the House, LJ (1861) 18; CJ (1861–62) 77; European Community Instruments, LJ (1972–73) 94; European Communities, LJ (1974) 214; European Community Secondary Legislation, CJ (1972–73) 95; European Secondary Legislation, etc, CJ (1974) 112; CJ (1974–75) 76. A committee has been given power to appoint a sub-committee to confer, CJ (1944–45) 79.
5 European Communities, LJ (1975–76) 24; European Secondary Legislation, CJ (1975–76) 40; Procedure, CJ (1975–76) 371; Practice and Procedure, LJ (1975–76) 615. SO No 127(11) (European Legislation and its sub-committees); SO No 129(6) (Sound Broadcasting); SO No 125(12) (Computer Sub-Committee of the Services Committee). For examples of such concurrent meetings, see Minutes of Evidence taken before a concurrent meeting of the Select Committee on European Legislation, etc (Sub-Committee II) (Commons) and the Select Committee on the European Communities (Sub-Committee B) [Lords] (1977–78) HL 149 and HC 69–iv and v; Sound Broadcasting, Proceedings, HC 691 (1977–78) p 7.
6 Sound Broadcasting, CJ (1977–78) 169; ibid (1979–80) 49; LJ (1977–78) 275; Computers (Sub-Committees) LJ (1976–77) 607; CJ (1976–77) 375.

CHAPTER 25

Witnesses and Parliament

This chapter deals with the practice relating to summoning witnesses before either House or a Committee of the whole House, and select committees of either House. No witness has been summoned before either House (or a Committee of the whole House) for many years. It is also comparatively rare for select committees of either House to use the power of formal summons to require the attendance of a witness: however the frequent appearance of witnesses as a result of a request by a Committee rests upon the formal powers possessed by both Houses which are described here.

Matters relating to misconduct before the House or a committee, disobedience of rules or orders of the House or a committee, and to the obstruction of witnesses are considered in chapter 9 (Contempts), especially pp 116–118, 131–132; the premature publication or disclosure of committee proceedings are also considered in that chapter, pp 122–124, and in chapter 24, pp 636–637.

MODE OF SECURING ATTENDANCE

Summons of witnesses by the Lords

Witnesses summoned to give evidence before the House of Lords or any Committee of the whole House are ordered to attend at the bar on a certain day, to be sworn; and they are served with the order of the House, signed by the Clerk of the Parliaments. If a witness is in prison, the person responsible for his custody is ordered to bring him to the House.[1] If the House has reason to believe that a witnesss is purposely keeping out of the way to avoid being served with the order, it has been usual to direct that the service of the order at his house shall be deemed good service.[2]

Peers, as witnesses, before the Lords

When the evidence of peers, peeresses or Lords of Parliament has been required, the Lord Chancellor has been ordered to write letters to them, desiring their attendance to be examined as witnesses;[3] but they ordinarily attend and give evidence without any such form.

Summons of witnesses by the Commons

Should the attendance of a witness be required, to be examined at the bar by the House of Commons, or by a Committee of the whole House, he is simply ordered to attend at a stated time;[4] and the order, signed by the Clerk

---

1 LJ (1836) 513, 558.
2 LJ (1834) 295, 358.
3 LJ (1834) 144.
4 CJ (1823) 240; ibid (1836) 338. For attendance before select committees in the Commons, see pp 627–631.

of the House, is served upon him personally, if he is in or near London; but if he is at a distance, it is forwarded to him by the Serjeant at Arms, either by post, or, in special cases, by a messenger. If the witness does not obey the order for his attendance he may be ordered to be sent for in custody of the Serjeant at Arms, and Mr Speaker may be ordered to issue his warrant accordingly;[1] or he may be declared guilty of a breach of privilege, and ordered to be taken into the custody of the Serjeant at Arms.[2]

The House on one occasion ordered the attendance of two witnesses forthwith, and the witnesses, who had been privately notified of anticipated intentions of the House and had placed themselves at the disposal of the Serjeant at Arms, were immediately brought to the bar by the Serjeant.[3]

If a witness whose attendance is desired by the House or by a select committee is serving a term of imprisonment the Speaker may be asked to issue his warrant, which is personally served upon the appropriate person responsible for the prisoner's custody by a messenger of the Serjeant at Arms and by which he is directed to cause the prisoner to be brought to the House to be examined.[4]

Attendance of Members

If the evidence of a Member is desired by the House, or a Committee of the whole House, he is ordered to attend in his place on a certain day.[5] But when the attendance of a Member as a witness is required before a select committee, the chairman sends to him a written request for his attendance. Pursuant to the resolution of 16 March 1688, 'if any Member of the House refuse, upon being sent to, to come to give evidence or information as a witness to a committee, the committee ought to acquaint the House therewith, and not summon such Member to attend the committee.'[6]

On occasion, Members have been ordered by the House to attend select committees.[7] There has been no instance of a Member persisting in a refusal to give evidence when ordered by the House to do so.[8]

A Member who has submitted himself to examination without any order of the House is treated like any other witness. When a Member's refusal to answer questions has been reported to the House by a select committee, the House has ordered that he should submit his objection to the committee.[9]

---

1 CJ (1840) 58.
2 CJ (1851–52) 147, 148, etc.
3 CJ (1946–47) 377; HC Deb (1946–47) 441, cc 2274–2276.
4 CJ (1940–41) 9; for the case of a Member in custody, see ibid (1939–40) 227. For recent examples of a prisoner attending a select committee: Report of the Select Committee on Conduct of Members , HC 490 (1976–77) xxii; Education, Science and Arts Committee, Minutes of Evidence, HC 45–II (1982–83) 128 ff.
5 CJ (1806) 386; ibid (1809) 17; ibid (1810) 21, 30, etc.
6 CJ (1688–93) 51.
7 CJ (1718–21) 403. In 1731 Sir Archibald Grant, a Member, was committed to the custody of the Serjeant at Arms 'in order to his forthcoming to abide the orders of the House', and was afterwards ordered to be brought before a committee, from time to time, in the custody of the Serjeant, CJ (1727–32) 851, 852.
8 On 28 June 1842 a committee reported that a Member had declined to comply with its request for his attendance. A motion was made for ordering him to attend the committee and give evidence; but, the Member having at last expressed his willingness to attend, the motion was withdrawn, CJ 1842, 438, 453, 458; see also Report on Precedents, ibid 449; HC 392 (1842). A Minister of the Crown has declined an invitation to give evidence before a select committee on the grounds that, according to the principle of collective Cabinet responsibility, another Minister, had direct ministerial responsibility for giving evidence on the matter in question on behalf of the Government, HC Deb (1975–76), vol 903, col 287.
9 CJ (1842) 227. See also the Memorandum by the Clerk of the House to the Select Committee on Procedure of 1977–78, HC 588–I (1977–78) p 15.

Attendance of Members of the other House

The most usual occasion when the attendance of a Member of the other House is required is when a select committee wishes to take evidence from him. (See p 526 and pp 629–630.) Under Standing Order No 120 the House of Commons has given a general leave to attend to any Member requested to attend as a witness before a Lords committee or its sub-committees, if the Member thinks fit. Under Lords Standing Order No 22 (Lords attendance at Commons Select Committees) any Lord requested by a committee of the Commons to attend as a witness before it or before any sub-committee appointed by it, is given leave to attend if he thinks fit. In the case of private bill committees the attendance of a Member of either House as a witness is also at his discretion.[1]

If the attendance of a Lord is desired to give evidence before the House of Commons, or any committee of the House of Commons,[2] other than a select committee or a sub-committee of a select committee, the Commons sends a message to the Lords, to request them to give leave to the Lord to attend as a witness. If the Lord is in his place when this message is received, and he consents, leave may be given for him to be examined, 'his lordship consenting thereto'; if the Lord is not present, the House gives leave for his lordship to attend 'if he think fit'.Exactly the same form is observed by the Lords, when they desire the attendance of a Member of the House of Commons.

Attendance by officers of either House

If either House wishes to examine any officer of the other House either before the House itself or before any select committee, a message requesting his attendance must be sent to the other House and leave given by it. When leave is given, the words 'if he thinks fit' which are used in the case of Members are omitted from the message in reply.[3]

Peers, not being Lords of Parliament

Peers who are not Lords of Parliament have been ordered by the Commons to attend as witnesses.

> Whether the attendance of a peer who is not a Lord of Parliament may be required by the Commons, and, if necessary, enforced by their own authority, is a matter upon which in the past the Houses have not agreed. The Commons have on two occasions ordered such peers to attend,[4] and they have attended accordingly. On the second occasion, however, the Lords took exception to the mode of summons, and (after a conference between the two Houses at which the Commons maintained that the right to decline, if they thought fit, to attend the House of Commons for the purpose of giving information upon inquiries instituted by that House was confined to peers who had seats in the House of Lords) resolved that it was the privilege of all peers, except such as had waived their privilege by

---

1 3 Hatsell 21n.
2 CJ (1826–27) 394; ibid (1833) 173, 179; For examples of the practice in select committees before there was a regular order, see eg ibid (1966–67) 492, 493, etc.
3 CJ (1969–70) 292; LJ (1981–82) 162, 339.
4 Earl of Balcarres, CJ (1778–80) 366; Lord Teignmouth, CJ (1806) 374.

becoming Members of the House of Commons, that the House of Commons had no right to enforce the attendance of peers, whether Lords of Parliament or not; and that it was the duty of the House of Lords to maintain and uphold the privilege of all such Peers, and to protect them against any attempt to enforce their attendance on the House of Commons contrary to such privilege.[1] This resolution, however, was not communicated to the Commons.

Inquiry to be previously ordered

Before any message requesting the attendance of a Member or an officer is sent to the other House, or any witness is otherwise summoned, the House should previously have directed an inquiry into the matter upon which evidence is sought.[2]

EXAMINATION OF WITNESSES

Examination of witnesses in the House: Lords

Lords of Parliament, and peers not being Lords of Parliament, and peeresses, are sworn at the Table of the House, by the Lord Chancellor;[3] and other witnesses who are to be examined by the House, or by a Committee of the whole House are sworn at the bar. An Irish peer, being a member of the House of Commons, is sworn at the bar as a commoner.[4] The Lords formerly claimed the privilege of being examined upon honour, instead of upon oath.[5] But this supposed privilege has long since been abandoned, and Peers are everywhere examined upon oath, even in the House of Lords itself. If counsel are engaged in an inquiry at the bar, the witnesses are examined by them, and by any Lord who may desire to put questions. When counsel are not engaged, the witnesses are examined by the Lords generally. A Lord of Parliament is examined in his place; and peers not being Lords of Parliament, and peeresses, have chairs placed for them at the Table.[6]

Examination of witnesses at the bar: Commons

Should a witness be examined by the House of Commons, or by a Committee of the whole House,[7] he must attend at the bar, which is then in

---

1 LJ (1805–6) 678, 699, 710, 733, 744, 779, 789, 805, 807, 812, CJ (1806) 465, 489, 503, 511, 525, 536; 2 Hatsell App 9. Colchester ii, 69, 73. 1 June 1825, 'The Chancellor, by Mr Cowper's advice, thought it necessary to have leave given by the House for the Archbishop of Dublin's attendance before the Commons' committee, although, not being on the rota, he has no seat in the House of Peers, or duty to discharge there', Colchester iii, 394.
2 On 31 March 1813 a motion being made for a message to the Lords for the attendance of Lord Moira to give information concerning the Princess of Wales, the Speaker desired the attention of the House to the proceeding as novel and unparliamentary; 'the rule being, according to all precedents, not to desire the attendance of witnesses of any sort, excepting upon a matter pending in the House, and which the House had previously resolved to examine'. The motion was superseded by reading the Orders of the Day, CJ (1812–13) 364; Colchester ii, 434.
3 LJ (1787–90) 68, 69; ibid (1845) 725; ibid (1854–55) 213.
4 Viscount Palmerston, 16 July 1844.
5 LJ (1685–91) 18; ibid (1731–36) 136.
6 LJ (1736–41) 303; see also ibid 100; ibid (1787–90) 69; ibid (1806–08) 172, 189, where Senators of the College of Justice in Scotland had chairs set for them at the bar, to be examined.
7 2 Hatsell, 140; but see CJ (1640–42) 26.

position. If the witness is not in custody, the mace remains upon the Table, when, according to the strict rule of the House, the Speaker should put all the questions to the witness, and Members should only suggest to him the questions which they desire to be put.[1] But, for the sake of avoiding the repetition of each question, Members are usually permitted to address their questions directly to the witness, which, however, are still supposed to be put through the Speaker.[2] When a witness is in the custody of the Serjeant at Arms, or is brought from any prison in custody, it is the usual practice for the Serjeant to stand with the mace at the bar. When the mace is on the Serjeant's shoulder, the Speaker has the sole management; and no Member may speak, or even suggest questions to the Chair.[3] In such cases, therefore, the questions to be proposed should either be put, in writing, by individual Members, or settled upon motions in the House, and given to the Speaker before the prisoner is brought to the bar.[4] If a question is objected to, or if any difference should arise in regard to the examination of a witness, he is directed by the Speaker to withdraw, before a motion is made or the matter is considered. In Committee of the whole House any Member may put questions directly to the witness. Where counsel are engaged, the examination of witnesses is mainly conducted by them, subject to the interposition of questions by Members; and where any question arises in regard to the examination, the parties, counsel and witnesses are directed to withdraw.

Members, Lords of Parliament, etc

Members of the House are examined in their places;[5] and peers, Lords of Parliament, the judges, and the Lord Mayor of London, have chairs placed for them within the bar, and are introduced by the Serjeant at Arms.[6] Peers sit down covered but rise and answer all questions uncovered. The judges and the Lord Mayor are told by the Speaker that there are chairs to repose themselves upon; which is understood, however, to signify that they may only rest with their hands upon the chair backs.[7]

Examination of witnesses before select committees

Witnesses are frequently invited, or occasionally summoned, to give evidence before select committees and committees on private bills (which, in the Lords, are select committees). Committees may only exercise such power when sitting within the United Kingdom, nor are witnesses summoned from overseas to give evidence (see p 630). Fuller information on the conduct of select committees is set out in the previous chapter and private bill committees are discussed in chapter 37.

---

1 CJ (1547–1628) 536.
2 Parl Deb (1857) 146, c 97; ibid (1858) 150, c 1063 ff.
3 2 Hatsell 141 n; HC Deb (1946–47) 441, c 2275.
4 2 Hatsell 142.
5 'Agreed that Members ought not to be brought to the bar unless when they are accused of any crime', CJ (1688–93) 46. On 12 January 1768 Mr Wilkes, being brought to the bar in custody, objected that he could not appear there without having taken the oaths; but his objection was overruled.
6 The same forms are observed when a peer desires to address the House, as in the case of Viscount Melville, 11 June 1805, Parl Deb (1805) 5, c 250; and of the Duke of Wellington, 1 July 1814, ibid (1813–14) 28, c 489; Abbot's Speeches 84; Colchester ii, 6–8.
7 2 Hatsell 148, where all these forms are minutely described.

Witnesses before select committees sit at a table facing the chairman. In select committees on private bills witnesses sit at the shorthand writer's table.

The degree of formality in the questioning of committees depends on the terms of reference of the committee and the subject matter of the questioning. However committees, being extensions of the House, possess substantial powers to require answers to questions.[1]

A witness is bound to answer all questions which the committee sees fit to put him,[2] and cannot excuse himself, for example, on the ground that he may thereby subject himself to a civil action,[3] or because he has taken an oath not to disclose the matter about which he is required to testify,[4] or because the matter was a privileged communication to him, as where a solicitor is called upon to disclose the secrets of his client;[5] or on the ground that he is advised by counsel that he cannot do so without incurring the risk of incriminating himself or exposing himself to a civil suit,[6] or that it would prejudice him as defendant in litigation which is pending,[7] some of which would be sufficient grounds of excuse in a court of law. Nor can a witness refuse to produce documents in his possession on the ground that, though in his possession, they are under the control of a client who has given him instructions not to disclose them without his express authority.[8] (For the treatment of matters *sub judice* see pp 624–625 and 377–378).

However, a witness who is unwilling to answer a question, after stating why he desires to be excused from answering, may appeal to the Chair whether in the circumstances, or for the reason stated by him, he ought to answer. He may also request that the whole or part of his evidence should not be published (see p 636 esp fn 1).

It is generally the case that members of select committees co-operate with the Chair and with each other in questioning witnesses in order more effectively to achieve the purposes for which the committee was appointed by the House. Thus a member of a committee seldom interrupts another member except to obtain elucidation of the question being asked or to contribute to the questioning. However, a question put to a witness may be objected to by a Member. Questions are usually objected to for much the same reasons as those offered by the parties or their counsel in a court of law, but Members are not confined to objections of this description.

If a question should be objected to, or if any difference should arise in regard to the examination of a witness, that witness is directed by the chairman to withdraw, and the committee proceeds to consider the matter. When the committee has come to a decision the witness is again called in, and the examination proceeds.[9]

---

1 These powers have been confirmed from time to time. For example in 1947 the House of Commons resolved 'that the refusal of a witness before a select committee to answer any question which may be put to him is a contempt of the House and an infraction of the undoubted right of this House to conduct any inquiry which may be necessary in the public interest', CJ (1946–47) 378. See too Privileges Committee Report, HC 138 (1946–47).
2 CJ (1946–47) 378.
3 Parliamentary Oath (Mr Bradlaugh) Committee, HC 226 (1880) p vi.
4 Parl Deb (1823) 9, cc 113, 119, 120, 493.
5 Parl Deb (1828) 18, c 968 ff.
6 Parl Deb (1806) 6, cc 353–359.
7 Loans to Foreign States Committee, HC 367 (1875) p. liii.
8 British South Africa Committee, HC 311 (1897) p 473.
9 Eg Proceedings of the Select Committee on the Official Secrets Acts, HC 173 (1937–38) p xlv.

When parties are allowed to call witnesses, the examination of such witnesses is mainly conducted by the parties themselves or their counsel, and objections are taken and argued before the committee in the same manner as in a court of law; but members of the committee may also participate in the examination, and object to questions in the same manner as when the inquiry is conducted exclusively by them. When any question arises in regard to the examination, the parties, counsel and witnesses are directed to withdraw. It is disorderly for either a Member or counsel to interrupt a witness whilst he is answering a question that has been regularly put to him.[1] Further information on the hearing of parties before select committees in the Commons and the assistance which may, in certain circumstances, be given by counsel is given in the previous chapter (see pp 631–632). In neither House may a select committee hear counsel unless authorised by the House (SO No 64) (Lords).

Conduct of witnesses before select committees. If a witness refuses to answer a question properly put to him, or to produce a paper which he has been directed to produce, the matter is usually reported to the House. In such cases the House has ordered the recalcitrant witness to attend at the bar, where he has been admonished by the Speaker as to the necessity of answering such questions as may be put by the committee.[2]

Similarly, witnesses who give false evidence,[3] prevaricate, present forged or falsified documents to a committee with intent to deceive the committee,[4] or attempt in any other way to deceive a committee, or who are guilty of disrespectful conduct to the committee in a state of intoxication[5] may be reported to the House to be dealt with as may be determined.

By section 1 of the Perjury Act 1911, where evidence is given upon oath, the giving of false evidence is punishable as perjury. The power of either House to punish for false evidence is not, however, superseded by this Act, and it may, therefore, imprison witnesses, as in any other case, upon its own authority; and if it appears that a conviction at law can also be obtained, it is competent to the House to direct the Attorney General to prosecute the offending witnesses for perjury.[6] Where evidence is not given upon oath, the giving of false evidence is punishable only as a contempt (see pp 116–118). Misconduct in the presence of either House, or of a committee, is considered in chapter 9.

Oaths administered by Lords' committees

By the Parliamentary Witnesses Act 1858, any committee of the House of Lords may administer an oath to the witnesses before such committee. In accordance with the resolution, 11 June 1857, 'that select committees, in future, shall examine witnesses without their having been previously sworn, except in cases in which it may be otherwise ordered by the House',[7] witnesses have only been sworn in the case of inquiries of a special character and select committees on private bills[8] (see p 937).

1 Parl Hist xxiv 864.
2 CJ (1833) 212, 218; ibid (1897) 361, 365; ibid (1946–47) 377.
3 CJ (1860) 230.
4 CJ (1889) 311, 346. For a fuller list of offences considered to have been contempts see p 116 and fns 4 to 14.
5 CJ (1852–53) 389.
6 CJ (1860) 258; ibid (1865–67) 239.
7 LJ (1857) 60; Committee on Administration of Oaths and Witnesses, Report, LJ (1857) 39.
8 Sweating System, LJ (1889) 19; Women's Royal Air Force, ibid (1919) 382; Registration and Regulation of Osteopaths Bill, ibid (1934–35) 32.

False evidence. Besides the infliction of punishment for perjury, false evidence before the Lords, prevarication or other misconduct of a witness is punishable as a contempt.[1]

Administration of oaths by Commons' committees

In pursuance of the recommendations of a select committee of 1869 the Parliamentary Witnesses Oaths Act 1871 was passed, empowering the House of Commons and its committees to administer oaths to witnesses, and attaching to false evidence the penalties of perjury. By Standing Orders Nos 114 and 140, oaths, and affirmations under the Oaths Act 1978, are administered to witnesses, before the House or a Committee of the whole House, by a Clerk at the Table; and before a select committee, by the chairman, or by the clerk attending the committee. It is not usual, however, for select committees to examine witnesses upon oath, except upon inquiries of a judicial or other special character.[2]

The procedures followed when witnesses withhold evidence or give false evidence are described in chapter 9.

EXPENSES OF WITNESSES

A witness is allowed travelling expenses actually incurred, and allowances for subsistence and loss of earnings on the same scale as that laid down by the Treasury for witnesses before royal commissions and government committees. Payment is made, in the Commons by the Fees Office, in the Lords by the Accountant, on the authority of the committee Clerk or a member of the staff of the committee acting on his behalf. A witness claiming expenses is required to fill in a prescribed form, based on that used in the public service, and authorized for the purposes of the House of Commons or the House of Lords by the Accounting Officer of the House.

The payment of travelling expenses and subsistence allowances to witnesses from abroad, who have been invited to give evidence before select committees, may be sanctioned under arrangements made by the House of Commons Commission or the House of Lords Committee Office. Under the

---

1 LJ (1810–12) 371, etc.
2 The Committee on Foreign Loans in 1875 was the first to examine witnesses upon oath under the Act; they were also so examined by the committees on Public Petitions 1878 (during its inquiry into the alleged forgery of signatures to certain petitions); Privilege (Tower High Level Bridge) and Mr Goffin's certificate 1879; Contagious Diseases Acts 1882 (during a particular branch of the inquiry); East India (Hyderabad Deccan Mining Company) 1888; Friendly Societies 1888; Privilege (Service of a Writ on a Member in the Outer Lobby) 1888; Irish Society and London Companies (Irish Estates) 1890; Shop Hours Bill 1892; British South Africa 1897; Royal National Lifeboat Institution 1897; Cottage Homes Bill 1899 (while inquiring into the manner in which the terms of a draft report submitted to them had been divulged to a newspaper); War Office Contracts 1900; Marconi's Wireless etc., Agreement 1912–13; Putumayo 1912–13; Navy and Army Canteens 1923; Office Secrets Acts 1937–38; Conduct of a Member 1940–41; Privileges 1941–42; idem, 1946–47. By an instruction, the committee on London Corporation (Charges of Malversation), 1887, was directed to take evidence on oath, CJ (1887) 97. In 1946–47 the Privileges Committee, in two separate inquiries, took evidence on oath, HC 36, 138, 142 (1946–47). In 1976–77 the Select Committee on the Conduct of Members took oral evidence on oath from several witnesses, CJ (1975–76) 589, HC 490 (1976–77). In 1987–88 the Trade and Industry Committee took evidence on oath from certain witnesses HC 732 (1982–88).

previous system, it was held that Treasury sanction was necessary before an invitation to witnesses from abroad involving expenditure, could be made.[1]

PROTECTION OF WITNESSES

While each House punishes misconduct with severity, it is careful to protect witnesses from the consequences of their evidence given by order of the House and the Witnesses (Public Inquiries) Protection Act 1892 applies to evidence given to committees of either House. On extraordinary occasions, where further protection has been deemed necessary to elicit full disclosures, Acts have been passed to indemnify witnesses from all the penal consequences of their testimony.[2] Committees have taken evidence from witnesses whose names are not divulged where there is reason to apprehend that private injury or vengeance might result from publication.[3]

An action for slander will not lie for statements made in evidence before a committee of the House of Commons.[4] For other provisions concerning the protection of witnesses, members and servants of committees, see Chapter 9.

---

1 Eg Parl Deb (1872) 212, cc 99–100. In 1873 the Committee on East India Finance resolved that the expenses of witnesses coming from India (not exceeding £10,000) should be paid out of the revenue of the United Kingdom, but the Treasury declined to act on this resolution, Second Report from the Select Committee on East India Finance, HC 194 (1873) pp 4, 6–9. The Treasury, on application from the Committee on British and Foreign Spirits, sanctioned a payment of £105 to two witnesses for work done for the committee, and in 1902 special allowances for experiments in connection with the ventilation of the House of Commons for the select committee on that subject HC 227 (1903), p vii. On another occasion, upon a special report from the Committee on the Army and Navy Estimates, and with the sanction of the royal recommendation, a grant was made to provide for the remuneration of accountants who might be employed, on behalf of the committee, to examine and audit the expense accounts of the army manufacturing departments HC 239 (1887) CJ (1887) 399, 407, 413. See also Committees on British South Africa, 1897; Training and Employment of Disabled Ex-Service Men, 1922; Capital Punishment, 1929–30.
2 Election Compromises, 1842, 5 & 6 Vict c 31; Sudbury Disfranchisement, 1843, 6 & 7 Vict c 11; Gaming Transactions, 1844, 7 & 8 Vict c 7.
3 See for instance committees on Home Work, HC 246 (1908) p xxii; Debtors (Imprisonment), HC 344 (1908) p viii; Violence in Marriage, HC 553–II (1974–75) pp 15–31. When a prisoner gave evidence to an inquiry by the Education Committee into prison education his name was not published HC 45–II (1982–83).
4 *Goffin v Donnelly*, 6. Q.B.D. 307, 50 L.J.Q.B. 303.

CHAPTER 26

Financial procedure—general

GENERAL PLAN OF CHAPTERS ON FINANCE

This and the four following chapters are intended to cover the ground of financial procedure. The present chapter describes briefly the financial relations between the Crown and Parliament and the items comprised in the financial procedure of Parliament, and sets out the scope and the general rules of financial procedure. Then follow chapters dealing, respectively, with ordinary annual expenditure (supply), new expenditure (financial resolutions), the raising of revenue (ways and means) and finally the financial relations of the House of Lords with the House of Commons.

FINANCIAL RELATIONS BETWEEN THE CROWN AND PARLIAMENT[1]

The Sovereign, being the executive power, is charged with the management of all the revenue of the State, and with all payments for the public service. The Crown, therefore, acting with the advice of its responsible ministers, makes known to the Commons the financial requirements of the government; the Commons, in return, grant such aids or supplies as are required to satisfy these demands; and they provide by taxes, and by the appropriation of other sources of the public income, the ways and means to meet the supplies which they have granted. Thus the Crown demands money, the Commons grant it, and the Lords assent to the grant: but the Commons do not vote money unless it is required by the Crown; nor do they impose or augment taxes, unless such taxation is necessary for the public service, as declared by the Crown through its constitutional advisers (see p 691).

The financial control of the House of Commons is exercised at two different levels. As an agent in the formation of policy, it authorizes the several objects of expenditure and the sums to be spent on each; it also authorizes the levying of taxes. On the level of administration, it satisfies itself that its expenditure decisions are duly carried out—in other words, that the sums it has granted, and no more, are spent for the purposes for which they were granted, and for no other purposes. For both sets of functions the House of Commons has, partly through its own procedure, and partly through legislation and administrative practice, secured appropriate machinery. The procedure and machinery for the control of financial policy—the presentation of estimates, the budget, the voting of estimates,

---

1 In relation to financial control, 'Parliament' means the House of Commons. The participation of the House of Lords is confined to assenting to such financial provisions of the House
of Commons as require statutory authorization.

the business of Ways and Means, and Consolidated Fund, Appropriation and Finance Bills—form the subjects of the chapters that follow.

FINANCIAL BUSINESS—INTRODUCTORY

Long term expenditure plans

The annual cycle of financial business in Parliament needs to be seen within the wider context of the Government's longer term expenditure plans, plans which cover a number of categories of expenditure not included in the Supply Estimates. Announcements about public expenditure plans for several years ahead have been made annually by successive Governments in Command Papers since 1969. The first such announcement, which follows the completion of the so-called public expenditure round within Government, is made by the Chancellor of the Exchequer in an 'Autumn Statement', usually in November. In addition to setting out the Government's assessment of general economic prospects, the Autumn Statement sets out in aggregate terms the Government's public expenditure plans for the following three financial years. These plans are related to each Government department; together with provision for a reserve and for other elements[1], they comprise the 'public expenditure planning total'. This figure is considerably larger than the Supply Estimates since it has included, for instance, all spending by local authorities and not simply central Government grants to local authorities[2]. It also includes expenditure not directly provided for in Supply Estimates, including the Social Security Fund.[3] More detailed information about planned departmental spending for future years has been given in Public Expenditure White Papers published in January. Following the recommendations of the Treasury and Civil Service Committee it is now proposed that much of the material which had previously been published in the Public Expenditure White Paper should be included in the Autumn Statement, while discussions continue on the precise arrangements for publishing more detailed information relating to individual Government departments.[4]

Debates have regularly been held in the House of Commons both on the Autumn Statement and on the Public Expenditure White Paper. Departmentally related select committees may take evidence and publish reports on the public expenditure plans and supply estimates relevant to the departmental administration which they examine. The Treasury and Civil Service Committee regularly reports on the totality of these plans before debates take place in the House.

The House is thus made aware of the longer term context in which public expenditure is planned, but its formal role in dealing with public spending continues to be based on its consideration of the annual Supply Estimates.

---

1 In recent years including privatisation proceeds.
2 The Government has announced that it intends to introduce a 'new planning total', excluding self-financed local authority expenditure, which will, however, continue to form part of the total of 'General Government Expenditure' in public expenditure documents (*see* Cm 441, July 1988: 'A New Public Expenditure Planning Total').
3 For 1988–89 while the public expenditure planning total was planned to be £157 billion, the amount to be voted in the Supply Estimates was £108 billion (Supply Estimates, 1988–89, Summary and Guide, Cm 328, p 7).
4 Financial Reporting to Parliament, Cm 375, May 1988.

ITEMS OF FINANCIAL BUSINESS

Expenditure

At the opening of a new session the Queen's speech refers to estimates for the public services which are to be laid before the House of Commons. These are the main Supply Estimates for the ensuing financial year starting on 1 April, and they are presented on or before Budget day.[1] Before that, however, supplementary estimates to cover unforeseen expenditure in the current year (the 'winter supplementaries') are likely to reach the House in November or December. Further supplementary estimates are presented to the House in February or March (the 'spring supplementaries'), by which time departments have a clear idea of how much money they need to obtain by way of supplementary grants to cover their operations up to 31 March.

As the Crown's requests for supply (submitted to the House of Commons in the form of estimates) are not finally voted until near the end of the session, some interim steps have to be taken to make sure that money is available for the service of the early part of the ensuing year. Before the new financial year opens on 1 April, therefore, votes on account must be agreed to, for the civil services, the defence services, the House of Commons administration and the National Audit Office. These are published in November or early December and are normally voted before Christmas. Each vote on account sets out the requirements as a lump sum sufficient for four to five months' expenditure (notionally covering the months from April to July or August when the balances to complete the sums required for the year are voted), and are calculated on the basis of the previous year's voted money.

In March the House also considers the amount, if any, by which the expenditure of any department in the previous financial year exceeded the amount of supply voted, including supplementary estimates, for that year. These so-called 'excess votes' are few in number. They represent a failure (maybe a blameworthy failure) by a department to keep its expenditure within the limit approved, in spite of the opportunities for presenting a supplementary estimate. It is because the excess expenditure has been incurred right at the end of the financial year—after the latest practicable time for getting a supplementary estimate voted—that it has to be carried over and voted as an excess vote in the following year.

Thus the House is presented before the end of March with estimates relating to three separate financial years, ie:

(a) any excess for the previous year;
(b) supplementaries for the closing months of the current year;
(c) estimates (including interim provision) for the coming year.

After 31 March the House has about four months before it rises for the summer recess in which to vote on the main Supply Estimates for the financial year that has now begun (less anything already voted on account). The first block of supplementary estimates in the financial year are usually presented in June or July (the 'summer supplementaries') together with any 'revised' estimates. They are voted at the same time as the main estimates.

---

1 The practice in recent years has been to present them on Budget day together with all the other Papers relating to the Budget.

Taxation

Between March and July the House also disposes of another major piece of financial business—the authorization of taxation to raise the money which it is being asked to grant to meet Government expenditure. In March or early in April the Chancellor of the Exchequer makes his Budget speech, including his proposals for new and varied taxes. These proposals provide the House with material for debate both at once and also later, when the Finance Bill (which gives permanent legislative effect to the proposals) is considered.

Accounts and Audit

Appropriation Accounts, which are audited by the Comptroller and Auditor General and the staff of the National Audit Office throughout the year, are formally rendered to him by about the end of September and laid before the House in the January following the end of the financial year to which they relate. A scrutiny of these Accounts and the audit of the Comptroller and Auditor General is carried out by the Committee of Public Accounts during the session (see pp 660–661).

SCOPE OF FINANCIAL PROCEDURE

Financial procedure is primarily concerned with the authorization of public expenditure sometimes equated to 'charges upon the public revenue' and of taxation, sometimes equated to 'charges upon the people'.

Charges upon the public revenue

A charge 'upon the public revenue' or 'upon public funds' now means an obligation to make a payment out of the Consolidated Fund or the National Loans Fund, ie an item of national expenditure. In relation to expenditure, financial procedure is, with one exception mentioned below, exclusively concerned with charges payable out of the two Funds. Charges upon the public revenue are divided into *charges payable out of moneys to be provided by Parliament*, ie moneys voted year by year[1] in response to demands presented in the form of estimates; and *charges payable directly out of the Consolidated Fund and the National Loans Fund*, ie moneys payable out of the Funds under statute without further parliamentary authority. In addition—and this is the exception just mentioned—under Standing Order No 46, 'the releasing or compounding of any sum of money owing to the Crown' (ie the writing off of any portion of a debt owed to the Consolidated Fund) is treated as a charge.

Charges upon the people

The term 'charge upon the people' is now primarily taken to connote any impost in the nature of a tax or customs duty the proceeds of which are payable into the Consolidated Fund (see pp 726–727). But in a secondary

---

1 Either form of charge upon the public revenue may, of course, be a single payment.

sense it also includes any burden upon local revenues. Financial procedure is concerned with the imposition of burdens upon local authorities' finances, because they are augmented by grants from central government funds (see p 714) and because they fall within the sphere of public finance with respect to which the Commons claim privilege against the Lords (see p 743). In other respects the rules of financial procedure are not applied to local revenues. The Speaker has ruled that the financial standing orders are concerned with *monetary* charges, and that precedents exist for the transference of *property* to the Crown without any resolution preceding a bill.[1]

Limitation of the scope of financial procedure

The rules of financial procedure are not applied to funds or levies which, though they may be public in the sense that they are regulated by statute or publicly administered, exist for sectional rather than national purposes. Examples of such funds and levies are the revenues of the Church Commissioners; funds created within an industry for purposes beneficial to the industry, and the contributions by which such funds are raised (see pp 730–731); and licences and fees charged by departments as payments for services rendered to the public (see p 731). To these may be added such local revenues as form part of distinct and self-balancing funds and the Social Security Fund (see p 717). All these matters are treated as outside the category of charges and as exempt from the rules of financial procedure set out below.

GENERAL RULES OF FINANCIAL PROCEDURE OF THE COMMONS

The general rules which govern the financial procedure of the House of Commons can be generally stated under four heads.

Rule 1. Legislative authorization and appropriation of charges. A charge has to be authorized by legislation; it must originate in the House of Commons (except to the extent that the Commons waive their privilege, or when a bill is brought from the Lords pursuant to Standing Order No 48(2)); and, if it constitutes a service paid for out of moneys provided by Parliament, must be appropriated in the same session as that in which the relevant estimate has been laid before the House.

Rule 2. The financial initiative of the Crown. A charge cannot be taken into consideration unless it is demanded by the Crown or recommended from the Crown.

Rule 3. Preliminary consideration of resolutions. A charge must first be considered in the form of a resolution, which, when agreed to by the House, forms a necessary preliminary to the bill or clause by which the charge is authorized.

Rule 4. Interval between stages of financial legislation. Not more than one stage of a bill founded upon a charging resolution can be taken on the

---

1 HC Deb (1933–34) 291, c 213.

same day. (See however p 709 for the practice in relation to Consolidated Fund Bills).

Rule 1.   Legislative authorization and appropriation of charges

In respect of supply and ways and means.   The rule that legislation is necessary to sanction grants of supply and ways and means is based on ancient constitutional usage. This rule is subject to statutory exceptions, mentioned below, whereby in certain cases provisional validity, and in other cases final validity, is given to resolutions of the House of Commons. The Commons from the earliest times have claimed predominant rights—privilege—in such bills, which were called 'bills of aids and supplies'. The right of the Lords to initiate such bills was denied; their power over them was reduced to the simple giving or withholding of assent; and a special enacting formula was employed for bills of aids and supplies which explicitly asserted the rights of the Commons. This formula is still used for the two modern classes of bills into which the old bills of aids and supplies have been differentiated, namely, Consolidated Fund and Appropriation Bills on the one hand, and, on the other, bills imposing taxation, the principal of which are the annual Finance Bills.[1]

Bills falling into either of these classes cannot be amended by the Lords without infringement of privilege. The modern procedure in respect of privilege arising out of the application of the bill form to the grant of supply is dealt with in chapter 30.

Although legislation is needed to give final sanction to parliamentary grants, a temporary and provisional validity is given to ways and means resolutions imposing taxation by the Provisional Collection of Taxes Act 1968 (first enacted in 1913) (see pp 734–736).

Specific legislative sanction is not required for the imposition of customs duties under powers conferred by the Import Duties Act 1958 and other Acts. The imposition of such duties is finally (not provisionally) authorized by a simple resolution of the House of Commons. The procedure governing the making of value added tax orders is contained in the Finance Act 1972.

Contingencies Fund.   An exception to the rule that Parliament must vote money for a service before any expenditure is incurred is provided by the Contingencies Fund. The Treasury can authorize issues out of this Fund up to a limit fixed by statute to meet expenditure in advance of the granting of authority by Parliament; at present the limit is 2 per cent. of the supply expenditure for the year ending on the previous 31 March authorized by Acts passed before that date.[2] The main circumstances in which the Fund is used are to meet expenditure (other than on new services) in excess of the amount granted in a vote on account; to meet (until a supplementary vote is available) expenditure on unforeseen new services; to meet (until a supplementary vote is available) expenditure in excess of the provisions on those subheads, such as grants in aid, which may not be financed from savings on other subheads; to meet further expenditure on existing services

---

1 In order to mark the fact that the grants which these bills embody are by the free gift of the Commons, the name of the Chairman of Ways and Means precedes the name of any Minister in the list of Members ordered to 'prepare and bring in' such a bill.
2 Contingencies Fund Act 1974.

when the cash provision on the vote is exhausted and to finance working balances over the turn of the financial year. The Accounts of the Fund are presented annually to the House of Commons in pursuance of an order for a return.

By propriety rather than by law no final charge is permitted to rest on the Fund, and Parliament is invariably asked to vote the necessary supply in due course to enable repayment to be made. If expenditure requiring specific legislation necessitates the use of the Fund, recourse to it is normally deferred until the bill has had a second reading.[1]

Appropriation of expenditure. The appropriation of the grants of Supply of the House of Commons to the services for which they are voted is secured annually by legislation, and is enforced outside Parliament by permanent machinery for administering and accounting for the sums issued to departments in accordance with the parliamentary grants.

Three important precepts of financial practice are implied in the appropriation of expenditure. (1) A sum appropriated to a particular service cannot be spent on another service. (2) The sum appropriated is a maximum sum. (3) It is available only in respect of charges which have arisen during the year in respect of which it has been appropriated by the relevant Act. As a consequence, any sum found to be saved on a vote at the end of a financial year must be surrendered to the Exchequer. (However, in the case of a grant in aid, that is a grant from voted money to a particular organization or body, any sums which remain unspent at the end of a financial year are not liable to surrender.)

Destination of revenue. Taxes are payable into the Consolidated Fund by virtue of section 10 of the Exchequer and Audit Departments Act 1866, which provides that the gross revenues collected by the Revenue Departments shall be paid, after deduction of certain payments such as drawbacks, into the Exchequer Account at the Bank of England. The moneys paid into the Exchequer Account form what is termed the Consolidated Fund. Any excess of payments into the Consolidated Fund over payments out of it must be paid into the National Loans Fund. The hereditary revenues of the Crown are directed to be paid into the Exchequer and made part of the Consolidated Fund under the Civil List Act 1952, s. 1. Other items of revenue are payable to the Exchequer under specific statutory provision. Receipts realized by departments in the course of their duties are not as a rule paid into the Exchequer, but are directed under the Public Accounts and Charges Act 1891, section 2 (2), to be applied in aid of their votes. The sums to be applied as 'appropriations in aid' are authorized annually by the Appropriation Act (see p 708).

Legislative authorization for objects of expenditure. The requirement of legislative sanction for expenditure for novel purposes initiated by financial resolutions depends as in the case of Supply upon practice. Charges for novel purposes are charges which require to be authorized by specific legislation. They fall into two classes. Either the charge thus initiated is intended to be payable 'out of money to be provided by Parliament', in which case it will be effectively imposed by the voting of a consequential

---

1 HC Deb (1974) 873, c 1250.

estimate, presented in the same or a succeeding session, and finally author-ized and appropriated by an Appropriation Act. Alternatively the charge is imposed directly 'upon the Consolidated Fund', in which case the Act which authorizes the charge is the authority also for the appropriation of the money necessary to make good the charge. By far the largest single item in the Consolidated Fund Standing Service is the payment to the National Loans Fund in respect of the service of the National Debt. Examples of other items are payments to the European Communities; payments to Northern Ireland of its share of 'reserved' taxes; the Civil List; salaries of the Speaker, of judges, of the Comptroller and Auditor General, of the Parlia-mentary Commissioner for Administration and the Data Protection Regis-trar; and the expenses of returning officers at parliamentary elections.

Rule 2. The financial initiative of the Crown

The long established and strictly observed rule of procedure, which ex-presses a principle of the highest constitutional importance, that no public charge can be incurred except on the initiative of the Crown, seems to be differently based in the case of Supply and Ways and Means, on the one hand, and of expenditure initiated by financial resolutions, on the other.

Supply and Ways and Means. Although it is sometimes connected with the standing order of 1713 (now No 46)—which reserves to the Crown the initiation of expenditure for novel purposes—the rule which withholds from the Commons the initiative in granting Supply and Ways and Means seems to rest upon constitutional practice which had become established long before the passing of that order. This practice may be expressed as the rule that a demand from the Crown invariably precedes a grant by the Commons.

When, with the commencement of parliamentary control over the Ex-chequer, the granting of Supply was differentiated into two functions—the voting of sums of money and the provision of revenue by taxation—it was accepted without question by the House of Commons that the rule applied to both of the now clearly distinguished functions of Supply and of Ways and Means, and to any business which belonged to either of these classes.[1]

In these matters the initiative is reserved to the Crown under consti-tutional practice and its exercise is implied in procedure rather than expressly asserted. An announcement that estimates will be laid before the House of Commons is contained in the Queen's speech at the opening of Parliament; they are presented 'by command' of Her Majesty; and the resolutions by which they are voted make them in terms grants to the Queen. In the case of Ways and Means resolutions for imposing taxes, the exercise of the royal initiative, otherwise unexpressed, is taken to be implied in the demand for Supply, through the old principle that no more money should be raised by taxation than was necessary to cover the Supply already voted by, or at any rate demanded from, the House of Commons.[2]

Expenditure authorised by resolutions. While the royal initiative in Supply and Ways and Means rests upon ancient constitutional usage, in respect of

---

1 Owing to the subordination of Ways and Means to Supply the rule was for long less strictly enforced in Committee of Ways and Means (see p 725).
2 Modern practice has extended the scope of Ways and Means (see p 727).

novel expenditure it is based on Standing Orders. The governing Standing Order is that now numbered 46.[1]

The constitutional importance of this standing order has always been recognized, but it is doubtful whether it can be said to have laid down any new constitutional principle. What it did was rather to recognize the principle underlying the long previously established practice whereby the demand of the Crown regularly preceded the grant of Supply, and to apply this principle to the action of the House in dealing with proposals for expenditure emanating elsewhere than from the Crown.

The intention underlying this procedure was in effect that the Queen's recommendation, signified by a Minister of the Crown, should be an exercise of the financial initiative analogous to the Crown's demand for Supply. If the Queen chose to recommend to the Commons a proposal of expenditure not originally made by herself, she could be regarded as adopting it as an addition to her demand for Supply. The new form was found convenient and, instead of being reserved for petitions, it was soon extended, without any formal change in the Standing Order, to motions, and particularly to motions emanating from Ministers and concerned with matters for which the Crown was responsible.

Rule 3. Preliminary consideration of resolutions

The ancient rule that financial matters must originate in a Committee of the whole House was abandoned in 1966 following the report of a Select Committee on Procedure. This had the effect of removing a stage from financial proceedings, but it left unchanged the need to obtain the authority of a resolution of the House before a charge can be considered in the form of a bill. Thus Consolidated Fund Bills are brought in upon Supply resolutions; Finance Bills and other taxing bills are brought in upon Ways and Means resolutions; and financial resolutions are necessary preliminaries to the consideration in committee of the provisions of other bills which impose charges.

Rule 4. Intervals between stages of financial legislation

The rule that not more than one stage of a financial bill shall be taken on the same day applies only to bills which are brought in on Ways and Means resolutions. It applies in practice only to taxation bills and is capable of being relaxed by order of the House. The third reading of a finance bill is often taken immediately after consideration when such an order has been made[2], and in 1979 a resolution was agreed to to enable the Finance Bill to be brought in and passed through all stages in one day before a dissolution.[3] On 19 July 1982 the House agreed to a Standing Order (No 54) which provides for proceedings on Consolidated Fund Bills and Appropriation Bills to be purely formal and for second and third readings to be taken at a single sitting.[4]

Enforcement of rules of financial procedure

The rules of financial procedure, whether based on practice or upon the standing orders, are strictly observed by the House of Commons; and any

1 Originally passed as a resolution in 1706 and made a standing order in 1713.
2 See e.g. CJ (1985–86) 476.
3 CJ (1978–79) 271.
4 CJ (1981–82) 481.

disregard of them would now only be due to misunderstanding of their applicability in a particular case, or to inadvertence.[1] Questions of interpretation are decided by the Speaker, or if they arise in committee, by the Chairman. In discharging its duty of disallowing any proceedings which would infringe the rules of financial procedure, the Chair relies in the last resort upon its power to decline to propose the necessary questions.

Unless the recommendation of the Crown enjoined by Standing Order No 46 has been signified, the Speaker cannot propose the question on a motion which comes within the scope of this standing order. Accordingly, if any motion is offered to be moved which requires but fails to receive the Queen's recommendation, it is the duty of the Chair to announce that no question can be proposed on the motion.[2]

When bills which should have been brought in on resolutions (see pp 736–738) have been introduced without such preliminary proceedings, the Speaker has declined to propose the necessary questions and the bills have not been proceeded with.[3] Similarly, the Speaker has intervened to prevent two stages of a bill introduced on tax-imposing resolutions being taken on the same day and proceedings on third reading taken inadvertently on the same day as the committee stage have been declared null and void.[4] In February 1986 proceedings in committee and on third reading of a bill at a previous sitting were declared null and void because the necesary financial resolution had not been passed.[5]

Relaxation of financial rules in urgent cases

On rare occasions the provisions of the financial standing orders have been over-ridden by an order of the House[6] (to which the Queen's recommendation was signified) providing that the requirements of some or all of the standing orders, and the practice of the House relating to the imposition of charges on the public revenue, should be deemed to have been complied with in respect of the provisions of a bill or of any Government amendment moved thereto (see also p 711).

APPLICATION TO AMENDMENTS OF RULES REGULATING FINANCIAL PROCEDURE

The House of Commons has long found it necessary to place restrictions on the moving of amendments in order to keep intact the principle of the financial initiative of the Crown.

The royal recommendation fixes the upper limits of a charge

The Crown's recommendation lays down the maximum amount of a charge and its object and purposes. An amendment infringes the financial initiative

---

1 See 3 Hatsell 177 and 167 n.
2 3 Hatsell 168; CJ (1808–09) 266.
3 HC Deb (1912) 35, c 1495, etc.
4 CJ (1956–57) 201.
5 CJ (1985–86) 155.
6 CJ (1938–39) 402, 405; ibid (1939–40) 138; ibid (1946–47) 373; ibid (1947–48) 188; ibid (1953–54) 96.

of the Crown, not only if it increases the amount, but also if it extends the objects and purposes, or relaxes the conditions and qualifications, expressed in the communication by which the Crown has recommended a charge. Accordingly no amendment to a motion for Supply is in order except a simple reduction of the amount demanded. For taxation, the incidence as well as the amount of the burden is implied by the Crown's initiative, and an amendment which would transfer a burden to taxpayers not previously liable is out of order accordingly. This standard is binding not only on private Members but also on Ministers, whose only advantage is that, as advisers of the Crown, they can present new or supplementary estimates or secure the royal recommendation to new or supplementary resolutions. In the case of Supply resolutions and financial resolutions, the Crown's recommendation is expressed formally to the resolutions of which notice has been given and accordingly they cannot be varied orally at the time that they are moved. In the case of Ways and Means resolutions notice is not required, and the Crown's recommendation is not formally signified; accordingly in the case of Ways and Means resolutions, if notice has been given, the form of the resolution may nevertheless be varied orally when it is moved.

If a financial or Ways and Means resolution is amended, it is the final version of the resolution which is effective and the charge imposed may not exceed the limits so laid down.

CHAPTER 27

Expenditure: Supply

This chapter (which is the first of four describing in detail the financial procedure of Parliament) is concerned solely with the procedure under which the ordinary expenditure of the year is demanded, voted, and sanctioned by legislation. It deals with the main varieties of estimates and the form in which they are presented; with the procedure for voting estimates; and with the Consolidated Fund Bills and Appropriation Bills which, respectively, authorize the issue of sums out of the Consolidated Fund and restrict their application both in scope and amount to the services for which Supply has been voted. Of the other kinds of expenditure, that on 'Consolidated Fund Services' is mentioned on p 691, while the authorization of expenditure on new purposes by special bills forms the subject of the next chapter.

1. THE SUPPLY ESTIMATES

DIFFERENT KINDS OF ESTIMATES

Estimates are divided into:

(1) Ordinary Annual Estimates (Main Estimates).
(2) Votes on Account.
(3) Supplementary Estimates.
(4) Excess Votes.

In the past demands for supply have also been met by votes of credit and by exceptional grants. These are described below on pp 702–703.

A. ORDINARY ANNUAL ESTIMATES (MAIN ESTIMATES)

In accordance with the royal direction the Supply estimates are annually laid before the House of Commons, stating the specific grants of money which will, during the current year, be required for the civil and defence services, for House of Commons administration and for the National Audit Office. On presentation, the estimates are ordered to be printed. It should be noted that, although presented 'by Command', the estimates are, unlike other command papers, presented not to both Houses of Parliament but to the House of Commons only, and are printed not at the instance of a department

695

but by order of the House; they are numbered as House of Commons papers and not in the series of command papers.

Presentation and publication of estimates

The Supply estimates for the forthcoming financial year have in recent years been presented and published on budget day together with the other financial papers. The publication of the estimates is accompanied by the presentation as a command paper of a memorandum upon all the estimates by the Chief Secretary to the Treasury. The memorandum contains tables giving, among other things, the overall total of the Supply estimates, and analyses the public expenditure content of the estimates and compares this with the public expenditure programmes as published in the latest White Paper on Public Expenditure. The public expenditure content of the estimates is also analysed in terms of economic classifications. The staff employed in central Government is analysed by main programme, by department and by function.

Form of the estimates

As the Sovereign is responsible for the presentation of the estimates of the public expenditure, the Crown, acting through its Ministers, controls, subject to the requirements of the Exchequer and Audit Departments Act 1866, the form in which the estimates are presented.[1] This control has devolved on the Treasury as the chief financial department, and as responsible under section 23 of that Act for the form of the accounts of each spending department—the form of an account being necessarily determined by that of the estimate, which is its 'precursor and foundation'.[2] Under established usage, however, important changes in the customary form of the estimates should not be made without the previous approval of the Committee of Public Accounts (see pp 660–661), and since 1921 of first the Estimates Committee,[3] then the Expenditure Committee and now the Treasury and Civil Service Committee, acting on behalf of the House of Commons; and, in deference to this principle, official alterations in the estimates are restricted to such rearrangements as involve no question of principle.[4] The committees themselves often initiate changes in the form of the estimates (see for example HC 1980–81 325 as a result of which considerable changes were made in the form of the Supply estimates for 1982–83).

The contents of the estimates

The estimates are limited to setting out only the sums which it is calculated will be paid in the current year, and do not show the value of assets held or

---

1 HC Deb (1963–64) 691, c 37.
2 Epit HC 154 (1937–38) p 212.
3 HC Deb (1921) 143, cc 1506–1507, 2079–2082.
4 Parl Deb (1890) 341, c 1517; see also Public Accounts Committee's Reports HC 333 (1867) p iii; ibid 350 (1881) p iii; ibid 405 (1888) p iv; ibid 71 (1890) p iv; ibid 361 (1890–91) p ix; ibid 288 (1904) p x ; ibid 179 (1913) p iii; ibid 115 (1916) p xxiii; ibid 125 (1923) p 31; ibid 27 (1968–69); see also Eighth Report of the Expenditure Committee, 1972–73, HC 209.

the liabilities outstanding from the previous financial year or to be spread over future years.

The principle underlying the classification of estimates is that each class of the estimates is designed to correspond to a separate programme as classified in the Government's Public Expenditure White Paper; as far as possible connected services appear together, and the estimates for the services controlled by a particular department are mainly grouped in the same class.

Each class is divided into a number of votes, on each of which it is possible for the House to take a separate decision (see p 704). Votes are units of appropriation (see p 690). They are drawn up on a departmental basis, and each vote specifies which department is accountable for it, but there may be several votes controlled by a single department.

The net cost only of administering a service is demanded in each vote; and, to arrive at its total cost, it is necessary to add first appropriations in aid (see pp 698–699) and second the value of services rendered by other departments, for instance, those for heating, lighting, accommodation, etc. These inter-departmental services are borne on the estimates of the Department of the Environment, etc, but a table showing the cost of other supporting services is printed with each class of the estimates.

The main Supply estimates for 1989–90 consisted of 167 votes, classified as follows:

Class	Department
I	Defence
II	Foreign and Commonwealth Office
IV	Ministry of Agriculture, Fisheries and Food
V	Trade and Industry
VI	Energy
VII	Employment
VIII	Transport
IX	DOE—Housing
X	DOE—Other environmental services
XI	Home Office and legal departments
XII	Education and Science
XIII	Arts and Libraries
XIV	Health
XV	Social security
XVI	Scotland
XVII	Wales
XVIII	Northern Ireland
XIX	Chancellor of Exchequer's departments
XX	Other departments
XX A	House of Commons
XX B	National Audit Office

(No estimate was presented for Class III—European Communities.)

Sub-division of votes

Each vote is divided into four parts:

Part I gives a formal description of the services to be financed from the vote, known as its 'ambit'. It also shows the net amount of money required for the coming financial year, the department or person(s) who will account for the vote and the amount allocated to it in the vote on account. The ambit is reproduced in the Appropriation Act and provides the statutory description in that Act of the purpose for which the Supply demanded in the estimate is granted. No voted expenditure can therefore be properly incurred on any service which is not covered by the ambit. The remaining parts of the vote give supporting detail. The only figure from the remaining parts which is reproduced in the Appropriation Act is the total figure for appropriations in aid—that is, receipts which, with the authority of Parliament, are used to finance some of the gross expenditure on the vote and therefore limit the amount which needs to be issued from the Consolidated Fund.

Part II of the vote analyses the gross and net provision sought in the Supply estimate by functional programme and by subhead. Within programmes related subheads may be further grouped into sections. These subheads themselves may be further analysed into different items and frequently include some explanatory narrative. The subheads of a vote are the headings under which the Treasury requires the expenditure to be accounted for. Departments may not redistribute the sums shown under the subheads of a Supply estimate without the agreement of the Treasury who, so long as the total gross and net amounts voted are not exceeded, may sanction the use of the savings under one subhead to meet excess expenditure under another—a process known as 'virement'. This discretion is not extended to cases where the proposed re-allocation is thought to be of such importance or to consti-tute so great a departure from the original Supply estimate that it ought to be brought specifically before Parliament by means of a supplementary esti-mate.

The figures shown in the subheads do not appear in the Appropriation Act. On 17 July 1984 certain subheads of votes in Classes II and XIV of the supply estimates were the subject of specific votes in advance of the resol-ution which included the balance of those votes. The votes concerned were not divided or distinguished in the subsequent Appropriation Act, and the power of virement was not affected.[1]

Part III gives particulars of receipts which are expected to be received in connection with the expenditure on the vote but which are to be paid into the Consolidated Fund and not appropriated in aid of the vote. Whether receipts are appropriated in aid or treated as Consolidated Fund extra receipts depends upon a variety of considerations including whether it is thought more appropriate to set a cash limit on gross or net expenditures. Because the total receipts appropriated in aid of each vote to the Supply estimates are reproduced in the Appropriation Act, any additional receipts received during the course of the year can only be appropriated in aid if the authority of Parliament is first sought through a supplementary estimate.

Part IV of each vote analyses the total in Part I of the vote by functional programme and type of expenditure, distinguishing between public and other expenditure and, within the former, between current and capital expenditure.

Appropriations in aid

As previously stated, the sum to be voted shown in Part I of an estimate is a net sum, being the difference between the total expenditure shown under

---

1 CJ (1983–84) 700.

the expenditure subheads in Part II and the receipts (if any) in respect of those subheads. These receipts, which arise in the course of business of a department (through fees or sales, etc), are, instead of being paid into the Consolidated Fund, directed by Treasury Minute under the Public Accounts and Charges Act 1891 to be appropriated in aid of the department's estimate as if they were money provided by Parliament for that purpose. The amount of its receipts which a department may use is limited and subject to Parliamentary control in the Appropriation Act, and any surplus actually received above the amount estimated to be received by a department is not applied as an appropriation in aid but is paid into the Consolidated Fund as 'extra receipts'.

Token votes and subheads

Receipts in the case of certain services, such as those of the Public Trustee, may be equal to or greater than the gross expenditure. In such a case, in order to maintain Parliamentary control over the gross expenditure, a 'token' estimate for a conventional sum—normally £1,000—is presented, receipts being appropriated in aid to an amount less by £1,000 than the gross expenditure on the service and the balance of receipts being paid as 'extra' receipts into the Consolidated Fund.

A token subhead is inserted in a main estimate when it is anticipated that a grant of money will be required for a service involving an extension of the ambit of Part I as previously defined, or when the amount of the grant cannot be precisely estimated, either because of its contingent nature or because, being a new service, insufficient detail is available. In such a case a 'token' sum is inserted under the appropriate subhead, together with the information so far available, and the expenditure actually incurred is financed either out of savings on the vote generally or by the subsequent presentation of a supplementary estimate (see also p 701).

Revised estimates

If it proves to be necessary to vary the terms of a vote (so as to alter the ambit of the vote, or even to alter materially the descriptions of a subhead) or to reduce the amount demanded, the original estimate is withdrawn and a revised estimate presented. This can, of course, only be done before the original estimate has been voted. According to modern practice it is rare to present a revised estimate for an increased amount. If an increased amount is required, the original estimate is proceeded with, and a supplementary estimate is presented unless the sum involved is exceptionally large, when a revised estimate may be presented to draw attention to this fact.[1]

Votes A

In addition to the ordinary defence estimates, the Secretary of State for Defence presents each February the Votes A for the Navy, Army and Air Force. These seek Parliamentary authority for the maximum numbers of personnel to be maintained for service with the armed forces during the following financial year. For historical reasons only a total number of

---

1 See revised estimate for Export Guarantees, 1972–73 (HC 198 (1971–72)).

officers, ratings and Royal Marines has to be authorized for Naval service, but for the Army and the Air Force separate authority has also to be given for the maximum numbers to be maintained in certain reserve forces.

B. VOTES ON ACCOUNT

Since the sums granted by Parliament to cover the estimated expenditure of a particular year are appropriated by statute to the service of that year only, it follows that any unexpended sums in the hands of the departments at the end of one financial year cannot be retained for use in the next, but must be surrendered to the Consolidated Fund. It is, accordingly, necessary to make provision in advance for the public service during the coming financial year. Various considerations—such as the undesirability of framing estimates too long in advance of the year to which they relate—combine to make it impossible to dispose of the estimates before the beginning of the financial year. Some provision of grants before the beginning of the year and in advance of complete parliamentary sanction is therefore necessary. Special estimates are presented seeking 'votes on account' which provide a total amount to cover the needs of the defence services, the civil services, House of Commons administration and the National Audit Office respectively for the requisite period of four or five months before complete provision will have been made by the passage into law of the Appropriation Act.

The operative part of the votes on account for the coming year is a demand for an aggregate sum representing standard proportions (approximately 45 per cent) of the amounts voted so far for the corresponding services in the current year, except where it is known that any particular amounts required will differ significantly from this standard provision.[1] In a schedule are given figures showing for each vote that will be included later in the ordinary estimates (1) the total net amount voted to date, and (2) the amount required to be voted on account.

Demands for grants on account are restricted to such services as have received the sanction of Parliament, but provision may also be made in respect of a service in respect of which specific legislation is currently before Parliament.

Votes on account before a dissolution

Grants on account may also be rendered necessary by a dissolution of Parliament. If the dissolution occurs in the earlier part of a session, it may be necessary to take votes on account sufficient to carry on all the civil and defence services until the new Parliament is able to consider the grant of Supply.[2]

The grants on account made necessary by a dissolution should be sanctioned by an Appropriation Act, passed before Parliament is dissolved,

---

1 See First and Second Reports of the Select Committee on Procedure (HC 410 and 411 (1968–69)) and Special Report from the Committee of Public Accounts (HC 27 (1968–69)).
2 CJ (1859) 158; ibid (1965–66) 130. Before the dissolutions in May 1929, 1955 and 1970, however, the whole of supply was voted, CJ (1928–29) 254; ibid (1954–55) 152; ibid (1969–70) 340. Before the May dissolutions of 1983 and 1987 all the main supply estimates were voted and incorporated into Appropriation Acts. The Summer supplementaries were voted and appropriated in the succeeding Parliaments.

applying in detail all the Supply voted in the expiring session in the same manner as at the close of an ordinary session; and the amount of Supply left unvoted is dealt with by the succeeding Parliament.[1] In 1979, when Parliament was dissolved on 4 April, an Appropriation Act was passed which appropriated the sums granted on account and certain supplementaries.

C. SUPPLEMENTARY ESTIMATES

A supplementary estimate may be presented either (1) for a further grant to an existing service, in addition to the sum already demanded for the current financial year, or (2) for a grant caused by a fresh occasion for expenditure that has arisen since the presentation of the sessional estimates, such as expenditure on behalf of a service newly imposed upon the executive government by statute, or to meet the cost created by an unexpected emergency.

The Spring supplementary estimates are, if possible, presented before the main estimates for the following year are published, as they enter into the figures of expenditure for the current year, which are repeated in those estimates for the purpose of comparison with the figures of expenditure for the coming year.

Token votes (supplementary)

The occasions on which a 'token' supplementary vote (normally £1,000) is required are the following:

(1) When it is desired to incur expenditure on a service which is not within the ambit of Part I of the existing vote, although the additional expenditure can be fully covered by savings on other subheads;

here a token sum is demanded, the additional expenditure being shown in gross under its appropriate subheads and the savings (allocated by subheads) shown as a deduction therefrom;

(2) if expenditure in excess of an original gross estimate can be covered by increased receipts, Parliamentary authority, necessary for the use of receipts in excess of those already appropriated in aid, is obtained by presenting a token supplementary estimate showing the increase in gross expenditure and, as a deduction, the increase in appropriations in aid;

(3) when it is necessary to secure Parliamentary authority for a new service, the cost of which is to be met by a special contribution from non-public sources; and

(4) when it is proposed to make a material change in the conditions under which an original grant has been voted, and even though the change in conditions may not require the specific approval of Parliament.

---

1 See also Appropriation Acts 1886 and 1974 (sess. I and II).

D. EXCESS VOTES

The need for an excess vote arises when a department has carried expenditure upon a service beyond the amount granted to that service, during the financial year for which the grant was made.[1]

Procedure on excess votes

Demands for excess grants are not brought before the House of Commons until the following steps have been taken. When the exact amount of the excess expenditure for the past financial year has been ascertained on the completion of the audit of the appropriation accounts, the Comptroller and Auditor General reports to the House and this report comes before the Committee of Public Accounts. After examination, the Committee makes a report to the House, if possible in February or early March of the financial year following that in which the excess occurred, setting out the various excesses, and stating the objections (if any) to their being approved. The Treasury then presents a Statement of Excesses, setting out all the instances of excess expenditure for the year in question, which is presented as a single vote for each branch of the estimates in which excess expenditure has occurred. If the Committee of Public Accounts reports that it sees no objection, the question on excess votes may be put without debate on a day not later than 18 March, pursuant to Standing Order No 53(3) (see p 707).[2] The vote is normally included in the March Consolidated Fund Bill,[3] and receives final sanction in the next Appropriation Act.

Votes of credit. Unexpected demands upon the resources of the United Kingdom, for example for a military undertaking, which on account of the magnitude or indefiniteness of the service cannot be stated with the detail given in an ordinary estimate, are brought before Parliament by an application, based on an estimate of the total sum required, for a vote of credit.[4] Sums obtained upon a vote of credit are, like other grants of supply, available solely during the financial year in respect of which the grant is made.[5]

The form of a vote of credit is a demand for a lump sum with the objects stated in very general terms. It is accounted for by the Treasury, which issues money to the departments in accordance with their requirements so far as

1 The House by resolution (CJ (1849) 190) has attached great importance to the duty of departments not to exceed the authorized limits to their expenditure. However the Committee of Public Accounts has also drawn attention to the danger of over-estimating in order to avoid an excess vote (eg HC 362 (1968–69), para 29).

2 Although the Public Accounts Committee frequently draws general conclusions from particular excess votes, there is no case of it objecting to a vote being granted.

3 On occasions, in order to give facilities for further discussion, excess votes have not been taken until a late date in the session, CJ (1902) 402; Parl Deb (1902) 104, c 296; CJ (1903) 378; see also ibid (1943–44) 152; ibid (1945–46) 311; ibid (1974) 293.

4 CJ (1882) 407; ibid (1885) 173; ibid (1914) 426; ibid (1914–16) 8, 66, 145, 206, 234, 281; ibid (1916) 8, 9, 88; ibid (1918) 25, 116, 177, 231; ibid (1938–39) 405; ibid (1939–40) 72, 176, 240; ibid (1940–41) 34, 140, 194; ibid (1941–42) 22, 58, 117, 160, 173; ibid (1942–43) 28, 107, 138, 179; ibid (1943–44) 25, 108, 149; ibid (1944–45) 24, 136; ibid (1945–46) 34. The practice of demanding a vote of credit by a message from the Crown has, since 1854, ibid (1854) 432, been discontinued.

5 Parl Deb (1884) 285, c 875.

they fall within the scope of the objects for which the vote of credit has been granted. During the war years 1914–18 and 1939–45 the services unconnected with the war were provided for by ordinary estimates, and no grants out of the vote of credit were applicable to such services. Several votes of credit were taken in each of those years, and each vote was confirmed by a Consolidated Fund Bill; in the war of 1914–18, the Appropriation Act was delayed till late in the autumn, but in the war of 1939–45 a second or third Appropriation Act was passed shortly before the end of the session.[1]

Under Standing Order No 53 questions for granting votes of credit are excluded from the questions which are required to be put without debate (see p 707).

Exceptional grants. Expenditure of an unusual character may be initiated in a variety of ways. The provision made for the Civil List on the demise of the Crown has regularly been made in response to a demand by message from the Sovereign under the sign manual[2] (see p 718). Any payments required have then been authorized by the Acts subsequently passed in response to the message and charged upon the Consolidated Fund accordingly. Grants to distinguished naval, military and air commanders have been made in response to a message,[3] but have been provided for by supply resolutions and the Appropriation Act. A similar course was taken in the case of the expenses attending the state funeral of Sir Winston Churchill.[4] The initiative has also come effectively from the Commons, when they have agreed to addresses, for example, for the erection of memorial statues[5] or (under former practice) for the conferring of some signal mark of Royal favour on retiring Speakers of the House,[6] with assurances that the House would make good the attendant expenses. Again the expenses were either borne on supply resolutions or were made charges upon the Consolidated Fund by ensuing Acts of Parliament.[7]

2. THE VOTING OF ESTIMATES

On 19 July 1982, following a report from the Select Committee on Procedure (Supply),[8] the House agreed to major alterations of standing orders which came into effect from the beginning of session 1982–83. Two principal changes were made. New procedures were adopted for considering the estimates; these are described in more detail in the following paragraphs. At the same time the previous arrangement of having so-called 'Supply Days' on which discussion of the estimates could in theory take place but which in

---

1 Eg in session 1941–42, the Appropriation Act received the Royal Assent on 6 August, the second Appropriation Act on 11 September and the third on 22 October.
2 CJ (1901) 60; ibid (1910) 171 (Civil Lists); ibid (1830–31) 719 (Duchess of Kent and Princess Alexandrina Victoria of Kent); ibid (1850) 539 (Duke of Cambridge); ibid (1857) 153 (Princess Royal); ibid (1863) 69 (Prince of Wales), resolutions agreed to nem. con; ibid (1889) 290 (Prince Albert Edward), etc.
3 CJ (1935–36) 207; ibid (1936–37) 258; ibid (1951–52) 307.
4 CJ (1964–65) 110.
5 See eg CJ (1976–77) 60.
6 See eg CJ (1970–71) 191; for current practice on the Speaker's retirement see p 18.
7 See eg Mr Speaker King's Retirement Act 1971, s 1(3).
8 HC 118 (1980–81).

practice were available for the debate of topics chosen by the Opposition,[1] was altered to take account of the reality of the situation. Instead a number of days were allotted for Opposition debates (see pp 261–262), without a specified relationship to the consideration of estimates.

Procedure under Standing Orders Nos 52 and 53

Standing Order No 52 provides for three days (one of which may be divided into two half days) specifically for the consideration of estimates recommended for debate by the Liaison Committee. The Liaison Committee may recommend that an estimate be debated only so far as one of its several purposes is concerned.[2] Standing Order No 53 provides for the voting of sums to be granted out of the Consolidated Fund without debate (or without further debate if they have been debated on the three allotted days). These two Standing Orders were formerly one and the division of the earlier Standing Order took place on 27 February 1986. That division recognized the practical difference between the House's functions of debating an estimate and of authorizing the issue of sums from the Consolidated Fund.

The basic purpose of the new Standing Orders is twofold. They enable the Government to obtain at regular intervals the finance necessary to carry on its essential business. At the same time they enable the House to devote a specific amount of time to consideration of selected estimates, and, equally importantly, to vote on such estimates and amendments thereto. They are framed in such a way as to recognise that the House cannot and will not discuss in detail all the numerous estimates described in the first part of this chapter. They also take account, through the role of the Liaison Committee (see p 658 and Standing Order No 131), of the need for the House to be given adequate information, by means of select committee reports or otherwise,[3] as to which estimates have topical interest and which features of such estimates merit a debate.

Timing of estimates days

The timing of the three days appointed for consideration of the estimates under Standing Order No 52 is flexible, the only proviso being that they must be taken before 5 August. It is thus possible for the House to devote all three days to the main estimates or to devote one, two or even all three days to the supplementary estimates. The determination of the pattern to be followed in any session is largely in the hands of the Liaison Committee, who will be guided by the nature of the particular estimates presented as well as by the workload of the individual select committees at any one time. Estimates days often coincide with the days on which the remaining estimates are voted under the 'guillotine' procedure (see p 707), but there is no procedural requirement for them to do so.

---

1 For a full description of the former procedures, see 19th edn, pp 728 ff.
2 For the effect of this procedure on the rules of debate see p 706.
3 In its choice of estimates to recommend for consideration the Liaison Committee is not limited to such estimates as have been commented upon in the reports of Select Committees.

Choice of estimates for debate and vote

Responsibility for determining which estimates are considered on each of the three allotted days, the order in which they are considered, and the time allotted to consideration of each estimate rests with the Liaison Committee (see pp 658 and 704). Under Standing Order No 131 the Committee is required to report its recommendations as to the allocation of time for consideration by the House of the estimates on any day allotted for that purpose. No formal provision is made for a time limit within which the Committee must report before the House considers the estimates; but if the Committee reports some days beforehand, adequate notice can be given to the House of which estimates are to considered and amendments can be tabled accordingly. A motion to agree with the report of the Committee may be made either at the beginning of proceedings on an allotted day or on a previous day,[1] and the question on it is put forthwith. Once agreed to, the recommendations of the Committee have the effect of an order of the House.[2]

Form of resolutions

Each estimate to be considered is placed before the House by a motion, which states the amount to be granted, and the particular service or services for which the sum is demanded. The amount to be granted is the total sum required for the service less any amount already granted by a vote on account and any appropriations in aid. The form the motion takes is 'That a sum, not exceeding £x be granted to Her Majesty out of the Consolidated Fund, to [complete the sum necessary to][3] defray the charge which will come in course of payment during the year ending on 31 March 19 . . for the services therein specified'. A motion for a vote on account states the total sum required; the amounts needed for each vote are set out in a schedule in the relevant papers.

Although it is the Liaison Committee which determines the order in which estimates are to be considered, the proposal of any motion must be made by a Minister in accordance with the rule of the House about the financial initiative of the Crown (see p 688). Motions to grant the sums concerned are customarily tabled in the name of the Financial Secretary to the Treasury.

Form of amendments

In accordance with the general rules of the House relating to financial procedure, no amendment to a motion for the grant of a sum is in order

---

1 See eg CJ (1985–86) 469.
2 SO No 131(2).
3 These words are inserted when a vote on account has been taken in respect of a service.

which seeks to increase the total sum to be granted.[1] A proposal to reduce an estimate is expressed in the form 'That Class X, Vote Y be reduced by £Z [in respect of Subhead –]', the words in square brackets being included if it is desired to draw attention to a particular item in that vote. Amendments may be tabled on behalf of a particular select committee which has considered and reported on that estimate or by any other Member. Any number of amendments may be tabled to a particular motion, but it is for the Chair to determine which if any of the amendments are to be selected.

Relevancy in debate

The normal rules of debate apply to consideration of the estimates; the main principle is that debate should be relevant to the matter which is contained in the estimate currently under discussion. On a main estimate it is in order to discuss the general policy which lies behind the demand for that particular sum of money. Where an amendment has been moved to reduce a particular item, or where a supplementary estimate is being considered, debate should be confined to the reasons why the reduction is sought or why the extra money is sought; nevertheless a motion for a token reduction can be used as a 'peg' for arguments for the increase or extension of a service.[2] In applying the rule of relevance the Chair also takes into account the recommendations of the Liaison Committee as agreed by the House. The Chair has ruled that, once the House has agreed to a report from the Liaison Committee, the recommendations therein have effect as if they were orders of the House.[3] The purpose of the procedure is not to permit discussions of general policy, as occurred under the previous 'Supply Days' procedure, but to focus attention on the need to grant, reduce or refuse to grant particular items of expenditure.

Voting individual estimates

On each of the three days allotted for consideration of the estimates, the time for debating each estimate recommended by the Liaison Committee is set out in the Report from that Committee and agreed to by the House. When the time allotted for a particular estimate has expired, the Chair does not put the question on the estimate or amendment currently before the House, but proceeds immediately to call a Minister to move the next estimate which is down for consideration. Under Standing Order No 52(5) the questions necessary to dispose of proceedings on the estimates set down for consideration on any allotted day are deferred until ten o'clock (though an amendment may be withdrawn either at the end of the relevant debate[4] or at ten o'clock). At that time therefore debate on the last estimate set down for consideration is interrupted. The Chair then proceeds to put successively the questions on any amendment or amendments selected to the first estimate considered, followed by the question on the estimate itself; the same procedure is followed immediately for the other estimates which have been

---

1 The Select Committee on Procedure (Supply) considered the possibility of allowing motions stating that 'in the opinion of the House' increases in a particular vote should be made, but recommended that such a motion should not be in order (HC 118 (1980–81) p xxiv).
2 CJ (1985–86) 483.
3 HC Deb 129 (1987–88) 129, c 207.
4 CJ (1982–83) 233.

considered. If an amendment is carried, the subsequent question put by the Chair on the estimate is 'That a sum, not exceeding £[A minus B], be granted' etc (where A is the original sum requested and B the reduction proposed in the successful amendment).

Voting the remaining estimates

Standing Order No 53(5) provides that at least two days' notice shall be given of the estimates which are to be put down for agreement by the House under the 'guillotine' procedure. Chapter 26 describes the financial time-table for each session, and Standing Order No 53 provides for the requisite sums to be voted at the appropriate time. In determining the total amount required for each financial year, account has to be taken of the amounts voted for particular estimates on any of the three allotted days; those totals are subtracted from the total amount sought. Under Standing Order No 53 the Speaker is required at ten o'clock to put the question that the total amount outstanding in respect of each financial year be granted, and in the case of the March guillotine that the appropriate numbers be maintained for defence services (the Votes A). It remains open to Members to vote against any of these questions but no amendment may be proposed, nor is it possible for Members to vote against any of the individual items or sub-totals which go to make up the total amounts put to the House under the Standing Order.

3. BILLS AUTHORIZING GRANTS OF SUPPLY

All grants of supply voted in respect of whatever estimate—ordinary, supplementary or excess—require to be authorized by legislation (see p 688). The bills for this purpose are known as Consolidated Fund Bills and are brought in upon the relevant estimates resolutions, and it is the duty of the Public Bill Office to prepare these bills for the Chairman of Ways and Means and the Treasury Ministers who are ordered by the House to bring them in. In so doing, the Office ensures, on behalf of the Speaker,[1] that the bills do not contain grants which have not originated in resolutions.

Consolidated Fund Bills

As stated on p 688 sanction of the issue of money immediately required for the public service is necessary every session before the final completion of financial arrangements enables the Appropriation Bill to be introduced. This sanction is given by Consolidated Fund Bills which are passed for the purpose of authorizing the Treasury to issue money out of the Consolidated Fund in pursuance of the Exchequer and Audit Departments Act 1866 and the Public Accounts and Charges Act 1891.

There are usually two Consolidated Fund Bills (any bill subsequent to the first in each session being distinguished by a number) in the period between the beginning of the session and the end of the financial year. Normally the first bill of the session is that incorporating[2] the defence, civil, House of Commons administration and National Audit Office votes on account, and

---

1 Report on Public Moneys, HC 279 (1857) p 27, sess. II; Todd II, 230.
2 See SO No 53(2).

the winter supplementary estimates, which have been voted on a day not later than 6 February. The second bill is usually that passed towards the end of March which authorizes the issue from the Consolidated Fund of sums to make good (1) further (spring) supplementary grants for the closing financial year; and (2) grants to make good excesses incurred in the previous financial year. Sometimes, however, when further grants need to be authorized, a separate Consolidated Fund Bill is introduced for this purpose early in the session.[1] Similarly, if additional grants are urgently required, further Consolidated Fund Bills may be brought in later in the session.[2]

A Consolidated Fund Bill consists of a special enacting formula which expresses the predominant share of the House of Commons in finance (see pp 442, 491), and clauses authorizing the Treasury to issue money out of the Consolidated Fund to make good Supply already granted. If the Supply is in respect of different years, the Supply for each financial year is embodied in a separate clause.

The Appropriation Act

The final Consolidated Fund Bill is the Consolidated Fund (Appropriation) Bill, which on enactment receives the title of the Appropriation Act. It supplements the Consolidated Fund Bills passed earlier in the session by authorizing the issue of the remaining sums for the service of the year, and to that extent its contents are similar to those of a Consolidated Fund Bill. But in addition it appropriates the money issued by it and by the preceding Consolidated Fund Bills of the session, vote by vote, to the services for which they were granted, in terms following those of Part I of each individual estimate; and authorizes the application, as appropriations in aid, of receipts to the amount specified.

Exceptionally the Appropriation Bills of 1974 and 1979 only appropriated moneys issued under previous Acts, since the reason for the bills was the imminent dissolution of Parliament and no further grants were required at the date of their introduction.

Since 1974 Appropriation Acts have also repealed spent Consolidated Fund and Appropriation Acts.

Appropriation to be completed each session

The principle of appropriation, the constitutional importance of which has been indicated in the previous chapter (pp 689–691), requires that all money issued from the Consolidated Fund should be appropriated by statute to the services for which it has been voted, and that the session should not be closed before this has been done. If it is intended to dissolve Parliament before Supply for the year has been provided, any grants on account that may be necessary must be appropriated by an Appropriation Act before the session is closed (see pp 700–701). If at any time during a session after the Appropriation Act has been passed further grants of money are voted, a second[3] or even a third[4] Appropriation Act may become necessary.

1 Eg Consolidated Fund Bill 1974–75, enacted as the Consolidated Fund (No 4) Act 1974.
2 Eg Consolidated Fund (No 2) Bill 1974, enacted as the Consolidated Fund (No 3) Act 1974.
3 CJ (1902) 493; ibid (1955–56) 390.
4 CJ (1941–42) 166, 178.

The prorogation or dissolution of Parliament without an Appropriation Act having been passed is a constitutional irregularity, as thereby all the grants of the Commons are nullified. The sums would have to be voted again in the next session, before a legal appropriation could be effected.[1]

Proceedings on Consolidated Fund and Appropriation Bills

Proceedings in the Commons. Under Standing Order No 54 agreed to by the House on 19 July 1982 which came into force from the beginning of the 1982–83 session, proceedings on a Consolidated Fund Bill or Appropriation Bill are purely formal. The question on second reading is put forthwith as soon as the order of the day is read, no order is made for the committal of the bill, and the question for third reading is then put forthwith.

Under the same Standing Order as soon as proceedings on the Bill are complete, the adjournment may be moved, and a series of private Members' debates takes place which may continue until nine o'clock the following morning (or eight o'clock if the motion is moved on a Thursday).[2] For the Standing Order to take effect, a Consolidated Fund or Appropriation Bill must stand as the first order of the day.

Proceedings in the Lords. Consolidated Fund Bills and Appropriation Bills are invariably certified by the Speaker of the House of Commons as 'money bills' under the Parliament Act 1911 (see pp 751–752) and they can therefore be submitted for the Royal Assent under that Act if they are not passed by the Lords within one month. In practice proceedings on Consolidated Fund and Appropriation Bills are often completed in one day in the Lords. Such bills are never committed; nor are they ordered to be printed by the Lords. On 3 March 1982 the House agreed to a report from the Procedure Committee which stated: 'While it is clear that it is neither unconstitutional nor contrary to the privileges of the Commons for the Lords to discuss and even to divide upon Consolidated Fund Bills, the House has as a matter of fact passed such Bills without such discussion or dissent for over seventy years and there is a general, though unwritten, convention that proceedings upon them are taken formally'.[3]

Royal Assent. For a description of the pronouncing of the Royal Assent by Commission to a bill of aids and supplies see p 529.

---

1 On the advice of Pitt in 1784, and of Lord Grey in 1831. The Commons, in 1784, resolved that the persons who acted on Supply grants unsanctioned by an Appropriation Act, would be guilty of a high crime and misdemeanour, CJ (1782–84) 858.
2 For a description of the previous procedure under which the second reading of Consolidated Fund Bills and Appropriation Bills was used as a vehicle for similar debates, but with the topic notionally linked to a particular item of expenditure contained in the bill, see 19th edn pp 745–747.
3 HL Deb (1981–82) 427, cc 1289–1290.

CHAPTER 28

Expenditure: financial resolutions

The procedure in respect of ordinary annual expenditure which is comprised in the estimates and is authorised for a single year by the Appropriation Act has been described in the preceding chapter. It remains to explain the procedure upon the other main branch of expenditure, expenditure for new purposes requiring to be authorized by specific enactment of less limited duration, which is initiated, as a matter of ordinary practice, by resolutions—'Financial Resolutions' or 'Money Resolutions', as they are called—with the recommendation of the Crown signified thereto. This expenditure, too (unless it is imposed as a direct charge on the Consolidated Fund or National Loans Fund), will have to be provided for in the supply estimates and authorized by the Appropriation Act, but on a recurrent basis. It should be added that the procedure about to be explained is applicable to certain matters which are not strictly expenditure but involve a loss to the Exchequer, such as the remission of debts owed to the Crown.

Application to new expenditure of the general rules of financial procedure

Before describing the varieties of new expenditure initiated by financial resolutions, it will be convenient to show how the general rules governing financial procedure in Parliament (see pp 688–689) are modified in their application to this class of expenditure.

(1) The legislative authorization, required by Rule 1, for such expenditure is given in each case by a bill which may originate in either House (though, if it originates in the House of Lords, the expedient for avoiding the infringement of privilege must be used) (see pp 745–746).
(2) The proof, required by Rule 2, that the charge is initiated by the Crown, is given either in the form of a message under the sign manual or (ordinarily) by means of a royal recommendation signified in writing by a Minister of the Crown to the resolution imposing the charge.
(3) The need for the initiation of expenditure by resolution (Rule 3) is the subject of this chapter.
(4) The intervals between stages of financial legislation, prescribed by Rule 4, are required only in the case of bills introduced upon resolution; since bills whose main purpose is to authorize expenditure are now invariably introduced under Standing Order No 48 (see p 721) the rule does not apply in their case.

Arrangement of chapter

Following the order of the previous chapter, the material of this chapter is arranged under the following heads:

(1) The varieties of expenditure which are initiated by financial resolutions.

(2) Procedure on financial resolutions.
(3) The procedure on the special bills which give legislative sanction to such expenditure.

Forms of proceeding for the initiation of expenditure

According to modern practice the form of proceeding by which expenditure for new purposes is initiated, and to which the Queen's recommendation is accordingly given, is a motion. This, when agreed to, becomes a resolution—hence the term 'financial resolution'. However, certain other proceedings in the House may also have implications of approval for public expenditure, and they are described here briefly accordingly.

Standing orders. A motion for the adoption *inter alia* of Standing Order No 51 and of Standing Order 156A (Private Business) was held to require the recommendation of the Crown because those standing orders exempted from compliance with the standing orders and practice of the House relating to provisions authorizing charges upon the public revenue, provisions of bills authorizing expenditure by a local authority which would or might operate to increase the amount of any exchequer equalization grant under Part I or Part II of the Local Government Act 1948.[1]

Business of the House motions. Business of the House or procedure motions, passed on rare occasions, usually of emergency, which have exempted bills from the necessity of compliance with the standing orders and practice of the House relating to provisions authorizing charges upon the public revenue (see p 693), have received the royal recommendation.[2]

Public petitions. The regular use of petitions for initiating expenditure has lapsed.[3] The effect of Standing Order No 46 has become purely negative—to prevent the reception of petitions 'for sums relating to public service'—and this result is reinforced by Standing Order No 47.

1. VARIETIES OF EXPENDITURE INITIATED BY FINANCIAL RESOLUTIONS

Since the normal form of procedure which is, subject to the unimportant exceptions mentioned, used for the initiation of expenditure is a resolution moved with the royal recommendation, it is necessary to indicate the kinds of expenditure and matters akin to expenditure which require this procedure. Such matters fall under the general heading of 'charges' (see p 687)—a term which in this connection has a highly technical meaning. It will be necessary to show at the outset that not all matters which *prima facie* involve expenditure are 'charges'.

---

1 CJ (1948–49) 18; see also ibid (1953–54) 336. This grant has been replaced by revenue support grant (see pp 714–715).
2 CJ (1938–39) 405; ibid (1939–40) 138; ibid (1946–47) 373; ibid (1947–48) 188; ibid (1953–54) 96; ibid (1965–66) 11.
3 Until the passing of the British Museum Act 1963 a petition from the Museum for a grant in aid was presented annually by the Home Secretary, who signified the royal recommendation (eg CJ (1962–63) 174).

Tests used to determine whether expenditure involves a 'charge'

It is not always easy to determine whether a particular proposal for expenditure actually imposes a charge and therefore requires the Queen's recommendation. The practice of the House has evolved certain tests for deciding this question, which may be summed up as follows. In order to constitute a charge upon public funds, expenditure must be (1) new and distinct; (2) payable out of the Consolidated Fund or the National Loans Fund; (3) effectively imposed.

(a) A charge must be new and distinct. The question may arise whether a proposal for expenditure or for increased expenditure is not already covered by some general authorization. The test for determining this question in the case of a substantive proposal, ie a provision in a bill, as introduced, is a comparison with existing law.

(i) Provisions in bills. The comparison of provisions in a bill with the law on the subject, as it exists, may show that, while such provisions undoubtedly involve expenditure, the power to incur such expenditure is covered by general powers conferred by statute.

Examples of expenditure which, as being covered by pre-existing legal powers, is not treated as a charge are given on pp 717–718. This standard of reference is readily applicable in the case of the large number of bills which are, in terms, amendments of previous statutes on the same subject. It may, however, be difficult to decide whether a provision for expenditure which proposes to finance that expenditure out of funds provided by statute for another purpose is or is not a 'new and distinct' charge (see p 716).

(ii) Proposals by way of amendment. Amendments must be judged in relation to existing law for the purpose of determining whether they involve charges in the same way as provisions contained in a bill as introduced and by reference to the financial resolution which authorizes the charges embodied in the bill as introduced. If financial resolutions are drawn in general terms they will cover amendments which would be out of order if the terms were drawn in precise detail. This is a matter which has given the House some concern in the past (see pp 723–724). The relation between a financial resolution and amendments to a bill is dealt with later in this Chapter (see p 722).

(b) Expenditure, to be a charge, must be payable out of the Consolidated Fund or National Loans Fund. This rule depends upon the provision of Standing Order No 46, which defines a charge upon the public revenue as either 'payable out of the Consolidated Fund or the National Loans Fund' or 'out of money to be provided by Parliament'. It excludes not only payments out of funds for public purposes which receive no grants from the Consolidated Fund, such as the revenues of the Church Commissioners, but also payments out of funds which are fed by grants from the Consolidated Fund, such as the Social Security Fund, see p 717 unless payments out of the Consolidated Fund may be thereby attracted. Apart from any such result, the imposition of burdens upon such funds, even to the point of reducing them to insolvency, involves no charge and may be initiated without the recommendation of the Crown.

The same rule excludes from the category of a 'charge' any method of financing expenditure by intercepting the proceeds of taxation or other sources of revenue before they are paid into the Consolidated Fund.

(c) A charge must be effectively imposed. The effective imposition of a charge has been extended by an amendment of Standing Order No 46 to include the imposition of charges upon 'money to be provided by Parliament' which before 1866 had been excluded, probably on the ground that it implied no immediate charge but only authorized the presentation of estimates. However, only resolutions specifically authorizing payments fall within the terms of the Standing Order and so require the royal recommendation. Resolutions cast in this form 'in the opinion of this House . . .'[1] or otherwise advocating rather than authorizing a charge escape that requirement.

All proposals for new expenditure are subjected to these tests for the purposes of deciding whether they require the Queen's recommendation.

It must be noted again that the same rules apply to charges proposed not only by way of resolution but also (except where so stated) by amendments to resolutions or bills, and to the increase of existing charges as well as to the imposition of new charges.

Matters requiring the Queen's recommendation

(a) Moneys to be provided by Parliament. The most frequent case of expenditure of this type is that of charges upon moneys to be provided by Parliament for salaries and other expenses caused by the imposition of novel duties upon the executive government by the legislation of the session.

A resolution authorizing such expenditure may be described shortly as a preliminary to the presentation of an estimate. It initiates the process of giving legislative sanction to annual expenditure for new purposes as yet unauthorized. The sanctioning of such expenditure thus undergoes two stages: (1) it is initiated by a money resolution imposing a charge payable 'out of moneys to be provided by Parliament' which receives confirmation by specific enactment; (2) it is subsequently presented to the House of Commons in the form of an estimate which receives final sanction in the Appropriation Act. Although a resolution of this type initiates no immediate charge, but is intended only to authorize the eventual presentation of an estimate, it is in view of the terms of Standing Order No 46 regarded as containing a 'charge' in the technical sense and could not be brought before the House without the recommendation of the Crown.

Instances of charges imposed upon moneys to be provided by Parliament occur in abundance every session. The following examples may be given:

(1) The expenses connected with the establishment of a new department.
(2) The expenses arising out of the imposition of new duties on an existing department or authority.

---

1 See, eg, motions relating to Members' Expenses, CJ (1956–57) 247; Votes and Proceedings (1987–88) 21 July 1987, pp 108 ff, etc. Cf p 718.

(3) Grants authorized to be paid, whether annually or otherwise, to specified bodies.
(4) Any proposal whereby the Crown would incur a liability or a contingent liability payable out of money to be voted by Parliament.
(5) The transfer of expenses from local revenues to estimates.

(b) Charges upon the Consolidated Fund. Another type of expenditure, initiated by money resolutions, examples of which occur in the legislation of every session, is the imposition of charges to be paid directly out of the Consolidated Fund. The following are categories of charges which require the Queen's recommendation:

(1) The imposition of an annual charge on the Consolidated Fund.
(2) Contingent or prospective charges on the Consolidated Fund (such as might arise from a Treasury guarantee).
(3) Issue of money from the Consolidated Fund to the Contingencies Fund.
(4) The making of advances out of the Consolidated Fund to be repaid out of moneys provided by Parliament.
(5) The authorization of a single payment out of the Consolidated Fund.

(c) Charges upon the National Loans Fund. Section 2 of, and Schedule 1 to, the National Loans Act 1968 transferred to the National Loans Fund almost all government lending to nationalized industries and other bodies in the United Kingdom which had hitherto been financed by advances out of the Consolidated Fund. These provisions of the National Loans Fund Bill were authorized by a financial resolution, and since 1 April 1968 any provision for new government lending to nationalized industries etc beyond existing authorized limits has required similar authorization.

(d) Charges upon local revenues. Formerly grants, known as rate support grants, were payable out of money provided by Parliament to local authorities, and Ministers were required[1] in fixing the level of grant to take into account the amount of relevant local authority expenditure. When a bill sought to confer new or enlarged functions on local authorities, in the absence of express provision in the bill to the contrary, the functions were held to impose a charge on the Consolidated Fund and to require a money resolution accordingly.

The Local Government Finance Act 1988 and the Abolition of Domestic Rates etc. (Scotland) Act 1987 replaced Rate Support Grant by Revenue Support Grant with effect from 1 April 1990. Under those Acts (in the latter case as amended by Schedule 6 to the Local Government and Housing Act 1989) there is no statutory obligation on Ministers to have regard to the level of local authority expenditure in determining the amount of grant. Nevertheless the expectation is that they will do so and this is held to justify a continued requirement for a money resolution in respect of provisions of a Bill which impose on local authorities duties involving them in significant expense.

(e) Remission or compounding of debts to Crown. The remission or compounding of a debt due to the Crown requires, under Standing Order

---

1 See Local Government Planning and Land Act 1980 and Local Government (Scotland) Act 1966

No 47, to be initiated by a resolution, and by practice it also requires the Queen's recommendation. Where provisions in a bill repeal a liability for future payment before any actual sum has become due they do not come within this rule[1]. Matters of the following description have required the royal recommendation:

(1) Extension of time for repayment of sums deposited under standing order (which would otherwise be forfeited).
(2) Repayment of sums deposited as security.
(3) Provision in a private bill for remitting or compounding sums due to the Crown.
(4) Extension of period within which sums issued to the Contingencies Fund are to be repaid to the Exchequer.
(5) Reduction of repayments due to the Consolidated Fund.
(6) Remission of statutory advances made by the Treasury.
(7) Compounding of debt to the Crown.
(8) Remission of statutory contributions from salaries.
(9) Reduction of the commencing capital debt of a nationalized industry to a Minister.

Remission of liability to duties is not regarded as remission of debt but as exemption from taxation, and does not require a resolution.

(f) Further charge by extension of time. Matters of the following description have also been treated as a charge:

(1) Transfer to Consolidated Fund of expenses chargeable upon moneys provided by Parliament.
(2) Extension for one year of building bonus (without increase of total grant).
(3) Continuation of expiring enactments involving expenditure.
(4) Extension of charge by inclusion of Act in Expiring Laws Continuance Bill.
(5) Increase of charge through postponement of date of day appointed for commencement of Act.
(6) Increase of period for making advances, without increase of total amount of liability.
(7) Provision for making a charge with retrospective effect, from a date before that on which the bill becomes law.

(g) Increase of charge by extension of purposes, etc. When a bill contains provisions extending the purposes of expenditure already authorized by statute, such provisions may require the Queen's recommendation. The following examples may be given:

(1) Extension of cases in which compensation can be paid.
(2) Extension of classes of insured persons or persons to whom allowances may be paid out of money provided by Parliament.

(h) Increase of amount of charge. When a bill contains provisions varying a formula for grant so that an increased payment would result, a money resolution is required.

---

1 Eg Petroleum Royalties Relief Bill (1983–84); Petroleum Royalties Relief and Continental Shelf Bill (1988–89).

(i) Variation of appropriation and diversion of revenue. Modern practice makes it unlikely that certain older decisions, exempting on technical
grounds charges from the requirements of financial procedure, would now
be upheld. In the case of taxation the principle has been clearly established
that the royal initiative is involved in any alteration of the incidence of a tax
(see p 728). It is likely that any similar action in the field of expenditure
would nowadays be regarded in the same light. Indeed in 1928 a bill which
proposed to substitute a new purpose for an existing statutory grant was
ruled out of order because it had not been introduced on a resolution
recommended by the Crown.[1] An amendment belonging to the category of
'variation of appropriation', ie one which seeks to divert expenditure authorized by a financial resolution from the purpose for which it was recommended by the Crown to another purpose, is always ruled out of order.

Matters involving money which do not require the Queen's recommendation

(a) Provisions involving the reduction of charges. No special form of
procedure applies to proposals to reduce existing charges, and they may be
moved in the House or in Committee without the royal recommendation.

A proposed reduction of a charge may consist in reducing its amount, or
restricting its objects, or inserting limiting conditions, or shortening the
period of its operation. The transference of a charge from the Consolidated
Fund to 'moneys to be provided by Parliament', ie its transformation from
an indefinitely continuing to an annually renewable charge (see pp 690–691)
may be regarded as an instance of reducing the duration of a charge.

The same principle applies in the case of amendments moved to a bill
which abolishes or reduces a charge authorized by existing law. Amendments to such a bill, which are designed to restore a portion or the whole of
the charge which the bill proposes to reduce or abolish, are in order without
the need of a preliminary financial resolution.

*(b) Charges on public funds other than the Consolidated Fund or the
National Loans Fund.* The imposition of charges on funds other than the
Consolidated Fund or the National Loans Fund does not require the royal
recommendation, unless it involves an increased payment out of one or
other of those Funds, or increases the liability (eg through a guarantee) upon
them, or automatically attracts a grant from moneys provided by Parliament
(see p 712).

The Social Security Fund is an example of this kind of fund; and proposals
to increase the benefits payable out of it do not require the royal recommendation. Thus successive Social Security Bills, which increased the
benefits payable out of the Fund (without increasing Exchequer contributions) have required no financial resolution. But any increase in
Exchequer contributions to the Fund or in social security grants payable out
of money provided by Parliament rather than out of the fund or in the
expenses incurred in administering them (unless so small as to be negligible;
National Insurance (Amendment) Bill 1955; National Insurance Bill 1956)

1 Empire Settlement Bill 1928. See also Northern Ireland Land Bill 1929 (which was ruled to
  require a financial resolution in respect of provisions varying the conditions of grants).

even though ultimately recoverable by the Exchequer must be recommended by the Crown.[1]

The existence of the Social Security Fund cannot be used by private Members as a means of evading the basic rule that a net charge cannot be imposed unless it is recommended by the Crown. Thus while it is permissible for a private Member to propose benefits or increases in benefits which are within the scope of social security legislation and to specify that the benefits are to be payable out of the Fund, it would not be in order to use the Fund for purposes other than those already covered by existing legislation, for example the cost of educational services.

Charges which are met by appropriations from the Consolidated Fund of Northern Ireland do not require the royal recommendation.[2]

(c) Expenditure covered by existing statutory authority. Where sufficient statutory authority already exists for payments to which bills relate, no further resolution and recommendation is required. Cases coming under the following heads have been held not to require further authorization.

(1) Transfer of charges from the Consolidated Fund to the estimates. The transfer to the estimates of a payment chargeable by law upon the Consolidated Fund amounts to converting the payment from a statutory standing charge to a payment which requires to be annually voted (see pp 690–691). Provisions and amendments of this nature are accordingly accepted without being recommended by the Crown.
(2) Liability (to pay damages) covered by existing law.
(3) Reimposition of a suspended charge.
(4) Charges in Consolidation Bills.
(5) Payment of costs by Crown.
(6) Widening the jurisdiction of a court or creating offences although they may have the effect of increasing the costs of the administration of justice.

(d) Exemption from penalties due to Crown. A bill which exempts persons or bodies from penalties which would otherwise be payable is not regarded as falling within the terms of Standing Order No 47.

(e) Implying but not imposing a charge. The fact that the abolition of a charge may imply that further legislation will be required to introduce some alternative charge does not create a requirement for royal recommendation of the abolition.

(f) Motions expressed as an opinion. Motions relating to the remuneration of Members have been put down in abstract form in order to allow Members to move amendments to increase the figures proposed in them. They cannot however provide the necessary authority for including any increased figures in the estimates. This can only be done by a further 'effective' resolution, which must bear the Queen's recommendation because contributions from Members' salaries towards their pensions are

1 Family Allowances and National Insurance [Money], CJ (1951–52) 218; National Insurance (Industrial Injuries) Bill 1956; National Insurance [Money], CJ (1954–55) 17.
2 See eg Fair Employment (Northern Ireland) Bills, 1975–76 and 1988–89; Disabled Persons (Northern Ireland) Bill 1988–89.

supplemented by Exchequer contributions; which are automatically increased when there is an increase in salaries.[1] Since the Queen's recommendation prescribes the maximum charge which can be imposed no amendment to increase this figure is in order (see pp 720).

2. PROCEDURE ON FINANCIAL RESOLUTIONS

Methods of signifying the exercise of the royal initiative

(a) Demands by message from the Queen under the sign manual. The object of such a message is usually to obtain a grant for the maintenance of the dignity and well-being of the Crown or for the reward of people who have rendered distinguished service to the State (see p 703). The message is formally presented to the House by a Minister of the Crown in the prescribed manner (see pp 558–559) and the reply of the Commons is to resolve to consider it on that or a future day. A Supply resolution stating the terms of the grant may be embodied in the Appropriation Act. Alternatively, an *ad hoc* motion of which notice appears on the Order Paper is moved, which afterwards becomes the basis of a special bill.

Messages seeking provision for the Civil List have ordinarily been referred to a Select Committee. When the Select Committee has reported, a resolution has been moved[2] upon which a bill making the appropriate provision has been founded.[3]

Demands made by message are presented to both Houses, the form of the message being varied so as to ask for a grant from the House of Commons and concurrence in such grant from the House of Lords.

In the Commons the terms of the royal message govern proceedings on the Civil List, and no amendment can be moved for extending the purposes for which provision is demanded.[4]

(b) Signification of Queen's recommendation by a Minister of the Crown. On other occasions, which form the great majority of cases, the Queen's recommendation is signified by a Minister of the Crown,[5] in writing to the Clerk of the House. A note indicating that the recommendation has been signified is included on the Order Paper. This practice has superseded the former custom by which a Minister signified the Queen's recommendation from his place in the House.[6]

---

1 HC Deb (1977–78) 952, cc 1333–1334.
2 CJ (1951–52) 239; ibid (1970–71) 448.
3 CJ (1951–52) 306 (Committee of the whole House, as then required), 312; ibid (1971–72) 76. The Civil List Act 1972, which resulted from the latter resolution, provided for payments until the end of the present reign and for six months thereafter (s 1), and for the sums in the Act and certain other sums to be capable of being increased by order (s 6). The Bill for the Civil List Act 1975 (which amended details of the 1972 Act) was presented in the ordinary way, without a preceding message, and the expenditure involved was authorized by a money resolution.
4 HC Deb (1935–36) 311, cc 1589–1590.
5 See p 560.
6 See Report from the Select Committee on Procedure 1965–66 (HC 122 (1965–66)). The change was effected from 14 December 1966 and the present procedure was first used on 20 January 1967.

Proceedings on financial resolutions

A financial resolution is not part of the proceedings on a bill and may therefore be taken at any time before the detailed consideration of the provisions of the bill which necessitate the resolution. Thus, although such resolutions are normally considered immediately after the second reading of bills, they have also been considered after presentation but before second reading,[1] during the committee stage,[2] before the report stage,[3] and before consideration of Lords amendments.[4]

Debate on a financial resolution is confined to the terms of the resolution itself and must not be extended to the related bill,[5] nor to the merits of matters excluded from the resolution.[6]

The function of the House in financial matters being restricted to the approval or the reduction of the expenditure under consideration, or an increase in the stringency of the terms and conditions of the charge thereby created, amendments must be directed to these objects.

An amendment proposing to substitute for the resolution an argumentative[7] justification for the refusal of the demand is out of order, as are also amendments proposed with a view to substituting an alternative scheme to that proposed with the royal recommendation.[8]

In accordance with the constitutional principle which reserves the initiative in finance to the Crown, the terms of the message under the sign manual or of the resolution recommended by the Queen for imposing a charge are treated as laying down a maximum charge, which amendments may reduce but may not extend, in respect of the amount of the expenditure, the area of its operation and the objects to which and the conditions under which it applies. Where the terms of a money resolution have recommended payment of a grant from public funds, it has been held that an amendment to substitute for that provision a repayable advance of public money was out of order, on the ground that the amendment changed the method of financing from that recommended by the Crown[9].

In respect of the degree of restriction imposed upon the House a difference arises as a result of the two methods of signifying the royal initiative.

Message under the sign manual. Where a message under the sign manual is received, opportunity may exist for the moving of amendments which, though they increase the charge authorized by the particular resolutions moved, do not exceed the terms of the royal message.[10] In the case of a royal demand to the Commons for new financial provision to be made for the Civil List (see p 462) the financial initiative of the Crown is contained in the royal

---

1 CJ (1974–75) 97, 99.
2 CJ (1963–64) 285.
3 Eg CJ (1985–86) 390.
4 Eg CJ (1985–86) 465.
5 HC Deb (1916) 83, c 1700; ibid (1917–18) 98, c 1136; ibid 99, c 423; ibid (1918) 106, c 1605; ibid (1921) 143, c 1132; ibid (1938–39) 343, c 1195; ibid (1946–47) 432, cc 886–892; ibid (1948–49) 462, cc 2239–2240.
6 HC Deb (1968–69) 772, c 1201.
7 Parl Deb (1901) 98, c 923; HC Deb (1910) 19, c 1624; ibid (1920) 134, c 1552; HC Deb (1936–37) 320, c 1035.
8 HC Deb (1917) 98, c 617.
9 HC Deb (1953–54) 525, cc 1753–1756.
10 Perceval ii, 303.

message under the sign manual which merely requests the House to 'adopt such measures as may be suitable for the occasion', without specifying any limits (cf pp 693–694).

On 9 July 1952, an amendment which proposed to remove the upper limit of expenditure laid down in the Government's Civil List motion was held to be in order because it fell within the wide terms of the royal message.

Resolution with Queen's recommendation. When the resolution which has received the Queen's recommendation is the resolution actually considered by the House, the power of amendment is strictly limited to reduction of the demand thereby made. This limitation on the power of proposing amendments applies equally to Ministers of the Crown as to private Members. If the Government itself wishes to extend, or to accept amendments extending, the charge thus proposed, it is necessary to withdraw the resolution and submit another containing the desired modification,[1] or at a later date to submit a second resolution.[2]

Proceedings on motions authorizing expenditure in connection with a bill are exempted from the 'Ten o'clock' rule until a quarter to eleven o'clock, or until the expiration of three quarters of an hour after the commencement of proceedings, whichever is the later (Standing Order No 14(1)(d)).

3. PROCEDURE ON BILLS SANCTIONING EXPENDITURE

After a charge, having been recommended by the Crown, has been agreed to, it still remains for it to receive legislative authorization by being embodied in an Act of Parliament.

Presentation under Standing Order No 48

Since the passage of Standing Order No 48 in 1938 bills whose main object is to create a charge, except Consolidated Fund Bills, may be presented or brought in by a Minister of the Crown in the same manner as bills which create a charge subsidiary to the main object. They may be proceeded with, if brought from the Lords, so long as they are 'taken up' (see p 467) by a Minister of the Crown. But they may not be introduced by a private Member. When bills are introduced under Standing Order No 48 the necessary money resolution may be considered after the second reading of the bill in the same way as are money resolutions relating to other bills. Bills presented under Standing Order No 48 are distinguished by a note at the top of the first page.

Bills which create a charge subsidiary to their main object do not need to be taken up by a Minister when brought from the House of Lords. The financial provisions of both types of bill require to be covered by money resolutions, as in the case of bills introduced into the House of Commons. Thus when a bill which, according to the rule, should have been founded upon a money resolution, has been presented or submitted in a motion for

---

1 CJ (1929–30) 165, 169. See also HC Deb (1930–31) 248, cc 1095–1149.
2 Eg CJ (1950–51) 249; ibid (1960–61) 147; ibid (1985–86) 465, etc.

leave under Standing Order No 19 by a private Member the Speaker has declined to allow the bill to be presented or to propose the necessary question, and the bill has not been proceeded with.[1]

The rule of practice that requires the stages of bills having as their main object the creation of a charge to be taken on different days (see p 692) does not apply to bills proceeded with under Standing Order No 48.

Italicized provisions

Before the clauses and provisions creating charges can be considered by the committee on the bill, a resolution sanctioning them must be passed in the manner described on pp 719–720.[2] In the copies of the bill as first printed, the clauses and provisions which directly create these charges are printed in italics to mark the fact that they do not unconditionally form part of the bill and that no question can be proposed thereon, unless they have been authorised by a financial resolution.[3] For bills introduced in the Lords see pp 745–746.

This rule applies specifically to the committee stage of the bill. On the second reading the House is not precluded from discussing the provisions printed in italics before the relevant financial resolution has been agreed to.[4]

The words printed in italics must be 'covered' by the relevant money resolution, ie the charge they authorize may not be larger in amount, or more extensive in purpose than the charge recommended by the Crown. If they are found not to be so covered, they may not be considered in committee until a further resolution covering the deficiency has been agreed to. Alternatively, the italicized words must themselves be amended so as to be brought within the terms of the resolution.[5]

On the other hand it has been held that the money resolution must not be more detailed than the terms of the corresponding clause in the bill as that might unduly restrict the power to move amendments (see pp 723–724).

Those clauses of a bill which do not propose a charge may be considered in committee before the resolution 'covering' the italicized clause or clauses has been reported and agreed to.[6]

This rule is enforced in committee by the refusal of the chairman to propose the question on a clause, schedule or amendment involving a charge, which is not completely covered by the money resolution related to the bill.[7] If a question has been proposed on an amendment, which in the

---

1 Political Contributions Bill, HC Deb (1969–70) 801, cc 410–413.
2 CJ (1883) 234.
3 Parl Deb (1865) 177, c 1308.
4 Parl Deb (1894) 24, c 185.
5 Local Government (Scotland) Bill 1928–29, cl 70; Unemployment Insurance (No 2) Bill 1929–30. In the latter case, to comply with the spirit of the rule, the necessary amendment was made at the beginning of the italicized words in cl 12(2).
6 Stg Co E, Proceedings (1949), Analgesia in Childbirth Bill, p 6; Mr T J Brooks' ruling, Stg Co Deb (1950–51) Co B, New Streets Bill, c 589.
7 Stg Co C, Proceedings (1969–70), Chronically Sick and Disabled Persons Bill, p 3; ibid (1978–79) Official Information Bill, p 4.

course of debate is shown to involve a charge not covered by the financial resolution, it is the duty of the Chair to intervene and rule it out of order.[1]

Interpretation of 'main object' in relation to a bill

In relation to the bill authorizing it, a charge varies from being the sole purpose of the bill to covering minor provisions of a bill which only incidentally involve expenditure.

For example, the European Communities (Finance) Bill in 1987–88 made new arrangements for payments to finance the Communities' budget and was therefore introduced under Standing Order No 48. At the other end of the scale, the expenditure involved may be purely administrative, as for example, in the Water Bill (as introduced) 1988–89.

A bill may have for its main object the creation of a new service which consists in the disbursement of public funds. Such a bill (eg the Legal Aid and Advice Bill 1948–49) is regarded as having the creation of the service rather than the charge as its main object. On the other hand a bill of which the main object is to extend such a service to new classes of persons or to relax the conditions upon which it is available (eg the Legal Aid Bill 1959–60) is regarded as having the creation of a public charge for its main object. Furthermore a bill may have several objects, of which some consist only in the creation of a charge, while others do not create a charge at all or only create one incidentally. In such cases it has to be considered whether the financial objects of the bill are sufficient to outweigh substantive provisions not primarily financial. Thus the main object of the Agriculture (Miscellaneous Provisions) Bill 1962–63 was considered to be that which consisted in increasing various kinds of grant to agriculture and the bill was accordingly introduced under Standing Order No 48. On the other hand the Housing Bill 1960–61 contained in addition to provisions for financial assistance for housing other provisions of sufficient importance to justify the bill's introduction without recourse to Standing Order No 48.

Stages after presentation

The ordinary rules of order, applicable to bills generally, such as the rules requiring relevancy to the subject matter of a bill, apply to debate on the stages of bills imposing charges.

(a) Amendments in committee (or on report). The general rules governing the admissibility of amendments in committee on such bills are those set out in the chapter on Public Bills, pp 490–493. No amendment may be moved in committee on a bill which would increase the charge beyond the limits authorized by the relevant money resolution, as recommended by the Crown and agreed to by the House. On the other hand, if the charge contained in the bill before the committee in any way falls short of the terms of the resolution recommended by the Queen (or initiated on a message from the Queen) and agreed to, it may be increased in amount or extended in area up to that limit.[2]

---

1 CJ (1916) 108; HC Deb (1916) 83, c 362; CJ (1918) 215; HC Deb (1918) 110, c 237; CJ (1919) 157; HC Deb (1919) 116, c 915; CJ (1920) 280; HC Deb (1920) 131, c 1900, etc.
2 Civil List Bill 1936, HC Deb (1935–36) 312, c 117; CJ (1935–36) 221.

(b) Restrictive effect of terms of money resolution. In view of the way in which the terms of a money resolution limit the scope and extent of the charging provisions of a bill, the Speaker has had occasion to deprecate an excessive amount of detail in the drafting of such resolutions as tending to restrict unduly the power of private Members to propose amendments.[1] The view of the Government on the proper practice in this matter has been laid down by a Treasury circular, communicated to the House on 9 November 1937 and accepted by the Speaker as conforming to the legitimate desires of the House[2]. There have, nevertheless, been several money resolutions since 1937 which have been drafted in considerable detail.[3]

The different kinds of expenditure which are regarded as charges have been tabulated in pp 713–716. The rules there stated are generally the same for amendments as they are for bills, with the substitution of the relevant money resolution for the existing law as the standard in relation to which the increase of a charge is ascertained.

1 HC Deb (1934–35) 295, c 1236.
2 HC Deb (1937–38) 328, cc 1593–1600; ibid (1939–40) 357, c 1193. See also ibid (1956–57) 569, cc 85–86.
3 See for example, Coal Industry [Money] CJ (1979–80) 632–633; Industry [Money] CJ (1980–81) 24; Electricity Bill [Money] Votes and Proceedings (1988–89), 13 January 1989.

CHAPTER 29

Ways and Means

This chapter gives an account of the procedure in considering Ways and Means—in other words, the provision of revenue to meet national expenditure and to forward the objectives of economic policy. Ways and Means are, of course, principally provided by the imposition of taxation, but also by the raising of loans and by provision made as occasion arises for the payment of sums of money into the Consolidated Fund or the National Loans Fund.[1]

Application to Ways and Means of the general rules of financial procedure

Before classifying in greater detail the various matters which are treated as Ways and Means—and also those which, though prima facie of the same kind, are not so treated—it will be convenient to show how the general rules governing financial procedure are modified in their application to Ways and Means.

(1) The legislative authorization, required by Rule 1 (see p 689), for Ways and Means is given principally by the annual Finance Bill, but also by special bills, the Ways and Means provisions in which must be covered by resolutions of the House of Commons.
(2) The proof, required by Rule 2 (see p 691), of the exercise of the Crown's initiative is not given expressly, but is, owing (as in the case of Supply) to historical causes, implied in the nature of the initiatory proceedings.
(3) The preliminary consideration of resolutions required by Rule 3 (see p 692), is followed in the Ways and Means resolutions upon which Finance Bills and other taxing measures are founded.
(4) The intervals between stages of financial legislation prescribed by Rule 4 (see p 692) are obligatory for the stages of the authorizing bills, although the House may on occasion by order dispense with such intervals.[2]

Arrangement of chapter

Following the order of the previous chapters the material of this chapter will be arranged under three main heads:

(1) The varieties of matters which fall within the scope of Ways and Means.
(2) Procedure on the business of Ways and Means.

---

1 The former Committee of Ways and Means, in which all ways and means business originated, was abolished on 24 October 1967. For the procedures followed before that date, see the 17th edn of this work.
2 Eg CJ (1985–86) 476.

(3) The procedure in considering the Finance Bill and other bills with associated Ways and Means resolutions.

1. THE SCOPE OF WAYS AND MEANS

Ways and Means must be initiated by a resolution. For historical reasons, referred to on p 691, a Ways and Means resolution is not recommended by the Crown, but it can only be moved by a Minister of the Crown[1] and, once moved, it has the same limiting effect upon amendments relating to 'charges upon the people' as a resolution recommended by the Crown has upon amendments relating to 'charges upon public funds', whether such amendments are offered by private Members or by Ministers. This effect is explained on p 723.

Instructions. An instruction is not used for the purpose of Ways and Means as an originating motion, but only as a formal link between a resolution agreed to by the House, and a bill already ordered to be brought in, usually in order to cover amendments which require to be authorized by such a resolution (see p 740). The effect of requiring for the initiation of Ways and Means a resolution moved by a Minister has been to rule out of order instructions for the purpose of initiating or increasing charges offered by private Members on Finance Bills and other bills imposing taxation.[2]

TESTS FOR DETERMINING WHETHER MATTERS INVOLVE CHARGES UPON THE PEOPLE

Matters which are covered by the term 'charges upon the people' may be briefly summarized as (1) the imposition of taxation, including the increase in rate, or extension in incidence, of existing taxation, (2) the repeal or reduction of existing alleviations of taxation such as exemptions or drawbacks, (3) the delegation of taxing powers within the United Kingdom, (4) the granting of borrowing powers and (5) provision for the payment into the Consolidated Fund or the National Loans Fund of receipts which do not arise from taxation. Matters of such kinds require to be authorized by the procedure outlined on p 732, whether they are original provisions in bills or are proposed by way of amendments to bills. Instances to be given below will be drawn from both bills and amendments. The question whether a particular matter involves a charge upon the people is more easily answered than the similar question in respect of charges upon public funds (see pp 712–713). But, as doubtful cases arise in practice, it will be convenient to mention briefly the tests which are applied in order to decide this question.

Charges upon the people are normally imposed generally and intended to be used for general purposes. Thus levies upon an industry the proceeds of which are intended to form a fund for the purposes of that industry have

---

1 A motion for a Committee of the whole House for the purpose of extending the probate duty offered by a private Member was withdrawn, Parl Deb (1844) 73, c 1052.
2 Parl Deb (1894) 24, c 1218; ibid (1901) 95, c 755.

been held in certain circumstances (see p 730) not to be charges. Fees imposed by Departments of State are regarded as charges if they are intended to cover the cost of a service previously paid for out of votes or the cost of imposing a new regulatory scheme. Subject to that, reasonable fees for services rendered are not normally regarded as charges, nor are fees intended to meet administrative expenses if they are subject to a defined and reasonable limit, and relate to the service rendered. Although impositions are not generally charges unless the proceeds are payable into the Consolidated Fund, the absence of a requirement for payment into the Consolidated Fund does not of itself prevent an imposition being treated as a charge.[1] This connotation excludes local taxation and loans and even burdens imposed by Parliament, the proceeds of which are payable to local funds. Finally, though the exclusion of tax provisions from the category of charges upon the people by reason of the existence of statutory powers already 'covering' them is unlikely, instances have occurred of loan provisions being excluded for that reason (see p 731).

The proposal of an alleviation of taxation, such as a drawback, does not involve a charge and does not require the special procedure appropriate to charges.

MATTERS INITIATED BY WAYS AND MEANS RESOLUTIONS

The following are examples of matters which require to be initiated in the form of a Ways and Means resolution by a Minister of the Crown.

(1) Taxation

A Ways and Means resolution is a necessary preliminary to the imposition of a new tax, the continuation of an expiring tax, an increase in the rate of an existing tax, or an extension of the incidence of a tax so as to include persons not already payers. According to present practice it is immaterial whether the tax is solely intended to provide revenue for the service of the year, or whether its primary purpose is to regulate imports or otherwise to forward public policy.

New taxation. New taxes and duties receive special treatment in two respects: (i) They may not come into force immediately under the Provisional Collection of Taxes Act 1968 (although security can be demanded in the case of new duties) (see p 735); (ii) New duties on separate commodities cannot be included in the same Ways and Means resolution (see p 735).

Continuation of an expiring tax. Most taxes are imposed indefinitely or for a period of years. But for the purpose of maintaining parliamentary control, the rates of which income and corporation tax are to be charged are imposed annually by successive Finance Bills. The extension of the duration of a tax requires a Ways and Means resolution.

---

1 A Ways and Means resolution was needed for a provision (which became s 49 of the London Regional Transport Act 1984) requiring the Greater London Council to pay grant for one year to London Regional Transport, although no money was payable into the Consolidated Fund, CJ (1983–84) 261.

Re-imposition of a repealed tax. The revival of a repealed or expired tax is treated in the same way as the imposition of a new tax; and consequently the resolution authorizing the re-imposition cannot become effective under the Provisional Collection of Taxes Act and cannot include several separate commodities. Thus Ways and Means resolutions were required when the 'new duties' imposed by the Finance (No. 2) Act 1915, allowed to lapse in 1924, were re-imposed by the Finance Act 1925 (CJ (1924–25) 176). Similarly a resolution was required when the duty on tea, abolished in 1929 (CJ (1928–29) 211), was re-imposed on a permanent basis in 1932 (CJ (1931–32) 156).

Increase in the rate of an existing tax. The increase in the rate of a permanent tax must be initiated by a resolution for that purpose in a Ways and Means resolution. The resolution may authorize the increase indefinitely[1] or for a limited period. Alterations of stamp duties, effected by private bills, which might result in the payment of increased duty in certain cases, have been regarded as a charge which requires authorization by resolution. They were initiated not as Ways and Means but by an *ad hoc* resolution, which required the signification of the royal recommendation.[2]

Extension of incidence of tax. A Ways and Means resolution is required to authorize the extension of a tax to new classes of tax-payers[3] or to commodities previously free of duty.[4]

(2) Repeal or reduction of alleviations of taxation

Ways and Means resolutions have been required in the following cases:

—Repeal of exemption from tax:

In the Crown Lands (No 2) Bill 1927, the repeal of an exemption from stamp duty.[5]

—Restriction of zero-rating for purposes of Value Added Tax:

The withdrawal of zero-rating from hot food supplied for consumption off the premises in the Finance (No 2) Bill, 1983–84.[6]

(3) Delegation of taxing powers within the United Kingdom

A proposal in an amendment to the Finance Bill to delegate powers of taxation to an authority other than the House has been ruled out of order.[7] But such delegation has sometimes been effected in bills founded on Ways and Means resolutions.[8] As to the power of the House of Commons

1 Tobacco Duties 1927, CJ (1927) 114; Hydrocarbon Oils, CJ (1930–31) 411.
2 Liverpool, London and Globe Insurance Company Bill [*Lords*], CJ (1904) 156, 160.
3 Finance No 2, 1931, CJ (1930–31) 415; Finance 1926, CJ (1926) 139.
4 Import Duties 1932, CJ (1931–32) 70–72.
5 CJ (1927) 105.
6 CJ (1983–84) 434.
7 HC Deb (1917–18) 95, c 828.
8 Abnormal Importations (Customs Duties) Bill 1931, CJ (1931–32) 28; Import Duties Bill 1932, CJ (1931–32) 74; Safeguarding of Industries Act 1921, s 2, CJ (1921) 145.

to delegate its function of taxation to another body, see the Speaker's remarks in the case of the Imports and Exports Regulation Bill 1919,[1] and the Abnormal Importations (Customs Duties) Bill 1931.[2]

(4) Grant of borrowing powers

Provisions in a bill authorizing the Crown to raise money by the issue of a loan require to be based on a Ways and Means resolution.[3] Temporary borrowing by Ways and Means advances and Treasury bills is authorized by permanent statutory provision.[4]

(5) Payments into the Consolidated Fund or the National Loans Fund

Taxes are payable into the Consolidated Fund under statute. The payment into the Consolidated Fund of receipts from a source other than taxation is authorized by a Ways and Means resolution; for example, fees under the Vehicle and Driving Licences Bill 1968–69[5] or for payments in respect of licences to supply electricity under the Electricity Bill 1988–89[6]. Since the substitution in 1968 of the National Loans Fund for the Consolidated Fund in certain enactments, payments into the National Loans Fund must be authorized in the same way; for example, sums received by the Minister by way of the repayment of the commencing capital debt under the Post Office Bill 1968–69[7].

When such receipts are minor matters incidental to the exercise of functions which involve expenditure, authority for their payment into the Consolidated Fund or the National Loans Fund usually, for the sake of convenience, forms part of the resolution authorizing expenditure; for example, repayments of and interest on advances under the Air Corporations Act 1969[8].

MATTERS, AKIN TO CHARGES UPON THE PEOPLE, NOT INITIATED BY WAYS AND MEANS RESOLUTIONS

(1) Local receipts

The rules of financial procedure do not apply to the receipts of local authorities, when they form the subject of legislation, unless, of course, they are in the form of grants from the Consolidated Fund. Provisions in bills dealing with local loans do not require authorization by Ways and Means resolution; nor do bills empowering local authorities to levy charges.

(2) Alleviation of taxation

Provisions for the alleviation of taxation are not subject to the rules of financial procedure. In the past the repeal or reduction of a tax, for instance,

---

1 HC Deb (1919) 122, c 213.
2 HC Deb (1931–32) 259, cc 719 ff.
3 War Loan Bill, CJ (1917–18) 193; ibid (1918) 153; Defence Loans Bill, CJ (1936–37) 130; National Loans Bill, CJ (1942–43) 89; Armed Forces (Housing Loans) Bill, CJ (1958–59) 21.
4 Exchequer Bills and Bonds Act 1866 and Treasury Bills Act 1877; cited collectively as Exchequer and Treasury Bills Acts 1866 and 1877.
5 CJ (1968–69) 37.
6 Votes and Proceedings (1988–89), 13 December 1988.
7 CJ (1968–69) 20.
8 CJ (1968–69) 221.

by the Finance Bill, has sometimes been preceded by a specific Ways and Means resolution.[1] This procedure is not necessary if the House has agreed to a resolution for the general amendment of the law but may be resorted to if the reduction is to have immediate effect under the Provisional Collection of Taxes Act 1968. Thus provisions for the repeal or reduction of taxation, the granting or extension of exemptions, the creation or increase of drawbacks, etc, can be presented in bills or inserted by amendment under the authority of the amendment of the law resolution. The effect of this principle on the power to move amendments to bills will be stated on p 740. This resolution is occasionally omitted when it is desired to restrict the scope of a Finance Bill to a minimum, as, for example, before the general election in 1974.

To escape the rules of financial procedure, a scheme for the alleviation of taxation must not include any incidental increase of the burden upon any taxpayer, however indirect or relatively insignificant that increase may be.[2] Since 1960, except when there is no amendment of the law resolution, it has been customary to include among the Budget resolutions one authorising any incidental or consequential changes to any duty or tax (including any changes having retrospective effect) which may arise from provisions designed in general to afford relief from taxation.[3]

(3) Levies upon an industry for its own purposes

Levies upon employers in a particular industry for the purpose of forming a fund used to finance activities beneficial to the industry are not normally regarded as charges. Provisions in the following bills (quoted by way of example) have been treated as falling within this rule: Coal Mines Control Agreement (Confirmation) Bill 1917; Coal Industry (Emergency) Bill 1919; Ministry of Mines Bill 1920; Cotton Industry Bill 1938; Sea Fish Industries Bill 1951; Transport Bill 1953; Betting Levy Bill 1960–61; Industrial Training Bill 1963–64; Countryside and Tourist Amenities (Scotland) Bill 1963–64; Football Betting Levy Board Bill 1972–73.

The Agriculture and Horticulture Bill 1963–64 imposed a levy on imports, not to raise revenue but in order to maintain a minimum price level. This levy was held to require a Ways and Means resolution. The Agriculture (Miscellaneous Provisions) Bill 1966–67 included a levy to provide payments to bacon curers. This, too, required a Ways and Means resolution. So did the Air Travel Reserve Fund Bill 1974–75, which required contributions from air travel organizers to a fund designed to compensate their customers for financial failure by the organizers. This was held to be a tax rather than a levy because, although it could be argued that the restoration of public confidence by the bill was beneficial to the industry the Government had absolute discretion to dispose of the assets of the Fund in the event of its being wound up, thus making it possible for the Consolidated Fund to benefit at the expense of the travel organizers.

---

1 Customs duties on antiques, CJ (1926) 137; on tea, ibid (1928–29) 211.
2 Thus on 12 April 1916 the chairman, in allowing an amendment to be moved in committee on the Finance (New Duties) Bill with the object of altering the method of levying a new tax, insisted that the amendment should be so framed as not to increase the charge that would be imposed on any individual payer of the tax, HC Deb (1916) 81, c 1812.
3 See CJ (1959–60) 176; ibid (1985–86) 270.

It was also decided that a Ways and Means resolution was required in the case of the Merchant Shipping Bill 1973–74, which imposed an obligation on importers of oil to contribute to an international fund for compensation for oil pollution damage. This impost was so clearly not for the benefit of the industry concerned that it was held to be a tax in spite of the fact that its proceeds were not payable into the Consolidated Fund.

Fees which were payable into a fund for the administration of a scheme managed by the industry were held not to require a Ways and Means Resolution (Animal Health and Welfare Bill 1983–84, c 12); but where the Agriculture Bill of 1985–86 required payment of further sums to the Consolidated Fund, intended to meet the cost of enforcement, resolution was required.

(4) Charges imposed for services rendered by departments

Payments which are intended to cover the expenses of a government department in performing services for the public or sections of the public and are retained by the department,[1] are not regarded as charges.[2] Such payments may take the form of fees or licences.

This rule is not allowed to legitimize charges so disproportionate to the cost of the services rendered or so broadly based as to amount to taxation.[3]

The Speaker has ruled that, in the case of a licence granted by a government department, the payment charged for the issue of the licence, if it is a small fee of an administrative character, should not be considered a charge upon the subject necessitating a Ways and Means resolution, but that if the fee charged did more than this, a Ways and Means resolution would be necessary.[4]

In view of this ruling a Ways and Means resolution has been regarded as necessary in any case where the charge for a fee or licence has been unduly high or without a defined limit.[5]

(5) Provisions authorized by existing law

Just as it has been ruled that provision for a charge upon public funds does not require the Queen's recommendation if it is a variant of and in substitution for a provision authorized by a previous statute (see pp 717–718), so it has been ruled that a scheme for raising a loan did not require to be preceded by a Ways and Means resolution, since it was covered by powers of borrowing conferred by a previous Act and in substitution for the particular scheme authorized by that Act.[6]

---

1 For the authority for this procedure, see p 690.
2 Recent examples are fees for import and export licences and certificates, cl 3 of the Agriculture Bill 1985–86; recovery of the expenses of the Nuclear Installations Inspectorate from licensees of nuclear sites, cl 2 of the Atomic Energy Bill 1988–89.
3 A Ways and Means charging resolution was required in respect of cl 1 of the Food and Environment Protection (Amendment) Bill 1988–89, where the amending provisions altered the basis of payments required so that manufacturers collectively met the cost of pesticide testing, where previously payment had been on a more limited basis.
4 HC Deb (1917–18) 100, c 164; ibid (1920) 136, c 1000.
5 Road and Rail Traffic Bill 1932–33, CJ (1932–33) 175; Whaling Industry (Regulation) Bill [Lords] 1933–34, CJ (1933–34) 295; Merchant Shipping (Safety Convention) Bill 1948–49, CJ (1948–49) 179.
6 See American Loan Bill 1914–16, HC Deb (1914–16) 74, cc 1219, 1272.

On the same analogy a tax authorized by a Finance Act and subsequently suspended has been re-imposed by a later bill without a Ways and Means resolution (Finance 1920, section 62 and Finance (No 2) 1915, section 49).

(6) Charges not effective till applied by subsequent legislation

Provisions in Finance Bills which alter the fiscal law may have the effect of increasing the charge upon the taxpayer, but this increase may be contingent upon the passing of subsequent legislation. In such a case a Ways and Means resolution is not required for the provision authorizing the increase, but for the provision which puts it into effect. The following instances may be mentioned: the abolition of the three years' average for the assessment of income tax by the Finance Bill 1926 (put into effect by the Finance Act 1927); the substitution of surtax for supertax by the Finance Bill 1927 (made effective by the Finance Act 1928); the imposition of pay-as-you-earn by the Wage-Earners' Income Tax Bill 1943 (made effective by the Finance Act 1944, section 19(2)). See also Finance Act 1947 (section 14(2)) which gave effect to various minor provisions relating to income tax contained in bills of the previous session. No Ways and Means resolution was needed to found a clause in the Finance Bill of 1967–68 which provided that if arrangements were made in such manner as Parliament might thereafter determine for the holding of a national lottery, nothing in any enactment relating to lotteries should make those arrangements unlawful.

2. PROCEDURE ON THE BUSINESS OF WAYS AND MEANS

In accordance with the provisions of the Standing Order (No 50 (1)), a Ways and Means motion may be made in the House without notice on any day, so soon as an address has been agreed to in answer to Her Majesty's speech.

It will be convenient to consider first of all the general rules of procedure on the business of Ways and Means, and then the special rules applicable to the 'budget' resolutions upon which the Finance Bill is founded.

GENERAL RULES OF PROCEDURE ON WAYS AND MEANS BUSINESS

Apart from the budget resolutions on which greater latitude is permitted (see p 734) each Ways and Means resolution is considered separately, and debate and amendment must be relevant to the resolution under consideration.[1]

When a resolution has been moved and proposed from the Chair it is in the same position with regard to potential amendment as a resolution recommended by the Crown. That is to say, it is not amendable in such a way as to increase the charge which it authorizes, whether such an amendment is

---

1 By general agreement a general debate has been allowed on the first of a series of resolutions in cases other than the budget resolutions. Import Duties, HC Deb (1931–32) 261, c 305; the resolutions preliminary to the Ottawa Agreements, ibid (1931–32) 269, c 43.

proposed by a private Member or by a Minister of the Crown. Examples of the restrictive effect of a Ways and Means resolution, once proposed from the chair, are stated below and on pp 740–741.

It has been held as contrary to precedent to proceed upon a Ways and Means motion unless notice of such an intention has been given to the House. This notice may, however, be given in general terms and as detailed notice of such a resolution is not required, though it is sometimes given when the public interest would not be thereby prejudiced, the Chair has allowed a resolution of which notice had been given to be moved in an altered form at the request of the Minister in charge.[1]

Inclusion of several duties in one resolution

Objection is taken to the inclusion of several new duties relating to different commodities in a single resolution.[2]

No objection applies to the imposition of a number of new duties of a similar kind,[3] or the renewal at an increased rate of a number of existing taxes,[4] by means of a single resolution.

Procedure on amendments

The established usage of the House, in the form and method of dealing with amendments, is followed on Ways and Means business; and every amendment must relate to the matter under consideration, and is governed by the rule of relevancy.

Taxing resolutions are normally moved without notice of their details and, if they form a series upon which a bill is to be brought in, the questions upon them are put forthwith upon all except the first. Amendments to such resolutions are rare in modern practice. However, if an amendment is offered, it is compared with the terms of the resolution proposed from the Chair, and is ruled out of order if it in any way increases the amount or extends the area of incidence of the charge defined in those terms. Similarly, in the case of a Ways and Means resolution which proposed to increase the amount authorized by law to be raised by loan for certain services, amendments for the purpose of extending the services were disallowed[5].

FINANCIAL STATEMENT AND BUDGET

The consideration of the annual financial statement made by the Chancellor of the Exchequer, and of the ensuing resolutions is the most important business of Ways and Means. This statement, familiarly known as 'the budget', is made when he has completed his estimate of the probable income and expenditure for the financial year[6]. In it he develops his views of the

---

1 Horticulture Products (Emergency Duties), HC Deb (1931–32) 260, c 783. For a resolution moved in a different form to that set out in the resolutions published on the day of the budget, see Resolution 26, Votes and Proceedings (1987–88) 21 March 1988.
2 HC Deb (1916) 83, cc 560, 771; ibid (1925) 183, cc 1015 ff. For an enabling Resolution see HC Deb (1931–32) 269, cc 153 ff.
3 CJ (1909) 151; HC Deb (1909) 4, cc 1467, 1737.
4 CJ (1901) 139; ibid (1916) 108.
5 HC Deb (1938–39) 344, c 59.
6 For a budget statement delivered in answer to a private notice question see HC Deb (1988–89) 149, cc 293–309.

resources of the country, communicates his calculations of probable income and expenditure, and declares whether the burdens upon the people are to be increased or diminished. The economic aspect of the budget is important and taxes are imposed for their effects upon the nation's economy as well as for raising revenue to meet the expenditure for the year. The annual Financial Statement and Budget Report is made available immediately at the conclusion of the budget speech, as are the terms of the budget resolutions.[1]

The resolutions which form the usual basis of the Chancellor's statement are the resolutions for the continuance, during the financial year, of income tax and corporation tax, and the imposition of any new duties or increases of permanent duties necessary for the purpose of adjusting the revenue to the expenditure of the year; and upon these and any other necessary resolutions, the bill is introduced which gives legislative effect to the financial purposes of the Government.

Special procedure on budget resolutions

The procedure in respect of the budget resolutions, on which the Finance Bill is introduced, differs from the ordinary procedure on Ways and Means resolutions since the House must be at liberty to consider the resolutions proposed by the Chancellor of the Exchequer as forming, together with existing taxation, a complete scheme of revenue to be debated as a whole; and must also be at liberty to consider expenditure in its relation to the burden of providing the necessary revenue. A general debate, which is on the broadest lines, is accordingly allowed, comprising all these resolutions and any financial resolutions[2] required to authorize the provisions of the resulting Finance Bill. To permit this, the debate takes place upon the first resolution proposed—generally that for the purpose of amending the fiscal law[3]—and continues for about four days at the end of which the question is put on the first resolution and, then, under Standing Order No 50(3) the questions are put forthwith upon all the resolutions upon which the Bill is to be brought in.[4] The consequences of this procedure are on the one hand to permit mature consideration of the budget resolutions (which by their nature must be secret until the financial statement is made) before the House is required to pronounce upon them, but on the other hand to prevent individual consideration of the resolutions and to deny the opportunity of amending any of the resolutions save the first. If two bills are founded on the same series of resolutions (see p 736), the first resolution for the second bill does not have to be put forthwith under Standing Order No 50(3), and a special motion needs to be passed at the commencement of public business to make this obligatory.[5]

Provisional collection of taxes

As explained above, the practice following the budget statement is for a general debate to take place on the first Ways and Means resolution (nor-

---

1 See eg HC Deb (1967–68) 761, c 251; ibid (1987–88) 129, c 993, etc.
2 Eg CJ (1911) 518; ibid (1982–83) 265 etc.
3 In 1929 the resolution for the repeal of the tea duty was used for this purpose, CJ (1928–29) 211; in the first budget of 1974–75 the resolution for the capital transfer tax, CJ (1974–75) 60.
4 Eg HC Deb (1968–69) 781, cc 991 and 782, c 170.
5 CJ (1974–75) 65.

mally that entitled 'amendment of the law') and for the questions to be put on all the resolutions upon which the Finance Bill is to be founded at the end of the last day of the budget debate. Provision has first to be made, however, for giving immediate provisional validity to those proposals which are to come into force (many of them on budget day itself) before specific statutory authority can be obtained. This is done under the terms of the Provisional Collection of Taxes Act 1968, as amended by section 1(5) of the Finance Act 1972, and under section 50 of the Finance Act 1973.

Section 5 of the Provisional Collection of Taxes Act provides that provisional validity may be given to specified budget resolutions by means of a single motion. This omnibus motion is made immediately after the conclusion of the budget speech and the question is put thereon forthwith under Standing Order No 50(2).[1] The budget resolutions thus given provisional force must be passed within the next ten days on which the House sits for their validity to be continued.

The Provisional Collection of Taxes Act does not apply to new taxes. In the case of income tax, value added tax, customs and excise duties, car tax, petroleum revenue tax and supplementary petroleum duty, section 1 provides for the renewal for a further period of any tax in force (with or without modifications) and for the variation or abolition of any existing tax. Section 3 of the Act provides for securing new duties of customs and excise.

Section 1 lays down that resolutions passed in March or April, which contain a declaration that it is expedient in the public interest that they should have statutory effect under the provisions of the Act, shall be valid until 5 August in that year, and such resolutions passed at other times of the year for a period of 4 months after the date on which they are expressed to take effect or, if no such date is expressed, after the date on which they are passed. A resolution ceases to have statutory effect however if a bill varying or renewing the taxes to which it relates is not read a second time by the House within the next twenty-five days on which the House sits after the resolution is agreed to. The resolution also ceases to have statutory effect in the event of a dissolution or prorogation of Parliament, or on the passage of an Act renewing or varying the tax,[2] or on the rejection of the provisions giving effect to the resolution. If the resolution is modified by the House it has effect as so modified. The application of the Act is limited by Section 1(8) to one resolution of the same effect during the same session. Section 50 of the Finance Act 1973 lays down broadly similar provisions in relation to changes in stamp duty.

Since section 1 relates only to pre-existing taxes and duties, it is necessary to make separate provision for the protection of the revenue to be obtained from new duties of customs and excise. Section 3 of the Act provides that in respect of new duties which have been imposed by means of resolutions as from a prescribed date, provision may be made for securing their collection from that date by the requiring of security in the case of customs duties and

---

1 See Mr Speaker's statement, HC Deb (1967–68) 761, c 251.
2 In 1981 an increase in the excise duty on hydro-carbon oil took immediate effect under the Provisional Collection of Taxes Act. When the ensuing Finance Bill was amended to provide for a lower rate of increase, it was further amended to provide that the full increase should have effect for the period between budget day and 2 July of that year (see Finance Act 1981, s 4).

by regulations to be made by the Commissioners of Customs and Excise in the case of excise duties.

3. FINANCE BILLS AND OTHER BILLS FOUNDED ON WAYS AND MEANS RESOLUTIONS

INTRODUCTION OF BILLS

When the Ways and Means resolutions and associated resolutions have been agreed to, the bills which they authorize are ordered to be brought in.

The resolutions on which a Finance Bill (and occasionally other taxing bills) is founded may comprise resolutions with the Queen's recommenda- tion as well as Ways and Means resolutions and procedure resolutions;[1] and the resolutions may have been passed on different days.[2] In such a case the usual practice is for the bill to be ordered when the last Ways and Means resolution is passed, with an entry in the Votes and Proceedings and Journal recording that it is based as well on earlier resolutions indicated by the days on which they were agreed to by the House.[3] The Members appointed to prepare and bring in the bill are then named and the bill is presented.

After the main resolutions have been passed and the bill has been ordered in, the House may agree to one or more further resolutions in order to authorize subsidiary provisions. Thus

(1) If such a resolution is agreed to after the bill has been presented and read the first time and before committal, an instruction is given to any committee to which the bill may be committed that it has power to make provision therein accordingly.
(2) If such a resolution is agreed to after the bill has been committed, the committee on the bill is instructed that it has power to make provision therein accordingly.
(3) If such a resolution is agreed to after the bill has been reported from a committee no instruction is required since the House does not need to instruct itself.

When a money resolution has been agreed to before a Finance Bill has been brought in the bill is regarded as founded on the money resolution as well as the Ways and Means resolutions; nevertheless, when such a money resolution has been agreed to at a later stage, no instruction has been given empowering a committee to make provision accordingly.[4]

Two bills have been founded on the same series of resolutions eg, in 1916 the Finance Bill, and the Finance (New Duties) Bill,[5] and in 1968 the Revenue Bill and the Revenue (No 2) Bill[6]. In each of these cases there was a resolution common to both bills. In other cases, however, there has been no common resolution, and each bill has been founded on separate resolutions in the series, eg in 1924 the British Sugar (Subsidy) Bill and the War Charges (Validity) Bill[7] and in 1974 the Finance Bill and the Oil Taxation Bill[8].

---

1 CJ (1936–37) 233; ibid (1953–54) 176; ibid (1982–83) 265 etc. For procedure resolutions, see p 739.
2 CJ (1952–53) 192.
3 CJ (1924) 182.
4 CJ (1974) 188.
5 CJ (1916) 48, 65.
6 CJ (1967–68) 65, 93.
7 CJ (1924–25) 45.
8 CJ (1974–75) 68–69.

Provisions in a bill which had been presented in the ordinary way, involving the payment of receipts into the Exchequer, which accordingly required to be authorized by a Ways and Means resolution, were regarded as authorized by one of the resolutions on which another bill (a Finance Bill) was founded, see the Currency and Bank Notes Bill 1928.[1]

RELATION OF BILLS TO WAYS AND MEANS RESOLUTIONS

Bills enacting provisions which require the preliminary authorization of Ways and Means resolutions should, in some cases, be ordered to be brought in upon such resolutions, but in other cases may be presented with these provisions printed in italics, subject to their being authorized by resolution before being considered in committee. The form of procedure appropriate in each case is decided on the same principles as those applied to bills authorizing expenditure (see pp 461–462). There is, however, much less room here for doubtful cases, as taxation for the revenue of the year is concentrated in a single bill, and even when taxation is not primarily for this purpose, it can hardly fail to be the main purpose of the bill which authorizes it, unless it is obviously insignificant.

Examples of subsidiary provisions in bills requiring Ways and Means resolutions are normally such matters as the payment of receipts into the Consolidated Fund, or the extension of the levy on independent television contractors to cable programme services, see the Cable and Broadcasting Bill 1983–84. Occasionally general taxing provisions in a bill (other than the Finance Bill, see p 736) have been treated as subsidiary; see the Speaker's ruling on Imports and Exports Regulation Bill 1919[2]. In the Land Commission Bill 1966–67 the imposition of betterment levy was regarded as subsidiary to the establishment of the Land Commission, and accordingly the Ways and Means resolution was agreed to after the second reading of the bill[3].

Bills founded on Ways and Means resolutions

When a bill is based on Ways and Means resolutions, all its provisions, and not only those which impose taxation, must be covered by the resolutions on which it is brought in.[4] Thus the resolutions on which the Finance Bill is brought in usually include a resolution providing for the general amendment of the fiscal law, which would not otherwise require to be moved as a Ways and Means resolution.[5] If, however, such a resolution is not included, the

---

1 CJ (1928) 121.
2 HC Deb (1919) 122, c 211.
3 CJ (1966–67) 62.
4 Eg Erskine Bridge Tolls Bill 1967–68.
5 In 1961, one of the resolutions upon which the Finance Bill was brought in related to Finance Bill (Procedure) (Isle of Man Act 1958). The inclusion of this resolution among the founding resolutions was necessitated by the fact that the provision to be covered was not essentially a matter of United Kingdom finance and therefore no resolution from the Committee of Ways and Means or a Committee of the whole House would have been appropriate to cover it (CJ (1960–61) 202).

scope for amendment of the bill is severely limited.[1] The Finance (Income Tax Reliefs) Bill 1977 was a purely relieving measure, brought in on specific resolutions covering the reliefs specified in the Bill. In the absence of an amendment of the law resolution no amendments extending the reliefs were in order. Sometimes the general resolution is so drawn as to exclude or restrict amendment of a particular tax.[2]

It has been decided that the 'Amendment of the Law' resolution is not sufficient authority for the inclusion in a Bill of a taxing provision not separately covered by a specific Ways and Means resolution; see the Speaker's ruling on Revenue Bill 1913[3].

If any provisions of a bill are found to go beyond the resolutions on which the bill is founded, further resolutions must be passed before those provisions are considered in committee on the bill,[4] or the bill must be amended so as to conform to the resolutions to which the House has agreed.[5]

Bills containing subsidiary Ways and Means provisions

The procedure on bills which contain subsidiary provisions necessitating Ways and Means resolutions (or Ways and Means provision incorporated into money resolutions, see p 729) is the same as that on bills containing subsidiary provisions involving expenditure. These provisions are printed in italics in the copies of the bills as presented, and cannot be considered in committee until the necessary Ways and Means resolutions have been passed.

Since the passing of Standing Order No 78 bills containing subsidiary Ways and Means provisions may be proceeded with by the Commons after being brought from the Lords. The Merchant Shipping Bill was introduced into the Commons in 1973–74 but failed to pass all stages. It was reintroduced into the Lords in 1974 and duly received the Royal Assent. On both occasions Ways and Means resolutions were passed by the Commons[6].

It is not the practice to print in italics provisions involving Ways and Means in bills brought from the Lords.

SCOPE OF FINANCE BILLS

The scope of a Finance Bill is not limited to the imposition and alteration of taxes for the purpose of adjusting the revenue of the year. It is not intended to be an annual Act in the same sense as the Appropriation Act, but normally includes many provisions of a permanent character for the regulation of fiscal machinery and other purposes. But, although the taxation it

---

1 Finance (No 2) Bill 1945 (CJ (1944–45) 138). Finance Bill 1955 (CJ (1954–55) 133). Finance Bill 1974–75 (CJ (1974–75) 65).
2 CJ (1948–49) 210; ibid (1950) 88; ibid (1951–52) 156; ibid (1961–62) 202, etc.
3 HC Deb (1913) 56, cc 319, 1010.
4 For the purpose of linking such a resolution with the bill to which it relates, the House on agreeing to the resolution orders an instruction to the committee on the bill enabling it to make provision accordingly. Instructions for this purpose may be ordered after the committee has begun consideration of the bill, CJ (1881) 240; ibid (1894) 204, 236; Parl Deb (1894) 24, c 1201.
5 CJ (1894) 204; Parl Deb (1894) 25, c 982; CJ (1914) 352; HC Deb (1914) 64, c 1973.
6 See also Antartic Minerals Bill [Lords] 1988–89, Children Bill [Lords] 1988–89 etc.

imposes may extend beyond the current financial year, a Finance Bill is regarded as exceeding its proper scope if it imposes a tax, payment of which is not to be demanded until after the close of the current financial year. However, when budget proposals have included advance proposals of this nature, resolutions have frequently been moved under the title 'Procedure (Future Taxation)' which have expressly authorized the inclusion of the proposals in the bill 'notwithstanding anything to the contrary in the practice of the House'.[1] Where supplementary Ways and Means resolutions have been moved during the passage of a Finance Bill similar procedure resolutions have been moved when appropriate.[2]

Provisions authorizing expenditure not essentially connected with national finance, or not incidental to the taxing or administrative provisions of a Finance Bill, are outside the scope of a Finance Bill, and their inclusion might justify an accusation of 'tacking' (see p 747). Where, however, it is considered desirable to insert in a Finance Bill a matter outside its normal scope, a resolution may be passed, again beginning with the words 'notwithstanding anything to the contrary in the practice of the House' to authorize the inclusion of the matter concerned.[3] It is the practice for such resolutions to be confined to matters not so far removed from central finance as to make their inclusion indefensible.[4]

DEBATE ON MAIN STAGES

Second reading

Debate of, and any amendments to, the question for the second and third reading of bills introduced on Ways and Means resolutions are governed by the ordinary rules of relevancy.[5] On the second reading of the Finance Bill, however, a general review of national finance is normally permitted.

Since the Finance Bill is invariably founded on Ways and Means resolutions at all its stages it constitutes exempted business under Standing Order No 14(1)(a).

Committee stage

It is now the normal practice for the Finance Bill to be divided between a Committee of the whole House and a standing committee by means of a motion made under Standing Order No 61 (3), except when dissolutions in the Spring have led to such bills being considered entirely in Committee of the whole House. The Finance Bill 1968 was the first such bill committed to a standing committee. In 1969 the Finance Bill was divided according to what has since become the normal practice. Before the amendment of Standing Order No 61 in 1967 Finance Bills and other bills for imposing taxes were required to be committed to a Committee of the whole House for their committee stage.

---

1 Eg CJ (1984–85) 337.
2 Eg CJ (1984–85) 549.
3 Eg CJ (1983–84) 443.
4 Eg CJ (1974) 66.
5 Parl Deb (1895) 33, c 1376; ibid (1903) 123, c 327; ibid (1905) 146, c 589; ibid (1906) 158, c 355; HC Deb (1918) 107, c 655; ibid (1919) 118, c 439; ibid (1920) 132, cc 1472, 1495.

Under Standing Order No 61 (3) Mr Speaker may permit a brief explanatory statement from the Member who makes and from one Member who opposes a motion to commit a bill to a standing committee in respect of some of its provisions and to a Committee of the whole House in respect of other provisions. Such a motion is made immediately after the second reading has been agreed to.

Amendments in committee and on report

Amendments in committee on the Finance Bill, and other bills founded on Ways and Means resolutions, are governed in the first place by the ordinary rules applicable to bills generally (see pp 490–493). The Finance Bill is in a rather special position owing to the characteristics mentioned above. The following points may be noted. When one of the resolutions on which a Finance Bill is founded is the customary 'Amendment of the Law' resolution, no instruction is needed to enable the committee to receive new clauses for the remission of taxes in force which are not dealt with by the bill. Where, however, there is no 'Amendment of the Law' resolution no amendment may be moved unless the relief proposed is covered by one of the Ways and Means resolutions on which the bill is founded. Nor may an amendment so covered exceed any figure prescribed in the relevant resolution[1].

When the 'Amendment of Law' resolution had been agreed to by the House in a restricted form so as to exclude the consideration of import duties imposed by another Act of the same session, amendments for the remission of those duties were not in order[2]. The 'Amendment of Law' resolution has regularly been agreed to in a restricted form which has secured since 1950 the partial exclusion of amendments proposing to reduce purchase tax[3] and since 1973, the partial exclusion of amendments relating to Value Added Tax[4].

Rules forbidding the increase of charges

Amendments must not exceed the scope, increase the amount or extend the incidence of any charge upon the people, defined by the terms of the Ways and Means resolutions by which the provisions proposed to be amended are authorized.[5] The rule is essentially the same as that in connection with financial resolutions explained on p 493. If it is desired to move new clauses or amendments which exceed the terms of the relevant Ways and Means resolutions, further resolutions must be passed, with instructions to the committee on the bill before such new clauses or amendments can be considered.[6]

If it is desired to recommit the bill and then proceed on the same day to the report stage, an order must be made to set aside the practice of the House regarding the interval between the stages of a money bill.[7]

---

1 HC Deb (1954–55) 540, cc 997–998.
2 CJ (1931–32) 177.
3 CJ (1950) 88.
4 CJ (1972–73) 191.
5 Parl Deb (1894) 24, c 1219; ibid (1901) 96, c 473; ibid (1904) 136, c 591; ibid (1904) 138, c 527; CJ (1909) 473; HC Deb (1909) 11, c 1763; ibid (1912–13) 41, cc 2425, 2451; ibid (1914) 64, c 690; ibid (1914–16) 75, cc 202, 204, 217; ibid (1916) 83, c 941; ibid (1919) 118, c 325.
6 CJ (1919) 135; ibid (1921) 259; ibid (1945–46) 293; ibid (1946–47) 254, 283, 294 etc.
7 CJ (1974) 276.

Charge in bill less than that authorized by resolution

When a tax is imposed in a bill, subject to alleviations of any kind which were not expressed in the resolution authorizing the tax, or for a shorter period than the period (if any) specified in the resolution, amendments are in order in committee on the bill to omit the alleviation[1] or extend the period[2] up to the limit laid down by the resolution.

Provisions reducing existing charges

The rule that the repeal or reduction of an existing tax, though it may be embodied in a Ways and Means resolution, is not subject to the rules of financial procedure, applies to the committee and also to the report stages of bills. Hence at these stages amendments are in order to reduce or omit drawbacks or other alleviations of existing taxes proposed by the bill.[3] Cases of unalloyed reduction of existing taxes should, however, be distinguished from cases where, in a Ways and Means resolution, an existing tax is increased in conjunction with the increase of an existing, or creation of a new, alleviation such as a drawback. In such a case, the new or increased alleviation could not be reduced or omitted without an increase of the whole charge, of which it is regarded as forming a limiting condition.

Third reading

While the normal rules relating to the scope of debate on third reading apply to the Finance Bill as much as to other bills, in practice some degree of latitude is frequently permitted.

Royal Assent

For a description of the pronouncing of the Royal Assent by Commission to a Finance Bill or other bill founded upon a Ways and Means resolution see p 529.

---

1 Eg HC Deb (1914–16) 75, c 218; ibid (1981–82) 22, cc 737–765 etc.
2 Ibid c 249.
3 HC Deb (1914–16) 76, c 1074; ibid (1917–18) 95, c 829.

CHAPTER 30

The House of Lords and charges

The financial powers of the House of Lords are limited, first by the ancient 'rights and privileges' of the House of Commons, and secondly by the terms of the Parliament Acts 1911 and 1949.

THE FINANCIAL FUNCTIONS OF THE LORDS

Concurrence in supplies and taxation

Stated generally, the role of the Lords in the grant of supplies for the service of the Crown, and in the imposition of taxation, is to agree, and not to initiate or amend. Thus, while the speech from the throne on the opening of a session is addressed to both Houses of Parliament, the demand for supply is directed to the Commons; and to the financial legislation which that demand creates the Lords must be a consenting party.[1]

Insistence by the Lords on the financial powers reserved to them

When the Lords, tacitly at any rate,[2] acquiesce in the Commons' claim to financial privilege, they in their turn claim the proper recognition of their constitutional responsibilities in the matter of finance, and insist upon all facilities which are necessary for the due exercise of their responsibilities. The following examples may be adduced:

Messages from the Crown for pecuniary aid

The Lords have taken exception if a message from the Crown for pecuniary aid is sent exclusively to the Commons,[3] and it is a long-established custom to present such messages to both Houses, if possible upon the same day, addressing the demand for the grant to the Commons, and desiring the concurrence of the Lords, a procedure which maintains the constitutional relations of the two Houses of Parliament in matters of Supply. The reply made by the Lords to the message is an address to the Crown, declaring their willingness to concur in the measures which may be adopted by the other House.[4]

---

1 But see Parliament Act 1911, s 1(1).
2 The Lords resolution of 1702 condemning the practice of 'tacking' (see p 747) virtually admits their inability to amend bills of supply.
3 Messages respecting the Civil List on 11 March 1936, 16 March 1937 and 18 November 1947 were presented to the Commons alone CJ (1935–36) 123, ibid (1936–37) 171, ibid (1947–48) 51.
4 LJ (1951–52) 195.

Consideration of public expenditure. The Lords also express their opinion upon public expenditure, and the method of taxation and financial administration, both in debate and by resolution, and they have investigated these matters by their select committees.[1]

RESTRICTIONS UNDER CONSTITUTIONAL USAGE

Basis of modern practice with respect to privilege

The modern practice in respect of the Commons' financial privileges is based upon the resolution of 1671 'That in all aids given to the King by the Commons, the rate or tax ought not to be altered by the Lords'; and that of 3 July 1678, 'That all aids and supplies, and aids to his Majesty in Parliament, are the sole gift of the Commons; and all bills for the granting of any such aids and supplies ought to begin with the Commons; and that it is the undoubted and sole right of the Commons to direct, limit, and appoint in such bills the ends, purposes, considerations, conditions, limitations, and qualifications of such grants, which ought not to be changed or altered by the House of Lords'.[2]

The principles expressed in the resolutions of 1671 and 1678 were restated and amplified by subsequent resolutions[3] of the Commons on two notable occasions in the financial history of the two Houses—in 1860 after the rejection by the Lords of the Paper Duty Repeal Bill and in 1910 after the rejection by the Lords of the Finance Bill 1909.

Local revenues within the scope of privilege

The Commons have long included not only bills dealing with the public expenditure and revenue but also bills which deal with local revenues or charges as matters to which their privilege extends. Hence they have claimed to waive their privilege in considering Lords Amendments to bills proposing a community charge[4] and have disagreed to Lords Amendments to such bills on grounds of privilege;[5] and they have similarly claimed to waive their privilege in respect of bills relating to other revenues such as land drainage rates where river boards were financed by contributions from local authorities and had power to levy charges on agricultural property.[6]

General but not public funds not within the scope of privilege

On the other hand the claim to an exclusive right over financial legislation asserted by the Commons has not been extended to bills dealing with funds set apart for the purposes of general, but not public, utility. Bills comprising

---

1 See eg HL 238–II (1984–85) pp 553, 702: Report of the Select Committee on Overseas Trade.
2 CJ (1667–87) 235, 509.
3 See Resolutions, CJ (1860) 360; Parl Deb (1860) 159, c 1383; and CJ (1910) 95.
4 Abolition of Domestic Rates Etc (Scotland) Bill 1986–87, Votes and Proceedings (1986–87), 13 May 1987.
5 Local Government Finance Bill 1987–88, Votes and Proceedings (1987–88), 20 July 1988.
6 Land Drainage Bill 1961 (CJ (1960–61) 306).

charges upon the property and revenues of the Church,[1] and bills applying to various purposes the fund created by the Irish Church Act 1870, have been received from the Lords by the Commons, or amended by the Lords, without objection on the ground of privilege.[2]

Actions which infringe privilege

With regard to the charges in respect of which they claim privilege, the Commons treat as a breach of privilege by the Lords not merely the imposition or increase of such a charge but also any alteration, whether by increase or reduction, of its amount or of its duration, mode of assessment, levy, collection, appropriation or management; and, in addition, any alteration in respect of the persons who pay, receive, manage, or control it, or in respect of the limits within which it is leviable.[3]

Bearing in mind the connotation hereby given to the term 'privilege' the Commons claim to 'privilege' may be analysed into:

(1) Restriction of the Lords' right to *initiate* bills.
(2) Restriction of the Lords' right to *amend* bills.
(3) Admission of the Lords' right to *reject* bills.

It is the function of the Speaker to direct the attention of the House, when occasion arises, to a breach of its privileges in bills or amendments brought from the Lords, and to direct the special entries to be made in the Journals by which the House, in respect of particular amendments, signifies its willingness to waive its privilege without thereby establishing a general precedent.

1. RESTRICTIONS ON THE LORDS' RIGHT TO INITIATE BILLS

The Commons are not prepared to consider bills sent from the Lords which contain provisions formally infringing privilege in any of the ways mentioned on p 743. Bills which thus infringe the privileges of the Commons, when received from the Lords, are either laid aside or postponed for six months.[4]

However the expedient for avoiding the formal infringement of privilege in Lords bills (the so-called 'privilege amendment', see pp 460, 745) is frequently resorted to, and is admissible even in the case of Lords bills whose main object is to create a charge upon the public revenue and which are

---

1 Church Endowment Bill 1843; Ecclesiastical Commissioners (England) Bill 1841; Bishopric of Manchester Bill 1847; Tithe Bill 1936.
2 Intermediate Education (Ireland) Bill [Lords] CJ (1878) 338; Arrears of Rent (Ireland) Bill; ibid (1882) 451.
3 See Speaker's rulings on Municipal Corporations (Ireland) Bill 1839, Parl Deb (1839) 50, c 3; Local Government (England and Wales) Bill 1893, Parl Deb (1894) 21, c 686; Public Libraries (Scotland) Bill 1920, HC Deb (1920) 133, c 368, Unemployment Insurance Act (1920) Amendment Bill 1921, ibid (1921) 138, c 2066; Police Pensions Bill 1921, ibid (1921) 144, c 1699; Unemployment Insurance (No 2) Bill 1924, ibid (1924) 176, c 2210; and the Commons claim to privilege in respect of a Lords Amendment to the Water Bill providing for the repayment of government grants, see Votes and Proceedings (1988–89), 3 July 1989.
4 CJ (1660–67) 311; ibid (1801) 88; ibid (1830–31) 905; ibid (1837) 659; ibid (1846) 724; ibid (1850) 458; ibid (1860) 308, 361; Parl Deb (1860) 159, c 539; CJ (1889) 304, 316; ibid (1950–51) 290; HC Deb (1950–51) 490, c 1246; CJ (1967–68) 106; HC Deb (1967–68) 758, c 1156.

brought down pursuant to Standing Order No 48(2) and proceeded with in the Commons pursuant to Standing Order No 78.

Relaxation of privilege by standing order

The Commons have by standing order relaxed their privilege in the following cases:

(a) Pecuniary penalties and fees. The claim to exclusive jurisdiction over charges imposed upon the people was formerly extended by the Commons to the imposition of fees and pecuniary penalties, and to provisions which touched the mode of suing for fees and penalties,[1] and to their application when recovered; and they denied to the Lords the power of dealing with these matters. The rigid enforcement of this claim proved inconvenient, and in 1849 the Commons adopted a standing order (now No 77) based on a resolution passed in 1831,[2] which waived their privileges on Lords bills or amendments dealing with pecuniary penalties, forfeitures, or fees, when the object of such penalties or forfeitures was to secure the execution of an Act; and when the fees imposed were not payable to the exchequer, or in aid of the public revenue.[3]

(b) Private legislation. Under Standing Order 191 the Commons have surrendered their privileges as far as they affect private bills sent from the House of Lords, which refer to tolls and charges for services performed, not being in the nature of a tax, or to local authorities' finance, or to sums payable by way of revenue support grant under the enactments relating to local government in England and Wales or in Scotland (see pp 714–715). Standing Order 191 is applied to provisional order bills by Standing Order 219 and to special procedure order bills by Standing Order 248A.

Privilege amendment

The expedient of a 'privilege amendment' is adopted when a bill containing provisions which deal with charges upon the people or upon public funds is proceeded with first in the Lords. This expedient was formerly limited to cases where the financial provisions were a subsidiary portion of a bill, and was not considered justifiable where such provision was the main purpose of a bill, whether it involved a charge upon public funds or merely upon local revenues. Since Standing Order No 78 was made in 1972, however, the Commons may proceed with a Lords bill, except a bill of aids and supplies, which would have as its main object the imposition or alteration of a charge upon the people or upon public funds but for the fact that it states that no such charge is imposed or altered, and provided that it is taken charge of in the Commons by a Minister of the Crown.[4]

The method of avoiding formal infringement of the Commons' privileges is for the Lords to insert a 'privilege amendment' on the third reading of a bill

---

1 8 March 1692, CJ (1688–93) 845; 3 Hatsell 126, 134.
2 CJ (1830–31) 477; ibid (1849) 557.
3 For the position with regard to private bills see p 978.
4 Eg Overseas Pensions Bill [Lords] 1972–73; CJ (1972–73) 154; Public Lending Right Bill [Lords] 1975–76, CJ (1975–76) 327; Commonwealth Development Corporation Bill [Lords] CJ (1985–86) 133.

in the form of a subsection added to the final clause of the bill. This subsection reads as follows: 'Nothing in this Act shall impose any charge on the people or on public funds, or vary the amount or incidence of or otherwise alter any such charge in any manner, or affect the assessment, levying, administration or application of any money raised by any such charge'. These words are marked by a thick black line in the margin of the bill when it is printed for the House of Commons, and the subsection is subsequently removed by an amendment in committee.

When Lords bills have been brought to the Commons without the privilege amendment incorporated in the text of the bill messages have been sent asking the Commons to return the bill.[1]

2. RESTRICTIONS ON THE LORDS' RIGHT TO AMEND BILLS

The Commons' resolution of 1678, cited on p 743, conceals, in its final clause, a very important distinction between two kinds of amendment by the Lords which, as breaches of privilege, are of very unequal moment in the eyes of the Commons. One of them is often tolerated, the other never. This distinction depends upon a distinction of kind in the bills amended. There is a certain kind of bill which descends from the earliest days of the Commons' history, and which is felt by them to embody privilege in its most essential form. This is the 'bill of aids and supplies.' Its modern counterparts are the Finance Bill for taxation and the Consolidated Fund Bill for expenditure. Any amendment by the Lords of such a bill, whether or not the amendment in itself involves interference with a charge, is regarded by the Commons as an intolerable breach of privilege.[2] In the case of any other bill, to be a breach of privilege, an amendment must in itself involve some interference in a charge; and such breaches of privilege the Commons feel themselves at liberty to accept, when they choose, with no more than a special record of the fact that they have waived their privilege. The practice is, therefore, treated here under the separate headings:

(1) Lords amendments to bills of aids and supplies.
(2) Lords amendments to other bills.

(1) Lords amendments to bills of aids and supplies

Such bills include, as stated above, the annual Finance and Consolidated Fund Bills.

So completely do the Lords accept the restriction resulting from the Commons' privileges upon their power to amend such bills, that they regularly refrain from going into committee on them. The last debate on a Consolidated Fund Bill was in 1907; since then proceedings have been purely formal.[3] The Lords have in the past preferred to accept a provision for the resumption of Irish grants, tacked to a supply bill of 1700, rather than

---

1 See LJ (1945–46) 196, 198; ibid (1978–80) 1139, 1152; ibid (1984–85) 190, 193. For an instance in the case of a private bill, see LJ (1974) 97.
2 3 Hatsell 153–154.
3 See First Report from the Select Committee on Procedure (Supply), HC 118–III (1980–81), pp 20–21. See also p 709.

cut out the provision, and to reject the Finance Bill of 1909 rather than amend it by the excision of the provisions to which they objected.

Since the start of the sessional series of Consolidated Fund Bills (1787) and Finance Bills (1860) these two kinds of bill for long embraced all the major instances of bills of aids and supplies. More recently however there have been certain bills for imposing customs duties or conferring power to levy tolls which have the characteristics of bills of aids and supplies. They are founded on Ways and Means resolutions and are drawn with a modified form of the special enacting formula devised in the seventeenth century for bills of aids and supplies. One such bill was the Safeguarding of Industries Bill 1921. The Commons disagreed to Lords amendments to the Bill, giving a single reason, namely 'because they infringe the sole and undoubted rights of the Commons to impose taxation.' But it was not claimed that the bill could not be amended at all without a breach of privilege, nor did the reason given include an assertion that the action taken by the Lords was unconstitutional.[1] Further bills of this character were the Abnormal Importations (Customs Duties) Bill 1931–32, the Severn Bridge Tolls Bill 1965, the Erskine Bridge Tolls Bill 1967–68, the National Insurance Surcharge Bill 1976–77, the Gas Levy Bill 1980–81 and the Oil Taxation Bill 1983–84.

Provisions 'tacked' to bills of aids and supplies. In former times, the Commons abused their right to grant supplies without interference from the Lords, by tacking to Supply bills provisions which, in a bill that the Lords had no right to amend, must either have been accepted by them unconsidered, or have caused the rejection of a measure necessary for the public service. This practice infringed the privileges of the Lords, no less than their interference in matters of Supply infringes the privileges of the Commons; it has been met by the Lords by Standing Order No 50, embodying a resolution of 9 December 1702:

> The annexing of any clause or clauses to a bill of aid or supply, the matter of which is foreign to and different from the matter of the said bill of aid or supply, is unparliamentary, and tends to the destruction of constitutional government.[2]

On no recent occasion have clauses been irregularly tacked to bills of supply.[3]

As for the modern equivalents of bills of aids and supplies, namely, Consolidated Fund and Finance Bills, the rules of order of the House of Commons exclude the possibility of foreign matter being tacked to such bills by way of amendment; and respect for constitutional practice prevents the inclusion of such matters among their original provisions.[4]

---

1 CJ (1921) 364; HC Deb (1921) 146, c 1695. See also Report on Tax Bills, HC 414 (1860); 3 Hatsell 141 n.
2 LJ (1701–05) 185.
3 Questions of tacking have been raised in connection with the Finance Bill 1976, HL Deb (1975–76) 372, cc 1225–1229; ibid (1977–78) 392, cc 6–44; ibid (1981–82) 431, cc 451–452. See also LJ (1976–77) 762–763.
4 On 19 July 1976 a suggestion of possible tacking was made in regard to cl 52 and Sch 6 of the Finance Bill, but the Speaker announced the following day that he had certified the Bill as a money bill. See HC Deb (1975–76) 915, cc 1290, 1520.

(2) Lords amendments to other bills infringing privilege

In the case of bills other than bills of aids and supplies, if the Lords return a bill with amendments which infringe the privileges of the Commons, the action open to the Commons, when the Speaker has called their attention to the breach of privilege, is according to the nature of the case, either to disagree with the amendments on the ground of privilege, or to agree with them, waiving privilege *pro hac vice*. They need not necessarily, however, be confronted with this choice. For just as in the case of the Lords bills, so in the case of Lords amendments to Commons bills, some part of the Commons' privilege remains in abeyance under standing order, and by the co-operation of both Houses certain expedients are in use for the purpose of avoiding formal infringement of privilege.

Rejection of amendments infringing privilege. When the Lords amendments are disagreed to by the Commons, and the amendments are in breach of the Commons' privileges, the disagreement is made on the ground of privilege alone; and in the message to the Lords from the Commons, communicating the reasons for their disagreement, the assertion of this claim usually takes the form of a statement that the amendments would interfere with the public revenue, or affect the levy and application of local revenues, or involve a charge on public funds, or alter the area of taxation, or alter the financial arrangements made by the Commons, or affect the administration of public funds, or otherwise infringe the privileges of the House, and that the Commons do not offer any further reason, 'trusting that the reason given may be deemed sufficient'.[1] This hint of privilege is generally accepted by the Lords, and the amendment is not insisted on.[2]

The Lords may offer amendments in lieu of amendments disagreed to by the Commons on the ground of privilege.[3]

On the Unemployment Insurance (No 2) Bill in 1929 the Lords returned a message to the Commons insisting upon certain amendments disagreed to by the Commons on grounds of privilege. Instead of ordering the reasons given by the Lords for insisting on their amendments to be laid aside, or deferring their consideration for three or six months, which was then held to be the correct procedure, the Commons did not insist on disagreement with the amendments, but proposed amendments to certain of them, to which the Lords agreed.[4]

Rejection by Commons of amendments infringing privilege in respect of the imposition of a charge. Amendments have been rejected in the Commons without debate when the Speaker has drawn the attention of the House to the fact that the amendments sought to impose a charge which had not been authorized by a financial resolution.[5]

---

1 Electricity Supply Bill CJ (1926) 417; Coal Bill, ibid (1937–38) 348; Wireless Telegraphy Bill, ibid (1948–49) 306; Housing (Slum Clearance Compensation) Bill, ibid (1965–66) 55, etc.
2 See the Lords debate on Lords Amendments to the Local Government Finance Bill 1987–88 disagreed to by the Commons for which privilege alone was, in this way, assigned as the reason for disagreement HL Deb (1987–88) 500, cc 168–189. See also HC Deb (1929–30) 234, c 1861; HL Deb (1983–84) 450, cc 346–349; ibid (1984–85) 463, cc 957–967; ibid (1985–86) 479, cc 416–421; ibid (1987–88) 501, cc 541–590.
3 See eg HL Deb (1984–85) 463, c 958.
4 CJ (1929–30) 179; HC Deb (1929–30) 234, c 1861.
5 HC Deb (1977–78) 948, cc 1801–1802, and 954, c 1011.

A new paragraph (3) was added on 30 March 1983 to Standing Order No 76, which provides that if the Speaker is satisfied that a Lords amendment imposes a charge upon the public revenue such as is required to be authorised by resolution of the House under Standing Order No 47, and that the charge has not been so authorized, he shall declare that he is so satisfied and the amendment shall be deemed to have been disagreed to.[1]

The Standing Order does not cover the case of a Lords Amendment which would impose a charge upon the people which has not been authorised by a Ways and Means resolution. Accordingly in such a case the Speaker has drawn the attention of the House to the infringement of privilege and has called upon the Member in charge of the bill to move forthwith that the House disagree to the amendment.[2]

Acceptance by the Commons of amendments infringing privilege. The Commons, when they so wish, 'waive privilege' in individual cases, and accept amendments by the Lords, so long as they do not materially infringe the privileges of the Commons.[3] In such cases they record their action by an entry inserted in the Journal, under direction from the Speaker. Formerly there were a variety of forms of entry, but since 1968 a standard form has been adopted, stating merely that the Commons are willing to waive their privileges.[4] Although such waiving is commonplace, it is not entirely a formality. Its significance continues to be recognized in the usual requirement of an allocation of time order for considering Lords Amendments. Under such an order the Speaker is required, when the 'guillotine' falls, to designate such of the Lords Amendments which remain to be considered as involve questions of privilege. After the House has disposed by separate questions of any ministerial motions relating to an amendment, questions are put for agreement with each of the remaining designated amendments separately from a question for agreement with all the rest of the Lords Amendments not previously disposed of.[5]

Amendments infringing privilege with respect to local revenue. The Commons now generally waive their claim regarding amendments made to bills that they have sent to the Lords, dealing with local revenues; more especially when those amendments affect charges upon the people incidentally only, and are made for the purpose of giving effect to the legislative intentions of the Commons.[6]

---

1 For such a declaration see Lords Amendments to the Education Reform Bill 1987–88, Votes and Proceedings (1987–88), 19 July 1988.
2 HC Deb (1984–85) 78, cc 220–222.
3 Cf HL Deb (1962–63) 252, cc 480–489.
4 CJ (1968–69) 72, 155, 282, 350, etc.
5 Eg CJ (1985–86) 516, etc. On occasion the order has required the remaining designated amendments to be disposed by a single question, eg CJ (1985–86) 528 etc.
6 See eg the extensive Lords Amendments to the Local Government Finance Bill, 1987–88, Votes and Proceedings (1987–88), 20 July 1988. However certain of the Lords Amendments which infringed privilege were disagreed to, and in those cases the customary privilege reasons were assigned. For a reason not based on privilege where privilege had been waived see Landed Property (Ireland) Bill 1847, CJ (1847) 594, 606.

Relaxation of privilege by standing order in the case of Lords amendments

Pecuniary penalties and fees. The Standing Order (No 77) referred to above (p 745) which relaxes the Commons' claim to privilege in matters affecting pecuniary penalties and fees applies to amendments made in the Lords as well as to bills originating in the Lords.

This standing order, therefore, relieves the Speaker of the duty of directing the attention of the House to Lords amendments dealing with the matters to which it applies.

Local revenues in private bills. Standing Order 191, which relaxes the Commons' privileges in respect of private bills sent from the Lords dealing with local revenues, applies equally to Lords amendments, dealing with similar matters, made to Commons bills. This standing order is extended to provisional order bills by Standing Order 219, to confirmation bills under the Private Legislation Procedure (Scotland) Act 1936 by Standing Order 228A, and to bills under the Statutory Orders (Special Procedure) Act 1945 by Standing Order 248A.

3. RIGHT TO REJECT BILLS RETAINED BY LORDS

The Lords may reject financial bills without infringing privilege.

The legal right of the Lords, as a co-ordinate branch of the legislature, to withhold their assent from any bill whatever, to which their concurrence is desired, is unquestionable; and in former times their power of rejecting a bill for granting aids or supplies to the Crown was expressly acknowleged by the Commons:[1] but, until the year 1860, though the Lords had rejected numerous bills concerning questions of public policy, in which taxation was incidentally involved, they had respected bills exclusively relating to matters of Supply and Ways and Means.

Adoption of the practice of an annual inclusive finance bill

Before 1860 it was not unusual for the repeal or imposition of separate classes of duties or taxes to be effected by separate bills, but the rejection by the Lords in that year of the Paper Duties Repeal Bill led the Commons to adopt the practice of including all the fiscal changes of each year in a general or composite bill.[2]

This practice had become accepted as normal by 1894, with the technical result that the rejection or restoration of a duty by the Lords would have been an amendment of a bill of aids and supplies—an inadmissible proceeding—instead of its rejection—a right which the Commons still admitted while thus reducing the power of exercising it to a practical impossibility.

Rejection by Lords of separate financial provisions in non-financial bills

The right of the Lords to reject a bill for granting aids and supplies to the Crown has been held to include a right to omit provisions creating charges

---

1 3 Hatsell 110–157; May, Const. Hist. i, 379; Report on Tax Bills, HC 414 (1860).
2 See Resolutions, CJ (1860) 360; Parl Deb (1860) 159, c 1383.

upon the people, when such provisions form a separate subject in a bill which the Lords are otherwise entitled to amend. The claim of privilege cannot, therefore, be raised by the Commons regarding amendments to such bills, whereby a whole clause, or series of clauses, has been omitted by the Lords, which, though relating to a charge, and not admitting of amendment, yet concerned a subject separable from the general objects of the bill.[1]

The Lords amended Part I of the Agricultural Land (Utilisation) Bill 1931, and Part III of the Land Commission Bill 1967 (which provided for a betterment levy). Then they left out these Parts in their entirety (one on report,[2] the other on third reading[3]). The Commons disagreed to the amendments leaving the Parts out and amended the words so restored to each bill. In both cases some of the Lords amendments, of which the Commons had taken informal notice, were included.[4]

LIMITATIONS IMPOSED BY THE PARLIAMENT ACT 1911

The practice of collecting all changes in taxation together and embodying them in a single composite finance bill made it impossible for the Lords to reject such a bill without destroying the financial provision of the year. The situation created by the Lords' rejection of the Finance Bill of 1909[5] resulted in the passing of the Parliament Act 1911 the financial provisions of that Act are set out below. (For the effect of the Act on bills not certified as money bills see p 533).

Definition of money bill

Section 1(2) of the Act defines a 'money bill'[6] as a public bill which in the opinion of the Speaker of the House of Commons contains only provisions dealing with all or any of the following subjects, namely, the imposition, repeal, remission, alteration, or regulation of taxation; the imposition for the payment of debt or other financial purposes of charges on the Consolidated Fund or the National Loans Fund,[7] or on money provided by Parliament or the variation or repeal of any such charges; Supply; the appropriation, receipt, custody, issue or audit of accounts of public money; the raising or guarantee of any loan or the repayment thereof; or subordinate matters incidental to those subjects or any of them. For the purposes of this definition the expressions 'taxation', 'public money', and 'loan' respect-

---

1 Coal Mines Bill 1930, in which they omitted two clauses setting up the Coal Mines Reorganization Commission. The Commons disagreed to the amendments to the Bill, with a reason based on merits and not on privilege.
2 LJ (1930–31) 218. When Part I was re-inserted, the Lords insisted on leaving out cl 1, establishing an Agricultural Land Corporation. This was treated as another 'separate subject' and the Commons did not insist on re-inserting it.
3 LJ (1966–67) 344.
4 CJ (1966–67) 325.
5 LJ (1909) 453; May, Const. Hist. iii, 353.
6 A 'money bill' should not be confused with a bill introduced under Standing Order No 48 (procedure on bills whose main object is to create a charge) (see p 721).
7 See s 1 of National Loans Act 1968.

ively do not include any taxation, money, or loan raised by local authorities or bodies for local purposes, matters which, on the other hand, are included within the scope of privilege.

Procedure in passing money bill

A 'money bill' which has been passed by the House of Commons and sent up to the House of Lords at least one month before the end of the session, but is not passed by the House of Lords without amendment within one month after it is so sent up, is, unless the House of Commons direct to the contrary,[1] to be presented for the Royal Assent and becomes an Act of Parliament on the Royal Assent being signified to it. A 'money bill' when it is sent up to the House of Lords, and when it is presented to Her Majesty, must be endorsed with the Speaker's certificate that it is a 'money bill'. Before giving this certificate the Speaker is directed to consult, if practicable, those two members of the Chairman's Panel (see p188) who are appointed for the purpose at the beginning of each session by the Committee of Selection.[2]

When the Speaker[3] has certified a bill to be a 'money bill' this is recorded in the Journal; and such certificate is conclusive for all purposes and may not be questioned in a court of law (section 3 of the Parliament Act 1911).

No serious practical difficulty has arisen in deciding whether a particular bill is or is not a 'money bill'; and criticism has seldom been voiced of the Speaker's action in giving or withholding his certificate. A bill which contains any of the enumerated matters and nothing besides is indisputably a 'money bill'. If it contains any other matters, then, unless these are 'subordinate matters incidental to' any of the enumerated matters so contained in the bill, the bill is not a 'money bill'.

The Speaker does not consider the question of certifying a bill until it has reached the form in which it will leave the House of Commons, and has declined to give his opinion on whether the acceptance of a proposed amendment would prevent a bill from being certified as a money bill.[4] Similarly in committee the chairman has declined to anticipate the Speaker's decision in this matter or to allow the effect of an amendment in this regard to be raised as a point of order.[5]

'Money bills' under Parliament Act and bills of aids and supplies

A 'money bill' within the meaning of the Parliament Act 1911 is not the same as a bill of aids and supplies. Included under the former term is the large and increasing class of bills which 'impose charges upon the Consolidated Fund or on moneys provided by Parliament.' A bill which is exclusively for this

---

1 In the case of a bill which by inadvertence has not been read the third time by the Lords within a month, as required by s 1(1) of the Parliament Act 1911, the Commons have ordered that the provisions of the subsection shall not apply, CJ (1933–34) 272. The Commons have also ordered that the provisions of s 1(1) of the Act should not apply in the case of a bill to which the Lords could not readily agree within the period of one month because of a Parliamentary recess, CJ (1972–73) 90, CJ (1975–76) 542. But when the Lords passed a money bill after the Commons had adjourned at the end of July, the bill received Royal Assent in the ordinary way in October without an order in the Commons to disapply s 1(1) of the Act (Rate Support Grants Bill 1985–86).
2 See, for example, HC Deb (1975–76) 915, c 1520.
3 A bill has been endorsed as being a 'money bill' by the Deputy Speaker, CJ (1914) 453; ibid (1947–48) 68; ibid (1950–51) 146.
4 HC Deb (1912–13) 41, c 2667. See also ibid (1911) 31, c 1209, ibid (1975–76) 915, c 1290.
5 HC Deb (1914–16) 72, c 1704.

purpose is held to be a 'money bill'. But it is not a bill of aids and supplies. On the other hand a bill of aids and supplies, such as a Finance Bill, is not necessarily a 'money bill' for it may and often does include provisions dealing with other subjects than those enumerated in the definition of a 'money bill'. In fact approximately half of the Finance Bills[1] sent to the Lords since the Parliament Act was passed have not been certified as money bills.

The Lords are debarred from amending bills of aids and supplies by the Commons' claim to privilege, and though rejection of these bills is permissible, it has virtually ceased to be practicable. The purpose of section 1 of the Parliament Act is to debar them from amending or rejecting 'money bills'. But section 6 of the Parliament Act provides that 'nothing in this Act shall diminish or qualify the existing rights and privileges of the House of Commons.' This in practice gives the Commons a choice of proceeding upon Lords amendments under their privileges or according to the procedure laid down by the Act, and consequently they are free to consider and, if they choose, accept amendments made by the Lords to a certified bill.[2] This result follows from the fact that, as stated above, 'money bills' include bills, the amendment of which by the Lords is not held by the Commons to be in itself a breach of privilege. But it would not be possible for the Commons, while agreeing to certain amendments made by the Lords to a certified bill and disagreeing to others, to secure the Royal Assent to the bill under the terms of section 1 of the Act.

1 See eg Finance Bills of 1980–81, 1981–82, 1982–83 and 1986–87.
2 CJ (1921) 347, 364; HC Deb (1921) 146, cc 835, 1689. See also Industrial Development (Ships) Bill 1969–70. Other certified Bills to which the Commons agreed to Lords Amendments were the Unemployment Assistance (Temporary Provisions) Extension Bill 1935–36; Inshore Fishing Industry Bill 1946; and the China Indemnity Bill 1925, where, before the Commons had ordered the amendment to be considered, the month specified in section 1 of the Parliament Act expired; the Commons, however, agreed to the amendment.

CHAPTER 31

Public petitions

Development of petitioning

Though the right to petition Crown and Parliament is of great antiquity and of importance to both constitutional and procedural development, this chapter is concerned only with the modern form of petitions to one or other of the Houses of Parliament, principally to the Commons, which grew up in the seventeenth century, when Parliament had come to be regarded as a political and legislative body rather than as the highest court of justice. Public petitions may pray for an alteration of the general law or the reconsideration of a general administrative decision, and they may also pray for redress of local or personal grievances; they are to be distinguished from petitions relating directly to private business (see chapters 33–37).

The rights of petitioners and the power of the House to deal with petitions were expressed in two resolutions of the Commons in 1669:

'That it is the inherent right of every commoner in England to prepare and present petitions to the House of Commons in case of grievance, and the House of Commons to receive the same';

'That it is an undoubted right and privilege of the Commons to judge and determine, touching the nature and matter of such petitions, how far they are fit and unfit to be received'.[1]

Until after the first Reform Act the procedure of the House of Commons imposed little restriction on the raising of debate on the presentation of petitions, which served as a method of introducing subjects from outside the House and could be used for obstructing other kinds of business. In view of the great increase of the number of petitions, which roughly coincided with a growth in demand for the time of the House from official sources, a series of Standing Orders was adopted in 1842, which, as subsequently amended, made the presentation of petitions a formal proceeding incapable, except in rare cases, of giving rise to immediate debate.

Form of petitions

Petitions to the House of Lords should begin, 'To the right honourable the Lords Spiritual and Temporal in Parliament assembled';[2] and to the House of Commons, 'To the honourable the Commons of the United Kingdom of Great Britain and Northern Ireland in Parliament assembled'. The

---

1 These resolutions of general import formed part of a group of resolutions, the rest of which related specifically to trading matters in the East Indies, and reflected a serious quarrel between the two Houses (*Skinner v East India Company*). In an effort to settle the controversy, the House later acceded to a royal command that the entire group of resolutions be erased from the Journal, CJ (1667–1687) 126. See also 3 Hatsell 240 n.

2 A petition intended for the previous Parliament will not be received; see Mirror of Parliament, 1831, vol 3, p 2199.

petition should continue: 'The humble petition of [here insert the name or other designation of the petitioner or petitioners] sheweth'. The general allegations of the petition are then set out and are followed by what is called the 'prayer', in which the particular object of the petitioner is expressed. The petition should conclude as follows: 'And your petitioners, as in duty bound, will ever pray, etc.' Finally, there will appear the signatures (or marks) of the petitioners and their addresses.

Remonstrances, etc. Without a prayer, a document will not be taken as a petition;[1] and a paper, assuming the style of a declaration,[2] an address of thanks,[3] or a remonstrance only, without a proper form of prayer, will not be received. In other cases, remonstrances respectfully worded, and concluding with a proper form of prayer, have been received:[4] but a document, distinctly headed as a remonstrance, though concluding with a prayer, has been refused.[5] A so-called memorial, properly worded, and concluding with a prayer, has been received.[6]

Signature, etc. In the Commons, a petition should be written upon parchment or paper; a printed,[7] lithographed,[8] or type-written[9] petition will not be received. In the Lords, however, a petition may be written, printed or typed on parchment or paper.[10] In both Houses, it must be signed[11] and at least one signature should be upon the same sheet or skin upon which the petition is written.[12] If petitions are presented without any signatures to the sheet on which they are written, they are not noticed in the Votes. The petition must have original signatures or marks, and not copies from the original,[13] nor signatures of agents on behalf of others, except in case of incapacity by sickness.[14] The signatures must be written upon the petition itself, and not pasted upon, or otherwise transferred to it.[15] Every signature must be accompanied by the address of the signatory.[16] Where a petition consists of more than one sheet, only those signatures will be considered valid which are written on sheets headed by the prayer of the petition or on the back of those sheets; but on every sheet after the first the prayer may be reproduced in print or by other mechanical process.[17] Petitions of corporations aggregate should be under their common seal.

---

1 CJ (1842) 470; Parl Deb (1842) 65, cc 1225 and 1227.
2 Parl Deb (1842) 60, c 640.
3 Parl Deb (1842) 64, c 423.
4 Parl Deb (1860) 159, cc 761, 1524; see also CJ (1812) 398; ibid (1821) 391.
5 Parl Deb (1843) 70, c 745.
6 Parl Deb (1878) 240, c 1682.
7 CJ (1792–93) 738; ibid (1812–13) 624, 648; ibid (1817) 128, 156.
8 Parl Deb (1840) 52, c 158.
9 Parl Deb (1897) 50, c 1297.
10 Companion to the Standing Orders (1989 ed.) p 184.
11 CJ (1822) 127.
12 CJ (1817) 128, 155; ibid (1822) 127; Parl Deb (1843) 66, c 1032; CJ (1845) 335; ibid (1854) 293.
13 CJ (1836) 576.
14 CJ (1667–87) 369, 433; ibid (1688–93) 285; ibid (1772–74) 800; Report, Public Petitions Committee, 1848, ibid (1847–48) 786.
15 Special Reports, Public Petitions Committee, CJ (1849) 283; ibid (1850) 79.
16 Order of reference to Public Petitions Committee, CJ (1944–45) 10, etc.
17 HC Deb (1942–43) 390, c 1113.

A petition must be in the English language, or accompanied by a trans-lation, which the Member who presents it states to be correct;[1] it must be free from interlineations or erasures.[2] No letters, affidavits or other docu-ments may be annexed to a petition,[3] and the sheets of the petition itself may not contain any extraneous matter such as appeals by the petitioners for subscriptions or financial support.[4]

Forgery or fraud. Any forgery or fraud in the preparation of petitions, or in the signatures attached, or the being privy to, or cognizant of, such forgery or fraud, is liable to be punished as a breach of privilege,[5] and is considered and dealt with by the House as a matter of privilege.[6] There have been frequent instances in which such irregularities have been discovered and punished by both Houses.[7] In some cases the House has satisfied itself by the rejection of the petition,[8] or by discharging the order for its lying on the Table.[9] A motion to that effect has been permitted without previous notice;[10] though a claim to draw attention, as a matter of privilege, to expressions in a petition presented at a previous sitting, has not been conceded.[11]

Character and substance of petitions

The language of a petition should be respectful and temperate and free from disrespectful language to the Sovereign[12] or offensive imputations upon the

---

1 CJ (1821) 173, 189; ibid (1845) 560.
2 CJ (1826–27) 118, 262; ibid (1831) 748. See also Special Report, Select Committee on Public Petitions, HC 228 (1972–73).
3 CJ (1826) 82; ibid (1826–27) 41; ibid (1856) 102.
4 HC Deb (1951–52) 501, c 1328 and Special Report of Public Petitions Committee, HC 286 (1951–52).
5 CJ (1772–74) 800.
6 Parl Deb (1878) 238, c 1741.
7 CJ (1825) 445; ibid (1826–27) 491, 561, 582; ibid (1829) 187; ibid (1834) 92; ibid (1843) 523, 528; LJ (1850), 367, 477; CJ (1851) 193, 289; ibid (1865) 157, 336; ibid (1878–79) 175, 180; LJ (1862) 300, 321, 378, 386; CJ (1887) 292, 306, 313.
8 CJ (1867) 345; Special Report of Public Petitions Committee 1872, ibid (1872) 370, 395. In sessions 1893–94 and 1912–13 special reports were made to the House recommending that certain petitions should be rejected, but no action was taken thereon by the House, HC 393 (1893–94) 533; HC 401 (1912–13), CJ (1912–13) 464.
9 Petitions from Dublin against the Sale of Intoxicating Liquors on Sunday (Ireland) Bill 1878, CJ (1878) 130, 139, 181, 184. Special Report, Public Petitions Committee, 1883, ibid (1883) 153.
10 Parl Deb (1876) 228, c 1400.
11 Parl Deb (1867) 187, c 14.
12 Parl Deb (1852) 122, c 863.

character or conduct of Parliament[1] or the courts of justice,[2] or other tribunal,[3] or constituted authority.[4]

Offensive expressions, not particularly affecting, though addressed to, the House itself may be regarded as disrespectful to the House.[5]

The language of a petition may be improper, not because of its being offensive in itself or indecorous in its terms, but because the statements of which it is the vehicle are not proper to be made by the petitioners, as, for example, where a petition refers to anything which may have been said by Members in debate in the House.[6]

The petition must set out a case in which the House has jurisdiction to interfere,[7] and must conclude with a prayer for such relief as is within the power of the House to grant.[8]

Where a petition, besides a prayer for relief which is not within the power of the House, prays also for something which is within its power, the petition will be received.[9]

If the prayer of the petition is within the power of the House to grant, the absurdity of it is no objection to the reception of the petition.[10]

A petition may not allude to debates in either House of Parliament,[11] or to intended motions, if merely announced in debate:[12] but when notices have been formally given and printed on the notice paper, petitions referring to them are received. The procedure on petitions praying for public money, etc, has already been described (see p 711). By Standing Order No 136, the usage under which the House refused to entertain petitions against a resolution or bill imposing a tax or duty for the service of the year, was discontinued. In the Lords, a petition relating to a bill before the Commons, which has not yet reached their House, or which has already been rejected will not

---

1 CJ (1826–27) 589; ibid (1829) 275. See also Parl Deb (1822) 6, c 1231, ibid (1823) 9, c 1253 for a petition containing offensive imputations against the Commons (and cf ibid (1849) 105, c 581, CJ (1840) 193 for the registration of a petition deliberately insulting the House); CJ (1874) 209 for the withdrawal of a petition reflecting on a select committee; CJ (1861) 364, 377, 381 for a petition charging a Member with fraud. A petition to the Commons containing language disrespectful of the Lords has been withdrawn (CJ (1837–38) 236), though another praying in temperate language for the abolition of the upper House was after debate received (CJ (1847–48) 384, Parl Deb (1847–48) 97, c 1055).
2 CJ (1821) 105. Printed copies of a petition were cancelled and the petition withdrawn in 1874, since imputations were made on the conduct of judges (CJ (1874) 276); and similar action was taken the following year against a petition which reflected on the House, the Speaker, the Lord Chief Justice and two senior judges (CJ (1875) 134, 145.
3 CJ (1821) 92; ibid (1828) 541.
4 CJ (1823) 431; ibid (1836) 698. A petition threatening to resist the law has not been allowed to lie on the Table (CJ (1831–32) 547).
5 Parl Deb (1836) 34, c 670; ibid (1831) 6, cc 292–294; ibid (1837–38) 40, cc 474–475.
6 Parl Deb (1830–31) 3, cc 1734–1736; ibid (1819) 40, c 150–151; ibid (1834) 24, c 1287; ibid (1840) 54, c 462; ibid (1826) 15, c 970.
7 Parl Deb (1817), 35, c 173; ibid (1830–31) 2, cc 654–655; ibid (1831–32) 9, c 1275; ibid (1831–32) 13, c 1115.
8 Parl Deb (1816) 33, c 215; ibid (1819) 40, c 910; ibid (1837–38) 43, c 803.
9 Parl Deb (1836) 33, c 326.
10 Parl Deb (1836) 34, cc 1042–1044.
11 CJ (1822) 150; ibid (1826–27) 604; ibid (1836) 616; ibid (1842) 259; ibid (1847–48) 406, 633; ibid (1850) 160; ibid (1854) 160. Parl Deb (1842) 63, c 192.
12 CJ (1830) 107; Parl Deb (1851) 114, c 820.

be received. In the House of Commons petitions have been received relating to bills which have already been read the third time in that House.[1]

Petition from person attainted

A petition has been received from persons attainted of treason in circumstances, however, which were too exceptional to establish any principle.[2]

Petitions from abroad

Petitions from British subjects resident abroad[3] as well as petitions from inhabitants of British colonies having local parliaments[4] have always been received; and also those of foreigners resident in this country.[5] In 1876, when a petition from inhabitants of Boulogne-sur-Mer, several of whom appeared to be British subjects, was offered, a select committee appointed to consider the matter did not advise its reception on the ground that it contained the signatures of French citizens as well as British subjects; and the petition was rejected.[6]

Receivability of petitions dependent upon the competence of Parliament

Petitions have been received from Dominions and colonies.[7] Following petitions to both Houses in 1935 from Western Australia for legislation to withdraw that state from the Commonwealth of Australia, and to recreate it as a self-governing colony, a joint committee[8] appointed to consider the receivability of the petition reported that the petition should not be received,[9] since it was contrary to constitutional conventions for the UK Parliament to interfere in such circumstances, save at the request of the government of the Dominion the constitution of the whole of which would be affected. Neither House took any action on the report of the joint committee.

More recently, petitions were received from Canadian Indians.[10]

Petitions for attendance of witnesses or production of evidence in a court of law

The presentation of a petition is the usual method of seeking the leave of the House for a Member to give evidence in a court of law touching proceedings

---

1 HC Deb (1956–57) 568, c 937.
2 Parl Deb (1849) 106, c 389.
3 From British residents in Dresden, Votes and Proceedings (1870) 102; Appendix to Votes (1870) 1 March 1970. From members of British and Foreign Anti-Slavery Society, Cuba, Votes and Proceedings (1874) 6 August 1974; from British citizens resident in: Venezuela, CJ (1980–81) 269; Sierra Leone, ibid 316; Belgium, ibid 331.
4 Eg CJ (1966–67) 103; HC Deb (1966–67) 756, c 178.
5 Provided that the subject of their complaint relates to the action of British, and not foreign, authorities, Parl Deb (1832) 13, c 1115.
6 HC 232 (1876); CJ (1876) 148, 181, 200; Parl Deb (1876) 228, c 1411.
7 A Petition from the inhabitants of Nova Scotia was received in 1868. A Petition from the British Migrants Association of Australia was received in 1932, Votes and Proceedings (1931–32) 14 April 1932. See also HC Deb (1948–49) 458, c 1049 (Newfoundland).
8 LJ (1934–35) 56; CJ (1934–35) 103.
9 HL 52, 75 (1934–35); HC 88 (1934–35).
10 CJ (1975–76) 85; ibid (1979–80) 236; ibid (1981–82) 121.

in the House or in a committee,[1] or for an officer of the House to give evidence or produce documents relating to such proceedings.[2] No petition is required for leave to refer in court to the reports and debates of the Commons, if there is no question of the evidence touching those proceedings or of the production of other documents (see pp 91–92). Following the presentation of a petition an appropriate motion may be made, without notice, for the leave of the House to be granted (see pp 323–324). Petitions of this sort are printed *in extenso* in Votes and Proceedings, and are not ordered to be printed pursuant to Standing Order No 135. Since the House alone can take action upon them, they are not transmitted by the Clerk of the House to a Minister of the Crown (see pp 762–763).

Presentation of petitions

Duty of Members in the presentation of petitions. Petitions are to be presented by a Member of the House to which they are addressed,[3] but, as was decided in 1894, a Member cannot be compelled to present a petition.[4] In consenting to present a petition to the House a Member does not necessarily commit himself to the views contained in it.[5] A Member who has not taken the oath or made affirmation cannot present a petition.[6]

According to established usage the Speaker does not present petitions to the House.[7] A Member must sign his name at the beginning of a petition he presents.[8]

Presentation of petitions from the corporation of London. Petitions from the corporation of London are presented to the House of Commons by the sheriffs, at the bar (being introduced by the Serjeant with the Mace),[9] or by one sheriff only, if the other be a Member of the House,[10] or unavoidably absent.[11]

A similar privilege granted in 1813 to the Lord Mayor of Dublin (and last exercised by him in 1916) may be regarded as having been overtaken by the independent status of the republic of Ireland.[12]

---

1 CJ (1948–49) 14; ibid (1966–67) 578; ibid (1967–68) 98; ibid (1981–82) 175.
2 CJ (1958–59) 313; ibid (1962–63) 201; ibid (1967–68) 125; ibid (1969–70) 153; ibid (1975–76) 428; ibid (1977–78) 442.
3 Parl Deb (1881) 263, c 1011.
4 *Chaffers v Goldsmid* [1894] 1 QB 186.
5 HC Deb (1968–69) 779, c 389.
6 Parl Deb (1881) 259, c 892; CJ (1882) 295.
7 A petition from persons resident in the constituency represented by the Speaker has been presented by another Member (HC Deb (1982–83) 47, c 537).
8 CJ (1884–85) 11; see also, ibid (1833) 190; ibid (1844) 284, Parl Deb (1844) 74, c 714. Notice being taken that a Member's name had been affixed to a petition without his authority, the petition was ordered to be withdrawn (CJ (1876) 141, Parl Deb (1876) 228, c 1320) and it has been ruled that the Member's name should be signed by his own hand, and that it is irregular to authorize another person to affix it Parl Deb (1876) 229, c 586.
9 MS Officers and Usages of the House of Commons, p 46; CJ (1947–48) 133.
10 CJ (1835) 506; ibid (1847–48) 122, 331, 731; ibid (1881) 248.
11 CJ (1820) 213; ibid (1839) 432. Other steps were taken in 1840 when both sheriffs were in the custody of the Serjeant at Arms (CJ (1840) 43, 82, 198).
12 CJ (1812–13) 209: see ibid (1916) 191.

Petitions on first day of session. Petitions are not received on the first day of a session, when the Queen's Speech is delivered.

Presentation of a petition from a Member. A peer or Member may petition the House to which he belongs; but if a Member desires to have a petition from himself presented to the House, he should entrust it to some other Member, as he will not be permitted to present it himself.[1] This rule, however, does not extend to cases in which a Member presents a petition signed by himself in his representative capacity as chairman of a local authority or of any public incorporated body.

Transmission by post. To facilitate the presentation of petitions, they may be transmitted through the post to Members of either House, free of charge, provided they are sent without covers, or in covers open at the sides, and do not exceed 32 ounces in weight.[2]

Irregularities in petitions. In both Houses it is the duty of Members to read petitions which are sent to them before they are presented and, if they observe any irregularity, to return them to the petitioners. In the House of Commons it is also now customary for Members to submit petitions to the Clerk of Public Petitions in the Journal Office for scrutiny before they give notice of formal presentation (see below). If any irregularity escapes detection at this time but is discovered when the petition is further examined, or if an irregular petition is presented by the informal method (p 762), no entry of the presentation is made in the Votes, although a footnote, to the effect that an informal petition is not noticed, appears in the Votes and Proceedings of that day.[3] More formal notice has been taken of irregularities in petitions, which have then not been received,[4] or been ordered to be withdrawn,[5] or rejected.[6] A Member who has reason to believe that the signatures to a petition are genuine is justified in presenting it, although doubts may have been raised as to their authenticity; but in such cases the attention of the House should be directed to the circumstance.[7]

A Member of the Commons wishing to present a petition gives notice by signing a list kept in the Table Office, not later than 12 noon on the day on which the Member desires to present the petition (before the rising of the House on Thursday for a presentation on Friday).

Presentation of petitions to the Lords

The practice with regard to petitions (other than those relating to judicial or private business or a claim to a peerage of Ireland) is governed in the Lords by Standing Order No 70. By the terms of this Standing Order no such petition shall be received by the House unless it is presented by a Lord and bears his signature. A Lord may deposit a petition with the Clerk of the

1 Parl Deb (1841) 59, c 476; HC Deb (1984–85) 80, c 597.
2 Post Office Act 1969, s 84(1)(b).
3 Eg Votes and Proceedings (1987–88) 973.
4 CJ (1841) 159; ibid (1849) 154; ibid (1850) 160; ibid (1854) 160; ibid (1856) 102.
5 CJ (1837–38) 236; ibid (1845) 335; ibid (1847–48) 633; ibid (1861) 364 (as containing libellous charges against a Member of the House and other parties).
6 CJ (1841) 193; ibid (1867) 345.
7 Parl Deb (1851) 117, c 399.

Parliaments or hand it in at the Table of the House during a sitting. In presenting a petition to the House a Lord may only read out the prayer and state the number of petitioners who have signed the petition. Petitions to which the Standing Order applies are not printed unless a Lord puts down a motion to debate it for a particular day. When a petition has been presented an entry recording the fact is made in the Minutes and Journals together with the prayer of the petition.[1] Petitions are rarely printed at length in the Journals unless they relate to proceedings of a judicial character or to peerage claims.[2]

Presentation of petitions to the Commons

Formerly comment and debate on petitions to the Commons and the general issues which they raised had been permitted; but the number had so much increased,[3] and the business of the House was so much interrupted by the debates which arose on receiving petitions,[4] that Standing Orders dealing with the matter were adopted in 1842 and 1853. In accordance with these orders, a Member, on the presentation of a petition, may make a statement as to the parties from whom it comes and the number of its signatures. He may read the prayer, and summarize the material allegations of the petition:[5] under Standing Order No 133 the petition will be read *in extenso* by the Clerk at the Table, if required.[6] Petitions have been had read on objection being taken to their contents.[7] If a petition conforms to the rules or practice of the House it is brought to the Table by the direction of the Speaker and is then placed in the bag behind the Speaker's chair.[8] No debate is permitted, except in the case of petitions relating to present personal grievance (see p 762), but points of order relating to the petition have been allowed to be raised.[9] Standing Order No 133 provides that on Mondays, Tuesdays, Wednesdays and Thursdays petitions are to be presented immediately after a member of the government has signified his intention to move, That this House do now adjourn, for the purpose of bringing the

---

1 LJ (1987–88) 510, 539, 583, 589, 803, 842, 866;ibid (1988–89) 112.
2 LJ (1976–77) 13.
3 In the following periods the number of public petitions presented to the House of Commons was: from 1828 to 1832, 23,283; from 1838 to 1842, 70,072; from 1868 to 1872, 101,573; from 1878 to 1882, 72,850; from 1888 to 1892, 50,141; from 1898 to 1902, 35,646; up to 1907, 27,853; to 1912, 24,414; to 1917, 1,332; to 1922, 245; to 1927, 1032; to 1931–32, 83; to 1936–37, 878; to 1941–42, 32; to 1951–52, 147; to 1961–62, 224; to 1969–70, 108; to 1974–75, 72; to 1980–81, 198; to 1986–87, 2498. The 1980's have witnessed a steady rise in the sessional number of petitions, though the number of separate topics raised by petitions in any one session has not increased commensurately. 33,742 petitions were presented in session 1893–94, a number exceeded only by the 33,898 of session 1843.
4 In 1833 and 1834, sittings from twelve to three were devoted to petitions and private bills.
5 HC Deb (1985–86) 88, cc 1187–1188: ibid (1987–88) 139, cc 1159, 1160.
6 Parl Deb (1845) 79, c 496; ibid (1849) 106, c 300; HC Deb (1948–49) 458, c 1814; ibid (1955–56) 558, c 1917; ibid (1973–74) 867, cc 1621–1622; ibid (1977–78) 953, c 860; ibid (1981–82) 997, cc 526–530.
7 Parl Deb (1861) 164, c 978; ibid (1870) 202, c 1307.
8 When a petition has been laid upon the Table, it is irregular for any Member to remove it, CJ (1850) 99.
9 Eg HC Deb (1951–52) 501, c 1327; ibid (1967–68) 759, cc 913, 942; ibid (1979–80) 985, c 679.

sitting to a conclusion, or after a Minister of the Crown has signified his intention to move, pursuant to the Standing Order relating to Sittings of the House (Suspended sittings), That the proceedings of this day's sitting be suspended.[1]

On Fridays, petitions are presented at the beginning of the day's sitting, which was the practice of the House in respect of all petitions until 1974.

Informal method of presenting petitions. If he prefers, a Member may present a petition duly signed by him, at any time during the sitting of the House, by placing it in the petition bag kept at the back of the Speaker's chair.

Discussion of petitions relating to present personal grievances. In the case of a petition complaining of a present personal grievance, calling, as an urgent necessity, for an immediate remedy, the matter contained in such petition may be brought into discussion on the presentation thereof (Standing Order No 134). Proceedings thereon are not to be interrupted at ten o'clock, and may be proceeded with, though opposed, until any hour.

Petitions held by the Speaker to comply with the terms of the Standing Order have concerned such grievances as tampering with the mails:[2] a petition concerning Mr A N Wedgwood Benn and the Viscountcy of Stansgate was received under the Standing Order and immediately referred to the Committee of Privileges.[3] In other circumstances the Speaker has ruled that petitions were not of such a character as to benefit from the provisions of the Standing Order.[4]

A Member will not be permitted, under cover of a motion for the adjournment of the House to bring under discussion the contents of a petition which he would be restrained by the Standing Order from debating:[5] but a personal explanation has been permitted, without any question being before the House, upon matters affecting a Member which have been alluded to in a petition.[6]

Proceedings following presentation of petition. Standing Order No 135 requires that all petitions (except those relating to present personal grievances) shall be printed. The Standing Order directs the Clerk of the House to transmit all petitions to a Minister of the Crown. Any observations that a Minister or Ministers may make in reply to a petition are to be laid upon the

---

1 A petition has been presented on Maundy Thursday before the interruption of business, immediately before a member of the Government moved, That this House do now adjourn, CJ (1974–75) 329.
2 Parl Deb (1844) 75, c 1264.
3 CJ (1960–61) 37, HC Deb (1960–61) 631, c 171.
4 Complaints of tampering with mail in the past (CJ (1844) 398, Parl Deb (1844) 75, c 894; injuries sustained and behaviour of the police (Parl Deb (1854–55) 139, c 453); borough contracts and the need for investigation (Parl Deb (1890) 345, c 1809); and illegal arrest and deportation (HC Deb (1923) 164, c 816); and see also ibid (1913) 56, c 2224.
5 7 July 1856 (Attorney General and the Bedford charities).
6 Parl Deb (1839) 48, c 226; ibid (1850) 109, c 235; and 7 July 1856.

Table by the Clerk of the House and ordered to be printed.[1] (For the procedure governing petitions for attendance of witnesses or production of evidence in a court of law, see pp 758–759). The number of signatures to a petition is no longer counted.

---

1 See eg CJ (1960–61) 122. Formerly, all public petitions stood referred to a Select Committee on Public Petitions. Details of the functions of this committee are to be found in earlier editions of this work (eg 19th edn, pp 821–822). The House sometimes ordered that petitions be referred to a select committee other than the Committee on Public Petitions (see pp 617, 665).

CHAPTER 32

Parliament, the European Communities and international assemblies

Part 1 of this Chapter relates to the United Kingdom's membership of the European Communities and the methods by which Parliament seeks to exercise an influence on Community affairs and notably in Community legislation. It includes a brief description of the four institutions of the Communities and certain other Community bodies, concentrating on matters relevant to parliamentary interest in the Communities' work. Part 2 discusses the Parliamentary Assembly of the Council of Europe, the Assembly of the Western European Union and the North Atlantic Assembly. Each of these bodies is attended by a delegation from the United Kingdom Parliament.

1. PARLIAMENT AND THE EUROPEAN COMMUNITIES

On 1 January 1973 the United Kingdom became a Member State of the three European Communities, namely, the European Coal and Steel Community (ECSC), the European Economic Community (EEC) and the European Atomic Energy Community (Euratom). The United Kingdom then accepted obligations by and under the various Community treaties to which the United Kingdom had acceded and which were given effect by the provisions of the European Communities Act 1972 (see also chapter 4, pp 57–58). These Treaties have from time to time been amended,[1] most recently by the Single European Act,[2] which came into force on 1 July 1987. The European Communities (Amendment) Act 1986 gave the Parliamentary approval necessary for United Kingdom ratification of the single European Act.

The principal amendments to the earlier treaties effected by the Single European Act place a duty on the Community to complete the internal market (as defined in that Act) by 31 December 1992, introduce new measures designed to speed up decision-taking particularly on matters related to the internal market and give formal expression to Community powers in certain areas of policy. The Act also gives an enhanced role to the European Parliament in certain respects. The Single European Act also

---

1 A consolidated text of the treaties establishing the European Communities as amended by subsequent treaties was published in September 1988 as Cm 455.
2 Published in May 1988 as Cm 372.

gives the European Council (see p 769) a specific Treaty basis and establishes a Treaty framework for European co-operation in the sphere of foreign policy.

INSTITUTIONS OF THE COMMUNITIES

The institutions were created by, and their powers and duties are described in, the Treaties as establishing the various communities. These Treaties amended from time to time. Other bodies, not defined as 'institutions' in the Treaties are described at pp 769–770 below.

Each of the Communities was established by a separate treaty (the ECSC in 1951 and the EEC and the Euratom in 1957) and each treaty made provision for the institutions of that Community. By virtue of the Treaty establishing a Single Council and a Single Commission of the European Communities of 1965 a Council of the European Communities was established to take the place of the Special Council of Ministers of the European Coal and Steel Community, the Council of the European Economic Community and the Council of the European Atomic Energy Community. The same Treaty also established a Commission of the European Communities to take the place of the High Authority of the European Coal and Steel Community, the Commission of the European Economic Community and the Commission of the European Atomic Energy Community. Each of the founding Treaties provided for an Assembly to exercise certain advisory and supervisory powers. By virtue of the Convention on certain institutions common to the European Communities of 1957, which was signed at the same time as the EEC and Euratom treaties, a single Assembly was established to exercise the powers and jurisdiction under the EEC and Euratom treaties; this Assembly also took over the functions of the Common Assembly of the ECSC. The 1976 Act concerning the election of the representatives of the Assembly by direct universal suffrage replaced certain of the provisions in the original treaties; these therefore lapsed. The Assembly was formally re-named the European Parliament by virtue of article 3 of the Single European Act. The 1957 Convention also established a single Court of Justice to exercise the powers and jurisdiction of the courts provided for under the EEC and Euratom Treaties; this also took over the functions of the Court provided for in the ECSC Treaty.

The Council

The Council[1] is made up of ministerial representatives of the Governments of Member States. Its actual composition varies according to the subject of the business under discussion, although Foreign Ministers (meeting as the General Affairs Council) assume a primary role in most major matters. In

---

1 The constitution and principal functions of the Council are set out in arts 26 to 30 of the ECSC Treaty, arts 145 to 154 of the EEC Treaty and arts 115 to 123 of the Euratom Treaty. References to the constitution and principal functions of the institutions in the footnotes in this part of the chapter are to the articles as set out in the original Treaties. The consolidated text referred to earlier incorporates under these articles the changes made subsequently as described above.

practice the Council is the pre-eminent legislative body within the Communities.[1] The Council normally meets in private[2] and its proceedings are not published, although a press statement is usually issued after each meeting summarizing its principal conclusions and decisions. Unless the relevant Treaty article otherwise prescribes, Council decisions are taken by simple majority. However, in most major policy areas, either a qualified (or weighted) majority or unanimity is prescribed.

One result of the Single European Act was an increase in the use of qualified majority voting and reduction in the need for unanimity, notably in relation to some internal market measures. Each Member State is understood to have the right to block any decision in respect of which the relevant Treaty base provides for majority voting if it asserts (and other Member States accept) that the proposed measure adversely affects its vital national interests.[3] In such cases, it is the practice for discussions in the Council to continue until a solution is found which can be adopted unanimously.

The Council is assisted in its work by a Committee of Permanent Representatives (COREPER), which consists of the Member States' Permanent Representatives to the Communities[4]. COREPER is responsible for preparing the work of the Council and carrying out tasks assigned to it by the Council. A proposal on which COREPER is able to reach full agreement will normally come before the Council for formal approval only.

The European Council, which brings together the Heads of State or of Government of the Member States is described at pp 769–770 below.

The Presidency of the Council of Ministers is held by each Member State in turn for a period of six months. The order in which Member States hold the office of President is set out in the Treaties. The formal responsibilities of the President are set out in the rules of procedure of the Council.

The Commission

The Commission is the executive organ of the European Communities. There are seventeen Commissioners, two each from France, the Federal Republic of Germany, Italy, Spain and the United Kingdom and one each from Belgium, Denmark, Greece, Ireland, Luxembourg, the Netherlands and Portugal. On appointment, Commissioners accept a Community responsibility and operate collectively: they are specifically enjoined by the Treaties to be completely independent and neither to seek, nor to take, instructions from any other body in the performance of their duties.

The basic functions and responsibilities of the Commission[5] are:

—to ensure that Member States apply the provisions of the Treaties and subsequent legislation and to take action seeking to rectify any breaches it identifies;

---

1 The Commission has legislative powers under some provisions of the Treaties; it also makes a substantial volume of implementing rules under powers conferred by Council measures.
2 Rules of Procedure of the Council, art 3(1).
3 HC Deb (1974) 875, c 453 and HC Deb (1985–86) 96, cc 389–390.
4 Such a proposal is known as an 'A' point.
5 The constitution and functions of the Commission are set out in arts 8 to 19 of the ECSC Treaty, arts 155 to 163 of the EEC Treaty and arts 124 to 135 of the Euratom Treaty.

—to initiate Community action, proposing policies and putting legislative proposals to the Council (which, in most policy areas, can act only upon such a proposal);

—to act as negotiator on behalf of the Communities in areas of Community competence; these include trade agreements and reciprocal arrangements with third countries;

—to implement Community policies, in accordance with the relevant provisions, including such powers of delegated legislation, inspection and supervision as are conferred on it by the Council;

—in the case of legislative proposals subject to the co-operation procedure (see p 769), to re-examine the Council's common position on the proposal if any amendments to it are proposed by the European Parliament, and to submit a re-examined proposal to the Council;

—to implement the budget of the European Communities.

The Court of Justice

The Court of Justice, consisting of thirteen judges assisted by six advocates-general, is the final arbiter on all legal questions submitted to it under the Community Treaties.[1] Its duty is to ensure that in the interpretation and application of the Treaties the law is observed. In this context, it may hear cases arising from disputes between Member States, between Member States and Community institutions, and between Community institutions and firms, individuals, or Community officials. It may hear proceedings initiated by Member States, the Commission, the Council, or, in certain circumstances, by the European Parliament,[2] or by individuals or firms on all of whom its rulings are binding. Its jurisdiction has two main strands. First, it can review the legality of the acts of the institutions, within limits set by the Treaties. Second, it can receive references from the courts of Member States to give preliminary rulings on the interpretation of the Treaties and on the validity and interpretation of acts of the institutions.

The workload of the Court has steadily increased over the years, causing substantial lengthening of the period between actions being started and the Court's decisions being given. The Single European Act therefore introduced[3] into the Treaties provision for a Court of First Instance to be added to the Court. The Court of First Instance is empowered to exercise at first instance the jurisdiction of the Court in certain specified areas chosen either because proceedings are likely to require scrutiny of complex facts or because they are of less major general interest. There is a right of appeal from its decisions to the European Court of Justice (on matters of law only). The Court of First Instance is not competent to hear and determine actions brought by Member States or Community institutions or to give preliminary rulings on questions referred from national courts.

---

1 The constitution and principal functions of the Court are set out in arts 31 to 45 of the ECSC Treaty, arts 164 to 192 of the EEC Treaty and arts 136 to 160 of the Euratom Treaty and the related statutes.

2 See, for example, Case 302/87 *European Parliament v Council*.

3 ECSC Treaty, art 32d, EEC Treaty, art 168a, Euratom Treaty art 140a. See also Council Decision 88/591/ECSC, EEC, Euratom, of 24 October 1988.

National courts are in general responsible for applying Community legislation, and Member States retain full competence over their national criminal law and over most areas of civil law.

The European Parliament

The European Parliament (formerly known as the Assembly) is the fourth institution of the European Communities. Its members are elected, by direct universal suffrage, for a term of five years beginning with the opening of the first session after the election. Electoral procedure is presently determined independently by each Member State;[1] the Parliament itself is required to draw up a proposal for a uniform electoral procedure to be used eventually in later elections.[2]

The total membership of the European Parliament is currently 518, of whom 81 represent United Kingdom constituencies (66 in England, 8 in Scotland, 4 in Wales and 3 in Northern Ireland). There is no restriction on a Member of either House of the United Kingdom Parliament also being a Member of the European Parliament.

General functions.   The general functions of the European Parliament are set out in the Treaties.[3] It has power to adopt its own rules of procedure[4] and has the duty to discuss in open session the annual general report submitted to it by the Commission[5] and to give a discharge to the Commission in respect of the implementation of the Community budget.[6] It also has power (by a two-thirds majority vote) to require the resignation of the members of the Commission as a body.[7] The admission of new Member States now requires the assent of the European Parliament[8] as does the conclusion of certain agreements between the Community and other states or international organisations.[9] The Parliament has a substantial role, set out in the Treaties, in establishing the Community budget.[10]

Under section 6 of the European Assembly Elections Act 1978 no treaty which provides for an increase in the powers of the European Parliament can be ratified by the United Kingdom unless it has been approved by an Act of Parliament.

Legislative functions.   The instances in which consultation of the European Parliament is formally required before the Council legislates are set out in the Treaties. The process of consultation with the Parliament has developed by practice beyond what is formally required and now extends to all proposals of importance. In addition, the Parliament has adopted rules

---

1 The procedure for United Kingdom elections is prescribed in the European Assembly Elections Act 1978.
2 The European Parliament adopted a Resolution on this subject in 1982 but it has not yet been acted on by the Council.
3 The constitution and principal functions of the Parliament are set out in arts 20 to 25 of the ECSC Treaty, arts 137 to 144 of the EEC Treaty and arts 107 to 114 of the Euratom Treaty.
4 EEC Treaty, art 142.
5 Ibid art 143.
6 Ibid art 206b.
7 Ibid art 144.
8 Ibid art 237 (as amended by the Single European Act).
9 Ibid art 238 (as amended by the Single European Act).
10 See eg, ibid, arts 203 and 204.

designed to ensure renewed consultation in certain circumstances[1] and a conciliation procedure for use in cases of important Community decisions where the Council intends to depart from the opinion of the Parliament.[2]

The involvement of the Parliament in the legislative process, since the coming into force of the Single European Act, may take one of two forms; the relevant Treaty article prescribes the appropriate form in each case. Where consultation is prescribed,[3] the Council is required to obtain the opinion of the European Parliament on the Commission's proposal before it proceeds to adoption. Where the co-operation procedure (introduced by the Single European Act) is prescribed,[4] the Council, after obtaining the opinion of the Parliament on the Commission proposal, reaches a common position. The common position is then communicated to the Parliament which may accept it, reject it, or propose amendments. If the Parliament has proposed amendments, the Commission then submits to the Council a re-examined proposal based on the common position and taking into account the amendments to it proposed by the Parliament. It forwards to the Council, with the re-examined proposal, those amendments of the European Parliament it has not accepted. The Council may then either adopt the Commission's re-examined proposal as it stands by a qualified majority, or adopt it in an amended form, including acceptance of amendments proposed by the Parliament which the Commission has not accepted, by unanimity. If it takes no action within a period of three months, the Commission re-examined proposal is deemed not to have been adopted. If the Parliament has rejected the common position, unanimity is required for the Council to adopt it definitively. All stages subsequent to adoption by the Council of a common position are subject to prescribed time limits.

The Parliament has adopted rules[5] to restrict the scope of amendments which may be moved to a common position.

Other bodies

The Treaties designate the four preceding bodies as the 'institutions' of the Community. However, there are a number of important bodies which are not institutions within the narrow definition used in the Treaties; some of these are described below.

The European Council. For many years the Heads of State or of Government of Member States have regularly met under this title. However, until the Single European Act came into force, there was no express treaty basis

---

1 Rules of Procedure, r 42.
2 Ibid r 43.
3 See for example, arts 14, 43, 75, 87, 100, 126–127, 130s, 201, 209, 235 and 236 of the EEC Treaty. The Euratom Treaty and the ECSC Treaty also contain provisions requiring the opinion of the Parliament to be sought under particular Treaty articles.
4 The relevant provisions are set out in the Single European Act, art 6. The procedure is set out in the EEC Treaty, art 149.
5 Rules of Procedure, r 51.

for such a body. That Act formally established[1] a European Council to bring together the Heads of State or of Government of the Member States and the President of the Commission and provided for them to be assisted by the Ministers for Foreign Affairs and by a Member of the Commission. It is required to meet at least twice a year.

Whilst the Single European Act did not invest the European Council with formal legislative powers, its deliberations and conclusions are often of great importance in determining the main lines of Community policy and a major influence upon the Council of Ministers.

The Court of Auditors. A Court of Auditors, consisting of twelve members, is responsible for examining the accounts of the Communities and is required to examine and to report on whether all revenue has been received and all expenditure incurred in a lawful and regular manner and on whether financial management has been sound.[2] The Court prepares an annual report which is published together with the replies of the institutions. It is also charged with assisting the European Parliament and the Council in exercising their powers of control over the implementation of the budget.

The Court of Auditors may also, at any time, submit observations on specific questions and deliver opinions at the request of one of the Community institutions.

The Economic and Social Committee. The Economic and Social Committee consists of 189 members drawn from employers' organizations, trade unions, consumers and other interests (although once appointed members are bound to act in a personal capacity and cannot accept outside instruction). The United Kingdom has 24 places on the Committee.[3] Apart from being consulted by the Council or the Commission on specific matters in accordance with the Treaties, it may be consulted in other cases where it is considered appropriate.

The Committee operates both in plenary session and through a series of specialised sections.

THE LEGISLATIVE PROCESS WITHIN THE COMMUNITIES

Community legislation is made either by the Council, generally on a proposal from the Commission, under powers conferred by the Treaties, or by the Commission, either under powers conferred on it directly by certain articles of the Treaties, or under authority delegated to it by the Council. The Single European Act added an obligation on the Council to confer on the Commission, in acts which the Council adopts, powers for implementation of the rules which the Council lays down, subject to certain conditions and exceptions.[4]

Forms of Community legislation

Irrespective of whether it is made by the Council on the proposal of the Commission or made by the Commission itself, Community legislation is divided into various types, which are defined in the Treaties.

---

1 Single European Act, art 2.
2 EEC Treaty, art 206a.
3 Ibid art 193.
4 Ibid art 145 as amended by the Single European Act, art 10. The Council exercised this power in its Decision of 13 July 1987 (87/373/EEC).

Article 189 of the EEC Treaty and article 161 of the Euratom Treaty are identical and read as follows:

> In order to carry out their task the Council and the Commission shall, in accordance with the provisions of this Treaty, make regulations, issue directives, take decisions, make recommendations or deliver opinions.
>
> A regulation shall have general application. It shall be binding in its entirety and directly applicable in all Member States.
>
> A directive shall be binding, as to the result to be achieved, upon each Member State to which it is addressed, but shall leave to the national authorities the choice of form and methods.
>
> A decision shall be binding in its entirety upon those to whom it is addressed.
>
> Recommendations and opinions shall have no binding force.

Article 14 of the ECSC Treaty reads as follows:

> In order to carry out the tasks assigned to it the High Authority [now the Commission] shall, in accordance with the provisions of this Treaty, take decisions, make recommendations or deliver opinions.
>
> Decisions shall be binding in their entirety.
>
> Recommendations shall be binding as to the aims to be pursued but shall leave the choice of the appropriate methods for achieving these aims to those to whom the recommendations are addressed.
>
> Opinions shall have no binding force.
>
> In cases where the High Authority [now the Commission] is empowered to take a decision, it may confine itself to making a recommendation.

Thus the definitions of the various types of legislation differ in the case of the ECSC from that of the other two Communities. In particular, a 'directive' under the EEC and Euratom Treaties has binding force equivalent to that of a 'recommendation' under the ECSC Treaty, while a 'recommendation' under the EEC and Euratom Treaties has no binding force. In fact, the amount of legislation with general effect emanating from the ECSC is very small and for the purposes of this chapter the terms used in the EEC and Euratom Treaties are used.

Regulations, directives and decisions of both the Council and the Commission must state the reasons on which they are based[1] including the legal basis. Some of the recitals in the preambular material will be directed to discharging this duty.

By far the largest categories of legislation are regulations and directives. So far as the United Kingdom is concerned, these derive their authority from section 2(1) of the European Communities Act 1972.

Although regulations are binding in their entirety and directly applicable, supplementary domestic provisions may be required to make them fully effective—for example provision for enforcement. Directives are binding upon Member States as to the results to be achieved but leave the form and methods of implementation to the national authorities.

In the United Kingdom, supplementation of regulations and implementation of directives is effected by:

(a) Acts of Parliament;

(b) regulations or Orders in Council made under section 2(2) of the European Communities Act 1972 for the purpose of implementing Community obligations;

---

1 EEC Treaty, art 190; Euratom Treaty, art 162. Art 15 of the ECSC Treaty imposes a similar obligation regarding decisions, recommendations and opinions of the High Authority.

(c) subordinate legislation made under an Act other than the European Communities Act 1972; or

(d) administrative action (in certain limited circumstances only).

Legislation adopted by the Council on a proposal from the Commission. Before legislation is proposed to the Council by the Commission, its provisions will sometimes have been discussed with national experts and where applicable, interested organizations, although such consultation is not obligatory under the terms of the Treaties. The roles of the European Parliament and of the Economic and Social Committee in the legislative process have been briefly discussed at pp 768–769, 770.

Following the formal submission of a proposal to the Council by the Commission, the proposed measure is considered by the Council of Ministers after preliminary consideration by their official representatives at various levels. Expert discussion takes place in Council Working Groups and a proposal is generally put to COREPER (see p 766) to try to narrow points of difficulty before it goes to the Council of Ministers.

The Commission may alter its proposal at any time before the Council has acted on it.[1] In practice, the Commission frequently submits an amended proposal where the European Parliament, in its opinion on the Commission's original proposal, has suggested amendments. The Commission may also submit an amended proposal to seek to facilitate agreement in the Council, or to take account of any relevant developments since the original proposal was submitted. In addition, successive drafts of a proposal are often worked out in the course of discussions at official level under the authority of the Presidency.

The procedures described above have as their aim the amendment of the Commission's proposals to meet the various national needs and to reconcile what may be conflicting national requirements with the Community objective being pursued. The text of a measure when finally adopted thus frequently differs, sometimes considerably, from the text as originally proposed by the Commission. The Council may only formally amend a proposal from the Commission (including any re-examined proposal submitted by the Commission under the co-operation procedure (see p 769)) by unanimity.

Regulations must be published in the Official Journal of the Communities[2] and appear in the Official Journal (OJ) 'L' series. In practice, all other legislative instruments of general importance are also so published.

Legislation adopted by the Commission. Legislation adopted by the Commission forms the overwhelming bulk of Community legislation. The power for the Commission to make such legislation on its own initiative stems largely from article 155 of the EEC Treaty which states that the Commission shall 'exercise the powers conferred on it by the Council for the implementation of rules laid down by the latter'. However, it also has certain direct powers under the Treaties, for instance, in relation to competition rules and state aids (under the EEC Treaty).

1 Ibid art 149.
2 Ibid art 191.

The bulk of Commission legislation is made up of measures for the day-to-day management of agricultural matters, made under powers delegated by Council measures relating to the Common Agricultural Policy.

European political co-operation

The Single European Act introduced formal European co-operation in the sphere of foreign policy.[1] The object of this endeavour is to formulate and implement a joint European foreign policy. To this end, the Member States have undertaken to inform and consult each other on any foreign policy matters of general interest so as to ensure that their combined influence is exercised as effectively as possible.

Ministers for Foreign Affairs are required to meet at least four times a year within the framework of European Political Co-operation and may also discuss foreign policy matters within the framework of Political Co-operation at meetings of the Council. The Commission and the European Parliament are both to be associated with the process. The Presidency of European Political Co-operation is held by the Member State holding the Presidency of the Council of Ministers.

A separate Secretariat for European Political Co-operation carries out its duties under the authority of the Presidency.

PARLIAMENTARY OVERSIGHT OF COMMUNITY MATTERS

Use of existing procedures. Since the accession of the United Kingdom to the Communities, many of the existing procedures in both Houses (already described in previous chapters) have been used to enable Members to exercise a measure of control and influence over those activities of the various bodies within the Communities which are most susceptible to some kind of scrutiny by a national Parliament. This is in addition to and distinct from the work of the European Parliament, the members of which are able to question, debate and in some degree to supervise the activities of the Council as a whole and of the Commission. In the United Kingdom Parliament it is the Ministers of the Government in their capacity as members of the Council (and with their responsibility for the activities of their officials at lower levels within the Council's machinery) to whom Members of both Houses look in order to seek to influence and control what is done by the institutions of the Communities.

For this purpose, traditional parliamentary practice has been used and adapted where necessary. Although it is no longer the practice in the Commons for any fixed part of the time allocated to oral questions to be given over to EEC matters, Ministers remain accountable to the House in this way for their Community activities. Use is made of ministerial statements to enable Parliament to be kept informed by members of the Government of their activities in the Council. It is the practice for the Government to present White Papers to Parliament describing developments in the Communities over each six month period.

---

1 Art 30.

Debates take place periodically in both Houses, not only on specific Community legislative proposals (see below) but also more generally on European Community matters.[1]

Procedures introduced following accession to the Community. Both Houses have established new machinery to exercise influence in relation to Community affairs, particularly as regards the activities of the Council, in view of the accountability of Ministers to Parliament for their activities in Council. To this end, all proposals for legislation made to the Council by the Commission are deposited in Parliament, as are any other documents which the Government considers to fall within the orders of reference of the committees established by both Houses (see below) to examine European legislation. Draft Commission legislation is normally deposited only on the rare occasions when it requires Council approval or confirmation. United Kingdom Ministers otherwise have no direct responsibility in relation to this legislation. The European Parliament seeks to exercise some supervision over implementing measures tabled in the Parliament by the Commission.[2]

The two Houses have each established Select Committees to examine the material described above. In the Lords the Committee is designated 'the Select Committee on the European Communities' and in the Commons 'the Select Committee on European Legislation' (for the full orders of reference of the Committees etc, see pp 582–583 and 657.) Although the orders of reference of the two Committees differ, their essential task is similar. They are both concerned with consideration of draft proposals by the Commission for legislation and other documents published (in most cases by the Commission) for submission to the Council or to the European Council and making recommendations to their respective Houses arising from their assessment of policy implications. The purpose of the work of the two Committees is to keep Parliament informed of the implications of all Community legislation which is due to come before the Council, so as to enable each House to bring any appropriate influence to bear upon members of the Government whose duty it is to deal with the legislation at the Council. Neither House has any power to amend or reject proposed Community legislation, but Ministers are expected to take into account the views expressed by each House.[3]

The texts of the documents which the two Committees examine are transmitted to both Houses by the Government shortly after they are received from the Secretariat of the Council. The Government then prepares a further document, known as an explanatory memorandum, which gives factual information about the Community document and its legal, financial and policy implications so far as the United Kingdom is concerned. In cases where a proposal is expected to come before the Council before a formal text can be deposited, the relevant Department usually prepares an explanatory memorandum (known as an 'un-numbered explanatory memorandum') describing the expected content of the proposal (often derived from Commission or Council working texts) and the implications as described above. Both Committees study these documents and if necessary

---

1 For example, it is usual in the Commons for the six monthly White Papers to be debated.
2 Rules of Procedure, r 53.
3 Minutes of Evidence to the First Report of the Select Committee on Procedure—HC 294 (1974–75) p 20 (Q 22).

they seek further information by way of oral or written evidence either from Government departments or from other bodies or individuals.

The Government has undertaken[1] to ensure that the House of Commons is informed of changes of substance in proposals involving major policy developments so that the Select Committee can report further on them. This information is normally provided in a supplementary explanatory memorandum, deposited in both Houses, which is then considered by the Committees.

The Lords Committee is required by its order of reference to make reports on those Community proposals which 'raise important questions of policy or principle', and on 'other questions to which the Committee considers that the special attention of the House should be drawn'. It has become usual practice for the Committee to make full reports, after receiving written and oral evidence, on the more significant Community proposals; to write a letter to the appropriate Minister on proposals which raise a single narrow issue (often a legal issue) or which are about to come before the Council and to make no report on the remaining proposals. In addition the Committee makes more general reports on aspects of Community policy or practice. The Committee recommends about half its reports for debate and submits the remainder to the House for information. The Government has undertaken to ensure that debates recommended by the Committee are held before the documents to which they relate are adopted by the Council.[2] In addition to its substantive reports, the Committee makes (usually fortnightly when the House is sitting) a Progress of Scrutiny Report listing the documents before the Committee and the stage which its scrutiny has reached, and giving details of recent reports and debates held or to be held on them.

The Commons Committee makes regular reports to the House covering every document which comes before it. The Committee informs the House whether in its opinion these documents raise questions of legal or political importance and what matters of principle or policy may be affected thereby, giving reasons for its decisions in cases where it considers this necessary. The Committee has the duty of recommending whether or not Community documents to which it has drawn attention as raising questions of legal or political importance should be further considered by the House (see below). This part of its work is rendered especially important by the fact that, by a resolution of the House of 30 October 1980, the Government is required, save where the Committee has indicated that agreement need not be withheld and in certain other closely defined circumstances, to find time for the consideration by the House of all draft legislative instruments recommended for debate by the Committee before Ministers give agreement to the relevant proposal in the Council.[3] If a Minister decides that the circumstances are such as to justify him in giving his agreement in the Council to such an instrument in advance of a debate being held, he is required by virtue of this resolution to explain the reasons for his decision to the House at the first

1 HC Deb (1975–76) 916, c 803.
2 HL Deb (1974–75) 354, c 641.
3 CJ (1979–80) 818–819. Before this, the requirement rested on a Government undertaking made when the committee was first established; HC Deb (1974) 872, cc 532–552 w; ibid 874, cc 1425–1429, 1547.

opportunity thereafter. The Government has also undertaken[1] to treat analogously all draft legislative instruments in respect of which scrutiny has not been completed. This undertaking has also been applied to scrutiny by the Lords Committee to the extent that a letter is written by a Minister to the Chairman whenever Council adoption occurs (including adoption by a majority vote when the United Kingdom has not voted in favour) before the Lords' scrutiny is complete.

The Commons and Lords Committees and their sub-committees have the power[2] to confer or to meet concurrently (see pp 670, 773–776). This power has been used on occasion.[3]

Legal advice to the Committee is given in the Lords by the Counsel to the Lord Chairman of Committees, and in the Commons by the Speaker's Counsel (see Standing Order No 127(3)).

Debate on Community documents. Debates held in the House of Commons in pursuance of the recommendations of the Select Committee on European Legislation may take place either on the floor of the House or in a standing committee on European Community Documents. The procedure for consideration of documents by a standing committee are described on pp 595–596. Documents debated on the floor of the House are often taken as exempted business under Standing Order No 14(1) after the moment of interuption when they may be debated for a maximum of one and a half hours (see pp 316–317). An analysis of the frequency of, and amount of time taken by, such debates is given on p 271. Documents recommended for further consideration by the House may also be considered in the context of more general debate on the subject in question; if, in such a case, the document concerned is not referred to in the motion a note stating that the document is relevant to the debate is included on the Order Paper[4]. The Select Committees sometimes indicates that a document, although not recommended for further consideration by the House, is in its opinion relevant to a debate on a particular topic; a similar note is included on the Order Paper in such cases also[5].

2. PARLIAMENT AND OTHER INTERNATIONAL ASSEMBLIES

This part of this chapter gives an account of the Parliamentary Assembly of the Council of Europe, the Assembly of Western European Union and the North Atlantic Assembly, each of which is attended by a delegation from the Parliament of the United Kingdom under treaties or other international agreements.[6] The formal relationship between each Assembly and the

---

1 Second Special Report of the Select Committee on European Legislation, Session 1985–86, (HC 400), App IV.
2 Standing Order No 127(11).
3 See, for example, HL 281 (Session 1975–76) and HL 149 (Session 1977–78) (concurrent taking of evidence).
4 Eg 14 March 1989.
5 Eg 2 March 1989.
6 Payment of expenses of delegations to the three Assemblies have been formally authorized by the House of Commons, CJ (1970) 159.

remainder of the organization of which it forms a part is also briefly described.

Since 1949 staff of both Houses have regularly provided temporary assistance at the three Assemblies. The United Kingdom delegations to the three Assemblies are accompanied by a secretariat drawn from the Overseas Office of the House of Commons.[1]

THE COUNCIL OF EUROPE

The Council of Europe was formed in 1949, on the recommendations of a Committee appointed by the Brussels Treaty Consultative Council 'to consider and report to Governments on the steps to be taken towards securing a greater measure of unity between European countries'. The signatories (Belgium, France, Luxembourg, Netherlands and the United Kingdom) of the Brussels Treaty of 1948 invited Denmark, Ireland, Italy, Norway and Sweden to confer with them in drafting a constitution; and Greece,[2] Turkey, Iceland, the Federal Republic of Germany, Austria, Cyprus, Switzerland, Malta, Portugal, Spain, Liechtenstein, San Marino and Finland were later invited to become Members, bringing the number of Member States of the Council of Europe to twenty-three.

The Council of Europe differs from the European Communities in the width of its membership and its general interest in all forms and fields of non-military co-operation. Its principal aim is set out in Article 1 of the Statute of the Council of Europe, which was signed in London in May 1949.

Article 1 states:
(a) the aim of the Council of Europe is to achieve a greater unity between its Members for the purpose of safeguarding and realising the ideals and principles which are their common heritage and facilitating their economic and social progress.

(b) This aim shall be pursued through the organs of the Council by discussion of questions of common concern and by agreements and common action in economic, social, cultural, scientific, legal and administrative matters and in the maintenance and further realisation of human rights and fundamental freedoms.

(c) Participation in the Council of Europe shall not affect the collaboration of its Members in the work of the United Nations and of other international organisations or unions to which they are parties.

(d) Matters relating to national defence do not fall within the scope of the Council of Europe.

Conditions of membership. The conditions for membership of the Council of Europe are set out in article 3 of the Statute. Every Member State must accept the principles of the rule of law and of the enjoyment by all persons within its jurisdiction of human rights and fundamental freedoms. It must also collaborate sincerely and effectively in realising the aim of the Council as specified in Article 1 of the Statute.

---

1 Resolution of the House of Commons (Services) Committee, 14 February 1966, approved by the Speaker.
2 Greece withdrew from the Council in December 1969, and was then suspended de facto from its right of representation. This position was confirmed de jure in December 1970 (see Committee of Ministers Resolution (70) 34). Greece was readmitted to the Council in November 1974.

Strasbourg is named in the Statute as the seat of the Council and has been the meeting place of the Assembly since its inauguration.

The Council of Europe consists of the following two organs: the Committee of Ministers and the Parliamentary Assembly.

The Committee of Ministers

Constitution. The Committee of Ministers is composed of Ministers for Foreign Affairs from each Member State. The Committee normally meets twice each year, but there are more frequent meetings of Ministers' Deputies, who are usually the Permanent Representatives to the Council of Europe of Governments of Member States. The chairmanship of the Committee of Ministers is held in turn by its members in the alphabetical order of their countries in English.

Under article 13 of the Statute the Committee of Ministers is 'the organ which acts on behalf of the Council of Europe'. The Committee of Ministers' executive function is largely complementary to the deliberative function of the Assembly. Under article 15(a) of the Statute, the Committee has the duty of considering, either on the recommendation of the Assembly or on its own initiative, the action required to further the aim of the Council of Europe. Such action includes the conclusion of conventions or agreements, and the adoption by Goverments of a common policy with regard to particular matters. The Committee of Ministers is empowered to make recommendations to member Governments, and subsequently to enquire what action has been taken on its recommendations.

For expert advice the Committee of Ministers relies on a number of expert committees dealing with the various aspects of the Council's work, notably legal affairs, human rights, economic and social affairs and public health, education and culture, and environment and local authorities.

Report of the Committee of Ministers to the Assembly. Although the Committee of Ministers has the power either to accept or to reject recommendations of the Assembly, it has to report to the Assembly on its activities and this statutory report is presented to the Assembly at each of its part-sessions by the Chairman of the Committee of Ministers.

The Parliamentary Assembly

The Parliamentary Assembly is the parliamentary organ of the Council of Europe. It is for the Committee of Ministers to consider, and, if they think fit, to take action on the Assembly's recommendations and for the Governments of Member States to give effect to them.

Sessions and credentials. Ordinary sessions are held every year, and are usually divided into three part-sessions, each lasting for about one week. Credentials of Representatives and Substitutes must be in the hands of the President of the Assembly not later than a week before the opening of a session.

Representation. The Parliamentary Assembly consists of 177 Representatives from twenty-three Member States, with a President elected by the

Assembly annually from among their number. The number of Representatives from each of the first ten Member States was laid down in the Statute, and subsequently when a country has been invited by the Committee of Ministers to become a Member, the number of Representatives which it is entitled to send has been indicated in the letter of invitation. Generally speaking the entitlement to Representatives is roughly in proportion to the Member States' population.[1]

Article 25 of the Statute as amended in 1970 provides that the Assembly shall consist of Representatives of each Member State elected by its Parliament from among the Members thereof, or appointed from among the Members of that Parliament in such manner as it shall decide, subject to the right of each Member Government to make any additional appointments necessary when Parliament is not in session and has not laid down the procedures to be followed in that case.

A Representative's term of office expires at the beginning of the ordinary session of the Assembly after that in respect of which he was appointed. However, it is usual to nominate a new United Kingdom delegation if a General Election causes a change of Government. Since 1949 the United Kingdom Representatives have been appointed annually by the Prime Minister, after consultation with the political parties. The composition of the delegation has broadly reflected the balance of parties in the House of Commons.[2] The names of the delegation are usually announced in a written reply to a Question tabled to the Foreign Secretary.[3] The composition of the delegation is altered by the same means when necessary.

A Representative who is prevented from attending a sitting of the Assembly may be replaced by a Substitute of the same nationality. Substitutes are appointed in the same manner as Representatives. In the absence of a Representative a Substitute may sit, speak and vote in his place and enjoy the same rights in the Assembly. Substitutes may be full members of committees.

Privileges and immunities. The Statute confers on Representatives in the territories of Member States such privileges and immunities as are reasonably necessary for the fulfilment of their functions. This includes immunity from arrest and legal proceedings in respect of words spoken or votes cast in the Assembly or its committees. In addition, a General Agreement on Privileges and Immunities (which the United Kingdom government has ratified)[4] confers on Representatives freedom from restriction in their movements to and from the Assembly's place of meeting; confirms the freedom from arrest and legal proceedings conferred by the Statute; and during a session of the Assembly grants to Representatives while on their own national territory the immunities accorded to Members of Parliament,

---

1 In 1989, the number of Representatives was, Austria 6, Belgium 7, Cyprus 3, Denmark 5, Finland 5, France 18, Federal Republic of Germany 18, Greece 7, Iceland 3, Republic of Ireland 4, Italy 18, Liechtenstein 2, Luxembourg 3, Malta 3, Netherlands 7, Norway 5, Portugal 7, San Marino 2, Spain 12, Sweden 6, Switzerland 6, Turkey 12, United Kingdom 18.
2 HC Deb (1950–51) 486, cc 32–33; ibid (1967–68) 763, cc 90–92.
3 Eg HC Deb (1987–88) 120, c 301 w.
4 SI 1960/442.

and exemption from arrest or prosecution while on the territory of other Member States. These last immunities may be waived by the Assembly and there is an exception in the case of Representatives found in the act of committing an offence.

Powers and agenda. The Parliamentary Assembly may discuss any matter within the aim and scope of the Council of Europe. It may make a Recommendation, or agree to an Opinion or a Resolution.

A *Recommendation* is addressed to the Committee of Ministers asking it to take certain action in pursuit of the aim of the Council. An *Opinion* contains the view of the Assembly in answer to a formal request from the Committee of Ministers for the expression of such a view on a matter specifically referred to it. A Recommendation and an Opinion require for their adoption a majority of two-thirds of the votes cast, comprising at least one-third of the Representatives of the Assembly. The formal expression of the opinion of the Assembly on a particular matter which does not call for action by the Committee of Ministers is termed a *Resolution*, for which a majority of votes cast is required.

Communications to the Assembly, whether from the Committee of Ministers or from any other body, and motions tabled by Representatives are normally referred to the appropriate committee before being debated in the Assembly. Debate subsequently takes place on the report of the Committee and on the draft Recommendations, Opinions or Resolutions which it contains.

Languages. The official languages of the Assembly are English and French; all its documents are produced in these two languages. Other languages, namely German and Italian, are recognized as working languages, both in the Assembly and in its Committees. A speech made in any one of these four languages is simultaneously interpreted into the other three languages.

Arrangement of seats. The Assembly is laid out in a half circle. Seating is arranged in alphabetical order with the aim of preventing Representatives from sitting in national delegations. Representatives normally speak from their own places. There is a tribune on the continental pattern which is reserved for Ministers who wish to address the Assembly and for other speakers who are not members of the Assembly.

Political groups. The formation of political groups within the Assembly has made possible to a limited degree the development of European, non-national shades of opinion on political questions. The Christian Democrat, Communist, European Democrat, Socialist, Liberal and Independent groups have gained recognition as such, and receive funds to support their activities.

Committees. At the beginning of each session the Assembly appoints thirteen general committees, which have the duty of considering and making reports on the main categories of Assembly business. The general committees are on Political Affairs; Economic Affairs and Development; Social and Health Affairs; Legal Affairs; Culture and Education; Science and

Technology; the Environment, Regional Planning and Local Authorities; Rules of Procedure; Agriculture; Relations with European Non-Member Countries; Parliamentary and Public Relations; the Budget and the Inter-governmental Work Programme; and Migration, Refugees and Demography. Special committees may be appointed for specific purposes.

Since 1949 the Assembly has appointed sessionally a Standing Committee to act on its behalf between sessions or part-sessions and to ensure the continuity of its work. The Standing Committee consists of the President of the Assembly as ex officio chairman, all the Vice-Presidents of the Assembly and chairmen of the general committees, and other members appointed by the Assembly. It meets several times a year, and is empowered to adopt Recommendations and Opinions on behalf of the Assembly when the Assembly is not sitting.

The representation of Member States on committees is roughly pro-portionate to their representation in the Assembly. At the same time as it nominates the members of committees, the Assembly also nominates an alternate for each member.

Committees sit in private. Committees and sub-committees meet between sessions or part-sessions at Strasbourg and in many other cities of Member States.

Budget. The budget of the Council of Europe is adopted annually by the Committee of Ministers after it has considered a draft budget submitted by the Secretary-General.[1] The Statute does not give the Assembly any auth-ority over the form or content of the budget of the Council, but administrat-ive arrangements have been made to enable the Secretary-General to incorporate in the draft budget without alteration the Assembly's proposals relating to its own operations. The Secretary-General retains the right not to accept any proposal made by the Assembly. But if he were to exercise that right, he would first consult the President of the Assembly and then inform the Committee of Ministers giving reasons for his decision.[2] The Assembly also expresses a view annually on the remainder of the Budget.

WESTERN EUROPEAN UNION

The Western European Union (WEU) deals primarily with defence mat-ters. It was set up under the modified Brussels Treaty in 1954. The seven member countries are Belgium, France, the Federal Republic of Germany, Italy, Luxembourg, the Netherlands and the United Kingdom. Like the Council of Europe the WEU comprises a Ministerial Council and an Assembly. Spain and Portugal have signed a Protocol for their Accession to the Treaty, which is awaiting ratification by all the Member States.

The Council

The Council of the seven Foreign Ministers meets at ministerial level and, more frequently, at ambassadorial level, when the Ministers are represented

---

1 Statute, art 38 (c).
2 These arrangements were put forward by the Secretary-General in January 1973 and were approved by the Standing Committee on 23 March 1973.

by the ambassadors in London of the six continental countries and a representative of the same rank from the British Foreign and Commonwealth Office. At ministerial level, the chairmanship of the Council is held by each country for a period of twelve months in turn in alphabetical rotation. At ambassadorial level, the Secretary-General of WEU is the permanent Chairman.

The Council has established an Agency for the Control of Armaments and the Standing Armaments Committee, both of which are based in Paris.

The Chairman of the Council is regularly invited to make an oral presentation of the Council's annual report to the Assembly. He may reply to matters raised in the general debate on the report which follows his presentation. The Council may receive questions from Representatives in writing on any matter which is relevant to the Brussels Treaty, or which has been submitted to the Assembly for an Opinion.

The Assembly

Representation. In accordance with the provisions of the modified Brussels Treaty, the Assembly of Western European Union is composed of the same Representatives and Substitutes of the seven Brussels Treaty Powers as those appointed to the Parliamentary Assembly of the Council of Europe.[1]

Term of office and sessions. The Assembly normally meets in the chamber of the French *Conseil Economique et Social* in Paris. The term of office of Representatives and Substitutes is the same as for the Parliamentary Assembly of the Council of Europe.

The Assembly must meet at least once during each calendar year; in practice it meets twice, usually in June and in December. The President may also convene extraordinary sessions either on his own initiative or at the request of the Council or of at least a quarter of the Representatives.

Privileges and immunities. The Council of WEU has adopted a text dealing with the status of Representatives to the Assembly.[2] Under its terms, no administrative or other restrictions are to be placed on Representatives or Substitutes in their free movement to or from the place of meeting of the Assembly. In matters of customs and exchange control, they are to be accorded the same facilities by their own government as would be accorded to senior officials travelling abroad on temporary official duty; and they are to be immune from official interrogation, arrest or legal proceedings in respect of words spoken or votes cast by them in the exercise of their

---

1 The number of Representatives are: Belgium 7, France 18, Federal Republic of Germany 18, Italy 18, Luxembourg 3, Netherlands 7, United Kingdom 18.
2 See SI 1960/444.

functions. During the sessions of the Assembly, during the sittings of its committees, and in travelling to and from such meetings, Representatives are to enjoy freedom from arrest and prosecution on the territory of other Member States. The Assembly may waive this last immunity, and it does not apply when the individual concerned is found committing, attempting to commit or having committed an offence.

Powers of the Assembly. Under the terms of its Charter the WEU Assembly carries out the parliamentary function arising from the application of the modified Brussels Treaty. In 1956 the Assembly agreed with the Parliamentary Assembly of the Council of Europe that on defence matters the latter should limit its activities to the political aspects of European security while the former would concentrate on military questions and possibly related political implications. The WEU Council transferred the social and cultural work of WEU to the Council of Europe in 1959.

The Charter also indicates the general method by which the WEU Assembly is to discharge its parliamentary function. Section V empowers the Assembly to make Recommendations or transmit Opinions to the Council of WEU on any matter consonant with the aims, and falling within the terms of reference, of Western European Union. If the Assembly prefers to adopt a Resolution on such a matter, it may do so and this will be transmitted as appropriate to international organizations, governments and national parliaments.

Like the Parliamentary Assembly of the Council of Europe the WEU Assembly is a consultative body and has no power to regulate the activities of the executive organ to which it is related.

The draft budget of the Assembly is prepared in committee, considered by the Assembly, and then transmitted to the Council for approval. The Assembly may also express its views on the approved budget of the Union, when it has been communicated to the Assembly.

Committees. Discussion of matters by the Assembly usually takes place on the report of the relevant committee. The Assembly is directed by the Charter to set up four committees—on Defence Questions and Armaments, General Affairs, Budgetary Affairs and Administration, and Rules of Procedure and Privileges. Other committees may be appointed as necessary, and committees have been set up on Scientific, Technical and Aerospace Questions, and for Parliamentary and Public Relations. Besides examining questions and documents referred to them by the Assembly, committees are also required to examine any action taken on Recommendations and Resolutions adopted by the Assembly.

The number of Representatives on each committee is limited according to a formula which takes account of the size of national delegations. An equal number of alternates is appointed to each committee who may replace Representatives of the same delegation in the case of their absence.

Languages. The official languages of the Assembly are English and French; all its documents are produced in these two languages. Speeches in the Assembly, however, may also be made in German, Italian and Dutch, and simultaneous interpretation is provided into all these five languages. In committees a member may speak in any of the five languages but simultaneous interpretation is only provided into English and French.

THE NORTH ATLANTIC ASSEMBLY

Members of both Houses have attended meetings of the North Atlantic Assembly (known until 1966 as the Assembly of NATO Parliamentarians) since its inception in 1955. The North Atlantic Assembly, unlike similar bodies previously mentioned in this chapter, has no statutory basis as the official consultative organ of the related intergovernmental organization. On the other hand, links between the Assembly and the North Atlantic Treaty Organization (NATO) have been strengthened; and in particular the North Atlantic Council (the highest authority of NATO) examines and comments on the recommendations and resolutions of the Assembly.

As the North Atlantic Treaty of 1949 not only brought into being a military alliance but also committed the signatories to developing political, economic, social and cultural co-operation among themselves, so the aims of the North Atlantic Assembly are to strengthen understanding and co-operation among the Member States of NATO.

The North Atlantic Assembly holds its main plenary session annually in the autumn. The secretariat of the Assembly is located in Brussels, but since 1969 it has been the practice for the Assembly's sessions to be held in different member countries.

Membership. The Assembly is composed of delegates from the national Parliaments of the sixteen Member States. There is no limit to the size of the delegations, but voting strengths are restricted.[1] The United Kingdom delegation is appointed by Ministers and announced in a Written Answer by a Minister in the Foreign and Commonwealth Office.

Structure. At its autumn plenary session the North Atlantic Assembly elects a President, three Vice-Presidents and a Treasurer from among the delegates. The Assembly hears addresses by Ministers and leading representatives of Atlantic and European organizations; it debates and adopts reports and recommendations made by its committees, and may forward them to NATO member governments and to the North Atlantic Council and other intergovernmental organizations.

There are at present five committees—namely, the Political Committee, the Defence and Security Committee, the Economic Committee, the Scientific and Technical Committee and the Civilian Affairs Committee. Sub-Committees may also be appointed.

Committees meet in the spring, and again on the occasion of the autumn plenary session. After the spring committee meetings a one-day plenary session has been held in recent years. It is not usual for committees to meet at other times during the year, though the sub-committees they appoint may meet more often.

In addition, the Assembly appoints a Standing Committee, composed of one delegate from each Member State. This committee is responsible for policy decisions including general oversight of the budget of the Assembly, for assigning working programmes to other committees, and for arranging

---

1 The current voting strength of each Member State is: Belgium 7, Canada 12, Denmark 5, France 18, Federal Republic of Germany 18, Greece 7, Iceland 3, Italy 18, Luxembourg 3, Netherlands 7, Norway 5, Portugal 5, Spain 12, Turkey 10, United Kingdom 18, United States of America 36.

the organization and agenda of plenary sessions. The Standing Committee normally meets at least three times each year.

The official languages of the Assembly are English and French.

Budget. The Budget of the Assembly is directly under the control of the Assembly itself. The Budget is prepared by the Standing Committee, who submits it to the Assembly for approval.

Almost the whole of the income of the Assembly derives from contributions by member countries. It is for each delegation (in practice, each government) to decide how its contribution is paid. In many countries the contributions are paid out of the parliamentary budget, but in several (notably France and the United Kingdom) contributions are paid in the form of an annual grant out of the budgets of the Ministries of Foreign Affairs. In addition to the national contributions, there is also a small annual subsidy from NATO.

PART III

Proceedings in Parliament: private business

CHAPTER 33

Preliminary view of private bills

INTRODUCTORY

Private legislation is legislation of a special kind for conferring particular powers or benefits on any person or body of persons—including individuals, local authorities, statutory companies, or private corporations—in excess of or in conflict with the general law. As such it is to be distinguished from public general legislation, which is applicable to the general community and is treated in Parliament on an entirely different basis.

Until comparatively recently private legislation was effected by means only of private bills and it was not necessary to have any general term to describe non-public legislation. Since the middle of the nineteenth century, however, other forms of private legislation have grown up, almost all as alternatives to private bills and designed to simplify, expedite, or cheapen such legislation. Nowadays, therefore, private legislation falls into several categories, which are treated in Parliament by different methods and may be classified as follows:

Private bills.

Bills for confirming Provisional Orders.

Orders subject to special parliamentary procedure under the Statutory Orders (Special Procedure) Acts 1945 and 1965, and bills presented in pursuance of those Acts.

Bills for confirming Provisional Orders under the Private Legislation Procedure (Scotland) Act 1936.

It is proposed in Part III first to describe the manner of passing private bills, with a reference to the other methods of legislation by which they have been or are being superseded, and then to deal in detail with these other methods in the order enumerated above.[1]

DISTINCTIVE CHARACTER OF PRIVATE BILLS

Private bills are bills for the particular interest or benefit of any person or body of persons, for example a public company or corporation or a local authority, and are therefore to be distinguished from legislation dealing with public policy which is of general application. This distinction extends to the manner of their introduction.

The essential difference in procedure between a public bill and a private bill is that, whereas a public bill is either presented direct to the House or introduced on motion by a Member of Parliament, a private bill is solicited

---

1 References in Part III to standing orders are to standing orders of the House of Commons (Private Business) unless otherwise stated. For the history of the individual standing orders, see Williams ii.

by the parties who are interested in promoting it and is founded upon a petition which must be duly deposited in accordance with standing orders.[1] Furthermore, the payment of fees by the promoters is an indispensable condition of its progress (see p 835).

History of private bills

The separation of legislative and judicial functions is a refinement in the principles of political government and jurisprudence. In the early history of Parliament, special laws for the benefit of private parties and judicial decrees for the redress of private wrongs were both founded on petitions and were not easily distinguishable in principle or in form. When petitions sought obviously for remedies which the common law afforded, the parties were referred to the ordinary tribunals, but in other cases Parliament exercised a remedial jurisdiction. Since the fifteenth century petitions of the latter type have been cast in the form of what are now known as private bills. Until the nineteenth century, probably most private bills were concerned with the affairs of individuals; there being no ordinary procedure for divorce or naturalization, many of them were bills for these purposes, and most of the others were concerned with the alteration of settlements and entails. From about 1700, however, a growing number of private bills were concerned with the construction of toll roads, canals, railways, reservoirs and other works, and with the local government of boroughs and other areas, such as vestries. In modern times, the greater and more important part of the private bills which come to Parliament are those promoted by local authorities and statutory undertakers for the better fulfilment of their functions by the conferring of powers which the ordinary law does not give them.

Peculiarity of proceedings on private bills

Before agreeing to exemption from or amendment of the general law in particular local circumstances, Parliament has always required proof, first of the need for the exemption or amendment, and secondly of the fact that the need is, at any rate in part, that of the promoters of the bill.[2] These two closely allied principles were fulfilled in the past by the petitioner for what would now be called a private bill appearing at the Bar of the House to which he had addressed his petition (normally the Commons) and adducing evidence in support of his case. Nowadays, the interest of the promoters in the bill is a matter on which the Speaker may rule at the time when the order for second reading of the bill is read,[3] and 'proof of need' is, as regards the detailed clauses of a private bill, normally assessed by committees of each House.[4]

Legislative and judicial functions of Parliament

In passing public (general) bills, Parliament acts strictly in its legislative capacity: it originates such measures of public policy as it considers appro-

---

1 For cases of urgent necessity, where an exception has been made and a private bill has been brought in otherwise than upon petition, see p 829.
2 See Report of the Joint Committee on the Promotion of Private Bills, HL 176, HC 262 (1959).
3 See pp 794, 798.
4 See p 909.

priate, it conducts inquiries, when necessary, for its own information, and enacts laws in accordance with its own judgment. Outside individuals have no direct participation in the conduct of the business or immediate influence upon the decision of Parliament.

In passing private bills Parliament still exercises its legislative functions, but its proceedings are also of a judicial character. The persons who are applying for powers or benefits appear as petitioners for the bill, while those parties who fear that their interests may be adversely affected by its provisions have the opportunity to oppose it. Many of the formalities of a court of justice are maintained; various conditions are required to be observed and their observance to be strictly proved; and if the parties do not meet such requirements, the bill will not be permitted to make further progress. If they abandon it and no other parties undertake its support, the bill is lost.[1]

In 1828 the Manchester and Salford Improvement Bill was abandoned in committee by its original promoters; its opponents, having succeeded in introducing certain amendments, undertook to take steps to secure its further progress. In another case, the committee would not allow this course to be taken.[2] In 1873, the committee on the Kingstown Township Bill, after the commissioners under their corporate seal had withdrawn from its promotion, refused to allow them to proceed with it as individuals. In the Horncastle Gas Bill 1876, the promoters and opponents came to an agreement in committee by which the opponents paid the promoters' costs and were given the conduct of the bill.

Jurisdiction of the courts

The Court of Chancery regarded the process of private legislation as akin to an ordinary lawsuit, and therefore took the view that its jurisdiction extended to restraining persons from petitioning for or against such bills.[3] This jurisdiction, frequently invoked in the nineteenth century, was claimed by analogy with the common injunction,[4] and was reaffirmed as recently as 1942.[5]

Despite this, however, there is no doubt that the courts have expressed their great reluctance to interfere, and have emphasized that the strongest possible arguments must be adduced to obtain relief.

In some cases judges have gone so far as to state that it is difficult to conceive of circumstances in which an injunction might be granted.[6] It would be difficult, indeed, to conceive of stronger grounds for proceeding than in

---

1 Cf p 918 for 'Parties not proceeding'.
2 Cork Butter Market Bill 1859, Minutes of Evidence, iii, 84.
3 *Heathcote v North Staffordshire Rly Co* (1850) 2 Mac & G 100; *Stevens v South Devon Rly* (1851) 13 Beav 58; *Lancaster and Carlisle Railway v London and North Western Rly* (1856) 2 K & J 203; *Re London, Chatham and Dover Rly Arrangement Act* (1869) 5 Ch App 671.
4 *Stockton and Hartlepool Rly Co v The Leeds and Thirsk and Clarence Rly Cos* (1848) 2 Ph 669.
5 *Bilston Corporation v Wolverhampton Corporation* [1942] Ch 391. Its validity has, however, been questioned. See Holdsworth *History of English Law XI* p 361, cf also 59 Law Quarterly Review (1943) 2; 71 ibid (1955) 336; and Hanbury *Modern Equity* (8th edn) p 610.
6 Eg Lord Cottenham LC, *Heathcote's case,* loc cit, p 109; Simonds J, *Bilston Corporation v Wolverhampton Corporation,* loc cit, p 393.

Bilston Corporation v Wolverhampton Corporation where the plaintiffs sought an injunction to restrain the defendants from petitioning against a bill in breach of an agreement which had been scheduled to a previous private Act and thus received statutory authority from the legislature itself.[1] But an injunction was nevertheless refused here. No guide as to the circumstances in which an injunction would be upheld can be obtained from precedent, since there appears to be no such case on record, although there are instances where an injunction was granted but dissolved on appeal.[2]

Instances may indeed be found where an injunction was granted to restrain the use of funds for the promotion of a private bill,[3] or to prevent parties from proceeding with a bill in their corporate capacity.[4]

Future applications to the court are likely to be extremely rare. Indeed the position of the courts has recently been exhaustively examined by the House of Lords in the case of *British Railways Board v Pickin*, when it was decided that the courts had no power to disregard an Act of Parliament, whether public or private, nor had they any power to examine proceedings in Parliament in order to determine whether the passing of an Act had been obtained by means of any irregularity or fraud[5] (see p 91).

Principles by which Parliament is guided

The union of the judicial and legislative functions is not confined to the forms of procedure, but is an important principle in the inquiries and decision of Parliament upon the merits of private bills. As a court, it inquires into and adjudicates upon the interests of private parties; as a legislature, it is concerned to safeguard the interests of the public. The promoters of a bill may prove beyond a doubt that their own interests will be advanced by its success and no one may complain of injury or urge any specific objection, but if Parliament considers that it may be damaging to the community as a whole, it has power to reject the bill or to impose conditions or restrictions which were not sought by the parties. In order to increase the vigilance of Parliament in protecting the public interest, the Chairman of Committees in the House of Lords and the Chairman of Ways and Means in the House of Commons are entrusted with the general supervision of private business (see pp 826–829, 890, 933–934), while Government departments are also required to scrutinize all private bills (see pp 890–891).

Private bills pass through same stages as public bills

Although private bills are examined by officers of the House and contested by the parties before committees, and are subject to notices, forms, and intervals unusual in other bills, when they come before either House, they

---

1 A Committee of the House of Commons has condemned such agreements as improper and of doubtful value: Special Report from the Committee on Group A of Private Bills, Bilston Corporation Bill, Supplement to the Vote 1942, p 7.

2 Eg *Heathcote v South Staffordshire Rly*, loc cit; *Stockton etc Rly Co v Leeds etc Rly Cos*, loc cit, *Re London, Chatham and Dover Rly Arrangement Act*, loc cit.

3 *Stevens v South Devon Railway Co* (1851) 13 Beav 48; see also *Attorney-General v Andrews* (1850) 2 Mac & G 225; *Attorney-General v West Hartlepool Improvement Commissioners* (1870) LR Eq 152.

4 *Attorney-General v Commissioners of the Township of Kingstown* (1873) IR Eq 383.

5 [1974] 1 All ER 609.

are treated at each stage as if they were public bills, although separate hours are allotted for their discussion. They are read as many times and similar questions are put,[1] except when any proceeding is especially directed by the standing orders, and in general the same rules of debate and procedure are maintained throughout.

In the same way, if any proceeding on a private bill is postponed on motion for six months, such postponement is equivalent to a rejection of the bill and no new bill for the same object may be introduced that session.

DIFFICULTY IN DETERMINING WHETHER CERTAIN BILLS SHOULD BE PUBLIC, PRIVATE, OR TREATED AS HYBRID

The distinction between public and private bills has been generally defined, but considerable difficulties often arise in determining to which description particular bills properly belong. Thus, upon a public bill, the question not infrequently arises whether it ought not more properly to have been introduced as a private bill (see pp 519–520 below) or treated as a hybrid bill (see pp 807–808 above); and private bills have often been objected to and have been debarred from proceeding on the ground that, from their scope or objects or from the principles involved in them, they should have been introduced as public bills.[2]

Before the general principles adopted in determining bills to be public or private are described, one point should be made clear. The petition on which a private bill is founded is a petition to the House of Commons, or in a few cases to the House of Lords; but the bill itself is in the form of a petition to the Crown. In practice no private bill is ever introduced by the Government, and it has been stated that the reason for this is that the Crown cannot petition itself.[3] A further reason may be found in the fact that a bill introduced by a Government department for the direct or indirect benefit of that department may well be presumed to be founded upon state policy and accordingly be more properly introduced as a public bill, despite the fact that in all other respects it may display all the characteristic features of a private bill.

No bill introduced by the Government and proceeded with as a hybrid bill can be cited as a precedent to show that a subsequent bill is of such a character that it ought to be treated as a public and not as a private bill. It may well be that such hybrid government bills as the London Water Bill 1902, the Port of London Bills 1903 and 1908, the London Passenger Transport Bill 1930-31 and the Transport (London) Bill 1968–69, dealt with matters of such far-reaching importance and extended to such wide areas that they ought in any case to have been introduced as public bills. There are two reasons why bills affecting private rights such as these are properly proceeded with as hybrid bills—first that, although in part they may be of a private nature, their main object is a public one; and secondly, that there

---

1 For the difference in practice on consideration of public and private bills, see p 924.
2 HC Deb (1938–39) 343, c 954 and cc 1091–1092; ibid (1958–59) 600, c 787; ibid (1959–60) 617, c 199; ibid (1978–79) 961, c 1211; ibid (1979–80) 977, c 1100; ibid (1983–84) 53, c 120; ibid (1985–86) 90, c 1075.
3 See 34 Halsbury's Laws of England, (4th edn) p 488.

may be no parties able and willing to present a petition. But, since the bills were introduced by the Government, the fact that they were introduced as public bills cannot be brought forward as an argument that bills of a similar nature, if not introduced by the Government, ought not to be introduced as private bills. In dealing, therefore, in this chapter with the question whether bills ought to be treated as public or private bills, this fact must be borne in mind. On the other hand, when a government bill has been proceeded with throughout as a public bill and not as a hybrid bill, this, though not conclusive evidence, is at any rate some indication that the subject-matter dealt with is of a public nature. With this caution, the principles which govern the subject and the examples which follow may now be considered.[1]

In general there are four principles which have been followed in determining that a private bill should not be allowed to proceed as such, but should be introduced as a public bill. These are as follows:

(1) That public policy is affected;
(2) That the bill proposes to amend or repeal public Acts. In these cases, the nature and degree of the proposed repeal or amendment have to be considered;[2] (see pp 802–803.)
(3) The magnitude of the area and the multiplicity of the interests involved;[3]
(4) The fact that the bill though partly of a private nature has as its main object a public matter (see above). In this case the fact that standing orders have to be complied with is often an important factor in deciding whether a bill should be a private bill. Thus in the case of the Registration of Clubs (London) Bill 1959, introduced as a private bill, no standing orders except those relating to the advertisement of the Bill were applicable. It was ruled that the Bill could not proceed as a private bill.[4]

Bills brought in by the Government for local purposes, etc

Bills which are brought in by the Government (dealing with Crown property, or with national and other works in different localities, etc), and which affect private interests, are introduced as public bills, and subsequently treated as hybrid bills.[5]

---

1 In pp 794–802, Government bills have been indicated as such in the text and distinguished with an asterisk (*) in the footnotes.
2 Parl Deb (1895) 30, c 708; ibid 38, c 335.
3 HC Deb (1938–39) 343, cc 950–954; ibid (1979–80) 977, c 1100.
4 HC Deb (1959–60) 617, cc 199–200.
5 Eg *Public Offices Site Bill 1882, and other *Public Offices (Sites), etc., Bills to 1946–47; *Crown Lands Bills 1906, 1927,1935–36; *Post Office (Sites) Bill, 1900, and other *Post Office (Sites) Bills to 1953–54; *North Killingholme (Admiralty Pier) Bills 1912–13, and 1930–31; *Invergordon Harbour (Transfer) Bill 1920; *Air Ministry (Croydon Aerodrome Extension) Bill 1924–25; *Festival of Britain (Supplementary Provisions) Bill 1948–49; *Park Lane Improvement Bill 1957–58; *Covent Garden Market Bill 1960–61; *British Museum Bill 1962–63; *Maplin Development Bill 1972–73; *Channel Tunnel Bills 1973–74, 1974, 1974–75, and 1985–86, 1986–87, 1987–88; *Chevening Estate Bill 1986–87; *Norfolk and Suffolk Broads Bill 1986–87, 1987–88; *Dartford-Thurrock Crossing Bill 1987–88. This does not apply to nationalized industries which have frequently promoted private bills.

Bills relating to London

The metropolis. Owing to the large area, the vast population, and the variety of interests concerned, bills which affect the entire metropolis used, as a rule, to be regarded as measures of public policy rather than of local interest. Such bills were usually, though not invariably,[1] introduced and proceeded with throughout as public bills[2] or were dealt with as hybrid bills.[3] Bills relating to the Metropolitan Police and to Metropolitan Magistrates Courts have always been public bills[4] and where any of the principles outlined on p 794 are involved the rule that bills affecting the metropolis should be introduced as public bills still applies.[5] In recent years, however, bills relating to detailed local government and allied matters in London have mostly been promoted by the former Greater London Council and statutory authorities such as the Port of London Authority, and have been private bills. Similarly, provisions relating to London Transport have been contained in private bills promoted by London Regional Transport and its predecessors.

Bills relating to the River Thames. Thames Conservancy Bills and other bills relating to that river are usually private bills. Thus the Thames Conservancy Bills of 1857, 1894, 1905, 1911, 1921, 1924, 1931–32 and 1958–59 were private bills, but the Thames Conservancy Bill 1864 was a hybrid bill introduced by the Government. The Thames Navigation Bill 1866, and the Thames River (Prevention of Floods) Bill 1877, were hybrid bills, but the Thames River (Prevention of Floods) Bill 1878–79 was a private bill.[6] In 1881 the Thames River Bill was introduced as a private bill, but, on exception being taken to it as a private bill, it was withdrawn and a public (hybrid) bill was introduced though not passed. In 1971–72 the Thames Barrier and Flood Prevention Bill was a private bill.

Port of London. The Port of London Bill 1903 was introduced by the Government and proceeded with as a hybrid bill, but, after being suspended, was withdrawn in the next Session. The Port of London Bill 1908, a

---

1 London Valuation and Assessment Bill 1895, Parl Deb (1895) 30, c 709.
2 *Metropolitan Sewers Bills 1848 and 1854; *Metropolis Local Management Act Amendment Bill 1858; Annoyance Jurors (Westminster) Bill 1861; *Metropolis Local Management Bill 1855; Metropolis Management Acts Amendment Bill 1875, and Metropolis Management and Building Acts Amendment Bills 1882 and 1890; Racecourses (Metropolis) Bill 1878–79; *Public Health (London) Bill 1890–91; Public Health (London) Act (1891) Amendment Bill 1893–94; *London Government Bill 1899.
3 *Metropolis Water Bill 1851 and Metropolis Water Supply Bill 1852; *Thames Embankment (North Side) Bill 1863, and Thames Embankment (South Side) Bill 1863; *Metropolis Gas Bill 1867, and Metropolis Gas (Surrey Side) Bill 1876; Metropolis Water Supply and Fire Prevention Bill 1874; Metropolis Toll Bridges Bill 1877; Thames Steam Navigation Regulation Bill 1880; *Metropolis Waterworks Purchase Bill 1880; *Hyde Park Corner (New Streets) Bill 1883; Metropolis Water Supply Bill 1891; Watermen's and Lightermen's Company Bill 1892. And cf *London Government Bill 1962, and CJ (1851) 191; ibid (1878) 13; ibid (1893–94) 487, 492; ibid (1895) 21, 44.
4 *Metropolitan Police Bills 1829 to 1934–35, etc; *Metropolitan Police Courts Bills 1839, 1840; Metropolitan Police Act 1839 (Amendment) Bill 1958; *Metropolitan Police Borrowing Powers Bill 1952; *Metropolitan Magistrates Court Bill 1959.
5 *Public Health (London) Bill 1890; Public Health (London) Bill 1935; *London Government Bills 1939 and 1962; and see Mr Speaker's ruling on the Registration of Clubs (London) Bill 1959, HC Deb (1959–60) 617, cc 199–200.
6 CJ (1878–79) 39.

Government bill which constituted the Port of London Authority, was also proceeded with as a hybrid bill, but bills promoted since then by the Authority have regularly been passed as private bills. The Port of London (Financial Assistance) Bill 1980 was introduced by the Government and passed as a public bill.[1]

City of London. Bills concerning only the City of London have generally been private bills solicited by the Corporation itself, which desired special legislation affecting its own property, interests, and jurisdiction.[2]

> Thus even the bill for establishing a police force within the City was brought in upon petition, and passed as a private bill;[3] and in 1863, when it was sought by the Government to repeal this Act by a public bill (for the amalgamation of the City and Metropolitan Police) without the notices required for a private bill, standing orders were not dispensed with and the bill was not permitted to proceed.[4] In 1919 the City of London Police Bill (to amend the enactments relating to the expenses of the police force of the City of London) was a hybrid bill introduced by the Government. Private bills also have been solicited for the reform of the Corporation itself,[5] while measures for the same object have been proposed by the Government in public bills.[6] Again, the Corporation and other parties sought, by means of private bills, to improve Smithfield Market, or to provide a suitable market for cattle,[7] but the Metropolitan Cattle Market was established by an Act which was brought in by the Government as a public bill and subsequently treated as a hybrid bill.[8] This Act, however, was amended in 1875 by a private Act,[9] and the Metropolitan Market and Foreign Cattle Market (Deptford) Bill in the same year was also a private bill.[10] Other bills, again, concerning the City of London, but at the same time affecting public interests, and involving considerations of public policy, have been introduced and passed as public bills.[11] The London Government Act 1963 specifically excepted the City of London from its provisions.

---

1 HC Deb (1979–80) 982, cc 1214–1216.
2 London (City) Small Debts Bills 1847 and 1847–48; London Corporation Bill 1849; Coal Duties (London and Westminster and Adjacent Counties) Bill 1851; London Bridge Approaches Bill, and City of London School Bill 1878–79; City of London (Various Powers) Bills 1900, 1911, 1912–13, etc, to 1986–87; City of London (Guild Churches) Bill 1951–52, etc.
3 London City Police Bill 1839, CJ (1839) 175.
4 *Metropolitan and City of London Police Amalgamation Bill 1863, CJ (1863) 173, 176, 195, 211. Cf also the London (City) Police Bill 1874 (a private bill), CJ (1874) 33.
5 CJ (1849) 15; ibid (1852) 57; Parl Deb (1852) 119, c 1035.
6 *London Corporation Bills 1856, 1859, 1860, CJ (1856) 114, Parl Deb (1856) 141, c 314; CJ (1859) 253, Parl Deb (1859) 154, c 946; CJ (1860) 28, Parl Deb (1860) 156, c 282. These bills were not proceeded with.
7 CJ (1847–48) 176; ibid (1851) 22, 26.
8 CJ (1851) 66, etc.
9 Metropolitan Central Markets (Smithfield) Act 1875.
10 Both these bills were promoted by the Corporation (CJ (1875) 11).
11 *Coalwhippers (Port of London) Bill 1843, 1846, and 1851; *Coal Trade (Port of London) Bill 1845; Ballast Heavers (Port of London) Bill 1852; *London Coal and Wine Dues Continuance Bill 1861; *London Coal and Wine (Duties) Continuance Bill 1863, 1867–68; and Coal Duties (London) Abolition Bill 1889, Parl Deb (1889) 336, c 701.

Bills relating to cities and counties, etc

A bill relating to a city or a county other than London is normally held to be a private bill, although some such bills have been treated as public bills on the grounds that they were measures of public policy.[1]

Edinburgh. Bills concerning Edinburgh have usually been private, but have sometimes been public, according to their objects and the circumstances connected with their introduction.[2] Since 1899 legislation which previously would have been private has been dealt with by means of provisional orders under the Private Legislation Procedure (Scotland) Act[3] (see chapter 39).

Bills applicable to several localities

A bill not affecting public policy may proceed as a private bill although it may apply to many localities, provided that the authorities concerned in the promotion of the bill have a joint interest in obtaining powers exercisable severally by each of them. Where, however, the joint interest amounts to nothing more than a common desire to obtain the same additional powers by authorities each of which could properly ask separately for such powers, it is doubtful whether the bill may properly proceed as a private bill.[4]

In 1856, the Local Dues on Shipping Bill (a government bill) was held to be properly a public bill. It proposed to abolish passing tolls, to transfer the harbours of Dover, Ramsgate, Whitby and Bridlington to the Board of Trade, to impose rates, and to repeal local Acts. Being a measure of general policy, its character was not changed by the fact that only these four harbours came under its operation.[5] In 1861, the Harbours Bill, also a government bill, was introduced and passed as a public bill. It affected the same four harbours and the local Acts under which they were administered, but otherwise dealt with so many matters of general legislation as to be unquestionably a measure of public policy.

As examples of private bills affecting several localities, the London Electric Supply Bill 1908, and the Green Belt (London and Home Counties) Bill 1938 may be quoted. Both of these bills were introduced as private bills, and proceeded without objection. The title of the latter bill indicates the joint interest of the several authorities concerned:— 'A Bill to make provision for the preservation from industrial or building development of areas of land in and around the administrative county of London; to confer powers for that purpose upon the London County Council and certain other local authorities and persons, and for other purposes.' On the other hand, the Home Counties (Music and Dancing)

---

1 See, for example, the bills relating to the administration of justice referred to in fn 5 on p 799; the bills relating to the sale of intoxicating liquors referred to in fn 6 on p 803; the Local Dues on Shipping Bill 1856 (below); and the Senior Public Elementary Schools (Liverpool) Bill 1939 (fn 3 on p 803).
2 CJ (1847) 113, 121; ibid (1852–53) 612, 613, 630; ibid (1857) 298, 302; ibid (1878–79) 32; ibid (1882) 27; ibid (1890–91) 54; ibid (1896) 28.
3 For a substituted bill, see Edinburgh Boundaries Extension and Tramways Bill [Lords] 1920.
4 See Reports of the Joint Committee on the Promotion of Private Bills, HL 176, HC 262 (1958–59); of the Committee on the British Transport Commission Bill 1959 (Reports on Private Bills 1959, p 59) and of the Chairman of Ways and Means on the Kent County Council Bill 1958 (Reports on Private Bills 1958, p 157) and p 799.
5 CJ (1856) 17, 72. The bill was not passed.

(Licensing) Bill 1926, which concerned the counties of Buckinghamshire, Essex, Hertfordshire and Kent and the county boroughs of Croydon, East Ham, and West Ham, was a public bill.

When a private bill was introduced in 1899 which proposed to deal with the rates leviable by certain harbour, dock and other authorities in different parts of the country, the Chairman of Committees in the House of Lords considered that this object ought to be attained either by a public bill or by separate private bills applying severally to the various ports, etc., and the bill was not proceeded with.[1] In 1911 another instance was afforded in the Local Authorities (Combined Drainage) Bill under which the law relating to drainage was to be altered in twenty-one widely separated boroughs and urban districts. The Chairman of Committees in the House of Lords again gave it as his opinion that the provisions of the bill ought either to be the subject of a public bill amending the general law or to be in the form of a series of private bills each affecting its own district; the bill was not proceeded with.[2] In 1959 the Speaker ruled that the National Association of Almshouses (Investment) Bill could not proceed as a private bill, and it was withdrawn.[3] For similar reasons, doubts were expressed by the Chairmen in both Houses, in special reports, and by the Lords committee on the bill, about the propriety of allowing the South-Eastern Gas Corporation Limited (Associated Companies) Bill 1939 to proceed as a private bill. It was subjected to certain conditions which were subsequently incorporated in standing orders designed to ensure that the consents of companies not themselves promoting a bill had been obtained. (see p 867).

Bills promoted by a county council jointly with, or on behalf of, district councils

A bill to confer powers on a county council and on district councils within the county may be promoted jointly by the county council and those district councils and may proceed as a private bill, since the promoting authorities share a joint interest in the good government of the county.[4] In some cases a bill of this kind has been promoted by a county council jointly with some district councils within the county and on behalf of other such district councils.[5]

Such a bill may also be promoted by the county council alone, and may proceed as a private bill, notwithstanding the general rule that a petitioner for a private bill may petition Parliament only on his own behalf. In such cases the district councils for whose benefit provisions are included in the bill are required by Standing Order 136A (HC) and Standing Order 124A (HL) to advertise those provisions locally and to pass a resolution in favour of their inclusion in the county council's bill.[6]

---

1 LJ (1899) 59.
2 LJ (1911–12) 126. See also p 804.
3 CJ (1958–59) 113.
4 See Report of the Joint Committee on the Promotion of Private Bills, HL 176, HC 262 (1958–59) and p 797 above.
5 Greater Manchester Bill [Lords] 1978–81.
6 In 1961 the operation of certain clauses in the Devon County Council Bill was excluded from those districts in the county which had not passed resolutions in favour of them.

These Standing Orders resulted from the report in 1959 of the Joint Committee on the Promotion of Private Bills,[1] which was appointed following the reports by the Chairman of Committees in the House of Lords[2] and the Chairman of Ways and Means in the House of Commons[3] on a bill promoted by Kent County Council in the previous session. That bill contained 442 clauses and 6 Schedules, fewer than 100 of which were intended to apply directly to the county council, the remainder being for the benefit of other local authorities in the county. County councils had been allowed since 1921 to take powers for other authorities within their area, but had never before attempted to do so on such a large scale.

Section 70 of the Local Government Act 1972 prohibits local authorities from promoting bills to form or abolish any local government area or to alter the status of any such area.[4]

Bills relating to the administration of justice in particular areas

Bills relating to the administration of justice and various public jurisdictions have often been treated as public or hybrid bills,[5] but they have also been solicited by the promoters as private bills.[6]

> On 10 March 1868 exception was taken to the Salford Hundred and Manchester (City) Courts of Record Bill, on the ground that it ought to have been introduced as a public bill, but it was shown by the Chairman of Ways and Means that the rules and precedents of the House justified its introduction as a private bill. In Session 1911 the Salford Hundred Court of Record Bill was introduced by the Government and was treated as a hybrid bill.[7]
>
> In 1871 the Court of Hustings (London) Abolition Bill, which proposed to establish a new superior court of law with jurisdiction not confined to the City of London, was not allowed to proceed as a private bill.[8] In 1959 objection was taken to the Criminal Justice Administration (Amendment) Bill, a public bill, on the ground that being purely local in character it should have been brought in as a private bill, but the objection was overruled.[9]

---

1 Op cit, para 23.
2 LJ (1957–58) 172. See also HL Deb (1957–58) 209, cc 233–247 and 473–540.
3 Reports on Private Bills (1957–58), p 157.
4 A bill for such a purpose, if introduced as a public bill, is referred to the Examiners (West Midlands County Council (Abolition) Bill, CJ (1981–82) 263).
5 Buckingham Summer Assizes Act 1849; *Newgate Gaol (Dublin) Act 1849; *Sheriff and Commissary Courts (Berwickshire) Act 1853; *Cinque Ports Acts 1855 and 1857; *Falmouth Borough Act 1865; County of Sussex Act 1865; Chester Courts Act 1867; *Glasgow Boundary Act 1871; *Bath City Prison Act 1871; *Berwickshire County Town Act 1903; Mayor's and City of London Court Bill [Lords] 1920, and *Chatham and Sheerness Stipendiary Magistrate Bill 1928–29, were passed as public bills. For bills relating to Metropolitan Magistrates Courts and the Metropolitan Police, see p 795. The *Belfast Municipal Boundaries Act 1853; County of Hertford and Liberty of St Alban Act 1874; and County of Suffolk Act 1904, were treated as hybrid bills.
6 Staffordshire Potteries Stipendiary Justice Acts 1839, 1871, and 1895; Yorkshire Registries, etc, Bill 1910; Pontypridd Stipendiary Magistrates Bill 1920; Lancashire Quarter Sessions Bill 1960–61.
7 CJ (1911) 292, 293. See also p 803 fn 1 (Liverpool Corporation Act 1921).
8 CJ (1871) 103, Parl Deb (1871) 204, c 1500.
9 HC Deb (1958–59) 600, cc 1497–1500.

In 1839 three Government measures were passed, as public bills, for improving the police in Manchester, Birmingham, and Bolton,[1] the provisions being compulsory upon those towns, in the interest of public order, and the chief commissioners of police being appointed by the Crown.[2] In 1908 a private bill was introduced for the purpose of transferring the powers and duties of the standing joint committee of the West Riding of Yorkshire to the county council, but on the order being read for its second reading Mr Speaker called the attention of the House to its provisions which were of too important a character to be dealt with by a private bill, and the bill was accordingly withdrawn.[3]

Bills concerning property owned by religious communities, colleges etc

Bills concerning detailed matters related to the property or powers of religious communities, colleges, etc, have usually been private, although Church bills of wider application have been public.

Thus in 1871 a bill for regulating the management of certain trust properties of the Presbyterian Church of Ireland was introduced into the House of Lords as a private bill, but objection being taken to legislation upon such a subject by means of a private bill, the bill was withdrawn, and a public bill for effecting the same object was passed by both Houses.[4] In 1876 the Methodist Conference Bill, in 1907 the United Methodist Church Bill, in 1928–29 the Methodist Church Union Bill, in 1938–39 the Methodist Church Bill, in 1951–52 the City of London (Guild Churches) Bill, in 1958–59 the Calvinistic Methodist or Presbyterian Church of Wales (Amendment) Bill and in 1971–72 and 1980–81 the United Reformed Church Bills were introduced and passed as private bills, the second, third and fourth of these being referred to select committees.[5] In 1905 a public bill—the Churches (Scotland) Bill—was introduced by the Government to provide for the allocation, between the Free Church and the United Free Church, of properties belonging to the former. It was a measure of general interest and of general application, but as it affected the property of individuals it was referred to the Examiners. They held, however, that the standing orders relating to private bills were not applicable to it, and it proceeded, and was passed, as a public bill.[6] In 1888 the Keble College Bill was rejected on third reading, on the ground that it was inexpedient to extend by a private bill, to a college exceptionally constituted, the exemption from the Mortmain Acts which was enjoyed by other colleges at Oxford and Cambridge.[7] In the same session the public Act consolidating the law relating to mortmain and to the disposition of land for charitable uses was passed.[8] By amendments made during its passage both Keble College and the Victoria University were included among the bodies for

---

1 *Manchester, *Birmingham, and *Bolton Police Bills 1839.
2 Parl Deb (1839) 50, c 141.
3 CJ (1908) 32.
4 Presbyterian Church (Ireland) Bill 1871, Parl Deb (1871) 204, c 1968. Cf also the Primitive Wesleyan Methodist Society of Ireland Regulation Bill 1871; Salvation Army Bill 1962–63.
5 CJ (1876) 28; ibid (1907) 8; ibid (1928–29) 91; ibid (1938–39) 52.
6 CJ (1905) 248, 259.
7 CJ (1888) 165, 166; Parl Deb (1888) 324, cc 1687 ff.
8 *Mortmain and Charitable Uses Act 1888.

whom a special exemption was provided,[1] and other bodies have since been added, by private bills, to the number of those to whom this exemption extends.[2]

Bills concerning public funds

A bill the sole object of which was the creation of a charge on public funds has not been allowed to proceed as a private bill.

In 1979 on the second reading of the Aberfan Disaster Fund Bill, Mr Speaker drew attention to the fact that the sole object of the bill was the creation of a charge on public funds, and ruled that such a bill could proceed only as a public bill. The bill was accordingly withdrawn.[3]

A bill concerning a government guarantee, even though it amended a private Act, has been a public bill.[4]

Bills apparently similar respectively regarded as public and private

A small distinction between two apparently similar bills is sometimes enough to constitute one a public and the other a private bill.

Thus in 1855 the Carlisle Canonries Bill, which suspended the appointment to the next vacant canonry, and directed the Ecclesiastical Commissioners to pay the income to the augmentation of certain livings at Carlisle, was treated as a public bill, as it related to the Ecclesiastical Commissioners, a public body holding certain church funds in trust for public purposes prescribed by law, and merely diverted the application of some of these funds from one purpose to another.[5] On the other hand, the South Shields Parochial Districts Bill was held to be a private bill, as it sought to appropriate to local purposes (namely, the increase of certain small livings at South Shields) a sum of £15,000 to which the Dean and Chapter of Durham had become entitled by the sale of lands for the execution of certain public works.[6] In 1872 a bill to vest the Rock of Cashel and the buildings and ruins thereon in trustees was brought in as a public bill, but, on its being referred to the Examiners, it was held that the

---

1 S 7; Parl Deb (1888) 330, cc 380–382, 437.
2 Liverpool University Act 1903; University of Leeds Act 1904; University of Sheffield Act 1905; University of Bristol Act 1909; University of Reading Act 1926; University of Nottingham Act 1949; University of Hull Act 1955; University of Leicester Act 1958, etc. As to exemptions from the Mortmain Acts provided for before the consolidating Act of 1888, see the Charitable Uses Act 1735, s 4; the Ecclesiastical Commissioners Act 1841, s 13; the University College, London, Act 1869; and Parl Deb (1888) 324, c 1689.
3 CJ (1978–79) 128; HC Deb (1978–79) 961, c 1211.
4 Red Sea and India Telegraph Bill 1861, CJ (1861) 36, etc; Denison 78. See also eg Western Highlands and Islands (Transport Services) Act 1928, Cunard (Insurance) Agreement Act 1930, North Atlantic Shipping Act 1961 and Port of London (Financial Assistance) Act 1980, for examples of public Acts entailing government support for private undertakings.
5 See also Newcastle Chapter Bill 1884. Since 1919 matters of this kind have been dealt with by Measure under the Church of England Assembly (Powers) Act 1919 (see pp 554–557) but the Act makes no provision for a special procedure for Measures of the nature of private bills.
6 See also Burnley Rectory Bill 1890; Hanover Chapel Bill, and Handsworth (Stafford) Rectory Bill 1890–91; Somersham Rectory Bill [Lords] 1933–34, which was a private bill though it affected money held by the Minister of Agriculture on behalf of Cambridge University.

standing orders relative to private bills which were applicable to the bill
had not been complied with and the Standing Orders Committee resolved
that such compliance should not be dispensed with.[1] In the following year
another bill for the same objects but empowering the Church Temporalities Commissioners and the secretary to the Commissioners of
Public Works in Ireland, with the consent of the Lord Lieutenant, to
transfer and assign the Rock and buildings to trustees, was similarly
introduced and was held to be a public bill, as it merely sought powers for
public bodies who already had a statutory interest in the property.[2] In
1902 the management of the Imperial Institute was transferred from the
existing corporation to the Board of Trade by means of a private Act, but
in 1916 when the management was transferred from the Board of Trade to
another government department, namely, the Colonial Office, recourse
was had to a public bill.[3] Further changes were made and the two previous
Acts repealed by another government bill in 1925 which was proceeded
with as a hybrid bill.[4] Other amendments were made by the Commonwealth Institute Bill 1957–58, which was a public bill introduced by the
Government.

Repeal of public Acts by private bills

It has been questioned whether public Acts may properly be repealed or
amended by a private bill; and the inconvenience of their repeal or amendment by an Act which, being passed as a private bill and being of a local
character, is not printed among the public general Acts, has sometimes been
urged as a reason for refusing to sanction this course.

In 1832 a public general Act (7 & 8 Geo 4, c 31) was amended, so far as the
city of Bristol was concerned, by means of a private Act. This case was
quoted by Mr Speaker, on 18 July 1864, when objection was taken to the
Metropolitan District Railways Bill on the ground that it amended the
Thames Embankment (a hybrid) Act 1862 and he ruled that no such
objection in point of order could be sustained.[5]

No rule, however, has been established which precludes the promoters of a
private bill from seeking the repeal or amendment of public Acts. A private
bill is itself an exception, in some degree, from the general law, or seeks for
some powers which the general law does not afford, and the fact that it

1 CJ (1872) 156, 157, 189, 198.
2 CJ (1873) 114, 115, 140.
3 *Imperial Institute (Management) Bill 1916.
4 *Imperial Institute Bill 1924–25.
5 Parl Deb (1864) 176, c 1619. Cf also the questions raised, in the Lords, on the Brokers' Bonds
  and Rent Bills 1864, ibid cc 408–411, the London (City) Tithes Act 1864, which repealed a
  public Act of Henry VIII, ibid 480; the Dover (Corporation) Harbour Bill 1887, ibid (1887)
  311, cc 656–668; and the Woolwich Borough Council Bill 1905, Parl Deb (1905) 146,
  cc 1075–1087; and, in the Commons, on the London Valuation and Assessment Bill 1895, the
  Belfast Corporation Bill 1896, and the Telegraph Act (1892) Amendment Bill 1899 (see
  pp 804–806).

provides for a repeal or an amendment of public Acts is far from always being a fatal objection to its being introduced as a private bill.[1]

The provisions of some public general Acts relating to public health are regularly amended, in some degree, with regard to particular localities, by means of private bills, and the Model Clauses and the earlier clauses upon which they are based (see pp 810–811) contain many provisions amending or superseding sections of public Acts. But the scope of the public Acts which a private bill proposes to repeal or to amend, and the nature and degree of the proposed repeal or amendment, have to be considered.[2]

Certain subjects considered unsuitable for private legislation

A private bill has sometimes been rejected, although properly introduced as such, because the House has resolved that the subject-matter was unsuitable for private legislation.

In 1854 the Manchester and Salford Education Bill was introduced as a private bill, but on the second reading an amendment was carried, declaring education supported by public rates to be a subject which ought not, at the present time, to be dealt with by any private bill.[3]

In 1865 the Liverpool Licensing Bill was brought in as a private bill. It was objected that, as the bill proposed to deal with the public revenues, it ought not to have been introduced as a private bill, but, as the bill was strictly local, and as the clauses relating to licence duties were printed in italics and reserved for the consideration of a Committee of the whole House, it was held that the bill was not open to any technical objection requiring its withdrawal.[4] On the second reading, however, an amendment was carried to the effect that the granting of licences for the sale of intoxicating liquors was a subject which ought not, at present, to be dealt with by any private bill.[5] Bills relating to the sale of intoxicating liquors on Sunday in particular counties have been introduced and treated as public bills[6] as have bills relating solely to the sale of liquor at airports.[7] In 1888 a bill to exempt Keble College from certain provisions of the general law was rejected on the grounds that it was inexpedient to proceed by private bill in this matter (see pp 800–801).

---

1 In 1894 two consolidation bills, the London Streets and Buildings Bill 1894 and the Thames Conservancy Bill 1894, were both passed as private bills, although in each case various public Acts were repealed. Part XIV of the Liverpool Corporation Act 1921 (a private consolidation Act) repealed and re-enacted the provisions of the Liverpool Court of Passage Acts 1893 and 1896 (public general Acts).

2 Contrast, eg, the London Valuation and Assessment Bill 1895, which the Speaker ruled ought to be introduced as a public bill, Parl Deb (1895) 30, c 708, and the Belfast Corporation Bill 1896, which was allowed to proceed as a private bill, ibid (1896) 38, c 335.

3 CJ (1854) 90. The Senior Public Elementary Schools (Liverpool) Act 1939 was introduced as a public bill because it made an exception in the Education Act 1921.

4 Parl Deb (1865) 177, c 655.

5 CJ (1865) 92. See also HC Deb (1959–60) 617, c 199 where similar objections were given as one reason for the Registration of Clubs (London) Bill not being allowed to proceed as a private bill.

6 Sale of Intoxicating Liquors on Sunday (Cornwall) Bills 1882 and 1883; ibid Durham, Yorkshire, Isle of Wight, Northumberland Bills 1883, etc.

7 Eg Licensing (Airports) Bill 1953, CJ (1953–54) 24.

There have also been cases where a committee on a private bill has reported that the subject-matter was unsuitable for private legislation.

In 1959 the Committee on the St Neots Urban District Council (Commons) Bill reported that, having regard to the recent report of the Royal Commission on Crown Land, private bills seeking to alienate common lands should not be introduced pending public legislation. The Committee therefore found the preamble not proved.[1] The Chairman of Ways and Means subsequently reported under Standing Order 85 (Power of Chairman of Ways and Means to report special circumstances, etc, to the House) on two bills, the Plymouth Corporation (Harrowbeer Aerodrome) Bill [Lords] in 1961 and the City of London (Various Powers) Bill in 1962, pointing out that some of the provisions of the bills impinged on the report of the Royal Commission.[2]

In July 1960 the Select Committee on the Esso Petroleum Company Bill (which later received Royal Assent) recommended that no further private bills for the construction of pipelines should be passed by the House. The following session the Trunk Pipelines Bill was introduced on petition and the Chairman of Ways and Means reported on it under Standing Order 85, drawing attention to the Select Committee's recommendation. The bill was withdrawn after debate on second reading[3].

Private bills objected to on the ground that they should have been public bills

Private bills have frequently been objected to on the ground that they should have been brought in as public bills. Many of these objections have been sustained by the Speaker and the bills have been withdrawn, or not proceeded with, but other bills have been allowed to proceed.

(1) Private bills withdrawn or not proceeded with

In 1895, objection was taken to proceeding with the London Valuation and Assessment Bill (introduced for the purpose of forming a common basis of imperial and local taxation) as a private bill, on the ground that it entirely changed the law of assessment and rating, and repealed numerous public Acts of Parliament. The Speaker stated that the Acts proposed in this instance to be repealed were of vast magnitude and covered a vast area, that the Bill affected not only local rating but imperial taxation, involved interests which were much more than local, and proposed to create a new Court of Record in the matter of assessment, and that, in view of its scope, it ought to be introduced as a public, and not as a private bill.[4]

In 1900 on the second reading of a private bill promoted by the Metropolitan Water Companies, the Speaker called the attention of the House to the large and important powers which were proposed to be conferred by it upon a public department (the Local Government Board), and which, according to the practice of the House, ought to be secured by a

---

1 Reports of Committees on Private Bills (1958–59), p 19.
2 CJ (1960–61) 87; ibid (1961–62) 137.
3 CJ (1960–61) 87, 208; HC Deb (1960–61) 639, cc 699–746.
4 CJ (1895) 32, 38. Parl Deb (1895) 30, c 706–710.

public rather than by a private bill, and the bill was accordingly withdrawn.[1]

In 1910 on the second reading of the Society of Apothecaries of London Bill, which had been introduced as a private bill, the Speaker drew attention to the fact that the bill sought to empower the Society to grant diplomas in sanitary science and public health, and for dentistry and dental surgery, and ruled that such matters should be dealt with by a public bill as they were public interests, and the bill was accordingly withdrawn.[2]

The London Rating (Site Values) Bill, which was presented in 1939, proposed to levy a rate which was ultimately to be met by the landlord, notwithstanding any existing or future contract to the contrary. It was objected that the bill ought to have been introduced as a public bill. The Speaker, after referring to the precedent of the London Valuation and Assessment Bill 1895, ruled that since the bill raised questions of public policy of great importance and affected interests of vast magnitude, it ought to have been introduced as a public bill, and could not proceed as a private bill.[3]

In 1959, on the second reading of the National Association of Almshouses (Investment) Bill, the Speaker called the attention of the House to the provisions of the Bill, which in his opinion raised such questions of public policy and were of such general application that the bill should not be allowed to proceed, and in 1960 on the second reading of the Registration of Clubs (London) Bill, the Speaker drew attention to these considerations and also to the fact that the bill proposed to amend and repeal provisions in public Acts recently passed. Both bills were accordingly withdrawn.[4]

In 1980, on the second reading of the Portsmouth City Council Bill, which proposed to prohibit the export of live animals through Portsmouth, the Speaker ruled that since the bill affected ports other than Portsmouth and raised the question of public policy with regard to the export of live animals, it could proceed only as a public bill. The bill was accordingly withdrawn.[5] Similar considerations arose on the Thames River Bill 1881 (p 795); West Riding County Council Bill 1908 (p 800); and the Aberfan Disaster Fund Bill 1979 (p 801).

In 1984, the Speaker declined to propose the question on the second reading of the Piece Hall, Halifax Bill because the provisions of the bill conflicted with the general law on Sunday trading.[6] Similarly, in 1986, the Speaker refused to allow the Lloyd's Bank (Merger) (Amendment) Bill to proceed because its terms were in conflict with recent industrial relations legislation.[7]

1 CJ (1900) 30, 124.
2 CJ ((1910) 31; HC Deb (1910) 14, c955.
3 HC Deb (1938–39) 343, c952 and 1091; CJ (1938–39) 78.
4 CJ (1958–59) 113; HC Deb (1958–59) 600, cc787–788; CJ (1959–60) 102; HC Deb (1959–60) 617, cc199–200.
5 CJ (1979–80) 343; HC Deb (1979–80) 977, c1100.
6 CJ (1983–84) 323; HC Deb (1983–84) 53, c120.
7 CJ (1985–86) 148; HC Deb (1985–86) 90, c1075.

(2) Private bills allowed to proceed

In 1896, on the second reading of the Belfast Corporation Bill (to extend the city of Belfast and for other purposes), it was objected that, as the bill dealt with very large interests, embraced a very large area, and also repealed important sections in certain public Acts, it ought not to have been introduced as a private bill. But the Speaker stated that, although the bill referred to a public matter, and sought to enact that public statutes should not apply or should be partially repealed, these provisions were not so numerous or so important as to necessitate its introduction as a public bill.[1]

In 1899, objection was taken to proceeding with the Telegraph Act (1892) Amendment Bill, which was a private bill to enlarge the powers of the National Telephone Company under the provisions of the Telegraph Act 1892 on the ground that the area affected was the whole of the United Kingdom, that the bill established a new jurisdiction, and that the powers asked for should be granted, if at all, to the Postmaster-General. But the Speaker pointed out that the bill was of far narrower application than the London Valuation and Assessment Bill 1895, and that it proposed under certain conditions and in certain places to exempt a company, carried on for purposes of profit, from the operation of a particular subsection of a public Act, and he held that it would be in order, and in accordance with the action of the House on other occasions, that the bill should proceed as a private bill.[2]

In 1919 objection was taken on its second reading to the British and Continental Bank Bill [Lords] proceeding as a private bill, on the ground that it appropriated the London assets of a Russian bank for the benefit of creditors through the London branch to the detriment of creditors through its Russian headquarters and branches, and in this way raised issues affecting international relations, but the Speaker ruled that the bill affected private interests and was properly introduced as a private bill although the bearing of its proposals on public interests could be discussed.[3]

Public bills introduced in place of private bills withdrawn

When a private bill is withdrawn because it has been ruled to affect public interests which should have been dealt with by a public measure, a public bill for the same purpose has frequently been introduced in its place and passed, but a bill, begun as a private bill, cannot be taken up and proceeded with as a public bill.[4]

---

1 Parl Deb (1896) 38, c 335, and see HC Deb (1959–60) 617, cc 199–200.
2 Parl Deb (1899) 67, cc 1335–1338.
3 HC Deb (1919) 122, c 1281. See also the Metropolitan District Railways Bill 1864 (p 802), the Salford Hundred and Manchester (City) Courts of Record Bill 1868 (p 799) and the London County Council (Co-ordination of Passenger Traffic) Bill 1929, HC Deb (1928–29) 225, cc 1032–1052.
4 Middlesex Industrial Schools Bill 1865, Denison 182.

Public bills objected to on the ground that they should have been private bills

Since the passing in 1883 of standing orders providing for the examination of public bills by the Examiners (see pp 520–521), very few bills have been objected to on the ground that they should have been brought in on petition, though objection has frequently been taken that they should have been referred to the Examiners. It is, in any event, a more difficult task to argue that a public bill should have been brought in as a private bill than vice versa since many bills will contain some element of public policy which, while insufficient to debar a bill from proceeding as a private bill should it be introduced as such, could equally justify its introduction as a public bill. Furthermore it would appear that bills of a private nature may be properly introduced as public bills if there are no parties able to petition Parliament: for example, the Suffolk County Council Committees (Borrowing Powers) Bill 1893–94, was so introduced and proceeded with as a hybrid bill, at a time when county councils (except the London County Council) were not empowered to promote bills. Hybrid bills hardly distinguishable from private bills have sometimes been brought in by private Members.[1] Thus, in the examples quoted, no recorded cases of public bills being successfully objected to on the ground that they should have been brought in upon petition will be found in recent years, though Members have been dissuaded from bringing in bills which might have been so objected to. The examples which follow show whether the objections have been overruled or have been sustained.

(i) Overruled. In 1873 a public bill was introduced for the protection and preservation of certain ancient monuments in various parts of the country, the monuments in question being enumerated in the schedule to the bill.[2] Objections were raised that, as the bill affected the property of persons upon whose land those monuments were situated, it should have been brought in as a private bill, but its nature and objects were obviously of a public character, and it concerned too many counties and localities to be treated as a private bill, nor were any of its objects such as are contemplated by the standing orders or referred to in them.[3]

In 1873 exception was taken to the Union of Benefices Bill on the ground that, as it deprived certain parishes of powers which they possessed under the Union of Benefices Act 1860, it ought to have been brought in as a private bill or to be treated as a hybrid bill, but it was held to be strictly a public bill.[4]

Other instances are: the Weighing of Grain (Port of London) Bill 1864,[5] the Brokers (City of London) Bill 1870,[6] and the Criminal Justice Administration (Amendment) Bill 1959 (p 799).

---

1 Orkney and Zetland Small Piers and Harbours Bill 1896; Fisheries Acts (Norfolk and Suffolk) Amendment Bill 1896; County of Suffolk Bill 1904; Remission of Surcharges (Dublin) Bill 1909; Mercantile Marine Memorial Bill 1927; Epsom and Walton Downs Regulation (Amendment) Bill 1953.
2 Ancient Monuments Bill, CJ (1873) 11, 13, 191, etc.
3 See also Parl Deb (1874) 218, c 574; ibid (1875) 223, c 879.
4 Parl Deb (1873) 214, cc 282, 507.
5 Parl Deb (1864) 176, cc 171–172.
6 CJ (1870) 83, 104, Parl Deb (1870) 202, c 740.

(ii) Sustained. In 1825 notice was taken that the Dunleary Harbour Bill and the College Lands Mortgage Bill ought to have been brought in upon petition and notices given as being private bills. In each case the order of the day was discharged and the bill withdrawn.[1]

ALTERNATIVES TO PROCEEDING BY PRIVATE BILL

As a result of the passing of Acts of Parliament under which alternatives to proceeding by private bill have been made available, parties are now enabled, for a large number of various purposes, to make use of the provisions of these Acts instead of having to apply for special powers by means of a private bill. This object has been achieved:

(1) by amendments in the general law which have facilitated various kinds of objects or furthered particular classes of undertakings or interests, and by the passing of general Acts the provisions of which may be applied to local authorities either by adoption by the local authority or by departmental order;

(2) by the establishment and extension of the system of provisional orders;

(3) by the institution of orders subject to special parliamentary procedure under the Statutory Orders (Special Procedure) Acts 1945 and 1965 and bills presented in pursuance of those Acts; and

(4) by the passing, in 1899, of the Private Legislation Procedure (Scotland) Act, since consolidated by the Private Legislation Procedure (Scotland) Act 1936.[2]

(1) Amendments in the general law and adoptive Acts

The following are some of the principal general Acts relating to matters which formerly have been the subjects of private Acts of Parliament: the Tithe Commutation Acts, the Acts for the enfranchisement of copyholds, the Joint Stock Companies Acts, the Acts for the regulation and management of railway companies, the Settled Estates and Settled Land Acts, the Acts relating to entail in Scotland, the Endowed Schools Acts, the Naturalization Act, the Divorce and Matrimonial Causes Acts, the Education Acts, the Municipal Corporation Acts, the Public Health Acts, the Local Government Acts for England and Wales and Scotland, the Water Act 1945, the Town and Country Planning Act 1947, the Trustee Investments Act 1961, the Local Government (Miscellaneous Provisions) Act 1976 and the Local Government (Miscellaneous Provisions) Act 1982.

(2) Provisional orders

By the various statutes which authorize procedure by provisional order, many of the government departments are empowered to make provisional orders, which are practically bills and which have only to be confirmed in an Act of Parliament in order to become law. Most of these orders confer

---

1 CJ (1825) 490 and 491.

2 For further short-lived experiments which to some extent superseded private bills see CJ (1929–30) 128, etc. (certified bills) and schemes under the Public Works Facilities Act 1930, s 1, which existed in Sessions 1930–31 to 1933–34; CJ (1930–31) 57, etc; CJ (1932–33) 22.

powers or secure objects for which a private bill was formerly necessary (see chapter 38). It should, however, be observed here that, in addition to their powers of making provisional orders, many government departments have also been invested with delegated powers of legislation in matters which would otherwise have been the subject of legislation by Act, and are empowered in numerous cases to make orders which are not provisional, that is to say which do not require confirmation in an Act of Parliament (see pp 538 ff).

(3) Special procedure orders

The provisional order system has itself been largely superseded by a system of special procedure orders under the Statutory Orders (Special Procedure) Acts 1945 and 1965. This differs from the provisional order system in that a confirming bill is not normally required. The Act protects private interests by providing for the deposit of petitions against the order, which may be considered by a joint committee in certain circumstances (see chapter 38).

(4) Private Legislation Procedure (Scotland) Act

By the Private Legislation Procedure (Scotland) Act which was passed in 1899, parties were provided with a new and compulsory procedure for obtaining parliamentary powers in regard to almost every matter affecting public or private interests in Scotland for which they were entitled to apply by means of a private bill. The special machinery, which thus virtually took the place of procedure by private bill, centres in the powers conferred by the Act upon the Secretary for Scotland (as he then was) of issuing orders which are subsequently confirmed by Parliament in a bill.

The Act of 1899 and an amending Act of 1933 were consolidated by the Act of 1936 which now governs procedure (see chapter 39).

CHAPTER 34

Preliminary proceedings in both Houses on private bills

DEPOSIT OF PETITIONS FOR BILLS

For every private bill—in whichever House it is eventually presented—a petition, signed by the parties (or some of them) who are promoters for the bill, must be duly deposited in the Private Bill Office of the House of Commons on or before 27 November, with a printed copy of the proposed bill annexed; and a printed copy of every such bill must also be deposited, on or before the same date, in the Office of the Clerk of the Parliaments, House of Lords.[1] For circumstances in which the deposit of a petition for a late bill may be authorized, see pp 829–830.

CONTENT AND FORM OF BILLS

In preparing their bills for deposit the promoters must be careful that no provisions are inserted which infringe standing orders, and that clauses which the standing orders require to be inserted are inserted.[2] If the bill is for any of the purposes to which the provisions of any of the 'Clauses Acts'[3] are applicable, those provisions are invariably incorporated by reference, subject to such exceptions and variations as may be thought necessary or desirable.

The principal 'Clauses Acts' are the Companies Clauses Consolidation, Lands Clauses Consolidation, and Railways Clauses Consolidation Acts, 1845, the Markets and Fairs Clauses, Commissioners Clauses, Harbours, Dock and Piers Clauses, Towns Improvement Clauses, Cemeteries Clauses, and Town Police Clauses Acts 1847, and the Electric Lighting (Clauses) Act 1899. These Acts, as stated in the preambles, were passed, 'as well for avoiding the necessity of repeating such provisions in each of the several Acts relating to such undertakings, as for ensuring greater uniformity in the provisions themselves.' Some of them are amended by subsequent Acts.

Model clauses

In 1948, in order to secure further uniformity in the drafting of private bills, an unofficial committee was appointed jointly by the Chairman of Committees in the House of Lords and the Chairman of Ways and Means in the

---

1 SO 2, 2A (HC); SO 2 and 38 (HL). Under SO 194A (HC) every petition for a private bill, together with the copy of the proposed bill annexed thereto, is open to inspection by all parties.
2 See eg SO 155 (HC).
3 See Bigg *Clauses Consolidation Acts*.

House of Commons. The purpose of the committee, which included the Counsel to the Lord Chairman, the Speaker's Counsel, representatives of Government departments and parliamentary agents, was to revise and consolidate earlier work on model bills and standard clauses.

In 1953 the committee published a volume of Model Clauses dealing with matters of local legislation such as lands, streets and buildings, sanitary matters, public buildings and parks, and other subjects which appeared frequently in private bills. Revised editions were published in 1957, 1960, 1963 and 1968. Introductions to the book point out that the inclusion of a clause in the book does not justify its inclusion in a bill.[1] It is merely a guide to the form in which, if included, the clause should be drafted. In the 1963 edition the two Chairmen explained that all clauses in a private bill require proof of local need.[2]

STANDING ORDERS (PRIVATE BUSINESS)

Compliance before presentation of bill

The requirements of the standing orders, which are to be complied with by the promoters of private bills before the bill is presented, were conveniently arranged by the Commons in 1847 in the following order; and a similar arrangement has since been adopted by the House of Lords:

(1) Notices by advertisement.
(2) Notices to owners, lessees, and occupiers.
(3) Documents required to be deposited and the times and places of deposit.[3]
(4) Plans, books of reference, sections, and cross-sections.

Compliance with these standing orders, so far as applicable, must be proved as respects every private bill, except a personal bill.

The requirements of the two Houses relating to notices and deposit of documents, plans, etc, are now, mutatis mutandis, practically identical.

Compliance after presentation of bill

In addition to the standing orders above alluded to, there are others (Standing Orders 60–68 of both Houses), the compliance with which is proved after the bills have been presented to Parliament (see pp 865–868).

Compliance proved before the Examiners

Compliance with the standing orders was formerly required to be separately proved—in the Commons, before the committees on petitions for private bills, and in the Lords, before the Standing Orders Committee. But in 1846

---

1 On the recommendation of the Joint Committee on Private Bill Procedure, HL 14, 58, HC 139 (1954–55). The Joint Committee on the Promotion of Private Bills also called attention to the words (see Report, HL 176, HC 262 (1958–59)).

2 See also Report of Joint Committee on Promotion of Private Bills, ibid para 17.

3 As to the custody, and as to facilities for the inspection of, documents directed to be locally deposited under the standing order cf the Local Government Act 1972 (ss 225, 228) and SO 27.

the House of Commons provided, by standing order, for the appointment of one or more 'Examiners of petitions for private bills',[1] instead of the committees previously appointed. A few years later, in 1854, the Lords resolved, 'That there shall be one or more officers of this House, to be called "the Examiners for standing orders",' to examine into certain of the facts required to be proved before their Standing Orders Committee; they then appointed as their Examiners the gentlemen who held the office of Examiners of petitions in the House of Commons; and finally, in 1858, they entrusted to these officers the same powers which they exercised as Examiners for the Commons. This arrangement has enabled the Examiners to take the evidence on behalf of both Houses simultaneously, and has removed the need for a double proof of all those orders, common to both Houses, with which parties, at extra expense and with an interval of some months between the proofs, were formerly obliged to prove compliance twice over. The two Examiners, therefore—appointed by the House of Lords and the Speaker—now conduct, for both Houses, the preliminary investigations formerly carried out separately in each House: they adjudicate upon all facts relating to the compliance or non-compliance with the standing orders: and, where they find that standing orders have not been complied with, the Standing Orders Committee in each House determines, upon the facts as reported by the Examiners, whether these orders ought or ought not to be dispensed with (see pp 819–822, 933).[2]

PERSONAL BILLS (STANDING ORDER 191A (HC); STANDING ORDER 3 (HL))

The standing orders of the two Houses relating to personal bills take account of the practice that such bills originate in the House of Lords (see p 943). Under Standing Order 3 (HL), when an application is made for leave to bring in a bill relating to 'the estate, property, status or style, or otherwise relating to the personal affairs, of an individual', the Chairman of Ways and Means in the House of Commons and the Chairman of Committees in the House of Lords may, on an application being made, certify that the proposed bill conforms to this description and that the standing orders relating to notices, dates of deposit, etc should not apply to it.[3] If the Chairmen so certify, the proceedings in the House of Lords are governed thereafter by the provisions of Part VII of the standing orders of that House (see pp 942–946). When the bill has been passed by the Lords, it is sent to the House of Commons and, in accordance with Standing Order 74 (HC), read the first time in that House and referred to the Examiners. If the Chairman of Ways and Means reports to the House that the bill as brought from the Lords relates to the estate, property, status or style, or otherwise relates to the personal affairs, of an individual and that the standing orders relating to

---

1 Now SO 69; and cf Report of Select Committee for Revision of the Standing Orders 1846, CJ (1846) 1262; and Williams i, 74.

2 Two additional Examiners were appointed in 1976–77 in connection with the examination of the Aircraft and Shipbuilding Industries Bill (CJ (1976–77) 44, 233; LJ (1976–77) 38, 355).

3 For private bills which have not been treated as name, estate, or personal bills, but on which it was reported that no standing orders were applicable, see Ascot Authority Bill [Lords], LJ (1913) 154; Rhodes Estate Bill [Lords], LJ (1916) 137; CJ (1916) 114.

notices, dates of deposit, etc, should not apply thereto, the order referring the bill to the Examiners is discharged and the bill is ordered to be read a second time. Subject to some special provisions in the standing orders (see pp 835, 840, 885), the bill then proceeds as an ordinary private bill.[1]

GENERAL LIST OF PETITIONS (STANDING ORDER 194 (HC))

When all the petitions for private bills, with printed copies of the bills annexed, have been deposited, on or before 27 November, in the Private Bill Office of the House of Commons, and printed copies of the bills have been deposited, on or before the same date, in the Parliament Office in the House of Lords (Standing Order 38 (HL)), 'The General List of Petitions for Private Bills' is prepared. The petitions are numbered, and arrangements are made for them to be heard by the Examiners, the convenience of the parties being the primary consideration in arranging the order in which they are heard.

MEMORIALS COMPLAINING OF NON-COMPLIANCE

In respect of petitions for bills numbered in the general list

When the time has expired for depositing documents and complying with other preliminary conditions, parties interested are enabled to judge whether the standing orders of the two Houses have been complied with. If it should appear to them that the promoters have neglected to comply with any of these orders, parties may prepare memorials, addressed to the Examiners, complaining of such non-compliance. These memorials, in respect of petitions for bills which have been deposited on or before 27 November, have to be deposited in the Private Bill Office of the House of Commons on or before 17 December, with two copies of each memorial for the use of the Examiners, as laid down by Standing Order 75 (HC). Under Standing Order 107A (HC), where the Examiners report that standing orders have not been complied with, only those parties who have deposited memorials may appear before the Standing Order Committee to argue that the standing orders concerned should not be dispensed with.

In respect of petitions for bills deposited after 27 November

Standing Order 75 (HC) also prescribes that memorials in respect of petitions for bills deposited after 27 November are to be deposited not later

1 In the case of the Valerie Mary Hill and Alan Monk (Marriage Enabling) Bill [Lords] (1984–85), the Speaker directed that the requirement to print the bill for its progress through the Commons should be dispensed with.

than the fourth day before the day appointed for the examination of the petition or, if the House is not sitting on that day, on or before the next day on which the House sits. Standing Order 78 (HL) prescribes that such memorials shall be deposited before twelve o'clock on the day preceding that appointed for the examination.

In respect of petitions for additional provision, etc

Standing Order 75 (HC) and Standing Order 78 (HL) also deal with memorials in respect of petitions for additional provision. The Commons' order also includes bills referred to the Examiners after second reading, bills brought from the Lords or bills presented by leave of the House in lieu of others withdrawn; while the Lords' order includes bills referred to the Examiners after first or second reading or by direction of the Chairman of Committees. All these memorials are to be deposited before twelve o'clock on the day preceding that appointed for the examination. Under Standing Order 75 (HC) and Standing Order 76 (HL), the Examiner is at liberty to entertain the memorial, although it is not signed by the party specially affected by the non-compliance with the standing orders.

Preparation of memorials

Memorials complaining of non-compliance are prepared in the same form, and are subject to the same general rules, as petitions to the two Houses (see pp 754–758), as well as to other special rules, which are noticed on pp 817–818.

Withdrawal of memorials

Standing Order 76A (HC) and Standing Order 79 (HL) provide that a memorialist may withdraw his memorial if he deposits a requisition, duly signed by himself or by the agent who deposited the memorial, in the Private Bill Office of the House of Commons or the Office of the Clerk of the Parliaments, as the case may be. Where a memorial has been signed by more than one person, any person who has signed may withdraw from the memorial by signing and depositing a similar requisition.

SITTINGS OF THE EXAMINERS

The public sittings of the Examiners begin on 18 December, unless that day falls on a Saturday or Sunday, in which case they begin on the Monday following, Standing Orders 71 (HC) and 70 (HL). Each Examiner sits separately and usually deals with half the total number of petitions.

Notice of examination

The Examiner is required by Standing Order 72 (HC) and Standing Order 71 (HL) to give at least seven clear days' notice of the day appointed for the examination of each petition.

Striking off and reinsertion of petitions (Standing Orders 72, 106 (HC))

If the promoters do not appear at the time when their petition is to be heard, the Examiner is required to strike the petition off the General List of Petitions. The petition cannot afterwards be reinserted on the list, except by order of the House; and if the promoters desire to proceed with the bill, they must deposit a petition, praying that the petition for the bill may be reinserted, and explaining the circumstances in which it was struck off. This petition will stand referred to the Standing Orders Committee, who will determine, upon the statement of the parties, whether or not the promoters have forfeited the right to proceed, and will report to the House accordingly.[1] If by the order of the House the petition for the bill is reinserted in the General List, the usual notice will be given by the Examiner, and the case will be heard at the time he appoints.

Statement of proofs

When the case is called, the agent soliciting the bill appears before the Examiner with a 'statement of proofs', showing all the requirements of the standing orders applicable to the bill which have been complied with, and the name of every witness, opposite each proof, who is to prove the matters stated therein. If the bill is opposed on the question of compliance with standing orders, the agents for the memorialists are required to enter their appearances[2] upon each memorial, at this time, in order to entitle them to be heard subsequently. Neither promoters nor memorialists are entitled to be heard by counsel.[3]

Formal proofs

In the meantime the 'formal proofs', as they are termed, proceed generally in the same manner, both in opposed and unopposed cases. Each witness is examined by the agent, who produces all affidavits and other necessary proofs, in the order in which they are set down in the statement, one fair copy of which is supplied for the Examiner, and another for the clerk to the Examiner. In addition to the proofs comprised in the statement, the Examiner may require such other explanations as he may think fit, to satisfy himself that all the orders of the House have been complied with.

---

1 CJ (1874) 73.
2 The appearance is a paper, which is previously obtained from the Private Bill Office, certifying that the agent has entered himself at that office as agent for the memorial. This appearance is given to the Clerk of the Examiners.
3 SOs 74A, 75 (HC); 76 (HL).

Proof by affidavit (Standing Order 77 (HC), Standing Order 80 (HL))

Under the standing orders of both Houses, the Examiner may admit affidavits in proof of compliance with the standing orders, or may require further evidence.

Unopposed cases

In an unopposed case the Examiner can at once give his decision whether the standing orders have, or have not, been complied with, and make his report accordingly.

Opposed cases

In an opposed case, when the formal proofs have been completed, the Examiner proceeds to hear the memorialists. The agents for the latter ordinarily take no part in the proceedings upon the formal proofs; but if they desire that any of the promoters' witnesses who have proved the deposit of documents, the service of notices, or other matters, should be detained for further examination, in reference to allegations of error contained in the memorials, the Examiner directs them to be in attendance until their evidence is required.

Attendance of witnesses

The attendance of witnesses is ordinarily secured by the parties themselves; but if the Examiner should report to the House that the attendance of any necessary witness, or the production of any document, cannot be procured without the intervention of the House, the House will make an order accordingly.[1]

Hearing of parties on a memorial (Standing Orders 75, 76 (HC), Standing Orders 76, 77 (HL))

Any parties are entitled to be heard by themselves or their agents upon a memorial, addressed to the Examiner, complaining of non-compliance with the standing orders, provided that the matter complained of be specifically stated in the memorial, that the party (if any) or his agent who may be specially affected by the non-compliance with the standing orders has signed the memorial and has not withdrawn his signature, and that the memorial has been duly deposited. In the case of certain bills which are referred to the Examiners under the 'Wharncliffe' standing orders of both Houses (pp 865–868), any proprietor or member of any company, society, association, or partnership, who has by himself, or by any person authorized to act for him in that behalf, dissented at any meeting called in pursuance of these standing orders, is entitled to appear and be heard by the Examiner by himself or his agent, upon a memorial addressed to the Examiner complaining of non-compliance with the 'Wharncliffe' standing orders.

---

1 Wandle Water and Sewerage Bill, CJ (1852–53) 257; Bristol and North Somerset Railway (Southern Extension) Bill, ibid (1866) 114, 127.

Specific statements of non-compliance required

Unless the matters complained of are specifically stated in the memorial, the memorialists are not entitled to be heard, and the utmost care is consequently required in drawing memorials. When a memorial complains of more than one breach of the standing orders, it is divided into distinct allegations. Each allegation should specifically allege non-compliance with the standing orders, and should state the circumstances of such alleged non-compliance, in clear and accurate language.

Preliminary objections

When the agent for a memorial rises to address the Examiner, the agent for the bill may raise preliminary objections to his being heard upon the memorial, on any of the grounds referred to in the standing orders, or on account of violations of the rules and usage of Parliament, or other special circumstances. Such objections are distinct from any subsequent objections to particular allegations. It has been objected, for example, that a memorial has not been duly signed so as to entitle the parties to be heard. No proof of the signatures, however, is required in any case, unless there should be some prima facie reason for doubting their genuineness. The same rule is applied to the fixing of a corporate seal.

Memorials subject to same rules as petitions

On 16 February 1846 an instruction was given to the committee on petitions for private bills (the predecessors of the Examiners) not to hear parties on any petition 'which shall not be prepared in strict conformity with the rules and orders of this House'.[1] As memorials addressed to the Examiner have taken the place of petitions to the House complaining of non-compliance with the standing orders, the Examiners have applied to them all the parliamentary rules applicable to petitions (see pp 754–758).

Preliminary objections to allegations

If no preliminary objection is taken to the general right of the memorialists to appear and be heard, or if the objection is overruled, the agent proceeds to read the first allegation in his memorial. Preliminary objections can be raised to any allegation; for example, that it alleges no breach of the standing orders; that it is uncertain, or not sufficiently specific; or that the party specially affected or his agent has not signed the memorial, or has withdrawn

---

1 CJ (1846) 147.

his signature. In connection with the latter grounds of objection, the signatures of parties specially affected are required in respect of such allegations only as affect parties personally, and in which the public generally has no interest. Thus if it is alleged that the name of any owner, lessee, or occupier of property has been omitted from the book of reference, or that he has received no notice, the Examiner will not proceed with the allegation, unless the party affected has himself signed the memorial. But the application of this rule depends on the particular circumstances of each case.

Objections on points affecting the public

There are, however, numerous grounds of objection which relate to matters concerning the more general public affected by the bill, and which do not therefore require the signatures of parties specially affected. Thus objections to the adequacy of newspaper notices, and objections to the accuracy of the plans, sections, and books of reference where the errors alleged can be clearly demonstrated in the documents themselves, or are separable from questions relating to personal property in lands and houses, have always been treated as public objections. The same principle has been applied to objections to the estimate, and to allegations that any documents have not been deposited in compliance with the standing orders. It is for public information and protection that all requirements of this character have to be complied with by the promoters of the bill; and any person is therefore entitled to complain of non-compliance on behalf of the public, without proving any special or peculiar interests of his own.

Questions of merits excluded

Allegations are to be confined to breaches of the standing orders, and may not raise questions about the merits of the bill, which are afterwards to be investigated by Parliament and by committees of both Houses. It may be shown, for example, that an estimate is informal, and not such an estimate as is required by the standing orders: but the inadequacy of the amount of the estimate is a question of merits, over which the Examiner has no jurisdiction.

DECISIONS OF THE EXAMINERS

Communication of Examiners' decisions

The Examiner decides upon each allegation, explaining to parties, whenever it is necessary, the grounds of his decision. The decisions of the Examiners upon the petitions for private bills are communicated to both Houses in the following form:

(a) To the House of Commons. By Standing Order 70 (HC) the Examiner is required to report to the House whether Standing Orders 4 to 59 have or have not been complied with in respect of every petition for a private bill. He thus reports to the House on petitions for bills which are to originate in the House of Lords as well as those which are to originate in the House of Commons (see pp 828–829). Where the standing orders have not been

complied with, he must also report the facts upon which his decision is founded and any special circumstances connected with the case.

(b) To the House of Lords. The provisions of Standing Order 72 (HL), which also apply to bills originating either in that House or in the House of Commons, prescribe that the Examiner should certify in each case whether the standing orders have or have not been complied with, such certificate to be deposited in the Office of the Clerk of the Parliaments. In cases of non-compliance he must report the facts upon which his decision is founded and any special circumstances.

Special report from the Examiners (Standing Order 79 (HC), Standing Order 81 (HL))

Under standing orders of both Houses, if the Examiner feels doubts as to the true construction of any standing order in its application to a particular case, he is to make a special report of the facts, without deciding whether the standing order has or has not been complied with. This report is referred to the Standing Orders Committee in each House.[1]

STANDING ORDERS COMMITTEE (HOUSE OF COMMONS)[2]

The composition of the Standing Orders Committee is prescribed by Standing Order 103 (HC). It consists of the Chairman of Ways and Means, who is ex officio chairman of the committee, the Deputy Chairmen, and eight members nominated by the Committee of Selection at the beginning of every session. The quorum of the committee is three, and the committee has the assistance of the Counsel to Mr Speaker.

Examiners' reports referred (Standing Order 104 (HC))

All the reports of the Examiners of Petitions for Private Bills in which they report that the standing orders have not been complied with are referred to the Standing Orders Committee, irrespective of whether the bills to which the reports relate are to originate in the Lords or in the Commons. The committee has to determine and to report to the House, in each case, whether the standing orders not complied with ought or ought not to be dispensed with, and whether, in its opinion, the parties should be permitted to proceed with their bill, or any portion of it, and upon what terms and conditions (if any).

When the Examiner has found that the standing orders have not been complied with in the case of a petition for a bill, and the Standing Orders Committee of the House in which the bill originates has reported that they

---

1 Great Grimsby Street Tramways Bill, CJ (1900) 64–5, 95, LJ (1900) 36, 70; Durham County Water Board Bill [Lords], CJ (1933–34) 49; Sunderland Corporation Bill (petition for additional provision), CJ (1934–35) 160, 173, LJ (1934–35) 142, 169; City of London (Tithes) Bill, CJ (1946–47) 56, 116, LJ (1946–47) 50, 106; British Transport Docks (Felixstowe) Bill, CJ (1975–76) 195, 217–18, LJ (1975–76) 221, 241. See also LJ (1914) 91 for similar proceedings in the case of a provisional order bill.
2 The Standing Orders Committee of the House of Lords is described on p 933.

should be dispensed with, the Standing Orders Committee of the second House does not defer its decision until the bill reaches its House, but at once considers and pronounces upon the Examiner's report also. By adopting this course it obviates the possibility of a promoter proceeding with his bill through the first House and then finding its subsequent progress barred by a different decision being given, upon its reaching the second House, from that of the Standing Orders Committee in the first House. In practice, the view taken by both committees in these cases has, as a rule, been the same.[1]

Examiners' special reports referred (Standing Order 104 (HC))

All special reports made by the Examiner are also referred to the Standing Orders Committee. In any case where the Examiner has made a special report under Standing Order 79 as to the construction of a standing order, the committee has to determine, according to its construction of the order, and on the facts stated in the report, whether the standing orders have or have not been complied with; and it either reports to the House that the standing orders have been complied with or, if not complied with, proceeds to consider whether the standing orders ought to be dispensed with and reports to the House accordingly.[2]

In 1901 a special report made by the Examiner regarding a provisional order bill (originating in the Commons) which had been referred to him by that House after being reported from a committee, was referred to the Standing Orders Committee who reported that no standing orders not previously inquired into were applicable.[3]

Proceedings of the Standing Orders Committee

According to the usual practice of the committee, written statements are prepared by the agent for the bill, and in opposed cases by the agent for the bill on the one side, and on the other by the agents for memorialists who have been heard by the Examiner. The statements are circulated by the agents to members of the committee and copies are deposited in the Chairman of Ways and Means' office in advance of the meeting. The committee, if it thinks fit, hears the agents or parties before deciding whether the standing orders ought or ought not to be dispensed with, and whether the parties should be permitted to proceed with their bill, and upon what terms and conditions (if any). The parties are called in and acquainted with the decision of the committee, which is afterwards reported to the House.

Under Standing Order 107A the committee is authorized, if it thinks fit, to hear only certain parties. If the committee is considering an Examiner's report or special report referred to it under Standing Order 104 (see above), it may hear the promoters of the bill and any memorialist who has appeared

---

1 For cases in which divergent views were taken, see Nottinghamshire and Derbyshire Traction, Petition for Bill, CJ (1946–47) 127, LJ (1946–47) 144; Great Northern London Cemetery (Crematorium), Petition for Bill, CJ (1952–53) 96, LJ (1952–53) 58; St. John d'el Rey Mining Company, Petition for Bills, CJ (1959–60) 166, LJ (1959–60) 170; Clerical, Medical and General Life Assurance Society, Petition for Bill, CJ (1959–60) 185, LJ (1959–60) 192; Great Yarmouth Borough Council Bill [Lords] (petition for additional provision), CJ (1980–81) 333, LJ (1980–81) 452.
2 CJ (1934–35) 160, 173; ibid (1946–47) 56, 116; ibid (1975–76) 195, 217.
3 CJ (1901) 302, 307, 318.

before the Examiner. If the committee is considering a petition praying that any of the standing orders be dispensed with (see p 841) or that a petition for a private bill be reinserted in the General List (see p 815), it may hear the petitioner and any parties who have presented petitions in opposition to the petition. Standing Order 107A allows parties to be heard by themselves or to be represented by their agent, but the resolutions of the committee normally limit the number of speakers to one from each party in support of their statements, if the committee thinks fit.[1] In some inquiries of a special character which have been referred to the committee, however, it has also examined witnesses[2] before it has agreed to its report.

In 1986, in the case of a hybrid bill with regard to which the Examiners had reported a non-compliance, certain parties opposing the bill, who had not appeared before the Examiners, were allowed to appear before the Standing Orders Committee, their petition against dispensing with the standing orders having been specially referred to the committee by the House.[3]

Principles by which the Standing Orders Committee is guided

The committee, in its report to the House, does not explain the grounds of its determination; but the principles and general rules by which it is guided may be briefly stated. The report of the Examiner being conclusive as to the facts, it is the province of the committee to consider equitably, with reference to public interests and private rights, whether the bill should be permitted to proceed. If the promoters appear to have attempted any fraud upon the House, or to be chargeable with gross or wilful negligence, they will have forfeited all claim to a favourable consideration. But assuming them to have taken reasonable care in endeavouring to comply with the orders of the House, and that their errors have been the result of accident or inadvertence, not amounting to culpable negligence, their case will be considered according to its particular circumstances. Broadly speaking the committee take into account three questions; first, whether it is in the public interest, apart from that of the promoters, that the standing orders should be dispensed with; secondly, whether the promoters have been negligent and, thirdly, to what extent parties other than the promoters will be adversely affected. According to the general view which it may take of the whole of the circumstances, the committee will report either that the standing orders ought not to be dispensed with, or that they ought to be dispensed with and parties be permitted (subject, or not subject, to any conditions) to proceed with their bill.

Standing orders dispensed with and leave given to parties to proceed

If the Standing Orders Committee reports that the standing orders ought to be dispensed with, the House, by agreeing with the committee's resolution,

---

1 The minutes of speeches delivered before the Standing Orders Committee have been reported to the House and ordered to be printed, CJ (1985–86) 371.
2 Edinburgh and Perth Railway Bill, CJ (1847) 226, 293; and evidence printed at the expense of the parties, Edinburgh and Northern Railway Bill, ibid (1849) 37, 48, 70; Great Central Railway (Grimsby Fish Dock) Bill, recommitted resolution, ibid (1912–13) 134, 155, 162.
3 CJ (1985–86) 345 (Channel Tunnel Bill); cf CJ (1900) 320 (Military Manoeuvres Bill).

gives the parties leave to proceed; and where any conditions are specified in the committee's report, the necessary compliance with them is required to be proved, in ordinary cases, before the committee on the bill,[1] or, in some special cases, before the Examiners,[2] or partly before the committee and partly before the Examiners.[3] The agreement of the House to reports that the standing orders ought to be dispensed with is given formally, without the need for a motion to be made.[4]

Standing orders not to be dispensed with

If the Standing Orders Committee reports that the standing orders ought not to be dispensed with, its decision is generally acquiesced in by the promoters, and is fatal to the bill. But in order to leave the question still open for consideration, the House agrees to those resolutions only which are favourable to the progress of bills, and passes no opinion upon the unfavourable reports, which are merely ordered to lie upon the Table.

No recommendation by Standing Orders Committee

In 1986 the Standing Orders Committee declined to make a recommendation on whether the standing orders should be dispensed with, on the grounds that the matter ought to be decided by the House; and the House subsequently ordered such a dispensation.[5]

Decision of Standing Orders Committee objected to in the House

Occasionally, exception has been taken to a decision of the Standing Orders Committee, and the House has ordered that the case be referred back to them for consideration.

In 1886, in the case of the Felixstowe, Ipswich, and Midlands Railway Bill, the committee having refused to recommend dispensation with the standing orders, its resolution was referred back to it; and the committee then reported that the standing orders should be dispensed with, subject to certain proofs being given before the Examiner, and that the committee on the bill should report how far this condition had been complied with.[6]

In the case of the Filey Gas and Water Bill 1898, a resolution of the committee was referred back on the motion of the chairman of the committee, as some misconception had arisen as to its meaning.[7]

In 1911, in the case of a petition for additional provision in the Macclesfield and District Railless Traction and Electricity Supply Bill [Lords], the committee reported that the standing orders ought not to be dispensed with. The resolution was referred back to the committee which was given

---

1 CJ (1854) 78; ibid (1904) 38, ibid (1945–46) 169; CJ (1980–81) 333.
2 CJ (1849) 70 (as to deposit of amended notices); ibid (1849) 81, 84 (of estimate, etc); ibid (1886) 205 (of amended plans).
3 British Tramways (Extensions) Bill, CJ (1904) 99, 105.
4 HC Deb (1988–89) 148, cc 509–510.
5 CJ (1985–86) 371, 386–387.
6 CJ (1886) 196, 205. Cf also ibid (1887) 234, 244, 255; ibid (1919) 149, 165, 219, 229; HC Deb (1919) 117, c 1979.
7 Parl Deb (1898) 55, cc 726–727.

power to inquire whether there were any special circumstances which rendered it just and expedient that the standing orders should be dispensed with in respect of the petition. The committee reported that the standing orders ought to be dispensed with provided that an advertisement in terms prescribed by the committee was published in a local newspaper.[1]

In 1912, the Examiner's report that the standing orders had not been complied with in the case of the petition for the Great Central Railway (Grimsby Fish Dock) Bill [Lords] was referred to the committee who reported that the standing orders ought not to be dispensed with. Its report was referred back to it and it was given the same powers as in the previous case. The committee made a special report to the House, that it had satisfied itself from evidence given that the work proposed in the bill was a matter of urgent public importance. It accordingly recommended that compliance with the standing orders should be dispensed with, but did not desire its decision to be regarded as a precedent.[2]

The House has also referred back to the committee a resolution refusing to dispense with a particular standing order in the case of a petitioner against a bill[3] (see p 841). Motions to refer back resolutions to the committee have occasionally been negatived.[4]

In certain exceptional cases an alternative course was taken. For example, where all parties consented or where there was an urgent necessity for the bill to be passed in the current session, the promoters sought leave to deposit another petition for a bill. The committee reported to the House upon this petition whether, in its opinion, the parties should have leave to deposit a petition for a bill;[5] and, unless such leave were refused,[6] the petition for a bill was deposited in the Private Bill Office, and was examined and endorsed by the Examiner in the same manner as if it had been originally deposited at the prescribed time. The standing orders, previously reported not to have been complied with, were taken to have been dispensed with; and, unless any further breaches were discovered,[7] the Examiner reported that the standing orders had been complied with.

Special reports from Standing Orders Committee

The Standing Orders Committee has on occasion made a special report to the House.

In 1920 the Examiner reported in the case of certain tramway bills that Standing Order 22 (now 25) had not been complied with, inasmuch as the consent of some local authorities had not been obtained to the proposed tramways. The committee made a special report to the House that it did not feel justified in exercising its discretion in the matter without direction

---

1 CJ (1911) 225, 241, 252.
2 CJ (1912–13) 85, 134, 155, 162.
3 CJ (1905) 61, 117, 128.
4 CJ (1884–85) 296; ibid (1905) 177.
5 Manchester and Southampton Railway, CJ (1847) 220, 228, 269; Bagenalstown and Wexford Railway, ibid (1854) 77, 89, 120, 135; South London Railway, ibid (1860) 69, 94; Hastings Western Water, ibid (1861–62) 92, 139.
6 Southam Railway, CJ (1863) 68, 102.
7 CJ (1847) 474.

from the House. A motion was made in the House in favour of dispensing with the standing orders, to which a reasoned amendment was moved. The question that the words proposed to be left out stand part of the question was negatived, but the insertion of the alternative words could not be proceeded with owing to the interruption of business under Standing Order No 9 (Public). Acting on these proceedings in the House, the committee at a subsequent meeting resolved 'that Standing Order 22 (now 25) ought not to be dispensed with; that the parties be permitted to proceed with their bill, on condition that all the provisions as to tramways, to which Standing Order 22 (now 25) relates and which have not been complied with, be struck out of the bill; that the committee on the bill do report how far such order has been complied with'.[1]

In 1923 the Examiners made a special report in the case of the petition for the Londonderry and Lough Swilly Railway Bill, stating that they felt doubts as to the due construction of the standing orders in relation to the petition, inasmuch as the bill applied to the Irish Free State and Northern Ireland and they were unable to find any instructions in the standing orders directing them to deal with such a case, and further reported that the standing orders, if they did apply, had not been complied with. The committee made a special report to the House stating that it entertained grave doubts as to whether it was competent for the promoters, a company domiciled in Northern Ireland, to apply for a private bill in the House, if the subject-matter of the private bill related to the Irish Free State, and asked for directions from the House. Further action, however, was not taken by the House.[2]

In 1924 a similar bill which originated in the House of Lords contained a clause safeguarding the interests of the Irish Free State and was allowed to proceed.[3]

In 1959, a special report in respect of the Humber Bridge Bill was made by the committee recommending that Standing Order 146, in so far as it related to the height of fences, should be re-examined.[4] In the same session, the committee made a special report about a letter which had come to its attention in connection with its consideration of the British Transport Commission Bill.[5]

In 1976 the Examiners made a special report stating that they felt doubts as to the due construction of certain standing orders in relation to the British Transport Docks (Felixstowe) Bill and to a memorial complaining of non-compliance. In view of the complexity and unusual nature of the problems raised by the Examiners the committee embodied its conclusions in a special report.[6]

1 CJ (1920) 11, 53, 121, 134, 135.
2 CJ (1923) 148, 160; HC 77 (1923).
3 CJ (1924) 276.
4 CJ (1958–59) 205.
5 CJ (1958–59) 208.
6 CJ (1975–76) 195, 217–218.

Other duties of Standing Orders Committee (Standing Orders 105, 106 (HC))

The proceedings of the Standing Orders Committee in regard to reports from the Examiners will be referred to again, incidentally, when bills referred to the Examiners after presentation (see p 865) and petitions for additional provision (see pp 830–831) are dealt with. Besides the Examiners' reports, however, there also stand referred to the committee all petitions, which have been deposited in the Private Bill Office, praying that any of the standing orders of the House may be dispensed with,[1] or that petitions for private bills, which have been struck off the General List by the Examiners, may be reinserted,[2] and all petitions opposing the same; and the committee reports its opinion upon such petitions to the House. Other matters, also, are sometimes referred to the Standing Orders Committee;[3] and its duties in reference to clauses and amendments which may be referred to it, in accordance with Standing Order 182, will be noticed later (p 923).

COMMITTEE OF SELECTION (HOUSE OF COMMONS)

Under Standing Order 109 the Committee of Selection,[4] which was first appointed by resolution in 1839,[5] consists of nine Members, of whom the quorum is three. Recent practice has been to nominate the members of the committee for the duration of a Parliament.

The duties of the Committee of Selection in relation to public committees have been described in chapter 24. Its duties in relation to private business are laid down in Standing Orders 103, 109–118, 124, 131, 217, 228, 229 and 243 (HC), and a general outline of its proceedings is all that need be given here. The committee is responsible for nominating and filling vacancies on:

(a) The panel from which committees on unopposed private bills are selected.
(b) Committees on opposed private bills.
(c) The Standing Orders Committee.
(d) The parliamentary panel of Members to act as Commissioners under the Private Legislation Procedure (Scotland) Act 1936.
(e) Members to serve on joint committees on Scottish provisional order bills.
(f) Members to serve on joint committees on petitions against special procedure orders.

If so ordered by the House, the committee also nominates members of select committees on private and hybrid bills and members to serve on joint

---

1 Cf below, p 841.
2 Cf above, p 815; see also Private Business (1958–59) p 205.
3 In 1882, petitions presented by certain parties, praying that the Blackrock and Kingstown Tramways Bill might be referred to the Examiner to inquire as to the legality of the sealed bill produced before him in the proof of compliance with standing orders, were referred to the Standing Orders Committee, who reported thereon to the House, CJ (1882) 81, 95.
4 The Committee of Selection of the House of Lords is described on pp 584, 936.
5 CJ (1839) 67.

committees on private bills and fill any vacancy occurring amongst such members. In the exercise of its various duties, the Committee of Selection is empowered by Standing Order 118 to send for persons, papers and records. Further details of the committee's activities will be described in connection with the committal of bills.

SUPERVISION OF PRIVATE BILLS BY CHAIRMAN OF COMMITTEES AND CHAIRMAN OF WAYS AND MEANS

Supervision by the Lord Chairman and his Counsel

The office of Chairman of Committees in the Lords was first constituted in 1800, when the House resolved that it would, 'at the commencement of every session, proceed to nominate a Chairman of Committees of this House'.[1] According to a further resolution, which was passed at the same time, and is now embodied in Lords Standing Order No 58 (Public), the Lord so nominated 'shall take the chair in all Committees of the whole House, and in all other committees of the House, unless the House otherwise directs'.[2] So far as they are conferred upon him by this and other standing orders, the powers and duties of the Lord Chairman in regard to private bills will be noticed below (see also pp 933–934). The practical character which his supervision of all private bills has acquired, however, is attributable in part to the fact that it was exercised for nearly fifty years before the House of Commons in 1848 adopted a similar system and in part to the duty, which in practice has long rested primarily with the Lord Chairman, of moving the several stages of private bills in that House. When he moves the second or third reading of a bill, his action is an assurance to the House that in his opinion there is no objection to the passing of that particular stage. If he entertains such an objection, the stage is moved by another Lord, the Chairman stating his objection in the course of debate before the sense of the House is taken.

If any Lord opposes the second or third reading of a private bill, the stage is moved by another Lord and not by the Chairman, who is thus left free to express his opinion in debate.[3]

The Counsel to the Chairman of Committees was first appointed shortly after the office of Chairman was constituted in 1800, and he became a permanent salaried officer of the House of Lords in 1808.[4]

Copies of bills introduced into either House supplied to Lord Chairman

To facilitate his examination of private bills, copies are supplied to the Lord Chairman and his Counsel, upon its first deposit, of every private bill proposed to be introduced into either House. Copies are again supplied to them of the bill, in its 'filled-up' form[5] as proposed by the promoters to be

---

1 LJ (1800) 636.
2 In the Chairman's absence, one of the Lords appointed each session to the panel of Deputy Chairmen takes his place.
3 Cf Parl Deb (1906) 153, c 1053; HL Deb (1913) 14, c 91; ibid (1975–76) 375, c 1664.
4 LJ (1806–08) 792.
5 Cf SO 123 (HL).

submitted to a committee, and at every other stage upon which it is amended, or proposed to be amended, in either House. This practice is convenient to promoters of a bill originating in the Commons.It enables them to prepare amendments to give effect, during the progress of their bill through that House, to the observations of the Lord Chairman and his Counsel; and, unless the bill is opposed, its subsequent progress through the House of Lords is both easy and expeditious owing to the facilities thus afforded, before the bill has passed the Commons, of securing the insertion of amendments suggested by the authorities in the Lords.

Supervision by Chairman of Ways and Means and Speaker's Counsel

For many years after this supervision of private bills had been instituted in the Lords, the House of Commons did not feel the need to adopt any similar arrangement of its own; but, as private business increased in importance, the House gradually entrusted to the Chairman of Ways and Means many duties analogous to those performed by the Chairman of Committees in the House of Lords; and since 1848 he has been charged with the supervision of all private bills.[1] Under Standing Order 82 of the House of Commons, it is his duty, with the assistance of the Counsel to Mr Speaker, to examine all such bills whether opposed or unopposed, and to call the attention of the House, and also of the chairman of the committee on every opposed private bill, to all points which may appear to him to require it (see also p 890). To facilitate this examination, copies of every bill as originally deposited are required to be laid before him and the Speaker's Counsel not later than the day after the Examiner has examined the petition for the bill. Copies of every bill, and of amendments made or proposed to be made in it, are also required under Standing Orders 84 and 86–88 to be laid before him and the Speaker's Counsel, at various later stages in its progress through the House of Commons. The Chairman's duties and powers under these and other standing orders, eg 85, 181, 182, will be outlined when these later stages are described. Like the Lord Chairman he also moves the stages of private bills in the House, though this does not commit him to any particular view about the bill. The Chairman's duties in respect of a private bill in which he had an interest have been discharged by the Deputy Chairmen.[2]

The Counsel to Mr Speaker was originally appointed to assist the Speaker generally in any legal questions coming before him and to discharge certain other duties in accordance with the report of a select committee of 1838. It was not until 1850, as a result of another select committee in that year, that he was regularly associated with the Chairman of Ways and Means to assist in the examination of private bills.[3]

---

1 See Report of Select Committee on the Method of improving Private Business Procedure, 1847–48; HC Deb (1932–33) 280, c 1172; ibid (1935–36) 315, c 1423; ibid (1955–56) 548, c 446; and Williams i, 101.
2 HC Deb (1980–81) 995, c 767; CJ (1980–81) 43.
3 See reports of the Select Committee (House of Commons) on Private Business, 1838 and 1851, second report of the Select Committee to inquire into the working of the Preliminary Inquiries Acts, 1850, Clifford ii, 799, and Williams i, 95 ff; and report of the Select Committee on House of Commons Accommodation, etc, HC 184 (1953–54) pp 146–147.

DIVISION OF BILLS BETWEEN THE TWO HOUSES BEFORE PRESENTATION (STANDING ORDER 81 (HC), STANDING ORDER 90 (HL))

On or before 8 January in each year, the Chairman of Ways and Means or the Counsel to Mr Speaker seeks a conference with the Chairman of Committees of the House of Lords or his Counsel, for the purpose of determining in which House the respective private bills shall be first considered. Since this power has been delegated to the Chairmen, their decision as to the House in which a bill shall originate is final.[1] The examination of all private bills by the Chairmen and their Counsel begins in practice at an earlier date, as soon as the bills have been deposited in November; and, for convenience, the division of the bills between the two Houses is usually decided each year before Christmas. In the House of Commons, if the Chairman is unable to act, or the office of Chairman is vacant, the Counsel to Mr Speaker is authorized to act in his stead.[2]

Formerly, by far the greater number of private bills necessarily originated in the House of Commons because, by the privileges of the Commons, every bill which involves any pecuniary charge or burden on the people, by way of tax, rate, toll, or duty, ought to be first brought into that House (see p 742 ff). But, in accordance with a resolution of 1858, which has been made a standing order (Standing Order 191 (HC)), the House of Commons does not now insist upon its privileges, with regard to any provision of a private bill brought from the House of Lords, or returned by that House with amendments, on the ground that the provision authorizes or affects any toll or charge for services performed (not being in the nature of a tax). Standing Order 191 is applied to provisional order bills (p 870) by Standing Order 219, to confirmation bills presented under the Private Legislation Procedure (Scotland) Act 1936 (p 972) by Standing Order 228A, and to bills presented under the Statutory Orders (Special Procedure) Acts 1945 and 1965 (pp 962–963) by Standing Order 248A. Standing Order 191 has been held to apply to turnpike, harbour drainage, and other similar bills,[3] but not to hybrid bills.[4] It has been ruled not to extend to clauses in an improvement bill, which proposed to impose a tax upon all insurance companies having policies upon houses within the borough.[5]

With the removal of this obstacle, the private bills proposed to be introduced are now divided as equally as possible between the two Houses with a

1 Speaker's ruling, Parl Deb (1900) 78, c 695. For Chairman's report, CJ (1937–38) 67; ibid (1947–48) 89; ibid (1978–79) 75, etc.
2 For report from Mr Speaker's Counsel, see CJ (1924) 36; ibid (1924–25) 46; ibid (1950) 25. For report from the First Deputy Chairman, see CJ (1980–81) 43.
3 Reading and Hatfield Road Bill 1859; Wexford Harbour Commissioners Bill 1861; Melton Mowbray Navigation Bill 1877; Dearne Valley Water Bill 1880.
4 Lee River Conservancy Bill 1868.
5 On 8 May 1873, the Speaker called attention to clauses of this character in the Bradford Improvement Bill, which had been brought from the House of Lords; but 'as the promoters were not responsible for the introduction of the bill into the other House, and had signified their intention to withdraw these clauses, he submitted to the House that this course would be sufficient under the circumstances to repair the irregularity'. Upon this condition the bill was allowed to proceed. CJ (1873) 194; Parl Deb (1873) 215, c 1676.

view to general convenience. Competing bills normally originate in one and the same House so as to be considered together; and where a bill has been rejected previously in one House, a subsequent bill with similar objects normally originates in that House. It has been the practice for personal bills and consolidation bills to originate in the Lords.

DEPARTURES FROM USUAL PROCEDURE ON PRIVATE BILLS

The standing orders which regulate the deposit of private bills have already been described (see p 810). Certain departures from these rules are, however, authorized in some instances. For a case when the petitions for certain bills were deemed to have been deposited and the bills taken pro forma to the stage reached before dissolution, see p 930.

There have also been instances of such urgent necessity for legislation that a private bill has been brought in on motion: the standing orders have been suspended by order of the House, and leave given to bring in the bill.[1] In another case, a bill was subjected to a special procedure, in accordance with an order of the House.[2]

Petitions for bills deposited after time

If parties who have not deposited a petition for the bill before 27 November desire to solicit a private bill during the current session, they may apply to the Chairman of Ways and Means in the House of Commons and the Chairman of Committees in the House of Lords for leave to deposit a petition for a bill, explaining both the circumstances in which they have been prevented from complying with the orders of the House as to the deposit of the petition for the bill at the proper time and the desirability in the public interest of the provisions[3] and indicating the reasons of urgency which make it undesirable for them to delay the deposit of a petition until the following session.[4] If the Chairmen approve this application,[5] they authorize the promoters to deposit the petition for the bill, and indicate the House in which the bill will originate. Thereafter the petition for the bill is formally endorsed by the Chairman of the House of origin[6] and duly deposited in the Private Bill Office of the House of Commons or the Office of the Clerk of the Parliaments as the case may be. The bill then proceeds in the usual manner.

---

1 East London Railway (Payment of Debts) Bill, CJ (1878) 320; Metropolitan Board of Works (District Railway) Bill, ibid (1883) 242; Manchester Ship Canal Bill, ibid (1887) 276; Hull, Barnsley, and West Riding Junction Railway and Dock (No 2) Bill, ibid (1889) 295; Lancashire Union Railway (Mines) Bill, ibid (1894) 218.
2 London Passenger Transport Board (Finance) Bill 1935, CJ (1934–35) 252.
3 In 1955, the Chairman refused the application of the Huddersfield Corporation for a late bill on the ground that the provisions sought had already been rejected by a committee on another private bill.
4 In 1947 the National Union of Journalists were refused permission for a late bill on the ground of lack of urgency. A similar decision was taken in the case of the proposed University of Buckingham Bill in 1987. See also Cumberland County Council and Middlesex County Council applications, p 830 below, fn 1.
5 Supplementary information is sometimes called for, eg the application for a late bill by the Falmouth Docks and Engineering Company in 1958.
6 SO 2A (HC); SO 97 (HL).

The endorsement of the Chairman does not, however, excuse the petitioners from the results of their failure to comply with the requirements of the standing orders governing the time for depositing petitions for bills; nor does it in any way prejudge the case before the Examiner or the Standing Orders Committee.

The Chairman of Ways and Means and the Chairman of Committees in the House of Lords have indicated their reluctance to endorse a petition for a bill which contained provisions additional to those of an urgent nature. Such petitions should accordingly be confined to matters of urgency and should not be made the occasion for the introduction of a 'general purposes' bill.[1]

PETITION FOR ADDITIONAL PROVISION

If, after the presentation of a private (but not a hybrid[2]) bill in the first House, any additional provision is desired to be made in the bill in respect of matters to which the standing orders are applicable, a petition for that purpose, with a printed copy of the proposed provisions annexed, may be deposited in the Private Bill Office of the House of Commons or the Office of the Clerk of the Parliaments. The deposit of a petition for additional provision is conditional upon the approval by the Chairman of Ways and Means or the Chairman of Committees of an application, similar to that made for a late bill (see p 829), for leave to deposit the petition. Under Standing Order 166A (HC) and Standing Order 73 (HL) respectively, a petition to either House for additional provision requires the approval of the appropriate Chairman; and no petition which relates to a bill brought from the first House may be received.

Under Standing Order 73 (HC) and Standing Order 73 (HL) the petition is referred to the Examiners of petitions for private bills, who are required to give at least two clear days' notice of the day on which it will be examined.

Memorials complaining of non-compliance with the standing orders, in respect of the petition, may be deposited in the Private Bill Office, or the Office of the Clerk of the Parliaments, as the case may be, together with two copies thereof, before twelve o'clock on the day preceding that appointed for the examination of the petition; and the Examiner may entertain any memorial, although the party (if any) who may be specially affected by the

---

1 Eg in the Cumberland County Council (Water, etc) Bill 1947 (which subsequently became the North Cumberland Water Board Act 1947) 'general purposes' provisions, not of an urgent nature, were not allowed to proceed. In 1949, also, the two Chairmen granted leave in respect of only one of several provisions for which application was made to introduce a late bill by the Middlesex County Council.

2 In 1958, an instruction was moved by the Government to the committee on the Park Lane Improvement Bill (a hybrid bill), empowering it to make certain amendments which would have required an additional provision had they been made to a private bill. The bill as amended was subsequently referred to the Examiners and, after they had found a non-compliance with standing orders, to the Standing Orders Committees of both Houses who reported recommending that the Bill should be allowed to proceed, CJ (1957–58) 147, 153, 169. Similarly, the committee on another hybrid bill, the Channel Tunnel Bill 1985–87, was given power by instruction to make alternative provision for access by road to the terminal area, CJ (1985–86) 512. In the event, it did not exercise such a power, although the select committee in the Lords subsequently amended the bill to include such a provision.

non-compliance has not signed it (Standing Orders 75 (HC); 76, 78 (HL)).

After hearing the parties, in the same manner as in the case of an original petition for a bill, the Examiner reports to the House whether or not the standing orders have been complied with; and if the Standing Orders Committee reports that those standing orders with which the Examiner reports a non-compliance should be dispensed with, the promoters have leave, upon the resolution of that committee being agreed to by the House, to introduce their additional provision, if the committee on the bill thinks fit[1] or subject to any stated conditions.[2]

The procedure for withdrawing a petition for additional provision depends upon the stage which that petition has reached. In the Commons, if the petition has been endorsed, but has not yet been examined by the Examiner, the promoters may withdraw the petition by informing the Private Bill Office of their intention not to proceed. If the Examiner's report has been referred to the Standing Orders Committee, and the promoters inform the committee of their intention not to proceed with their petition, the committee has reported the fact to the House.[3] If at a later stage the promoters no longer wish to proceed with the provisions contained in the petition, they inform the committee on the bill accordingly.

WITHDRAWAL OF BILLS IN COMMONS

In the House of Commons, when a bill has been presented and read the first time, and any order as to its further stages has been made, if the promoters do not wish to proceed, that order is discharged by the House and a further order to withdraw the bill is made.[4] If the promoters decide not to proceed further with a petition for a bill, after the Examiner has reported non-compliance with the standing orders, and the report has been referred to the Standing Orders Committee, an order is made by the House, discharging the reference to the committee and withdrawing the petition for the bill.[5] In another case, the promoters informed the Standing Orders Committee that they did not intend to proceed with their bill, and the committee reported the fact to the House.[6] Where no such reference has been made, the promoters inform the Private Bill Office of their intention not to proceed, and a notice to that effect appears in Private Business.[7]

If the bill has originated in the Lords, no order is now made by the House for its withdrawal, but the order for the second reading or other stage is discharged;[8] a notice may also appear in Private Business that the bill will

---

1 CJ (1904) 79, 85; ibid (1937–38) 174; ibid (1947–48) 215, etc.
2 CJ (1934–35) 173.
3 CJ (1955-56) 32.
4 CJ (1929-30) 182, 184; ibid (1936-37) 193; ibid (1954–55) 115, ibid (1956–57) 106; ibid (1958–59) 188; ibid (1977–78) 179; Votes and Proceedings (1987–88), 8 February 1988.
5 CJ (1928–29) 122.
6 CJ (1905) 38.
7 Private Business (1936–37) 64, 65; ibid (1950) 5; ibid (1969–70) 55; ibid (1971–72) 45, 55; ibid (1978–79) 99; ibid (1988–89) 21, 31, 69.
8 Barmouth Urban District Council Bill [Lords], CJ (1938–39) 327; Mountbatten Estate Bill [Lords], ibid (1948–49) 291.

not be further proceeded with.[1] For withdrawal of bills in the House of Lords, see p 942.

PARLIAMENTARY AGENTS

The persons by whom the promotion of private bills, and the conduct of proceedings upon petitions against such bills, are carried out, are parliamentary agents. An important distinction is made between those parliamentary agents who are entitled to practise both in promoting and opposing bills and those who may oppose bills only. The former, who are normally members of existing firms of parliamentary agents, must apply for inclusion in the permanent register (Roll A) of parliamentary agents to the Speaker, who must first be satisfied that they are persons with practical knowledge of the Standing Orders and procedure of the House of Commons regulating private business. While an individual petitioner against a private bill may choose to conduct his case in person, societies or groups of persons may authorize an agent who is not on Roll A to act on their behalf in opposition to a specific bill. Such agents must attend the Private Bill Office to sign the sessional register (Roll B) of parliamentary agents, their registration ceases to be valid at the close of the session in which it was effected and, unless they are solicitors or have previously been registered as parliamentary agents, their application must be accompanied by a certificate of respectability from a member of parliament, justice of the peace, barrister or solicitor.

Rules relating to parliamentary agents and petitioners

Various duties and responsibilities are imposed by the orders of both Houses upon parliamentary agents; and in both Houses rules have been laid down to be observed by the officers of the House, and 'by all parliamentary agents and solicitors engaged in prosecuting proceedings in the House upon any petition or bill'.

These rules were originally laid down by the Speaker, by authority of the Commons in 1837,[2] and have been revised at intervals. In December 1952, new sets of rules, which slightly modified the previous system, were approved and issued by the Chairman of Committees in the Lords and the Speaker in the Commons. These rules are set out below in the form in which they were further revised and reissued in the Commons in 1982:[3]

1. In these rules—
    'bill' means—
    (a) any private bill;
    (b) any public bill with respect to which one of the Examiners of Petitions for Private Bills has reported that any of the Standing Orders numbered 4 to 68 relating to Private Business are applicable,
    and includes a provisional order or certificate against which a petition has been presented;
    'solicitor' includes a solicitor in England, Scotland or Northern Ireland and a writer to the signet;

---

1 Private Business (1938–39) 361.
2 CJ (1836) 819; ibid (1837) 113.
3 HC 397 (1981–82).

the expressions 'special procedure petition' and 'special procedure order' have the same respective meanings as in the Standing Orders numbered 238 to 248A relating to Private Business;

the expression 'counter-petition' has the same meaning as it has in Standing Order 244 (counter-petitions) relating to Private Business;

the expression 'petitioner in person' means a person who is engaged in opposing a bill or special procedure order on his own behalf and not on behalf of any other person.

2. There shall be kept in the Private Bill Office a register of the persons entitled to practise as parliamentary agents distinguishing those entitled so to practise both in promoting and opposing bills and those entitled so to practise in opposing bills only.

3. No person shall be entitled to practise as a parliamentary agent unless he is so registered:

Provided that a person so registered, if a member of a firm, may carry on his business as parliamentary agent under the name and style of the firm notwithstanding that one or more other members of the firm are not so registered, but partnership with a person who is so registered shall not entitle any partner not so registered to practise as a parliamentary agent.

4. No person shall be registered or admitted as a petitioner in person until he has subscribed before one of the clerks in the Private Bill Office a declaration in such form as the Speaker may prescribe engaging to obey and observe the orders and practice of the House of Commons and any rules prescribed by the Speaker, and also to pay and discharge from time to time when demanded all fees and charges due from the parties for whom he shall act or as the case may be from him.

5. Any person either before or after he has subscribed such a declaration shall, if required by the Speaker, enter into a recognisance or bond in a penal sum not exceeding £500, with two sureties each for half the penal sum, to observe the said declaration.

6. In the case of a firm, it shall suffice if one member of the firm subscribes the required declaration and enters into the required recognisance or bond on behalf of the firm.

7. No fee shall be payable in respect of the said declaration, recognisance, bond or registration.

8. No applicant shall be qualified to be registered as a parliamentary agent entitled to practise both in promoting and opposing bills unless he satisfies the Speaker that he has practical knowledge of the standing orders and procedure of the House of Commons regulating private business.

9. The Speaker may, if he thinks fit, appoint an advisory committee and refer to that committee for advice any question arising as to the qualifications of any applicant for registration.

10. No person shall be qualified to be registered as a parliamentary agent entitled to practise as such, in opposing bills only, unless he is actually employed in opposing a bill, and the registration shall cease to have effect on the close of the session in which it was effected.[1]

11. Any person possessing the required qualifications shall be entitled to be registered unless the Speaker otherwise directs:

Provided that unless he is a solicitor or has been previously registered as a parliamentary agent he must on his first application for registration produce to one of the clerks of the Private Bill Office a certificate of his respectability from a Member of Parliament, a justice of the peace, a barrister, or a solicitor.

12. Every application for registration must be in writing.

---

1 The requirement that any such agent should be registered anew if the bill were carried over to the next session was waived in the case of the Channel Tunnel Bill 1985–87, CJ (1985–86) 601.

13. No person's name shall be printed on any bill, as a parliamentary agent for such bill, unless and until his name has been duly inscribed upon the register of parliamentary agents.

14. No notice, except a notice given by a petitioner in person relating to his petition, shall be received in the Private Bill Office for any proceeding upon a petition or bill, until an appearance to act as the parliamentary agent upon the same shall have been entered in the Private Bill Office; in which appearance shall also be specified the name of the solicitor (if any) for such petition or bill.

15. Before any person desiring to appear by a parliamentary agent shall be allowed to appear or be heard upon any petition against a bill, an appearance to act as the parliamentary agent upon the same shall be entered in the Private Bill Office; in which appearance shall also be specified the name of the solicitor and of the counsel who appear in support of any such petition (if any counsel or solicitor are then engaged), and a certificate of such appearance shall be delivered to the parliamentary agent, to be produced to the committee clerk.

16. Except in cases where a bill is promoted or a petition is presented by two or more companies, bodies or persons separately interested, one parliamentary agent or firm of agents only shall be allowed to appear and to be heard in the proceedings on the bill on behalf of the promoters or the petitioners.

17. In case the parliamentary agent for any petition or bill shall be displaced by the solicitor thereof, or such parliamentary agent shall decline to act, the responsibility of such agent shall cease in respect of any fees incurred after that time upon a notice being given to the clerks in the Private Bill Office, and a fresh appearance shall be entered upon such petition or bill.

18. No written or printed statement relating to any bill shall be circulated within the precincts of the House of Commons[1] without the name of a parliamentary agent or petitioner in person attached to it, who will be held responsible for its accuracy.

19. The sanction of the Chairman of Ways and Means is required to every notice of a motion prepared by a parliamentary agent, for dispensing with any standing order of the House.[2]

20. A parliamentary agent shall not divide with or pay to any client, or any solicitor, clerk, officer, or servant of any client, any moneys which the agent at any time receives in respect of his costs, charges and expenses in promoting, opposing or otherwise dealing with any bill or provisional order, or give any commission or gratuity to any person in respect of his employment as a parliamentary agent.

21. Every parliamentary agent and solicitor or petitioner in person conducting proceedings in Parliament before the House of Commons shall be personally responsible to the House, and to the Speaker, for the observance of the rules, orders, and practice of Parliament, as well as of any rules which may from time to time be prescribed by the Speaker, and also for the payment of the fees and charges due and payable under the standing orders.

22. Any person registered as a parliamentary agent who shall act in violation of the orders and practice of the House of Commons or who shall be guilty of professional misconduct of any kind as a parliamentary agent shall be liable to an absolute or temporary prohibition to practise as a parliamentary agent at the discretion of the Speaker.

23. No person who has been suspended or prohibited from practising as a parliamentary agent or who otherwise than at his own request has been struck off the roll of solicitors or disbarred by any of the Inns of Court shall be allowed to be entered or retained on the register without the express authority of the Speaker.

---

1 Ie the Vote Office. See HC Deb (1957–58) 591, cc 31–34.
2 This includes motions to suspend proceedings on a bill from one session to another. See motions on Milford Haven Bill 1959, subsequently withdrawn, Private Business, 1958–59, p 341 ff.

24. These Rules shall apply with the necessary modifications to agents for special procedure petitions, agents for ministers of the crown responsible for laying special procedure orders before Parliament, agents for applicants for such orders and agents for counter-petitions and to petitioners in person in relation to special procedure orders.

Registry of agents (Standing Order 192 (HC))

The name and place of business of the parliamentary agent soliciting a bill are entered in the registers in the Private Bill Office, which are open to public inspection.

Members and officers of the House disqualified as agents

Besides these regulations, there are certain disqualifications for parliamentary agency. Members may not be agents, though they can deposit petitions on behalf of parties (see p 839). No officer or clerk in the service of either House is allowed to transact private business before the House, for his emolument or advantage, either directly or indirectly.[1]

Unqualified persons not entitled to call themselves parliamentary agents

In 1949 the Speaker drew the attention of the House to the fact that certain persons were representing themselves as parliamentary agents, without possessing the necessary qualifications. He referred to the rules on the subject, and stated that any person contravening them was liable to be dealt with by the House for a contempt.[2]

FEES PAYABLE ON PRIVATE BILLS

The fees which are chargeable in either House upon the various stages of private bills,[3] and are payable by the several parties promoting or opposing such bills, are specified in Appendix (C) to the standing orders of the House of Lords and in the Table of Fees annexed to the private business standing orders of the House of Commons.

Following a recommendation of the Joint Committee on Private Bill Procedure, 1954–55, the fees charged by both Houses were revised in 1956 and, mutatis mutandis, made identical.[4]

Half fees may be charged for proceedings in the two Houses on personal bills and bills relating to charitable, religious, educational, literary or scientific purposes from which no private profit or advantage is derived, and applications for such concessions in the House of Commons are submitted to the Speaker for his approval.[5]

---

1 HC 648 (1833) p 9; HC 606 (1835) pp 17, 19. Cf also Clifford ii, 878; Report, etc, of Joint Committee on Parliamentary Agency, HC 360 (1876); and O C Williams, *The Clerical Organization of the House of Commons*, pp 179–189, 234–235, 261–267.
2 HC Deb (1948–49) 464, c 1665.
3 For fees payable on provisional order bills and on special procedure orders, see p 964.
4 CJ (1955–56) 420; LJ (1955–56) 455.
5 Fees were remitted in both Houses without any petition in the case of the Red Cross and Order of St John Bill [Lords] in 1918. In 1604, counsel was assigned to a party, in a private bill, *in forma pauperis,* he 'being a very poor man', CJ (1547–1628) 241.

It is declared by the Commons in the Table of Fees that the 'fees shall be charged, paid and received at such times, in such manner and under such regulations as the Speaker shall from time to time direct'.

Hybrid bills

Fees are also chargeable on hybrid bills, though in some special cases, or where the objects of the bill were mostly of a public nature, they have been remitted; and petitioners against hybrid bills are charged with fees.[1]

Collection of fees

In both Houses there are officers whose special duty it is to take care that the fees are properly paid by the persons responsible; and the Speaker and the Chairman of Committees have power to prohibit, either absolutely or temporarily, an agent, who defaults in the payment of the fees of the House, from practising in that capacity (see Rules 21 and 22, p 834). Petitioners in person who have defaulted may be prevented from petitioning on a matter of private business on a future occasion until outstanding fees are paid.[2]

Application

All moneys arising from the fees may be treated as an appropriation in aid of the vote for the offices of the respective House, and an estimate of the amount is made annually for this purpose.

TAXATION OF COSTS

In connection with the passing of private bills, mention must also be made of the assessment and certification ('taxation') of the costs incurred by the promoters, opponents, and other parties. Before 1825 no provision was made by either House, as it was in courts outside, for the taxation of costs incurred by petitioners in Parliament. In 1825, an Act was passed to establish such a taxation in the Commons,[3] and in 1827, another Act was passed to effect the same object in the Lords.[4] Both these Acts, however, were defective, and were subsequently repealed. Under the present statutes[5] regulating the taxation of costs in each House a regular system of taxation has been established.

Taxing officers

In each House there is a taxing officer, having all the necessary powers of examining the parties and witnesses on oath, and of calling for the production of books or writings in the hands of either party to the taxation.

---

1 For the definition of a private bill in connection with which fees are chargeable, see the Table of Fees approved by the House in 1864 and quoted in Williams vol II, p 273.
2 Private ruling, 7 December 1977.
3 6 Geo 4, c 123.
4 7 & 8 Geo 4, c 64.
5 House of Commons Costs Taxation Act 1847 and House of Lords Costs Taxation Act 1849, as amended and applied by the Parliamentary Costs Act 1865 and the House of Commons Costs Taxation Act 1879, s 17 of the Perjury Act 1911, and s 7 of the Statutory Orders (Special Procedure) Act 1945.

Lists of charges

Lists of charges have been prepared in each House, in pursuance of these Acts, defining the charges which parliamentary agents, solicitors and others will be allowed to charge for the various services usually rendered by them. These charges were revised in 1956 following a recommendation by the Joint Committee on Private Bill Procedure, 1954–55. There have been subsequent increases in the amounts of fees authorized by both Houses. Lists of charges are printed for distribution to all persons who may apply for them.

Applications for taxation

Any person upon whom a demand is made by a parliamentary agent or solicitor for any costs incurred in respect of any proceedings in the House, or in complying with its standing orders, may apply to the taxing officer for the taxation of such costs. Any parliamentary agent or solicitor who may be aggrieved by the non-payment of his costs may apply, in the same manner, to have his costs taxed, preparatory to the enforcement of his claim. The client, however, is required by the Act to make this application within six months after the delivery of the bill. But the Speaker in the Commons, or the Clerk of the Parliaments in the Lords, on receiving a report of special circumstances from the taxing officer, may direct costs to be taxed after six months have expired.

Costs in both Houses taxed together

The taxing officer of either House is enabled to tax the whole of a bill brought before him for taxation, whether the costs relate to the proceedings of that House only, or to the proceedings of both Houses; and also other general costs incurred in reference to the private bill or petition. Each taxing officer may request the other, or the proper officer of any court, to assist him in taxing any portion of a bill of costs. The proper officers of the courts may, in the same manner, request the assistance of the taxing officer of either House in the taxation of parliamentary costs; such costs when taxed and settled are returned by the taxing officer, with his opinion thereon, to the officer who made the request.[1]

When costs have been awarded by a committee on a private bill to one party against another, and the losing party has objected to items in the bill of costs presented to it, the taxing officer has heard both parties before reaching a decision.[2]

Certificate to have the effect of a warrant to confess judgment

Except when costs have been taxed at the request of the taxing officer of a court outside Parliament, the taxing officer, if requested so to do by the parties, reports his taxation in the Commons to the Speaker, and, in the Lords, to the Clerk of the Parliaments. If no objection be made within twenty-one days after such report, either party may obtain from the Speaker or from the Clerk of the Parliaments, as the case may be, a certificate of costs

---

1 House of Lords Costs Taxation Act 1849, s 12.
2 Wallasey Corporation's objections to bill of costs of Wallasey Embankment Commissioners, heard on 25 November 1958.

allowed, which in any action brought for the recovery of the amount so certified, will have the effect of a warrant of attorney to confess judgment, unless the defendant shall have pleaded that he is not liable to the payment of the costs.

Costs of provisional and special procedure orders

By the House of Commons Costs Taxation Act 1879 the powers of the taxing officer were extended to costs in respect of provisional orders and bills promoted by public authorities, and oppositions to public bills. The powers of the taxing officers of both Houses were further extended to special procedure orders by section 7 of the Statutory Orders (Special Procedure) Act 1945. The taxing officer of the House of Commons is required to tax costs incurred in respect of any provisional order if requested to do so by a Secretary of State and costs incurred in respect of a special procedure order if requested to do so by the minister responsible for the order.[1]

1 House of Commons Costs Taxation Act 1879, s 2. Statutory Orders (Special Procedure) Act 1945, s 7 (2).

CHAPTER 35

Petitions in favour of, against, or relating to private bills in the House of Commons; and the Court of Referees

PRESENTATION AND WITHDRAWAL OF PETITIONS
(Standing Orders 171, 171A, 172, 173, 219)

All petitions in favour of or against or otherwise relating to private bills or bills to confirm provisional orders[1] are presented to the House, not in the same way as public petitions, but by depositing them in the Private Bill Office, where they may be deposited by a Member,[2] party, or agent. Under Standing Order 172 a copy of any petition so deposited must be supplied by the agent for the petition to any interested party who applies and pays for it, not later than the day after that on which the application and payment is received. Any petitioner may withdraw his petition on a requisition to that effect being deposited in the Private Bill Office, signed by himself or by the agent who deposited the petition;[3] and, where any such petition has been signed by more than one person, any person who has signed may withdraw from the petition by signing and depositing a similar requisition.

By long-standing practice, Government departments do not petition either in favour of or against private bills. A report on the bill may be made by any interested Minister and, if the committee on the bill thinks fit, a departmental officer may be heard in explanation of it.[4] It is not clear, however, that a Government department—more particularly one set up by statute—can in no circumstances petition Parliament. Departments have in the past petitioned against private bills,[5] and in rare instances leave has been given by the House for departments, though they have not presented a petition,[6] to appear by counsel before a committee on the bill.[7]

---

1 This chapter does not apply generally to petitions against confirmation bills presented under the Private Legislation Procedure (Scotland) Act 1936, for which see ch 39. For petitions against special procedure orders, see ch 38.
2 A Member does not register as a parliamentary agent when depositing a petition against a bill on behalf of other parties. See Private Business (1955–56) 179; ibid (1982–83) 21. Depositing a petition, however, makes him liable for the fees incurred in so doing.
3 Cf the proceedings on the Thames Conservancy Bill, CJ (1894) 121; on the Thames Tunnel, etc, Bill (Group 2), 12 and 13 June 1860; and on the South Yorkshire, etc, Railway Bill (Group 8), 27 June and 1 July 1890.
4 See pp 896–897.
5 Eg Petition of the Commissioners of Works against the Clapham Junction and Paddington Railway Bill 1893. Also, a Petition of the Duchy of Cornwall was presented against the Plymouth and South West Devon Water Bill 1969–70.
6 For an example of a department being refused a hearing by a committee because no petition had been deposited, see Minutes of Evidence, Group A, 13 and 14 March 1902.
7 Eg to the War Office, Lee Conservancy Bill, CJ (1900) 106.

PETITIONS IN FAVOUR OF PRIVATE BILLS

Petitions in favour of private bills are not normally referred to the committee as the petitioners are not parties to the bill. On one side are the promoters, and on the other petitioners against the bill. Petitioners in favour of the bill can claim no hearing before the committee, except as witnesses called by the promoters. Counsel may allude to the presentation of such petitions in argument, but may not examine witnesses in respect of their contents or signatures. Parties wishing to range themselves on the side of promoters and against petitioners do so by presenting petitions against alterations, though this does not necessarily entitle them to be heard before the committee (see pp 906–907).

PETITIONS AGAINST PRIVATE BILLS

Petitions to be presented before a prescribed time (Standing Orders 171A, 217)

Petitions against a private bill originating in the House of Commons, for which the Examiner has reported that standing orders have been complied with and which is not a bill the examination of the petition for which has been adjourned until after 20 January, must be presented on or before 30 January. Petitions against any other private bill, with a few exceptions, must be presented not later than the tenth day after the first reading of the bill.[1] The exceptions are petitions against a bill after it has been reported from a committee; petitions against a personal bill; or petitions complaining of amendments proposed in the filled-up bill (see pp 889–890), of any proposed additional provision, or of any matter which has arisen during the progress of the bill before the committee. A petition against an alteration or a petition against an additional provision may be deposited at any time before the committee has reported the bill to the House.

Petitions against a bill to confirm a provisional order, originating in the Commons, must be deposited not later than the seventh day after that on which notice is given of the day on which the bill will be examined or, if the House is not sitting on that day, not later than the next day on which the House sits.

The time limit for depositing petitions against personal bills, which normally originate in the Lords, is subject to directions by Mr Speaker[2] as are proceedings in the Commons generally on personal bills.[3]

Petitions to stand referred to committee on the bill and right of audience (Standing Orders 126, 127, 217)

Under Standing Order 126 every petition against a private bill (or bill to confirm a provisional order) which complies with the requirements of Stand-

---

1 When 30 January falls on a Sunday, the petitions required to be presented on or before that day have to be presented on or before 29 January. If the last day of a period prescribed for presenting any other petition falls on a day on which the House is not sitting, the time is extended by the provisions of SO 171A to the next day on which the House sits.
2 For examples, see Private Business (1962–63) 225, (1971–72) 133, (1974–75) 201 and (1984–85) 119.
3 SO 191A. For procedure upon personal bills see pp 812–813.

ing Order 171A (see above), and every petition in which the petitioners complain of amendments as proposed in the filled-up bill, of any proposed additional provision or of any matter which arises during the progress of the bill before the committee, stand referred to the committee on the bill,[1] if they have been deposited in accordance with the standing orders.[2]

Under Standing Order 127 the promoters of an opposed private bill are entitled to be heard before the committee on the bill by themselves, their counsel, or agents in favour of the bill and against any petitions against the bill. Similarly petitioners against the bill, subject to the rules and orders of the House, and to the prayer of their petition, are entitled to be heard upon their petition by themselves, their counsel, or agents (see p 904). It should be noted that this does not apply to petitioners against alterations, for whose rights of audience see pp 906–907.

Petitions presented after time

If a petition is presented after the time limit, the only way in which the petitioners can obtain a hearing is by presenting a petition, praying that the standing orders be dispensed with in their case, and that they may be heard by the committee. The petition will stand referred to the Standing Orders Committee; and if the petitioners are able to show any special circumstances which entitle them to such consideration and, particularly, that they have not been guilty of negligence, the standing orders may be dispensed with.[3]

When the Chairman of Ways and Means has ordered an unopposed bill to be treated as opposed (see p 890), the House has ordered that petitions against the bill presented within a specified period should be referred to the committee on the bill.[4]

In 1905 the Standing Orders Committee having reported, in the case of a petitioner against the Great Northern (Ireland), etc, Railways Bill, that Standing Order 128 (now 171A) ought not to be dispensed with, the House ordered that the committee's resolution be referred back to it, to consider whether under the circumstances of the case the standing order should be dispensed with; but the committee again resolved that it should not.[5]

Death of petitioners

Where petitioners have died after the deposit of their petitions, their sons, or their agents or executors, have petitioned to be heard, and, on the report of the Standing Orders Committee, have been permitted to appear and be

---

1 For petitions against bills 'substituted' for orders under the Private Legislation Procedure (Scotland) Act 1936, see ch 39.
2 When part of a petition had been omitted by mistake, and afterwards added, it was ruled that such part was not referred to the committee, Parl Deb (1846) 83, c 487.
3 Standing Orders Committee report, That SO 128 (now 171A) ought to be dispensed with, CJ (1904) 48; ibid (1932–33) 69; ought not to be dispensed with, ibid (1904) 235; ibid (1933–34) 93; ibid (1941–42) 62. For a petition to dispense with SO 171A presented and subsequently withdrawn, together with a petition for not dispensing with that standing order, see Private Business (1982–83) 93, 105, 109.
4 CJ (1901) 240; ibid (1911) 81. See also CJ (1907) 422, for an instruction to a committee to which an unopposed bill had been recommitted to hear witnesses.
5 CJ (1905) 61, 117, 128.

heard upon the petitions of the deceased petitioners,[1] or to deposit a new petition after the time limited.[2]

Grounds of objection to be specified (Standing Order 128)

No petition will be considered which does not distinctly specify the grounds on which the petitioners object to any of the provisions of the bill. The petitioners can be heard only on the grounds so stated. If the grounds are not specified with accuracy, the committee may direct a more specific statement to be given, in writing, but limited to the grounds of objection which had been inaccurately specified; but this power has been seldom exercised.[3]

LOCUS STANDI OF PETITIONERS AGAINST PRIVATE BILLS

It is now necessary to describe the procedure for adjudicating upon formal objections, on the part of promoters, to petitions against a private bill, and upon the petitioners' rights to be heard before the committee appointed to deal with the bill. Prior to 1864, any such question was heard and determined in both Houses—as it is still in the Lords—by the committee on the bill. Considerable objection was raised to this practice on the ground of its inconvenience and expense, counsel and witnesses having often been kept in attendance on behalf of petitioners who were adjudged, at the eleventh hour, to have no claim to be heard. To meet these objections, and at the same time to introduce greater uniformity and certainty into the decisions upon these important points, the adjudication of questions of locus standi as regards private bills[4] was entrusted by the Commons in 1865 to the 'Referees of the House on Private Bills', who had been constituted by a standing order passed in the preceding year.[5]

COURT OF REFEREES ON PRIVATE BILLS

Constitution and duties (Standing Orders 89, 90)

The Court of Referees consists of the Chairman of Ways and Means, the Deputy Chairmen, and the Counsel to Mr Speaker, with not less than seven

---

1 Petition of F L Hopkins against the Lincolnshire Estuary Bill, CJ (1851) 226, 233. See also the proceedings in the committee on the Great Western Railway (Steam Vessels) Bill, 29 June 1909 (Group 5 of Railway Bills), for the circumstances and conditions under which certain persons who were parties to, and had contributed to the cost of, a petition against the bill, although they were not signatories thereof, were allowed to be heard upon the petition, when the persons who had signed it did not enter an appearance upon it.

2 Petition of the Duke of Portland against the Ardrossan and Glasgow Railway Bill (CJ (1854) 206, and Suppl. to Votes, 1854, p 606). Petition of C Morrison against the Metropolitan Inner Circle, etc, Railway Bill (CJ (1878) 112), and Private Business (1878) p 188, etc.

3 Cf., upon this point, the recommendation of the Select Committee on Private Business (HC 378 (1902) p ix).

4 For locus standi of petitioners against hybrid bills, see p 523; of petitioners against special procedure orders, p 961; of petitioners against confirmation bills under the Private Legislation Procedure (Scotland) Act 1936, p 974.

5 See also HC 108 (1876); CJ (1876) 101, 120; HC 378, (1902) App 9; Clifford ii, 804–813; Williams i, 144–161, for other information as to the Referees.

other Members of the House, who are appointed by the Speaker for such periods as he thinks fit.[1] Three Referees are enough to constitute each court.

The duty of the Court of Referees is to determine the rights of petitioners against private bills[2] to be heard, though without prejudice to the power of the committee to whom the bill is referred to decide any question relating to such rights arising incidentally in the course of its proceedings.[3]

Standing Order 90, which defines the jurisdiction of the Court of Referees, is applied by Standing Order 215 to petitions against bills to confirm provisional orders.

Rules of procedure (Standing Orders 91, 91A)

The practice and procedure of the Court, the times of sitting, order of business, and the forms and notices required in its proceedings are prescribed by rules framed by the Chairman of Ways and Means and subject to alteration by him as occasion may require. These rules and alterations must be laid on the Table of the House and are published.[4]

Under Standing Order 91A, a petitioner is entitled to be heard before the Court by himself, his counsel or agent in support of his right to be heard on his petition. Similarly the promoters are entitled to be heard by themselves, their counsel or agent in opposition to the petitioner. Only one counsel, however, may appear in support of the petitioner and one in opposition.

By Standing Order 215, the proceedings of the Court in relation to petitions against a bill for confirming a provisional order are to be conducted in like manner as in the case of a private bill, and are subject to the same rules and orders of the House, so far as they are applicable.

Notice by promoters of intention to object

By one of the rules made by the Chairman of Ways and Means under Standing Order 91, the promoters of a bill who intend to object to the right of petitioners to be heard against it are to give notice of such intention, and of the grounds of their objection, to the clerk to the Court and to the agents for the petitioners, not later than the eighth day after the day on which the petition was actually deposited in the Private Bill Office;[5] but the Court may permit such notices to be given under special circumstances after the prescribed time has expired.[6] Such notices may also be withdrawn by notice in writing given in the Private Bill Office, and a copy thereof must be served upon the agents for the petitioner on the same day.

---

1 Members of the Court of Referees are normally appointed for the duration of a Parliament; see, eg Private Business (1987–88) 29.
2 For an example of the locus standi of petitioners against an additional provision, see Minutes of Proceedings on the Sunderland Corporation Bill 1934–35 (Group H). Cf also the petition of Coventry Corporation 'against alterations' in the London, Midland and Scottish Railway Bill, 1934–35 (Minutes of Proccedings, Group B).
3 But see below, p 859, for locus standi of petitioners against private bills committed to select committees and to joint committees.
4 The present rules are dated 29 June 1953, HC 208 (1952–53).
5 The time allowed for serving such notices of objection is exclusive of the day on which the petition was deposited, S 6, App 97; 2 C & S 2. It has been ruled that the service of such notices by post is not sufficient, but under certain circumstances it has been allowed, S 7, App 98; 3 C & R 376.
6 Permission granted, R & M 173; not granted, R & S 11, 159.

Where the jurisdiction of the Court of Referees does not apply, as is the case with bills committed to a select committee or joint committee of both Houses, and the promoter of a private bill, hybrid bill or provisional order confirmation bill intends to object to the locus standi of a petitioner, notice of the intended objection, stating the grounds, is deposited in the Private Bill Office and served on the petitioner or his agents at least five clear days before the first sitting day of the committee on the bill (who consider questions of locus standi in such cases).

Manner of hearing locus standi cases

If no one appears in support of the petition before the Court of Referees, the locus standi of the petitioners is disallowed.[1] If the petitioners appear—their petition against the preamble or clauses of the bill, the statement of objections to their right to be heard, and the bill itself being before the court—the counsel or agent for the petitioners supports their claim; and the counsel or agent for the promoters is heard in reply—the speeches being thus limited to one on each side. For the purposes of argument on questions of locus standi, the allegations of a petition are ordinarily admitted: but where the right of petitioners to be heard depends upon special facts which are disputed, they may be called upon to give prima facie evidence in support of their case.[2]

If the petitioners have called evidence in support of their prima facie case, the promoters are not permitted to call rebutting evidence.[3] Recorded divisions are not normally taken; the Chairman counts the votes and declares the result by a majority. The Chairman has a vote (as in a court of law) but no casting vote. The Court of Referees has now no power to award costs.[4]

Locus standi limited to points alleged in petition

Some petitioners pray to be heard against the preamble and clauses of the bill, some against certain clauses only; and others pray for the insertion of protective clauses, or for compensation for damage which will arise under the bill. The locus standi of a petitioner is always limited to the points alleged in his petition.[5] It is often still further limited by a decision of the court disallowing him a locus standi except against some only of those provisions to which he objects in the bill. In giving its decision in such cases the court limits the petitioner's locus standi, not to certain portions of his petition, but to certain portions of the bill.[6] When the parties have come to an agreement before the court, the locus standi of the petitioners is usually disallowed except to the extent to which the agreement goes,[7] or a limited locus standi is

1 S 8, App 91.
2 S 11, 12, App 93; 1 C & S, App 41; 3 C & R 155, 316, 319; 1 S & A 294. If a witness's attendance can only be obtained by order of the House, the House makes the order (CJ (1866) 116–117).
3 1 S & A 197–198.
4 1 C & S 7.
5 1 C & S App 6; Metropolitan District Railway Bill 1868.
6 Cf 2 C & R 130; 2 S & A 191; 1 B 70; [1936–60] LSR 3.
7 2 S & B 11.

allowed,[1] but in some cases no order is made.[2] In other cases the court, in allowing a general or 'unlimited' locus standi against a bill, have left the relevancy of some of a petitioner's allegations for the determination of the committee.[3]

Entitlement to locus standi: general principles

When its jurisdiction began in 1865, the Court of Referees took as the basis of its practice the principles and precedents contained in the decisions, regarding thc locus standi of petitioners, that had previously been given by individual committees; and it reduced to a system, as far as possible, thc rules affecting the rights of petitioners to be heard. In the course of time this system has been modified, not only by the interpretations and decisions of the court itself, but by the additions and alterations that have been made in the standing orders relating to locus standi. Generally speaking, it may be said that petitioners are not entitled to a locus standi unless it is proved that their property or interests are directly and specially affected by the bill, whether a private bill or a bill to confirm a provisional order other than a provisional order under the Private Legislation Procedure (Scotland) Act 1936.[4] But so many exceptional circumstances naturally arise in each instance that, in the following pages, nothing beyond a brief review can be given of the more important types of case determined by the court. For more detailed information, the reader must consult the invaluable series of 'Locus Standi Reports', to which frequent references are here given, and especially the introductory chapters prefixed to 1 and 2 Clifford and Stephens' Reports.[5]

Landowners' locus standi

It has been laid down, as an established practice, that the owners of land proposed to be compulsorily taken—and also the lessees and occupiers on whom, as on owners, the notices required by the standing orders of both Houses are to be served—should always be heard against both the preamble and the clauses of a bill.[6]

It has been ruled that a petitioner whose petition alleges that his land is taken and who prays to be heard against the preamble and clauses of the bill may be heard against the bill generally, even though his petition does

---

1 2 S & B 70.
2 2 S & B 18, 54.
3 1 C & R 47; 2 ibid 130. And cf R & S 117–120, 330; 2 S & A 182.
4 See SO 215 which applies to bills confirming provisional orders, the practice and procedure of the House as to the determination of questions of the locus standi of petitioners against private bills and specifically applies thereto the relevant standing orders. What follows in this chapter respecting locus standi can therefore be taken as applying to such confirming bills equally as to private bills. In the case of provisional orders under the Private Legislation Procedure (Scotland) Act 1936 questions of locus standi are decided by the Commissioners holding the inquiry under that Act (see s 6 (2)).
5 For reports of cases of locus standi decided by the Court of Referees in 1865 (the first year of its jurisdiction) and in 1866, cf S. For the years covered by subsequent reports of cases, see the Table of Abbreviations under C & S, C & R, R & M, R & S, S & A, S & B, B, [1936–60] LSR and [1960–83] LSR.
6 London and North Western Railway Bill 1868, 1 C & S, App 62, 63 (known as the 'post' case); 3 C & R 481.

not allege that he will be injured and though it contains no reference to the preamble except in the prayer of the petition.[1]

The same unlimited ('landowner's') locus standi has also been granted to the owners of minerals,[2] and to the lord of a manor,[3] claiming to be heard against bills affecting their property or rights; to magistrates and councillors having an interest in the lands or a right to gravel on the foreshore, within their burgh or barony;[4] and to other petitioners who have been held to 'have an interest' in land proposed to be taken.

In all such cases the Court of Referees determines—according to the circumstances which necessarily vary in each instance—whether petitioners have such an interest in land as to entitle them to a landowner's locus standi; or to what extent and with what restrictions they may claim a hearing.[5]

Even in the case of an omnibus bill, that is to say, a bill in which the promoters seek powers for a number of various objects or different undertakings, whether promoted by a public authority or a railway or other company, the general locus standi allowed to a petitioner as a landowner has enabled him, however little of his land is taken, to be heard against the whole bill; and in cases where the promoters have desired more particularly to exclude him from being heard on any save certain provisions of a bill, the Court have generally refused so to limit his locus standi.[6]

A landowner has been granted a general locus standi against an omnibus railway bill, however limited his interest;[7] and a landowner, whose land was to be taken, has been held to have a general locus standi against a general improvement bill.[8]

In 1891, however, and again in 1903, when granting the usual 'landowner's locus standi', against the whole of a railway (various powers) bill,

---

1 Cf Resolution of General Committee on Railway and Canal Bills 1861, 1 C & R 207; 3 ibid 301, 457.
2 1 C & R 221; 3 ibid 46.
3 S App 95; 1 C & S 39; 2 ibid 89; 2 C & R 109, 212.
4 1 S & A 15.
5 1 C & R 158 (owners of pavement in front of house in Glasgow); R & S 328–330 (commoners where railway line proposed across common lands); R & M 313 (owners of property not taken, but injuriously affected, by proposed railway); 1 S & B 67, 104–105 (telephone company owning wires carried on brackets or posts); 2 S & A 184 (owners of bed and foreshore of river though right of user vested in river Commissioners); 1 S & B 29 (owners of ferry proposed to be acquired compulsorily by local authority); 1 S & B 121 (coal owners entitled under agreement to rights in respect of a water way); S App 120; 2 C & R 34 (mineral owners objecting to provisions relating to tolls); 1 C & R 215–6; 3 ibid 55 (owners and occupiers of land in reasonable proximity to canal proposed to be stopped up); S 17; 1 C & R 270 (owners of equitable interest where legal estate vested in trustees); 2 C & R 193; 3 ibid 156; R & S 45 (owners of land affected by underpinning though land outside limits of deviation); 2 S & A 55 (promoters of bill to complete purchase of land treated as owners thereof)—see however 2 S & A 144; R & S 320 (owners of colliery against authorization of enlargement of reservoir alleged to endanger life and property in colliery); 1 S & A 116; 2 ibid 16, 117 (owners of land in proximity to site of proposed sewage works but outside limits entitling them to notice under SO 17).
6 2 C & R 130; 2 S & A 15, 123, 182, 230; and cf 2 ibid 73–75; 1 S & B 127. But see 1B, 55–57.
7 London and North Western Railway Bill 1868, 1 C & S App 62, 63 (the 'post' case); 2 C & S 37; R & S 117, etc (petitions of railway companies as landowners); 1 C & R 221; 2 ibid 130; R & S 67; 2 S & A 182–183, etc (petitions of other landowners).
8 1 C & S 19, App 49; 1 C & R 158; 2 ibid 69–70, etc.

to a petitioner whose land was taken under a part only of the bill, the court expressly declared that, in doing so, it did not intend to influence the committee, who would deal with the petitioner's interest as affected by the bill, in judging what might or might not be considered as material.[1] In 1902, the locus standi of a petitioning landowner, a railway company, against an improvement (omnibus) bill promoted by an urban district council, was limited to those parts of the bill under which the company's land was taken or their interests affected.[2]

In the case of a bill for the abandonment of a railway not completed within the time for which compulsory powers had been granted, the owner of land upon the route has not been allowed a locus standi,[3] except in some cases where it has been shown that he has sustained special damage.[4] Lessees of minerals beneath a line proposed to be abandoned have been refused a locus standi.[5]

In the case of a bill for an extension of time, the owners of land authorized by a former Act to be taken, and already contracted for with the company, have been refused a hearing, on the ground that they were merely creditors,[6] and this has been held to apply even where a notice to treat has been served under the previous Act but no contract signed.[7]

In the case of a bill providing, not for an extension of time, but for a revival of the expired powers of a company, a locus standi has been allowed to another railway company[8] or a landowner[9] as if the bill were the original bill; but it has been refused in a similar case when, the money for the purchase of his property under the original Act having been paid into court, the petitioner's legal interest in it had passed into the hands of the promoters.[10] On the other hand the owners of land which was proposed to be taken by a bill but which was subject to compulsory powers of purchase, though not actually taken, by another company, have been held to have a locus standi, as not being yet divested of their right as owners.[11]

Locus standi of bodies representing associations, etc

The locus standi of bodies representing trades, businesses and interests in a locality is dealt with by Standing Order 95, which confers on the Court of Referees a discretion of granting a locus standi to such bodies if they allege that the trade, business or interest will be injuriously affected by provisions

1 R & S 117 (railway company petitioning against an omnibus railway bill); 2 S & A 182 (London County Council, as landowner, against Metropolitan District Railway (Various Powers) Bill; and cf 1 C & R 47–48; R & S 330 (Cardiff, etc, Bill).
2 2 S & A 104. See also 1 B 55.
3 1 C & S 27; 2 C & R 40; 3 ibid 78, 399, 403.
4 1 C & S 28; 2 C & R 231; R & M 139.
5 1 C & S 28–29.
6 S App 110; 1 C & S 31, App 37; 3 C & R 315; R & M 133; R & S 330. Cf. as exceptional cases, R & S 224; 1 C & S 29, 32; 2 C & R 100; R & M 67, 113; 1 S & A 1; 1 S & B 48; R & M 59, 187; R & S 330–333; 1 C & S 28, 34; R & M 89; 1 S & A 261; 2 S & A 39–40; 1 S & B 157.
7 [1936–60] LSR 13.
8 R & M 89; 1 S & B 114, 157.
9 1 C & S 36, App 35; 1 S & A 261.
10 1 C & R 219–20.
11 1 C & R 207.

contained in the bill in question.[1] The standing order further provides that
bodies representing amenity, educational, travel or recreational interests
may be granted a locus standi if they allege that the interest they represent
will be adversely affected to a material extent.[2]

Locus standi on the ground of contingent damage

In accordance with the general principle that, to entitle them to a locus
standi, petitioners should prove that their property or interests are directly
and specially affected by a bill, petitioners whose property was not taken,
but who contended that they would be adversely affected by the close
proximity of a railway, have on several occasions been refused a hearing.[3]

In some exceptional cases, however, of special danger, disturbance, or
injury, petitioners so affected have been allowed a hearing;[4] and owners
and occupiers of houses who complained that their property, although
untouched, would be injured or shaken by a proposed line, have been
heard and have obtained protective clauses.[5] The owners of property in
proximity to a proposed railway, claiming to be heard on the ground of
injury from vibration, have in some cases been granted,[6] and in others
been refused,[7] a locus standi. It has been laid down as a general principle
that a landowner or inhabitant cannot claim a locus standi on the ground
that proposed works will destroy the beauty or salubrity of a place;[8] but in

---

1 The locus standi of such bodies was first dealt with by standing order in 1884 (CJ (1884) 349).
This SO was replaced by an SO of wider scope (CJ (1904) 414) which is substantially
reproduced by SO 95. For decisions of the Court of Referees see 1 S & A 202, 225, 229; 2 S &
A 221; 1 S & B 68, 97, 113, 152; 2 ibid 54; 2 S & A 228; 1 S & B 42, 126; 2 ibid 3; 1 B 21, 79, 98;
[1936–60] LSR 9, 18; [1960–83] LSR 10 (locus standi of Federation of Civil Engineering
Contractors and Contractors' Plant Association allowed). For a decision of a select committee on a hybrid bill, see the Special Report from the Select Committee on the Charlwood
and Horley Bill, HC 55 (1973–74) (locus standi of Horley and District Chamber of Commerce
disallowed).
2 Para (2) of the standing order, relating to amenity and other interests, was added on 1 April
1968. For decisions of the Court of Referees, see [1960–83] LSR 15 (locus standi of Friends of
the Earth Ltd disallowed); ibid 25 (locus standi of Transport 2000 North London and South
London disallowed); Harwich Parkeston Quay Bill 1985–86 (locus standi of Harwich Mayflower Trust and Harwich Mayflower Developments Ltd disallowed); King's Cross Railways
Bill 1988–89 (locus standi of Victorian Society and others allowed; locus standi of Joint
Committees of National Amenity Societies and others disallowed). For decisions of the Lord
Chairman of Committees and the Chairman of Ways and Means under the Statutory Orders
(Special Procedure) Act 1945, see County Borough of Bournemouth (Turbary Common)
Appropriation Order 1971, CJ (1972–73) 42 (locus standi of the Dorset Rights of Way Group
allowed; locus standi of the Bournemouth and Poole Amenity Society disallowed), and
Redcar-Marske-Saltburn Compulsory Purchase Order 1979, CJ (1980–81) 480 (locus standi
of the Save the Stray Committee disallowed); Exeter-Launceston-Bodmin Trunk Road
(Okehampton By-pass) Compulsory Purchase Orders 1984, CJ (1984–85) 26 (locus standi of
the Dartmoor Preservation Association, etc, allowed). For a decision of a select committee
on a hybrid bill, see the Special Report from the Select Committee on the Channel Tunnel
Bill, HC 195 (1974) (locus standi of the Railway Development Association and the Railway
Invigoration Society disallowed).
3 S 26–28, App 101, 102, 117; 1 C & S App 45; 1 C & R 80; 2 ibid 38, 124, 249; 3 ibid 86; R & M
208; 2 S & A 123–124, 157; 1 S & B 2; Shoreham Harbour Bill 1986.
4 1 C & S 40–44; 2 C & R 2, 14, 75.
5 2 C & S 189; 1 C & R 46; R & S 44–45; 2 S & A 90.
6 2 S & A 100, 126, 128; King's Cross Railways Bill 1989 (petition of Jim Brennan).
7 2 S & A 65, 192; King's Cross Railways Bill 1989 (petitions of Eileen Tegg and Nicholas
Holliman).
8 1 C & R 203; 3 ibid 30, 125; 1 S & A 264, 330; 2 ibid 157; 1 B 28.

two cases, occurring in 1891, petitioners claiming to be heard upon such grounds were granted a locus standi.[1] The owners of glass works, and the owners of business premises, who apprehended injury from the obstruction of light by proposed works, have also been heard, their case being considered sufficiently exceptional to justify a departure from the general principle of previous decisions—that landowners can be heard only when their land is actually taken or interfered with.[2] The trustees of a hospital who alleged that, although no land was to be taken by a railway, great injury would arise to the patients from the noise and vibration of passing trains, have been refused a locus standi.[3] The trustees of a church, alleging that the services would be interfered with by the proximity of a railway, have in one case been refused, and in another been allowed, a hearing upon that ground. In both cases they were allowed a locus standi on the further ground of obstruction of access.[4] In numerous cases, petitioners complaining of interference with their access to their premises, or to the sea, or other waterside, have been allowed a locus standi, although their property was not directly affected.[5] It has been held that the displacement of population, involved by a bill, was not a sufficient ground for allowing a school board to be heard in opposition.[6]

Locus standi against bills affecting water and water supply

The locus standi of river boards and landowners in opposing bills affecting water and water supply is regulated by Standing Order 99. By that order the Court of Referees has a discretion to grant a locus if it is alleged that under the provisions of the bill the river or any water or water supply of which the river board or landowners may legally avail themselves will be diminished or seriously affected.[7]

By Standing Order 100 the Court also has a discretion to allow a locus standi to land drainage authorities who allege that their district will be injuriously affected by the provisions of a bill authorizing the abstraction or impounding of water, or the discharge of water into watercourses within their district.[8]

---

1 Local Government Provisional Order Bill 1891 (R & S 127). Manchester, Sheffield, and Lincolnshire Railway (Extension to London, etc) Bill 1891 (R & S 130 ff). In the latter case a locus standi was granted to owners, occupiers, etc., whose property was not taken, but who claimed that its amenity would be injured by the proposed line.
2 1 C & R 258; and cf. R & S 213–214; 2 S & A 235–236.
3 North British Railway Bill 1877 (2 C & R 54); London and North-Western Railway Bill 1889 (R & M 263). The petitioners in this case obtained a locus standi and a protective clause before a committee in the House of Lords.
4 2 C & R 249; R & S 139; and cf 2 S & A 58, 235–236, and 1 S & B 148 (locus standi disallowed).
5 2 C & R 139, 197; 3 ibid 60, 70, 226; R & M 46, 145; R & S 20, 23, 137–139, 151–152, 212; and cf R & M 92; 2 S & A 210–212; 1 S & B 109.
6 3 C & R 182, 185. And as to other and later cases where particular grounds, on which petitioners claimed a hearing, were not held to be sufficient for granting a locus standi, cf 2 S & A 206, 214–216.
7 For cases under the SO see (locus standi allowed) 2 S & A 88, 117; 1 S & B 8, 51, 160; 2 ibid 64, 73; (limited locus standi allowed) 2 S & A 162; 2 S & B 83; (locus standi disallowed) 2 S & A 205, 207, 227; 1 S & B 160.
8 [1936–60] LSR 1 (limited locus standi allowed).

Locus standi against amalgamation bills

In the case of amalgamation bills a larger latitude than usual is generally allowed to opponents.[1] The general ground upon which petitioners have been admitted to oppose amalgamation bills is that the amalgamation itself will injuriously affect them, and not that they can show any grievance resulting from past legislation.[2]

Locus standi on the ground of competition (Standing Order 92)

It was formerly held, as a parliamentary rule, that competition did not confer a locus standi; but in course of time this rule was considerably relaxed, and numerous exceptions were, in practice, admitted; and under a standing order, originally passed in 1853 (now Standing Order 92), petitioners have generally been admitted to be heard against a bill on the ground of competition, the Court of Referees, in the exercise of its discretion under this standing order, allowing[3] or refusing[4] a locus standi, according to its opinion of the extent and directness of the competition in respect of which the petitioners claim to be heard. In cases where it was only proposed to improve an existing competition, a locus standi has not been allowed,[5] but where the nature of the competition is changed (eg by becom-

---

1 1 C & R 240; 2 S & A 116.
2 1 C & R 77–78. Cf also 1 C & R 240–247; 3 ibid 58, 97, 404; R & S 240, 334; 1 S & A 90, 173; 2 ibid 113, 139. For cases of amalgamation bills on the following subjects see eg 1 C & R 73 (canal); 3 ibid 15, 319 (docks); 1 ibid 28, 112; R & S 217; 1 S & A 145 (docks and railway); 2 C & S 218; 1 C & R 141 (gas); 3 ibid 38 (tramways); 1 ibid 59; 2 ibid 307 (water).
3 Locus standi allowed: to railway companies, dock owners etc., against railway, dock, etc, bills, 3 C & R 371; R & M 87; 2 S & A 52, 224; 1 S & B 24–25, 26, 27, 39, 76, 81, 82, 83; 2 ibid 23, 49; and (limited), 1 ibid 86. To steamboat owner against a railway bill, 2 S & A 107. To corporation owning tramways against railway bill seeking power to run omnibuses, 1 S & B 38. To promoters of a new tramway against a link in existing lines affecting the proposed line, 1 S & B 138. To steam tramway companies, etc, against railway bills, 3 C & R 285, 471. To railway companies against tramways, steam tramways, or electric tramways bills, 2 S & A 57; 3 C & R 455; 1 S & A 242; 2 ibid 23, 118, 245. To omnibus companies against tramways bills, 1 C & S, App 120; 2 ibid 87–89; 2 S & A 19; 1 S & B 73. To owners of a bridge or pier against bills authorizing another bridge or pier, R & S 23; 2 S & A 5, 249. To gas, etc, companies, 2 C & S 100; 1 C & R 50; 2 ibid 229; 3 ibid 109; 1 S & B 18, 20,49,71, 89,98; 2 ibid 67, 91; and (limited), 2 S & A 249; 1 S & B 129; 2 ibid 78. And to other petitioners, 1 S & A 170, 202, 298; 2 ibid 81, 177, 201, 210; 1 S & B 68, 102; 2 ibid 57, 86. See also 1 S & B 35–38, where a locus standi was given to petitioners on account of the novel character of the scheme proposed. Limited locus standi allowed, 1 S & B 47.
4 Locus standi disallowed: To railway companies against railway or dock bills, 2 S & A 160; 1 S & B 92, 150. And against tramways or electric tramways bills, 2 C & S 142; 1 C & R 13; 2 S & A 149; R & S 242; 1 S & A 157, 322. To electric railway company against power to run omnibuses in a railway company's bill, 1 S & B 24. To hotel keepers, 3 C & R 23, and to railway-carriage makers, 2 C & R 50, against powers sought in a railway company's bill. To cab proprietors against a tramways bill, 2 C & R 323. To owners of a bridge, 2 C & R 89; R & S 36; 1 S & A 195. To gas or water companies, 1 S & A 46; 2 S & A 38, 194. To a corporation supplying gas, 1 S & B 162. To electric supply companies, 2 S & A 181, 189, 200, 226; 1 S & B 15; 2 ibid 104. And to other petitioners, 3 C & R 131; 1 S & A 250; 2 ibid 29, 169, 233; 1 S & B 103.
5 2 C & R 133; 3 ibid 225, 378; R & M 118, 197; R & S 242; 2 S & A 150.

ing aided by rates or exchequer grants),[1] or where a tunnel is proposed to take the place of a ferry,[2] a locus standi has been allowed. By an extension of this principle, where the nature of the competition, eg concessionary fares on public service vehicles, may not adversely affect a petitioner in the district covered by the bill, but may create precedents to his ultimate disadvantage, a locus standi has been allowed.[3]

A railway company has been granted a limited locus standi against a bill authorizing another company to take lands which the petitioners had scheduled for the purposes of a bill that they themselves were promoting.[4]

It has been held that the promoters of a bona fide application to a government department for a provisional order should be entitled to a locus standi against a bill for a competing scheme, conditional only on the application not being actually rejected before the hearing of the bill in committee.[5]

In the case of a bill authorizing a railway company to own and run steamboats, the claim of steamship owners' associations to a locus standi has frequently been considered by the Court of Referees; and a locus standi against such a bill has been granted, on the ground of competition, to other railway companies,[6] to dock companies,[7] to steam packet companies,[8] and to merchants or shipowners trading to ports affected,[9] but has been refused where the interests of such petitioners were not considered to be sufficiently affected to entitle them to be heard on this ground.[10]

Locus standi of 'frontagers' against a tramway bill (Standing Order 102)

In the case of a tramways bill, the locus standi of the petitioners commonly known as 'frontagers' is dealt with by Standing Order 102. By that order a locus standi as of right is conferred on owners, lessees and occupiers of premises in any street or road along which a tramway is proposed to be constructed, who allege that the construction or use of the tramway will injuriously affect them in the use or enjoyment of their property or in the conduct of their trade or business. Further, the Court of Referees is given a discretion to grant a locus standi to owners, lessees and occupiers of prem-

---

1 Proceedings of the committee on the Sunderland Corporation Bill 1935, where the committee, acting under SO 97 (now 90) allowed a locus standi to petitioners against an additional provision. The petition being against an additional provision and *not against the bill* the question of locus standi was determined not by the Court of Referees, but by the committee on the bill. See also Minutes of Evidence of Lords Committee on Coventry Corporation Bill, 19 March 1958.
2 1 B 44.
3 1 B 21; Minutes of Evidence of Lords Committee on Coventry Corporation Bill, 19 March 1958.
4 1 S & A 176. Cf also 2 ibid 91; 2 C & S 242.
5 1 C & R 234, 235; 3 ibid 100, 114; and cf 1 S & A 301; 2 ibid 248; 1 S & B 55.
6 1 S & A 229; 2 ibid 135; 1 S & B 150.
7 R & M 270; 1 S & B 39.
8 R & M 197; 2 S & A 107; and cf R & M 100.
9 R & M 241–242, 251, 270; and cf R & S 346; 2 S & A 25, 216–221, 223.
10 R & M 241, 270; R & S 111; 2 S & A 109, 115, 174.

ises which, though not situated in such street or road, have access materially dependent thereon.[1]

Locus standi of county and municipal authorities etc (Standing Orders 96–101)

Of the six standing orders (Standing Orders 96 to 101) which deal with the locus standi of county, municipal and other public authorities, two (Standing Orders 97 and 98) grant locus standi as of right, the others are of a discretionary nature. Standing Order 97 confers the right on the council of any district or London borough alleging that their city, district or borough may be injuriously affected by the provisions of any bill relating to the lighting or water supply thereof or the raising of capital or the borrowing of money for any such purpose.[2] Standing Order 98 confers the right on the council of any county alleging that the county or any part thereof may be injuriously affected by the provisions of any bill relating to the water supply of any area whether within or without the county, or proposing to authorize the construction or reconstruction of a tramway along any road within the county to the maintenance or repair of which the county council contribute.[3]

But Standing Order 96 is the principal standing order which confers on the Court of Referees a general power of granting a locus standi to any local authority[4] of any area, the whole or any part of which is alleged in the petition to be injuriously affected[5]. The same order authorizes the grant of a locus standi to any inhabitants of the area of a local authority, and it is this locus of inhabitants which has been the chief source of dispute before the court.[6]

---

1 The latter part of SO 102, conferring the right to grant a discretionary locus, was added in 1903 to a standing order originally passed in 1870 (see CJ (1870) 221) and amended in 1886 (see CJ (1886) 281). For decision of the court with reference to this part of the SO see 2 S & A 237.
2 For the interpretation of this SO see R & S 125–127; 2 S & A 106. The question whether the words 'relating to' are to be construed as meaning 'affecting' was discussed in 2 S & B 15, 42. The word 'alleging' implies allegation of facts, 2 S & B 102.
3 Locus standi allowed: 2 S & A 47; 1 S & B 44; [1936–60] LSR 4 (against waterworks bill); 2 S & A 63; 2 S & B 35, 100 (against tramways bills); locus standi disallowed: 2 S & A 46 and 53. Locus standi limited: 1 S & A 85–90; 2 ibid 164–165.
4 For definition of 'local authority' see SO 1. That definition is wide enough to cover all the authorities to which two standing orders 136 and 138 (consolidated during the revision of 1945 into SO 96) applied, and has made obsolete numerous decisions of the Court of Referees as to the scope of those orders.
5 Loss of prospective benefit, arising out of the choice of one site for a railway terminal rather than another, has been held not to constitute injurious affection: King's Cross Railways Bill 1988–89 (petitions of the London Boroughs of Newham, Tower Hamlets and Waltham Forest). On this point, see also 1 C & R 2.
6 2 C & R 78; 3 ibid 382, 442; R & M 110; R & S 72, 221; 1 S & A 312; 2 C & S 84 ff; [1936–60] LSR 14 (Hastings 'Save our Trolleys' Committee, locus standi disallowed: insufficient interest). And cf R & S 60 ff; 1 S & A 326; 2 ibid 11, 239, 240, 242, 251. In the following cases a locus standi was allowed: R & S 227, 337 (extension of time bills); R & S 34, 237, 327; 1 S & A 9, 47, 154, 273, 334; 2 ibid 119; 1 S & B 6, 8, 9, 27, 31, 50, 100, 101; 2 ibid 1, 26, 46, 61, 73, 86, 94, 97. To road authorities of adjoining districts, against clause in bill authorizing corporation

Of the other standing orders dealing with the locus standi of public authorities, Standing Order 99 relating to river boards, and Standing Order 100 relating to land drainage authorities, have already been described (p 849). Standing Order 101 enables a locus standi to be granted to conservators having the control, regulation or management of any forest, common or open space alleged to be injuriously affected by the bill against which the petition is presented.

Locus standi of consumers of gas and water

In many cases, consumers of gas and water have been admitted to oppose gas and water bills affecting the area of supply in which they are consumers,[1] and in deciding such cases the court will have regard to the volume of interest concerned.[2] But where the petitioners were only affected in common with other ratepayers they have not been allowed a locus standi.[3] A locus standi has also been refused to residents in a new district which it was proposed to supply with gas, on the ground that they were not compelled to use the gas to be supplied or restrained from manufacturing their own.[4]

Locus standi of shareholders, preference shareholders, and 'dissentients' at a 'Wharncliffe' meeting (Standing Order 93)

The doctrine that shareholders or members of a corporate body are legally bound by the acts of the majority used frequently to be invoked as a ground of objection to the locus standi of individual shareholders who had petitioned against a bill promoted by the corporate body in which they held

---

to run omnibuses outside the borough, 1 S & B 13. Limited locus standi allowed, 1 S & B, 42, 84; 2 ibid 27, 43. Locus standi disallowed, 1 S & A 216, 328, 329; 2 ibid. 33, 141, 165, 177, 181, 213, 223, 225, 234–235; 1 S & B 23, 63, 75; 2 ibid 16, 37, 50, 63, 71, 89; in the case of extension of time bills, 1 S & B 33, 107; 2 ibid 17, 100, 101; and cf 2 S & A 241; and Parl Deb (1904) 136, c 92–106 (petition of J Taylor against Maidenhead Bridge Bill 1904). Inhabitants whose right to be heard was objected to on the ground that they were represented by the local authority, have been granted a locus standi, 2 C & R 47, 52; 1 S & A 254; 1 S & B 140. In some cases, however, where a local authority has also petitioned against a bill, a locus standi has been refused to inhabitants if they were not of a representative character, R & S 72; 2 S & A 64, or if the points they urged were similar to those urged in the local authority's petition, 2 C & S 5. Cf, however, below, for the case of consumers of gas or water. For a decision of the Lord Chairman of Committees and the Chairman of Ways and Means under the Statutory Orders (Special Procedure) Act 1945, see Welsh Water Authority and North West Water Authority (Alteration of Boundaries) Order 1979, CJ (1979–80) 550 (locus standi allowed).

1 1 C & R 17, 51, 135, 141, 143, 213; 2 ibid 9, 10; 3 ibid 40, 118; R & M 12 (water), 137, 191 (gas); R & S 53; 1 S & A 254; 2 S & B 19, 52, 65, 84. A landowner has been granted a locus standi against a bill transferring the supply of water from a corporation to a new company, 1 S & B 118.
2 2 S & B 19, 65. See also ibid 76.
3 1 C & R 144.
4 1 C & R 267; 2 ibid 78.

shares. In 1853 the House passed a standing order which, as reproduced by the first part of Standing Order 93, runs:

> Where a bill is promoted by an incorporated company, society, association or partnership, members thereof shall not be entitled to be heard before the committee against the bill, unless their interests, as affected thereby, are distinct from the general interests of the company, society, association or partnership.

The earliest decisions of the Court of Referees were therefore founded, in cases of this kind, upon the nature of the petitioners' interest, and the manner in which it is affected by the provisions of the bill.[1] The importance of these decisions has largely disappeared as the result of the passing in 1876 of a standing order (now a proviso to Standing Order 93) securing the locus standi of petitioners who have dissented at a 'Wharncliffe' meeting (for which, see pp 865–868).

For many years before the adoption of this standing order by the Commons a similar rule prevailed in the Lords; and shareholders who had dissented from the bill at the meeting called in pursuance of the Wharncliffe order were expressly permitted to be heard, and were even heard without such dissent.

It appears at present to be the case that any shareholder who has dissented at a Wharncliffe meeting is entitled to be heard on his petition,[2] but that if he has not so dissented he is entitled to be heard only if his interest, or the interest of the class of shareholders of which he is a member, is different from that of the general body of shareholders.

Locus standi of local electors and other persons represented

Closely akin to the position of shareholders is that of petitioners who—in the capacity in which they petition—may be held to be represented by a local authority or other body. Electors, for example, have not been allowed to be heard, as such, against a bill promoted by a corporation,[3] or other local authority,[4] to which they pay a charge. It should be noted, however, that this does not necessarily apply to cases where the bill is promoted by another local authority of which the petitioners are not electors but which may affect them as local taxpayers or residents (see below). By an analogy with local electors, individual members of bodies whether corporate or unincorporated have been refused a hearing against bills promoted or approved by those bodies.[5]

> In 1901, individual freemen of the Watermen and Lightermen's Company, petitioning against the Thames Piers and River Service Bill, were refused a locus standi, although the governing body of the company—by whom, it was contended, they were represented—had not petitioned.[6]

1 3 C & R 77; 1 C & S, App 8; R & M 181; cf also 1 C & S 103; 1 C & R 43, 51, 102; 2 ibid 101, 169, 273; 3 ibid 91; R & M 3, 155, 162, 225.
2 See, eg Private Business (1969–70) 205 (National Trust Bill [Lords]).
3 1 C & R 211; 3 ibid 376–377; R & M 74; R & S 287; 1 S & A 316; 2 ibid 126, 243–245; 1 S & B 58.
4 2 C & S 97, 265; 1 C & R 196; 2 ibid 9; 1 S & A 129; 2 ibid 41.
5 Committee on Queensferry Passage Bill, Group 13, 1848; Committee on Mersey Docks and Harbour (New Works) Bill, Group J 1858; R & M 288–289.
6 2 S & A 82.

On the other hand, owners who petitioned against a bill promoted by a corporation[1] or local authority,[2] and imposing upon their property a new liability to rates,[3] have been granted a locus standi, having special interests which were not considered to be represented by the promoting body, though in the case of the Ilkley Local Board Bill 1871, the Court of Referees determined that certain petitioners, being owners of property and rate-payers, could not be heard against the bill, being represented by the board by whom the bill was promoted.[4] In the case of a borough extension bill opposed by a rural sanitary authority, not only owners but ratepayers within the part of the district proposed to be added to the borough have been heard in opposition, as well as the authority itself, their interests being considered sufficiently distinct to entitle them to a separate hearing.[5]

> In 1904 a locus standi was granted to two railway companies who claimed to be heard as ratepayers against the Wolverhampton Corporation Bill on the grounds that they were affected differently from other ratepayers and that they desired to ask for differential rating.[6] In 1897 the rating author-ities of two parishes were granted a locus standi, limited to the question of rating, against a railway bill, in addition to the superior authority of the larger district of which these parishes formed a part.[7]

Locus standi against bills brought from the Lords

A petitioner who has not opposed a bill in the other House is not precluded from being heard upon his petition in the House of Commons;[8] but the locus standi of petitioners has been disallowed, where they have consented, in the other House, to protective clauses.[9]

Petitioners who had tendered a clause in the House of Lords which was rejected by the committee, and who had then accepted two other clauses, with alterations suggested by themselves, were held not to be precluded from a hearing before the committee of the Commons, as the clauses they had accepted were of minor importance, and had only been acquiesced in conditionally upon the acceptance of their own clause, which had been rejected.[10] If the parties agree to abide by the decision of the committee in one House they will not be heard in the other: but if they have not so agreed[11] it is otherwise.

---

1 2 C & S 121; 1 C & R 211, 229; 2 ibid 149, 233; R & M 76–78; R & S 349; 2 S & A 175; 1 S & B 142; 2 ibid 30 (limited), 69.
2 1 C & R 196, and cf R & S 276–278; 1 S & A 39, 139; 2 ibid 72; 1 S & B 77; [1936–60] LSR 21.
3 The locus standi thus given to an owner has also been given to the leaseholder (for a substantial terms of years) of property rendered liable to increased taxation, R & S 349–353.
4 2 C & S 97. Cf also 3 C & R 376–378; R & M 73; R & S 276; 2 S & A 153; 1 S & B 3, 65; 2 ibid 30, 84.
5 2 C & R 47; R & M 77. But cf 2 S & A 228–229.
6 2 S & A 254. See also 2 S & B 76. But cf 1 S & B 1, 54, 129.
7 1 S & A 222. Cf also 2 S & A 11, 12.
8 S, App 162.
9 S, App 95; 2 C & R 27; R & S 39; 2 S & A 85.
10 1 C & R 275.
11 Whitehaven, Cleator etc Railway Bill 1875, 1 C & R 200.

By Standing Order 130 of the Commons, reproducing a standing order originally passed in 1888,[1] it is expressly provided that—

A petitioner against a bill originating in the House of Lords who has discussed clauses in that House shall not on that account be precluded from opposing the preamble of the bill in this House.

Parties are occasionally precluded from opposing a bill by some special circumstance, such, for example, as an undertaking to this effect given to the promoters. However in 1892 petitioners who had been precluded, under an agreement with the promoters, embodied in an Act of Parliament, from opposing a bill which was first introduced in the Lords, were granted a locus standi against it in the Commons, the bill having been so materially amended by the Lords' committee that, as brought down to the second House, it was held no longer to be the bill which the petitioners were bound not to oppose.[2]

Locus standi objected to on ground of want of precision or informality

An objection which inter alia has sometimes been taken to the locus standi of a petitioner is, that the allegations of his petition are not sufficiently specific;[3] but the Court of Referees have rarely refused a locus standi for this reason alone,[4] and, as already pointed out (see p 842), Standing Order 128 expressly enables the committee on a bill to require a petitioner to give in a more specific statement of the grounds of his opposition.

An analogous objection that has frequently been taken to the locus standi of petitioners is that their petition is informal, according to the rules and orders of the House applicable to petitions generally (see chapter 31), or as specially applicable to petitions against private bills.

The informality which has been the most fruitful source of disputes before the Court of Referees has been with reference to the signature of petitions.[5]

---

1 CJ (1888) 449.
2 R & S 231–232.
3 Suppl to Votes, 1847–48, p 322; 1849, p 173; 1851, pp 103, 108, 109, 110; Minutes of Committees, 1857, ii, p 707; 1 C & R 22, 201; 3 ibid 50, 81, 442; R & M 213.
4 1 S & A 341; and cf 1 C & R 207; 3 ibid 301, 457 (landowners' petition); 2 S & A 106 (petition of local authority under SO 134A (now 97)); 1 S & B 43, 100, 134, 143.
5 Locus standi allowed: 1 C & S App 7 (Petition signed by majority of committee appointed to conduct opposition to the bill); 1 C & R 272; 1 C & S App 3–4 (petition signed by Chairman of committee of board of guardians acting as rural sanitary authority under resolution of the sanitary authority, the guardians in their capacity as sanitary authority having no common seal); R & M 14, 270–271 (petition signed by persons on behalf of company when the authority to sign was proved to the satisfaction of the court although no allegation to that effect contained in petition); R & S 163 (vicar and churchwardens authorized to sign at public meetings); 1 S & B 138 (petition signed by two of the promoters of competing bill on behalf of all the promoters); 2 C & R 25, 261; 3 ibid 316; R & M 14 (petition of company signed by directors without special authority); 1 C & R 72 (petition of landowner signed by agent holding a general power of attorney for the administration of the estate); but evidence of authority not allowed where agent had no power of attorney, 3 C & R 155. Locus standi disallowed: S App 97 (petition signed by some only of a body of trustees); S App 174 (petitioner subscribing petition for other parties); 1 C & R 117 (petition signed by chairman of Commissioners containing no allegation that he was authorized to sign on their behalf).

The Court of Referees has declined to inquire into the genuineness of the signatures to a petition, that being a matter for the consideration of the House.[1]

Locus standi and the 'filled-up' bill

The bill before the Court of Referees during its consideration of a case is the bill as deposited, not the 'filled-up' bill (see pp 889–890) as proposed to be amended and submitted to the committee by the promoters; and a petitioner is not refused a locus standi because the promoters undertake, by amendments in the filled-up bill, to meet his objections to the bill as deposited,[2] but has uniformly been allowed to go before the committee to see that this undertaking is carried out.[3] The Court has thus supported the right of landowners to be heard where their lands were proposed to be taken by the bill as deposited.

On the other hand a person who objected to an amendment proposed in the 'filled-up' bill would petition not against the bill but against the alterations of the bill, and the committee on the bill would have to determine his locus standi.

Locus standi of petitioners against a consolidation bill

In the case of a consolidation bill, the locus standi of a petitioner is not allowed where he is affected not by the bill but by the provisions of a former Act;[4] or where no fresh powers affecting the property of a petitioner are sought by the bill;[5] and the decision in the Birmingham Corporation (Consolidation) Bill 1883, whereby petitioners were allowed to be heard against the provisions of the Acts proposed to be consolidated, would appear to be inconsistent with the general practice.[6] The injury alleged must not be one due to past legislation, untouched by the bill, but injury which is or may be occasioned under the bill, either for the first time, or in aggravation of injury already suffered.[7]

Pure consolidation bills now usually originate in the House of Lords and are referred to a joint committee, to which the petitions against such a bill stand referred (see also p 888).

Miscellaneous cases of locus standi

Cases sometimes arise before the Court of Referees where locus standi is claimed on exceptional grounds, and are decided on their individual facts.

---

1 1 C & R 119; 2 ibid 321. Cf the special report from the committee on the Glasgow Municipal Extension Bill 1879, which inquired into the genuineness of the signatures to a petition against the bill, and refused a hearing to the parties appearing before it on the petition, CJ (1878–79) 176.
2 The bill as deposited, however, has been considered by the Court of Referees to include such amendments as the Standing Orders Committee shall have required to be made in it as a condition of its proceeding; Renfrew Burgh etc Bill CJ (1898) 75; 1 S & A 274; Airdrie, etc, Tramways Bill, CJ (1900) 55; 2 S & A 2.
3 1 C & R 78; R & S 341–342, 352; 1 S & A 19–20.
4 Suppl to Votes, 1847, ii, 1070, 1113; 3 C & R 28, 58, 96, 97; R & S 208; 1 S & A 100; 2 ibid 71, 230.
5 2 C & R 207; R & M 26, 70; R & S 1, 56, 93.
6 3 C & R 257.
7 1 C & S 95; [1936–60] LSR 13.

For example, a telephone company, who alleged that the propinquity of an electric tramway (authorized, but not made) would injure their work by induction and who desired to ask for protective clauses in a bill for the extension of time for its completion, was granted a locus standi on the ground of the change which had taken place in the scientific knowledge and practical application of electricity.[1]

Again, petitioners using a canal for the purposes of traffic have claimed, sometimes successfully,[2] and sometimes unsuccessfully,[3] to be heard against a bill for the purchase of the canal by a railway company.

A locus standi has also been granted to petitioners against a clause in a bill, on the ground that the clause would establish a precedent.[4]

Where petitioners and promoters have placed different constructions upon an ambiguously worded clause, the Court of Referees has declined to pronounce upon its legal effect, but, giving the petitioners the benefit of the doubt, has allowed them a locus standi to be heard before the committee.[5]

A locus standi has not been granted to a petitioner who claimed to be heard as the prospective parliamentary candidate or local councillor for a constituency or ward within the area affected by a bill[6] or for local branches of political parties[7].

REVISION BY THE HOUSE OF DECISIONS OF REFEREES

In some instances where a locus standi against a private bill has been disallowed by the Court of Referees, the petitioners' case has been brought before the House by a motion to instruct the committee on the bill to hear them.

Such a motion was made in 1872 with regard to petitioners (the Corporation of London) against the Thames Embankment, North, Bill, but was negatived on division.[8] In 1890, an instruction was similarly moved to direct the committee on the North British, etc, Railway Companies Bill to hear certain petitioners who had been refused a locus standi; and although the motion for an instruction was withdrawn, the case of the petitioners was referred back on the motion of the Chairman of the Court to the Court of Referees, who reheard it and granted them a locus standi.[9] A motion to refer back to the Court the case of the 'Save our Trolleys' Committee, who had petitioned against the Hastings Tramways Bill [Lords] 1957, was withdrawn.[10]

1R & S 102, 167, 242, 259; 2 S & A 34, 77. Cf ibid 62, 86, 98. For other cases where the decision was based on the fact whether the existing law did or did not afford sufficient protection, see R & S 242–245, 256–258, 262; 1 S & A 108, 282; 2 S & A 69, 145, 193, 237, 241; 1 S & B 48, 54, 106, 115; 2 S & B 8.

21 C & S App 66, 126.

31 C & R 150.

41 B 21, 79. See also Minutes of Evidence of Lords Committee on Coventry Corporation Bill, 19 March 1958.

5R & M 59; R & S 137, 339. Cf 2 S & A 48 (disallowed).

6[1960–83] LSR 22, Shoreham Harbour Bill 1986.

7King's Cross Railways Bill 1989 (petitions of Hampstead and Highgate Constituency Labour Party and others).

8CJ (1872) 159; Parl Deb (1872) 210, c 1808. Cf also notice of instruction (not moved) on the Maidenhead Bridge Bill, Private Business, 1904, p 560; CJ (1904) 257; Parl Deb (1904) 136, cc 92–106, 1060–66.

9CJ (1890) 257–58; Parl Deb (1890) 343, cc 1181–1185; R & S 52–53.

10Private Business (1956–57) 225, 234 and 237. See also Private Business (1988–89) 228, 368.

PETITIONERS AGAINST PRIVATE BILLS COMMITTED TO SPECIALLY CONSTITUTED COMMITTEES

Where a private bill is specially committed to a select committee nominated partly by the House and partly by the Committee of Selection (see pp 825–826), the locus standi of petitioners against the bill[1] depends upon whatever order as to petitions is made by the House when committing the bill. In some such cases the House has ordered that, 'subject to the rules, orders, and proceedings of the House', all petitioners against the bill,[2] or all the petitioners whose petitions shall have been deposited before a specified time,[3] should be heard by the committee; or, that such petitioners 'as would otherwise have a locus standi',[4] or 'whose locus standi may be sustained',[5] should be heard; and in these cases the petitioners' locus standi is determined by the Court of Referees. But, more commonly, the House has ordered select committees upon a private bill to hear all the petitioners against the bill,[6] or all petitioners whose petitions shall be deposited within a specified time;[7] and in such cases it has been held that the jurisdiction of the Court of Referees is superseded by the order of the House.[8]

PRIVATE BILL COMMITTEES INSTRUCTED BY THE HOUSE TO HEAR CERTAIN PETITIONERS

In 1864 permissive instructions were given to an ordinary private bill committee on a group of metropolitan railway bills to allow the promoters of certain competing schemes (which the House had ordered not to be proceeded with in that session) to be heard upon their petitions, if duly deposited against particular bills before the committee.[9] In 1869 all the metropolitan street tramways bills were considered by one committee, and it was ordered that all petitioners against any of the said bills be heard, without reference to any question of locus standi.[10] In 1905 a mandatory instruction was given, directing the committee on the North East London Railway Bill to hear the promoters of another scheme who had deposited a petition against the bill, and whose locus standi was about to be contested before the

---

1 See p 844 for rules about notice of intention to object to locus standi in these cases.
2 CJ (1895) 53; ibid (1898) 172; ibid (1959–60) 265; ibid (1961–62) 190.
3 CJ (1899) 96. Cf also CJ (1890–91) 330.
4 CJ (1893–94) 233; ibid (1899) 83. In both these cases a time before which the petitions had to be presented was specified.
5 CJ (1882) 166 (all petitions presented during the session); ibid (1893–94) 84 (all petitions presented before a specified time).
6 CJ (1878) 62; ibid (1881) 466; ibid (1883) 323. In the case the York (Micklegate Strays) (recommitted) Bill, the House ordered that the 'parties interested' should be heard before the select committee, CJ (1907) 422.
7 All petitions presented during the session: CJ (1871) 65; ibid (1872) 312; or within the time limited by standing orders: CJ (1886) 69; ibid (1888) 330; or before a specified time: CJ (1875) 230; ibid (1909) 104; ibid (1928) 66 (Joint Committee), 148 (Joint Committee); ibid (1928–29) 125, 180 (Joint Committee). An order that has been made, referring to the committee petitions presented before a specified time has subsequently been suspended in favour of particular petitioners, CJ (1892) 136; ibid (1899) 89, 234, 238.
8 Commercial Gas Bill 1875, 1 C & R 149–150.
9 CJ (1864) 167, 190.
10 CJ (1868–69) 63. See also CJ (1852–53) 572, Suppl to Votes, 1852–53, p 999; CJ (1909) 282; ibid (1910) 210.

Referees.[1] In 1913 the petitions of certain societies against a clause of a private bill and the relative part of the preamble presented five clear days before the meeting of the committee on the bill were ordered to be referred to the committee,[2] and in 1914 the council of a metropolitan borough was permitted to appear upon the allegations contained in its petition against a bill promoted by two railway companies, while the committee was also instructed that it might determine how far the powers of one of these companies to supply electricity should be limited.[3]

Petition specially referred by House to Private Bill Committee

On 17 May 1849 a petition from the Attorney General against a private bill was brought up and read; and it being stated that it was essential to the public interest that it should be referred to the committee on the bill, the standing order requiring all such petitions to be deposited in the Private Bill Office was read and suspended, and an instruction given to the committee to entertain the petition.[4]

---

1 CJ (1905) 231. Cf also the notice of instruction (not moved) on the Weaver Navigation Bill 1893, Private Business (1893–94) p 510; and R & S 312.
2 CJ (1913) 144. See also ibid (1914) 80, 141.
3 CJ (1914) 93.
4 CJ (1849) 302.

CHAPTER 36

Proceedings in the House of Commons on private bills

GENERAL

The proceedings in the House of Commons on a private bill will now be followed, step by step, from its presentation in that House, in the order in which particular rules are to be observed by the parties or enforced by the House or its officers. This statement of the various forms of procedure is introduced by a few observations explanatory of the general conduct of private business in the House of Commons.

Giving of notices in connection with private business

It has been stated elsewhere that the public business for each day is set down in the order book, either as notices of motions or orders of the day; but the notices in relation to private bills (except those which a Member desires to move in relation to private business in the House) are required to be delivered at the Private Bill Office, at specified times, by the agents soliciting the bills. These notices will each be described in their proper places; but Standing Order 209 applies to all of them alike as well as to deposits—they must be deposited between eleven and five o'clock (or, on a Friday, between half-past nine and three o'clock) on any day on which the House sits, or between eleven and one on any day on which the House does not sit,[1] excluding Sundays and bank holidays. After any day on which the House has adjourned beyond the following day, no notice may be given for the first day on which it is next to sit.

If notice not duly given, proceedings void. If any stage of a bill is proceeded with when the notice has not been duly given, or the proper interval allowed, or if notice is taken of any other informality, the proceeding will be null and void, and the stage must be repeated.[2]

Notices printed in the Votes. All notices are open to inspection in the Private Bill Office, but for the sake of greater publicity and convenience

---

1 It is normal practice for agents intending to deposit such notices on a Saturday to notify the Private Bill Office in advance.
2 CJ (1845) 423; ibid (1846) 167; ibid (1851) 75; ibid (1852) 157; ibid (1867) 66; ibid (1878) 61; ibid (1884) 57; ibid (1945–46) 360.

they are also printed with the Votes. The private business to be taken on a particular day appears in the appropriate place in the order paper for that day (see pp 277–281).

Private business

The time at which matters relating to private bills are considered by the House has already been stated in chapter 16. To entitle a motion to be heard at the time of private business, it must relate to a private bill before the House, or strictly to private business in some other form. Motions for the amendment of the standing orders relative to private business, and matters indirectly connected with the private business of the House, are also taken into consideration at the time of private business.[1]

On 30 April 1895 a proposed amendment to one of the standing orders relative to private business was not permitted to be moved at the time of private business, on the ground that it dealt simply with general questions relating to the conduct of railway companies. The Speaker stated that amendments to those standing orders, if taken at that time, must relate directly to the subject-matter of private bills and not to the general conduct of the companies who promoted the bills.[2] Similarly, a proposed general instruction to all committees on railway bills has not been permitted to be moved at the time of private business, on the ground that the proposed motion raised a question of general policy.[3]

As a result of the passing of the Local Government Act 1948 amendments were required both to the public business and to the private business standing orders (see p 869), and it was found convenient that these should be discussed together. The House accordingly ordered that the motion relevant to the amendments might be made at the time of public business notwithstanding that it related in part to the private business standing orders.[4] The same procedure was followed after the passing of the Local Government (Financial Provisions) (Scotland) Act 1954.[5] On that occasion, however, Standing Order 51 (Application of public money standing orders to private bills, etc), which brought private bills within the scope of the standing orders relating to public money subject to certain exemptions, was amended to extend those exemptions to any category of bills prescribed by the private business standing orders. The effect of this amendment was to avoid a recurrence of the need to move amendments simultaneously to both public and private business standing orders relating to public money.

Deferment of stages of private bill, etc, if opposed

Under Standing Orders 174 and No 16 (Public), no opposed business may be proceeded with during the time of private business, but must be deferred

---

1 Eg CJ (1854) 396; ibid (1935–36) 367; ibid (1974–75) 622, etc. See also HC Deb (1979–80) 978, cc 1074–1075 and 1268.
2 Parl Deb (1895) 33, cc 116–118.
3 The Speaker's private ruling, 26 March 1895.
4 CJ (1948–49) 18.
5 CJ (1953–54) 333.

until such time as the Chairman of Ways and Means may appoint.[1] Business not reached by the end of the time for private business stands over to the next sitting, or in the case of business which has been opposed, to the next sitting other than a Friday.[2] Opposed business includes any proceedings on a private bill or confirming bill which have been deferred so long as notice of an amendment stands upon the notice paper in the form of a notice of motion on second reading, consideration or third reading of a bill, provided that no such notice of motion may stand upon the notice paper for more than seven days unless renewed.

The procedure on objection being taken to an item of private business has already been described (see p 278). Under Standing Order 174(5) and Standing Order No 16(5) (Public), when opposed private business has been set down by direction of the Chairman of Ways and Means for consideration at seven o'clock, that direction includes the setting down of any motion contingent directly or otherwise thereupon, eg instructions moved after second reading, to committees on the bills.

Conduct of bills by Members

The forms and proceedings in the offices of the House, connected with the progress of a bill, are managed by the agent for the bill, and by the officers of the House; but, in the House itself, orders upon a private bill are obtained by a motion made by a Member and a question proposed and put, in the usual manner, from the Chair; and, except when opposed, motions relating to private bills are subject to the general rules of the House regarding motions (see pp 321 ff). The various stages of private bills, when taken at the time of private business, are moved formally in the House by the Chairman of Ways and Means as also are amendments, etc, desired by the promoters. However, when a bill has been set down by the Chairman for consideration at seven o'clock, once the order of the day has been taken up by the Chairman, its second reading or any later stage is moved by a Member who has agreed to act on behalf of the promoters.

Private bill registers (Standing Order 192)

Every proceeding of the House upon a private bill is entered in the Votes and Journals; and, in the Private Bill Office, registers are also kept, which are open to public inspection daily, and in which all the proceedings, from the petition to the passing of the bill, are recorded.

1. PROCEEDINGS FROM PRESENTATION TO COMMITTEE STAGE

After these explanations, the proceedings in the House are described in the order in which they usually occur.

---

1 He may appoint no day. See HC Deb (1961–62) 664, c2 and ibid (1976–77) 936, c278.
2 No opposed private business may be taken on a Friday (SO 174(3)).

PRESENTATION OF BILL (STANDING ORDER 163)

A private bill is presented to the House by being deposited in the Private Bill Office. It must be laid upon the Table of the House by one of the clerks of that office on the next sitting day.[1]

Where, in respect of a petition for a private bill, the Examiner has reported that the standing orders have been complied with, the bill itself must be presented to the House on 21 January, or, if the House is not sitting on that day, on the first sitting day thereafter, or if the Examiner's report is laid on the Table on or after 21 January, on the first sitting day after the report was so laid. Where the Examiner has reported non-compliance and the House, on considering the report from the Standing Orders Committee that the standing orders ought to be dispensed with, gives leave to the parties to proceed with their bill, the bill must be presented not later than the following day, or, if leave was given before 21 January, on that day, or if the House is not sitting on that day, on the first sitting day thereafter.

Where the Examiner has made a special report under Standing Order 79 (see p 819) in respect of a petition for a private bill, the date of presentation depends upon the decision reached by the Standing Orders Committee. If the Standing Orders Committee decides that the standing orders have not been complied with and the House, on considering a report from that Committee that the standing orders ought to be dispensed with, gives leave to the parties to proceed with the bill, the bill must be presented not later than the following day, or, if such leave was given before 21 January, on that day, or if the House is not sitting on that day, on the first sitting day thereafter. If, however, the Standing Orders Committee reports that the standing orders have been complied with, the bill must be presented to the House not later than the following day, or if the report was made before 21 January, on that day, or if the House is not sitting on that day, on the first sitting day thereafter.

Printing of private bills (Standing Orders 38, 164, 164A, 168)

Every private bill must be printed, and printed copies[2] delivered on or before 27 November at the Vote Office for the use of Members and in the Private Bill Office for the use of agents and others interested. The Speaker has permitted this requirement to be dispensed with in the case of a personal bill (see p 813). For purposes of presentation a private bill must be printed on A4-size paper in the same style as public bills[3] and enclosed in a cover of parchment, upon which the title is written; the short title of the bill, as first entered in the Votes, must correspond with that at the head of the advertisement. This copy of the bill is called the 'House Copy'.[4]

Standing Order 168 provides that 'subject to the provisions of Standing Order 156A (see p 870), all charges in any way affecting the public revenue,

---

1 By the Speaker's private ruling of October 1945, private bills are presented by the Clerk of the House, and it is no longer necessary for Members to present, or have their names printed on the back of, such bills.

2 These copies must have bound up with them any financial memoranda stipulated under SO 169 (see below).

3 Speaker's order of 24 June 1984.

4 On 20 February 1846 the solicitor and agent for a bill petitioned for leave to add schedules which had been accidentally omitted from the printed copies of the bill, and the House allowed the parties to make the alteration, CJ (1846) 183, 185 (Southport Improvement Bill).

which occur in the clauses of any private bill, shall be printed in italics'. (This differs from the arrangement for public bills, see p 468.) Also, under Standing Order 164A the name of any company, society, association, or partnership, not being promoters of the bill, upon which powers are conferred or whose constitution is to be altered, must be expressed in the title of any bill originating in the Commons to which Standing Order 64 applies (see pp 867–868).

Financial memorandum required in certain cases (Standing Orders 169, 219)

Every private bill or bill to confirm a provisional order which involves, or in respect of which there has been promised, a grant from any Government department, must, on presentation, have bound with it a printed statement in the form of a financial memorandum describing the grant and showing the amount thereof. No such memorandum is, however, required when the question of a Government grant arises by reason only that the bill contains provisions of the types mentioned in Standing Order 156A (see p 870), nor is one necessarily required merely because the bill involves expenditure from public funds.

First reading (Standing Order 166)

When 'laid on the Table of the House' a private bill is deemed to have been read the first time on the day on which it is so laid, and is ordered to be read a second time, and is recorded in the Journal as having been so read and ordered.

Lords bills read the first time and referred to the Examiners (Standing Orders 74 and 166). A private bill brought from the House of Lords is deemed to have been read the first time on the day on which it is received from that House, and it is recorded in the Journal as having been so read. It is thereupon referred to the Examiners, before whom compliance with such standing orders only as have not been previously inquired into has to be proved. For the procedure on personal bills, see pp 812–813.

Bills referred to the Examiners under Standing Order 61 (HC and HL). Whenever any alteration has been made in any work authorized by any bill in respect of which a plan and section are required under Standing Order 27 to be deposited, during its progress through the House in which it originates, proof has to be given before the Examiner, when the bill reaches the second House, of compliance with certain conditions which are specified in detail in the standing order. These conditions correspond to those with which compliance has to be proved, before the presentation of such a bill, under the preliminary standing orders already mentioned, including notices to, and obtaining consents from, owners, lessees and occupiers of land through which the alteration is to be made.[1] Compliance with this order is not necessary when alterations have been made upon a petition for additional provision in the first House.

Bills referred to the Examiners under the 'Wharncliffe' Orders (Standing Orders 62–67 (HC and HL)). Under what are known as the 'Wharn-

---

1 Cf Committee on South Eastern Railway Bill 1889.

cliffe' standing orders,[1] bills conferring particular powers upon companies constituted by Act of Parliament or otherwise have to be referred, in both Houses, to the Examiners for proof that the bills have been duly approved of by the proprietors or members of the companies concerned, in the manner prescribed in the orders.[2] Similarly, under Standing Order 68, where a bill proposes to set up a company, proof must be given to the Examiners that the bill has the agreement of any person named in it as a director, etc. The particular provisions of this standing order and of the six 'Wharncliffe' orders are practically identical in both Houses, and are described here in their House of Commons form. The 'Wharncliffe' orders fall into three pairs, namely, Standing Orders 62 and 65, 63 and 66, and 64 and 67, the second order of each pair dealing with the same subject as the first order of the pair when the bill originates in the second House, or when provisions, of a kind specified in the order, have been inserted in that House. In the first House such bills are referred to the Examiners after second reading for proof of compliance with these standing orders. In the second House, when such a bill is referred to the Examiners after first reading, proof is given (if necessary) that there has been compliance with these standing orders.[3]

Consents of proprietors of statutory companies promoting bills (Standing Orders 62 and 65). These orders provide that, where a bill is promoted by a company constituted by Act of Parliament, proof is to be given to the Examiner that the several requirements of the standing order relating to the meeting of proprietors, and the approval by such proprietors holding at least three-fourths of the paid-up capital of the company represented by the votes at the meeting, have been complied with. Provision is also made that, where the company carries on two or more separate undertakings and portions of the capital are allocated so as to be exclusively applicable to the several undertakings, separate meetings of the proprietors of the capital so allocated to separate undertakings shall be held so far as the bill relates to any such separate undertaking.

Both this pair and the following pair of orders contain requirements with regard to notice to be given of meetings (Standing Orders 62 and 65 only), the use of proxies, the holding of a poll if demanded, and the recording of proceedings at meetings. Provision is made for the modification of the requirements as regards notice of late bills. Further, while Standing Order 62 refers to all such bills originating in the Commons, Standing Order 65 refers to

> every bill brought from the House of Lords in which provisions have been inserted in that House, empowering the promoters thereof, being a company constituted by Act of Parliament to execute, undertake, or contribute towards any work other than that for which it was originally established, or to sell or lease their undertak-

---

1 Named after Lord Wharncliffe who was largely responsible for framing the first order of this nature and for its adoption in 1838 by the House of Lords. See Williams i, 162–168.
2 For the right of proprietors, etc, dissenting under SOs 62–68, to be heard before the Examiners, cf SO 76, and above, p 816.
3 For the practice regarding hybrid bills see pp 520–521.

ing, or any part thereof, or to enter into any agreements with any other company for the working, maintenance, management, or use of the railway or works of either company, or any part thereof, or to amalgamate their undertaking, or any part thereof, with any other undertaking, or to purchase any other undertaking, or part thereof, or any additional lands, or to abandon their undertaking, or any part thereof, or authorizing or enacting the dissolution of the promoting company, or in which any such provisions originally contained in the bill have been materially altered in that House.

Consents of members of registered companies, etc, promoting bills (Standing Orders 63 and 66). These orders apply to a bill promoted by any company, society, association, or partnership, whether a company within the meaning of the Companies Act 1985 or otherwise constituted (and not being a company to which the preceding order applies). If the promoting company is a company within the meaning of the Companies Act 1985, proof must be given before the Examiner that the bill has been approved by a special resolution of the company. If the company, etc, has been otherwise constituted, proof must be given that the bill has been consented to by three-fourths in number and (where applicable) in value of the proprietors or members present and voting at a meeting convened by notice. Moreover, if the bill relates to a separate class of proprietors or members as distinct from the proprietors or members generally, the approval of that class must be proved. While Standing Order 63 refers to all such bills originating in the Commons, Standing Order 66 refers to

> every bill brought from the House of Lords, in which provisions have been inserted in that House empowering or requiring the promoters thereof, being a company, society, association, or partnership, whether a company within the meaning of the Companies Act 1985 or otherwise constituted (and not being a company to which the preceding order applies), to do any act not authorized by the memorandum and articles of association, or other instrument constituting or regulating the company, society, association, or partnership, or authorizing or enacting the abandonment of the undertaking, or any part of the undertaking, of such company, society, association, or partnership, or the dissolution thereof, or in which any such provisions originally contained in the bill have been materially altered in that House.

Also, by Standing Order 66, where consent, as mentioned in Standing Order 63, has been given 'subject to such additions, alterations and variations as Parliament may think fit to make therein,' it is not necessary to obtain any further approval or consent in respect of any provisions inserted in the bill in the Lords, unless the committee on the bill otherwise decides.

Consents of members of companies, etc, not being promoters, in the case of certain bills (Standing Orders 64 and 67). These two orders were made in 1940 to meet the case of a bill promoted by a company controlling other companies and to provide that meetings should be held to obtain the consent of the proprietors or members of all the companies concerned.[1] The orders provide that where any bill contains provisions conferring any powers upon, or altering the constitution of any company, society, association or partnership named in the bill but not being the promoters thereof, compliance with Standing Orders 62, 63, 65 and 66, as the case may be, shall be proved as

---

1 CJ (1939–40) 249, 250; HC Deb (1939–40) 365, cc 1407–1410 (South-Eastern Gas Corporation Limited (Associated Companies) Bill). See also pp 797–798.

though any such company, etc, were the promoters, so far as the aforesaid provisions are concerned; but the orders are not to apply to any bill so far as its provisions are for the protection of the company, etc, or relate to a proposal either for the compulsory acquisition by or transfer to the promoters of the whole or part of the undertaking or assets of the company, etc, or for the imposition of any duty or obligation upon, or the limitation of any power of, the company etc.

> In 1954 representations were made by the opponents of the Kent Water Bill that the bill 'conferred powers' upon certain water companies by transferring other water undertakings to them; that these transfers did not impose 'any duty or obligation' within the meaning of the proviso to Standing Order 64; and that the consents of members of the companies concerned should therefore be obtained before the bill could proceed. After hearing the parties, the Chairman of Ways and Means decided that Standing Order 64 was not applicable, and the bill was accordingly not referred to the Examiners after second reading.

By Standing Order 164A the name of any company, etc, upon which powers are to be conferred or whose constitution is to be altered by the bill must be expressed in the title of any bill to which Standing Order 64 applies; and by Standing Order 44 where any such company, etc, carries on an undertaking for the supply of water, either a printed copy of the bill or notice in writing of its provisions must be delivered or sent to the clerk of the council of each county or district and to the town clerk of each city or borough which comprises the whole or any part of the area within which the company, etc, supply water.

SECOND READING

Interval between first and second reading (Standing Order 170)

Between the first and second reading of a private bill, there must be not less than four clear days.

Notice of second reading (Standing Order 198)

The agent for the bill is required to give not less than three clear days' notice in writing to the Clerks in the Private Bill Office, of the day proposed for the second reading, and no such notice may be given until the day after that on which the bill has been ordered to be read a second time. If it should afterwards be discovered that such notice had not been duly given, the proceedings upon the second reading will be declared null and void.[1]

Notice of second reading must be given for a day not later than the eighth day after first reading, unless the bill has been brought from the House of Lords and referred to the Examiners. In that event, notice of second reading may be given for a day not later than the eighth day after the bill has been ordered to be read a second time. If the House resolves to adjourn beyond

---

1 North Union Railway (Horwich Branch) Bill, CJ (1846) 371.

the eighth day, the notice may be given for the day to which the House has adjourned or the following day.[1]

Bill examined in Private Bill Office (Standing Orders 196, 197)

Meanwhile the House copy of the bill is in the custody of the Private Bill Office, where the bill is examined as to its conformity with the rules and standing orders of the House.

Provisions in private bills, or petitions for additional provision, imposing charges

Bills other than those affecting grants to local authorities. It has already been explained (see p 468) that any clauses and provisions, incidentally contained in a public bill, which create a charge on the consolidated fund or on the national loans fund or on the public revenues, or which impose a tax on the people, have to be sanctioned by a resolution of the House, the recommendation of the Crown being signified. Before the committee on a bill (other than a bill affecting only grants to local authorities) can consider the matter, similar proceedings are necessary with regard to any such provision when contained in a private bill or proposed, whether by amendment[2] or upon a petition for additional provision,[3] to be inserted in a private bill. The procedure follows that for financial resolutions relating to public bills, but proceedings are taken at the time of private business.[4]

> In 1882, the East London Railway Bill, after having been considered as amended, was re-committed to a Committee of the whole House, with an instruction to make provision pursuant to the resolution that had been reported from the committee on East London Railway [Repayment of Deposits] and agreed to by the House.[5]

A bill suspended during its passage through the Commons may not rely on a financial resolution passed in the previous session.[6]

Bills affecting grants to local authorities. The Local Government Finance Act 1988 (see p 714) has made a fundamental alteration in the method of financing exchequer grants to local authorities as a consequence of which new expenditure by a local authority might lead to increases in the grants which it receives. To avoid the necessity for compliance with the financial procedure of the House in each individual case, three standing

---

1 In 1962, the agents for the Runcorn and District Water Bill failed to give notice for second reading of the Bill until after seven days (as was then prescribed) had elapsed. The House agreed to a motion by the Chairman of Ways and Means permitting the agents to rectify the matter, CJ (1961–62) 265; see also, ibid (1867–68) 289; ibid (1936–37) 267.
2 City of Westminster Bill (receipts from fixed penalties payable into Consolidated Fund), Votes and Proceedings (1986–87), 7 May 1987, HC Deb (1986–87) 115, cc 935–936, 940.
3 National Loan Fund Life Assurance Society Bill (stamp duty on memorials), CJ (1854–55) 217, 221, 225, 229; Law Life Assurance Society Bill (stamp duty on memorials), ibid (1863) 312, 316, 327, 330; Land Securities Company Bill (stamp duty on mortgage debentures), ibid (1864) 116, 122, 126, 127.
4 See eg CJ (1967–68) 132, Votes and Proceedings (1987–88), 17 May 1988.
5 CJ (1882) 242, 254.
6 Covent Garden Market Bill 1965–66, CJ (1964–65) 255; ibid (1965–66) 14; Yorkshire Water Authority Bill 1985–86, CJ (1984–85) 594; ibid (1985–86) 20.

orders (Standing Order No 51 (Public) and Standing Orders 156A and 156B (Private); originally passed in November 1948, as a consequence of the Local Government Act 1948) cover bills authorizing expenditure by a local authority.[1] By virtue of these orders it is not necessary, in the case of a private bill, to comply with the standing orders and practice of the House relating to charges upon the public revenue, by reason only that the bill contains provisions of the kind mentioned which would or might operate to increase the sums payable by way of exchequer grant.[2] The manner in which control over certain of these charges on the public revenues is maintained by the Crown is described below (see p 901).

Bills containing provisions referred to in Standing Order 156A are exempt from the provisions of Standing Order 168 (charges affecting public revenue to be printed in italics) (see pp 864–865), and Standing Order 169 (attachment of financial memoranda to certain bills) (see p 865), and enjoy the relaxation of the Commons' privileges contained in Standing Order 191 (tolls and charges not in the nature of a tax) (see p 828).

House of Lords and charges upon the people in private bills

The House of Commons will not allow the Lords to be concerned in the levy of any charge upon the people; but a considerable change in modern practice has resulted from the operation of Standing Order 191, by which the Commons do not insist on their privileges in regard to clauses referring to tolls and charges for services performed (not being in the nature of a tax), and to sums payable by way of exchequer grant to local authorities in England and Wales or in Scotland.

Bills withdrawn and bills presented in lieu of bills withdrawn (Standing Orders 74, 75, 214)

If the bill be improperly drawn[3] the House may order it to be withdrawn. If, when a bill is withdrawn, leave is given to present another,[4] the bill so presented is distinguished from the first bill by being styled No 2 and, having been read the first time, is referred to the Examiners. Not less than two clear days' notice is given of the examination, and memorials may be deposited before twelve o'clock on the day preceding that appointed. The Examiner inquires whether the standing orders, which have not been previously inquired into in respect of the first bill, have been complied with in respect of the No 2 bill, and reports accordingly to the House, when the bill proceeds in the ordinary course.

---

1 See HC Deb (1948–49) 457, cc 1275–1288; CJ (1948–49) 18, 19. The Standing Orders have been amended from time to time to take account of changes in the law; see eg Votes and Proceedings (1980–81) 14 April 1981.

2 For the effect of these orders upon provisional order bills, see p 956; upon bills presented under the Statutory Orders (Special Procedure) Act 1945, see pp 962–963; upon Scottish confirmation bills, see p 972.

3 Eg the Birkenhead Corporation (Improvement etc) Bill 1881, where the Committee on the Bill made a Special Report that the alterations proposed in the 'filled-up' bill were too extensive. CJ (1881) 153, 166.

4 CJ (1844) 187–188, 211; ibid (1849) 71, 118, 320; ibid (1851) 209; ibid (1852–53) 289; ibid (1881) 153, 166.

In 1845, the Speaker called the attention of the House to the Midland Railway Branches Bill, which contained a clause, giving compulsory power to take lands, of which no notice had been given, and without the proper plans, sections, and estimates having been deposited according to the standing orders. The order for the second reading was discharged, and the bill referred to the committee on petitions for private bills (the predecessors of the Examiners). This committee found that the standing orders had not been complied with; and it was thereupon instructed to inquire by whom, and under what circumstances, the violation of the standing orders had been committed. Its report upon this point was referred to the Standing Orders Committee, who determined that the standing orders ought not to be dispensed with; and the bill was not proceeded with.[1]

Debate on second reading

The second reading of a private bill corresponds with the same stage in other bills, and in agreeing to it the House affirms the general principle, or expediency, of the measure. There is, however, a distinction between the second reading of a public and of a private bill: a public bill being founded on reasons of state policy, the House, in agreeing to its second reading, accepts and affirms those reasons; but the expediency of a private bill, being mainly founded upon allegations of fact, which have not yet been proved, the House, in agreeing to its second reading, affirms the principle of the bill conditionally, and subject to the proof of such allegations before the committee. Where, irrespective of such facts, the principle is objectionable, the House will not consent to the second reading; but otherwise, the expediency of the measure is usually left for the consideration of the committee.[2] This is the first occasion on which the bill is brought before the House otherwise than pro forma, or in connection with the standing orders; and if the bill is opposed on its principle, now is the proper time for attempting its defeat. If the second reading is deferred for three or six months, or if a reasoned amendment is carried (see p 475),or if the bill is rejected, no new bill for the same object can be offered until the next session (see pp 468–469).

Limitation of scope of debate on Second Reading. The following examples illustrate the limits which have been placed on the scope of debate on the second reading of private bills.

On the second reading of the Liverpool and London and Globe Insurance Company Bill 1904, the Speaker ruled that a Member could not move an amendment that would raise the general policy and the state of the general law as to alterations of the articles of association of insurance companies, but that he might have an opportunity of arguing against the bill on those lines.[3]

On the second reading of the Fishguard and Rosslare Railways and Harbours Bill 1913, it was ruled that it was inadmissible to discuss the

---

1 CJ (1845) 169, 219, 247, 262, 385, 419.
2 Cf also Minutes of Committee on Mersey Conservancy and Docks Bill 1857; and Parl Deb (1857) 147, c 133.
3 Parl Deb (1904) 133, c 1259.

action of a company which was only a subscriber to the undertaking authorized by the bill.[1]

On the second reading of the Lancashire and Yorkshire Railway Bill 1913, the Speaker ruled that regulations put into force by the company in common with other companies could not be discussed on that particular bill, but should be dealt with by a general bill.[2]

On the second reading of the London County Council (Money) Bill 1927, the Speaker declined to allow discussion of the alleged grievances of certain temporary employees who were performing work of a permanent character.[3]

On the second reading of the Luton Corporation Bill 1969, which was to authorize the Corporation to raise money by the issue of bills, the Speaker would not permit debate on the objects upon which the money might be spent.[4]

In 1949, the Speaker was asked for his ruling on the scope of debate on the British Transport Commission Bill 1949, as being the first private bill promoted by a nationalised industry to be discussed in the House. He ruled that the Bill was a general purposes bill, and that, in view of the position of the British Transport Commission, the debate could extend beyond the contents of the Bill, although it must remain related to its purpose, and not traverse the constitution and powers of the Commission which had already been settled by Parliament.[5]

Subsequent rulings[6] on successive bills promoted by the British Transport Commission and by one of its successors, the British Railways Board[7] reaffirmed and amplified the ruling given in 1949: if the bill was of wide content, debate upon the whole administration of the management responsible for the matters contained in the bill was in order; but if the provisions of the bill related only to railways, debate could not extend to other activities of the Commission such as road transport, inland waterways or hotels.

COMMITTAL (STANDING ORDER 109)

Every private bill, after being read a second time and committed, stands referred to the Committee of Selection, whose duties in this connection are described fully on pp 882–888, below. A bill which is referred to the Examiners after second reading is not committed, however, until the Examiners have reported compliance with any standing orders not previously inquired into or, if the standing orders have not been complied with, the Standing Orders Committee have resolved that such standing orders should be dispensed with, and the House has agreed to this resolution,[8] or if, on

---

1 HC Deb (1913) 52, cc 654–655.
2 HC Deb (1913) 52, cc 654–655.
3 HC Deb (1927) 206, c 1974. Cf HC Deb (1929) 226, cc 2343–2344; ibid (1935–36) 308, cc 1868–1869; ibid 334, c 268; ibid (1940–41) 367, c 997; ibid (1943–44) 402, cc 1176–1177.
4 HC Deb (1968–69) 778, cc 845, 848.
5 HC Deb (1948–49) 461, cc 1765–1766.
6 HC Deb (1950) 473, c 655; ibid (1950–51) 485, c 514; ibid 487, c 1760; ibid (1951–52) 497, c 105; ibid (1952–53) 512, c 1362; ibid (1953–54) 524, c 282, etc
7 HC Deb (1962–63) 672, c 1162.
8 CJ (1914–16) 73; ibid (1928–29) 140.

considering a special report from the Examiners (see p 819), the Standing Orders Committee has resolved that standing orders have been complied with, or that standing orders have not been complied with and ought to be dispensed with, and the House has agreed with either of these resolutions. Instances of departure from the ordinary procedure on the committal of a private bill are given on pp 886–888.

INSTRUCTIONS

Time for moving instructions

After a bill has been read a second time, an instruction may be given by the House, if it thinks fit, for the guidance of the committee on the bill. An instruction may be moved after an opposed bill set down for consideration at seven o'clock has been read a second time, or may be considered independently of the motion for second reading (see p 279).[1] The procedure followed in relation to instructions is described on p 485.

When a bill is referred to the Examiners after its second reading, an instruction is moved not 'to the committee on the bill', but 'to any committee to which the bill may be referred',[2] since compliance with the further standing orders must be proved or the standing orders must be dispensed with, before the bill can be committed.

If a bill has been reported, and is subsequently recommitted, an instruction may similarly be given to the committee on the recommitted bill.[3]

Principles of instructions to private bill committees

The origin of instructions and the principles which underlie their proposal in connection with public bills have been fully described in chapter 21.

In considering how far these principles may relate to instructions in respect of private bills, four important distinctions must be observed. First, Standing Order No 63 (Amendments in committee), which gives a general power to committees to make such amendments in bills as they think fit, provided they be relevant to the subject-matter of the bill, does not apply to committees on private bills. Secondly, the process of petitioning for an additional provision provides machinery for the incorporation in a private bill of amendments which would otherwise be inadmissible (see below); whereas, in a public bill, it is impossible for a committee to make amendments which go beyond the scope of those contemplated by Standing Order No 63 (Amendments in committee), unless an express instruction has been given by the House. Thirdly, Standing Order 175, which is described in detail below, prevents the moving of instructions, when they seek to authorize amendments which could normally only be made by means of an additional provision. Fourthly, an instruction to a private bill committee may be mandatory or permissive. A mandatory instruction defines the course of action which a committee must follow and leaves them no option in the exercise of their functions with regard to the particular matter which is

---

1 CJ (1903) 99; ibid (1928–29) 146; HC Deb (1928–29) 225, cc 514, 1724–1726; CJ (1932–33) 282; ibid (1974) 183.
2 Private Business (1984–85) 246.
3 CJ (1921) 342.

the subject of the instruction.[1] Though for that reason mandatory instructions have sometimes been deprecated,[2] they are frequently proposed and given to committees. A permissive instruction confers on a committee powers to consider matters relevant to the subject-matter of the bill, which would not otherwise be within their competence, or would not come within the ordinary scope of their inquiry. An amendment to alter the form of a permissive instruction standing on the notice paper into a mandatory instruction without notice, has been refused.[3]

Power of committee to make amendments

A committee on a private bill is precluded from admitting provisions which are beyond the scope of the bill as delimited by the clauses and schedules annexed to the petition for the bill. It is within its competence, however, to make amendments in the bill which are within those purposes, though such amendments, necessarily, must not enlarge the powers sought by the bill. One of the chief effects of this rule is to prevent the insertion by a committee of provisions affecting the property and interests of persons who would have been entitled to object if such provisions had been included in the bill as originally deposited. Where, after a bill has been presented, it is desired to insert such provisions, the promoters are required to proceed by petition for additional provision (see pp 830–831), and opponents, therefore, are given an opportunity to voice their objections.

Standing Order 175 and its effect on instructions

Instances have occurred in the past where attempts have been made, by means of an instruction, to require or empower a committee to insert provisions which might affect the property and interests of outside parties, although they would not have received the protection to which they are entitled under the standing orders. This practice was deprecated, because it was an evasion, if not of the letter, at least of the spirit of the standing orders; and for this reason, on more than one occasion, an instruction was ruled out of order. An instruction of this nature, whether mandatory or permissive, has been specifically prohibited by Standing Order 175, passed on 17 December 1936, which in its present form states:

> Where it is sought by a proposed instruction to authorize or require a committee on a private bill to make an amendment in the bill, Mr Speaker, if he is of the opinion that the amendment is such that it could not have been inserted except upon a petition for additional provision, shall decline to propose the question on the instruction to the House.[4]

It will be seen that the effect of this standing order is far-reaching, and many instructions to private bill committees which were allowed in the past

---

1 For cases where a committee has been unable fully to carry out a mandatory instruction, see Special Report from the Committee on the British Transport Commission Bill, CJ (1959–60) 207, and Special Report from the Committee on the Esso Petroleum Company Bill, CJ (1959–60) 300; HC 280 (1959–60).
2 Parl Deb (1894) 25, cc 1067–1068; ibid (1900) 80, cc 180, 195; HC 378 (1902) pp v and vii, Qns. 42–67, 1137.
3 Parl Deb (1890–91) 350, c 1825.
4 CJ (1936–37) 66; HC Deb (1936) 318, c 2591.

would now be regarded as contravening the standing order and so be inadmissible. Broadly speaking, therefore, no instruction can be moved to a committee on a private bill, seeking to introduce amendments which enlarge the powers sought by the bill, or which affect private interests.[1] This does not apply to a hybrid bill.[2] Subject to this overriding standing order, the question whether an instruction is or is not in order depends on principles deduced from the rulings of the Chair which are examined in detail below and differs according to whether the instruction is mandatory or permissive.

Mandatory instructions

Mandatory instructions to committees on private bills may be divided into three categories:

(1) Instructions directing the committee to insert definite provisions in a bill or to require safeguards or security before passing certain provisions, or directing the taking of certain evidence.

   (a) In 1888 an instruction was given to the committee on the Brixton Park Bill, to provide that the purchase of the park should not be made till the opinion of the ratepayers of Lambeth had been taken on the desirability of the purchase.[3]

   (b) In 1893, the committee on the Weaver Navigation Bill was instructed to insert a clause requiring the trustees to come to Parliament within two years with such a bill as would enable Parliament to deal with the whole question of the trust.[4]

   (c) In 1896 an instruction was given to the committee on the London County Council (Vauxhall Bridge Tramways) Bill to take the evidence of the police upon the question of traffic.[5]

   (d) In 1902 the committee by whom the London United Electric Railways Bill and the Piccadilly, City, and North-East London Railway Bill were considered, was instructed to take security, in each case, from the undertakers for the completion of the whole scheme of railways comprised in each bill.[6] The first of these two bills was withdrawn while before the committee;[7] and, on the second, the committee made a special report stating that the conditions imposed by the instruction of the House could consequently not be complied with, and that the preamble could not therefore be proved.[8]

   (e) In 1918 the committee on the Londonderry Corporation Bill was instructed to insert a clause in the bill limiting the borrowing powers of the corporation for certain purposes to a specified sum, until they had taken the necessary steps to introduce within the next two sessions of Parliament a bill for the extension of the city boundaries.[9]

   (f) An instruction was given to the committee on the London County

---

1 HC Deb (1929) 226, c 355.
2 CJ (1957–58) 91, ibid (1985–86) 512.
3 CJ (1888) 105. Cf also CJ (1888) 166.
4 CJ (1893–94) 339.
5 CJ (1896) 68.
6 CJ (1902) 361.
7 CJ (1902) 443.
8 CJ (1902) 447; Parl Deb (1902) 113, c 1142, etc.
9 CJ (1918) 23.

Council (Charing Cross Bridge) Bill 1929, to insert clauses or obtain an undertaking from the promoters to secure by competition, or otherwise, designs for the bridge and for the architectural treatment of the viaducts.[1]

(g) An instruction was moved directing the committee on the North Wales Hydro-Electric Power Bill 1952, to make provision in the Bill for the protection of the Snowdonia National Park and access thereto by restoring to local planning authorities the planning powers which the bill took from them and by requiring the Minister of Housing and Local Government to appoint an amenity committee to advise himself, the local planning authorities and the electricity authority; but after debate the motion was withdrawn.[2]

(h) In 1956 an instruction was given to the committee on the British Transport Commission (No 2) Bill to insert a temporary provision in the bill against further deterioration of the Kennet waterways and appliances.[3]

(i) In 1960, an instruction was given to the committee on the Esso Petroleum Company Bill to amend the bill to ensure adequate safeguards to the interests of owners, lessees and occupiers of lands likely to be affected. A motion for an instruction directing the committee to make provision for safeguarding items of archaeological interest discovered during the works proposed by the bill was withdrawn after debate.[4]

Other matters which have been the subject of mandatory instructions are superannuation and provident funds,[5] workmen's trains and fares,[6] amount of charge in excess of authorized fares and workmen's fares,[7] assimilation of fares on new railways to those on existing lines,[8] erection of trolley vehicle equipment,[9] abstraction of water from a canal[10] and the payment by the promoters of certain costs to an individual.[11] An instruction has also been given to a committee to secure a hearing for persons who might not otherwise be entitled to give evidence.[12]

(2) Instructions directing the committee to omit definite provisions from a bill.

Instructions to this effect were given to the committee on the London County Council Bill 1890,[13] the Wolverhampton Corporation Bill 1891,[14] the Colne Corporation Bill, and other bills in 1905,[15] the Mersey Railway Bill 1906,[16] the Manchester Corporation (General Powers) (recommitted)

---

1 CJ (1929–30) 201.
2 CJ (1951–52) 176.
3 CJ (1955–56) 224.
4 CJ (1959–60) 265.
5 CJ (1900) 284; ibid (1901) 76, 90, 257, 278; ibid (1902) 82; ibid (1904) 250.
6 CJ (1902) 324, 360.
7 CJ (1920) 87.
8 CJ (1923) 34.
9 CJ (1922) 89.
10 CJ (1959–60) 160.
11 CJ (1904) 257; Parl Deb (1904) 136, c 1060.
12 CJ (1922) 50 (Provisional Order Bill).
13 CJ (1890) 194.
14 CJ (1890–91) 94.
15 CJ (1905) 54, 60, 68, 69.
16 CJ (1906) 186.

Bill 1921,[1] the Sunderland Corporation and the London County Council (Money) Bills 1935,[2] the British Transport Commission (No 2) and the Leeds Corporation Bills 1956,[3] the Oldham Corporation Bill 1960,[4] and the West Midlands County Council Bill [Lords] 1979,[5] the Greater London Council (Money) Bill 1984[6] and the Greater London Council (General Powers) Bill 1985.[7] Other similar instructions have been given to strike out clauses relative to milk supply other than model clauses,[8] and to strike out provisions increasing any statutory maximum price of gas or modifying existing statutory provisions as to the relating of price to dividend.[9] In 1974 an instruction that certain sums in the Greater London Council (Money) Bill should be reduced was moved, the motion being negatived on division.[10]

Standing Order 175 would prevent the moving of an instruction if the provision to be struck out were one limiting the powers of the promoters.

(3) Instructions directing the committee to inquire into and, in certain cases, to report upon matters which in the opinion of the House are relevant to the bill, or can be suitably investigated in connection therewith.

(a) In 1884 an instruction was moved to direct the committee on the Dublin, Wicklow, and Wexford Railway Bill to inquire and report whether the proposed railway would injuriously affect an open space in Dublin, and on its being objected that the committee already possessed the powers to be conferred by the instruction, the Speaker said that the instruction, being mandatory, was perfectly in order.[11]

(b) In 1884 an instruction was given to the committee on the Ennerdale Railway Bill, to inquire and report whether the proposed railway would interfere with the enjoyment of the public, and of visitors to the Lake District, by injuriously affecting the scenery.[12]

(c) In 1896 the committee on the City and South London Railway Bill was instructed to consider whether any, and, if any, what provisions could reasonably be made for the preservation of the Church of St. Mary Woolnoth without preventing the construction of the railway.[13]

(d) The committees on the Belfast Water Bill and the Sheffield Corporation Bill 1912, were instructed to take into consideration Standing

---

1 CJ (1921) 342.
2 CJ (1934–35) 139, 234.
3 CJ (1955–56) 224, 238.
4 CJ (1959–60) 264.
5 CJ (1978–79) 148.
6 CJ (1983–84) 609.
7 CJ (1984–85) 459.
8 CJ (1908) 80.
9 CJ (1918) 136, 176, 186.
10 CJ (1974) 183.
11 CJ (1884) 190; Parl Deb (1884) 287, c875; cf also CJ (1896) 55, 174; ibid (1899) 185; ibid (1902) 366; ibid (1913) 143, 208.
12 CJ (1884) 70; cf also CJ (1897) 224; Parl Deb (1897) 49, cc339–353.
13 CJ (1896) 169.

Order 184a (now 159), as if the bill authorized the construction of works.[1]

(e) In 1920 a committee on two water bills was instructed to consider the desirability in the public interest of joint utilization and control of certain sources of water supply by the promoters of the bills and an existing water company.[2]

(f) Instructions were given to the committees on the Southend-on-Sea Corporation Bill 1926,[3] the Buxton Corporation Bill 1927,[4] the Bognor Urban District Council Bill 1928,[5] and the Chester Corporation Bill 1929,[6] to have regard to section 56 of the Public Health Act 1925 in their consideration of a particular provision of the bill.

(g) The committee on the Adelphi Estate Bill 1933 was instructed to consider the effect of the bill on the architectural and artistic aspect and other amenities of the river front, to hear such evidence as it thought fit, and to provide that drawings of any new building should be approved by the Royal Fine Art Commission or other suitable body.[7]

(h) In 1957, an instruction was moved to direct the committee on the London County Council (Money) Bill to obtain certain undertakings from the promoters, but was withdrawn.[8]

(i) In 1959, an instruction was moved to direct the committee on the Torquay Corporation (Water) Bill to inquire into the depletions of the water resources of Dartmoor and allied matters, and to hear such evidence as the committee might think fit on the subject. The motion was negatived.[9]

(j) In 1987, an instruction was given to the committee on the London Docklands Railway (Beckton) Bill to report to the House on the evidence presented to it on the adequacy of the proposed railway to meet likely demands arising out of development in the area of the Royal Docks.[10]

Permissive instructions

A permissive instruction has been moved frequently in the past, empowering the committee to introduce amendments cognate to the general purposes of the bill; but in view of the restrictions imposed by Standing Order 175 in 1936, it is not easy to see how an instruction of this kind could be framed so as to be in order. It may be broadly said, therefore, that, apart from matters affecting the procedure of the committee,[11] permissive instructions are now

---

1 CJ (1912–13) 46.
2 CJ (1920) 250.
3 CJ (1926) 257.
4 CJ (1927) 44.
5 CJ (1928) 33.
6 CJ (1928–29) 109.
7 CJ (1932–33) 273, 282.
8 CJ (1956–57) 203.
9 CJ (1958–59) 145.
10 Votes and Proceedings (1987–88), 10 December 1987.
11 In 1958, the committee on four water bills was given a permissive instruction empowering them to consolidate the bills or parts thereof if they thought fit, CJ (1957–58) 254. In 1960 a notice of motion was given to suspend SO 136 and empower the committee on the Devon Water Bill to hear evidence from the Exeter Corporation but was subsequently withdrawn. See Private Business (1959–60), pp 209, 215.

confined to those empowering the committee to inquire into matters which are relevant to the subject-matter of the bill, or which can be suitably investigated in connection therewith.

(a) In 1879 an instruction was given to the committee on the Liverpool Lighting Bill (promoted by the corporation) empowering it to inquire and report as to the conditions under which lighting by electricity should be sanctioned by Parliament in the case of local authorities or public companies.[1]

(b) In 1878 an instruction was given to the committee on the Manchester Corporation Water Bill, empowering it to consider the requirements of the populations between Manchester and the Lake District, whence was to come the proposed supply.[2]

(c) In 1892, the committee on the Birmingham Corporation Water Bill received an instruction empowering it to inquire and report whether it was necessary to extinguish the rights of commoners and others over the large district proposed to be taken for the collection of the water to be supplied under the bill. Exception was taken to the instruction, as being unnecessary, but was over-ruled by the Speaker.[3]

(d) In 1894 an instruction was given to the committee on the Furness Railway Bill, empowering it to inquire whether it was expedient to abolish certain dues.[4]

(e) In 1902 the committee on the North Metropolitan Tramways Bill was empowered to inquire, if it saw fit, as to the company's existing night service of cars. An amendment proposed with the object of making this instruction mandatory instead of permissive was negatived.[5]

(f) In 1909, 1910, and 1911 instructions were given to the committees on various water bills empowering them to inquire whether adequate provision was made by the bill for the supply of water at reasonable rates to the agricultural community and to any persons whose existing supply might be affected by the proposed works, and to insert clauses compelling the promoters to provide such supply.[6]

Inadmissible instructions[7]

The restriction placed upon the moving of instructions by Standing Order 175 has already been observed but, even in cases to which that standing order does not apply, there are frequently other grounds upon which an instruction may be disallowed.

(1) An instruction is out of order if it seeks to traverse the decision of the House in rejecting a reasoned amendment on the second reading of the bill.

An instruction was put down to the London and North Western Railway (Steam Vessels) Bill 1898, which proposed that the powers given to the

1 CJ (1878–79) 87, and for later proceedings in this case, ibid 112, 124, 314.
2 CJ (1878) 68; cf also CJ (1919) 67.
3 CJ (1892) 97; Parl Deb (1892) 2, c 626.
4 CJ (1894) 74.
5 CJ (1902) 131; Parl Deb (1902) 105, cc 972–974.
6 CJ (1909) 67, 75, 76; ibid (1910) 52, 66, 89, 144; ibid (1911) 140, 164. See also CJ (1914) 99.
7 Prefatory words in the nature of a preamble to an instruction have been ruled out of order. Notices of Motion 1904, pp 1621, 1676.

company should remain in force for fourteen years. The Speaker ruled that the instruction raised again the precise question which had been raised by an amendment on the second reading of the bill, proposing that the powers should not be permanent. The House having debated and decided against that amendment, the question could not be raised again.[1]

(2) A permissive instruction is unnecessary and out of order if it proposes to confer powers which the committee is already able to exercise.

An instruction was put down to the London and North Western Railway (Steam Vessels) Bill 1898, which was to give permanent powers to the railway company with regard to traffic between Holyhead and Ireland, empowering the committee to regulate the traffic on the Holyhead and Chester line in connection with the steamship traffic. The Speaker ruled that this was a matter within the power of the committee, and that the instruction was not needed and was, therefore, out of order.[2]

(3) An instruction is out of order, if the objects which it proposes are clearly of an impractical kind, or if its terms are too vague to afford definite directions to the committee.

(a) On 3 May 1898, an instruction offered to the Fishguard and Rosslare Railway Bill, by which it was proposed to direct the committee to insert such clauses as would secure the commercial interests of the city and port of Cork, etc, was privately ruled out of order on the ground that it was too vague and gave no definite instruction to the committee.[3]

(b) On 31 March 1903, by a private ruling, the Speaker also disallowed, upon the same ground, an instruction by which it was proposed to direct the committee on the Midland and Belfast and Northern Counties Railways Bill, to inquire and report whether, in the absence of provisions as to a proper steamship service and as to rates and fares, the bill would affect the trade and commerce of Londonderry, without compensating advantages.[4]

(4) An instruction is out of order if it imposes an unreasonable restriction on the discretion of the committee. An instruction has also been ruled out of order which would prevent a committee leaving out a clause contained in a bill as presented.

(a) In 1901, an instruction, on the Great Eastern Railway Bill, was ruled out of order by the Speaker, who said that it proposed to give a mandatory direction to the committee to set aside the form of a clause prescribed by standing order with regard to houses of the working classes, and that such a course would be an abuse of instructions.[5]

(b) A mandatory instruction was ruled out of order in 1909 on the ground that it dictated to a committee the express terms of a clause to be inserted in the bill before the committee had had an opportunity of considering the bill.[6]

---

1 Parl Deb (1898) 56, c 1514; cf also Parl Deb (1901) 90, c 1536.
2 Parl Deb (1898) 56, c 1514; cf also Parl Deb (1894) 26, c 116; ibid (1899) 68, c 940. In the last case the instruction was moved and withdrawn.
3 Private Business (1898) p 306.
4 Private Business (1903) p 207; cf also Parl Deb (1902) 111, c 442.
5 Parl Deb (1901) 91, c 54.
6 HC Deb (1909) 4, c 1300; cf also HC Deb (1929) 225, c 2087.

(c) In 1909, several mandatory instructions, directing the committees on certain water and railway bills to insert in the bills clauses which were set out in the instructions, were removed from the paper in accordance with private rulings of the Speaker.[1] In the case of the water bills, a permissive instruction was moved in general terms.[2]

(d) In 1949, the Bolton Corporation Bill, as presented, contained a clause giving power to provide a residential hotel. Subsequently the promoters agreed with certain opponents to strike out the clause in the filled-up bill. Notice was thereupon given of an instruction to the committee on the bill to make provision that the Bolton Corporation be authorized to provide and carry on a residential hotel.[3] The Speaker ruled privately that this instruction was not in order.

(5) An instruction is out of order if it deals with a question of public policy which, regard being had to the object and purposes of a private bill, should more properly be the subject of a public bill.

(a) In 1892 the Eastbourne Improvement Act (1885) Amendment Bill was introduced to repeal a section, for the prohibition of processions on Sunday, which had been secured by the corporation of Eastbourne in their Act of 1885; and notice was given of a mandatory instruction to the committee on the bill to insert further clauses, exempting Eastbourne from the operation of the provision contained in the Roman Catholic Relief Act 1829, under which Roman Catholic ecclesiastics were practically prohibited from participating in processions. The Speaker stated that the proposed clauses could not be engrafted on the private bill before the House; and that it would be out of order by an instruction on the bill in question to seek the repeal, in the instance of a particular town, of provisions contained in the general law and passed in the interests of public policy.[4]

(b) On 8 March 1892 notice was given of an instruction to the committee on the South Eastern Railway Bill, to inquire into and report on the accommodation etc, supplied to third-class passengers on the railway. The Speaker privately informed the Member in whose name it stood that the instruction was not in order, on the ground that the remedy (if legislation were needed) should be sought in a general statute applicable to all railways alike; that this would be a matter of general policy to be considered at the time, not of private but of public business; and that it would be contrary to the practice of the House to single out the bill of a particular company and impose on it alone conditions applicable to railways generally.

(c) On 26 March 1895 the Speaker ruled privately that a proposed motion for a general instruction to every committee on any railway bill directing them to inquire and report whether the Board of Trade had any complaint regarding the promoting company in respect of the Railway Regulation (Servants' Hours) Act 1893 or of the conciliation powers under the Railway and Canal Traffic Acts, raised a question

---

1 Private Business (1909) pp 138–39, 174–75, 228.
2 CJ (1909) 67.
3 Private Business (1948–49) p 59.
4 Parl Deb (1892) 2, c 627.

of general policy and ought not to be brought on at the time of private business.[1]

(d) On 3 March 1898, notice having been given of an instruction to direct the committee on the Great Northern Railway Bill to provide for an increased number of workmen's trains (to which there was no reference in the bill), the Speaker intimated to the Member who had given notice of the motion that the question was one of general policy affecting all railways, and that there being nothing in the bill to which it was germane, the proposed instruction could not be moved.

(e) In 1923, an instruction on the London, Midland and Scottish Railway Bill to insert a clause to repeal a statutory provision requiring a certain level crossing to be kept closed for road traffic was ruled out of order as repealing part of a public Act, namely, the Regulation of Railways Act 1842.[2]

Instructions to divide bills

An instruction is necessary and may be given to divide a bill into two or more bills.[3]

(a) In 1915, in order that the unopposed portions of the bill might proceed as a separate bill, the London County Council (General Powers) (suspended) Bill was recommitted to the Local Legislation Committee with an instruction to divide it into two bills and to report the bills, without amendments, except such as were consequential upon the division.[4]

(b) In 1910, in the case of certain bills each of which was promoted by and dealt with several gas companies for a common purpose, objection was taken to the difficulty imposed by this method of procedure upon opponents who were necessarily interested in the proposals of only one company. To meet this objection the committee was instructed to consider on the request of any petitioners the expediency of dividing the bills, and in the case of one bill to hear separately the case of the promoters.[5]

NOMINATION OF COMMITTEES

It has already been stated that every private bill, after being read a second time and committed, stands referred under the terms of Standing Order 109

---

1 For other similar rulings on instructions, see Parl Deb (1894) 26, c 561; ibid (1896) 39, c 1707; ibid (1901) 91, c 55; ibid (1901) 97, cc 1312–1313; ibid (1929) 226, c 355.
2 HC Deb (1923) 165, c 811.
3 CJ (1872) 165.
4 CJ (1914–16) 180–181; HC Deb (1915) 73, c 2.
5 CJ (1910) 192, 193, 242; HC Deb (1910) 18, c 575, 597.

to the Committee of Selection, whose constitution and general functions have been described on pp 825–826. A more detailed account is now given of the allocation of bills amongst committees, and the nomination of Members selected to serve on private bill committees.

Committees on Unopposed Bills (Standing Orders 111 and 132)

Every unopposed bill is referred by the Committee of Selection to the Committee on Unopposed Bills, which consists of seven members, namely the Chairman of Ways and Means (who is ex officio chairman, but by practice does not attend), the Deputy Chairmen, and four members, who are selected from time to time, by the Chairman of Ways and Means, from a panel appointed by the Committee of Selection at the beginning of every session. The Chairman of Ways and Means has power to select from the panel one additional member to act as chairman at every sitting of a committee on an unopposed bill at which neither he nor either Deputy Chairman is present.[1] The committee has the assistance of the Counsel to Mr Speaker. The quorum of the committee is three. The time and date of the first meeting of the committee on a bill are fixed by the Chairman.

Committees on opposed bills (Standing Orders 109–114)

The Committee of Selection will not treat a bill as an opposed bill unless a petition has been presented against the bill in accordance with Standing Order 171A (see p 840) and has not been withdrawn, or unless the Chairman of Ways and Means reports to the House, in accordance with Standing Order 85, that the bill, though unopposed, ought to be treated as opposed (see p 890). If the Chairman so acts, the bill again stands referred to the Committee of Selection, in accordance with Standing Order 112.

The Committee of Selection appoints committees to consider opposed bills and fixes the time of the first sitting of committees (subject to the provisions of Standing Order 177).

The Committee may also form into groups such bills as may be conveniently submitted to the same committee and name the bill or bills which are to be taken into consideration at the first sitting of the committee on any such group.[2] They may also remove a bill from a group or transfer a bill from one group to another.

Composition of committees (Standing Order 111). The committee on every opposed private bill consists of four members having no local or other interest in the bill or bills referred to them. It is not the practice to appoint Members who have spoken on the second reading of the bill. When appoint-

---

1 Under this provision, two or more committees on unopposed bills may sit concurrently, the progress of unopposed bills being thus expedited. See the sessional order of 16 December 1937, CJ (1937–38) 69; HC Deb (1937) 330, cc 1305–1307, and the report of the Chairman of Ways and Means made in pursuance thereof, CJ (1937–38) 111; also sessional order of 5 December 1938, CJ (1938–39) 37. The provisions of these sessional orders were incorporated in SO 132 in 1945 and amended in 1948 and 1951. Up to the present it has not been found necessary for two unopposed bill committees to sit concurrently.
2 In March 1958, the Committee heard representations from the agents for four competing water bills before deciding which should be considered first.

ing the committee, the Committee of Selection nominates one of the four members chairman of the committee. A committee to which an opposed bill is referred has the assistance of the Speaker's counsel where the bill is promoted by a local authority and proposes to create powers relating to police, sanitary or other local government matters in conflict with, deviation from or excess of the provisions of the general law (Standing Order 123).[1]

Members of committees on opposed bills to sign declaration (Standing Order 120). Each member of a committee on an opposed private bill, before he is entitled to attend and vote, is required to sign a declaration that his constituents have no local interest, and that he has no personal interest, in the bill, and that he will never vote on any question which may arise without having duly heard and attended to the evidence relating thereto. (For procedure where a member subsequently discovers that he has a direct interest see p 892.)

Notice to be given to members to serve on committee (Standing Order 115). Notice of his appointment must be given to each member of a committee on any opposed private bill, and at the same time a blank form of the declaration (see above) is transmitted to him, with a request that it may be forthwith returned properly filled up and signed.

Members returning no answer (Standing Order 116). If a Member neglects to return the declaration in a reasonable time, or does not send a sufficient excuse, the Committee of Selection will report his name to the House, and he may be ordered to attend the committee on the bill;[2] or to attend the House in his place, where, on offering sufficient apology for his neglect, he will be ordered to attend the committee.[3]

Members refusing to attend. If the Committee of Selection is dissatisfied with a Member's excuse, it will require him to serve upon a committee, when his attendance will become obligatory, and if necessary will be enforced by the House.

On 5 May 1845 a Member did not attend a committee on a group of railway bills to which he had been nominated, and his absence was accordingly reported to the House in the prescribed manner.[4] He stated to the House that a correspondence had taken place between the Committee of Selection and himself, in which he had informed them that he was already serving on two public committees, and that his serving on the railway group committee was incompatible with those duties. But the House ordered him to attend the railway committee.[5]

In 1846 the Committee of Selection, not being satisfied with the excuses of Mr Smith O'Brien, nominated him a member of a committee on a

1 This provision was first made by the sessional order of 16 December 1937, CJ (1937–38) 69; HC Deb (1937) 330, cc 1305–1307.
2 CJ (1847–48) 590, 627; ibid (1860) 138; ibid (1862) 91; ibid (1865) 369 (in this case no order was made).
3 CJ (1860) 94, 99, 106.
4 See pp 892–893 as to SO 122 under which a report must be made to the House of the absence of members of committees.
5 CJ (1845) 399; Parl Deb (1845) 80, c 166.

group of railway bills in the usual manner. He did not attend the committee; his absence was accordingly reported to the House; and he was ordered to attend the committee on the following day. Being again absent, his absence was again reported; he attended in his place in the House and stated that he refused to attend the committee; upon which he was declared guilty of a contempt, and was committed to the custody of the Serjeant at Arms.[1]

One Member substituted for another (Standing Order 117). The Committee of Selection has the power to discharge any Member or Members from a committee, and substitute an equal number of other Members. It is not normal practice, however, to discharge Members from a committee while a bill is under consideration.

On 3 July 1979, when the chairman of a committee fell ill shortly after they had started proceedings on a bill, the Committee of Selection forthwith appointed another Member in his place as Chairman, the parties having signified their agreement to this course.[2]

In March 1985, a member of the Joint Committee on the Exeter-Launceston-Bodmin Trunk Road (Okehampton By-pass) Compulsory Purchase Orders 1984 raised in the House a point of order concerning the scope of the orders, a matter which he had previously queried in the committee. As he felt that this action could throw doubt upon his impartiality, he voluntarily withdrew from membership of the committee and the Committee of Selection agreed to replace him for its remaining proceedings.[3]

In January 1986, a member of the committee on the Felixstowe Dock and Railway Bill, who had several times been reported to the House for being absent from its sittings, finally declared that she would take no further part in its proceedings. The Committee of Selection appointed another member in her place, but he in turn indicated that he was not prepared to attend. The House then gave leave for the committee to sit with a quorum of two for the remainder of its proceedings.[4]

Interval between committal of opposed private bill and sitting of committee (Standing Order 177)

An interval of not less than six clear days is required to elapse between the committal of an opposed private bill and the first sitting of the committee. The required interval between the committal of an opposed personal bill and the first sitting of the committee is not less than three clear days. Subject to this order, the Committee of Selection, as already stated, is empowered by

1 Special report of Committee of Selection, CJ (1846) 566, 582, 602–603; Parl Deb (1846) 85, cc 1071, 1152, 1290, 1300, 1351; ibid (1846) 86, cc 966, 1198. For more recent cases in which Members, reported absent from a private bill committee, have been ordered to attend, see CJ (1900) 297, 305; ibid (1902) 382; ibid (1903) 197; ibid (1905) 67; ibid (1924) 249. For a case in which the Serjeant at Arms reported his inability to serve a Member with the order of the House for his attendance upon a committee, see CJ (1914) 240, 241.
2 Minutes of Evidence of Committee on City of London (Various Powers) Bill, 3 July 1979, pp 13–14.
3 HC Deb (1984–85) 74, cc 333–334; Minutes of Evidence of the Joint Committee, 5 March 1985, pp 1–2.
4 HC Deb (1985–86) 91, cc 1013–1046.

Standing Order 113 to fix the time for holding the first sitting of the committee on every opposed private bill.

Departures from ordinary procedure in committal of private bills

In all these matters the Committee of Selection ordinarily proceeds in compliance with the standing orders; but where any departure from the standing orders, or the usual practice of the committee, is deemed advisable, or where, for any other reason, a particular mode of dealing with any bill is desired by the House, special orders have been made, or special directions to the Committee of Selection have been given.

> For example, the House has directed the Committee of Selection to refer two or more bills to the same committee,[1] or to form all the bills of a certain class into one group;[2] to refer a bill to another committee;[3] to remove a bill from a group, and refer it to a separate committee;[4] to withdraw a bill from one group and place it in another;[5] or to refer a bill to the Chairman of the Committee on Standing Orders, and two other Members.[6] Transferences of this kind, however, are now usually carried out by the Committee of Selection without directions from the House. Leave has also been given to the Committee of Selection to appoint the first meeting of committees on an earlier day than the standing orders would otherwise allow,[7] or forthwith;[8] or not to fix the sitting of committees upon certain classes of bills until a later period;[9] or otherwise dealing with the first meeting of committees.[10] In 1855 the Westminster Land Company Bill was added to a group of private bills directly, by order of the House, without the intervention of the Committee of Selection; and an instruction was given to the committee on the bill to sit and proceed forthwith if it should think fit.[11]
>
> In Session 1929–30, in order to secure greater expedition, the Lord Privy Seal was empowered to certify bills which contained provisions relating to works the execution of which would substantially contribute to the early relief of unemployment. Where such a bill contained other provisions also, it was divided, the certified provisions proceeding separately as a certified bill, and the remaining provisions standing referred to the Committee of Selection or the Local Legislation Committee. The progress of the certified bills was regulated by the order of the House.[12]
>
> In Sessions 1978–79 and 1979–80 notice was given of motions to refer several clauses of three local authority general powers bills to a Committee of the whole House. The Chairman of Ways and Means drew the

---

1 CJ (1845) 95, 224; ibid (1846) 460; ibid (1851) 280; ibid (1868–69) 48, 63.
2 CJ (1849) 248.
3 CJ (1845) 607.
4 CJ (1850) 351.
5 CJ (1850) 418.
6 Rock Life Assurance Company Bill, CJ (1868–69) 137.
7 CJ (1865) 405; ibid (1866) 490; ibid (1867) 427; ibid (1946–47) 320; ibid (1950) 168.
8 CJ (1847–48) 700; ibid (1850) 513; ibid (1852) 300; ibid (1948–49) 328.
9 CJ (1850) 72, 84; ibid (1851) 67.
10 CJ (1854) 406; ibid (1856) 256; ibid (1857–58) 119, 254, 303.
11 CJ (1854–55) 279. Cf also CJ (1867–68) 158.
12 CJ (1929–30) 129. For bills certified in whole or in part, see CJ (1929–30) 147, 263, 308, 321, 322.

attention of the House to the inconveniences of agreeing to such a motion.[1]

Bills referred to specially constituted committees

Private bills dealing with subjects which, in the opinion of the House, are of special interest or importance, are sometimes referred to a select committee nominated partly by the House and partly by the Committee of Selection, or otherwise specially constituted.[2] The numbers of such a committee and the proportions in which it has been nominated by the House and the Committee of Selection have varied. A few committees have been nominated entirely by the House[3] or entirely by the Committee of Selection.[4] Private bills have also been committed to a select committee on a hybrid bill.[5]

Unless the question for committing a private bill to a select committee is agreed to, the bill stands referred to the Committee of Selection in the ordinary way.[6]

Private bills committed to a joint committee

Private bills, either singly or in conjunction with other bills, are sometimes committed to a joint committee.[7] This course is usually adopted for consolidation bills (see pp 667–669, 888), and has been adopted for competing bills, a number of bills on the same subject, bills on which the Government has announced that, in its view, a joint committee would be in the public interest and bills in respect of which the promoters and a substantial body of the opponents are agreed in asking that a joint committee should be substituted for the ordinary procedure.[8]

The Commons members are usually nominated by the Committee of Selection,[9] though on some occasions they have been nominated by the

---

1 Private Business (1978–79) pp 85 ff; ibid (1979–80) pp 13 ff; HC Deb (1978–79) 964, cc 345–350); SO No 31 (Public) was subsequently amended to extend the Speaker's power of selection to motions of this kind.
2 Since 1900 the following bills have been referred to select committees: London County Council (Electric Supply) Bills 1906 and 1907; United Methodist Church Bill [Lords] and York (Micklegate Strays) Bill [Lords] 1907; Great Northern, Great Central, and Great Eastern Railways Bill 1909; London County Council (General Powers) (Pt VI), City of London (Various Powers) (Pt III), and Glasgow Corporation (Celluloid) Bills 1914; Alexander's Restitution Bill [Lords] 1916; Methodist Church Union and Methodist Church Union (Scotland) Bills 1929; City of London (Guild Churches) Bill 1951–52; Esso Petroleum Company Bill 1959–60 and Letchworth Garden City Corporation Bill (1961–62).
3 CJ (1907) 416, 422; ibid (1916) 82.
4 CJ (1867–68) 66, 74; ibid (1900) 101; ibid (1914) 80–81.
5 CJ (1867) 205, 207, 209; ibid (1875) 216; ibid (1882) 55, 56, 89; ibid (1912–13) 381, 393.
6 Cf CJ (1872) 75; ibid (1873) 73.
7 Since 1900 the following private bills, originating in the Commons, have been committed to joint committees: Dublin Corporation and Clontarf Urban District Council Bills 1900; Metropolitan Water Board (Various Powers), and Metropolitan Water Board (Charges etc) Bills 1907; Thames Conservancy Bill 1911; several dock and harbour bills in 1919; Metropolitan Water Board (Charges), Thames Conservancy, and Lee Conservancy Bills 1921; seven railway (Road Transport) bills in 1928; South Suburban Gas (Consolidation) Bill 1928; six railway (Air Transport) bills in 1929. For hybrid bills committed to joint committees, see p 522.
8 See HL Deb (1928–29) 73, cc 207–210; HL Deb (1953–54) 186, cc 1233–1250; and Report of Joint Committee on Private Bill Procedure, HL 14, 58–I (1955), HC 139–I (1955) para 53.
9 CJ (1900) 141, 172; ibid (1928–29) 180.

House itself;[1] and power is usually given to the committee to send for persons, papers, and records. The number of members appointed by each House is now ordinarily four or five. The ordinary rules of locus standi are superseded by an order referring to the committee all petitions in favour of or against the bill which have been presented during the session,[2] or a certain number of days before the meeting of the committee,[3] or before a specified date.[4] When a joint committee was appointed to consider a bill or bills originating in the House of Lords, it was formerly not the practice of the House of Commons to make any order regarding the hearing of the promoters or opponents of the bill before the committee. In Session 1934–35, however, it was decided that directions as to the hearing of promoters and opponents, similar to those given by the Lords to their members, should in future be given by the Commons to their members also. The members of a joint committee on a private bill do not sign the declaration required of members of an ordinary private bill committee (see p 892), and their absence is not reported to the House. The procedure in a joint committee on a private (or hybrid) bill follows that of a select committee of the Lords[5] on a private bill (see pp 936 ff), where that procedure differs from that of select committees of the Commons.

Resolutions by one House proposing that bills should be committed to a joint committee have been disagreed to by the other House.[6]

Joint Committee on Consolidation Bills. Private consolidation bills usually originate in the House of Lords and are referred to the Joint Committee on Consolidation Bills (see pp 667–669).

In the two Sessions 1928 and 1928–29, two joint committees were appointed, one of which, the Joint Committee on Private Bills (Consolidation), was 'to consider all private bills for the exclusive purpose of consolidating the provisions of existing private Acts of Parliament'.[7] In Session 1929–30, one joint committee only was appointed, to deal with both public and private bills.[8] In Session 1937–38 a Joint Committee on Consolidation Bills was set up, to which, in accordance with a further resolution agreed to by both Houses, all private consolidation bills were referred.[9] Each of these committees was directed not to take into consideration any petition against a private bill which sought to alter the existing law.[10]

---

1 CJ (1873) 178–179; cf also CJ (1908) 184; ibid (1920) 224 (provisional order bill); ibid (1927) 219 (hybrid bills).
2 CJ (1873) 178–179.
3 CJ (1900) 141.
4 CJ (1928–29) 180.
5 The following bills, originating in the Lords, have been committeed to joint committees: three railway amalgamation bills in 1900; Metropolitan Water Board (New Works) Bill [Lords] 1911; one gas and water and three water bills in 1921; and Dover Gas Bill [Lords] 1928.
6 CJ (1908) 79, 102; CJ (1928–29) 150, 168; CJ (1953–54) 130, 172.
7 CJ (1928) 87, 157, 184, 187; ibid (1928–29) 34, 66, 116, 127.
8 CJ (1929–30) 29, 34, 41, 54.
9 CJ (1937–38) 47, 57, 70, 78.
10 The Shropshire, Worcestershire and Staffordshire Electric Power (Consolidation) Bill [Lords] 1938 and the Dover Harbour (Consolidation) Bill [Lords] 1954, were considered by the Joint Committee on Consolidation Bills. The Middlesex County Council Bill 1944, and Croydon Corporation Bill 1959, which were mainly consolidation bills but with elements of amendment, were considered by the Committee on Unopposed Bills.

Proceedings in the second House on bills committed to a joint committee. The committee stage of a private bill which has been considered by a joint committee is dispensed with in the second House. *In the House of Lords* the committee stage of a bill originating in the House of Commons is negatived, so that the bill proceeds to its third reading after being read a second time.[1] *In the House of Commons*, a bill which originated in the Lords has usually been ordered to lie upon the Table, after the standing orders relative to the committal of private bills have been suspended;[2] or the orders relative to both committal and report have been suspended, and the bill ordered to be read the third time.[3]

> The London Building Bill [Lords] 1930, and the Shropshire, Worcestershire and Staffordshire Electric Power (Consolidation) Bill [Lords] 1938, which had been considered by joint committees, were committed in the House of Commons for the purpose of introducing amendments of a drafting character, and considered by the Committee on Unopposed Bills, and reported with amendments from that committee.[4]

Notice of first sitting of committee on private bill (Standing Order 199)

With regard to any private bill which stands referred in the ordinary way to the Committee of Selection, at least four clear days' notice is given in the Private Bill Office (and published among the notices relating to private business) of the day and hour appointed for the first sitting of the committee on an opposed bill; one clear day's notice is given of the first sitting on a recommitted bill and one day's notice of the first sitting on an unopposed bill. Where the first sitting of a committee on a bill is deferred, notice is given in the Private Bill Office of the day to which the sitting is deferred.[5]

Amendments to conciliate interested parties

Before the meeting of a committee on a private bill, the promoters may, by proposing amendments of their own, seek to conciliate parties who are interested, and to avert opposition.

'Filled-up' bill to be deposited (Standing Orders 137, 200)

Before the sitting of a committee on a private bill, certain proceedings must be taken by the promoters. The agent is required to deposit in the Private Bill Office a 'filled-up' bill, as proposed to be submitted to the committee, and signed by himself, two clear days before the meeting of a committee on an opposed bill, and the day before the meeting of a committee on an unopposed bill. A copy of the proposed amendments is to be furnished by the promoters, one clear day before the sitting of the committee, to parties petitioning against the bill who apply for it.

---

1 LJ (1911–12) 276, 288; ibid (1919) 174, 185; ibid (1955–56) 119, 122.
2 CJ (1911) 367; ibid (1921) 273, 311, 332; ibid (1928) 275; ibid (1928–29) 182; ibid (1953–54) 139.
3 CJ (1900) 363, 371; cf also CJ (1920) 377 (provisional order bill).
4 CJ (1929–30) 400, 418; ibid (1937–38) 302, 312.
5 For an instance of the suspension of SO 199, see CJ (1948–49) 328.

Under Standing Order 137, copies of the filled-up bill must be laid before each member of the committee at the first sitting on the bill.

In 1845 certain committees upon bills reported that no filled-up bill had been deposited by the agent as required, and that the committee had therefore declined to proceed with the bill, and had instructed the chairman to report the circumstances to the House.[1] In those cases the committees were revived and given leave to sit and proceed on a certain day, provided that the filled-up bill had been duly deposited.[2]

Submission of bills to the Chairman of Ways and Means (Standing Orders 82, 84, 85)

The duty of the Chairman of Ways and Means under Standing Order 82 to examine all private bills, whether opposed or unopposed, with the assistance of the Counsel to Mr Speaker, has already been described (see pp 826–827 above). Under Standing Order 85 he is at liberty, at any time, to report any special circumstance regarding any private bill,[3] or to inform the House that any unopposed bill should be treated as an opposed bill[4] (see also p 883). For this reason, the agent is not only required to lay copies of the original bill before the Chairman of Ways and Means and the Speaker's Counsel; it is also provided by Standing Order 84 that one clear day before the day appointed for the consideration of the bill by a committee, copies of the bill, as proposed to be submitted to the committee, must be laid before the Chairman and Counsel, duly signed by the agent, together with copies of any of the estimates and statements deposited in accordance with Standing Orders 45 or 46. Copies of opposed or recommitted bills must be so laid at least two clear days before the day appointed for the consideration of the bill in committee. In the House of Lords, copies of the bill, as proposed to be submitted to the committee on the bill in the Commons, are also laid before the Chairman of Committees and his counsel (see p 827); and a simultaneous examination of the bill is consequently proceeding in both Houses. Amendments are suggested or required by the authorities in both Houses, which are either agreed to at once by the promoters, or after discussion are insisted upon, varied, modified, or dispensed with.

Scrutiny by public departments

In accordance with the provisions of Standing Order 39, a printed copy of every private bill must be deposited on or before 4 December with the Treasury and certain public departments. The other departments, with which bills relating to various subjects must be deposited, are also set out in this standing order; while Standing Orders 60 and 180 prescribe similar deposits which must be made at later stages, and Standing Order 158

---

1 CJ (1845) 261, 281, 302. Cf also the objection raised regarding the filled-up bill in committee on the Truro etc Railway Bill (Group 2, 18 April 1894).
2 CJ (1845) 270, 302, 304.
3 CJ (1935–36) 220, 223; ibid (1939–40) 163; ibid (1960–61) 87; ibid (1961–62) 137; ibid (1975–76) 412; ibid (1976–77) 157; Reports on Private Bills (1957–58) p 157.
4 CJ (1901) 238; ibid (1906) 271; ibid (1911) 51; ibid (1922) 106; ibid (1930–31) 267, 299, 336; ibid (1931–32) 164; ibid (1932–33) 67; ibid (1935–36) 309; ibid (1955–56) 295; ibid (1977–78) 168.

requires notice to be given to the Attorney General of a bill which deals with charities and educational institutions. This provision enables the various public departments to obtain early knowledge of the contents of private bills and to decide whether, in respect of any bill, a report to the House on matters under the jurisdiction of their respective Ministers is called for. The officials of these departments are in frequent communication with the promoters of bills, and the influence which they exercise, both by such consultation and by reports to Parliament, serves to ensure protection of Crown or public rights and the observance of public Acts governing any matter to which a private bill relates. Reports are deemed to have been presented to the House if copies are deposited in the Private Bill Office (Standing Order 144). They may deal with either or both the preamble and general policy relating to the bill and questions of administrative detail arising on the clauses.[1] They may also include recommendations that clauses should be inserted in the bill to secure the protection of Crown or public interests. (See also pp 896–897 for the procedure on reports from government departments.)

The committee on the Kent County Council Bill 1959 reported that 'it would be helpful to Committees if Departments would indicate their views on a clause even where they have no recommendation to make in respect of it, and requested also that Departments should indicate where appropriate the number of precedents for a clause'.[2] This practice has subsequently been followed.

Limits to amendments before sitting of the committee

When the amendments consequent upon these various proceedings have been settled, the proposed amendments and clauses are inserted in the filled-up bill (see pp 889–890); but care must be taken, in preparing these amendments, that they are within the purposes of the bill (see p 874), that they involve no infraction of the standing orders, and are not excessive in extent. If the contents are not within the scope of the bill, the proper course is for the promoters to present a petition for additional provision (see pp 830–831).

Where it was proposed to leave out the greater part of the clauses in the original bill, and to insert other clauses, the Chairman of Ways and Means submitted to the House that the bill should be withdrawn.[3] The Report of the Committee on the Wallasey Corporation Bill 1958 deprecated the practice of submitting further substantial amendments to the committee after the filled-up bill had been deposited.[4] Frequently, however, in committees on opposed bills, the promoters, after hearing the evidence, propose substantial amendments to meet points raised by petitioners.

---

1 For cases where the propriety of reports dealing with questions of policy has been disputed, see Minutes of Evidence, Group B, Coventry Corporation Bill, 22 July 1942, p 36; Minutes of Evidence, Group A, East Grinstead Gas and Water Bill, 29 May 1945, pp 11–12.
2 Reports of Committees on Private Bills (1959–60), p 133.
3 Bristol Parochial Rates Bill, CJ (1845) 535; Birkenhead Corporation (Improvement, etc) Bill, CJ (1881) 153, 166, and cf Porthleven Harbour Bill, CJ (1869) 180.
4 Reports of Committees on Private Bills (1957–58), p 67.

2. COMMITTEE STAGE AND SUBSEQUENT PROCEEDINGS

The proceedings of committees on private bills are governed by certain standing orders, of which some are applicable only to committees on opposed bills, some only to unopposed bills and others to all committees. Standing Orders 120 to 128 and 130 to 131A refer to committees on opposed bills, Standing Orders 132 to 134 to committees on unopposed bills, and Standing Orders 135 to 139, 141, 142, 144 to 147, 150 and 152 to 162[1] to committees on bills, whether opposed or unopposed. The provisions of the more important of these standing orders are first explained, before proceedings in committee are described.

STANDING ORDERS RELATING TO COMMITTEES ON OPPOSED BILLS

Declaration of members (Standing Order 120)

No committee on an opposed private bill, or group of bills, can proceed to business until the required declaration (see p 884) has been signed by each of the members.[2]

> On 28 February 1860 leave was given by the House to the committee on Group 1 of Railway Bills to sit and proceed to business, notwithstanding that one of the members (who had received notice of his appointment to the committee) had not signed the required declaration.[3]
> On 9 July 1900 the committee on Group J of Private Bills having proceeded with the business referred to it, although one of the members of the committee (who was reported absent) had failed to sign his declaration, the House ordered that the proceedings before the committee should notwithstanding 'be deemed to be, and be, valid'.[4]

If a member who has signed this declaration should subsequently discover that he has a direct interest in a bill, or in a company who are petitioners against a bill, he will withdraw from the committee, after stating the fact, and may, if necessary, be discharged by the House (or by the Committee of Selection) from further attendance.[5]

Quorum (Standing Orders 121, 122)

The committee may not proceed if more than one of the members is absent, unless by special leave of the House; and no member of a committee on an opposed private bill may absent himself, except in case of illness, or by leave of the House.[6] Suspension from the service of the House does not exempt a Member from serving on a committee on a private bill to which he has

---

1 SOs 129, 140, 143, 148 and 149 have been repealed.
2 CJ (1854) 207; ibid (1862) 258.
3 CJ (1860) 94.
4 CJ (1900) 304, 305; Parl Deb (1900) 85, c 939. See also CJ (1911) 341; HC Deb (1911) 28, c 1024; CJ (1913) 75.
5 CJ (1845) 386; ibid (1846) 904; ibid (1892) 398; ibid (1945–46) 277.
6 CJ (1850) 418.

previously been appointed.[1] Members absenting themselves are reported to the House at its next sitting.

Formerly the House ordered such members to attend the next sitting of the committee,[2] but if their absence was occasioned by illness,[3] domestic anxiety,[4] or other sufficient cause,[5] no such order was made.[6]

Members not present within one hour of the time of meeting are also reported to the House.[7]

If the chairman is absent, the member next in rotation on the list of members, who is present, acts as chairman.

If at any time more than one of the members is absent, the chairman suspends the proceedings, and if, after one hour, more than one member is absent, the committee is adjourned to the next day on which the House shall sit, when it meets at the hour at which it sat on the day of the adjournment. If, after a committee has been formed, a quorum of members cannot attend, the chairman reports the circumstances to the House, which may make such orders as are necessary to enable proceedings to continue.[8]

Entering of appearances

The parties respectively promoting and opposing a bill are required to enter appearances on the day on which the bill is to be considered (see p 904 below).[9]

A committee on a group of bills take first into consideration the bill or bills named by the Committee of Selection; and appoints the day on which it will consider each of the other bills, and on which it will require the parties promoting and opposing to enter appearances. The committee clerk is to give at least two clear days' notice of such appointment, in the Private Bill Office; and if the committee defers the consideration of any bill, notice is given of the day to which it is deferred (Standing Order 124). It is the usual practice of the committee to consider the several bills in the group in the order set out on the printed list; and this practice is not departed from, unless sufficient grounds be shown for a different arrangement of the business.[10]

The agent for each petition against a bill must be prepared with a certificate from the Private Bill Office that he has entered an appearance upon the petition. This document is delivered to the committee clerk on the first day on which the bill is set down for consideration by the committee and, unless it be produced, the petition will be entered in the Minutes as not appeared

---

1 SO No 43(5) (Public).
2 CJ (1900) 297, 305; ibid (1930–31) 228.
3 CJ (1903) 94; ibid (1947–48) 179; ibid (1980–81) 465.
4 CJ (1905) 208, 217.
5 CJ (1900) 305.
6 Occasionally the House has discharged an absent member from further attendance (CJ (1854–55) 294), but cf p 885.
7 CJ (1953–54) 237; ibid (1979–80) 614; ibid (1985–86) 140; Votes and Proceedings (1987–88), 26 April 1988.
8 CJ (1890) 402; ibid (1897) 143. See also Parl Deb (1899) 67, c 27; CJ (1964–65) 348, 351; ibid (1985–86) 175.
9 For the case of a hybrid bill in respect of which this requirement was modified by order of the House, see CJ (1985–86) 398.
10 Minutes of Committees 1857, vol II, p 634.

upon.[1] A petitioner may suspend or withdraw his appearance at any time during the proceedings by application to the clerk of the committee; a suspension takes effect on the day following the application and while suspended he is charged no fees.

When opposed bills become unopposed (Standing Order 131)

If no parties appear on the petitions against an opposed bill, or, having appeared, withdraw their opposition before the evidence of the promoters is begun, the committee is required to refer the bill back, with a statement of the facts, to the Committee of Selection, which treats it as an unopposed bill.

> Where the bill has been one of a group of bills and the opposition has been withdrawn, an instruction has been given to the committee on the group to sit and proceed with the bill.[2]
>
> In 1911, the Local Government Provisional Orders (No 3) Bill became unopposed after evidence had been taken, and, through inadvertence, was referred back to the Committee of Selection; but the original committee was revived by order of the House for its further consideration.[3]

In 1985, where the sole petitioners, in consideration of amendments submitted to the filled-up bill, decided not to pursue their objections, the committee nevertheless met to determine the petitioners' application for costs.[4]

Reference of petitions to committee (Standing Order 126)

Standing Order 126 provides that all petitions presented against a bill, or complaining of amendments in the filled-up bill or of any proposed additional provision, subject to their compliance with the standing orders and the rules of the House, stand referred to the committee on the bill; and copies of all such petitions are to be laid before each member of the committee. Under Standing Order 172 copies of any petition against or otherwise relating to a bill must, on application and payment by any interested party, be supplied to him by the agent for the petition (see pp 839–841).

STANDING ORDERS RELATING TO THE COMMITTEE ON UNOPPOSED BILLS

The composition of the committee on unopposed bills has already been described (p 883). Two other standing orders relate to procedure before this committee.

Member if interested not to vote (Standing Order 133)

No member of a committee on an unopposed bill in which he is locally or otherwise interested may vote on any question that may arise, but he may attend and take part in the proceedings of the committee.

---

1 Minutes of Committee on Pontypool Gas and Water Bill 1890, vol 2, Group C.
2 CJ (1870) 72; ibid (1871) 218.
3 CJ (1911) 280.
4 Minutes of Evidence of Committee on Harrogate Stray Bill, 23 April 1985.

Right of promoters to be heard (Standing Order 134)

The promoters of an unopposed private bill are entitled to be heard before the committee in favour of the bill by themselves or their agents. This order, a corollary of Standing Order 127 with regard to opposed bills (see p 902), was first made in 1945, though the practice had long existed.

STANDING ORDERS RELATING TO COMMITTEES ON BILLS WHETHER OPPOSED OR UNOPPOSED

Whether the bill is opposed or unopposed, there are various standing orders which are binding upon the committee on every private bill, and others which relate only to particular classes or descriptions of bills. It is the duty of every committee to take care that the provisions required by the standing orders to be inserted in private bills are included in them wherever they are applicable. This may be effected in some cases by the incorporation of general Acts.

Method of deciding questions (Standing Order 135)

All questions before committees are decided by a majority of votes; and, whenever the votes are equal, the chairman has a second or casting vote.

Copies of 'filled-up' bill to be laid before members (Standing Order 137)

Copies of the bill, as proposed to be submitted to the committee, are to be laid before each member at the first meeting of the committee, ie with the amendments proposed by the promoters indicated. It should be noted that these amendments are not binding on the committee which has discretion whether or not to accept them. Where they result from an agreement between promoters and petitioners, or parties who might otherwise have petitioned, however, it is usual for the committee to accept them.[1]

Minutes of proceedings (Standing Orders 138, 145)

The names of the members attending each committee are entered by the committee clerk in the minutes of proceedings; and when a division takes

---

1 See remarks of the Chairman of Ways and Means on the Bolton Corporation Bill 1949 (HC Deb (1948–49) 464, cc 1104–1105 and p 911). Cf, however, Gloucester Corporation Bill 1958, where the Commons committee on the Bill reversed an agreement to which the Lords committee had given effect. On the application of the promoters, the clause was withdrawn on consideration.

place the clerk takes down the names of the members, distinguishing on which side of the question they respectively vote. The minutes of proceedings are laid upon the Table of the House with the report of the committee in accordance with Standing Order 145, but are not printed. They are open to inspection by Members only.

Proof of compliance with certain standing orders only (Standing Order 139)

Unless the House so orders, a committee is precluded from examining into compliance with Standing Orders 4 to 68, which are directed to be proved before the Examiners.

Practically the only case in which such an order is given is where the House (on the report of the Standing Orders Committee) allows parties to proceed with their bill, provided that they prove compliance before the committee with particular requirements with which they had neglected to prove compliance under the preliminary standing orders before the Examiners.[1]

When any special inquiry relating to the standing orders is involved, however, the matter has been referred to the Examiners rather than to the committee (see p 822).

Ministerial reports (Standing Orders 144, 146, 147, 156B, 158)

All reports made by a Minister of the Crown on a private bill stand referred to the committee on the bill. A committee must not begin to consider a private bill relating to a charity or an educational institution until a report on the bill by the Attorney General has been presented to the House[2] nor can a provision authorizing expenditure affecting grants payable to local authorities be authorized unless a departmental report approving such expenditure has been presented under Standing Order 156B. (For further details see p 901 and for contents of reports generally, see pp 890–891).

> The Joint Committee on Private Bill Procedure 1954–55 recommended that Ministers' reports should as a rule be made available to all interested parties not less than fourteen days before the committee of the first House sits on the bill. When by agreement of the parties, the committee sits less than fourteen days after the second reading of a bill, the report should be issued as soon as possible after second reading.[3] This recommendation was accepted by the Government.[4]

It has for a long time been the practice for officers of public departments to attend committees considering private bills on which their Ministers have made reports. Committees on private bills are debarred by Standing Order 136 from receiving, without express authority from the House,[5] any evidence except that adduced by the parties entitled to be heard (see p 902); so

---

1 CJ (1854) 78, and Suppl to Votes, 1854, pp 581–582.
2 For examples of non-compliance with this standing order and subsequent remedial action by the House, see p 899, fn 1.
3 HL 14, 58–I (1954–55), HC 139–I (1954–55).
4 HC Deb (1955–56) 557, c 1150.
5 In 1909 a mandatory instruction was given to the Select Committee on the Great Northern, Great Central and Great Eastern Railways Bill to hear the Board of Trade and any other Government department by counsel and witnesses, CJ (1909) 103.

that departmental officers have no absolute entitlement to speak to the practice and policy of their department. If, however, a ministerial report contains a recommendation, the committee is authorized by Standing Order 144, if it thinks fit, to hear an officer of the department in explanation of the report. Similarly, under Standing Order 147, committees may, if they think fit, hear officers of departments on bills containing provisions relating to level crossings. It is, in fact, normal practice for committees to hear departmental officers if they wish to add anything to their reports. Committees are required by Standing Orders 144 and 156 to notice ministerial recommendations in their reports to the House and, if they do not accept them, to state their reasons.

Other documents referred to committee

Other documents, such as correspondence with a government department,[1] or minutes of evidence taken before committees on bills in former sessions,[2] or the current session,[3] may also be referred to the committee on a bill.

Agreements (Standing Order 157)

Where any agreement is to be sanctioned by any bill, such agreement has to be printed as a schedule to the bill.[4]

It would appear that the rules concerning amendments to agreements scheduled to public bills (see p 493) have not been applied to private bills. Amendments may be made in the House of Lords because under Standing Order 129 (HL), any agreement scheduled to a private bill must contain a clause declaring that agreement to be made subject to such alterations as Parliament may think fit to make therein (see p 940).[5]

STANDING ORDERS RELATING TO COMMITTEES ON CERTAIN KINDS OF BILLS

Bills affecting fencing of bridges and railway, tramroad or tramway bills

Fencing of bridges (Standing Order 146). Where in any bill it is proposed to construct a bridge for carrying a public carriage-road, the bill is to require the erection of a good and sufficient fence on each side of the bridge.[6]

Level crossings (Standing Order 147). The committee on a bill may not allow the construction of a railway or tramroad so as to cross a railway,

---

1 CJ (1857–58) 160, 161, 166. Cf also LJ (1854) 256.
2 CJ (1857) 156, 173, 205, 235; ibid (1862) 267; ibid (1867) 218, 221; ibid (1890–91) 218.
3 CJ (1845) 536; ibid (1900) 289.
4 For a case in which, and the conditions upon which, compliance with this standing order was dispensed with, see CJ (1912–13) 42, 263.
5 In 1946 an agreement printed as a schedule to the Bucks Water Board Bill was altered by amendments made to a clause of the bill by a committee on unopposed bills. A special report indicated the reasons for the amendments. Suppl to Votes, 1945–46, p 45.
6 For comments on this standing order, see Special Report of Committee on Humber Bridge Bill 13 May 1959, Reports of Committees on Private Bills (1958–59) pp 68–69. The former requirements in the standing order relating to alterations in the level of roads were repealed on 6 February 1980.

tramway, tramroad or public carriage-road on the level, or the construction of a tramway so as to cross a railway on the level, unless a report from the Secretary of State for Transport is laid before the committee, and the committee, after considering the report and hearing an officer of the department, if it thinks fit, recommends the level crossing, giving reasons and facts. In every clause authorizing a level crossing the number of lines of rails authorized to be made at such crossing is to be specified.

Statement of length of line (Standing Order 150). In every railway, tramroad or tramway bill the length of the line is to be set forth in a clause describing the works, with a statement whether each tramway is a single or a double line.

Distance between passing vehicles when used on tramway (Standing Order 152). Where double lines are indicated on the plan deposited in respect of a tramway bill, provision is to be made that there is a distance of not less than 15 inches between the sides of the widest carriages and the engines to be used, when passing one another.

Restriction on power of acquisition of tramways by local authorities (Standing Order 153). No powers are to be given to any local authority to construct, acquire, take on lease or work any tramway beyond the limits of their district, unless it is in connection with a tramway which belongs to them or which they are authorized to construct, acquire, or work, and unless the committee on the bill determines that, having regard to the special local circumstances, such powers ought to be given. If the committee so determines, it must specify what portion of the tramway will be beyond the district of the local authority to whom such powers are given; and it must insert a protective clause (in terms indicated in the standing order) conferring upon the local authority, in whose district it will be situate, an eventual option of purchasing such tramway or portion of tramway, unless it reports, stating its reasons, that such a clause is not required.

Running powers in tramways bills (Standing Order 154). Where a local authority is empowered to work tramways belonging to it or authorized to be acquired by it, it may also be empowered to enter into agreements for running powers over any tramways in connection with those that it so works. But the committee on the bill must make provision for the approval of such agreements by the Secretary of State for Transport and for the observance of certain other conditions, and must report the circumstances specially to the House.

Bills affecting charities or educational foundations (Standing Order 158)

Provision is made by Standing Order 158 that, with certain exceptions, private bills affecting charities and educational foundations in England shall not be considered in committee until a report from the Attorney General on the bill has been presented to the House.[1]

Accommodation for workmen on works (Standing Order 159)

Standing Order 159 enjoins a committee on a bill which authorizes the construction of works elsewhere than in London to inquire, if in its view the scale of the proposed works makes an inquiry desirable, into the provision made in the bill for proper housing and sanitation for persons employed in constructing the works, and for their treatment in cases of sickness, infectious disease or accident. If the committee considers that more housing or services should be provided, it must insert in the bill amendments which will have the effect of securing such provision. This standing order has been applied by instruction to a bill as if it were a bill authorizing the construction of works.[2]

Compensation water (Standing Order 160)

Two requirements are laid by Standing Order 160 upon a committee on a bill for impounding or abstracting the whole or any part of the water of any river or stream. Where a dam is to be constructed, it must inquire into the expediency of providing that the water to be supplied in compensation should be given in a continuous flow throughout the twenty-four hours of the day. In any other case, it must inquire whether provision ought to be made for limiting the quantity to be abstracted, and report accordingly. The standing order also lays down the considerations to which the committee should have regard in determining what, if any, provision should be made.

Limits of burial ground, gas works, etc, to be defined (Standing Order 161)

In every bill for making gas works or sewage works, or works for the manufacture or conversion of the residual products of gas or sewage, or electric generating station, or for making, constructing or extending any sewage farm, cemetery, burial ground, crematorium, destructor, or hospital for infectious diseases, there is to be a clause defining the lands in or upon which the same is to be made or constructed.

Bills relating to water companies (Standing Order 162)

In every bill in which an existing water company is authorized to raise additional capital, provision is to be made for the offer of such capital by auction or tender, unless the committee reports, stating its reasons, that such provision ought not to be required. Though the auction clause is invariably inserted in water bills, it is now the usual practice to insert clauses enabling the company to issue shares to consumers and employees at the

---

1 Where this standing order was found not to have been complied with, the proceedings of the committee have subsequently been validated by order of the House: Hastings Borough Council Bill, Votes and Proceedings (1987–88) 1 February 1988; Birmingham City Council Bill, ibid, 20 October 1988.
2 CJ (1912–13) 46.

current market price, and subject to such conditions as the department concerned may impose to issue shares for subscription by the public.

Application of money to be recited in local authorities' bills (England and Wales) (Standing Order 155)

Where a bill authorizes a local authority in England or Wales to borrow money for any matter within the jurisdiction of the Secretary of State for the Environment, the proposed application of the money for permanent works (except so far as the borrowing power is to be exercised subject to the sanction of the Secretary of State) is to be recited in the bill, and to be proved before the committee. Copies of the estimates of expenditure and statements required to be deposited under Standing Orders 45 and 46 are also to be laid before the committee.

Bills promoted by local authorities (Standing Order 156)

The committee on a bill promoted by, or proposing to confer powers on, a local authority, is required to consider the clauses of the bill with reference to certain considerations set out in Standing Order 156. The most important are whether the bill assigns a period for the repayment of any loan or for the redemption of any charge or debt exceeding sixty years or any period disproportionate to the duration of the works to be executed or to any other objects of the loan, charge or debt, and whether the bill gives borrowing powers for purposes for which such powers already exist or may be obtained under any public Act, without subjecting the exercise of the powers to the consent of a government department. The committee must report on these points, in particular whether a term for repayment or redemption exceeding sixty years has been allowed (with the reasons therefor) and whether a ministerial report on the bill has been referred to it and in what manner its recommendations (if any) have been dealt with.

In considering any provisions in the bill as to borrowing powers and powers relating to police, sanitary, and local government matters, the committee must have regard to the provisions as to such powers in existing general Acts; and it must report specially upon these and other points specified in the standing order[1] including any special circumstances of which, in the opinion of the committee, the House should be informed. These have included reasons for disallowing[2] or amending clauses;[3] for allowing the withdrawal of clauses,[4] and for awarding costs against a promoter[5] and have drawn attention to cases where the committee considered there had been infringements of standing orders[6] or of statutes[7] or to apparent abuses of private bill procedure.[8] (See also pp 917–918 (special reports from committees)).

---

1 See the sessional order of 16 December 1937, CJ (1937–38) 69, and the Chairman of Ways and Means's remarks, HC Deb (1937) 330, cc 1305–1306. See also CJ (1938–39) 37.
2 Reports of Committees on Private Bills (1957–58) p 133.
3 Ibid (1960–61) p 21.
4 Ibid (1957–58) p 67.
5 Ibid (1957–58) p 68.
6 Ibid (1957–58) p 68.
7 Ibid (1957–58) p 37.
8 Ibid (1957–58) pp 37–39; (1958–59) pp 56, 59–60, 96.

Bills affecting grants to local authorities (Standing Order 156B)

Where a bill contains any provision authorizing expenditure by a local authority which would or might operate to increase the sums payable by way of exchequer grants, and the standing orders and practice of the House relating to charges upon the public revenue have not been complied with (see pp 869–870), the committee must, subject to a proviso, insert a clause providing that such expenditure shall not be taken into account for the purpose of determining the aggregate amount of such grants. The proviso to Standing Order 156B permits the omission of the clause where a report on the bill made by the Secretary of State for the Environment or the Secretary of State for Scotland recommends that the expenditure sanctioned by the bill should be taken into account under the Acts.

This standing order preserves the initiative of the Crown when charges upon the public revenue arise from local expenditure, notwithstanding the terms of Standing Order 156A (see p 870). Where a private bill promoted by a local authority contains provision for new expenditure which may lead to an increase in exchequer grant, a recommendation contained in a report by one of the Ministers mentioned above is substituted for the Queen's recommendation signified in the usual manner (see pp 691–692) as a condition which precedes the charge being sanctioned by the committee on the bill.

It has been indicated[1] that where a local authority is seeking powers which are not entirely novel, the Minister's recommendation will be given as a matter of course.[2] It should be remembered that where such recommendation is given the committee on the bill is not bound by it, but is still at liberty to insert the saving clause if it thinks fit, just as it is open to the House to reject a financial motion despite the Queen's recommendation.

Standing Order 156B does not apply to provisional order bills or to bills to confirm special procedure orders. Such bills, however, unlike the generality of bills both public and private, can be introduced only by a Minister of the Crown.

PROCEEDINGS IN COMMITTEE

The various matters which are required by the standing orders to be reported upon by committees or to be proved before them, and the provisions required to be inserted in particular bills having been considered, the general proceedings of committees upon private bills must now be briefly

---

1 HC Deb (1948–49) 457, cc 1286–1287.
2 Since SO 156B was passed in 1948, the Minister's recommendation has been withheld only from certain provisions in the Birmingham Corporation Bill 1955, and the Leicester Corporation Bill 1955, which authorized expenditure on special travel facilities; see Reports of Committees on Private Bills (1955–56) pp 12 and 41.

x

explained. These are partly regulated by the usage of Parliament, partly by standing orders, and partly by statute.

Committee's power to hear evidence (Standing Order 136). By this order, first made in 1945, it is declared that a committee is not empowered, without express authority from the House, to hear evidence other than that which may be tendered by the parties entitled to be heard.[1] Standing Order 134 specifies the parties entitled to be heard before the committee on an unopposed bill and Standing Order 127 the parties so entitled before the committee on an opposed bill.

Visits to sites. Committees on private bills do not normally have power to adjourn from place to place. In recent years, however, committees on opposed private bills,[2] select committees on hybrid bills[3] and joint committees on special procedure orders[4] and Scottish order confirmation bills[5] have frequently been given power by the House to visit the sites of works proposed in the bills or orders concerned. In addition committees on two substituted bills have been given power to adjourn from place to place and one of these committees used this power both to visit Shetland and to hold all its meetings to hear evidence in Edinburgh.[6]

(1) Committees on unopposed bills

The constitution of committees on unopposed bills, which is laid down by Standing Order 132, has already been described (see p 883). Their proceedings are more brief and less formal than those of a committee on an opposed private bill; but, because there are no opponents of the bill, a special responsibility devolves on the committee in its consideration of the preamble and provisions of the bill to ensure that the interests of the public are properly safeguarded and that the bill conforms with the standing orders of the House. This responsibility is imposed chiefly upon the Chairman of Ways and Means, who is ex officio chairman of the committee when present, and who, being an officer of the House as well as a Member, is entrusted with the special duty of examining, with the assistance of Mr Speaker's Counsel, every private bill, whether opposed or unopposed. The promoters therefore have to prove the preamble, to the satisfaction of the committee, by the production of the necessary evidence which is usually not taken upon oath, and by such explanations as may be required of them. They have to satisfy the committee as to the propriety of and the need for the several

1 In 1960, a committee sought leave of the House to hear other evidence by means of an instruction but the matter was not pressed. See Private Business (1959–60) pp 209, 215.
2 Eg Committees on Hampshire (Lyndhurst By-pass) Bill [Lords] (Votes and Proceedings (1987–88), 12 May 1988) and City of London (Spitalfields Market) Bill (Votes and Proceedings (1987–88), 14 June 1988).
3 Eg Select Committees on Channel Tunnel Bill (CJ (1985–86) 398) and Norfolk and Suffolk Broads Bill (Votes and Proceedings (1986–87), 4 March 1987).
4 Eg Joint Committee on Exeter-Launceston-Bodmin Trunk Road (Okehampton By-pass) Compulsory Purchase Orders (CJ (1984–85) 339).
5 Eg Joint Committee on Lothian Region (Edinburgh Western Relief Road) Order Confirmation Bill (CJ (1985–86) 170).
6 Committee on the Zetland County Council Bill (CJ (1972–73) 295). The Committee on the Orkney County Council Bill did not use the power to adjourn from place to place (CJ (1974) 70).

provisions of the bill (see p 909); that all the clauses required by the standing orders are inserted in the bill; and that such standing orders as must be proved before the committee have been complied with. Counsel are not heard, the promoters' case being presented by the agent for the bill.

On 4 May 1906, the committee on the Mid-Oxfordshire Gas Bill, after hearing the evidence, announced that it considered the finance of the bill so unsatisfactory that, on grounds of public policy, it declared the preamble of the bill not proved, and reported accordingly to the House.[1]

In 1936, the committee on the Ministry of Health Provisional Order (Helston and Porthleven Water) Bill, not being satisfied with the case put before it, adjourned the consideration of the bill until an inquiry had been held by the Ministry of Health. On the receipt of the report of the inquiry the bill was approved by the committee and reported to the House.[2] On other occasions when the committee has not been satisfied with the case as presented, it has adjourned consideration for further evidence[3] and in other cases has made a special report.[4]

In 1948, the committee considered that the order contained in the Ministry of Health Provisional Order (Bradford) Bill was not a proper object for the exercise of the powers of section 303 of the Public Health Act 1875, under which it had been made. It therefore reported to the House that in its opinion the order ought not to be confirmed, the bill being reported without amendment.[5]

In 1955, the committee considered that the order contained in the Ministry of Housing and Local Government Provisional Order (Mortlake Crematorium Board) Bill made an improper use of the powers of the Mortlake Crematorium Act 1936, under which the order was made. It therefore reported that in its opinion the order ought not to be confirmed. The bill was reported without amendment.[6]

In 1956, during consideration of the North-East Surrey Crematorium Board Bill [Lords] by a committee on unopposed bills, it was brought to their notice that a petition had been deposited complaining of a matter which had arisen during the progress of the bill before the committee. The committee adjourned further consideration of the bill and made a special report to the House.[7]

It has been stated above (p 890) that the Chairman of Ways and Means is empowered by Standing Order 85 to inform the House that in his opinion any unopposed private bill should be treated as an opposed bill. He can exercise this power, whether or not the committee on unopposed bills has

---

1 CJ (1906) 163. For other cases where the preamble has not been proved see Northam UDC Bill (CJ (1968–69) 187), Yorkshire Derwent Water Bill (CJ (1969–70) 315), and Ross and Cromarty County Council Bill (CJ (1974–75) 473).
2 CJ (1935–36) 319.
3 Reports of Committees on Private Bills (1960–61) p 99.
4 Reports of Committees on Private Bills (1957–58) p 3.
5 CJ (1947–48) 304.
6 CJ (1955–56) 62.
7 CJ (1955–56) 289.

begun to consider the bill.[1] Under Standing Order 112, if such a report is made to the House, the bill stands again referred to the Committee of Selection, and is then dealt with as an opposed bill.

(2) Committees on opposed bills

Committee room: when open and when cleared. When counsel are addressing the committee, or while witnesses are under examination, the committee room is an open court;[2] but when the committee is about to deliberate, all the counsel, agents, witnesses, and strangers are ordered to withdraw, and the committee sits with closed doors. When it has decided any question, the doors are again opened, and the chairman acquaints the parties with the decision of the committee, if it concerns them.

Parties appear before the committee. The first proceeding of a committee on an opposed bill, when duly constituted, is to call in all the parties. The counsel in support of the bill appear before the committee. The petitions against the bill, upon which an appearance has been taken out, are read by the committee clerk; and the counsel or agents appear in support of such petitions.[3] If an appearance has not been taken out on any petition, the opposition of the petitioners is held to be abandoned.

Appearances upon petitions against bill. If parties have neglected to enter their appearance at the proper time, they will not be entitled to be heard.[4] In some special cases, however, indulgence has been granted to them.[5]

An appearance paper has been allowed to be amended, where it stated that a petition praying to be heard against the preamble related to clauses only.[6] The responsibility for the conduct of a petition has been transferred by one agent to another.[7] For the suspension and withdrawal of appearances see pp 893–894 above.

Appearance upon petitions on matters arising in committee. Where petitions complain of matters arising during the sitting of the committee, or of amendments proposed to be made in the bill, appearances are allowed to be entered as the occasion arises.[8]

In the case of the Glasgow Corporation Tramways Bill 1879, which after being referred to a group as an opposed bill became unopposed, a petition

---

1 CJ (1906) 271; Private Business (1906) p 647; CJ (1922) 106; ibid (1935–36) 309; ibid (1955–56) 295; ibid (1983–84) 628, where a petition against alterations had been deposited.
2 But see Minutes of Evidence Group A on the Kent Electric Power Bill, 21 May 1941, for an occasion when a committee sat in private for reasons of public security, and on the Dartford-Thurrock Crossing Bill (a hybrid bill), 17 November 1987, for reasons of commercial confidence.
3 Before cases of locus standi were heard by the Court of Referees (see pp 842–843) it was also usual at this time to intimate that objections would be raised to the hearing of petitioners. This is still the proper occasion for raising a similar objection to hearing petitioners against a hybrid bill.
4 See pp 893–894; Suppl to Votes, 1853, p 829. Minutes of Committees on Opposed Bills, 1857, vol II, p 793.
5 Minutes of Evidence of Committee on London Docklands Railway (City Extension) Bill, 20 May 1986, p 24.
6 Minutes of Committee, Group 3 (5 July) 1859.
7 Private Business (1953–54) 186; ibid (1954–55) 48; ibid (1962–63) 125; ibid (1987–88) 275, etc.
8 See also SO 126 and p 894.

was deposited complaining of matters which had arisen during the sitting of the committee on unopposed bills. The Chairman of Ways and Means presented a report from the committee on this circumstance, and the bill was recommitted to the former committee.[1]

Preliminary objections. When the parties are before the committee, the senior counsel for the bill opens the case for the promoters. A preliminary objection has sometimes been raised by petitioners to proceeding further with the bill.[2] These objections, however, have not usually been sustained. Usually they have referred to questions inherent in the principle and inception of the bill, and as such might have been raised on its second reading. As the bill has been referred by an order of the House to a committee for consideration, the strong presumption is that the duty of the committee is to deal with the bill on its merits. Preliminary objections have sometimes been sustained when they have arisen on matters which have occurred after the second reading of a bill.

Proceedings in support of the preamble. Unlike the practice in regard to public bills (see pp 498–499) the preamble of a private bill is usually considered first unless the bill is for a variety of purposes, in which case consideration of the preamble or the parts not relevant is normally postponed until after the consideration of the various clauses, those which are opposed on petition being taken first. (See also p 909.) If the preamble is opposed, counsel addresses the committee more particularly upon the general expediency of the bill, and then calls witnesses to prove every matter which will establish the truth of the allegations contained in the preamble. The witnesses may be cross-examined by the counsel or agent who appears in support of the several petitions against the preamble, but not, as to the general case, by counsel or agent of parties who object only to certain provisions in the bill. Cross-examination is confined to matters comprised in the petitions, except when it is sought to discredit a witness. After the cross-examination, each witness may be re-examined by the counsel in support of the bill.

Rules as to the hearing of petitioners against the preamble. As already stated (see p 894) all petitions against a private bill, which have been deposited in accordance with the standing orders, stand referred to the committee; and such petitioners, subject to the rules and orders of the House, must be heard upon their petition. Unless petitioners pray to be heard against the preamble, however, they are not entitled to be heard, or otherwise to appear in the proceedings of the committee, until the preamble has been disposed of. Nor will a general prayer against the preamble entitle a petitioner to be heard against it, if his interest be merely affected by certain clauses of the bill.[3] Petitioners, however, have been heard against the preamble of a bill, although the word 'preamble' was not in the prayer of

---

1 CJ (1878–79) 229, and Minutes of Group 11, 13 and 23 May 1879.
2 Birmingham (Corporation) Water Bill 1875; Stockton and Middlesborough Corporations Water Bill 1876; Hammersmith and Fulham Recreation Ground Bill 1884 (sustained); Great Forest of Brecknock Bill 1893; Local Government Provisional Orders (No 15) Bill 1903; Sale of Bread (London) Bill 1905, etc.
3 Suppl to Votes, 1843, p 131; ibid 1850, pp 45, 199, etc Petitioners, however, who pray to be heard against certain clauses and so much of the preamble as relates thereto, have frequently been heard on the preamble.

their petition, when their intention was clearly shown by the context.[1] The proper time for urging objections to parties being heard against the preamble is when their counsel or agent first rises to put a question to a witness, or to address any observations to the committee. The counsel for the bill having been heard and all the witnesses in support of the preamble having been examined, the case for the promoters is closed.

Proceedings in support of petitions against the preamble. When petitioners appear against the preamble, their counsel or agent either opens their case or reserves his speech until after the evidence. Witnesses may be called and examined in support of the petitions, cross-examined by the counsel for the bill, and re-examined by the counsel or agent for the petitioners; but counsel and agents can be heard, and witnesses examined on behalf of petitioners, only in relation to matters referred to in their petitions.[2]

Where there are numerous parties, appearing on separate interests, the committee makes such arrangements as it thinks fit for hearing the different counsel.[3] For competing bills, see pp 907–909.

Proceedings on petitions against alterations. Petitions against alterations (see p 840) are not infrequently presented by parties who object to alterations which are proposed to be made in the bill in committee, and which might affect them. Such petitions may contain objections to amendments proposed by the promoters and included in the 'filled-up' bill (including additional provisions), or to amendments that either have been or, it is anticipated, will be requested by petitioners or made by the committee.

The procedure for considering such petitions in a committee depends on the circumstances. If the petitioner is objecting to amendments proposed by the promoters, he has a right to be heard after the case for the promoters on the relevant part of the bill has been closed. If, however, he is objecting to amendments requested by other petitioners against the bill, two courses of procedure are possible. Should the promoters be opposed to the requested amendments, they are held to be fully competent to defend their bill without the intervention of the petitioner against alterations, and it is not usual for the petitioner against alterations to be heard.[4] If the promoters are disposed to leave the decision entirely to the committee or to concede the requested amendments, then the petitioner against alterations assumes the task of defending the bill in this respect in the place of the promoters. In such circumstances petitioners against alterations have been heard to make their case for the bill as originally presented before the petitioners against the bill have argued their case for the amendments they propose. If, however, the committee is disposed to agree to the proposed amendments, it may, before

1 Minutes of Committees on Opposed Bills 1856, vol I, p 65.
2 Glasgow and South Western Railway (No 2) Bill, and South Wales Railway (Monmouth) Bill 1853; Suppl to Votes, 1852–53, pp 721, 1339; Minutes of Committees on Opposed Bills 1856, vol I; Railway and Canal Bills, p 56, etc.
3 Suppl to Votes 1852–53, p 1031.
4 Minutes of Evidence of Committees on Private Bills, 1904, vol I, p 175. Cf, however, SO 127(2).

taking a decision, give the petitioner against alterations an opportunity of stating his case (which may not be the same as that of the promoters) and of producing any new and relevant evidence.

Under Standing Order 90 the jurisdiction of the Court of Referees extends only to petitions against private bills. The locus standi of petitioners against alterations is therefore decided by the committee on the bill.

Hearing of witnesses and departmental representatives. In general, the normal rules of evidence apply, though witnesses are allowed to refer to a proof of evidence. Departmental representatives may be heard at any convenient part in the proceedings; they are not witnesses and may not be cross-examined, but the Chairman, if he thinks fit, may allow questions to be put to a departmental representative if addressed through him.[1]

Reply of counsel for the bill. When the speeches and evidence in support of petitions against the preamble are concluded, counsel for the bill replies on the whole case. If a petitioner has not called witnesses or put in any document, counsel for the bill has no right of reply; but if a petitioner puts in a document, or even, without putting it in, cross-examines the promoters' witnesses upon it, this generally entitles the promoters to a reply. In some cases this reply is restricted; for example, where the petitioner refers to any Act of Parliament[2] or judgment of a court, or to the decision, proceedings, or report of a committee of either House of Parliament or other similar body, the reply must be limited to the particular document quoted. It has been held that, where there are several petitioners, only one of whom has adduced evidence, the reply of counsel for the promoters must be confined to the case of that one petitioner.[3] Any documents, or minutes of evidence on bills of a previous session which may have been referred to the committee, may be commented on by counsel without objection, and considered by the committee; but reference to such document by a petitioner does not entitle the promoters to a reply.

Question upon preamble. When the arguments and evidence upon the preamble have been heard, the room is cleared, and a question is put, 'That the preamble is proved,' which is resolved in the affirmative or negative, as the case may be.

It is usual to prove in sections the preamble of an omnibus bill, or bill for the authorization of several separate undertakings. The question that 'so much of the preamble as relates thereto' is put and decided by the committee with regard to each section. Where there is no opposition to the preamble of a bill with several purposes, it is usual to postpone the preamble until after consideration of the clauses.[4]

Competing bills. Where there are competing bills in the same group, the cases are heard together, and the decision of the committee is postponed until after it has heard the evidence in support of and against all the bills. The

---

1 Eg Minutes of Evidence, Committee on Zetland County Council Bill 1973.
2 Eg Minutes of Evidence, Committee on South Essex Waterworks Bill, 4 April 1962, p 47.
3 Suppl to Votes, 1852–53, p 720.
4 A committee has for convenience deferred final consideration of one part of the preamble until it had heard the arguments relating to the other parts and has then announced its decisions, Kent Water Bill, Minutes of Evidence, 19 May 1954, pp 48–49.

procedure is as follows when there are two or more competing bills (the additional procedure required, when there are more than two such bills, being placed in square brackets):

(i) The counsel for Bill No 1 opens his case in a statement explanatory of the purposes of his bill and calls his witnesses, who are subject to cross-examination by the counsel for Bill No 2 [and for Bill No 3], and by the counsel for the other petitioners against Bill No 1.

(ii) The case of these petitioners against Bill No 1 is then heard, their counsel calling evidence and having the right to address the committee either before or after the examination of the witnesses, but not twice.

(iii) The counsel for Bill No 2 next opens his case in a statement explanatory of the purposes of his bill, and calls his witnesses, who are subject to cross-examination by the counsel for Bill No 1 [and for Bill No 3], and by the counsel for the other petitioners against Bill No 2.

(iv) The case of the petitioners against Bill No 2 is then heard. When, however, the same petition has been presented against both [or all] the competing bills, the committee instead of hearing the petitioners against each of the bills at separate times, may hear them against both [or all] the bills after the counsel for the last of the competing bills has made his opening statement and called his evidence, but before he proceeds to sum up his case in reply.[1]

[(iva) Counsel for Bill No 3 here opens his case in a statement explanatory of the purposes of his bill, and calls his witnesses, who are subject to cross-examination by the counsel for Bills No 1 and No 2, and by the counsel for the other petitioners against Bill No 3.

(ivb) The case of these petitioners against Bill No 3 is then heard, subject to the qualification made by the second sentence of (iv) above.

(ivc) The counsel for Bill No 3 then sums up the case for his own bill as against the other competing bills and in reply to the evidence adduced in opposition to his bill.]

(v) The counsel for Bill No 2 then sums up the case for his own bill as against the other competing bill [or bills], and in reply to the evidence adduced in opposition to his bill.

(vi) The counsel for Bill No 1 then replies on the whole case. The committee then gives its decision on the preambles of both [or all] the bills, and subsequently considers the clauses of the bill [or bills] of which the preamble is declared to be proved.[2]

The Committee on the Derby Corporation, Sheffield Corporation, and

---

1 See Minutes of Proceedings, Group F, Thames River Steamboat Service Bill and Thames Steamboat Trust Bill, 26 April 1904; Minutes of Proceedings, Group 5, Invergarry etc, Railway Bill; North British etc, Railway Bill 11–22 March 1897.

2 For two competing bills, see Thames Steamboat Trust Bill and Thames River Steamboat Service Bill (Group F) 1904; Cork City Railways etc, Bill and Cork Link Railways Bill (Group 5) 1906; Glasgow Boundaries (substituted) Bill and Clydebank Burgh Extension etc (substituted) Bill (Group E) 1925; Birmingham Extension Bill and West Bromwich Corporation Bill (Group B) 1927; Rochdale Canal Bill and Lancashire County Council (Rochdale Canal Bridges) Bill (Group A) 1952. For three competing bills, see Brecon etc, Railway Bill, Alexandra, etc, Docks and Railway (General Powers) Bill, and Barry Railway Bill (Group 3) 1907. For four competing bills, see Bucks Water Board Bill, South Bucks and Oxfordshire Water Bill, Reading and Berkshire Water etc Bill and Mid-Wessex Water Bill (Group B) 1958.

Leicester Corporation Water Bills 1899 were empowered by an instruction of the House (passed on the motion of the chairman of the committee) to consolidate the bills; and accordingly, having formally passed the preambles of the three bills, they struck out all the clauses, and proceeded to consider a consolidated bill (against which the parties petitioning against all three bills were heard), and to report this consolidated bill (Derwent Valley Water Bill) to the House.[1]

In a few cases, the committee has considered each bill separately, although deferring its decision on the preamble of each bill until the case on the last bill had been concluded.[2] Occasionally, too, where the subject-matter of bills in the same group has been partly the same, committees have heard the cases separately, but have deferred their decision till after the conclusion of the last case.

Decision on preamble. The committee calls in the parties and acquaints them with its decision regarding the preamble; and, if the preamble is proved, they then go through the bill clause by clause.

Clauses considered. Where petitioners appear against a clause, or propose amendments, they are heard in support of their objections or amendments, as they arise; or opposed clauses may be postponed and considered at a later period in the proceedings, if the committee thinks fit. It is usual to consider clauses opposed on petition first and those which are the subject of comments in reports from Departments next. The amount of proof of need which a committee will require for the various clauses of a bill must obviously vary, but the Joint Committee on the Promotion of Private Bills suggested in 1959 that a stringent proof should be required in the case of those clauses which are unprecedented, which impose penalties or create criminal offences or which involve expenditure of local tax-payers' money.[3] Well-precedented and generally acceptable clauses may sometimes be allowed without special mention, but even model clauses (see pp 810–811) which are generally in this category, have not infrequently been disallowed where adequate need for them has not been shown to the committee.[4]

By Standing Order 136A, a committee considering clauses in a bill promoted by a county council which confer powers upon district councils within the county cannot accept proof that the clauses are needed unless a certificate is produced to the effect that a resolution in favour of the clauses has been passed by an absolute majority of the council of the local authority after due local advertisement of the relevant provisions.[5]

In accordance with the rules of the House in committee in dealing with a public bill, when all the clauses of the bill have been disposed of, new clauses may be offered either by members of the committee or by the parties.

---

1 CJ (1899) 229, 267, and Minutes of Proceedings, Group B, 24 April, 7, 8, 9 June 1899.
2 For proceedings of committees in the Lords, on the London Electric Power Bills 1905 and on the Penllwyn and other Welsh Railway Bills 1906, and other competing bills, see p 938.
3 Report of Joint Committee on Promotion of Private Bills 1958–59, para 15.
4 Eg Kent County Council Bill 1958; see Reports of Committees on Private Bills 1957–58, p 133.
5 In 1962, the committee on the Devon County Council Bill refused to allow a clause conferring powers on district councils to apply to an urban district which had not passed the resolution required by the standing order. The operation of other clauses was excluded by the bill itself for the same reason.

Alternative clauses. An alternative clause prepared by petitioners is frequently produced and considered in connection with a clause which is formally before the committee, and which may be amended or negatived in consequence.

Counsel may claim the right of reply when they have brought up a new clause; but a distinction should be drawn in this respect between a purely alternative clause and a new clause; such an alternative clause is produced only in support of the argument against, and is virtually an amendment to, a clause already formally before the committee, and it should be treated as an amendment only, without any right of reply; while counsel proposing a new and substantive clause for the consideration of the committee, when no other clause was before it, would not be so limited.

Admissible clauses and additional provisions. The power of a committee to admit clauses or amendments has already been described (see p 874). If, however, a committee is of opinion that provisions which would necessitate a petition for additional provision should be inserted in the bill, the further consideration of the bill can be postponed, in order to give the parties time to petition the House for additional provision[1] (see pp 830–831). It should be noted, however, that additional provisions may not be obtained in the second House. Similarly, and as a consequence of this, it is a well-established rule that a clause conferring powers upon the promoters struck out in one House should not be re-inserted in the other, and restrictive amendments imposed by one House on the promoters are not reversed by the other.[2]

In one instance a restrictive amendment has been reversed by the other House. A clause in the West Midlands County Council Bill [Lords] 1979, which provided for the control of acupuncturists, was amended in committee in the Commons so as to exempt petitioners from its provisions. The Lords disagreed to the amendment, on which the Commons did not insist.[3]

A committee has refused to entertain a clause which the promoters of a bill had agreed upon with another company and proposed to insert in the bill, even when it appeared that the petition of that company had been withdrawn, on condition of the introduction of that clause. In such cases, however, which are of rare occurrence, a committee has sometimes consented to the promoters calling witnesses representing the company con-

1 London and North Western Railway (Northampton Branch) Bill, Suppl to Votes, 1853, p 964; and ibid p 1255; Bradford Tramways etc, Bill, Suppl to Votes, 1899, p 1341; Ossett Corporation Bill, Minutes of Proceedings (Group B), 11 April 1938; CJ (1937–38) 203; Bucks Water Board Bill, CJ (1957–58) 217; Special Report from the Committee on the Lloyd's Bill, CJ (1980–81) 464; London Docklands Railway (Beckton) Bill, Minutes of Evidence, 15 March 1988.
2 In 1956, the committee on the Gloucestershire County Council Bill deleted an amendment which had previously been made by the House of Lords at the request of the promoters to give effect to an agreement between them and petitioners. Doubts were expressed as to the validity of this and the promoters obtained leave to withdraw the amended clause on consideration; CJ (1955–56) 220, Minutes of Evidence, 22 February 1956, Gloucestershire County Council Bill [Lords].
3 Committee on the West Midlands County Council Bill [Lords], Minutes of Evidence, 13 and 14 March 1979; Lords Minutes (1979–80) 31 January 1980; HL Deb (1979–80) 404, cc 997–1003; CJ (1979–80) 394; HC Deb (1979–80) 979, cc 322–344.

cerned,[1] or has offered to obtain power from the House to hear the company, notwithstanding the withdrawal of its petition.[2] In other cases the parties affected have been refused a hearing.[3]

The latter issue has been raised indirectly in the House. The Bolton Corporation Bill 1949, as presented, had contained a clause authorizing the Corporation to provide a residential hotel. Subsequently, as a result of negotiations with opponents, the promoters agreed to strike out the clause in the 'filled-up' bill, and the committee on the bill made the necessary amendment. On the consideration stage, a motion was made to recommit the bill to a Committee of the whole House in respect of a clause couched in terms similar to the clause already left out in committee (re-committal was necessary since the provisions of the clause involved a charge upon the rates, see pp 714–715). The Chairman of Ways and Means, in advising the House to reject the motion, drew attention to the serious consequences which might ensue in future negotiations on private legislation, if promoters were to be compelled to insert a clause which they had previously agreed to leave out.[4] The motion to recommit the bill was negatived.[5]

In the case of the Urmston Urban District Council Bill 1949, where a petition had been withdrawn as a result of a similar undertaking given by the promoters, the committee on the bill made a special report stating that although it had felt obliged to accept the position, it nevertheless regretted the omission of the powers contained in the clause and wished to draw the attention of the House to their desirability.[6]

By contrast, in the London County Council (General Powers) Bill 1961, the promoters, having included a clause on street trading in the bill at the request of certain metropolitan borough councils, proposed, in the 'filled-up' bill, to delete it because one borough council objected, and the committee on the bill accepted this amendment. On consideration of the bill, the House agreed to a motion to re-insert a slightly different provision on street trading.[7]

Enforcement of pledges. A committee has also inserted clauses compelling a railway company, under penalty of a suspension of its dividends, to apply to Parliament in the next session, for a bill to authorize the construction of a line of railway which the company had pledged itself to make.[8] The preamble of a bill has also been negatived, on proof that it was a violation of a pledge previously given by a company.[9]

1 Colne Corporation Bill 1905 (Minutes of Evidence, Police and Sanitary Committee, vol XIV, pp 42–48, 3 April).
2 Thames Tunnel Railway Bill, Minutes of Group 2, 1860, pp 84–88.
3 British Transport Commission (No 2) Bill 1956, Minutes of Evidence, 1955–56, pp 1–2.
4 HC Deb (1948–49) 464, cc 1104–1105.
5 CJ (1948–49) 231.
6 CJ (1948–49) 252.
7 HC Deb (1961–62) 661 cc 1039–1080.
8 London and South Western Railway Act 1855; Suppl to Votes 1854–55, pp 251–253. Cf in this connection, Report of Select Committee on Railways (Ireland) Amalgamation Bills, CJ (1899) 373–374.
9 Mid-Sussex etc, Railway Bill (Group 3) 1860. Yorkshire Woollen District Transport Bill, Minutes of Evidence (Lords) 22 March 1961.

Preamble of bill not proved. If the proof of the preamble is negatived, the committee reports to the House that the preamble has not been proved.[1]

It has been ruled that when a committee has resolved that the preamble of a private bill has not been proved, and ordered the chairman to report, it is not competent for it to reconsider and reverse its decision, but that the bill should be recommitted for that purpose.[2] This course, however, of recommitting a bill of which the committee has reported the preamble 'not proved' is unusual and requires a strong case to be made out for its adoption.[3]

In 1902, the promoters of the South Eastern and London, Chatham, and Dover Railways Bill, a bill with several purposes, were unable to accept the provisions suggested by the committee in one opposed portion, 'Railway No 1', of the bill. The committee therefore reported that the preamble of the whole bill, including other and unopposed portions, was not proved. The bill was recommitted with an instruction to the committee to reconsider its decision upon so much of the preamble as did not relate to Railway No 1; and the committee subsequently reported that it had done so and had found the preamble proved except in so far as it related to Railway No 1.[4]

In several other instances where compromises have afterwards been effected, and the promoters have consented to make amendments, the bills have been recommitted for that purpose.[5]

In 1913, the Local Legislation Committee decided that so much of the preamble of the East Ham Corporation Bill as related to Part II, which constituted East Ham a county borough, was not proved. The chairman in announcing the committee's decision stated that it would welcome the reconsideration of its decision by the House in view of the novelty and importance of the questions raised. The bill was recommitted to the same committee with an instruction to reinsert these provisions, if it thought fit, either with or without modifications, and the committee reinserted the powers asked for.[6]

In the same year, owing to the lateness of the session, the promoters of the Electric Lighting Provisional Orders (No 6) Bill [Lords] decided not to proceed with one of the orders contained in the bill relating to Kingstown. The committee on the bill reported to this effect. The House thereupon recommitted the Bill to the committee for the purpose of reinstating the Kingstown order, gave the committee power to divide the bill into two bills dealing with the opposed and unopposed order respectively, and ordered that the bill for confirming the opposed order should stand referred to the Committee of Selection.[7]

---

1 In 1836 the committee on the Durham (South West) Railway Bill was ordered to reassemble, 'for the purpose of reporting specially the preamble, and the evidence and reasons, in detail, on which it came to the resolution that the preamble had not been proved', CJ (1836) 396.
2 CJ (1857–58) 209; ibid (1924–25) 179, London County Council (Tramways and Improvements) Bill, where the committee was instructed to reconsider its decision on the preamble.
3 Cf the proceedings in the House on the Piccadilly, City, and North East London Railway Bill 1902, Parl Deb (1902) 113, c 1154, and on the City of London (Various Powers) Bill 1961, HC Deb (1961–62) 661, cc 1080–1116.
4 CJ (1902) 306, 314, 330, 343; Parl Deb (1902) 110, c 759. And cf the proceedings on the North Cornwall Railway Bill 1894, CJ (1894) 103, 108, 121; and Dublin and Central Ireland Electric Power Bill 1908, ibid (1908) 132, 201, 212.
5 CJ (1874) 225; ibid (1877) 177; ibid (1924–25) 179.
6 CJ (1913) 189, 283, 293; HC Deb (1913) 55, c 2132; HC 267, (1913) pp iii, xxi, xxvi.
7 CJ (1913) 305, 337, 354, 359–360; HC Deb (1913) 56, c 1374.

In 1976 the Committee on the Hampshire County Council (Haslar Bridge) Bill found the preamble not proved without having heard evidence in support of the allegations contained in it. The bill was recommitted to the Committee of Selection with an instruction to refer it to a new committee.[1]

Alterations in preamble. Alterations may be made in the preamble, subject to the restriction which applies to any other amendment, that it is not inconsistent with the purposes of the bill (see p 874), or with the standing orders of the House applicable to the bill. The chairman of the committee is, however, required by Standing Order 142 to report such alterations and to state the reasons for making them.

Award of costs in certain circumstances to petitioners against or promoters of a private bill. In 1865 the important principle of restraining vexatious litigation by awarding costs was first introduced. Under the Parliamentary Costs Act 1865,[2] when a committee (in either House of Parliament) on a private bill decides that the preamble is not proved, or inserts any provision, or strikes out or alters any provision already in the bill, for the protection of any petitioner, and further unanimously reports that one or more of the petitioners against the bill have been unreasonably or vexatiously subjected to expense in defending their rights, such petitioner or petitioners are entitled to recover their costs (or such part of them as the committee thinks fit) from the promoters.[3] On the other hand, when a committee unanimously reports that the promoters have been vexatiously subjected to expense by the opposition of petitioners, the promoters are entitled to recover costs from those opponents;[4] but it is provided that no landowner who bona fide, at his own sole risk and charge, opposes a bill which proposes to take any part of his property, shall be liable to any costs in respect of his opposition.

It has been held that the Act has been duly complied with, if all the members of the committee present at the hearing of the case, provided that

---

1 CJ (1975–76) 412, 415.
2 28 & 29 Vict c 27.
3 Costs granted to petitioners: Great Western Railway Bill, CJ (1866) 328; Brecon etc, Railway Bill, ibid (1867) 109; Thames Embankment etc, Bill, ibid (1867–68) 193; Stockton-on-Tees, etc, Improvement Bill, ibid (1868–69) 149; Great Eastern etc (Metropolitan Railways etc) Bill, ibid (1870) 93; North Eastern Railway (Additional Powers) Bill, ibid (1874) 126; Metropolitan Railway Bill, and North British Railway (General Powers) Bill, ibid (1881) 102, 191; Hull Extension etc, Bill, ibid (1882)177; Great Eastern Railway (General Powers) Bill and Swindon, Marlborough, and Andover Railway Bill, ibid (1883) 183, 198; Sunderland etc, Water Bill, and Metropolitan Outer Circle Railway (Extension of Time) Bill, ibid (1890–91) 161, 390; Dublin Southern District Tramways Bill, ibid (1893–94) 467; Manchester, Sheffield, and Lincolnshire Railway Bill, ibid (1896) 187; Great Northern Railway (No 1) Bill, ibid (1902) 197; Oldham Corporation Bill, ibid (1909) 173; Newcastle-upon-Tyne Corporation Bill, ibid (1911) 307; Sunderland Corporation Bill, ibid (1934–35) 242; Wallasey Corporation Bill, ibid (1957–58) 241; British Transport Commission Bill, ibid (1961–62) 189; Portland Deepwater Quays Bill, LJ (1974) 248; Harrogate Stray Bill, CJ (1984–85) 393.
4 Costs granted to promoters: North British Railway (Coatbridge etc) Bill, CJ (1866) 327; Hull Docks Bill, ibid (1867) 108; London, Blackwall etc, Railway Bill, ibid (1870) 93; Tivy Side Railway Bill, ibid (1872) 212; Ely and Bury etc, Railway Bill, ibid (1875) 319; Skegness etc, Tramways (Abandonment) Bill, ibid (1886) 206; Folkestone, Sandgate etc, Tramways Bill (in which case the petitioners had been offered a protective clause by the committee), ibid (1890–91) 139 and Minutes of Evidence (Group 2), 5 and 6 March 1891; Bank of Bolton Bill, CJ (1895) 231; Buxton Urban District Council Bill, ibid (1902) 275.

they form a quorum, have unanimously reported in the manner prescribed for entitling parties to recover costs.[1]

When costs are awarded, special mention of the award is made in the report on the bill, which is endorsed with the words 'Costs awarded' and is ordered to be printed. The costs awarded by a committee have to be taxed by the Taxing Officer of the House if the parties so apply (see pp 836–838).

Award of costs in case of provisional order bills. By section 2 of the Parliamentary Costs Act 1871 committees (in either House) upon bills for confirming provisional orders may award costs in like manner, and under the same conditions, as in the case of a private bill.[2] The question of costs is, however, decided by a majority of a joint committee under the Private Legislation Procedure (Scotland) Act 1936 (see p 974).

Award of costs in case of special procedure orders. The provisions of the Parliamentary Costs Act 1871 are applied to orders considered by a joint committee under the Statutory Orders (Special Procedure) Act 1945, by section 7 of the latter Act. A joint committee on a special procedure order has, accordingly, the same powers in this respect as a committee of either House in relation to a provisional order bill.[3]

Cases where costs have and have not been awarded. Although, since 1865, costs have been awarded in numerous cases, (see p 913 above) they have more frequently been refused; and in other cases, owing to the circumstances in which it has been made, the application for costs has not been entertained by a committee. In one case the promoters having informed the committee on a bill, in the Commons, that it was not their intention to proceed with it,[4] a petitioner applied to the committee to report that, the promoters not having adduced evidence, the preamble was not proved, and to consider an application for costs. The committee, however, decided to report that the parties had stated that it was not their intention to proceed with the bill and that the question of costs could not consequently be entertained.[5]

> In 1899, the committee on the London and North Western Railway (New Railways) Bill found that the preamble, in so far as it related to certain railways, was proved, subject to certain terms desired by petitioners; but the promoters, in preference to accepting the conditions imposed, withdrew that portion of the bill, and the committee thereupon acceded to an application for costs made by petitioners.[6] A similar situation occurred in respect of the Wallasey Corporation Bill 1958. The committee reported to the House that it felt bound to accede to the promoters' request to

---

1 Minutes of the Police and Sanitary Committee (consisting of nine members, with a quorum of five), Lancaster Corporation Bill 1888 etc.
2 Costs granted to petitioners: Local Government Provisional Orders (Atherton, etc) Bill, CJ (1877) 426; Tramways Orders Confirmation (No 2) Bill, ibid (1878) 258; Ancient Monuments Preservation Order Confirmation (No 1) Bill, LJ (1914) 208; to promoters: Allotments Provisional Order Bill, CJ (1890–91) 368; Electric Lighting Provisional Orders (No 3) Bill, ibid (1912–13) 279.
3 No costs have yet been awarded.
4 Cf p 918 below (parties not proceeding with their bill).
5 Abbotsbury Railway Bill 1873. And cf also Portsea Island Reclamation Bill 1871.
6 CJ (1899) 209.

withdraw the disputed clause from the bill, since to refuse permission might have prejudiced the remainder of the bill, which contained valuable provisions, but it affirmed that, in its view, it was desirable that the clause as amended by it at the request of the petitioners should be enacted and awarded costs to one of the petitioners who had applied for them.[1]

When one of the orders contained in the Local Government Provisional Orders (No 15) Bill 1895 was withdrawn by the parties promoting it, costs were granted to petitioners.[2]

In the case of two bills,[3] the promoters struck out in the filled-up bill certain provisions objected to by petitioners, who nevertheless applied for costs; but the committee refused the application in both cases. In another similar case, however, the petitioners were awarded 30% of their costs.[4]

In 1883, the South Kensington Market Bill was withdrawn in the House on the first day appointed for its consideration by a committee, and parties who had petitioned against it applied for costs; but the committee, not having considered the bill, decided that it had no power to grant costs. A similarly unsuccessful application was made in 1898, by petitioners against the Taff Vale Railway Bill, which was withdrawn by the promoters after the appearances had been entered and parties were in attendance before the committee.[5]

In 1880, before the committee upon the Pier and Harbour Provisional Orders Bill, no parties having appeared in support of the Weymouth Pier Order, certain petitioners applied for costs against the promoters; but the committee decided that, as the consideration of the scheme had not been entered upon, the case did not come within the words of the Act as to the granting of costs.[6]

The only petitioners against the North Metropolitan Electric Power Supply Bill 1905 did not appear before the committee on the bill and the promoters applied for costs against them; but the committee decided that, as the bill had to be referred back as unopposed for consideration by the Committee on Unopposed Bills, they were not in a position to hear evidence in proof of the preamble, nor, consequently, to entertain an application for costs.[7]

Summons of witnesses before private bill committees. The attendance of witnesses before select committees has already been described (see pp 628 ff). The power given to those committees of sending for persons, papers, and records is not, however, entrusted to ordinary committees on private bills.[8] The parties are, by Standing Orders 127 and 134, given the right to tender evidence and are generally able to secure the attendance of their own witnesses, without any summons or other process, and a large proportion of all the witnesses examined attend professionally. When, how-

---

1 CJ (1957–58) 241; Reports of Committees on Private Bills (1957–58) p 67.
2 CJ (1895) 330.
3 North Staffordshire Railway Bill 1879 (Minutes of Group 4, 14 May 1879); British Railways Bill 1975 (opposed bill committee in Lords).
4 Minutes of Evidence of the Committee on the Harrogate Stray Bill, 23 April 1985.
5 Minutes of Group 4, 15 June 1898.
6 34 & 35 Vict c 3: and Minutes of Group E, vol II, p 171, 24 June 1880.
7 Minutes of Group L, vol II, 6 July 1905. Cf SO 113 (HL) (see pp 936–937).
8 In 1896 a motion to give a private bill committee this power was made but was withdrawn, London County Council (Vauxhall Bridge Tramways) Bill, CJ (1896) 68–69.

ever, it becomes necessary to compel the attendance of an adverse or
unwilling witness, or of any official person who would otherwise be unable
to absent himself from his duties, application is made to the committee,
who, when satisfied that due diligence has been used, that the evidence of
the witness is essential to the inquiry, and that his attendance cannot be
secured without the intervention of the House, directs a report to that effect
to be made to the House,[1] upon which an order is made for the witness to
attend and give evidence,[2] or to attend and produce particular documents,[3]
before the committee. The limitation imposed by Standing Order 136 on the
committee's power to call for evidence has already been noticed (p 902).

Examination upon oath. By the Parliamentary Witnesses Oaths Act 1871,
any committee of the House of Commons is empowered to administer an
oath to witnesses examined before it;[4] and witnesses before opposed private
bill committees are examined on oath. A committee has made a special
report stating that, in its opinion, a witness had been guilty of perjury.[5]

Duties of chairman when reporting private bill. Besides the matters,
already referred to (see pp 897–901), which are required by the standing
orders of the House of Commons to be reported upon by a committee,
particular duties are imposed by standing order on the chairman of the
committee on every private bill (whether opposed or unopposed) as to
recording the proceedings of the committee and reporting them to the
House. Under Standing Order 141 he must sign 'the committee bill', which
incorporates all the amendments made by the committee, and initial the
several clauses added in the committee. Finally, under Standing Order 142,
he must report to the House whether the allegations of the bill have been
found to be true; and, if the preamble has been amended, why that amendment was necessary and whether the allegations contained in the preamble,
as amended, have been found to be true. If the promoters inform the
committee that they do not intend to proceed with the bill,[6] the chairman
must report accordingly.

Minutes of evidence. Under Standing Order 131A, whenever copies of the
minutes of the evidence taken before an opposed bill committee are
required, they are to be duplicated at the expense of the parties. The
standing order also provides that the Chairman of Ways and Means may
authorize the printing of minutes of evidence if the promoters apply to him,

---

1 This report for the attendance of a witness on an opposed bill is made by the Chairman of
  Ways and Means in cases where the committee on the bill has not yet met, CJ (1900) 290; ibid
  (1901) 78, 121, 128; ibid (1921) 109; or has adjourned, ibid (1899) 265.
2 CJ (1871) 228 (for attendance of a prisoner); ibid (1872) 99; ibid (1921) 94.
3 CJ (1874) 98; ibid (1924–25) 333; ibid (1929–30) 276, 278 (where the order was subsequently
  discharged).
4 See p 682 above. Committees of the House of Commons had been previously empowered, by
  s 1 of the Parliamentary Witnesses Act 1858, to administer an oath to witnesses upon a private
  bill, and, by s 3 of the Parliamentary Costs Act 1871, to witnesses upon a provisional order
  bill. Both of these sections were rendered unnecessary, and were repealed, by the Parliamentary Witnesses Oaths Act 1871. For the power of committees in the Lords to administer
  oaths, see s 2 of the Parliamentary Witnesses Act 1858, and p 937 below.
5 CJ (1860) 230.
6 See also p 918.

not less than six clear days before the first meeting of the committee, for permission to print instead of to duplicate. By the Speaker's order of 5 February 1957, the expense of the duplicating or printing is to be divided among the several parties in such proportions as may be agreed upon by them;[1] and where the minutes of evidence are duplicated or printed, the agent for the promoters of the bill is required to deposit two copies in the Private Bill Office. If any Member gives notice in the Private Bill Office, before the first sitting of the committee on the bill, that he requires copies, the agent for the promoters arranges for these to be supplied. No charge is made unless a large number of copies is required.[2]

Minutes of evidence taken before committees in former sessions, or in the same session, are sometimes referred to committees on private bills (see p 897).

Although the minutes of evidence taken before committees on private bills are not laid upon the Table, they are available to Members and may be quoted in debate in the House.[3]

Special Reports from private bill committees. If matters should arise in the committee, apart from the immediate consideration of the bill referred to it, which it desires to report to the House, the committee directs the chairman to make a special report accordingly.[4] The House may also instruct the committee on a private bill to make a special report.[5]

Recommendations by committees. If a committee wishes to record a decision on a matter in respect of which it is unable to amend the bill (because to do so would be to incorporate provisions outside the purposes of the bill (see p 874)), it can do so by making a recommendation which is incorporated either in a special report or in the report upon the bill required

---

1 The cost of shorthand-writing is apportioned, the promoters bearing half the attendance fee and the recording of evidence and all the cost of recording the speeches; the other half of the attendance fee and of the costs of transcription of evidence being met by the House.
2 HC Deb (1952–53) 516, cc 2103–2106; ibid 517, cc 205–206; ibid (1975–76) 911, cc 1296–1316.
3 Speaker's ruling, HC Deb (1981–82) 24, cc 451–452.
4 Special reports from committees on opposed private bills: recommending general legislation or inquiry upon particular questions, CJ (1895) 119, ibid (1904) 268, and ibid (1951–52) 206; on electrical traction (tramways) in London, ibid (1898) 281; on electrical undertakings and Board of Trade, ibid (1902) 183; on participation of railway companies in service of road transport, ibid (1922) 195; giving reasons for the rejection of a bill, ibid (1929–30) 325; Reports of Committees on Private Bills (1958–59) 19; Votes and Proceedings (1987–88), 26 July 1988. From committees on unopposed bills: on water supply in rural districts, CJ (1933–34) 138; giving reasons for amendments to a scheduled agreement concerning compensation to directors, ibid (1945–46) 215; regretting the omission of a clause which the promoters had requested be left out as the result of an agreement with opponents, ibid (1948–49) 252; on discriminatory charges for shipping, Reports from Committees on Private Bills (1957–58) p 134; on whether joint promotions should be required in respect of powers sought for parties other than the promoters, ibid (1958–59) pp 59–60; on the drafting of a provisional order bill (CJ (1974–75) 206). From a joint committee on a provisional order bill, on conditions of borough extension, CJ (1920) 276; on a special procedure order, on highway routes passing through National Parks, CJ (1984–85) 251. For other examples of special reports from private bill committees on their treatment of a bill, or on special circumstances etc, see CJ (1935–36) 146, 243; ibid (1941–42) 113; ibid (1946–47) 265; ibid (1952–53) 201; ibid (1955–56) 57, 289, 377; ibid (1956–57) 191; ibid (1957–58) 97; ibid (1958–59) 94, 130, 189, 199, 208, 289; ibid (1970–71) 479; ibid (1980–81) 464; ibid (1983–84) 251, 744; Votes and Proceedings (1988–89), 9 March 1989.
5 Votes and Proceedings (1987–88), 10 December 1987.

by the standing orders.[1] Parties are informed of such recommendations by the committee.[2]

Report that 'Parties do not proceed', etc.

If parties acquaint the committee that they do not desire to proceed further with the bill,[3] this fact is reported to the House; and an order is then made that the bill be withdrawn[4] or, merely, that the report do lie upon the Table.[5] In 1902, a committee having reported that the parties did not intend to proceed with their bill, notice was given of a motion to recommit the bill; but the Speaker ruled that such a motion would be out of order, on the ground that a private bill was the property of the promoters and that the House could not compel them to proceed with it against their wish.[6] This, however, does not apply to the separate parts of a bill which can only be withdrawn by the promoters with the leave of the committee. If the committee refuses leave to withdraw[7] a clause or clauses or insert amendments unacceptable to the promoters, the latter have the alternative of abandoning the bill as a whole, and this course of action has on occasion been taken.[8]

Adjournment of committees on opposed bills to be reported (Standing Order 125).

It is the duty of committees on opposed bills to report to the House the bill that has been referred to them, and not by long adjournments to withhold from the House the outcome of their proceedings; and therefore it has been prescribed by standing order that every committee on an opposed private bill shall report specially to the House the cause of any adjournment over any day on which the House sits.[9] If any attempt of this nature is made to defeat a bill, the House will interfere to prevent it. Thus, in 1825, the committee on a private bill having adjourned for a month, was 'ordered to meet tomorrow, and proceed on the bill';[10] and again, on 23 March 1836, the House being informed that a committee had adjourned till 16 May, ordered

---

1 Reports on Private Bills 1953–54, p 69.
2 Minutes of Evidence, Kent Water Bill 1954, p 577.
3 In 1824 the committee on the South London Docks Bill reported that, following a protracted examination of witnesses, the promoters desired leave to withdraw their bill, and that the chairman had been instructed to move for leave (which was accordingly given) to lay the minutes of evidence before the House (CJ (1824–25) 445, 449).
4 CJ (1850) 510; ibid (1876) 372.
5 CJ (1874) 98; ibid (1894) 184; ibid (1902) 443; ibid (1904) 97, 123. For a special report relative to a bill with which the promoters did not proceed, see CJ (1922) 195.
6 London United Electric Railway Bill, CJ (1902) 443; and the Speaker's private ruling, 29 October 1902. See also Parl Deb (1905) 150, c 329; and p 791 above).
7 London Midland and Scottish Railway Bill 1935. See also Salford Corporation Bill, Minutes of Evidence 1909; Plymouth Corporation Bill, Minutes of Evidence 1903, vol 14, p 1.
8 Glasgow Waterworks Bill 1848 (Minutes, p 97); Plymouth Corporation Bill 1903 (in House of Lords) etc. For a case where the promoters of an omnibus bill decided not to proceed with one portion of which the committee had found the preamble proved subject to conditions, see London and North Western etc (New Railways) Bill, CJ (1899) 209. The committee on the Wallasey Corporation Bill 1958, which was also a bill conferring general powers, gave leave to the promoters to withdraw a clause which it had amended in a way unacceptable to the promoters, but made a special report saying that it had done so only to avoid prejudicing the other provisions of the bill and awarded costs against the promoters (see p 891 above).
9 CJ (1890–91) 371; ibid (1935–36) 136; ibid (1947–48) 210, 255; ibid (1953–54) 182, 214, etc.
10 CJ (1825) 474.

it 'to meet tomorrow, and proceed on the bill'.[1] Frequent or long adjournments may put the parties to considerable expense and inconvenience, and for this reason also they are avoided as far as possible. In practice committees sit rarely on Fridays and infrequently on Mondays.

Committees revived. If a committee adjourned without naming another day for resuming its sittings,[2] it was formerly held that it had no power of reassembling without an order from the House giving the committee leave to sit and proceed on a certain day.[3] However, it is now common practice for committees to adjourn 'beyond the next sitting day' and to resume proceedings without the need for an order to revive them.

PROCEEDINGS ON PRIVATE BILLS BEFORE SPECIALLY CONSTITUTED COMMITTEES

Where a private bill has been referred, in departure from the ordinary procedure, to a select committee nominated partly by the House and partly by the Committee of Selection, or otherwise specially constituted (see p 887), the proceedings are generally similar to those of ordinary private bill committees.[4] But in such a committee the chairman—in accordance with a resolution of the House of 25 March 1836 and with the established rules of Parliament regarding select committees (see p 623) — can vote only when there is an equality of voices, and the members do not sign the declaration required by Standing Order 120 (see p 884),[5] nor are they subject to the requirements of the standing orders as to attendance on private bill committees[6] (see pp 892–893).

REPORT OF BILL

Every private bill as amended in committee to be printed and delivered (Standing Orders 179, 203)

When the report has been made out and agreed to by the committee, the committee clerk delivers in to the Private Bill Office 'the committee bill'

---

1 CJ (1836) 195. Cf also the debate on the instruction, directing the committee on the Manchester Ship Canal Bill to report the bill before a specified day, CJ (1887) 291; Parl Deb (1887) 316, cc 24–34.

2 CJ (1902) 401, 440; ibid (1955–56) 293.

3 For leave given to committees to sit on a day on which the House is not sitting, see pp 625–626 above; and CJ (1897) 337 (leave given to committee on Group 9, to sit on a Saturday) etc.

4 Such committees, in common with private bill committees, have the power of examining witnesses on oath (p 916 above).

5 In the committee on the Southampton Docks Bill 1892, one member was a director of the dock company, and another held shares in the South Western Railway Company (the purchasing company). A member of the London County Council was a member of the committee on both the London County Council (General Powers) Bill and London Improvements Bill 1893; see debate on the latter bill, Parl Deb (1893) 14, cc 30, 36. Cf also the debate regarding the committee on Electric Power Bills 1900, Parl Deb (1900) 80, cc 1053–1059.

6 In 1900, when certain electric power bills were committed to a select committee of seven members, nominated by the Committee of Selection, an order was made by the House that the committee should be subject to the standing orders relative to the proceedings of committees on opposed bills (except that fixing the number of members), CJ (1900) 101; Parl Deb (1900) 80, cc 206, 900, 1053–1059.

(p 916). In strict conformity with this authenticated copy, the bill, as amended by the committee, is required by the standing orders to be printed at the expense of the promoters in the same style as the House copy deposited under Standing Order 164 (p 864).[1] When printed, copies of the amended bill must be delivered to the Vote Office, for the use of Members, three clear days at least before the consideration of the bill; and agents, when they give notice in the Private Bill Office of the day for the consideration of the bill, must produce a certificate from the Vote Office of the delivery of the amended printed bill on the proper day.[2] The copy of the amended bill, printed and covered in like manner as the House copy, must be deposited in the Private Bill Office where it is examined by the clerks of that office and endorsed as so examined. It then takes the place of the former House copy.

Bills withdrawn or referred to Examiner after report

Sometimes the alterations made by the committee to a bill have been so numerous and important as almost to make it a different measure from that originally brought before the House. In such cases the House has sometimes required the bill to be withdrawn and another bill presented, which has been referred to the Examiners. Thus, on 21 May 1849, on the report of the Holme Reservoirs Bill, notice being taken that almost the whole of the bill as brought in had been omitted, and a new set of clauses introduced, the bill was ordered to be withdrawn.[3] But, unless there has been great irregularity, the later and better practice has been to refer the bill as amended to the Examiners, 'to inquire whether the amendments involve any infraction of the standing orders'.[4] If the Examiner reports that there is no infraction of the standing orders, the bill proceeds without further interruption; but if he reports that there has been such an infraction, his report, together with the bill, will be referred to the Standing Orders Committee who reports whether the standing orders ought or ought not to be dispensed with.[5]

Similar motions to refer hybrid bills as amended in committee to the Examiners have been made. The motion to refer the Smithfield Market Bill 1860 was negatived,[6] but the motions to refer the Metropolitan Foreign Cattle Market Bill 1868 and the Park Lane Improvement Bill 1958 (a Government bill) were agreed to.[7] The Toll Bridges (River Thames) Bill 1876 underwent so many important alterations in committee

---

1 In 1959 during a printing strike, SO 179 was suspended on the motion of the Chairman of Ways and Means. Bills which had been amended in committee did not have to be reprinted, but the amendments made had to be indicated on the copies available for Members. CJ (1958–59) 276.
2 Order of the Clerk of the House, 30 March 1844.
3 CJ (1849) 320, 382. See also CJ (1881) 153, 166, where the committee on the Birkenhead Improvement Commissioners etc Bill made a special report that the alterations proposed in the 'filled-up' bill were too extensive and the bill was ordered to be withdrawn.
4 For a provisional order bill referred, as amended, to the Examiners, see CJ (1901) 302, 307, 318.
5 Dublin Central Tramways Bill, CJ (1877) 366, 378, 399; and Milford Docks Bill, ibid (1874) 141, 142, 153 (the bill was referred with an instruction to the Examiners to report whether a specified standing order had been complied with, in reference to clauses inserted in committee).
6 CJ (1860) 370.
7 CJ (1867–68) 223, ibid (1957–58) 147.

as to be substantially a new bill, and its opponents urged that it ought to be withdrawn. But the second reading of the bill had been postponed, while a select committee was considering the whole subject-matter of the bill; and when that committee had reported, the bill was read a second time and committed; and the report of the committee (together with other reports upon the same subject) was referred to the committee on the bill. These proceedings were regarded by the committee as in the nature of an instruction, and amendments had therefore been made, of a comprehensive character, founded upon previous inquiries and recommendations. Under these exceptional circumstances, the Speaker suggested that the House would probably consider that the committee had not so far exceeded its powers as to require the withdrawal of the bill. But as private rights and interests were concerned in the bill and in the amendments made by the committee, he recommended that it should be referred to the Examiners. This was accordingly done; and though it appeared that in respect of some of the amendments the standing orders had not been complied with, the Standing Orders Committee reported that they ought to be dispensed with, and the bill was allowed to proceed through all its further stages.[1]

The Channel Tunnel Bill 1986–87 was referred to the Examiners in respect of amendments made during its passage through the Lords. The Standing Orders Committee reported that the relevant standing orders ought not to be dispensed with, but the House subsequently resolved to the contrary and the Lords amendments were agreed to.[2]

Recommittal of private bill

Sometimes private bills, reported from a committee, have been recommitted;[3] and, unless the House has otherwise directed, the recommitted bill has stood referred, in the ordinary way, to the Committee of Selection.[4] Usually, however, when a private bill is recommitted, it is referred specifically 'to the former committee';[5] and no Member can then sit, unless he had been duly qualified to serve upon the original committee on the bill.[6] In other cases a private bill has been recommitted to a Committee of the whole

1 CJ (1876) 354, etc; Parl Deb (1876) 230, cc 1679–1680; Mr Speaker Brand's Note-book.
2 Votes and Proceedings (1986–87) 13, 16 and 21 July 1987.
3 See also p 926 for recommittal on third reading.
4 Dublin Corporation Bill, CJ (1896) 406, 409, where the minutes of evidence before the former committee were referred to the committee on the recommitted bill; Edinburgh Boundaries Extension and Tramways Bill [Lords], with an instruction to the committee to have regard to the findings of a joint committee on a provisional order bill with regard to borough extensions, CJ (1920) 293. In committing this bill to the former committee, the Committee of Selection gave notice that it was not proposed to take further evidence but that counsel on either side would be heard, Private Business (1920), p 433. See also p 913 for a bill recommitted to the Committee of Selection with an instruction to refer it to a new committee.
5 See p 912 for bills recommitted for further consideration of its decisions by a committee. Though the County of South Glamorgan (Taff Crossing) Bill 1986, being a suspended bill, could not for that reason be recommitted, it was in fact committed to a committee consisting of the same members who had considered it in the previous session, Votes and Proceedings (1986–87), 12 March 1987.
6 Leave has been given for the committee to sit and proceed with two members, CJ (1887) 166; ibid (1894) 278; or with a quorum of two, ibid (1856) 256. On the Warrington etc, Railway (recommitted) Bill 1853, the committee had leave to proceed with three members, but another was afterwards added by the House, CJ (1852–53) 690, 698.

House,[1] or to a select committee nominated partly[2] or entirely[3] by the House. Unless the bill is recommitted by the House with express reference to particular provisions,[4] the whole bill is open to reconsideration in committee.[5] By Standing Order 199 (see p 889), one clear day's notice is to be given to the clerks in the Private Bill Office of the meeting of the committee on a recommitted bill; and a filled-up bill, as proposed to be submitted to the committee, on recommittal, is to be deposited by the agent in the same office, two clear days before the meeting of the committee.[6]

Proceedings on and after report of private bill (Standing Order 178)

Every private bill reported from a committee, if amended in the committee, is ordered to lie upon the Table. If it has not been amended, it is ordered to be read the third time. If, however, the committee reports that the allegations of the bill have not been proved to its satisfaction, or that the parties promoting the bill have informed the committee that it is not their intention to proceed further, the bill is ordered to lie upon the Table.

The bill reported to the House is the bill as amended in committee. The report made by a committee upon a railway, tramroad or tramway bill, or a bill promoted by a local authority, or a bill upon which an instruction has been given by the House or a recommendation has been made in a ministerial report, is ordered to be printed, and is made available to Members.[7] If not printed they are open to inspection only by Members of the House.

Interval between report and consideration of bill (Standing Order 181). Not less than three clear days are required to intervene between the report and consideration of a bill ordered to lie upon the Table.

Bill as amended laid before Chairman of Ways and Means, etc (Standing Orders 86, 180, 181). Three clear days, at least, before the consideration of a bill, a copy of the bill, as amended in committee, is to be laid by the agent before the Chairman of Ways and Means and the Counsel to Mr Speaker, and is also to be deposited with every department and office at which it was deposited under Standing Orders 39 and 40.

---

1 Sheffield Corporation Bill, CJ (1900) 358; Farmers' Estate Society (Ireland) Bill, ibid (1847–48) 782. And see p 869 above. For an occasion where a motion to recommit a private bill to a Committee of the whole House was negatived, see CJ (1948–49) 231; for the reasons therefor, see p 911 above.
2 Lochearnhead etc, Railway Bill 1897 (recommitted to a select committee nominated partly by the House and partly by the Committee of Selection), CJ (1897) 223–224.
3 CJ (1901) 374, 381, 389; ibid (1907) 416, 422.
4 Tyneside Tramways etc, Bill, CJ (1904) 278; Corporation of London (Bridges) Bill, ibid (1911) 272; Manchester Corporation (General Powers) Bill [Lords] in respect of a clause, with an instruction to strike out the clause, ibid (1921) 342; Nottingham Corporation Bill [Lords] in respect of two clauses, ibid (1924–25) 354. See also West Midlands County Council Bill [Lords], CJ (1979–80) 89, 329; HC Deb (1979–80) 969, cc 691–758; and County of South Glamorgan (Taff Crossing) Bill (1986–87), Votes and Proceedings (1986–87), 12 March 1987.
5 CJ (1901) 192.
6 SO 200. See, however, CJ (1924–25) 354, where these standing orders were suspended.
7 The Chairman of Ways and Means deferred consideration of the Mid-Wessex Water Bill, set down for 17 March 1959, until the report of the committee on the Bill was printed so that it should be available to Members.

If a bill does not contain the several provisions required by the standing orders or contains any provisions which contravene standing orders, the Chairman of Ways and Means must inform the House or signify the same in writing to the Speaker before the bill is considered.

Notice of consideration of bill (Standing Order 201). Not less than one clear day's notice, in writing, is required to be given by the agent for the bill to the clerks in the Private Bill Office of the day proposed for the consideration of every private bill ordered to lie upon the Table.

Rules as to amendments proposed to be moved on consideration, etc, of bill. When the promoters intend to offer any clause, or to propose any amendment on the consideration of any private bill ordered to lie upon the Table—or any verbal amendment on the third reading—notice is required, under Standing Order 204, to be given to the clerks in the Private Bill Office, not less than one clear day previously. Standing Order 87 provides that, on the day on which notice is given, the clause or amendment is to be laid before the Chairman of Ways and Means and the Counsel to Mr Speaker. Under Standing Order 183, where the Chairman of Ways and Means considers that prints of any such amendment or new clause should be made available to Members, he may give directions for it to be printed, and these directions may include a requirement that any clause proposed to be amended shall be printed in extenso, with every addition or substitution in distinctive type, and the omissions included in brackets, and underlined. The expense of printing is borne by the promoters. If any clause or amendment is proposed by a Member, independently of the parties concerned in the bill, he may give notice either to the clerks at the Table or to the clerks in the Private Bill Office. The notice appears in Private Business. For convenience, when notice of extensive amendments has been given by Members, any amendments proposed by the promoters have also been printed and the expense has been borne by the House.[1]

By Standing Order 182, no clause or amendment may be offered by the promoters on the consideration of a bill, if the Chairman of Ways and Means has informed the House or signified in writing to the Speaker that, in his opinion, it is such that it ought not to be entertained by the House without referring it to the Standing Orders Committee, whereupon the clause or amendment stands referred to that committee.

Proposed clauses or amendments referred to Standing Orders Committee (Standing Orders 182, 107). If a clause or amendment is referred to the Standing Orders Committee, there can be no further proceeding until its report has been brought up. The report must state whether or not the clause or amendment may properly be adopted by the House, or whether the bill should be recommitted.

---

1 Private Business (1979–80) pp 70–73.

PROCEEDINGS ON CONSIDERATION AND THIRD READING

Unlike a public bill, a private bill, if it has been amended, is considered (see Standing Order 178) on question put,[1] and to this question amendments may be moved, for example, to secure the consideration of the bill on a later day or its recommittal. A reasoned amendment irrelevant to the provisions of the bill has been ruled out of order.[2] A private bill is not now considered unless it has been amended in committee (Standing Order 178).

Debate on consideration and third reading

Debate on the question for consideration of a private bill, as reported from a committee, or for its third reading has been confined by rulings from the chair within narrower limits than the debate on second reading. Not only have attempts to raise questions of general policy been ruled out of order[3] (see pp 871–872), but debate on the later stages has been restricted to the matters contained in the bill.[4] Thus a motion to recommit a bill with reference to matters outside its scope has been refused,[5] while new clauses and amendments have been held to be out of order on the same ground.[6]

Amendments on consideration

On the consideration of a private bill new clauses or amendments may be introduced, subject to the restrictions imposed by Standing Order 182, which requires certain amendments proposed by the promoters first to be referred to the Standing Orders Committee; by Standing Order No 73 (Public) and Standing Order 175, which when read together provide that no amendment may be proposed on report which could not have been made in committee except upon petition for additional provision; and by the practice of the House regarding charges upon the people (see p 493).

The following procedure is now used for dealing with amendments on consideration and verbal amendments on third reading, proposed by the promoters, and Lords amendments. When the title of the bill is read, the Chairman of Ways and Means either moves the amendments formally, or, on rising to move, indicates to the House the nature of the amendments, for example, that they are only of a drafting nature, that no objection need be taken to them or that he recommends them to the House. The amendments

---

1 For cases in which the question, 'That the bill, as amended, be now considered' was negatived, see CJ (1967–68) 353 and ibid (1974–75) 515.
2 HC Deb (1910) 19, c 943.
3 Parl Deb (1895) 32, cc 1605–1607; ibid (1901) 97, c 1312; see also the Speaker's ruling on a new clause, HC Deb (1938) 334, cc 268–271; HC Deb (1955–56) 548, cc 446–447, cf, however, HC Deb (1957–58) 591, cc 475–537.
4 Parl Deb (1895) 32, c 705; ibid (1895) 33, c 781; HC Deb (1910) 17, c 1273; ibid (1910) 18, c 276; ibid (1910) 19, c 1844, 1847; ibid (1914) 60, c 1116, 1119, 1124; ibid (1966–67) 749, c 173; ibid (1968–69) 786, cc 313–314; on a provisional order bill, ibid (1918) 107, c 815. For similar rulings on bills presented under the Private Legislation Procedure (Scotland) Act, see Parl Deb (1908) 198, c 443; HC Deb (1910) 19, c 1855; ibid (1919) 122, c 1025; ibid (1935–36) 312, c 2108.
5 HC Deb (1910) 19, c 1842.
6 Parl Deb (1891) 353, c 555.

are then put from the Chair in a single question. The duty of the Chairman of Ways and Means under Standing Orders 182 and 183, with regard to amendments on consideration and third reading (see p 924), and under Standing Order 186, with regard to Lords amendments (see p 927), remains unaffected. When the amendments are not printed, copies of them may be obtained from the Vote Office and inspected in the Private Bill Office,[1] and a notice to this effect appears on the order paper. Amendments proposed by Members are dealt with in the ordinary way in the order in which they appear in the bill[2] (see p 504). Where amendments are proposed both by Members and by the promoters, it has sometimes been found convenient for all the amendments to be printed and dealt with in the order in which they appear in the bill, the promoters' amendments being moved formally and, where appropriate, in groups, in which case each group is put from the Chair in a single question.[3]

Bill ordered to be read the third time

After a bill has been considered, it is ordered by the House to be read the third time.

Entry of amendments on consideration or third reading (Standing Order 206)

When amendments are made by the House on the consideration of a bill, or verbal amendments on the third reading, they are entered by one of the clerks in the Private Bill Office upon the House copy of the bill, as amended in committee. This copy, as amended, is signed by him, and preserved in the office.

Notice of third reading of a private bill (Standing Order 205)

Not less than one clear day's notice, in writing, is required to be given by the agent for the bill to the clerks in the Private Bill Office of the day proposed for the third reading; and this notice may not be given until the day after the bill has been ordered to be read the third time.

Third reading of a private bill (Standing Order 184)

On the third reading, verbal amendments only may be made, and in other respects this stage is the same as for public bills (see p 509 and SO (Public) No 75). The House finally approves of the entire bill, with all the alterations made since the second reading, before it is passed and sent up, or returned, to the House of Lords (see p 510).

---

1 HC Deb (1981–82) 24, cc 191 and 367.
2 See HC Deb (1937–38) 334, c 315; CJ (1962–63) 252 and Private Business (1962–63) pp 241, 244, 249 and 258; ibid (1972–73) p 164 b; ibid (1973–74) pp 41–47; ibid (1987–88) pp 104–107.
3 HC Deb (1979–80) 977, cc 101–123.

Recommittal on third reading

The order for the third reading of a bill has sometimes been discharged, and the bill has been recommitted[1] or the question for the third reading of the bill has been amended by an order to recommit the bill.[2]

Queen's consent

The third reading is usually the stage at which the Queen's consent is signified, by a Privy Councillor, to any bill affecting the property or interests of the Crown, or Duchy of Lancaster; and the consent of the Prince of Wales, as Duke of Cornwall, or, if he is not of age, of the Queen on his behalf.[3]

> On 20 April 1852, notice being taken that Her Majesty's interest was concerned in the Rhyl Improvement Bill, and that her consent had not been signified thereto, the proceedings on the third reading of the bill, on a previous day, were ordered to be null and void.[4] On 19 November 1987, however, where the Queen's consent had been properly obtained in respect of the Felixstowe Dock and Railway Bill but had not been notified to the House, the bill was allowed to proceed.[5]

Stages taken by mistake

Where a bill has been read a second time by mistake the order then made 'That the bill be now read a second time' has been discharged on a later day, and another day appointed for the second reading,[6] or the bill has been referred back to the Examiners.[7] An order for committal has also been discharged, and the bill referred to the Examiners.[8] In similar circumstances the proceedings on consideration of a bill have been declared null and void, and another day has been appointed for its consideration[9].

> On 8 May 1945, the Commercial Gas Bill and the South Suburban Gas Bill were brought from the Lords, read the first time, and referred to the Examiners. On 10 May a message from the Lords was received and taken into consideration, explaining that the bills had been taken to the Commons by mistake, and requesting their return. The House ordered that the bills should be returned and discharged the order of reference to the Examiners.[10]
> On 10 April 1974 the Clerical, Medical and General Life Assurance Bill was brought from the Lords, read the first time and referred to the Examiners. On 2 May a message from the Lords was received, explaining that the bill had been sent to the Commons before an amendment to avoid questions of privilege had been made, and requesting its return. The

---

1 CJ (1851) 202, 209; see also Votes and Proceedings (1986–87), 12 March 1987.
2 CJ (1897) 324; ibid (1911) 272; ibid (1921) 342. See also CJ (1924) 343 where the amendment for recommittal was negatived.
3 CJ (1845) 513; ibid (1877) 245; ibid (1929–30) 451; ibid (1952–53) 213; ibid (1970–71) 266, etc.
4 CJ (1852) 157. See Blackwater (Youghal) Wooden Bridge Bill, ibid (1866) 423.
5 HC Deb (1987–88) 122, c 1233.
6 CJ (1872) 135; ibid (1884) 57.
7 CJ (1875) 72; ibid (1878) 61.
8 CJ (1945–46) 192.
9 CJ (1912–13) 186; ibid (1927) 270.
10 CJ (1944–45) 123.

Commons ordered that the bill should be returned and discharged the order of reference to the Examiners.[1]

Bill examined before being sent to the Lords (Standing Order 207)

No private bill is permitted to be sent up to the House of Lords until the fair printed bill has been endorsed as examined by the clerks in the Private Bill Office against the bill as read the third time. Private bills, like public bills, are endorsed by the Clerk of the House on being sent to the Lords.

LORDS AMENDMENTS (Standing Orders 88, 186, 208)

If the bill is subsequently returned from the Lords with amendments, notice is to be given, in the Private Bill Office, not less than one clear day before they are to be considered. If the promoters intend to propose amendments thereto, a copy of such amendments is to be deposited; and no notice of their intention may be given by the promoters until the day after that on which the bill has been returned from the Lords. Copies of such amendments are also to be laid before the Chairman of Ways and Means and the Counsel to Mr Speaker, before two o'clock on the day before that on which it is proposed to consider the Lords amendments. As the Lords amendments may relate to matters which might be construed to involve an infringement of the privileges of the Commons, and the amendments proposed to them may be in the nature of consequential amendments (see pp 510–512), the Speaker's sanction must be obtained before they are proceeded with. Before Lords amendments or any amendments to Lords amendments are taken into consideration, the Chairman of Ways and Means may direct that they be printed at the expense of the promoters, if he considers that prints should be made available for the use of Members;[2] and where a clause has been amended or a Lords amendment is proposed to be amended, that it should be printed in extenso, with every addition or substitution in distinctive type, and omissions included in brackets and underlined.

Towards the end of a session the consideration of Lords amendments is sometimes expedited by the suspension of Standing Order 208 for the remainder of the session,[3] or, when an extension of the session into the autumn is contemplated, until the summer adjournment.[4] Similar orders have also been made for particular bills.[5]

Commons' privileges infringed by the Lords

With private bills as with public bills, the same principles apply as to the infringement of the Commons' privileges by the Lords except in so far as

---

1 CJ (1974) 84 and 106.
2 See HC Deb (1955–56) 544, c 179.
3 CJ (1921) 338; ibid (1922) 297; ibid (1928–29) 232; ibid (1929–30) 474; ibid (1944–45) 155; ibid (1955–56) 82.
4 CJ (1937–38) 380; ibid (1946–47) 338; ibid (1952–53) 289 etc.
5 CJ (1914–16) 123; ibid (1947–48) 388; ibid (1951–52) 381; ibid (1954–55) 153; ibid (1972–73) 454.

they are modified by Standing Order 191 (see also p 828). If a private bill, which contains provisions creating a charge (other than a charge sanctioned by Standing Order 191) or imposing a tax, originates in the Lords, those provisions are struck out in that House on third reading,[1] the bill is sent down to the Commons with blanks, and the words are reinserted by the Commons, after the necessary resolution authorizing them has been agreed to (see pp 745–746). When an amendment, involving privilege is made by the Lords to a bill originating in the Commons, the Speaker brings it to the attention of the House, and it is for the House to decide whether it is willing to waive its privileges. If it is willing, the amendment is agreed to with a special entry in the Journal.[2]

GENERAL PROVISIONS

Every stage of a private bill in the Commons has now been described, with the standing orders and proceedings applicable to each. In conclusion, it may be added that, under Standing Order 188, except in cases of urgent and pressing necessity, no motion may be made to dispense with any sessional or standing order of the House, without due notice, and by rule 19 of the rules relating to parliamentary agents (see p 834), every notice of motion to dispense with any standing order prepared by an agent requires the sanction of the Chairman of Ways and Means.

Standing orders suspended

Standing orders are not infrequently suspended, if good cause is shown, to permit bills—more especially bills brought from the other House at a late period of the session—to proceed without the usual intervals and notices.[3]

SUSPENSION OF BILLS TILL FOLLOWING SESSION

Where a dissolution of Parliament is anticipated before the private business of the session has been disposed of, it has been customary for both Houses to make orders enabling the promoters of private bills and provisional order bills to suspend further proceedings, and to afford facilities for their proceeding further with the same bills in the first session of the next Parliament.[4] In a similar manner orders have also been made, late in the session, following application by the promoters to the Chairman of Ways and Means, in order that particular bills might be suspended and proceeded with in the next session of the same Parliament,[5] though such an order is not always

---

1 LJ (1929–30) 43 (Birmingham Corporation (General Powers) Bill).
2 CJ (1890) 575; Parl Deb (1890) 348, cc 963–965; CJ (1929–30) 482; HC Deb (1930) 242, c 235.
3 See eg SO 170 (interval between first and second readings), CJ (1950) 133; SO 198 (notice of second reading), CJ (1946–47) 320; SOs 86, 179, 180 (consideration), CJ (1944–45) 168; ibid (1955–56) 263; SO 205 (notice of third reading), CJ (1947–48) 376; Votes and Proceedings (1987–88), 10 November 1987; cf also p 885 (committal) and p 927 (Lords Amendments).
4 LJ (1982–83) 341–342 and CJ (1982–83) 361–363; Lords Minutes (1986–87) and Votes and Proceedings (1986–87), 12 May 1987.
5 CJ (1985–86) 574–576, Votes and Proceedings (1987–88), 8 and 10 November 1988.

made by the House,[1] and the Chairman is generally unwilling to entertain an application for a suspension motion where a bill originating in the Commons has not received a second reading by the end of a normal session.

The precedents indicate that where the suspension is from one Parliament to the next,[2] one order is made for all the bills to be suspended, but where the suspension is from one session to the next in the same Parliament, a separate order is made for each bill pending.[3] The suspension is equally effective for a new session of the same Parliament or for a new Parliament.[4]

Motions to suspend bills originate in the House in which the bill is at that moment, and a message is sent to the other House to acquaint them of the resolution passed. If the other House has already passed the bill it makes parallel orders, but if it has not yet received the bill it concurs with the orders made by the first House. Orders have also been made for the suspension of a hybrid bill[5] and for the suspension of private business standing orders relating to a hybrid bill.[6]

The rule that no Member may speak twice to the same question has been relaxed in the case of a suspension motion to permit a Member who has already spoken to move amendments to it (see pp 341–342).[7]

In the next session the agent for the suspended bill deposits in the Private Bill Office a copy of the bill together with a declaration that the bill is in the form required by the order of the House. If the bill has been brought from the Lords in the previous session and amended, the order provides for it to be reintroduced in the form in which it was brought from the Lords and to be committed to the Chairman of Ways and Means with an order that he should make the same amendments as were made by the committee on the bill in the previous session.[8] In other cases the order provides that the deposited bill should be the same in every respect as the bill at the last stage of proceedings in the previous session.

A bill may be suspended before being reported from the committee to whom it has been referred.[9]

---

1 See proceedings on Kent River Board (Harbour of Rye) Bill 1962, CJ (1961–62) 313; Ashdown Forest Bill [Lords] 1973, CJ (1972–73) 490; Cromarty Petroleum Order Confirmation Bill 1976, CJ (1975–76) 572.
2 See fn 4, p 928.
3 See fn 5, p 928.
4 HC Deb (1977–78) 955, cc 340–341.
5 Port of London Bill, CJ (1903) 421; London Passenger Transport Bill, ibid (1930–31) 444, 446 and ibid (1931–32) 322; Channel Tunnel Bill, ibid (1985–86) 600 and Votes and Proceedings (1986–87), 13 May 1987.
6 Relating to the Channel Tunnel Bill, CJ (1973–74) 160.
7 HC Deb (1977–78) 955, cc 338–339.
8 CJ (1957–58) 299; ibid (1972–73) 436, 447; ibid (1978–79) 262; ibid (1980–81) 523; Votes and Proceedings (1987–88), 10 November 1988.
9 CJ (1957–58) 296; ibid (1980–81) 482; Votes and Proceedings (1987–88), 8 November 1988.

Further suspension of bills

When the time available in the next session has not sufficed for the consideration of suspended bills, they have been further suspended, either collectively or singly, until the following session.[1]

Revival of bills after dissolution or prorogation

In the case of an unexpected dissolution, orders have been made early in the new Parliament enabling private bills which had not received the Royal Assent to be reintroduced, and taken pro forma to the stage reached before dissolution.[2] A similar order has been made in relation to a hybrid bill.[3] In the latter case the order was framed in such a way as to render unnecessary any further money or ways and means resolution.

At the end of the 1987–88 session an unusual number of suspension motions met with objection and had to be put down for debate shortly before prorogation. The Government tabled a motion to exempt the business from the ten o'clock rule but in the event did not move it, with the result that several suspension motions failed through lack of time. In these exceptional circumstances orders were made in the new session to enable each of the outstanding bills to be proceeded with.[4]

JOINT COMMITTEE ON PRIVATE BILL PROCEDURE

In January 1987 a Joint Committee was established to examine the processes of enacting private legislation and to consider, in particular, whether there were matters at present effected by private bills which could be more appropriately dealt with in some other way, and whether any changes were desirable in private bill procedure or in procedures under the Private Legislation Procedure (Scotland) Act 1936 or the Statutory Orders (Special Procedure) Act 1945. The Report of the Joint Committee, which contained a variety of recommendations as to the need for private legislation in particular cases and for certain procedural changes, was published in October 1988.[5] It was subsequently debated in both Houses,[6] but none of its proposals had been implemented by July 1989.

---

1 Eg, Zetland County Council Bill, CJ (1972–73) 436, ibid (1973–74) 159–60. Felixstowe Dock and Railways Bill, CJ (1984–85) 610, ibid (1985–86) 581, Votes and Proceedings (1986–87), 12 May 1987. For a hybrid bill, see CJ (1930–31) 444, 446 and ibid (1931–32) 322 (London Passenger Transport Bill); Channel Tunnel Bill, CJ (1985–86) 600–601; Votes and Proceedings (1986–87), 13 May 1987. For a case in which an order suspending a bill was made applicable to a later session, see CJ (1921) 363, 405 (Ministry of Health Provisional Order (Cardiff Extension) Bill).
2 HC Deb (1974–75) 880, cc 382–383; LJ (1974–75) 54–55.
3 Channel Tunnel Bill, CJ (1974–75) 58.
4 Votes and Proceedings (1987–88), 10 November 1988 and HC Deb (1987–88) 140, cc 543–583; Votes and Proceedings (1988–89), 1 December 1988.
5 HL 97, HC 625 (1987–88).
6 HC Deb (1988–89) 151, cc 474–548; HL Deb (1988–89) 507, cc 1180–1212.

CHAPTER 37

Proceedings in the House of Lords on private and personal bills; Royal Assent and classification of private Acts

INTRODUCTORY

As already mentioned (see p 810), all private bills are founded on a petition. The modern practice is that such petitions are presented in the House of Commons.[1] The petitions are deposited in that House by 27 November, and under Standing Order 38[2] a copy of each of the bills to which the petitions relate is deposited in the Parliament Office on or before the same day. On or before 8 January, under Standing Order 90, the Chairman of Committees and the Chairman of Ways and Means and their respective Counsel meet and apportion the bills between the two Houses. The normal practice is for half the bills, as near as may be, to be allotted to each House. Formerly the only private bills which could originate in the Lords were those not affecting rates, tolls or duties, but the relaxation in the privileges of the Commons (see p 745) and the desire to equalize the pressure of private business upon the two Houses have led to the present more convenient arrangement which has already been described (see p 828). The subsequent proceedings upon private bills in the two Houses are similar, and have already been described, so far as they relate to the House of Commons, in chapters 35 and 36. In the present chapter it is, therefore, only necessary to describe those points in which procedure in the Lords differs from that in the Commons. Since 1945, the standing orders of the two Houses have been made as nearly as possible the same; in particular the standing orders, compliance with which is to be proved before the Examiners, are now almost identical.

Where a proposed private bill relates to the estate, property, status or style, or otherwise to the personal affairs of an individual, an application may be made to the Chairman of Committees under Standing Order 3 to certify that the proposed bill is of that nature and that Standing Orders 4–68 should not apply to it. Personal bills are dealt with on p 942.

---

1 For certain exceptions, see p 932 below.
2 The references in this chapter to the standing orders are to those of the House of Lords unless otherwise stated.

A. PRIVATE BILLS

Petitions for bills (Standing Orders 2 and 97)

In the case of a 'late bill' which is to be introduced in the House of Lords, a petition for the bill, with a copy of the bill annexed, is presented to the House and referred to the Examiner. Similarly, a petition for additional provision (which can only be presented in the first House) is presented to the House of Lords if the bill to which it relates was introduced in that House. For the powers of the Chairman of Committees to authorize a late bill, see pp 829–830.

After they have been presented, such petitions are referred to the Examiner who, as a matter of course, has to report non-compliance with standing orders so far as they relate to times for deposit and service and publication of notices. In the case of late bills, the Standing Orders Committee, to whom the report is referred, decides whether the circumstances of the case are such that the standing orders may be dispensed with and leave be given to introduce the bill.[1] The Chairman of Committees also has power to sanction the presentation of a petition for additional provision (see pp 830–831). Such petitions are also referred to the Standing Orders Committee, which normally allows them if unopposed.[2]

Proceedings before the Examiners (Standing Orders 69–83)

Any parties may appear before the Examiners and be heard, by themselves or their agents, upon a memorial addressed to the Examiner; and witnesses may be examined under the same conditions as in the Commons (see pp 816–817).

Every bill brought from the Commons is referred, under Standing Order 74, after first reading, to the Examiners, before whom compliance with such standing orders as have not been previously inquired into is proved. As regards petitions for additional provision, Standing Order 73 lays down procedure similar to that in the Commons (see p 814). The Examiner is required to give two clear days' notice of his examination of a bill or of a petition for additional provision. Memorials in respect of any bill referred to the Examiners after first reading, or by direction of the Chairman of Committees, or in respect of any petition for additional provision (see p 830), or any petition for leave to bring in a late bill deposited after 27 November, are deposited under Standing Order 78, with two copies, in the office of the Clerk of the Parliaments before noon on the preceding day.

All certificates of the Examiners are under Standing Order 82 to be laid upon the Table of the House not later than the first sitting day after their deposit in the office of the Clerk to the Parliaments.[3]

---

1 Epping Forest (Waterworks Corner) Bill, LJ (1966–67) 505, 527, 543; Falmouth Container Terminal Bill, ibid (1969–70) 238, 293, 303; Clifton Suspension Bridge Bill, ibid (1985–86) 168, 195, 229.

2 In 1952, a petition for an additional provision in the Kingston-upon-Hull Corporation Bill was opposed and rejected by the Standing Orders Committee. LJ (1951–52) 151.

3 The proceedings of the Examiner in respect of hybrid bills (SO 83) are similar to those in the Commons (see p 520).

The 'Wharncliffe' Orders. In the case of certain bills, there are additional standing orders with which compliance is proved before the Examiner at a later stage. These are the 'Wharncliffe' Orders already described on pp 865–868, which mutatis mutandis are the same for both Houses.

Bills brought from the other House, notices and deposits (Standing Orders 60 and 61). Compliance must also be proved with the requirements of certain standing orders which are similar in both Houses and which relate to the deposit with various public departments of bills brought from the Commons, if such bills have been amended on consideration in that House or if alterations have been made in works to be authorized by the bill.

Standing Orders Committee (Standing Orders 84–89)

The Standing Orders Committee is appointed at the beginning of every session, and consists of the Chairman of Committees, who is always chairman, and such other Lords as are named by the House. Three Lords, including the chairman, are a quorum in opposed cases, while by practice in unopposed cases the Chairman of Committees acts alone. Three clear days' notice is to be given of the meeting of the committee.

Every certificate from the Examiner stating that the standing orders have not been complied with, or any special report made by him,[1] is referred to the committee. The committee reports whether the standing orders ought to be dispensed with, and upon what terms and conditions, if any. The committee is specially empowered by Standing Order 88 to hear the parties affected by any standing order referred to in the Examiner's certificate or special report, provided that such parties have duly deposited a statement (which is strictly confined to the points reported upon by the Examiner) of the facts to be submitted to the committee. Such statements are lodged in the office of the Clerk of the Parliaments not later than three o'clock on the second day after the order for the meeting of the committee is made, or one o'clock, if that day is a Saturday. In practice, the agents of the parties are invariably heard on their statements by the committee in the Lords; but, under the standing order, no party may enter into any matter not referred to in his statement.

The Chairman of Committees

Mention has already been made (see p 826) of the supervision of private bills by the Chairman of Committees in the House of Lords. Specific standing orders (Standing Orders 90–93) give him powers to confer with the Chairman of Ways and Means for determining the allocation of bills between the two Houses, to report that an unopposed bill should proceed as an opposed bill, to direct the House's attention to special circumstances and to any proposed instruction to a committee to make an amendment which could only have been proposed (by the promoters) in a petition for additional provision.[2] These powers are similar to those conferred on the Chairman of Ways and Means by Standing Orders 81, 82, and 85 (HC) respectively (see

---

1 Sunderland Corporation Bill (petition for additional provision) LJ (1934–35) 142, 152, 169.
2 Under SO 175 (HC), the Speaker must decline to propose the question on such an instruction.

p 827). The Chairman of Committees is also empowered by Standing Order 95 to name the Lords to form committees on opposed private business.

First reading (Standing Order 98)

No private bill originating in the Lords may be read a first time until the Examiner has certified compliance with the standing orders, or the Standing Orders Committee has reported that the standing orders have been complied with; and no such bill is to be read a first time later than the seventh day on which the House sits for public business after such certificate or report. Where, after a certificate of non-compliance from the Examiner, the Standing Orders Committee has reported that the standing orders ought to be dispensed with, the bill is read a first time not later than the seventh sitting day after the House has agreed that the bill shall be allowed to proceed.

A private bill brought from the Commons is read a first time forthwith.

Petitions against private bills (Standing Orders 101–103)

Under Standing Order 101 the final date for presenting petitions against private bills introduced in the Lords is 6 February. In the case of bills brought from the Commons and late bills and in certain other circumstances, petitions against bills must be deposited not later than the tenth day after that on which the bill was read a first time.

If the period allowed for presenting petitions, except those which are required to be presented by 6 February, expires during any recess of the House, it is (by Standing Order 201A) extended to the first sitting day after the recess. Any petitioner can withdraw his petition on the deposit of a requisition to that effect in the Office of the Clerk of the Parliaments, signed by the agent depositing the petition. A petitioner can similarly withdraw from a petition signed by other persons besides himself (Standing Order 103). Standing Order 102 provides for the supply of copies of the petition by the agent concerned to parties and to the agent for the bill.

Second reading

The second reading of a private bill, in contrast to that of a public bill, does not affirm the principle of the bill. It merely gives approval for the bill and the principle to be considered by a committee. For this reason it is unusual for a debate to take place on the second reading of a private bill in the Lords and it is even more unusual for a private bill to be rejected at second reading.[1]

Instructions

Instructions to the committee on the bill are moved after second reading. They should not fetter the discretion of the committee in dealing with the bill; hence instructions of a mandatory nature, ordering the committee to

---

1 The last private bills rejected at second reading were the North Devon Water Bill and the North Devon Electric Power Bill in 1937, HL Deb (1936–37) 104, cc 894–929.

amend the bill in a particular way, are not generally made by the House,[1] though instances of this type of instruction have occurred.[2]

In 1918 the House passed an instruction to the Select Committee on the St Olave's Church, Southwark, Bill to amend the bill in a particular manner, in spite of warnings from the Chairman of Committees that 'this House is usually reluctant to fetter its committees with instructions which tie their hands in considering a bill on its merits' and that the giving of such instructions is 'quite out of accord with the ordinary procedure' of the House.[3] The Committee obeyed the instruction but, in a special report, declared that 'they feel it their duty to represent to the House that the result must be the dropping of the bill' and strongly recommended to the House the adoption of a different course. One of the alternatives recommended by the committee was adopted by the House after long debate on third reading.[4] On the third reading a noble Lord said: 'There has been much difficulty in dealing with this bill and . . . it has arisen from a course having been taken which, as the Lord Chairman pointed out on the second reading, was without precedent in this House—the course, that is, of giving a rigid instruction to one of your Lordships' committees as to what they ought to do'.

Instructions which would direct the committee to have regard to matters which would already (either under the standing orders or because they are raised in a petition against the bill) be considered by it, have been refused by the House.[5] The more usual type of instruction in recent times may be said to be of a cautionary nature. For example, the committee on a bill is sometimes instructed not to grant certain powers unless satisfied that certain matters of public policy (eg food production) have been adequately safeguarded, or that certain objections of a public nature have been considered.[6] Instructions have occasionally been given to an unopposed bill committee.[7]

Commitment

Private bills after second reading are normally committed, if opposed, to a select committee. Standing Order 100 prohibits commitment, in the case of bills referred to the Examiners after second reading, until the Examiners or the Standing Orders Committee have made a favourable report, to which

---

1 St Mildred's Churchyard Bill, HL Deb (1925) 60, c 501.
2 Middlesborough Corporation Bill, LJ (1932–33) 128; Birmingham Corporation Bill, ibid (1934–35) 133; Poole Corporation Bill, ibid (1936–37) 201; Manchester Corporation Bill, ibid (1961–62) 103. And cf LJ (1892) 112 (general instruction to committees on railways bills of session 1892).
3 HL Deb (1918) 29, cc 219, 431.
4 HL Deb (1918) 29, cc 1119, 1147.
5 Esso Petroleum Company Bill, LJ (1960–61) 33; Kent River Board (Harbour of Rye) Bill, ibid (1961–62) 133; Clywedog Reservoir Joint Authority Bill, ibid (1962–63) 163.
6 Tees Valley and Cleveland Water Bill, LJ (1966–67) 234; Brighton Marina Bill, ibid (1966–67) 687–688; Saint Mary, Hornsey, Bill, ibid (1967–68) 474; Saint Saviour, Paddington, Bill, ibid; Calderdale Water Bill, ibid (1968–69) 132; Lloyds Bill, ibid (1981–82) 215; Swanage Yacht Haven Bill, ibid (1986–87) 355.
7 Saint Dionis Backchurch Churchyard Bill and Saint Nicholas Acons Churchyard Bill, LJ (1962–63) 163; British Railways (Selby) Bill, ibid (1978–79) 282; London Transport Bill, ibid (1979–80) 1103; Severn-Trent Water Authority Bill, ibid (1982–83) 283 (this bill was subsequently committed to a select committee).

the House has agreed. For the practice of both Houses in regard to the commitment of private bills to joint committees, see p 887.[1]

Select committees on private bills

Membership (Standing Order 104). Each select committee to which a private bill is committed consists of five members. In two instances, however, the committee has been increased to seven.[2]

Appointment of members (Standing Order 95). The Chairman of Committees usually selects and proposes to the House the members of the select committee and names the chairman; but the Committee of Selection performs this function if in the opinion of the Chairman of Committees it should do so or if two or more members of the Committee of Selection request it.[3]

Interests (Standing Order 96). Any Lord is exempted from serving on a committee on any bill in which he has an interest though if his interest is only a remote or minor one it is the practice for him to declare it at the beginning of the committee's proceedings and, if the parties have no objection, to continue to sit. A Lord may be excused from serving on a committee for special reasons, to be approved in each case by the House.

Attendance of members (Standing Orders 105 and 106). Every member 'shall attend the proceedings of the committee during the whole continuance thereof' (Standing Order 105). But if any member is unable to attend, the committee may, with the consent of all the parties, sit in his absence, provided that the number of the committee is not less than four and that the committee reports the fact to the House when the House next sits (Standing Order 106).[4] No Lord who is not a member of the committee may take part in its proceedings.

Equality of votes on a division in a committee. If for any reason, such as the unavoidable absence of a member of the committee, opinions are equally divided as to whether a bill should proceed or not, the practice is to allow the bill to proceed.[5] The Lord in the chair has no casting vote.

Report of causes of adjournments (Standing Order 108). Every committee on an opposed bill must report to the House the cause of any adjournment over any day on which the House is to sit.

Withdrawal of opposition (Standing Order 113). If no parties appear on their petitions against a bill or on petitions against alterations, or, having

---

1 For private bills which have been committed to a joint committee, see p 888, and for proceedings after second reading in the Lords on bills originating in the Commons which have been so committed, see p 889.
2 Tees Valley and Cleveland Water Bill (LJ (1966–67) 243); Calderdale Water Bill (LJ (1968–69) 253).
3 The Committee of Selection selected the members of the committee on the Lloyd's Bill, LJ (1981–82) 232.
4 Brighton Marina Bill, LJ (1967–68) 144. The select committee on the Swanage City Council Bill adjourned *sine die* because not all the parties consented to the committee sitting as four members in the absence of the fifth member, LJ (1984–85) 356.
5 First Report from the Select Committee on the Procedure of the House of Lords (1962–63) HL 123.

appeared, withdraw their opposition before the evidence of the promoters has been opened, or if their locus standi is disallowed, the committee is required to report accordingly to the House. The bill is then dealt with as if originally unopposed and, unless there is an outstanding application for costs before the select committee, is committed to an unopposed bill committee. But nothing contained in this order prevents the committee 'from requiring the preamble of a bill to be proved in any case in which an application for costs has been made'.

Hearing and evidence (Standing Orders 109 and 110). Petitions against bills are automatically referred to committees, and the parties may be heard by themselves, their counsel or agents. The proceedings of a Lords' committee on a private bill differ in no material point from those of a committee in the Commons (see p 901), except as to questions of locus standi and the method of dealing with the unopposed parts of the bill, for which see below.

By section 2 of the Parliamentary Witnesses Act 1858 (21 & 22 Vict c 78), any committee of the House of Lords may administer an oath to the witnesses examined before them. The practice on private bills is that witnesses in opposed proceedings are always sworn, but witnesses in an unopposed bill committee are not sworn, except the witness who formally proves the preamble.

Witnesses may be examined, either upon the preamble, against particular clauses, or in support of new clauses or amendments. Parties may be similarly heard upon their petitions against alteration in the bill. Witnesses are examined in chief by counsel, cross-examined and re-examined. When the case for and against the preamble (if opposed) has been concluded, and if the committee is of the opinion that the bill should proceed, the opposed clauses of the bill are gone through in the same manner, and the bill is then ordered to be reported to the House by the Lord in the chair with or without amendment. Every opposed private bill on which a select committee has reported that the bill should be allowed to proceed is recommitted to an unopposed bill committee (see p 939) for consideration of the unopposed provisions; but no decisions made by a select committee may be varied by an unopposed bill committee.

Visits to sites. A select committee may, if it thinks fit, visit the site affected by a private bill.[1]

Locus standi of petitioners (Standing Order 114). Questions on the locus standi of the petitioners against a bill are heard by the committee to which the bill is referred. In this respect the House of Lords has preserved the original practice of both Houses, which was abandoned by the House of Commons in 1865, when the Court of Referees was established (see p 842); but the House of Lords, like the House of Commons, has passed several standing orders (Standing Orders 115 to 120), some of which are mandatory and some permissive, regulating the locus standi of petitioners in certain cases. Moreover, the House may give directions, either by suspending certain of the standing orders relating to locus standi, or by giving an

---

1 For example, Epsom and Walton Downs Regulation Bill 1982; Felixstowe Dock and Railway Bill 1988, Hampstead Radio Station Bill 1988.

instruction to the select committee, which may in particular cases modify the rules relating to locus standi.

In the case of the Adelphi Estate Bill 1933, as a result of an undertaking given by the Chairman of Committees in debate on the second reading, an Instruction directing the committee to amend the bill in certain particulars was not moved, and the standing order limiting the time within which petitions against the bill might be deposited was suspended so as to allow the hearing of certain petitioners.[1]

On the Greater London Council (Money) Bill 1976 the select committee disallowed the locus standi of all petitioners but nevertheless met to consider an instruction and, having obtained power to hear evidence other than that tendered by the parties, took evidence from some of the unsuccessful petitioners.[2]

Competing bills. In the case of competing bills the practice of select committees of the House of Lords has not conformed to the procedure employed in the Commons (see p 907).

The Select Committee on the London Electric Power Bills in 1905 and on the Penllwyn and other Welsh Railway Bills in 1906 considered each bill separately, though deferring its decision on the preamble of each bill until the case of the last bill had been concluded. In 1955, the Chatham and District Water Bill and the Sevenoaks and Tunbridge Wells Water Bill competed with certain parts of the Kent Water Bill; all the bills were considered by the same select committee. By agreement between the parties, a complicated procedure was devised, which is outlined on pp 1021–1022 of the 17th edition of this work.

Costs. Committees of the House of Lords have the same powers as those of the House of Commons to award costs (see pp 913–915).

Special reports. It is usual for a select committee to make a special report on a bill if the House has given the committee upon the bill an instruction, or if the bill, though unopposed, has been referred by the Chairman of Committees to the select committee, or if any point arises during their consideration of the bill which they think merits such treatment.[3]

Unopposed bills referred by the Chairman of Committees to a select committee

Standing Order 92 gives the Chairman of Committees power to refer an unopposed bill to a select committee.[4] This standing order has also been

---

1 HL Deb (1933) 86 cc 1220, 1225; LJ (1932–33) 138.
2 LJ (1975–76) 623, 632.
3 For a special report on costs, see British Railways (No 2) Bill (1981–82) HL 23. For a special report from a select committee on unopposed provisions, see Greater Manchester Bill, LJ (1979–80) 953. For special reports made by an unopposed bill committee, see Saint Dionis Backchurch Churchyard Bill and Saint Nicholas Acons Churchyard Bill, ibid (1962–63) 237–238; British Railways (Selby) Bill, ibid (1979–80) 40. For special reports on hybrid bills, see Maplin Development Bill, LJ (1972–73) 626; Channel Tunnel Bill, ibid (1986–87) 352; Dartford-Thurock Crossing Bill, ibid (1987–88) 516.
4 Esso Petroleum Bill, LJ (1960–61) 33; Brighton Marina Bill, ibid (1966–67) 695; Saint Mary, Hornsey, Bill, ibid (1968–69) 17; Saint Saviour, Paddington, Bill, ibid (1968–69) 17; Severn-Trent Water Authority Bill, ibid (1982–83) 298.

interpreted as giving power to the Chairman to refer parts of a bill to a select committee, including unopposed parts of opposed bills.[1]

Where a select committee is considering an unopposed bill thus remitted to it by the Chairman of Committees, the promoters are frequently represented only by their agents, though in other respects, so far as applicable, the procedure appropriate to an opposed bill is followed.

Rejection of bill by select committee

A select committee rejects a private bill by reporting to the House 'That it is not expedient to proceed further with the bill'. This report is ordered to lie on the Table, and the bill is thereupon dropped from the list of bills in progress.[2]

Unopposed bill committees

Unopposed bills committed to unopposed bill committees (Standing Order 121). Every private bill which has not been petitioned against is committed to an unopposed bill committee. Bills against which petitions were presented but later withdrawn are also so committed. Bills which have become unopposed by reason of the provisions of Standing Order 113, except bills which the Chairman of Committees has under Standing Order 92 reported to the House should proceed as an opposed bill, are also committed to an unopposed bill committee. An unopposed bill committee consists of the Chairman of Committees and, if the Chairman sees fit, such Deputy Chairmen as he may select. No other Lord may take part. The committee is assisted by the Counsel to the Chairman of Committees. In the absence of the Chairman, one of the Deputy Chairmen acts in his place.

By virtue of Standing Order 122 (which is equivalent to Standing Order 134 of the House of Commons) the promoters of an unopposed private bill are entitled to be heard before the committee by themselves or their agents or, in cases where the unopposed bill committee consists of the Chairman of Committees and any Deputy Chairmen, by counsel. There also normally attend the representatives of those Ministers who have sent in reports on, or who are concerned with, the bill, and witnesses of the promoters who can answer any points that have been raised by such reports or by the Chairman of Committees or his Counsel.

Committees on bills whether opposed or unopposed (Standing Orders 123–146)

Copies of filled-up bill to be laid before the Chairman of Committees (Standing Order 123). Copies of filled-up bills and of estimates and statements deposited under Standing Orders 45 or 46 must be submitted to the Chairman of Committees before the day appointed for the consideration of the bill in committee; and in the case of an opposed or recommitted bill such

---

1 LJ (1955–56) 74.
2 For Commons bills rejected by select committees, see Birmingham Corporation Bill, Walsall Corporation Bill and West Bromwich Corporation Bill (LJ (1955–56) 74, 321); for Lords bills so rejected, see Plymouth Corporation (Harrowbeer Aerodrome) Bill, LJ (1960–61) 255; Yorkshire Woollen District Transport Bill, ibid (1961–62) 157; Milford Haven Conservancy Bill, ibid (1964–65) 223; Hamapstead Radio Station Bill, ibid (1987–88) 691.

copies must be so laid not less than two clear days before the day so appointed.

Powers of committees, and their limitations. By Standing Order 124 a committee is not empowered, without express authority from the House, to hear evidence other than that tendered by any parties entitled to be heard[1] (see p 902); by Standing Order 125 a committee is prohibited from examining into the compliance with such standing orders as are directed to be proved before the Examiners; and by Standing Order 126 a committee may admit affidavits in proof of any allegation, deed or document mentioned or set forth in a bill or its schedule.

Reports of public departments (Standing Order 127). All reports upon a private bill or its objects by any public departments or by the Attorney General stand referred to the committee on the bill, who may, if it thinks fit, hear an officer of the department in explanation of the report. Such officers are not sworn and may not be cross-examined before a select committee by counsel, though the effect of this latter prohibition is circumvented in practice by the chairman of the committee putting questions to them on behalf of counsel. Since the representatives of departments are not on oath, they should not comment on or traverse evidence as to fact given by sworn witnesses.

Agreements (Standing Order 129). Any agreement scheduled to a bill must contain a clause declaring that it is made subject to such alterations as Parliament may think fit to make to it; but if the committee makes any material alteration in an agreement, any party to the agreement may withdraw from it.

Arrangements between parties and undertakings given in committee (Standing Order 130). It is a condition of acceptance by any committee of (a) any arrangement between the promoters of a private bill and any other party appearing or (b) any undertaking given to the committee by or on behalf of the promoters or any such other party, that any difference arising between the parties concerned shall, after the discharge of the committee, be determined by the Chairman of Committees.

Action to be taken by committees on certain bills (Standing Orders 131–146). Committees on certain private bills are required to take particu-

---

1 For cases where authority to hear evidence other than that tendered by parties entitled to be heard has been given, see Welland and Nene (Empingham Reservoir) and Mid-Northamptonshire Water Bill, LJ (1969–70) 150; Coity Wallia Commons Bill, ibid (1975–76) 401; Greater London Council (Money) Bill, ibid 623; London Transport Bill, ibid (1979–80) 1126; Severn-Trent Water Authority Bill, ibid (1982–83) 301; London Docklands Railway (City Extension) Bill, ibid (1985–86) 661.

lar actions. There are similar standing orders in the House of Commons (see pp 897–901). Standing Orders 131–139 relate to bills affecting fencing of bridges and railway, tramroad and tramway bills; Standing Orders 140 and 141 relate to local government bills and Standing Orders 142–146 relate to bills affecting charitable institutions, accommodation for workmen, water bills and gas works, etc bills.

Recommitment of private bills

Recommitment to Committee of the whole House (Standing Order 94). In order to ensure attention to bills affecting public interests, the Chairman of Committees may propose that any private bill be recommitted to a Committee of the Whole House:[1] but no private bill so recommitted is, by reason of such commitment, allowed to proceed as a public bill.

Deposit of amended bills (Standing Order 147)

A copy of every private bill as amended in committee must be deposited not less than three clear days before the third reading at every office at which it was deposited under Standing Orders 39 and 194, or would be required to be deposited under those orders if it had been originally introduced in the form in which it emerged as amended in committee. Proof of compliance with this standing order is given by depositing a certificate in the office of the Clerk of the Parliaments.

Private bills to be reprinted (Standing Order 128). All private bills which have been amended in committee are reprinted as amended before the third reading, unless the Chairman of Committees considers that reprinting the bill is unnecessary.

Report stage

Normally no report stage is held in the House. Private bills are reported to the House from a select committee or from an unopposed bill committee merely by means of an entry in the minutes of proceedings of the House as soon as the formalities consequent upon their amendment in committee have been completed; or, if they have not been amended, as soon as the committee has considered them.

When a special report (see p 938) is made, a motion to take note of it may be moved.[2]

Third reading

Amendments may be moved on third reading (Standing Orders 148 and 149) provided that notice has been given in the Parliament Office one clear day

---

1 Oriental Bank Corporation Bill, LJ (1873–74) 318; Nottingham Corporation Bill, ibid (1882) 170.
2 A motion to take note of the special report on the County of South Glamorgan Bill was amended so that certain provisions rejected by the select committee were recommitted; LJ (1975–76) 48–49. A motion to take note of the special report of the select committee on the West Midlands County Council Bill was amended to the effect that certain proposed amendments rejected by the committee should be made on third reading; LJ (1977–78) 814.

before the third reading. The Chairman of Committees is not normally prepared to move amendments on third reading unless he is satisfied that the consent of all parties has been given. The promoters' agents make available in the Printed Paper Office typed copies of the amendments.

Private bills are occasionally debated on third reading and may, less frequently, be opposed.[1] When amendments on general grounds are to be moved these are ordered to be printed by the House.

Proceedings after third reading

When a bill has been read a third time and passed, it is sent to the Commons; or, if it is a bill brought from that House, it is either returned with amendments, or a message is sent to acquaint the Commons that it has been agreed to without amendment. The ordinary proceedings in the Commons on amendments made by the Lords to private bills originating in the Commons are described in chapter 36. In the event of disagreement between the Houses the same forms are observed as for public bills (see pp 514 ff). In the case of private bills, however, the second house will not make a bill more onerous (except on the promoters) than it was when it left the first house (see p 910).

Commons amendments (Standing Order 150)

Copies of Commons amendments to Lords bills and of amendments proposed by promoters to such amendments must be laid by the agent before the Chairman of Committees not later than two o'clock on the day when such amendments are to be considered by the House.

Withdrawal of bills

Private bills may be withdrawn at any stage during their passage through the House.[2]

Bills relating to Northern Ireland (Standing Order 200)

Standing Order 200 applies the Standing Orders to a bill which relates wholly or partly to Northern Ireland, subject to such adaptations and modifications as may be prescribed by the Chairman of Committees or by the Standing Orders Committee; but nothing in Standing Order 200 is taken as implying any extension of the cases in which bills relating to Northern Ireland may properly be promoted in the United Kingdom Parliament.

B. PERSONAL BILLS (Standing Orders 151–174)

Definition (Standing Order 151)

Standing Order 151 defines as 'personal bills' all private bills relating to the estate, property, status, or style, or otherwise relating to the personal

---

1 British Transport Docks (Felixstowe) Bill 1986 (a Commons bill), LJ (1975–76) 817 and Swanage Yacht Haven Bill 1987, LJ (1987–88) 234, were rejected at third reading. Anglesey Marine Terminal Bill, LJ (1971–72) 123 and Greater Manchester Bill, ibid (1979–80) 1184, were opposed on third reading.
2 LJ (1974) 295; ibid (1984–85) 147.

affairs, of an individual, which have been certified as such under the provisions of Standing Order 3 (see pp 812–813).[1] By virtue of Standing Order 3, Standing Orders 4–68 do not apply to personal bills. By Standing Order 174 all relevant standing orders relating to private bills are applied, so far as applicable, to personal bills, subject to any directions by the Chairman of Committees. Proceedings on personal bills are subject to general or special directions given from time to time by the Chairman of Committees.

All personal bills are introduced in the House of Lords. Few such bills have been promoted in recent years because many of the purposes for which such bills were commonly sought—notably divorce—have been provided for or made obsolete by public general legislation. The only personal bills to have passed the Personal Bills Committee since 1975 have been bills to authorise marriage between persons falling within the prohibited degrees of affinity. The first of a series of bills for this purpose was passed in 1980.[2] Such bills seem likely to be more rare in future because of the wide relaxation in the general law governing this matter made by the Marriage (Prohibited Degrees of Relationship) Act 1986.[3] Since the 1986 Act came into force there have, however, been two successful marriage enabling bills authorizing marriages that would not have been permissible under that Act.[4]

By Standing Order 199, where a private bill contains clauses or provisions of the nature of a personal bill, the Chairman of Committees may direct that the relevant provisions of Part VII of the standing orders (relating to personal bills) shall apply; this may include a direction that the bill be printed.

Preliminary stages

Petitions for bills (Standing Orders 152, 153, 167). The promoters deposit in the Office of the Clerk of the Parliaments a petition for leave to bring in the bill. The petition contains a copy of the proposed bill and is signed by one or more of the parties. The bill cannot proceed until the Chairman of Committees has certified that the proposed bill comes within the definition referred to above (see p 812). If an infant has an interest in the proposed bill, the Chairman of Committees may require him to be represented in any proceedings on the petition or on the bill by a guardian appointed by the Lord Chancellor.[5]

The Personal Bills Committee (Standing Order 154). The Personal Bills Committee is appointed at the beginning of every session; and every petition

1 Until 1945 personal bills affecting estates were subject to a distinct procedure but, apart from the provisions of SOs 162 to 172, this is no longer the case.
2 Edward Berry and Doris Eileen Ward (Marriage Enabling) Bill (1979–80), John Francis Dare and Gillian Loder Dare (Marriage Enabling) Bill (1981–82), and Hugh Small and Norma Small (Marriage Enabling) Bill (1981–82). For other recent examples of personal bills, see Lucas Estate Bill (1962–63) and Wellington Estate Bill (1971–72).
3 1986, c 16.
4 George Donald Evans and Deborah Jane Evans (Marriage Enabling) Bill (1986–87) and John Ernest Rolfe and Florence Iveen Rolfe (Marriage Enabling) Bill (1986–87).
5 Bury Estate Bill, LJ (1927) 148; Grosvenor Estate Bill, ibid (1932–33) 195; Tatton Estate Bill, ibid (1936–37) 267.

for a personal bill, as soon as certified by the Chairman of Committees, stands referred to the committee. The committee consists of seven Lords, including the Chairman of Committees, and three is the quorum. The committee, after hearing the promoters, their counsel or agents, reports to the House whether the objects are proper to be enacted by a personal bill, whether the provisions thereof are proper for carrying its purposes into effect, and what amendments, if any, are required. If the bill is approved by the committee, the Chairman signs a copy of the bill, which includes any amendments recommended. A copy of the committee's report and of the amended bill are supplied to the agent for the bill.

Proceedings in the Personal Bills Committee (Standing Orders 166, 167)

A personal bill is seldom opposed because of the requirement imposed on the committee on the bill by Standing Order 166 to be satisfied that all parties concerned consent to the consequences of the bill. It is, however, open to the Personal Bills Committee to report that the consent of any such party may be dispensed with on account of remoteness of interest or for any other reason. There is no provision in standing orders for opponents of a personal bill to appear before the Personal Bills Committee. An adverse report by the Personal Bills Committee would in practice be fatal to the bill, which would be struck from the list of Bills in Progress. The Personal Bills Committee has reported adversely on the ground that a proposed bill should be the subject of general legislation. The committee reported adversely on the Warrender Estate Bill in 1954 on the ground that its purpose was the avoidance of estate duty; and it is now customary for the promoters of a bill which will alter a settlement to obtain a statement from the Treasury Solicitor to the effect that the government does not oppose the bill.

Scottish personal bills (Standing Order 155)

If the petition is for a bill affecting private interests in Scotland, there is an additional stage. The Personal Bills Committee is required to refer the petition to two judges of the Court of Session. The judges summon the parties, hear evidence and take 'such proof of the allegations' contained in the proposed bill 'and such consents of the parties interested, and such acceptances of trusts as may be tendered to them'. They then report to the Personal Bills Committee 'the state of the case, and their opinion thereon, under their hands, and what amendments (if any) are required in the bill'. If they approve the proposed bill, they sign a copy containing the required amendments (if any). This report is delivered by the parties to the Chairman of Committees for submission to the Personal Bills Committee, which is precluded from reporting to the House on the petition for the bill until it has received and considered the report.

No petition has been referred to the judges of the Court of Session since the establishment of the Personal Bills Committee. The Warrender Estate Bill 1954 seemed to come within the scope of Standing Order 155; but, at the insistance of the promoters, the petition was dealt with by the Personal Bills Committee without reference to the Court of Session. Indeed, unless a proposed bill were exclusively concerned with Scottish affairs, it is difficult to see how Standing Order 155 could be made to work satisfactorily.

First reading of personal bills (Standing Order 156)

No personal bill may be read a first time until the report of the Personal Bills Committee has been made to the House.

Proceedings after first reading (Standing Orders 157, 162)

Subject to the directions of the Personal Bills Committee, a copy of every personal bill must be delivered before second reading to every person concerned, or, in case of infancy, to the guardian or next relation of full age not concerned in the consequences of the bill. Where the bill affects an estate, the promoters must, before second reading, give notice of the bill to every mortgagee of the estate.

Petitions against personal bills (Standing Order 158)

Petitions against personal bills are presented at such times as the Chairman of Committees, in each case, having regard to all the circumstances, may direct.

Commitment of personal bills (Standing Orders 159, 160, 161)

With the exception of marriage enabling bills, unopposed personal bills are committed to an unopposed bill committee and proceed as unopposed private bills; but the Chairman of Committees is given power to report that, in his opinion, an unopposed personal bill should be proceeded with as an opposed bill. Every personal bill which is opposed or on which the Chairman of Committees has so reported is referred to a select committee of five Lords, and is proceeded with as an opposed private bill. No committee, other than the Personal Bills Committee, may sit on a personal bill until ten days after second reading.

In the case of those personal bills which allow the marriage of persons otherwise prohibited by reason of a relationship of affinity ('marriage enabling bills'), the House has agreed that the second reading of the bill should normally be taken formally and that it should then be referred to a select committee consisting of the Chairman of Committees, a Bishop and two other Lords.[1] The committee to which the bill is committed examines the promoters of the bill on oath in private and calls for any other evidence which it considers relevant to deciding the question whether the bill should proceed.[2]

Committees on personal bills (Standing Orders 164 to 167 and 170 to 172)

The committee to whom a personal bill is committed (which must be distinguished from the Personal Bills Committee to whom the petition is referred) has the following specific duties imposed upon it by standing orders:

(1) Where the bill is for an exchange of settled estates, and contains a schedule of the estates and their value as required by Standing Order 164, the committee must require proof of the schedule.

---

1 HL Deb (1985–86) 475, cc 709–711.
2 Select Committee on the George Donald Evans and Deborah Jane Evans (Marriage Enabling) Bill, LJ (1986–87) 7, 44.

(2) The committee must be satisfied by evidence that all parties concerned in the consequences of the bill have consented to its provisions, subject to the following exceptions:

  (a) no proof is required if the Personal Bills Committee has reported that proof may be dispensed with;

  (b) if the petitioners for, and consenting parties to, a bill relating to an entailed estate are together competent to bar the entail, the consent of remaindermen after the petitioners and those parties is not required;

  (c) if the bill is promoted by a tenant in tail under age, or if a person under age is a consenting party to the bill by his guardian, the consent of a remainderman is dispensed with if the Lord Chancellor or Lord Keeper has appointed a person specially to assent or dissent from the bill on behalf of the minor;

  (d) Standing Orders 170 to 172 contain provisions for the consent of persons to personal bills relating to entailed estates in land or heritable subjects in Scotland.

(3) The committee must take the consent in person of trustees through whose hands money is to pass, unless they are trustees to preserve contingent remainders only.

The committee, unless otherwise required by standing orders, may take evidence on affidavit.

ROYAL ASSENT[1]

The proceedings on Royal Assent have already been described in chapter 21 (pp 527–529), but certain details relating only to Private Acts may here be given.

Private Acts declared public. For some centuries the promoters of certain private bills were in the habit of inserting a clause to the effect that 'this Act is to be deemed and taken to be a public Act'. The object of these words was to enable the Acts to be judicially noticed by the courts without being specially given in evidence. But one of the effects of such words in a bill was that the bill received the Royal Assent in the form 'La Reyne [or Le Roy] le veult'. Private bills which did not contain a formula declaring them to be public Acts received the Royal Assent in the form which properly answered the petition contained in the beginning of private bills: 'Soit fait comme il est désiré'. The practice, however, of declaring private bills to be public Acts had, by the middle of the nineteenth century, become so general that Lord Brougham in 1850 deemed it convenient to introduce a bill 'for shortening the language of Acts of Parliament', one effect of which was that in future every private bill should be deemed and taken to be a public Act on receiving the Royal Assent, unless the contrary were expressly provided and declared in the bill.[2] The effect of this provision is that all private bills, save personal bills, receive the Royal

1 In this and the following section the words 'Private Act' are used in their ordinary colloquial sense to mean 'a private (or personal) bill which has received the Royal Assent'.
2 13 & 14 Vict c21, s7. This Act was replaced by the Interpretation Act 1978, which contains the same provision.

Assent in the form 'La Reyne [or Le Roy] le veult'. Personal bills continue to receive Royal Assent in the form 'Soit fait comme il est désiré'.

CLASSIFICATION OF PRIVATE ACTS

The present system

At present (subject to the one exception mentioned below), all private Acts are printed after Royal Assent by the Queen's Printer. They are classified as follows:

(1) In one series, which is given chapter numbers in lower case Roman figures, there are listed:

  (a) Private Acts other than personal Acts; and
  (b) 'Public Acts of a local character', which include Provisional Order Confirmation Acts, Scottish Order Confirmation Acts passed under the Private Legislation Procedure (Scotland) Act 1936 and Pier and Harbour Order Confirmation Acts.

  Such Acts are numbered in the order in which they receive Royal Assent.

(2) Personal Acts are given a chapter number in italic arabic figures.

Unprinted personal Acts, which are now virtually obsolete, can be given in evidence in the courts of law only from copies of the Rolls of Parliament authenticated in the Parliament Office.

Private Acts are not published as annual volumes but they are listed and indexed in 'The Local and Personal Acts' which is published annually by the Stationery Office.

Past systems

The present system dates back to 1869, and was the result of the passage of Lord Brougham's Act (see above).

Before 1798 the 'Local and Personal Acts declared public' were printed and published in the same sessional volumes as the public general Acts. Until 1752 they were numbered in upper case roman numerals in one series indiscriminately with the public Acts, and from 1753 and 1797 they were numbered after the public Acts still in upper case roman numerals.

From 1798 the local and personal Acts were printed separately from public Acts: until 1814 they were numbered in arabic numerals and from 1815 in lower case roman numerals.

The private Acts not declared public were not printed by the Queen's Printer, but were listed and given arabic numbers in the sessional volumes.

CHAPTER 38

Provisional orders and special procedure orders

INTRODUCTORY

The system of legislation by provisional order and special procedure order enables government departments to deal with many undertakings with which Parliament would otherwise be asked to deal ab initio in a private or public bill. The origin of the provisional order method is to be found in the desire to lighten the expense of promoters, and in the necessity of containing the number of private bills which come before committees of both Houses. The aim of the Statutory Orders (Special Procedure) Act 1945 was to ensure that, during the reconstruction period after the war, government policy in certain spheres, particularly water, was not obstructed or delayed by private interests, while retaining safeguards for the latter.[1]

The earliest method of replacing private bills was found in the adoptive Act,[2] the purpose of which was to apply generally provisions contained in a number of individual local Acts, and after the report of select committees in 1846 and 1847 a number of 'Clauses Acts'[3] were passed. Use was also made of the preliminary local inquiry[4] and in 1846, again as a result of the report of the select committee of 1846, the Preliminary Inquiries Act was passed. This Act compelled local inquiries to be made by officers of the Commissioners for Woods, Forests, Land Revenues, Works and Buildings, or of the Admiralty, before an application for a private bill was made to Parliament. This procedure is now obsolete.

The Public Health Act 1848 set up the General Board of Health, who could send out inspectors to make an inquiry in any district, and could then in certain cases make a provisional order applying parts of the Act to the district; in other cases parts of the Act were applied by Order in Council. The first provisional orders under this Act received the Royal Assent in the session of 1850.

The system lasted for ten years, till the Public Health Act was amended by the Local Government Act of 1858. This Act, which could be adopted in localities, authorized the establishment of local boards, who were enabled in such matters as the compulsory purchase of land to apply to the Secretary of State for a provisional order. The Secretary of State was then to institute a local inquiry and, if the proposal was justified, to bring the resulting provisional order before Parliament in a confirming bill. What is practically the present method of making provisional orders had thus been evolved by

---

1 See White Paper on a National Water Policy 1944 (Cmd 6515).
2 Eg Lighting and Watching Act 1833.
3 Eg Harbours Docks and Piers Clauses Act 1847; Town Police Clauses Act 1847.
4 Eg Inclosure Act 1845.

1858. In subsequent years the practice became more firmly established, and the power of granting a provisional order was gradually extended to other government departments.

A minor variant upon the provisional order system was the introduction of 'Special Orders'. Of these by far the most numerous were those relating to gas and electricity undertakings. The relevant Acts were the Electricity (Supply) Act 1919 and the Gas Regulation Act 1920. The distinction between the special orders and provisional orders was that whereas special orders which required parliamentary sanction,[1] obtained it by means of an affirmative resolution, provisional orders obtained it by means of a confirming bill. All statutory powers to make special orders which required the sanction of Parliament were repealed by 1948, although the statutory use of the term still survives in certain instances where parliamentary approval is not required for the validity of the orders.[2]

These two systems of provisional order bill and private bill legislation were extended in 1945 by a third, that of special procedure orders. The Statutory Orders (Special Procedure) Act 1945 was based on two assumptions: first, that Parliament would from time to time be asked to confer powers to make orders for purposes which had hitherto been dealt with by private legislation in the form either of private or of provisional order bills; and secondly, that provision was necessary for a newer and quicker procedure designed to secure effective parliamentary control over the exercise of such powers both in respect of broad questions of national policy and in respect of questions of detail affecting private individuals. It combined certain features both of the provisional order and of the special order systems, but introduced a new feature in drawing a distinction between objections based on broad policy and those based on individual interests. The Act came into operation on 1 June 1946.[3]

SCOPE OF THE PROVISIONAL ORDER AND SPECIAL PROCEDURE ORDER SYSTEMS

A large number of enactments existed under which provisional order making powers were granted during the latter half of the nineteenth century and the first half of the twentieth. Under section 8(1) of the Statutory Orders (Special Procedure) Act 1945 and the second schedule thereto certain of these powers (contained in Acts passed in 1944 and 1945 and including the Water Act 1945) were converted to special procedure order making powers. Section 8(3) of the Act also provided that if at any time after the commencement of the Act an address was presented to His Majesty by both Houses of Parliament praying that the provisions of the Act should be applied in substitution for provisional order making powers contained in any enactment passed before the commencement of the Act, His Majesty might by Order in Council make provision for that purpose; and any such Order in

---

1 Some special orders took effect without approval by Parliament; eg certain orders made under the National Health Insurance Act 1936.
2 Towns Improvement Clauses Act 1847, ss 132–136; Burgh Police (Scotland) Act 1892, ss 306–315.
3 For the debate on the second reading of the bill for this Act, see HC Deb (1945–46) 414, cc 1374–1420. See also the 1944 White Paper on a National Water Policy, Cmd 6515, and HC Deb (1943–44) 401, cc 33–35.

Council might adapt or modify any enactment to such extent as might be expedient in consequence of the order. An Order in Council[1] was made in December 1949 under this power, after the necessary preliminary approval by Parliament had been given. This Order converted to the special procedure order system all the most fruitful sources of provisional orders remaining, with the exception of those made under the Private Legislation Procedure (Scotland) Act 1936. As far as future legislation is concerned, section 1(1) of the Statutory Orders (Special Procedure) Act 1945 provided that where by any Act passed thereafter, power to make or confirm orders was conferred upon any authority, and provision was made requiring that any such order should be subject to special parliamentary procedure, then the provisions of the 1945 Act should apply in relation to any order so made or confirmed. A number of Acts containing such provisions have since been passed, and no powers to make provisional orders have been conferred by public Acts since 1945.[2] However, one conversion from provisional order to special procedure order, made in 1949, has after criticism in both Houses[3] subsequently been restored to provisional order procedure.[4] This related to the amendment of local enactments under section 303 of the Public Health Act 1875. In 1965 certain amendments were made in the procedure to be followed in Parliament upon orders made under the 1945 Act, by the Statutory Orders (Special Procedure) Act of that year.

Provisional Order Bills: enabling provisions

The position then at present is that very few powers relating to England and Wales remain to make provisional orders which require confirmation by confirming bill, and no such bills have been introduced since 1980. A brief résumé of the enabling Acts which have not been affected is given below.

Provisional orders: miscellaneous powers. Existing powers to make orders which may be submitted to Parliament include those contained in the General Pier and Harbour Acts 1861 and 1862, the Commons Act 1876, the Fishery Harbours Act 1915, the Railways Act 1921, the Public Health (Drainage of Trade Premises) Act 1937, and, as a result of the order restoring provisional order procedure referred to above, section 303 of the Public Health Act 1875, as re-enacted by section 317 of the Public Health Act 1936. Private Acts also may contain powers to make provisional orders.

The application of the Statutory Orders (Special Procedure) Act 1945 is determined by section 1(1) of the Act as regards subsequent Acts, by the second schedule to the Act as regards certain pre-existing Acts specified by name, and by the power given under section 8(3) of the Act to make Orders in Council substituting special parliamentary procedure for pre-existing powers to make provisional orders. A list of the later Acts which apply the provisions of the 1945 Act may be found in the Index to the Statutes under the heading 'Statutory Instruments', sub-heading 'Special Parliamentary

---

1 Statutory Orders (Special Procedure) (Substitution) Order 1949 (SI 1949 No 2393).
2 Except by s 87(3) of the London Government Act 1963, which has since been repealed by the Local Government Act 1985.
3 In debates on motions to annul the Leicester (Amendment of Local Enactments) Order, 1959, HL Deb (1958–59) 215, cc 906–922; HC Deb (1958–59) 604, cc 727–754.
4 By the Statutory Orders (Special Procedure) (Substitution) Order 1962 (SI 1962 No 409).

Procedure orders'. Considerable changes were made by the First Schedule to the Statutory Orders (Special Procedure) (Substitution) Order 1949, and in particular the following powers to make provisional orders are covered by the procedure:

(a) powers under the Housing Acts for compulsory purchase in respect of commons, open spaces and allotments; and

(b) the powers under section 240 of the Local Government Act 1972 to make provisional orders.

Provisional orders in Scotland. Under the Private Legislation Procedure (Scotland) Act 1936, the Secretary of State for Scotland possesses very extensive powers of making orders that are submitted to Parliament for confirmation in a bill (see pp 965–975 below).

PRELIMINARY PROCEEDINGS: PROVISIONAL AND SPECIAL PROCEDURE ORDERS

Before their presentation, Parliament takes no cognizance either of provisional orders or of special procedure orders; there are no standing orders regulating proceedings on a special procedure order before its presentation, and, with one or two exceptions mentioned later, the standing orders regulating the preliminary proceedings in the promotion of a private bill are not applicable to provisional order bills. Those interests, however, which in the case of a private bill are protected by the standing orders, do not suffer; for in this respect the government department takes the place of Parliament, and secures the observance of rules and regulations—similar in nature and effect to the standing orders—as to notice by advertisement of the objects of the order, notice to owners and occupiers, consents, deposit of documents and other similar matters. The preliminary proceedings on provisional orders are governed by the enabling Act; on special procedure orders they are governed either by the first schedule to the Statutory Orders (Special Procedure) Act 1945, or, where the new system is substituted for a previous provisional order making power, by the requirements of the original enabling Act.

An important and very frequent feature in departmental procedure in both types of orders is the preliminary local inquiry, which, under the first schedule to the 1945 Act and many of the provisional order enabling Acts, may have to be held into the merits of the provisions proposed to be authorized by the order. In some cases dealing with provisional orders, this inquiry is obligatory; while in others the inquiry is only held if thought expedient, or if—as in the case under the first schedule to the 1945 Act—an objection has been made to the order and has not been withdrawn. The inquiry is usually held in the locality affected by the proposed order, after due notice, by an officer of the department, or other properly qualified person, who makes a report on the case to the department.

These preliminary proceedings, however, being departmental and unconnected with the practice of Parliament, will not be described in detail. For the necessary procedure in each case, reference must be made to the special provisions of the relevant Act, and to the instructions issued by the government department empowered to deal with the particular subject.

PROCEDURE IN PARLIAMENT ON BILLS FOR CONFIRMING PROVISIONAL ORDERS

The procedure followed in Parliament upon bills for confirming provisional orders may be shortly stated. It applies to all such bills with a few exceptions, already noticed, where a different procedure in part or in whole is expressly prescribed. The bills are presented as public bills in either House according to the discretion of the department responsible for them.

The standing orders of both Houses relating to bills confirming provisional orders—referred to for the purposes of the standing orders as confirming bills—are Standing Orders 178 to 186 (HL) and 211 to 219 (HC). The provisions of these orders, allowance being made for slight variations due to differences in general practice, lay down almost identical procedure. Standing Orders 178 (HL) and 211 (HC) define the meaning of 'confirming bill' in the orders which follow, and exclude from their operation provisional orders issued under the Private Legislation Procedure (Scotland) Act 1936, and bills to confirm such orders (see chapter 39).

First reading and reference to examiners

Under Standing Orders 182 (HL) and 216 (HC) no confirming bill, originating in either House, is to be presented after 15 May except during a session which begins before that date in the same year.[1] After first reading all such bills are referred to the Examiners, before whom compliance with two standing orders must be proved. The first of these orders, Standing Orders 179 (HL) and 212 (HC) lays down requirements as to deposits of plans, etc, at the appropriate office of the respective House whenever such plans have been deposited at a public department in relation to a provisional order or to any order which, although not provisional as made, became provisional after being made. The second order—Standing Orders 180 (HL) and 213 (HC)—applies to confirming bills Standing Order 47 (of both Houses) providing for the deposit of statements, showing the number of houses on the land and the number of persons residing in those houses, when power to acquire land is proposed to be conferred, revived or extended by a private bill. By Standing Orders 181 (HL) and 214 (HC) the Examiner must give at least two clear days' notice of the date of examination, and he may not give notice until after the bill has been printed by order of the House. He is required to report whether the two preceding orders have or have not been complied with, stating his reasons and any special circumstances if his report is adverse; and the appropriate standing orders relating to the examination of private bills are applied to this examination. Standing Orders 181 (HL) and 214 (HC) also provide for the deposit of memorials complaining of non-compliance; for the Examiner's power to entertain a memorial even though not signed by the person specially affected; and for examination as to compliance when the first House has inserted in a confirming bill provisions to which, had the bill been a private bill, the standing orders would apply.

---

1 For a suspension of this provision in the Commons, see CJ (1921) 208.

Second reading

In the Lords, Standing Order 183 provides that no confirming bill may be read a second time until the Examiner or the Standing Orders Committee, as the case may be, has reported that the standing orders have been complied with, or the House, following a favourable report from the Standing Orders Committee, has agreed that standing orders should be dispensed with.

In the Commons, as soon as the Examiners report that no standing orders are applicable or that the standing orders applicable to the bill have been complied with, or, in the case of non-compliance, as soon as the House agrees to a resolution reported by the Standing Orders Committee that the standing orders should be dispensed with, a confirming bill is ordered to be read a second time on a future day. If the standing orders have not been complied with and are not dispensed with, no further proceedings take place on the bill unless the House takes further action in the matter. On second reading and other stages in the House, Members may object in the same way as to a private bill. Opposed provisional order bills are treated as opposed private business and may be set down by the Chairman of Ways and Means for debate at seven o'clock under the terms of Standing Order No 16 (Public) and Standing Order 174.

Committee stage

The deposit of petitions against confirming bills and proceedings in committee on such bills are regulated on similar lines but in slightly varying forms by Standing Orders 184 and 185 (HL) and 217 (HC). *In the Lords,* petitions against such bills must be presented on or before the seventh day after the second reading, or on or before the seventh day after first reading of a bill brought from the Commons. Every confirming bill, as respects any unopposed orders, is referred to an unopposed bill committee to be dealt with in the same way as an unopposed private bill and, as respects any opposed orders, is referred to a select committee of five Lords and proceeded with as an opposed private bill. By Standing Order 186 (HL) certain other standing orders relating to private bills are made applicable to confirming bills (powers of the Chairman of Committees, and printing and withdrawal of petitions). Confirming bills are then considered in a Committee of the whole House.

In the Commons under Standing Order 217 confirming bills, after second reading, are committed and stand referred to the Committee of Selection.[1] Standing Order 217 also applies to confirming bills a number of other standing orders relating to the committee stage of private bills, especially those dealing with the powers of the Committee of Selection and the proceedings of committees on opposed and unopposed bills. Where one or more only of the several orders contained in a confirming bill are opposed, however, Standing Order 217 specifically provides that the Committee of

---

1 For confirming bills which have been referred to a joint committee, see Railway Rates and Charges PO Bills, CJ (1890–91) 129; (1892) 62; Canal Rates, Tolls, and Charges PO Bills, CJ (1893–94) 251; (1894) 123; (1895) 230; (1896) 50; Ministry of Health PO (Birkenhead Extension) Bill [Lords] and (Widnes Extension) Bill [Lords], CJ (1920) 224, 251; or to a select committee, see Government Departments (Transfer of Powers) PO Bills, CJ (1889) 268; Local Government PO (Poor Law) Bill, CJ (1893–94) 313; Trade Boards Act PO Bills, CJ (1913) 174; (1914) 247.

Selection may refer the bill to the committee on unopposed bills which is to divide the bill into two bills, the first containing the opposed and the second the unopposed orders. The committee is then to refer the opposed bill back to the Committee of Selection.[1]

The time before which petitions against confirming bills have to be deposited has already been stated (see p 840), and petitions which have met this requirement stand referred to the committee on the bill. Standing Order 215 brings confirming bills within the jurisdiction of the Court of Referees (see p 842) and requires that the proceedings of the Court are to be conducted in the same manner as for a private bill and be subject to the same rules and orders of the House so far as they are applicable. Instructions to committees on such bills are governed by the same principles as instructions to committees on private bills[2] (see pp 873–875).

In committee on an opposed provisional order bill where one order only is scheduled to the bill, the consideration of the preamble and clauses of the bill is postponed until the scheduled order has been considered. Procedure follows that on a private bill, but the question put on the conclusion of the case is 'That the order be confirmed' or 'be confirmed subject to modifications'. If more than one order is scheduled to the bill, the question 'that the order be confirmed' is put separately at the conclusion of the case on each order. Where any order is confirmed subject to modifications, the committee then makes the necessary amendments. After all the orders have been considered, the preamble and clauses of the bill are agreed to or amended and agreed to and the bill is ordered to be reported to the House.[3] Standing Order 217 requires the committee to report whether each order contained in the bill should or should not be confirmed.

Amendments to confirming bills

In either House the committee to which a confirming bill is referred may amend the order if the proposed amendment is of such a nature that it would have been within the powers of the department by which the order was made to incorporate it in the order as issued. Such amendments are made in the text of the scheduled order, and a consequential amendment is made in the confirmatory clause in the bill itself.[4] But no new matter should be introduced in the scheduled order which would be inconsistent with or go beyond the public notice and advertisement for the purpose of the order required by the Act in pursuance of which the order is issued or by regulations made under that Act. It has also been held undesirable that new matter of this kind should be introduced into the confirming bill.[5]

---

1 This order (then 208A) has been suspended and an instruction given to the Committee of Selection to refer one order in a bill to a particular committee, see CJ (1909) 162.
2 For a mandatory instruction to divide a bill into two portions (before SO 217 existed), see CJ (1893–94) 313, and Parl Deb (1893) 12, c 1230; also Parl Deb (1904) 136, c 109. For other instructions, see inter alia, CJ (1893–94) 359; Parl Deb (1896) 39, cc 941–948; CJ (1899) 284; Parl Deb (1899) 73, cc 414–431.
3 For a special report, see CJ (1920) 276.
4 Contrast s 1 of Ministry of Health PO Confirmation (Leicester and Warwick) Act 1935 with s 1 of Ministry of Health PO Confirmation (Cumberland and Lancaster) Act 1935, and see Pier and Harbour Provisional Order (Fishguard and Goodwick Harbour) Act 1975.
5 Local Government Provisional Orders (No 7) Bill, CJ (1901) 290, 302, 307, 318, 323, and Minutes of Evidence, Group N, 19–28 June and 2 July 1901.

Later stages

Confirming bills are not usually reprinted as amended unless important amendments have been inserted or some other reason makes this desirable.[1]

In the Lords, after being reported from a Committee of the whole House, confirming bills proceed as public bills. *In the Commons,* on being reported, a confirming bill is ordered to be considered,[2] if amended, or, if not amended, to be read the third time, on the following (or a future) day.[3] It may be noted here that Standing Order 224 (Examination of public bills by Examiners) does not apply, but that Standing Order 156A (Modification of practice as to charges on public revenue), Standing Order 169 (Attachment of financial memoranda to certain bills) and Standing Order 191 (Tolls and charges not in the nature of a tax) do apply to bills for confirming provisional orders. For provisions in a confirming bill which create a charge upon the people or upon the public revenues, see p 869.

Parliament Act

A bill for confirming a provisional order is expressly excluded from the operation of the Parliament Act 1911.

Suspension of provisional order bills

Provisional order bills have, from time to time, been suspended at the end of a session[4] in the same way as private bills and with certain minor differences follow the same procedure (see pp 928–930). The declaration that the bill is the same in every respect as the bill at the last stage of proceedings in the previous session is required to be made by or on behalf of the Minister responsible for the bill.

PROCEDURE IN PARLIAMENT ON SPECIAL PROCEDURE ORDERS

Presentation of orders

After the requirements as to preliminary proceedings have been complied with, the Minister concerned is required to give not less than three days' notice in the London Gazette of his intention to lay the order before Parliament. The order, when laid, must be accompanied by a certificate from the Minister certifying that the preliminary requirements have been complied with. Where there has been no local inquiry, the certificate must contain a statement to that effect.[5] The standing orders[6] require the further

---

1 For an occasion when such a bill was reprinted see CJ (1974–75) 206, 211.
2 For a provisional order bill which was recommitted with an instruction to reinstate an order which had been reported 'Parties do not proceed,' see p 912 and CJ (1913) 305, 337, 354; for a bill recommitted to a select committee, see CJ (1901) 374.
3 Sometimes consideration and third reading are taken on the same day, CJ (1928–29); ibid (1930–31) 157, etc.
4 For examples of suspended provisional order bills, see p 959n (s) and p 960, n (s) of the 18th edn of this work.
5 Statutory Orders (Special Procedure) Act 1945, s 2
6 SO 239 (HC), 205 (HL).

deposit of copies of the order and certificate in the Private Bill Office and Vote Office of the House of Commons and in the Office of the Clerk of the Parliaments. Copies must also be made available to members of the public on application to the Minister unless the order is required to be printed and sold under the Statutory Instruments Act 1946. Unless the Minister has initiated the order, the name and address of the person on whose application the order has been made must be endorsed on all copies of the order which are laid, deposited or made available.

Deposit of plans

If, under a special procedure order, it is proposed to authorize the compulsory acquisition or use of land, or if an order relates to any works or any area of land or water, and the works or area are described by reference to a map or plan, a copy of the map or plan must be deposited in each House when the order is laid.[1]

Petitions relating to orders

Petitions may be presented to either House against the order within a period of twenty-one days[2] beginning with the day on which the order is laid before Parliament, or, if the order is laid on different days before the Houses, from the later of the two days.[3] The Act provides for two types of petition. Petitions praying for particular amendments to be made in the order must specify the amendments and are called petitions for amendment. A petition against the order generally must not be included in a petition for amendment, but may be contained in a separate petition, called a petition of general objection.[4] Petitions of both types are presented by being deposited in the Private Bill Office of the House of Commons or in the Office of the Clerk of the Parliaments. They must be endorsed in accordance with the standing orders and prepared and signed in strict conformity with the rules and orders of each House.[5] Not later than the day following that on which the petition is presented, copies must be deposited in the appropriate office of the other House and at the office of the Minister who laid the original order. Copies must also be delivered or sent by registered post to the applicant or applicants for the order, and made available to any member of the public on application to the petitioner or his agent.[6] Petitions which are duly presented to either House stand referred for examination to the Lord

---

1 SO 239A (HC), 205A (HL).
2 The period was extended from fourteen to twenty-one days by the Statutory Orders (Special Procedure) Act 1965, s 1(2). If this period expires when Parliament is dissolved or prorogued or when either House is adjourned for more than four days, it is extended to expire on the first day thereafter on which the House sits, and a recall of Parliament at a date earlier than that fixed originally at the time the House adjourned does not count for this purpose; SO 247 (HC), 213 (HL).
3 S 3(1).
4 S 3(2).
5 In February 1958 a petition signed by power of attorney against the Derwent Water Order 1957 was certified by the Chairmen as proper to be received.
6 SO 240 (HC), 206 (HL).

Chairman of Committees and the Chairman of Ways and Means.[1] The standing orders relating to the withdrawal of petitions against private bills are applied to the withdrawal of petitions against special procedure orders.[2]

Within a period of seven days beginning with the day on which the petition is presented, the Minister concerned or the applicant for the order may deposit a memorial addressed to the two Chairmen objecting to the petition being certified as proper to be received (see below); or if the petition has been presented as one for amendment, the memorialist may object that it is, in fact, a petition of general objection. Provisions as to further deposits and delivery of copies of the memorial to the petitioner or his agent are set out in the standing orders. Memorials, like petitions, may be withdrawn.[3]

As soon as is practicable after the expiry of the petitioning period, and of the period allowed for memorials objecting to petitions, the two Chairmen are required by section 3(3) of the Act to take into consideration all petitions referred to them, and if they are satisfied that the provisions of the Act and of standing orders have been complied with, they must certify that the petition is proper to be received, and is either a petition for amendment or a petition of general objection.[4]

If a memorial has been duly deposited, the Chairmen must give notice of the time and place at which they will consider the petition and memorial. A similar notice is required, although no memorial has been deposited, if on first consideration they are not satisfied that a petition should be certified as proper to be received, or if it is presented as a petition for amendment and they are not satisfied that it is such.[5] If such a notice is given by the Chairmen, parties have a right to be heard by themselves or their agents at the subsequent meeting for consideration of the petitions and memorials; counsel may not, however, be heard except by leave of the two Houses. The conduct of the meeting is regulated by the Chairmen, who decide according to the circumstances of each case which party should open the proceedings. It is usual for a transcript to be made[6] but not reported to either House.

If in the opinion of the Chairmen a petition presented as a petition for amendment involves amendments such as would constitute a negative of the main purpose of the order, they must, if the petition is otherwise proper to be received, certify it as a petition of general objection, unless the petitioner satisfies them that not all of the amendments are affected by their decision. If so satisfied, the Chairmen may direct the deletion of so much of the petition as requires amendments constituting a negative of the main purpose of the order, and certify the remainder of the petition as a petition for amendment.[7]

---

1 Under SO 238, the Chairman of Ways and Means can delegate his powers to a deputy. This course was adopted when the Chairman was himself a petitioner against an order, HC Deb (1958–59) 606, c 1355. See also p 827.
2 SO 245 (HC), 211 (HL).
3 Ibid.
4 The Chairmen have declined to certify a petition as proper to be received, on the ground that the standing order requiring the deposit of a copy of the petition with the Minister and the applicant had not been complied with, CJ (1952–53) 318, LJ (1952–53) 291. They have also declined to certify a petition in which the petitioners did not pray to be heard, CJ (1980–81) 480.
5 SO 242 (HC), 208 (HL).
6 The cost of shorthand-writing is apportioned, half the attendance fee and half the cost of the transcript being borne by the two Houses and the other costs by the memorialist.
7 S 3(4).

A memorialist objecting to petitions against the Mid-Northamptonshire Water Board Order 1948, based part of his objection on the ground that the sum total of the amendments required by several individual petitions were such as to constitute a negative of the main purpose of the order; it was accordingly claimed that each individual petition should be certified as one of general objection. The two Chairmen nevertheless certified the petitions as petitions for amendment. Similar arguments were addressed to the Chairmen on behalf of the Minister of Housing and Local Government in objecting, on memorial, to petitions against the Wolverhampton Water Order 1958. In this case, the petitioners sought to substitute a joint water board for the merging of one water authority in another, as the order proposed. The amendments would have involved serving new notices on those affected. The two Chairmen nonetheless certified the petitions as petitions for amendment.

Power is given to the Chairmen to determine questions of locus standi in connection with their examination of special procedure petitions.[1]

The Chairmen are required by the Procedure Act to report to both Houses on petitions against every special procedure order. Their report must state whether any petitions have been received against the order; and if petitions have been so received they must set out which petitions, if any, have been certified as proper to be received, and whether each petition has been certified as a petition for amendment or a petition of general objection.

Where the Chairmen have certified a petition against an order as a petition for amendment, a counter-petition may be presented within fourteen days of the Chairmen's report to both Houses. Such counter-petitions have a function similar to petitions against alterations in the case of private bills, and are in the form of a complaint that an amendment or amendments prayed for in a petition against the order will affect the interest of the person presenting the counter-petition. They are presented to the House to which the original petition complained of has been presented, by being deposited in the Private Bill Office of the Commons, or the Office of the Clerk of the Parliaments in the Lords. Counter-petitions must be prepared and signed in strict conformity with the rules and orders of each House. There are equivalent requirements under the standing orders, as with petitions, regarding endorsements, further deposits, delivery of copies and withdrawals.[2] Counter-petitions are not referred to the two Chairmen for examination.

It is not necessary for a counter-petitioner to present separate petitions against each of the petitions to which he wishes to object.[3]

Proceedings following Chairmen's report

Within a period of twenty-one days[4] beginning with the date on which the report of the two Chairmen is laid, any Member of either House may move, after notice, that the order be annulled. Such motions in the Commons are

---

1 S 9(d); SO 242(3) (HC), 208(3) (HL) and see p 848, n (2).
2 SO 244, 245 (HC), 210, 211 (HL).
3 Two counter-petitions were presented against petitions for amendment of the Derwent Water Order 1957, one objecting to two of the petitions and the other to three of the petitions, see Private Business 26 February 1958.
4 In reckoning this period no account is taken of any time during which Parliament is dissolved or prorogued or during which both Houses are adjourned for more than four days; s 4.

exempted business and may be entered upon after ten o'clock, even though opposed (see p 243). If a motion for annulment is carried, the order thereupon becomes void, and no further proceedings may be taken thereon.[1] A new order may, however, be laid afresh before Parliament.

If neither House has resolved that the order be annulled within the period of twenty-one days of the Chairmen's report, the further progress of the order depends upon the state of petitions, if any, against the order. If the Chairmen have certified any petitions as proper to be received, and if neither House has resolved that the petition or petitions of general objection (if any) be not referred to a joint committee,[2] a committee stage will be required. If no such petitions are outstanding, the order comes into operation at the expiry of the twenty-one day period mentioned above, or on such later date as may be specified in the order.[3]

Under the Procedure Act, there is no method of inserting an agreed amendment in a special procedure order once that order has been laid before Parliament, without recourse to the machinery of a joint committee.[4]

Joint committee stage

The circumstances in which a committee stage may be required have been described above. The only committee that is competent under the Procedure Act is a joint committee of both Houses. It must consist of six members, three from each House, nominated by the Chairman of Committees in the Lords in pursuance of Standing Order 95 and by the Committee of Selection in the Commons. To this committee there stand referred:

(1) All petitions for amendment duly certified by the Chairmen.[5]
(2) All petitions of general objection duly certified by the Chairmen and not withheld by either House.[6]
(3) All counter-petitions duly deposited.[7]

By the standing orders of both Houses,[8] the petitioner is entitled to be heard before the committee by himself, his counsel or agent. A similar entitlement is given to the Minister responsible for the order, or, in certain circumstances, the applicant for the order. An applicant may be heard in lieu of the Minister, if the Minister gives due notice[9] that he desires his rights in this respect to be exercised by the applicant, who must be specified in the notice. Counter-petitioners, however, have not an automatic right to be heard, but may be heard by themselves, their counsel or agent, only if the

---

1 S 4(3).
2 For an example of such a resolution, see CJ (1975–76) 381.
3 S 4(3).
4 When all the parties were agreed that effect should be given to a petition for amendment of the Maidstone (Extension) Order 1954, the order was withdrawn and a new amended order was laid by the Minister, CJ (1953–54) 119, 331; LJ (1953–54) 116, 126, 351. See also minutes of evidence on the Bolton Water Order 1962, 29 January 1963, where the Joint Committee held that it was precluded from inserting an amendment altering the date of operation of the Order.
5 S 4(2).
6 S 4(1) and 4(2).
7 SO 244(1) (HC), 210(1) (HL).
8 SO 243(1) (HC), 209(1) (HL).
9 In accordance with the terms of SO 243(2) (HC), 209(2) (HL).

committee is satisfied that an amendment prayed for by the original petition may affect the interest of the counter-petitioner.[1] The minutes of evidence taken before the committee are required to be reported to both Houses.[2]

The procedure of the committee follows that of a joint committee on a private bill (see pp 887–888), so far as such procedure is relevant, and subject to the following important considerations.

Since it is the petitions themselves which are primarily referred to the committee, the order stands referred only for the purpose of the consideration of the petitions.[3] In consequence, the onus of proof lies not upon the promoters of the order to establish its necessity, but upon the petitioners to prove the facts of their case. After a short explanatory statement by counsel for the minister or applicant, therefore, the proceedings in committee have been opened by counsel for each of the petitioners in turn, and they are followed by counsel for the minister or applicant. If the minister or applicant calls evidence, the petitioner may call further evidence in rebuttal on which the minister or applicant may comment, but the petitioner has in all cases a right of reply.[4]

The explanatory statement must, by Standing Order 244, be agreed between the parties beforehand.[5] If not so agreed, it is dispensed with and the petitioner opens the proceedings. The explanatory statement may also be dispensed with in the case of petitions of general objection, since the petition being against the whole of the order, the latter is fully explained by counsel for the petitioner in making his case against it.[6]

It would appear from the specific language of Standing Orders 209 (HL) and 242(3) (HC) and from the power given to the Chairmen by the Act and the standing orders regarding the determination of locus standi questions, that it is not open to the committee to entertain any objections as to the locus of any petitioners. There would appear to be no bar to a similar objection before the committee in respect of counter-petitioners, but, since they have not in any event an absolute right of audience, such an objection would merely be one of the factors on which the committee would base its decision whether to hear the counter-petitioners.

The committee is empowered to report an order either without amendment or with such amendments as it thinks expedient to give effect, either in whole or in part, to any petition for amendment referred to it, and with such consequential amendments, if any, as it may think proper.[7] If the committee is satisfied that effect ought to be given to a petition of general objection, it is

---

1 SO 244(5) (HC), 210(5) (HL). For occasions when counter-petitioners have been heard, see minutes of evidence of Joint Committee on the Mid-Northamptonshire Water Board Order 1948, p 2–7, and of the Joint Committee on the Wolverhampton Water Order 1958. See also minutes of evidence on the Derwent Water Order 1957, where the case, after a brief opening statement on behalf of the Minister making the order, was left by him to be fought between the counter-petitioners and the petitioners.
2 SO 243(3) (HC), 209(1)(d) (HL).
3 S 5(1).
4 SO 243.
5 See Minutes of Evidence of Joint Committee on petitions against the Herefordshire Water Order 1959, and cf ibid on petition against the Newhaven and District (No 1) Water Order 1962. (No statement agreed).
6 See Minutes of Evidence of Joint Committee on petition against the Great Ouse River Board (Old West Internal Drainage District) Order 1952, pp 1–4.
7 S 5(1).

empowered by the Procedure Act to report the order with amendments, notwithstanding that the petition is one of general objection.[1]

If after considering a petition of general objection, the committee is of opinion that the order ought not to take effect, it is required to report that the order be not approved.[2]

The Act provides that subject to standing orders (which are silent upon the point), the report of a joint committee in respect of any special procedure order (including any special report which such a committee may decide to make[3]) shall be laid before both Houses of Parliament.

Operation of orders

Special procedure orders come into operation as follows:

Where there has been no joint committee. If there has been no joint committee and neither House has resolved that the order be annulled during the resolution period, the order comes into operation on the expiry of the resolution period, or on such later date as may be specified in the order (see p 960).

Where an order is reported by a joint committee without amendment. Where an order is reported by a joint committee without amendment, it comes into operation on the date on which the report of the committee is laid before both Houses, or on such later date as may be specified in the order.[4]

Where an order is reported by a joint committee with amendments. Where an order is reported by a joint committee with amendments, if the responsible Minister considers that it should take effect as so amended, the order, as amended, is brought into operation on such date as the Minister may determine by giving notice thereof in the manner prescribed by the standing orders.[5]

If the Minister considers that it is inexpedient to bring into effect an order which has been amended by a joint committee, he may withdraw the order by giving notice in the manner prescribed by the standing orders. A copy of this notice must be laid before both Houses within four days from its publication.[6] Where a joint committee has reported that an order be not approved, the order may not, in any event, take effect unless confirmed by Act (see below).

PROCEDURE IN PARLIAMENT ON BILLS TO CONFIRM SPECIAL PROCEDURE ORDERS

Standing Orders 156A (HC), relating to the relaxation of financial practice (see pp 869–870) and 191 (HC), relating to the relaxation of Commons'

---

1 S 5(2).
2 S 5(2).
3 Eg Special report of the Joint Committee on the Exeter-Launceston-Bodmin Trunk Road (Okehampton By-pass) Compulsory Purchase Orders 1984, CJ (1984–85) 365, LJ (1984–85) 254.
4 S 6(1).
5 S 6(2); SO 248(1) (HC), 214(1) (HL). The standing orders require notice to be given, according to the circumstances, in the *London Gazette*, the *Edinburgh Gazette*, and local newspapers.
6 SO 248(2) (HC), 214(2) (HL).

privileges (see p 828), are applied to all bills to confirm special procedure orders.[1] There is no requirement as to the special clause to be inserted under the provisions of Standing Order 156B (HC).

Bills to confirm orders amended by a joint committee

Where an order has been amended by a joint committee, the responsible Minister may, instead of withdrawing it, submit it to Parliament in a confirming bill. The bill must set out the order as amended in committee and is treated as a public bill. After presentation, however, there is no second reading or committee stage; the bill proceeds immediately to the report stage when amendments may be moved, and is thereafter read the third time. It is then sent to the second House where a similar procedure is followed.[2]

Bills to confirm orders which a joint committee has rejected

Where a joint committee has reported that an order be not approved, a bill may be presented for its confirmation. The order is here set out in the bill as it was referred to the committee, and the bill is treated in all its stages as if it were a public bill. Its future course differs according to whether there are any outstanding duly certified petitions for amendment of the order.

Where there are outstanding petitions for amendment

Where a duly certified petition for amendment has not been dealt with by the joint committee, the bill after presentation is read the second time and referred to the original joint committee for consideration of the petition. After being reported from the committee, it is considered on report and read the third time. In the second House, it is deemed to have passed all stages up to and including committee.[3]

Where there are no petitions for amendment outstanding

Where no such petition has been so certified, the bill receives only a report and third reading stage in either House.[4]

SPECIAL PROCEDURE ORDERS RELATING ONLY TO SCOTLAND

An attempt has been made to assimilate the procedure on orders relating only to Scotland, so far as possible, to that followed under the Private Legislation Procedure (Scotland) Act 1936 (see chapter 39). There are, therefore, considerable differences in procedure from special procedure orders relating to England and Wales,[5] most of which affect the progress of the order before its presentation.

---

1 SO 248A (HC).
2 S 6(4). For an example see proceedings on the Mid-Northamptonshire Water Board Order Confirmation (Special Procedure) Bill 1949.
3 S 6(5)(a).
4 S 6(5)(b). For an example see proceedings on the Okehampton By-pass (Confirmation of Orders) Bill 1985–86, HC Deb (1985–86) 86, c 710, 87, cc 36, 140–223.
5 These differences are set out in s 10 of the Statutory Orders (Special Procedure) Act 1945.

Procedure on orders before presentation

Before any such order is made or confirmed by the responsible Minister (who will usually be the Secretary of State for Scotland), the requirements of the enabling Act with respect to the service of notices must be complied with, and further notices must be inserted in the Edinburgh Gazette.[1] The latter notices must specify the time within which, and the manner in which, objections may be made to the application or to the proposed order. If any objection is duly made and not withdrawn (other than an objection which the Minister considers frivolous or which relates to a matter which can be dealt with by an arbiter by whom compensation is assessable), or if for any reason the Minister considers an inquiry necessary, an inquiry is directed to be held by Commissioners under the Private Legislation Procedure (Scotland) Act 1936 and the provisions of that Act, with minor variations, apply to the subsequent inquiry.[2] The provisions of the Act which apply to the making of general orders are extended to cover the making of general orders to regulate the proceedings of such inquiries.

If the Minister is not prepared to accept the recommendations of the Commissioners on the order, he may present to Parliament a bill for the confirmation of the order. The further proceedings on a bill of this nature are governed by section 9 of the Scottish Procedure Act (see p 973).

A statement by the Minister must accompany any order or bill laid before, or presented to, Parliament. This statement, which is in lieu of the certificate accompanying orders not extending solely to Scotland, must specify any objections made to the order and not withdrawn; it must also state whether an inquiry has been held, and, if no inquiry has been held, what objections there were, if any, which in the opinion of the Minister were frivolous or related to matters which could be dealt with by an arbiter.

Procedure on orders after presentation

Following their presentation to Parliament, the procedure on Scottish orders is the same as for English or Welsh orders. It should be noticed that the Minister has two opportunities of introducing a confirming bill for an order extending to Scotland only: he may introduce a bill if dissatisfied with the recommendations of the Commissioners, and he may also bring in a bill if the order is amended or reported as not approved by a joint committee of both Houses.

FEES AND TAXATION OF COSTS[3]

The standing orders of both Houses prescribe the fees to be paid on the various stages both of provisional order bills and special procedure orders. For proceedings before the Court of Referees or any committee of either House the same fees are charged to applicants for provisional order bills and opponents of them as are charged for private bills. For the powers of the taxing officer of the House of Commons in relation to provisional order bills and special procedure orders, see p 838.

---

1 And in certain circumstances, in a local newspaper; see s 10(2).
2 For these inquiries see pp 969–971.
3 For the power of committees to award costs see pp 913–915.

CHAPTER 39

Private legislation procedure (Scotland)

The Private Legislation Procedure (Scotland) Act 1936 provides the machinery and prescribes the method by which parties must now proceed when they desire 'to obtain parliamentary powers in regard to any matter affecting public or private interests in Scotland for which they would have been entitled, before the commencement of the Private Legislation Procedure (Scotland) Act of 1899 to apply by a petition for leave to bring in a private bill'. The 1936 Act, which may conveniently be referred to as the 'Procedure Act', consolidates and supersedes the original Private Legislation Procedure (Scotland) Act of 1899 and an amending Act of 1933. Under the system so set up, instead of presenting a petition for a private bill, parties 'shall proceed'—to quote the directions of the Procedure Act—'by presenting a petition to the Secretary of State, praying him to issue a provisional order in accordance with the terms of a draft order submitted to him or with such modifications as shall be necessary'.[1]

Scope of Procedure Act

The special procedure upon orders under the Procedure Act, and upon the bills for their confirmation, differs from the procedure upon the ordinary provisional orders and provisional order bills described in the last chapter, because its object is to provide an inquiry in Scotland, instead of at Westminster, before commissioners taken from a panel primarily parliamentary, and at the same time to preserve in the two Houses of Parliament the final control of the legislative proposals. There is, moreover, an important difference of scope. The objects that can be obtained through an ordinary provisional order are confined, by the particular enabling Act under which it is granted, within very specifically defined limits; but the objects to be obtained through an order under the Procedure Act comprise almost every matter in Scotland in regard to which parties are entitled to seek parliamentary powers by the means of a private bill. The only objects expressly excepted are specified in section 16 of the Act, which provides that the Act 'shall not apply to estate bills', and shall not

> affect the right of any person to apply for or the power of the Board of Trade or the Minister of Transport, or the Electricity Commissioners, or any other department to make or confirm provisional or other orders under the provisions of any Act for the time being in force and passed prior to the twenty-ninth day of July 1933, or the procedure therein specified.

---

1 S 1(1); for the development of this procedure, see the Select Committee's Report on the Private Bill Procedure (Scotland) Bill, HC 307 (1898), especially the evidence of Lord Balfour of Burleigh and cf Report and Minutes of Evidence of the Select Committee on the Private Legislation Procedure (Wales) Bill, HC 243, Q 1165 (1904). As to local authorities promoting or opposing orders etc, under the Act, see s 11, which embodies, in the process of consolidation, the repealed s 2 of the County Councils (Bills in Parliament) Act 1903.

Private legislation affecting 'Scotland and elsewhere'

Under section 1(4) of the Procedure Act, promoters may make a representation to the Secretary of State that they 'desire to obtain parliamentary powers to be operative in Scotland and elsewhere, and that it is expedient that such powers should be conferred by one enactment by reason of the fact that it is necessary to provide for the uniform regulation of the affairs of an undertaking or institution carried on or operating in Scotland and elsewhere'. Thereupon the Secretary of State and the Chairmen consider the representation and, if of opinion that the powers (or some of them) would more properly be obtained by promoting a private bill than by the duplicate process of a bill for England and a draft order for Scotland, they notify their decision in the London and Edinburgh Gazettes, and they report it to Parliament. When this is done, the restriction in section 1(1) of the Procedure Act ceases to apply as regards any powers to which the decision relates.[1] Standing orders ensure that the representation under section 1(4) is submitted to the Secretary of State in good time before the deposit of the bill.[2]

The 'General Orders'

The provisions of the Procedure Act are supplemented, and the proceedings under it regulated in detail, by a number of 'general orders' made (in accordance with its provisions) by the Chairman of Committees of the House of Lords and the Chairman of Ways and Means in the House of Commons, acting jointly with the Secretary of State, and laid before Parliament.[3] As the main purpose of the Act is to provide, for promoters in Scotland, a special machinery and procedure to replace the proceedings on a private bill in its preliminary and committee stages, these general orders will be found to correspond very largely to the standing orders of both Houses by which those stages are governed. The notices, deposits, and other preliminary requirements are, generally speaking, the same;[4] and, in practice, the parliamentary Examiners appointed under standing orders act as the Examiners assigned for the purposes of the Act.[5] Provision is also made for the incorporation, in any provisional order under the Act, of those general Acts or clauses which would be incorporated in it if it were a private bill.[6]

1 S 1(4). In view of s 1(1) it might be argued that there is a presumption that a private bill does not extend to Scotland unless expressed so to extend; if therefore, in pursuance of s 1(4), a bill is to extend to Scotland as well as England, it may be well that it should state expressly that it shall so extend. See s 22 of the Methodist Church Act 1939; see also s 4 of the Royal Society for the Prevention of Cruelty to Animals Act 1940, though it may be doubtful whether the latter Act falls within s 1(1) of the Procedure Act ('in regard to any matter affecting public or private interests in Scotland').
2 SO 231 (HC), 193 (HL). For cases when this provision has been set aside as to time, see CJ (1968–69) 33; ibid (1971–72) 101. In the case of the United Reformed Church Bill 1980, no such representation having been submitted before the deposit of the bill, the promoters subsequently made their representation in respect of a petition for additional provision.
3 S 15, 18.
4 GO 4–64. By GO 118 and 119, the provisions both of the Parliamentary Documents Deposit Act 1837, as to documents deposited under the standing orders, and, mutatis mutandis, of the Parliamentary Deposits Act 1846, as to money deposits in relation to private bills, are made applicable to the documents similarly deposited and to the money deposits similarly required under the general orders.
5 S 13; GO 1.
6 S 15(2); GO 117.

Application for a provisional order

Petitions for the issue of a provisional order must be deposited at the Scottish Office, London, together with a draft of the proposed order, on or before 27 November, or on or before 27 March.[1] A copy of the draft order must also be deposited with the Clerk of the Parliaments, the Private Bill Office of the House of Commons, the Treasury and other prescribed public offices.[2]

Petitions against

Petitions against a proposed provisional order, except those of dissentient petitioners (ie petitioners who have dissented at any meeting called in pursuance of General Order 75), must be deposited not later than six weeks after 11 December or 11 April, ie the final dates for the publication of notices.[3]

Report by the Chairmen (Lords and Commons)

When the extent of opposition offered to the proposed provisional orders has thus been indicated, the draft orders applied for are taken into consideration, and are reported upon, by the Chairman of Committees of the House of Lords and the Chairman of Ways and Means in the House of Commons,[4] who throughout the Act are referred to as 'the Chairmen'.[5] The Chairmen's report upon each of the draft orders is made to the Secretary of State, and a copy is laid before Parliament.[6] If in the opinion of the Chairmen the provisions or some provisions of a draft order 'relate to matters outside Scotland to such an extent, or raise questions of public policy of such novelty and importance that they ought to be dealt with by private bill and not by provisional order'[7] they report their objection; thereupon the Secretary of State must without further inquiry refuse to issue the provisional order (or the portion of it) to which objection is thus taken. In that event, however, it is open to the promoters to proceed by way of a private bill—described as a 'substituted bill'—for those powers which, by reason of the Chairmen's objection under section 2(2) of the Act, they are debarred from seeking through their proposed provisional order.[8]

When considering the draft orders and making their report to the Secretary of State, the Chairmen are empowered by section 2(1) of the Act to

---

1 GO 2.
2 S 1(2); GO 38, 39.
3 GO 75. The time is extended for any dissentient at the 'Wharncliffe' meeting (see pp 865–868) held under GO 58–63, who would otherwise be precluded from presenting a petition in time. Provision is also made (in GO 77) for petitioners who complain of matters arising subsequently during an inquiry held under the Act.
4 The Act provides that 'with a view to such report', the Secretary of State shall forthwith inform the Chairmen of any objections, etc, that have been duly made to the provisions of an order, s 2(1).
5 They are so described in s 1(4) and in SO 225 (HC) and 187 (HL).
6 S 2(1), (3); SO 227 (HC), 189 (HL).
7 S 2(2). The Chairmen have reported that a draft provisional order ought to be introduced as a public bill, see Post Office Site (Glasgow) Order, CJ (1908) 37 (cf Post Office Site (Glasgow) Act 1908); and Church of Scotland Order, CJ (1930–31) 309.
8 S 2(4); SOs 225, 232 (HC), 187, 194 (HL). Where the Chairmen have reported that part only of a provisional order applied for should proceed as such, promoters can proceed with that part accordingly and embody the rest of their original scheme in a private bill. In some instances they have not elected to promote a bill in substitution for the part of their proposed order to which the Chairmen have objected, Off J 1902–3, p 28, 1903–4, p 24, 1940–46, p 81 and 1953–54, p 19.

determine all matters of practice and procedure.[1] In practice they invite the deposit, by a specified date, of representations relevant to a possible objection on their part under section 2(2). If representations are made, the Chairmen hear the agents for the parties making representations and the agents for the promoters in reply.

Procedure for promotion of substituted bills

The promoters are required to communicate their intentions within a prescribed time to all opponents and must satisfy the Examiners that they have duly done so.[2] If they decide to proceed with a substituted bill, they must deposit copies of the bill in every public office where they had previously been obliged to deposit copies of their proposed provisional order.[3] They must also satisfy the Examiner that the bill so deposited does not contain any provisions not contained in the order for which it is substituted;[4] and they must give any additional notices that may be required in connection with it under the standing orders.[5] Subject to these conditions, however, the notices and deposits for the proposed order are held to have been served and made for the substituted bill, compliance or non-compliance with the preliminary general orders being regarded as equivalent to compliance or non-compliance with the corresponding standing orders.[6] The petition for the proposed provisional order is taken as the petition for the substituted bill. The petitions deposited against, or in favour of, the draft order are transmitted from the Scottish Office, London, and are received by the House in which the bill originates as petitions against, or in favour of, the substituted bill;[7] the relevant standing order of the House of Lords adds that no petitions relating to bills originating in that House, other than petitions so deposited, may be received. Petitions against, or in favour of, the bill in the second House follow the normal rules for petitions against private bills (see pp 840 and 934). The Chairmen determine, as with private bills, in which House the substituted bill is to originate;[8] and its subsequent course is identical with that of a private bill. Where the order, for the whole or a part of which a bill is substituted, is one of those applied for on or before 27 March, it is competent for the promoters to deposit their substituted bill on or before the ensuing 27 November;[9] but most substituted bills so applied for have been introduced and passed, either with or without a suspension of the standing orders, before the ordinary time of prorogation.[10] Substituted bills have been suspended until the following session in the same way as private bills.[11]

---

1 SO 226 (HC), 188 (HL).
2 S 2(4); GO 75; SO 233 (HC), 195 (HL).
3 SO 232 (HC), 194 (HL).
4 SO 234 (HC), 196 (HL).
5 S 2(4).
6 SO 233 (HC), 195 (HL).
7 SO 235 (HC), 197 (HL).
8 CJ (1903) 16; ibid (1904) 31, etc
9 SO 232 (HC), 194 (HL). And cf. the proceedings on the Hutcheson's Hospital and Hutcheson's Educational Trust Bill (in substitution for a provisional order applied for on or before 17 April 1903), LJ (1903) 157; ibid (1904) 18, 21; Off J 1903–4, p 24. Cf also proceedings on the Ross and Cromarty County Council Bill 1974–75.
10 Eg Loch Leven Water Power Bill 1901, CJ (1901) 201, 206, 334, 420; Scottish Ontario etc Company Bill 1903, ibid (1903) 208, 291, 376, 412, etc.
11 Zetland County Council Bill, CJ (1972–73) 436, ibid (1973–74) 159–160.

Proceedings before Examiner on proposed provisional order

Every draft order as originally applied for is referred by the Secretary of State to the Examiners, one or other of whom reports to him and to the Chairmen whether the 'preliminary' general orders have or have not been complied with. In the case of a non-compliance the Examiner also reports to the Chairmen the grounds for his decision;[1] and, within a prescribed time, it is competent for the promoters to apply by memorial to the Chairmen praying them to dispense with any general order with which they have failed to comply. The Chairmen's decision (to grant or refuse this dispensation) is final; and if, in granting a dispensation, they attach any conditions to it, the draft order cannot be proceeded with until the Examiner has reported that these conditions have been satisfied.[2]

Issue of provisional order

When the Chairmen have reported that a proposed provisional order may proceed, and there has been a due compliance with the general orders, the Secretary of State takes the application for the order into consideration.[3]

Proceedings on orders on which an inquiry is held

If a provisional order is opposed,[4] or if the Secretary of State considers that inquiry is necessary even though there is no opposition, he directs an inquiry (into the propriety of making and issuing the provisional order applied for) to be held by commissioners sitting in Scotland.[5]

Appointment of commissioners for inquiry. The commissioners appointed on these inquiries are drawn from three panels formed under the Act. Two of these are 'parliamentary' panels, and consist of not more than fifteen Members of the House of Lords selected and proposed by the Chairman of Committees, and not more than twenty-five Members of the House of Commons selected and proposed by the Committee of Selection.[6] The third or 'extra-parliamentary' panel is nominated every five years by the Chairmen and the Secretary of State, and consists of twenty 'persons qualified by experience of affairs to act as commissioners'; and any casual vacancy occurring in this extra-parliamentary panel is filled by the Chairmen acting

1 GO 67.
2 S 3(2); GO 68.
3 S 3(1).
4 No provisional order is considered as opposed unless the petitions against it (see p 967) have been properly deposited, GO 75.
5 S 3(1). In 1901 an inquiry was directed to be held on the Arizona Copper Company Ltd, provisional order, although (no petition having been duly presented against it) it was not an opposed order, Off J 1900–1, pp 3, 12, 38; HC 243, Q 126 (1904). Similarly, in 1988, the Secretary of State directed an inquiry to be held in relation to the City of Glasgow District Council Order, notwithstanding the fact that the only remaining petition was withdrawn shortly before the inquiry was due to commence. The inquiry on two opposed provisional orders in 1902 was deferred and was not directed to be held until 1904, Off J 1901–2, pp 25, 89; Parl Deb (1902) 109, cc 1179–1185; PLR ii, 48, and iv, 29, 61. The time and place of each inquiry are fixed by the chairman of the commissioners appointed to hold it, due notice being given to the parties concerned, s 6(1); GO 74; and cf HC 243, Qs 961, 2638–9 (1904).
6 S 5(2); SO 228 (HC), 190 (HL).

jointly with the Secretary of State.[1] When an inquiry is directed to be held on a proposed order or group of orders, the Chairmen of both Houses constitute a commission for the purpose by selecting four Members from the two parliamentary panels, taking two Members, when it is found feasible to do so, from the panel of each House, and nominating one of the four as chairman of the commissioners.[2] If the Chairmen of both Houses are unable to appoint all the commissioners for an inquiry from the two parliamentary panels, recourse is then had to the third or extra-parliamentary panel, the Secretary of State taking from it sufficient Members to make up the required number of commissioners.[3] If a casual vacancy occurs in the chairmanship or among the members of a commission, the Secretary of State is empowered to fill it from any of the three panels.[4]

Proceedings before commission on inquiry. The proceedings before a commission are analogous to those before a private bill committee in either House of Parliament. The commissioners are similarly restricted from inquiring into matters to be proved before the Examiner,[5] and are required to sign similar declarations before proceeding to business.[6] The manner in which particular classes of undertakings or proposals are to be dealt with and reported upon is similarly conditioned and prescribed;[7] and the rules for the attendance, voting, and adjournment of the commissioners,[8] and for the 'filled up' and the signed copy of the order, etc[9] are the same *mutatis mutandis* as for a private bill committee. Any recommendations made by the Chairmen of both Houses, or by any Minister of the Crown, with regard to a proposed order, are always referred to the commissioners and must be mentioned in their report; and the commissioners may, if they think fit, hear an officer of the department concerned in explanation of any ministerial report.[10] If the commissioners do not agree with a recommendation contained in any ministerial report they must state in their report to the Secretary of State their reasons for dissenting from it.[11] The commissioners must also report whether they have inquired into the allegations of each provisional order referred to them, and, if the preamble has been amended, they must report the amendment, the grounds for making it and whether the allegations contained in the preamble have been found to be true.[12]

In addition, the commissioners are empowered to enforce the attendance of witnesses and the production of papers.[13] Any person who has petitioned

1 S 4, and cf Off J 1904–5, p 29.
2 S 5(1), (3). If need be, three or all of the commissioners may be members of the same parliamentary panel; see s 5(4).
3 S 5(5), which also suggests that circumstances might arise in which all the commissioners might be taken from the extra-parliamentary panel; such a course would in practice be unlikely and indeed, if possible, would be avoided; Off J 1964–65, p 19; ibid 1984, p 11.
4 S 5(6), and cf Off J 1913–14, p 27. The occurrence of a dissolution of Parliament does not debar any member of the parliamentary panels from continuing to act in an inquiry on which he has already been appointed as a commissioner, s 5(7).
5 GO 87.
6 S 5(8); GO 79.
7 GO 98–99, 102, 104–115.
8 S 10(5), (6); GO 80–84, 86.
9 GO 85, 95.
10 S 6(4); GO 93; cf also s 17; Off J 1964–65, p 20; ibid 1985, p 6.
11 S 6(4); GO 93.
12 GO 91.
13 S 10; GO 78.

in the prescribed manner is entitled to appear in opposition to an order;[1] but the commissioners, whose decision on any question of locus standi is final, may not allow a locus to any person who is not thus entitled to be heard, except upon special grounds and subject, at the commissioners' discretion, to the payment of costs or to other conditions.[2]

Report of commissioners. The commissioners must sit, as far as possible, from day to day till their inquiry is finished. They then report to the Secretary of State,[3] recommending that the order should be issued as prayed for, or that it should be issued with modifications,[4] or that it should be refused. If they report that the order should not be made, the Secretary of State must refuse to issue it; otherwise he makes the order as prayed for, or with whatever modifications may appear to be necessary having regard to the recommendation of the commissioners, of the two Chairmen, and of any Minister of the Crown.[5]

Proceedings on order on which no inquiry is held

If there is no opposition to a proposed order (or opposition has been formally withdrawn before an inquiry has been held),[6] and if the Secretary of State does not consider an inquiry necessary, he makes the order as prayed for, or 'with such modifications as shall appear to be necessary having regard to' recommendations from the Chairmen and from Ministers of the Crown. But in dealing with a draft order on which no inquiry is held, he is to 'have regard to' the instructions which the general orders give to a commission in the case of an inquiry; and the promoters, on due notice being given them, must appear before him or his representative to give whatever proofs, and to produce whatever evidence or documents, may be required in regard to their proposed order.[7]

Procedure on provisional orders when modified

Wherever any modifications are made in any draft order as originally applied for,[8] the order is referred again, in its modified form, to the Examiners in the same manner as the original draft order.[9] And before finally making and issuing an order as modified, the Secretary of State must cause copies of it to be deposited, for not less than fourteen days, in the Office of the Clerk of the Parliaments and the Private Bill Office of the House of Commons, at the Treasury, and at all the offices where the draft order was

---

1 S 6(3); GO 76, 77.
2 S 6(2); GO 91; Off J 1900–1, p 45. Cf PLR i, 60, 61; HC 243, Q 333 (1904). See s 6(6) and SR & O 1946 (No 2170) for the Scale of Costs Order made thereunder.
3 S 6(5).
4 When they report that an order should be issued with modifications—the most common case—they must submit a copy of the order showing the modifications they recommend: s 6(5); Off J 1965–66, p 18.
5 S 8(1).
6 GO 78A; Off J 1900–1, p 76; ibid 1953–54, p 39; ibid 1965–66, p 5.
7 S 7; GO 73 and 116.
8 S 1, 7, 8(1); GO 68.
9 GO 68. The Examiners then report 'No further General Orders applicable', or 'Further General Orders complied with' or 'not complied with', as the case may be. Cf Off J 1904–5, pp 37, 65, etc.

originally deposited, and must again have regard to any recommendations that may be made by the Chairmen and Ministers of the Crown.[1]

Procedure upon bills to confirm orders

The confirmation bill, requisite to give validity to any provisional order under the Act, is presented to Parliament as soon as practicable after the order is made and issued,[2] notice being given as for other provisional order bills. Bills for confirming provisional orders, like private bills, may be set down by the Chairman of Ways and Means for debate on second reading or later stages at seven o'clock.[3] The Act creates a cardinal distinction, in respect of their passage through Parliament, between bills for the confirmation of those orders (whether opposed or unopposed) upon which an inquiry by commissioners has been held, and bills to confirm those unopposed orders upon which no inquiry has been held.[4] The bills to confirm orders upon which no inquiry has been held[5] proceed under section 7 of the Act. The bills to confirm orders upon which an inquiry has been held[6] proceed under section 9. Under Standing Order 228A (HC), the following standing orders of the House of Commons are made applicable to bills proceeding both under section 7 and section 9 of the Act: Standing Order 169 (Attachment of financial memoranda to certain bills), Standing Order 191 (Tolls and charges not in the nature of a tax), Standing Order 218 (Proceedings in House on confirming bills), and Standing Order 156A (Modification of practice as to charges on public revenue). The Queen's consent is not required to be signified to bills to confirm orders.

Procedure on bills to confirm orders on which no inquiry has been held (section 7)

A bill presented to confirm any order upon which no inquiry has been held is deemed to have passed all the stages up to and including committee.[7] Consequently, in the House in which the bill originates the order for its consideration is made immediately upon its presentation, and after it has been considered and read the third time, it is sent to the second House in the ordinary way.[8] In the second House a precisely similar course is followed. The order for the consideration stage is made immediately on the bill being brought from the first House, and the subsequent proceedings are the same

---

1 S 7, 8(1); GO 97.
2 S 7, 8(3); and cf Off J 1904–5, p 88. The Secretary of State determines in which House it shall originate, see HC 243, Q 154 (1904).
3 HC Deb (1971–72) 843, cc 213–221; ibid (1973–74) 866, cc 279–330; ibid (1985–86) 88, cc 354–387, 89, cc 72–106.
4 Ss 7, 8(1), 9.
5 Under this description is included any bill to confirm an order which has been referred to and reported from a commission, but with regard to which (owing to the non-appearance of opponents or to other causes) the commissioners have reported that they have not inquired into its allegations. Such a bill, being one to confirm an order upon which no inquiry has been held, proceeds under s 7 of the Act, Glasgow Corporation (Tramways and General) Order Confirmation Bill 1901, CJ (1901) 343.
6 S 8(1).
7 S 7(2).
8 CJ (1985–86) 51, 61, 68, etc.

as upon any ordinary public or provisional order bill.[1] Confirmation bills proceeded with under section 7 have occasionally been amended on consideration.[2]

Procedure on bills to confirm orders on which inquiry has been held (section 9)

The procedure for a bill to confirm any order upon which an inquiry has been held is prescribed by section 9 of the Act.[3] A bill of this description, on being presented in the House in which it originates, is read the first time in the ordinary way; but immediately after presentation, an opportunity is given for a petition to be presented, which may lead to a further inquiry being held by a parliamentary committee. If no petition is then presented, it would appear that no opportunity is subsequently given during the passage of the bill through Parliament of referring it to a committee.[4]

Committal of bill to a joint committee

The Procedure Act provides that if, within seven days after the presentation in the first House of a bill on which an inquiry has been held, a petition is presented against any order comprised in the bill,[5] a Member or Lord may then give notice of a motion to refer the bill to a joint committee of both Houses.[6] Where a petition is presented against the order, therefore, it rests with the House in which the confirmation bill originates to decide whether a further inquiry by a parliamentary committee shall be granted. If a motion for a joint committee is made and carried in that House, the bill stands referred to a joint committee of both Houses of Parliament.[7] The opponent, subject to the practice of Parliament, may then appear and oppose by himself, his counsel or agent; and counsel or agent may be heard in support of the order.

Constitution and procedure of joint committee. The joint committee so appointed consists of six members, three from each House, the Lords members being named by the Chairman of Committees in pursuance of Standing Order 95 and the Commons members being nominated by the

1 CJ (1984–85) 626, 639, 642.
2 CJ (1935–36) 116; CJ (1979–80) 122.
3 By s 16(1) of the Act, the procedure prescribed in s 9 is also made applicable, 'with the necessary modifications', to bills for the confirmation of orders made by the Secretary of State under the Acts passed prior to 1899. These bills have proceeded under s 9 of the Act except that they have been referred after first reading to the Examiners.
4 See p 974.
5 In practice it has not been usual to include in a confirmation bill more than one order issued under the Act.
6 The time at which such a motion may be made is immediately after the bill is read a second time in the House in which it originated, North British Railway Order Confirmation Bill, CJ (1908) 467. In the House of Commons the motion for a joint committee, if objected to, would be treated as opposed private business (see pp 279–281). Cf CJ (1901) 225, 231 (Arizona Copper Co Ltd Order Confirmation Bill); ibid (1904) 224, 240 (Leith Corporation Tramways, Order Confirmation Bill). For a debate on such a motion, see HC Deb (1950) 477, cc 2550–2566.
7 S 9(1). Leith Corporation Tramways Order Confirmation Bill, CJ (1904) 240, 246; Lothian Region (Edinburgh Western Relief Road) Order Confirmation Bill, CJ (1985–86) 65.

Committee of Selection.[1] The joint committee hears and determines any question of locus standi;[2] and it may by a majority award costs, the taxation and recovery of which are to be secured in the manner prescribed by the Parliamentary Costs Act 1865[3] (see p 913).

Subsequent procedure on bill in first House

The report of the joint committee when made is laid before both Houses of Parliament.[4] If the committee reports that the order ought to be confirmed, the bill is ordered, if amended, for consideration—or, if not amended, for third reading—and is sent in due course to the second House.

Procedure in first House on bills when no joint committee is appointed

If no petition is presented against the order, or if a petition is presented but a motion for a joint committee is either not made or not carried,[5] the confirmation bill in the House in which it originates is deemed to have passed the stage of committee. The order for its consideration is made immediately after its second reading (or after any unsuccessful motion for a joint committee), and after being considered and read the third time the bill is sent to the second House.[6]

Procedure in second House upon bills to confirm order on which an inquiry has been held

The procedure in the second House upon a bill to confirm an order upon which an inquiry has been held differs according to whether a joint committee has or has not been appointed in the first House.

Procedure when joint committee has been appointed in first House. If on a motion made and carried in the first House, the bill has been referred to a joint committee, after being brought from the House in which it originates, it is read the first time and second time. Between these two stages no such length of time need intervene as is necessary in the first House for petitions because a second joint committee cannot be appointed. Thereafter the bill is deemed to have passed the stage of committee, and is ordered to be read the third time.[7]

It may be noted that where such a bill originates in the Lords, no opportunity is provided for amending it (except verbally) during its subsequent passage through the Commons where Standing Order No 75 (Public) forbids any amendments which are not merely verbal on the third reading.

Procedure when joint committee has not been appointed in first House. Where there has been no joint committee in the first House, the

---

1 SO 229 (HC), 191 (HL).
2 S 9(1); PLR iv, 15.
3 S 9(3). Cf Constable, pp 94–95.
4 S 9(2); CJ (1985–86) 220, LJ (1985–86) 186.
5 CJ (1985–86) 90.
6 S 9(4); CJ (1985–86) 90, 186, 187; Votes and Proceedings (1986–87) 27, 28, 29 January 1987.
7 SO 230 (HC), 192 (HL).

second House procedure in the Lords differs somewhat from that in the Commons.

(a) *In the Commons* the bill after being read the first time is ordered to be read a second time, and is deemed to have passed the stage of committee;[1] it is then ordered in consecutive stages to be considered and read the third time.[2]

(b) *In the Lords* the bill after first reading is deemed to have been read a second time and reported from the committee, and is ordered to be considered on report; thereafter it proceeds to its third reading in the normal manner.

As in the previous case no interval is given in the second House for the presentation of petitions, and it would appear that it is not competent for a Member to move that the bill should be referred to a joint committee, although the language of the Act is not entirely clear on this point.[3] In the House of Lords there would, in any event, be no opportunity for such a motion, because, by practice, a separate second reading stage is dispensed with.

---

1 Note by Mr Speaker 10 August 1904.
2 The Edinburgh and District Water Order Confirmation Bill was brought from the Lords on 7 August 1914, and passed through all its stages in the House of Commons on the same day, CJ (1914) 430, HC Deb (1914) 65, c 2146. The stages of consideration and third reading have been taken on the same day, CJ (1923) 324.
3 S 9(4); Parl Deb (1901) 94, c 536; ibid (1901) 97, c 979; ibid (1907) 179, cc 1148–1149; HL Deb (1916) 21, cc 512 and 525–526.

House of Commons standing orders relative to public business (July 1989)

The Speaker

1. Election of the Speaker. (1) Whenever it is necessary to proceed forthwith to the choice of a new Speaker in consequence of Mr Speaker having ceased for any reason to be a Member of this House, the chair shall be taken by that Member, present in the House and not being a Minister of the Crown, who has served for the longest period continuously as a Member of this House.

(2) Whenever it is necessary to proceed to the choice of a new Speaker in consequence of an intimation to Her Majesty by Mr Speaker of his wish to relinquish that office then Mr Speaker shall continue to take the chair and shall perform the duties and exercise the authority of Speaker until a new Speaker has been chosen, whereupon he shall leave the chair and shall cease to perform those duties and to exercise that authority and Mr Speaker Elect shall take the chair accordingly:

Provided that, if when this House proceeds to choose a new Speaker the unavoidable absence of Mr Speaker has been announced, Mr Deputy Speaker shall forthwith leave the chair and the chair shall be taken in accordance with the provisions of paragraph (1) of this order.

(3) A Member taking the chair under the provisions of paragraph (1) of this order shall enjoy all those powers which may be exercised by Mr Speaker during proceedings under paragraph (2) thereof.

(4) When a motion has been made, in accordance with the provisions of this order, that a certain Member do take the chair of this House as Speaker, a question shall be proposed on that motion and the question on any further such motion shall be put as an amendment thereto.

Deputy Speaker and Chairmen

2. Deputy Chairmen. At the commencement of every Parliament, or from time to time, as necessity may arise, the House may appoint two Deputy Chairmen of Ways and Means, who shall be known respectively as the First and the Second Deputy Chairman of Ways and Means, and who shall be entitled to exercise all the powers vested in the Chairman of Ways and Means, including his powers as Deputy Speaker.

3. Deputy Speaker. (1) The Chairman of Ways and Means or a Deputy Chairman shall take the chair as Deputy Speaker, when requested so to do by Mr Speaker, without any formal communication to the House.

(2) Whenever the House shall be informed by the Clerk at the Table of the unavoidable absence or the absence by leave of the House of Mr Speaker,

the Chairman of Ways and Means shall perform the duties and exercise the authority of Mr Speaker in relation to all proceedings of this House, as Deputy Speaker, until Mr Speaker resumes the chair or, if he does not resume the chair during the course of the sitting, until the next meeting of the House, and so on from day to day, on the like information being given to the House, until the House shall otherwise order:

Provided that if the House shall adjourn for more than twenty-four hours the Chairman of Ways and Means shall continue to perform the duties and exercise the authority of Speaker, as Deputy Speaker, for twenty-four hours only after such adjournment.

(3) Whenever the House has been informed by the Clerk at the Table of the unavoidable absence or the absence by leave of the House both of Mr Speaker, and of the Chairman of Ways and Means, the First Deputy Chairman of Ways and Means shall perform the duties and exercise the authority of the Speaker in accordance with paragraph (2) of this order; and if the House should be so informed of the unavoidable absence or the absence by leave of the House of the First Deputy Chairman also, the Second Deputy Chairman shall perform those duties and exercise that authority.

4. Chairmen's Panel. (1) Mr Speaker shall nominate, at the commencement of every session, not fewer than ten Members to act as temporary chairmen of committees when requested by the Chairman of Ways and Means.

(2) The Members nominated in accordance with the preceding paragraph together with the Chairman of Ways and Means and the Deputy Chairmen of Ways and Means shall constitute the Chairmen's Panel.

Members (Introduction and Seating)

5. Affirmation in lieu of oath. Every person returned as a Member of this House may make and subscribe a solemn affirmation in the form prescribed by statute instead of taking an oath.

6. Time for taking the oath. Members may take and subscribe the oath required by law at any time during the sitting of the House, before the orders of the day and notices of motions have been entered upon, or after they have been disposed of; but no debate or business shall be interrupted for that purpose.

7. Seats not to be taken before prayers. No Member's name shall be affixed to any seat in the House before the hour of prayers; and Mr Speaker shall give directions to the doorkeepers accordingly.

8. Seats secured at prayers. Any Member having secured a seat at prayers shall be entitled to retain the same until the rising of the House.

Sittings of the House

9. Sittings of the House. (1) The House shall meet on Mondays, Tuesdays, Wednesdays and Thursdays at half-past two o'clock and will first proceed with private business, motions for unopposed returns, questions and ballots for notices of motions.

(2) No motion for the adjournment of the House shall be made on Monday, Tuesday, Wednesday or Thursday until all the questions asked at the commencement of public business shall have been disposed of, and, save as provided in paragraph (1) of Standing Order No 20 (Adjournment on specific and important matter that should have urgent consideration), no Member other than a Minister of the Crown may make such a motion on any day before the orders of the day or notices of motions shall have been entered upon.

(3) At ten o'clock on Mondays, Tuesdays, Wednesdays and Thursdays, the proceedings on any business then under consideration shall, save as otherwise provided in paragraph (1) of Standing Order No 14 (Exempted business), be interrupted; and, if the House be in committee, the chairman shall leave the chair, and report progress and ask leave to sit again; and if a motion has been made for the adjournment of the House (unless that motion is included in a motion to be made after the interruption of business under paragraph (2) of Standing Order No 14 (Exempted business)), or of the debate, or in committee that the chairman do report progress, or do leave the chair, every such motion shall lapse.

(4) On the interruption of business the closure may be claimed; and if moved, or if proceedings under Standing Order No 35 (Closure of debate) be then in progress, Mr Speaker or the chairman shall not leave the chair until the questions consequent thereon and any further question, as provided in Standing Order No 35 (Closure of debate), have been decided.

(5) An order of the day not disposed of before the termination of a sitting shall be deferred to such day being a day on which the House ordinarily sits as the Member in charge of that order may appoint and any order of the day not reached before the termination of a sitting shall, unless the Member in charge of the order has given other instructions to the Clerk at the Table, stand over until the next sitting.

(6) After the business under consideration at ten o'clock has been disposed of, no opposed business shall be taken, save as provided in Standing Order No 14 (Exempted business).

(7) The House shall not be adjourned except in pursuance of a resolution or by Mr Speaker in pursuance of paragraph (3) of Standing Order No 10 (Sittings of the House (suspended sittings)) or Standing Order No 45 (Power of Mr Speaker to adjourn House or suspend sitting):

Provided that, when a substantive motion for the adjournment of the House has been made at or after ten o'clock Mr Speaker shall, after the expiration of half an hour after that motion has been made, adjourn the House without putting any question.

10. Sittings of the House (suspended sittings). (1) On Monday, Tuesday and Wednesday, a motion may be made after ten o'clock by a Minister of the Crown, 'That the proceedings of this day's sitting be suspended', and the question thereon shall be put forthwith; and if the question be agreed to in the House, a motion may immediately thereafter be made, 'That this House do now adjourn', and at the conclusion of the debate on that motion and in no case later than half an hour after the motion has been made, the motion shall lapse, and Mr Speaker shall suspend the sitting till ten o'clock on the following morning, or, if it be after midnight, till ten o'clock in the morning of the same day.

(2) If the question on a motion, made likewise in a committee of the whole House, 'That the proceedings of the committee be suspended', be so decided in the affirmative, the chairman shall leave the chair and make a report to that effect, whereupon Mr Speaker shall forthwith put the question, 'That the proceedings of this day's sitting be suspended', and the House shall proceed thereon in accordance with the provisions of paragraph (1) of this order, and, if the question be agreed to, a motion for the adjournment of the House may be made and the sitting shall afterwards be suspended as aforesaid; but, if that question be negatived, the House shall immediately again resolve itself into the committee.

(3) On the resumption of the sitting the House shall forthwith resume the suspended proceedings and may afterwards proceed with the remaining business of the sitting which has been suspended:

Provided that—

(a) on a motion being made by a Minister of the Crown, 'That this House do now adjourn', Mr Speaker shall put the question thereon forthwith; or

(b) on the conclusion of the business Mr Speaker shall adjourn the House without putting any question; or

(c) if the business has not been concluded before two o'clock, Mr Speaker shall interrupt the proceedings at that hour and the debate or further consideration of the bill shall stand adjourned, or, if the House be in committee, the chairman shall leave the chair and report progress and ask leave to sit again, and Mr Speaker shall thereafter adjourn the House without putting any question.

11. Friday sittings. (1) The House shall meet on Fridays at half-past nine o'clock, and will first proceed with private business, petitions, and motions for unopposed returns.

(2) Standing Orders No 9 (Sittings of the House) and No 14 (Exempted business) shall apply to the sittings on Fridays with the omission of paragraph (1) of Standing Order No 9 (Sittings of the House) and with the substitution of references to half-past two o'clock, a quarter past three o'clock and four o'clock for references to ten o'clock, a quarter to eleven o'clock and half-past eleven o'clock respectively.

(3) In the application of Standing Order No 15 (Prayers against statutory instruments, &c (negative procedure)) to the sittings on Fridays there shall be substituted references to four o'clock for references to half-past eleven o'clock.

(4) At eleven o'clock Mr Speaker may interrupt the proceedings in order to permit questions to be asked which are in his opinion of an urgent character and relate either to matters of public importance or to the arrangement of business, statements to be made by Ministers, or personal explanations to be made by Members.

(5) If the House is in committee at eleven o'clock, on an occasion when Mr Speaker's intention to permit such questions, statements or explanations has been made known, the chairman shall leave the chair without putting any

question, and report that the Committee have made progress and ask leave to sit again.

(6) The House, when it meets on Friday, shall, at its rising, stand adjourned until the following Monday without any question being put.

12. Earlier meeting of House in certain circumstances. (1) Whenever the House stands adjourned and it is represented to Mr Speaker by Her Majesty's Ministers that the public interest requires that the House should meet at a time earlier than that to which the House stands adjourned, Mr Speaker, if he is satisfied that the public interest does so require, may give notice that, being so satisfied, he appoints a time for the House to meet, and the House shall accordingly meet at the time stated in such notice.

(2) The government business to be transacted on the day on which the House shall so meet shall, subject to the publication of notice thereof in the order paper to be circulated on the day on which the House shall so meet, be such as the government may appoint, but subject as aforesaid the House shall transact its business as if it had been duly adjourned to the day on which it shall so meet, and any government order of the day and government notices of motions that may stand on the order book for any day shall be appointed for the day on which the House shall so meet.

(3) In the event of Mr Speaker being unable to act owing to illness or other cause, the Chairman of Ways and Means, or either Deputy Chairman, shall act in his stead for the purposes of this order.

Arrangement and Timing of Public and Private Business

13. Arrangement of public business. (1) Save as provided in this order, government business shall have precedence at every sitting.

(2) Twenty days shall be allotted in each session for proceedings on opposition business, seventeen of which shall be at the disposal of the Leader of the Opposition and three of which shall be at the disposal of the leader of the second largest opposition party; and matters selected on those days shall have precedence over government business provided that—
   (a) two Friday sittings shall be deemed equivalent to a single sitting on any other day;
   (b) on any day other than a Friday, not more than two of the days at the disposal of the Leader of the Opposition may be taken in the form of four half days, and one of the days at the disposal of the leader of the second largest opposition party may be taken in the form of two half days; and
   (c) on any such half day proceedings under this paragraph shall either—
      (i) lapse at seven o'clock if not previously concluded, or
      (ii) be set down for consideration at seven o'clock and, except on days on which private business has been set down for consideration under the provisions of paragraph (5) of Standing Order No 16 (Time for taking private business), shall be entered upon at that time:
   Provided that on days on which business stands over until seven o'clock under the provisions of Standing Order No 20 (Adjournment on specific and

important matter that should have urgent consideration) proceedings under this sub-paragraph shall not be entered upon until such business has been disposed of, and may then be proceeded with for three hours, notwithstanding the provisions of Standing Order No 9 (Sittings of the House).

(3) For the purposes of this order 'the second largest opposition party' shall be that party, of those not represented in Her Majesty's Government, which has the second largest number of Members elected to the House as members of that party.

(4) Private Members' bills shall have precedence over government business on ten Fridays in each session to be appointed by the House.

(5) On and after the seventh Friday on which private Members' bills have precedence, such bills shall be arranged on the order paper in the following order:

consideration of Lords amendments, third readings, consideration of reports not already entered upon, adjourned proceedings on consideration, bills in progress in committee, bills appointed for committee, and second readings.

(6) The ballot for private Members' bills shall be held on the second Thursday on which the House shall sit during the session under arrangements to be made by Mr Speaker, and each bill shall be presented by the Member who has given notice of presentation or by another Member named by him in writing to the Clerks at the Table, at the commencement of public business on the fifth Wednesday on which the House shall sit during the session.

(7) Private Members' notices of motions and private Members' bills shall have precedence, in that order, over government business on ten Fridays in each session to be appointed by the House.

(8) On four days other than Fridays in each session to be appointed by the House private Members' notices of motions shall have precedence until seven o'clock and, if not previously concluded, the proceedings thereon shall lapse at that hour and the House shall then proceed with government business.

(9) Ballots for private Members' notices of motions shall be held after questions on such Wednesdays as may be appointed by the House in respect of motions having precedence on Fridays and on such days as may be appointed by the House in respect of motions having precedence on days other than Fridays. Notice of a subject to be raised on any motion for which a ballot is held in pursuance of this paragraph may be given at the Table or in the Table Office not less than nine days before the day on which the notice of motion is to have precedence.

(10) Until after the fifth Wednesday on which the House shall sit during the session, no private Member shall give notice of a motion for leave to bring in a bill under Standing Order No 19 (Motions for leave to bring in bills and nomination of select committees at commencement of public business) or for presenting a bill under Standing Order No 58 (Presentation and first reading).

14. Exempted business. (1) The following business may be proceeded with at any hour though opposed, shall not, save for the purpose of moving a motion pursuant to paragraph (2) of this order, be interrupted at ten o'clock, and if under discussion when business is postponed under the provisions of any standing order may be resumed, though opposed, after the interruption of business:

(a) proceedings on a bill brought in upon a ways and means resolution or any Consolidated Fund Bill or Appropriation Bill;

(b) proceedings in pursuance of any Act of Parliament, save in so far as Standing Order No 15 (Prayers against statutory instruments, &c (negative procedure)) otherwise provides, and proceedings on European Community documents, but Mr Speaker shall put any questions necessary to dispose of such proceedings not later than half-past eleven o'clock or one and a half hours after the commencement of those proceedings, whichever is the later:

Provided that, if Mr Speaker shall be of opinion that, because of the importance of the subject matter of the motion, the time for debate has not been adequate, he shall, instead of putting the question as aforesaid, interrupt the business, and the debate shall stand adjourned till the next sitting (other than a Friday);

(c) proceedings in pursuance of any standing order of this House which provides that proceedings though opposed may be decided after the expiration of the time for opposed business;

(d) proceedings on a motion authorising expenditure in connection with a bill:

Provided that any questions necessary to dispose of the proceedings on such a motion shall be put at a quarter to eleven o'clock or three-quarters of an hour after the commencement of those proceedings, whichever is the later.

In this paragraph, and in Standing Orders No 84 (Constitution of standing committees), No 86 (Nomination of standing committees) and No 102 (Standing Committees on European Community Documents), 'European Community documents' means draft proposals by the Commission of the European Communities for legislation and other documents published for submission to the Council of Ministers or to the European Council whether or not such documents originate from the Commission.

(2) If a notice of motion in the name of a Minister of the Crown stands upon the order paper at the commencement of public business to the effect that any specified business may be proceeded with at this day's sitting though opposed—

(a) until any hour;

(b) until a specified hour; or

(c) until either a specified hour or the end of a specified period after it has been entered upon, whichever is the later,

or in a form combining any or all of these effects in respect of different items of business, the motion shall stand over and may not be made until after the interruption of business and shall then be proceeded with, though opposed, in accordance with the following paragraphs of this order provided that on any day on which Mr Speaker is directed to put questions at ten o'clock pursuant to paragraph (5) of Standing Order No 52 (Consideration of estimates), any such motion shall stand over until those questions have been decided.

(3) If the business interrupted is included in the business specified in the motion or in paragraph (1) of this order, Mr Speaker shall, immediately after the interruption of business, or if the House has been in committee, before any day is named for the House again to resolve itself into that committee, call upon the Minister to move his motion and the question thereon shall be put forthwith, and after that question has been decided the consideration of the business interrupted shall be resumed if such business is included in the business specified in paragraph (1) of this order or if the question be resolved in the affirmative.

(4) If the business interrupted is not included in the business specified in the motion or in paragraph (1) of this order, Mr Speaker shall call upon the Minister to move his motion at the conclusion of any proceedings arising on the interruption of business under the provisions of Standing Order No 9 (Sittings of the House) but before the resumption of any proceedings postponed under Standing Order No 16 (Time for taking private business) or No 20 (Adjournment on specific and important matter that should have urgent consideration).

(5) If a motion made under either of the two preceding paragraphs be agreed to, the business so specified shall be proceeded with as if it were included in the business specified in paragraph (1) of this order, save that—
  (a) business which may be proceeded with until a specified hour may not if opposed be entered upon or resumed after that hour and the proceedings thereon if not previously concluded shall be interrupted at that hour;
  (b) when proceedings on such business have been postponed under the provisions of Standing Order No 20 (Adjournment on specific and important matter that should have urgent consideration), such business may be proceeded with after the specified hour for a further period of time equal to the duration of the proceedings upon the motion under the said Standing Order No 20; and
  (c) the proceedings upon business which may be proceeded with until either a specified hour or the end of a specified period after it has been entered upon, whichever is the later, shall if not previously concluded be interrupted at that hour or at the end of that period, as the case may be.

(6) Not more than one motion under paragraph (2) of this order may be made at any one sitting and after any business proceeding under the provisions of this order is disposed of after ten o'clock, the remaining business of the sitting shall be dealt with according to the provisions of Standing Order No 9 (Sittings of the House) applicable to business taken after ten o'clock.

15. Prayers against statutory instruments, &c (negative procedure). (1) No proceedings on a motion to which this order applies shall be entered upon at or after half-past eleven o'clock.

(2) If such a motion is under consideration at half-past eleven o'clock, Mr Speaker shall forthwith put any question which may be requisite to bring to a decision any question already proposed from the chair:

Provided that, if he shall be of opinion that—
(a) owing to the lateness of the hour at which consideration of the motion was entered upon, or
(b) because of the importance of the subject matter of the motion,
the time for debate has not been adequate, he shall interrupt the business and the debate shall stand adjourned till the next sitting (other than a Friday).

(3) A debate which has been adjourned under paragraph (2) of this order shall not be resumed later than eleven o'clock, but shall stand further adjourned till the next sitting (other than a Friday), and the foregoing provisions of this paragraph shall apply to any debate which has been further adjourned under this paragraph as if the further adjournment were an adjournment under paragraph (2) of the order.

(4) The motions to which this order applies are—
(a) any motion for an humble address to Her Majesty praying that a statutory instrument be annulled, and any motion that a draft of an Order in Council be not submitted to Her Majesty in Council, or that a statutory instrument be not made,
(b) any motion that, or for an humble address to Her Majesty praying that, any other document which may be subject to proceedings in the House in pursuance of a statute be annulled, or cease to be in force, or be not made.

16. Time for taking private business. (1) On Mondays, Tuesdays, Wednesdays and Thursdays the time for private business shall end not later than a quarter to three o'clock and business entered upon and not disposed of at that hour shall be deferred to such time as the Chairman of Ways and Means may appoint. Business not reached shall stand over to the next sitting, or in the case of opposed business until the next sitting other than a Friday.

(2) During the time of private business, opposed business shall not be proceeded with but shall be deferred to such time, other than a Friday, as the Chairman of Ways and Means may appoint.

(3) Opposed business shall include any proceedings on a private bill or a confirming bill which have been deferred under paragraph (2) of this order, so long as a notice of an amendment stands upon the order paper in the form of a notice of motion (other than a notice of motion in the name of the Chairman of Ways and Means) on second reading, consideration or third reading of such bill:
Provided that no such notice of motion shall stand on the order paper for more than seven days unless renewed.

(4) No opposed business shall be taken on a Friday.

(5) Business deferred under paragraphs (1) and (2) of this order shall be considered at the time of private business on the day appointed unless the

Chairman of Ways and Means directs that such business shall be set down for seven o'clock on any specified Monday, Tuesday, Wednesday or Thursday, and business so set down (including any motion contingent directly or otherwise upon any item of such business) shall be taken in such order as the Chairman of Ways and Means may determine:

Provided that business so set down shall be distributed as nearly as may be proportionately between the sittings on which government business has precedence and other sittings.

(6) On any day specified under paragraph (5) of this order at seven o'clock or as soon thereafter as any motion for the adjournment of the House under Standing Order No 20 (Adjournment on specific and important matter that should have urgent consideration) has been disposed of, the business set down by direction of the Chairman of Ways and Means shall be entered upon and may be proceeded with subject to the provisions of Standing Order No 9 (Sittings of the House).

Notices of Questions, etc

17. Questions to Members. (1) Notices of questions shall be given by Members in writing to a Clerk at the Table or to the Table Office.

(2) Questions shall be taken on Monday, Tuesday, Wednesday and Thursday, after private business has been disposed of, and not later than a quarter to three o'clock.

(3) No question shall be taken after half-past three o'clock, except questions which have not been answered in consequence of the absence of the Minister to whom they are addressed, and questions which have not appeared on the paper, but which are in Mr Speaker's opinion of an urgent character, and relate either to matters of public importance or to the arrangement of business.

(4) A Member who desires an oral answer to his question shall distinguish it by an asterisk, but subject to paragraph (5) of this order notice of any such question must appear at latest on the notice paper circulated two days (excluding Sunday) before that on which an answer is desired.

(5) Questions received at the Table Office before half-past two o'clock on a Monday or Tuesday on which the House is sitting may, if so decided by the Member, be put down for oral answer on the following Wednesday or Thursday respectively:

Provided that this paragraph shall not apply to questions received on the first day of a session nor to questions received on the day on which the House first meets pursuant to Standing Order No 12 (Earlier meeting of House in certain circumstances).

(6) Notice of a question shall not be given for oral answer on a day later than ten sitting days after the date of notice.

(7) If a Member does not distinguish his question by an asterisk, or if he is not present to ask it, or if it is not reached by half-past three o'clock, the Minister to whom it is addressed shall cause an answer to be printed in the Official Report of the Parliamentary Debates, unless the Member has

before half-past three o'clock signified his desire to postpone the question. A Member who, while not desiring an oral answer to his question, desires that the answer to it shall be printed in the Official Report on the day for which notice has been given, shall distinguish it with the letter W, and the Minister shall cause the answer to be so printed:

Provided that the minimum notice for such a question shall be the same as that prescribed for questions for oral answer.

(8) Whenever the House stands adjourned to a day other than the next day (not being a Saturday or Sunday)—

(a) if the day to which the House stands adjourned is a Monday, notices of questions for oral answer on that Monday shall not be received later than half-past four o'clock on the preceding Thursday; and notices of questions for oral answer on the Tuesday following shall not be received later than half-past four o'clock on the preceding Friday;

(b) if the day to which the House stands adjourned is a Tuesday, notices of questions for oral answer on that Tuesday or the Wednesday following shall not be received later than half-past four o'clock on the preceding Friday;

(c) if the day to which the House stands adjourned is a Wednesday, notices of questions for oral answer on that Wednesday shall not be received later than half-past four o'clock on the preceding Friday; and notices of questions for oral answer on the Thursday following shall not be received later than half-past four o'clock on the preceding Monday;

(d) if the day to which the House stands adjourned is a Thursday, notices of questions for oral answer on that Thursday shall not be received later than half-past four o'clock on the preceding Monday; and

(e) if the day to which the House stands adjourned is a Friday, notices of questions for oral answer on the following Monday shall not be received later than half-past four o'clock on the preceding Thursday:

Provided that this paragraph shall not affect the provisions of paragraphs (4) and (5) of this order if the House should sit on any day on which they are applicable.

(9) Any questions tabled for written answer on a day on which this House does not sit by reason of the continuance of a previous sitting shall be deemed to be questions for written answer on the next sitting day and shall appear on the order paper for that day.

18. Notices of motions, amendments and questions. A notice of a question, or of an amendment to a motion standing on the order paper for which no day has been fixed or of the addition of a name in support of such a motion or amendment, which is given after half-past ten o'clock in the evening shall be treated for all purposes as if it were a notice handed in after the rising of the House.

Motions for Bills and Select Committees

19. Motions for leave to bring in bills and nomination of select committees at commencement of public business. (1) On Tuesdays and Wednesdays, and if given by a Minister of the Crown, on Mondays and Thursdays, notices of motions for leave to bring in bills, and for the nomination of select committees, may be set down for consideration at the commencement of public business. Mr Speaker, after permitting, if he thinks fit, a brief explanatory statement from the Member who makes and from a Member who opposes any such motion respectively, shall put either the question thereon, or the question, 'That the debate be now adjourned'.

(2) With respect to a private Member's motion for leave to bring in a bill under this order—

    (a) notice shall be given in the Public Bill Office by the Member in person or by another Member on his behalf, but on any one day not more than one notice shall be accepted from any one Member;

    (b) no notice shall be given for a day on which a notice of motion under this order already stands on the paper;

    (c) no notice shall be given for a day earlier than the fifth or later than the fifteenth sitting day after the day on which it is given;

    (d) not more than one such notice shall stand on the paper in the name of any one Member for a day within any period of fifteen sitting days.

Motions for the Adjournment of the House

20. Adjournment on specific and important matter than should have urgent consideration. (1) On Monday, Tuesday, Wednesday and Thursday a Member rising in his place at the commencement of public business may propose, in an application lasting not more than three minutes, to move the adjournment of the House for the purpose of discussing a specific and important matter that should have urgent consideration. If Mr Speaker is satisfied that the matter is proper to be so discussed, the Member shall either obtain the leave of the House, or, if such leave be refused, the assent of not fewer than forty Members who shall thereupon rise in their places to support the motion, or, if fewer than forty Members and not fewer than ten shall thereupon rise in their places, the House shall, on a division, upon question put forthwith, determine whether such motion shall be made.

(2) If leave is given or the motion is so supported or the House so determines that it shall be made the motion shall stand over until the commencement of public business on the following day (or, on Thursdays, until the commencement of public business on the following Monday) when proceedings upon it shall be interrupted after three hours, or, if Mr Speaker directs that the urgency of the matter so requires, until seven o'clock on the same day.

(3) A Member intending to propose to move the adjournment of the House under the provisions of this order shall give notice to Mr Speaker by twelve o'clock, if the urgency of the matter is known at that hour. If the urgency is not so known he shall give notice as soon thereafter as is practicable. If Mr Speaker so desires he may defer giving his decision upon whether the matter is proper to be discussed until a named hour, when he may interrupt the proceedings of the House for the purpose.

(4) In determining whether a matter is proper to be discussed Mr Speaker shall have regard to the extent to which it concerns the administrative

responsibilities of Ministers of the Crown or could come within the scope of ministerial action. In determining whether a matter is urgent Mr Speaker shall have regard to the probability of the matter being brought before the House in time by other means.

(5) Mr Speaker shall state whether or not he is satisfied that the matter is proper to be discussed without giving the reasons for his decision to the House.

(6) Debate on motions made under this order may include reference to any matter that would be in order on a motion to take note of the subject under discussion, and a motion may be made under this order notwithstanding the fact that a motion for the adjournment is already before the House or is proposed to be made.

(7) Proceedings on any business postponed at seven o'clock under this order may be resumed at the conclusion of proceedings on the aforesaid motion for the adjournment of the House unless such motion is agreed to, shall not be interrupted, except as provided in paragraph (2) of Standing Order No 14 (Exempted business), may be proceeded with for such further period of time as would have been permissible under any orders of the House at seven o'clock had no such motion then been made, and shall not be subject to the provisions of any such orders with regard to the disposal of the business until the conclusion of the said period.

21. Adjournment of House to facilitate business of select or standing committees. In order to facilitate the business of select or of standing committees a motion may, after two days' notice, be made by a Minister of the Crown at the commencement of public business, in either of the following forms:

   (a) 'That this House do now adjourn' (in which case, if the question thereon be not previously agreed to, Mr Speaker shall put the question half an hour after it has been proposed), or

   (b) 'That this House do now adjourn till seven o'clock this day' (in which case the question thereon shall be put forthwith):

Provided that if, on a day on which notice of a motion in the terms of paragraph (a) of this order stands on the paper, leave has been given to move the adjournment of the House at seven o'clock for the purpose of discussing a specific and important matter that should have urgent consideration, or opposed private business has been set down by direction of the Chairman of Ways and Means, the motion shall be made in the terms and subject to the procedure prescribed by paragraph (b) of this order.

22. Periodic adjournments. Whenever a motion shall have been made by a Minister of the Crown for the adjournment of the House for a specified period or periods, any questions necessary to dispose of proceedings shall be put three hours after they have been entered upon, if not previously concluded.

Orders of the Day

23. Orders of the day to be read without question put. Upon Mr Speaker's direction, the Clerk shall read the orders of the day, without any question being put.

24. Order of disposing of orders of the day. The orders of the day shall be disposed of in the order in which they stand upon the paper, the right being reserved to Her Majesty's Ministers of arranging government business whether orders of the day or notices of motion in such order as they think fit.

25. When chair to be left without question put. Whenever an order of the day is read for the House to resolve itself into a committee other than a committee on a bill, Mr Speaker shall leave the chair without putting any question, and the House shall thereupon resolve itself into such committee.

Rules of Debate

26. Anticipation. In determining whether a discussion is out of order on the ground of anticipation, regard shall be had by Mr Speaker to the probability of the matter anticipated being brought before the House within a reasonable time.

27. Seconders. No motion or amendment shall require to be seconded before the question thereon is proposed from the chair.

28. Powers of chair to propose question. (1) When a Member is in the course of making a motion or moving an amendment at any stage of proceedings on a bill, a Member rising in his place may claim to move, 'That the question be now proposed', and, unless it shall appear to the chair that such motion is an abuse of the rules of the House, the question, 'That the question be now proposed', shall be put forthwith.

(2) This order shall apply in committee only when the Chairman of Ways and Means or either Deputy Chairman is in the chair.

29. Debate on the motion for the adjournment of the House. Notwithstanding the practice of the House which prohibits in a debate on a motion for the adjournment of the House any reference to matters requiring legislative remedy, Mr Speaker may permit such incidental reference to legislative action as he may consider relevant to any matter of administration then under debate when enforcement of the prohibition would, in his opinion, unduly restrict the discussion of such matter.

30. Questions on amendments. When an amendment has been moved, the question to be proposed thereon shall be, 'That the amendment be made', except that—

(1) when to the question 'That a bill be now read a second time (or the third time)' an amendment has been moved to leave out the word 'now', the question shall be, 'That the word "now" stand part of the question'; and

(2) on the twenty days allotted under paragraph (2) of Standing Order No 13 (Arrangement of public business),
  (a) where to any substantive motion an amendment has been moved by a Minister of the Crown to leave out a word or words and insert (or add) others, the question shall be, 'That the original words stand part of the question', and, if that question be passed in the negative, the question 'That the proposed words be there inserted (or added)' shall be put forthwith;
  (b) if such amendment involves leaving out all the effective words of the

motion Mr Speaker shall, after the amendment has been disposed of, forthwith declare the main question (as amended or not as the case may be) to be agreed to.

31. Selection of amendments. (1) In respect of any motion or any bill under consideration on report or any Lords amendment to a bill, Mr Speaker shall have power to select the amendments, new clauses or new schedules to be proposed thereto.

(2) In committee of the whole House, the Chairman of Ways and Means and either Deputy Chairman shall have the like power to select the amendments, new clauses or new schedules to be proposed.

(3) Mr Speaker, or in a committee of the whole House, the Chairman of Ways and Means or either Deputy Chairman, may, if he think fit, call upon any Member who has given notice of an amendment, new clause or new schedule to give such explanation of the object thereof as may enable him to form a judgment upon it.

(4) For the purposes of this order, motions for instructions to committees on bills, motions to commit or re-commit bills and motions relating to the proceedings on bills shall be treated as if they were amendments under paragraph (1) of this order.

(5) The powers conferred on Mr Speaker by this order shall not be exercised by the Deputy Speaker save during the consideration of the estimates.

32. Calling of amendments at end of debate. If on the last day on which the motion for an address in answer to Her Majesty's Speech is debated in the House an amendment proposed to the said motion shall have been disposed of at or after the expiration of the time for opposed business, a further amendment selected by Mr Speaker may thereupon be moved, and the question thereon shall be put forthwith.

33. Debate on dilatory motion. When a motion is made for the adjournment of a debate or of the House during any debate or of further consideration of a bill or of the Lords amendments to a bill or that the chairman do report progress, or do leave the chair, the debate thereupon shall be confined to the matter of such motion; and no Member, having made any such motion, shall be entitled to make any similar motion during the same debate.

34. Dilatory motion in abuse of rules of House. (1) If Mr Speaker, or the chairman, shall be of opinion that a dilatory motion is an abuse of the rules of the House, he may forthwith put the question thereupon from the chair, or he may decline to propose the question thereupon to the House or the committee.

(2) For the purposes of this order the expression 'dilatory motion' shall include a motion for the adjournment of a debate, or of the House, during any debate, or of further consideration of a bill or of the Lords amendments to a bill, or that the chairman do report progress or do leave the chair.

35. Closure of debate. (1) After a question has been proposed a Member rising in his place may claim to move, 'That the question be now put,' and, unless it shall appear to the chair that such motion is an abuse of the rules of the House, or an infringement of the rights of the minority, the question 'That the question be now put', shall be put forthwith.

(2) When a question 'That the question be now put' has been decided in the affirmative, and the question consequent thereon has been decided, a Member may claim that any further question be put which may be requisite to bring to a decision any question already proposed from the chair, and if the assent of the chair, as aforesaid, be not withheld, any question so claimed shall be put forthwith.

(3) This order shall apply in committee only when the Chairman of Ways and Means or either Deputy Chairman is in the chair.

36. Majority for closure or for proposal of question. If a division be held upon a question for the closure of debate under Standing Order No 35 (Closure of debate) or for the proposal of the question under Standing Order No 28 (Powers of chair to propose question), that question shall not be decided in the affirmative unless it appears by the numbers declared from the chair that not fewer than one hundred Members voted in the majority in support of the motion.

Divisions

37. Procedure on divisions. (1) If the opinion of Mr Speaker or the chairman as to the decision of a question is challenged he shall direct that the lobby be cleared.

(2) After the lapse of two minutes from this direction he shall put the question again, and, if his opinion is again challenged, he shall announce the names of tellers.

(3) After the lapse of at least six minutes from this direction he shall direct that the doors giving access to the division lobbies be locked.

38. Voting. (1) A Member may vote in a division although he did not hear the question put.

(2) A Member is not obliged to vote.

39. Division unnecessarily claimed. Mr Speaker or the chairman may, after the lapse of two minutes, if in his opinion the division is unnecessarily claimed, take the vote of the House, or committee, by calling upon the Members who support, and who challenge his decision, successively to rise in their places; and he shall thereupon, as he thinks fit, either declare the determination of the House or committee, or name tellers for a division.

40. Quorum. (1) If it should appear that fewer than forty Members (including the occupant of the chair and the tellers) have taken part in a division, the business under consideration shall stand over until the next sitting of the House and the next business shall be taken.

(2) The House shall not be counted at any time.

Order in the House

41. Irrelevance or repetition. Mr Speaker or the chairman, after having called the attention of the House, or of the committee, to the conduct of a

Member, who persists in irrelevance, or tedious repetition either of his own argument or of the arguments used by other Members in debate, may direct him to discontinue his speech.

42. Disorderly conduct. Mr Speaker or the chairman shall order any Member or Members whose conduct is grossly disorderly to withdraw immediately from the House during the remainder of that day's sitting; and the Serjeant at Arms shall act on such orders as he may receive from the chair in pursuance of this order. But if on any occasion Mr Speaker or the chairman deems that his powers under the previous provisions of this order are inadequate, he may name such Member or Members, in which event the same procedure shall be followed as is prescribed by Standing Order No 43 (Order in debate).

43. Order in debate. (1) Whenever a Member shall have been named by Mr Speaker, or by the chairman, immediately after the commission of the offence of disregarding the authority of the chair, or of persistently and wilfully obstructing the business of the House by abusing the rules of the House or otherwise, then, if the offence has been committed by such Member in the House, Mr Speaker shall forthwith put the question, on a motion being made, 'That such Member be suspended from the service of the House'; and, if the offence has been committed in a committee of the whole House, the chairman shall forthwith suspend the proceedings of the committee and report the circumstances to the House; and Mr Speaker shall on a motion being made forthwith put the same question, as if the offence had been committed in the House itself.

Proceedings in pursuance of this paragraph, though opposed, may be decided after the expiration of the time for opposed business.

(2) If any Member be suspended under paragraph (1) of this order, his suspension on the first occasion shall continue for five sitting days, and on the second occasion for twenty sitting days, including in either case the day on which he was suspended, but, on any subsequent occasion, until the House shall resolve that the suspension of such Member do terminate.

(3) Not more than one Member shall be named at the same time, unless two or more Members, present together, have jointly disregarded the authority of the chair.

(4) If a Member, or two or more Members acting jointly, who have been suspended under this order from the service of the House, shall refuse to obey the direction of Mr Speaker, when severally summoned under Mr Speaker's orders by the Serjeant at Arms to obey such direction, Mr Speaker shall call the attention of the House to the fact that recourse to force is necessary in order to compel obedience to his direction, and the Member or Members named by him as having refused to obey his direction shall thereupon and without any further question being put be suspended from the service of the House during the remainder of the session.

(5) Suspension from the service of the House shall not exempt the Member so suspended from serving on any committee for the consideration of a private bill to which he may have been appointed before his suspension.

(6) Nothing in this order shall be taken to deprive the House of the power of proceeding against any Member according to ancient usages.

44. Members suspended, &c, to withdraw from precincts. Members who are ordered to withdraw under Standing Order No 42 (Disorderly conduct) or who are suspended from the service of the House under Standing Order No 43 (Order in debate) shall forthwith withdraw from the precincts of the House, subject, however, in the case of such suspended Members, to the provisions of paragraph (5) of Standing Order No 43 (Order in debate).

45. Power of Mr Speaker to adjourn House or suspend sitting. In the case of grave disorder arising in the House Mr Speaker may, if he thinks it necessary to do so, adjourn the House without putting any question, or suspend the sitting for a time to be named by him.

45A. Short speeches. (1) Mr Speaker may announce at the commencement of public business that, because of the number of Members wishing to speak in a debate on one of the matters specified in paragraph (2) of this order, he will call Members either between six o'clock and ten minutes before eight o'clock or between seven o'clock and ten minutes before nine o'clock on Monday to Thursday sittings, and between half-past eleven o'clock and one o'clock on Friday sittings, to speak for not more than ten minutes; and whenever Mr Speaker has made such an announcement he may, between those hours, direct any Member who has spoken for ten minutes in such a debate to resume his seat forthwith.

(2) This order shall apply to debates on:
 (a) the second reading of public bills;
 (b) matters selected under paragraph (2) of Standing Order No 13 (Arrangement of public business) for consideration on allotted opposition days;
 (c) motions in the name of a Minister of the Crown; and
 (d) motions for an address in answer to Her Majesty's Speech.

Public Money

46. Recommendation from Crown required on application relating to public money. This House will receive no petition for any sum relating to public service or proceed upon any motion for a grant or charge upon the public revenue, whether payable out of the Consolidated Fund or the National Loans Fund or out of money to be provided by Parliament, or for releasing or compounding any sum of money owing to the Crown, unless recommended from the Crown.

47. Certain proceedings relating to public money. Any charge upon the public revenue whether payable out of the Consolidated Fund or the National Loans Fund or out of money to be provided by Parliament including any provision for releasing or compounding any sum of money owing to the Crown shall be authorised by resolution of the House.

48. Procedure upon bills whose main object is to create a charge upon the public revenue. (1) A bill (other than a bill which is required to be brought in upon a ways and means resolution) the main object of which is the creation of a public charge may either be presented, or brought in upon an order of the House, by a Minister of the Crown, and, in the case of a bill so presented or brought in, the creation of the charge shall not require to be authorised by a resolution of the House until the bill has been read a second time, and after the charge has been so authorised the bill shall be proceeded with in the same manner as a bill which involves a charge that is subsidiary to its main purpose.

(2) The provisions of paragraph (1) of this order shall apply to any bill brought from the Lords, of which a Minister of the Crown has informed the Clerks at the Table of his intention to take charge.

49. Restriction on receipt of petitions relating to public money. This House will not receive any petition for compounding any sum of money owing to the Crown, upon any branch of the revenue, without a certificate from the proper officer or officers annexed to the said petition, stating the debt, what prosecutions have been made for the recovery of such debt, and setting forth how much the petitioner and his security are able to satisfy thereof.

50. Ways and means motions. (1) A ways and means motion may be made in the House without notice on any day as soon as an address has been agreed to in answer to Her Majesty's Speech.

(2) A Minister of the Crown may without notice make a motion for giving provisional statutory effect to any proposals in pursuance of section 5 of the Provisional Collection of Taxes Act 1968; and the question on such a motion shall be put forthwith.

(3) When the question has been decided on the first of several motions upon which a bill is to be brought in for imposing, renewing, varying or repealing any charge upon the people, the question on each such further motion shall be put forthwith; and proceedings in pursuance of this paragraph, though opposed, may be decided after the expiration of the time for opposed business.

51. Application of public money standing orders to private bills, &c. In relation to private bills, provisional order bills and bills introduced under the Private Legislation Procedure (Scotland) Act 1936, or the Statutory Orders (Special Procedure) Act 1945, the standing orders relating to public money shall have effect subject to any exceptions prescribed by the standing orders of this House relating to private business.

52. Consideration of estimates. (1) Three days, other than Fridays, before 5th August, shall be allotted in each session for the consideration of estimates set down under the provisions of paragraph (2) of Standing Order No 131 (Liaison Committee); and not more than one day so allotted may be taken in the form of two half days, not being Fridays.

(2) On any such day—
   (a) consideration of estimates or reports of the Liaison Committee relating thereto shall stand as first business; and
   (b) other business may be taken before ten o'clock only if the consideration of estimates has been concluded.

(3) On any such half day—
   (a) proceedings on consideration of estimates or reports of the Liaison Committee relating thereto, standing as first business, shall be interrupted at seven o'clock; or
   (b) notwithstanding the provisions of paragraph (2) of this order, con-

sideration of estimates or reports of the Liaison Committee relating thereto may be set down for consideration at seven o'clock and shall be entered upon at that time:

Provided that on days on which business stands over until seven o'clock under the provisions of Standing Order No 20 (Adjournment on specific and important matter that should have urgent consideration) or has been set down for that hour under the provisions of Standing Order No 16 (Time for taking private business) proceedings under this sub-paragraph shall not be entered upon until such business has been disposed of and may then be proceeded with for three hours, notwithstanding the provisions of Standing Order No 9 (Sittings of the House).

(4) On any day or half day allotted under this order, questions necessary to dispose of proceedings (other than a dilatory motion) on the estimates on which debate has been concluded shall be deferred until the hour prescribed under paragraph (5) of this order.

(5) At ten o'clock on an allotted day or half day, or as soon thereafter as proceedings under the proviso to paragraph (3)(b) of this order have been disposed of, Mr Speaker shall put, successively, any questions deferred under paragraph (4) of this order, and any questions necessary to dispose of proceedings on all other estimates appointed for consideration on that day.

53. Questions on voting of estimates, &c. (1) On any day to which the provisions of paragraphs (2), (3) or (4) of this order apply Mr Speaker shall at ten o'clock put the questions on—
  (a) any outstanding vote relating to numbers for defence services for the coming financial year;
  (b) the total amount outstanding in respect of each financial year to be granted out of the Consolidated Fund for the purposes defined in the related votes.

(2) The provisions of paragraph (1) of this order shall apply on a day not later than 6th February, if any of the following total amounts have been put down for consideration:
  (a) votes on account for the coming financial year;
  (b) supplementary estimates for the current financial year which have been presented at least seven clear days previously.

(3) The provisions of paragraph (1) of this order shall apply on a day not later than 18th March, if any of the following numbers or total amounts have been put down for consideration:
  (a) votes relating to numbers for defence services for the coming financial year;
  (b) supplementary estimates for the current financial year which have been presented at least seven clear days previously;
  (c) excess votes, provided that the Committee of Public Accounts has reported that it sees no objection to the sums necessary being provided by excess vote.

(4) The provisions of paragraph (1) of this order shall apply on a day not later than 5th August, if the total amount of estimates which are still outstanding has been put down for consideration.

(5) At least two days' notice shall be given of the votes which are to be put down for consideration under paragraphs (2), (3) or (4) of this order.

(6) The provisions of this order shall not apply to any vote of credit or votes for supplementary or additional estimates for war expenditure.

54. Consolidated Fund Bills. (1) On any day on which the second reading of a Consolidated Fund or an Appropriation Bill stands as the first order of the day, the question thereon shall be put forthwith upon the reading of that order, no order shall be made for the committal of the bill and the question for third reading shall be put forthwith.

(2) At the conclusion of proceedings on a Consolidated Fund or an Appropriation Bill, a member of the Government may move 'That this House do now adjourn', the motion shall not lapse at ten o'clock, or be interrupted at that hour save for the purpose of moving a motion pursuant to paragraph (2) of Standing Order No 14 (Exempted business), may be proceeded with at any hour, though opposed, and if proceedings have not been concluded by nine o'clock in the morning at that sitting, the motion shall lapse at that hour:

Provided that if the sitting shall have commenced on a Thursday, the motion shall lapse at eight o'clock in the morning.

55. Contracts to be approved by resolution. In all contracts extending over a period of years, and creating a public charge, actual or prospective, entered into by the government for the conveyance of mails by sea, or for the purpose of communications beyond sea, there shall be inserted the condition that the contract shall not be binding until it has been approved of by a resolution of the House. Proceedings in pursuance of this order, though opposed, may be decided after the expiration of the time for opposed business.

56. Contracts to be laid on Table. Every such contract, when executed, shall forthwith, if Parliament be then sitting, or if Parliament be not then sitting, within fourteen days after it assembles, be laid upon the Table of the House, accompanied by a minute of the Lords of the Treasury, setting forth the grounds on which they have proceeded in authorising it.

57. Contracts to be confirmed by public Act. In cases where any such contract requires to be confirmed by Act of Parliament, the bill for that purpose shall not be introduced and dealt with as a private bill, and power to the government to enter into agreements by which obligations at the public charge shall be undertaken shall not be given in any private Act.

Public Bills

58. Presentation and first reading. (1) A Member may, after notice, present a bill without previously obtaining leave from the House to bring in the same.

(2) When a bill is presented either in pursuance of an order of the House or under the provisions of paragraph (1) of this order, the bill shall be read the first time without any question being put, shall be ordered to be read a second time on such day as the Member presenting it shall appoint, and shall be ordered to be printed.

(3) If a Member informs the Clerks at the Table of his intention to take charge of a bill which has been brought from the Lords, the bill shall be deemed to have been read the first time on the day on which the Member so informs the Clerks, and to have been ordered to be read a second time on such day as he shall appoint, and shall be recorded in the Journal of the House as having been read the first time and ordered to be read a second time on the day so appointed, and shall be ordered to be printed.

59. Bills which are *prima facie* hybrid. (1) Where a public bill (not being a bill to confirm a provisional order or certificate) is ordered to be read a second time on a future day, and it appears that the standing orders relating to private business may be applicable to the bill, the Examiners of Petitions for Private Bills shall be ordered to examine the bill and they shall proceed and report with all convenient speed whether the said standing orders are applicable thereto. If they find that the standing orders are applicable, they shall further report whether they have been complied with.

(2) If the Examiners report that any standing order applicable to the bill has not been complied with, and the Standing Orders Committee report that such standing order ought not to be dispensed with, the order of the day relating to the bill shall be discharged.

60. Amendment on second or third reading. (1) If on an amendment to the question 'That a bill be now read a second time (or the third time)' it is decided that the word 'now' stand part of the question, Mr Speaker shall forthwith declare the bill to be read a second or the third time as the case may be.

(2) When the question has been proposed 'That a bill be now read a second (or the third) time and the question on any amendment to leave out all the words after 'That' and insert other words has passed in the negative, the main question shall be put forthwith.

61. Committal of bills. (1) When a public bill (other than a Consolidated Fund or an Appropriation Bill, or a bill for confirming a provisional order) has been read a second time, it shall stand committed to a standing committee unless the House otherwise order.

(2) A motion to commit a bill to a committee of the whole House or to a select committee or to a special standing committee, or a motion that it is expedient that a bill be committed to a joint committee of Lords and Commons, may be made by any Member and if made immediately after the bill has been read a second time shall not require notice, and, though opposed, may be decided after the expiration of the time for opposed business, and the question thereon shall be put forthwith.

(3) A motion to commit a bill to a standing committee in respect of some of its provisions and to a committee of the whole House in respect of other provisions may be made by the Member in charge of the bill and, if made immediately after the bill has been read a second time, shall not require notice, and may, though opposed, be decided after the expiration of the time for opposed business. If such a motion is opposed, Mr Speaker after permitting, if he thinks fit, a brief explanatory statement from the Member who makes and from a Member who opposes the motion shall, without permitting any further debate, put the question thereon.

(4) If the question on a motion made under paragraph (2) or paragraph (3) of this order is negatived, Mr Speaker shall forthwith declare that the bill stands committed to a standing committee.

62. Notices of amendments, &c, to bills. Whenever the House is adjourned for more than one day, notices of amendments to bills, new clauses or new schedules or of amendments to Lords amendments received in the Public Bill Office at any time not later than half-past four o'clock on the last day on which the House is not sitting (excluding any Saturday, Sunday, bank holiday or public holiday in England) may be accepted as if the House were sitting.

63. Amendments in committee. All committees to which bills may be committed or referred for consideration on report shall have power to make such amendments therein as they shall think fit, provided they be relevant to the subject matter of the bill: but if any such amendments shall not be within the long title of the bill, they shall amend the long title accordingly, and report the same specially to the House.

64. Committee of whole House on bill. Whenever an order of the day is read for the House to resolve itself into a committee on a bill, Mr Speaker shall leave the chair without putting any question, and the House shall thereupon resolve itself into such committee, unless notice of an instruction to such committee has been given, when such instruction shall be first disposed of.

65. Postponement of preamble. In a committee on a bill the preamble shall stand postponed until after the consideration of the clauses and of any schedules.

66. Questions not to be put on words in italics. In a committee on a bill no questions shall be put for inserting words already printed in italics.

67. Debate on clause or schedule standing part. If, during the consideration of a bill in a committee of the whole House, the chairman is of opinion that the principle of a clause or schedule and any matters arising thereon have been adequately discussed in the course of debate on the amendments proposed thereto, he may, after the last amendment to be selected has been disposed of, state that he is of this opinion and shall then forthwith put the question 'That the clause (or, the clause, as amended) stand part of the bill' or 'That this schedule (or this schedule, as amended) be the schedule to the bill' as the case may be.

68. Procedure on offer of new clause. When a Member has brought up a clause in committee on a bill or on consideration of a bill on report, it shall be read the first time without any question being put, but no clause shall be offered on consideration of a bill on report without notice.

69. Report of bill from committee of whole House. At the close of the proceedings of a committee of the whole House on a bill the chairman shall report the bill forthwith to the House, and when amendments shall have been made thereto, a day shall be appointed for taking the bill as amended into consideration, unless the House shall order it to be taken into consideration forthwith.

70. Consideration of bill as amended in committee of whole House. When the order of the day for the consideration of a bill, as amended in a committee of the whole House, has been read, the House shall proceed to consider the same without question put, unless the Member in charge thereof nominates a future day for its consideration or a motion shall be made to re-commit the bill in whole or in part.

71. Report of bills committed to standing committees. Save as provided in Standing Order No 92 (Consideration on report of certain bills by a standing committee) every bill committed to and reported from a standing committee, whether amended or not, shall be considered on report by the House, and the provisions of Standing Order No 70 (Consideration of bill as amended in committee of whole House) shall apply to such consideration.

72. Re-committal of bill. If a motion to re-commit a bill as a whole be made, Mr Speaker shall permit a brief explanatory statement of the reasons for such re-committal from the Member who makes, and a brief statement from a Member who opposes, any such motion, and shall then put the question thereon.

73. Amendments on report. Upon the consideration of a bill on report no amendment which could not have been proposed in committee without an instruction from the House may be proposed unless it has been authorised by a resolution of the House.

74. Debate on bill reported from standing committee. When a bill has been committed to a standing committee, or has been so committed in respect of some of its provisions, then, on consideration on report of the bill or such of its provisions as were so committed, the rule against speaking more than once shall not apply to the Member in charge of the bill or to the mover of any amendment or new clause in respect of that amendment or clause.

75. Third reading. No amendments, not being merely verbal, shall be made to any bill on the third reading.

76. Lords amendments. (1) Lords amendments to public bills shall be appointed to be considered on a future day, unless the House shall order them to be considered forthwith.

(2) When the order of the day for the consideration of Lords amendments to a public bill has been read, the House shall proceed to consider the same without question put, unless the Member in charge thereof nominates a future day for their consideration.

(3) If Mr Speaker is satisfied that a Lords amendment imposes a charge upon the public revenue such as is required to be authorised by resolution of the House under Standing Order No 47 (Certain proceedings relating to public money) and that such charge has not been so authorised, on reaching that amendment, Mr Speaker shall declare that he is so satisfied and the amendment shall be deemed to have been disagreed to and shall be so recorded in the Journal.

77. Pecuniary penalties. With respect to any bill brought to this House from the House of Lords, or returned by the House of Lords to this House, with amendments, whereby any pecuniary penalty, forfeiture, or fee shall be authorised, imposed, appropriated, regulated, varied, or extinguished, this House will not insist on its ancient and undoubted privileges in the following cases:

(1) when the object of such pecuniary penalty or forfeiture is to secure the execution of the Act, or the punishment or prevention of offences;
(2) where such fees are imposed in respect of benefit taken or service rendered under the Act, and in order to the execution of the Act, and are not made payable into the Consolidated Fund, or in aid of the public revenue, and do not form the ground of public accounting by the parties receiving the same, either in respect of deficit or surplus;
(3) when such bill shall be a private bill for a local or personal Act.

78. Privilege (bills brought from the Lords). The House may proceed with any public bill brought from the Lords except a bill of aids and supplies provided that—
(a) it is so framed that no charge upon the people or upon public funds, unless it be such a charge as is defined in Standing Order No 77 (Pecuniary penalties), is imposed or altered; and
(b) in the case of a bill which, if it were not so framed, would have as its main object the imposition of alteration of such a charge, a Minister of the Crown has informed the Clerk at the Table of his intention to take charge of it.

79. Temporary laws. The precise duration of every temporary law or enactment shall be expressed in a distinct clause or subsection of the bill.

80. Business Committee. There shall be a committee, to be called the Business Committee, consisting of the Chairman of Ways and Means, who shall be chairman of the committee, and not more than eight other Members to be nominated by Mr Speaker in respect of each bill to which this order applies. The quorum of the committee shall be four. The committee—
(a) shall, in the case of any bill in respect of which an order has been made by the House, allotting a specified number of days or portions of days to the consideration of the bill in committee of the whole House or on report, divide the bill into such parts as it may see fit and allot to each part so many days or portions of a day so allotted as it may consider appropriate; and
(b) shall report its resolution (or resolutions) to the House, and on a motion being made for the consideration of such report the question thereon shall be put forthwith and on consideration of the said report the question 'That this House doth agree with the committee in its resolution (or resolutions)' shall be put forthwith and, if that question be agreed to, any such resolution shall have effect as if it were an order of the House.
Proceedings in pursuance of this sub-paragraph, though opposed, may be decided after the expiration of the time for opposed business.

81. Allocation of time to bills. If a motion be made by a Minister of the Crown providing for an allocation of time to any proceedings on a bill Mr Speaker shall, not more than three hours after the commencement of the proceedings on such a motion, put any question necessary to dispose of those proceedings.

Committees of the whole House
82. When chairman leaves chair without question put. When the chairman

of a committee of the whole House has been ordered to make a report to the House, he shall leave the chair without putting any question. Every such report shall be brought up without any question being put.

83. Chairman to report resolutions when reporting progress. When the chairman of a committee of the whole House has been directed to report progress, or has left the chair to report progress in pursuance of Standing Order No 9 (Sittings of the House), he shall, if the committee has come to any resolution, so acquaint the House before reporting progress.

Standing Committees

84. Constitution of standing committees. (1) As many standing committees shall be appointed as may be necessary for the consideration of bills or other business committed or referred to a standing committee.

(2) Subject to the provisions of Standing Order No 95 (Scottish Standing Committees), the bills committed and statutory instruments or draft statutory instruments or European Community documents as defined in Standing Order No 14 (Exempted business) or measures under the Church of England Assembly (Powers) Act 1919 and instruments made under such measures referred to a standing committee shall be distributed among the committees by Mr Speaker.

(3) In all but one of the standing committees to which bills other than bills provided for in Standing Order No 95 (Scottish Standing Committees) are committed or referred government bills shall have precedence.

(4) Government bills allocated to a particular standing committee shall be considered in whatever order Her Majesty's Ministers may decide.

85. Chairmen of standing committees. (1) The chairman or chairmen of each standing committee shall be appointed by Mr Speaker from the Chairmen's Panel.

(2) Mr Speaker may change the chairmen so appointed from time to time.

(3) When more than one chairman is appointed to a standing committee any of the chairmen so appointed may exercise the powers conferred by paragraph (3) of Standing Order No 89 (Procedure in standing committees).

(4) The Chairmen's Panel, of which three shall be a quorum, shall have power to consider matters of procedure relating to standing committees and to report its opinion thereupon to the House from time to time.

(5) Any Member of a standing committee may, at the request of the chairman of the committee, act as chairman for not more than a quarter of an hour on any one occasion:
    Provided that such Member shall not exercise the powers conferred on the chairman of a standing committee by paragraph (3) of Standing Order No 89 (Procedures in standing committees).

86. Nomination of standing committees. (1) Save in the case of—
    (a) the Scottish Grand Committee,
    (b) the Welsh Grand Committee, and
    (c) a standing committee for the consideration of a bill on report,

the Committee of Selection shall nominate not fewer than sixteen nor more than fifty Members to serve on each standing committee for the consideration of each bill allocated or referred to it, or for the consideration of statutory instruments or draft statutory instruments or European Community documents as defined in Standing Order No 14 (Exempted business) or measures under the Church of England Assembly (Powers) Act 1919 and instruments made under such measures referred to it.

(2) In nominating such Members the Committee of Selection shall have regard to the qualifications of those Members nominated and to the composition of the House, and shall have power to discharge Members from time to time and appoint others in substitution for those discharged:
Provided that—
   (i) for the consideration of any public bill certified by Mr Speaker as relating exclusively to Scotland or of a public bill (or part of a public bill) ordered to be considered by a Scottish standing committee, the committee shall be so constituted as to include not fewer than sixteen Members representing Scottish constituencies;
   (ii) for the consideration of any public bill relating exclusively to Wales, the committee shall be so constituted as to include all Members sitting for constituencies in Wales.

87. Attendance of law officers and ministers in standing committees. (1) Mr Attorney General, the Lord Advocate, Mr Solicitor General and Mr Solicitor General for Scotland, or any of them, being Members of the House, though not members of a standing committee, may take part in the deliberations of the committee, but shall not vote or make any motion or move any amendment or be counted in the quorum.

(2) In a standing committee which is to consider a bill brought in upon a ways and means resolution any Minister of the Crown, being a Member of the House, though not a member of the standing committee, may take part in the deliberations of the committee, but shall not vote or make any motion or move any amendment or be counted in the quorum.

88. Meetings of standing committees. (1) A standing committee to which a bill or other business has been committed shall meet to consider such business on the day and at the hour named by the Member appointed chairman of the committee in respect of that business. If the consideration of the business is not completed at that sitting the committee shall meet further to consider the business on such days of the week (being days on which the House sits) as may be appointed by the committee at half-past ten o'clock, unless the committee otherwise determines:
Provided that no standing committee shall sit between the hours of one o'clock and half-past three o'clock in the afternoon, except as hereinafter provided.

(2) If a standing committee is not previously adjourned, the chairman shall adjourn the committee without putting any question at one o'clock:
Provided that—
   (i) if, in the opinion of the chairman, the proceedings on a bill or other business could be brought to a final conclusion by a short extension of the sitting, he may defer adjourning the committee until a quarter past one o'clock;

(ii) if proceedings under Standing Order No 35 (Closure of debate) be in progress at the time when the chairman is required to adjourn the committee under this paragraph, he shall not adjourn the committee until the question for the closure of debate, the question or questions consequent thereon and on any further motion as provided in that standing order, have been decided.

89. Procedure in standing committees. (1) Except as provided in Standing Order No 94 (Scottish Grand Committee) the quorum of a standing committee shall be seventeen or one third of the number of its members excluding the chairman, whichever is the less; and in calculating the quorum fractions shall be counted as one.

(2) Strangers shall be admitted to a standing committee unless the committee otherwise orders.

(3)(a) Any notice of an amendment to a bill which has been committed or referred to a standing committee, or to a motion relating to a document referred to a committee under paragraph (4) of Standing Order No 102 (Standing Committees on European Community Documents), shall stand referred to the committee, and the chairman shall have the like powers as are given to Mr Speaker, the Chairman of Ways and Means and either Deputy Chairman respectively by Standing Order No 31 (Selection of amendments).

(b) Standing Orders No 28 (Powers of chair to propose question), No 35 (Closure of debate) and No 36 (Majority for closure or for proposal of question) shall apply to standing committees, except that the number necessary to render the majority effective for the closure or for the proposal of the question shall be the number prescribed as the quorum by paragraph (1) of this order.

(c) The chairman of a standing committee shall have the like powers as are given to a chairman of a committee of the whole House under the following standing orders:
No 34 (Dilatory motion in abuse of rules of House)
No 41 (Irrelevance or repetition)
No 67 (Debate on clause or schedule standing part).
(d) The following standing orders shall apply to standing committees:
No 107 (Quorum of select committee)
No 110 (Entry on minutes of proceedings of select committee)
No 111 (Minutes of proceedings to be laid on the Table).

(4) On a division being called in the House or a committee of the whole House the chairman of a standing committee shall suspend the proceedings of the committee for such time as will, in his opinion, enable Members to vote in the division and return to the committee.

(5) All standing committees shall have leave to print and circulate their proceedings with the Vote.

90. Second reading committees. (1) A motion, of which at least ten days' notice has been given, may be made by a Minister of the Crown at the commencement of public business, that a public bill be referred to a second reading committee, and the question thereupon shall be put forthwith; and if, on the question being put, not fewer than twenty Members rise in their places and signify their objection thereto, Mr Speaker shall declare that the noes have it:

Provided that no such notice shall be given until the bill has been printed and delivered to the Vote Office.

(2) A motion, of which at least ten days' notice has been given, may with the leave of the House be made by the Member in charge of a private Member's bill at the commencement of public business on any day when private Members' bills or notices of motions have precedence under the provisions of Standing Order No 13 (Arrangement of public business), that the said bill be referred to a second reading committee, and the question thereupon shall be put forthwith. If such a motion be agreed to, any order that the said bill be read a second time which stands on the paper for that or any subsequent day shall be discharged. No such motion shall be made before the seventh Friday on which private Members' bills have precedence and no such notice shall be given until the bill has been printed and delivered to the Vote Office.

(3) A second reading committee shall be a standing committee.

(4) A second reading committee shall report to the House either that it recommends that the bill ought to be read a second time or that it recommends that the bill ought not to be read a second time, and in the latter case it shall have power to state its reasons for so recommending.

(5) When a second reading committee shall have made a report to the House in respect of a bill referred to it under paragraph (2) above, the bill shall be ordered to be read a second time upon a future day.

(6) Upon a motion being made for the second reading of a bill reported from a second reading committee, the question thereon shall be put forthwith.

91. Special standing committees. (1) A special standing committee to which a bill has been committed shall have power, during a period not exceeding 28 days (excluding periods when the House is adjourned for more than two days) from the committal of the bill, to send for persons, papers and records, and, for this purpose, to hold up to four morning sittings of not more than three hours each. At not more than three sittings oral evidence may be given and, unless the committee otherwise orders, all such evidence shall be given in public. Oral evidence shall be printed in the Official Report of the committees' debates together with such written evidence as the committee may order to be so printed.

(2) For the sittings referred to in paragraph (1) of this order, and notwithstanding the provisions of paragraph (1) of Standing Order No 85 (Chairmen of standing committees), Mr Speaker may appoint any Member other than a Minister of the Crown as chairman of a special standing committee.

(3) Except as provided in the foregoing paragraphs, the standing orders relating to standing committees and Standing Orders No 109 (Withdrawal of

documents before select committee), No 113 (Entry of questions asked), No 117 (Witnesses and evidence (select committees)) and No 118 (Publication of evidence (select committees)) shall apply to any special standing committee.

(4) The question on any motion made by a Minister of the Crown to extend the period of 28 days mentioned in paragraph (1) of this order may be decided after the expiration of the time for opposed business.

92. Consideration on report of certain bills by a standing committee. (1) A bill which has been considered by a second reading committee or by the Scottish Grand Committee in relation to the principle of the bill may be referred for consideration on report to a standing committee or to the Scottish Grand Committee, as the case may be, upon a motion made after notice by a Minister of the Crown at the commencement of public business, and the question on such motion shall be put forthwith; and if, on the question being put, not fewer than twenty Members rise in their places and signify their objection thereto, Mr Speaker shall declare that the noes have it.

(2) A standing committee to consider bills on report shall consist of not fewer than twenty nor more than eighty Members, to be nominated by the Committee of Selection to serve on the committee for the consideration of each bill referred to it; and in the nomination of such Members, the Committee of Selection shall have regard to their qualifications and to the composition of the House:

Provided that, for the consideration of all public bills relating exclusively to Wales, the committee shall be so constituted as to include all Members sitting for constituencies in Wales.

(3) Any committee to which a bill is referred under this order shall report to the House that it has considered the bill and has made amendments or has made no amendment thereunto, as the case may be; and the bill so reported shall be ordered to be read the third time upon a future day.

93. Public bills relating exclusively to Scotland. (1) If, after any public bill has been printed, whether introduced in this House or brought from the House of Lords, Mr Speaker is of opinion that its provisions relate exclusively to Scotland, he shall give a certificate to that effect:

Provided that a certificate shall not be withheld by reason only that a provision of that bill amends Schedule 1 to the House of Commons Disqualification Act 1975 or Schedule 1 to the Northern Ireland Assembly Disqualification Act 1975.

(2) On the order for the second reading of any such bill being read, a motion may be made by a Minister of the Crown, 'That the bill be referred to the Scottish Grand Committee', and the question thereupon shall be put forthwith; and if, on that question being put, not fewer than ten Members rise in their places and signify their objection thereto, Mr Speaker shall declare that the noes have it.

(3) A bill so referred to the Scottish Grand Committee shall be considered in relation to the principle of the bill, and shall be reported as having been so considered to the House and shall be ordered to be read a second time upon a future day.

(4) On the order for the second reading of any such bill being read, a motion may be made by a Minister of the Crown, 'That the bill be committed to a Scottish Standing Committee (or a special standing committee)', and the question thereupon shall be put forthwith:

Provided that this paragraph shall not apply in the case of any bill to the second reading of which notice of an amendment has been given by not fewer than six Members.

(5) If such a motion shall have been agreed to, the bill shall be deemed to have been read a second time, and shall be committed to a Scottish Standing Committee (or a special standing committee).

(6) Proceedings in pursuance of paragraphs (2) and (4) of this order, though opposed, may be decided after the expiration of the time for opposed business.

94. Scottish Grand Committee. (1) There shall be a standing committee to be called the Scottish Grand Committee which shall consider—
- (a) bills referred to it for consideration in relation to their principle under paragraph (2) of Standing Order No 93 (Public bills relating exclusively to Scotland);
- (b) bills referred to it under Standing Order No 92 (Consideration on report of certain bills by a standing committee);
- (c) Scottish estimates referred to it under Standing Order No 96 (Scottish estimates); and
- (d) specified matters referred to it under Standing Order No 97 (Matters relating exclusively to Scotland).

(2) The Scottish Grand Committee shall consist of all the Members representing Scottish constituencies, of whom a quorum shall be ten.

(3) Whenever any bill, estimate or matter has been referred to the Scottish Grand Committee, a motion may be made by a Minister of the Crown that, in the course of its consideration thereof, the Committee may meet in Edinburgh on any specified Monday at half-past ten o'clock, and the question on that motion shall be put forthwith; and if, on the question being put, not fewer than twenty Members rise in their places and signify their objection, Mr Speaker shall declare that the noes have it:

Provided that nothing in this order shall prevent the committee from considering the same bill, estimate or matter on other days at Westminster.

95. Scottish Standing Committees. (1) For the consideration of bills certified by Mr Speaker as relating exclusively to Scotland and committed to a standing committee or bills committed to a Scottish Standing Committee not more than two standing committees may be appointed.

(2) Government bills shall have precedence in one such standing committee.

96. Scottish estimates. A motion may be made by a Minister of the Crown at the commencement of public business to the effect that the estimates or any part of the estimates for which the Secretary of State for Scotland is responsible be referred to the Scottish Grand Committee, and the question thereon shall be put forthwith; and if such motion be agreed to, the Committee shall consider the estimates so referred to it in any session on at least six days in that session and shall from time to time report only that it has considered the said estimates or any of them.

97. Matters relating exclusively to Scotland. (1) A motion may be made by a Minister of the Crown at the commencement of public business to the effect that a specified matter or matters relating exclusively to Scotland be referred to the Scottish Grand Committee for its consideration, and the question thereon shall be put forthwith; and if, on that question being put, not fewer than ten Members rise in their places and signify their objection thereto, Mr Speaker shall declare that the noes have it.

(2) If such a motion be agreed to, the Scottish Grand Committee shall consider the matter or matters to it referred on not more than six days in a session, and shall report only that it has considered the said matter or matters.

98. Welsh Grand Committee. (1) There shall be a standing committee to be called the Welsh Grand Committee, which shall consider—
 (a) bills referred to it; and
 (b) such specified matters relating exclusively to Wales as may be referrred to it;
and shall consist of all Members sitting for constituencies in Wales, together with not more than five other Members to be nominated by the Committee of Selection, which shall have power from time to time to discharge the Members so nominated by it and to appoint others in substitution for those discharged.

(2) A motion, of which at least ten days' notice has been given, may be made by a Minister of the Crown at the commencement of public business, that a public bill be referred to the Welsh Grand Committee, and the question thereupon shall be put forthwith; and if, on the question being put, not fewer than twenty Members rise in their places and signify their objection thereto, Mr Speaker shall declare that the noes have it:
 Provided that no such notice shall be given until the bill has been printed and delivered to the Vote Office.

(3) The Committee shall report to the House either that it recommends that the bill ought to be read a second time or that it recommends that the bill ought not to be read a second time, and in the latter case it shall have power to state its reasons for so recommending.

(4) Upon a motion being made for the second reading of a bill reported from the Committee, the question thereon shall be put forthwith.

(5) A motion may be made by a Minister of the Crown at the commencement of public business to the effect that a specified matter or matters relating exclusively to Wales be referred to the Welsh Grand Committee for its consideration, and the question thereon shall be put forthwith.

(6) If such a motion be agreed to, the Committee shall consider the matter or matters to it referred and shall report only that it has considered the said matter or matters.

99. Northern Ireland Committee. (1) There shall be a Standing Committee to be called the Northern Ireland Committee which shall consider such specified matters relating exclusively to Northern Ireland as may be referred to it and shall consist of all Members sitting for constituencies in Northern Ireland, together with not more than twenty-five other Members to be nominated by the Committee of Selection, which shall have power from time to time to discharge the Members so nominated by it and to appoint others in substitution for those discharged.

(2) A motion may be made by a Minister of the Crown at the commencement of public business to the effect that a specified matter or matters relating exclusively to Northern Ireland be referred to the Northern Ireland Committee for its consideration and the question thereon shall be put forthwith.

(3) If such a motion be agreed to, the Committee shall consider the matter or matters referred to it and shall report only that it has considered the said matter or matters.

100. Standing Committee on Regional Affairs. (1) There shall be a Standing Committee to be called the Standing Committee on Regional Affairs which shall consider any matter or matters relating to regional affairs in England which may be referred to it.

(2) All Members sitting for constituencies in England shall be members of the Standing Committee, together with not more than five other Members to be nominated by the Committee of Selection, which shall have power from time to time to discharge the Members so nominated by it and to appoint others in substitution for those discharged, and the provisions of Standing Order No 87 (Attendance of law officers and ministers in standing committees) shall not apply.

(3) A motion may be made by a Minister of the Crown at the commencement of public business to the effect that a specified matter or matters relating to regional affairs in England be referred to the Standing Committee for its consideration, and the question thereon shall be put forthwith; and if, on the question being put, not fewer than twenty Members rise in their places and signify their objection thereto, Mr Speaker shall declare that the noes have it.

(4) The Committee shall consider the matter or matters referred to it on a motion 'That the Committee has considered the matter or matters'; and the Chairman shall put any question necessary to dispose of the proceedings on such a motion, if not previously concluded, when the Committee has sat for two and a half hours after the commencement of those proceedings; and the Committee shall thereupon report to the House that it has considered the matter or matters without any further question being put.

(5) Six shall be the quorum of the Committee.

101. Standing Committees on Statutory Instruments, &c (1) There shall be one or more standing committees, to be called Standing Committees on Statutory Instruments, &c, for the consideration of statutory instruments or draft statutory instruments referred to them.

(2) Any member, not being a member of such a standing committee, may take part in the deliberations of the committee, but shall not vote or make any motion or move any amendment or be counted in the quorum.

(3) Where—

(i) a Member has given notice of a motion for an humble address to Her Majesty praying that a statutory instrument be annulled, or of a motion that a draft of an Order in Council be not submitted to Her Majesty in Council, or that a statutory instrument be not made, or that the House takes note of a statutory instrument, or

(ii) a Minister of the Crown has given notice of a motion to the effect that a statutory instrument or draft statutory instrument be approved,

a motion may be made by a Minister of the Crown at the commencement of public business, that the said instrument or draft instrument be referred to such a committee, and the question thereupon shall be put forthwith; and if, on the question being put, not fewer than twenty Members rise in their places and signify their objection thereto, Mr Speaker shall declare that the noes have it.

(4) Each committee shall consider each instrument or draft instrument referred to it on a motion, 'That the committee has considered the instrument (or draft instrument); and the chairman shall put any question necessary to dispose of the proceedings on such a motion, if not previously concluded, when the committee shall have sat for one and a half hours (or, in the case of an instrument or draft instrument relating exclusively to Northern Ireland, two and a half hours) after the commencement of those proceedings; and the committee shall thereupon report the instrument or draft instrument to the House without any further question being put.

(5) If any motion is made in the House of the kind specified in paragraph (3)(i) or (3)(ii) of this order, in relation to any instrument or draft instrument reported to the House in accordance with paragraph (4) of this order, Mr Speaker shall put forthwith the question thereon and proceedings in pursuance of this paragraph, though opposed, may be decided after the expiration of the time for opposed business.

(6) The provisions of this order shall apply to measures under the Church of England Assembly (Powers) Act 1919 and instruments made under such measures as if such measures and such instruments were statutory instruments; and the notice referred to in paragraph (3)(ii) of this order may, in respect of such measures and instruments, have been given by any Member.

102. Standing Committees on European Community Documents.
(1) There shall be one or more standing committees, to be called Standing Committees on European Community Documents, for the consideration of European Community documents (as defined in Standing Order No 14 (Exempted business)) referred to them.

(2) Any member, not being a member of such a standing committee, may take part in the deliberations of the committee, but shall not vote or be counted in the quorum.

(3) Where notice has been given of a motion relating to a European Community document, a motion may be made by a Minister of the Crown at the commencement of public business, that the said document be referred to such a committee, and the question thereupon shall be put forthwith; and if, on the question being put, not fewer than twenty Members rise in their places and signify their objection thereto, Mr Speaker shall declare that the noes have it.

(4) Each committee shall consider each such document referred to it on a motion made by a Minister of the Crown to which amendments may be moved, and the chairman shall interrupt proceedings, if not previously concluded, when the committee shall have sat for two and a half hours after the commencement of those proceedings. Thereafter, notwithstanding the provisions of paragraph (2) of Standing Order No 88 (Meetings of standing committees), he shall forthwith put successively—

(a) the question on any amendment already proposed from the chair;
(b) the question on any other amendments selected by the chair which may be moved;
(c) the main question (or the main question, as amended).

The Committee shall thereupon report the document to the House, together with any resolution to which it has come, without any further question being put.

(5) If any motion is made in the House in relation to any document reported to the House in accordance with paragraph (4) of this order, Mr Speaker shall forthwith put successively—

(a) the question on any amendment selected by him which may be moved;
(b) the main question (or the main question, as amended);

and proceedings in pursuance of this paragraph, though opposed, may be decided after the expiration of the time for opposed business.

103. Business sub-committees. (1) Whenever an order has been made by the House allocating time to the proceedings of a standing committee on any bill which has been allocated or committed to it, the order shall stand referred to that committee, and shall be considered by a sub-committee thereof to be called the business sub-committee.

(2) A business sub-committee shall consist of the chairman or one of the chairmen of the committee (who shall be chairman of the sub-committee) and seven members of the committee, to be nominated by Mr Speaker as soon as may be after such an order has been made; the quorum of the sub-committee shall be four, of whom the chairman so nominated shall be one; and the sub-committee shall have power to report from time to time to the committee.

(3) A sub-committee shall report to the committee its resolutions upon—

(a) the number of sittings to be allotted to the consideration of the bill;
(b) the allocation of the proceedings to each sitting; and
(c) the time at which any proceedings, if not previously concluded, shall be brought to a conclusion.

(4) All such resolutions shall be reported to the committee at the commencement of the next sitting of the committee and shall be recorded in the minutes of the proceedings of the committee.

(5) Whenever a sub-committee has made a report to the committee, the Member in charge of the bill may forthwith move 'That this committee do agree with the business sub-committee in its resolution (or resolutions)'; and the question on such a motion shall be put forthwith.

(6) If the question is agreed to, the resolution (or resolutions) shall have effect as though included in the order aforesaid, but if it is negatived the

resolution (or resolutions) shall stand re-committed to the business sub-committee.

Select Committees

104. Nomination of select committees. (1) Any Member intending to propose that certain Members be members of a select committee, or be discharged from a select committee, shall give notice of the names of Members whom he intends so to propose, shall endeavour to ascertain previously whether each such Member will give his attendance on the committee, and shall endeavour to give notice to any Member whom he proposes to be discharged from the committee.

(2) No motion shall be made for the nomination of members of select committees appointed under Standing Order No 130 (Select committees related to government departments), or for their discharge, unless—
   (a) notice of the motion has been given at least two sitting days previously, and
   (b) the motion is made on behalf of the Committee of Selection by the chairman or another member of the committee.

105. Lists of Members serving on select committees. Lists shall be fixed in some conspicuous place in the Committee Office and in the lobby of the House of all Members serving on each select committee.

106. Sittings of committees. All committees, other than committees of the whole House, shall have leave to sit at any time on any day on which the House sits, but may not otherwise sit during any adjournment of the House, without the leave of the House, and such leave shall not be moved for without notice.

107. Quorum of select committee. (1) A select committee may not proceed to business unless a quorum be present; and if at any time during the sitting of a select committee a quorum shall not be present, the clerk of the committee shall bring this fact to the notice of the chairman, who shall thereupon suspend the proceedings of the committee until a quorum be present, or adjourn the committee.

(2) In determining whether the requisite number of Members is present to form the quorum the chairman shall be counted.

108. Strangers (select committees). (1) A select committee shall have power, if it so orders, to admit strangers during the examination of witnesses.

(2) A sub-committee appointed by such a select committee shall have a like power except as that committee otherwise orders.

109. Withdrawal of documents before select committee. No document received by the clerk of a select committee shall be withdrawn or altered without the knowledge and approval of the committee.

110. Entry on minutes of proceedings of select committee. The names of the Members present at each sitting of a select committee and, if a division takes place, the name of the proposer of the motion or amendment, the question put, and the respective votes thereupon of the Members present shall be entered on the minutes of the proceedings of the committee.

111. Minutes of proceedings to be laid on the Table. The minutes of the proceedings of a select committee shall be laid on the Table of the House during the session to which they relate, unless the committee proposes to bring them up with a report in a following session of the same Parliament.

112. Entry on minutes of evidence of select committee. The names of Members present at each sitting of a select committee shall be entered on the minutes of evidence, if any.

113. Entry of questions asked. To every question or series of questions asked of a witness under examination in the proceedings of a select committee, and at the beginning of each page of the minutes of evidence, there shall be prefixed the name of the inquiring Member.

114. Administration of oath in select committee. Any oath taken or affirmation made by any witness before a select committee may be administered by the chairman, or by the clerk attending such committee.

115. Power to report opinion and observations. Every select committee shall have leave to report to the House its opinion and observations upon any matters referred to it for its consideration, together with the minutes of the evidence taken before it, and also to make a special report of any matters which it may think fit to bring to the notice of the House.

116. Select committees (reports). All select committees shall have power to authorise the Clerk of the House to supply copies of their reports to officers of government departments, to such witnesses who have given evidence to committees or to their sub-committees as those committees consider appropriate, to lobby journalists, and to such other press representatives as the committee thinks fit, after those reports have been laid upon the Table but not more than forty-eight hours before the intended time of publication of such reports.

117. Witnesses and evidence (select committees). (1) All select committees having power to send for persons, papers and records shall have power to publish the names of persons who have appeared as witnesses before them, and to authorise the publication by the witnesses concerned or otherwise of memoranda of evidence submitted by them.

(2) Mr Speaker shall have power to authorise such publication in the case of any such select committee which is no longer in existence.

118. Publication of evidence (select committees). When evidence has been given before a select committee meeting in public, no complaint of privilege will be entertained on the ground that it has been published before having been reported to the House.

119. Select committees (adjournment of the House). Whenever the House stands adjourned for more than two days, and any select committee having power to sit notwithstanding any adjournment of the House shall have agreed to a report, or shall have resolved that its minutes of proceedings should be printed or that the minutes of evidence taken before it or before any sub-committee appointed by it or any papers laid before it should be reported to the House and printed, it shall have power to direct the printing of such report, minutes or papers, and such printing shall be under the authority of the House; and any such reports, minutes or papers shall be deemed to have been reported to the House and shall be laid upon the Table when the House next sits.

120. Members (attendance at Lords select committees). Any Member requested by a committee appointed by the Lords to attend as a witness before it or before any sub-committee appointed by it shall have the leave of this House so to attend, if the Member think fit.

121. Committee of Privileges. (1) There shall be a Committee of Privileges.

(2) The Committee of Privileges shall consist of seventeen Members.

(3) The committee shall have power to send for persons, papers and records.

(4) The quorum of the committee shall be six.

(5) Unless the House otherwise orders, each Member nominated to the committee shall continue to be a member of it for the remainder of the Parliament.

122. Committee of Public Accounts. (1) There shall be a select committee to be called the Committee of Public Accounts for the examination of the accounts showing the appropriation of the sums granted by Parliament to meet the public expenditure, and of such other accounts laid before Parliament as the committee may think fit, to consist of not more than fifteen Members, of whom four shall be a quorum. The committee shall have power to send for persons, papers and records, to report from time to time, and to adjourn from place to place.

(2) Unless the House otherwise orders, each Member nominated to the committee shall continue to be a member of it for the remainder of the Parliament.

123. Joint Committee on Consolidation, &c, Bills. (1) There shall be a select committee, to consist of twelve Members, to join with the committee appointed by the Lords as the Joint Committee on Consolidation, &c, Bills, to consider—

    (a) consolidation bills, whether public or private;
    (b) Statute Law Revision Bills;
    (c) bills prepared pursuant to the Consolidation of Enactments (Procedure) Act 1949, together with any memoranda laid pursuant to that Act and any representations made with respect thereto;
    (d) bills to consolidate any enactments with amendments to give effect to recommendations made by one or both of the Law Commissions, together with any report containing such recommendations;
    (e) bills prepared by one or both of the Law Commissions to promote the reform of the statute law by the repeal, in accordance with Law Commission recommendations, of certain enactments which (except in so far as their effect is preserved) are no longer of practical utility, whether or not they make other provision in connection with the repeal of those enactments, together with any Law Commission report on any such bills; and

(f) any Order in Council laid or laid in draft before the House where an affirmative resolution is required before it is made, or is a condition of its continuance in operation, and which but for the provisions of the Northern Ireland Act 1974 would, in the opinion of the Committee, have been enacted by a consolidation bill, whether public or private, or by a Statute Law Revision Bill.

(2) The committee shall have power to send for persons, papers and records; and to sit notwithstanding any adjournment of the House.

(3) Two shall be the quorum of the committee.

(4) Unless the House otherwise orders, each Member nominated to the committee shall continue to be a member of it for the remainder of the Parliament.

124. Statutory Instruments (Joint Committee). (1) A select committee shall be appointed to join with a committee appointed by the Lords to consider—

(A) every instrument which is laid before each House of Parliament and upon which proceedings may be or might have been taken in either House of Parliament, in pursuance of an Act of Parliament, being—
  (a) a statutory instrument, or a draft statutory instrument;
  (b) a scheme, or an amendment of a scheme, or a draft thereof, requiring approval by statutory instrument;
  (c) any other instrument (whether or not in draft), where the proceedings in pursuance of an Act of Parliament are proceedings by way of an affirmative resolution; or
  (d) an order subject to special parliamentary procedure;
     but excluding any Order in Council or draft Order in Council made or proposed to be made under paragraph 1 of Schedule 1 to the Northern Ireland Act 1974;

(B) every general statutory instrument not within the foregoing classes, and not required to be laid before or to be subject to proceedings in this House only, but not including measures under the Church of England Assembly (Powers) Act 1919 and instruments made under such measures:

with a view to determining whether the special attention of the House should be drawn to it on any of the following grounds:
  (i) that it imposes a charge on the public revenues or contains provisions requiring payments to be made to the Exchequer or any government department or to any local or public authority in consideration of any licence or consent or of any services to be rendered, or prescribes the amount of any such charge or payment;
  (ii) that it is made in pursuance of any enactment containing specific provisions excluding it from challenge in the courts, either at all times or after the expiration of a specific period;
  (iii) that it purports to have retrospective effect where the parent statute confers no express authority so to provide;
  (iv) that there appears to have been unjustifiable delay in the publication or in the laying of it before Parliament;
  (v) that there appears to have been unjustifiable delay in sending a notification under the proviso to section 4(1) of the Statutory

Instruments Act 1946, where an instrument had come into operation before it has been laid before Parliament;

(vi) that there appears to be a doubt whether it is *intra vires* or that it
appears to make some unusual or unexpected use of the powers
conferred by the statute under which it is made;

(vii) that for any special reason its form or purport calls for elucidation;

(viii) that its drafting appears to be defective;

or on any other ground which does not impinge on its merits or on the policy
behind it; and to report its decision with the reasons thereof in any particular
case.

(2) The quorum of the committee shall be two.

(3) The committee shall have power to appoint one or more sub-committees severally to join with any sub-committee or sub-committees
appointed by the committee appointed by the Lords; and to refer to such
sub-committee or sub-committees any of the matters referred to the committee.

(4) The committee and any sub-committee appointed by it shall have the
assistance of the Counsel to Mr Speaker and, if their Lordships think fit, of
the Counsel to the Lord Chairman of Committees.

(5) The committee shall have power to sit notwithstanding any adjournment of the House and to report from time to time, and any sub-committee
appointed by it shall have power to sit notwithstanding any adjournment of
the House.

(6) The committee and any sub-committee appointed by it shall have power
to require any government department concerned to submit a memorandum
explaining any instrument which may be under its consideration or to depute
a representative to appear before it as a witness for the purpose of explaining
any such instrument.

(7) The committee and any sub-committee appointed by it shall have power
to take evidence, written or oral, from Her Majesty's Stationery Office,
relating to the printing and publication of any instrument.

(8) The committee shall have power to report to the House from time to
time any memorandum submitted to it or other evidence taken before it or
any sub-committee appointed by it from any government department in
explanation of any instruments.

(9) It shall be an instruction to the committee that before reporting that the
special attention of the House be drawn to any instrument the committee do
afford to any government department concerned therewith an opportunity
of furnishing orally or in writing to it or to any sub-committee appointed by it
such explanations as the department think fit.

(10) It shall be an instruction to the committee that it shall consider any
instrument which is directed by Act of Parliament to be laid before and to be
subject to proceedings in this House only, being—

(a) a statutory instrument, or a draft of a statutory instrument;

(b) a scheme, or an amendment to a scheme, or a draft thereof, requiring
approval by statutory instrument; or

(c) any other instrument (whether or not in draft), where the proceedings in pursuance of an Act of Parliament are proceedings by way of an affirmative resolution;

and that it have power to draw such instruments to the special attention of the House on any of the grounds on which the Joint Committee is empowered so to draw the special attention of the House; and that in considering any such instrument the committee do not join with the committee appointed by the Lords.

(11) Unless the House otherwise orders, each Member nominated to the committee shall continue to be a member of it for the remainder of the Parliament.

125. Select Committee on House of Commons (Services). (1) There shall be a select committee to advise Mr Speaker on the control of the accommodation and services in that part of the Palace of Westminster and its precincts occupied by or on behalf of the House of Commons, and to report thereon to the House.

(2) The committee shall consist of twenty Members.

(3) The quorum of the committee shall be five.

(4) the committee shall have power to send for persons, papers and records, to sit notwithstanding any adjournment of the House, to adjourn from place to place, and to report from time to time.

(5) The committee shall have power to invite any specially qualified person, whom it may select, to attend any of its meetings in an advisory capacity on any architectural or related matters.

(6) The committee shall have power to appoint sub-committees and to refer to such sub-committees any of the matters referred to the committee.

(7) The quorum of every such sub-committee shall be two.

(8) Every such sub-committee shall have power to send for persons, papers and records, to sit notwithstanding any adjournment of the House, to adjourn from place to place, subject to the approval of the Committee, and to report to the committee from time to time.

(9) The committee shall have power to report from time to time the minutes of evidence taken before sub-committees.

(10) Any sub-committee which may be appointed to deal with the organisation of, and the provision of services in, the Library shall have the assistance of the Librarian.

(11) Any sub-committee which may be appointed to consider the organisation of the services in the Refreshment Department shall have power to appoint specialist advisers for the purpose of particular inquiries, either to supply information which is not readily available or to elucidate matters of complexity within the sub-committee's order of reference.

(12) Any sub-committee on computers that may be appointed shall have power to join with any sub-committee thereon that may be appointed by the Select Committee of the House of Lords on House of Lords Offices, and to appoint specialist advisers either to supply information which is not readily available or to elucidate matters of complexity relating to the matter referred to it.

(13) Unless the House otherwise orders, each Member nominated to the committee shall continue to be a member of it for the remainder of the Parliament.

126. Select Committee on the Parliamentary Commissioner for Administration. (1) There shall be a select committee to examine the reports of the Parliamentary Commissioner for Administration, of the Health Service Commissioners for England, Scotland and Wales and of the Parliamentary Commissioner for Administration for Northern Ireland, which are laid before this House, and matters in connection therewith; and the committee shall consist of nine Members of whom the quorum shall be three.

(2) The committee shall have power—
  (a) to send for persons, papers and records, to sit notwithstanding any adjournment of the House, to adjourn from place to place, and to report from time to time; and
  (b) to appoint specialist advisers to supply information which is not readily available or to elucidate matters of complexity within the committee's order of reference.

(3) Unless the House otherwise orders, each Member nominated to the committee shall continue to be a member of it for the remainder of the Parliament.

127. Select Committee on European Legislation. (1) There shall be a select committee to consider draft proposals by the Commission of the European Communities for legislation and other documents published for submission to the Council of Ministers or to the European Council whether or not such documents originate from the Commission, and to report its opinion as to whether such proposals or other documents raise questions of legal or political importance, to give its reasons for its opinion, to report what matters of principle or policy may be affected thereby, and to what extent they may affect the law of the United Kingdom, and to make recommendations for the further consideration of such proposals and other documents by the House.

(2) The committee shall consist of sixteen Members.

(3) The committee and any sub-committee appointed by it shall have the assistance of the Counsel to Mr Speaker.

(4) The committee shall have the power to appoint specialist advisers for the purpose of particular inquiries, either to supply information which is not readily available or to elucidate matters of complexity within the committee's order of reference.

(5) The committee shall have power to send for persons, papers and records; to sit notwithstanding any adjournment of the House; to adjourn from place to place; and to report from time to time.

(6) The quorum of the committee shall be five.

(7) The committee shall have power to appoint sub-committees and to refer to such sub-committees any of the matters referred to the committee.

(8) Every such sub-committee shall have power to send for persons, papers and records; to sit notwithstanding any adjournment of the House; to

adjourn from place to place; and to report to the committee from time to time.

(9) The committee shall have power to report from time to time the minutes of evidence taken before such sub-committees.

(10) The quorum of every such sub-committee shall be two.

(11) The committee or any sub-committee appointed by it shall have leave to confer and to meet concurrently with any committee of the Lords on the European Communities or any sub-committee of that committee for the purposes of deliberating and of examining witnesses.

(12) Unless the House otherwise orders, each Member nominated to the committee shall continue to be a member of it for the remainder of the Parliament.

128. Select Committee on Members' Interests. (1) There shall be a select committee to examine the arrangements made for the compilation, maintenance and accessibility of the Register of Members' Interests; to consider any proposals made by Members or others as to the form and contents of the Register; to consider any specific complaints made in relation to the registering or declaring of interests; to consider what classes of person (if any) other than Members ought to be required to register; and to make recommendations upon these and other matters which are relevant.

(2) The committee shall consist of thirteen Members.

(3) The committee shall have power to send for persons, papers and records; to sit notwithstanding any adjournment of the House; and to report from time to time.

(4) The quorum of the committee shall be five.

(5) Unless the House otherwise orders, each Member nominated to the committee shall continue to be a member of it for the remainder of the Parliament.

129. Select Committee on Sound Broadcasting. (1) There shall be a select committee to give directions and perform other duties in accordance with the provisions of the Resolution of the House of 26th July 1977 in relation to sound broadcasting, and to make recommendations thereon to the House.

(2) The committee shall consist of six Members.

(3) The committee shall have power to send for persons, papers and records; to sit notwithstanding any adjournment of the House; to adjourn from place to place; and to report from time to time.

(4) The quorum of the committee shall be two.

(5) The committee shall have power to appoint specialist advisers either to supply information which is not readily available or to elucidate matters of complexity relating to the matters referred to it.

(6) The committee shall have leave to confer and to meet concurrently with any committee of the Lords on sound broadcasting for the purpose of deliberating and of examining witnesses.

(7) Unless the House otherwise orders, each Member nominated to the committee shall continue to be a member of it for the remainder of the Parliament.

130. Select committees related to government departments. (1) Select committees shall be appointed to examine the expenditure, administration and policy of the principal government departments set out in paragraph (2) of this order and associated public bodies, and similar matters within the responsibilities of the Secretary of State for Northern Ireland.

(2) The committees appointed under paragraph (1) of this order, the principal departments of government with which they are concerned, the maximum numbers of each committee and the quorum in each case shall be as follows:

Name of committee	Principal government departments concerned	Maximum numbers of Members	Quorum
1. Agriculture	Ministry of Agriculture, Fisheries and Food	11	3
2. Defence	Ministry of Defence	11	3
3. Education, Science and Arts	Department of Education and Science	11	3
4. Employment	Department of Employment	11	3
5. Energy	Department of Energy	11	3
6. Environment	Department of the Environment	11	3
7. Foreign Affairs	Foreign and Commonwealth Office	11	3
8. Home Affairs	Home Office	11	3
9. Scottish Affairs	Scottish Office	13	5
10. Social Services	Department of Health and Social Security	11	3
11. Trade and Industry	Department of Trade and Industry	11	3
12. Transport	Department of Transport	11	3
13. Treasury and Civil Service	Treasury, Management and Personnel Office, Board of Inland Revenue, Board of Customs and Excise	11	3
14. Welsh Affairs	Welsh Office	11	3

(3) The Foreign Affairs Committee, the Home Affairs Committee and the Treasury and Civil Service Committee shall each have the power to appoint one sub-committee.

(4) There may be a sub-committee, drawn from the membership of two or more of the Energy, Environment, Trade and Industry, Scottish Affairs, Transport, and Treasury and Civil Service Committees, set up from time to time to consider any matter affecting two or more nationalised industries.

(5) Select committees appointed under this order shall have power—
  (a) to send for persons, papers and records, to sit notwithstanding any adjournment of the House, to adjourn from place to place, and to report from time to time;
  (b) to appoint specialist advisers either to supply information which is not readily available or to elucidate matters of complexity within the committee's order of reference;
  (c) to report from time to time the minutes of evidence taken before sub-committees;
  (d) to communicate to any other such committee its evidence and any other documents relating to matters of common interest; and

(e) to meet concurrently with any other such committee for the purposes of deliberating, taking evidence, or considering draft reports;

and the sub-committees appointed under this order shall have power to send for persons, papers and records, to sit notwithstanding any adjournment of the House, and to adjourn from place to place, and shall have a quorum of three.

(6) Unless the House otherwise orders, all Members nominated to a committee appointed under this order shall continue to be members of that committee for the remainder of the Parliament.

131. Liaison Committee. (1) A select committee shall be appointed, to be called the Liaison Committee—
   (a) to consider general matters relating to the work of select committees, and
   (b) to give such advice relating to the work of select committees as may be sought by the House of Commons Commission.

(2) The committee shall report its recommendations as to the allocation of time for consideration by the House of the estimates on any day or half day which may be allotted for that purpose; and upon a motion being made that the House do agree with any such report the question shall be put forthwith and, if that question is agreed to, the recommendations shall have effect as if they were orders of the House.

Proceedings in pursuance of this paragraph, though opposed, may be decided after the expiration of the time for opposed business.

(3) The committee shall have power to send for persons, papers and records, to sit notwithstanding any adjournment of the House, and to report from time to time.

(4) Unless the House otherwise orders, each Member nominated to the committee shall continue to be a member of it for the remainder of the Parliament.

(5) The quorum of the committee shall be six.

Public Petitions

132. Presentation of petitions. Every Member offering to present a petition to the House, not being a petition for a private bill, or relating to a private bill before the House, shall confine himself to a statement of the parties from whom it comes, the number of signatures attached to it, and the material allegations contained in it, and to reading the prayer of such petition.

133. No debate on presentation of petition. Every petition presented under Standing Order No 132 (Presentation of petitions) not containing matter in breach of the privileges of this House, and which, according to the rules or usual practice of this House, can be received, shall on Mondays, Tuesdays, Wednesdays and Thursdays be brought to the Table after a member of the government shall have signified his intention to move, 'That this House do now adjourn', for the purpose of bringing the sitting to a conclusion, or after a Minister of the Crown shall have signified his intention to move, pursuant to Standing Order No 10 (Sittings of the House (suspended sittings)), 'That the proceedings of this day's sitting be suspended', and proceedings under this order shall not be interrupted at ten o'clock, and Mr Speaker shall not allow any debate, or any Member to speak upon, or in relation to, such petition; but it may be read by the Clerk if required.

134. Petition as to present personal grievance. In the case of a petition presented under Standing Order No 132 (Presentation of petitions) and complaining of some present personal grievance, for which there may be an urgent necessity for providing an immediate remedy, the matter contained in such petition may be brought into discussion on the presentation thereof and proceedings under this order shall not be interrupted at ten o'clock and may be proceeded with, though opposed, until any hour.

135. Printing of petitions and of ministerial replies. All petitions presented under Standing Order No 132 (Presentation of petitions), and not proceeded with under Standing Order No 134 (Petition as to present personal grievance), shall be ordered to lie upon the Table and to be printed, and the Clerk of the House shall transmit all such petitions to a Minister of the Crown and any observations made by a Minister or Ministers in reply to such petitions shall be laid upon the Table by the Clerk of the House and shall be ordered to be printed.

136. Petitions against imposition of tax. Petitions against any resolution or bill imposing a tax or duty for the current service of the year shall be henceforth received, and the usage under which the House has refused to entertain such petitions shall be discontinued.

Parliamentary Papers

137. Presentation of command papers. If, during the existence of a Parliament, papers are commanded by Her Majesty to be presented to this House at any time, the delivery of such papers to the Votes and Proceedings Office shall be deemed to be for all purposes the presentation of them to this House.

138. Presentation of statutory instruments. Where, under any Act of Parliament, a statutory instrument is required to be laid before Parliament, or before this House, the delivery of a copy of such instrument to the Votes and Proceedings Office on any day during the existence of a Parliament shall be deemed to be for all purposes the laying of it before the House:

Provided that nothing in this order shall apply to any statutory instrument being an order which is subject to special parliamentary procedure or to any other instrument which is required to be laid before Parliament, or before this House, for any period before it comes into operation.

139. Notification in respect of certain statutory instruments. When any communication has been received by Mr Speaker, drawing attention to the fact that copies of any statutory instrument have yet to be laid before Parliament, and explaining why such copies have not been so laid before the instrument came into operation, Mr Speaker shall thereupon lay such communication upon the Table of the House.

Witnesses in House

140. Administration of oath in House. Any oath taken or affirmation made by any witness before the House, or a committee of the whole House, may be administered by the Clerk.

Strangers

141. Duties of Serjeant at Arms with respect to strangers. (1) The Serjeant at Arms attending this House shall take into his custody any stranger whom he may see, or who may be reported to him to be, in any part of the House or gallery appropriated to the Members of this House, and also any stranger who, having been admitted into any other part of the House or gallery, shall misconduct himself, or shall not withdraw when strangers are directed to withdraw, while the House, or any committee of the whole House, is sitting.

(2) The power conferred upon the Serjeant at Arms by paragraph (1) of this order may, if the chairman so directs, be exercised in respect of strangers present at sittings of select and standing committees.

142. Places to which strangers are not admitted. No Member of this House shall presume to bring any stranger into any part of the House or gallery appropriated to the Members of this House while the House, or a committee of the whole House, is sitting.

143. Withdrawal of strangers from House. (1) If at any sitting of the House, or in a committee of the whole House, any Member shall take notice that strangers are present, Mr Speaker, or the chairman (as the case may be), shall forthwith put the question, 'That strangers do withdraw,' and such question, though opposed, may be decided after the expiration of the time for opposed business:

Provided that Mr Speaker or the chairman may, whenever he thinks fit, order the withdrawal of strangers from any part of the House.

(2) An order that strangers do withdraw shall not apply to members of the House of Lords.

Letters

144. Custody of letters addressed to Members. To prevent the intercepting or losing of letters directed to Members of this House, the postmaster of the House or other persons appointed by the Post Office shall attend daily (Sundays excepted) for the delivery and redirection of all letters arriving in course of post and shall take care, during their stay there, to deliver the same to the several Members to whom they shall be directed, or to their known servant or servants, or other persons bringing notes under the hands of the Members sending for the same.

145. Directions to officers in charge of letters. The said officers shall, upon their going away, lock up such letters as shall remain undelivered.

146. Mode of dealing with letters directed to House. When any letter or packet directed to this House shall come to Mr Speaker, he shall open the same; and acquaint the House, at its next sitting, with the contents thereof, if proper to be communicated to this House.

Index

Bold figures indicate the most important references to a subject.

1025

Chairman of Ways and Means (Commons)
—*continued*
closure, powers, 405–8
committee of whole House, in, 585–7
Court of Referees, 842
decisions, no appeal from, to Speaker, 586
Deputy, 187–8
impartiality, 187
leaves chair, 499, **587–8**
meeting of House, power to give notice of
earlier, 187, **224**
presents bills, 707
private business duties, 277–81, **827–8**, 863,
883, 890
reflections upon, 127, **325**, 379
resignation, 187
rulings by, 5, 187
salary, 18
secretary to, 195
Speaker's absence, and, 185–6
Speaker's counsel and, 190, **827–8**
Standing Orders Committee, 819
Statutory Instruments Reference Committee, 541
temporary chairmen, 188, 585
Temporary Deputy Chairman, 188
unopposed private bills, duties, 883
Chairmen
closure in committee of whole House,
405–8
committees of the whole House, in, 585–7
joint committees, 667
private bill committees, 885, 895, 916
reflections on, 127, **325**, 379
select committees, **620–3**, 653
questions to, 286
standing committees, 596–7, 601–3
sub-committees, 639
temporary, 188, 585
closure powers, House, in, 405
select committees, 621–2
standing committees, 597
Chairmen's Panel, 188, 597, 600, 752
Chambers of the two Houses, 165–7
Chancellor of the Exchequer
budget, 687, **733–5**
Chiltern Hundreds, and, 50–1
Channel Islands, Measures and, 555
Chaplain, Speaker's, 198
prayers by, 229, **275**
Charges upon the people
amendments affecting, 495–6, 740
definition, 687–8
Lords amendment imposing, 749
Lords omit provisions imposing, 750–1
private bills creating, 869–70
standing committees, in, 606–7
tests for determining, 726–7
Charges upon the revenue
amendments affecting, 693–4, 722
definition, 687
diversion of revenue, 716
Lords amendment imposing, 512–3, **748–9**
motion to bring in a bill entailing, refused,
464

Charges upon the revenue—*continued*
private bills creating, 869–70
select committee resolutions recommending, 641–2
tests for determining, 712–3
Chief Opposition Whip, 18, 201
Lords, in, 203
Chief Whip, 202
Chiltern Hundreds, 31, **50–52**, 231
Chubb v Salomons, 91
Church Commissioners, 49, 688, 712
questions to, 286
Church of England
clergy disqualification, **45–6**, 54
Measures, 554–7
copyright, 89n
printing, 535
Royal Assent, 527
standing committees on, 594–5
time provided for, 269
questions about, in Lords, 437
**Church of England Assembly (Powers) Act
1919,** 244, **554**
**Church of Scientology of California v John-
son-Smith (1972),** 157
Citation clauses, 440, 500
Civil Contingencies Fund. *See* CONTINGENCIES
FUND
City of London
bills concerning, 796
Member for, 167n
petitions from, 759
Civil List, 462, 560–1, 703, **719**
Civil List Act 1952, 690
Civil servants
disqualification of, 47–8
evidence from, 576, 629
Lords committees, assistance to, 578
Clauses Acts, 810
Clauses of bill in Commons, 442
adequate discussion of principle, **403**, 496,
601
charge, creating a, 606, **721**
citation, 440, 500
closure on words of (former procedure),
408
discussed together, 496–7
division, 487
'expenses', **468**, 495
'Henry VIII', 539
instructions, received pursuant to, 496
leave out, amendments to, 492, 504
negatived, 486
new, 492, **497**, 502–4
selection of, 404
postponement of, 487–8
printed as amended, 501–2
private bill committee, 909–11
question on, 496–7
subsections, amendment to leave out, 495
table (arrangement of clauses), 442
taken out of order, 487
transfer of, **487**, 504

Committees, Select (Commons)—
continued
evidence—*continued*
  premature publication of, 86, 123, **636–7**
  publication of, by witness or otherwise, 86, 89, 124, 637
  'sidelining', 635–6
  sub-committees, of, 640
  vote office and Library, 635
examination of witnesses, 679–81
expert assistance, 640–1
functions and history, 611–2
government departments, on, 655–6
government replies to reports of, 649–50
hybrid bills committed to, 521–4
inquiries, scope of, 618–20
instructions to, 482, 484, 617, **618–20**, 653, 896n
interests, declaration of, 385
meetings and sittings, 620, 625–7
  listed on Order Paper, 207
members—
  addition and discharge, 310, 616–7
  attendance, record of, 625
  charges made against, 637
  decline to serve, 616
  list of, 616
  nomination, 309–10, 465, 613–6, 640
  number of, 613
  personal interest, 615, 620
  places in Chamber, 167
  presence of other, 632–3
  senior, 620
  unsworn, 231
minutes of proceedings, **625**, 646
oaths, 635, **682**
opinion, power to report, 641
order of reference, 618–20
other House—
  communications with committee of, 670
  members of, as witnesses, before, 677
overseas—
  meeting, 626–7
  witnesses from, 630–1, 682–3
papers—
  other House, from, 617
  power to send for, 630
  reference of, 617
  withdrawal or alteration of, 118, 637
parties, hearing of, 631–2
Parliament, nominated for duration of, 612
Parliamentary Privilege, on, 83, 86, 93, 108n, 110
peers as witnesses, before, 629, 677
persons, papers and records, power to send for, 627–30
petitions referred to, 617n, 763n
precincts of House, beyond, 116, 626–7
previous question, 620
private bill committees, distinguished from, 613
private bills, before, 919
private bills referred to, 887

Committees, Select (Commons)—
continued
privilege, reporting breaches of, 124, 141–3
proceedings, in, 620–53
proceedings, premature publication of, 86, 123–4, 636, **648–9**
proceedings, printed, **625**, 646
proceedings referred to, 375
prorogation, effect of, 648
quasi-judicial matters, on, 615, 624
questions—
  addressed to chairman, 286
  inadmissible, 634–5
  objected to, 680
quorum, 623–4
regularly appointed, 655–62
reports—
  advance copies, 649
  amendments, 642–3
  confidential final revise copies, 649
  debate on, 651–2
  draft, 86, 642–3
  evidence, 633–7
    unreported, debate on, 375
  expenditure, advocating, 641–2
  government replies to, 649–50
  impugning, 156
  members only, printed for, 646
  memoranda to Government instead of, 647
  minority, 644–5
  not agreed upon, 645
  opinion, 641
  Order Paper, mentioned on, 207
  premature publication, 123–4, 649
  presentation, 645–7
  public bills, on, 653–5
  publication of, 648–9
  recommitted, 652
  several presented, 645
  special, 643, 647, 654
  sub-committees, 639, **644**
  unfinished inquiries, **648**, 654
resolutions, 643–4
  rescinded, 623
  returns of statistics, 652–3
scope of deliberations, 618–20
secret, 633
selection of amendments, 622
senior member, 620
sessional, **612–3**, 648
sittings and meetings, 620, 625–7
slander, no action for, 683
smoking, 620
specialist advisers, 640–1
standing order, appointed in pursuance of, 612, **655–62**
statutory instruments, 552–3
strangers, admission of, 632
  misbehaviour, 171n, 633
sub-committees, 637–40
  reports, 639, **644**
sub judice, matters, 624–5
suspension, 623, 624

Perjury Act 1911, 681
Personal
  bills. *See* BILLS, PERSONAL
  explanations
    Commons, **304–6**, 349, 374
      Fridays, 273
    Lords, **421**, 435
    Official Report, to correct, 212
  pecuniary interest, or
    Commons, 120–1, **354–9**
      declaration and registration, **384–90**, 659
      private bill committees, 884, 892, 894
      select committees, 615–6
      standing committees, 605–6
    Lords, 432–3
      private bill committees, 936
Persons, Papers and Records, power to send for, 627–31
Persons under twenty-one, disqualification
  Commons, 40–1
  Lords, 38
Petitioners
  death, 841–2
  protection of, 89, 132–3
Petitioning candidates, disqualification of, 46–7
Petitions against
  hybrid bills, 522
  hybrid instruments, 550
  personal bills, 840, 945
  private bills—
    appearances on, 904
    Court of Referees, 842–3
    death of petitioners, 841–2
    forgery of signatures, 142
    government departments, by, 839
    late, 841
    locus standi. See LOCUS STANDI
    Lords, House of, 934, 937
    parties not appearing, 893–4
    preamble, 905–6
    referred to committee, 840–1, 894
    right of audience, on, 840–1
    specially referred to committee, 859–60
    time for presentation, 839–40
    withdrawn, 839, 894
  provisional order bills, 954
  Scottish provisional orders, 967
  special procedure orders, 957–62
Petitions against alterations, 841, 906
Petitions, election, 30, 36, 53, 178
Petitions for
  additional provision, 830–1
    instructions, and, 873, 874–5
    memorials against, 814, 830
    not obtainable in second House, 910
  evidence, production of, 91, 758–9
  personal bills, 943
  private bills—
    deposit, 810, 839
    general list, 813

Petitions for—*continued*
  private bills—*continued*
    government departments, by, 793, 839
    late, 829–30, 932
      memorials against, 813–4
    Lords, presented to, 932
    memorials, **813–4**, 816–7, 830–1
    withdrawal, 831, 839
Petitions in favour of private bills, 840
Petition, Speaker's, 70–1, 227
Petitions, Public, (Commons), 754–63
  abroad, from, 758
  abuse of right, 116–7, 118
  bag for, 762
  bills, relating to, 757–8
  committee (former) on, 763n
  declaration of interest, 385
  development of, 754
  discussion of, 762
  evidence, for production of, 758–9
  exempted business, 242, 762
  expenditure, 560, 711
  forgery 756
  form of, 754–8
  Fridays, 273, 317
  irregularities in, 755–8, 760
  limit on numbers coming to present, 170
  London, from corporation of, 759
  Member, from, 760
  number of, 761n
  observations by Minister of the Crown on, 762–3
  post, transmission by, 760
  present personal grievance, 762
  presentation of 317–8, 759–60, 761–2
  printing of, 762–3
  privilege, affecting, 136, 762
  select committees, referred to, 576
  signature of, 755–6, 760
  standing committees, not received by, 607
  tampering with, 118
  Votes and Proceedings, 206
  witnesses, for attendance of Members or Officers as, 323–4, 758–9
Petitions, Public, (Lords)
  bills, relating to, 757–8
  development of, 754
  form, 754–5, 760
  Lords, from, 760
  presentation, 423, 760–1
Pickin, British Railways Board v (1973), 91, 157, 536n, 792
Pitt, case of Colonel (1734), 79n
Points of Order (Commons)
  divisions, during, 366
  fraudulent, 397
  introduction of Member, during, 299
  right to raise, 396–7
  rulings from the Chair, to obtain, 5, 397
  speaking twice on, 371
  statements, treated as, 298

Wilkes, case of (1763), 75, 113, 209
Williams, case of Sir William (1684), 147
Withdrawal in Commons
  additional provisions, petition for, 831
  amendments, 332, 490
    because out of order, 340, 495, 722
  bills, private, **831–2**, 870, 918, 920–1
    because should be public bill, 800, 801,
      804–5
  bills, public, 360, 468, **471–2**, 480, 486, 563,
    693
  disorderly expressions, 381, **394**
  early day motions, 325
  Members, of, 140–1, **394–5**, 397–9, 586
  memorials, **814**, 958
  motions, 332
  new clauses, **497**, 504
  notices of motions, 303, 325
  papers, 215, 360, 637
  petitions relating to private bills etc., 831,
    839, 859
  questions to Ministers, 284
  statutory instruments, motions for, 549
  strangers, 173, 306
    committee of the whole House, 587
    standing committee, 603
Withdrawal in Lords
  bills, private, 942
  bills, public, 444, **446**
  memorials, **814**, 958
  motions, 427
  strangers, 435
Witnesses, 675–83
  absconding, 676
  affirmation, making, 682
  arrest of, 102, 131
    by House, 676
  attendance, 117–8, **627–30**, **675–8**
  bar, examined at, 678–9
  civil servants, 576, 629
  corruption, 132
  counsel, and, 678, 681
  discussions, informal, persons having, not
    treated as, 641
  evidence, false, giving, 116, 141–2, 681
  evidence, premature publication of, 122–4,
    636
  examination of, 635, 678–9
  Examiners, before, 816
  expenses, 682–3
  freedom from arrest, 102
  hybrid bill committees, before, 523
  indemnified, 683
  intimidation, 132
  legal proceedings against, 132
  Lords, as, 629, 675, 677–8, 679

Witnesses—*continued*
  Members as—
    before other House, 576, 629, 677, 679
    courts, in, 91, 100
      petition for, 758–9
    House or committees, before, 629,
      676–7, 679
  misbehaviour of, 116, 136, **681**
  oaths, 681–2, 916, 937
    refusal to take, 116
  obstruction of, 131–3
  officers of Parliament, as—
    committees, in, 576, 629, 677
    courts, in, 91, 758–9
  overseas, from, 630–1, 679, 682–3
  prisoners, 675, 676, 679
  private bill committees, before, 907, **915–6**,
    937
  protection of, 92, 102, 132, 683
  publication of Select Committee evidence,
    by, 122–4, **636–7**
  questions to, objected to, 680
  refusing to answer questions, 116, 141–2,
    680–1
  refusal to attend when summoned, 117,
    628, 676
  Scottish provisional orders, 970
  select committees, 576–7, 627–30, 679–81
  Serjeant at Arms and, 675–6
  summons, absconding to avoid, 142
  summons of, 675–6
    private bill committees, 915–6
  tampering with, 132
Witnesses (Public Inquiries) Protection Act
  1892, 131
Woolsacks, 166, 173–4
Words of heat (Lords), 435
Writs
  attachment, of, 99, 114
  habeas corpus, **107–8**, 109, 146, 149, 150,
    153
  new, for election of Members, 29–31
    Clerk of the Crown and, 29, 32–3
    Deputy Speaker, and, 185
    issue of, 32–3
    members appointed to issue, 32–3
    motions for, 233, **276–7**, 306
    recess, during, **31–3**, 51, 53
    return of, 33–5
    supersedeas to, 31
    suspended, 37
  Parliament, summoning, 58–9, 221
  Queen's, 8
  summons to Lords, 5n, 42, 420

Yeoman Usher of the Black Rod, 178
  See also BLACK ROD
Younge, Thomas, case of (1455), 71n